Authorised issue 1999 for Mixing GmbH, Neckarsulm, Germany
Cartography: © Falk Verlag
Photos: Corel Professional Photos, PhotoDisc, project photos
Printed in Slovenia

Content

Legend

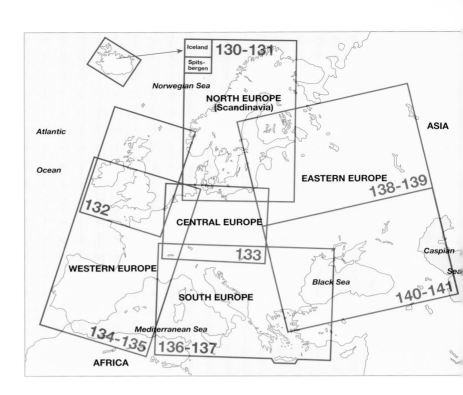

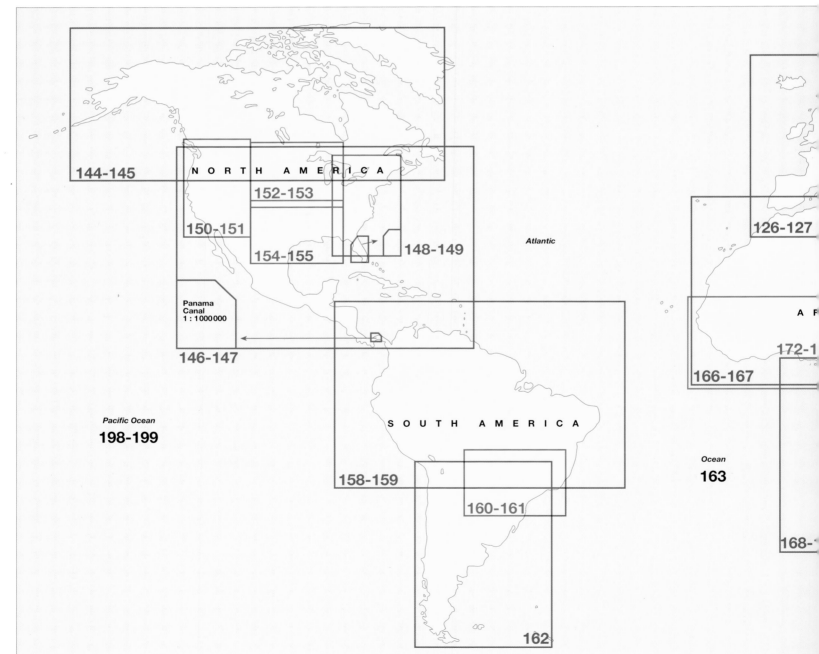

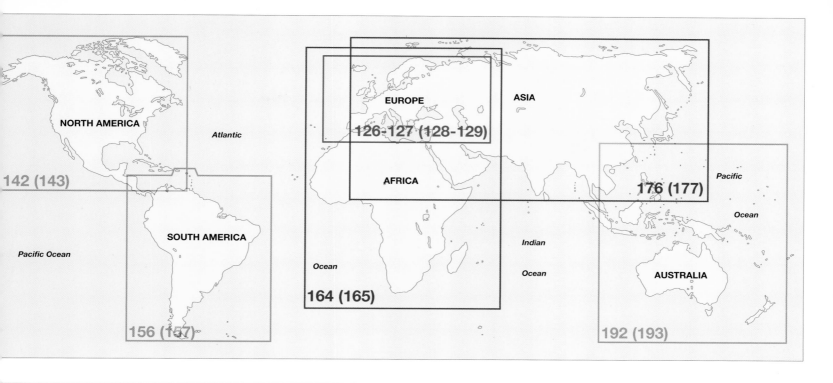

142 (143)

NORTH AMERICA

Atlantic

Pacific Ocean

SOUTH AMERICA

156 (157)

EUROPE

126-127 (128-129)

ASIA

AFRICA

Ocean

Indian

Ocean

164 (165)

176 (177)

Pacific

Ocean

AUSTRALIA

192 (193)

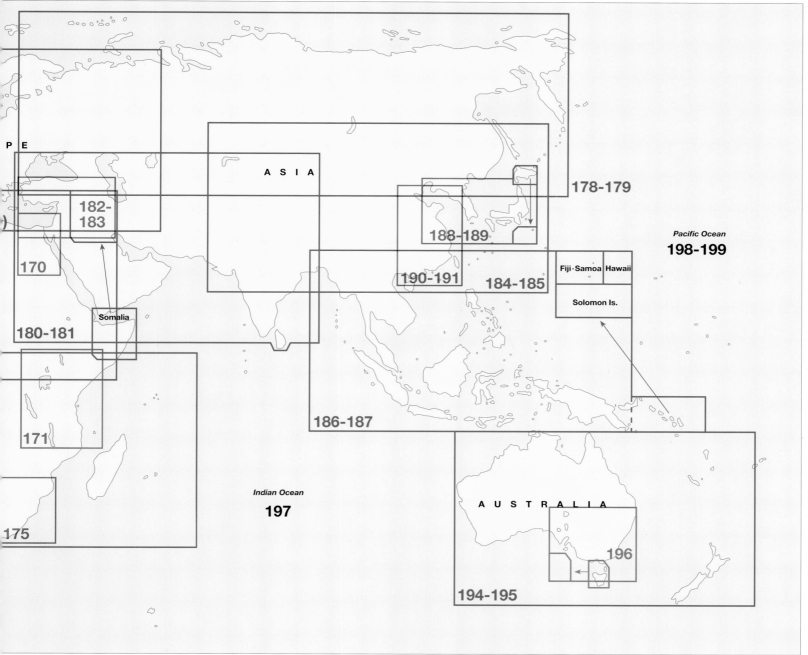

P E

A S I A

178-179

182-
183

188-189

Pacific Ocean

198-199

170

190-191

184-185

Fiji·Samoa Hawaii

Solomon Is.

Somalia

180-181

171

Indian Ocean

197

186-187

AUSTRALIA

175

196

194-195

Map overview

Planet Earth

Stars and galaxies

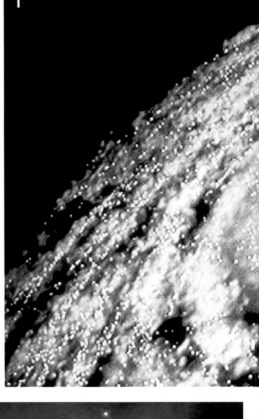

A star-filled sky on a clear night has provided mankind with a fascinating spectacle since time immemorial. For our ancestors the night sky was a realm of myths, legends and the supernatural; for us, however, space probes and giant telescopes have made breathtaking views of the universe and scientific discussions on its secrets possible. In spite of all that we know, we are still awed by the wonders of the heavens. The planet Earth represents a mere speck of dust in the immense expanse of space.

The origins of the Universe

According to a generally accepted theory, our universe originated about 15 billion years ago. A mighty explosion or "big bang" signalled the moment the universe came into being. Space, time and matter originated from literally out of nowhere.

In the 1920's, the American astronomer E.P. Hubble found the explanation for the continually expanding universe. He proved that our galaxy, the Milky Way, has been drifting through the universe for billions of years, moving further and further away from its neighbouring galaxies. Billions of cubic metres of new space come between the galaxies and push them further apart each day. The farther apart they are from each other, the quicker they move away from each other and the quicker the distance grows between them. But the reverse is also true; that the further back in time one goes, the closer they must have been to each other. Ultimately this means that in the beginning the universe must have been incredibly dense. All matter must have been unified in one place from which the universe eventually exploded.

Today the universe has taken on vast dimensions. The most distant recognizable objects at the moment are quasars which are about 12 billion light-years away. A light-year refers to the distance a ray of light can travel in one year. The speed of light is c. 300,000 km/sec. Cosmic background radiation (called "3-K-radiation") is considered to be further evidence for the Big Bang Theory. 3-K-radiation is electromagnetic radiation left over from the beginning of the universe (corresponding to 3 K above absolute zero; zero degrees Kelvin is minus 276 °C Celsius).

Einstein, in 1916, used his Theory of Relativity to prove that large masses such as the Sun through their gravitation can cause the curvature of light, thereby creating the belief that the universe is the form of a bent shape that cannot be represented pictorially. There are two possibilities for the future of the universe according to the Theory of Relativity: the "Big Crunch" (massive collapse) after reaching its maximum extent, or the currently favoured possibility that its further expansion will continue with diminishing velocity.

Galaxies

Galaxies are believed to have completed their formation process an estimated 5 billion years after the Big Bang. While the universe was still young and had not expanded so far, the galaxies must have been far closer together than they are today. Indeed, the farther back one looks into the past, the closer they were. Collisions and the melting down of galaxies were the result. This could happen to our galaxy, the Milky Way, which is moving towards Andromeda, our neighbouring galaxy within the "Local Group" that is 1.7 million light-years away. Our Milky Way system belongs to the "Local Group" which is a cluster of galaxies with around 30 known members: 3 large spiral systems (our Milky Way with its large and small Magellanic Clouds as companions, the Andromeda system with two smaller companions and the spiral cloud M33), 10 elliptical and 4 irregular systems. The nearest cluster of galaxies is the Virgo Cluster with around 3000 members. The unimaginably large number of galaxies, clusters of galaxies and vast clusters in the sponge-like structure of the universe is not known. However, the variety of known forms that galaxies can take extends from ball-like galaxies to elliptical stellar systems, from spiral clouds and barred spirals to entirely irregular shapes. The shape also reflects the speed which the process of formation required. With galaxies (the Milky Way system) it results in the formation of sun and planets.

Stars

Stars, in contrast to planets, are self-illuminating heavenly bodies. From any one observation point on the Earth, only about 2,500 can be seen with the naked eye, as it is impossible to see the whole world at one time. Were it possible to see all the stars with a so-to-speak globally naked eye, there would be about 6,000. With a powerful telescope there are up to 10^{22}

1 *Spiral galaxy: areas with young bright stars and gas clouds which are formed in long spirals around galaxies.*

2 *The "birth place" of the stars, extensive gas and dust clouds, are to be found in many places in space*

3 *The northern heavens with the Pole Star (Polaris) in the centre*

4 *The Hubble Space Telescope orbits 600 km above the Earth*

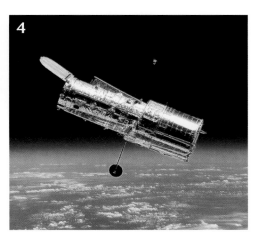

4

3

face temperatures (spectral class) of stars are plotted against their luminosities (absolute brightness). The "main line" stars, including the Sun, are differentiated from the other stars, which have greater luminosity, i.e. a larger surface, and are called "giants", by the relationship between surface temperature and spectral class. When a star grows old, it moves from the main sequence into the area of the giants and supergiants. At the end of its life, it shrinks to become a "white dwarf".

Constellations

The confusing multiplicity of stars in the night sky has always stimulated man to look for orientation in the stars. Thus stars in the sky were arranged into figures which became the constellations that were used for astrology and religious purposes, as well as for navigation and to compile calendars. The appearance of the star Sirius at dawn warned the Egyptians that the flooding of the Nile was drawing closer. The constellations that we use today date back not only to the Greeks, but also to the Egyptian and Babylonian cultures of Antiquity and Pre-antiquity. Today there are 88 internationally recognised historical constellations, 31 in the northern, 45 in the southern celestial sphere, and 12 on both sides of the Celestial Equator.

to be seen. Stars are distributed in different ways; they form open or galactic stellar clusters, and ball-like stellar clusters. Due to their being a great distance away, stars appear only as specks of light. Yet they are created in different ways and have corresponding characteristic qualities regarding luminosity, radius, temperature, mass, spectral class, density, energy production, speed of rotation, magnetic field and chemical composition. Until the introduction of astrophysics, they were categorized by their stellar position and brightness. Then they were categorized by their spectrums. Fundamental information on the state and development of stars is given by the "Herzsprung-Russell-Diagram," named after its developers. It is a graph on which the sur-

The Sun and the planets

The Sun, a star typical of the main sequence, is the central sphere in the solar system and rules over its orbiting satellites as a huge glowing ball of gas without fixed boundaries. It consists of 78% hydrogen, 20% helium and 2% other elements. Solar energy depends on nuclear reactions in its core, that produce temperatures of around 15 million degrees. Light from the Sun requires 8 minutes to reach us. Only during a spectacular eclipse of the Sun can the eye discern the corona, a ring of light that envelopes the Sun and is far above its surface. The visible yellow disc of the Sun is called the photosphere and its surface is granular and constantly changing (granulation).

Prominence, gases that appear on the periphery of the Sun as bright fiery fountains and are up to 1 million km high, escape from out of the chromosphere, a layer that looks like red-glowing flames between the photosphere and corona. The most noticeable phenomenon on the Sun is its short-lived sunspots, which are at a lower temperature and appear as dark regions, have a strong magnetic field and extend to 50,000 km. Their frequency shows an 11 year maximum (sunspot cycle).

Origins of the Solar System

Our solar system is part of the Milky Way and came into being about 4.6 billion years ago from a vast cloud of dust and gas. This collapsed into a flat rotating disc with the proto-sun at its centre. Within this cosmic disc, smaller bodies (planetesimal) kept forming ever larger globes that picked up material (accre-

tion) until they became the planets that we know today. Our solar system consists of nine planets and their moons, as well as numerous smaller planet-like fragments (planetoids) that orbit the Sun.

The distances of the planets from the Sun influence their chemical and physical properties. The heavier elements condensed and solidified at high temperatures close to the Sun during the formation of the solar system. The lighter elements, such as helium and hydrogen, were flung into the outer regions of the solar system. Thus the planets have been categorized into two groups according to their composition. The inner planets (Mercury, Venus, Earth and Mars) form a "terrestrial earth-like" group, because they a have a solid crust, are rich in iron and silica and of a high density. The group of giant outer planets (Jupiter, Saturn, Uranus and Neptune) are designated as "sun-like", because they are low density planets, have high concentrations of helium and hydrogen, and are gaseous. Pluto is an in-between type.

In contrast to stars, the planets do not shine themselves; they merely reflect the sunlight. They orbit the Sun according to Kepler's laws on circular and elliptically-shaped orbits. At the same time they all spin on their own axes.

The Inner Planets

Mercury: From an earthly perspective, the closest and second smallest planet in the solar system cannot be distinguished very well from the Sun, and therefore can only be observed with the naked eye when it is close to the horizon. Because there is no atmosphere to protect the surface of Mercury from shocks, it is characterized by a moon-like landscape that is scarred with craters. Unlike our Moon, Mercury has a large but not entirely solidified iron core that makes the creation of a very weak magnetic field possible, and contributes to the planet's high density, which is 98% that of the Earth's.

Venus: The immediate neighbour of the Earth is the so-called Morning or Evening Star, because it only climbs a few degrees above the horizon. Its brilliance originates from the extremely dense atmosphere that consists of 97% carbon-dioxide and produces a pressure on the surface of Venus which is 90 times greater than that which the Earth's atmosphere produces. The clouds of sulphur-dioxide on Venus mix with the carbon-dioxide and the remaining water-vapour to produce an extreme greenhouse effect that drives the temperatures on the surface of Venus up to 475 °C. The surface is covered with deep valleys,

high mountains, craters and high plateaux.

Mars: The "red" planet is the most earth-like object in the inner solar system: axis tilt, rotation time, seasonal cycles and weather patterns are comparable. Even the poles are covered in ice. Noticeable river and erosion structures testify to prior bodies of water on this dried-up, life-threatening desert planet. Temperature differences, volcanic activity, meteor collisions and movements in the crust have affected the surface structure of Mars.

The outer Planets

Jupiter: The largest planet is surrounded by a mighty, turbulent atmosphere, that even through an amateur telescope enables numerous details to be seen, for example the "big red spot" which is a violent tornado larger than the Earth. The American Voyager probe registered winds of up to 500 km/h in the upper cloud zone. The body of Jupiter is in essence fluid. High temperature and pressure cause the hydrogen close to the centre to take on metallic qualities. This explains its powerful magnetic field. Of Jupiter's 12 orbiting moons, Galileo discovered the four largest ones. On the surface of the moon "Io", the Voyager probe registered constant heavy volcanic activity.

Saturn: Because of its free-flowing ring system of about 1,000 individual rings with a diameter of 280,000 km, Saturn is considered the most beautiful planet in the solar system. The main elements of its atmosphere are hydrogen, helium, methane and ammonia. Toward the centre, liquid hydrogen joins up to a core of stone and metal.

Uranus: Uranus was discovered by F.W. Herschel in 1781. It appears to be "rolling" because its axis is tilted at 60° to its axis of spin. Depending on its position to the Earth, one looks at the north and then the south pole of the planet respectively. There is a mantle of ice around what is thought to be a solid core. Above this is the curve of the atmosphere composed of oxygen, helium and methane.

Neptune: This planet was discovered by J.G. Galle in 1846. Around a solid core of stone, that has some metallic properties, there is a solid mantle of dry ice. Storm winds race at speeds of over 600 km/h. through an atmosphere composed of hydrogen, helium and methane.

Pluto as a special case

The outermost known planet in the solar system is a special case within the solar system. It has indeed a lower density that speaks for being "sun-like", but on the other hand its size and surface of rock and ice banish it to the "terrestrial" planets. Discovered by C. Tombaugh in 1930, Pluto presents many puzzles.

The Solar System

1 Sun	3 Venus	5 Mars	7 Jupiter	9 Uranus	11 Pluto
2 Mercury	4 Earth	6 Asteroids	8 Saturn	10 Neptune	

The silent companion

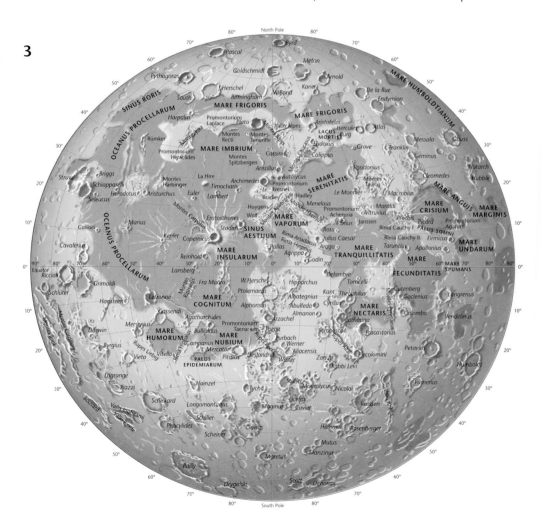

The Moon was worshipped by many cultures because it illuminated the frightening darkness of the night. Its regular recurring light patterns (moon phases) were the basis for the first calendar (moon calendar). Earth and Moon form a double system. The Moon goes around the Earth in an almost circular orbit. With one rotation around the Earth, the Moon turns once around itself, so that always one and the same side of the moon is visible.

Origins

There are four theories as to how the Moon originated 4.4 to 4.8 billion years ago. These are that it either split away from the Earth through the force created by the Earth's rotation; or that it was a separate body captured by the Earth's gravity; or that it was formed out of a cloud of planetesimal while in orbit around the Earth, or finally that it was formed from debris thrown off when a cosmic object the size of Mars struck the young and not yet solidified Earth. A lot of attention has been given to the latter, the Collision Theory. The fragments flung out after the collision formed smaller moons, that then later became the Earth's Moon.

Surfaces

When the Moon is full, it is possible, with the naked eye, to perceive light and dark patches on the Moon's surface. These correspond to high plateaux, craters and circles of mountains. After observing the Moon through his newly-invented telescope in 1610, Galileo maintained that the dark spots were large "seas". He named them Maria (Lat. Mária, stress on the first syllable mare = sea). In fact they are lava-filled basins that were formed when meteors (small planets or planetesimal) collided with it during an early stage of the solar system's creation. The interior of these craters were filled with molten lava. The largest crater is the Oriental Mare on the dark side of the Moon, with a diameter of 965 km, and the

deepest crater is Newton (7,000-8,850 m). The lighter regions he described as Terrae (lands), because they are highlands that rise above the Mare. The mountain chains around the "seas" exceed the height of mountains on Earth. With a small telescope it is possible to make out the form of various valleys and even crack-like "grooves". Geologically the Moon has been considered dead for around three billion years, because neither volcanic eruption nor earthquake nor landslide has been substantiated since then. Today detectable shocks still stem from colliding meteorites. Because there is no atmosphere, there is no water, no life, no protective shell from meteorite collisions and dangerous radiation from the Sun, no sound, only slight weathering by extreme temperature fluctuations.

The Moon Phases

The Moon is not a light-emitting body; it merely reflects the sunlight. Depending on its position in respect to the Sun and the Earth, the part visible from the Earth of the sun-lit side of the Moon varies. This is what we know as the cycle of Moon phases: full moon, decreasing half-moon, crescent moon, new moon. It takes about 29.5 days for the Moon to complete a cycle of phases from new moon to new moon, called a "synodic month." Because the Moon takes the same amount of time for its own rotation as it takes for one revolution around the Earth, the same side of the Moon always faces the Earth.

Eclipses

In many cultures, eclipses are considered to be highly significant celestial signs. Eclipses can only happen when the middle point of the Sun, Earth and Moon fall into an approximately direct line. A lunar eclipse occurs when the Earth is between the Sun and the Moon, and the Moon passes through the Earth's shadow. Lunar eclipses can only occur when there is a full moon, because the Moon can then pass into the

2

1 *Solar eclipse: the Moon moves between the Earth and the Sun. A corona is visible at the side*

2 *Neil Armstrong was the first person to set foot on the Moon in 1969*

3 *The Earth side of the Moon with the large oceans which are visible as dark spots to the naked eye*

4 *The dark side of the Moon, which can only be seen from space*

umbra shadow of the Earth, where it disappears into the black night. It usually occurs twice a year and moreover can only be observed on the dark side of the Earth. A total lunar eclipse is only possible when the Moon passes through the core shadow of the Earth. Depending on the position of the Moon, it may only be partially covered by the Earth's shadow. This is called a partial lunar eclipse. During a lunar eclipse, the temperature on the surface of the Moon decreases sharply, because the visible part is no longer illuminated. A solar eclipse occurs when the Moon moves between the Earth and the Sun, so that the Moon's umbra shadow passes over the Earth. A solar eclipse can only happen when there is a new moon and it is directly between Earth and Sun.

Solar eclipses occur around the world about five times every two years. There are distinctions between total, annular and partial solar eclipses.
In a total eclipse, the Moon in its elliptical orbit comes closest to the Earth. The Moon's disc therefore appears larger than the Sun's disc, and can completely cover the Sun and cast an umbra shadow on the Earth's surface. Outside of the core shadow, one can observe a partial solar eclipse.
In an annular eclipse, the Moon is at its greatest distance from the Earth, so that it appears smaller and it does not completely cover the sun. The umbra shadow does not reach the Earth's surface: a ring of light remains uncovered.
The solar eclipse on 11th August 1999, the only total eclipse in the 20th century in Europe and the last one in the 2nd millennium, is considered to be the Central European event of the century. The Moon's core shadow on the Earth's surface is a good 100 km wide. The next total solar eclipse in Europe is on 3rd October 2005. Any one place can experience a total solar eclipse for up to 7 minutes at the most. Even a 6 minute one is a rare event. In 585 BC the Greek philosopher, Thales of Milet, accurately predicted a solar eclipse.
Tides are caused by the gravitational pull of the Moon in connection with that of the Sun. The Moon produces three-fifths of the tidal effect due to its proximity to the Earth, the Sun the remaining two-fifths of the effect. This gravitational pull raises the level of the Earth's water surface by a few metres. When there is a new or full moon, the gravitational pull of the Sun and Moon are added together to create a spring tide with a stronger flood. In the first and last quarters of the Moon's phases, the gravitational pull of the Sun and Moon do not work together which leads to a low neap tide.

4

The blue planet

Our Earth's ability to support life is fascinating and absolutely unique in the solar system. Only on the Earth are the conditions fulfilled for life to exist and develop further. In antiquity, the geocentric view of the world prevailed, so that the Earth, being something special, was seen as the centre of the universe. The planets moved through diverse orbits in the firmament. Not until the 16th century was this view of the world dispelled by the astronomer Copernicus, who saw the Sun as being at the centre.

Present day astronomy is based on his theories. Space travel brought the impressive evidence that the Earth is a sphere. In 1961, the Russian cosmonaut, Yury Gagarin, was the first person to circle our home planet in a satellite. Geometrically however, the Earth is not a globe, but an ellipsoid, because it is flattened slightly at the poles and bulges a little at the Equator.

Origins and evolution of the Earth

The connection between the formation of our Earth 4.5 billion years ago and the formation of the solar system is that they were both formed out of the same rotating, collapsing, interstellar dust cloud with the Sun at its centre. There are two different theories about the later stages of the Earth's formation, because the construction of the shell still poses riddles. The Hot Accretion Theory (accretion = collection of material) states that the Earth was created out of a hot primordial mist. A core rich in iron formed as a result of the Earth's molten state at a very early stage. Deposits of silica formed on the core later creating layers.

According to the Cold Accretion Theory, a solid terrestrial globe of a homogeneous nature was first formed. Through the decay of radioactive el-

ements, the inner Earth heated up to melting-point. The lighter elements rose upward and collected in layers of different chemical composition, whereas the heavier elements sank through gravitation toward the interior and formed the heavy core of the Earth. Then the Earth cooled from the outside inwards and the solid crust and the mantle resulted.

The actual history of the Earth is classified into different epochs that lead from the Ancient Stone Age (Precambrian Period) through the Old Stone Age (Palaeolithic Period) and the Middle Stone Age (Mesolithic Period) to the New Stone Age (Neolithic Period). Fossils of animals and plants preserved in stone are fascinating evidence of the history of the evolution of life. When fossils characterize certain segments of the Earth's history, we call them pioneering fossils. The first appearance of man occurred in the New Stone Age (Pleistocene Period).

Construction of the Earth

An approximately 35 km thick crust forms a solid outer shell around the Earth. Beneath the oceans it is considerably thinner than under the continents. The interior of the Earth has a structure of concentric shells. The outermost crust consists primarily of silica and alumina and therefore gets the name "sial"; the inner crust, called "sima", is named after its main elements silica and magnesium. The mantle or "sifema" is a shell named after its main elements silica, iron and magnesium. The partially liquid upper mantle reaches a depth of 900 km, and joins onto the lower solid mantle which goes a further distance to reach a depth of 2,900 km. The Earth's core, called "nife", composed of nickel and iron, reaches a depth of 2,900 to 6,370 km; the outer core reaches 2,900.-5,100 km

and is glutinous; the inner core is solid. The nearer to the centre of the Earth, the greater the temperature and pressure. Temperatures of 5,000 °C prevail at the centre of the Earth's core, which is 6,370 km beneath the Earth's surface.

Atmosphere

Without an atmosphere, the layer of air enveloping the Earth could not support life. The atmosphere is classified into different layers. The closest layer stretches from the Earth's surface upwards to a height of 10 km (at the poles) and 17 km (at the Equator) and is known as the troposphere. This layer is what is actually responsible for our weather and is characterized by a decreasing temperature of 6.5 °C per km of height, as well as by the forming of cloud and precipitation. The stratosphere, which contains mainly ozone, lies above the troposphere. This ozone layer protects all life on the Earth from harmful ultraviolet radiation (UV rays) emitted by the sun. In recent years a "hole" has formed in the Ozone Layer as the result of man's tratment of the environment. This has caused mankind to rethink basic questions about his relationship to nature. The mesosphere covers the Earth from a height of about 50 to 80 km and is composed of a mixture of gases: 78% nitrogen, 21% oxygen, 1% inert gas (e.g. argon, neon, helium), carbon-dioxide, ozone, water-vapour and aerosol particles. The ionosphere forms a thick blanket (thermosphere) at a height of roughly 80 to 600 km, that refracts and reflects radio waves and produces a spectacular phenomenon called the "Northern or Polar Lights".

1

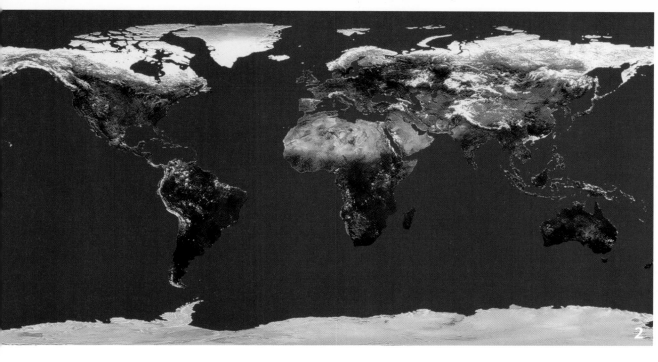

2

The concentration of ions steadily increases up to a height of 1.000 km. The exosphere forms the outermost layer in the interplanetary space in which uncharged atoms can reach a breakaway speed and thus fly off into outer space.

The Earth's rotation

For billions of years our planet has orbited through a universal vacuum. People observed the sky and observed that the Sun, Moon, planets and stars rose and set. These movements, however, only appear to be happening, because in reality they do not move; every 24 hours the Earth completes one spin on its axis (rotation) from west to east, and causes day and night. The Earth takes 365 days, 5 hours, 48 minutes and 46 seconds to go round the Sun in an almost circular ellipse (revolution). The rotation of the Earth started during its formation within the solar system. This primordial force went into a spinning motion and was transmitted to both the Sun and its planets.

Seasons

The axis of our planet is tilted at an angle of 23.5° away from the Equatorial plane (ecliptic tilt). The position of the axis itself hardly changes at all in its rotational orbit around the Sun; it is as good as rigid. Over the course of a year the gradually changing position of the Earth to the Sun causes the seasons. That is why not all parts of the Earth can be shone on evenly at the same time. When the northern hemisphere is tilted toward the Sun and hit by stronger sunlight, then it is summer in the northern hemisphere as well as polar day in the Arctic circle. Polar day is a period of months when a zone in the Arctic is hit with constant sunlight. Simultaneously it is winter in the southern hemisphere and polar night in the Antarctic. A six-month rhythm later tilts the northern hemisphere away from the Sun, so that it is winter in the northern hemisphere and polar night in the Arctic region.

The future of the Earth

If the laws that govern our solar system remain fundamentally unchanged, then there will be an Earth for several billion years to come. In five billion years the Sun will nonetheless have converted all of its nitrogen supply into helium and have inflated into a giant star 60 million km across with a luminosity a thousand times greater than at present. The rising temperatures will cause the Earth's atmosphere to evaporate into outer space and life will no longer be possible. As the temperature on the Sun continues to rise, the incredibly huge Sun will devour the planets Mercury and Venus, and in the end the Sun's surface will reach the present-day orbital path of the Earth. The Earth itself will then orbit the Sun as a burnt planet.

3

Atmosphere
Earth´s Crust
Mantle
Outer crust
Inner crust

Continental crust
Lithosphere
Oceanic crust
Magma
Asthenosphere

The Earth in figures	
The surface of the Earth	510.1 Mio. km^2
of which water	362.0 Mio. km^2
of which dry land (including lakes)	148.1 Mio. km^2
mean distance to the Sun	149.6 Mio. km
diameter at the Equator	12,756.32 km
diameter between the Poles	12,075.55 km
widest radius at the Equator	40,075.161 km
widest radius at the Meridian	40,007.86 km
mass	6 x 10^{27} g
average density (at the core up to)	5,52 g/cm^3 (12 g/cm^3)
mean annual temperature	14°C

Tectonics
the Earth's movements

Since the formation of our restless mother Earth, imperceptible movements have been producing constant but indubitable change to its outward appearance. One glance at a map of the world and it becomes clear that the continents fit together like a jigsaw puzzle.

The east coast of South America and the west coast of South Africa best exemplify this concept. Similarities between stone found on the west African and the Brazilian coast, as well as surprising similarities between the fossils on both continents, led the German scientist Alfred Wegener (1880 - 1930) to formulate his famous theory on how continents move, called the "continental drift". From this idea of "Sea-Floor-Spreading" the theory of plate tectonics, as it is known today, was developed. Wegener suspected the cause of continental drift lay in astronomical forces. Today, however, we know that the forces in the Earth's interior are responsible for the drifting of the plates, which can total 20 cm per year.

At the beginning of the Palaeozoic era (Old Stone Age) the continents were distributed very differently from today. The land-masses moved over the Earth's surface, came to rest against neighbouring fragments, until during the Permian age, 225 million years ago, the continents drew so close to each other that a relatively stable global continent emerged called Pangaea. It broke apart during the further course of the Earth's history. In the outermost layer of the Earth's crust geologically significant processes occur that lead to these plate movements.

Causes of the Plate Movements
Tectonics is the study of the Earth's crust, its construction and the forces and processes that led to its present-day outward appearance. The outermost layers of the Earth are responsible for these movements. They are categorized in two main types. The uppermost stratum is called the "lithosphere" and is the cool and rigid layer that we can see and observe. It encompasses the Earth's crust, as well as parts of the upper mantle. On average it can reach a thickness of up to 100 km, but is thicker in continental regions

than under the ocean. Under this rigid lithosphere lies a hotter and therefore less rigid "asthenosphere", that can be altered by forces from within the interior of the Earth. The asthenosphere produces the effect of a gliding layer on which the solid plates of the lithosphere move. In the lithosphere six large plates can be identified (Pacific plate, Antarctic plate, Indo-Australian plate, American plate, African plate, Eurasian plate) and several smaller ones. The Pacific plate consists of almost completely oceanic lithosphere, the other large plates in contrast are primarily continental lithosphere. At present these plates move at their edges at a rate of about 1 to 20 cm per year either towards each other, away from each other or just past each other.

Plate Edges
The three sorts of plate edges can be distinguished from each other by the direction of their movement. The constant direct head-on collision of two plates leads to **converging**, so-called **destructive** plate edges. If both are continental plates, the Earth's crust is pushed up into inland mountain chains – a process that takes millions of years. The Himalayas are the result of the powerful forces between the Eurasian and the Indian plates. If one is an oceanic plate and the other is a continental plate, the oceanic one most often pushes itself under the continental one, it "dives" under into a subduction zone. The continental plate, on the other hand, pushes up and folds into a chain of mountains. This buckling effect is characterised by deep sea trenches bordering on young fold mountains. As a typical example, the Andes Mountains with the parallel running Atacama Trench formed by the collision of the American plate and the Nazca plate. If the subduction

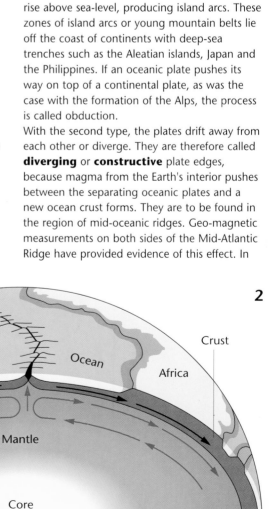

zone lies in the middle of the ocean, one oceanic plate pushes underneath another oceanic plate and buckles into mountains that rise above sea-level, producing island arcs. These zones of island arcs or young mountain belts lie off the coast of continents with deep-sea trenches such as the Aleatian islands, Japan and the Philippines. If an oceanic plate pushes its way on top of a continental plate, as was the case with the formation of the Alps, the process is called obduction.

With the second type, the plates drift away from each other or diverge. They are therefore called **diverging** or **constructive** plate edges, because magma from the Earth's interior pushes between the separating oceanic plates and a new ocean crust forms. They are to be found in the region of mid-oceanic ridges. Geo-magnetic measurements on both sides of the Mid-Atlantic Ridge have provided evidence of this effect. In

Deep sea trenches

The Andes

South America

Atlantic

Ocean

Africa

Crust

Mantle

Core

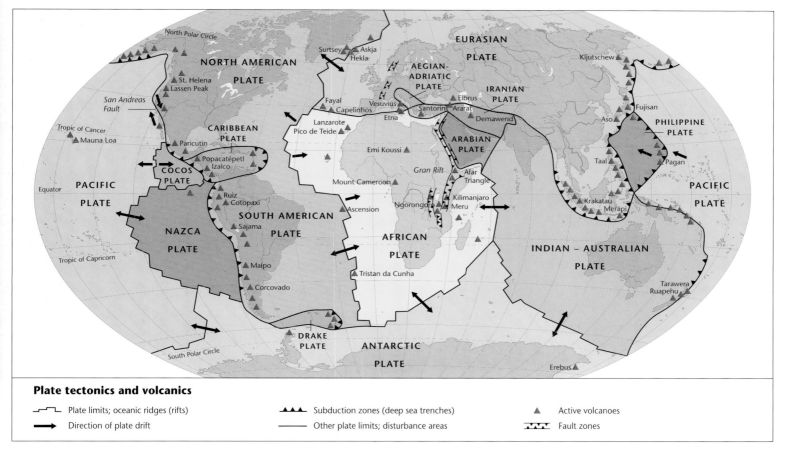

Plate tectonics and volcanics

- ⌐‾L Plate limits; oceanic ridges (rifts)
- ▲▲▲ Subduction zones (deep sea trenches)
- ▲ Active volcanoes
- → Direction of plate drift
- — Other plate limits; disturbance areas
- ⋀⋀⋀ Fault zones

1 Earthquake-proof steel construction: Flat Iron Columbus Tower in San Francisco

2 Schematic structure of tectonic movements

3 Danger of collapse after an earthquake: four-storeyed house near San Francisco

the area of the Atlantic, the ocean floor has been moving apart for 180 million years and has pushed the originally connected continents of Europe and Africa away from America. When continental plates separate from each other, a trench is formed, e.g. the Jordon Trench in the Red Sea. The East African Trench system could represent the beginning stage of continental disintegration.

With the third type, the plates just brush past each other, without new lithosphere being formed or old being destroyed. They are therefore called **conserving** or **conservative** plate edges. The San Andreas Fault is an example of this.

Plate tectonics are the result of the slow creeping movements of the lithosphere over the asthenosphere. Earthquakes and volcanic eruptions occur mainly on the edges of tectonic plates. The belt-like distribution of volcanoes can be traced along tectonic lines, where the Earth's crust is very weak. Forces from the Earth's interior that form the surface of the Earth through volcanic activity, earthquakes and mountains are called endogenic forces.

Oceans *and the larger islands*

The Earth is an anomaly within our planetary system, because only here are found large bodies of water which are essential to the evolution of life. The Earth appears as a blue planet because so much of the planet's surface is dominated by oceans. In fact, 71% of the Earth's surface is covered by water. Aerial photos, taken from space, show how impressive this is.

Oceans

The largest bodies of water are found in the southern hemisphere. The oceans of the world are classified by continental landmasses into the Atlantic, Pacific and Indian Oceans. The smaller seas that extend into mainland areas are classified into channels, straits and sounds, bays, gulfs and seas. The ocean floor has a phantastically varied relief. Surrounding the mainland at a depth of up to 200 m, there are flat continental shelves that drop off abruptly into the depths of the ocean deep-sea basins (to a depth of between 4000-6000 m), deep-sea trenches (e.g. the Mariana Trench in the Pacific 11,034 m below sea-level and thus the deepest point on planet Earth) and mid-ocean ridges; these make up an ocean floor that is just as diversified and bizarre as the structural variety of the landmasses. The creation of these huge forms on the bottom of the ocean can be explained by the Tectonic Plate Theory.

The salt content of the ocean is on average 3.5 %. For different parts of the Earth's liquid surface, the concentration of salt in a body of water varies depending on how much freshwater reaches it from rivers and the rate of evaporation in the area.

The Sun's rays hit the surface of the oceans and warm it up. The temperature drops as one moves from the Equator towards the poles. Wind, currents and tides keep the oceans' waters in constant motion. Planetary wind circulation is a contributing factor in the creation of ocean currents. Ocean currents that flow away from the Equator in the direction of the poles are called warm in contrast to the surrounding volumes of cooler water. As a continuation of the warm Equatorial current, the Gulf Stream, Europe's distant source of heat, transports masses of warm water from the Equatorial regions to the North Cape. Therefore the winter temperatures in Western Europe are higher than its latitudinal norm. The waters that flow in the opposite direction are called "cold currents". The seas have been used by mankind since early times as a transport route and as a source of food and raw materials. Fishing and salt extraction from seawater were carried out by ancient civilisations. Today, mankind's careless use of the oceans causes ever-increasing harm to this underwater world.

The constructive and destructive forces of the oceans can be seen along the coasts, the battle zone between land and sea. The bizarre steep coasts stand most clearly as a testament to the incredible strength of breakers.

Islands

Although islands are simply pieces of land surrounded by water, they have the power to fuel romantic dreams and hold people spellbound by their beauty. As steep rock needles that rise up out of the ocean or as rounded ridges only a few metres above sea level, islands take on a wide spectrum of appearances.

Continental islands along the coast that sit on a continental shelf are primarily what is left over from a formerly connected landmass. Continental islands mostly have geological as well as biological similarities to the neighbouring mainland. Oceanic islands were created either by tectonic forces (volcanic islands) or are a coral formation. In tropical seas along the edges of the continental shelf (socle) **fringing reefs** can be found that have been formed by tiny coral organisms. They can only live in oxygenated, nutrient rich sea water, whose surface temperature does not fall below 20 °C. **Barrier reefs** lie flat along the tropical coasts and are separated from the shore by a saltwater lagoon. The Great Barrier Reef off the coast of eastern Australia is the largest in the world. Circular coral reefs, called **atolls**, are usually formed by the gradual subsidence of an extinct volcano, the coral growing up where the coast once lay. A circular rampart-like reef surrounds a flat lagoon.

The Seychelles with their snow-white beaches, bizarre granite rocks and deep blue lagoons and rich flora and fauna are famous as an ideal holiday destination for tourists and a tropical sea mecca for divers to the north of Madagascar. Around 40 of the islands consist of granite and similar rock, are hilly and fall steeply to the sea. The other 60 flat coral atolls in contrast scarcely poke above sea-level. The islands are surrounded by reefs populated with colourful fish. Behind them are calm lagoons with heavenly beaches. The volcanic island of Hawaii emerged out of the depths of the ocean from a depth of 5,000 m below sea-level to a towering height of 4,000 m above.

1 Signs of movement: cracks in the lava on a volcanic island in the Galapagos

2 A paradise for sportsmen: huge breakers off Hawaii

3 The famous cliffs of the Seven Sisters in Sussex, England

4 Magical underwater world: the Great Barrier Reef off the east coast of Australia

The largest islands	sq km
Greenland	2,130,800
New Guinea	771,900
Borneo	754,000
Madagascar	587,000
Baffin Island	507,451
Sumatra	425,000
Honshu	227,414
Victoria Island	217,290
Great Britain	216,777
Ellesmere Island	196,236
Celebes	189,200
New Zealand, South Island	150,718
Java	118,000
New Zealand, North Island	114,453
Newfoundland	108,860
Cuba	105,007
Luzon (Philippines)	104,688
Iceland	103,100
Mindano (Philippines)	94,630
Ireland	84,403
Hokkaido	77,900
Sakhalin	76,400
Hispaniola	76,192

Oceans	area in Mil. sq km
Atlantic Ocean	106
Indian Ocean	75
Pacific Ocean	180

Continent	area in Mil. sq km
Asia	44
Africa	30
North and Central America	24
South America	18
Antarctica	14
Europe	10
Australia	9

Santorin, one of the Greek islands of the Cyclades group, belongs to a chain of volcanoes that lie on the edge of the zone where the African plate is disappearing under the Aegean plate at a speed of 2 to 4 cm per year. The 400 m deep and 83 km wide sea is nothing more than a gigantic caldera: the volcanic basin was formed after a series of devastating eruptions that made the volcanic cone collapse. The volcanic island of Krakatau in the Sunda Strait, Indonesia, also belongs to an island arc that marks the "swallowing zone" on the border between the Indo-Australian and the Pacific plates. Island plant and animal kingdoms exhibit special features. Certain species are endemic, that means are only found in those regions. One example is the Galapagos Islands which is called "Tortoise Island", because of its unique fauna including giant tortoises, iguanas, penguins and Darwin's finches. It was here that Darwin formulated his Theory of Evolution.

out of Earth's depth

Numerous myths are connected with mountains spewing fire, which is interpreted both as a blessing and a curse. Despite the disastrous effects volcanoes inflict, they captivate mankind nonetheless. They are praised as the home of the gods or worshipped is if they were gods themselves and therefore offered sacrifices. Mount Fujiyama (3,776 m), a dormant volcano and the symbol of Japan, can be seen from 13 different provinces. Anyone who wants to be considered truly Japanese, should climb once in his lifetime to the top of where the gods make their home, Mount Fujiama.

Volcanoes

Volcanic activity occurs principally along the edges of tectonic plates – the weakest zone in the Earth's crust. Volcanoes are created when magma, a mixture of gases and hot liquefied rock, pushes through cracks in the Earth's crust as lava onto the Earth's surface. Ash and slag collect around the main vent and form a crater. A ring shaped crater, called a caldera, is formed through a collapse or when a strong eruption catapults the top of an existing cone off.

We differentiate between active, dormant and extinct volcanoes. Even after centuries of inactivity, volcanoes can suddenly erupt, as was the case of Pinatubo on 9.9.1991 in the Philippines. Most of the active volcanoes are found in the region of the Pacific Ocean. **Andesitic volcanoes** are found in areas where the Earth's surface is being pushed together. They take their name from the Andes. **Basaltic volcanoes** are found where surfaces are pulling apart. Very runny lava material forms a basaltic volcano; in Hawaii there are many broad low ones. When an andesitic volcano is being formed, hardened lava often clogs the vent.

Eruptions can be violent as the blockage is blasted free, as in the eruption of Mt. St Helens in North America in 1980. Mount Vesuvius, that towers up behind Naples with its twin peaks, is also an example of this type. In 79 AD it buried the city of Pompeii under 6 - 10 m of ash in one eruption.

Although intensive observation through volcanology is undertaken throughout the world, the exact time of an eruption is very difficult to predict. Volcanoes give off warning signals long before they erupt through various phenomena connected with the rising up of the magma in the Earth's interior. Intense pressure can be registered in the surrounding layers of rock that cause cracks to form and an earthquake to happen. There are observable changes in the Earth's magnetic fields and an intensified escape of volcanic gases.

Large cities, such as Naples, Yokohama, Jakarta and Honululu, were built in the immediate vicinity of a volcano. The lava, that through weathering had became fertile soil, led to dense settlement of the volcano's slopes. Volcanic rock, such as basalt, is a good material for road building.

Geysers and other post-volcanic formations

Even after the actual volcanic eruption, there is post-volcanic activity that can be observed in following centuries. Hot springs, or geysers, are the most well-known and spectacular. As soon as the boiling point in the ascent passage is reached, they discharge jets of hot water into the air at regular intervals. The largest collection of geysers and hot springs in the world is to be found in Yellowstone National Park in the USA. Around 200 geysers, many of them only 1 to 2 m high, present a natural display of strength and beauty. "Old Faithful" reliably discharges an explosive column of steam and hot water in a fountain to a height of up to 50m at hourly intervals.

The volcanic origin of Iceland is denoted by frequent volcanic activity and numerous hot springs. Some of them are geysers. On Iceland, the warmth is used to heat homes and hothouses. The Northern Island of New Zealand offers a natural spectacle with its volcanic highland (Ruapehu 2,802 m) that is blessed with geysers and thermal springs. Other post-volcanic phenomena include Solfatara (Ital. solfo = sulphur steam springs containing sulphur with tem-

1 Volcanic eruption on Mauna Ulu, Hawaii

2 The ruins of Pompeii, destroyed in 79 AD. In the background is Vesuvius, whose last major eruption occurred in 1944

3 Already cooled lava on a road close to the Aloi Crater, Hawaii

4 A path through the volcanic ash covered area around the Kilauea Crater

peratures between 100 and 200 °C), Fumarole ("exhalation of gas", steam springs with temperatures between 200 and 800 °C) and Moffette (carbon-dioxide emissions at temperatures under 100 °C).

Earthquakes

The best-known earthquake zone in the world is the San Andreas Fault, which runs in a straight line through California. The plate edges of the North American plate and the Pacific plate, so called conservative plates edges, push against each other. Quakes on the plate edges are named after their formation process, tectonic quakes (90 % of all earthquakes). San Fransisco, the city that awaits death, lives under the constant threat of the next big earthquake.

Earthquakes can also be categorized according to how they originate. Volcanic quakes (7 % of all quakes) are closely connected with volcanic activity. Collapsing quakes (3 % of the cases) originate from the collapsing of hollow spaces. The force of an earthquake can be measured with a seismograph and given a rating on the Richter scale from one upwards. Quakes under 4 are considered as weak, quakes with a rating of 8, on the other hand, are destructive. The strongest shakes and shocks occur at the epicentre – the place directly above the focus of the earthquake which is located in the depths of the earth's crust or in the uppermost part of the mantle. Earthquake focus points are frequently located at a depth of about 20 km. Also in the surrounding region, the earthquake zone, the quakes can be clearly felt. Earthquakes last from a few seconds to a maximum of four minutes.

Hills and caverns

Mountains and caves are a source of unending fascination to mankind and awaken the imagination. Shrouded in mystery, the highest mountain peaks in the world are considered to be the roof of the world or home of the gods. Hidden places within the Earth, caverns or caves, were the realm of dwarfs in myths and fairy tales, who wanted to lock up their treasures in the darkness. Mountains are easily visible from a great distance, but the discovery of caves may well depend on chance.

Caves

Thousands of caves lie widely distributed around the world, and new ones are still being found. **Primary caves**, large hollow spaces or cavities in rock, may have been formed during the rock's formation itself, such as bubble and lava caves in volcanic rock or reef caves in coral reefs. Most caves, however, are formed as **secondary caves** by outside forces, called exogenic forces, on already formed rock. Examples are caves formed by breakers or formed through marine erosion, such as the Blue Grotto on Capri. Landslide caves are formed through the falling in of masses of stone along clefts. The largest caves are formed by water dissolving rock, especially in limestone mountains. Karst is the name given to formations above and below the ground that were created through the mechanical or chemical effect of water on porous limestone. The karst caves sometimes form very complicated cave systems. Stalactites (like icicles) that grow from above can connect with stalagmites (like pillars) that grow from the floor.

Speleology, or the study of caves, involves their exploration as well as research regarding their settlement. Prehistoric man used caves as shelter, refuge and living quarters. Famous cave paintings such as the ones in Altamira made during the New Stone Age bear witness to these

early cultures. Uluru (Ayers Rock), a sandstone monolith south-west of Alice Springs, is unique. The largest monolith on Earth (9.4 km circumference, 2.4 km wide, 3.6 km long and 348 m high) it is the most famous mountain and the symbol of Australia. Countless myths and legends surround it. It is worshipped by the native population, the Aborigines, as a sanctuary. They believe it to be a giant sleeping whale formed out of a sand dune and call it Uluru. "Weathered caves" were formed in the cleft sandstone with mica outcrops, in which the Aborigines met and worshipped the gods. Artistic rock drawings steeped in mystery preserve the symbols, history and myths of the Aborigines.

Mountains

The surface of the Earth's crust is the result of a manifold game of strength. The soft brows and ridges of the highlands do not excite the bystander as much as the rocky bluffs, sharp ridges and steep, towering peaks of majestic high mountains. The highest mountains in the world, the Himalayan Mountains, present 14 peaks over 8000 m. The longest mountain system in the world are the Cordilleras, which are over 15,000 km long. This fold mountain system on the west coast of North and South America extends from Alaska to Tierra del Fuego.

Mountains were formed through inner (**endogenic**) forces and immediately altered by outer (**exogenic**) forces. Fold mountains originated from the huge hollows of **geosynclines** (Geosyncline: a slowly sinking piece of the Earth's crust) that were near the coast and flooded by the sea. Sediment was deposited and mountains formed during relatively calm times. These were then folded and in part pushed above one another and raised. Mountains formed in this way were immediately subject to the forces of erosion (temperature extremes, wind, water and ice), destroyed and modelled. **Old fold moun-**

tains were fold mountains that through erosion over a period of millions of years became worn down to a hump. Through forces from the Earth's interior they were sometimes lifted again and broken into individual clods. The raised clods form **horsts**; those which sank form basins, trenches, rifts or hollows.

During the course of the Earth's history there were several epochs of mountain formation. We distinguish three mountain formation periods since the Earth's Old Stone Age; the Caledonic (end of the Silurain period: the Scandinavian Mountains, Scotland), the Varistic (during the carboniferous period: fold mountains in central

1 Ice age cave paintings from Altamira, Spain

2 The large stalactite cavern in Carlsbad, USA

3 This stalagmite has been growing for over a thousand years in a Mayan pot, Belize

4 Panorama of the Grand Teton National Park, Rocky Mountains, USA

5 Torres del Paine, Chile

6 Close up of Uluru (Ayers Rock), Australia

7 The roof of the world: Mount Everest, Nepal

Europe), and Alpidic mountain formation (tertiary: the present-day high mountains of the Earth, such as the Alps, Pyrenees, Himalayas, Apennines, Atlas, Carpathian, Caucasus and the North and South American west coast mountains).

Climatic conditions change not only from Equator to pole but also with increasing elevation. The intensity of the sun's rays, in particular the harmful UV rays, increases with elevation, while air pressure and temperature simultaneously decrease. In high mountains areas, the elevation determines the type of vegetation. Whereas in the Alps the snow-line lies at an altitude of 2,600 m, in the Andes on the Equator at this height plant varieties of a temperate latitude such as potatoes and barley can be cultivated. The snow line there is at 5,000 m.

The young mountains of the Himalayas, which means "home of the snow" have little snow in comparison with other high mountains in the world. The New Zealander, Edmund Hillary, and Sherpa Tenzing Norgay, were the first to climb to the top of the 8,848m peak of Mount Everest. Countless mountaineers before and after them have paid for their attempts with their lives.

Glaciers offer a natural spectacle; in high mountain ranges above the snow-line, ice-flows are formed that slowly flow down into the valley and melt below the snow-line. The meltwater collects in a glacial stream.

Earth's deepest caves	Depth in m
Réseau du Foillis	1 455
Gouffre de la Pierre-Saint Martin	1 325
Jubiläumsschacht	1 320
Sistema Huautla	1 250
Sneschnaja peschtschera	1 200
Gouffre Berger	1 198
Sima Liquerda	1 192
Mammuthöhle	1 170
Batman-Schacht	1 160
Sistema Badalona	1 104
Schneeloch	1 101
Sima G.E.S.M.	1 098
Réseau des Aiguilles	980
Garma Ciega/Sumidero de Cellarga	970
Gouffre Jean-Bernard	934
Gouffre André Touya	930

our lifelines

Rivers have always been a lifeline for settlement and transport. Massive rivers dominate the countryside of various zones of the Earth. At their source they are still small and insignificant, along their path they are joined by tributaries, near the sea they reach gigantic dimensions. A river forms its bed depending on the gradient of its descent. The volume of water and the amount and type material carried also play a significant role. The rocks in the subsoil are subject either to erosion or sedimentation. This results in differing valley forms.

Canyons and fjords

A special kind of valley is the canyon. As in the case of a **gorge**, the water completely fills up the lowest part of the valley so that there is no valley floor, only steep banks. The slopes do not even out since horizontal layers of sedimentary rock form projecting steps due to the differing resistance factors of the stone. The most famous example of this type of valley is the Grand Canyon in the USA, breathtaking on account of its vast dimensions and varying formations and colours. It took millions of years for the Colorado River to create this gigantic natural phenomenon. The typical and very prominent meanderings in the river began at the time when the river snaked across the land only a few metres above sea-level. Then at the period when the land was pushed up, the river remained caught in its old bed and carved out the gorge. The result is a picture book of the Earth's history, a chronicle showing the different layers of rock from the beginning of the Middle Stone Age through to the Ancient Stone Age.

Fjords are impressive land formations. During the Ice Age northern Europe was covered by huge ice sheets. The glaciers transformed what were river valleys into U-shaped troughs, into which the sea forced its way after the melting of the ice. The Norwegian fjords offer unspoilt nature covering large stretches of land.

Delta formation

In a wide valley with only a slight gradient, a river will **meander** many times like a snake in the grass. On the outside of a bend in the river the water is fastest and therefore also the strongest, and through its power a steep escarpment is formed. On the inside, where the water flows slowest, there is a build-up of deposited material, a soft flat **slip-off slope** is formed and **oxbow lakes** can result. In the lower courses of the river where the gradient is gentle, fine sediment and suspended matter are deposited. Some rivers form a **delta** into the sea.

Grandiose delta formations can be seen in the rivers Mississippi, Ganges, Brahmaputra, Hwangho, Nile and Po.

Waterfalls

The bubbling and cascading splendour of a large waterfall is a mystical natural wonder. Rivers work unceasingly to remove the unevenness in their paths by erosion. Waterfalls are a sign that a river cannot be very old. Most are found in mountains where ice from the last Ice Age melted about 10,000 years ago or are still covered by glaciers. The water falls over one or more steps (cascades) into the depths. The speed of the current and consequently the erosive force of the river at these points is particularly strong.

The Iguaçu Falls are in the mountains of southern Brazil. The river divides up into countless arms and falls into a deep gorge forming 275 waterfalls. What makes it so spectacular is less the height of the falls (only 60 to 80 m), than their extraordinary width. The rumbling volumes of water collect in a 20 m wide and more than 1 km long gorge, called "Garganta del Diabola", "The Devil's Jaws". The appearance of waterfalls

Largest inland lakes	Area in sq km	depth in m
Caspian Sea	371 001	1 000
Upper Lake	82 103	405
Lake Victoria	69 483	81
Lake Aral	64 501	68
Lake Tanganyika	32 893	1 417
Lake Baikal	31 499	1 620
Lake Ladago	17 703	225
Lake Titicaca	8 288	281

1 Satellite picture of the Ganges delta in Bangladesh

2 Fjord cut deep into the mountain in Alaska

3 Impressive view at Crater Lake National Park, USA

4 Fantastic play of form and colour in the Grand Canyon, USA

High Waterfalls	Height of falls
Angel Falls, Venezuela	970 m
Yosemite Falls, California	739 m
Cuqueán Falls, Venezuela	610 m
Sutherland Falls, New Zealand	580 m
Roraima Falls, Guayana	457 m
Gavarnie Falls, France	422 m
Tugela Falls, Rep. South Africa.	411 m
Krimmler Waterfalls, Austria	380 m
Giessbach Falls, Switzerland	300 m

River	Continent	Length in km	Flows into
Nile (with the Kagera)	Africa	6 671	Mediterrenean
Amazon	South America	6 518	Atlantic Ocean
Mississippi (with the Missouri)	North America	6 030	Atlantic Ocean
Yangtsekiang	Asia	6 000	East China Sea
Ob (with the Irtysch)	Asia	5 400	Kara Sea
Hwangho	Asia	4 845	Yellow Sea
Mekong	Asia	4 500	South China Sea
Amur (with the Argun)	Asia	4 444	Sea of Okhotsk
Lena	Asia	4 440	Laptev Sea
Congo	Asia	4 374	Atlantic Ocean

how the largest lakes in the world, such as Lake Victoria, were formed.

Thousands of years ago people settled on the shores of the largest inland lake in Africa, Lake Victoria which is full of fish. It is, in comparison with other large lakes, only of moderate depth (40 m on average and 84 m at its deepest point). This lake, located in the basin of the African highland and with innumerable islands and extensive marshlands, is one of the few large waters to remain unpolluted. Because it is so shallow, the wind is able to mix the water of the lake vertically and even the deepest areas are always supplied with oxygen. Thus fish can live in all parts of the lake, which is impossible in the deep trench lakes in East Africa.

The deepest lakes are to be found in tectonic faults which formed trenches in the Earth's crust (Lake Baikal, the deepest lake on Earth, the Dead Sea, Lakes Tanganyika and Nyasssa in East Africa).

Picturesque and perfectly circular lakes fill the craters of countless volcanoes.

Man-made reservoirs are used for drinking water and energy, regulation of the water level and irrigation.

changes constantly. The Horseshoe Falls (54 m high) on the east bank of the Niagara are also fascinating with their receding up-river erosion.

Inland lakes

Lakes form in depressions and hollows in the Earth's surface. They are formed either through deepening or damming up. Most lakes were formed by glacial erosion, moraine deposits, meandering rivers and meltwater from ice blocks (dead ice). Large lakes are therefore found in regions that were covered with glaciers in geologically recent times (Pleistocene), such as the Great Lakes in North America, in northern Europe and northern Asia. The lake system of the Five Great Lakes on the border between Canada and the USA form the largest connecting area of freshwater in the world. Connected to the Atlantic by the St. Lawrence Seaway, they are also the most important commercial inland waterway on Earth.

In places where tectonic forces pushed up or lowered the Earth's crust, **synclines** or troughs were formed, that filled up with water. This is

and vegetation belts

The Earth's climate has always influenced plant, animal and human life in that they adapted to the prevailing conditions. Burgeoning settlements sprang up in areas with a favourable climate. Climatically inclement regions remain deserted and empty. In this way the climate sets a natural limit to human activities.

Weather – Weather Conditions – Climate

Under the term **weather** we understand the momentary combination of meteorological elements: the temperature, the air-pressure, the humidity, the wind, the precipitation and the cloud cover in one particular place. The weather

has been known to change hourly in some particular areas. **Weather conditions** refers to weather that is similar over a period of days or weeks. **Seasonal weather** prevail during a particular time of year and reoccur regularly. **Climate** is the umbrella word for the totality of the atmospheric conditions and activity that have been observed in a particular place or region over a long period of time. Science classifies climate according to main types that vary from polar to tropical climates. A **climatic zone** refers to large regions of the Earth where the main climatic elements of precipitation and temperature are the same during the course of a year. The climatic conditions on the Earth dictate which plants can grow. The Earth can also be classified into large **vegetation zones** that are closely dependent on the climatic zones. When distinguishing between large vegetation and climatic zones certain essentials need to be observed: Their occurrence is not just influenced by the Sun's rays, which are to a large extent dependent on the geographical latitude; the distribution of land and water surfaces, the height above sea-level, the shape and form of the land

and the influence of ocean currents also all play a role, just as the location on either the east or west side of the continent does too. The snow covered peaks of the Himalayas (a), the desert regions of the Sahara (b), and Florida with the famous sunbathing paradise in Palm Beach (c), are all on the same degree of latitude.

The Tropics

Tropical climates can be classified into two branches. The constantly humid always wet tropics and the humid summer, seasonally wet tropics. The constantly humid tropics lie on both sides of the Equator. The 1,500 mm of precipitation is evenly distributed over the whole year, but has an absolute maximum during the two rainy periods. Taken overall it can be said that the hallmarks of this climate are the consistently high air humidity and temperature. The average

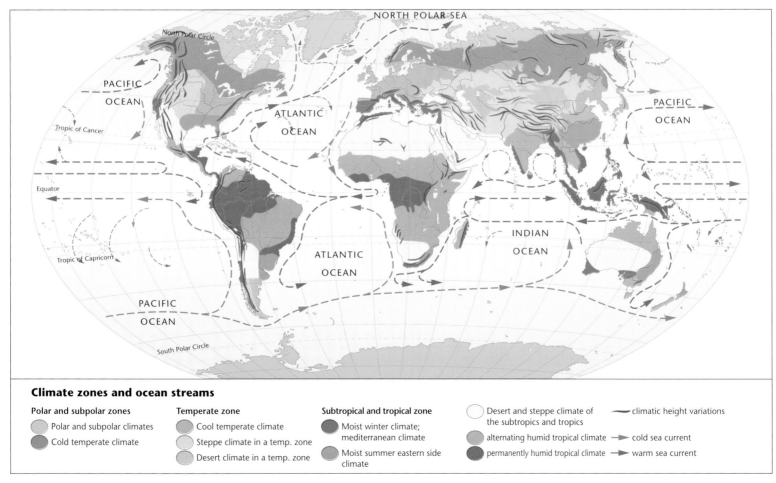

Climate zones and ocean streams

Polar and subpolar zones	Temperate zone	Subtropical and tropical zone	
◯ Polar and subpolar climates	◯ Cool temperate climate	◯ Moist winter climate; mediterranean climate	◯ Desert and steppe climate of the subtropics and tropics — climatic height variations
◯ Cold temperate climate	◯ Steppe climate in a temp. zone	◯ Moist summer eastern side climate	◯ alternating humid tropical climate → cold sea current
	◯ Desert climate in a temp. zone		◯ permanently humid tropical climate → warm sea current

annual temperature is 25 °C. The fluctuation in average monthly temperatures during a year amounts to 6 °C at most. Hence there are no seasons, only a variation in temperature between day and night of about 10 °C. During the course of a day there are patterns that can be determined, so that we can speak of a "time of day climate". Under these conditions the growth possibilities for vegetation are excellent. The vegetation belt of luxuriant green tropical rain forest with its immense wealth of plant species and levels of vegetation occurs here naturally. The humid summer tropics are typified by alternating rainy and dry periods. The closer one gets to the tropics, the longer the dry period lasts. Of the two rainy periods close to the Equator, only one is experienced close to a tropic. During the day high fluctuations in temperature are recorded. Moving out of the Equatorial trop-

ical rain forest belt towards the Tropics of Capricorn and Cancer, one finds a vegetation belt of tropical savannahs and deserts. The rule is: The longer the dry season lasts, the more sparse the plant growth is, the more the plants have to adapt to the dry conditions.

In a humid savannah the landscape is covered with tufts of grass that grow above the head, and richly mixed deciduous forests. In the dry season the trees sometimes shed their foliage. In a dry savannah, the landscape is covered in an even grass carpet and has thin forests. The plants have adapted to the dryness by forming hard leather-like leaves as well as roots and stems that can hold water.

In the thorny savannah grass cover has become patchy. Characteristic are the individual trees that through an umbrella-like crown are able to adapt to the dry conditions. Precipitation no

longer falls on the outermost edge of the tropics. The savannah changes into tropical desert, which extend into the subtropical zone. Even in the desert life is possible, however, only for plants that can survive a dry spell lasting several years. After a rare rainfall the desert blooms with green.

The Subtropics

A subtropical climate is something between a tropical and a temperate climate. As an essential difference between tropical and subtropical regions, the latter has **seasons** instead of a rainy and dry period as experienced in the tropics. On either side of the Tropics of Capricorn and Cancer hot summer semi-deserts and desert regions (Sahara, Arabian Peninsula, Central Australian) are found. There are two differing types of climate on the same line of latitude: the **humid winter Mediterranean climate** and the **humid summer or always humid eastern climate**. The Mediterranean climate is characterized by hot, dry summers with an average temperature of 25 °C during the summer months, whereas in the winter it is rainy with cooler temperatures. Thus we speak of rainy winter regions. This climatic region on the west side of the continents can produce evergreen plants. They protect themselves against evaporation with small, thick, hairy, leathery leaves. Pine, laurel and cypress are characteristic trees. The humid winter evergreen forests in the Euro-

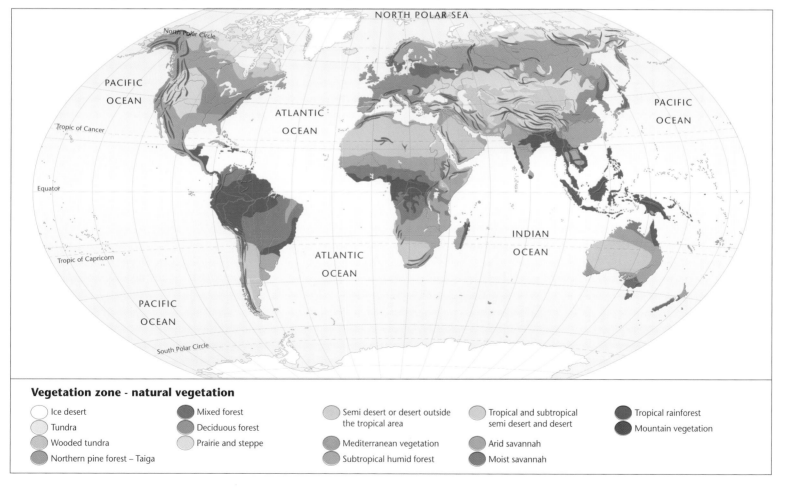

Vegetation zone - natural vegetation

- Ice desert
- Tundra
- Wooded tundra
- Northern pine forest – Taiga
- Mixed forest
- Deciduous forest
- Prairie and steppe
- Semi desert or desert outside the tropical area
- Mediterranean vegetation
- Subtropical humid forest
- Tropical and subtropical semi desert and desert
- Arid savannah
- Moist savannah
- Tropical rainforest
- Mountain vegetation

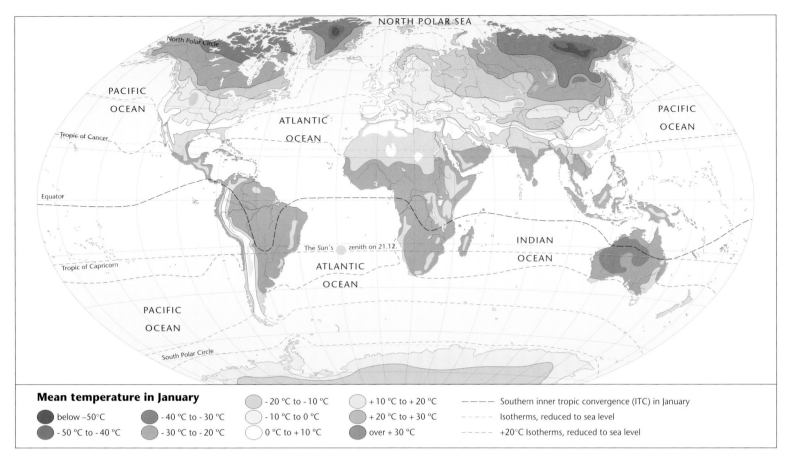

Mean temperature in January

● below –50 °C	● - 40 °C to - 30 °C	○ - 10 °C to 0 °C	● +20 °C to +30 °C
● - 50 °C to - 40 °C	● - 30 °C to - 20 °C	○ 0 °C to +10 °C	● over +30 °C
	● - 20 °C to - 10 °C	● +10 °C to +20 °C	

– – – Southern inner tropic convergence (ITC) in January
– – – Isotherms, reduced to sea level
– – – +20°C Isotherms, reduced to sea level

pean part of the Mediterranean have been cut down to a large extent.

The humid summer or always humid eastern climate is found on the eastern side of the continents. The eastern part of the continents receives humidity in the summer too, and as such is always humid. So the always humid forests enriches the landscape of the subtropics with bamboo and magnolia and luxuriant shrubs.

The Temperate Climate

A temperate climate has four seasons. It is characterized by distinct differences in temperature between summer and winter, and prevailing westerly winds. The west side of the continents receive precipitation from prevailing west winds all year round; one speaks of an ocean climate. The following rule holds true: The closer a place is to the sea, the less the temperatures fluctuate on an annual average. Bodies of water have a moderating effect on temperature. On the other hand, as one moves farther away from the ocean one speaks of a continental climate (inland climate) in the interior of large mainland areas. The temperature fluctuations during the course of a year increase with the distance from the ocean. The summer temperatures become higher, the winter temperatures lower.

In Europe there are the following divisions:
1. an oceanic climate in Western Europe
2. a continental climate in Eastern Europe
3. a central European climate forming a transi-

tion with mild oceanic influences in the west and slight continental characteristics in the east. The deciduous and mixed forests that originally existed in oceanic and central European climates have, to a large extent, been cut down and the area turned into cultivated land. A continental climate has steppes, extensive grassland that is almost without trees and shrubs in the moderate as well as the subtropical zones. The prairies of North America or the

steppes in the interior of Asia are an example. Decisive is that the moisture is no longer sufficient for forests to grow.

Sub-Polar Zone

In a sub-polar climatic zone and the transition to the polar zone, there is a zone of boreal (the north wind) coniferous forests with pine, spruce and larch. In Siberia these forests are called taiga. The number of days in Siberia with moderate

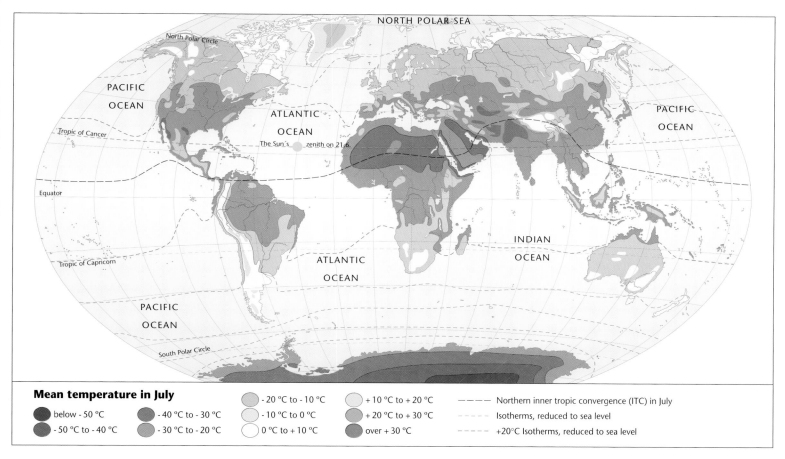

Mean temperature in July

- below - 50 °C
- - 50 °C to - 40 °C
- - 40 °C to - 30 °C
- - 30 °C to - 20 °C
- - 20 °C to - 10 °C
- - 10 °C to 0 °C
- 0 °C to + 10 °C
- + 10 °C to + 20 °C
- + 20 °C to + 30 °C
- over + 30 °C
- ——— Northern inner tropic convergence (ITC) in July
- - - - - Isotherms, reduced to sea level
- - - - - +20°C Isotherms, reduced to sea level

temperatures of over 10 °C fall to a mere 120 days per year. The long cold winter is interrupted only by a short warm summer. Due to its extreme continental nature there is very little precipitation. In the southern hemisphere this zone does not exist, because there is no large landmass at this particular latitude.

Polar Zone

Within the Polar Circle the change from polar day to polar night and the low average temperatures characterize this climatic zone. There are less than 30 days per year of average temperatures of over 10 °C. Tundra, treeless vegetation of lichens, mosses, grass and low shrubs can be found here. Life threatening ice deserts lead to the polar caps.

Climatic Changes

The Earth's climate is influenced by the continual changes that take place over time and in space. The climatic events in the troposphere (weather bearing layer of the atmosphere) are held in a delicate balance that has formed the present-day climatic zones. However, they did not always exist in this form. In the history of the Earth long warm periods were interrupted time and again by ice ages. Fossils and also cave drawings give us hints to the climates of the past. Is it possible to speak about climatic changes during the course of the Earth's history? In a historical time frame they are merely climatic fluctuations for which there have been various attempts at clarification.

Causes for Fluctuations

One cause could be the fluctuations in the Sun's energy that reaches us in the form of rays. The Sun's rays are not even, but are influenced by violent eruptions on the Sun. These fluctuations underlie an 11 year cycle that is reflected in weather patterns. Another cause could be the reduction in the atmosphere's ability to allow rays from the Sun to penetrate because fine ash from volcanic eruptions orbit around the troposphere for years. This causes a corresponding decrease in average temperatures.

Man's interference with nature has become a noticeable factor that is playing an increasing role in climatic change. Since industrialization began in Europe at the end of the 18th century, the composition of the atmosphere has worsened due to emissions (emanation of polluted air). Greenhouse gases (carbon-dioxide, nitrogen, methane, CFC) increasingly cause changes. Thus the carbon-dioxide content in the atmosphere has increased by 25% in the last 100 years. The concentration of carbon dioxide in the atmosphere has the effect of a glass window in a greenhouse. Sunlight reaches the Earth, but radiation back into the universe is prevented.

The Earth is warming up and the greenhouse effect results. The world-wide average temperature has risen by about 0.5 °C during this same period. According to a computer simulation, by the year 2030 the temperature may rise by a further 1.2 °C. The world-wide rise in the tem-

① *Picture from space: a hurricane over the Atlantic Ocean off the east coast of Florida*

perature means that the polar ice caps and glaciers can further melt leading to a corresponding rise in the sea-level and the flooding of flat coastal lowlands around the world. This would mean the flooding of large areas throughout the world. The most obvious example is that of Holland which is already protected by dykes. Either the dykes would have to be raised or the land reclaimed originally from the sea would again return to sea.

El Niño

It has not been established whether El Niño is caused by man's interference with natural processes connected with global warming. El Niño, a climatological anomaly, that has its starting point in the Central and East Pacific, has been made responsible for numerous regional weather extremes and natural catastrophes.

El Niño (Spanish for boy, allusion to the Christ child) occurs in intervals of three to nine years and is particularly fierce during the Christmas period, that is the summer time in the southern hemisphere.

magnificient ecosystems

Nicknamed "green hell" or "white man's grave", tropical rain forests are at all events an extraordinary ecological system. The wealth of plant and animal species here is unique in the world; a manifold living space that is increasingly threatended by people with commercial interests.

The Hothouse Climate and the Wealth of Species

Tropical climates are classified into the constantly humid (always humid) tropics and the humid summer (changeably humid) tropics. An isotherm of 20 °C is the standard boundary for the tropics. The region of constantly humid tropical weather (inner tropics) lies on both sides of the Equator 5 ° north and south in latitude and has low air pressure and still winds (calm).

In the ITC (inter tropical convergence zone), rising masses of hot air are the cause of high precipitation throughout the entire year (min. 1,500 mm/year). An oppressive sultriness prevails with constant high temperatures of 24 ° to 28 °C. There are no seasons, only a fluctuation in temperature between day and night. Because the course of the day follows a set rhythm, one speaks of a "time of day" climate. These climatic conditions have a paralysing effect on Europeans. On the other hand, this hothouse climate provides the always humid, always green tropical rain forests with a superlative cover of vegetation.

Different "storeys" of vegetation are the result of competition between the plants for sunlight. At the bottom there is a layer of shrubs and foliage that prefer the shade, on the second level trees of an average size force their way through the undergrowth. A thick roof of leaves from the medium size trees form the third level. Only solitary 60 m giant-sized trees that stand on pillar-like, board shaped roots, tower above all else on the fourth level. The wealth of plants and animals is unique in this world. There are colourful plants such as flamingo plants, orchids and African violets, well-known as house-plants, as well as over 100 different species of tree per hectare, among them tropical woods such as teak, palisander, mahogany and ebony. Creepers climb through all of the levels.

All phases of growth can be found immediately next to each other: buds, ripe fruit, withered and green leaves all on the same plant.

This occurs throughout the year, because foliage loss is distributed over the course of the whole year and not limited to autumn as in temperate latitudes, hence the term "evergreen". The impenetrable thicket is populated by huge snakes such as the anaconda, capuchin and other types of monkey, humming birds and colourful parrots. On the ground beetles, snails, frogs, ants, all larger than in Europe, take advantage of the food on offer, namely insects, fruits and other small animals. Life in immeasurable extensiveness and in abundance!

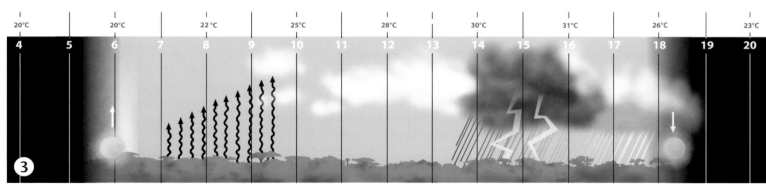

Living space of the native population

In spite of its riches, the rain forests have never been densely populated; it is the home of native people who roam in small groups through the forests as hunters and collectors. The Pygmies, who grow to a height of only 140 cm, still practise this traditional lifestyle. They are a form of African society ideally suited to their environment. Nature supplies them with all they require. Their motto is using without destroying! Other tribal groups, such as the Bantus in Africa

1　Fallen giant trees are immediately overgrown

2　Brightly coloured: the red-eyed tree frog

3　The day in the Tropics: mornings evaporation, after-noons rain

4　About the size of a squirrel: marmoset in the Amazon rain-forest, Brazil

5　Morning mist over Lacan-dona Rainforest, Chiapas, Mexico

6　Schematic diagram of the levels of a rainforest

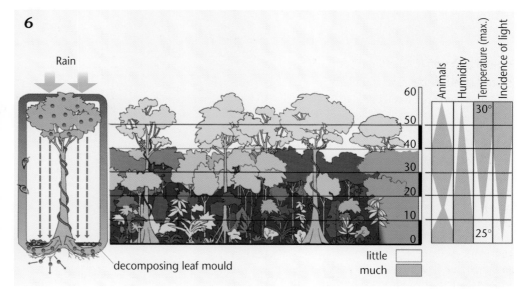

Rain

decomposing leaf mould

little
much

Animals | Humidity | Temperature (max.) | Incidence of light

30°

25°

or the Indians in the Amazon Basin, have developed a simple form of farming. Small fields are prepared by cutting and burning trees. Between the stumps they loosen the soil with a stick made out from a branch or a primitive hoe and sow corn, peanuts and rice or plant shoots of banana, palms or manioc. Originally these tribal people cultivated only as much as they needed to survive (self-sufficiency or subsistence farming).

The valuable mineral nutrients in the soil are soon washed away by the heavy precipitation. After two to three years the yield decreases and they make a new village and new fields in a new area. A poorer sort of degenerated secondary forest grows on the fallow lands and can be cleared again after about 25 years. If this pattern continues, only coarse grass and shrubs will be able to grow on the barren ground.

Destruction of the rain forests

A section of rain forest the size of a football pitch disappears irreversibly every second; that is 30 million hectares per year. Causes for the destruction are the growing demands in industrial countries for tropical wood for furniture and construction. More and more land is being cleared for plantations that produce sought-after tropical crops: kautshuk, bananas, pineapples and cocoa, and at higher elevations, also coffee.

In order to open up and exploit the rich mineral deposits (e.g. petroleum, iron ore, copper, nickel, manganese, gold), transport routes are built that cut deeply into the forests. Often road building is only the beginning of harsh clear cutting. The rain forests already laid to waste in this way in the Amazon would cover the area of several European countries put together.

This kind of large-scale and quick destruction process by mankind disturbs the food-chain as well as the hydrologic cycle. The unrelenting heavy rains pelt and wash away the soil (ground erosion). Luxuriant vegetation no longer holds the water and so local precipitation decreases in regions that have been cleared on a large-scale and the water table sinks. These local changes influence atmospheric circulation which in its turn influences the world's climate. The damage caused by this destruction affects not only the native people living in this region, but all mankind.

harsh living conditions

Arabs called the deserts "Bahr bela ma"- seas without water. Hot and dry, empty and hostile, deserts make up 15% of the surface area on the continents. They stretch either like a belt around the Earth or extend across specific areas. A common characteristic is the extreme all year round aridity. Strong evaporation outweighs the minimal precipitation. According to their origin, three types of "genetic" deserts can be defined.

Desert Types

Tropical deserts are formed due to tropical air circulation. The dry Passat trade-winds on their way to the Equator do not have an opportunity to enrich themselves with moisture or give off rain, so that widespread deserts result. This almost world-wide trade-wind belt of deserts lies between the tropics (23.5° north and south latitude). The Sahara, the Thar and the Arabian Deserts belong to this type.

Rain-shadow deserts are created when a trade-wind passes over an area of water and absorbs moisture, and then deposits the rainfall on the windward side of the mountain as it is forced to rise, so that the leeward side of the mountain remains dry. Precipitation decreases over the land to the west (Kalahari, Australian deserts).

Coastal deserts are found on the western coast of continents. Cold ocean currents (Bengali Stream off the west coast of Africa, Humbold Stream off the west coast of South America) and buoyant cold water made choppy by land winds, cause the moisture in the sea air to condense before it can reach the coast (Namib, Atacama Deserts).

Continental deserts, or inland deserts, are located at greater latitudes in the interior of the continent, in enclosed basins, on the leeward side of high mountains and in areas far from the sea on large landmasses (Great Plains in the USA, Gobi desert, Tarim Basin).

Sahara – the largest desert in the world

Sand as far as the eye can see, no water, no life! The real picture does not correspond to that of a flat sand-covered desert plain. Diversity and contrasts characterize this desert, which covers over 9 million sq km and is the largest connected desert in the world. (To give an idea of its size, Australia and Oceania cover 8.5 million sq km). Three different types of desert form the unique, fascinating and manifold appearance of this desert.

Desert forms

The stone, rock or gravel deserts (Hamada) are not what we generally think of as being desert, nonetheless they make up roughly 70% of all desert areas. Naked, sometimes towering rock faces or jagged rock fragments, products of exposure to the elements, dominate the landscape. Daily temperature extremes lead to quick weathering. The heating of the stone to 80°C by day and drastic cooling at night to minus temperatures have the effect of an explosive charge. Large areas of rubble surround mountains and highlands that appear to be standing with their foothills in debris.

The Tibetan rubble and gravel deserts (Serir) present another phenomenon. Flat basins covered with gravel and rubble were formed due to the fact that while Europe was experiencing an ice age, the Sahara was blessed with regular rainfall. The rivers transported gravel and sand into the plains. Today the dry riverbeds indicate the existence of a former wetter climate. When-

ever it rains after years of drought, the dry valleys are flooded with mud, rock fragments, gravel and sand.

Sandy deserts, that make up a mere 15 to 20% of the Sahara, are formed when nearby sandstone mountains supply the desert with ample quantities of sand through wind erosion. When wind speeds reach a certain peak, various bizarre

1 The mojawe desert: unending variety of forms

2 Fruit in the middle of the drought: the date cactus

3 Brilliant camouflage adapted wonderfully to the hard desert life: the desert iguana

4 Camels can go for up to 17 days without water

5 The large ears of the desert fox function above all as a cooling system for the blood circulation

People in the Desert

From far off, desert travellers saw a green island. It was an oasis! Oases can be utilized intensively through clever irrigation systems. There are different types, depending on the origin of the water: ground water oases in which the ground water collects in hollows or basins or rises in artesian wells. Source oases can be found at the foot of wet mountains. River oases are fed by "foreign" rivers, that is rivers that come from areas with a lot of precipitation. The Ancient Egyptians have the river oasis of the Nile Valley to thank for their advanced civilisation. The main crop, the date palm, stands with its feet in water and its head in the fiery heat.

The nomads, called "men of the desert", moved from water-hole to water-hole with their camel herds, offered caravans protection and did good trade with the oasis farmers. Their traditional lifestyle, based on ecological methods, has been radically changed by the discovery of oil. Lorries travelling along well-laid desert roads as well as air transport have reduced the significance of caravan transport and most nomads have now settled down. The oases are suffering from overpopulation and all of its social and economic evils.

types of sand-dunes are formed. Fearsome hurricane-like desert winds create billowing clouds of dust and sand that have the effect of a sandblaster that can reduce a boulder to the size of a "toadstool".

The living desert

In spite of hostile conditions, plants and animals are able to live permanently in the desert using strategies adapted to drought. Underneath the desert floor there are particularly effective root systems, corms and seeds capable of germinating after years when they come into contact with moisture. They turn the desert into a flow-

ering, green paradise for a short time. Many desert plants are so formed that transpiration is reduced. Some can hold large quantities of water, while others continue to live even if the upper part appears to be dead.

Similar principles apply to desert animals. In order to survive, they remain in underground caves or tunnels, are only active at night, and in cases where water supplies really fail, they fall into a motionless state of preservation. Desert foxes and hares are protected by their pelts from sunrays that are too strong. Their long ears function like a cooling system. Reptiles "swim" through the upper, not-so-hot layers of sand.

Largest deserts	Area
Sahara (Africa)	9 Mil. sq km
Libyan Wüste (Africa)	2 Mil. sq km
Kalahari (Africa)	1 Mil. sq km
Gobi (Asia)	1 Mil. sq km
Great Sandy Desert (Australia)	520 000 sq km
Gibson Desert (Australia)	330 000 sq km
Victoria Desert (Australia)	300 000 sq km

Life close to the Poles

The ice-covered polar caps of the Arctic and Antarctic are clearly visible from outer space. The cold deserts, where polar day and polar night prevail, stretch from the polar circles (66°33 north and south latitude) to the pole. The ice shell over Greenland and the Antarctic and the almost completely frozen Arctic Ocean appear to rule out human life and activity. Yet under the most extreme of conditions within the polar circles, there are people who have made this inhospitable place their permanent home or who were drawn by research to the region.

Antarctica – continent of extremes

The continent of extremes and superlatives was the loneliest continent for thousands of years because it was far away and could not be reached by transport routes. The lowest imaginable temperatures (minus 70 °C in winter) and the most extreme wind speeds prevail on the largest connected ice mass in the world. 90% of the world's ice masses lie in the Antarctic; only 10% in the Arctic. Antarctica encompasses 14 million sq km and comprises the landmass around the South Pole, its companion islands and shelf ice. The landmass alone totals 12.5 million km^2 (Europe has 10 million sq km). An ice shell with an average depth of 2 000 m, but 4 770 m at its thickest part, covers the continent like an ice cap. This inland ice region is the result of millions of years of precipitation which fell as snow and solidified into ice in the extreme temperatures. The inland ice is pushing itself away from the crown of its ice cap on all sides towards the world's oceans. Glaciers are sliding down the slopes of the mountains into the valleys. The edge of the in-

land glacial ice is breaking off into the sea, glaciers are "calving" The edge of the inland ice coves the continental shelf as shelf ice. The Ross Shelf, the largest expanse of shelf ice, takes in an area as large as France. Drift-ice moves around the continent like a belt of sheet-ice floe. When ice masses, either above or below sea-level, push over or under each other, they form pack-ice.

Life in the Antarctic

Only lichens and mosses are able to survive on the Antarctic continent. In contrast, the animal kingdom thrives along the coasts and in the open sea. The penguin is the most characteristic animal of the Antarctic; seals, sea-lions and whales have adapted to the extreme living conditions. Huge swarms of krill, plankton and tiny shellfish that live in the cold and very nutritious seawater offer a source of food rich in protein. Despite the extreme inclemency, explorers and researchers continue to try to penetrate the secrets of this continent, which was first discovered in 1820. In 1911-1912 an expedition to the South Pole by the Norwegian Amundsen and the British Scott took place. Amundsen reached the goal first on his dogsledge, because Scott's motorized sledge kept stalling due to the murderous cold.

40 winter research stations house the researchers who come from all over the world. Not only scientific, but also national and economic interests underlie the research. There are deposits of important raw materials such as petroleum, natural gas, titan, iron, copper, chrome, platinum, gold, coal, uranium and manganese. There are also strategic reasons that make the inhospitable continent interesting. It is the only piece of land left that has yet not been divided among the nations of the world. Seven countries have territorial claims on it: Norway, Australia, New Zealand, Argentina, France, Chile and the United Kingdom. In light of these circumstances, steps have been taken to protect this unique, untouched continent at an international level. The Antarctica Treaty signed in 1959 laid down the exclusive peaceful use of the southern polar region and prohibits military activity. The extraction of mineral deposits has been renounced until at least 2041.

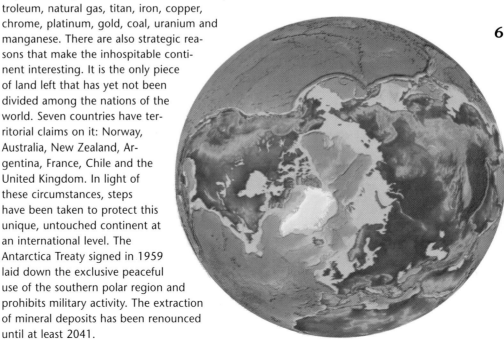

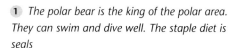

1 *The polar bear is the king of the polar area. They can swim and dive well. The staple diet is seals*

2 *Start of a weather balloon from a research station in the Antarctic*

3 *The Eskimos are the only people on Earth who spend the whole year in polar areas*

4 *Penguins live mainly in the southern polar areas as well as in the south west of South America*

5 *The king of the air in the southern polar areas: the albatross with its wingspan of nearly 3 metres*

6 *The northern hemisphere: adjoining ice masses are found mainly on the coasts of continents as well as on Greenland*

7 *The southern hemisphere: 90 % of all ice on the Earth are found in the Antarctic. The whole continent is covered by an ice mass with an average depth of 2,000 m*

5

Arctic

The Arctic encompasses the landmasses (8 million sq km) and areas of sea (18 million sq km) that lie around the North Pole. The Arctic Ocean, over 4,000 m deep, is covered almost the whole year round with a layer of ice that has an average of 2 to 3 m. Greenland is covered with the largest inland ice sheet in the northern hemisphere; it has a maximum depth of 3 200 m.

The underlying rock is only visible along the edges where high protrusions tower over the icy surface. Blocks of ice break off from the edges of the inland ice to form icebergs that are carried south by ocean currents. In summer these icebergs can reach a latitude of 36 ° N and be a danger to shipping (for example, the sinking of the Titanic 14th April 1912).

7

The scanty tundra vegetation covers a belt up to 200 km wide in northern Europe, along the Siberian Arctic Ocean coast to the Bering Strait, and in North America from Alaska to Labrador. In the region of Hudson Bay this belt is called "Barren Grounds". The permafrost thaws superficially only in the summer; its surface changes into an impassable muddy area.

In the Arctic, native people such as the Eskimos and Lapps, developed hunting and collecting cultures in the New Stone Age, and lived in harmony with the environment. Europeans and Americans brought an end to their ancient lifestyle when they started extracting raw materials from the land. The construction of the Alaskan Pipeline represented an arrogant attack on the life of the native people and the ecological balance. Petroleum from the largest oilfield in North America (also with a rich natural gas deposit) in Prudhoe Bay on the edge of the Arctic Ocean is pumped over 1,280 km through a pipeline across Alaska to Valdez on the Pacific coast. The untouched landscape, that man had only developed to an extent of 10% , and was a hunting and game reserve, that had always provided for the inhabitants, was destroyed.

The Origins *of Mankind*

In anthropology, the term race refers to any of several large subdivisions of mankind into physically distinctive groups. On the basis of inherited physical features (colour of skin, shape of eyes and nose, colour and type of hair etc.) a racial group can be clearly differentiated. Often a race has a natural geographical home. The almost 6 billion people that now populate the Earth have, according to our present knowledge, a common origin.

The first stages of Man

Since the revolutionary Theory of Evolution by the English Charles Darwin (1809-1882), the acceptance of the statement in the Bible that mankind originated from one act of creation is no longer acceptable. We must accept, however, that a close family relationship exists between man and anthropoids (primates). Through a process of natural selection and mutation, man has evolved into what he is today. Decisive was whether altered forms (mutations) were better suited to their environment than their predecessors. The better adapted gene asserted itself over the less adaptable old one (natural selection). The ability to stand upright is considered to be the transition from the animal stage to the level of the human being. The evolution from primates, who were related to us, into actual human beings with the ability to think, spanned over a long period and was certainly not a straightforward process. On the contrary, several groups existed side by side, before some of them died out and others continued the line of development. Despite intensive research, it is still not possible to put an exact date to man's first appearance on the planet. The oldest finds of human ancestors come from the steppes of East Africa. Savannahs replaced wide areas of African forest due to a global cooling and our ancestors, the Hominids, had to adapt their lifestyle to the open land. It is possible that they developed an upright posture to enable them to see over the long grass.

From Homo habilis to Homo sapiens sapiens

"Homo habilis" (skilled person), who lived on the steppes of East Africa 2 – 3 million years ago, was probably the earliest form of the human race, the first example of the genus "Homo". His ability to think rationally was so highly developed that he could make simple cutting and scraping tools out of stone. "Homo erectus" (upright person), who can be traced back to around 300,000 years ago, was the next highest form in the history of evolution. As hunters and collectors they formed nomadic groups, hunted together, shared their spoils and huddled in caves for protection. A considerable step forward in the history of human development is the mastering of fire. Remains of "Homo erectus" were not only found in Africa, but also

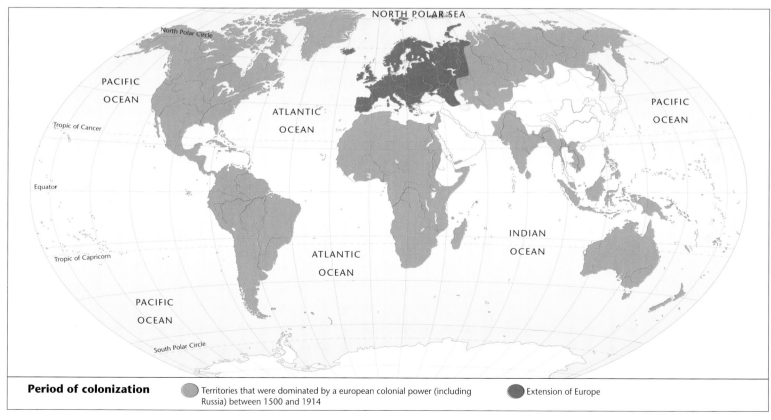

Period of colonization   Territories that were dominated by a european colonial power (including Russia) between 1500 and 1914   Extension of Europe

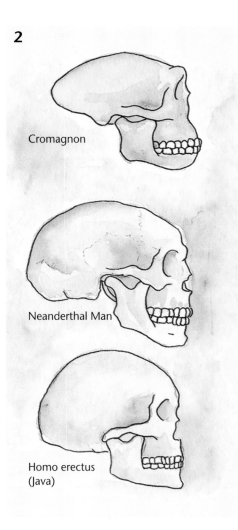

Cromagnon

Neanderthal Man

Homo erectus
(Java)

1 Multicoloured cave
paintings with bison
cows in labour, sur-
rounded by bison,
Altamira, Spain

2 The shape of skulls
provide information
about the development
of Man

3 Useful when it's
very hot: the broad
nose is suited to the
high humidity

4 Insulating fat layers
protect against the
freezing cold

in Europe and East Asia. The oldest fossils of this sort found in Java prove that "Java people" lived there approximately 1 million to 700,000 years ago. The regional diversity of "finds" indicates that migrations must have taken place that would be impossible today with the present distribution of water and land. For example, there was a land bridge from Asia to America, because the Bering Strait had not been submerged in water at that time.

"Homo erectus" developed into "Homo sapiens" (a man endowed with the powers of reasoning, or wise man), an advanced type of human being that left behind many traces. The most famous example is "Homo neanderthalis". Neanderthal man, who lived 100,000 to 35,000 years ago used fire, made tools and clothing, put burial gifts into the graves of their dead and performed religious cult activities. From his origins in Asia or Eastern Europe, he spread into Europe, Russia and North Africa. Neanderthal man, only a sub-branch in the evolution of humanity, died out about 35,000 years ago during the last Ice Age and was replaced by a new genus of mankind.

"Homo sapiens sapiens" refers to present-day man, and in contrast to earlier humans, we are able to express ourselves artistically. The true forerunner of the present-day human race is the Cro-Magnon Man, whose cave paintings found in Lascaux (France) and Altamira (Spain) date back 15,000 years, depicting their environment using artistic symbolic representations, prove their civilisation to have been considerably advanced. The exact evolutionary path which has led to man's present-day appearance is not yet known in great detail.

Races

The Ice Ages played a decisive role in the development of races. Because vast areas were covered in snow and ice, people were forced to migrate and adapt to a new environment. So due to regional isolation and varying demands on life, one group of primitive man eventually developed into several different races with common hereditary features and a common living area.

We classify the different human races into Old Level Races, that are seen as an old form of "Homo sapiens", such as the Aborigines in Australia with their sloping forehead, protruding lower jaw and receding chin, and into Large Races (Caucasoid, Mongoloid and Negroid), as well as into Contact or Mixed Races.

The Negroid are a prime example of a tropical race. Climate-conditioned selection not only necessitated pigmentation, but also favoured the flat shaped nose that is better suited to high air humidity. Since the last Ice Age, Caucasoids have been found in Europe and North Africa. The pronounced variations in skin colour are explicable through the process of climate-conditioned selection (protection from the sun's rays). Skin colour becomes darker as one moves from the north to the south. Mongoloids have also adapted excellently to the cold steppes. They have a stocky build, an insulating layer of fat under their skin, and a small nose and flat ears that resist the cold well. Contact and Mixed Races developed in large contact zones between the Large Races and the Old Level Races. Classifications of this kind, though, remain as simplified theories, because in view of worldwide mobility, distinctions are becoming increasingly blurred and now there are countless mixed forms. For example, Caucasoids have spread throughout the world since the great voyages of discovery took place; African Negroids were taken to America as slaves. European colonization even pushed the Australoids into the inner desert steppes of Australia.

Population
and life expectancy

The Earth, the innate living space of mankind, is only available to its population to a very limited degree. Two-thirds of the Earth's surface can be immediately discounted, because it is covered by water. The mainland also has regions that are unsuitable for permanent settlements even to modern man with his highly developed technical means.

Population distribution

Natural factors such as climate, soil, relief, vegetation and water-supply, put limits on where people can live and work. Areas with extreme cold and ice-cover are not suitable for permanent habitation and neither are desert regions. Temperate and subtropical zones with their mild climate, fertile soil, and lush fauna and flora meet all the natural requirements of mankind. However, even today in South and East Asia, in the north-east of the USA, in Europe and in the Lower Nile Valley, very large masses live right next to huge unpopulated desert or polar regions.

The very first population centres and advanced civilisations developed in the low-lying plains of the world, where the climate is warm and favourable. Ancient Egyptian civilization on the Nile delta and the Babylonians in the fertile Mesopotamian area are evidence of this. At that time, people were even more dependent than today on natural factors, such as arable land, pastureland and, above all, on a water-supply.

Migration

In the 15th and the 16th century the Europeanization of the Earth began. Settlements concentrated along the coasts of Africa, South America, North America and Australia, and from there colonization spread noticeably.

The colonisation of America is the largest population movement in the history of the world. There are only an estimated one million native Indians in the USA, in comparison with a total population of 248 million. Even today whole ethnic communities leave their homeland time and time again. These migrations are caused by emigration, refugee movements and the migration of workers. The reasons lie in push and pull factors. All crises in the world, as well as environmental and natural catastrophes, produce a push factor, because they put streams of refugees in motion. A strong pull effect is created by the highly developed countries of the western world.

Population density

Population density (the number of people living in 1 sq km) is highest in areas of the world where there is employment. It is possible to distinguish whether an area with a very dense population developed due to its agricultural potential (Java, the Nile Delta, Indus plain, Hwango plain), or as a result of industrialization. Areas with the highest population density are found in Europe, the eastern part of the USA, and in large parts of South and East Asia. About three-quarters of the world's population inhabit only 7% of the mainland, because populations concentrate into small, favourable regions. The population density figure does not, however, show the real distribution in countries with large areas of land. Thus Australia with a low population density has dense centres that stand in sharp contrast to nearby areas devoid of human life.

Urbanization in industrial countries

National and international migrations lead to a

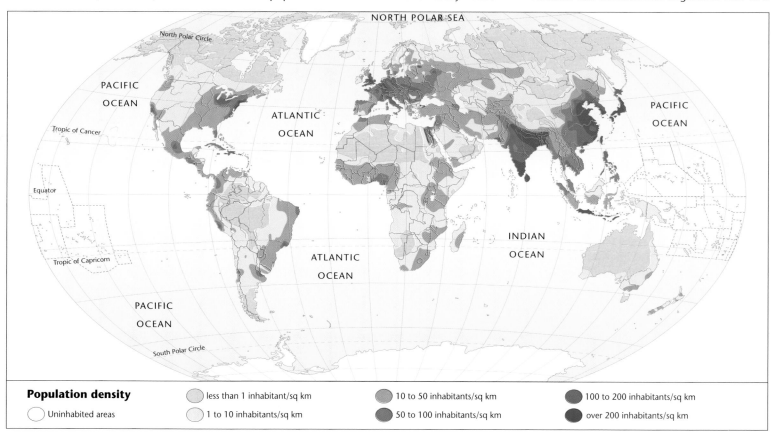

Population density			
Uninhabited areas	less than 1 inhabitant/sq km	10 to 50 inhabitants/sq km	100 to 200 inhabitants/sq km
	1 to 10 inhabitants/sq km	50 to 100 inhabitants/sq km	over 200 inhabitants/sq km

constant world-wide increase in urbanization. An over-proportional growth of cities goes along with a rapid population growth. In the industrial areas of central and western Europe this development began in the 19th century and continued in the population concentrations of Eastern Europe, Japan, China and the USA. Thus industrial areas sprang up in the vicinity of coal deposits in the middle of England, North-eastern France, the Ruhr in Germany, and in Eastern North America, and created ever larger cities. In the Middle Ages and at the beginning of modern times, cities bore individual characteristics, such as a royal seat, a cathedral or a university, but through industrialization their outward appearance and population structure changed.

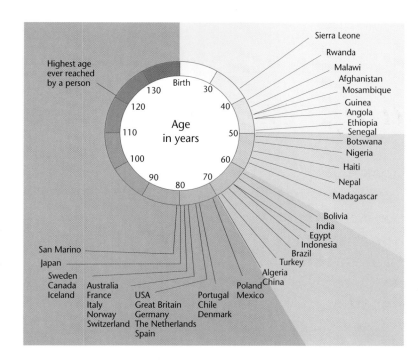

Life expectancy clock: the life expectancy is used as an indication of the quality of life in a country and shows a great variety world-wide

Urbanisation in developing countries

Around 45% of the Earth's population live in cities. 30% of that number applies to developing countries. The urbanization process started later in developing countries than it did in industrial nations, but nonetheless it is happening with explosive force and speed. Large cities attract above all poor people from the surrounding rural areas, who hope to find better work and earn more money, partake in the advantages of city life, improve their opportunities for better education or to use social and health services. In the slums on the outskirts of the cities, there are job shortages and an abundance of crime, catastrophically unhygienic conditions and a lack of social and educational institutions. The proportion of slum inhabitants to the total population increases annually; over 80% in Cairo and a good 30% in Rio de Janeiro live in slums. The poverty stricken rural population fleeing the country is indicative of structural problems in social, political and economic fields in developing countries. It is calculated that in the year 2010 far more than half of mankind will live in cities. In 1800 it was barely 3%, in 1900 it was around 15%.

World-wide urbanization

The huge world-wide increase in the population of large cities leads to the formation of densely populated industrial regions with more than a million inhabitants, called agglomeration or urban sprawl. By the year 2000 it is estimated that there will be more than 400 cities of this size. Adequate infrastructure needs to be created for the rise in population numbers. Tremendous traffic problems, growing environmental problems through industrial and air pollution and ever-growing mountains of rubbish provide the world's big cities with considerable tasks.

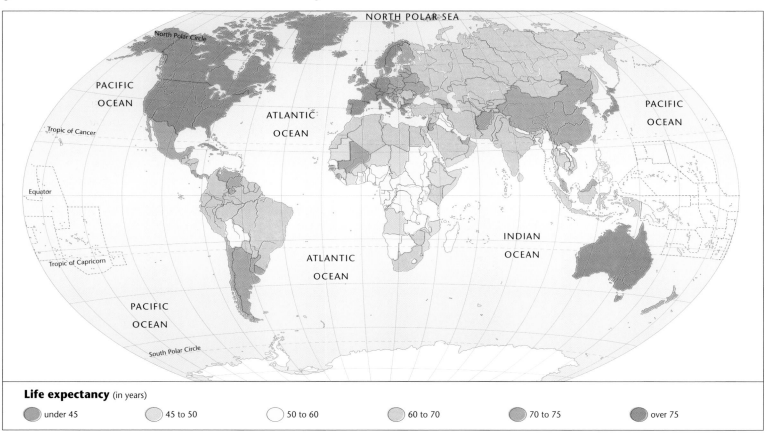

Life expectancy (in years)

◯ under 45   ◯ 45 to 50   ◯ 50 to 60   ◯ 60 to 70   ◯ 70 to 75   ◯ over 75

Mineral deposits
and energy production

Mineral, rock and chemical compound deposits represent an important basis for man's economic strength. Some raw materials were so important that prehistoric cultures were named after them (Stone, Bronze and Iron Age).
The number of raw materials used has multiplied during the course of man's history. Not all raw materials can be found in one land, so that at an early stage a flourishing trade developed in the sought-after substances. Precious metals such as gold and silver had a special attraction and often led to warlike conflicts. For industrial countries an adequate supply of raw materials is of the utmost importance today.

Raw Materials

The number of raw materials used has multiplied during the course of man's history. Not all raw materials can be found in one land, so that at an early stage a flourishing trade developed in the sought-after substances. Precious metals such as gold and silver had a special attraction and often led to warlike conflicts. For industrial countries an adequate supply of raw materials is of the utmost importance today. Because mining in industrial countries has become increasingly unprofitable due to high mining costs and low quality deposits, industrialists have become dependent on imports from developing countries. They, in turn, have to export in order to earn foreign currency for their economic development and, among other things, for repayment of credits and for urgently required imports. Raw material prices and trade politics provide a potential for conflict worldwide. Problems arise above all in countries that are over-dependent on one export, for example Chile (copper) or Bolivia (zinc).

Distribution and developing of deposits

The distribution of mineral deposits follows geological regularity round the world; different types of deposit are restricted to certain zones of the Earth's crust. On many occasions mankind had to go to uninhabited areas in order to make use of them. Considerable changes in the landscapes are the result. Whole cities sprang up with the

exploitation of ore-mines in the North American Cordilleras. After the mines had been exhausted, the city was abandoned and turned into a ghost town. The extraction of mineral deposits on the edge of or outside established settlements has always been connected with immigration.
In most European industrial countries the mining of many raw materials has become unprofitable.
While in the old industrial countries the mineral deposits were intensively worked for centuries, in developing countries the tapping of new raw materials is still possible.
Exploration companies operate against great difficulties. They go to greater depths, remoter areas and use more and more complicated techniques for mining. One example is the economic opening up of inhospitable Siberia with its immeasurable reserves of raw materials but hostile climate and settlement conditions. Nowadays ecological considerations such as environmentally-friendly mining, processing and use, as well as recycling possibilities and disposal, play an increasing role. Development and transport costs come on top of that. These factors limit the use of the raw materials that are globally available in ample amounts.

Energy

An increasing demand for energy sources developed with industrialization in the 19th century. The various primary and secondary sources of energy are classified according to whether they are solid, liquid, gas or atomic. The prime sources of energy – coal, petroleum, natural gas, uranium ore and hydroelectric power – can be used in their natural form, while secondary

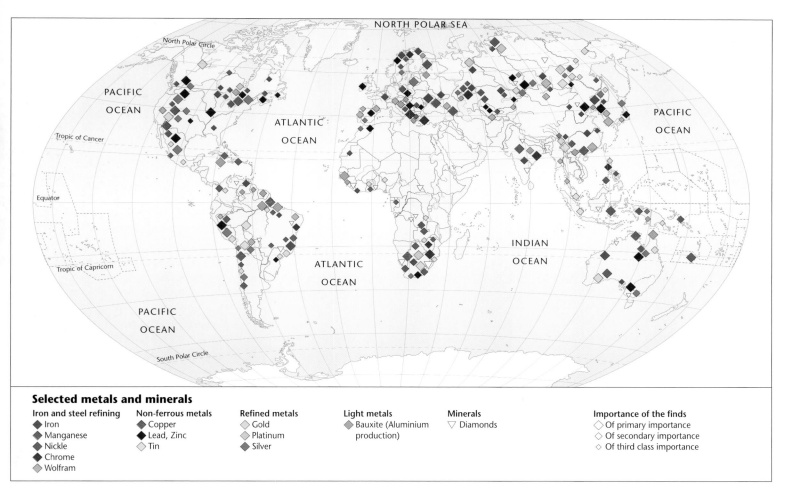

Selected metals and minerals

Iron and steel refining
◆ Iron
◆ Manganese
◆ Nickle
◆ Chrome
◆ Wolfram

Non-ferrous metals
◆ Copper
◆ Lead, Zinc
◇ Tin

Refined metals
◇ Gold
◇ Platinum
◇ Silver

Light metals
◆ Bauxite (Aluminium production)

Minerals
▽ Diamonds

Importance of the finds
◇ Of primary importance
◇ Of secondary importance
◇ Of third class importance

1 *Oil drilling in the North Sea off the coast of Falmouth, England. The exploration, developments werking on these fields have brought the British government a valuable source of revenue*

2 *Wind energy is already widely used in Denmark and the USA*

3 *Thomas Edison opened the first public electricity station in 1882 close to New York*

4 *The cooling towers of atomic power stations belong to the modern industrial landscape*

sources of energy have to undergo a transformation process first (electricity, heating oil, petrol). The use of the primary sources of energy – coal, petroleum and natural gas, completely revolutionized the economic principles of man. In contrast, for thousands of years renewable energy forms, such as sun, water, wood, as well as human and animal muscle power, were the only sources of energy.

Fossil fuels

The use of fossil fuels laid the tracks for industrialization in the 19th century. The collective term "fossil fuels" refers to sources of energy that were formed from organic plant and animal substances millions of years ago and is now stored in the Earth in the form of peat, brown and pit-coal, petroleum and natural gas. They are irrevocably burnt to produce energy. Fossil deposits are limited, not renewable, and will at some time be exhausted. They provide over 90% of the world's energy requirements at present. Man has risked the opening up of petroleum deposits in the icy deserts of Canada, Alaska and Siberia, as well as in hot deserts and on off-shore oilrigs near the coast.

Alternative energy

The knowledge that the supply of fossil fuels is limited and environmentally-friendly attitudes have caused people to rethink the issues and therefore to step up the search for alternative forms of energy. Whilst nuclear power is increasingly seen as bad, mankind is becoming more conscious of regenerative energy forms, such as hydroelectric, wind and solar energy, and energy from the Earth's warmth (biowarmth). The amount of energy man uses continues to increase. The problem really lies in the fact that a minority of well off industrial countries uses the largest share of energy and four-fifths of the oil deposits and one half of the natural gas reserves are in developing countries!

trade and world traffic

Trade and transport are inseparable. The volume and direction of traffic streams reflect the dimensions of trade. In order to bring sought-after goods from their places of manufacture to their end consumers, natural routes by river and over land were used or created. Thus trade routes for the silk trade were established between the Mediterranean area and China.

Development of international trade

International trade, the world-wide exchange of goods, had little significance in terms of volume before industrialisation. Only the sea powers Great Britain, the Netherlands, Spain and Portugal upheld trade relationships between their colonies and the homeland. The stream of goods served the business interests of the colonizers. The slave trade also played an important role. With cheap goods European trade partnerships bought slaves in Africa, who were then sold to America. Slave labour made possible the export of large quantities of valuable raw materials such as sugar-cane, spices and cotton to Europe. Industrialization has shaped world trade into its present form.

We understand "international products" to be goods that have significance over and above national interests. This would include petroleum as the most important, but also goods such as cotton, peanuts, tea, cocoa, sugar, coffee and bananas. No other international product has such an effect on the economy as petroleum. Industrialization is dependent on this "black gold", without which business could not function. Petroleum has this absolute pre-eminence in world trade, because the distribution of its deposits and consumption around the world is so varied. Industrial countries dependent on petroleum do not have productive mineral deposits available to them, so that brisk trade with the oil-producing often developing countries is required. Developing countries try to use revenues from the export of oil to finance the building up of their own industry.

The flow of goods and international trade powers

The main flows of goods can be broken down into main routes for the transport of raw materials, and the transport of finished and semi-finished products. Economically weak regions are characterised by the predominant export of raw materials, economically strong regions in contrast import raw materials and export high-grade finished products, such as machinery, electrical goods or cars that fetch a high price. Developing countries that are heavily dependent on imports from industrialised nations are often highly indebted, because costly foreign exchange is required to buy finished goods. The large volume of trade in raw materials flows from only a few places in the world to the east coast of the USA, to Europe and Japan. Japan has next to no mineral deposits but is compensated by a highly skilled work force and large investments in research and development. With agricultural products, however, the story is different; they are

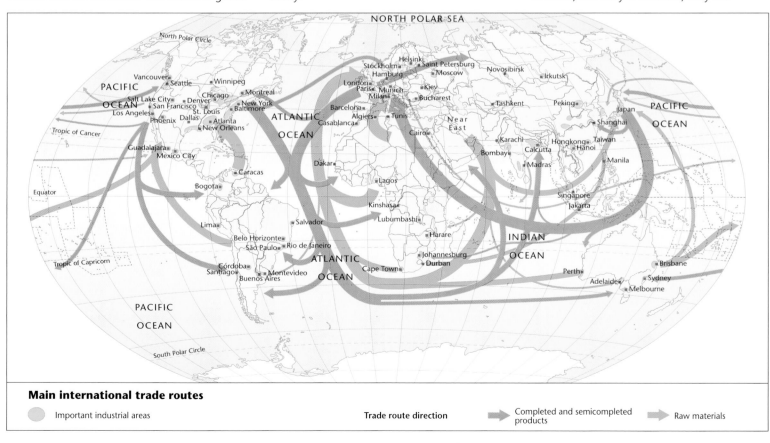

Main international trade routes

◯ Important industrial areas	**Trade route direction** ➡	➡ Completed and semicompleted products ➡ Raw materials

exported by both highly industrialized countries such as the USA and Canada, and developing countries.

The three most important world trade powers are the USA, Germany and Japan. The world trade balance is considered to be a good yardstick. From it the value of and the relationship between a country's imports and exports can be calculated. If exports exceed imports then the trade balance is said to be positive, there is an export surplus. The three world trade powers export overall around one-third of all exported goods in the world. The world market price is formed by the forces of supply and demand according to a framework of pliant rules in the commodity markets of world trade centres such as New York and London. The higher the demand is or the scarcer the supply is, the higher the price is. In commodity forward

exchanges goods are bought before the harvest in speculation that after the harvest they can be sold more profitably.

International traffic

An extensive transportation network by water, on land and in the air spans the globe. People, products, capital and news reports are transported within a short time around the world. The most important goods shipped by sea are crude oil (40 % of sea traffic), coal, mineral oil products, iron ore and grains.

One of the most important sea-ways from East Asia and the Persian Gulf led through the Suez Cannel to Europe until the Six Day War in 1967. Its blockade until 1975 forced ships to take an expensive roundabout way around the Cape of Good Hope. In order to hold ground against price-cutting pressures, ever larger ships were developed, in particular the supertankers. They created a transport advantage, but also a danger to the environment. Crude oil that has spilled out into the oceans in tanker disasters has led to whole coasts being contaminated.

The importance of container traffic is increasing steadily, because an ever greater proportion of shipments are high-grade industrial goods. The

1 *Container terminals handle the bulk of the worldwide goods flow. Some Asians and European ports now specalize in Container and the necessary hinterland*

2 *With 610 million trips abroad in 1997, tourism is increasingly an important source of income in the world market*

proportion of bulk goods (raw materials) meanwhile is decreasing. Containers are packing and transport units that are a prerequisite for a quick turnover of goods. International ports such as Rotterdam, the largest port in the world, or Hong Kong, the largest container port in the world, have specialised and have become centres for international traffic. International air traffic registers strong growth. In 1997, 2.45 billion people and 23.3 million tonnes of freight were transported. The role played by tourism should not be underestimated. In international tourism more than 610 million trips abroad were recorded for 1997. For many developing countries tourism is of vital economic significance because there are scarcely any alternatives for earning foreign currency or for work-places.

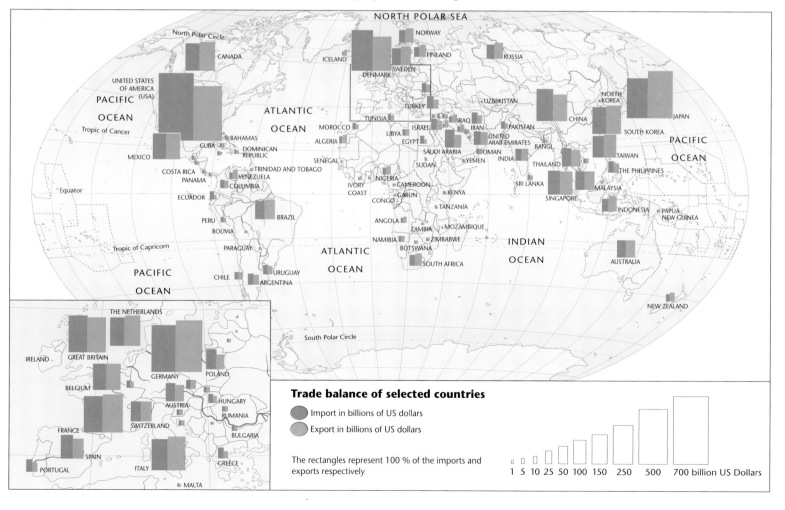

Trade balance of selected countries

- Import in billions of US dollars
- Export in billions of US dollars

The rectangles represent 100 % of the imports and exports respectively

1 5 10 25 50 100 150 250 500 700 billion US Dollars

Buildings and structures

Early on skyscrapers were praised as man-made "natural wonders" and compared to a range of jagged mountains bordering deep canyons.

Skyscrapers

New York with its famous Manhattan skyline is considered to be the epitome of a modern metropolis. With Manhattan, composed to a large extent of skyscrapers of over 100 storeys, the very idea of how a city should look has completely changed. It is not by chance that New York is called the "capital of the world". It was here that a break with architectural tradition took place on an impressive scale. The invention of a new type of building – the high-rise building- was the catalyst for this development. The self-supporting steel structure is the most significant technical achievement that has revolutionized architecture in the 19th and 20th century. Precisely calculated, exactly positioned steel girders take on the functions of outer walls as well as the supporting beam. This construction principle enables a reciprocal use of the static lines of force. Only after this invention did it become possible to build really high buildings. The gravitational force of brickwork was overcome and the supporting wall was replaced with a steel frame. A rigid steel frame is the key to skyscraper construction, the walls simply "hang" from the frame (curtain walling). Thus the old dream of a "glass tower" could be realised by simply fastening panes of glass (like thin layers of skin) to the steel frame. Also the invention of the electric elevator (1853 Elisha Otis at the industrial exhibition in New York) was decisive for the triumph of skyscrapers. Prior to the lift, the number of stories a building had was limited to six.

Skyscrapers in the New World

Not only high land prices, but also aspirations for prestige and power lay behind the construction of such high buildings. Skyscraper facades reflect these aspirations. Thus the Gothic window tracery of the Woolworth Building (1913), one of the first skyscrapers in New York, was given the nickname "cathedral of trade". This name effectively symbolized the aspirations at the time not just to build functional buildings, but rather to create representative architectural objects. The palazzo (palace) style of the renaissance with its classical pillars and pilasters (or-

namental columns set into a wall) was considered as the perfect look for a representative building when high-rise construction started in Chicago. The appearance of the city today reflects this style in the "skyscraper palazzo". In New York, the city of skyscrapers, architects did not take to the palazzo but rather the tower as their standard, something like the Campanile of Piazza Ducale in Venice or Dutch Gothic towers. Skyscrapers are signs of economic power and entrepreneurial spirit. Up to 90% of the office space in skyscrapers is occupied by corporate enterprise, banks, insurance companies, media companies, advertising agencies and lawyers. Against this backdrop we can say that yesterday's best is out of date today and today's best will be surpassed tomorrow.

The skyscraper with all its technology, an invention of the New World, gave the modern large city a new look and created a built-up environment where the green of nature plays an insignificant role. In New York, Central Park has the effect of a last small paradise. New York is still the city with the most skyscrapers; the highest, however, are now going up in Asia. Modern cities will increasingly become skyscraper cities, such as can be seen in Hong Kong, Johannesburg, Sao Paulo and Toronto.

Skyscrapers of the Old World

While the highest concentration of skyscrapers is in large American cities, European metropolises keep their historical city centres almost free of them. The contrast between the Old and New World is nowhere else so clearly seen. The architectural features of the core of large European cities consist primarily of buildings with a maximum of six storeys. Thus downtown Paris with its countless historical buildings attracts visitors from all over the world. The skyscrapers in Paris, as in other European cities, are concentrated on the outskirts of the metropolis. La Défense to the west of Paris is an example of this. Downtown Frankfurt with its skyscrapers is

an exception in the European arena. Europe's largest office and service centre emerged there. The Commerzbank Tower (259 m) and the Exhibition Tower (256 m) are the tallest buildings in Europe. The architecture symbolizes Frankfurt's development as an important international financial centre.

Metropolises

The concept of a metropolis, as well as the towering size of the city, covers its central function and dominating role in the overall system of cities. Some metropolises have been transformed during the course of industrialization from industrial, financial and service sector hubs into economic decision making centres, such as the world metropolises of New York, London and Tokyo. Other core cities group around Tokyo, which has become a world metropolis in East Asia. Yokohama, Kawasaki and Chiba form a huge agglomeration in the shape of a horseshoe around Tokyo Bay.

Chicago, Paris, Los Angeles, Toronto, Amsterdam, Frankfurt, Hong Kong, Sydney, Zurich, San Francisco and Singapore in a second hierarchy of metropolises are international financial centres worth mentioning.

1 The epitome of the modern metropole: the famous Manhattan Skyline

2 Central Park, New York

3 Rome: buildings are kept to low levels, typical for the European city

4 Skyscrapers increasingly dominate the picture of Far East cities, here in Singapore

5 La Défense, dormitory town at the gates of Paris: European cities grow taller especially in the outer districts

Conurbations	Inhabitants
Tokyo (Japan)	26,800,000
São Paulo	16,400,000
New York (USA	16,300,000
Mexico City (Mexico)	15,600,000
Shanghai (China)	15,100,000
Bombay (India)	15,100,000
Los Angeles (USA)	12,400,000
Peking (China)	12,400,000
Calcutta (India)	11,700,000
Seoul (South Korea)	11,600,000

Skycrapers	Height in m
Petronas Towers, Kuala Lumpur, Malaysia	451
Sears Tower, Chicago, USA	443
Jinmao Tower, Shanghai, China	420
World Trade Center, New York, USA	417

The largest cities		Population
Europe	Moscow	8,718,000
	London	7,074,300
	Istanbul	7,774,100
	St. Petersburg	4,837,000
	Berlin	3,458,700
Asia	Chong-qing	15,300,000
	Shanghai	13,000,000
	Peking	10,800,000
	Seoul	10,229,200
	Bombay	9,925,800
	Jakarta	9,341,400
Australia	Sydney	3,879,400
	Melbour-ne	3,283,000
	Brisbane	1,520,600
Africa	Cairo	6,800,000
	Luanda	2,250,000
	Kinshasa	4,655,000
	Alexandria	3 380 000
America	São Paulo	9,839,400
	Mexico City	11,707,000
	New York	7,380,900
	Lima	6,479,000
	Rio de Janeiro	5,551,500

In developing countries, the increasing number of people fleeing the rural areas has led to an ever greater concentration of people in capital cities. Capitals are by far the largest economic centres of a country, where foreign companies often also have offices. The building up of infrastructure often cannot keep pace with the growth in the city's population, so that huge slums are formed as a result.

45

imposing constructions

Bridges and tunnels testify to the creativity of man, his ability to overcome natural spatial obstacles with corresponding innovative ideas and the use of ever more complicated materials.

From the beginning to stone bridges

Bridges are a fascinating sign of human imagination and creativity. They are as old as mankind and their development took thousands of years to progress from the primitive suspension bridge (rope bridge) to far more advanced constructions. The development of the bridge is at the same time bound up with the development of the person who is going to use it. The simple stepping stones in the water for man and animals and light loads later became a pontoon bridge made of boats tied together. Finally wooden footbridges were the forerunners of the mighty stone bridges of ancient Rome. Important ruins of Roman bridge construction can be found particularly outside of Italy, where bridges and aqueducts in conquered territories are a testimony to the might that was once there.

The decline of the Roman Empire also meant the end of a century-old tradition in engineering skills. Only with the construction of the much praised bridge of Avignon in 1180, were master builders of the Middle Ages successful in creating a work that was worthy of the Romans (the ruins still stand today).

The dream holiday destination of Venice has about 400 bridges, more than any other city in the world. Most of the canals are so small that they can easily be spanned by small bridges. The largest waterway, the Grand Canal, constantly produces problems for pedestrians and traffic. Many wooden bridges preceded the present-day Rialto Bridge, before the permanent bridge of stone was finally built in 1591. The bridge, with a clearance of 6.4 m was high enough for a magnificent official gondola to pass underneath it and at the same time flat and wide enough to offer space for shops. History abounds around the Bridge of Sighs that connects the palace to the state prison. The prisoner who was sentenced to death knew the glimpse out the bridge's window on his way over would be his last, and inevitably a sigh would be heard to escape him as he was led to his execution.

From iron bridges to cable-stayed bridges

The Industrial Age gave us the first iron bridge. Cast iron, as a revolutionary new material that does not occur naturally in the environment, was first used in bridge building. The iron bridge in Coalbrookdale, England, led the way with a span

of almost 30 m over the Severn and is a cultural monument of UNESCO. The form was borrowed from the method used when constructing in stone.

Cast iron proved soon after to be a problematic material that held out well under pressure, but could not withstand traction. Construction and finishing changed with the emergence of rolled steel and mankind was no longer restricted to cast forms. The method for constructing steel finally allowed for the bold hanging constructions, where a suspension mechanism is hung on a high mast. With cable-stayed bridges, technical designers are able to span enormous distances that enrich the landscape from an aesthetic and creative point of view. The combination of concrete and iron in the method for constructing reinforced concrete has made the construction of bridges possible with unheard-of simplicity in recent times, such as the Europe Bridge, 190 m in height (bridge on the Innsbruck-Brenner motorway over the Sill Gorge), which is the highest bridge in Europe. A large number of modern and bold bridge constructions fit harmoniously into the landscape today; for example the Golden Gate Bridge in front of the skyline of San Francisco or the Bosporus Bridge (suspension bridge

between two continents). For just one year the Store-Baelt Bridge, a connection between the Danish islands of Fyn and Zealand, completed in 1997, was the longest bridge in the world. In 1998 the Akashi-Kaikyo Bridge, that connects the islands of Honsho and Shikoku, took away the first place from the Danes. This bridge was con-

1 The most famous suspension bridge in the world: the Golden Gate Bridge in San Francisco

2 The cablestayed bridge: the Queen Elisabeth II Bridge, Dartford, England

3 Tunnel through the Diamond Head volcano on Honululu

4 A traditionally built lifting bridge: the Tower Bridge in London

5 The Ironbridge in Coalbrookdale (England), the world's first iron bridge

6 Spanning the Canale Grande in Venice since 1591: The Rialto Bridge

Longest suspension bridges	Length in m
Akashi-Kaikyo Bridge, Japan	1990
Store Bælt Bridge	1624
Humber Estuary, Great Britain	1410
Ts`ing Ma, China	1377
Verrazano Narrows, North America	1298
Golden Gate Bridge, North America	1280
Höga Kusten, Sweden	1210
Mackinac Straits, North America	1158

Tunnels	Length in km
Seikan Tunnel (Japan)	53.9
Eurotunnel (Great Britain/France)	49.9
Dai Shimizu (Japan)	22.2
Simplon (Italy/Switzerland)	19.8
Shin Kanmon (Japan)	18.7
Apennin (Italy)	18.5
St Gotthard Tunnel (Switzerland/Italy)	16.3
Rokko (Japan)	16.3
Furkapass (Switzerland)	15.4

structed to withstand earthquakes, which within a radius of 150 km can reach a rating of 8.5 on the Richter scale.

Tunnels

In antiquity tunnel building provided a water supply or was a secret passage out of a fortress. As a transport route, tunnels offer the possibility to overcome obstacles such as mountains, rivers or steep coastal regions. It is impossible to imagine a world without tunnels through the Alps, because they shorten and facilitate connections through this impassable mountain region. The first rail tunnel through the Alps was the 1,430 m long Simmering Steel Tunnel (1848-1854), the longest road tunnel is the Gotthart Tunnel, 16.3 km long (1980). The longest tunnel of all is the Seikan Tunnel in Japan, measuring 53.90 km. The Euro Tunnel, completed in 1994, is valued as a millennium construction project and milestone for the European Union. The English Channel is a strait that separates England from France. The idea to connect England and France with a tunnel had been contemplated for over 200 years. The commuter train "Le Shuttle" can make the journey from Folkestone in England to Coquelles near Calais in France in only 35 minutes. Cars and lorries are loaded in a very short time onto large double-decker waggons.

the world's time and date zones

Time Zones

The creation of times of day and seasons is a natural phenomenon but time zones are "man-made" divisions that became necessary because of world-wide trade and transport routes. When they were introduced, no one knew about "jet-lag". This upset can appear in travellers who pass through several time zones on their flight and experience considerable upsets because of the disruption to their biological clock.

Local time

Not everywhere in the world is it the same time of day. Time is set according to the position of the Sun at noon. The Sun reaches all the places that lie on the same meridian (line of longitude) and its highest position at the same time. It is noon at the same time in all these places. Every place should actually have its own time, or local time. However, in this age of international trading, this would lead to considerable confusion.

World Time

It was agreed in 1884 to split the Earth into fixed time zones, within each of which it was the same time. With the invention of the loco-motive (first steam-engine in 1804 in England), timetables with exact times became necessary. This "Railway Time" became Greenwich Time. Because the observatory in Greenwich was the world authority for time calculation, it was agreed that "Greenwich Mean Time" should be the standard for world time (UT universal time). Many astronomical observations are given in world time.

Zone Times

The zone times correspond respective to Greenwich Time at 12 o'clock noon. For middle Europe, mMiddle European Time is valid for the 15° line of longitude east of Greenwich, the place where the geographical zero meridian passes. Further time zones for Europe are West European time and East European time.
Per 15° of geographical longitude, there is an hour's difference. The 24 hours of the day with 15° divisions result in the 360° longitude around the Earth. With one rotation of the Earth, a circle is closed and therefore a day is complete. These schematic 15° divisions can be maintained without significant deviations. On the mainland, administrative borders and national borders have to be taken into consideration. Countries with a large east-west spread have several time zones, e.g. the USA (6), Australia (3). In China there is only Peking Time instead of four different zones. Some countries like India or Iran have special times that differ from the zone time by about half an hour.

Date Line

With a flight around the world from east to west, in the opposite direction to the rotation of the Earth, a day can be gained. By flying through each zone you gain one full hour, with one revolution around the Earth you gain 24 hours and therefore one whole day. If the trip goes in a west to east direction, the same day is counted twice. In order to balance out this difference, man has created the International Date Line that passes vertically through the Pacific ocean and follows the 180° longitude with the exception of a few deviations. If you pass over the date-line on your way east, you have to set your date one day back, with a trip in a westerly direction you need to set the date ahead by one day. Summer time, which has been introduced in some countries, has not been taken into consideration on maps. During summer the clocks are set one hour forward.

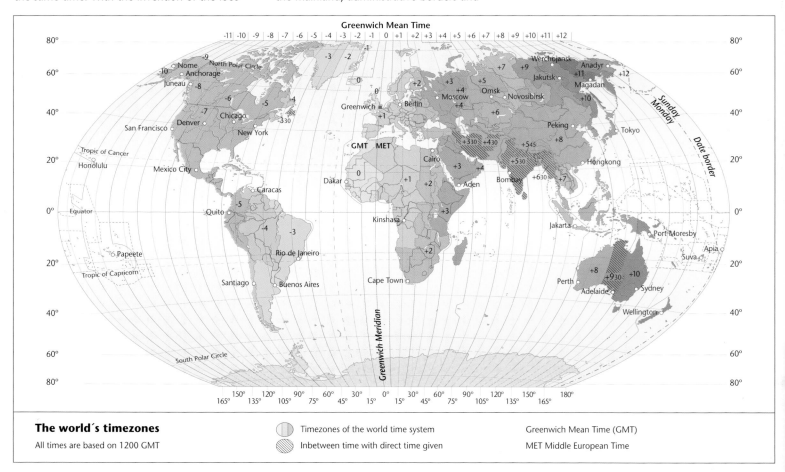

The world´s timezones
All times are based on 1200 GMT

Timezones of the world time system
Inbetween time with direct time given

Greenwich Mean Time (GMT)
MET Middle European Time

The countries of the world

All the countries of the world are listed on the following
pages in alphabetic order. A table provides information
about each country, listing its population figures, area in
sq km, capital, form of government, pro capita earnings,
currency as well as language and religion. Information
about history and economy of the individual country as
well as its topography are listed seperately.
The countries are listed under the international form.
This means, for example, that Croatia is listed under
Hrvatska and Georgia under Sakartvelo. When the country
is sought under its English name the original form of the
country is also listed.

Afghanistan

Afğānistān
Afghanistan
(AFG)

Population: 24.2 million (37 per sq km)
Area: 652,225 sq km
Capital: Kabul
Political system: Islamic republic
Languages: Dari, Pushtu (both official), Uzbekish
Religion: almost 100% Muslim (Sunni 80%, Shi'ite 20%)
GNP: under US$ 800 per head
Currency: 1 afghani = 100 puls
Industries: agriculture, fruit-growing, cattle-breeding; coal, petroleum, natural gas, lapislazuli

History: Settled by Iranian tribes since 2000 BC. The Afghan emirate was founded in 1747. Later it came under British influence. In 1919 it became an independent kingdom and has been a republic since 1973. In 1979 the Soviets marched in; they withdrew in 1989. Since 1992 there has been fierce civil war. Since 1994 Sunni Fundamentalists, called the Taliban, have taken part in the civil war. All peace negotiations have failed; the Taliban's position in the country is unstable.
Topography: The central highland of sparsely covered steppe and gravel desert is bordered by high Hindu Kush Mountains to the east, elsewhere by hilly landscapes and plains.
Economy: The civil war has virtually brought the economy to a standstill. Over 70% of the industrial basis has been destroyed.
Afghanistan, the world's largest opium producer in 1997, is one of the poorest countries in the world.

Al Arabiyah as Suudiyah
Saudi-Arabia
(KSA)

Population: 19.4 million (9 per sq km)
Area: 2,240,000 sq km
Capital: Riyadh
Political system: Islamic absolute monarchy
Languages: High Arabic (official), Arab dialects
Religion: Sunni Muslim 98%, Shi'ite minority
GNP: under US$ 10,000 per head
Currency: 1 rial = 100 hallalas
Industries: oil, petroleum products

History: In the 7th century AD the prophet Mohammed, who founded the Islamic religion, united various Bedouin tribes who spread Islam throughout the Arabic world very quickly after his death. In the 16th century parts of the peninsula were conquered by the Ottomans. Since the 18th

century, the Saud Dynasty has ruled and is still in power. In 1932 the Kingdom of Saudi-Arabia was founded.
Topography: This state covers a large part of the Arabian peninsula. It borders on the Red Sea to the west and on the Persian Gulf to the east. Stony and sandy deserts complete the picture.
Economy: Saudi-Arabia, thanks to the enormous mineral deposits in the Persian Gulf, is the largest exporter of petroleum in the world; crude oil and

petroleum products make up 90% of the export balance. Power and wealth is used, among other things, for the development of agriculture, which now supplies not only their own needs, but even yields enough to export. Every year 3 million Muslims go on a pilgrimage to the sacred cities in Mecca, which is the sacred duty of all muslims to do once in their life.

Al Bahrayn
Bahrain
(BRN)

Population: 599,000 (847 per sq km)
Area: 707 sq km
Capital: Manama (Al-Manamah)
Political system: absolute monarchy
Languages: High Arabic (official), English
Religion: 90% Muslims (Shi'ite 60%, Sunni 40%), Christian and Hindu minorities
GNP: under US$ 10,000 per head
Currency: 1 Bahrain dinar = 1000 fils
Industries: above all petroleum and petroleum products

History: In antiquity this area was a trading post for the Sumerians and Babylonians. In the 16th century it was occupied by the Portuguese and after that by the Persians. From 1816 until their declaration of independence in 1971, it was a British protectorate. It is a member of the Arab

League and has been under the absolute rule of the same Emir government since 1961.
Topography: This Persian Gulf state comprises 33 islands of which only 3 are permanently inhabited. The main island is Bahrain; it has a desert landscape with sand dunes and salt deserts.
Economy: The climate and the nature of the soil make agriculture virtually impossible. However, thanks to the oil deposits, the economic situation is excellent. Attempts are being made to improve the industrial base and service sector in preparation for the time when the oil has been exhausted.

Albania → Shqipëria

Marocco

1 Moroccan camel driver with one of his "ships of the desert", vital even today

2 Contains one of the most valuable commodities of the land: water towers in Kuwait City

3 Wind and weather formed this imposing "cauliflower" in the Algerian Sahara over thousands of years of painstaking effort

4 Morocco: The town of Tinrhir in the High Atlas. Irrigation transforms the desert into flowering countryside

stable situation many tourists now avoid this former holiday destination.

Topography: The Sahara desert covers a large part of this country. Highlands and mountains (Atlas, Tell Atlas, Ahaggar, Tassili) complete the picture. The majority of settlements are to be found along the 1 300 km long Mediterranean coast.

Economy: Exports include natural gas and petroleum from the vast inner reaches of the Sahara. A 40% share of GNP is derived from industry and the service sector. A mere 15% comes from agriculture.

Al Jazā'ir
Algeria
DZ

Population: 28.7 million (12 per sq km)
Area: 2,381,741 sq km
Capital: Algiers (El Djazaïr)
Political system: presidential republic
Languages: High Arabic (official) , Arabic, Berber, French
Religion: almost 100% Sunni Muslim
GNP: US$ 1,520 per head
Currency: 1 Algerian dinar = 100 centimes
Industries: natural gas, petroleum, cork, agriculture

History: Phoenicians, Carthaginians and Romans settled here successively and it was under Arab rule from the 7th to the 15th century. In 1830 the French conquest began. From 1881 until 1962 Algeria belonged to France; there were embittered battles for independence until it was granted in 1962. There have been recurring periods of unrest since 1990, due in particular to Islamic fundamentalism. Due to the politically un-

Al Kuwayt
Kuwait
KWT

Population: 1.5 million (89 per sq km)
Area: 17,818 sq km
Capital: Kuwait
Political system: Emirate (absolute monarchy)
Languages: High Arabic (official), Arabic dialects
Religion: Muslim (Sunni 55%, Shi'ite minority 40%)
GNP: over US$ 10,000 per head
Currency: 1Kuwait dinar = 1000 fils
Industries: oil

History: The ancestors of the present day inhabitants came at the beginning of the 18th century from the western part of the Arabian Peninsula and established a trading centre, which became very important for both ships and caravans. Since 1756 the Sabah family have ruled this land, but from 1899 until independence was granted in 1961, Kuwait remained a British protectorate. As a trading centre it lost significance at the end of the 19th century, until in 1938 oil was discovered and a turning point came. In 1990 Kuwait was invaded by Iraqi troops, and in the ensuing 1991 Golf War, Iraq was driven out by UN troops.

Topography: From the Bay of Kuwait on the coastal plains of the Persian Gulf, the land runs westward into an area of sand dunes and sandstone plateau. Kuwait also comprises the islands of Failaka, Bubiyan and Warba at north-east corner of Arabian Peninsula.

Economy: Through the discovery of oil, Kuwait has become a rich country, although it is dependent on foreign labour. Oil makes up 95% of the export balance; the land is not really arable due to the climate; almost all food has to be imported.

Al Maghrib
Morocco
MA

Population: 27 million (59 per sq km)
Area: 458,730 sq km
Capital: Rabat
Political system: parliamentary monarchy
Languages: High Arabic, (official) , Berber, various Arabic dialects
Religion: over 90% Sunni Muslim
GNP: US$ 1,290 per head
Currency: 1 dirham = 100 centimes
Industries: dates, figs, cork, wood pulp, wine, olives, citrus fruit, tourism

History: In prehistoric times this was Phoenician territory and later the location of Carthage. From 42 AD it belonged to the Romans, then to the Vandals, then in the 6th century to Byzantium and at the end of the 7th century to the Arabs. From the 11th to 15th century this land experienced its cultural heyday under various Berber dynasties, until the Spanish and Portuguese invaded.
Since the 16th century Arabian monarchs have ruled, except when Morocco was a French Protectorate from 1912 to 1956. Morocco, which has a parliamentary monarchy that in practical terms is closer to an absolute monarchy, is nevertheless one of the most liberal Islamic countries.

Topography: To the north, Morocco borders on the Mediterranean Sea, to the west on the Atlantic. Beyond the fertile coastal plains traversed by rivers in the north-west, the Middle and High Atlas mountain chain crosses the land from northeast to south-west, as well as the Anti-Atlas. To the east the land falls to steppe country and then to the Sahara desert. The area of the West Sahara long remained a source of discussion in Moroccan politics.

Economy: Apart from the largest phosphate deposits in the world, Morocco also has iron, lead, ores and oil. This wealth of minerals forms the basis for the domestic chemical and metal industry, which employs around 40% of Moroccans. Wool and skins from cattle-farming are turned into carpets and leather goods and then exported. About a third of the population live below the poverty line.

Al Misr
Egypt
ET

Population: 59.2 Mill. (59 per sq km)
Area: 1,002,000 sq km
Capital: Cairo (Al-Qahirah)
Political system: presidential republic
Languages: High Arabic (Official), Arabic, Nubic and Berber
Religion: 90% Sunni Muslim, Coptic Christian 5%
GNP: US$ 1,080 per head
Currency: 1 Egyptian pound = 100 piaster
Industries: natural gas and petroleum products, agriculture (wool, sugar-cane, grain); textiles, heavy and chemical industries; tourism

History: The advanced culture of the Egyptians dates from the 3rd millennium BC, with Libyan, Persian and Assyrian rule from the 1000 BC. From 30 BC it was a Roman province and the largest grain supplier to ancient Rome. An Arab conquest in 640 AD led to the conversion to Islam. The Ottoman Conquest took place in 1517, the Napoleon conquest in 1798. The Suez Canal opened in 1869, and from 1914 it was a British protectorate. In 1922 Egypt became an independent kingdom, and since 1953 it has been a republic. Israel has had a peace treaty with Egypt since 1979 following constant heated conflicts.

Topography: The fertile valley of the Nile - the longest river in Africa (6671 km) - has always determined life in Egypt. The valley is bordered to the west by the Libyan Desert and to the east by the Arabian Desert and the Sinai Peninsula.

Economy: Agriculture constitutes just 20% of the gross national product. Egypt is becoming

more and more an industrial nation. A considerable source of income is tourism; the main attractions are the ancient sites of advanced civilisation in Egypt (the Pyramids, Sphinx, etc). Due to terrorist attacks however, Egypt has suffered a noticeable decline in numbers of tourists in the recent past.

Argelia › *Al Jaza´ir*

Al Urdunn
Jordan
JOR

Population: 4.3 million (48 per sq km)
Area: 89,342 sq km
Capital: Amman
Political system: parliamentary monarchy
Languages: High Arabic (official), English, Bedouin
Religion: over 90% Sunni Muslim
GNP: US$ 1,650 per head
Currency: 1 Jordanian dollar = 1000 fils
Industries: Potash, phosphates (fertilisers), citrus, vegetables, cattle rearing products

History: The Nabataeans settled in this area in the 4th century BC and it was closely connected to Israel. In 64 BC it became the Roman province of Arabia, from the 7th century it belonged to the Syrians and from 1517 until 1918 to the Ottoman province of Damascus. From 1920 it was under a British mandate and in 1946 gained independence. A parliamentary monarchy was established in the 1952 constitution. King Hussein who ruled from 1952 until 1999, led his land

through war and economic difficulties, and strove hard to bring some peace into the area. A sign of this success was the negociation and signing of a peace treaty with Israel in 1994.

Topography: Jordan possesses a narrow link to the Red Sea. Israel and the Dead Sea form the border to the west. The major part of the land is covered with hilly forest adjoined by the Syrian Desert in the east.

Economy: The greater part of this country is not arable and mineral deposits are rare. Main exports are chemical products, phosphates and potash. Almost three-quarters of the population work in the service sector. Jordan is one of the poorest of the Arab countries. Tourists are welcomed and many are especially attracted by the archaeological sites of Petra, the capital of the Nabataeans and the provincial capital of the Romans from 3rd century BC until the 1st century AD.

_____Angola Angola

1 At a height of over 3000 metres this stone bridge winds its way through the inhospitable mountainous desert in Yemen

2 "Palace on the Rocks" (Dar Al Hajjar) near Sana, the capital of Yemen

3 Life in the sun and wind: Egyptian merchant in Cairo

4 Abu Simel, Egypt: two rock temples, which Ramses II (1290-1224 BC) had built between the first and second rapids on the west bank of the Nile

industry is one of the most important sources of revenue.

Al Yaman
Yemen
(ADN)

Population: 15.7 million (29 per sq km)
Area: 536,869 sq km
Capital: San'a
Political system: Islamic republic (authoritarian)
Languages: High Arabic (official), Yemenis, Bedouin dialect, south Arab languages
Religion: 99% Muslim (Sunni 63%, Shi'ite 37%)
GNP: US$ 380 per head
Currency: 1 Yemen rial = 100 fils
Industries: petroleum products, cotton, coffee, grapes, vegetables

History: In the 1000 BC the Minaers people lived here, then from 900 BC the Sabaer, who became rich trading in spices. One of their rulers was the Queen of Sheba, who is mentioned in the Bible. In 628 AD Yemen became Islamic, which led to the outbreak of numerous civil wars. From 1517 until 1635 and from 1890 this country was under Ottoman rule. In 1918 North Yemen was made into a kingdom with the help of the British.
After a military putsch in 1962 it became a republic. The British-controlled south separated in 1967 and formed a socialist republic. Although the process took a long time, the two states were united again in 1990.
Topography: The west coast borders on the Red Sea, the south coast on the Gulf of Aden and the Arabian Sea. Inland from the rather narrow coastal plains there are mountains which lead to desert on the Saudi-arabian border.

Economy: Because almost one-third of the population earn oil dollars, there is a shortage of labour in other fields in this largely underdeveloped country. Relatively good results are still produced in agriculture, but mainly through the cultivation and export of the illegal drug kat (a quarter of the GNP).

Andorra
Andorra
(AND)

Population: 71,000 (152 per sq km)
Area: 468 sq km
Capital: Andorra la Vella
Political system: parliamentary principality
Languages: Catalan (official), Spanish, French
Religion: Catholic (almost 100%)
GNP: over US$ 9,000 per head
Currency: 1 French frank = 100 centimes; 1 Spanish peseta = 100 centimos
Industries: sheep-breeding, tourism

History: From the 13th century it was ruled jointly by Spain and France, from the 17th century by France alone. Since 1993 the mini-state has been a sovereign principality.
Topography: Three high valleys to the east of the Pyrenees are surrounded by 3 000 m high mountain ranges.
Economy: Agriculture and industry are only possible under difficult conditions in a country where almost half the land lies above the tree-line. Almost 80% of the work force is in the service sector; and with 8 million tourists a year, the tourist

Angola
Angola
(ANG)

Population: 11.1 million (9 per sq km)
Area: 1,246,700 sq km
Capital: Luanda
Political system: presidential republic
Languages: Portuguese (official), various Bantu languages
Religion: Christian
GNP: US$ 270 per head
Currency: 1 Kwanza Reajustado
Industries: agriculture (coffee, sugar, tobacco, sisal); natural gas and iron-ore.

History: Some of the Angolan people who originally lived here were taken to Brazil as slaves by the Portuguese from 1483 onwards, others were subjugated when the country became a Portuguese province. Since independence in 1975, civil war has destroyed parts of both the country and thousands of its population. The 1994 peace process has repeatedly been put in jeopardy by the UNITA (National Union for the Total Independence of Angola).
Topography: The north-western coastal region is covered with rainforest and develops into savannah and desert to the south-west. The central highland is bounded by the Lunda Threshold in the north-east, by the Zambezi Basin in the southeast, and by the Congo Basin to the north. Angola has nine national parks with animal reserves.
Economy: Roughly three-quarters of the inhabitants work in agriculture. Crude-oil is the most important source of foreign currency.

Antigua and Barbuda

Antigua and Barbuda
Antigua and Barbuda
(AG)

Population: 66,000 (150 per sq km)
Area: 442 sq km
Capital: St. John's
Political system: parliamentary monarchy
Languages: English (official), Creole
Religion: Christian (mostly Anglican),
20% Catholic
GNP: US$ 7,330 per head
Currency: 1 Eastern Caribbean dollar =
100 cents
Industries: tourism, vegetables, wool, sugar
cane

History: Some of the indigenous Indian population that Columbus discovered in 1493 were
taken as slaves, others wiped out. From 1623
English people settled in the area.
Since 1981 the islands have been independent;
the head of state is still the British monarch as the
islands could not sustain themselves without outside assistance.
Topography: The state consists of the islands
Antigua (280 sq km), Barbuda (160 sq km) and
Redonda (uninhabited, 1 sq km); they are consti-
tuted of limestone and coral with volcanic outcrops and luxuriant vegetation.
Economy: 80% of the inhabitants are employed
in tourism which comprises 50% of the gross national product.

Argentina
Argentina
(RA)

Population: 35.2 million (13 per sq km)
Area: 2,780,400 sq km
Capital: Buenos Aires
Political system: presidential republic
Languages: Spanish (official), Indian languages
Religion: 91% Catholic
GNP: US$ 8,380 per head
Currency: 1 Argentinian peso = 100 centavos
Industries: agricultural products (foodstuffs, meat)

History: Indian tribes settled here from c. 9000
BC. The north-west was conquered by the Incas
in 1480 AD. The area came under Spanish rule in
1515. In 1810 the autonomous government of
Buenos Aires came into being, in 1816 indepen-
dence from Spain was declared by the United
Provinces of Río de la Plata, known from 1860 as
Argentina. In 1862 Buenos Aires became a part of
Argentina, likewise Patagonia in 1881. From 1930
military dictators ruled one after the other; a de-

mocracy was first established in 1983 after the
Falkland conflict, which also drew attention to
the number of people who were missing, pre-
sumed kidnapped and tortured by the military
junta in the period 1973-1983. An official apol-
ogy and compensation was proclaimed, although
there are still mothers who protest in the hope of
hearing something of their still missing sons.
Topography: The vast country is bounded to
the west by the high and mighty Andes mountains; the highest peak is the Aconcagua, 6 960 m.

The Patagonian plateau extends to the south and
an area of rain forest between the Paraná and
Uruguay rivers lies to the north. The most heavily
populated area is the central lowland, the Pampa,
which is a fertile steppe.
Economy: The processing of agricultural products and the plastics and mechanical engineering
industries are of importance; however, around
two-thirds of the gross domestic product is derived from the service sector.

Armenia › *Hayastan*

As Sudan
Sudan
(SUD)

Population: 27.2 million (11 per sq km)
Area: 2,505,813 sq km
Capital: Khartoum (Al-Khartum)
Political system: Islamic republic (military)
Languages: High Arabic (official), Sudanese Ara-
bic, over 100 African languages
Religion: Sunni Muslim 70%, animist 20%,
Catholic 5%, Protestant 5%
GNP: under US$ 800 per head
Currency: 1 Sudanese dinar = 100 piaster
Industries: cotton, sesame seed, cattle

History: In ancient times this land, at that time
known as Nubia, had close ties to its neighbour

Egypt. In 1000 BC the state of Kush came into
existence and lasted until almost the 5th century,
keeping up the traditions of Egypt.
After 640 AD three Christian states were formed
out of it and from 1200 AD the area was converted to Islam. These varied influences led to the
development of a completely independent culture. From the 19th century the British were the
colonial rulers in Sudan. In 1956 they granted its
independence; due to the civil war between the
Arab-dominated north and the African-rooted
south, however, Sudan has become weak. There
has been continuous civil war, with each side
blaming the other for the misery caused to the
population and dementing any rumours of
peace.
Topography: Geographically, Sudan is the
largest country in Africa. In its interior, basin-like
countryside extends around the flood area of the
White Nile; to the east the Ethiopian highlands
rise and form a divide to the Red Sea. To the
north lie the Nubian and Libyan deserts, and in
the south, the Imatong mountains, covered with
rainforest, form the border.
Economy: Almost half of the area is made up of
desert and this is expanding annually. Civil war
and natural catastrophes have led to high foreign
debt, the inflation rate for 1995/96 being over
160%. Without aid from abroad, this country
would be unable to survive.

1 Colourful and un-
conventional: appart-
ments in Buenos
Aires, capital of
Argentina

3 The famous
Iguaçu Falls on the
border between
Argentina and Brazil

2 Splendidly adorn-
ed working animal:
the camels in the
Sudanese caravans
transport mainly
salt and spices

4 Unique and
unmistakable in
its design: Sydney
Opera House,
built in 1973

Australia
Australia
(AUS)

Population: 18.3 million (2 per sq km)
Area: 7,628,300 sq km
Capital: Canberra
Political system: federal constitutional
monarchy
Languages: English (official), Aboriginal lan-
guages
Religion: 70% Christian (27% Catholic, 22%
Anglican), Muslim, Buddhist, Hindus
GNP: US$ 20,090 per head
Currency: 1 Australian dollar = 100 cents
Industries: Food (cereals, beef, veal, mutton,
lamb, sugar), wool, mineral coal, iron-ore, indus-
trial products, machines

History: The Aborigines arrived on the continent
during the last Ice Age. The first Europeans set
foot on Australian soil in 1606. The island was
used as a convicts' colony between 1788 and
1869. Immigrants started arriving in 1793, and a
gold-rush led to massive immigration in 1851.
The founding of the Commonwealth of Australia
took place in 1901, and the British monarch remains the head of state to this day. A new wave
of immigration from Europe started after World
War II. Only recently have the Aborigines been

accepted as citizens with equal rights and first
steps taken to apologize and make amends for
the ruthless colonisation through compensation
and the return of their lands.
Topography: More than two-thirds of Australia,
the smallest of the five continents, is made up of
desert, covering the west and the almost uninhabited interior. The north is comprised of savannah, with mangroves and rainforest along the
coast. The Barrier Reef along the east coast and
the many national parks attract numerous tourists
looking for unspoilt nature.
Economy: The sparsely populated land has a
high standard of living and education. Over two-
thirds of the people work in the service sector.
Besides foodstuffs and combustibles, important
exports include high-grade industrial goods.
Australia is the world's leading producer of wool.

Austria › Österreich

Azarbaycan
Azerbaijan
(AZ)

Population: 7.5 million (88 per sq km)
Area: 86,600 sq km
Capital: Baku (Baki)
Political system: presidential republic
Languages: Turkic, Azerbaijan/Azeri (official),
Russian, Armenian
Religion: Shi'ite Muslim
GNP: US$ 480 per head
Currency: 1 Azerbaijan-manat = 100 gepik
Industries: agriculture, petroleum, metals

History: Azerbaijan was a Roman province for a
brief period; from the 7th century it became Is-

lamic. It was ruled by the Mongols for 300 years.
In 1813 Russia and Persia divided Azerbaijan between themselves. The Azerbaijan Soviet Republic
was founded in 1920. It declared independence
in 1991 and was admitted to the CIS. Numerous
conflicts with the neighbouring country of Armenia over a mountainous area almost only inhabited by Armenians, called Nagomo-Karabakh,
makes peace difficult to attain.
Topography: This land is bordered to the north
by high and to the west by lower Caucasus
mountains, and to the south as far as Iran with
mountains, and to the east by the Caspian Sea.
Economy: Although the country possesses great
mineral and ore deposits and a good agricultural
system, there have been great economic difficulties in recent years due to an extremely high interest rate and high unemployment (30% in the
early 90's). Over 90% of the population live
below the poverty line.

Bahamas
Bahamas
(BS)

Population: 284,000 (20 per sq km)
Area: 13,940 sq km
Capital: Nassau
Political system: parliamentary monarchy
Languages: English (official), Creole
Religion: 31% Baptist, 16% Anglican, 16%
Catholic, 5% each Pentecost, Methodists
GNP: over US$ 9,000 per head
Currency: 1 Bahama dollar = 100 cents
Industries: tourism, crude oil, chemical
products

History: It was here in 1492 that Columbus set
foot on American soil for the first time. The Spanish displaced all the Indian inhabitants as forced
labour to Cuba and Hispaniola.
In the 17th century the uninhabited islands were
taken by the English as a crown colony. The Bahamas have been independent since 1973 and
the head of state is still the British monarch.
Topography: This state is comprised of around
700 large to tiny islands, of which 30 are inhabited. There are also innumerable reefs and cliffs.
Economy: Agriculture is almost impossible due
to the geographical conditions. Fishing and
tourism provide the main source of income in the
Bahamas.Tourism is the main source of revenue
for the Bahamas. Favourable legislation makes
this tropical paradise a tax haven.

Bahrain › Al Barayn

Bălgarija
Bulgaria

(BG)

Population: 8.5 million (75 per sq km)
Area: 110,994 sq km
Capital: Sofia (Sofija)
Political system: presidential republic (socialist pluralist)
Languages: Bulgarian, Turkish
Religion: 86% Bulgarian Orthodox Christian, 13% Sunni Muslim
GNP: US$ 1,190 per head
Currency: 1 lew = 100 stótinki
Industries: mining (iron-ore, brown coal), tobacco, wine, machinery, timber, chemicals

History: A first Bulgarian Empire existed from 680 till 1018, a second from 1185 until 1330. After that it came under Serbian rule and from 1396 was a part of the Ottoman Empire for 500 years. With the help of Russia it broke away from Turkish rule in 1878 but found itself entangled in a European power struggle, became an independent kingdom in 1908 but could not maintain its predominance in the Balkans. In 1946 it proclaimed itself the People's Republic of Bulgaria. It experienced a similar turn of events like other Eastern-bloc states in 1989 and has been a parliamentary republic since 1991.
Topography: The Danubian Plain, the north Bulgarian lowlands and the Balkan Mountains make up this country. The Black Sea coast was a favourite holiday destination until the turn-around; at present tourism is severely retarded because of the disastrous economic situation.
Economy: Bulgaria's transition from an agricultural to an industrial state was begun in the post War period but is now in difficulties due to the similar collapse of communist supported economies in Eastern Europe. Former trading partners are themselves experiencing difficulties and Bulgaria is searching for strong trading partners within the EU.

Bangladesh
Bangladesh

(BD)

Population: 121.6 million (825 per sq km)
Area: 147,570 sq km
Capital: Dhaka
Political system: parliamentary republic (restricted democracy)
Languages: Bengali (official), diverse Indo-Aryan, Mundari, Mon-Khmer languages
Religion: 87% Muslim, 12% Hindus
GNP: US$ 260 per head

Currency: 1 taka = 100 poisha
Industries: textiles, (clothing, knitted goods, jute)

History: Between 1757 and 1947 Bengal belonged to India, which was still a British colony at that time. When India gained its independence, the land was divided: west Bengal stayed as part of India and east Bengal became part of Pakistan. After a flood catastrophe in 1970 there was a rebellion. In 1971 East Bengal separated from Pakistan and declared itself the Republic of Bangladesh. The first democratically elected government has been in office since 1991.
Topography: The unprotected coast and the heavy precipitation from the Himalayas flowing into the huge Ganges river mean an almost annual flooding catastrophe for Bangladesh. The terrible consequences of this are widescale flooding which brings death, starvation and disease to this economically struggling country.
Economy: Bangladesh is one of the poorest nations in the world. Half of the population are underemployed and the illiteracy rate is over 60%. Around two-thirds of the labour force work in agriculture.

Barbados
Barbados

(BDS)

Population: 264,000 (614 per sq km)
Area: 430 sq km
Capital: Bridgetown
Political system: parliamentary monarchy
Languages: English (official), Bajan
Religion: 40% Anglican, other diverse Christian idenominations and sects
GNP: under US$ 10,000 per head
Currency: 1 Barbados dollar = 100 cents
Industries: tourism, sugar, rum, syrup, electronic components

History: The indigenous population, Arawak Indians, were taken as slaves by the Spanish at the beginning of the 16th century. When the English arrived in 1625 they found an uninhabited island which they immediately made a crown colony. In 1966 Barbados gained independence, but has maintained the British lifestyle. Many people came to the UK in the 60s due to the labour crisis in the UK economy.
Topography: Most easterly island of the Lesser Antilles in the West Indies; surrounded by coral reefs; subject to hurricanes.
Economy: Climate and landscape make this island a holiday paradise for tourists. The country's legislation makes it a tax haven for investors.

Three-quarters of the employed earn their living in the service sector, of which tourism forms a considerable part.

Belarus'
Belarus

(SU)

Population: 10.2 million (50 per sq km)
Area: 207,595 sq km
Capital: Mensk (Minsk)
Political system: presidential republic (emergent democracy)
Languages: Belorussian, Russian
Religion: Russian Orthodox 60%, Catholic 8%, with Baptist and Muslim minorities
GNP: US$ 2,070 per head
Currency: 1 Belarus rouble = 100 kopecks
Industries: agricultural machinery, electrical goods, metal processing, peat, fertilizers

1 Belize: Testimony to the advanced level of Mayan sculpture: relief in slate, 7th-9th century AD

3 Magnificent beaches are the chief asset of Barbados, the most easterly island of the Lesser Antilles

2 The Atomium, symbol of the Brussels World Exhibition in 1958, is 110 metres high, representing an alpha iron crystal enlarged a billion times

4 Bulgaria: After liberation from Turkish rule, the Alexander Newski church in Sofia was rebuilt

History: White Russia belonged in medieval times to the Kiev Rus, which was the first east Slavic state. It fell into numerous principalities, came under Lithuanian and Polish influence in the 14th century and formed its own language from them. In the 18th century it fell into the hands of the Russians but the cultural influence of the Poles remained intact, until in the 19th century the Russian tsarist policies took hold. In 1919 the White Russian Socialist Soviet Republic emerged, joining the USSR in 1922. In 1991 White Russia declared independence; it is one of the three founders of the CIS.

Topography: This extensive area of flat land is typical of a landscape formed during an ice age; it is marked by extensive areas of water (lakes, rivers, canals) as well as marshes and moorland. Only on the White Russian Ridge does one find hills.

Economy: White Russia is left with few economic options because the land is relatively poor, suited solely to cattle-farming, and lacks mineral deposits. Skilled workers, however, have helped towards a specialization in industry of which me-

chanical engineering and metal processing are the main branches and this knowledge is exported to the various member states of the CIS.

Belgïe/Belgique
Belgium
B

Population: 10.1 million (333 per sq km)
Area: 30,528 sq km
Capital: Brussels
Political system: parliamentary monarchy
Languages: Flemish, Walloon, German
Religion: 81% Catholic, Muslim, Jewish, Protestant
GNP: US$ 26,440 per head
Currency: 1 Belgian frank = 100 centimes
Industries: industrial goods (machinery, motor vehicles, chemical, iron and steel products)

History: Flanders was one of the most important trading centres in Europe at the end of the Middle Ages. Later the region fell under foreign rule for a long time. From the 16th century it changed hands frequently between the Spanish, Austrian, French and Dutch. Belgium has been an independent kingdom since 1830, a federal state since 1933, whose three regions (Flanders, Wallonia and Brussels) each have their own parliaments and governments. NATO and the EU have their headquarters in Brussels.

Topography: Fertile coastal marshland and heath are to the north-west; central rolling hills rise eastward; hills and forest are to the southeast (Ardennes). The main attraction for tourists are the coastal resorts and the picturesque medieval cities such as Ghent and Bruges.

Economy: Agricultural yields are high. When it comes to exports, the products from the indus-

trial regions of the Meuse and Sambre play the most important role.
Two thirds of Belgians are employed in the service sector. Belgium has the most extensive railway network in the world.

Belize
Belize
BH

Population: 222,000 (10 per sq km)
Area: 22,965 sq km
Capital: Belmopan
Political system: parliamentary monarchy
Languages: English (official), Creole, Spanish
Religion: 58% Catholic, 28% diverse Protestant
GNP: US$ 2,700 per head
Currency: 1 Belize dollar = 100 cents
Industries: agriculture (sugar-cane, bananas, cacao), tourism

History: This country belonged to the Mayan civilisation until the Spanish conqueror Cortez appeared. In the 17th century the British settled here and made it a crown colony in 1869 called British Honduras.
The name Belize came into use in 1973. British troops helped to secure the peace during the transition to independence which the colony declared in 1981.

Topography: This south-eastern part of the Yucatán Peninsula is covered in rain and mangrove forests. The coastal area is swampy and comprises numerous lagoons. There are 1000 m high mountains in the south.
There is a 300 km long coral reef along the coast with many islands.

Economy: Agricultural goods, primarily sugar and cocoa account for 90% of the export bal-

Benin

ance. Tourism is taking on an increasingly important role. Over half of the population works in the service sector.

Bénin
Benin
DY

Population: 5.6 million (50 per sq km)
Area: 111,622 sq km
Capital: Porto Novo (official), Cotonou (de facto)
Political system: presidential republic (socialist pluralist)
Languages: French (official), 47% Fon, 9% Yoruba, 6 other major tribal languages
Religion: 60% animist, 20% Catholic, 12% Muslim
GNP: US$ 350 per head
Currency: CFA franc
Industries: cotton, petroleum and its byproducts, coffee, palm products, peanuts

History: From the 17th century this region was a possession of the Dahomey Kingdom. Dahomey formed part of French West Africa from 1899. In 1960 the colony gained independence. After a coup d'état in 1975, a people's republic was declared and the name was changed from Dahomey to Benin. The first free elections took place in 1991.
Topography: A hot and humid marshy region with coastal lagoons to the south, a fertile highland that leads to a plateau to the north, the Niger Basin is to the north-east, semi-arid to the north.
Economy: A third of the population is engaged in agriculture which, because of mismanagement, plays an increasingly minor role, both for home-demands and export. Attempts at rescuing the country from its financial crisis by gearing up tourism have not been tremendously successful.

Bhutan
Bhutan
BHT

Population: 715,000 (15 per sq km)
Area: 46,500 sq km
Capital: Thimphu
Political system: constitutional monarchy (absolute)
Languages: Dzongkha (official), Sharchop, Bumthap, Napali, and English
Religion: over 70% Buddhist, over 20% Hindus
GNP: US$ 390 per head
Currency: 1 ngultum = 100 chhetrum
Industries: fruits and vegetables, electricity, timber, distilled spirits

History: Princely Indian rule was overthrown in the 9th century by Tibetan conquerors. The state of Bhutan was founded in 1553. In the 19th century the British co-operated in the establishment of a hereditary monarchy that still survives today; now it governs together with the national assembly.
Topography: Occupies the southern slopes of the Himalayas and is surrounded by impressive mountain peaks (highest point: Kalha Gangri , 7554 m). It is a small country between India and China and very hard to reach. Between the mountain chains there are fertile valleys and rain forests.
Economy: 94% of the inhabitants work in agriculture which meets the requirements of the land. Timber is exported to neighbouring India. It is slowly opening up to tourism.

Bolivia
Bolivia
BOL

Population: 7.5 million (6.9 per sq km)
Area: 1,098,581 sq km
Capital: Sucre (official), La Paz (de facto)
Political system: presidential republic (emergent democracy)
Languages: Spanish, Aymara, Quechua (all official), also Guarani
Religion: over 90% Catholic

GNP: US$ 830 per head
Currency: 1 boliviano = 100 centavos
Industries: agriculture, mining (zinc, gold, tin, silver), petroleum, natural gas

History: The indigenous Indians, like everywhere else on the continent, were suppressed by the colonists. At the end of the 18th century the native inhabitants revolted against the Spanish for the first time, which led to the founding of a republic in 1825. In this century the history of Bolivia has been characterised by changing military dictatorships, guerrilla warfare and attempts at democracy. A democratically elected government has been in office since 1982.
Topography: The Bolivian Andes form the border to the west; they encompass a 3 000 to 4 000 m high plateau. The lowland to the east leads to the Amazon Basin in the north and to the flatland (La Plata) in the south. In the Andes on the border to Peru, Lake Titica, which lies 3 810 m above sea-level, is the highest navigable stretch of water in the world.
Economy: Various metals, oil and natural gas, as well as timber and soya are important exports. In addition the illegal cultivation of coca plays an

1 Young woman of the Yoruba tribe in Benin

2 Rio de Janeiro (Brazil) with the Sugarloaf Mountain in the background

3 The royal palace in Benin

4 Picture of the landscape of a strange planet: rock formations near La Paz, Bolivia

5 The Kalahari semi-desert covers more than 80% of the land in Botswana

Industries: citrus fruits and vegetables, iron and steel, leather goods, textiles. Due to civil war the economy is not functioning.

History: At the beginning of the Middle Ages there was an independent principality here; the Ottomans conquered Bosnia in 1463, Herzegovina in 1482. From 1878 this area came under Austro-Hungarian administration, from 1908 under Austro-Hungarian rule. From 1918 it belonged to the kingdom of Serbia, Croatia and Slovenia, from 1929 to the kingdom of Yugoslavia, and after World War II to the Yugoslavian Federation. It declared its independence in 1991 and has since then been involved in a civil war between Serbs, Croats and Muslims, that has now become a holy war and is still continuing in parts of the former Yugoslavia.

Topography: Partly forested, partly barren, mountainous country in central Europe. Agriculture is only possible in a few fertile valleys.

Economy: The country has rich mineral deposits, a well-developed industrial sector and tourist attractions; however, the civil war has almost fully paralysed the economy. Unemployment has reached 80%; they could not survive without aid from abroad.

History: This country was organised into various Tswana Kingdoms until the colonial period. From 1885 it was a British protectorate and in 1966 it achieved independence.

Topography: Around 80% of the land is covered by the Kalahari desert, which lies on a high plateau. Farming is only possible in the southeast. A fifth of the land is covered with national parks.

Economy: Thanks to the diamond fields in the Kalahari, Botswana is the world's second largest diamond exporter. The most important form of farming, cattle-farming, is continually under threat by severe droughts.

Brasil
Brazil

BR

Population: 161.3 million (19 per sq km)
Area: 8,547,404 sq km
Capital: Brasilia
Political system: federal presidential republic (democracy)
Languages: Portuguese (official), around 180 Indian languages
Religion: 75% Catholic, 10% other Christian religion, Indian faiths
GNP: US$ 4,400 per head
Currency: 1 real = 100 centavos
Industries: coffee, sugar, soya beans, timber, motor vehicles, metals, precious stones

History: The first traces of settlement stem from the 8th century BC and from 900 BC there are signs of a settled population. The Spanish, who arrived here in 1500, followed soon after by the Portuguese, set up huge sugar plantations, enslaved the native population and brought 4 to 5 million African slaves to this land as an additional work force. In the 17th century Brazil was made a viceroy kingdom of Portugal. In 1822 it became an independent kingdom; in 1889 the monarchy was abolished and a republic was established when, on account of the abolition of slavery,

important role. Foreign investment was possible when the state monopoly of oil was ended in 1996. Although half of the population work in agriculture, it is not sufficient to meet the requirements of the country. Transport costs for imports and exports are high because Bolivia does not have access to the sea.

Bosna i Hercegovina
Bosnia-Herzegovina

BIH

Population: 4.5 million (88 per sq km)
Area: 51, 129 sq km
Capital: Sarajevo
Political system: democratic presidential republic
Languages: Serbian variant of Serbo-Croatian
Religion: 44% Sunni Muslim, 31% Serbian Orthodox, 17% Catholic
GNP: under US$ 800 per head
Currency: 1 convertible mark

Botswana
Botswana

RB

Population: 1.4 million (2.5 per sq km)
Area: 581, 730 sq km
Capital: Gaborone
Political system: presidential republic (democratic)
Languages: English (official), Setswana and Batu
Religion: 50% Christian, 50% animist
GNP: US$ 3,115 per head
Currency: 1 pula = 100 thebe
Industries: diamonds, iron-ore, coal, agriculture (beef), copper, nickel

Brunei

there was an uprising of the large landowners. After a military putsch in 1964, Brazil was ruled by a dictator for over 20 years. A democratically-elected civilian president has been in office since 1985.

Topography: Brazil is the fifth largest country in the world. The land is bounded to the east by the densely populated Atlantic coast, to the north by the dense tropical Amazon rain forest with its network of rivers, and to the south-west by the Amazon lowland rain forest area, that is being threatened by ruthless clearing although efforts are now being made to curb this practice.

Economy: Brazil's economic power was founded formerly on sugar-cane and coffee plantations; today cattle-breeding plays an ever increasing role. There are rich mineral deposits, above all, iron and manganese, that have not nearly been fully exhausted yet.

The highly developed industrial sector chiefly produces motor vehicles and parts, but textiles and leather goods are also made. In addition to the beaches near Rio de Janeiro and the famous carnival celebrations, tourists are attracted to the Amazon basin and the Iguaçú waterfalls in the south-west.

Brunei
Brunei
(BRU)

Population: 290,000 (50 per sq km)
Area: 5 765 sq km
Capital: Bandar Seri Begawan
Political system: Islamic monarchy (absolute)
Languages: Malay (official), Chinese, English, Iban
Religion: 67% Muslim, Buddhist, 15% Daoist and Confucian , 10% Christian
GNP: over US$ 9,000 per head
Currency: 1 Brunei dollar = 100 cents
Industries: natural gas, oil and mineral oil products

History: An independent Islamic sultanate from the 15th century, it became a British protectorate in 1888. The country was occupied by the Japanese from 1941 to 1945 and after the war it became a British colony. In 1959 a first attempt was made to achieve autonomy and it was finally gained in 1984. The head of state is the sultan as absolute monarch.

Topography: The country comprises two separate parts on the north-west coast of Borneo. The hilly interior is covered by tropical rain forest; the densely populated coast on the South China Sea consists predominantly of mangrove swamps and coral beaches.

Economy: The country's wealth can be almost solely attributed to its rich mineral deposits: Over 90% of export revenues are derived from the exploitation of petroleum and natural gas. Agriculture plays a very minor role; the majority of goods are imported.

Bulgaria › Bălgarija

Burkina Faso
Burkina Faso
(BF)

Population: 10.6 million (39 per sq km)
Area: 274,200 sq km
Capital: Ouagadougou
Political system: presidential republic
Languages: French (official), about 60 native Sudan lang. spoken by 90% of population
Religion: 50% animist, 43% Muslim, 12% Christian
GNP: US$ 230 per head
Currency: CFA franc
Industries: cotton, gold, live-stock and animal products

History: In the 11th century the Mossi people founded the kingdom of Ouagadougou. In the 19th century the French conquered this area and made it a colony of French West Africa after World War I, known as Haut-Senegal-Niger or Upper Volta. In 1932 it was divided up between Sudan, Niger and the Ivory coast. Since 1960 it has been independent.

Topography: The dry savannah in the interior is the most inhabited part, moist savannahs are found along the south-west border; it is semi-arid to the north, with hills to west and south-east. Tourists come for the national parks.

Economy: Over 90% of the population work in agriculture. Their main export is cotton. There is very little industry.

Burma › Myanmar

Burundi
Burundi
(BU)

Population: 6.4 million (231 per sq km)
Area: 27,834 sq km
Capital: Bujumbura
Political system: (one-party military) presidential republic
Languages: Kirundi and French (both official), Kiswahili
Religion: 65% Christian, 35% animist
GNP: US$ 170 per head

1

Currency: 1 Burundi franc = 100 centimes
Industries: agriculture (fruits, livestock, coffee)

History: Originally inhabited by the Twa pygmies, it was taken over by the Bantu Hutus in the 13th century and overrun in the 15th century by the Tutsi. In 1884 the long rule of the Tutsi ended and it became a colony of German East Africa.

From the end of World War II until independence in 1962 it was under Belgian administration. In 1966 the monarch was deposed and replaced with a dictatorship, and in 1976 a military dictator took over.

Since 1990 there has been an effort towards democratisation. Bloody conflicts between Hutus and Tutsis are a recurrent political occurrence.

Topography: The interior of the country comprises both humid and dry savannahs. In the north-west tropical rainforest is to be found and Lake Tanganyika forms the border to the southwest.

Economy: Almost 60% of the population work in agriculture. The main export is coffee. There are transport problems because of its landlocked status, which is in part responsible for their difficult economic situation.

1 Mother and child: terracotta figure of the Bantus who live in the south of Cameroon

2 Mosque of the Sultan of Brunei: thanks to the plentiful supply of oil, this small country is one of the richest in the area

3 Endless expanses of unspoilt scenery in Banff National Park, a nature reserve of over 6600 sq km, established in 1885 in the province of Alberta, Canada

4 Typical wooden house high up in the Rocky Mountains, British Columbia, Canada

Cabo Verde
Cape Verde
CV

Population: 389,000 (97 per sq km)
Area: 4,033 sq km
Capital: Praia
Political system: presidential republic (socialist pluralist state)
Languages: Portuguese (official), Portuguese Creole dialect
Religion: Catholic 95%, animist
GNP: US$ 1,010 per head
Currency: 1 Cape Verde escudo = 100 centavos
Industries: fish and fish products, shoes, bananas, salt

History: In 1975, after the "Carnation Revolution" in Portugal, the Cape Verde people declared their independence.
Topography: The 15 volcanic islands (9 are inhabited) that lie on the west coast of Africa, are infertile and mountainous; there are also luxuriant valleys with dense vegetation.
Economy: The island republic could not exist without development aid and the support of its citizens who live outside the country (over 50%).

Because the low rainfall in this area makes it one of the driest countries on Earth, 90% of all food has to be imported. The most important sources of income are fishing and fish processing.

Cambodia › Kâmpŭchéa

Cameroon
Cameroon
CAM

Population: 13.6 million (29 per sq km)
Area: 475,442 sq km
Capital: Yaoundé
Political system: presidential republic
Languages: French, English (both official), Bantu, Fang, Duala, Ful, etc.
Religion: animist 40%, Catholic 35%, Muslim 22%, Protestant 18%
GNP: US$ 610 per head
Currency: 1CFA franc = 100 centimes
Industries: petroleum, coffee, cocoa, cotton, timber, rubber, gold, bananas

History: This country, that was inhabited by various races, was used by the Portuguese and the Dutch as a trading centre for the slave trade in

the 15th century. In 1854 this territory became a German colony and was ruled by France and Britain after World War I: the western part went to the British colony of Nigeria, the French part became an independent unit that won independence in 1960. In 1970 it became the "United Republic of Cameroon."
Topography: The country's border to the southwest is the Atlantic coast and the farthest northeasterly point borders on Lake Chad. The Atlantic coastal lowlands gradually rise to highland, ending in the Adamawa Highlands, and still futher north the land descends towards the Chad Basin.
Economy: About 200 tribes that speak 150 different languages live in Cameroon, some of them preserving their traditional way of life. Over two-thirds of the population work in agriculture; important export articles include coffee, cocoa , timber, rubber, cotton, bananas and palm products. A third of the export balance is achieved from oil.

Canada
Canada
CDN

Population: 29.9 million (3 per sq km)
Area: 9,958,319 sq km
Capital: Ottawa
Political system: parliamentary monarchy
Languages: English, French (both official), European and Indian languages.
Religion: Catholic 45%, Protestant 28%, Jewish and Muslim minorities
GNP: US$ 19,020 per head
Currency: 1 Canadian dollar = 100 cents
Industries: wheat, timber, pulp and paper, fish, furs, oil, metals, motor vehicles, machinery, chemicals

61

Česká Republika
Czech Republic

History: The indigenous Canadians, Indians and Inuit (Eskimos) migrated here 20,000 years ago from Asia. From the beginning of the 17th century the British and French founded colonies in the Canadian area and disputed the other's right to rule. In 1931 this country became politically independent. The British monarch is still the Canadian head of state. The French defend their cultural and religious independence; this conflict is reflected in the bilingual nature of this country.

Topography: In terms of area this is the second largest country on Earth. It is bounded by the Atlantic coast and Appalachian hills to the east and the Pacific to the west, where the land rises the Canadian Rocky Mountains. The Great Plains, interspersed with many lakes, run centrally from south to north; they trail off north-easterly towards Hudson Bay. The northern frontier on the Arctic Ocean is formed by an Arctic island world.

Economy: Canada is one of the richest nations in the world. Extensive forests and pastureland provide for profitable timber and cattle-farming, but only 3% of Canadians are engaged in farming. Exports include motor vehicles, machinery and other industrial goods, petroleum and grain also play an important role. Tourists are attracted by the wide open spaces, the low population density and the unspoilt countryside and national parks.

Cape Verde › Cabo Verde
Central African Republic ›
République centrafricaine

Če"ská Republika
Czech Republic
CZ

Population: 10.3 million (13 per sq km)
Area: 78,866 sq km
Capital: Prague (Praha)
Political system: (emergent) republic
Languages: Czech (official), Slovak
Religion: no denomination 40%, Catholic 39%, Protestants 2%, other 19%
GNP: US$ 4,740 per head
Currency: 1 Czech koruna = 100 heller
Industries: machinery, vehicles, chemicals, iron and steel, coal

History: This area had already been settled in the 6th century by the Slavs. In the 9th century the Czechs and the Slavs formed a large Moravian Empire. Bohemia and Moravia, the area where the Czechs settled, recognised the German Kaiser as their supporter. In the 14th century Prague became the capital of the Holy Roman Empire, in 1348 the first German university was founded. In 1526 the Bohemian Kingdom fell to the House of Habsburg. After World War I the Czechs and the Slavs joined up to form the Czechoslovakian Republic. From 1939 until 1945 Bohemia and Moravia came under German Protectorate, afterwards the republic again started anew. In 1968 the course of reform in this land ("Prague Spring") was overthrown by the Soviet troops marching in. Since the end of the 60's there have been new efforts toward reform. After the breaking up of the Eastern-bloc in 1989, the

Czechs and the Slavs separated from each other in 1992 and autonomous republics were formed.

Topography: A large part of this country consists of mountains and hills. To the west the Erzgebirge and the Bohemian forest form a natural border to Germany, to the north the Sudeten Mountains form a border to Poland. To the south there is a lowland; here the Danube forms the border to Hungary.

Economy: Heavy industry, based on rich mineral deposits, was important even in the times of the Hapsburg Monarchy. Today, along with mechanical engineering, it forms the main pillars of the Czech economy. Other important industries include: glass, textiles, foodstuffs and luxury items, as well as chemical and electronic industries. Privatization of former state-owned concerns has boosted the economy.

Chad → Tchad

Chile
Chile
RCH

Population: 14.4 million (19 per sq km)
Area: 756,626 sq km
Capital: Santiago de Chile (Santiago)
Political system: presidential republic
Languages: Spanish (official), Indian languages
Religion: 77% Catholic, 13% Protestant
GNP: US$ 4,860 per head
Currency: 1 Chilean Peso = 100 centavos
Industries: mining (above all copper), pulp and paper, industrial products

History: This country was conquered in 1544 by the Spanish. In 1818 it achieved independence. From then on the people fought uninterruptedly against control by powerful landowners. In 1973 the socialist president Allende was murdered and a military junta led by General Pinochet introduced a regime of terror. Not until 1989 were there free elections and a return to democracy. In 1998 General Pinochet was arrested in the UK and held whilst extradition proceedings were initiated against him. Spain had applied to have him extradited for the murder of Spanish citizens in Chile.

Topography: Chile stretches along the Pacific coast for a length of 4230 km, from the middle of South America down to Tierra del Feugo on the southern tip of the continent. Despite its length, Chile has an average width of only 190 km (400 km at its widest point, narrowing down to 90 km).

1 The "Charles Brid-
ge" over the River
Moldau in Prague:
the Gothic bridge,
with the famous
statues begun by
P. Parler, one of the
city's important
monuments

2 The riddle of the
ancestral statues on
the Easter Islands
remains unsolved to
this day

3 The Osorno vol-
cano (2,660 m) on
Lake Llanquihue
(south Chilean Andes)

4 Belvedere Court-
yard in the Vatican
City

5 Vatican City has
no regular armed
forces; here the fa-
mous Swiss Guards
regiment

This gives Chile one of the strangest shapes of all
the nations on Earth. The large north-south ex-
tensions and the variations in elavation explain
the extreme climatic variations from the icy
southern point to the desert region to the north.
Economy: Chile is the largest exporter of copper
in the world. Not even a quarter of the land is
arable, so that almost all that is produced is for
their own consumption. Because practically the
whole country consists of coast, it is natural that
fishing and fish processing is a big industry.

China, People's Republic → Zhongquo

Choson
North-Korea
(DVRK)

Population: 22.4 million (183 per sq km)
Area: 122,762 sq km
Capital: Pyongyang (P'yongyang)
Political system: people's republic
(communism)
Languages: Korean
Religion: no denomination almost 70%,
Buddhist, Confucian (underground)
GNP: under US$ 1,000 per head
Currency: 1 won = 100 chon
Industries: machinery, vehicles, electronic
goods, mining (coal, iron, copper)

History: From the very beginning, the history of
Korea was closely linked with neighbouring China
and Japan. From 1910 till 1945 Korea found itself
under Japanese occupation; afterwards Soviet
troops occupied the northern part of the country,
that in 1949 became independent as the Democratic People's Republic of Korea. The imposing
personality in North Korea was Kim Il Sung, party
leader (since 1946) and prime minister (since

1948). For over 40 years he determined the fate
of this land and tried, among other things, to extend its frontiers during the Korean War between
1950 till 1953. Since Kim's death in 1994, his son
Kim Jong II, has tried to continue his father's
work.
Topography: North Korea makes up the northern part of the Korean Peninsula between the Sea
of Japan and the Yellow sea and a part of the Chinese mainland. In the north of the predominantly
mountainous country, the Kama Highland is to
be found; to the south towards the Yellow Sea,
the land becomes flatter and low ridges and wide
plains predominate.

Economy: Increasing political isolation has led to
economic stagnation. Agriculture, in which one-
third of the population work, produces their own
requirements. Mining and industrial products are
virtually the sole exports; machinery and labour-
intensive methods hinder effectiveness. The supply situation, burdened with bad planning and
extremely high arms expenditures, was further
set back by natural disasters in 1995 and 1996.

Città del Vaticano
Vatican City
(VV)

Population: 455 (1034 per sq km)
Area: 0.44 sq km
Political system: absolute Catholicism (elected
monarchy)
Languages: Latin, Italian (both official)
Religion: catholic 100%
Currency: Vatican city lira, Italian lira

History: The first church to honour the apostle
Peter and the first residence of the Pope were
built within the city of Rome in the 3rd century.
In the 8th century the Pope succeeded in extend-
ing his secular power; the church state achieved
its greatest period of expansion at the beginning
of the 16th century. In 1929 the Vatican won
recognition as a sovereign state; the Pope, who is
elected for life, rules in the political and religious
centre of the Catholic church.
Topography: The smallest state in the world lies
within the city limits of the Italian capital, Rome.
The Vatican Palace, the basilica and square of
St. Peter's, and the Vatican Museums attract
many pilgrims and tourists every year.
Economy: The Vatican finances itself through
holdings, donations, and the sale of coins and
postage stamps, and possesses a trade and business monopoly.

Colombia

Colombia
Colombia

(CO)

Population: 37.4 million (33 per sq km)
Area: 1,141,748 sq km
Capital: Bogotá (Santa Fe de Bogotá)
Political system: presidential republic (emergent democracy)
Languages: Spanish (official), Indian languages
Religion: 95% Catholic
GNP: US$ 2,140 per head
Currency: 1 Colombian peso = 100 centavos
Industries: coffee, petroleum products, bananas, flowers, emeralds, cocaine, tobacco

History: The advanced Indio culture of the Muiscas and the Chibchas with their highly developed craftsmanship of gold, nourished the greed for El Dorado (the land of gold) in the Spanish discoverers. Columbus incidentally, after whom this country is named, never set foot here! This Spanish colony, together with Venezuela, declared independence in 1819 as the Republic of Gran Columbia. Since 1886 Columbia has been a parliamentary presidential democracy. Civil wars, terrorist activity, and the drug Mafia have shaken this land ever since.
Topography: The Andes, in places as high as 5 000 m, run from north to south, separating the flat coastland to the west from the plains (llanos) to the east; the Magdelana River runs north to the Caribbean Sea. Colombia also comprises the islands of Providencia, San Andrés and Mapelo.
Economy: Columbia is the second largest exporter of coffee. Less well-known is that it is also the second largest exporter of flowers. Oil and petroleum products make up almost a third of the foreign-trade balance. Bananas, tropical fruits and sugar-cane, as well as cattle-farming, play an important role, but the biggest role of all is played by the illegal cultivation and export of marihuana and cocaine.

Comores
Comoros

(COM)

Population: 505,000 (271 per sq km)
Area: 1862 sq km
Capital: Moroni
Political system: Presidential republic (authoritarian nationalism)
Languages: Arabic (official), Comorian (Swahili and Arabic dialect), Makua, French
Religion: Muslim (official) almost 100%, Catholic 14%
GNP: US$ 450 per head

Currency: 1 Comorian franc = 100 centimes
Industries: Copra, vanilla, cocoa, sisal, cloves

History: The first settlers probably came from the Malaysian-Polynesian area, followed by Persians and Arabs. In 1886 the neighbouring island of Mayotte, which had been a French protectorate, became a part of Comoros and in 1912 they joined together and formed one colony.

In 1974 it won its independence (without Mayotte) and has been an Islamic republic ever since.
Topography: The Comoros group consists of three large and two smaller islands that are of volcanic origin. Rainforest covered mountains and mangrove coasts, coral reefs and palm beaches, characterize this land.
Economy: Three-quarters of the population work in agriculture and can cover half of their own needs. The most important export articles are vanilla and cloves.

Congo, Dem. Rep. › Choson
Congo, Rep. ›
Taehan-Min´guk

Costa Rica
Costa Rica

(CR)

Population: 3.4 million (67 per sq km)
Area: 51,060 sq km
Capital: San José
climate: tropical
Political system: presidential republic (liberal democracy)
Languages: Spanish (official), English, Creole and Pidgin
Religion: 89% Catholic, 8% Protestant
GNP: US$ 2,640 per head
Currency: 1 Costa-Rica-colón = 100 céntimos
Industries: coffee, bananas, chemical products, machinery

History: Originally occupied by Guaymi Indians, the area was turned into a Spanish province during the 16th century and the Indians were almost completely ousted. In 1838 the province became independent and in 1848 a republic. Since 1871 the government has been democratically elected. Costa Rica has had fewer conflicts to report in its history than other countries in this region.
Topography: The inland valley is the most populated area, on the Pacific side there is savannah and forest, on the Caribbean side tropical rain forest. The state at the "waist" between North and South America is one of the most beautiful countries in the world.

1 *The quintessence of exotic life: Colombian dancers on the beach at Santa Marta*

2 *Ivory Coast: Mask of the Dan, a Mande tribe living in the north-west of the country*

3 *Coconuts, possibly the most exotic of all tropical fruits, are cultivated in Costa Rica mainly for the country's own consumption*

4 *Over 90% of the Cuban tobacco production is still in the hands of over 200,000 small farmers*

Economy: Columbus dubbed Costa Rica the area with rich coasts; but the hope for valuable mineral deposits was not fulfilled. Important exports are coffee, bananas, sugar and beef – goods that are subject to extreme price fluctuations and thus account for an unstable economy.

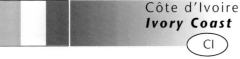

Côte d'Ivoire
Ivory Coast
CI

Population: 14.3 million (45 per sq km)
Area: 32,462 sq km
Capital: Yamoussoukro
Political system: one-party presidential republic
Languages: French (official), Baoulé, Bété, Diula, Senufo
Religion: 60% animist, 27% Muslim, 20% Christian
GNP: US$ 660 per head
Currency: CFA franc
Industries: cocoa, coffee, timber, cotton

History: The indigenous kingdoms of the Mali in the north and the Ashanti in the south ruled over this land. Missionaries brought it under European influence from the 17th century and in 1893 it became a French colony. A resistance movement against the French decree to forced labour on the plantations led this colony to independence in 1960.
Topography: The coastal rain forest to the south is used for intensive agriculture and rises to a 300 to 400 m plateau, covered by damp savannahs.
Economy: Agricultural products are at the top of the list of exports. The country is the world's biggest producer of cocoa.

Croatia ▸ **Hrvatska**

Cuba
Cuba
C

Population: 11 million (99 per sq km)
Area: 110,860 sq km
Capital: Havana (La Habana)
Political system: socialist republic (communist)
Languages: Spanish
Religion: no denomination 56%, Catholic 40%
GNP: under US$ 3,000 per head
Currency: 1 Cuban peso = 100 centavos
Industries: sugar, tobacco, coffee, nickel, fish, rum

History: The Arawaks and other tribes who had settled on the island were practically eradicated by the Spanish who took possession of Cuba in 1492 through forced labour and illness; from 1513 African slaves were imported as a work force.
After US military intervention in 1898 the Caribbean island came under American influence. After the Cuban Revolution in 1959, Cuba became the first socialist state in South America, led to this day by Fidel Castro.
After the break up of the communist world it has tried to hold its course but is becoming increasingly open to tourism.
Topography: Cuba, the largest island in the western Antilles, is divided by three high mountain ranges (almost 2 000 m), between which a marshy plain stretches in the east, and a higher-lying hilly region to the west.
Economy: Before the revolution, 80% of the country's export balance came from sugar. Today it is not quite 40%, which makes Cuba the third largest producer of sugar-cane in the world.
A further important export is nickel-ore and of its agricultural products, the world famous Cuban-cigar tobacco plays an important role (still

banned in the USA). Around a million tourists come annually to Cuba bringing foreign currency to the country.

Cyprus
Cyprus
CY

Population: 740,000 (80 per sq km)
Area: 9251 sq km
Capital: Nicosia (Levkosia)
Political system: presidential republic
Languages: Greek, Turkish (both official), English
Religion: Greek Orthodox 80%, Sunni Muslim 19%
GNP: over US$ 9,000 per head
Currency: Cyprus pound = 100 cents
Industries: citrus, grapes, raisins, Cyprus sherry, potatoes, clothing

History: This small island state in the Mediterranean Sea looks back on a changeable history of foreign rulers. As early as the 6th century BC, Stone Age civilizations left their traces behind; from 3000 BC copper finds turned this island into a trading centre. From 1500 BC Cyprus fell to the Egyptians, in the 13th century BC to the Greeks, in 1050 BC to the Assyrians, then again to the Egyptians and from 535 it came under Persian rule. From 333 BC the island belonged to Alexander the Great's Empire, in 295 BC it was a Ptolemian province and in 58 BC it was taken over by the Romans. From 395 till 1184 Cyprus belonged to the Byzantine Empire, then it was briefly independent until the conquest by the crusading troops of Richard the Lionheart in 1181. It was sold to a French dynasty and fell to Venice in 1489. From 1570 Cyprus found itself under Turkish rule, in 1878 it became a British Protectorate and a British colony in 1925. In 1960 it gained independence but the conflict between Greek and Turkish Cyprus has ended in the splitting of Cyprus in two. Through a UN mandate soldiers patrol the border to prevent further conflicts.

Topography: The Messaria plain in the central region is enclosed by mountains to the north and the south.

Economy: Agriculture, in which about 10% of the Cyprus population work, is the most important branch of industry; half of the export balance comes from processed agricultural products for the food industry. The second most important branch is the textile industry. Until the land was divided, tourism was an important economic factor, but due to the unstable political situation, the number of tourists has decreased, because many of the historical sites lie on the north of the island, which is occupied by the Turks.

Czech Rep. → Česká Republika

Danmark
Denmark
DK

Population: 5.3 million (122 per sq km)
Area: 43,094 sq km
Capital: Copenhagen (Krbenhaven)
Political system: parliamentary monarchy (liberal democracy)
Languages: Danish
Religion: 90% Lutheran
GNP: US$ 32,100 per head
Currency: 1 Danish krone = 100 qre
Industries: machinery and motor vehicles, meat and dairy produce, textiles, tourism

History: The original home of the Danes was Sweden where they emigrated from in the 5th century. Harold Bluetooth unified Denmark and converted it to Christianity in the 10th century. Until the 16th century the Danes expanded their predominance within the Baltic realm more and more; later they had to concede it bit by bit until after World War II only their present small territory remained. Since 1953 Denmark has been a parliamentary monarchy.

Topography: Comprises the Jutland peninsula and about 500 islands (100 inhabited); the land is flat and cultivated; sand dunes and lagoons on the west coast and long inlets (fjords) on the east coast; the main island is Sjaelland (Zealand), where Copenhagen is located.

Economy: Denmark is a modern welfare state with a highly developed industrial base and specialised agriculture.

Deutschland
Germany
D

Population: 81.9 million (229 per sq km)
Area: 357,021 sq km
Capital: Berlin
Political system: parliamentary federal republic
Languages: German
Religion: 34% Protestant, 33% Catholic
GNP: US$ 28,870 per head
Currency: 1 DM = 100 pfennig
Industries: motor vehicles, machinery, electronics and chemical products

History: After the crowning of Charlamagne as Kaiser (800 AD) many different tribes were united in the Holy Roman Empire (1st German Reich). Throughout the 12th century Popes and German Kaisers struggled to outdo each other in the fight for power.
After the Thirty Years War (1618-1648) the empire split up into numerous small principalities. Bismarck founded the 2nd German Reich in 1871.
Germany came out of World War I (1914-1918) the loser. In 1933 began the National Socialists' reign of terror, that led to the Holocaust, and only came to an end when Germany lost World War II (1939-1945). In 1949 the Allies divided the country into the Federal Republic of Germany and the German Democratic Republic. Since the re-unification in 1990 Germany comprises 16 federal states, that are governed by a Bundestag (Federal German Parliament) and a Bundesrat (Council of Constituent States).

Topography: This country is bounded to the north by the North Sea and the Baltic Sea, in the south by the Bavarian Alps; slowly rising hills lead southward from the coast down to the Harz Mountains, to the Black Forest and the Alps. The rivers Rhine, Weser and Elbe flow north, the

Danube flows south-east and were, even in earlier times, important trade routes, and are still important routes with the completion of the Rhine-Main-Danube system. As a travel destination, Germany is best known for its wealth of cultural attractions and its historic sites, including the Black Forest.

Economy: Around two-thirds of Germans are employed in the service sector. Germany belongs to the most significant industrial nations in the world. The most important exports include industrial goods such as machinery, motor vehicles and chemical products, but also iron, steel and textiles are manufactured. A further substantial economic factor is tourism, above all in the recreational areas in the Alps, the low mountains and the coast, as well as culturally interesting cities.

1 *The island of Cyprus, deforested since antiquity and only reforested at the beginning of the 20th century. (Forest now covers 18.5% of the land)*

2 *The statue of the little mermaid in the centre of Copenhagen's harbour, Denmark*

3 *Monument to Goethe and Schiller by Ernst Rietschel (1857), Weimar, Germany*

4 *The Dresden "Zwinger", a complex for court festivities begun in 1711*

5 *A small roadside altar in Calderón, Ecuador*

Basin that runs along the coast is one of the hottest spots in the world.

Economy: Although three-quarters of the population work in agriculture, this accounts for only 3% of the GDP. Three-quarters of the GDP is achieved through the ports: the French army has an important military base here, and container shipping plays an ever increasing role.

Dominica
Dominica
(WD)

Population: 74,000 (99 per sq km)
Area: 750 sq km
Capital: Roseau
Political system: parliamentary republic (liberal democracy)
Languages: English (official), French Creole
Religion: 80% catholic, 13% other christians
GNP: US$ 3,090 per head
Currency: 1 east Caribbean dollar = 100 cents
Industries: agriculture (bananas, cocoa, coconuts, citrus fruits)

History: The indigenous Indians, the Caribs, put up strong resistance to intruders. It was not until 1805 that this island became a British colony. In 1987 full independence was achieved.

Topography: This mountainous Windward Island that makes up part of the Lesser Antilles is of volcanic origin.
Rain forest, numerous lakes and waterfalls, palm beaches of black-lava sand and a national park with over 100 different kinds of birds give the visitor the impression of having found a tropical paradise.

Economy: Dominica is one of the poorest islands in the Caribbean. The greatest source of revenue is from agriculture; the export of bananas accounts for almost 50% of foreign trade. Tourism

has not made any impact; cruise tourism is the sole source of revenue for the state coffers.

Dominican Republic → República Dominicana

Ecuador
Ecuador
(EC)

Population: 11.6 million (43 per sq km)
Area: 272,045 sq km
Capital: Quito
Political system: presidential republic (emergent democracy)
Languages: Spanish (official), Quechua, Jivaro, and other Indian languages
Religion: 93% Catholic
GNP: US$ 1,500 per head
Currency: 1 sucre = 100 centavos
Industries: crude oil, bananas, coffee, industrial products

History: As long as 10,000 years ago Indian tribes lived here. The tribes of northern highland Ecuador formed the Kingdom of Quito about 1000 AD. It was conquered by the Incas in the 15th century and in 1534 the Spanish invaded and colonised it. Ecuador was liberated in 1822 and gained independence in 1830 after long battles, but ongoing power struggles with big landowners left it politically and economically unstable.

Topography: The equator crosses the heavily populated coastal plain that rises sharply to the Andes mountains (highest peak: 6267 m, Mt. Chimborazo). There is flat low-lying rain forest to the east, bordering on Peru. The Galapagos Islands, that lie 1000 km off the coast, also belong to Ecuador.

Economy: Around a quarter of the inhabitants live below the poverty line.

Djibouti
Djibouti
(DJI)

Population: 619,000 (27 per sq km)
Area: 23,200 sq km
Capital: Djibouti
Political system: presidential republic (authoritarian nationalism)
Languages: Arabic, French (official), Somali, Afar
Religion: 95% Muslim
GNP: under US$ 3,000 per head
Currency: 1 Djibouti franc 100 centimes
Industries: cattle-farming products (leather, pelts), coffee, salt

History: Afar nomads, who had been converted to Islam, settled in this country. The French annexed it as the colony of French Somaliland in 1896. An independent Republic of Djibouti emerged in 1977.
Unrest continues here because of conflicts between the Afar and Issar peoples, and because of an influx of refugees streaming in from Ethiopia.

Topography: Over 90% of the land surface consists of deserts and steppes. The Tadjoura

Estonia

Eesti
Estonia
(EST)

Population: 1.4 million (32 per sq km)
Area: 45,227 sq km
Capital: Tallinn
Political system: parliamentary republic (emergent democratic)
Languages: Estonian (official), Russian
Religion: strongly Lutheran
GNP: US$ 3,080 per head
Currency: 1 Estonian krone = 100 senti
Industries: cattle-farming fishing, textiles, wood (paper, furniture)

History: This small Baltic state was under foreign rule for a long time: in 1219 the Danes arrived, in 1561 the Swedish, in 1721 the Russians. In 1918 it obtained its independence only to find in 1940 that the Soviets marched in and took control. In 1991 Estonia finally declared its independence.
Topography: The landscape of this flat land is characterised by water: in the land's interior rivers and lakes, marshes and moorland are predominant. Over 1500 islands, many of which are very tiny, extend beyond the deeply indented Baltic coastline.
Economy: Stock-farming is a decisive factor in agriculture. The herring catch in the Baltic plays an important role. The most important branch of industry is oil slate extraction and processing.

Egypt › Al Misr

pendence and upon attainment found itself in a long history of struggles for power, government changes, military putsches and civil wars. Although the peace treaty in 1992 ostensibly ended the civil war, the democratically elected government has been left to struggle with the aftermath and the restoration of order.
Topography: The remains of Mayan limestone pyramids lie on the narrow mangrove forested coastal plain that gives way to fertile hills. The central highland, which is enclosed by the Cordilleras, is the most densely populated area. With its seven active volcanoes, it is one of the most earthquake prone areas in the world.
Economy: At times coffee has made up to an 80% share of the export balance. In addition to that, San Salvador has developed into the second largest producer of cotton in the world. Their self-sufficiency is in danger due to the monoculture and half the population is underemployed.

El Salvador
El Salvador
(ES)

Population: 5.8 million (276 per sq km)
Area: 21,041 sq km
Capital: San Salvador
Political system: presidential republic (emergent democracy)
Languages: Spanish (official), Nahuati, Indian languages
Religion: 92% Catholic, 8% Protestant
GNP: US$ 1,700 per head
Currency: 1 El Salvador colón = 100 centavos
Industries: coffee, sugar, cotton, chemical products

History: Long before the arrival of the Spanish in 1542 this province had been ruled by the Pipil Indians. They were however defeated by the Spanish who went on to subjugate the province despite strong opposition and added it to the province of Guatemala. In 1821 it strove for inde-

Ellas
Greece
(GR)

Population: 10.4 million (79 per sq km)
Area: 131,960 sq km
Capital: Athens (Athínai)
climate: Mediterranean
Political system: parliamentary republic
Languages: Greek
Religion: Greek Orthodox 97%
GNP: US$ 11,460 per head
Currency: 1 drachma = 100 lepta
Industries: tobacco, wine, currants, sultanas, fruit, vegetables, olives, olive oil, textiles, aluminium, tourism

History: The prevailing Minoan culture of 2600BC was superseded by the Mycenaean culture from 1600 BC. In 776 BC the first Olympic games took place in Greece. In 395 AD it became a part of the Byzantine Empire, in the 15th century a part of Turkey. In 1832 it became a sover-

eign monarchy, in 1924 a republic. In 1935 it returned to being a monarchy, and various military dictators exercised their power. Since 1974 Greece has been a democratic republic, in 1981 it became a member of the EEC.
Topography: The cleft mainland, as well as the many islands, are mountainous and covered with forest. The beaches on the Mediterranean Sea and the ancient cultural sites are the main attractions for tourists.
Economy: Industrial products make up more than a 50% share of the export balance. Apart from tourism, a further major source of foreign currency is the Greek trade fleet, which is the largest in the EU and one of the largest in the world. Traditional agriculture is becoming less significant, even though this country is still the third largest producer of olive oil in the EU.

Equatorial Guinea ›
Guinea Equatorial

desert climate. The most populated area is the highland to the north, where sufficient rainfall makes agriculture possible. To the south the lowland is desert-like.

Economy: The long-standing war of liberation has had disastrous consequences: 50% unemployment, 80% illiteracy. The infrastructure has been almost completely destroyed by war.

España
Spain
E

Population: 39.2 million (78 per sq km)
Area: 504,782 sq km
Capital: Madrid
Political system: parliamentary monarchy
Languages: Spanish (Castilian official),Basque, Catalan, Galician, Valencian, Majorcan
Religion: Catholic 96%
GNP: US$ 14,350 per head
Currency: 1 peseta = 100 céntimos
Industries: machinery, vehicles, food, tourism

History: Cave paintings prove that Spain was already inhabited in 20,000 BC. From 900BC on the indigenous Iberian people were joined by the Celts, who migrated there. This country was repeatedly conquered and colonised: in the 11th century BC by the Phoenicians, in the 5th century BC by the Carthaginians, from 218 BC by the Romans, from 711 AD by the Moors . In the 4th century the Christianisation of Spain began, from 1031 Christian kingdoms began to re-conquer Spain. In 1492 foreign rule ended, from 1512 there was a united Spain, that through the possession of large parts of the New World became a world power. Its powerful position was lost when in 1588 the Armada was defeated. In 1931 Spain became a republic; in 1936 a putsch by General Franco threw the country into civil war that ended in a victory for the fascists and their dictators. Only with Franco's death in 1975 and the ef-

forts made by King Juan Carlos did this country find its way back to democracy.

Topography: This land is bordered by the Atlantic to the north and the south-west, to the east and south-east by the Mediterranean Sea. Inland almost the entire country is mountainous; to the north there are forests, to the south steppe vegetation. The territories of Spain include the islands of Mallorca, Menorca and Ibiza, as well as the Canary Islands.

Economy: The industrial centre for steel and chemicals, which contribute 60% to the export balance, is found along the northern coastal area, as well as the area around the capital Madrid. Southern Andalusia supplies European countries with early fruits and vegetables. Around 60% of the Spanish work in the service sector. Tourism is a significant source of foreign currency; in 1997 nearly 65 million foreigners came to visit Spain, chiefly the Balearic and Canary Islands, and the beaches on the Mediterranean coast.

Estonia › *Eesti*
Ethiopia › *Ityop´ya*

Fiji
Fiji
FJI

Population: 803,000 (44 per sq km)
Area: 18,376 sq km
Capital: Suva
Political system: democratic republic
Languages: English (official), Fijian, Hindi
Religion: 44% Methodist, 40% Hindus, 8% Muslim
GNP: US$ 2,470 per head
Currency: 1 Fijian dollar = 100 cents
Industries: sugarcane products, tinned fish

Eritrea
Eritrea
ER

Population: 3.6 million (312 per sq km)
Area: 121,144 sq km
Capital: Asmara
Political system: republic
Languages: Tiginya, Arabic (official), Amharic (official)
Religion: 50% Muslim, 50% Eritrean Orthodox, animist
GNP: under US$ 780 per head
Currency: 1 nakfa = 100 cents
Industries: coffee, salt, citrus fruits, grains, cotton

History: This nomad land was made an Italian colony in 1890, came under British administration after World War II and, in 1962, it became an Ethiopian province. In 1993 it obtained independence only after much resistance and fighting.

Topography: The north-eastern coastline borders on the Red Sea. The coastal area is almost uninhabited because of the excessive heat of the

Finland

History: Settlers from south-east Asia presumably came to the main islands in about 2000 BC. The islands were first discovered by Europeans in 1643 and made into a British crown colony in 1874. The British introduced large scale sugar cane production. In 1970 independence was declared, although Fiji remained in the Commonwealth. After a military coup in 1987 it became a republic and left the Commonwealth. They rejoined after introducing a new constitution in 1997.

Topography: Comprises 844 Melanesian and Polynesian islands and islets with coral reefs (about 110 inhabited); they are mountainous, volcanic and comprise tropical rain forest and grassland. Endless South Sea beaches and friendly local people make it a favourite holiday choice.

Economy: Sugar-cane plantations, as well as fishing and fish-processing, are the pillars on which exports stand but the richest source of foreign currency is tourism.

Finland
Finland
(FIN)

Population: 5.1 million (15.2 per sq km)
Area: 338,144 sq km
Capital: Helsinki (Helsingfors)
Political system: democratic parliamentary republic
Languages: Finnish 93%, Swedish 6% (both official), small Saami minorities
Religion: Lutheran 86%, Eastern Orthodox 1.2%
GNP: US$ 23,240 per head
Currency: Finn markka = 100 penniä
Industries: metal, engineering projects (ice breakers and oil rigs), wood, paper, cellulose

History: The Finns were under Swedish rule from the 12th to the 18th century. After constant wars the Swedish had to hand over Finland to the Russians in 1809. In 1918 Finland became an independent republic. After World War II it maintained close contact with the Soviet Union. Since the sixties it has attached importance to contacts with the West and in 1995 it joined the EU.

Topography: Finland borders on the sea, namely the Gulf of Finland to the south and the Gulf of Bothnia to the west. Numerous small islands lie along the coast. Most of the country is forested and covered with lakes (about 60,000) which are a tourist attraction. The flat to hilly countryside is dotted with numerous marshlands. Lapland-like tundra lies to the north.

Economy: Lumber and metal processing form the industrial basis of the economy. The tradi-

tional sectors of the Finnish economy are agriculture (rearing of dairy stock) and logging (the processing of wood into furniture, paper and cellulose). Shipbuilding also plays an important role. Industry is highly developed.

France
France
(F)

Population: 58.3 million (107 per sq km)
Area: 543,965 sq km
Capital: Paris
Political system: Parliamentary presidential republic
Languages: French (official), regional dialects: Basque, Breton, Catalan, Provençal
Religion: Roman Catholic 78%, Muslim 6%
GNP: US$ 26,270 per head
Currency: 1 French franc = 100 centimes
Industries: wheat, fruit, vegetables, wine, cheese, iron and steel, automobiles, aircraft, chemicals, jewellery, silk, lace tourism

History: There is proof that the first traces of settlement date back to 50,000 BC. Greeks, Celts, Romans and Germans conquered parts of this land from about 600 AD. France became a state in its own right with the division of the Frankish Empire by the Treaty of Verdun in 843. Constant confrontations with the British ended in 1453 with them being driven out. An aggressive period of absolute monarchy followed, that reached its zenith with the "Sun King" Louis XIV, who between the years of 1643 and 1715 fought against a united Europe. The French Revolution gave Europe and finally the world the impulse to revolution and brought the middle-classes into power. In 1799 Napoleon Bonaparte proclaimed himself emperor of France in a coup d'etat and declared war on Europe. After various revolutions and counter-revolutions the Third Republic was proclaimed. France fought on the side of the Allies during World War I and II. As a result of the Indo-Chinese War (1946-1954), it lost its colonies. In

1957 France joined the European Community. From 1958 on, Charles de Gaulle made his mark as president on the politics of his country. In 1968 the student demonstrations that began in Paris gave an impulse world-wide towards political change.

Topography: A flat but often hilly landscape (Central Massif) stretches between the Alps to the east, between the Mediterranean Sea and Pyrenees to the south, and between the Atlantic to the west and north. The large rivers of the Rhône, Seine and Loire were important transport routes to the Mediterranean Sea and the Atlantic Ocean respectively, even in early times. Tourists are attracted to two main areas: the coasts with their resorts and the charming Loire Valley with its numerous castles. The cultural and business centre is Paris for the French and tourists alike.

Economy: Although France is still considered to be a land of wine and fine food, it is not longer just an agrarian state, but rather one of the top ten industrial nations. Only 5% of the population

work in agriculture, but almost 70% work in the service sector. High-grade consumer goods (fashion, perfume, etc.) make up 15% of the export balance. Trading partners are, above all, other EU countries.

1 Boat race in local traditional costume on the river Tammerkoski in Tampere, Finland

2 Gustave Eiffel constructed the tower in Paris in 1885-1889

3 Local shopping: a typical Parisian street scene

4 Tribal chief at a meeting in Ghana

5 The River Gambia, the most important trade route in the state of Gambia

Gabon
Gabon
G

Population: 1.1 million (4.2 per sq km)
Area: 267,667 sq km
Capital: Libreville
Political system: presidential republic (authoritarian nationalism)
Languages: French (official), Fang, Bantu
Religion: Christian (Catholic 52%, 7,8% Protestant), animist 40%
GNP: US$ 3,950 per head
Currency: CFA franc
Industries: petroleum, manganese, uranium, timber

History: The Portuguese set up trading centres here in the 15th century and so did other European powers afterwards. The indigenous Bantu population were the victims of slave hunters. The colonisers' interests extended to raw materials such as ivory and fine woods. This land became a French colony in 1885, gained independence in 1960, but nonetheless maintains in close contact with France.
Topography: Along the west coast on the Atlantic there are large mangrove forests mixed with coastal savannah areas which run parallel and rise up to a hilly forested interior. High plateaux lie to the north. Important cultural attractions for Gabon and its visitors are Lambaréné and the jungle hospital founded by Arnold Schweizer in 1913.
Economy: Gabon is one of the richest African countries. Petroleum makes up 80% of the export balance, and timber from the rain forests also plays a large part.

Gambia
Gambia
WAG

Population: 1.1 million (102 per sq km)
Area: 11,295 sq km
Capital: Banjul
Political system: presidential republic (liberal democracy)
Languages: English (official), Mandinka, Wolof, Fula and other native languages
Religion: Muslim 85%, Christian 10%
GNP: under US$ 800 per head
Currency: 1 dalasi = 100 bututs
Industries: ground nuts, peanuts, palm oil, fish

History: From the 8th century there were a number of kingdoms within this district; from the 12th century it was a part of the large Mali Empire; from 1765 it was a British colony; from 1965 an independent commonwealth state, from 1970 a republic. In 1994 there was a military putsch and in 1996 it was granted a new constitution and free elections.
Topography: Gambia is the smallest country in Africa, surrounded on all sides by the neighbouring country of Senegal. It consists of nothing but mangrove forests that flank the embankment of the river Gambia and measures hardly 50 km at its widest point.
Economy: 80% of the population work in agriculture and cultivate various sorts of grain for their own consumption, as well as peanuts for export. 15% of the GNP is produced through tourism.

Georgia → *Sakartvelo*
Germany → *Deutschland*

Ghana
Ghana
GH

Population: 17.5 million (74 per sq km)
Area: 238,535 sq km
Capital: Accra
Political system: presidential republic
Languages: English (official), and other African languages
Religion: animist 35%, Muslim 16%, Christian 60% (Protestant 40%)
GNP: US$ 360 per head
Currency: 1 cedi = 100 pesewas
Industries: coffee, cocoa, timber, gold, diamonds, manganese, bauxite

History: From the 12th to the 14th century the northern part of the country belonged to various different large and wealthy kingdoms. At the end of the 17th century the powerful and expanding Ashanti kingdom was established in the area of present day Ghana. The Ashanti dealt in gold and the slave trade with the Europeans, until in the 19th century the British ended the slave trade and declared the coastal area a British crown colony (the Gold Coast). Although little by little they subjugated the country, they could not break the Ashanti's will for independence. In 1957 Ghana was the first country in black Africa to gain independence.
Topography: This country borders on the Gulf of Guinea to the south. The coastal lagoons give way inland to grasslands, followed by tropical rainforest in the western lying Ashanti highland. Ghana is bisected by the river Volta and has the huge Volta reservoir to the east.
Economy: Rich mineral deposits and cocoa formerly bestowed great wealth on Ghana. Due to a fall in price on the world market and political unrest due to constantly changing governments, the economy went awry. During the early eighties it weakened further on account of a famine and an influx of refugees.

Greece → *Ellas*

Grenada

Grenada
Grenada
(WG)

Population: 99, 000 (287 per sq km)
Area: 344 sq km
Capital: St. George's
Political system: parliamentary monarchy (emergent democracy)
Languages: English (official), French and English Creole
Religion: Catholic 53%, Anglican 14%, Adventist and Pentecostal 15%
GNP: US$ 2,880 per head
Currency: 1 east Caribbean dollar = 100 cents
Industries: cocoa, nutmeg, bananas, mace, turism and financial services

History: The warring Carib tribes fought off European settlers for a long time but had to concede their island to Britain in 1877 and a crown colony was established. Universal suffrage was introduced in 1951 and self administration followed in 1967. In 1974 independence was granted. A "People's Revolutionary Government" came to power in 1979 through a putsch. In the early Eighties appeals were made by its neighbours about Grenada's connection to Cuba and the fear of it becoming communist. The USA invaded Grenada in 1983 and remained there until 1989.
Topography: Many cruisers make a call at this forested volcanic island with tropical beaches. It belongs to the Lesser Antilles.
Economy: The "Spice Island" includes its main export article, the nutmeg, in its coat of arms. Other than nutmeg, bananas and cocoa are cultivated. Tourism is a source of income that is gaining in significance as are the financial services sector.

Guatemala
Guatemala
(GCA)

Population: 10.9 million (100 per sq km)
Area: 108,890 sq km
Capital: Guatemala City
Political system: democratic presidential republic
Languages: Spanish (official), 40% speak Mayan Quiché languages (20 kinds)
Religion: Catholic 80%, Protestant 19%
GNP: US$ 1,470 per head
Currency: 1 quetzal = 100 centavos
Industries: coffee, sugar, bananas, beef, tourism

History: Guatemala was the centre of the Mayan Culture until the Spanish conquered and colonised it in 1524. Since independence was gained in 1821, dictators have governed here, and more often than not exercised a reign of terror. A democratically elected government has been in power since 1986. The long-standing civil war was ended in 1996 by a peace agreement.
Topography: This Central American country borders not only on the Pacific Ocean but also on

the Caribbean Sea. The highlands of the Sierra Madre join onto the Pacific coastal plains to the south; behind them the Central American Andes border the northern flatland with its rainforest. It is of tourist interest because of the well preserved relics of the Indian and Mayan cultures which brings in many much needed foreign currency.
Economy: Coffee, sugar and bananas are the main export articles, and to a lesser extent cotton, vegetables and cardamom. Almost 60% of the population work in agriculture and cultivate beans and maize on small plots for their own consumption. The military's reign of terror has driven out many Indians and destroyed social and economic structures and now over 90% of the population live below the poverty line.

Guinea Ecuatorial
Equatorial Guinea
(GQ)

Population: 410,000 (15 per sq km)
Area: 28,051 sq km
Capital: Malabo (Bioko)
Political system: presidential republic
Languages: Spanish (official), Bubi, Noowe, Fang
Religion: 99% Catholic
GNP: US$ 530 per head
Currency: CFA-franc
Industries: wood, cocoa, cloth fibres

History: The islands of Bioko and Pagalu were discovered in about 1470 and, together with the strips of coast on the mainland, were used by the Portugese as an intermediate stopping point for the slave trade. The islands belonged to Spain from 1778 and to the mainland from 1885. Independence was gained in 1968; the ruling dictator was overthrown in a military putsch in 1979.
Topography: The mainland area of Mbini is mountainous and consists of savannah and rainforest, and there are mangrove marshes on the coast. There are volcanic islands along the coast, the largest of which is Bioko.
Economy: Almost half of the GNP is derived from agriculture. Over 40% of the inhabitants work in the service sector. Although Equatorial Guinea possesses raw oil reserves offshore, these

① *A cemetry outside the gates of Ciudad Vieja, Guatemala*

② *The Great Jaguar Temple in Tikal, the pre-Columbian Mayan settlement (about 700 AD), only rediscovered in the 19th century in the rainforest lowlands of North Guatemala*

③ *Popular with cruise tourists on account of its heavenly beaches: the "spice-island" Grenada, which belongs to the Lesser Atilles*

④ *Typical mixtures of colour and design in handicrafts from Guatemala*

resources have scarcely been developed due to the shortage of finances and the ability to tap these resources. This is also true for the potential profits to be gained from fishing in the offshore areas.

Guinée
Guinea
RG

Population: 6.7 million (28 per sq km)
Area: 245,857 sq km
Capital: Conakry
Political system: presidential republic
Languages: French (official), African Mandinka languages
Religion: Muslim 95%, Christian 10%, animist 5%
GNP: US$ 560 per head
Currency: 1 syli or guinea franc = 100 caris
Industries: coffee, rice, palm kernels, alumina, bauxite, diamonds, gold

History: The original inhabitants, thought to be Pygmies, were driven out by the Mande. In the Middle Ages this region belonged to the wealthy countries of Ghana and Mali, until the Islamic Fulbe founded their own powerful empire there. The French found the inhabitants to be arrogantly resistant; not until 1898 was it possible to make it into a colony. In 1959 the colony gained independence through a referendum. It was to suffer under a one-party system with a bloody regime, that in 1984 was brought to an end by a military putsch. Since 1991 Guinea has been a presidential democracy.
Topography: A marshy area on the Atlantic coast in the west gives way to a highland region from where the rivers Senegal, Niger and Gambia spring. The surface of the land becomes flatter to the east, and is covered by savannah to the north-east and by rain forest to the south-east.

Economy: Guinea is the second largest producer of bauxite in the world and has rich mineral deposits at its disposal. Although more than 80% of the population work in agriculture, their self-sufficiency is not guaranteed. The infrastructure is poorly developed and makes the transition to a market economy difficult.

Guiné-Bissau
Guinea-Bissau
GNB

Population: 1 million (30 per sq km)
Area: 36,125 sq km
Capital: Bissau
Political system: presidential republic
Languages: Portuguese (official), Crioulo (a Portuguese dialect), Fulani
Religion: 60% animist, 30% Muslim, 8% Christian
GNP: US$ 250 per head
Currency: CFA franc
Industries: rice, coconuts, peanuts, cashews, fish, timber

History: This region was declared a Portuguese possession in 1466. In the 16th century the Portuguese dealt in the slave trade from here. In 1879 Guinea-Bissau became a Portuguese colony and in 1973 it fought and won independence. In 1980 a coup d'état temporarily brought an end to their parliamentary democracy. Not until 1994 were there free elections again.
Topography: A wide coastal plain with mangrove swamps and rivers leads inland to fresh water swamps, then to the east to a humid savannah and to hilly country in the south east.
Economy: More than 80% of the population works in agriculture; they run cattle-farms and cultivate grains for their own consumption, as well as peanuts and cashews. 80% of the export

balance is derived from cashew for export. This country has few mineral deposits and its infrastructure is only minimally developed.

Guyana
Guyana
GUY

Population: 839,000 (4 per sq km)
Area: 214,969 sq km
Capital: Georgetown
Political system: presidential republic (democratic)
Languages: English (official), Hindi, Urdu, Amerindian, Indian lang.
Religion: Protestant 34%, Hindus 33%, Catholics 20%, Muslims 8%
GNP: US$ 690 per head
Currency: 1 Guyanese dollar = 100 cents
Industries: sugar, rice, rum, timber, bauxite, shrimps, molasses

History: From the 15th century onwards, British, Dutch and French fought for control of this region and in 1814 divided it between themselves. In 1831 the western part was made into the crown colony of British-Guyana. In 1966 it attained independence and in 1980 the only socialist constitution in South America. Indians that immigrated there comprise 50% of the population. In 1978 this country hit the headlines when in Jonestown over 1000 members of a fanatical North American sect all committed suicide.
Topography: 80% of this extremely sparsely populated land is covered by rain forest. Mountain chains border onto fertile coastal plains to the west and the south.
Economy: Sugar and rice are produced for export; only 2% of the land is under cultivation. Mining products such as bauxite, manganese and diamonds make up one third of the export balance. A poor transport system hinders access to markets.

Armenia

Population: 3.7 million (127 per sq km)
Area: 29,800 sq km
Capital: Yerevan
Political system: presidential republic
Languages: Armenian (official), Russian
Religion: mainly Armenian Gregorian Christians
GNP: US$ 630 per head
Currency: 1 dram = 100 luma
Industries: metal, precious and semi-precious stones

History: In the 7th century Persians and Turks quarrelled over this region, in the 19th century Russia tried to conquer it, but without success. In 1922 Armenia was divided into a Turkish and a Soviet part. It was the first country in the area to adopt Christianity. Armenia gained independence in 1991 and is a member of the CIS.
Topography: Armenia is bordered to the west by the Ararat highland and to the north by the lower Caucasus. In the south-east, Lake Seva forms the centre of an area of very low-lying land. The vegetation is predominantly steppe and semi-desert in character.
Economy: The transition from a Soviet planned economy to a market economy has led to problems. The working population is evenly split between agriculture, industry and the service sector. The bottling of mineral water is an important industry.

Population: 7.3 million (264 per sq km)
Area: 27,750 sq km
Capital: Port-au-Prince
Political system: presidential republic
Languages: French, Creole (both official)
Religion: Catholic 80%, Voodoo cult 70%, Protestant 10%
GNP: US$ 310 per head
Currency: 1 gourde = 100 centimes
Industries: coffee, cocoa, cotton, toys, textile and light industry

History: In this former French colony, Haiti was proclaimed the first independent "Negro Republic" in 1804.
After a turbulent history of dictators and military putsches, peace appears to have returned since the USA intervened to reinstate a toppled president in 1994. Many Haitians have sought to es-

cape the poverty in the poorest of lands by illegal crossing into the USA.
Topography: Haiti takes in one-third of the Caribbean island of Hispaniola. The landscape is marked by mountains and savannahs that stretch across the country.
Economy: Agriculture cannot cover all their own needs, even though two-thirds of the population are engaged in farming. Coffee and cocoa are cultivated for export. The lion's share of the export balance comes from light industry such as electronics.

Population: 6.1 million (54 per sq km)
Area: 112,492 sq km
Capital: Tegucigalpa
Political system: democratic presidential republic (democratic)
Languages: Spanish (official), Indian languages
Religion: Catholic 90%
GNP: US$ 660 per head
Currency: 1 lempira = 100 centavos
Industries: coffee, bananas, seafood, rosewood, mahogany

History: From the 5th to 9th centuries the Mayas established a settlement in Copán, the ruins of which are a major tourist attraction today. The Indian tribes inhabiting the region strongly resisted the encroachments of the Spanish, but in vain, and in 1524 the Spanish colonised the region. In 1821 Honduras declared independence and joined up with other Central

American provinces to form the "United Provinces of Central America." In 1838 it left this coalition and has been an independent republic ever since. The often brutal dictatorships led to repression amongst the people and only since 1984 has there been any sort of stability within the country.
Topography: This country borders to the north on the Caribbean Sea along a stretch known as the Mosquito Coast, to the south on the Pacific. The populated areas are primarily the mild valleys of the Central American Andes.
Economy: Honduras is known as "the Poorhouse of Central America." Plentiful but undeveloped mineral deposits and an underdeveloped industrial basis make Honduras almost completely dependent on banana exports, and are thus affected by price fluctuations in the world market. In the recent past, coffee, fish and seafood have become the second pillar of their economy.

Population: 4.7 million (84 per sq km)
Area: 56,610 sq km
Capital: Zagreb (Agram)
Political system: presidential republic (emergent democracy)
Languages: 76% Croatian (official), Serbian
Religion: 76% Catholic, 11% Serbo-Orthodox
GNP: US$ 3,800 per head
Currency: 1 kuna = 100 lipa
Industries: machinery, motor vehicles, chemical products, agriculture

History: From the 7th century AD south Slavic tribes settled here. From 925 till 1102 Croatia

4

1 This realistic semi-relief portrait dates back to the classical period of Mayan art (300-600 BC), Copán, Honduras

2 Wholesale market in Eriwan, capital of Armenia

3 Roman amphitheatre in Pula/Istria, a part of Croatia

4 The famous Minangka building on Sumatra, the second largest of the Sunda islands, which belong to Indonesia

4 Shiva as the "god of dance", symbol of his power over the cosmos. Bronze figure, India

5

India
India
(IND)

Population: 945.1 million (288 per sq km)
Area: 3,287,263 sq km
Capital: New Delhi
Political system: federal parliamentary republic
Languages: Hindi, English, as well as 17 regional languages (all official), numerous other languages.
Religion: 80% Hindus, 11% Muslim
GNP: US$ 380 per head
Currency: 1 Indian rupee = 100 paise
Industries: tea, textiles, machinery, tourism

History: The highly advanced Indus Valley Civilisation, that predominated from 2600 BC, was superseded in the 15th century BC by Aryan nomads who came from the north. In the 12th century AD India's transition to Islam began. During its heyday from 1526 till 1605, the Mongolian Empire held sway over India. In 1858 India became a British colony. The Indian fight for independence started at the end of the 19th century and was continued from 1920 onwards through Mahatma Gandhi's method of peaceful revolution. In 1947 India gained its independence.
Topography: India is a subcontinent with three very different land zones: the Himalayan Mountains to the north-east, an adjoining low-lying plain with the great rivers of the Indus and the Ganges and a highland to the south, and the coastal strips on the Arabian Sea and the Indian Ocean.
Economy: Indian is the world's largest tea exporter. Around two-thirds of the population work in agriculture. In spite of their quite highly developed industrial basis, India is a developing country; the rate of illiteracy is almost 50%. The textile industry constitutes just about a quarter of the export balance. Numerous nature reserves and historically and culturally significant monuments make tourism the most important economic fac-

tor. The Indian film industry is, incidentally, the largest in the world, but has virtually no value on the world market.

Indonesia
Indonesia
(RI)

Population: 197 million (104 per sq km)
Area: 1,904,443 sq km
Capital: Jakarta
Political system: presidential republic (authoritarian nationalistic)
Languages: Bahasa Indonesian (official), Javanese, numerous Malayo-Polynesian and Papua-languages
Religion: 87% Muslim, 10% Christian
GNP: US$ 1,080 per head
Currency: 1 rupiah = 100 sen
Industries: petroleum, natural gas, timber, textiles, tourism

History: Between the 7th and the 15th centuries this region was ruled by vast Hindu-Buddhist empires. In the 13th century the influence of Islam started to penetrate the area. From the 16th to the 19th centuries the Dutch conquered the entire region in order to gain control of the spice trade. After a short period of Japanese occupation during World War II, Indonesia became an independent republic in 1949. This densely populated region has been subject to countless bouts of unrest and rebellion ever since.
Topography: This country comprises around 13,600 islands, which are to a large extent mountainous; half of them are inhabited; the largest ones are Java, Sumatra, Sulawesi and Borneo. A favourite holiday destination is the island of Bali.
Economy: Over half of the population works in agriculture; the land can produce enough for its

was an independent country, thereafter it fell under Ottoman rule until 1918. The Slovenian region that belonged to the Ottomans in the 16th and 17th centuries became a part of Croatia at the beginning of the 18th century. Dalmatia, the thin coastal strip plus islands, still belonged to the Republic of Venice in the 18th century. Austria conquered it and only in 1918 did it become a part of Croatia . The Istrian Peninsula, on the northern Adriatic coast, has today been added to this country. From 1918 this region was a part of the " Kingdom of Serbia, Croatia and Slovenia," that in 1945 became the Republic of Yugoslavia. With the disintegration of Yugoslavia in 1990, a bloody civil war flared up, and in 1991 Croatia declared independence. In 1995 the war came to an end with the Dayton agreement.
Topography: 600 islands lie to the west of the Adriatic coast. The strip of coast rises towards the Dinaric Mountains, that run in a north-east direction, and then descend to a low-lying plain which is crossed by the rivers Save, Danube and Drau.
Economy: Important export goods are machinery, motor vehicles and chemical products. The once thriving holiday area along the Adriatic coast is seldom visited any more; urgently needed foreign currency has stopped coming in due to the decrease in tourism.

Hungary → Magyarorszag
Iceland → Island

own needs now, and coffee, cocoa, rubber and palm oil are produced for export. Indonesia is one of the largest petroleum producers in the world. In contrast, the rich mineral deposits have hardly been mined.

Īrāk
Iraq
IRQ

Population: 21.3 million (49 per sq km)
Area: 438,317 sq km
Capital: Baghdad
Political system: presidential republic (one-party socialist)
Languages: high Arabic, (official), several languages among others Kurdish
Religion: 95% Muslim (60% Shi'ite, 37% Sunni)
GNP: under US$ 3,000 per head
Currency: 1 Iraqi dinar = 1000 fils
Industries: relies strongly on oil

History: Over 8000 years ago the Sumer peoples settled in the area between the two rivers Euphrates and Tigris, formerly called Mesopotamia, and built the first cities on earth. In the 2nd and the 1st millennium BC the Babylonians and the Assyrians ruled there, in the 6th century BC the Persians. In the 7th century AD Baghdad became the capital of Islam. In the 13th century the Mongols invaded the region. From the 16th century Mesopotamia was part of the Ottoman Empire. After World War I, the British supported the founding of an Iraqi kingdom which became independent in 1932. In 1958 the monarchy under King Faisal was overthrown and a republic established. In 1980 an eight year long war started with its neighbour Iran. This seriously damaged the oil export industry of both countries and also affected the world oil market. In 1990 Iraq made the headlines when the dictator Saddam Hussein marched into Kuwait and the Gulf War started.
Topography: In the south-east this country possesses a narrow access to the Persian Gulf. In the interior of the land, a fertile area extends over the Euphrates and Tigris region; to the west and south-west desert and semi-desert link up.
Economy: Iraq has at its disposal the second largest petroleum wells in the world; petroleum makes up 90% of the export balance. War damages, as well as the economic embargo inflicted on Iraq after the attack on Kuwait, left the economy on the brink of ruin. So much money has, however, been invested in the development of agriculture, industry and transport sinews that a quick recovery has been made from the crisis and an end to the embargo is being discussed.

Īrān
Iran
IR

Population: 62,5 million (38 per sq km)
Area: 1,684,000 sq km
Capital: Teheran (Tahran)
Political system: Islamic presidential republic (authoritarian)
Languages: Persian (official), other Iranian languages
Religion: 99% Muslim (92% Shi'ite, 7% Sunni)
GNP: under US$ 3,00 per head
Currency: 1rial = 100 dinars
Industries: petroleum, natural gas, carpets, caviar

History: In about 3000 BC this region was ruled by the Elam, in about 1500 BC the Medes and the Persians took it by force and founded the Achaemen Empire. In 331 BC Alexander the Great conquered Persia. In 637 AD it was conquered by the Arabs – the transition to Islam had begun. In the following centuries the Turks, Mongols, Afghans and Russians successively forced their way in. In 1906 Iran was given its first constitution. In 1979 the Shah was driven out by an Islamic revolution under the Ayatollah Khomeini, who, as the religious and political leader, insisted on strict Islamic principles. This also led to strained relationships with other countries.
Topography: The country borders to the north on the Caspian Sea, to the south and the south-west on the Persian Gulf. The Elburs Mountains, reaching up to 5 604 m, are on the coast of the Caspian Sea; in the west the Sagros Mountains form a natural border to Iraq. Between the mountains are dry plateaux and large salt deserts.
Economy: Almost 90% of export quotas are filled through petroleum and its products. Agriculture is only possible with the help of irrigation; only 10% of the land is cultivated. Persian rugs are as important as ever for export. Around 4 million square meteres of carpet are produced every year and produces sufficient wool to meet its market needs.

Ireland
Ireland
IRL

Population: 3.6 million (52 per sq km)
Area: 70,273 sq km
Capital: Dublin (Baile Atha Cliath)
Political system: parliamentary republic
Languages: Irish Gaelic, English (both official)
Religion: 88% Catholics, 3% Anglican

GNP: US$ 14,710 per head
Currency: 1 Irish pound (Ir£) = 100 pence
Industries: machinery, chemical products, dairy products, tourism

History: Settlements can be traced back to the 3rd millennium BC. In about 400 BC Celts settled on the land. In 1534 British rule over the island soon led to the suppression of the Irish Catholics. From 1845 until 1849 a terrible famine (the Potato Famine) caused Irish people to leave their country in thousands. In 1921 the Irish Free State emerged and in 1937 it gained independence as the Independent Free State of Eire. In 1949 it became a republic and left the Commonwealth, but in 1973 joined the EU. In 1998 the Northern Ireland Peace Treaty was signed and is intended to bring peace in the northern part of the island.
Topography: This island in the North Atlantic, whose northern corner, Northern Ireland, belongs to Britain, consists mainly of rolling green pastureland with highlands to the north and south.

1 Golden dome of a mosque in Najaf, about 150 kilometres south of Baghdad, Iraq

2 Always a friendly smile. Typical pub in Ireland

3 Enjoying a water-pipe, Isfahan, Iran

4 At regular intervals the geysers in Iceland spew their hot fountains high into the air

5 The leaning tower of Pisa, constructed of six galleries of columns, is about 55 metres high

Languages: Italian, regional German, French (all official)
Religion: 90% Catholic
GNP: US$ 19,880 per head
Currency: 1 Italian lira = 100 centesimi
Industries: machinery, aeroplanes, textiles, leather goods, tourism

History: Early settlements have been proven to date back to the Stone Age. In 1200 BC various Indo-Germanic tribes forced their way into this peninsula. In the 8th century BC the Etruscans founded numerous city states in Italy. The legend has it that Rome was founded by Romulus and Remus in 753 BC. The Roman Empire grew to be the most powerful in its time and at times ruled the entire Mediterranean area. Their empire fell in the 4th century when it came under the successive rules of the Ostrogoths, Byzantines and Lombards. Venice, Milan and other cities formed independent city states which gave this country the fine cultural heritage in the Renaissance and the Baroque periods. Only in 1861 did a United Kingdom of Italy emerge. After World War II, Italy, which had been a German ally under the dictator Mussolini, became a founding member of NATO and the EU.
Topography: The Apennine Mountains run the entire length of the "boot" of Italy. To the north the Alps form the Italian border. The peninsula is surrounded by the Adriatic and Tyrrhenian Seas. The islands of Sardinia and Sicily as well as Elba and Capri belong to Italy.
Economy: The Italian automobile industry, mechanical engineering and the leading Italian fashion houses are the most important pillars of the foreign trade balance. With 56 million foreign visitors annually, Italy is one of the favourite holiday countries; not only on account of the rich culture and the sunny Mediterranean beaches, but also because Italian lifestyle and cuisine are among the best in the world.

Currency: 1 Icelandic krone = 100 aurar
Industries: fishing, livestock, aluminium

History: Celtic monks first settled on this island in the 9th century, followed by Norwegians. In 930 AD the first democratic gathering took place and a parliament, Althing, was founded - the first of its kind. From 1264 the island was first under Norwegian and then Danish rule. An independent Republic of Iceland was proclaimed in 1944 and the old parliamentary traditions were reinstated.
Topography: This volcanic island, that borders on the Polar Circle, is partially covered with glaciers. Volcanoes (27 are still active), hot springs, geysers and sparse vegetation complete the picture. Iceland is the most sparsely populated country in Europe; more than 90% of the population live in the cities along the south coast.
Economy: Fishing is their main source of income; it makes up 70% of the export balance and gives them a high standard of living. Hydroelectric power and numerous hot springs provide them with their energy requirements. Iceland is also beginning to enjoy increased popularity as a tourist attraction with its volcanoes and geysers.

Economy: This typically agrarian country with cattle-breeding as its main industry has been transformed into a modern industrial state; mechanical engineering, chemical products, computers and textiles form the most important sectors of the economy. Only 10% of the population are still engaged in agriculture, in contrast over 60% are in the service sector. Tourism is a primary industry; the unspoilt countryside, historic old cities and blossoming pub culture prove to be particularly attractive.

Ísland
Iceland

IS

Population: 270,000 (2.6 per sq km)
Area: 103,000 sq km
Capital: Reykjavík
Political system: parliamentary republic
Languages: Icelandic
Religion: 93% Lutheran
GNP: US$ 26,580 per head

Israël → _Yisra´el_

Italia
Italy

I

Population: 57.3 million (190 per sq km)
Area: 301,323 sq km
Capital: Rome (Roma)
Political system: parliamentary republic

Ityop'ya
Ethiopia

ETH

Population: 58.2 million (51 per sq km)
Area: 1,133,380 sq km
Capital: Addis Ababa (Adis Abeba)
Political system: Federal Republic (socialist democratic)
Languages: Amharic (official), Semitic, Tigrinya, Orominga, Arabic
Religion: 45% Sunni Muslim, 40% Ethiopian Orthodox
GNP: US$ 100 per head
Currency: 1 birr = 100 cents
Industries: coffee, petroleum products, gold

History: The bones of "Lucy" were found on Ethiopian soil; she lived 3 to 4 million years ago and is one of the oldest known ancestors of man. In 1000 BC descendants of the legendary kingdom of Saba (southern Arabia) settled here and founded the kingdom of Aksum, that in 330 AD converted to Christianity and obstinately resisted all attempts of being converted to Islam. This region known then as Abyssinia ("mix of races") succeeded in fighting off colonisation. A long war of independence with the province of Eritrea and a terrible drought has shaken this land over the last few decades.
Topography: The Great Rift Valley runs from the south-west to north-east through the Ethiopian Highlands; to the east are plains. The Danakil Desert is located on the border to Eritrea.
Economy: Famine and starvation have always haunted this country because it is overpopulated. Although three-quarters of the population are engaged in agriculture, it is not possible to provide for even their most basic needs. Forestry and overcultivation have spoilt the soil. The main export is coffee.

Ivory Coast › Côte d´Ivoire

Jamaica
Jamaica

JA

Population: 2.5 million (232 per sq km)
Area: 10,991 sq km
Capital: Kingston
Political system: parliamentary monarchy (constitutional)
Languages: English (official), Creole
Religion: 56% diverse Protestant, 5% Catholic, 5% Rastafarian
GNP: US$ 1,600 per head
Currency: 1 Jamaican dollar = 100 cents

Industries: aluminium, bauxite, sugar, tourism, rum and coffee

History: After the Spanish had eradicated practically all of the indigenous population, they introduced African slaves as forced labour in 1517, to work on the huge sugar plantations which were run by Europeans.
In 1655 the British captured the island and in 1866 it was made into a crown colony. Jamaica has been an independent democracy since 1962.

Topography: Two-thirds of the surface of the island are covered with 500 m high limestone plateaux with caves and waterfalls. To the east the Blue Mountains rise to a height of 2000 m. On the coast there are white beaches and lagoons.
Economy: An important source of foreign currency is tourism. About two-thirds of the population work in the service sector. Jamaica is the third largest exporter of bauxite in the world; the extraction of bauxite in argillaceous earth destroys just that heavenly landscape that tourists come in search of. In recent years the cultivation of the traditional crop, sugar-cane, has declined sharply, because of a better earning potential with industry and tourism.

Japan › Nippon
Jordan › Al Urdunn

Jugoslavija
Yugoslavia

YU

Population: 10.5 million (104 per sq km)
Area: 102,173 sq km
Capital: Belgrade (Beograd)
Political system: federal republic (authoritarian military)
Languages: Serbo-Croat (official), Albanian, Macedonian, Slovenian etc.
Religion: 44% Sebro-Orthodox, 31% Catholic, 12% Muslim
GNP: under US$ 3,000 per head
Currency: 1 Yugoslavian new dinar = 100 para
Industries: industrial products, agricultural products, textiles

History: In about 1000 BC the Illyrians and the Thracians came to this area; over the course of the centuries Greeks, Slavs, Hungarians, Ottomans and Austrians followed. In 1918 the Kingdom of the Serbs, Croats and Slovenians was created. In 1945 Yugoslavia became a federal communist republic. In 1991 Croatia and Slovenia declared independence. This led to the outbreak of conflicts of nationality among the communist oppressed areas. In 1992 a new Yugoslavia (Serbia with Kosovo and Montenegro) was proclaimed; peace has, however, not been the result.
Topography: Serbia and Montenegro comprise what is left of Yugoslavia. Montenegro borders on the Adriatic Sea. The interior of the country is mountainous.
Economy: The war that has been going on for a number of years now has caused their main source of income, tourism, to almost completely dry up. Unemployment was at 40% in 1997, and the inflation rate at 120% in 1995 – nonetheless, it is better than in 1989 when it rose to 2500%. A trade embargo was lifted in 1996 so that heavy industry had a chance to recover and the rich mineral deposits could be used.

Jumhurii Tojikistan
Tajikistan

TJ

Population: 5.9 million (41 per sq km)
Area: 143,100 sq km
Capital: Dushanbe
Languages: Tajik (official), Russian, Uzbek

1 _Papyrus boat on Lake Tana, Ethiopia_

2 _Hand-made straw hats at the market in Port Antonio, Jamaica_

3 _Yugoslavian folk-lore singers in national costume_

4 _Angkor, a ruined site in Cambodia, which was an impor-tant centre of the Khmer kingdom in the 9th and l0th cen-turies. It is the might-iest construction in south-east Asia, mea-suring approximately 1,300 x 1,500 me-tres with a moat 200 metres in width_

Political system: presidential republic (socialist pluralist)
Religion: predominantly Sunni Muslim
GNP: US$ 340 per head
Currency: 1 Tajikistani rubel = 100 kopeken
Industries: metals and metal products, textiles, uranians

History: During the pre-Christian era Tajikistan was inhabited by a people who belonged to the Indo-European language group. Over the centuries many empires held claim to this region: the Persians, the Greeks, the Macedonians, the Arabs, the Mongolians and the Uzbeks; the latter leaving clear traces on the culture of Tajikistan. In the 19th century the Russians forced their way into inner Asia and in 1924 Tajikistan became a Soviet republic. In 1990 Tajikistan declared independence and joined the CIS. The heated civil war continues between the Orthodox communists and the democratic Muslims in spite of the 1997 peace treaty.
Topography: This mountainous country borders on China to the east and Afghanistan to the south. 90% of the land is higher than 1000 m. The Pamir Mountains in the south-east comprise treeless mountain ranges with innumerable glaciers; it is here that Pik Kommunisma (7 483 m), the highest peak of the CIS is located. Settlements are found along the mountain valleys. This country is very prone to earthquakes.
Economy: The mountainous nature of the landscape makes agriculture as well as the development of any infrastructure and industry difficult. The cultivation of cotton and the textile industry based on it are particularly important for export but the arable land is becoming saline due to the irrigation of the cotton fields. Mining and the

processing of mineral goods account for 50% of exports. Tajikistan is the poorest country in the CIS. It does however, have excellent airfields, a byproduct of the war and clashes with its neighbours. These were built by the USSR.

Kâmpǔchéa
Cambodia
K

Population: 10.2 million (57 per sq km)
Area: 181,035 sq km
Capital: Phnom Penh (Phnum Pénh)
Political system: parliamentary monarchy (communism)
Languages: Khmer (official), Vietnamese, Chinese
Religion: over 90% Buddhist
GNP: US$ 300 per head
Currency: 1 riel = 100 sen
Industries: wood, tropical milks, textiles, pepper, rubber

History: Of the peoples that had originally settled in the 1st century AD on the lower part of the river Mekong, it was the Khmer in the 6th century that created a powerful empire which encompassed present day Vietnam, Cambodia, Laos, Thailand and Burma. The capital of the Khmer Empire, Angkor, was abandoned in the 15th century and the region conquered successively by the Cham, Siamese and Vietnamese. In 1863 Cambodia became a French protectorate. A resolution was passed to give Cambodia its independence at the Geneva Conference in 1954. After a civil war, the Vietnam War and a period of "Stone Age communism" under the Khmer

Rouge, a peace agreement was signed in 1991, but this has not yet led to political stability.
Topography: Mountain chains border on this country to the west and the north. The low-lying and hilly landscape of the Mekong Basin stretches to the east, the land is otherwise of alluvium with many mangrove forests.
Economy: Almost three-quarters of the working population are engaged in agriculture with rice as the staple crop. The number of underemployed is roughly 50%. Important export goods, other than lumber and rubber, include iron, steel and textiles.

Kazakstan
Kazachstan
KZ

Population: 16.4 million (6 per sq km)
Area: 2,717,300 sq km
Capital: Astana (official), Almaty/Alma Ata (de facto)
Political system: presidential republic (emergent democracy)
Languages: Kazakh (official), Russian
Religion: 50% Muslim, 50% Christian
GNP: US$ 1,350 per head
Currency: 1 tenge = 100 tiin
Industries: oil and petroleum products, mining, agriculture

History: By the 6th century Turkish and Mongolian tribes had already settled in this region. It was conquered by the Russians in 1822. After violent fighting in 1920, the Kirgis Autonomous Socialist Soviet Republic came into existence. Later in 1936, it joined the USSR. In 1991 Kazikhstan declared its independence and joined the CIS.
Topography: South Siberian steppes stretch to the north; adjoining semi-desert and desert

Kenya

stretch to the south. To the south-east the land rises into the foothills of the Tian Shan and Altai Mountains to a height of 5 000 m. To the west lie the lowlands of the Caspian and Turanian Basin. In the centre lie the 1 500 m high Kasakh Uplands with innumerable salt water lakes.

Economy: Rich mineral deposits (among them petroleum, copper, chrome and manganese) provide the basis for industry in Kazakhstan, important branches being petrochemicals and mechanical engineering. The northern steppes are partly used for huge wheat and sunflower cultivation.

Kenya
Kenya
EAK

Population: 27.3 million (47 per sq km)
Area: 580,367 sq km
Capital: Nairobi
Political system: presidential republic (authoritarian nationalism)
Languages: Kiswaheli (official), Kikuyu, Masai and other tribal languages
Religion: 60% animist, 26% Catholic, 7% Protestant, 6% Muslim
GNP: US$ 320 per head
Currency: 1 Kenya shilling = 100 cents
Industries: coffee, tea, petroleum products, tourism

History: Early ancestors of man lived here 3 million years ago. Phoenician seafarers had already visited its coast in the pre-Christian era. Around 1000 AD Arabs settled on the coast and the interior was inhabited by Bantu tribes (Luos, Somal, etc.). At the beginning of the 16th century the Portuguese took possession of the region, followed in 1729 by the Ottoman sultan. In 1895 Kenya became a British protectorate. In 1963, after heavy battles (among them Mau-Mau resistance at the beginning of the 50's), independence was declared. The one-party system has been going through a process of democratisation since 1982.

Topography: This east African country borders on the Indian Ocean to the south-east; the low-lying coastal land leads westwards to infertile highlands and the Great Rift Valley. Kenya borders on Lake Victoria to the west.

Economy: Although almost 80% of Kenyans work in agriculture, it produces only 30% of the gross national income; in contrast the service sector (in particular tourism) produces nearly 60%. Cattle-farming plays an important role, alongside the cultivation of coffee, tea, sugar-cane etc. on plantations.

Kiribati
Kiribati
KIR

Population: 82,000 (101 per sq km)
Area: 810 sq km
Capital: Bairiki
Political system: presidential republic
Languages: English (official), Gibertese (I-Kiribati)
Religion: 53% Catholic, 39% Protestant, 2% Bahai
GNP: US$ 920 per head
Currency: 1 Australian dollar/Kiribati = 100 cents
Industries: copra, fish and fish products, tourism

History: These islands were inhabited even in the pre-Christian era. In 1892 the Gilbert Islands were put one by one under British protectorate. In 1979 all the Micronesian people resident on the Gilbert Islands were granted independence; they are members of the Commonwealth. Most of the population refer to themselves as Gibertese and the island communities are frequently led by women who are instrumental on the small farms.

Topography: This country, to which the Christmas Islands also belong, comprise 33 flat, scarcely habitable coral islands (the highest point is 3 m!).

Economy: The economy relies heavily on the export of coconuts and coconut products, so that even a slight alteration in the world price has a great effect on the island's economy. Another export industry is fish and seaweed processing. The people are very poor and frequently migrate to the capital in search of jobs. Seldom do they find employment there and so they wander back to their village or farm. The government is introducing legislation to try to alleviate the situation but migration and even emigration may seem a more welcoming prospect than unemployment and poverty. Nowadays tourism contributes 20% of the GNP and a weekly flight from Honolulu is envisaged to help the tourist industry.

Korea, North › ***Choson***
Korea, South ›
Taehan-Min´guk
Kuwait → ***Al Kuwayt***

Kyrgyzstan
Kyrgyzstan
KS

Population: 4.5 million (23 per sq km)
Area: 198,500 sq km
Capital: Bishkek (Biškek)
Political system: presidential republic (emergent democracy)
Languages: Kyrgyz, Russian (both official)
Religion: predominantly Sunni Muslim

GNP: US$ 550 per head
Currency: 1 Kirgistan som = 100 tyin
Industries: mineral deposits, sheep-rearing, textile industry

History: The Turkish and Mongolian nomad tribes, who later became the Kiris, came under Russian rule in 1830.
From 1917 onwards Kirgistan belonged to the Turkestan Autonomous Socialist Soviet Republic; in 1935 it became a part of the USSR. In 1991 Kyrgyzstan proclaimed its independence and joined the CIS.

Topography: Over half of this central Asian country lies in the Tian Shan Mountains on the Chinese border at a height of over 3 000 m. Steppes, deserts, semi-deserts and tundra characterize this land.

Economy: In this extremely dry land only 7% of the surface area is used for agriculture. Pastureland is used primarily for rearing sheep for their wool, which along with locally produced cotton and silk, is processed in their textile industry.

Lao
Laos
LAO

Population: 4.7 million (20 per sq km)
Area: 236,800 sq km
Capital: Vientiane (Viangchan)
Languages: Lao (official), minority languages

1 *Amboseli National Park in Kenya with Kilimanjaro, 5,895 m, (Tanzania) the highest mountain in Africa*

2 *Young Samuru warrior, Kenya*

3 *Reclining Buddha, Bhuddist art in Laos*

4 *Richly ornamented house facade in Riga, the capital and only large city in Latvia*

5 *In Kiribati nets and ropes are made from the leaves of the panadus tree*

protectorate and in 1917 a part of French Indo-China. In 1954 Laos gained independence.
The civil war between East and West (communist and pro-western forces) was temporarily a second arena for the Vietnam War. During this war, Laos was heavily bombed by the US forces. In 1973 all foreign troops were withdrawn after a cease-fire agreement. In 1975 the king abdicated and Laos chose to start a period of "gentle socialism", maintaining good contacts with non-socialist states.
Topography: Laos is the only south-east Asian country that does not have a route to the ocean. To the west, the Mekong river forms a natural boundary, to the east there is the Annamese Cordillera, to the north the Chinese Mountains and to the south the Cambodian plains. The landscape is characterised by hills and plateaux with gorges and alluvial plains inbetween.
Economy: Laos is one of the poorest Asian nations, but can, nonetheless, guarantee its self-sufficiency with its own staple foods (namely rice). Almost 80% of the population works in agriculture, but farming is made difficult by the rough and irregular gradient of the land. This involves intensive work with low productivity. Here rice is grown on terraces as in many other Asian countries. The large areas of timber (teak, bamboo, rattan) account for 40% of export income; an important illegal export is opium, gold and precious stones.

Political system: people's republic (communism, one-party state)
Religion: 58% Buddhist, 34% tribal religions
GNP: US$ 400 per head
Currency: kip
Industries: timber and wood products, coffee, textiles

History: Migrating Lao tribes from south China settled along the Mekong river and were united into an Empire in 1353, that reached its greatest extent in the 17th century and collapsed shortly afterwards. At the beginning of the 19th century it became a Siamese province, in 1893 a French

Latvija
Latvia
LV

Population: 2.4 million (39 per sq km)
Area: 64,589 sq km
Capital: Riga (Rīga)
Political system: parliamentary republic (emergent democracy)
Languages: Latvian (official), Russian
GNP: US$ 2,300 per head

Religion: 55% Lutheran, 24% Catholic, 9% Russian-Orthodox
Currency: 1 lats = 100 santims
Industries: agriculture, machinery, motor vehicles, timber and wood products

History: From the beginning of the 13th century the Teutonic knights took possession of this region. At the end of the 18th century it came under Russian rule. After the fall of the tsar, Latvia declared independence in 1920, but in 1940 Latvia was taken into the Soviet Union as a constituent republic. Latvia again declared independence in1991. Since 1995 it has been a member of the Council of Europe.
Topography: The shape of the land along the Baltic Sea coast was formed by the last Ice Age. Hilly landscapes and plains strewn with moors and lakes characterize Latvia.
Economy: In this former almost completely agrarian state, under 20% of the population work in agriculture today. Latvia is on its way to becoming a modern industrial state producing machinery, motor vehicles and electronic equipment for export. Latvia has a well-developed transport network at its disposal.

Lebanon › Lubnan

Lesotho
Lesotho
LS

Population: 2 million (67 per sq km)
Area: 30,000 sq km
Capital: Maseru
Political system: parliamentary monarchy
Languages: Sesotho, English (both official)
Religion: 44% Catholic, 30% Protestant
GNP: US$ 660 per head
Currency: 1 loti = 100 lisente
Industries: wool, mohair, textiles and shoes, machinery

Liberia

History: The Sotho, who were driven out of South Africa, settled here at the beginning of the 19th century and negotiated a British protectorate in 1867 under their then ruling king, King Moshosho the First, after the defeat by the South African Boers and Lesotho became a British colony in 1884. In 1966 this state declared independence. After gradually freeing itself from the Republic of South African and the 1986-1993 dictatorship, Lesotho is today a parliamentary monarchy.

Topography: Lesotho is completely surrounded by South Africa and predominantly over 2 000 m high; the Drakensberg Mountains that lie to the north-east are in places over 3 000 m high, and none of the land is under 1 000 m; cultivation is mainly on the plateau to the west.

Economy: This mountainous region is not suited to arable farming, but angora goats have turned Lesotho into one of the largest exporters of mohair. The economy is dependent on South Africa, without whom it would be cut off from the outside world. Without the income of its citizens working in South Africa, it could not survive and around 38% of the male working population work in South Africa.

Liberia
Liberia
LB

Population: 2.8 million (29 per sq km)
Area: 97,754 sq km
Capital: Monrovia
Political system: presidential republic (emergent democracy)
Languages: English (official), Gola, Kpelle, Mande etc.
Religion: 70% animist, 20% Muslim, 10% Christian
GNP: under US$ 800 per head
Currency: 1 Liberian dollar = 100 cents
Industries: iron-ore, kautshuk, timber

History: Liberia is the oldest republic in Africa. From 1821 freed American slaves were settled in this region and in 1847 Liberia was granted independence. Liberia nevertheless continued to co-operate closely with the USA. Social tensions led to a military putsch in 1980, which ended with the assassination of president Doe in 1990. Groups of rebels have fought each other ever since. In 1997 a new president was elected.

Topography: From the flat coastal plain on the Atlantic, the land climbs in several steps to the Upper Guinea Threshold; the coastal savannahs give way to areas of rain forest.

Economy: Raw materials, in particular, iron-ore (50% export quota), rubber (20%) and tim-

ber (20%) are exported. Falling prices on the world market have driven Liberia into an economic crisis, since the economy is largely dependent on a small number of export goods. Civil war since 1990 has made the situation even worse.

Libya
Libya
LAR

Population: 5.1 million (3 per sq km)
Area: 1,755,500 sq km
Capital: Tripoli (Tar~bulus)
Political system: Islamic socialist people's republic (one-party state)
Languages: high Arabic (official), Arab Maghrein dialect, Berber and Nilo-Saharan
Religion: 97% Muslim
GNP: under US$ 10,000
Currency: 1 Libyan dollar = 1,000 dirham
Industries: petroleum, natural gas

History: Cave drawings verify that this region was already inhabited 5 000 years ago. In a later era Phoenicians and Greeks settled along the coast. In the 1st century BC the Romans occupied the region, followed by Vandals, Byzantians, Spanish and Ottomans. This area of land was an Italian colony in 1911 when the Italians ousted the Turks. A UN was approved and Libya became an independent monarchy in 1951. However, 18 years later, in 1969, the ruling monarch, King Idris, was toppled in a putsch by Ghadafi. In 1981 the USA shot down 2 Libyan aircraft over the Gulf of Sirte, and this began a series of violent acts, including the shooting of a British policeman in London and the US bombing of Libya.

Topography: Desert covers 90% of the region, only a narrow strip of coast is fairly fertile. The Tibesti Massif rises to a height of over 2 000 m.

Economy: A mere 2% of the land area is arable and, more often than not, only through irrigation. The wealthy deposits of oil discovered in the 50's make up 90% of the export total; the foreign currency has allowed Libya to develop its agriculture, industry and water supply.

Liechtenstein
Liechtenstein
FL

Population: 31000 (194 per sq km)
Area: 160 sq km
Capital: Vaduz
Political system: parliamentary monarchy (constitutional)
Languages: German (official), Alemannic dialect
Religion: 83% Catholic, 7% Protestant
GNP: over US$ 9,000 per head
Currency: 1 Swiss franc = 100 rappen
Industries: machinery, motor vehicles, technical goods, foodstuffs

History: In 1719 this district became a principality. It has been an independent state since 1866, and is allied to Switzerland through an economic, monetary and customs duty agreement. Switzerland is also responsible for the military defence of Liechtenstein.

Topography: Liechtenstein lies in the Alps between Switzerland to the west and Austria to the east; the Rhine forms a natural boundary to the west.

Economy: This tiny country is a tax oasis with innumerable "letterbox firms," but in addition possesses highly specialised industries (e.g. dentures) as well as other half finished goods and has highly developed banking services.

Lietuva
Lithuania
LT

Population: 3.7 million (57 per sq km)
Area: 65,300 sq km
Capital: Vilnius
Political system: presidential republic

Languages: Lithuanian (official), Russian, Polish, Belorussian
Religion: predominantly Catholic
GNP: US$ 2,280 per head
Currency: 1 litas = 100 centas
Industries: heavy engineering, electrical goods, shipbuilding, cement, food processing

History: Lithuanian princes extended their boundaries in the 14th century reaching, at times, almost as far as Moscow and the Black Sea. In 1384 a union was formed with Poland that existed for 400 years. In 1795 Russia occupied Lithuania. In 1940 it became a Soviet republic. In 1991 Lithuania was the first country in the former USSR to declare independence.
Topography: This largest of the three Balkan republics exhibits the typical features of a landscape formed by glaciers. Countless lakes, moors and forests cover the plains that stretch between the low rolling hillsides of the north and south-east. A flat strip of coast with sand dunes borders on the spit of land called the Kursiu Marios lagoon on the Baltic Sea.
Economy: At the beginning of the nineties, industry suffered a temporary but significant setback through the transition from a planned to a market economy. Lithuania exports a wide variety of industrial products: minerals, textiles, machinery and technical products, animals and animal products, foodstuffs, timber and tobacco.

Lubnan
Lebanon
RL

Population: 4 million (390 per sq km)
Area: 10,452 sq km
Capital: Beirut (Bayrã)
Political system: parliamentary-presidential republic (emergent democracy)
Languages: Arabic (official), Lebanese-Syrian and Palestinian dialect of Arabic, Armenian, Kurdish
Religion: 60% Muslim (35% Shi'ite, 25% Sunni), 40% Christian
GNP: US$ 2,970 per head
Currency: 1 Lebanese pound = 100 piaster
Industries: paper products, textiles, jewellery

History: From the 12th to the 8th century BC the Phoenician Empire flourished here. As traders they controlled practically all of the Mediterranean area, and later under the rule of the Assyrians and the Persians this domain was maintained. Only in 64 BC with the arrival of the Romans mean the decline of the Phoenician culture begin. Later this region was merged into the Ottoman Empire, after World War I it was made into a French protectorate and in 1943 granted independence. In 1975 constant battles with neighbouring Israel and Syria escalated into a civil war that went on until 1990. The 30,000 Syrian soldiers that are still stationed there have not been able to end the conflicts.
Topography: The narrow plain on the Mediterranean coast climbs to the Lebanon Mountains, where it joins onto the Bequaa Plain. To the east Mount Hermon (2814m) and the Antilebanon Mountains rise above the Syrian border.
Economy: Civil war has brought the economy and infrastructure to a standstill. Agriculture produces 10% of gross national income, industry just over 20%. The most important export arti-

cles include paper products, jewellery and worked precious metals.

Luxembourg
Luxembourg
L

Population: 416,000 (161 per sq km)
Area: 2,586 sq km
Capital: Luxembourg (Lëtzebuerg)
Political system: parliamentary republic (liberal democracy)
Languages: Letzeburgesch, German, French (all official)
Religion: 95% Catholic
GNP: US$ 45,360 per head
Currency: 1 Luxembourg franc = 100 centimes
Industries: banks, various industrial goods

History: The history of Luxembourg began with the building of a fortress in the area of the present day capital. In 1354 it was declared a duchy. From 1443 it successively fell into the hands of the Burgundans, the Habsburgs, the French, the Dutch and the Belgians. In 1867 independence was gained. It belongs to the founding members of the EU and NATO.
Topography: This small country between Begium, France and Germany is covered by a part of the Ardennes to the north, Lorraine to the south and to the south-east the river Moselle forms the boundary to Germany.
Economy: Luxembourg is the seat of numerous EU institutions as well as the location of around 150 foreign banks. Three-quarters of the population are employed in the service sector. In contrast, the once very important heavy industry has lost most of its significance.

Macedonia → Makedonija

Madagascar

Madagascar

Madagascar
Madagascar
(RM)

Population: 13.7 million (23 per sq km)
Area: 587,041 sq km
Capital: Antananarivo / Tananarive
Political system: presidential republic (one-party socialist)
Languages: Malagasy, French (both official), Howa
Religion: over 50% animist, 25% Catholics, 20% Protestant
GNP: US$ 250 per head
Currency: 1 Madagascar franc = 100 centimes
Industries: coffee, graphite, fish, textiles, spices

History: Madagascar was colonised over 2000 years ago by Africans and Indonesians. They were joined from the 12th century by Muslim traders. In 1896, in spite of strong resistance, the island was made into a French colony. It was one of the first colonies to achieve independence in 1958. Socialist military governments have led to much unrest. After the first democratic elections for 18 years in 1993, the Chief of government, Ratsiraka was ousted, only to be reelected 3 years later in 1996 as the President.

Topography: This island, that lies just off the south-eastern coast of Africa, is the fourth largest in the world. Its central highland (up to 3000 m) falls steeply to the east through rainforest to the coast, to the west more gradually. The unique animal and plant world has been threatened by clearing and is one of the most endangered ecosystems in the world.

Economy: Three-quarters of the population are employed in agriculture; industry and infrastructure are under-developed. Coffee, fish, textiles and minerals such as graphite, are among the most important export goods. Madagascar leads the world market in vanilla and cloves; it is among the 15 poorest countries in the world.

Magyarország
Hungary
(H)

Population: 10.1 million (110 per sq km)
Area: 93,030 sq km
Capital: Budapest
Political system: parliamentary republic
Languages: Hungarian
Religion: 68% Catholic, 25% Protestant
GNP: US$ 4,340 per head
Currency: 1 forint = 100 filler
Industries: machinery, motor vehicles, mining and chemical products

History: Hungarians were originally a nomadic society of horsemen, who migrated here from the area between the Volga and Urals. Their language bears no resemblance to the languages of the neighbouring countries, only to Finnish. In the 13th century they were one of the most powerful peoples in Europe. In the 16th century the western part of the country went to the Habsburgs, who in the 17th century also took possession of the rest of Hungary, previously conquered by the Turks. In 1867 Hungary became independent, but still belonged to the double monarchy of the Austro-Hungarian Empire. After their defeat in World War I, Hungary lost two-thirds of its land area. In 1946 it became a republic and under Soviet pressure was given a communist government. In 1956 student demonstrations calling for the reinstatement of Imre Nagy as Minister President and the withdrawal of soviet troops had succes; Nagy was reinstated and immediately announced Hungary's withdrawal from the Warsaw Pact. The success was however, shortlived; three days later Soviets troops suppressed the movement and 25,000 members of the opposition, supporters and protesters were killed. Kádár was made minister president. Afterwards they achieved a form of gentle communism which occasionally permitted privatisation and freedom of travel. 1989 it was proclaimed a republic; in 1990 the first free elections took place. 1997 Hungary joined NATO and in 1998 it began negotiating entry to the EU.

Topography: The Great Hungarian Plain that lies to the east of the Danube encompasses most of the land. The Bekoney Forest, Lake Balaton and the Transdanubian Highlands are to the west.

Economy: The transition from planned to market economy means that industry, in particular heavy industry so important for export, urgently requires modernisation. A mild climate and good soil provide ideal conditions for agriculture and cattle-farming. Only 8% of the Hungarians work in agriculture but they produce enough to feed the majority of the population. In 1997 half the Hungarians lived below the poverty line but now the economy is experiencing an upswing once again. The tourist industry is still very important and largely unaffected by the economy.

Makedonija
Macedonia
(MK)

Population: 1.9 million (77 per sq km)
Area: 25,713 sq km
Capital: Skopje
Political system: republic
Languages: Macedonian (official), Albanian, Turkish, etc.

Religion: 67% Macedonian-Orthodox, 30% Muslim
GNP: US$ 990 per head
Currency: 1 denar = 100 deni
Industries: textiles, tobacco, metals

History: Present day Macedonia is only a fraction of its former size. In the early Middle Ages it was taken over first by the Bulgarians, in the 11th and 12th centuries by Byzantium, in the 13th and 14th centuries by the Serbians, and from 1389 for 500 years by the Ottoman Empire.
In 1912-1913, Macedonia was divided between Greece and Turkey. In 1918 the area became part of Serbia in the newly created Yugoslavia. With the founding of the People's Republic of Yugoslavia in 1945, Macedonia also became a republic in its own right. In 1991 it declared its independence.

Topography: The primarily mountainous landscape falls to the south-east down to the Vardar Basin. Around a third of the country is covered in forest. Three lakes on the border to Albania and Greece attract tourists, in particular the citizens of Macedonia.

Economy: In addition to the mining of the rich iron-ore deposits, metal working, textile and leather industries are particularly significant. It must be said that Macedonia is one of the economically most backward states in the region although there was an interim improvement between 1996 and 1998. Small farmers cultivate mainly tobacco, fruits, vegetables, wine and rice.

1. *The Hungarian Parliament building on the Danube, Budapest*

2. *Chameleon in Madagascar. Many species of animals are found only on this unique island and are threatened to becoming extinct due to forest clearing*

3. *Fishing village on Lake Malawi, one of Africa's largest inland waters and abundant in fish*

4. *Peasant working in a paddy field, Malaysia. Only since the end of the 1980s have industrial products begun to exceed agricultural products in the trade balance*

1993 a referendum voted for a multi party political system and, in 1994, Banda and the Malawi congress Party were defeated in elections.

Topography: Over two-thirds of this long, thin country, measuring 900km from north to south, and between 80 and 160 km in width, is covered by dry highland. The east African Rift Valley runs the length of the country and contains Lake Malawi, from where the Zambesi flows.

Economy: Malawi is one of the ten poorest countries in the world. It has virtually no mineral deposits and 90% of its export balance comprises agricultural products (70% from tobacco). 90% of the population works in agriculture.

Malawi
Malawi
(MW)

Population: 10 million (85 per sq km)
Area: 118,484 sq km
Capital: Linongwe
Political system: presidential republic
Languages: Chichewa, English (official), Lomwe, Yao, Seno, Chitumbuka
Religion: 58% Protestant, 17% Catholic, 10% animist
GNP: US$ 180 per head
Currency: 1 Malawi-kwacha = 100 tambala
Industries: tobacco, tea, sugar

History: In the 16th and 17th centuries Bantu tribes migrated to this area and displaced or eradicated the native population and founded the Kingdom of Malawi. Later the South African Ngoni and the Yao, who dealt with the Arabs in slave trade, forced their way in. In 1875 Scottish missionaries arrived and in 1891 it became a British protectorate. In 1964 independence was proclaimed and Dr. Hastings Banda took control of the state. The one party system that he introduced forbade any criticism; critical opponents were arrested and tortured. In 1992 international aid to Malawi was stopped because of this regime. In

Malaysia
Malaysia
(MAL)

Population: 20.5 million (62 per sq km)
Area: 329,758 sq km
Capital: Kuala Lumpur
Political system: elected monarchy (liberal democracy)
Languages: Malay (official), English, Chinese, Indian and local languages
Religion: 53% Muslim, 17% Buddhist, 12% Chinese religions, 7% Hindus, 7% Christians
GNP: US$ 4,370 per head
Currency: 1 Malaysian ringgit = 100 sen
Industries: machinery, crude oil, tin, forest and agriculture products

History: The original inhabitants were Malaysian farmers, who in the first century AD were joined by Chinese and Indian traders, who turned their settlements into successful trading metropolises. The greatest of them was Malakka, which in 1419 proclaimed itself a kingdom. In 1511 the Portuguese conquered the area and in 1641 so did the Dutch, who in1824 exchanged it with the British and by 1930 all of the Malaysian states on the peninsula were under a British protectorate. In 1957 an independence movement led to the

creation of the "Federation of Malaysia." In 1963 Malaysia comprised Malaya, Sabah, Sarawak and Singapore (Singapore left the federation in 1965). Today this country is ruled by a king who is chosen by the upper house for a period of five years.

Topography: Malaysia is made up of two separate parts that are separted by the South China Sea: West Malaysia, on the Malaysian peninsula, and East Malaysia, 600 km away on the northern tip of the island of Borneo, which otherwise belongs to Indonesia. Both parts of the country are mountainous and covered to a great extent by rain forests.

Economy: Malaysia is rich in mineral deposits and natural resources. It is not only the world's largest producer of tin, but also produces 60% of the world's palm oil products. Other important exports include rubber, crude oil and various metals. The former agrarian state is being industrialized very quickly; since the end of the 80's industrial products have contributed more to the gross national income than agriculture. Malaysia is still a developing country with class discrimination between rich Chinese and poor Malaysian people.

Maledives
Maledives
(MV)

Population: 256,000 (859 per sq km)
Area: 298 sq km
Capital: Malé
Political system: presidential republic
Languages: Moldavian-Divehe (Sinhalese dialect), English
Religion: practically 100% Sunni Muslim
GNP: US$ 1,080 per head
Currency: 1 rufiya = 100 larri
Industries: fish and fish products, tourism

Mali

History: In ancient times the Maldives were already inhabited, probably by the Sinhalese, and from the 9th century it came under Arab influence. In 1141 a Ceylonese prince was crowned king. This island kingdom was able to maintain its sovereignty for a long time but eventually became a British protectorate in 1887. In 1965 it gained independence.

Topography: The island state of the Maldives encompasses 19 atolls. Altogether there are 2000 coral islands, of which 191 are inhabited. Practically the only form of vegetation on the islands is the coconut palm tree. Apart from the white beaches, tourists specially esteem the underwater life of the coral reefs.

Economy: The main source of income is tourism, over 50% of the population work in the service sector. Fish and fish products make up 80% of the export balance.

Mali
Mali
(RMM)

Population: 9.9 million (8 per sq km)
Area: 1,240,192 sq km
Capital: Bamako
Political system: presidential republic
Languages: French (official), Bambara, Songhai-Jerma, Manding, Arabic, Ful
Religion: 80% Sunni Muslim, 18% animist
GNP: US$ 240 per head
Currency: 1 CFA franc = 100 centimes
Industries: cotton, gold, cattle-breeding and livestock products

History: The Mali Empire was one of the early advanced civilisations in this part of Africa, that were very rich and extremely well-organised. In the 14th century their frontiers stretched well beyond those of the present day. In 1870 the French began to conquer the area and in 1904 made it a part of French West Africa - the borders had been established on the drawing-board at the Berlin African Conference in 1884.
In 1960 this country gained independence and tried a form of "Mali Socialism." In 1968 there was a military putsch due to the poor economic situation. Since 1992 a democratically elected president has been in office. Many decisions are made by a few members of leading, influential families.

Topography: The northern part of the country is covered by the Sahara Desert, then comes a dry savannah. Moist savannah and forests are only to be found in the south. In the centre of the country the Niger basin delta produces fertile alluvial plains.

Economy: Over 80% of the population are employed in agriculture; the most important export is cotton. Further economic development is difficult due to poor infrastructure in a vast land that is subject to an unfavourable climate with terrible droughts.

Malta
Malta
(M)

Population: 373,000 (1180 per sq km)
Area: 315 sq km
Capital: Vallette
Political system: parliamentary republic (liberal democracy)
Languages: Maltese, English (both official), Italian
Religion: 93% Catholic
GNP: under US$ 10,000 per head
Currency: 1 Maltese lira = 100 cents
Industries: machinery, textiles, tourism

History: This island was inhabited in the Stone Age; megalithic sites are proof of this. In 1000 BC the Phoenicians settled here. They were followed by Carthaginians, Romans, Byzantians, Arabs and others, all of whom were interested in Malta's good strategic position, which lies between North Africa and Europe in the Mediterranean Sea.
In 1530 the Emperor Carl V gave the island over to an order of knights. In 1798 it was conquered by Napoleon and two years later the British came as colonisers. Political self administration was granted in 1947, followed by independence in 1964. Malta's constitution is obliged to absolute neutrality.

Topography: In addition to the main island, the smaller islands of Gozo (67 sq km) and Comino (3 sq km) are also part of Malta. The hilly to mountainous islands have sparse vegetation.

Economy: Infertile soil and a lack of mineral deposits force the Maltese to concentrate on industry and tourism. Alongside machinery and transport equipment, the main export goods are industrial and chemical products.

Marshall Islands
Marshall Islands
(MH)

Population: 57,000 (314 per sq km)
Area: 181 sq km
Capital: Majuro (Dalap-Uliga-Darrit)
Political system: constitutional republic
Languages: English (official), Micronesian languages

Religion: predominantly Christian
GNP: US$ 1,890 per head
Currency: 1 US dollar ($) = 100 cents
Industries: fish and fish products, copra

History: In 1886 the Marshall Islands were declared a German protectorate. In 1914 they were occupied by the Japanese. During World War II they were taken over and administered by the USA. Between 1946 and 1958 the Americans carried out 23 atomic tests on the Bikini and Eniwetok atolls.
Since 1986 the Marshall Islands were partially independent, but after 1990 became a completely independent republic because the USA gave up their UN mandate.

Topography: The state consists of two island groups that comprise 30 atolls. There are a total of 1100 islands altogether which stretch over a distance of 1200 km in the Pacific Ocean.

Economy: The wealth of fish around the islands is not only an important source of food for their own consumption but also a basis for their fish processing industry that produces exports. Profits from the coconut product, copra, also play an

1 White beaches and fantastic under-water life have made tourism the Maldives' chief source of income

2 Young girl from the Fulani tribe, Central Mali

3 This pyramid in Chichén Itzá, Mexico, dating back to the 11th century, was dedicated to the god Kukulkan. It is one of the most important temples of the Mayas

important role. The cultivation of fruits and veg-etables covers nearly all their own needs.

Mauritania → Mawritaniyah

Mauritius
Mauritius
MS

Population: 1.2 million (556 per sq km)
Area: 2,040 sq km
Capital: Port Louis
Political system: presidential republic
Languages: English (official), French Creole and other dialects
Religion: 52% Hindus, 30% Christian, 13% Muslim
GNP: US$ 3,710 per head
Currency: 1 Mauritius rupee = 100 cents
Industries: textiles, sugar-cane, tourism

History: This uninhabited island was made into a trading post first by the Dutch and then by the French. In 1810 it fell into English hands. Since 1968 it has been an independent state. The pop-ulation are the descendants of black slaves and those Chinese and Indians who came to the country as cheap labour in 1835 on the abolition of slavery and there was fighting between the two groups in 1969. A republic was claimed in 1992.
Topography: Mauritius lies east of Madagascar in the Indian Ocean. It is a volcanic island sur-rounded by innumerable coral islands and has a steep coast that rises to a central high plateau. White sandy beaches and nature reserves turn these islands into a tourist paradise.
Economy: Mauritius with its well-developed in-frastructure is today a modern welfare state. The main pillar of foreign trade is the textile industry, the second sugar-cane.
Mauritius is an associate member of the EU and has succeeded in attracting foreign firms to the area through low taxes and is developing into an important banking factor with offshore banking.

Mawritaniyah
Mauretania
RIM

Population: 2.3 million (2 per sq km)
Area: 1,030,700 sq km
Capital: Nouakchott
Political system: presidential republic
Languages: High Arabic, (official), various Niger and Congo languages
Religion: 97% Sunni Muslim
GNP: US$ 470 per head
Currency: 1 ouguiya = 5 khoums
Industries: fish and fish products, iron-ore, gyb-son

History: Originally this area was inhabited by black farmers. In the 3rd century Arabs and Berber forced their way in. In the 11th century the Almoravids conquered and converted it to Islam. After the decline of this empire in the 12th century, part of Mauritania remained as part of Morocco, the other part became a part of Mali. From 1934 to 1960 Mauritania was a French colony that was administrated from Senegal. Slavery was only abolished in 1980. Ethnic con-flicts between Moors and black Africans still cause problems. After a long dictatorship, free elections first took place in 1992 under the pressure of western creditors. The ruling military ruler, Presi-dent Maaouya Ould Taya was elected back to his office. The African population tend to support the government party, whereas the Moorish popula-tion tend to support the parties in exile.
Topography: The Atlantic coastal plain is joined in the south by the thorny Sahel Savannah. Far-ther to the north, the sandy and stony desert of the Sahara which covers two-thirds of the land, climbs to a sandstone plateau in the far north-east. The Senegal river in the south-west forms the border to neighbouring Senegal.
Economy: Not even 1% of the land is arable; the only areas being on the banks of the Senegal and a few oases in the south. The most important ex-port is iron-ore which is mined in the north.

México
Mexico
MEX

Population: 93.1 million (48 per sq km)
Area: 1,953,162 sq km
Capital: Mexico City (Ciudad de México)
Political system: presidential republic (federal democracy)
Languages: Spanish (official), Indian and Mayan languages
Religion: 90% Catholic, 5% Protestant
GNP: US$ 3,670 per head
Currency: 1 Mexican peso = 100 centavos
Industries: electronics and electrical engineer-ing, motor vehicles, machinery

History: The first settlements can be traced back to 20,000 BC. Many different peoples and tribes lived in this area and we are reminded even today of this advanced civilisation by the numerous mo-numents. The Mayan culture reached its zenith from 900 to 600 BC. In 1370 the Aztecs founded the lagoon city of Tenochtitlan (on the site of present day Mexico City) and subjugated the neighbouring tribes. In 1519 the Spanish subju-gated Montezuma, the Aztec ruler, destroyed their city of Tenochtitlan and other cultural mon-uments, and made the inhabitants slaves. After a long fight Mexico gained independence in 1821 and was an empire until 1823. It lost its northern part to the USA in the border war from 1845-1853. It again had an emperor in the Austrian archduke, Maximilian, from 1864 to 1867. In the 1910 Mexican Revolution, rebellious farmers suc-cessfully fought for free elections and instigated a very advanced constitution, resulting in a social and economic upswing for Mexico.
Topography: The land between the Gulf of Mexico and the Pacific Ocean borders to the north on the USA and to the south on Guatemala and Belize. To the north-west, the peninsula known as Lower California runs parallel to main-land Mexico with the Gulf of California inbe-tween. Running from north to south, mountains enclose the central plateau. Its highest point is

Micronesia

Citlaltepetl, 5 700 m; better known is Popocate-petl, 250 m lower. Tropical rain forest grows on the Yucatan Peninsula, which lies in the Gulf of Mexico and borders on the Caribbean. The capital city and the artefacts of ancient Mexican civilisations and the legendary beaches (e.g. Acapulco, Tampico) are the main attractions for tourists.

Economy: The greatest share of exports is made up by industrial products such as electronics and electrical equipment, motor vehicles and machinery, as well as textiles. In contrast, traditional mining has waned in significance, even though it is the second largest producer of silver in the world, and has other mining products of significance. The demand for oil is becoming more and more important; Mexico is in fourth place in world oil production. Fuel production accounts for 10% of exports. Mexico still has many poor inhabitants who consider crossing the border to the USA as a way out of poverty. Mexico, the USA and Canada have signed trading agreements which may make these attempts superfluous.

Micronesia
Micronesia
(FSM)

Population: 109,000 (156 per sq km)
Area: 700 sq km
Capital: Colonia (official); Palikir (de facto)
Political system: federal republic
Languages: English (official), Micronese and Polynese languages
Religion: 50% Catholic, 45% Protestant
GNP: US$ 2,070 per head
Currency: 1 US dollar = 100 cents
Industries: fish, tourism

History: Virtually nothing is known about the highly advanced civilisation whose monuments can be seen on the island of Pohnpei. In 1686 this group of islands came under Spanish rule and in 1899 was sold to Germany. After World War I it came under Japanese trusteeship and after World War II under the USA. Since 1990 Micronesia has been an independent republic that maintains close links to the USA.

Topography: The state comprises 4 island groups (Chuuk, Pohnpei, Yap and Kosrae) with a total of 607 mountainous volcanic islands and flat coral islands that spread over an area of 2.6 million sq km in the Pacific.

Economy: The most important source of export income is fishing which makes up 90% of the export balance. The main buyer is Japan. This country is dependent on imports and financial help from the USA.

Moçambique
Mozambique
(MOC)

Population: 18 million (23 per sq km)
Area: 799,380 sq km
Capital: Maputo
Political system: presidential republic (one-party socialist)
Languages: Portuguese (official), Kisuaheli, Makua, Nyanja etc.
Religion: 70% animist, 30% Catholic, 10% Muslim
GNP: US$ 80 per head
Currency: 1 metical = 100 centavos
Industries: crabs and prawns

History: During the 1st century AD Bantu people settled in this area and founded several kingdoms. From the 7th century the region fell under Arabian influence. In 1497 the Portuguese took control over part of the coast and at the Berlin Conference in 1884/85 the borders of this territory were demarcated as they still are today.
In 1964 a national independence movement took up arms and in 1975 gained independence. The non-stop civil war from 1976 until 1992 damaged Mozambique badly and it is still recovering with outside financial and humanitarian aid. The devastation is slowly being repaired although many skilled workers fled the land.

Topography: A belt of wide, flat tropical lowland runs along the coast on the Indian Ocean, bordered by low-lying plateaux to the north-west and mountains to the west. There is a low plateau that is traversed by rivers to the north.

Economy: Infrastructure and industry have been almost completely destroyed by civil war; this applies in particular to the transport routes, ports and railways that were previously intensively used by neighbouring countries, but also to the mining of raw materials. Important exports at present are crustaceans such as crabs and shrimps.

Moldova
Moldovia
(MD)

Population: 4.3 million (128 per sq km)
Area: 33,700 sq km
Capital: Chisinau (ChiŌin|u/Kischinjow)
Political system: presidential republic (emergent democracy)
Languages: Moldavian, allied to Romanian (official), Russian, Hungarian, Gagau
Religion: predominantly Russian-Orthodox
GNP: US$ 590 per head

Currency: 1 Moldau leu = 100 bani
Industries: foodstuffs, tobacco, wine and tobacco

History: In the 14th century the principality of Moldovia was united with Northern Bessarabia. From the 14th century the whole area came under Turkish rule. In 1812 it fell to Russia; then in 1918 to the Romanians. In 1940 the southern part was annexed by the Ukraine; the main part became an independent Soviet Republic. In 1991 Moldovia declared its independence and joined the CIS. An attempt to rejoin Rumania failed. In the elections of 1993, Moldavia returned the Communist Party.

Topography: The flat, dry steppe to the south climbs to the centre of the region to an area of mainly forested hills; to the north there is fertile steppe. The climate is one of long, warm summers and mild winters.

Economy: The mild climate made the Republic of Moldovia into the "bread basket" of the USSR. Even today tobacco, wine, fruits and sunflowers are cultivated and exported. Half of the population works in agriculture. Mineral deposits are not forthcoming and industry is underdeveloped.

1 Demonstration of dancing in a cultural centre in Pohnpei, Micronesia

2 Horse breeder at a horse fair, Mongolia

3 Innumerable and ornately decorated towers of the Shwedagon Pagoda in Yangon, Burma

4 The Yacht harbour and skyline of Monaco

Topography: The tiny city state on the Mediterranean coast is surrounded by almost vertical chalk cliffs. The colour of the sea gives it its name, Cote d'Azur. The climate is typically mild.
Economy: This country, that abolished income tax in 1865, attracts wealthy people from all over the world; not even 20% of the inhabitants are from Monagascans. Besides tourism and the casinos for which Monaco is world famous, small and medium-sized businesses are a source of income. Among other things, cosmetics and foodstuffs are produced.

Monaco
Monaco
MC

Population: 32,000 (16,410 per sq km)
Area: 1.95 sq km
Capital: Monaco-Ville
Political system: parliamentary republic (constitutional monarchy)
Languages: French (official), English, Italian, Monegasish
Religion: 90% Catholic, 6% Protestant
GNP: over US$ 10,000 per head
Currency: 1 French franc = 100 centimes
Industries: tourism

History: The Phoenicians in 600 BC and the Romans in 2nd century BC used this place as a port. In 1911 possession was granted to Genoa. In 1912 it formed a customs union with France. Since 1297 the principality of Monaco has been ruled by the Grimaldis (lords of the noble house of Genua).
In 1792 the mini-state was proclaimed a republic, but nevertheless united with France one year later. In 1815 Monaco gained independence. Until 1860 it was under the protection of Sardinia, then France took over that function and in 1865 Monaco joined in a customs and currency union with France.

Mongol Uls
Mongolia
MGL

Population: 2.5 million (1.6 per sq km)
Area: 1,566,500 sq km
Capital: Ulan-Bator (Ulaanbaatar)
Political system: republic (communism)
Languages: Khalkha Mongolian (official), Russian, Chinese, Turkic languages
Religion: 90% Buddhist, animist (Shamanism), Muslim
GNP: US$ 360 per head
Currency: 1 Tugrik = 100 mongo
Industries: copper and molybdan-ore, cattle-rearing

History: The vast Empire of the Mongols belonged successively to the Huns, Awaras and Uiguras, until in 1206 Genghis Khan united it into one empire. The Mongolian Mounted Armies extended the frontiers of the empire to encompass almost all of Asia and Asia Minor as far as the Baltic Sea and the Adriatic. Towards the end of the 13th century the empire started to break up. Southern Mongolia became a part of China and

Northern Mongolia (roughly the area occupied by present day Mongolia) became a part of Chinese external territory in 1691. With Russian support in 1911 Outer Mongolia declared itself independent. In 1924 the People's Republic of Mongolia was founded. In 1990 the first free elections took place and since 1992 they have had a new constitution changing the name simply to Mongolia.
Topography: This state between China and Russia is one of the most sparsely populated countries in the world. Desert and highland steppe depict the landscape. There are high forested mountains to the north-west and the Altai Mountains to the west, the Gobi Desert is to the south.
Economy: The areas of steppe are vast natural meadows that are used traditionally for animal farming. Rich mineral deposits are partly exported and partly used in local industry, which is still considered to be growing. The transition from planned to market economy presents problems.

Morocco › Al Maghrib
Mozambique › Moçambique

Myanmar
Burma
MYA

Population: 45.8 million (68 per sq km)
Area: 676,552 sq km
Capital: Yangon (formally Rangoon)
Political system: socialistic republic (military)
Languages: Burmese (official), minority languages
Religion: 87% Buddhist, 6% Christian, 4% Muslim
GNP: under US$ 800 per head
Currency: 1 kyat = 100 pyas
Industries: rice, timber, fish

History: Myanmar (Burma) is strongly influenced by Buddhism, which arrived in this area from India in 200 BC. From the 1st century AD Mongol tribes founded various Empires here and in the 9th and 10th centuries, Burmese from Tibet conquered this territory. In the 13th century the

1

Namibia

Mongols came back and after them the Thai people. From the 14th century, Burma started breaking up into different empires that fought with each other despite occasional efforts towards unification. In 1753 a unified Burma was achieved nonetheless though brutal force. The British conquered this land in three wars and in 1886 declared it to be a province governed by British India. However, in 1937 they made it into a crown colony. In 1942 Japan occupied Burma. In 1948 Burma won its independence. A military regime has ruled over Burma ever since.

Topography: The central low-lying plains around the river basin of the Irrawaddy and Chinwin rivers are framed to the west by the Gulf of Bengal and the Arakan Mountains, and to the east by the O Shan Plateau.

Economy: The largest area of rice cultivation in the world is here on the Irrawaddy Delta. In addition to basic agriculture exports, precious woods such as teak, play an important role. The population's economic situation is extremely serious; lack of supplies and no infrastructure, and the thoughtless clearing of the forests, create real worries for the future.

Namibia
Namibia
NAM

Population: 1.5 million (2 per sq km)
Area: 824,292 sq km
Capital: Windhoek
Political system: presidential republic (democratic)
Languages: English (official), Afrikaans (spoken by 60% of the white pop.), Bantu
Religion: 62% Protest, 20% Catholic, animist
GNP: US$ 2,250 per head
Currency: 1 Namibia dollar = 100 cents
Industries: diamonds and mineral products, agricultural products

History: Shepherds, farmers and cattle-breeders of various tribes populated this land, when in the middle of the 19th century the first European traders and missionaries appeared in the country. In 1884 it became the German colony of South-West Africa. After World War I it came under the administration of the South African Union. After a long-standing war of liberation, South Africa gave in to UN pressure: only in 1990, as second to last African country, did Namibia achieve independence.

Topography: The Namib Desert connects onto the coastal strip on the Atlantic Ocean, then the land climbs sharply to a hilly plateau in the centre of the country. The thorny savannah landscape of

the Kalahari Basin runs to the east. Tourists are attracted by the nature reserves.

Economy: Mining products make up the lion's share of exports, diamonds alone make up one-third of it. Almost half of the population work in agriculture and stock farming. Meat and pelts are produced for export. The Namibian economy has not yet recovered from the long war of independence and its separation from South Africa although the country now encourages tourism.

Nauru
Nauru
NAU

Population: 11,000 (516 per sq km)
Area: 21.3 sq km
Capital: Yaren
Political system: presidential republic (liberal democracy)
Languages: Nauruan, English (both official)
Religion: 60% Protestant, 30% Catholic
GNP: US$ 13,000 per head
Currency: 1 Australian dollar = 100 cents
Industries: phosphates

History: The native population of Nauru belong to the same ethnic group as the Polynesians. In 1888 this island, together with the Marshall Islands, was made into a German colony. With time, the influence that Christian missionaries had there grew. After World War I, Nauru came under the administration of Australia, New Zealand and Great Britain until independence was achieved in 1968, but with the exception of the years between 1942 and 1945, when it was occupied by Japan for a brief period during World War II.

Topography: Nauru is just one island that borders on coral reef.

Economy: Their affluent welfare state can be attributed to the abundance of phosphate on the island, the essential ingredient in the manufacture of fertilizer. Sources, however, are being fast depleted and efforts are being made to build up

a shipping business and to create new sources of income through capital investments.

Nederland
The Netherlands
NL

Population: 15.5 million (371 per sq km)
Area: 41,865 sq km
Capital: Amsterdam (official), The Hague (de facto)
Political system: parliamentary monarchy (constitutional)
Languages: Dutch
Religion: 36% Catholic, 19% Reformed Dutch, 7% other Protestants, 3% Muslim
GNP: US$ 25,940 per head
Currency: 1 Dutch guilder = 100 cents
Industries: machinery, chemical products, mineral oil

History: After centuries of changing foreign rulers, the Republic of the United Provinces of the Netherlands was founded under the rule of the House of Orange in 1581.
In the 16th and 17th centuries, the Netherlands were the greatest sea and trading power in Europe. Right up to the present day this relatively small country has had considerable power thanks to its possessions overseas.

Topography: Over a quarter of the surface area lies below sea-level and has been reclaimed and is protected by dykes. The Netherlands contains the mouths of five important rivers.
The North Sea coast is strewn with a dune belt, to the north the West Frisian Islands lie in a row along the coast. One sixth of the country's surface area is covered by inland waters (lakes, rivers and canals). To the south the lowland joins the lower Ardennes and the northern edge of the Rhein Schiefergebirge.

Economy: Classic exports are still cheese, tulips and herrings, but agriculture nowadays is in the hands of highly specialised modern enterprises. Dutch industry has suffered noticeable losses like

1 Sandwich Harbour: reeds growing at the narrow crossing point between the Atlantic Ocean and the desert, Namibia

3 The Dutch town of Leiden, between Amsterdam and The Hague

4 The Roof of the World: Mt. Everest, 8,848 m, is the highest mountain in the world, Nepal

2 Young Dutch girl wearing the gown of a countess from the Middle Ages

everywhere else since the end of the 70's, but to off-set that there is oil and natural gas mining in the North Sea, which is enjoying considerable growth. The port of Rotterdam is the largest in the world.

Nepal
Nepal
NEP

Population: 22 million (150 per sq km)
Area: 147,181 sq km
Capital: Kathmandu
Political system: parliamentary monarchy
Languages: Nepali (official), Indo-Arian and Tibeto-Burman
Religion: 90% Hindus, 5% Buddhist
GNP: US$ 210 per head
Currency: 1 Nepalese rupee
Industries: jute and jute products, carpets, textiles, furs, skins

History: It is said that from around 1000 to 700 BC, the Mongolian Newar and Indian tribes settled in the Kathmandu Valley. In 563 BC Buddha, who was later to become the founder of Buddhism, was born in Lumbini Gautama. In the 3rd century BC a long history of Indian influence in this area began. In 1768 an Indian ruler, King Prithi Narayan Shah, united the small principalities into the Kingdom of Nepal that was quickly able to expand its borders; in a war with Britain from 1814 to 1816 they were pushed back. In

1846 an authoritarian regime came into power that in 1951 was overthrown with the help of India; the king was again absolute ruler. Not until 1990, after a bloody uprising, did Nepal become a parliamentary monarchy.
Topography: This Himalayan country extends between China to the north and India to the south. Here one finds some of the highest peaks in the world, such as Mount Everest, 8846 m. high. The very high Himalayas in the north give way to the Himalayan foothills and the Siwali mountain range to the south. The most densely populated and most intensively cultivated area is the Kathmandu Valley in the interior.
Economy: Nepal is one of the poorest countries in the world. Over 90% of the population work in agriculture. Above all through stockfarming can they produce pelts and skins for export. Tourism is taking on increasing significance as a source of income, where trekking in the mountains is almost more attractive than visiting the numerous old cities of cultural interest.

Netherlands → Nederland

New Zealand
New Zealand
NZ

Population: 3.6 million (13 per sq km)
Area: 270,534 sq km
Capital: Wellington
Political system: parliamentary monarchy (constitutional)
Languages: English (official), Maori
Religion: 22% Anglican, 16% Presbyterian, 15% Catholic, Maori Church
GNP: US$ 15,720 per head
Currency: 1 New Zealand dollar = 100 cents
Industries: dairy products, meat, timber and wood products

History: Around 1000 years ago Maori people from Polynesia settled on these islands. From the

18th century Europeans arrived. In 1840 Britain acquired sovereign rights over the land. Since 1907 New Zealand has been independent de facto, but officially only since 1931. It is a member of the Commonwealth and the head of state is the British monarch.
Topography: The country comprises two large islands that lie in the south-west Pacific. The New Zealand Alps stretch along the length of the southern island. To the east the landscape is hilly and along the southern coast there are fjords, off which lies Stewart Island. On the northern island, where the capital Wellington is situated, there is volcanic highland with geysers, hot springs and active volcanoes. The country's territories also encompass a large area in the Arctic and an administrative area in the South Pacific.
Economy: New Zealand became a welfare state very early. The rearing of sheep and cattle which dominate the landscape, makes up one-third of the export balance – in the middle of the 60's it was 90%. Industrial products are gaining in significance. With the letting-go of the motherland, Great Britain, New Zealand has had to look for new trading partners in Japan, the Near East and the USA. Tourism is an increasingly important source of foreign currency; travellers looking for unspoilt nature and wide open spaces have their dreams fulfilled.

Nicaragua
Nicaragua
NIC

Population: 4.5 million (37 per sq km)
Area: 120,254 sq km
Capital: Managua ·
Political system: presidential republic (emergent democracy)
Languages: Spanish (official), Indian languages
Religion: 89% Catholic, 5% Protestant, animist
GNP: US$ 380 per head
Currency: 1 cordoba = 100 centavos
Industries: coffee, seafood, meat, sugar, bananas

Niger

*Niger*_____

History: Originally this area was inhabited by various Indian tribes of which the most important lived on the shores of Lake Nicaragua. In 1550 this region was annexed to Guatemala. In the 17th century it came under British protectorate. In 1821 Nicaragua declared independence and joined other Central American countries to form the United States of Central America. From 1936 it came under the dictatorship of the Somoza family until they were overthrown in 1979 by left-wing rebels, the Sandinistas. Consequently a civil war broke out between the Sandinistas and Contras (counter-revolutionaries supported by the USA), that did not end till 1990. In 1996 free elections were held in which Arnoldo Alemán Lacayo of the Constitutional Liberal Party won against the former president, Daniel Ortega Saavedra of the Sandinistan National Freedom Front.

Topography: To the west a chain of volcanoes connects up with the densely populated coastal plain on the Pacific. The land descends to the Nicaraguan Basin, then climbs to the Central American Cordilleras. It falls to the east to the wide low-lying Caribbean plain, that is covered in rain forest and traversed by numerous rivers. To the south, on the border to Costa Rica, there is the huge Lake Nicaragua.

Economy: Civil war and natural catastrophes (1972 earthquake, 1988 hurricane) have wreaked havoc with the Nicaraguan economy. What roads there are, are in a very poor state. A project to build a connecting canal to the two coasts has been proposed. With very little industry and an unemployment rate of over 50%, poverty in this land is great. Coffee, sugar-cane and bananas are cultivated for export. Staple foods are also grown for their own consumption.

Niger
Niger
(RN)

Population: 9.3 million (7 per sq km)
Area: 267,000 sq km
Capital: Niamey
Political system: presidential republic (military)
Languages: French (official), Hausa, Songhai-Dsherma, Fulbe, Tamashagh, Kanouri
Religion: 80% Sunni Muslim, over 10% animist
GNP: US$ 200 per head
Currency: 1 CFA franc = 100 centimes
Industries: uranium, cattle

History: In the pre-Christian era highly developed civilisations existed in this region. Later it belonged to the Mali and then to the Songhai Empires. Conversion to Islam began in the 10th century. Despite strong resistance, the French

made the region a colony in 1922. In 1958 it became an autonomous republic within the French commonwealth and in 1960 it acquired full independence. In 1974 a terrible drought brought an end to a regime that enriched itself while its people starved. The military dictatorship that followed was in power until 1990, when an attempt at democracy started to take hold. In 1996 there was another military putsch.

Topography: The Tenere and Air Mountains join up with the Niger Basin to the south and the Chad Basin to the south-east. The deserts and sandy highlands of the Sahara stretch to the north and north-west. Only a small zone irrigated by the Niger and located along the southern border is suitable for agriculture.

Economy: The fall in the price of uranium, the main export, and a three-year-long drought have caused a serious economic crisis; parts of the country are suffering from starvation.

Nigeria
Nigeria
(WAN)

Population: 114.5 million (124 per sq km)
Area: 923,768 sq km
Capital: Abuja
Political system: presidential republic
Languages: English (official), Kwa languages, Ful, Hausa etc.
Religion: 45% Muslim, 26% Protestant, 12% Catholic, 11% African Christian, animist
GNP: US$ 240 per head
Currency: 1 naira = 100 kobo
Industries: petroleum

History: Artistic sculptures found in the cities Ife and Benin are evidence of an ancient and advanced civilisation in Nigeria; the earliest date back to about 500 BC. The Kingdom of Benin had its heyday between the 15th and the 17th century and was not conquered by the British

until 1897. Since independence in 1960, the Biafra War that ended in 1970 and numerous coup d'état have weakened the country politically.

Topography: The mangrove coast on the Gulf of Guinea changes into virgin forest; then the land climbs to the North Nigerian Plateau in the interior, which is made up of savannahs, steppes and deserts. To the south-east and south-west there are hills and to the north-west a plain. The third longest river in Africa, the Niger, flows through the land in a north-south direction and forms a 24,000 sq km delta.

Economy: The oil deposits that were discovered at the beginning of the 60's in the Niger Delta have bestowed prosperity upon Nigeria, the country with the largest population in Africa. However the fall in the price of oil in the early 80s has had dramatic consequences for Nigeria. The formerly good road system has fallen into disrepair through lack of available cash, inland flights have dwindled and the economy is also suffering, as oil exports make up over 90% of Nigeria's oil balance.

Nippon
Japan
(J)

Population: 125.7 million (333 per sq km)
Area: 377,820 sq km
Capital: Tokyo (Tokyo)
Political system: parliamentary monarchy (constitutional)
Languages: Japanese
Religion: Shinto, Buddhist (often combined 80%)
GNP: US$ 40,940 per head
Currency: 1 yen (¥) = 100 sen
Industries: machinery, motor vehicles, electrical goods

History: In 20,000 BC people already lived in this area. From 350 AD various cultures unified to form an empire, that from the 6th century was in lively contact with China and came under the in-

1 *Nigerian girl cleaning corn. The wind separates the lighter chaff from the grain*

2 *The castle town of Matsumoto in Nagano on Honshu, the largest of the four main Japanese islands*

3 *Brightly decorated bus in Karachi, Pakistan*

fluence of Buddhism. From 1630 Japan isolated itself completely from the outside world and did not re-open its doors to trade and contact with other countries until 1853. Wars with Russia and China at the turn of the last century turned Japan into a world power. In World War II the USA dropped two atom bombs over Japan and forced them to capitulate. In 1947 Japan was given a new constitution; the emperor, once a god-like ruler, now has only a representative function.

Topography: This mountainous island empire encompasses alongside the four main islands around 500 small and innumerable tiny islands. Hot springs and around 40 active volcanoes are reminders of the volcanic origin of this earthquake danger zone. Virgin countryside is hard to find in this densely populated and highly industrialised land.

Economy: Japan is one of the most wealthy nations in the world. Japanese cars, electrical components and electronics are greatly sought-after items particularly in Germany and the USA but also in neighbouring China and Korea. Other than that, Japan owns one of the world's largest fishing fleets.

ous small kingdoms united into an empire that soon afterwards fell apart. In the 9th to the 11th century, the Norwegian Vikings undertook seafaring conquests to England, Iceland, Greenland and North America.

From the 11th century the region gradually fell under Danish rule. In 1814 Sweden won Norway in a war. In 1905 Norway obtained independence. Norway is one of the founding members of NATO.

Topography: The landscape was determined by the Ice Age and is predominantly mountainous. The mountains descend gradually eastwards to the Swedish border, but steeply to the west. There are numerous islands and skerries along the fjord-gouged west coast. There is a narrow coastal plain to the south.

Economy: Despite the fall in oil prices at the beginning of the 80's, their main exports are oil and natural gas, which guarantee the country's wealth. Water resources are used for the production of electricity, which is used for national industry and exported to neighbouring countries. Other pillars of the economy are fishing and logging. Because only 3% of the land is arable, most foodstuffs have to be imported.

Currency: 1 shilling =100 groschen
Industries: machinery, motor vehicles, iron, steel, tourism

History: From the 13th century Austria belonged to the Habsburg Empire, that wore the German Kaiser's crown for centuries. In 1804 Austria become an empire in its own right, that formed a double monarchy with Hungary. In 1918 the Republic of Austria was proclaimed.
From 1939 to 1945 Austria allied with the Germans to form the German Reich. In 1945 the second republic was founded, that in 1955 recovered its sovereignty. In 1995 Austria joined the EU.

Topography: The Alps make up almost two-thirds of the country, the highest mountain, Grossglockner, is 3798 m high. The Viennese Basin lies to the east, the foothills of the Alps are to the north-east; fields and meadows are to be found between the Danube and its tributaries.

Economy: Although less than half of the land is arable, the country's own requirements for agricultural products can almost be met. Timber and forestry also play an important role. A variety of industries make up the lion's share of the export balance. Iron-ore and brown coal are the chief mining products. Foreign visitors come in their millions (almost 24), drawn equally by the mountains and the varied cultural attractions.

Norge
Norway
N

Population: 4.3 million (13 per sq km)
Area: 323,758 sq km
Capital: Oslo
Political system: parliamentary monarchy
Languages: Norwegian (official), Saami in Lappland
Religion: 89% Protestant
GNP: US$ 34,510 per head
Currency: 1 Norwegian crone
Industries: petroleum and natural gas, machinery, motor vehicles

History: This area was already inhabited in 3000 BC by Saami and other nomads. In 872 AD, vari-

Oman › Saltanat Uman

Österreich
Austria
A

Population: 8 million (96 per sq km)
Area: 83,858 sq km
Capital: Vienna (Wien)
Political system: democratic parliamentary republic (federal)
Languages: German, Slavic, Croatian (all official)
Religion: 78% Catholic, 5% Protestant, 2% Muslim
GNP: US$ 28,110 per head

Pākistān
Pakistan
PK

Population: 133.5 million (168 per sq km)
Area: 796,095 sq km
Capital: Islamabad
Political system: Islamic republic (emergent democracy)
Languages: Urdu, English (both official), Punjabi, Sindhi, Pashtu, Balutchi, Braui, etc.
GNP: US$ 480 per head

Palau

Religion: almost 100% Muslim (75% Sunni, 20% Shi'ite)
Currency: 1 Pakistani rupee = 100 paisa
Industries: cotton and cotton material, rice, leather and leather goods

History: There was an ancient and advanced civilisation here 5000 years ago. Throughout the ages Persian and Indian Empires left behind traces of their existence. An independent state of Pakistan came into being only in 1947, when the former colony of British India was divided. At that time West and and East Pakistan were separated by a 1500 km long Indian land mass. In 1971, after a civil war, East Pakistan declared indepence as Bangladesh. Politically the country is not at rest.
Topography: To the south, Pakistan borders on the Arabian Sea. The Indus Lowland dominates the south-east and the east. The Karakorum mountains and the Himalayas lie to the north, where the highest peak, 8611m, is Mount Godwin Austen/K2. In the south-west there are foothills and tableland.
Economy: Only one-third of the land is arable; thanks to an ingenious irrigation system the country's own requirements for agricultural products can be met. The cotton crop provides material for production into cloth and yarn and has become their most important export article. Pakistan is the world leader in carpet exports.

Palau
Palau
PAL

Population: 17,000 (34 per sq km)
Area: 508 sq km
Capital: Koror
Political system: presidential republic
Languages: Palau, English (both official), Angaur, Japanese, Tobi, Sonsorol
Religion: 41% Catholic, 25% Protestant, 25% animist
GNP: under US$ 10,000 per head
Currency: 1 US dollar = 100 cents
Industries: seafood, coconuts, tourism

History: This island group was inhabited as early as the 10th century BC by Micronesians. At the end of the 19th century it came under Spanish rule, but was a German colony from 1898 to 1918. In 1947 it found itself under American trusteeship. Only in 1994 did it gain independence; there is an association agreement with the USA.
Topography: The mini-state comprises 6 island groups with a total of 241 islands, some mountainous, others with dense vegetation, and coral atolls.
Economy: Processed seafood and coconut products, such as copra, are their main exports. Tourism and the textile industry are in their infancy. This country is dependent on economic help from the USA.

Panamá
Panama
PA

Population: 2.6 million (35 per sq km)
Area: 75,517 sq km
Capital: Panama City
Political system: presidential republic (emergent democracy)
Languages: Spanish (official), Indian languages
Religion: 96% Catholic, 2% Protestant
GNP: US$ 3,080 per head
Currency: 1 balboa = 100 centimos
Industries: bananas, crabs, coffee

History: From the 16th century the native Indian population were conquered by the Spanish and pushed onto reserves. In 1821 this country broke away from Spain and joined the Republic of Greater Columbia. In 1903 the USA helped Panama to gain independence, securing in return the zone bordering the Panama Canal, which was completed in 1914. From the year 2000 onwards, Panama will have sole control over the canal. Recent history in Panama is one of turbulence with one US intervention.
Topography: Panama borders on the Caribbean Sea to the north, to the south on the Pacific. To the west and east it is framed by chains of mountains. The Panama Canal connects the Pacific Ocean and the Caribbean Sea at the narrowest point in Central America.
Economy: The country's income is visibly increasing step-by-step with the hand-over of the canal; almost two-thirds of the population work in the service sector. Important exports are bananas, coffee, cocoa, hemp, coconuts and shrimps.

Papua New Guinea
Papua New Guinea
PNG

Population: 4.4 million (9 per sq km)
Area: 462,840 sq km
Capital: Port Moresby
Political system: parliamentary monarchy
GNP: US$ 1,150 per head

Languages: English, Pidgin, Motu (all official), over 700 Papua languages
Religion: 58% Protestant, 33% Catholic, animist
Currency: 1 kina = 100 toea
Industries: gold, copper-ore, petroleum, timber, copra, coffee, tea, coconut and palm oil

History: Archaeological finds verify that these islands have been inhabited for at least 50,000 years. Some tribes live today just as they did in the Stone Age. Not until the 19th century were parts of the country colonised by the Germans, British and Dutch. After World Wars I and II, Australia was granted a League of Nations mandate and then a trusteeship over parts of the area. In 1975 this country was given its independence which has not as yet secured a lasting peace in the region.
Topography: The region comprises the eastern part of the island of New Guinea that borders on Indonesia, as well as numerous Pacific islands that lie to the east. The central highland on New Guinea is surrounded by coastal plains. The landscape is characterised by rain forest and savannahs.
Economy: The region has a wealth of mineral deposits and is one of the most important producers of gold in the world, but has an underdeveloped industrial base and insufficient access to world markets due to poor transportation routes. Agriculture is carried out to supply the country's own demands, though this has been threatened by recent droughts.

1 One of the most important waterways in the world: the 81.6 kilometre long Panama Canal

2 Three-quarters of the population of New Guinea live in the eastern part of the island

3 Not until 1911 were the ruins of Machu Pichu, Peru, discovered. This city of the Incas at a height of 2,900 m, was never entered by the Spanish

4 Filipino boy drinking straight from the coconut shell

independent republic. Paraguay has been unable to maintain peace because of dictators, civil wars and wars with their neighbouring countries Brazil and Bolivia. The situation appears to have stabilised somewhat since the last dictator, Stroessner, was overthrown.

Topography: This country, that lies in the centre of South America, is bounded to the east on the border to Brazil by hills and plateaux, and to the west by the plains of the Gran Chaco. The interior of the country encompasses the Paraguay River Valley and surrounding marshlands.

Economy: In this land so difficult to access, one-third of the population works in agriculture. The greater part of the export balance is made up by soya beans, cotton, vegetable oil, timber and wood products, tobacco, meat, skins and hides. For their own consumption rice, corn, and cassava are cultivated. A further source of income is hydroelectricity, produced in collaboration with Brazil and Argentina.

Paraguay
Paraguay
PY

Population: 4.9 million (12 per sq km)
Area: 406,752 sq km
Capital: Asuncion
Political system: presidential republic
Languages: Spanish, Guarani (both official)
Religion: 94% Catholic
GNP: US$ 1,850 per head
Currency: 1 Guarani = 100 céntimos
Industries: soya beans, cotton, vegetable oil

History: The native Indian inhabitants, the Guaraní, were subordinated by the Spanish conquerors when this area was annexed to the Spanish viceroyalty of Peru in 1543. From the 17th century Jesuit missionaries built self-governing Indian settlements and supported them in every possible way. The Jesuits were, however, brutally driven out by the Spanish in 1767, but not before they had succeeded in founding the "theology of liberation", which was so important for Latin America. In 1813 Paraguay proclaimed itself an

civilisations. From about 1200 AD the Incas extended their empire further and further into this area and set up a well organised social system to provide for the state. This empire was brutally crushed by the Spanish from 1531. In 1824 the Peruvians succeeded in liberating themselves from the Spanish colonists. Right up to the present day the crass difference between rich and poor, and more recently, the activity of the terrorist organisation "Shining Path", have caused serious problems.

Topography: The Andes Mountains (reaching almost 7000 m) follow along the Pacific coastal plains to the east; farther east they merge with the foothills of the Andes and to the north with the upper Amazon basin.

Economy: The land is rich in mineral deposits (e.g. silver, copper) that are exported as raw materials and finished goods. Fishing and fish processing are also significant; fish oil and fishmeal make up 15% of the export balance. The large number of poor who live below the poverty line is offset by a small and extremely rich elite. The region suffers from a lack of adaquate work for its people.

Perú
Peru
PE

Population: 24.2 million (19 per sq km)
Area: 1,2845,216 sq km
Capital: Lima
Political system: presidential republic
Languages: Spanish, Quechua, Aymara (all official)
Religion: 89% Catholic, 3% Protestant, animist
GNP: US$ 2,420 per head
Currency: 1 new sol = 100 centimes
Industries: worked and raw metals, fish products, petroleum and associate products

History: In about 900 BC the Chavín civilisation existed in northern Peru. Until the first millennium, the Tiahuanaco civilisation, famous for its monolithic constructions, predominated, followed by the artistically skilled Nazca and Moche

Pilipinas
Philippines
RP

Population: 71.8 million (240 per sq km)
Area: 300,000 sq km
Capital: Manila
Political system: presidential republic
Languages: Tagolo (Filopino, official), English and Spanish, Cebuano, Ilocano, Panay-Hiligaynon etc. (nearly 1000 in all)
Religion: 84% Catholic, 6% Independent Philippine Church, 5% Muslim, 4% Protestant
GNP: US$ 1,160 per head
Currency: 1 Philippine peso = 100 centavos
Industries: electrical machines and semi-conductors, textiles

Polska
Poland

History: People lived here as early as 22,000 BC and during the following millenniums many different tribes and tribal groups settled on the islands and left their mark there. In the 16th century Spanish conquerors took possession of the area. At the end of the 19th century the Philippines came under the supervision of the USA and gained independence in 1946. In 1986 the dictator, Ferdinand Marcos, was overthrown and a "freedom constitution" adopted; economic and political prosperity has not been forthcoming and the attempted military putsches continued, albeit unsuccessfully until now.

Topography: This region encompasses over 7000 partly mountainous, partly volcanic, large, small and tiny islands in the north-eastern part of the Malaysian Archipelago and is the second largest group of islands after Indonesia.

Economy: Despite rich mineral deposits and plenty of arable land, 30% of the Philipinos live below the poverty line – 80% of the country's wealth is in the hands of 20% of the population. Local industry has specialised in electrical semiconductor products and machinery as well as textiles, which together make up half of the export balance. The transfer of money by Philipinos working abroad (e.g. sailors) is a significant economic factor. Tourism has developed into a further important source of foreign currency.

Polska
Poland
PL

Population: 38.6 million (124 per sq km)
Area: 312,685 sq km
Capital: Warsaw (Warszawa)
Political system: parliamentary republic
Languages: Polish
Religion: 91% Catholics
GNP: US$ 3,230 per head
Currency: 1 zloty = 100 groszy
Industries: machinery and motor vehicles, coal products, chemical products

History: From the 6th century Slavs migrated to this area. In the 10th century the tribes living in the heart of Poland joined forces and formed the Kingdom of Poland, which had its heyday in the sixteenth century. From the 18th century the neighbouring countries of Russia, Prussia and Austria divided the country up so often that it scarcely existed. In 1918 the republic of Poland was declared, but in 1939 it was invaded by Germany and again taken over. In 1945 the present-day borders were fixed. A communist people's republic was proclaimed, and after decades of un-

rest, it came to an end in 1989, after massive demonstrations often led by Lech Walesa, leader of the Polish Worker's Union "Solidarity". Walesa was elected as the first president and received the Noble Peace Prize for his work. Poland was one of the first former Warsaw Pact countries to enter Nato.

Topography: The Vistula River runs through the middle of the country to the North Sea coast. East of the Vistula there are low-lying plains and to the west gentle mountains. To the south the Tatra, Carpathian and Sudetan Mountains form the limits of the country.

Economy: The transition from a planned to a market economy appears to have gone well, but has also led to poverty and unemployment. The main pillar of the economy is local heavy industry that causes considerable environmental problems. 60% of the land is used for agriculture, mainly to supply the country's own demands and retaining its unique charms.

Portugal
Portugal
P

Population: 9.9 million (108 per sq km)
Area: 92,345 sq km
Capital: Lisbon (Lisboa)
Political system: parliamentary republic
Languages: Portuguese
Religion: 90% Catholic
GNP: US$ 10,160
Currency: 1 escudo = 100 centavos
Industries: textiles, shoes, machinery, motor vehicles, tourism

History: In about 5500 BC the Mesolithic civilisation dominated this area. In about 900 BC the Celts invaded, followed in the 6th century BC by the Phoenicians and in 201 BC by the Romans. In the 3rd century Portugal converted to Christian-

ity; in the 4th century German tribes penetrated the area, in 711 the Moors. In 1143 Portugal became an independent kingdom. In 1494 Spain and Portugal divided up the the recently discovered New World between themselves. From 1580 until 1640 Portugal was ruled by Spain; from 1807 until 1811 France occupied the area and in 1910 Portugal was declared a republic. In 1926 a military dictator came into power who was not toppled until the "Carnation Revolution" in 1974. In 1975 Portugal's African colonies became independent. In 1986 Portugal became a member of the EU.

Topography: Lowlands traversed by countless rivers follow the Atlantic coast of the Iberian Peninsula, inland the Sierra de Estrêla mountains rise to a height of 2000 m and run south into the rolling hills of the Algrave.

Economy: The most important branch of the economy is the textile industry; clothing and shoes make up 30% of the exports. Heavy and chemical industries are becoming more significant.

Traditional exports such as wine, cork and tropical fruits play a diminishing role; only 12% of the Portuguese work in agriculture, which comprises a mere 5% of the gross national income. Tourism is gaining in importance as a source of foreign currency, attempting, however, to avoid the Spanish-style mass tourism.

Qatar
Qatar
Q

Population: 658,000 (58 per sq km)
Area: 11, 427 sq km
Capital: Doha (Ad-Dawhah)
Political system: absolute monarchy
Languages: High Arabic (official), Persian, Urdu and other Indo-Arab languages

3

1 The port of Danzig in Poland; view of St. Mary's Church (1343-1502), which had to be almost completely rebuilt after World War II

3 Unique rock formation in Praia da Rocha, Algarve, Portugal

4 Accordeon player on Madeira, an island belonging to Portugal about 500 km off the coast of north-west Africa

Religion: over 90% Sunni Muslim
GNP: over US$ 10,000 per head
Currency: 1 Qatar riyal = 100 dirham
Industries: petroleum, natural gas

History: Sheikhs of the al-Thani family have ruled here since the 18th century. In 1868 Qatar became an independent sheikhdom and in 1872 part of the Ottoman Empire. In 1916 it became a British protectorate achieving full independence in 1971. The Sheikh al-Thani is still the absolute monarch.
Topography: Qatar is a small, flat peninsula in the Persian Gulf on the east coast of Arabia. To the south the land is covered with salt marshes, to the east by a chalk plain, to the west by a region of rolling hills.
Economy: This country lives from oil and its natural gas deposits are considered the largest in the world. Sponsorship (foreigners are not allowed to open businesses, local partners have to be employed) guarantees prosperity for the country.

República Dominicana
Dominican Republic

(DOM)

Population: 7.9 million (165 per sq km)
Area: 48,422 sq km
Capital: Santo Domingo
Political system: democratic presidential republic
Languages: Spanish
Religion: 90% Catholic
GNP: US$ 1,600 per head
Currency: 1 Dominican peso = 100 centavos
Industries: tourism, sugar, coffee, iron-ore

History: When Columbus discovered the Caribbean in 1492 and gave this island the name Hispaniola (Little Spain), Arawak and Carib Indians lived there, but they were soon after eradi-

cated by the Spanish. Following a brief period of independence in 1821, it was occupied as the "Negro Republic" by Haiti until a successful revolt resulted in the establishment of the Dominican Republic in 1844.
Topography: This country comprises the eastern two-thirds of the island of Hispaniola; a central mountain range with fertile valleys of sugarcane makes up the picture. The sandy white beaches attract many tourists.
Economy: It takes third place in the race for most favoured Caribbean holiday spot; 60% of the tourists come from the USA. Mining products as well as sugar and coffee are the chief exports.

Rép. centrafricaine
Central African Republic

(RCA)

Population: 3.3 million (5 per sq km)
Area: 622,984 sq km
Capital: Bangui
Political system: presidential republic
Languages: Sangho, French (both official), Fulani, Ubangi, and Swahili
Religion: 57% animist, 35% Christian, 8% Muslim
GNP: US$ 310 per head
Currency: 1 CFA franc = 100 centimes
Industries: diamonds, coffee, timber, cotton, tobacco, uranium

History: From the 16th century this area was largely depopulated through the trading of slaves by Arabs and Europeans. It was colonised by the French at the end of the 19th century, exploited and depopulated further and finally – under international pressure – granted independence in 1960. In 1965 a reign of terror began, when through a military coup d'état the "Emperor" Bokassa, a dictator, came to power; in 1979 he

was overthrown. Since then the country has been subjected to recurring periods of unrest, which led to French intervention.
Topography: In the centre of the country, the Asande plateau separates the Chad from the Congo Basin. In the south there are dense tropical rain forests, which give way northwards to wet then dry savannah.
Economy: Agriculture in which almost 80% of the population is active, produces enough for self-sufficiency; coffee and cotton are the only crops cultivated for export. Gold and diamonds are also mined but do not appear in the export balance due to the fact that they are smuggled out of the country. This country is dependent on the support of France, who maintains two military bases.

Rép. Dém. du Congo
Democratic Republic of Congo

(ZRE)

Population: 45.2 million (19 per sq km)
Area: 2,344,885 sq km
Capital: Kinshasa
Political system: presidential republic
Languages: French (official), over 400 African languages
Religion: 42% Catholic, 25% Protestant, 15% other Christians, 2% Muslim, animist
GNP: US$ 130 per head
Currency: 1 new Zaire =100 makuta
Industries: mining (diamonds, copper, cobalt), petroleum, coffee, palm oil

History: From the 15th century this area of land was made up of a number of African kingdoms. In 1884/85 the land was allocated to King Leopold II of Belgium as a type of private possession, which he allowed to be brutally exploited by trading partners. In 1908 it became a colony of the Belgian government. In 1960 it gained independence, but fell into chaos and civil war that was ended by the dictator Mobutu in 1965. He remained in power until 1997, after which Zaire

République du Congo
Republic of Congo

changed its name to the Democratic Republic of Congo. The Zaire population elected a new president, Laurent Kabila and are awaiting democratic electins in 1999.

Topography: The narrow coastal plain on the Atlantic joins in the east onto the swampy rain forest covered lowland of the Congo basin. This country is bounded to the east by the foothills of the Great Rift Valley with many lakes, to the south by the Lunda plateau. In the west the rivers Ubangi and Congo/Zaire form the border to the neighbouring Republic of Congo.

Economy: The former Zaire is one of the poorest and most highly indebted countries in Africa. People at different levels of development live in this vast multinational state that is as large as West and Central Europe combined. Despite rich mineral deposits and a favourable climate, this country is having to fight the consequences of decades of mismanagement and high population growth.

République du Congo
Republic of Congo
(RCB)

Population: 2.7 million (8 per sq km)
Area: 342,000 sq km
Capital: Brazzaville
Political system: presidential republic
Languages: French (official), Lingala etc.
Religion: 54% Catholic, 50% animist
GNP: US$ 670 per head
Currency: 1 CFA franc
Industries: crude-oil, fine woods, cocoa, tobacco, bananas, sugar

History: The Batéké and Bakongo, the original inhabitants, co-operated with the European colonisers and supplied them with slaves, but opposed their attempts at colonisation. In 1891 this region was nevertheless made into a colony of the French Congo, together with Gabon. In 1960 it gained independence and in 1970 became a socialist people's republic. Since 1990 it has been going through a process of democratisation under the democratically elected president Lissouba.

Topography: To the east, the Ubangi and Congo/Zaire form the border to neighbouring Democratic Republic of Congo (formerly Zaire). To the north-east this country takes in a portion of the Congo Basin, in the east the Batake plateaux, and to the west there is flat to rolling coastland.

Economy: The republic is heavily dependent on petroleum which makes up 80% of the export balance. Because development in agriculture has

been neglected in favour of industrialisation, basic staple foodstuffs have to be imported and the once so important export of coffee, cocoa and cotton has declined. Two-thirds of the population live in the only cities of significance, Brazzaville and Pointe-Noire.

România
Romania
(RO)

Population: 22.6 million (95 per sq km)
Area: 238,391 sq km
Capital: Bucharest (Bucureşti)
Political system: parliamentary republic
Languages: Romanian (official), Hungarian, German
Religion: 87% Romanian Orthodox, 4% Reformed
GNP: US$ 1,600 per head
Currency: 1leu = 100 bani
Industries: textiles, metals, oilfield equipment, machinery

History: The principalities of Walachia and Moldavia ,dating from the 14th century, fell during the 15th and 16th centuries to the Ottoman Empire, which from 1711 till 1821 leased them out to the Greeks. They then fell under the influence of the Russians and Austrians, until in 1856 the Russian protectorate ended. In 1859 the two principalities united and in 1881 formed the Kingdom of Romania. After World War II, under pressure from the Red Army, it became a people's republic. From 1965 onwards Romania suffered under the dictator CeauÕescu who, in his

poverty-stricken country, lived in wasteful opulence. In 1989 the dictator was overthrown and later executed. In 1991 Romania became a republic.

Topography: The Carpathian mountain range makes its way through the centre of the country. The Transylvanian Alps lie to the west, the Moldavian River Valley, embedded in a hilly landscape, lies to the north-east; the Walachia Lowlands stretch across the south. To the south-east the Danube flows via a wide delta into the Black Sea.

Economy: Almost 60% of former government enterprises are now in private hands. The mining of mineral deposits (various ores, oil, natural gas) serves as a basis for the chemical and metal processing industries, which along with the textile industry, play an important role. Corn, wheat, fruit and wine are intensively cultivated.

Rossiya
Russian Federation
(RUS)

Population: 147.7 million (9 per sq km)
Area: 17,075,400 sq km
Capital: Moscow (Moskva)
Political system: presidential republic (emergent democracy)
Languages: Great Russian (official), languages of the other nationalities

98

St Christopher and Nevis

1 The famous cathedral of St. Peter and Paul, St. Petersburg, Russia

2 Bran Castle, the castle of Dracula, Transsylvania, Romania

3 Young girl from Cilibia, Romania

4 One of the most popular holiday resorts: the island of St. Lucia in the Lesser Antilles

Religion: predominantly Russian Orthodox
GNP: US$ 2,410 per head
Currency: 1 rouble = 100 kopecks
Industries: petroleum, natural gas, machinery and industrial products

History: In the 9th century various eastern Slavic tribes formed a loose alliance. In the 10th century the area was converted to Christianity, whereafter it came under Mongolian rule until well into the 14th century, whilst the principality of Moscow gradually gained significance. In the 15th century a powerful tsarist empire with its centre in Moscow arose; its heyday in the 18th century was brought to an end in 1917 by the "October Revolution" and Russia ended its participation in the First World War via the Treaty of Brest-Litovsk in 1918 with the western Allies. In 1922 the USSR was founded and became the second largest "super power" after the USA. After the disintegration of the Soviet Union in 1991, Russia comprised 21 autonomous republics.
Topography: This country, with the largest area of land in the world (almost twice the size of the USA), encompasses various geographical and climatic zones: from a subtropical climate on the Black Sea to that of Arctic tundra in the north. The country borders to the south-west on the Black and Caspian Seas, to the north-west on the Baltic Sea, to the north on the Arctic Ocean and the East Siberian Sea, and to the east on the Pacific. The Caucasus forms a natural border between the Black and Caspian Seas, and the eastern European lowlands stretch out to the west. Still further east, the Urals divide the land into a European and an Asian part. East of the Urals, the west Siberian lowland is enclosed by mountains and highlands to the east and south-east, and similarly by tundra to the north and north-east.
Economy: The transition from a planned to a market economy has plunged well-developed industries and agriculture into a difficult crisis. Rich mineral deposits are available, as is – considering the gigantic size of the country – a well-developed transportation system. Russia, as heir to the Soviet Union, has serious problems to cope with.

Land reform is just as necessary as reorganisation of supplies; their next aim will have to be the privatisation of state-owned enterprises and becoming competitive in the world market.

Rwanda
Rwanda
(RWA)

Population: 6.7 million (255 per sq km)
Area: 26,338 sq km
Capital: Kigali
Political system: presidential republic
Languages: Kinyarwanda, French, English (all official), Kiswahili
Religion: 50% Christian, 50% animists, 10% Muslims
GNP: US$ 190 per head
Currency: 1 Rwandan franc = 100 centimes
Industries: coffee, tea, pyrethrum

History: The incessant war that has been going on between the Hutu and the Tutsi people dates back to the 15th century when the Tutsi subjugated the indigenous Hutu population. During the colonial period it came under German and then Belgian rule. In 1962 Rwanda gained independence.
A bloody civil war erupted between the Hutu and the Tutsi population in 1994. Thousands were killed and thousands more fled to refugee camps.
Topography: The central highland of Rwanda gives way to a plateau with lakes to the east, the Kargera rift to the north-east, the mountainous border of the Central African Trench that falls sharply to the western border to Zaire and Mount Virunga, a volcano, is to the north-west.
The vegetation consists primarily of rain forests and humid savannahs. Bamboo forests are found in the uplands.
Economy: After the bloody massacres in 1994, the economy came practically to a standstill and despite aid programmes is only slowly recovering. Rwanda is the most densely populated country in Africa; overpopulation and undernourishment

create great problems. There is no direct access to the sea and the transportation system is underdeveloped, so that the transport of goods is expensive and difficult. The main exports include coffee, tea, tobacco, cotton.

Saint Kitts and Nevis
St Christopher and Nevis
(KN)

Population: 41,000 (157 per sq km)
Area: 262 sq km
Capital: Basseterre
Political system: parliamentary monarchy
Languages: English (official), an English dialect of Creole
Religion: 36% Anglican, 32% Methodist, 11% Catholic, and almost 40 other religious groups
GNP: US$ 5,870 per head
Currency: 1 East Caribbean dollar = 100 cents
Industries: machinery and vehicles, sugar and associated products, tourism

History: In around 1500 the British took possession of these islands inhabited by Caribs, and in 1623 founded their first colony in the West Indies, successfully defending it against the claims made by Spain, France and Holland . Only in 1983 did this country gain independence. Self administration was granted first in 1967 by the British Government and full independence followed in 1983. The smaller island of Nevis has unsuccessfully striven for independence from the larger St Kitts; for the present they alternately appoint the head of government.
Topography: These Caribbean Islands lie to the east of Puerto Rico in the Atlantic. Nevis is a huge volcanic cone and on St Kitts (short for St Christopher) a narrow peninsula joins onto a central mountainous region.
Economy: The traditional export of sugar-cane still makes up one-third of the export balance, half of which is obtained through machinery and motor vehicle construction. Foreign currency is also earned from cruise tourists.

Saint Lucia
St Lucia

Saint Lucia
St Lucia
(WL)

Population: 158,000 (256 per sq km)
Area: 616 sq km
Capital: Castries
Political system: parliamentary monarchy
Languages: English (official), Patois
Religion: 80% Catholic
GNP: US$ 3,500 per head
Currency: 1 east Caribbean dollar = 100 cents
Industries: agricultural products, tourism

History: The indigenous Caribs put up an embittered resistance to the encroachments made by the European conquerors, but were defeated in 1650 by the French. From then on the French and English fought each other for the island, rule over which changed hands more than 20 times, until in 1814 the French were forced to give in to the British. In 1979 St Lucia was granted independence.
Topography: This volcanic Caribbean island has rolling hills along the coast and mountains inland. Luxuriant vegetation, long sandy beaches and excellent hotels are what make St Lucia a holiday paradise.
Economy: The most important export is bananas, but the most significant source of foreign currency is tourism: in 1996 half a million tourists visited the island.

Saint Vincent
St Vincent
(WV)

Population: 112,000 (288 per sq km)
Area: 389 sq km
Capital: Kingstown
Political system: parliamentary monarchy
Languages: English (official), Creole English, French patois
Religion: 75% Protestant, 9% Catholic
GNP: US$ 2,370 per head
Currency: 1 east Caribbean dollar = 100 cents
Industries: bananas, copra, sweet potatoes, tourism

History: The native Caribs fought off the invasion attempts of the English and the French long and hard until the island became a British possession in 1814. In 1979 this group of islands gained independence.
Topography: The Caribbean islands are of volcanic origin. Other than the main island , St. Vincent (345 sq km), with its volcanic mountains,

100

the state comprises several smaller islands of which seven are inhabited.
Economy: The main export product is bananas as well as arrowroot, a plant from which starch is extracted for use in paper production. Small farmers cultivate coconuts, bread-fruit, pineapples and peas for their own consumption. This region is difficult to reach and therefore not well-developed for tourism; but notwithstanding it had almost a quarter of a million foreign visitors in 1996.

Sakartvelo
Georgia
(GE)

Population: 5.4 million (78 per sq km)
Area: 69,700 sq km
Capital: Tbilisi
Political system: presidential republic
Languages: Georgian (official), Russian
Religion: mostly Georgian Orthodox (separated from Russian Orthodox in 1917)
GNP: US$ 850 per head
Currency: 1 lari = 100 tetri
Industries:: agriculture (e.g. tea etc.), hydroelectricity, mining (e.g. manganese, mineral coal etc.), heavy industry, tourism

History: In ancient times this region was consecutively under Persian, Greek and Roman influence and stood from the 4th century under the protection of the Byzantine Empire. In the 7th century it was invaded by the Arabs, who from the 9th century unified the country and had their heyday lasting into the 13th century. In the 13th and 14th century it was laid to waste by the Mongols and divided between the Turks, Persians and Russians. In 1918 it declared itself an independent republic and was shortly afterwards annexed by the Soviet Union. In 1991 Georgia announced its renewed independence, and in 1993 joined the CIS. Confrontations between the Islamic minori-

ties of the Abchas and Osset cause unrest. The former Soviet Foreign Minister, Edward Shevardnadse was elected as President in 1995.
Topography: This land borders on the Black Sea to the west. To the north there are the Greater and to the south the Lesser Caucasian Mountains. To the east there are dry forests and grass steppes. The resorts on the subtropical coast, the winter sport resorts in the mountains, as well as 15 wild-life reserves, are traditional tourist locations.
Economy: Georgia was in its day the most important supplier of tea to the USSR; apart from that, intensive farming produces wine, fruit, tobacco and grain. Another pillar of the economy is mineral deposits including oil, cobalt and vanadium. The oil resources have not been tapped and Georgia still relies upon Russia for its oil. Around half of the population work in the service sector and only 30% live from tourism.

Saltanat 'Uman
Oman
(OM)

Population: 2.1 million (7 per sq km)
Area: 309,500 sq km
Capital: Muscat (Masquat)
Political system: absolute monarchy (sultanate)
Languages: High Arabic (official), Arabic, Urdu and other Indian languages
Religion: 85% Muslim (75% Ibadhi), 15% Hindus
GNP: US$ 10,000 per head
Currency: 1 rail omani = 1000 baizas
Industries: petroleum, machinery, copper, dates

History: This region, inhabited by different tribes since 2500 BC, was annexed in the 7th century to the Islamic Empire and until the 18th century governed by Imams. It was conquered and held by the Portuguese for a short period and came under British protectorate in 1890. In 1951 inde-

① *Jewish synagogue
in the old part of
Tiflis, Georgia*

② *Copra, a coconut
product, from which
coconut oil and fat
are made, is the most
important export of
Samoa*

③ *Switzerland:
Panorama of the old
part of Bern, the
capital of the Canton
of Bern, founded in
1191*

pendence was gained. The present-day governing dynasty has ruled since the 18th century.
Topography: From the narrow coastal strip on the Gulf of Oman to the north-east, the land climbs to a height of 3 000 m in the Oman Mountains; to the east and south they border on the Arabian Sea. To the west the Rub al Khali Desert stretches across the country.
Economy: The current ruling sultan is using the profits from the export of oil (80% of export income) in order to develop the capital city into an economic and administrative centre and to improve the quality of the streets, irrigation and school system. Prosperity has dampened religious and tribal conflicts in the country.

Samoa
Samoa, Western
(WS)

Population: 172,000 (61 per sq km)
Area: 2,831 sq km
Capital: Apia (on upper island)
Political system: parliamentary monarchy
Languages: Samoan, English (both official)
Religion: 71% Protestants, 22% Catholics
GNP: US$ 1,170 per head
Currency: 1 tala = 100 sene
Industries: copra, cocoa, tourism

History: Unlike other countries, the social and cultural identity of the Samoan people (of Polynesian origin) was not destroyed during colonisation and forms the basis of their present-day society. The first Polynesian inhabitants landed in Samoa around 1000 BC.
This area was divided between Germany and the USA in 1899; the German western part came under the supervision of New Zealand from 1920. In fact, New Zealand occupied the island and New Zealand then agreed to carry out a UN mandate resulting in West Samoa's independence in 1962, the first of the polynesian islands to attain independence.

Topography: Other than the main islands of Savai'i and Upolu, seven other smaller often uninhabited islands belong to this group that are of volcanic origin. The inland area is dominated by rain forest; the coastal strips are arable.
Economy: Farming and fishing supply basic food requirements. The most important export is the coconut product, copra, out of which coconut oil and fat is made. In addition to that cocoa and bananas are produced for export.

San Marino
San Marino
(RSM)

Population: 25,000 (413 per sq km)
Area: 61 sq km
Capital: San Marino
Political system: parliamentary republic
Languages: Italian (official)
Religion: 93% Catholic
GNP: no details
Currency: Italian lira, San Marino lira
Industries: arts and crafts, tourism

History: Ever since the monastery of San Marino was first mentioned in a document in 885, this mini-state succeeded in achieving and maintaining its independence from the 4th century AD under various rulers. Since 1862 there has been a customs union with Italy, although San Marino has always strongly resisted joining Italy. San Marino allied itself with Axis powers in the Second World War, it declared its neutrality in 1943. From 1978 until 1992, San Marino had the only elected communist government in Western Europe.
Topography: The smallest republic in Europe is basically made up of a chalk rock surrounded by hills, closed in on all sides by Italian territory.
Economy: Alongside agriculture and small skilled trades and handicrafts, tourism is the most important source of income. Tax advantages attract many firms to the area. A popular gimmick of this tiny republic are their own special stamps.

São Tomé e Príncipe
***São Tomé
and Principe***
(STP)

Population: 135,000 (135 per sq km)
Area: 1,001 sq km
Capital: São Tomé
Political system: presidential republic
Languages: Portuguese (official), Crioulo, Fang (Bantu)
Religion: 93% Catholics, 3% Protestant, animism
GNP: US$ 330 per head
Currency: 1 dobra = 100 cêntimos
Industries: cocoa, coffee, copra, palm oil

History: In 1470 the uninhabited islands were discovered by the Portuguese, who as colonial rulers, transported convicts, slaves and later forced labourers as manpower there. In 1975 this country fought for and won its independence.
Topography: The group of islands of volcanic origin lie close to the equator off the coast of Gabon, and consist of the two main islands, which give the country its name, and a few smaller islands.
Economy: Cocoa plantations cover the countryside; the crop makes up 90% of the export balance. Since democratisation in 1990, an effort has been made to create new sources of income to supplant the ecologically harmful and economically risky one-crop system; fishing, tourism and more varied farming are being promoted.

***Saudi-Arabia* → *Al Arabiyah
as Suudiyah***

Schweiz/Suisse
Switzerland
(CH)

Population: 7 million (171 per sq km)
Area: 41,285 sq km
Capital: Bern
Political system: parliamentary federal republic

Sénégal
Senegal

Languages: 65% German, 18% French, 12% Italian, 1% Romansch (all official)
Religion: 46% Catholic, 40% Protestant
GNP: US$ 44,350
Currency: 1 Swiss franc = 100 rappen/centimes
Industries: machinery and appliances, chemical and pharmaceutical products, tourism

History: As early as in the 11th Century, the Habsburgs tried to reduce the power of the Swiss Cantons. In 1291 the cantons of Schwyz, Uri and Unterwalden formed the Swiss Confederation, which in 1874 became a federal state. The 1874 constitution is still valid and obliges Switzerland to absolute neutrality. Not until 1990 were women granted the right to vote. In 1996 researchers discovered that Swiss banks still held accounts with "Nazi gold"; in view of this, the Swiss government has agreed to pay the money to the Holocaust Fund.

Topography: The surface of the land consists entirely of mountains: the Alps to the south, low mountains in the centre and the Jura to the north. To the south Switzerland has access to Lakes Maggiore, Lucerne, Geneva and Constance.

Economy: Switzerland has hardly any mineral deposits and is unable to meet its own requirements for energy and staple foods. These deficits are offset by highly specialised industries; high-grade products (watches, precision instruments, medicine, materials and chocolate) are much sought-after export articles. Swiss banks attract financial investors and tourists come on account of the mountains and excellent cuisine. Switzerland is one of the world's richest nations.

Sénégal
Senegal
SN

Population: 8.5 million (43 per sq km)
Area: 169,722 sq km
Capital: Dakar
Political system: presidential republic (emergent socialist democracy)
Languages: French, Wolof (both official), Mande and other African languages
Religion: 95% Muslim, 5% Christian, animist
GNP: US$ 570 per head
Currency: 1CFA franc = 100 centimes
Industries: fish and fish products, peanuts, cotton, phosphates

History: In the 19th century the races living in the region, the Fulani, Fulbe, Diola, Malinkas and Seres, fell under the rule of the Islamic Wolofs, who even today still hold the supremacy

in Senegal. Europeans had set up trading posts in the area from the 15th century. Colonial rulers changed regularly, until in 1791 the French took possession of the region. They gave the country independence in 1960 but Senegal became a real practising democracy first in 1983.

Topography: This country on the outermost point of west Africa lies within the Sahel zone. To the north the Senegal River forms the border to Mauritania. Plains rise to hills in the south-east, and swamp and tropical forest cover the south-west. To the south Gambia forms an enclave within Senegal.

Economy: Peanuts no longer form the basis of the Senegal economy, but do make up a 16% share of the export quota. The number one export product is fish and fish products. The most important trading partner is the former colonial ruler, France. Because of their monoculture and the many droughts in the Sahel Zone, this country is dependent on the import of staple foods.

Seychelles
Seychelles
SY

Population: 77,000 (170 per sq km)
Area: 454 sq km
Capital: Victoria
Political system: presidential republic (one-party socialist)
Languages: Creole, English, French (all official)
Religion: 90% Catholic, 8% Anglican
GNP: US$ 6,850 per head
Currency: 1 Seychelles rupee = 100 cents
Industries: tourism, fish, copra, cinnamon, refinery products

History: In 1742 these uninhabited islands were taken as a possession by the French and populated with African slaves. After the abolition of slavery and the British conquest of the region in 1810, an Indian labour force was brought in. In 1976 they achieved independence, and since then they have become a model African country.

Topography: This island group in the Indian Ocean consists of over 90 islands, of which not even half are inhabited. The larger islands are mountainous and have scanty vegetation.

Economy: The most important source of income is "gentle" tourism, by which they do their best to provide tourists with an intact ecosystem and animal kingdom.
Fisheries, coconut products and industries currently being established create further sources of income. Thanks to the stable political situation, an exemplary infrastructure has been built up with schools, transportation routes and health and social security systems.

Shqipëria
Albania
AL

Population: 3.2 million (114 per sq km)
Area: 28,748 sq km
Capital: Tirana (Tiranë)
Political system: presidential republic
Languages: Albanian (official language), Greek, Macedonian and others
Religion: Muslim 70%, Orthodox 20%, Catholic 10%
GNP: US$ 820 per head
Currency: 1 lek = 100 quindarka
Industries: textiles, shoes, natural gas, tobacco products

History: Albania belonged first to the Roman and then to the Byzantine Empire. The kingdom of Albania was founded in 1272 but fell under Ottoman rule from 1502. Since 1912 it has been independent and from 1946 a people's republic, that has, however, become more and more isolated and broken its contacts with the former USSR and China. Since 1990 it has opened up to

① *Senegal: 80% of the population live from agriculture, although only 12% of the country is farmed*

② *11th century Greek-orthodox church near Saranda, Albania*

③ *Dry straw in the fertile valley of River Soca on the Slovenian border to northern Italy*

④ *Golden statue of Buddha from a temple in Singapore*

Languages: Malay (nat. tongue), Chinese, Tamil, English (all official)
Religion: 32% Buddhist, 22% Daoist, 15% Muslim, 13% Christian, 3% Hindus
Currency: 1 Singapore dollar = 100 cents
Industries: machinery, vehicles, electronic products

History: When Stamford Raffles purchased the island for the British East India Company in 1819, only a few fishermen's families lived there. A significant trading port developed over the following years and in 1867 it was made into a British crown colony. In 1963 it gained independence and formed a federation with Malaysia that collapsed as early as 1965.
Topography: This island lying off the coast of Malaysia consists of flatland to the south and east, while the centre and the south-west are hilly.
Economy: Singapore is often called the "Switzerland" of South East Asia and in terms of their standard of living, could soon be a match for the Alpine country. This small island with no energy or raw materials of its own has developed into a modern technological and financial centre.

the outside world, but has been shaken by civil war-like conditions and is not at peace.
Topography: The geographical picture is of a mountainous highland (more than 40 peaks over 2 000 m high), huge lakes and 175 km of Adriatic coast.
Economy: The disastrous consequences of the planned economy are still being felt. Almost 40% of revenues come from agriculture. Other than its neighbouring countries, Germany is one of its trading partners.

Sierra Leone
Sierra Leone
(WAL)

Population: 4.6 million (65 per sq km)
Area: 71,740 sq km
Capital: Freetowm
Political system: presidential republic
Languages: English (official), various Mande languages, Temne, Limba, Krio
Religion: strongly animist, 39% Muslim, 8% Christian
GNP: US$ 200 per head
Currency: 1 Leone = 100 cents
Industries: mining (diamonds, bauxite), rutile, cocoa

History: In the middle of the 16th century the British set up trading posts along the coast and sold the natives as slaves. In 1797 the British anti-slave movement allowed freed slaves to settle here. In 1808 the coastal area became a British crown colony and in 1896, despite violent resistance, the hinterland also came under British protectorate. In 1961 it was given independence. Since then politics have been characterised by struggles for power; due to terrorist acts and putsches in recent times, streams of refugees have been leaving the country. The country is currently governed by Major Koroma after a coup in 1997.
Topography: From the forested plains along Atlantic coast, the land climbs to the east over several steep steps to the Lower Guinea Threshold. Many rivers run through this mainly savannah region.
Economy: The disastrous political situation has brought the economy practically to a stand-still. Rice, millet, and cassava for their own consumption, and coffee, cocoa and palm kernels are harvested for export. Mining products such as rutile (a titanium ore), diamonds and bauxite make up 80% of the export quota.

Singapore
Singapore
(SGP)

Population: 3 million (4,701 per sq km)
Area: 684 sq km
Capital: Singapore
GNP: US$ 30,550 per head
Political system: parliamentary republic (liberal democracy)

Slovenija
Slovenia
(SLO)

Population: 1.9 million (98 per sq km)
Area: 20,253 sq km
Capital: Ljubljana
Political system: republic (emergent democracy)
Languages: Slovene (official), Serbo-Croat, Hungarian, Italian
Religion: 71% Catholic, 2% Serbo-Orthodox
GNP: US$ 9,240 per head
Currency: 1 tolar = 100 stotin
Industries: motor vehicles, machinery, steel, woollen textiles, livestock, timber, grain

Slovenská Republika
Slovac Republic

History: From 1283 until 1918 Slovenia was a part of the Habsburg Empire. Later it declared independence and helped establish the "Kingdom of Serbia, Croatia and Slovenia". In 1945 it became a constituent republic of Yugoslavia. In 1991 Slovenia was the first constituent republic to leave the federation and became an independent republic.

Topography: The most northerly republic of the former Yugoslavia borders to the north on the Alps, to the west on the Adriatic. Characteristic of the landscape are the karst mountains and the forested hills.

Economy: After independence Slovenia had to struggle with difficult economic problems: transition from a planned to a market economy, collapse of east European markets, war damages etc. In the meantime the economy has nevertheless recovered to such an extent that Slovenia's entry to the EU is being discussed.

Slovenská Republika
Slovak Republic
SK

Population: 5.3 million (109 per sq km)
Area: 49,034 sq km
Capital: Bratislava
Political system: republic (emergent democracy)
Languages: Slovak (official) Hungarian, Czech
Religion: 60% Catholic, 10% atheist, 8% Protestant, 22% other
GNP: US$ 3,410 per head
Currency: 1 Slovak krone = 100 heller
Industries: machinery, motor vehicles, chemical products

History: As of 1918 Slovakia became the smaller part of the federation of Czechoslovakia. From 1939 to 1945, under the protectorate of Germany, it experienced a kind of artificial autonomy, but became part of socialist Czechoslovakia again after World War II. Slovakia has been a sovereign state since 1993. Since then it has marked by inner-political arguments between President Kovàc and the head of government, Mecás.

Topography: The landscape is primarily mountainous, with river basins between the ranges. The wooded mountains of the High Tatra lie to the north and there is a fertile lowland in the Danube Valley to the south.

Economy: The transition from a planned to a market economy and the separation from its larger partner, the Czech Republic, have led to economic problems. Heavy and armament industries are developed most and contribute the greatest share of exported goods.

Solomon Islands
Solomon Islands
SOL

Population: 389,000 (14 per sq km)
Area: 27,556 sq km
Capital: Honiara
Political system: parliamentary monarchy
Languages: English (official), Pidgin English, 80 Polynesian and Melanesian languages
Religion: 48% diverse Protestants, 34% Anglican, 19% Catholic
GNP: US$ 900 per head
Currency: 1 Salomon dollar = 100 cents
Industries: fish products, palm oil, timber, cocoa, copra

History: The islands inhabited by Melanesians since at least 1000 BC were discovered in 1568 but seemed to be unimportant and were almost immediately forgotten. The northern Solomon Islands were taken as a possession by the Germans in 1885 whilst those in the south came became a British proctorate in 1893. In 1942 the islands were occupied by the Japanese, but they were forced to leave after heavy fighting and the USA occupied the islands in 1943. The islands were granted their independence in 1978, but retain the Queen as head of state.

Topography: The numerous islands, over 1000 in all, are almost all inhabited. They are volcanic and stretch for over 1000 km in two long island chains in the Pacific Ocean. The area is prone to cyclones, the last major one occurring in 1986.

Economy: Agriculture and forestry are the main sources of income. Sweet potatoes, taro and yams, fruit and vegetables are cultivated for their own consumption. The ubiquitous coconut palms provide palm oil and copra for export. The most important export, however, is timber; in second place come fish and fish products.

Somalia
Somalia
SP

Population: 9.8 million (15 per sq km)
Area: 637,657 sq km
Capital: Mogadishu
Political system: presidential republic (one-party socialist)
Languages: Somali (official)
Religion: almost 100% Sunni Muslim
GNP: under US$ 800 per head
Currency: 1 Somali shilling = 100 centesimi
Industries: bananas, livestock, skins and hides, fruit

History: As early as 1500 BC the Egyptians had trade connections with present-day Somalia. The nomads of Somalia migrated here from the 10th century onwards and drove out the native Oromos and Bantus. In 1885 the land was divided between England, Italy and Ethiopia. Independence came in 1960 to the British and Italian parts; from 1977 to 1978 Somalia went to war with its neighbouring country over the Ethiopian part which caused immense numbers of refugees.

Topography: The continent's most easterly state on the horn of Africa occupies a coastal plain of narrow cleft hills on the Gulf of Aden. The lowland to the south-east is covered with dry savannahs that are used for cattle-farming.

Economy: Banana plantations and huge cattle herds each contribute about 40% to the export quota. Three-quarters of the population work in agriculture and cultivate among other things corn, millet and sugar-cane for there own consumption.

South Africa
South Africa
SA

Population: 37.6 million (31 per sq km)
Area: 1,219,080 sq km
Capital: Pretoria (official), Cape Town (de facto)
Political system: republic
Languages: Afrikaans, English, Ndebele, North and South Sotho, Setswana, Swati, Tsonga, Venda, Xhosa, Zulu (all official)
GNP: US$ 3,520 per head

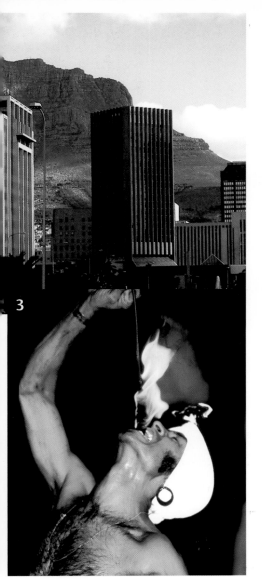

① *Cape Town in South Africa: view of the famous Table Mountain (1,092 m)*

② *Young girl from the island of Malaita, the second largest of the Solomon Islands after Guadalcanal*

③ *Fire-eater in Kandy in the central mountains of the island of Sri Lanka, formerly Ceylon*

④ *In Sri Lanka special forms of Indian art were developed that are found nowhere else (Hindu temple)*

rolling plateaux ("Veld") adjacent to the Kalahari Desert to the north and the Limpopo Basin to the north-east. Kruger National Park lies to the east on the other side of the Drakensberg Mountains – one of the main tourist attractions of the country.
Economy: South Africa has one of the richest mineral deposits in the world at its disposal. It was already famous for gold and diamonds in the last century. For the mining of chrome, platinum, uranium and manganese, South Africa holds one of the first three places world-wide. Heavy, chemical and consumer goods industries, as well as mechanical-engineering, have developed remarkably recently. Modern methods are being employed in agriculture, specializing in the culti- vation of corn and wheat; lambswool and pelts (Persian lamb) are traditional export products.

Spain → España

Sri Lanka
Sri Lanka
CL

Population: 18.3 million (279 per sq km)
Area: 65,610 sq km
Capital: Colombo
Political system: presidential republic (liberal democracy)
Languages: Sinhala, Tamil (both official), Malay, English
Religion: 70% Buddhist, 16% Hindus, 8% Muslim, 7% Catholic
GNP: US$ 740 per head
Currency: 1 Sri Lanka rupee = 100 Sri Lanka cents
Industries: Industrial products, tea, coconut products, rubber

History: Sri Lanka considers itself to be the land of Buddha's doctrine. Written history begins with the year 483 BC, the year of Buddha's death and the arrival of an Indian prince. For one and a half thousand years Anuradhapura was the capital and centre of Buddhism and the Singhalese civili-

sation. In 993 AD the Tamils conquered this capital and extended their empire over this region. Colonial rulers include: the Portuguese from 1505, the Dutch from 1658 and the British from 1796. The last king of this country so long broken up into different kingdoms was overthrown in 1815. In 1948 independence was gained by Ceylon, as it was then called, and in 1972 the Socialist Republic of Sri Lanka was proclaimed. A bloody civil war between the Sinhalese and the Tamils which started in 1983 and is still continuing to this day, despite several peace initiatives. In 1993 President Kumaratunga was elected as president.
Topography: The island just off the southernmost tip of India is surrounded by coastal lowlands that climb in steps to a mountainous central region. The climate is excellent for tea growing.
Economy: Industrial products, in particular textiles, make up three-quarters of exported goods. 15% of its export income is thanks to Sri Lanka's famous Ceylon tea.
40% of the population work in the service sector; trade and tourism are gaining increasing significance.

Sudan → As Sudan

Suriname
Surinam
SME

Population: 432,000 (2.6 per sq km)
Area: 162,265 sq km
Capital: Paramaribo
Political system: presidential republic (emergent democracy)
Languages: Dutch (official), Hindi, Java, Sranang, Tongo, Saramaccan
Religion: 27% Hindus, 23% Catholics, 20% Muslim, 19% Protestant, animist
GNP: US$ 1000 per head
Currency: 1 Surinam gulden = 100 cents

Religion: 40% Dutch Reformed Church, 11% Anglican, 8% Catholic, 25% other Christian
Currency: 1 rand = 100 cents
Industries: mining (diamonds, gold, platinum, uranium), iron and steel, copper, machinery, maize, sugar, fruit, wool

History: The oldest bones found in South Africa suggest that settlements date back to 1.5 million years ago. In 1500 BC the western part was inhabited by Khoi-Khoin ("Hottentots") and San ("bushmen"). In around 300 AD Bantu tribes immigrated from the north. In 1652 Cape Town was founded by the Dutch. From the 19th century this land was fought over by the British and the Boers (Dutch, German and Huguenot stock). The union of South Africa was formed in 1910. The apartheid system of strict racial discrimination, in practice beforehand, was officially introduced in 1948. Sanctions from abroad and unrest within the country led to the 1990 abolition of apartheid. Nelson Mandela, the main figure in the anti-apartheid movement become president, stepping down in 1999. The ANC, who opposed the white regime won the government elections.
Topography: This country on the southernmost tip of Africa climbs from a low narrow coastal margin on the Atlantic and Indian Oceans to higher countryside. The interior consists of low

Suriyah
Syria

Industries: aluminium, bauxite, timber, rice, shrimps

History: The native Indian population were joined by English settlers from 1651. In 1667 the English handed it over to the Dutch, who brought black slaves to the region. When slavery was abolished in 1863, manpower arrived from India, Java and China. The mixture of people, languages and religions is still noticeable within present-day society. Surinam gained independence in 1975. Temporarily it has had a military government and even today the army still has considerable influence.

Topography: Surinam lies on the northern coast of South America. The coastal plains that are criss-crossed with rivers join onto a wide loam and sand plain and then the land climbs towards the mountainous area of virgin forest in Guyana. A humid, practically impenetrable jungle covers three-quarters of the country.

Economy: Bauxite products, such as argillaceous earth and aluminium, constitute two-thirds of the export quota. The arable land is mainly covered with huge rice fields; the country produces 10% of the export quota through rice, and a further 10% with fisheries (predominantly with shrimps).

Suriyah
Syria
SYR

Population: 14.5 million (78 per sq km)
Area: 185,180 sq km
Capital: Damascus (Dimashq)
Political system: presidential republic (socialist)
Languages: High Arabic (official), Syrian Arabic, Kurdish, Armenian
Religion: 90% Muslim (70% Sunni, 16% Islamic sects), 9% Christian
GNP: US$ 1,160 per head
Currency: 1 Syrian pound = 100 piaster
Industries: petroleum, cotton, cereals, phosphates, tobacco

History: Syria is a land with an ancient civilization; in the 14th century BC the first alphabet came into being there. In the 7th century BC it became a part of the Roman Empire and was converted to Christianity. From the 7th century the Islamic conquest started; later European knights arrived on crusades. Egyptians, Mongols and Ottomans followed and ruled over the land until the end of World War I. In 1916 Syria was occupied by French troops then in 1941 by the Allies. In 1946 it fought for and won its independence. Conflicts with its neighbours Israel and Lebanon cause recurrent unrest.

Topography: The coastal plain along the Mediterranean Sea joins onto the Alawite Mountains to the east, and is followed by the Syrian tableland with its fertile valleys and then the Syrian Desert. The landscape is characterised by steppes and desert.

Economy: Petroleum and petroleum products make up two-thirds of the export quota, a further 9% is achieved with textiles and clothing, 5% with raw cotton. High armament costs and extreme underemployment create an unstable economic situation.

Sverige
Sweden
S

Population: 8.8 million (20 per sq km)
Area: 449, 964 sq km
Capital: Stockholm
Political system: parliamentary republic
Languages: Swedish (official), Finnish, Saami
Religion: 89% Swedish Lutheran (official)
GNP: US$ 25,710 per head
Currency: 1 Swedish krone = 100 öre
Industries: machinery and vehicles, aircraft, ball-bearings, drills, missiles, electronics, petrochemicals, textiles, furnishings, glass, paper, iron, steel, tourism

History: At the beginning of the 9th century Swedish Vikings on the warpath sailed to the Baltic region and eastern Europe. From 1389 to 1520 Sweden was united under a Danish Dynasty with Denmark and Norway.
Since 1523 Sweden has been an independent kingdom. During the Thirty Years War (1618 to 1648) Sweden extended its empire far into Europe. In the 18th century Sweden went to war with Russia and in the 19th century participated in the Napoleonic wars.
Since the 19th century Sweden has kept to a strict policy of neutrality and has developed into a model welfare state.

Topography: To the east the land borders on the Baltic Sea, to the west on the eastern slopes of the Scandinavian Mountains, which form the border to Norway. To the south the Central Swedish Basin is adjoined by hilly countryside pitted with lakes. Sweden is two-thirds covered with forest.

Economy: Sweden is one of the wealthiest countries in the world. Rich ore deposits form the basis of the often highly specialised metal processing industry.
The logs from the vast forests are processed locally into cellulose and paper. Hydroelectric

power plants provide the necessary energy for industry. Over 70% of the population work in the service sector.

Swaziland
Swaziland
SD

Population: 926,000 (53 per sq km)
Area: 17,363 sq km
Capital: Mbabane
Political system: parliamentary monarchy
Languages: Siswati/Isizulu, English (both official)
Religion: 72% Protestant, 5% Catholics, Bantu
GNP: US$ 1,210 per head
Currency: 1 lilangeni = 100 cents
Industries: sugar, canned fruit, wood pulp, asbestos, tourism

History: At the beginning of the 19th century the Swasi, a South-east Bantu group, conquered the Sotho inhabitants of this region and set up a kingdom with influential chieftains; a British protectorate in 1906 did little to change the existing social order. In 1968 the country achieved its sovereignty. Since 1978 this country has again been ruled in the traditional way, through tribal councils and a single ruler.

Topography: This country, the second smallest on the African mainland, borders to the east on Mozambique, and is otherwise surrounded by South Africa. Mountainous to hilly countryside with forests, savannahs and dry savannahs characterize this country.

Economy: In the central highlands corn, cotton, tobacco and pineapples are cultivated for their own consumption; an important export is sugar. The timber from the richly forested hillsides contribute 20% to the export balance. Swaziland is economically dependent on its neighbour South Africa: too few jobs are available in Swaziland, so that many people are forced to work in South Africa. On the other hand, Swaziland is a favourite holiday destination for South Africans; at the beginning of the 90's there were 1.6 million visitors from abroad.

Sweden → **Sverige**
Switzerland → **Schweiz**
Syria → **Suriyah**
Tajikistan →
Jumhurii Tojikistan

① The 12th century
Kalmar Castle with
its five towers lies
off the mainland of
South Sweden on an
island and served as
a sea fortress

② Prayer in the
Temple of Matsu in
Lugang, Taiwan

③ Masai warriors in
Tansania

④ Skyline and
mountainous hinter-
land of the Seoul,
one of the largest
and most important
economic centres of
the Far East

Taehan-Min'guk
South Korea
(ROK)

Population: 45.5 million (495 per sq km)
Area: 99,268 sq km
Capital: Seoul
Political system: presidential republic (emer-
gent democracy)
Languages: Korean
Religion: traditionally Buddhist (24%),
18% Protestant, 6% Catholic
GNP: US$ 10,610 per head
Currency: 1 won = 100 chon
Industries: steel, ships, chemicals, electronics,
textiles, shoes, machinery, plywood, fish

History: From the very beginning the history of
Korea has been closely knit with the neighbouring lands of China and Japan. From 1910 to 1945
the entire area was occupied by Japan. In 1945 it
was split up; in 1948 the US controlled south
achieved independent republic status. After the
Korean War, in which North Korea tried to extend its borders, South Korea came under a military dictatorship until 1987, when a democratic
constitution was adopted.
Topography: The southern part of the Korean
Peninsula is surrounded by the waters of the
Japanese Sea to the east and the Yellow Sea to
the west. Over 3000 islands extend off the coast
to the south. The geography of the land is primarily mountainous with flat to hilly country to
the west.
Economy: Since the 60's South Korea has experienced a true economic miracle. With the transition to modern technology and new production
methods, their industries have become extremely
competitive in the world market; these include
machinery, ship building, electrical goods, electronics and chemicals, as well as textiles and
clothing Their basic needs can be covered
through the cultivation of the staple food, rice.
Over half of the population works in the service
sector. In the 90's their economy became dis-
tressed due to the fall in prices on the world market, the recession in Europe and growing Asiatic
competition.

Taiwan
Taiwan
(TW)

Population: 21.4 million (596 per sq km)
Area: 36,000 sq km
Capital: Taipei (T'aipei)
Political system: presidential republic
Languages: Mandarin Chinese (official),
southern Chinese Min and Hakka
Religion: 43% Buddhist, 34% Daoist,
8% I-Kuan Taoist

GNP: US$ 12,838 per head
Currency: 1 new Taiwanese dollar (NT$) =
100 cents
Industries:: rice, electronics (computer parts)

History: The indigenous Malayo-Polynesian population were repressed by the mainland Chinese
from the 13th century. Portuguese, Spanish and
finally the Dutch made the island their trading
centre.
In 1662 the Dutch were driven out by the mainland Chinese, in 1683 the island was made into a
province of mainland China, in 1895 it was ceded
to Japan and from 1945 again belonged to China.
In 1949 the Guomindang government took refuge from Mao Zedong by transferring its seat of
government from Beijing to Taiwan and declared
itself the sole representative of all China. There
has been tension with the People's Republic of
China up to the present day. Taiwan insists on its
independence and opposes Chinese efforts at re-
unification.
Topography: Inland the wooded mountain
peaks are over 3000 m high. In the east the
slopes fall steeply to the sea, in the west a wider
lowland strip of coast meets the sea.
Economy: Rice is cultivated for their own consumption on terraced slopes. Taiwan is above all
a modern industrial country, whose inhabitants
enjoy relative prosperity. The main export is electronic components; almost 40% of the population is employed in this industry.

Tanzania
Tanzania
(EAT)

Population: 30.4 million (32 per sq km)
Area: 945,087 sq km
Capital: Dodoma (official), Daressalam (de facto)
Political system: presidential republic
Languages: Kiswahili, English (both official),
Bantu and Nitolish
GNP: US$ 170 per head

Tchad *Chad*

Religion: 35% Muslim, 33% Catholic, 13% Protestant, animism
Currency: 1 Tanzanian shilling = 100 cents
Industries: coffee, cotton, cashews nuts, cloves, tea, tobacco, diamonds

History: Arabs and Persians settled on the coast and nearby islands and traded from there with the tribes in the interior of the land, whose civilization was highly developed in respect of art and writing. In the 16th century the Portuguese occupied the region, but were driven out in the 17th century by the sultanate of Oman. At the end of the 19th century, in a dispute with Britain over possession of the mainland, Germany won the mainland and made it a colony, whilst the island of Zanzibar went to Britain in exchange for Heligoland. After World War I, the German colony (then Tanganyika) was administered as a British League of Nations mandate. In 1964 Tanganyika and Zanzibar united and proclaimed their independence as the United Republic of Tanzania. It attempted its own form of socialism; in 1992 a multi-party system was introduced into the former one-party state.

Topography: The western border is formed by the Great Rift Valley and Lakes Malawi and Tanganyika, the northern border by Lake Victoria. Serengeti National Park and the Ngorongoro Crater lie east from there and Mount Kilimanjaro (5895 m), the country's highest peak, is on the border to Kenya. To the east, islands extend off the coastal lowlands, the largest being Zanzibar.

Economy: The basis for the economy has always been agriculture. Their agricultural self-sufficiency is guaranteed. Coffee, cotton, cashews and cloves are cultivated for export.
The economy of Tanzania has been weakened through mismanagement, the fall in prices in the world market, 40% unemployment and lack of infrastructure. Tourism is also beginning to play a new part in the economy.

Tchad
Chad
(TCH)

Population: 6.6 million (5 per sq km)
Area: 1,284,000 sq km
Capital: Ndjamena
Political system: presidential republic (emergent democracy)
Languages: French, High Arabic (both official), Sara, Baguirmi, Boulala, Tibbu-Gorane
Religion: 50% Muslim 20% Catholic, 10% Protestant, animism
GNP: US$ 160 per head

Currency: 1 CFA franc = 100 centimes
Industries: cotton, livestock, meat, hides, skins, peanuts

History: The northern part of this region was under Libyan rule for centuries. Called Kanem when the Arabs settled in the 7th to 13th centuries, the area later became known as Bornu and in the 19th century was conquered by Sudan. From 1913 a province of French Equatorial Africa, Chad became an autonomous state in 1960 within the French commonwealth.
Since then there has been no end to the struggles for power.

Topography: The character of the land is marked by the deserts and savannahs of the Sahara, Sehel and Sudan.
Agriculture is only possible in the plains flooded by the Chari and Logone rivers, as well as Lake Chad area to the south; over half of the population live in these areas.

Economy: Chad is one of the poorest and least developed countries in the world and has neither a good transportation system nor any industry worthy of note. The only export worth mentioning is cotton, which, due to a fall in price in the world market, does not bring in nearly as much income as formerly.
Uranium, ore, oil and gas deposits cannot be exploited, because no money is available for their development. Chad, a country plagued by constant war, is dependent on help from abroad.

Thailand
Thailand
(T)

Population: 60 million (117 per sq km)
Area: 513,115 sq km
Capital: Bangkok (Krung Thep)
Political system: parliamentary monarchy
Languages: Thai (official), Chinese, Malay
Religion: 94% Buddhist, 4% Muslim
GNP: US$ 2,960 per head
Currency: 1 baht = 100 stangs
Industries: machinery, rubber, tin, rubies, textiles, maize, tapioca, rice

History: In the 4th century BC a farming community living in this region was displaced by the Mon (a Buddhist culture). They were followed by the Khmer who experienced their heyday in the 11th to 13th centuries; later it was overrun by Thai people from southern China, who acquired a vast empire. In 1350, after a change in rule, Siam experienced its economic and cultural heyday; it never fell under colonial rule; in 1767, however, the Burmese took over. The present dynasty dates from 1782. In 1932 the absolute monarchy was overthrown in a coup and a constitutional monarchy established, that in spite of many military governments, remains on the throne.

Topography: The flood plains of the Menam River on the Malakka Peninsula to the south is the most densely populated area. The Indian mountain chains are to the north; the Korat Plateau to the east runs gradually downward to the Mekong River Valley. The Mekong forms the border to Laos to the east and north-east.

Economy: Only superficially can Thailand be considered an "economic miracle" – the gap between rich and poor, country and city is too great. One third of the population live below the poverty line. As the only non-communist country in Indo-China, it was always generously supported by the West, but since the middle of the 90's it has been in an economic crisis. Thailand is on the verge of changing from being an agricul-

1 View of one of the countless temples (called "wats") in Bangkok, Thailand's capital city. In the foreground a statue of Buddha

3 Young woman from the main island Tongatapu, Tonga, a state consisting of approximately 400 coral and volcanic islands

2 Stretching the neck by wearing rings is still one of the most conspicuous rituals performed by Thai women

4 Rum and sugar cane are no longer so important as export goods. Tourism and oil now ensure Trinidad's prosperity

tural to an industrial country; machinery already constitutes 40% of exports. Over 7 million foreign visitors (1996) make tourism one of the most important sources of foreign currency, but mass tourism unfortunately brings problems, too. After years of rapid economic growth, the structural crisis became evident in 1996, which, together with political instability, led to the withdrawal of foreign investors.

Togo
Togo
TG

Population: 4.2 million (75 per sq km)
Area: 56,785 sq km
Capital: Lomé
Political system: presidential republic (one-party socialist)
Languages: French, Kabre, Ewe (official), Gur, Fulbe, Yoruba, Haussa
Religion: 50% animist, 22% Catholic, 15% Muslim, 13% Protestant
GNP: US$ 300 per head
Currency: 1 CFA franc = 100 centimes
Industries: Phosphates, cocoa, coffee beans, coconuts, cotton

History: This region on the former "slave coast" fell under German protectorate in 1884. After World War I the region was divided and administered into a British and a French part. The British part was integrated with Ghana; the French part gained independence in 1960 as the Republic of Togo. Lt-Gen Eyadéma, who came to power through a putsch, has been its ruler since 1967. In 1998 he was re-elected even though a new constitution in 1993 called for the introduction of democratisation.
Topography: This narrow west African country, that lies between Ghana and Benin, has a small part of Atlantic coast (53 km) on to which hillsides and then a mountainous sandstone plateau join. The humid savannah to the south changes into dry savannah farther north.

Economy: The rich phosphate deposits bestowed Togo with unexpected wealth in the 70's. Half of the export volume is still phosphate despite the fall in price on the world market. The development of profitable industry has failed on the whole; important export products are non-processed products such as raw cotton and green coffee. Togo is one of the poorest countries in the world today.

Tonga
Tonga
TO

Population: 97,000 million (130 per sq km)
Area: 748 sq km
Capital: Nuku'alofa
Political system: constitutional monarchy (absolute)
Languages: Tongan (official), English
Religion: 70% Protestant, 20% Catholic
GNP: US$ 1,70 per head
Currency: 1 pa'anga =100 seniti
Industries: fish, vanilla, coconut oil

History: The original inhabitants were the Polynesians. The history of the kings of Tonga dates back to the 10th century when a priest king ruled. The present dynasty, founded in 1831, encouraged the spread of Christianity and granted a constitution. Tonga, the only South Pacific state recognised by Europe in the middle of the 19th century, was under British protectorate from 1900 and gained full independence within the Commonwealth in 1970.
Topography: Tonga consists of around 170 coral and volcanic islands, of which only 36 are inhabited. The majority of the population live on the main island of Tongatapu.
Economy: The most important branch of the economy has always been agriculture, that partially covers their own needs; nonetheless a lot of food has to be imported. The traditional export product, copra, is nowadays processed into coconut oil and then exported.

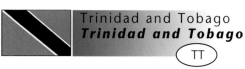

Trinidad and Tobago
Trinidad and Tobago
TT

Population: 1.2 million (253 per sq km)
Area: 5,128 sq km
Capital: Port-of-Spain
Political system: presidential republic (democratic)
Languages:
Religion: 40% Christian, 24% Hindus, 6% Muslim
GNP: US$ 3,870 per head
Currency: 1 Trinidad and Tobago dollar = 100 cents
Industries: petroleum products, chemicals, steel, sugar, cocoa

History: The Spanish took possession of Trinidad in 1498 and the native population was quickly eradicated. In 1797 it was captured by the English in the Spanish/English war. The neighbouring island of Tobago changed hands almost 30 times and in 1814 was ceded to Britain and in 1889 became a British crown colony along with Trinidad. In 1962 independence was granted within the Commonwealth. In 1976 the former monarchy became a presidential republic; full independence was achieved in 1987. An unsuccessful putsch was attempted by the black Muslim sect in 1990. In 1995, Basdeo Panday became the first prime minister of the island of South Asian origin. The aim of his coalition government is to fight unemployment, crima and racial discrimination.
Topography: The two islands lie off the coast of Venezuela. Three parallel mountain ranges run the length of Trinidad, the largest island of the Lesser Antilles. Tobago is mountainous.
Economy: The traditional Caribbean export products, rum and sugar, have only a secondary function now. Petroleum and petroleum products

make up half of the export balance; the oil is extracted in the country itself and also imported from Venezuela to be further processed in refineries. Tourism also brings money into the country; in 1996 there were almost 270,000 visitors from abroad. Tobago has heavenly beaches, while the less attractive Trinidad is the carnival stronghold of the Caribbean.

Tunis
Tunisia
TN

Population: 9.1 million (56 per sq km)
Area: 163,610 sq km
Capital: Tunis
Political system: presidential republic (emergent democracy)
Languages: High Arabic (official), Tunisian Arabic, French, Berber
Religion: 99% Sunni Muslim
GNP: US$ 1,930 per head
Currency: 1 Tunisian dinar = 1000 millimes
Industries: textiles, leather goods, phosphate, chemicals, olive oil

History: Carthage, which was founded by the Phoenicians in the 8th century BC, was a powerful city long before Rome. In 146 BC, after the third Punic War, the region was colonised by the Romans. In the 7th century Tunisia came under Arab rule and Islamic influence, until in 1574 it became a part of the Ottoman Empire. In 1881 it became a French protectorate. In 1956 full independence as a republic was gained and Bourguiba, as an authoritarian president nonetheless, led the country on a western course. Since his fall from power a democratization process has been initiated.

Topography: This north African country has a section of the Atlas Mountains to the north, on to which steppes and desert landscape join in the south. Tunisia borders on the Mediterranean Sea to the north and the east; at the most northerly point Sicily is less than 140 km away.
It is the smallest of the three Maghreb countries which comprise Marocco, Algeria and Tunisia.

Economy: Traditional handicrafts such as textiles, carpets and leather goods make up 50% of the export balance, though today they are mainly manufactured industrially. The most important agricultural exports are wine and olive oil. Tunisia is also a main producer of phosphate which is used as a fertilizer. It is mined in mines at Gapsa.Tourism is a significant source of foreign currency. The resorts on the Mediterranean coast and desert tours attracted almost four million visitors from abroad in 1996.

Türkiye
Turkey
TR

Population: 62.6 million (80 per sq km)
Area: 779,452 sq km
Capital: Ankara
Political system: parliamentary republic (democratic)
Languages: Turkish (official), Kurdish, Arabic
Religion: 99% Sunni Muslim
GNP: US$ 2,830 per head
Currency: 1 Turkish pound/lira = 100 kurus
Industries: cotton, yarn, textiles, steel, iron, citrus fruits, tobacco, tourism

History: The people of Asia Minor fought against the Greeks in the Trojan War. From the 6th century BC this region fell repeatedly under Persian rule. In 333 BC Alexander the Great conquered it and from 190 BC Roman influence spread. The Ottoman Turks, driven out of central Asia by the Mongols, overran Asia Minor in 1299, conquered Constantinople in 1453, and in the 16th century experienced their heyday; from the 18th century this gradually declined. In 1920 Ataturk, its first president, founded the independent Republic of Turkey and laid the framework for a new legal code and westernisation. After three military putsches (1960, 1971 and 1980), Turkish politics have been dominated by problems with the Kurdish minority and fundamentalist Muslims. Foreign policy is marked by the continuing conflict with Greece, in particular over Cyprus and the Aegean Islands. UN troops patrol the Turkish-Greek border on Cyprus. Turkey wishes to gain membership to the EU, but has so far been rejected due to its policy towards its minorities, violations of human rights and its weak economy.

Topography: Turkey consists of a very small European and a very large Asiatic part, which are connected with each other in Istanbul by two bridges over the Bosporous. To the west, countless islands lie off the Mediterranean and Aegean coasts. The Anatolian highlands are in the interior of the country, which borders on the Black Sea with a lowland margin in the north-west and the Ponti mountains in the east, and with coastal plains and the Taurus mountains in the south-west on the Mediterranean.

Economy: Agriculture makes up only a 6% share of the export figures; the major part is produced for their own consumption. The Turkish textile industry contributes one quarter to the export balance. The most important source of foreign currency comes from money transferred by Turkish people living and working abroad, as well as tourism (in 1997 almost 10 million tourists).

Turkmenistan
Turkmenistan
TM

Population: 4.5 million (9 per sq km)
Area: 488,100 sq km
Capital: Ashkhabad
Political system: presidential republic (socialist pluralist)
Languages: Turkmen (official), Russian
Religion: predominantly Muslim
GNP: US$ 940 per head
Currency: 1 Turkmenistan manat = 100 tenge
Industries: gas, cotton, sheep, carpets

History: Turkmenistan, populated by nomadic tribes, was subjugated by the Russians from 1869. After becoming the autonomous republic of Turkestan in 1918, it became a constituent republic of the USSR in 1925. In 1991 independence was declared and it joined the CIS, but continued to have a communist Government.

Topography: This central Asian country borders to the west on the Caspian Sea, to the north the Karakum Desert lowland and to the west desert and dry steppes.

1 The imposing Colosseum of El Djem, north of Sfax, Tunisia

2 Dwellings built into the mountainside, Cappadocia, central Anatolia, Turkey

3 On the tip of the Istanbul peninsula, Suleiman I extended the Serai complex to create a palace town (Top-Kapi)

4 Young woman in traditional dress, Zaporozhye, Ukraine

Economy: Since independence an effort has been made towards a smooth transition to a market economy. Because only 2% of the land is arable, most foodstuffs have to be imported. The most important export is gas; the country has large deposits of natural gas and petroleum. Cotton grown with the help of irrigation is manufactured in the domestic textile industry.

GNP: not available
Currency: 1 Australian dollar = 100 cents
Industries: copra, fish, handicrafts, stamps

History: The islands, which were inhabited by Polynesians, were invaded by Samoans in the 16th century. In the 19th century a slave trade was set up with South America. Originally known as the Ellice islands, they fell under British protectorate from 1892 and became a colony in 1915. They reverted to the name Tuvalu upon gaining full independence in 1978.
Topography: Tuvalu is a coral atoll in the Pacific with nine islands that form a circle; of these one is uninhabited. The island with the largest population is Funafuti. Many Tuvalus work on Kiribati, take wives there and there is a Kiribati community on Tuvalu. Life is however, still marked by the strong communal life and it is still hard for many.
Economy: Apart from coconut palms scarcely anything grows on the barren ground. Copra and fishing are therefore - apart from money transferred by islanders living abroad - the only source of income for the inhabitants. Tuvalu is among the poorest and least developed countries and could not survive without foreign support.

Religion: 40% Catholic, 26% Protestant, 5% Muslim, animists
Currency: 1 Ugandan shilling = 100 cents
Industries: coffee, gold, cotton, tea, copper

History: The Bugandu Empire was one of the richest and most powerful in Africa. The British made use of the organisational and power structures that equalled their own to extend their area of influence. In 1894 the region became a British protectorate, and in 1962 it gained independence. The dictator Idi Amin, who came to power in a 1972 putsch, ruled a reign of terror and virtually destroyed the country. Since 1986 the situation has begun to stabilise.
Topography: The major part of the country consists of high plains (1,000 to 3,000 m) that are bordered to the east and west by mountain ranges. To the south-east the land has a share of Lake Victoria.
Economy: With improvements in the political situation, the economy is also improving. Coffee has always been an important export; it contributes 70% to the export balance. Amongst other crops, corn and millet are grown. Over 80% of the population work in agriculture. There is not enough money to develop industry or to train skilled workers (40% illiteracy).

 Tuvalu Islands
Tuvalu
(TUV)

Population: 10,000 (385 per sq km)
Area: 26 sq km
Capital: Funafuti
Political system: parliamentary monarchy (liberal democracy)
Languages: Tuvaluan, English (both official)
Religion: 98% Protestant Church of Tuvalu

 Uganda
Uganda
(EAU)

Population: 19.7 million (82 per sq km)
Area: 241,139 sq km
Capital: Kampala
Political system: presidential republic (liberal democracy)
Languages: Kiswahili, English (official), Luganda, west and east Nilotish as well as Bantu
GNP: US$ 300 per head

 Ukrayina
Ukraine
(UA)

Population: 50.7 million (84 per sq km)
Area: 603,700 sq km
Capital: Kiev
Political system: presidential republic
Languages: Ukrainian (official), Russian
Religion: predominantly Russian Orthodox
GNP: US$ 1,200 per head

United Arab Emirates

Currency: 1 griwna = 100 kopecks
Industries: heavy industry, mining (coal, minerals), oil

History: The state, founded in the 9th century in Kiev, is considered to be the nucleus of the Russian Empire. In 1240 it was destroyed by the Mongols. Later the region fell under Polish and Lithuanian rule and from 1654 was taken over by Russian tsars. In 1918 an independent people's republic was proclaimed, but soon after was conquered by the Soviet Red Army and in 1919 made into a communist Soviet republic, that in 1922 became a part of the USSR. In 1991 it joined the CIS.

Topography: The Ukraine borders to the south on the Black Sea and consists predominantly of plains. The mixed forests to the north-west change into marshland, followed by a zone of wooded steppe and then a true steppe area.

Economy: The former "granary of the Soviet Union" is still a region for the cultivation of grain, potatoes, sugar-beet and other agrarian crops. The backbone of the economy is nevertheless heavy industry based on the rich mineral deposits of the land. The "black economy " is said to make up to 60% of economic activity; price increases and currency depreciation have given rise to a flourishing barter system. The nonpayment of wages and pensions has led to growing social unrest amongst the population. In June 1997 the miners went on strike. The IMF and other international organizations granted new loans to the Ukraine in 1997.

United Arab Emirates
United Arab Emirates
(UAE)

Population: 2.5 million (33 per sq km)
Area: 77,700 sq km
Capital: Abu Dhabi
Political system: federally elected monarchy
Languages: High Arabic (official), Arabic, Hindi, Urdu, Farsi
Religion: 96% Muslim, 3% Christian, Hindu
GNP: over US$ 10,000 per head
Currency: 1 dirham = 100 fils
Industries: petroleum, natural gas, fish, dates

History: Abu Dhabi, Dubai, Ash Sariqah, Ajman, Umm al Qaywayn, Ra's al Khaymah and al Fujayrah, the seven Sheikhdoms on the southern coast of the Persian Gulf, which was feared as the "pirate coast" at the beginning of the 19th century, came under British control in 1853. In 1971 the Emirates became independent and established a federation.

Topography: This state lies on the east coast of the Arabian Peninsula, and with the exception of a narrow coastal strip of salty marshland, is made up almost entirely of Rub al Khali Desert; to the north-east the land climbs to the Oman Mountains.

Economy: This country is the third largest oil producing country in the world and lives mainly from the extraction and processing of petroleum and natural gas. It is one of the richest countries in the world. Agriculture in this desert country is almost non-existent. An estimated three out of four inhabitants are foreign workers from India.

United Kingdom
United Kingdom
(UK)

Population: 58.7 million (242 per sq km)
Area: 242,900 sq km
Capital: London
Political system: parliamentary monarchy
Languages: English, Welsh, Gaelic
Religion: Anglican 57%, other Protestants 15%, Catholic 13%, Muslim, Jewish, Hindu
GNP: US$ 19,600 per head
Currency: 1 pound sterling (£) = 100 pence
Industries: cereals, rape, sugar beet, potatoes, meat (products), dairy products, electronic and scientific equipment, oil and gas, petrochemicals, pharmaceuticals, aircraft and automobiles

History: Early Britain was conquered from 400 BC by the Celts, from 43 BC by the Romans, from

the 5th century by the Anglo-Saxons and from 1066 by the Normans. In the following centuries England extended its predominance throughout the world and in the 18th century set up a vast colonial empire, but after World War II had to grant independence little by little. The UK is burdened with the Northern Ireland conflict. The "splendid isolation" or island mentality of the British is diminishing: in 1973 the UK joined the EEC and the Channel Tunnel has been built.

Topography: This island, that lies in the North Sea, is separated from the European mainland by the English Channel. Various islands, groups of islands, as well as Northern Ireland belong to the UK. The countryside is characterised by rolling

① Palace in Dubai, capital of the United Arab Emirates on the Persian Gulf

② Big Ben and the Houses of Parliament in London, capital of the United Kingdom and Northern Ireland

③ The Statue of Liberty on Liberty Island, New York, USA

④ Skyline of Manhattan, in the background the World Trade Centre, 412 m high

hillside, in Scotland and Wales by low mountains. The Gulf Stream provides the UK with a mild, wet climate.

Economy: Over 80% of the export balance is achieved through industry, although only a fifth of the population work in it – in contrast almost three-quarters work in the service sector. The UK has large deposits of coal, petroleum and natural gas at its disposal.

United States of America
United States of America
USA

Population: 256.2 million (27 per sq km)
Area: 9,80,155 sq km
Capital: Washington
Political system: presidential republic (liberal democracy)
Languages: English, Spanish (both official)
Religion: 26% Catholic, 16% Baptist, 6% Methodist, 4% Lutheran, 2.6% Jewish, 2% Presbyterian, 1.5% Orthodox, 0.5% Muslim
GNP: US$ 28,020 per head
Currency: 1 US dollar = 100 cents
Industries: machinery, motor vehicles, chemicals and pharmaceutical products, consumer goods

History: Nearly 1.5 million native Indian inhabitants with highly developed civilisations lived in numerous tribes and nations throughout North America. Within a short time after the discovery of America by white settlers, the Indians were

eradicated, driven out and decimated through illness and alcohol or displaced onto reserves. All the European colonial powers fought to gain control of this huge country. In 1776 the Declaration of Independence initiated an era of constant expansion for the United States that continued throughout the nineteenth century. In the American Civil War (1861-1865), the northern states asserted the abolition of slavery over the southern states. In the 20th century the USA grew to become a leading economic and military world power, strengthening their position by their intervention in both World Wars and numerous other wars (e.g. Korea, Vietnam, Gulf War).

Topography: This third largest country in the world stretches over 4500 km from the Atlantic in the east to the Pacific in the west, and over 2 500 km from the Canadian border in the north to the Caribbean in the south. It covers four time zones and all the climate zones except that of the tropics. The coastal plains on the Atlantic and Gulf of Mexico follow in a westerly direction to the rolling hills of the Appalachians, the Great Plains, the Rocky Mountains, a basin and plateau landscape, the coastal cordillera and the coastal strip on the Pacific. Alaska, which lies to the north-west of Canada, and the Hawiian Islands far west of Mexico, also belong to the USA.

Economy: The USA is a highly developed industrial and agrarian country that makes good use of its wealth of raw materials and good climactic conditions. Almost three-quarters of the population now work in the service sector, which also produces three-quarters of the gross national in-

come. Agriculture and cattle-farming are carried out using the most technically advanced methods, but only employ 2% of the Americans; one quarter of the population work in industry. This holiday country attracted almost 50 million visitors from abroad in 1997.

Uruguay
Uruguay
ROU

Population: 3.2 million (18 per sq km)
Area: 176,215 sq km
Capital: Montevideo
Political system: presidential republic (democratic)
Languages: Spanish
Religion: 78% Catholic, 2% Protestant
GNP: US$ 5,760 per head
Currency: 1 Uruguay peso = 100 centesimos
Industries: meat, wool, rice, textiles, leather goods

History: When the region was discovered at the beginning of the 16th century, the native inhabitants, especially the Charrua Indians, offered strong resistance to the attempts made to colonize and convert them. In the end they could not prevent the country being annexed to the Spanish viceroyalty of Rio de la Plata in 1776. In 1811 a war of liberation began, that led to Uruguay being annexed to Portuguese Brazil. In 1925, however, Uruguay was able to proclaim independence.

Uruguay is still feeling the after-effects of reforms introduced by President Batlle at the beginning of the 20th century. In the seventies and eighties it suffered under a military dictatorship; in 1989 the first free elections took place.

Uzbekistan

Topography: To the west the Uruguay River and the estuary of the Rio de la Plata form the border to Argentina. The gentle rolling hillside to the north turns southwards into an area of moist grassland (pampa).

Economy: Only 13% of the population work in agriculture, but produce around 90% of the export balance, mainly through animal-farming products such as meat and wool, but also rice, wheat, corn, sugar-cane and other agricultural products, that are for the most part processed by local industry before being exported. This country has hardly any natural resources.

Uzbekistan
Uzbekistan
(UZR)

Population: 23.2 million (52 per sq km)
Area: 447,400 sq km
Capital: Tashkent
Political system: presidential republic (socialist pluralist)
Languages: Uzbek (official), Russian
Religion: predominantly Sunni Muslim
GNP: US$ 1,010 per head
Currency: 1 Uzbekistan sum = 100 tijin
Industries: cotton, silk, gold, natural gas, rice, dried fruit, vines

History: The Uzbeks, a nomadic Turkish race, were united in the 14th century into a tribal force, and in the 17th century the Uzbek states of Buchara, Chiwa, and Kokand were founded.
After 1860 the region came under Russian influence; the Uzbek Empires were annexed or came under Russian protectorate with all efforts at autonomy being suppressed.
In 1924 it was made into a constituent republic of the USSR. In 1991 Uzbekistan declared independence and joined the CIS.

Topography: Four-fifths of the country are covered by the Kylsyl Kum Desert. The foothills of the Tianshan and Altai Mountains which form the border to the east and the Ustyurt Plateau to the west. The western area bordering onto Turkmenistan is formed by the Amu Darya River that flows into the Aral Sea in the northern part of the country.

Economy: The most important export products are cotton, with which almost half of the export balance is made up, and gold which accounts for one fifth.
Agriculture is only possible at oases or with the aid of irrigation; rice, fruit and wine do not even cover their own needs. Sheep-rearing and silkworm-farming supply the textile industry with wool, skins (caracul sheep) and silk.

Vanuatu
Vanuatu
(VU)

Population: 173,000 (14 per sq km)
Area: 12,190 sq km
Capital: Port Vila
Political system: parliamentary republic (democracy)
laBislama, English, French (both official), over 100 Melanesian languages
Religion: 32% Presbyterian, 17% Catholic, 11% Anglican, Cargo Cults, Animism
GNP: US$ 1,290 per head
Currency: 1 vatu = 10 centimes
Industries: copra, beef, timber, fish, coffee, cocoa

History: In 1840 Presbyterian and Church of England missionaries came to this island that was originally inhabited by Polynesians. From the 20th century, French and British jointly administered the "New Hebrides", that in 1980 were granted independence. When the state opted in favour of socialist ideologies and against atom bomb tests, it did not make itself very popular with its neighbours or the ex-colonial French rulers.

Topography: This country in the Pacific Ocean off the coast of Australia comprises around 80 mountainous and volcanic islands with volcanoes

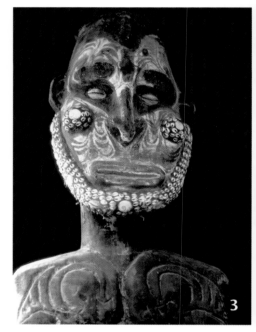

that are occasionally active, as well as coral islands.

Economy: The main export is, as in colonial times, the coconut product copra, which constitutes more than 40% of the export balance. Different kinds of vegetables are cultivated for their own consumption and cattle-farming is carried out; beef constitutes almost one fifth of the export balance.

Vatican City ›
Città del Vaticano

Venezuela
Venezuela
(YV)

Population: 23.3 million (25 per sq km)
Area: 912,050 sq km
Capital: Caracas
Political system: presidential republic (federal democracy)
Languages: Spanish (official), Carina, Goajiro, Guaraúno, Pemón, and other Indian languages

1 *Uzbekistan: woman in traditional dress, Termez, near the border to Afghanistan*

2 *Unusual road sign for European drivers: "Beware of camels crossing the road"*

3 *Making use of the wealth of shells: sculpture on the south Pacific island state of Vanuatu*

4 *The water falls 970 m to its depths: the Angel waterfalls in the south-east of Venezuela*

Religion: 93% Catholic, 5% Protestant
GNP: US$ 3,020 per head
Currency: 1 Bolivar = 100 centimo
Industries: petroleum and natural gas, aluminium, iron ore, timber, petrochemicals, coffee, gold

History: This region, inhabited by the Carib and Arawak Indians, was dubbed "Little Venice" by the Spanish conquerors, because the Indians on Lake Maracaibo lived in houses built on stilts above the water. In 1717 this region was annexed along with Ecuador, Colombia and Panama to their kingdom of "New Granada."
In 1821 Venezuela, as well as the rest of the middle and northern parts of central America, fought and won its freedom under the leadership of Símon Bolivar. Along with Ecuador and Columbia, Venezuela declared independence as "Greater Colombia", but in 1830 broke with the union and in 1864 became a federal republic. After a long period of civil wars and dictatorships, democratic stability has been achieved since 1958.
Topography: Venezuela lies on the north coast of South America where many islands dot the coast. To the north-west, in the flat area around Lake Maracaibo, there are large oil fields; the Venezuelan Andes run south from there. The Orinoco River Valley with low-lying plains and tableland of the Llanos divides the land in a east-westerly direction, to the south-east lie the foothills of the Guyana mountains.
Economy: Venezuela has been extracting petroleum for over 100 years; today petroleum and natural gas still constitute almost 80% of the export volume. The fall in the price of oil during the eighties nonetheless made a reorientation necessary, and so Venezuela is devoting itself increasingly to the mining of its rich mineral deposits, above all iron ore. The service industries are also an increasing sector, making up 56% of the economy. Venezuela is one of the richest countries in South America, but like almost everywhere else on this continent, the difference between rich and poor is crass.

Viet Nam
Vietnam
VN

Population: 73.3 million (228 per sq km)
Area: 331,114 sq km
Capital: Hanoi (Ha Noi)
Political system: socialist republic (communism)
Languages: Vietnamese (official), French, English, Khmer, Chinese, tribal
Religion: 55% Buddhist, 5% Catholic
GNP: US$ 290 per head
Currency: 1 dong = 100 xu
Industries: crude oil, coal, rubber, apatite, rice, clothing and shoes

History: In contrast to all the other south east Asian countries that were influenced early on by India, Vietnam was ruled by China from 111BC for one thousand years. Not until 929 AD did this region become independent and able to extend its area of influence southwards. Towards the end of the 16th century it split into north and south parts, which at the beginning of the 19th century were united for a brief while. In the second half of the 19th century it was occupied little by little by the French, who right from the start met with bitter resistance. In 1946 Vietnam declared independence, in 1954 the French were finally beaten in the battle of Dien Bien Phu and the division of Vietnam into north and south was confirmed at the Geneva Indo-China Conference. The Vietnam war, with the USA supporting the losing south,

ended in 1975 with north Vietnam uniting the two parts under a communist government. From 1979 to 1989 Vietnam occupied neighbouring Cambodia – a move that led to military conflicts with China.
Topography: Vietnam is a long, narrow strip of land on the South Chinese Sea. The mainly mountainous country is interrupted by the Red River delta in the north and the Mekong delta in the south. The Annam cordillera, with a height of over 3 000 m, runs in a north-south direction.
Economy: War, high arms expenditure and a planned socialist economy have seriously harmed the country. Since the end of the eighties, however, a slow but noticeable economic recovery has taken place. In the agriculturally higher yielding south, rice, not only the most important staple food, but also an export which product, is cultivated – Vietnam is the third largest exporter of rice in the world. Mineral deposits and heavy industry are concentrated in the north; the most important export is crude oil which constitutes 20% of the export balance.

Westsahara
Western Sahara
DARS

Population: 252,146 (1 per sq km)
Area: 252,120 sq km
Capital: El Aaiun
Political system: republic
Languages: High Arabic (official), Spanish, Hassani
Religion: almost 100% Sunni Muslim
GNP: not available
Currency: Sahara pesete (official), general currency in use is the Moroccan dinar
Industries: phosphate, fish

Yisra'el
Israel

History: This region was already inhabited in the middle Stone Age. The original inhabitants, the Tuareg people, nomads of Berber origin, were joined increasingly by Arabs from the 7th century onwards.

Until the seventies, the region of present day West Sahara was the largest possession of Spain in Africa. After the Spanish had withdrawn, the neighbouring countries of Morocco and Mauritania partitioned the land and a guerrilla war began. A referendum under supervision of the UN Security Council is to decide on whether independence or union with Morocco is best.

Topography: The desert country is very thinly populated; on the Atlantic coast there are rich fishing grounds, in the west large phosphate mines.

Economy: not available due to the pending elections.

Yemen → Al Yaman

Yisra'el
Israël
IL

Population: 5.6 million (259 per sq km)
Area: 21,946 sq km
Capital: Jerusalem (Yerushalayin/Al-Ouds)
Political system: parliamentary republic
Languages: Hebrew, Arabic (official), Yiddish
Religion: 81% Jewish, 14% Muslim
GNP: US$ 15,870 per head
Currency: 1 new shekel =100 agorot
Industries: machinery, aircraft, diamonds, citrus fruit, electronics, fertilizers, petrochemicals

History: Israeli tribes had settled and maintained their own state as far back as 1900 BC, until in 135 AD the Jews were driven out by the Romans. In 1948 the state of Israel was founded by European Jews who had returned to the region of their former homeland. The Arabs that lived there and in the neighbouring countries confronted them with constant war. In 1993 the passing of the Gaza-Jericho agreement has led to the introduction of a peace process.

Topography: To the north-east of the country there are highlands bordering on the Mediterranean Sea; to the east the border is formed by the Dead Sea and the Jordan Trench. The entire southern area is covered by the Negev Desert.

Economy: Cut diamonds and industrial goods such as machinery, motor vehicles and electronic goods make up the greatest share of the export balance. Agriculture is only possible through irrigation; despite this, basic requirements for fruits and vegetables can almost be met. The biblical

and historical cities attract numerous tourists who bring foreign currency to the country.

Yugoslavia → Jugoslavija

Zambia
Zambia
Z

Population: 9.2 million (12 per sq km)
Area: 752,614 sq km
Capital: Lusaka
Political system: presidential republic
Languages: English (official), Bantu dialects
Religion: 72% Christian, 27% animist
GNP: US$ 360 per head
Currency: 1 kwacha =100 ngwee
Industries: copper, cobalt, lead, zinc, manganese, emeralds, tobacco

History: The domain ruled by a number of ancient African Empires fell under the influence of the British from the 19th century. The region of present-day Zambia was given the name of Northern Rhodesia and in 1891 became a British protectorate. In 1953 Northern and Southern Rhodesia (now Zimbabwe), as well as Nyasaland (now Malawi) were united into the Federation of Rhodesia and Nyasaland. In 1964 Northern Rhodesia became the independent Republic of Zambia. After struggles for power and a period of quasi-dictatorship, a new constitution was adopted and free elections took place.

Topography: Zambia consists predominantly of high plateaus with towering isolated mountains. There are swamps and flood plains on the Zambesi, which forms the border to Zimbawe and Namibia in the south. The Victoria Falls attract numerous tourists.

Economy: The rich copper, cobalt and manganese deposits, that aroused the interest of the British colonial rulers in the past, dominate exports – copper alone makes up 70% of the export balance. The main export countries are Japan, France, Thailand and India. Energy requirements

1 On the way to prayers: an inhabitant of Jerusalem's old town, Israel

2 School children under the shade of a tree, Zimbabwe

3 The Great Wall of China is the longest protective construction in the world, 2,450 km long. It was begun around 220 BC. It exists in its present form since the 15th century

4 Zimbabwe: this frightening mask is only worn in ritual dances

are met through hydroelectric power plants at the Victoria Falls and at the Kariba Dam. There is very little industry and agriculture cannot cover even basic food requirements. Therefore, food (8%), industrial goods (37%), machines and equipment (35%) and fossil fuels (18%) are imported mainly from South Africa, but also from Europe, the USA, Japan and the neighbouring Zimbabwe.

Zhongquo
China, People's Republic of (VRC)

Population: 1221.7 million (128 per sq km)
Area: 9,572,395 sq km
Capital: Peking (Beijing)
Political system: communist peoples republic
Languages: Chinese (Putonghua), including Mandarin (official) and Cantonese and other dialects, 55 languages from national minorities
Religion: atheist (officially), traditionally Buddhist, Taoist, and Confucianism; Muslim
GNP: US$ 750 per head
Currency: 1 Renminbi yaun (RMBY) = 10 jiao
Industries: tea, silk, cotton, electronics and light industrial goods, oil, tungsten

History: Prehistoric man (Peking man) lived in this area as far back as 500,000 BC. 3000 BC was the height of the Yangshao culture; in 1776 BC the first Chinese Dynasty, the Shang Dynasty, arose. After 221 BC China developed into a mighty empire; the Great Wall of China was built. From 1280 China came under Mongolian rule and from 1644 it came under the rule of the Manchu Dynasty, that continued until the empire fell in 1911. 1946 saw the beginning of the Chi-

nese civil war between the communists under Mao Tse Tung and the Guomindang, that ended in 1949 with the foundation of the People's Republic of China. One of the most important political leaders following Mao was Deng Xiaoping, who died in 1997. At the beginning of the 90s he began to relinquish some of his political functions to Jiang Zemin, China's present head of state. He continues Deng's hardline policy against the democracy movement and political liberalisation.
Topography: This huge country, in which over a billion people live, is practically a self-contained continent, difficult to access; in the east its border is a 14,000 km long coast on the Pacific Ocean comprising low lying fertile plains. In the west the Himalayas and to the north the Gobi Desert form natural borders to inhospitable regions.
Economy: The 20 % of the population who work in agriculture are able to supply the country. As a cheap labour land, China produces electronic goods and clothing for export. After opening its borders, tourism has gained importance; the ancient cities draw increasing numbers of tourists.

Zimbabwe
Zimbabwe (ZW)

Population: 11.2 million (29 per sq km)
Area: 390,757 sq km
Capital: Harare
Political system: presidential republic (one-party socialist)
Languages: English (official), Fanagalo, Bantu

Religion: animist, 17% Protestant, 14% African Christian, 14% Catholic
GNP: US$ 610 per head
Currency: 1 Zimbabwe dollar = 100 cents
Industries: tobacco, cotton, coffee, mining (gold, silver, asbestos, nickel, copper)

History: The indigenous tribes were ruthlessly driven out when in 1891 the region fell under British protectorate. In 1923 Southern Rhodesia, as it was called then, became a British colony. The British felt the independence that had been called for since the sixties could only be granted if the Africans were given equal rights. The white minority opposed the movement and Southern Rhodesia declared itself unilaterally independent. Only after a long struggle against the white minority did the region finally gain independence in 1980 as the Republic of Zimbabwe.
Topography: The central highland with savannah vegetation descends in stages in the north to the Zambezi Basin, in the south to the Limpopo Basin. To the east there are highlands , to the west the country has a share of the Kalahari. The Victoria Falls to the north on the border to Zambia are the greatest toursit attraction.
Economy: Agriculture is able to provide the country with sufficient food and grows tobacco, cotton, coffee and other products for export. Rich mineral deposits, in particular gold, but also copper, chrome and iron are exported and also provide a good basis for heavy industry, which, by African standards, is well-developed. The hydroelectric power plant on the Kariba Dam provides the country with energy. Price and tax increases have been the cause of unrest in recent times.

Abbreviations used in the Maps

Abbr.	Meaning	Abbr.	Meaning
A....;...	Alpes, Alpen		Gulf (bays, gulfs)
ad.	adası	GA	Georgia
Ág.	Ágia, -ios	G.^{a}	Gora
Aig.^{lle}	Aiguille(s)	G.^{d}	Grand
AK	Alaska	G.$^{de(s)}$	Grande(s)
Akr.	Akreotérion	-geb.	-gebirge
AL	Alabama	G.^{fe}	Golfe
AO	Autonome Oblast	Gl.	Glacier
AR	Arkansas	-gl.	-gletscher
Arch.	Archipelago	-gn.	-ingen
Arr.	Arroyo	G.^{ng}	Gunung
Austr.	Australia	G.^{ng}-g.^{ng}	Gunung-gunung
Aut.	Autonomous	Gr.	Groß, -er, -e, -es
AZ	Arizona	-gr.	-gruppe (mountains)
B.	Bad, Basin, Bay		-graben (waters)
Ban.	Banjaran	G.^{ral}	General
Bat.	Batang	G.^{t}	Great
-b.	-bach	-h.	-hafen
Bel.	Belyi, -aja-, -oje, -yje	H.^{d}	Head
Bg(e).	Berg(e)	-hfn.	-hofen
-bg(e).	-berg(e)	-hgn.	-hagen
-bğ.	-burg	HI	Hawaii
B.^{io}	Balneario	-hm.	-heim
Bol.	Bol'šoj, -aja, -oje, -ije	-h.^{n}	-horn
Bos.	Bosanski, -a, -e	Hon.	Honduras
Bras.	Brazil	H.^{s}	Hills
-br(n).	-brücke(n)	-hsn.	-hausen
B.^{t}	Bukit	Htr.	Hinter
C.	Cape	-hvn.	-hoven
Č.	Český, -ká, -ké	...I.	Insel, Island
CA	California	I....	Isle
Can.	Canal	Î....	Île
C.^{bo}	Cabo	IA	Iowa
C.^{d}	Ciudad	I.^{a}	Ilha
Chan.	Channel	Î.^{a}	Îsola
Chin.	China	ID	Idaho
chr.	chrebet	IL	Illinois
C.$^{l(e)}$	Coll(e)	I.$^{la(s)}$	Isla(s)
C.^{ma}	Cima	IN	Indiana
CO	Colorado	Ind.	India
Col.	Colombia	I.^{s}	Islands
Coll.^{s}	Collines	Î.^{s}	Îles
Cor.	Coronel	Isr.	Israel
Cord.	Cordillera	It., Ital.	Italy
C.^{po}	Capo	J.	Jabal
Cr.	Creek	-j.	joch; joki
C.Rica	Costa Rica	Jap.	Japan
C.^{ro}	Cerro	Jord.	Jordans
CT	Connecticut	Juž.	Južnyj, -aja, -oje
Cuch.	Cuchilla	-K.	-kopf
D.	Danau	-kan.	-kanal
Dağl.	Dağlari	-kchn.	-kirchen
DC	District of Columbia	Kep.	Kepulauan
DE	Delaware	-kfl.	-kofel
Den.	Denmark	Kgl.	Kogel
Dép.	Département	-kgl.	-kogel
-df.	-dorf	km.	Kilómetro
Ea.	East	Kl.	Klein
Ec.	Ecuador	Kör.	Körfezi
E^{ción}	Estación	Kr.	Krasno, -yj, -aja, -oje
E. G.	Equatorial Guinea	KS	Kansas
f.	fontein	KY	Kentucky
Fd.	Feld	L.	Lake
-fd(e)	-felde(e)	LA	Lousiana
-fdn.	-felden	-lbn.	-leben
Fed.	Federal	L.^{d}	Land
F.^{êt}	Forêt	-l.^{d}	-land
Fj.	Fjord	Lim.	Limnē
-fj.	-fjord	L.^{le}	Little
FL	Florida	L.^{oa}	Lago(a)
Fr.	France, French	L.$^{una(s)}$	Laguna(s)
F.^{rte}	Fuerte	M.	Monte
F.^{t}	Fort	MA	Massachusetts
F.^{tin}	Fortín	Mal.	Malyj, -aja, -oje
G.	Gölü (lakes);		

Abbr.	Meaning	Abbr.	Meaning
M.^{as}	Montanhas	Ra.	Range
Mc.	Mac	Ra.^{s}	Ranges
MD	Maryland	R.^{ca}	Rocca
ME	Maine	Reg.	Region
Mex.	Mexico	Rep.	Republic
M.$^{gne(s)}$	Montagne(s)	Res.	Reservat
MI	Michigan	RI	Rhode Island
MN	Minnesota	Riv.	River
MO	Missouri	-riv.	-rivier
MS	Mississippi	S.	San
MT	Montana	...(-)S.	(-see) See
Mt.	Mount	S. Afr.	South Africa
M.^{t}	Mont	S.^{ai}	Sungai
M.^{ti}	Monti	SC	South Carolina
Mt.^{n}	Mountain	Sd.	Sund
Mt.^{s}	Mountains	S.^{d}	Sound
M.$^{t(s)}$	Mont(s)	SD	South Dakota
n.	nos	S.^{ei}	Sungei
Nat.	National-	Sev.	Severnyj, -aja, -oje
Nat.-P(ark)	Nationalpark	S.^{i}	Sidi
NC	North Carolina	Sl.`	Slovenski, -a, -e
ND	North Dakota	S.^{nia}	Serrania
N.^{do}	Nevado	Sp.	Spitze
Ndr.	Nieder	-sp.	-spitze (mountains);
NE	Nebraska		-sperre (waters)
Neth.	Netherlands	S.$^{ra(s)}$	Sierra(s)
NH	New Hampshire	Sred.	Srednе, -ij, -'aja, eje
Nic.	Nicaragua	S.^{rra}	Serra
Niž.	Nižnij, -'aja, -eje, -ije	St.	Sankt
nizm.	nizmenost'	S.^{t}	Saint
NJ	New Jersey	-st.	-stadt (cities, towns);
NM	New Mexico		-stein (mountains)
Norw.	Norway	Sta	Santa
Nov.	Novo, -yj, -aja, -oje	Star.	Staryj, -aja, -oje
NV	Nevada	S.^{te}	Sainte
N.^{va}	Nueva	S.th	South
NY	New York	-stn.	-stetten
N. Z.	New Zealand	st.^{n}	stein
o.	ostrov	S.^{to}	Santo
Ob.	Ober	Str.	Street
Obl.	Oblast	Tel.	Teluk
OH	Ohio	Ter.	Territory
OK	Oklahoma	TN	Tennessee
OR	Oregon	T.^{ng}	Tanjung
Ou	Ouèd	TX	Texas
o-va	ostrova	U. K.	Unitede Kingdom
oz.	ozero	Unt.	Unter, -ere
P.	Port (cities, towns);	USA	United States
	Paß (passes);	UT	Utah
	Pulau (islands)	V.	Volcán
PA	Pennsylvania	V^{a}	Vila
Pan.	Panama	VA	Virginia
Pass.	Passage	V.^{an}	Volćán
P.^{c}	Pic	vdchr.	vodochranilišče
P.^{co}	Pico	Vel.	Veliki, -aja, -oje
Pen.	Peninsula	Ven.	Venezuela
per.	pereval	Verch.	Verchne, -ij, -'aja, -eje, -ije
P.$^{it(e)}$	Petit(e)	V.ey	Valley
P.$^{k(s)}$	Peak(s)	V.^{la}	Villa
Pl.^{a}	Planina	vozvyš.	vozvyšenost'
Pl.^{au}	Plateau	VT	Vermont
-pl.^{au}	-plateau	W.	West
Port.	Portugal	(-)W.	(-wald) Wald
p-ov	poluostrov	-w	-witz
P.-p.	Pulau-pulau	WA	Washington
Pr.	Prince	-wd(e).	-wald(e)
Prov.	Province, Provincial	W.^{di}	Wadi
P.^{rto}	Puerto	WI	Wisconsin
P.^{so}	Passo	-wlr.	weiler
P.^{t}	Point	WV	West Virginia
P.$^{t(e)}$	Point(e)	WY	Wyoming
P.^{ta}	Punta	zal.	zaliv
P.^{to}	Porto	Zap.	Zapadnaja
P.^{zo}	Pizzo	zapov.	zapovednik
R	Rio		

Symbols

River, stream		Railroad	
Drying river, stream		Primary railroad	} on larger scale maps
Intermittent river, stream		Secondary railroad	
Canal		Suspended cable car	
Canal under construction		Railroad under construction	
Waterfall, rapids		Train ferry	
Dam		Tunnel	
Fresh-water or salt-water lake with permanent shore line		Major highway	
Fresh-water or salt-water lake with variable or undefined shore line		Expressway	} on larger scale maps
Intermittent lake		Expressway under construction	
Well in dry area		Caravan route, path, track	
Swamp, Bog		Ferry	
Salt marsh		Pass	
Flood area		Airport, Airfield	
Mud flat			
Reef, Coral reef			
Glacier		International boundary	
Average pack ice limit in summer		Boundary of autonomous area	
Average pack ice limit in winter		Boundary of subsidiary administrative unit	
Shelf ice		MADRID	National capital
Sand desert, gravel desert, etc.		Salem / Nachičevan'	Principal cities of subsidiary administrative units

Place			Locality				
	LONDON	over 1,000,000 Inhabitants		L.-HARROW		Inhabited spot, station	
	BRISBANE	500,000 -1,000,000 Inhabitants		BR.-IPSWICH		Ruins	
	ROSTOCK	100,000 - 500,000 Inhabitants		R.-WARNEMÜNDE		Castle, fort	
	Segovia	50,000 - 100,000 Inhabitants				Monastery, church	
	Douglas	10,000 - 50,000 Inhabitants					
	Ansó	unter 10,000 Inhabitants				Monument	
						Lighthouse	
						Nature reserve	

Type Styles

VENEZUELA	Independent country		GOBI / Mallorca / Devon	Physical regions and islands
Tirol	Subordinate administrative unit			
(Port.) (Port.)	Political affiliation		OCÉANO / North Sea / Volga	Hydrography
VALENCIA / Cáceres / Dover	Places		Devil's Hole	Ocean basin, trench, ridge etc.
ATLAS / Causses	Mountain		2834	Altitude and depth in meters
Snowdon	Mountain, cape, pass, glacier			Depth of lakes below surface

Altitudes and Depths

1:15,000,000 and smaller	>10000	10000	8000	6000	4000	2000	200	0 Depr. 0	200	500	1000	2000	3000	4000	5000	> 5000 m
	>32809	32809	26247	19685	13124	6562	656	0 Depr. 0	656	1640	3281	6562	9843	13124	16405	>16405 ft

1:5,000,000 to 1:7,500,000	>10000	10000	8000	6000	4000	2000	200	0 Depr. 0	100	200	500	1000	2000	3000	4000	5000	> 5000 m
	>32809	32809	26247	19685	13124	6562	656	0 Depr. 0	328	656	1640	3281	6562	9843	13124	16405	>16405 ft

1:1,000,000	> 200	200	100	40	20	0 Depr. 0	100	200	300	500	700	1000	1500	2000	2500	3000	> 3000 m
	> 656	656	328	131	66	0 Depr. 0	328	656	984	1640	2297	3281	4921	6562	8202	9843	> 9843 ft

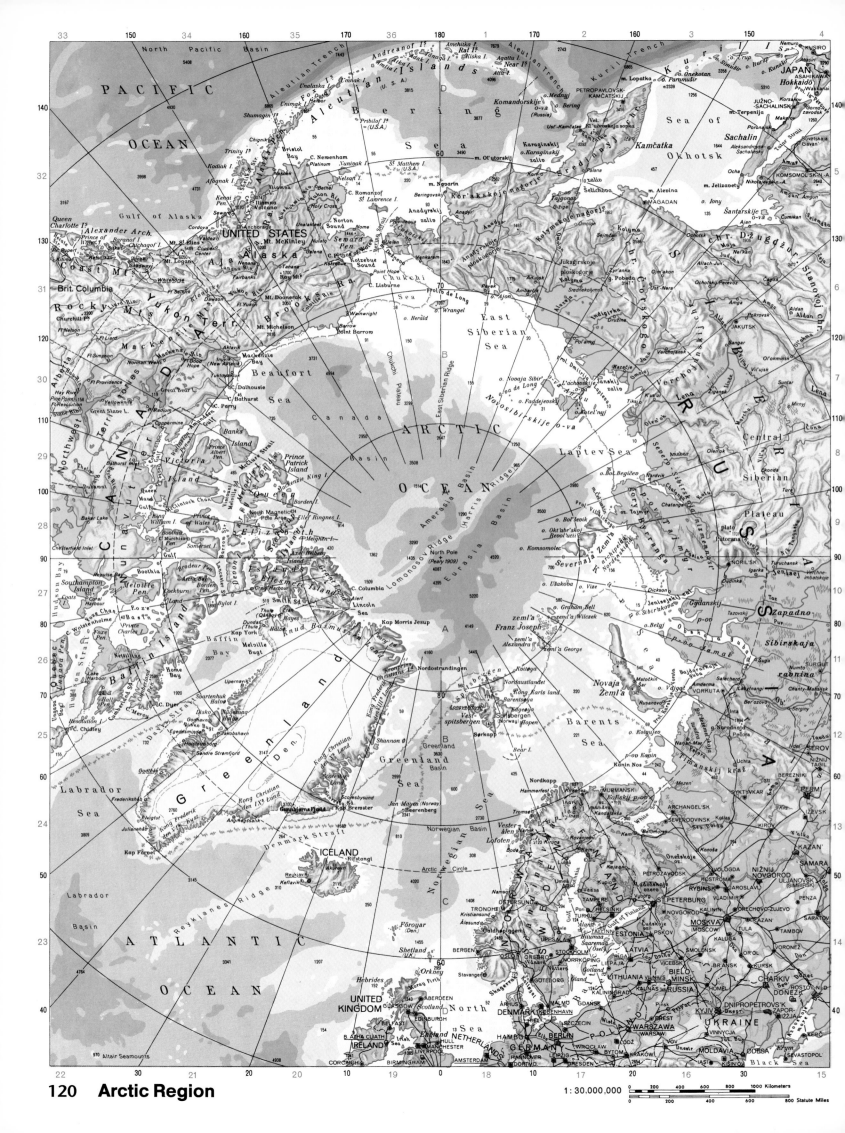

1 : 30,000,000

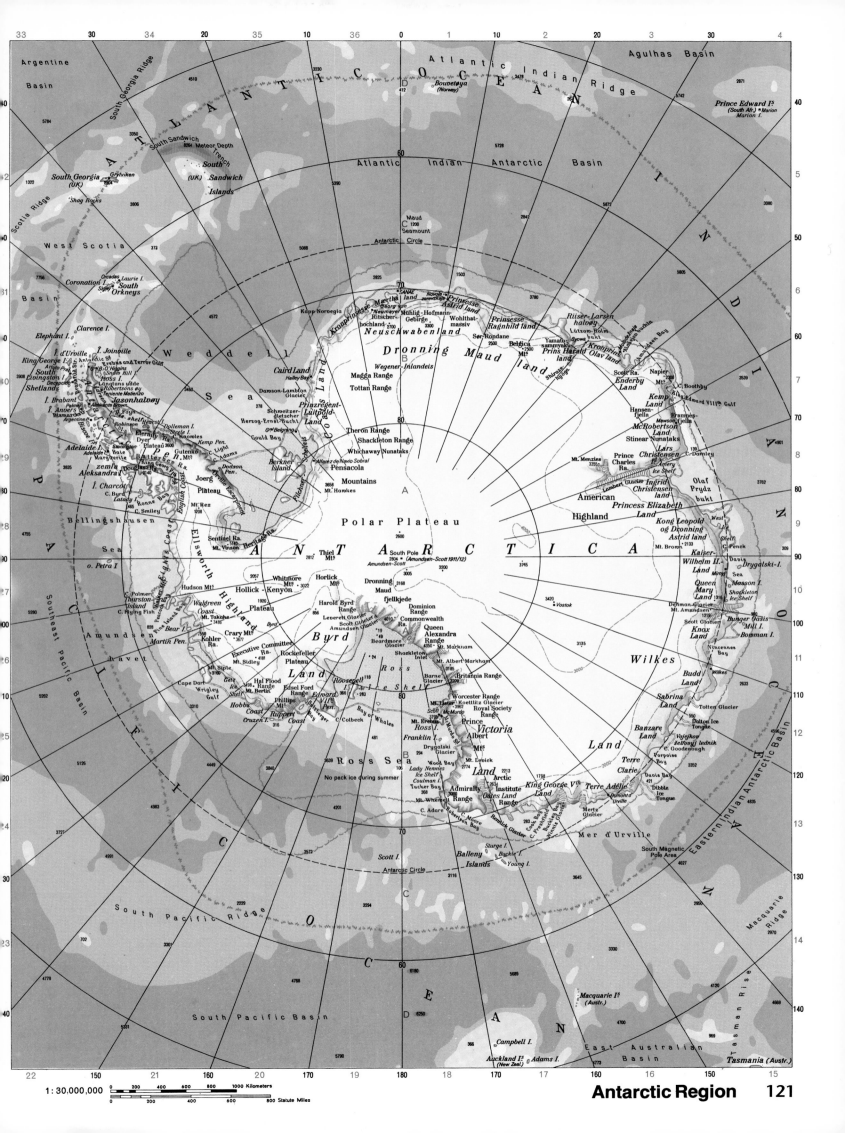

Antarctic Region 121

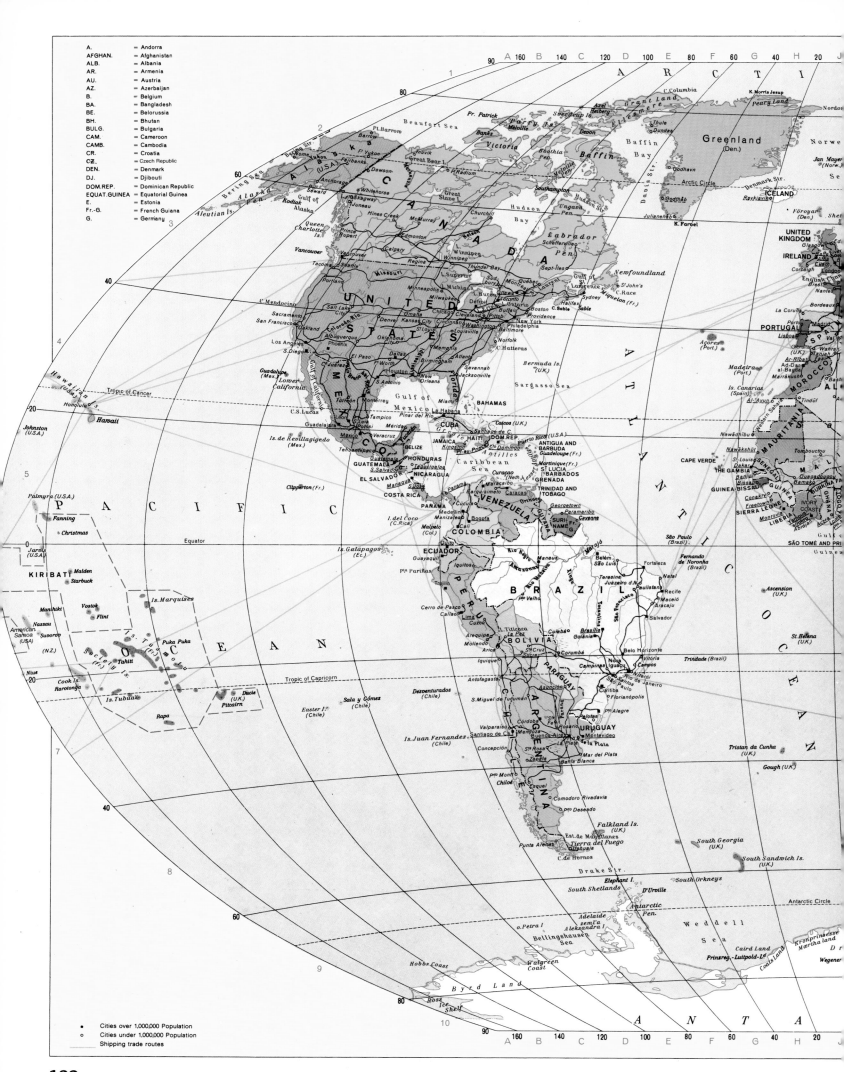

A. = Andorra
AFGHAN. = Afghanistan
ALB. = Albania
AR. = Armenia
AU. = Austria
AZ. = Azerbaijan
B. = Belgium
BA. = Bangladesh
BE. = Belorussia
BH. = Bhutan
BULG. = Bulgaria
CAM. = Cameroon
CAMB. = Cambodia
CR. = Croatia
CZ. = Czech Republic
DEN. = Denmark
DJ. = Djibouti
DOM.REP. = Dominican Republic
EQUAT.GUINEA = Equatorial Guinea
E. = Estonia
Fr.-G. = French Guiana
G. = Germany

■ Cities over 1,000,000 Population
○ Cities under 1,000,000 Population
— Shipping trade routes

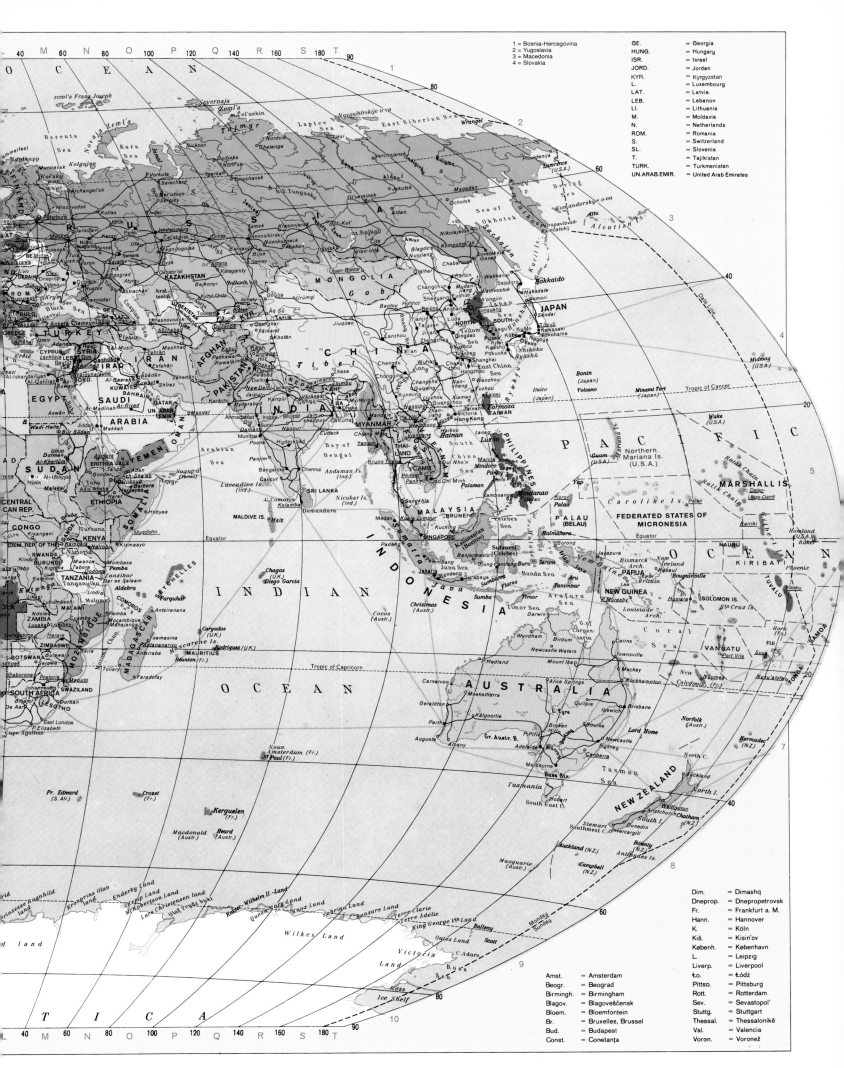

1 = Bosnia-Hercegovina		GE.	= Georgia
2 = Yugoslavia		HUNG.	= Hungary
3 = Macedonia		ISR.	= Israel
4 = Slovakia		JORD.	= Jordan
		KYR.	= Kyrgyzstan
		L.	= Luxembourg
		LAT.	= Latvia
		LEB.	= Lebanon
		LI.	= Lithuania
		M.	= Moldavia
		N.	= Netherlands
		ROM.	= Romania
		S.	= Switzerland
		SL.	= Slovenia
		T.	= Tajikistan
		TURK.	= Turkmenistan
		UN.ARAB.EMIR.	= United Arab Emirates

Dim.	= Dimashq
Dneprop.	= Dnepropetrovsk
Fr.	= Frankfurt a. M.
Hann.	= Hannover
K.	= Köln
Kiš.	= Kisin'ov
Københ.	= København
L.	= Leipzig
Liverp.	= Liverpool
Ło.	= Łódź
Pittsb.	= Pittsburg
Rott.	= Rotterdam
Sev.	= Sevastopol'
Stuttg.	= Stuttgart
Thessal.	= Thessaloníkē
Val.	= Valencia
Voron.	= Voronež

Amst.	= Amsterdam
Beogr.	= Beograd
Birmingh.	= Birmingham
Blagov.	= Blagoveščensk
Bloem.	= Bloemfontein
Br.	= Bruxelles, Brussel
Bud.	= Budapest
Const.	= Constanţa

World, political   123

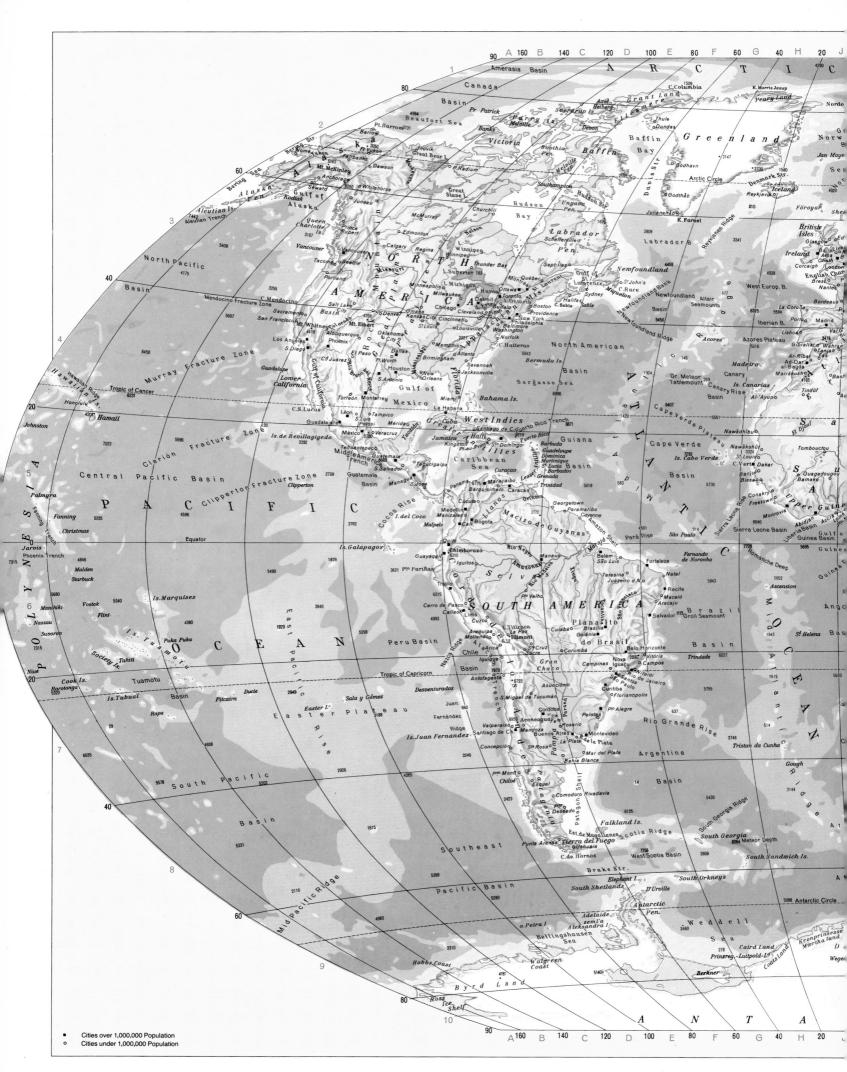

Cities over 1,000,000 Population
Cities under 1,000,000 Population

Dim. = Dimashq
Dneprop. = Dnepropetrovsk
Fr. = Frankfurt a. M.
Hann. = Hannover
K. = Köln
Kiš. = Kišin'ov
København. = København
L. = Leipzig
Liverp. = Liverpool
Ło. = Łódź
Pittsb. = Pittsburg
Rott. = Rotterdam
Sev. = Sevastopol'
Stuttg. = Stuttgart
Thessal. = Thessalonikē
Val. = Valencia
Voron. = Voronež

Amst. = Amsterdam
Beogr. = Beograd
Birmingh. = Birmingham
Blagov. = Blagoveščensk
Bloem. = Bloemfontein
Br. = Bruxelles, Brussel
Bud. = Budapest
Const. = Constanţa

1:15,000,000

Europe, political 127

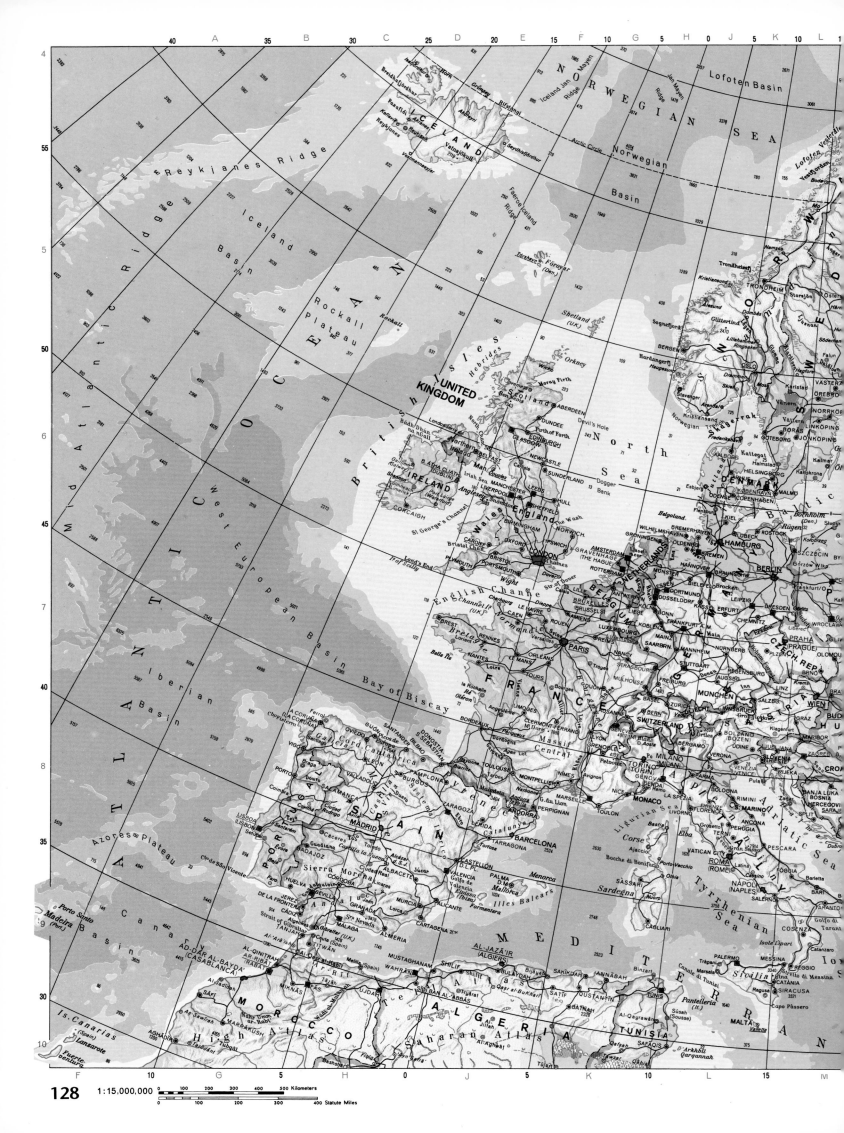

2 Nachicevan to Azerbaijan

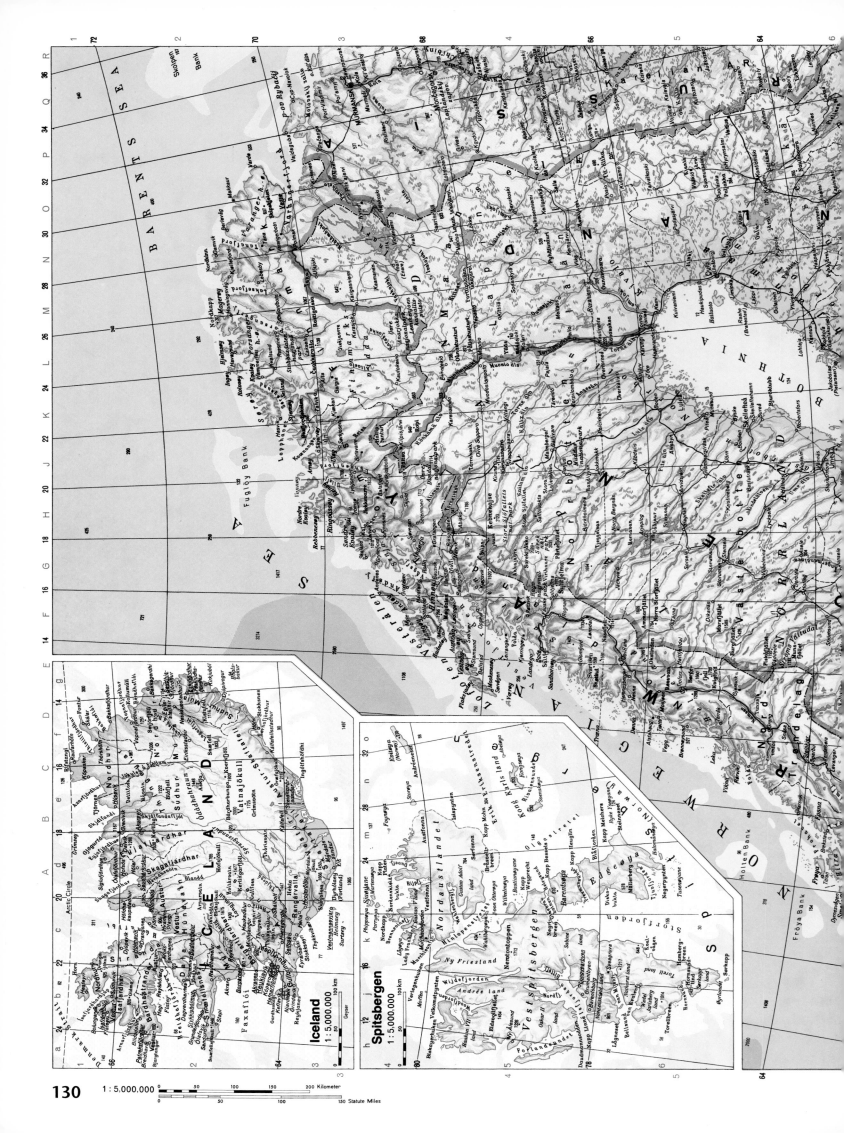

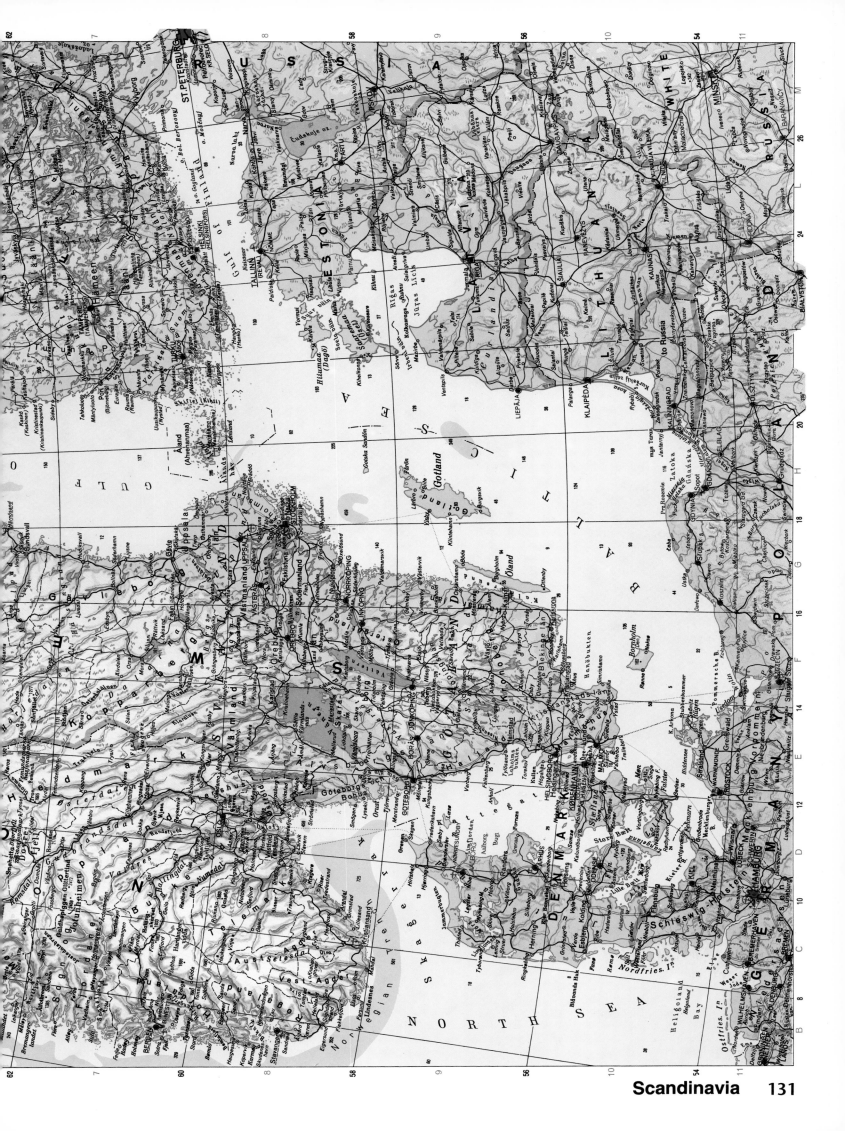

132 British Isles

1 : 5,000,000

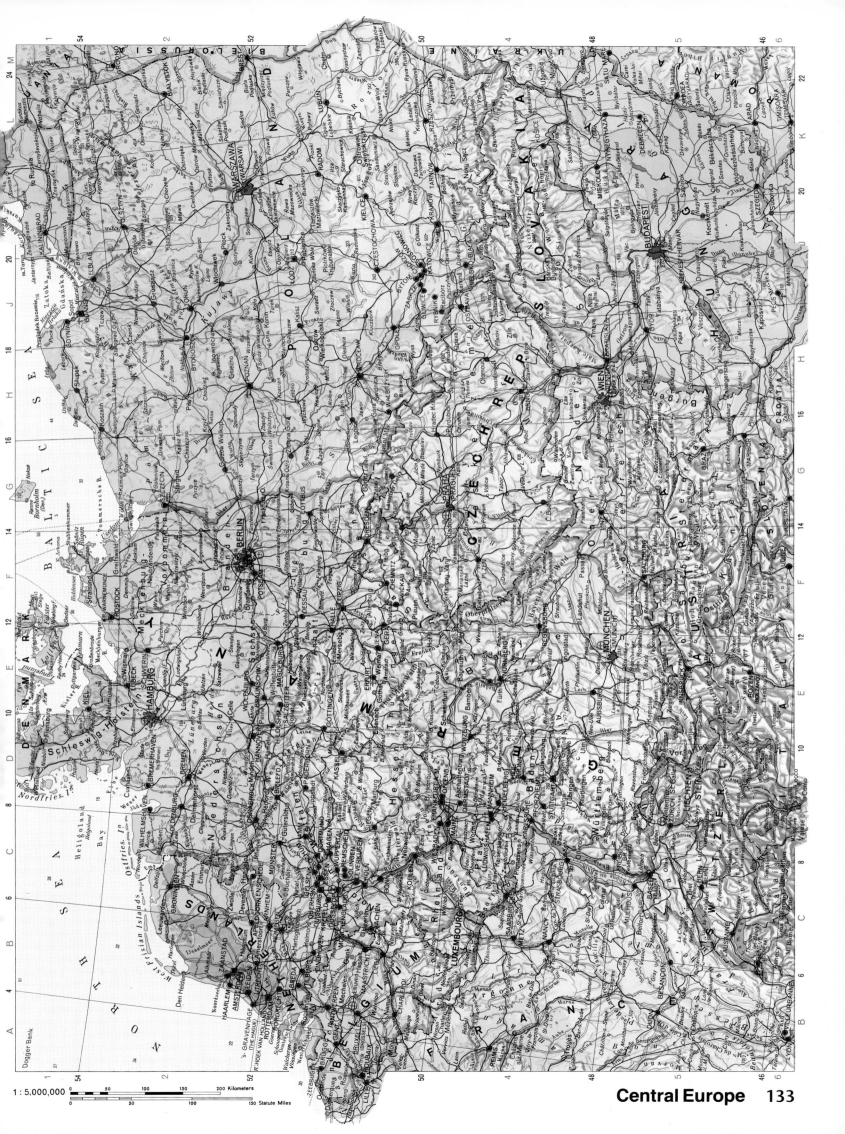

1 : 5,000,000

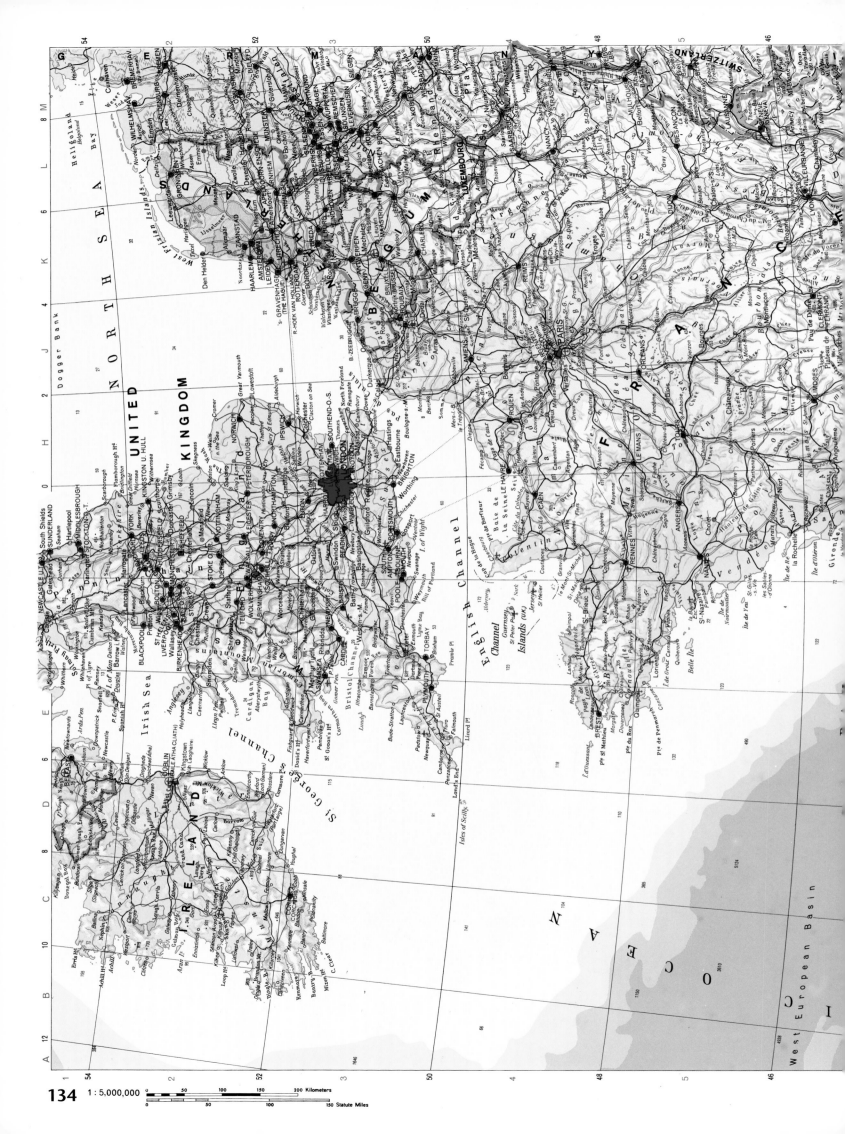

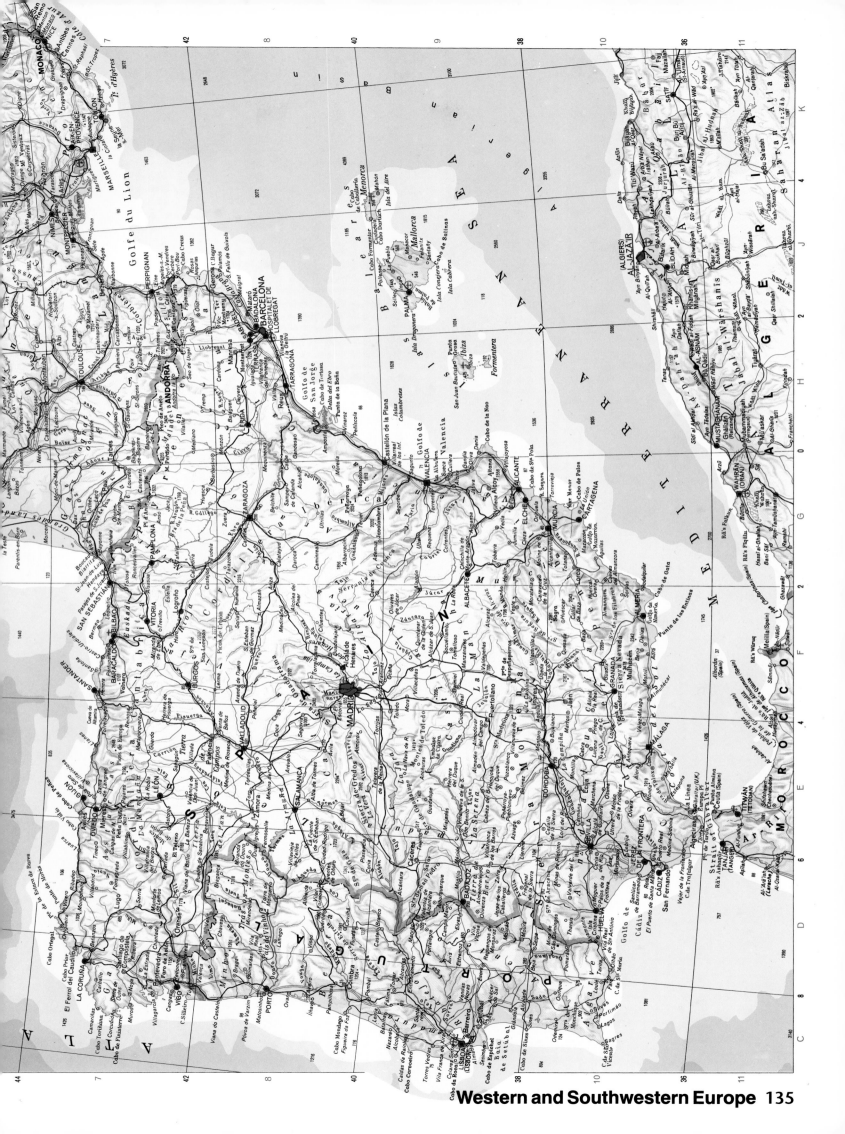

1 : 5,000,000

50   100   150   200 Kilometers

0   50   100

0   50   100   150 Statute Miles

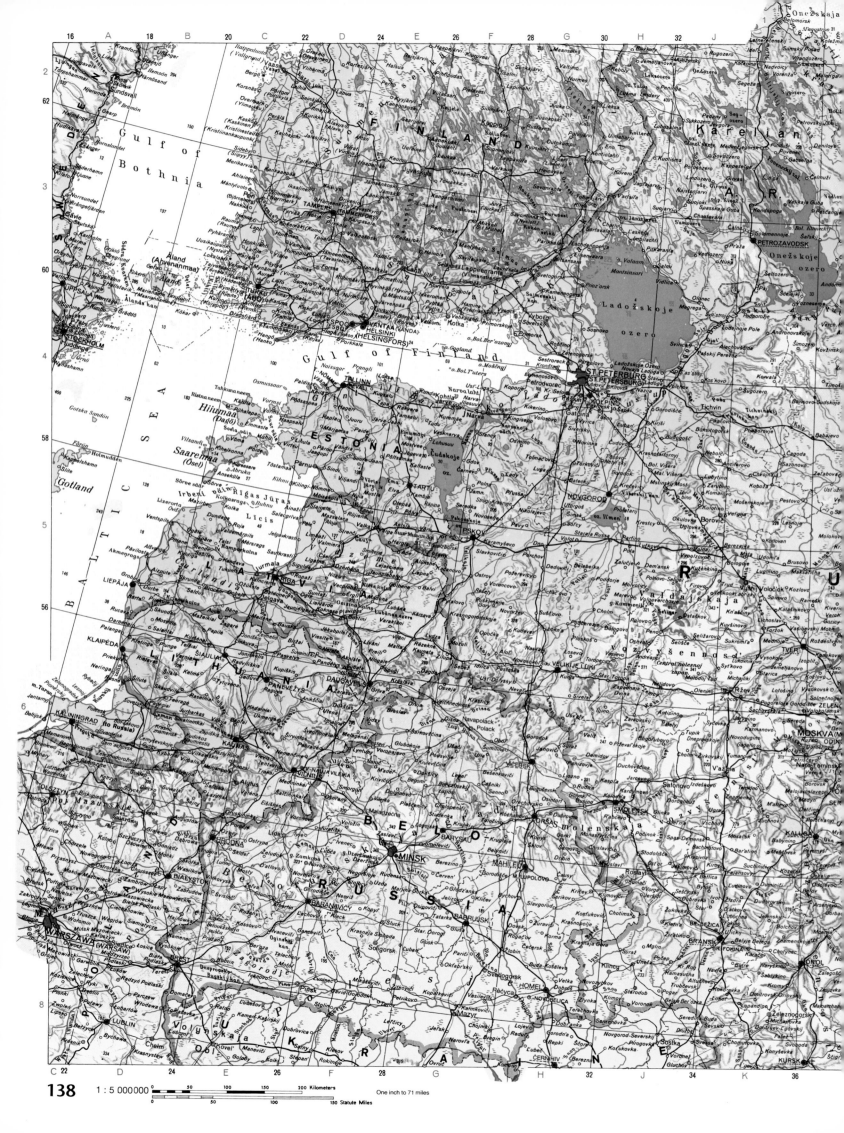

1 : 5 000 000

50   100   150   200 Kilometers

One inch to 71 miles

50   100

150 Statute Miles

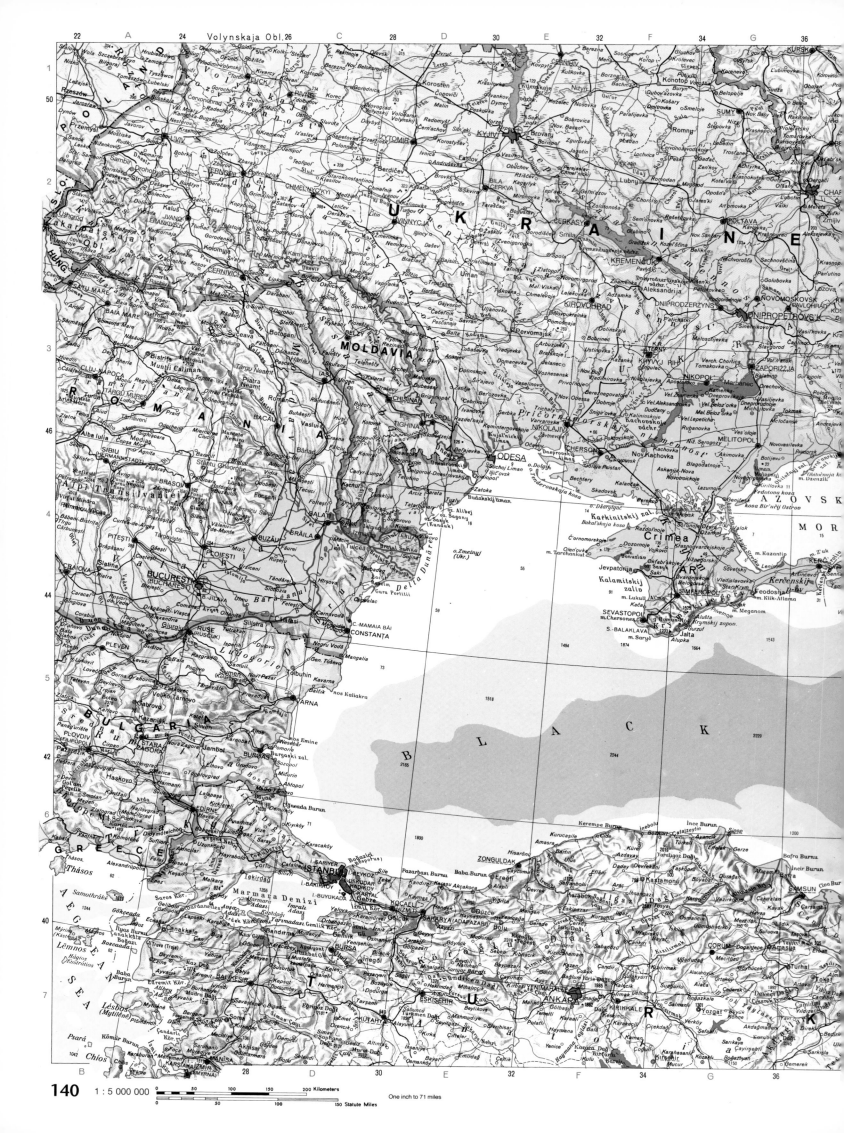

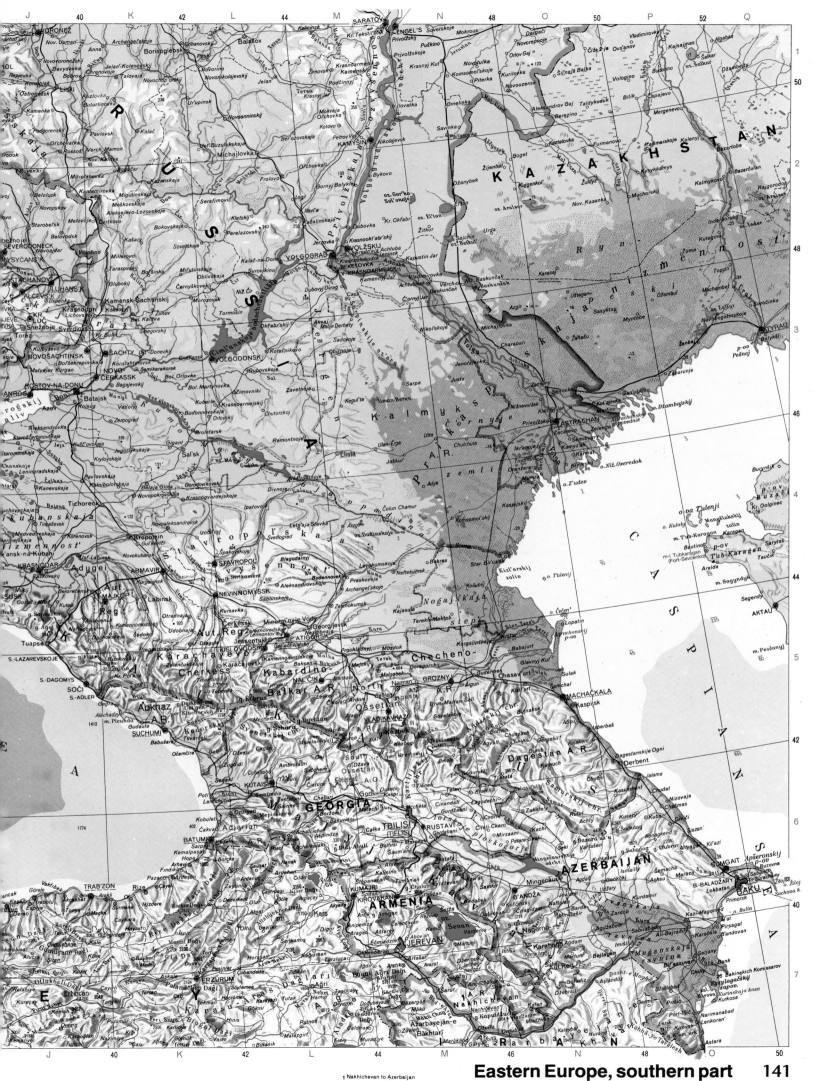

↑ Nakhichevan to Azerbaijan

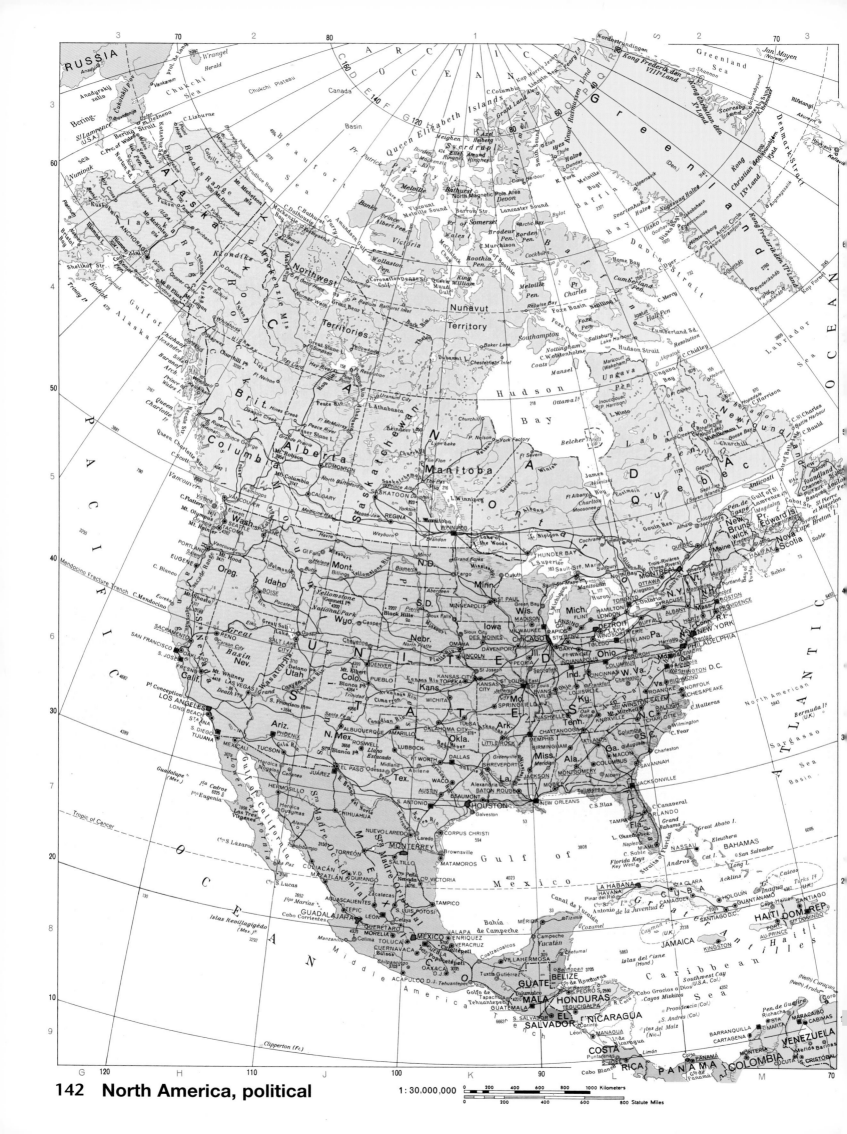

142   **North America, political**

1 : 30,000,000

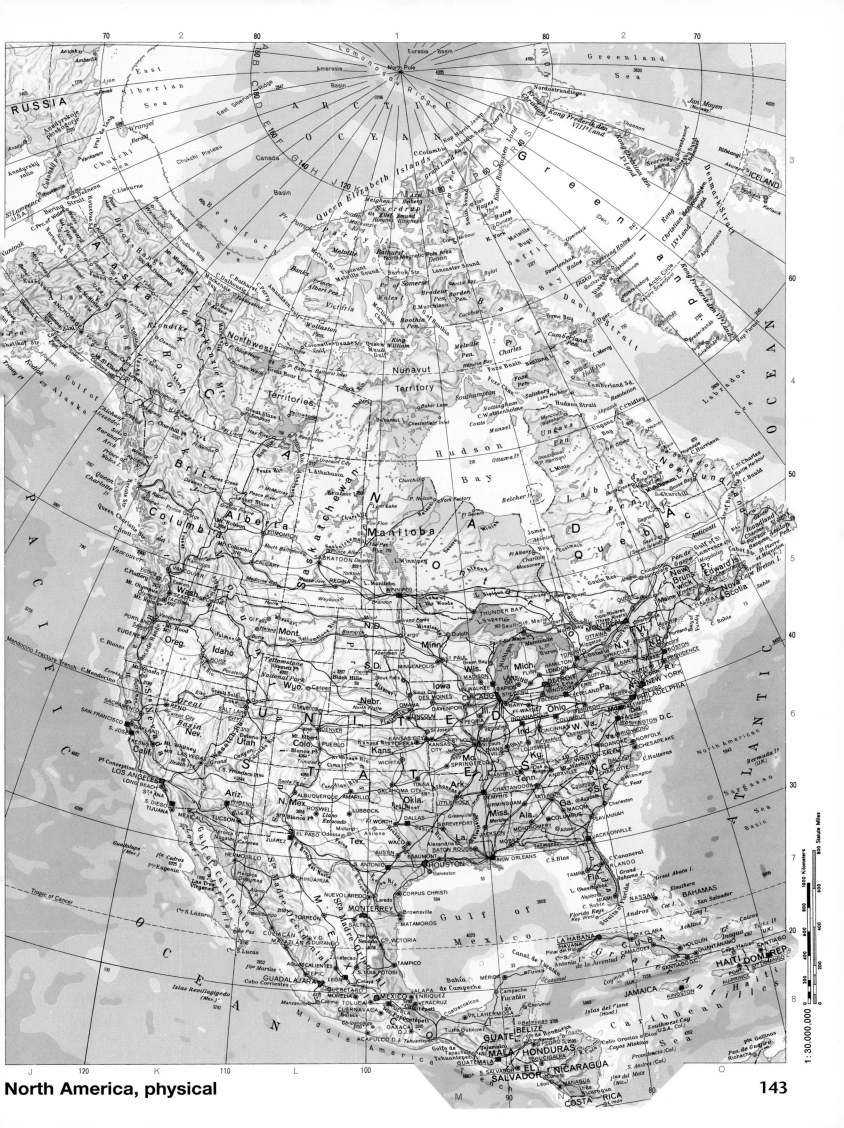

North America, physical

Panama Canal
1:1,000,000

1:15,000,000

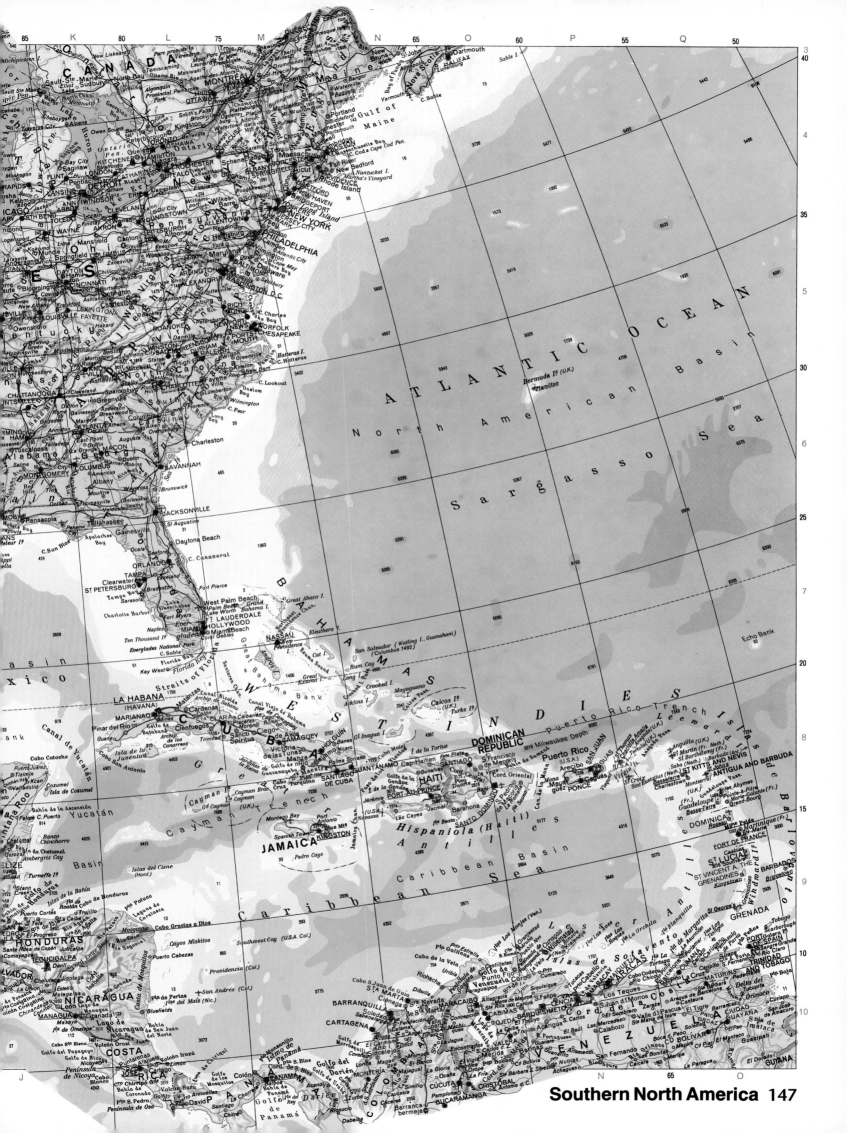

Southern North America 147

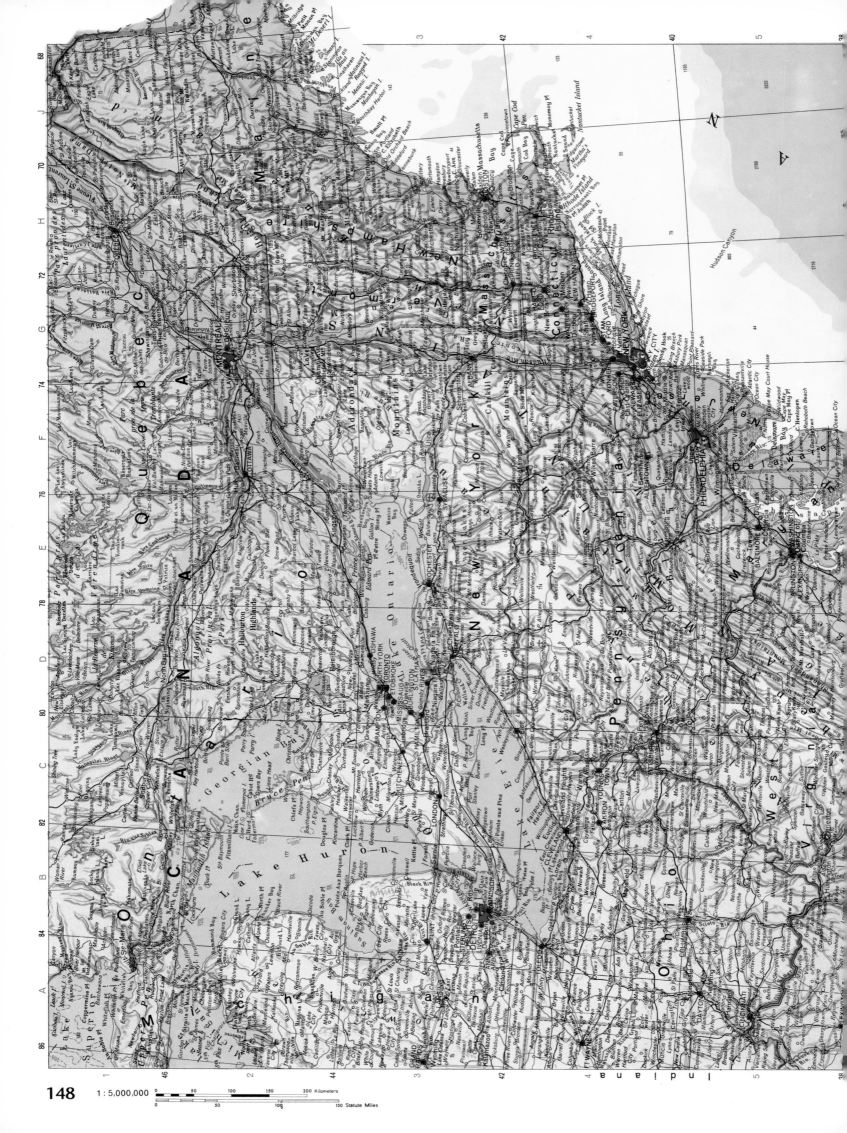

1 : 5,000,000

0   50   100   150   200 Kilometers

0   50   100   150 Statute Miles

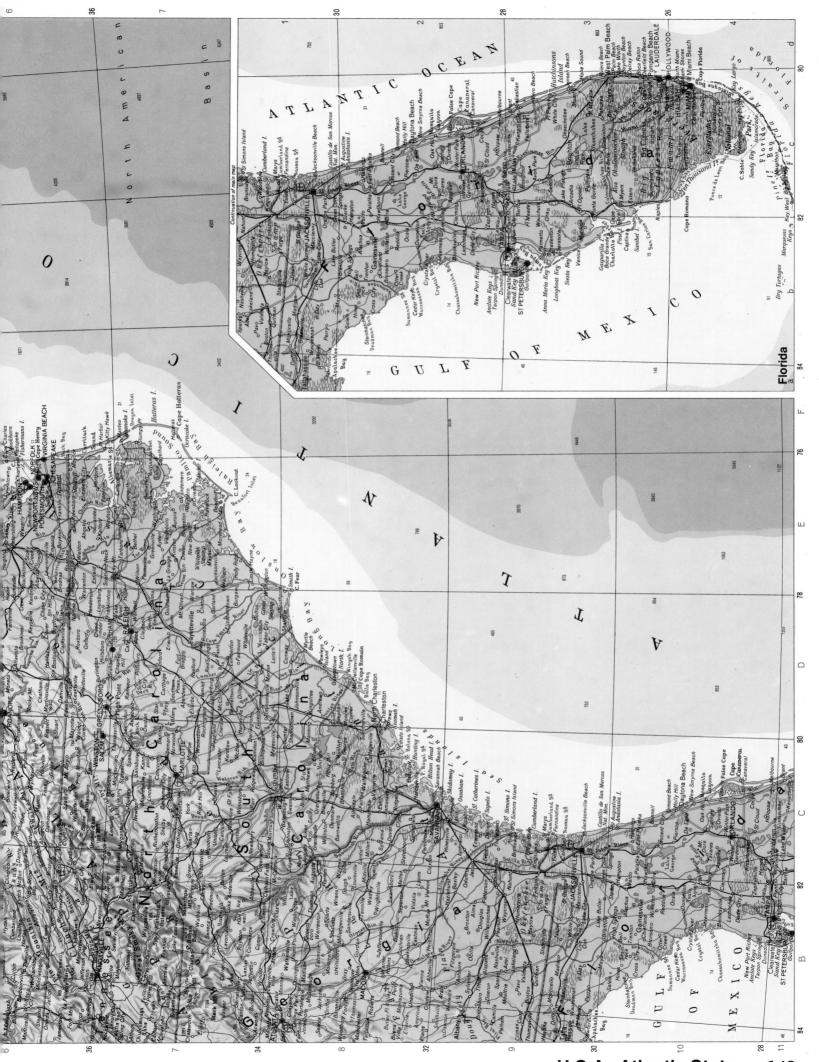

U.S.A., Atlantic States   149

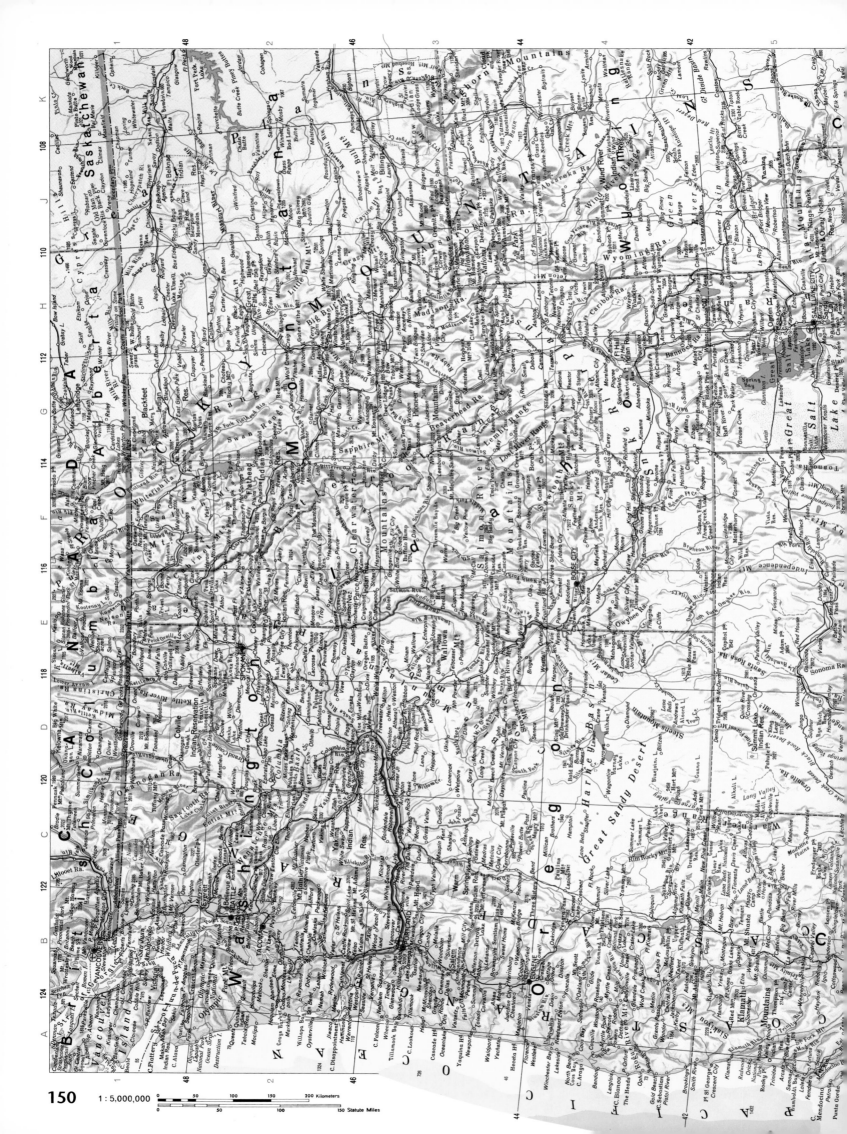

150

1 : 5,000,000

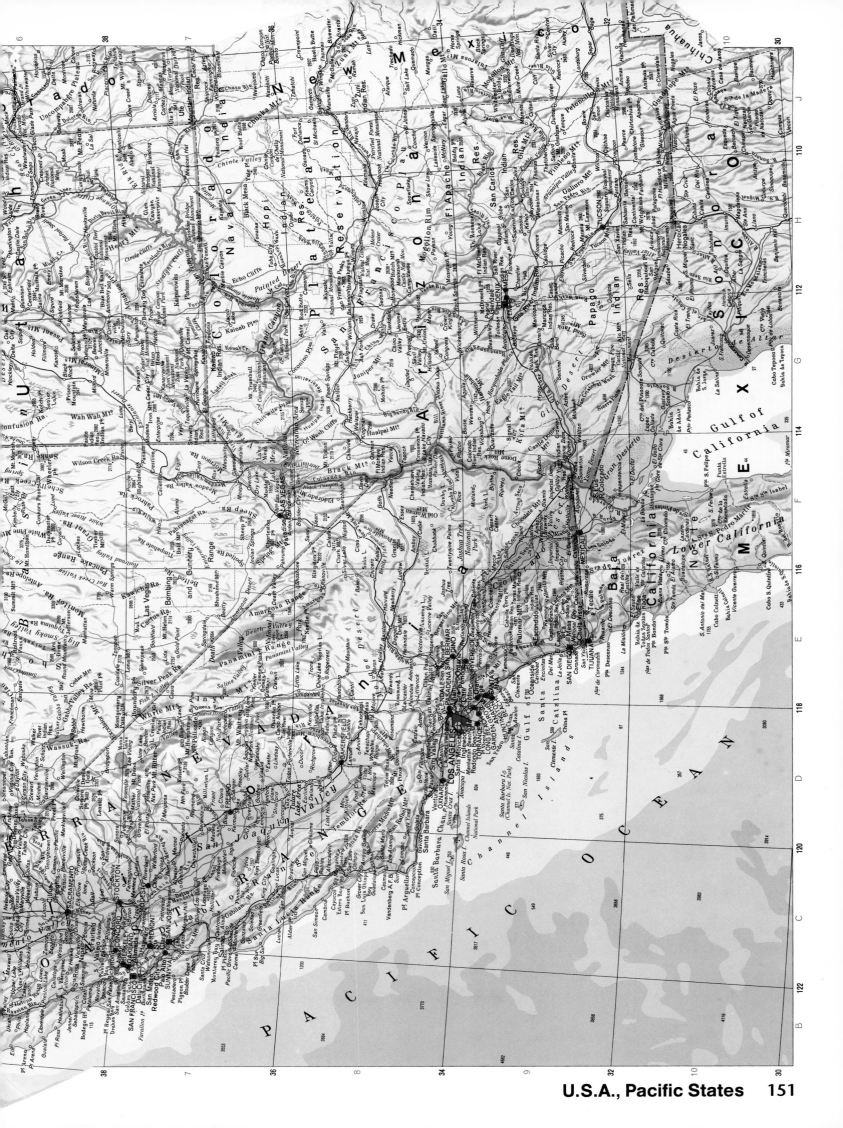

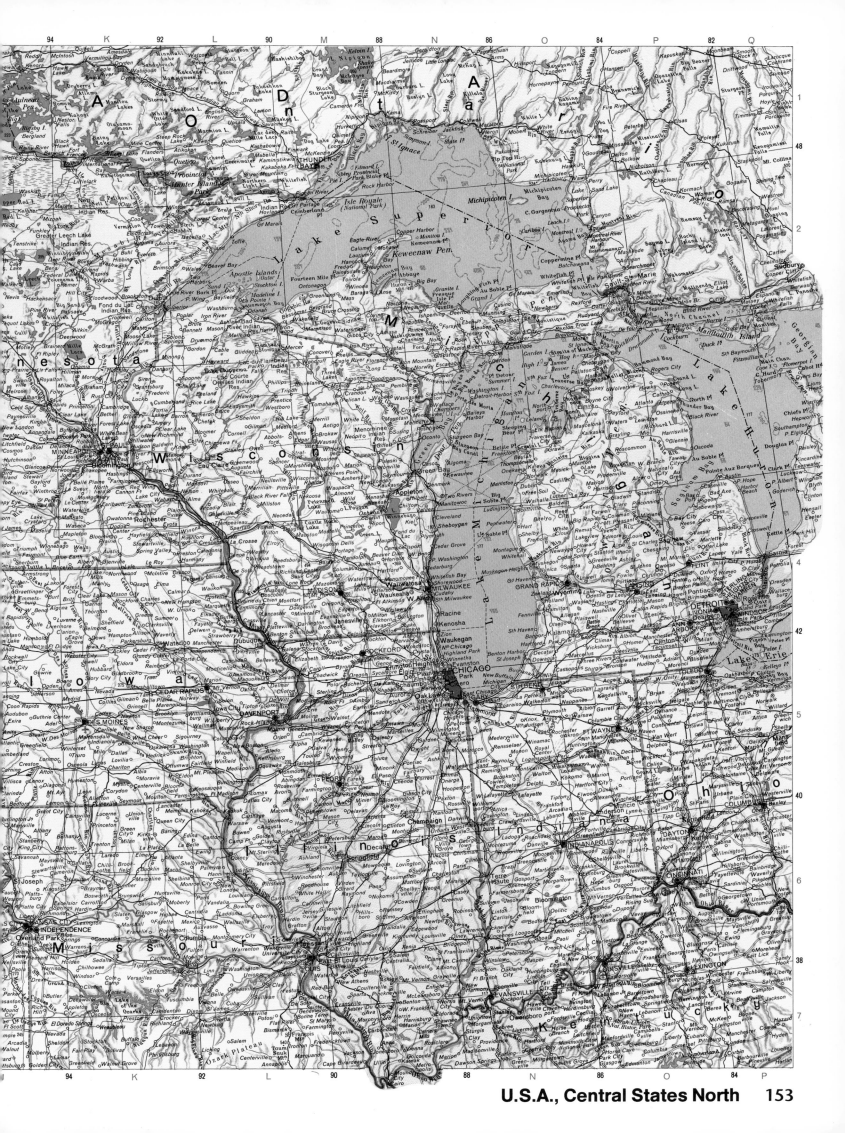

U.S.A., Central States North   153

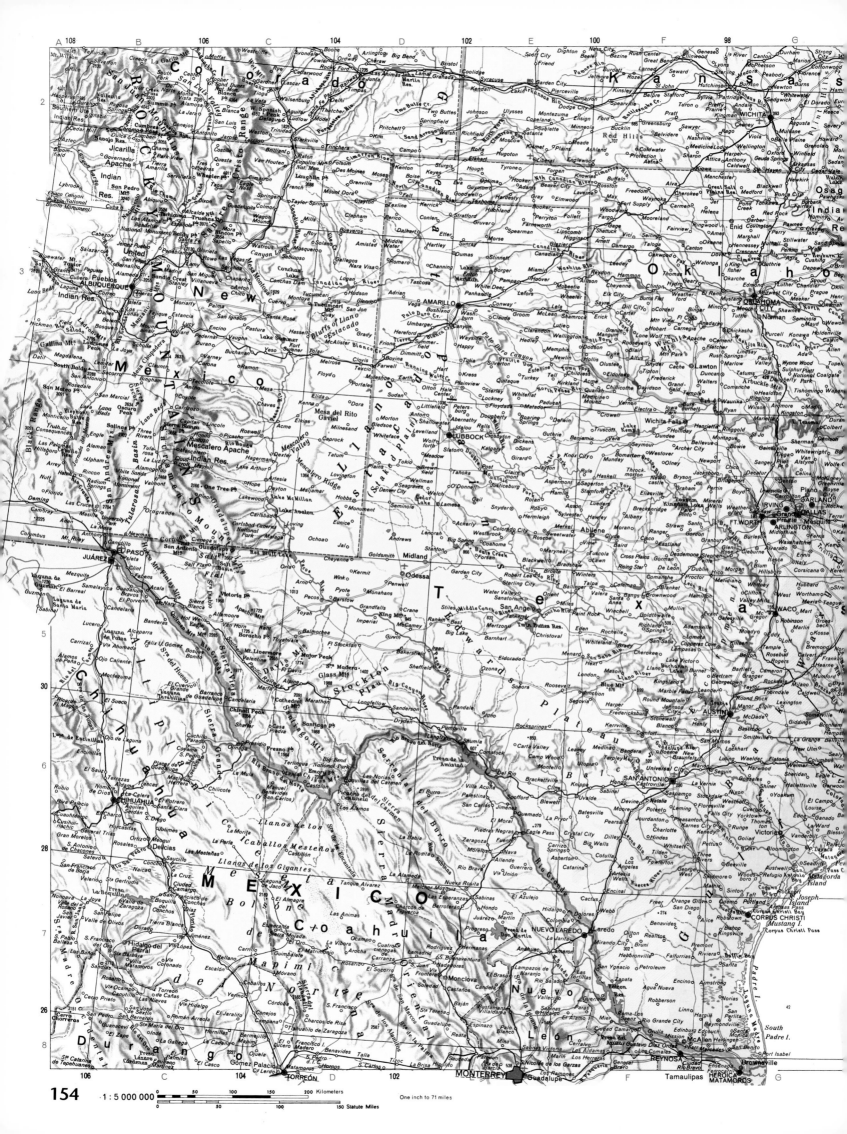

156   **South America, political**

1:30,000,000

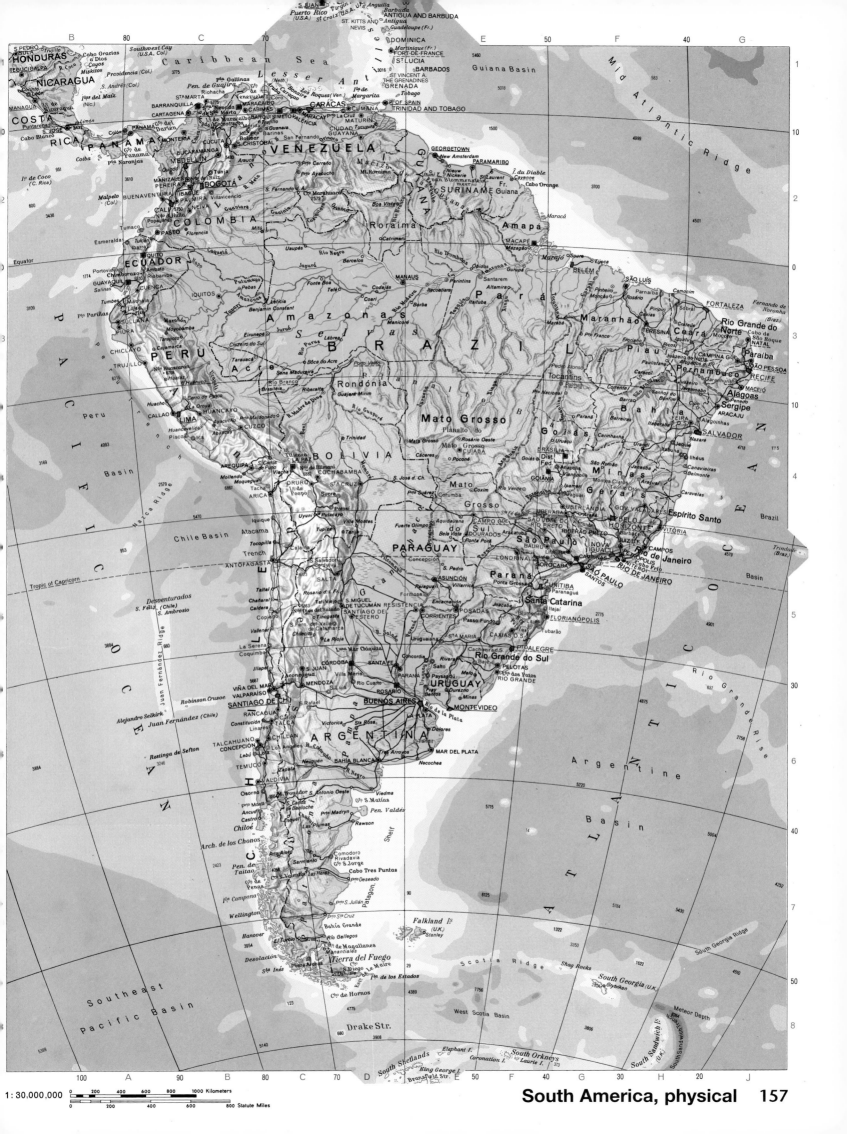

South America, physical 157

Northern South America 159

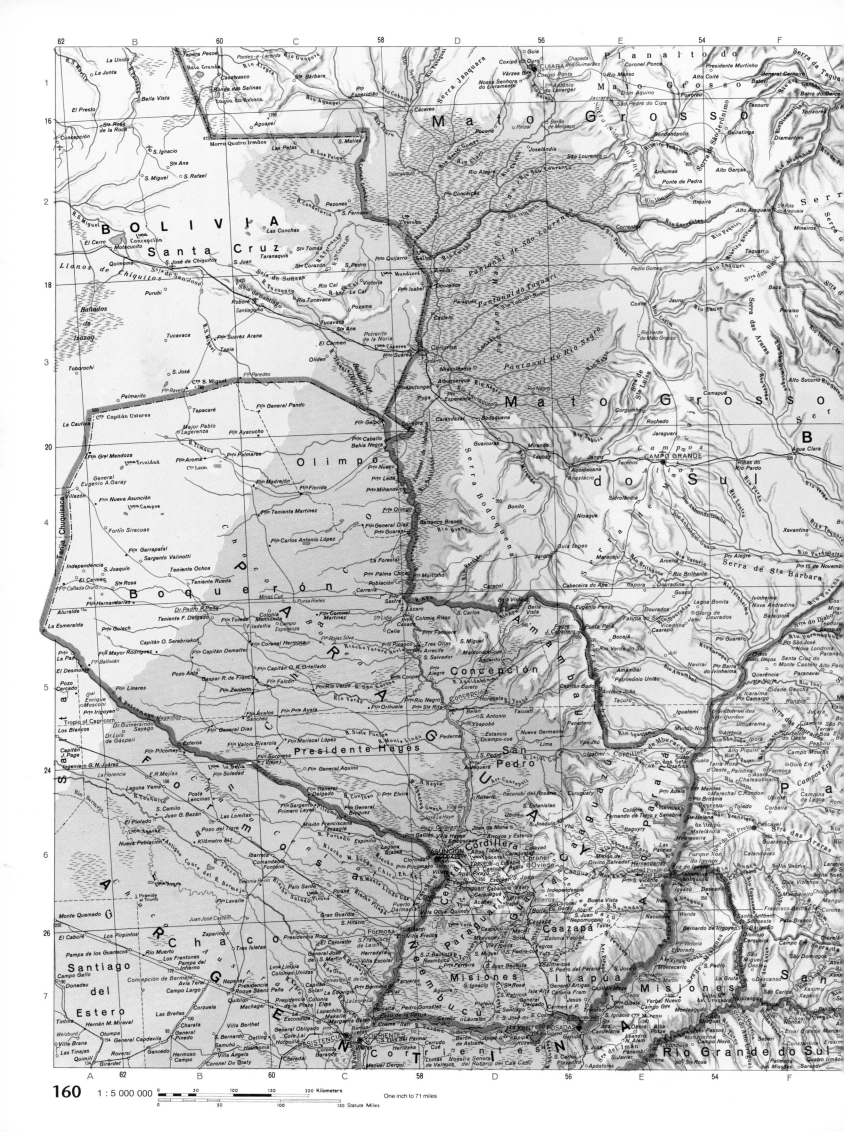

160   1 : 5 000 000

0   50   100   150   200 Kilometers

0   50   100   150 Statute Miles

One inch to 71 miles

Southern Brazil and Paraguay 161

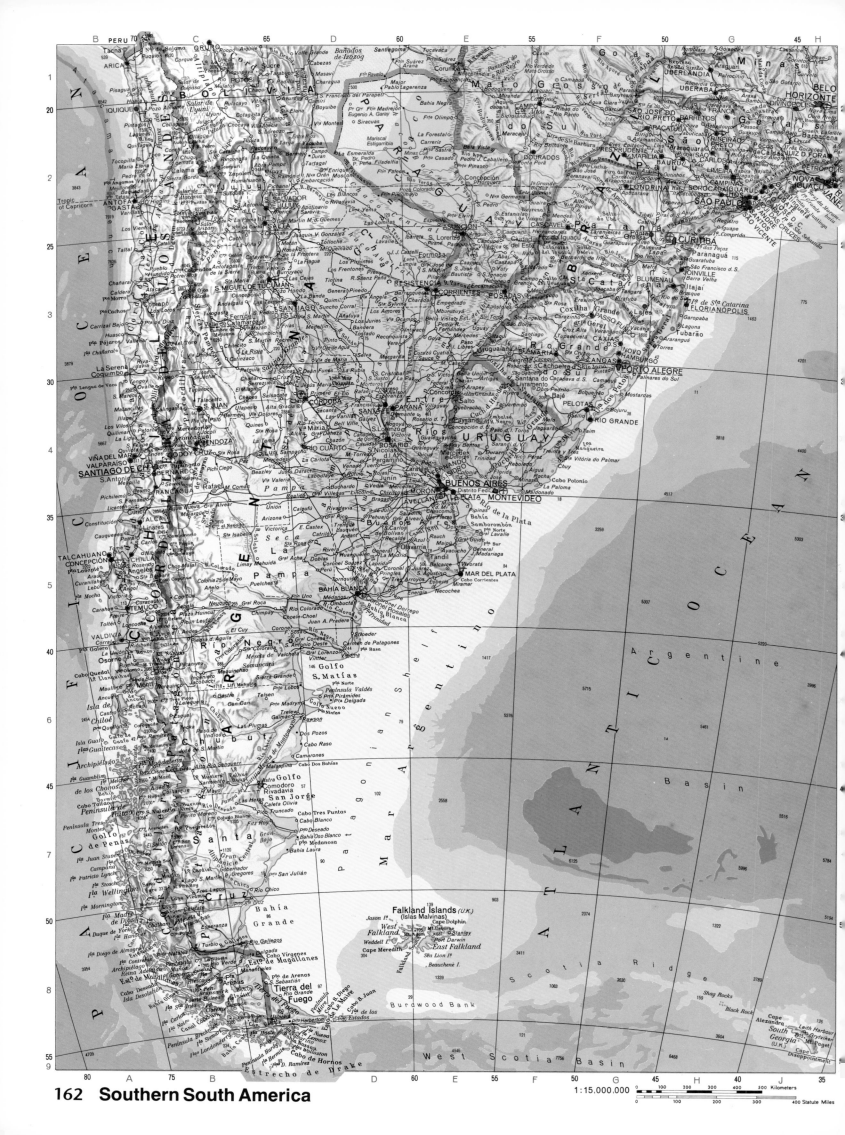

1:15,000,000

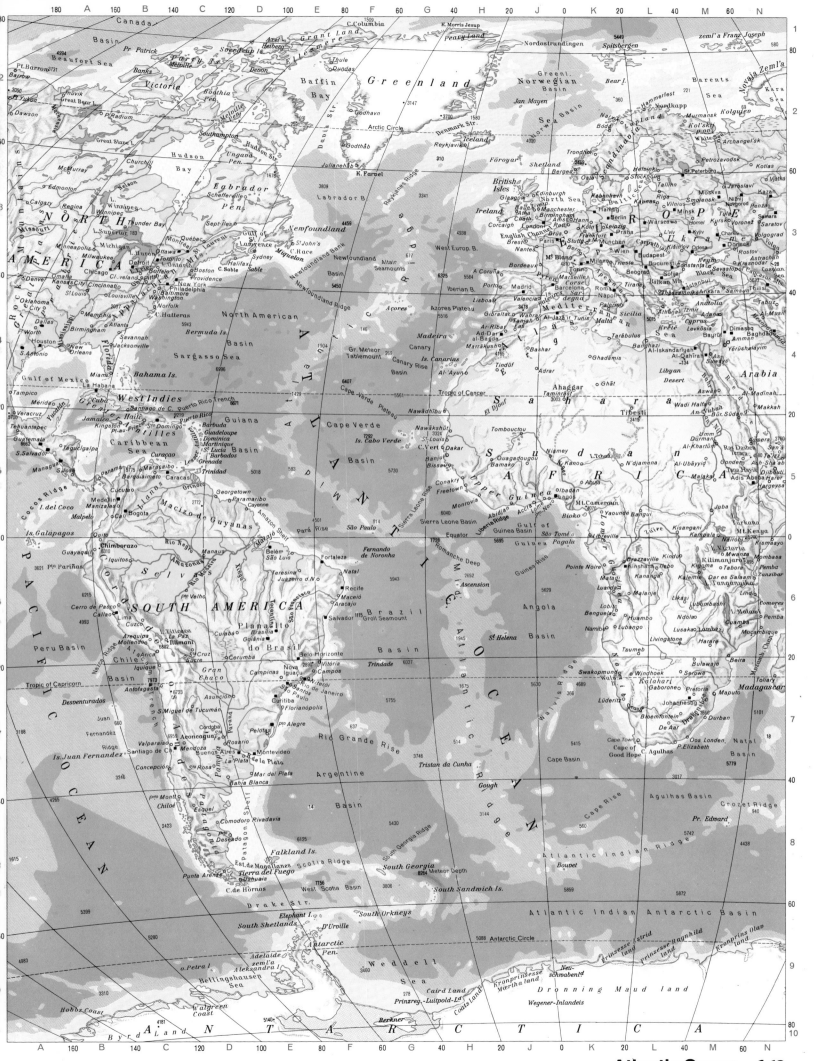

Africa, political

1:40,000,000

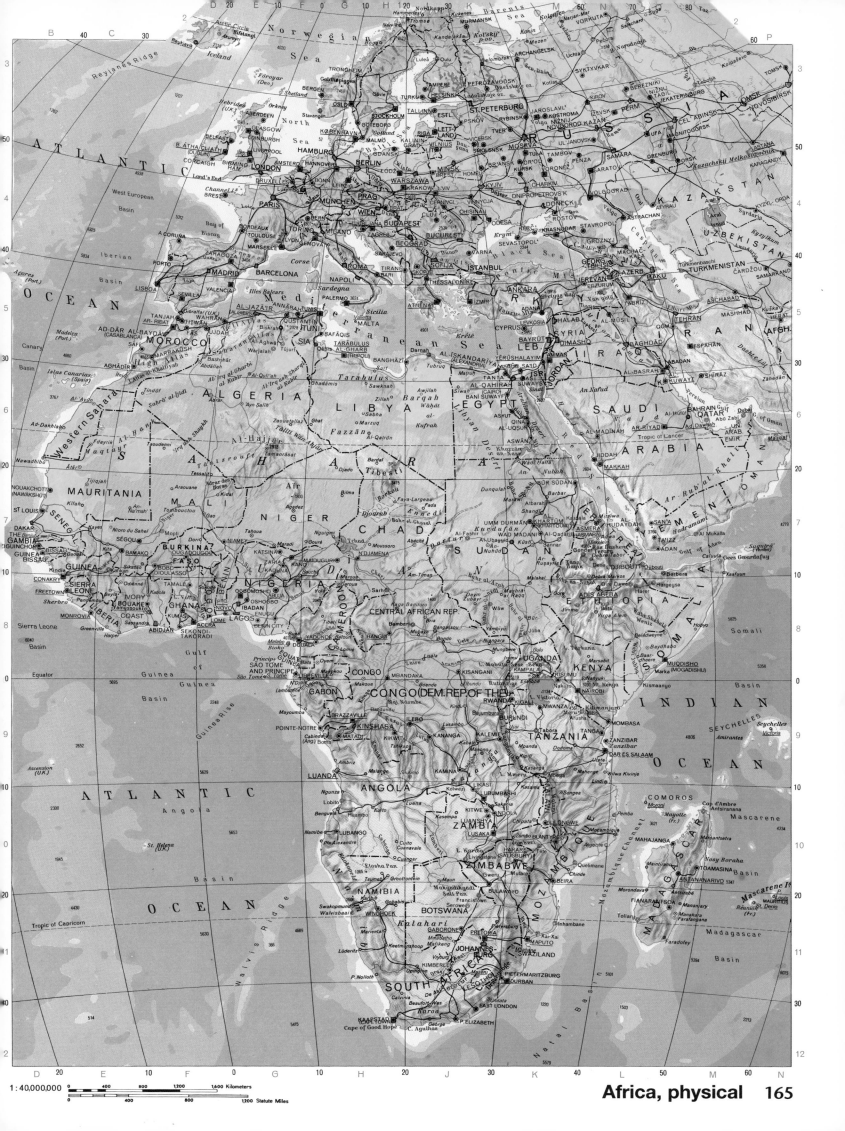

Africa, physical   165

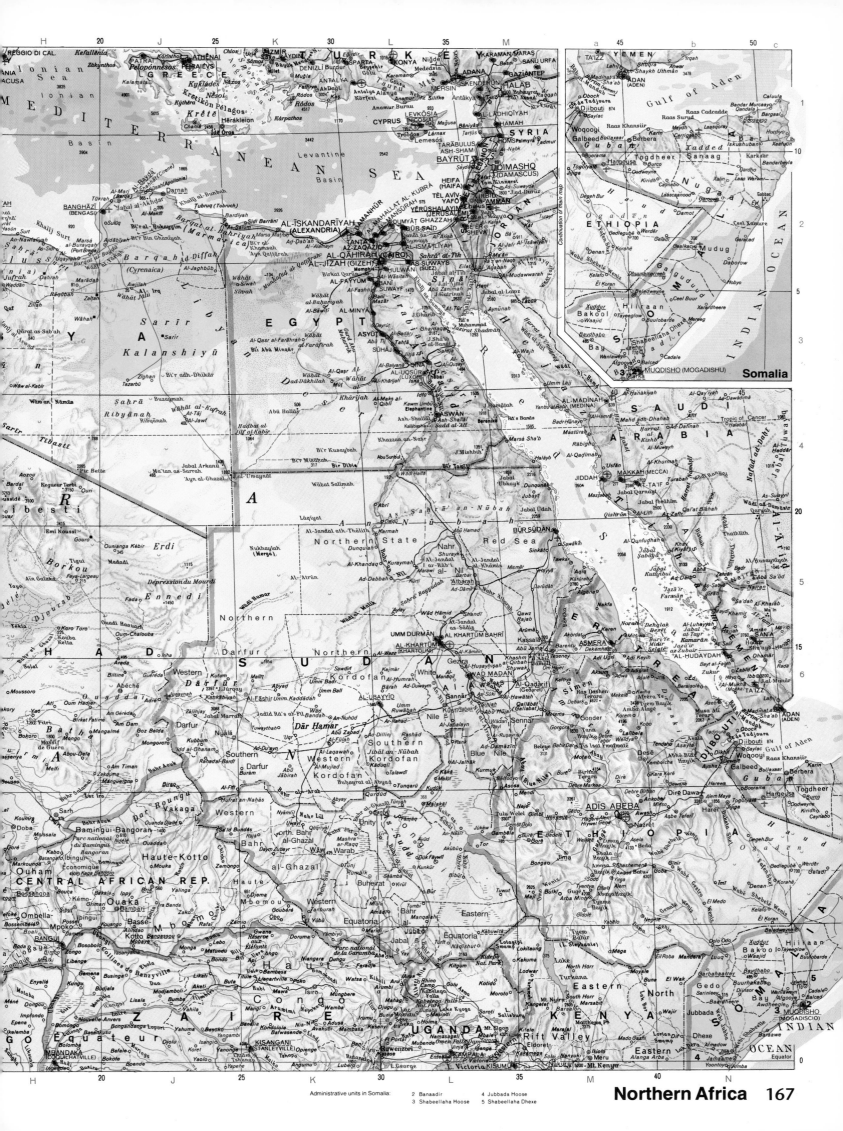

Administrative units in Somalia:
2 Banaadir
3 Shabeellaha Hoose
4 Jubbada Hoose
5 Shabeellaha Dhexe

Somalia

Southern Africa 169

Administrative units in Zimbabwe

1 Matabeleland North	4 Manicaland	7 Mashonaland West
2 Matabeleland South	5 Mashonaland East	8 Midlands
3 Masvingo	6 Mashonaland Central	

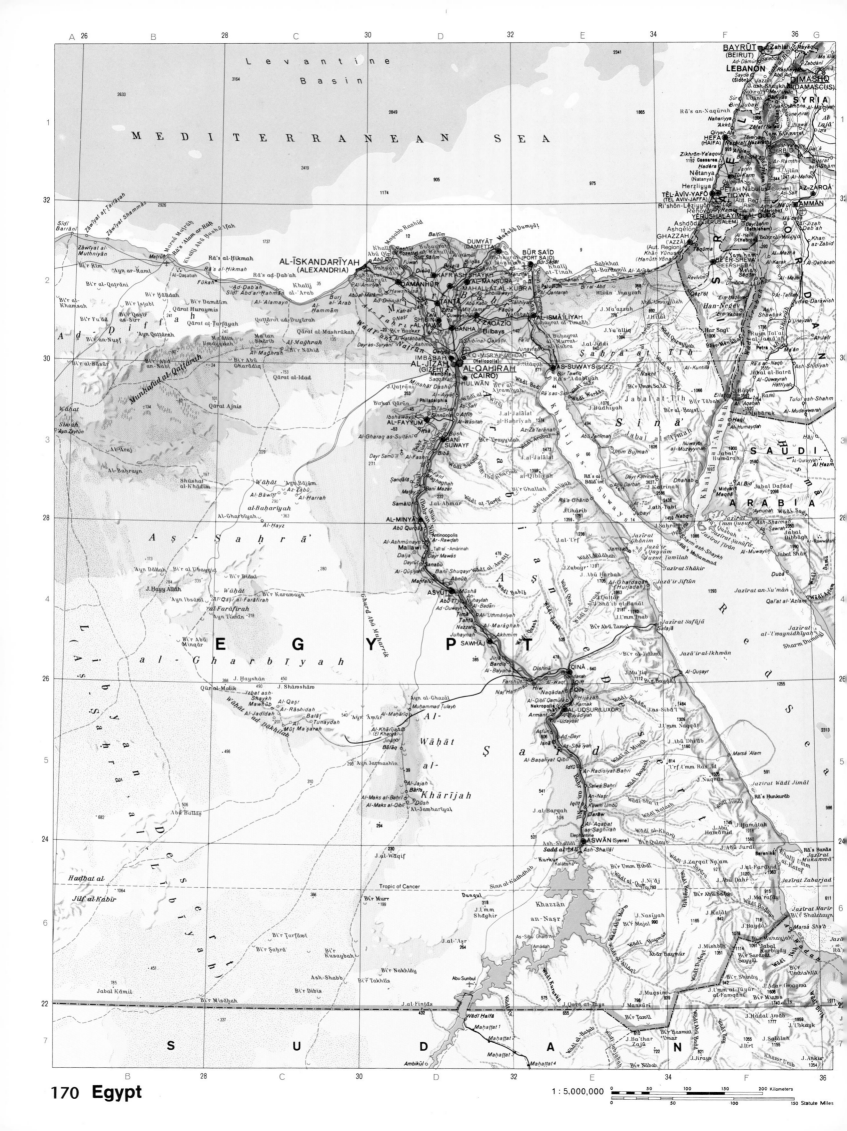

170 Egypt

1 : 5,000,000

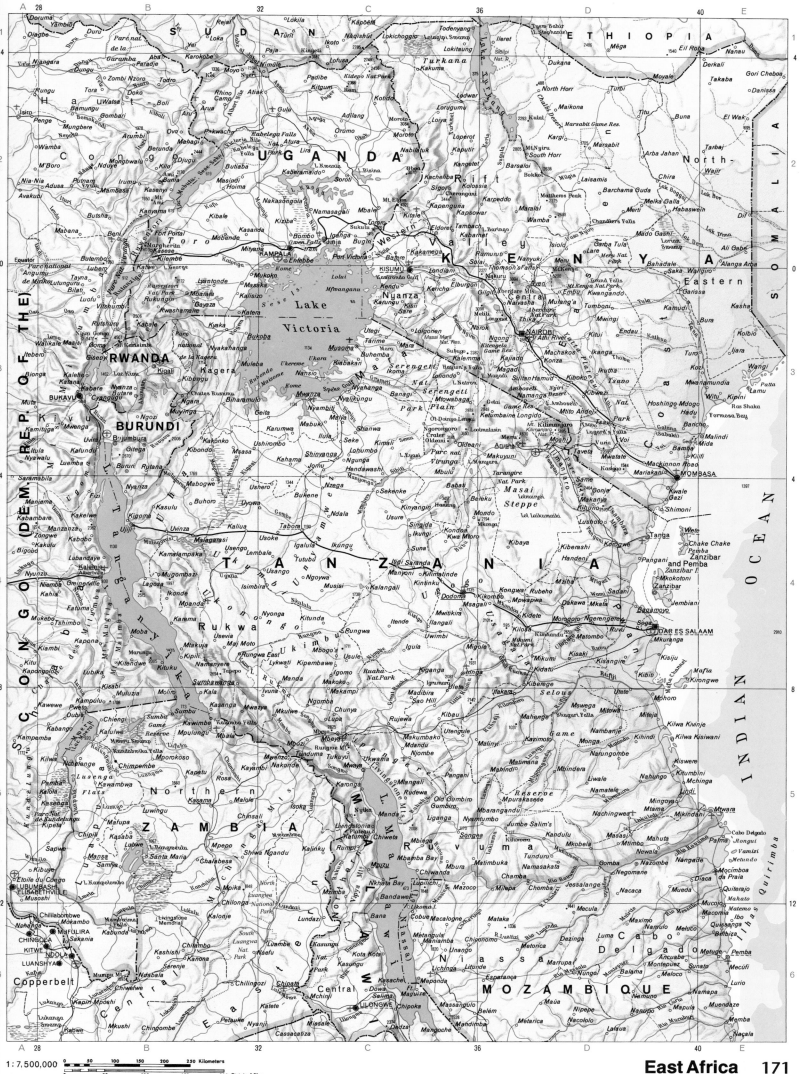

1 : 7,500,000

0 50 100 150 200 250 Kilometers

One inch to 107 miles

0 50 100 150

200 Statute Miles

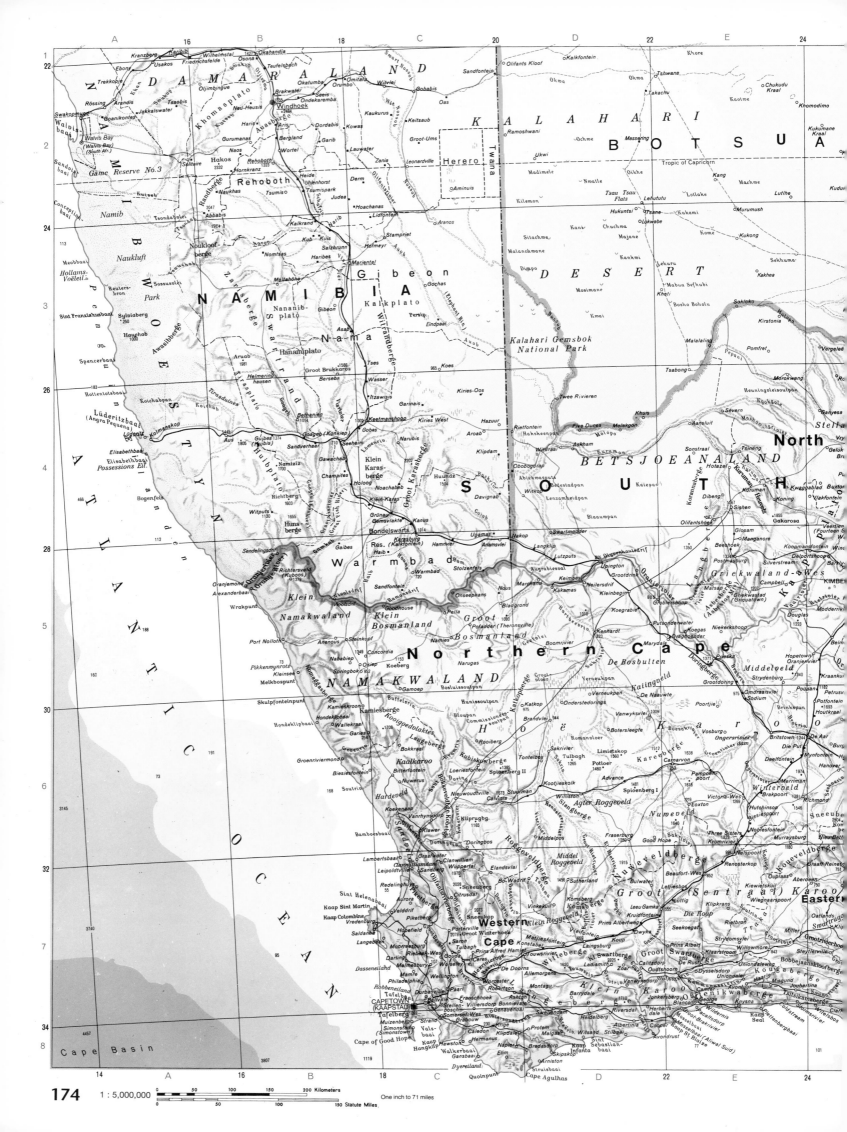

1 : 5,000,000

One inch to 71 miles

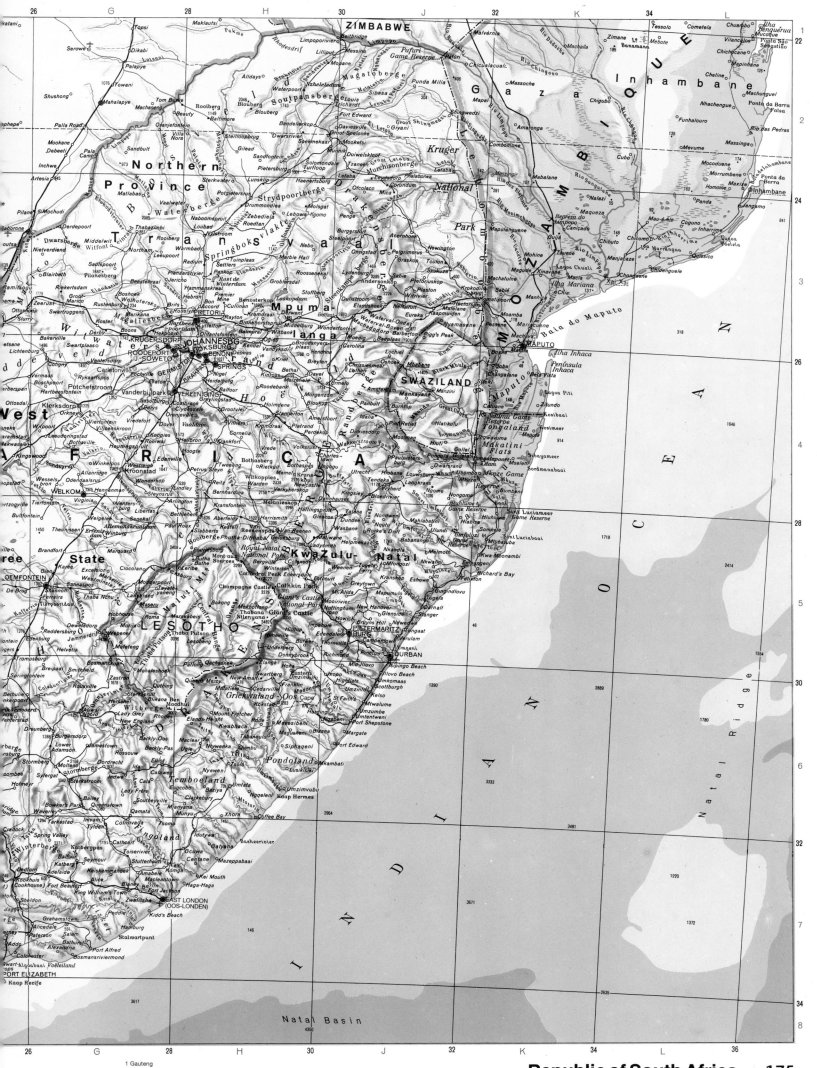

Republic of South Africa   175

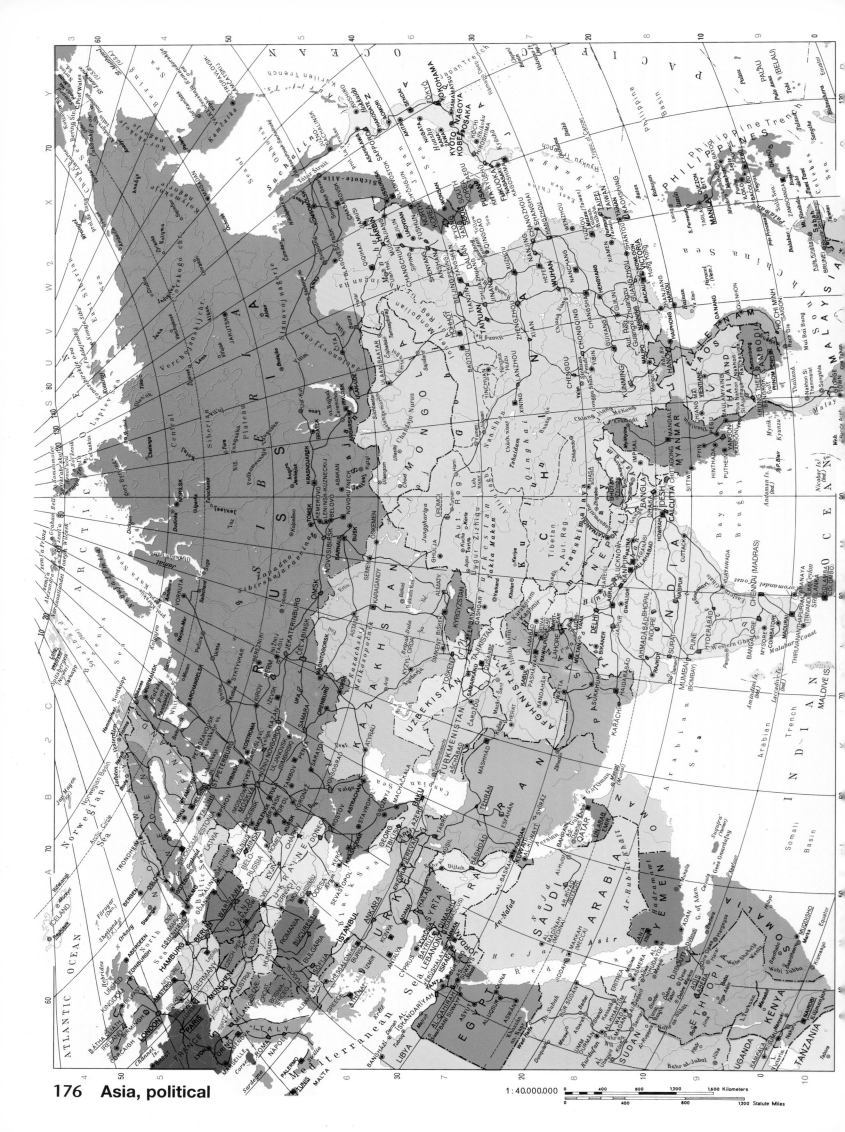

176 Asia, political

1 : 40,000,000

Asia, physical 177

178

Administrative units in the ex Soviet Union:
1 Komi- Permyak Aut. Area
2 Udmurt A.R.
3 Marij El A.R.
4 Chuvash A.R.
5 Mordovian A.R.
6 Tatar A.R.
7 Bashkir A.R.
8 Kyrgyzstan
9 Altaj A.R.
10 Khakass A.R.
11 Ust'- Ordynsky- Buryat Aut. Area
12 Aginsky-Buryat Aut. Area
13 Jewish Aut. Reg.

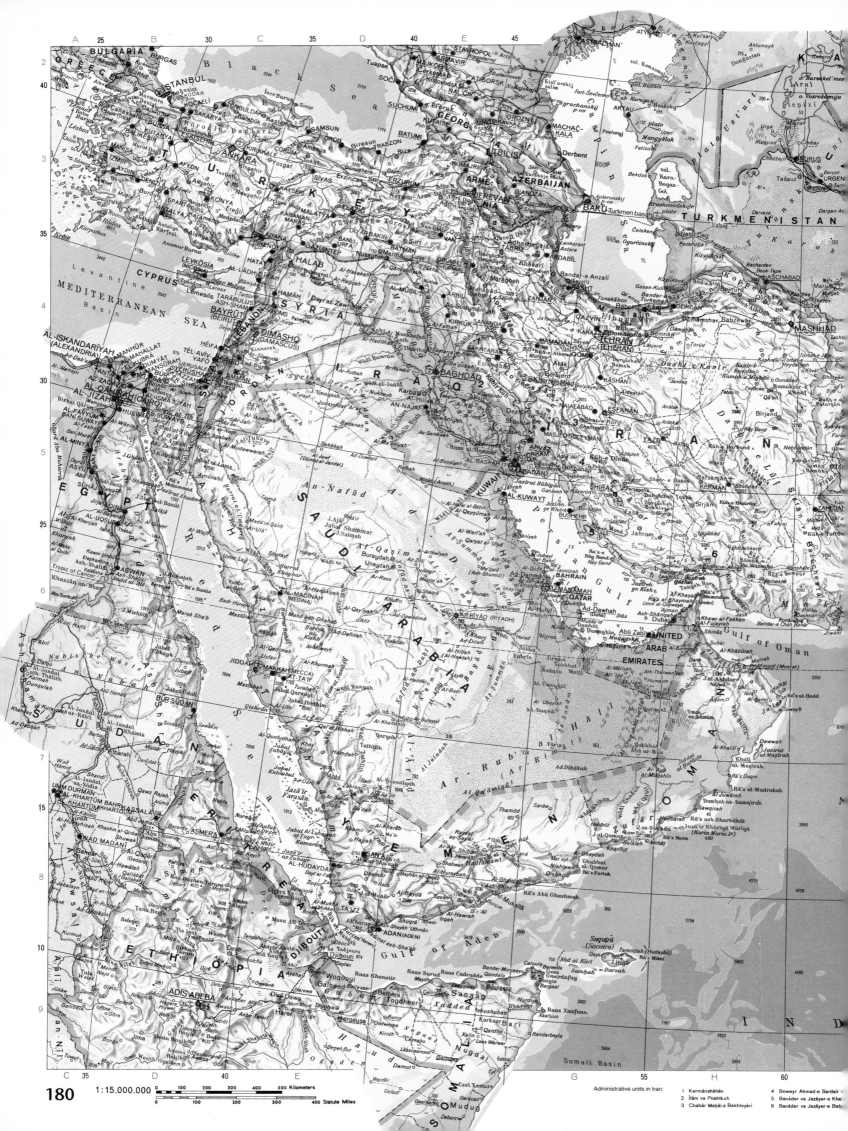

1:15,000,000

Administrative units in Iran:

1 Kermānshāhān
2 Ilām va Poshtkuh
3 Chahār Mahāl-e Bakhteyārī
4 Bowyer Ahmad-e Sardsir
5 Banāder va Jazāyer-e Kha
6 Banāder va Jazāyer-e Bah

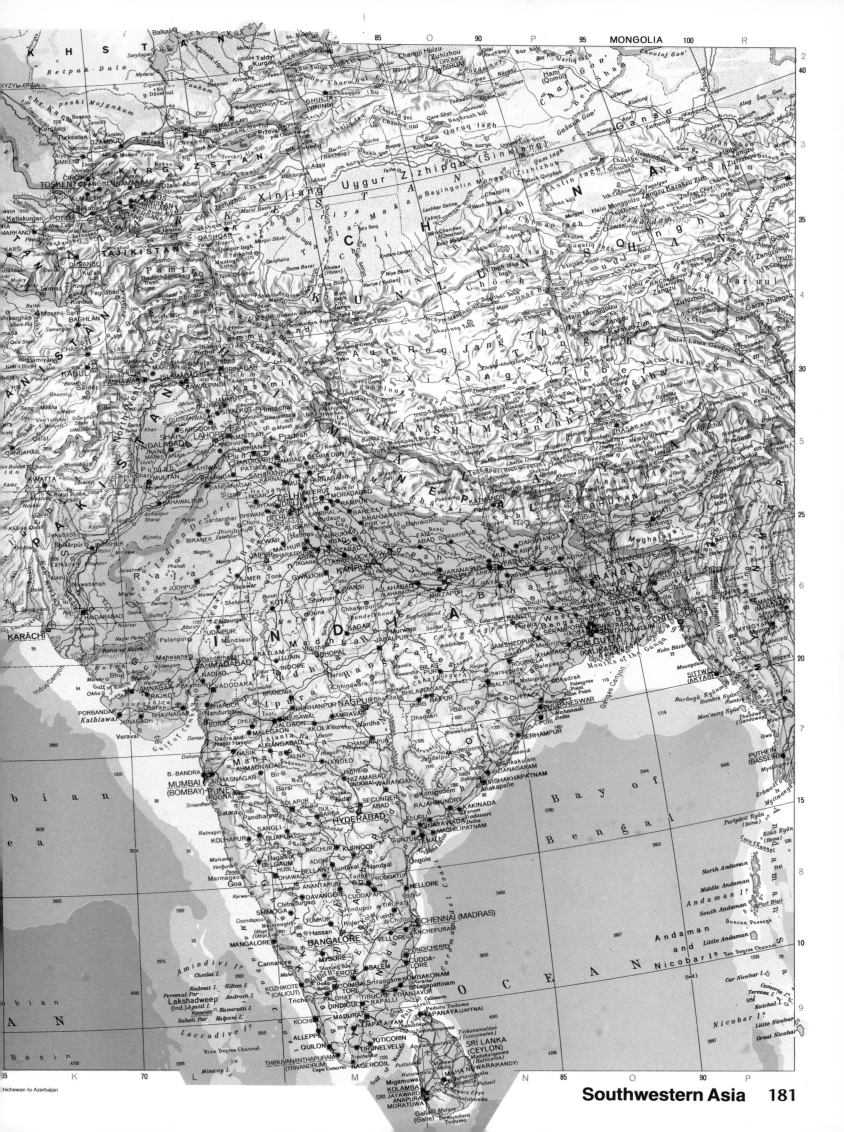

182 1:5,000,000

Near East

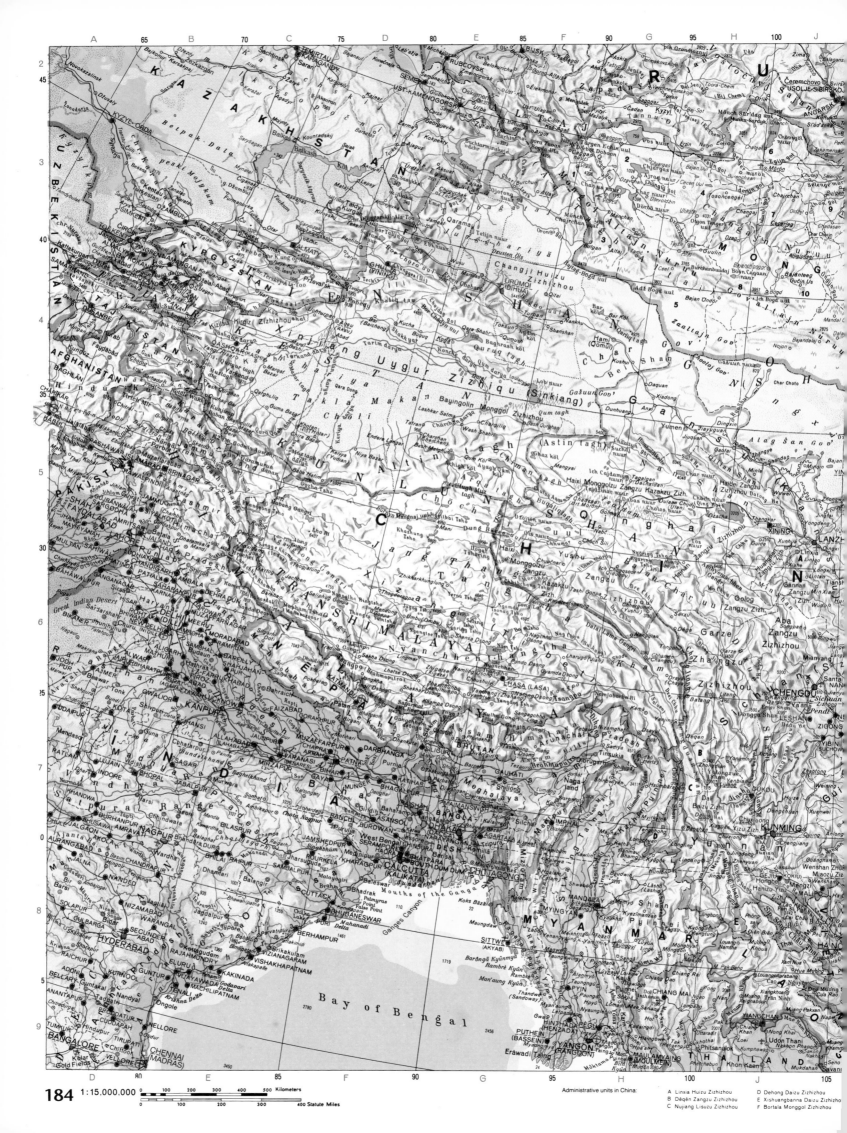

Administrative units in Mongolia:

1 Bajan Ölgij	4 Dzavchan	7 Archangaj	10 Övörchangaj	13 Dundgov'	16 Dornogov'
2 Uvs	5 Gov'altaj	8 Bajan Chongor	11 Selenge	14 Omnogov'	17 Suchbaatar
3 Chovd	6 Chövsgöl	9 Bulgan	12 Töv	15 Chentij	18 Dornod

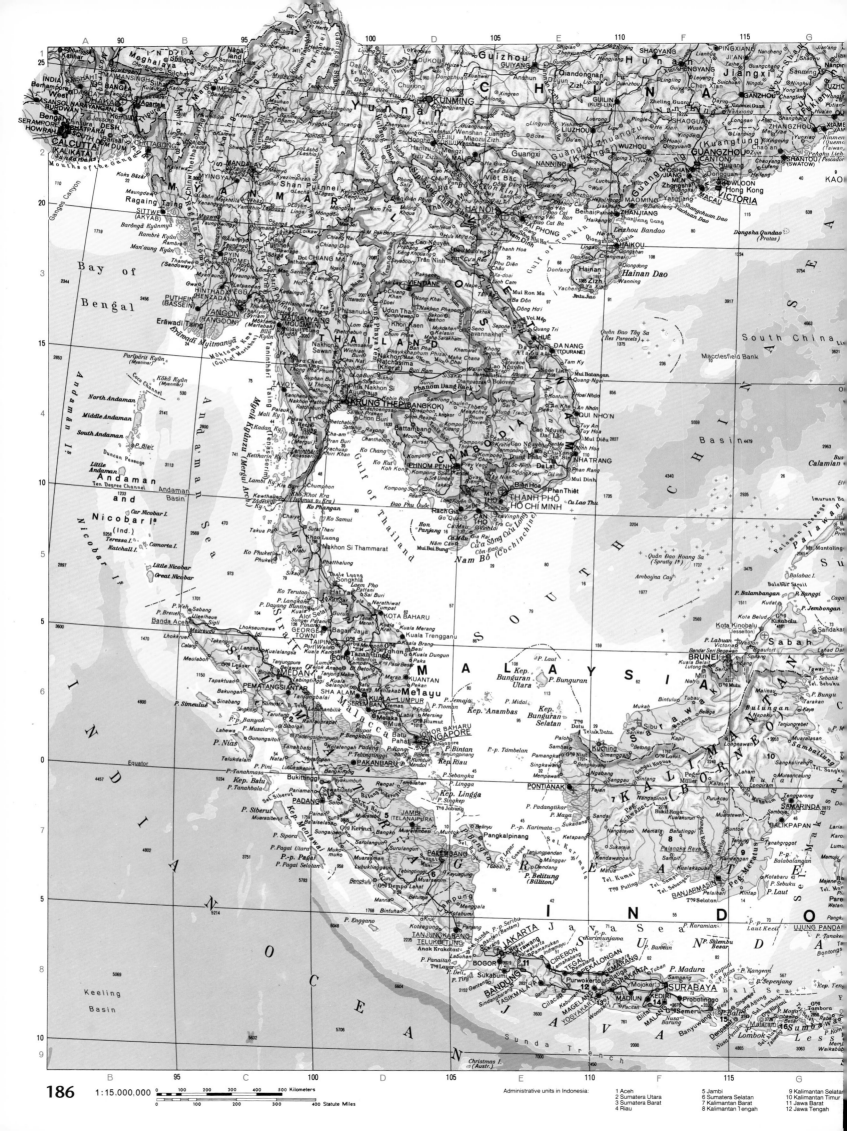

1 : 15,000,000

100   200   300   400   500 Kilometers

100   200   300   400 Statute Miles

Administrative units in Indonesia:

1 Aceh	5 Jambi	9 Kalimantan Selatan
2 Sumatera Utara	6 Sumatera Selatan	10 Kalimantan Timur
3 Sumatera Barat	7 Kalimantan Barat	11 Jawa Barat
4 Riau	8 Kalimantan Tengah	12 Jawa Tengah

Southeast Asia 187

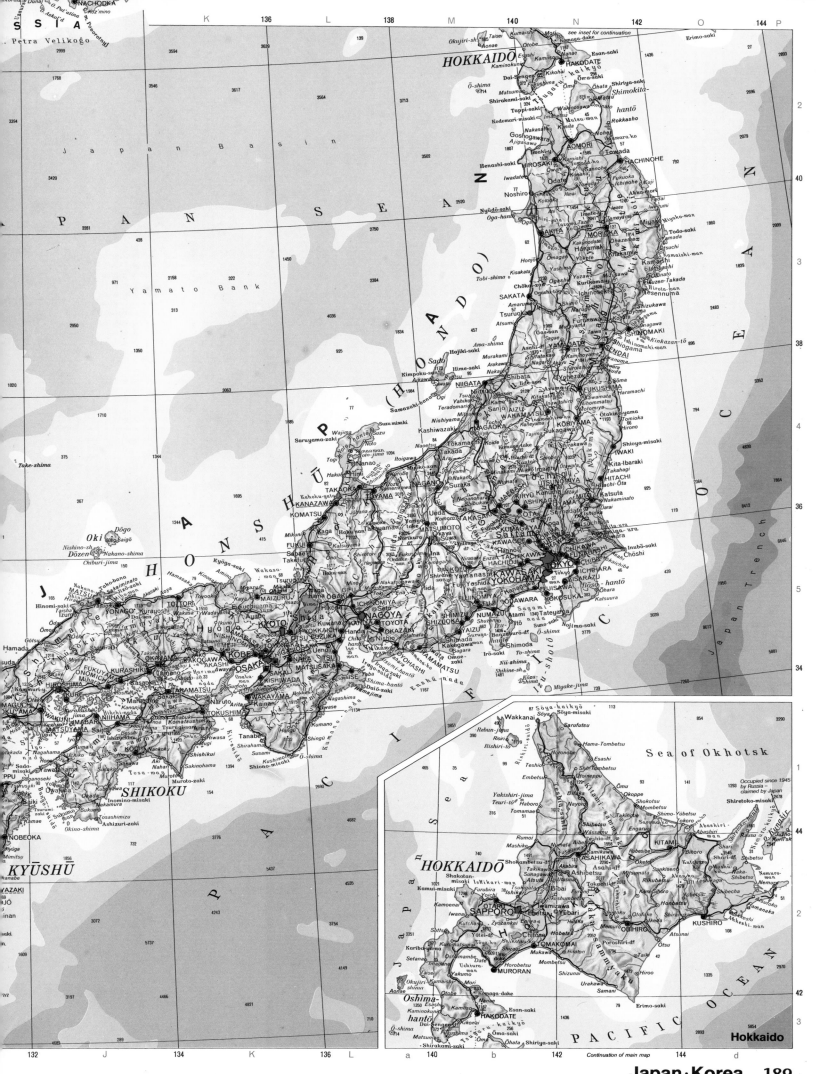

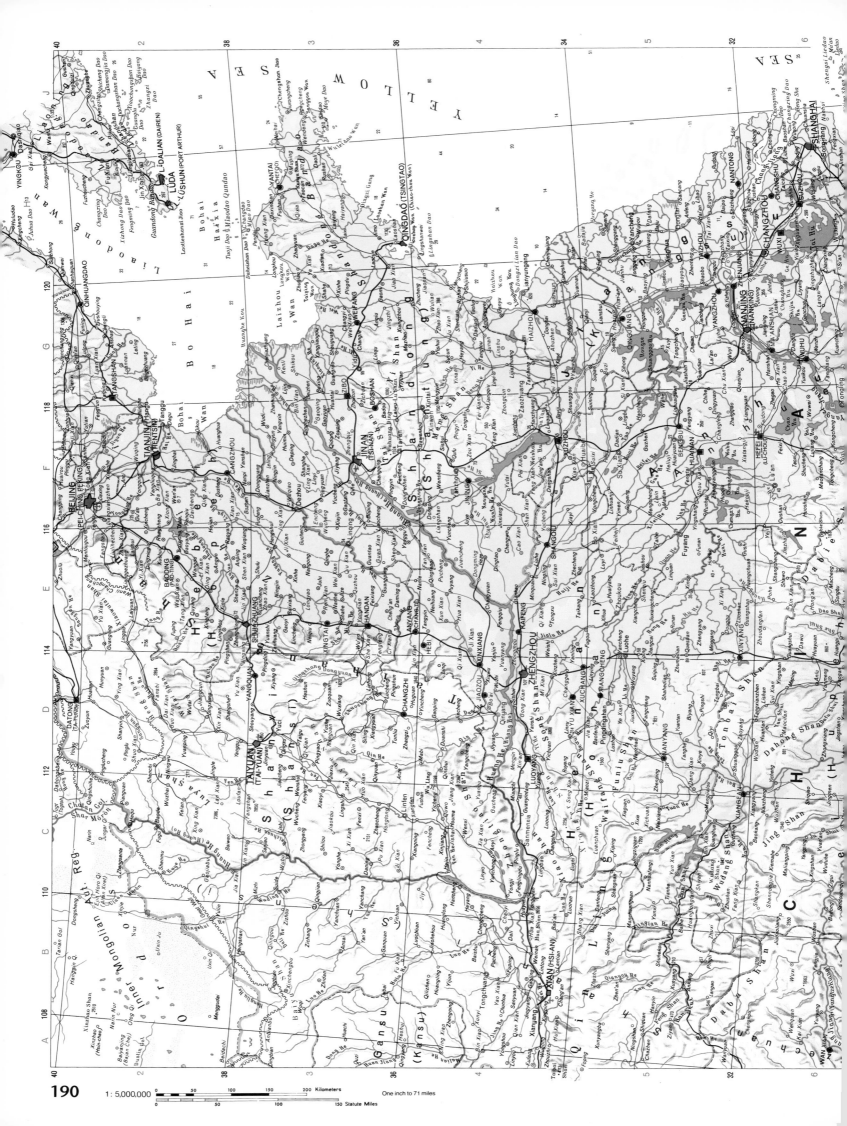

190

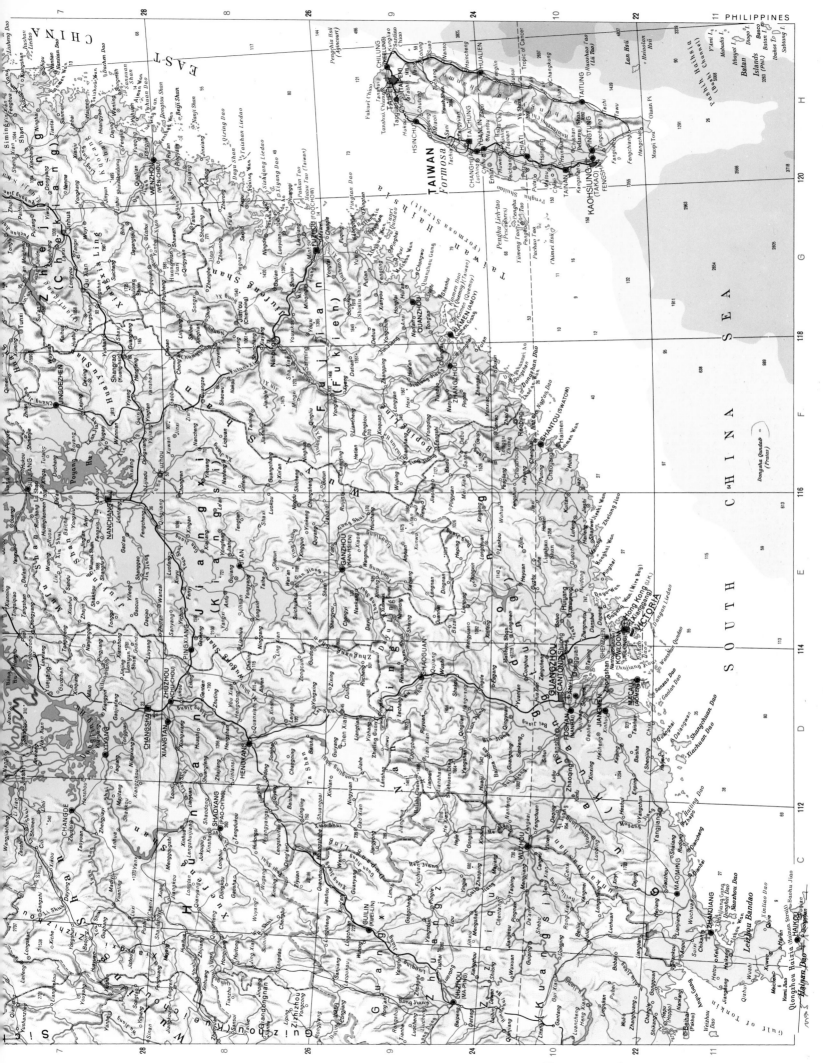

Eastern China · Taiwan   191

1 : 30 000 000

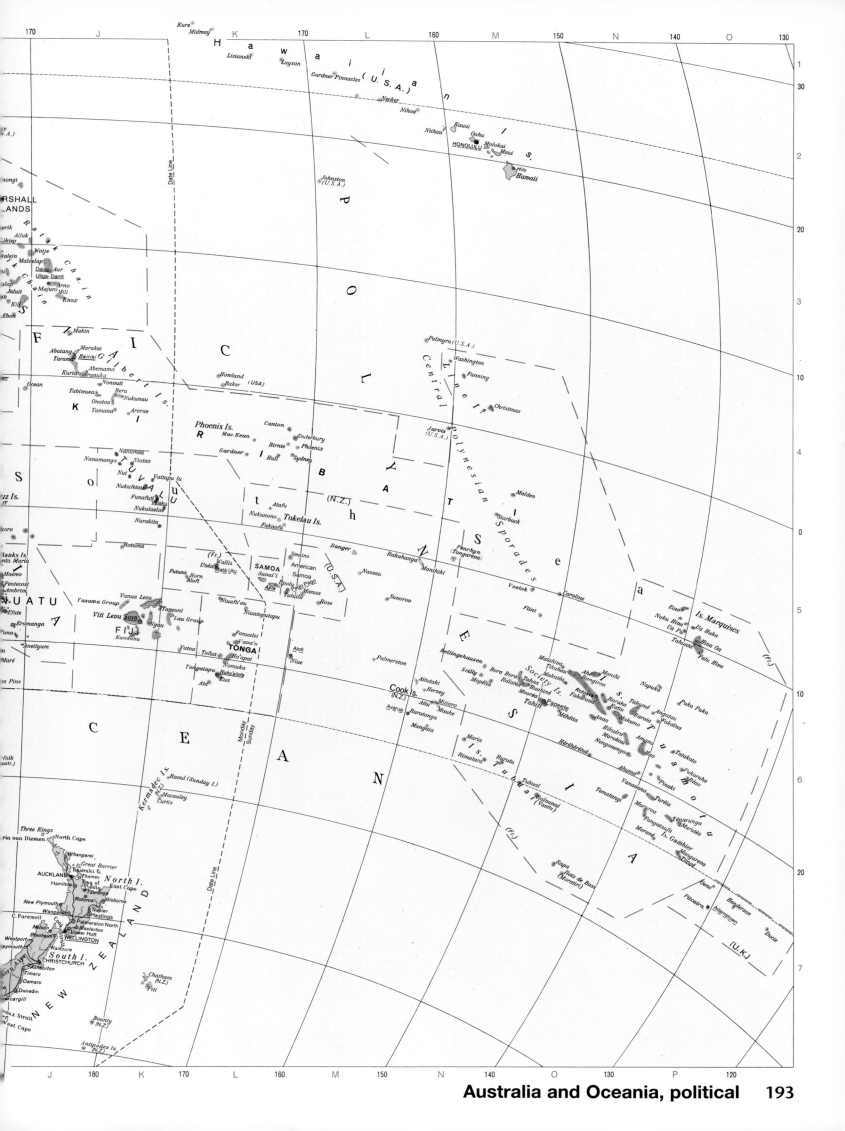

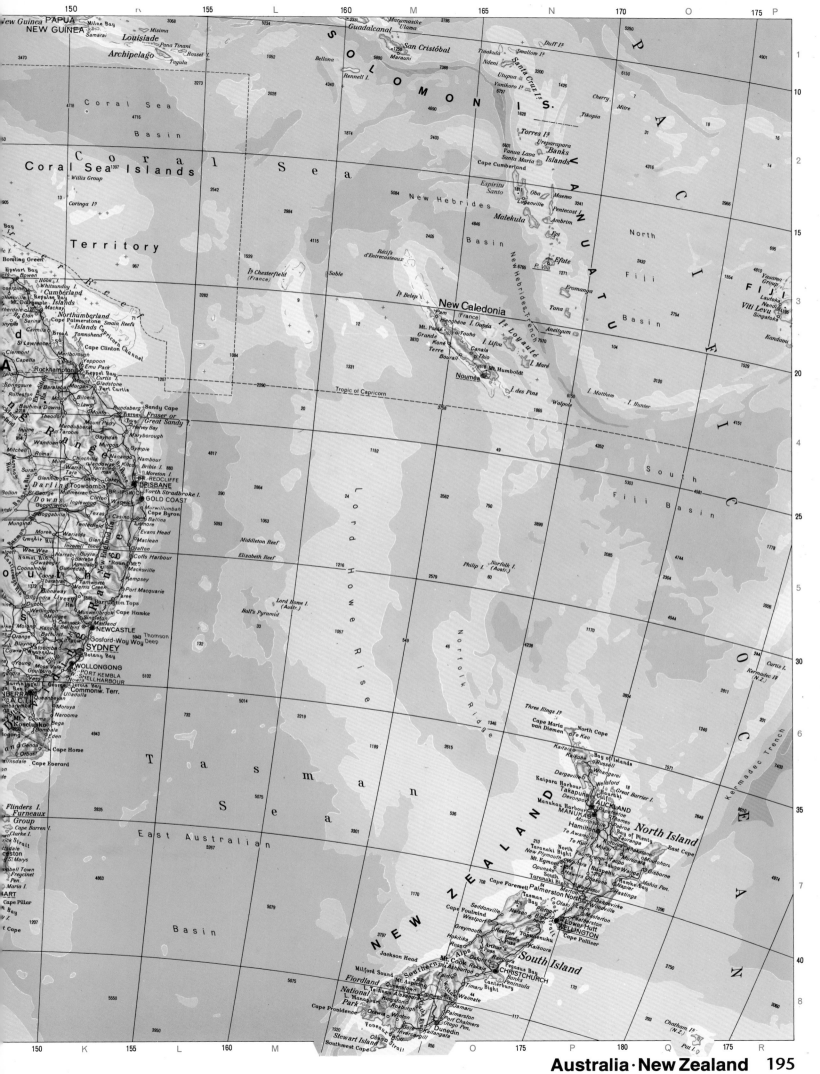

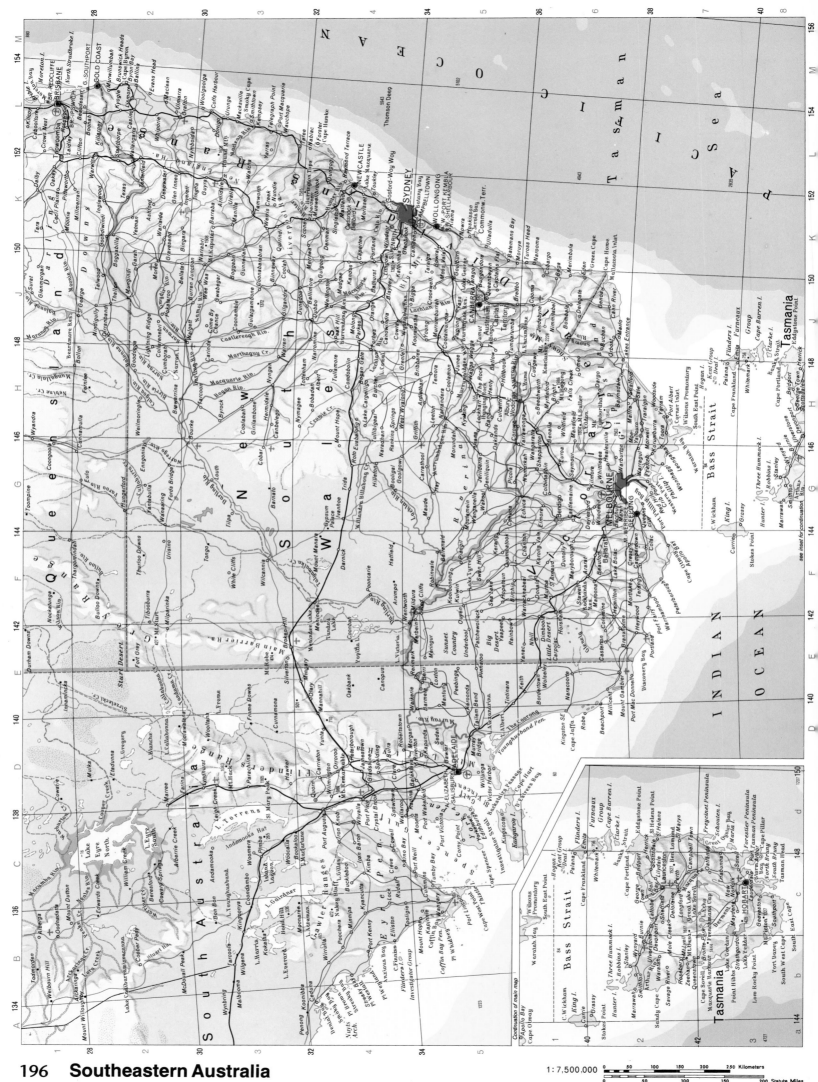

Southeastern Australia

1 : 7,500,000

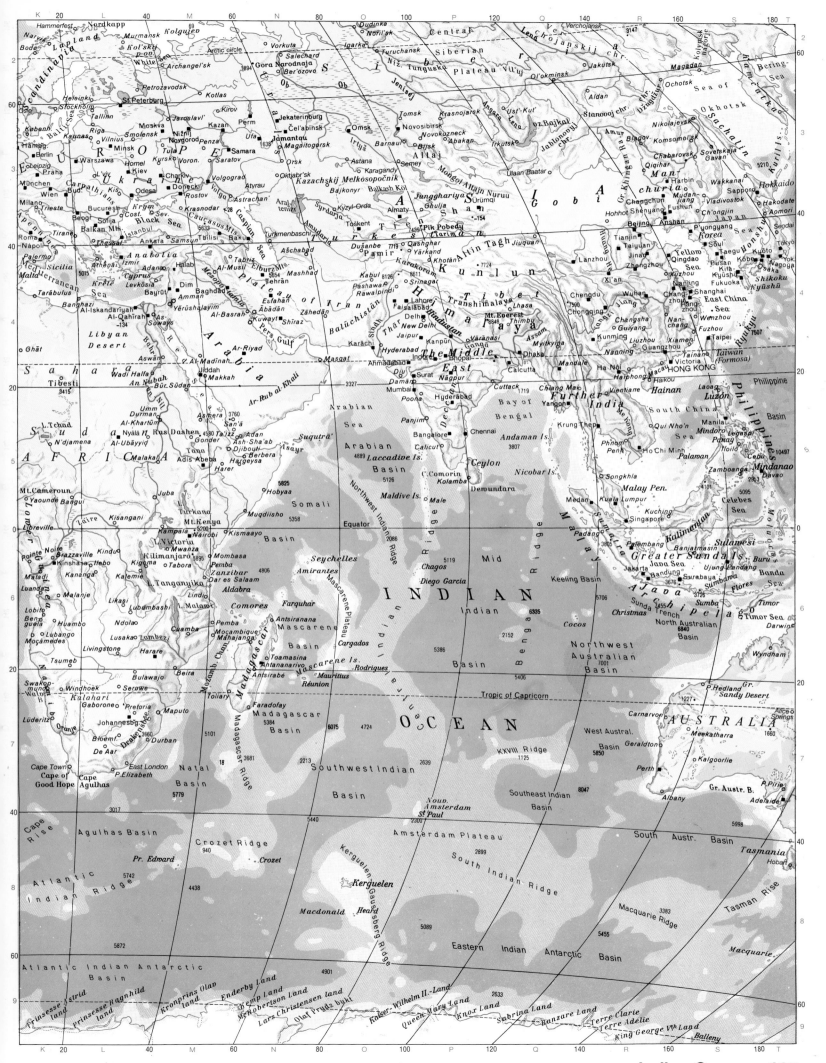

Scale at the center meridian 1 : 57 500 000

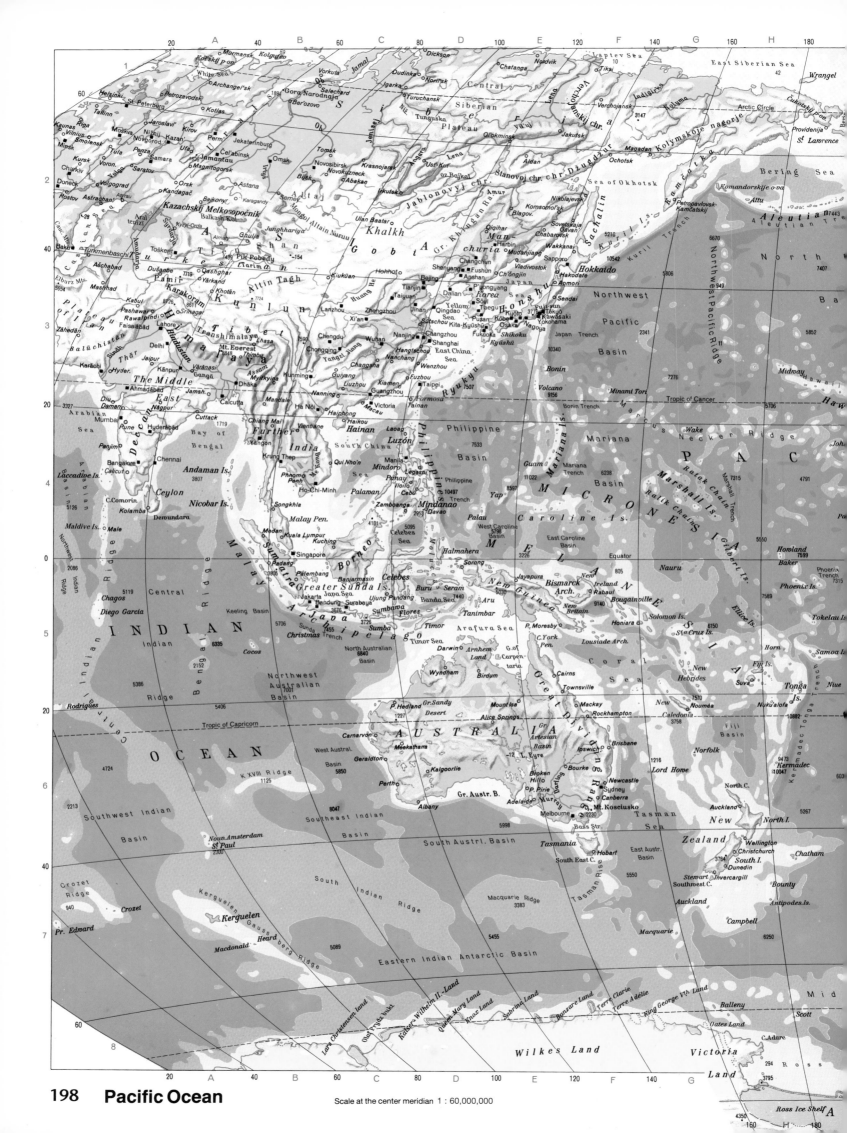

Scale at the center meridian 1 : 60,000,000

Index

The index contains all the names that appear within the international map section.
It is ordered alphabetically.
The umlauts ä, ö and ü have been treated as the letters a, o and u, and the ligatures æ, œ, as ae and oe.
The first figure after the name entry is the page number of the single or double page where the name being looked up is to be found. The letters and figures after the page reference refer to the grid in which the name is located or those grid sections through which the name extends. In the case of places (cities and towns), the positions of the place symbols are also included in the grid coordinates given.
The names that have been abbreviated on the maps are listed unabbreviated in the index. Only with U.S. place names have the official abbreviations been inserted accorded to common U.S. practice, e.g. Washington, D.C. The alphabetical sequence includes also prefixes, e.g. Fort, Saint. The determinative element of geographical names follows behind, e.g. Mexico, Gulf of –; Wight, Isle of – or the name of the city behind that of a suburb, e.g. Fremantle, Perth –. Official supplements to place names are included in the alphabetization. They may follow the name proper, e.g. Châlons-en-Champ. or be added in parenthesis, particularly in German speaking areas, e.g. Kempten (Allgäu).
To a certain extend official second name forms, linguistic variants, renamed places and other secondary designations are listed in the index with reference to the name form used in the map, e.g. Kamien Pomorski = Cammin in Pommern; Meran = Merano; Siam = Thailand.
To differentiate identical name forms mainly motor vehicle nationality letters for the respective countries have been added in brackets following these names:

A	Austria	ET	Egypt	MW	Malawi	SCV	Vatican City
AFG	Afghanistan	ETH	Ethiopia and Eritrea	N	Norway	SD	Swasiland
AL	Albania	F	France	NA	Netherlands Antilles	SF	Finland
AND	Andorra	FJI	Fiji	NIC	Nicaragua	SGP	Singapore
AUS	Australia	FL	Liechtenstein	NL	Netherlands	SME	Suriname
B	Belgium	GB	United Kingdom	NZ	New Zealand	SN	Senegal
BD	Bangladesh	GCA	Guatemala	P	Portugal	SP	Somalia
BDS	Barbados	GH	Ghana	PA	Panama	SU	former
BG	Bulgaria	GR	Greece	PAK	Pakistan		Sovjet Union
BH	Belize	GUY	Guyana	PE	Peru	SY	Seychelles
BOL	Bolivia	H	Hungary	PL	Poland	SYR	Syria
BR	Brazil	HK	Hong Kong	PNG	Papua New Guinea	T	Thailand
BRN	Bahrein	HY	Burkina Faso	PY	Paraguay	TG	Togo
BRU	Brunei	I	Italy	Q	Qatar	TJ	China
BS	Bahamas	IL	Israel	RA	Argentina	TN	Tunisia
BUR	Myanmar(Burma)	IND	India	RB	Botswana	TR	Turkey
C	Cuba	IR	Iran	RC	Taiwan	TT	Trinidad and Tobago
CDN	Canada	IRL	Ireland	RCA	Central African	USA	United States
CH	Switzerland	IRQ	Iraq		Republic	VN	Vietnam
CI	Ivory Coast	IS	Iceland	RCB	Congo	WAG	Gambia
CL	Sri Lanka	J	Japan	RCH	Chile	WAL	Sierra Leone
CO	Colombia	JA	Jamaika	RFC	Cameroun	WAN	Nigeria
CR	Costa Rica	JOR	Jordan	RH	Haiti	WD	Dominica
CS	Czech Rep. and	K	Cambodia	RI	Indonesia	WG	Grenada
	Slovakia	KWT	Kuwait	RIM	Mauritania	WL	Saint Lucia
CY	Cyprus	L	Luxembourg	RL	Lebanon	WS	Samoa
D	Germany	LAO	Laos	RM	Madagascar	WV	Saint Vincent
DK	Denmark	LAR	Libya	RMM	Mali	Y	Yemen
DOM	Dominican Republic	LB	Liberia	RN	Niger	YU	former Yugoslavia incl.
DY	Benin	LS	Lesotho	RO	Romania		Slowenia, Croatia,
DZ	Algeria	M	Malta	ROK	South Korea		Bosnia-Herzegowina
E	Spain	MA	Morocco	ROU	Uruguay		and Macedonia
EAK	Kenya	MAL	Malaysia	RP	Philippines	YV	Venezuela
EAT	Tanzania	MC	Monaco	RSM	San Marino	Z	Zambia
EAU	Uganda	MEX	Mexico	RU	Burundi	ZA	South Africa
EC	Ecuador	MS	Mauritius	RWA	Rwanda	ZRE	Congo, Dem. Rep.of the
ES	El Salvador	MVR	Mongolia	S	Sweden	ZW	Zimbabwe

To differentiate identical name forms among others the following symbols are used

▲	Mountain	⊙	Island	∅	Ruin
∪	Bay, Gulf	∧	Cape	≈	Lake
~	River	≅	Landscape, Region	★	State
▲▲	Mountain Range	●	City, Town, Locality	☆	administrative Unit
∩	Peninsula	⇄	Pass		

abenraa 133 DE 1
achen 133 C 3
alborg 130-131 CD 9
alborg Bugt 130-131 CD 9
alen 133 E 4
anekoski 130-131 L 6
ansluit 174-175 E 4
ar,De - 168-169 F9
arau 133 D 5
are 133 D 5
avasaksa 130-131 KL 4
a [WAN] 166-167 F 7
a [ZRE] 168-169 GH 2
ā' al-Qūr, Wādī - 182-183 J 7
ā ar-Rūs, Sabkhat 180-181 GH 6
ad 184-185 E 3
ādān 180-181 F 4
ādān, Jazīreh - 182-183 N 7-8
ādeh 180-181 G 4
adiânia 160-161 H 2
aeté 160-161 K 3
aeté, Rio - 160-161 K 3
agnar Qi = Xilin Hot 184-185 M 3
aí 162 E 3
aji 172-173 G 3
ajo Peak 150-151 J 7
akaliki 172-173 H 4
akan 178-179 R 7
alak 172-173 G 2
an 178-179 S 6
ancay 158-159 E 7
anga 172-173 H 5
anrherit, I-n- 166-167 F 5
ā Sa'ūd 180-181 EF 7
ashiri 184-185 RS 3
ashiri-wan 188-189 d 1-2
asiri = Abashiri 184-185 RS 3
au 186-187 N 9
ay 166-167 M 6
aya Hayik 166-167 M 7
aza 178-179 R 7
a Zangzu Zizhizhou 184-185 J 5
babis 174-175 B 2
beville 134-135 HJ 3
beville, AL 154-155 N 5
beville, GA 148-149 B 8-9
beville, LA 154-155 JK 5-6
beville, SC 148-149 B 7
botsford, WI 152-153 L 3
bottabad = Ebuṭṭābād 180-181 L 4
cásia, República Autónoma da - 140-141 K 5
cásia, Répubiiva Autónoma da - = 16 ◃ 126-127 R 7
chasia, Repubblica Autonoma dell' = 16 ◃ 126-127 R 7
chasische Autonome Republik 140-141 K 5
chaska Autonomiczna Republika 140-141 K 5
cházie 140-141 K 5
chazische Autonome Republiek 140-141 K 5
chazskaja Avtonomnaja Respublika = Abchasische Autonome Republik 140-141 K 5
chasia, Republica Autonoma = ◃ 126-127 R 7
od al-'Azīz, Jabal - 182-183 HJ 4
od al Kūrī 180-181 G 8
odāllah 166-167 D 2
od Allāh, Khawr - 182-183 N 8
dānān 182-183 M 6
dānān, Rūdkhāneh-ye 182-183 M 6
d an-Nabī, Bi'r - 170 B 2-3
dulino 178-179 J 7
odullah = Minā' 'Abd Allāh 182-183 N 8
éché 166-167 J 6
écher = Abéché 166-167 J 6
ed-Larache, El - = Al-Ādib al-'Arsh 166-167 F 3
eg, I-n- 166-167 D 4
eløya 130-131 n 5
engourou 166-167 D 7
eokuta 166-167 E 7
ercorn = Mbala 168-169 H 4
ercrombie, ND 152-153 H 2
erdare Mountains 168-169 J 2-3
erdare National Park 171 D 3
erdeen [AUS] 196 K 4
erdeen [GB] 132 EF 3
erdeen [ZA] 168-169 F 9
erdeen, ID 150-151 G 4
erdeen, MD 148-149 E 5
erdeen, MS 154-155 L 4
erdeen, NC 148-149 D 7
erdeen, SD 146-147 G 2
erdeen, WA 146-147 B 2
erdeen Lake 144-145 R 5
erfeldy [ZA] 174-175 H 5
ergavenny 132 E 6
ernathy, TX 154-155 E 4
ert, Lake - 150-151 CD 4
erystwyth 132 D 5
essinien = Äthiopien 166-167 MN7
esszínia = Etiópia 166-167 MW 7
ez' 178-179 L 4
hā 180-181 E 7
hār 182-183 N 4
ház Autonóm Köztársaság 140 K 5
hē Bid Hayik 166-167 N 6
ia 172-173 G 4
iaḍ, Râss el - = Rā's al Abyaḍ 166-167 FG 1
id al-'Arsh, Al- 166-167 F 3
idjan 166-167 CD 7
iekwasputs 174-175 D 4
i Hill 172-173 G 3
ilene KS 152-153 H 6
ilene, TX 146-147 FG 5
ingdon, IL 152-153 L 5
ingdon, VA 148-149 BC 6
ingdon = Isla Pinta 158-159 A 4
insk 140-141 J 4
iqulu, NM 154-155 B 2
isko 130-131 H 3
isynia = Etiopia 166-167 MN 7
itibi, Lake - 144-145 UV 8
itibi River 144-145 U 7-8
jasia, República Autónoma de 140-141 K 5
khaz Autonomous Republic 140-141 K 5
khazie, République Autonome d' 140-141 K 5
nūb 170 D 4
o = Turku 130-131 K 7
oisso 172-173 E 4
omé = Abomey 166-167 E 7
omey 166-167 E 7
ong-Mbang 166-167 G 8
onnema 172-173 G 4

Aborigen, pik - 178-179 cd 5
Aboso 172-173 E 4
Abou-Deïa 166-167 H 6
Aboû eḍ Ḍouhoûr = Abū aẓ-Ẓuhūr 182-183 G 6
Abov' an 140-141 M 6
'Abr, Al- 180-181 F 7
Abraham Lincoln National Historical Park 152-153 O 7
Abrantes 134-135 CD 9
Abra Pampa 162 CD 2
Abreojos, Punta - 146-147 CD 6
'Abrī 166-167 L 4
Abrolhos, Arquipelago dos - 158-159 M 8
Abruka 138-139 D 4
Abruzzen = Appennino
Abruzzese 136-137 E 4-F 5
Abruzzes = Appennino
Abruzzese 136-137 E 4-F 5
Abruzzi 136-137 EF 4
Absaroka Range 146-147 D 2-E 3
Absarokee, MT 152-153 B 3
Abu 180-181 L 6
Abū 'Ajāj = Jalib Shahab 182-183 M 7
Abū al-Ḥaṣīb 182-183 MN 7
Abū al-Maṭāmir 170 CD 2
Abū' Aweiqila = Abū' Uwayjilah 170 EF 2
Abū aẓ-Ẓuhūr 182-183 G 5
Abû Ballâṣ 166-167 K 4
Abū Ḍahr, Jabal - 170 F 6
Abū Dārah, Rā's - 170 G 6
Abū Darbah 170 E 3
Abū Dhi'āb, Jabal - 170 F 5
Abû Durba = Abū Darbah 170 E 3
Abu Gharādiq, Bi'r - 170 C 2-3
Abū Ghashwah, Rā's - 180-181 G 8
Abū Ḥādd, Wādī - 170 F 7
Abû Ḥaggâg = Rā's al-Ḥikmah 182-183 BC 7
Abū Ḥajār, Khawr - 182-183 L 7
Abū Ḥamad 166-167 L 5
Abū Ḥamāmid, Jabal - 170 F 5
Abū Ḥammān 182-183 J 5
Abū Ḥarbah, Jabal - 170 E 4
Abū Ḥashūifah , Khalīj - 170 BC 2
Abû Ḥjâr, Ḥōr - = Khawr Abū Ḥajār 182-183 L 7
Abū Hujar 166-167 LM 6
Abuja 166-167 F 7
Abū Jābirah 166-167 K 6
Abū Jaḥaf, Wādī - 182-183 K 6
Abū Jamal 166-167 M 5
Abū Jamal, Jabal - 166-167 M 6
Abū Jīr 182-183 K 6
Abū Jīr, Wādī - 182-183 K 6
Abū Jurdī, Jabal - 170 F 6
Abū Kabīr 170 D 2
Abū Kamāl 180-181 DE 4
Abû Khârga, Wâdī - = Wādī Abū Kharjah 170 DE 3
Abū Kharjah, Wādī - 170 DE 3
Abukuma-sammyaku 188-189 N 4
Abū Maris, Sha'īb - 182-183 L 7
Abū Marw, Wādī - 170 E 6
Abū Minqār, Bi'r - 166-167 K 3
Abū Muḥarrik, Ghurd - 166-167 KL 3
Abunã 158-159 FG 6
Abuná, Río - 158-159 F 7
Abū Qīr 170 D2
Abū Qīr, Khalīj - 170 D 2
Abū Qurqāṣ 170 D 4
Abū Rijmayn, Jabal - 182-183 H 5
Abū Sa'fah, Bi'r - 170 F 6
Abū Ṣaida = Abū Ṣaydat Ṣaghīrah 182-183 L 6
Abū Salmān 182-183 M 7
Abū Ṣaydat Ṣaghīrah 182-183 L 6
Abū Shalīl 182-183 K 5
Abū Shlīl = Abū Shalīl 182-183 K 5
Abû Sinbil = Abu Sunbul 166-167 L4
Abū Ṣkhair = Abū Ṣuhayr 182-183 L 7
Abū Ṣuhayr 182-183 L 7
Abu Sunbul 166-167 L 4
Abū Tīj 166-167 L 3
Abū 'Uwayjilah 170 EF 2
Abū Zabad 166-167 K 6
Abū Ẓabī 180-181 G 6
Abū Zanimah 166-167 L 3
Abū Zawal, Bi'r - 170 E 4
Abû Zenīma = Abū Zanimah 166-167 L 3
Abyaḍ 166-167 K 6
Abyaḍ, Ar-Rā's al- 166-167 A 4
Abyaḍ, Rā's al- 166-167 FG 1
Abyay 166-167 K 7
Abymes, les - 146-147 O 8
Abyssinie = Éthiopie 166-167 MN 7
A Coruña = La Coruña 134-135 C 7
Acadia = Acadie 144-145 XY 8
Acadia National Park 148-149 J 2
Acadie 144-145 XY 8
Acahay 160-161 D 6
Acajutla 146-147 HJ 9
Acala, TX 154-155 C 5
Acámbaro 146-147 FG 7
Acandí 158-159 D 3
Acaponeta 146-147 EF 7
Acapulco de Juárez 146-147 FG 8
Acará 158-159 K 5
Acaraí, Serra - 158-159 H 4
Acaraú 158-159 LM 5
Acaray, Rio - 160-161 E 6
Acarigua 158-159 F 3
Accomac, VA 148-149 F 6
Accra 166-167 DE 7
Aceh = 1 ◃ 186-187 C 6
Achalciche 140-141 L 6
Achalkalaki 140-141 L 6
Achsu 140-141 O 6
Achluba 140-141 N 3
Achlubinsk 140-141 NM 2
Achter-Indië 124-125 OP 5
Achter Roggeveld = Agler Roggeveld 174-175 D 6
Achty 140-141 N 6
Achtyrka 140-141 G 1
Achur' an 140-141 L 6
Aci Göl 182-183 CD 4
Ačinsk 178-179 R 6
Ačisu 140-141 N 5
Acıpayam 182-183 C 4
Acireale 136-137 F 7
Acklins Island 146-147 LM 7
Acme, LA 154-155 K 5
Acme, NM 154-155 C 4
Acme, TX 154-155 F 3
Ackerly, TX 154-155 E 4
Ackerman, MS 154-155 L 4
Ackley, IA 152-153 K 4
Acomayo 158-159 E 7
Aconcagua [RCH, ▲] 162 C 4
Acopiara 158-159 M 6
Açores 165 D 5
Açores, Patamar dos - 124-125 HJ 4
Açores, Seuil des - 124-125 HJ 4

Acornhoek 174-175 J 3
Àcqui Terme 136-137 C 3
Acraman, Lake - 194-195 FG 6
Acre 158-159 EF 6
Acre = 'Akkō 182-183 F 6
Acre,Rio - 158-159 F 6
Acri 136-137 G 6
Acton 148-149 C 3
Acton, CA 150-151 D 8
Açú, Rio - = Rio Piranhas 158-159 M 6
Açungui 160-161 H 6
Acworth, GA 148-149 A 7
Ačinsk 178-179 R 6
Achacachi 158-159 F 8
Achaguas 158-159 F 3
Achaïa 136-137 JK 6
Achao 162 B 6
'Achârá, El - = Al-'Asharah 182-183 J 5
Acharnai 136-137 K 6
Achegour 166-167 G 5
Achelôos 136-137 J 6
Acheng 184-185 O 2
Acherusia = Zonguldak 180-181 C 2
Achigh Köl 184-185 F 4
Achill 132 A 5
Achill Head 132 A 4-5
Acton, MT 152-153 B 3
Ada [GH] 166-167 E 7
Ada, OK 146-147 G 5
Ada, NM 152-153 H 2
Ada, OH 152-153 P 5
'Adabiyah, Rā's - 170 E 3
Adado, Raas - = Raas Cadcadde 166-167 b 1
Adafir 166-167 BC 5
Adairsville, GA 154-155 N 3
Adakale = Ardanuç 182-183 K 2
Adak Island 120 D 36
Adale = Cadale 166-167 b 3
Adalia = Antalya 180-181 C 3
Ādam 180-181 H 6
Adam, Monte - = Mount Adam 162 DE 8
Adam, Mount - 162 DE 8
Adama = Nazrēt 166-167 M 7
Adamana, AZ 150-151 HJ 8
Adamantina 158-159 JK 9
Adamaoua 166-167 G 7
Adamaua = Adamaoua 166-167 G 7
Adamawa 172-173 HJ 3
Adamello 136-137 D 2
Adam Peak 150-151 E 5
Adampol = Polonezkőy 182-183 C 2
Adams, MA 148-149 G 3
Adams ND 152-153 GH 1
Adams NE 152-153 H 5
Adams, NY 148-149 EF 3
Adams, OK 154-155 E 2
Adams, Cape - 121 B 130-131
Adams, Mount - 146-147 B 2
Adams Island 121 D 17
Adam's Peak = Samānaḷakanda 180-181 N 9
Adamstown 192-193 OP 7
Adamsville, AL 154-155 M 4
Adamsville, TN 154-155 L 3
Adamsville, TX 154-155 F 5
'Adan 180-181 F 8
Adana 182-183 F 4
Adapazarı = Sakarya 180-181 C 2
Adare, Cape - 121 B 18
Adavale 194-195 HJ 5
Adda 136-137 C 3
Addâr, Râss - = Rā's aṭ-Ṭib 166-167 G 1
Addis Alem = Alem Gena 166-167 M7
Addison, NY 148-149 E 3
Addison = Webster Springs, WV 148-149 C 5
Addisz Abeba = Adīs Abeba 166-167 M7
Addy, WA 150-151 E 1
Addo 174-175 F 7
Adel, GA 148-149 B 9
Adel, IA 152-153 J 5
Adel, OR 150-151 D 4
Adelaide [AUS] 194-195 GH 6-7
Adelaide [ZA] 174-175 G 7
Adelaide Island 121 C 29-30
Adelaide Peninsula 144-145 R 4
Adelaide River 194-195 F 2
Adelanto, CA 150-151 E 8
Adélie, Terre - 121 C 14-15
Adélie Land = Terre Adélie 121 C 14-15
Adelsberg = Postojna 136-137 F 3
Adem = 'Adan 180-181 F 8
Adem, Golfo de 180-181 F 8
Ademuz 134-135 G 8
Aden NM 154-155 B 4
Aden = 'Adan 180-181 EF 8
Aden, Golfe d, 180-181 F 8
Adén, Golfo de - 180-181 F 8
Aden, Golfo di - 178-179 F8
Aden, Golf van - 180-181 F 8
Aden, Golf von - 180-181 F 8
Aden, Gulf of - 180-181 F 8
Adendorp 174-175 F 7
Ádeni-öböl 180-181 F 8
Adeńska, Zatoka - 180-181 F 8
Adenský záliv 180-181 F 8
Aderesso Rapides 172-173 E 3
Adghar = Adrār 166-167 DE 3
Ādhār, Rā's - 166-167 G 1
Adharbayejān-e- Bākhtarī 180-181 EF 3
Ādharbāyejān-e-Khāvarī 180-181 EF 3
Adi, Pulau - 186-187 K 7
Adib al-'Arsh, Al- 166-167 F 3
Àdige 136-137 D 3
Ádige Autonóm Terület 140-141 JK 4
Adigej Autonome Region 140-141 JK 4
Adigezia, Provincia Autonoma dell' = 9 ◃ 126-127 Q 6 - R 7
Adīgrat 166-167 MN 6
Adiguey, Oblast Autónoma de - 140-141 JK 4
Adiguey, República Autónoma de - = 17 ◃ 126-127 R 7
Adī Keyih 166-167 MN 6
Adilang 171 C 2
Adilcevaz 182-183 K 3
Adin, CA 150-151 C 5
Aḍiriyāt, Jabal al- 182-183 G 7
Adirondack Mountains 146-147 M 3
Adīs Abeba 166-167 M 7
Adīs Dera = Dirē 166-167 M 6
Adī Ūgrī 166-167 M 6
Adıyaman 182-183 H 4
Adjarian Autonomous Republic 140-141 KL 6
Adjarie, République Autonome d' 140-141 KL 6
Adler, Soči - 140-141 J 5
Admar, Irq - 166-167 F 4

Admer, Erg d' = 'Irq Admar 166-167 F4
Admiralicji, Wyspy - = Admiralty Islands 186-187 N 7
Admiralitätsinseln = Admiralty Islands 186-187 N 7
Admiralitní ostrovy = Admiralty Islands 186-187 N 7
Admiralty Gulf 194-195 DE 2
Admiralty Inlet [CDN] 144-145 TU 3
Admiralty Inlet [USA] 150-151 B 1-2
Admiralty Island 144-145 K 6
Admiralty Islands 186-187 N 7
Admiralty Range 121 B 17
Admont 133 G 5
Adome 172-173 EF 4
Adonara, Pulau - 186-187 H 8
Ādoni 180-181 M 7
Adour 134-135 G 7
Adra 134-135 F10
Adramúttion = Edremit 180-181 B 3
Ādrār 166-167 DE 3
Adraskan, Daryā-ye - = Hārūt Rōd 180-181 J 4
Adré 166-167 J 6
Adrī 166-167 G 3
Àdria 136-137 E 3
Adrian, MI 152-153 O 5
Adrian, MN 152-153 J 4
Adrian, OR 150-151 E 4
Adrian, TX 152-153 D 3
Adrianopel = Edirne 180-181 B 2
Adriatic Sea 136-137 E 3-H 5
Adriatisches Meer 136-137 E 3-H 5
Adriatische Zee 136-137 E 3-H 5
Adriatyckie, Morze- 136-137 E 3-H 5
Adscharische Autonome Republik 140-141 KL 6
Adua 186-187 J 7
Adua = Adwa 166-167 M 6
Aduma 172-173 GH 3
Adusa 168-169 G 2
Advance 174-175 D 6
Adventura , Banco - 136-137 DE 7
Adventure, Banco - 136-137 DE 7
Adventure Bank 136-137 DE 7
Adventurebank 136-137 DE 7
Adwa 166-167 M 6
Adyča 178-179 a 4
Adygei Autonomous Region 140-141 JK 4
Adygejskaja Avtonomnaja Oblast' = Adygische Autonome Region 140-141 JK 4
Adygejski Obwód Autonomiczny 140-141 JK 4
Adyghéens, Région Autonome des - 140-141 JK 4
Adygische Autonome Region 140-141 JK 4
Adyk 140-141 M 4
Adžamka 140-141 F 2
Adžarskaja Avtonomnaja = Adscharische Autonome Republik 140-141 KL 6
Adžaristan, Repubblica Autonoma dell' = 17 ◃ 126-127 S 8
Adž Bogd uul 184-185 GH 3
Adzharia, Republika Autónoma de 140-141 KL 6
Adzharia, República Autónoma de - 140-141 KL 6
Adzjarische Autonome Republiek 140-141 KL 6
Adžarská autonomni republika 140-141 KL 6
Adžarska Autonomiczna Repulika 140-141 KL 6
Adzsár Autonóm Köztársaság 140-141 KL 6
Aegean Sea 136-137 L 5-M
Aetna, KS 154-155 F 2
Ærø 130-131 D 10
'Afag 182-183 L 6
Afallah 166-167 B 5
Afam 172-173 G 4
Afanasjevo 138-139 T 4
Afántu 136-137 N 7
Afars et Issas = Djibouti 166-167 N6
Afasto 172 173 G 1
Afeganistão 180-181 J 4-L 3
Afféry 172-173 DE 4
Afganistán 180-181 J 4-L 3
Afganistan 180-181 J 4-L 3
Afganisztán 180-181 J 4-L 3
Afghánistán 180-181 J 4-L 3
Afghanistan 180-181 J 4-L 3
Afgooye 166-167 ab 3
Āfhjalar = Āqchalar 182-183 L 5
'Afif 180-181 E 6
Afikpo 166-167 F 7
Aflāj, Al- 180-181 F 6
Afmadow 166-167 N 8
Afogados da Ingàzeira 158-159 M 6
Afognak Island 144-145 F 6
Afram 172-173 E 4
Afrēra Ye-Tyew Hayik 166-167 N 6
África 124-125 J-L 9
Africa 124-125 J-L 5
África 124-125 J-L 5
Africa 124-125 J-L 5
Africa del Sudoeste = Namibia 168-169 E 7
Africa del Sud-Ovest = Namibia 168-1 157 E 7
África do Sul, República da - 168 F-H 8
African Island 168-169 M 3
Afrika 124-125 J-L 5
'Afrin 182-183 G 4
Āfrineh 182-183 M 6
Afrique 124-125 J-L 5
Afrique du Sud 168-169 F-H 8
Afryka Południowo-Zachodnia = Namibia 168-169 E 7
Afşin 182-183 G 3
Afton, IA 152-153 J 5
Afton, OK 154-155 H 2
Afton, WY 150-151 H 4
Afuá 158-159 J 5
'Afūla 182-183 F 6
Afyon 180-181 C 3
Aga = Aginskoje 178-179 VW 7
Ağaçören 182-183 EF 3
Agadem 166-167 G 5
Agades = Agadez 166-167 F 5
Agadez 166-167 F 5
Agādir = Aghādīr 166-167 BC 2
Ägadische Inseln = Ìsole Ègadi 136-137 DE 6
Agadji 172-173 F 4
Agadyr' 178-179 N 8
Agai Burját Autonóm Körzet 178-179 V 7
Agaie 166-167 F 7
Ägäis = Ägäisches Meer 136-137 L 5-M 7
Ägäisches Meer 136-137 L 5-M 7
Agalega Island 168-169 N 5
Agalta, Sierra de - 146-147 J 8-9

Agamor 172-173 F 1
Agan 178-179 O 5
Agapa 178-179 Q 3
Agar, SD 152-153 F 3
Agarā = Agra 180-181 M 5
Agartala 180-181 P 6
Agata, ozero - 178-179 R 4
Agate, CO 152-153 E 6
Agathonêsion 136-137 M 7
Agats 186-187 L 8
Agatti Island 180-181 L 8
Agattu Island 120 D 1
Agawa Bay 152-153 O 2
Agbélouve 172-173 F 4
Agboville 166-167 D 7
Agdam 140-141 N 7
Agdaš 140-141 N 6
Agde 134-135 J 7
Agdžabedi 140-141 N 6
Agen 134-135 H 6
Agere Ḥiywer = Hagerē Hiywet 166-167 M7
Aghādīr 166-167 BC 2
Āghā Jarī 180-181 FG 4
Aghwāṭ, Al- 166-167 E 2
Ağın 182-183 H 3
Agin-Boerjatmongolen , Agincourt = Péng-chia Yü 190-191 HJ 9
Autonome Gebied der - 178-179 V 7
Agin-Burjatmongolen, Nationalkreis der - 178-179 V 7
Agiński Buriacki Okręg Autonomiczny 178-179 V 7
Aginskoje 178-179 VW 7
Aginskoje, Circ. Nat. Buriatodi = 11 ◃178-179 V 7
Aginský burjatský autonomní okruh 178-179 V 7
Aginsky-Buryat Autonomous Area 178-179 V 7
Ágios Geṓrgios 136-137 KL 7
Ágios Iōánnēs, Akrōtḗrion - 136-137 LM 8
Ágios Nikólaos 136-137 LM 8
Ağlasun 182-183 D 4
Agnew 194-195 D 5
Agnone 136-137 F 5
Agnes Baraka 172-173 H 1
Agnibilekrou 172-173 E 4
Agochi = Aoji 188-189 H 1
Agoj, gora 140-141 J 4
Agout 134-135 J 7
Agra 180-181 M 5
Agra OK 154-155 G 3
Agrachanskij poluostrov 140-141 NO 5
Agram = Zagreb 136-137 FG 3
Ağrı [TR] 180-181 E 3
Agrigento 136-137 E 7
Agrinion 136-137 J 6
Agròpoli 136-137 F 5
Agryz 178-179 J 6
Agter Roggeveld 174-175 D 6
Água Boa 160-161 L 2-3
Água Branca, Chapada da - 160-161 L 1-2
Agua Caliente Indian Reservation 150-151 E 9
Água Clara [BR] 158-159 J 9
Agua Fria River 150-151 G 8-9
Aguán, Rio - 146-147 J 8
Agua Nueva 162 BC 4-5
Agua Nueva, TX 154-155 F 7
Aguapei, Rio - [BR, São Paulo] 160-161 G 4
Agua Prieta 146-147 DE 5
Aguaray Guazú, Rio - 160-161 D 6
Aguascalientes[MEX, ●] 146-147 F 7
Aguascalientes[MEX, ⭑] 146-147 F 7
Àguas da Prata 160-161 J 4
Águas Formosas 158-159 L 8
Águas Vermelha 160-161 M 1
Águeda, Rio - 134-135 D 8
Agüerito 160-161 D 5
Aguga 171 C 2
Aguila, AZ 150-151 G 9
Aguglie, Bacino di - 124-125 L 8
Aguglie, Capo di - 168-169 F 9
Aguglie, Dorsale di - 124-125 K 8
Aguilar, CO 152-153 D 7
Águilas 134-135 G 10
Aguirre 160-161 D 7
Aguja, Punta - 158-159 C 6
Agujas, Cabo - 168-169 F 10
Agujas, Cuenca de - 124-125 L 8
Agulhas, Bacia das - 124-125 L 8
Agulhas Basin 124-125 L 8
Agulhas, Cabo das - 168 F 9
Agulhas, Cape - 168-169 F 10
Agulhas, Kaap - 168-169 F 10
Agulhasbecken 124-125 L 8
Agulhasbekken 124-125 L 8
Agulhas Negras 158-159 K 9
Agung,Gunung - 186-187 G 8
Agunrege 172-173 F 3
Agusan 186-187 J 5
Agvali 140-141 N 5
Ägypten 166-167 KL 3
Ahaggar = Al-Hajjār 166-167 EF 4
Ahaggar, Tassili Oua n' = Tāsīlī Wān al-Hajjār 166-167 E 5-F 4
Ahar 182-183 M 3
Ahar Chāy 182-183 M 3
Ahé 192-193 N 6
Ahır Dağı 182-183 G 4
Ahırlı = Karaburun 182-183 B 3
Ahlat 182-183 K 3
Ahlat = Yusufeli 182-183 J 2
Ahmadabad [IND] 180-181 L 6
Aḥmadābād [IR] 182-183 M 4
Aḥmadī, Al- = Minā' al-Aḥmadī 182-183 N 8
Ahmadnagar 180-181 LM 7
Aḥmadpūr Sharqi 180-181 L 5
Aḥmar, Jabal al- 170 D 3
Ahmednagar = Ahmadnagar 180-181 LM 7
Ahoada 172-173 G 4
Ahogayegua, Sierra de - 146-147 b 2-3
Ahoskie, NC 148-149 E 6
Ahtopol 136-137 MN 4
Ahunui 192-193 N 6
Āhūrān 182-183 M 6
Åhus 130-131 F10
Ahuzhen 190-191 G 4
Ahvāz 180-181 F 4
Ahvenanmaa = Åland 130-131 HJ 7
Aḥwar 180-181 F 8
Ahwaz = Ahvāz 180-181 F 4
Aia, L' = 's-Gravenhage 134-135 AB 2
Āībak = Samangān 180-181 K 3
Aibetsu 188-189 c 2
Aichi 188-189 L 5
Aidin = Aydın 180-181 B 3
Aígina [GR, ⊙] 136-137 K 7
Aígina [GR, ●] 136-137 K 7
Aigion 136-137 JK 6

Aigle, Chaîne de l' 133 GH 3
Aigle, l' 134-135 H 4
Aiguá 162 F 4
Aigues-Mortes 134-135 JK 7
Aiguilles, Bassin des - 124-125 L 8
Aiguilles, Cap des - 168-169 F 10
Aigun = Aihun 184-185 O 1
Ai He 188-189 E 2
Ai Ho = Ai He 188-189 E2
Aihsien = Yacheng 184-185 K 8
Aihui 184-185 O 1
Aija 158-159 D 6
Aikawa 188-189 LM 3
Aiken, SC 146-147 K 5
Aileron 194-195 F 4
'Ailī, Sha' ib al- = Sha' ib al- 'Aylī 182-183 H 7
Ailinginae 192-193 H 3
Aim 178-179 Z 6
Aimorés 158-159 L 8
Aimorés, Serra dos - 158-159 L 8
Ain 134-135 K 5
'Ain, Wādī al- = Wādī al-'Ayn 180-181 H 6
'Ainabo = Caynabo 166-167 b 2
'Ain al Mugshin, Al- = Al'Ayn al-Muqshin 180-181 GH 7
Ainaži 138-139 DE 5
Aïn-Beïda = 'Ayn Baydā, 166-167 F 1
Aïn-ben-Tili = 'Ayn Bin Ṭīlī 166-167 C3
'Aïn Diouâr = 'Ayn Dīwār 182-183 K 4
Aïn Galakka 166-167 H 5
Aïn-Salah = 'Ayn Ṣāliḥ 166-167 E 3
Aïn-Sefra = 'Ayn Ṣafrā 166-167 DE 2
Ainsworth, NE 152-153 FG 4
Aïn-Témouchent = 'Ayn Tamūshanat 166-167 D 1
Aioi 188-189 K 5
Aiquile 158-159 F 8
Aïr ou Azbine166-167 F 5
Airan Köl = Telijn nuur 184-185 F 2
Aire, Isla del - 134-135 K 9
Air Force Island 144-145 W 4
Aisch 133 E 4
Aisega 186-187 g 6
Aishihik 144-145 J 5
Aisne 134-135 J 4
Aitana 134-135 G 9
Aitape 186-187 M 7
Aitkin, MN 152-153 K 2
Aiud 136-137 K 2
Aiun, El - = Al-'Ayūn 166-167 B 3
Aiuruoca 160-161 K 4
Aiwan Wan 190-191 H 7
Aix-en-Provence 134-135 KL 7
Aix-les-Bains 134-135 KL 6
Āīzāl = Aizawal 180-181 P 6
Aizawal 180-181 P 6
Aizpute 130-131 J 9
Aizpute 138-139 C 5
Aizu-Wakamatsu 184-185 QR 4
Aizu-Wakamatu = Aizu-Wakamatsu 184-185 QR 4
Ajā, Jabal - 180-181 E 5
'Ajabshīr 182-183 L 4
Ajaccio 136-137 C 5
Ajadar 140-141 J 2
Ajaguz 178-179 P 8
Ajaj, Wādī - 182-183 J 5
'Ajājā 182-183 J 4
'Ajam, Al- 182-183 G 6
'Ajam, El- = Al-'Ajam 182-183 G 6
Ajan [SU, ~] 178-179 R 4
Ajan [SU, ● Pribrežnyj chrebet] 178-179 a 6
Ajan [SU, ● Sibirskoje ploskogorje] 178-179 U 6
Ajana 194-195 BC 5
Ajanka 178-179 g 5
Ajanta Range 180-181 M 6
Ajax Mountain 150-151 G 3
Ajdābiyah 166-167 J 2
Ajedabya = Ajdābiyah 166-167 J 2
Ājī Chāi = Rūd-e Āqdogh Mīsh 182-183 M 4
Ajigasawa 188-189 MN 2
Ājīn 182-183 M 5
Ajjer, Tassili n' = Tāsīlī Wan Ahjār 166-167 F3
Ajkino 138-139 R 2
'Ajlūn 182-183 FG 6
'Ajlūn, Jabal - 182-183 FG 6
'Ajmah, Jabal al- 166-167 L 3
'Ajmān 180-181 GH 5
'Ajmī 182-183 L 5-6
Ajnis, Qārat - 170 BC 3
Ajo, AZ 150-151 G 9
Ajo Mountains 150-151 G 9
Ajon, ostrov - 178-179 g 4
Ajrag nuur 184-185 GH 2
'Ajramīyah, Bi'r al- 170 DE 3
Ajtos 136-137 M 4
Akabar 172-173 F 2
Akabira 188-189 c 2
Akdemii, zaliv - 178-179 a 7
Akadien = Acadie 144-145 XY 8
Akaishi-sammyaku 188-189 LM 5
Akalkot 180-181 M 7
Akan ko 188-189 cd 2
Akantarer, I-n- 166-167 E 5
Akanyaru 171 B 3
Akasaki 188-189 J 5
'Akāsh, Wādī - = Wādī 'Ukāsh 182-183 J 5-6
Akashi 188-189 K 5
Akasi = Akashi 188-189 K 5
Äkäsjoki 130-131 KL 4
Akayu 188-189 N 3
Akcaabat 182-183 H 2
Akcadag 182-183 GH 3
Akçadağ 182-183 GH 3
Akçakale 182-183 H 4
Akçakoca 182-183 D 2
Akçakoyumla 182-183 G 4
Akçan = Sakavi 182-183 J 3
Ak Çay 182-183 C 4
Akchar = Āqshar 166-167 B 4
Ak Dağlar 180-181 BC 3
Akdağlar 182-183 FG 3
Akdağmadeni 182-183 F 3
Akera 140-141 N 7
Akershus 130-131 D 7-8
Aketi 168-169 F 2
Akhḍar, Jabal al- [LAR] 166-167 J 2
Akhḍar, Jabal al- [Oman] 180-181 H 6
Akhisar 182-183 BC 3
Akhmim 170 DE 4
Aki 188-189 J 6
Akik = 'Aqiq 166-167 M 5
Akimiski Island 144-145 UV 7
Akimovka 140-141 G 3
Akıncı Burnu 182-183 F 4
Akıncılar 182-183 B 2
Akita 184-185 QR 4
Akjoujt = Aqjawajat 166-167 B 5
Akkajaure 130-131 G 4
Akka-mori 188-189 N 2
Akkeshi 188-189 d 2

Akkeshi wan 188-189 d 2
'Akkō 182-183 F 6
Akköy 182-183 B 4
Akku =Çaldere 182-183 G 2
Akkuş 182-183 G 2
Akkerman = Belgorod - Dnestrovskij 140-141 DE 3
Aklavik 144-145 J 4
Akmal'-Abad = Gižduvan 178-179 L 9
Ak-Mečet' = Kzyl-Orda 178-179 M 9
Akmeņrags 138-139 C 5
Akmolinsk = Celinograd 178-179 MN 7
Akniste 138-139 EF 5
Akō 188-189 K 5
Akōbō = Akūbū 166-167 L 7
Akola 180-181 M 6
Akonolinga 166-167 G 8
Akor 172-173 D 2
Akordat 166-167 M 5
Akören 182-183 E 4
Akosombo Dam 172-173 F 4
Akoupé 174-173 E 4
Akpatok Island 144-145 X 5
Akpınar = Çınar 182-183 J 4
Akranes 130-131 bc 2
Akrar 130-131 b 2
Ākre = 'Aqrah 182-183 K 4
Akrítas, Akrōtḗrion - 136-137 JK 7
Akron, CO 152-153 E 5
Akron,IA 152-153 H 4
Akron, IN 152-153 NO 5
Akron, OH 146-147 K 3
Akrōtḗri 136-137 L 8
Akrōtēríu, Kólpos - 182-183 E 5
Akša 178-179 V 7
Aksaj [SU,~] 140-141 N 5
Aksai [SU,●] 140-141 LM 3
Aksakovo 138-139 TU 6
Akşar 182-183 K 2
Aksaray 182-183 EF 3
Akşehir 180-181 C 3
Akşehir Gölü 182-183 D 3
Akseki 182-183 D 4
Aks'onovo-Zilovskoje 178-179 VW 7
Aksoran, gora - 178-179 O 8
Akstafa 140-141 M 6
Aksu [SU] 178-179 N 7
Aksu [TR] 182-183 G 4
Aksu = Aqsu 184-185 E 3
Aksuat 178-179 P 8
Aksubajevo 138-139 S 6
Aksu Çay 182-183 D 4
Aksum 166-167 M 6
Akša 178-179 V 7
Aktanyš 138-139 TU 6
Aktau 140-141 P 5
Aktöbe 178-179 K 7
Aktogaj 178-179 O 8
Aktumsyk 178-179 K 8
Aku 172-173 G 4
Akūbū 166-167 L 7
Akulurak, AK 144-145 CD 5
Akune 184-185 OP 5
Akure 166-167 F 7
Akureyri 130-131 de 2
Akuse 172-173 EF 4
Akwaibom 172-173 GH 4
Akwanga 172-173 GH 3
Akwawa 172-173 EF 4
Akwizgran = Aachen 133 C 3
Akyab = Sittwe 186-187 B 2
Akyaka 182-183 K 2
Akyazı 182-183 D 2
Ål 130-131 C 7
Alabama 146-147 J 5
Alabama River 146-147 J 5
Alaca 182-183 F 2
Alacadağ 182-183 DE 4
Alacahan 182-183 G 3
Alacahöyük 182-183 F 2
Alachadzy 140-141 JK 5
Alaçam 182-183 F 2
Alachua, FL 148-149 b 2
Aladağ 182-183 K 3
Ālādāgh, Reshteh - 180-181 H 3
Ala Dağlar [TR, ▲▲] 182-183 F 4
Alagoas 158-159 M 6-7
Alagoinhas 158-159 M 7
Alagir 140-141 LM 5
Alagón 134-135 D 9
Alag Šan Gov' 184-185 J 4
Alajuela 146-147 K 9-10
Alakol', ozero - 178-179 P 8
Alalaú, Rio - 158-159 G 5
'Alamar-Rūm, Rā's - 170 B 2
'Alamayn, Al- 166-167 K 2
Alameda, CA 150-151 BC 7
Alameda, ID 150-151 G 4
Alameda, NM 154-155 B 3
Alameda, La - 154-155 DE 6
Alamo, ND 152-153 E 1
Alamo, NV 150-151 F 7
Alamo, Cerro - 150-151 EF 10
Álamo, El - [MEX, Baja California] 150-151 EF 10
Álamo, El - [MEX, Nuevo León] 154-155 F 7
Alamogordo, NM 146-147 E 5
Alamo Lake 150-151 G 8
Alamo River 150-151 F 9
Alamos 146-147 E 6
Alamosa, CO 146-147 E 4
Ålamos de Peña 154-155 B 5
Ālāmūt 182-183 O 4
Åland [SF, ⊙] 130-131 HJ 7
Åland [SF, ⭑] 130-131 HJ 7
Åland [SF, ilha] 130-131 HJ 7
Åland [SF, unidade administrativa] 130-131 HJ 7
Åland, Fosa de - 130-131 H 7
Åland, Fossa de - 130-131 H 7
Åland, Fossa delle 130-131 H 7
Åland, Fosse d' 130-131 H 7
Åland-mélység 130-131 H 7
Ålandsdiep 130-131 H 7
Ålands hav 130-131 H 7-8
Ålandstief 130-131 H 7
Alanga Arba 168-169 JK 2
Ālanmyō 186-187 C 3
Alanya 180-181 C3
Alaotra, Lac - 168-169 L 6
Alapaha, GA 148-149 B 9
Alapaha River 148-149 B 9
Alapajevsk 178-179 L 6
Alaplı 182-183 D 2
Ālappi = Alleppey 180-181 M 9
Alāq 166-167 B 5
Alarcón 134-135 FG 9
Alas, Selat - 186-187 G 8
Alasca 144-145 E-H 4
Alasca, Golfo do 144-145 G-J 6
Alaşehir 182-183 C 3
Alašejev buchta 121 C 5
Alashtar 182-183 MN 6
Alaska 144-145 F-H 4
Alaska, Golfe d' 144-145 GH 6
Alaska, Golfo de - 144-145 GH 6
Alaska, Golfo di - 144-145 G-J 6
Alaska, Golf van - 144-145 GH 6
Alaska, Golf von - 144-145 GH 6

Alaska, Gulf of - 144-145 GH 6
Alaska, Zatoka - 144-145 G-J 6
Alaska Highway 144-145 H 5
Alaska Peninsula 144-145 DE 6
Alaska Range 144-145 F-H 5
Alàssio 136-137 C 3-4
Alašejev buchta 121 C 5
Alaszka 144-145 E-H 4
Alaszkai-öböl 144-145 G-J 6
Al' at 140-141 O 7
Alatri 136-137 E 5
Alatyr' [SU, ~] 138-139 P 6
Alatyr' [SU, ●] 178-179 H 7
Alausí 158-159 D 5
Alava, Cape - 150-151 A 1
Alaverdi 140-141 M 6
Alayunt 182-183 D 3
Alazani 140-141 N 6
Alazeja 178-179 d 3-e 4
Alazejskoje ploskogorje 178-179 c 4
Alba 136-137 C 3
Albacete 134-135 FG 9
Alba de Tormes 134-135 E 8
Alba lulia 136-137 K 2
Albanese Alpen = Alpet e Shqipërisë 136-137 HJ 4
Albánia 136-137 J 5
Albania 136-137 J 5
Albânia 136-137 HJ 5
Albanië 136-137 H 4-5
Albanie 136-137 H 4-5
Albánie 136-137 J 5
Albanien 136-137 H 4-5
Albany 194-195 C 6-7
Albany, CA 150-151 B 7
Albany, GA 146-147 K 5
Albany,KY 154-155 N 2
Albany, MN 152-153 J 3
Albany, MO 152-153 J 5
Albany, NY 146-147 LM 3
Albany, OR 146-147 B 3
Albany, TX 154-155 F 4
Albany River 144-145 U 7
Albarracín 134-135 G 8
Albatros Island 168-169 NO 6
Albatross Bay 194-195 H 2
Albarkaïzé 172-173 F 2-3
Albayrak 182-183 KL 3
Albemarle, NC 148-149 C 7
Albemarle = Isla Isabela 158-159 A 5
Albemarle Sound 148-149 EF 6
Albenga 136-137 C 3
Alberche 134-135 E 8
Alberdi 160-161 CD 7
Alberga 196 B 1
Alberga, The - 194-195 FG 5
Alberrie Creek 196 C 2
Albert [AUS] 196 H 4
Albert, Lake - 194-195 GH 7
Albert, Parc national - = Parc national Virunga 168-169 G 2-3
Alberta 144-145 NO 6
Alberta, VA 148-149 E 6
Albertinia 174-175 D 8
Albertkanaal 134-135 J 3
Albert Lea, MN 146-147 H 3
Albert Markham, Mount 121 AB 17-15
Albert Nile 168-169 H 2
Alberton, MT 150-151 F 2
Albertville 134-135 L 6
Albertville = Kalemie 168-169 G 4
Albi 134-135 J 7
Albia, IA 152-153 K 5
Albin, WY 152-153 D 5
Albina 158-159 J 3
Albino 136-137 CD 3
Albion, IL 152-153 M 6
Albion, IN 152-153 O 5
Albion, MI 152-153 O 4
Albion, MT 152-153 D 3
Albion, NE 152-153 GH 5
Albion, NY 148-149 DE 3
Al-Biqā 182-183 = 4 ◃ 6 b
Alborán 134-135 F 11
Ålborg 130-131 CD 9
Ålborg Bugt 130-131 D 9
Alborz, Reshteh Kūhhā-ye - 180-181 G 3
Albufera, La - 134-135 GH 9
Albuquerque, NM 146-147 EF 4
Albuquerque, 160-161 D 3
Alburquerque 134-135 D 9
Al-Buraymi 180-181 H 6
Albury-Wodonga 194-195 J 7
Alcácer do Sal 134-135 C 9
Alcalá de Guadaira 134-135 E 10
Alcalá de Henares 134-135 F 8
Alcalá la Real 134-135 F 10
Alcalde, NM 154-155 BC 2
Àlcamo 136-137 E 7
Alcañiz 134-135 G 8
Alcántara 134-135 D 9
Alcántara [BR] 158-159 L 5
Alcantarilla 134-135 G 10
Alcañiz 134-135 G 8
Alcaparra 154-155 BC 5
Alcaraz 134-135 F 9
Alcaraz, Sierra de - 134-135 F 9
Alcarría, La - 134-135 F 8
Alcatrazes, Ilha dos - 160-161 K 6
Alcázar de San Juan 134-135 F 9
Alcázarquivir = Al-Qaṣr al-Kabīr 166-167 C1
Alcester Island 186-187 h 6
Alčevs'k 140-141 J 2
Alcira 134-135 G 9
Alcira [RA] 162 D 4
Alcoa, TN 154-155 O 3
Alcobaça 134-135 C 9
Alcobaça [BR] 158-159 M 8
Alcolea del Pinar 134-135 FG 8
Alcoota 194-195 F 4
Alcorn College, MS 154-155 K 5
Alcova, WY 152-153 C 4
Alcoy 134-135 G 9
Aldabra Islands 168-169 L 4
Aldağ [TR, ▲] 182-183 F 4
Aldağ [TR, ●] 182-183 F 4
Aldamas, Los - 154-155 F 7
Aldan [SU, ~] 178-179 Z 6
Aldan [SU, ●] 178-179 XY 6
Aldano-Učurskij chrebet 178-179 Y 6
Aldanskoje nagorje 178-179 X-Z 6
Aldeburgh 132 GH 5
Alder, MT 150-151 GH 3
Alderney 132 E 7
Alder Peak 150-151 C 8
Alduş = Temsiyas 182-183 H 3
Alechovščina 138-139 JK 3
Aledo, IL 152-153 L 5
Aleg = Alaq 166-167 B 5
Alegre 160-161 M 4
Alegrete 162 E 3-4
Aleï, I-n- 166-167 D 5
Alejandra, Cabo - = Cape Alexandra 162 J 8
Alejandría = Al-Iskandarīyah 166-167 KL 2
Alejandro Selkirk 157 B 6
Alejsk 178-179 P 7

Aleksandra, mys - 178-179 ab 7
Aleksandra I, zeml'a 121 C 29
Aleksandrija 140-141 F 2
Aleksandria = Al-Iskandariyah 166-167 KL 2
Aleksandro-Nevskij 138-139 N 7
Aleksandrov 138-139 N 6
Aleksandrov Gaj 140-141 O 1
Aleksandrovka [SU, Rostov 140-141 J 3]
Aleksandrovsk [SU, Rossijskaja SFSR] 138-139 V 4
Aleksandrovsk = Belogorsk 178-179 YZ 7
Aleksandrovskoje [SU, Zapadno-Sibirskaja nizmennost'] 178-179 OP 5
Aleksandrovskoje [SU, Stavropol'] 140-141 K 3
Aleksandrovskoje [SU, Stavropol'] 140-141 L 4
Aleksandrovsk-Sachalinskij 178-179 bc 7
Aleksandrów Kujawski 133 J 2
Aleksandry, zeml'a - 178-179 FG 1
Aleksejevka [SU, Kazachskaja SSR] 178-179 N 7
Aleksejevka [SU, Rossijskaja SFSR Belgorod] 140-141 J1
Aleksejevka [SU, Rossijskaja SFSR - Samara] 138-139 S 7
Aleksejevka [SU, Rossijskaja SFSR - Samara] 138-139 S 7
Aleksejevka [SU, Rossijskaja SFSR Saratov] 196 QR 7
Aleksejevo-Lozovskoje 140-141 K 2
Aleksejevsk = Svobodnyj 178-179 YZ 7
Aleksin 138-139 L 6
Aleksinac 136-137 JK 4
Álem 130-131 G 9
Aleman, NM 154-155 B 4
Alemanha 133 DF 2
Alem Gena 166-167 M 7
Alem Maya 166-167 N 7
Além Paraíba 158-159 HJ 5
Alençon 134-135 H 4
Alenquer [BR] 158-159 HJ 5
Alentejo 134-135 C 10-D 9
Alenuihaha Channel 186-187 ef 3
Alenz 182-183 J 4
Aléoutiennes, Fosse des - 120 D 35
Alepo = Halab 182-183 G 4
Aleppo = Halab 182-183 G 4
Alert 120 A 25
Alerta 158-159 E 7
Alès 134-135 K 6
Alessàndria 136-137 C 3
Alessándria = Al-Iskandariyah 166-167 KL 2
Ålesund 130-131 AB 6
Aleucki, Rów - 120 D 35
Aleutas, Fossas das - 120 D 35
Aléutengraben 120 D 35
Aleuten Trench 120 D 35
Aleutiana, Fosa das - 120 D 35
Aleutian Islands 120 D 35-1
Aleutian Range 144-145 E 6-F 5
Aleutine, Fossa delle 120 D 35
Aleutka 184-185 T 2
Aleutskij přikop 120 D 35
Alevina, mys - 178-179 cd 6
Aleviskik = Samandağ 182-183 F 4
Alexander, ND 152-153 E 2
Alexander, Kap - 144-145 WX 2
Alexander, Point - 194-195 G 2
Alexander Archipelago 144-145 E 6-K 5
Alexander City, AL 154-155 MN 4
Alexandra [NZ] 194-195 N 9
Alexandra, Cape - 162 J 8
Alexandra = Umzinto 174-175 J 6
Alexandria, IN 152-153 O 5
Alexandria, MN 152-153 J 3
Alexandria, SD 152-153 H 4
Alexandry 178-179 FG 1
Alexandra Fiord 144-145 VW 2
Alexandra land = zeml'a - Aleksandry 178-179 FG 1
Alexandretta = İskenderun 180-181 D 3
Alexandrette = İskenderun 180-181 D 3
Alexandria [AUS] 194-195 G 3
Alexandria [RI] 136-137 L 4
Alexandria [ZA] 168-169 G 9
Alexandria, LA 146-147 H 5
Alexandria, VA 146-147 L 4
Alexandria = Al-Iskandariyah 166-167 KL 2
Alexandrie = Al-Iskandariyah 166-167 KL 2
Alexandrina, Lake - 194-195 GH 7
Alfambra 134-135 G 8
Alfarez de Navio Sobral 121 A 132-35
Alfatar 136-137 M 4
Alfeiós 136-137 J 7
Ålfotbreen 130-131 A 7
Alfred, ME 148-149 H 3
Alfredo Chaves 160-161 M 4
Alga 178-179 K 8
Algabas 140-141 Q 1
Ålgård 131 A 8
Algarve 134-135 CD 10
Algeciras 134-135 E 10
Algeciras 138-139 N 7
Alger = Al-Jazā'ir 166-167 E 1
Alger, MI 152-153 O 4
Algeria 166-167 D-F 3
Algerian Basin 128-129 J 8-K 7
Algérie 166-167 D-F 3
Algerisch-Provenzialisches Becken 128-129 J 8-K 7
Algerije 166-167 D-F 3
Algerijns-Provençaals Bekken 128-129 J 8-K 7
Algéro = Al-Jazā'ir 166-167 E 1
Algiers = Al-Jazā'ir' 166-167 E 1

Algiersko-Prowansalski, Basen- 134-135 J 10-L 8
Algir = Al-Jazā'ir 166-167 E 1
Algoabaai 168-169 G 9
Algoa Bay = Algoabaai 168-169 G 9
Algodones 150-151 F 9
Algoma, OR 150-151 C 4
Algoma, WI 152-153 N 3
Algona, IA 152-153 JK 4
Algonquin Provincial Park 144-145 V 8
Alhambra, CA 150-151 DE 8
Alhucemas = Al-Husaymah 166-167 D1
Alhucemas, Islas de - 134-135 F 11
'Ali, Sadd al- 166-167 L 4
Aliákmon 136-137 JK 5
'Ali al-Garbi 182-183 M 6
Ali-Bajramly 140-141 O 7
Alibardak = Mermer 182-183 J 3
Alibej, ozero - 136-137 O 3
Alibej, ozero - 140-141 F 4
Alibey Adasi 182-183 B 3
Alibori 172-173 F 3
Alibunar 136-137 J 3
Alicante 134-135 GH 9
Alice 174-175 G 7
Alice, TX 146-147 G 6
Alicedale 174-175 G7
Alice, Punta - 136-137 G 6
Alice Springs 194-195 FG 4
Aliceville, AL 154-155 LM 4
Alicudi 136-137 F 6
Ali Gabe 171 E 2
Aligar = Aligarh 180-181 M 5
Aligarh 180-181 M 5
Aligüdarz 182-183 NO 6
Alihe 184-185 N 1
Alikovo 138-139 Q 6
Alima 168-169 DE 3
Alindao 166-167 J 7-8
Alingsås 130-131 E 9
Alipur Duar 180-181 O 5
Aliquippa, PA 148-149 C 4
Alisal, CA 150-151 C 7
Alitus = Alytus 138-139 J 6
Aliwal-Noord 168-169 G 9
Aliwal Suid = Mosselbaai 168-169 G 9
Aljaška 144-145 E-H 4
Aljašský zállv 144-145 G-J 6
Alkali Desert 150-151 EF 5-6
Alkali Flat 150-151 DE 5
Alkali Lake 150-151 D 5
Alkamari 172-173 H 2
Alkmaar 134-135 K 2
Allach-Jun' 178-179 a 5
Allada 166-167 E 7
Allagash, ME 148-149 J 1
Allagash River 148-149 J 1
Allahabad [IND] 180-181 N 5
Allaire, Banc - 146-147 BC 7
Allaire, Banco - 146-147 BC 7
Allaire, Banco di 146-147 BC 7
Allaire, mèlcina - 146-147 BC 7
Allairebank 146-147 BC 7
Allaire-pad 146-147 BC 7
Allakaket, AK 144-145 F 4
Allaküeküber Dağları 182-183 K 2
Allamoore, TX 154-155 C 5
Allanmyo = Ālanmyó 186-187 C 3
Allanridge 174-175 G 5
Alldays 174-175 H 2
'Allāqi, Wadi al- 170 E 6
Allegan, MI 152-153 O4
Alleghenies = Allegheny Mountains 146-147 K 4-L 3
Allegheny Mountains 146-147 K 4-L 3
Allegheny Plateau 146-147 K 4-L 3
Allegheny River 148-149 D 4
Allemagne = Deutschland 133 D-F 2-4
Allemagne, Baie d' 133 C 1
Allemanskraaldam 174-175 G 5
Allemorgens 174-175 D 7
Allen, OK 154-155 G 3
Allendale, SC 148-149 G 8
Allen Park, MI 152-153 P 4
Allenstein = Olsztyn 133 K 2
Allentown, PA 146-147 L 3
Alleppey 180-181 M 9
Aller 133 D 2
Allerheiligenbaai = Baía de Todos os Santos 158-159 M 7
Allerheiligenbai = Baía de Todos os Santos 158-159 M 7
Allerton, IA 152-153 K5
Alliance, NE 146-147 F 3
Alliance, OH 148-149 C 4
Allier 133 J 5
Alligator Sound 148-149 EF 7
Allison, IL 152-153 K 4
Allison, TX 154-155 EF 3
Alliston 148-149 D 2
Alma 134-135 J 6
Alma [CDN, Quebec] 144-145 W 8
Al'ma [SU] 136-137 F 2
Alma, AR 154-155 H 3
Alma, GA 148-149 B 9
Alma, KS 152-153 H 6
Alma, MI 152-153 O 4
Alma, NE 152-153 G 4
Alma, WI 152-153 M 3
Alma-Ata = Almaty178-179 O 9
Almada 134-135 C 9
Almadén 134-135 E 9
Alma, Lake = Harlan County Resevoir 152-153 G 5-6
Almalyk 180-181 KL 2
Almanor, Lake - 150-151 C 5
Almansa 134-135 G 9
Almanzora 134-135 F 10
Almaty 178-179 O 9
Almazán 134-135 F 8
Almeida 134-135 D 8
Almeida Campos 158-159 K 8
Almeirim [BR] 158-159 J 5
Almena, KS 152-153 G 5
Almenara [BR] 158-159 LM 8
Almendralejo 134-135 D 9
Almeria 134-135 F 10
Almeria, Golfo de - 134-135 F 10
Al'metjevsk 178-179 J 7
Almirante Brown [Antarktika] 121 C 30-31
Almo, ID 150-151 G 4
Almodóvar del Campo 134-135 E 9
Al Moktar 172-173 G 2
Almond, WI 152-153 M 3
Almont, CO 152-153 E 4
Almont [CDN] 148-149 E 2
Almorox 134-135 E 8
Almota, WA 150-151 E 3
Almuñécar 134-135 F 10
Almus 182-183 G 2
Almyrós 136-137 K 6
Alnasi 138-139 T 5
Alnwick 132 F 4

Alofi 186-187 b 1
Aloha, OR 150-151 B 3
Aloja 138-139 E 5
Aloʻ 138-139 G 5
Alonso, MO 150-161 G 6
Alonnêsos 136-137 KL 6
Alor, MO 154-155 K 2
Alor Setar 186-187 CD 5
Alotau 186-187 NO 9
Aloysius, Mount - 194-195 E 5
Alpen 128-129 KL 6
Alpena, MI 146-147 K 2
Alpena, AR 154-155 J 2
Alpena, SD 152-153 G 3
Alpercatas, Rio - 158-159 KL 6
Alpes 128-129 KL 6
Alpes Albaneses = Alpet e Shqipërisë 136-137 HJ 4
Alpes Cárnicos 136-137 E 2
Alpes Carnics 133 F 5
Alpes Carniques 136-137 E 2
Alpes Cottiennes 134-135 G 6
Alpes Dolomiticos = Dolomiti 136-137 DE 2
Alpes Graies 134-135 L 6
Alpes Julianos 136-137 EF 2
Alpes Julianas 136-137 EF 2
Alpes Juliennes 136-137 EF 2
Alpes Maritimes 134-135 L 6
Alpet e Shqipërisë 136-137 HJ 4
Alpha 194-195 J 4
Alpha, IL 152-153 L 5
Alphonse Island 168-169 M 4
Alpi 128-129 KL 6
Alpi Carniche 136-137 E 2
Alpi Giulie 136-137 EF 2
Alpine, AZ 150-151 J 9
Alpine, TX 154-155 C 5
Alpine, ID 150-151 H 4
Alpinópolis 160-161 J 4
Alpi Transilvanici 136-137 KL 3
Alps 128-129 KL 6
Alpu 182-183 D 3
Alpy 136-137 A 3-E 2
Alpy Australijskie = Snowy Mountains 194-195 J 7
Alqūsh 182-183 K 4
Alroy Downs 194-195 G 3
Als 130-131 C 10
Alsace 134-135 L 4-5
Alsácia 133 C 4-5
Alsasko 134-135 L 4-5
Alsasua 134-135 FG 7
Alsazia 134-135 L 4-5
Alschwangen = Alšvanga 138-139 D 6
Alsea, OR 150-151 B 3
Alstahaug 130-131 DE 5
Alsunga = Alšvanga 138-139 C 5
Alšvanga 138-139 C 5
Alta 130-131 J 3
Alta, IA 152-153 J 4
Altaelv 130-131 K 3
Alta Gracia [RA] 162 CD 4
Altagracia [YV] 158-159 E 2
Altaï = Altaj 184-185 E F 1
Altai = Altaj 178-179 PQ 7
Altaï-pad 146-167 PQ 7
Altai, Cima del - 124-125 H 2-3
Altair, Cume de - 124-125 H 3
Altairkuppe 124-125 H 3
Altair-Ondiepte 124-125 H 2-3
Altair Seamounts 124-125 H 2-3
Altair, Sommità di - 124-125 H 3
Altaj, Autonoma Region = 8 - ⊲178-179 Q 7
Altaj, Autonomous Region - 9 - ⊲178-179 Q 7
Altaj, Autonome Republiek - 9 - ⊲178-179 Q 7
Altaj, Région Autonome - 9 - ⊲178-179 Q 7
Altaj, República Autónoma de - 9 - ⊲178-179 Q 7
Altaj-hegyvidéki Autonóm Terület 178-179 Q 7
Altaj Mongolski = Mongol Altajn Nuruu 184-185 H-L 2
Altajn Nuruu = Mongol Altajn Nuruu 184-185 F-H 2
Altajská republika = 8 - ⊲178-179 Q 7
Altamaha River 146-147 K 5
Altamira [BR] 158-159 J 5
Altamira, Cueva de - 134-135 E 7
Altamont, IL 152-153 M 6
Altamont, OR 150-151 BC 4
Altamont, WY 150-151 H 5
Altamura 136-137 G 5
Altan Xiret = Ejin Horo Qi 190-191 BC 2
Altar Valley 150-151 H 10
Alta Vista, KS 152-153 H 6
Altavista, VA 148-149 D 6
Altay 184-185 F 2
Altdorf 133 D 5
Altenburg 133 F 3
Alter do Chão [BR] 158-159 HJ 5
Altevatn 130-131 H 3
Alt-Fennern = Vändra 138-139 F 4
Altheimer, AR 154-155 K 3
Altinekin 182-183 E 3
Altinhisar 182-183 F 4
Altinkaya Baraji 182-183 F 2
Altınópolis 160-161 J 4
Altınözü 182-183 G 4
Altin Tagh 184-185 EF 4
Altintaş 182-183 CD 3
Alto Adige 136-137 D 2
Alto Anapu, Rio - 158-159 J 5
Alto Araguaia 160-161 F 2
Alto Atlante 166-167 CD 2
Alto Coité 160-161 F 2
Alto Egipto = As-Sa'id 166-167 L 3-4
Alto Garças 158-159 J 8
Alto Longá 158-159 L 6
Alto Molócuè = Molócuè 168-169 J 6
Altônia 160-161 F 5
Altoona, PA 146-147 L 3
Alto Paraguai 158-159 H 8
Alto Paraná [PY] 160-161 E 6

Alto Parnaiba 158-159 K 6
Alto Piquiri 162 F 2
Alto Rio Doce 160-161 L 4
Alto Rio Senguerr 162 BC 6-7
Alto, TX 154-155 H5
Alton, MO 154-155 K 2
Altô Sucuriú 160-161 F 3
Altos [PY] 160-161 D 6
Alt-Pebalg = Vecpiebalga 138-139 EF 5
Alt-Schwaneburg = Gulbene 138-139 F 5
Altsohl = Zvolen 133 J 4
Altuchovo 138-139 JK 7
Altunhisar = Ortaköy 182-183 F 4
Āltūn Kūprī 182-183 L 5
Alturas, 178-179 F 9
Altus, OK 146-147 G 5
Altyagač 140-141 O6
Altyn Tagh = Altin tagh 184-185 EF 4
Altyševo 138-139 Q 6
Alucra 182-183 H 2
Alūksne 138-139 F 5
Alumine 182 B 5
Alung Gangri 184-185 E 5
Alupka 140-141 G 4
Aluradde 160-161 A 5
Alušta 140-141 G 4
'Aluula = Caluula 166-167 c 1
Alva, FL 148-149 c 3
Alva, OK 154-155 F 2
Alvalade 134-135 C 9-10
Alvand, Kūh-e - 180-181 FG 4
Alvar = Alwar 180-181 M 5
Alvarado 146-147 GH 8
Alvarado, TX 154-155 G 4
Alvarães 158-159 G 5
Álvares Machado 160-161 G 5
Álvaro Obregón = Frontera 146-147 H 8
Älvdal 130-131 D 6
Älvdalen 130-131 F 7
Älvesta 130-131 F 9
Alvin, TX 154-155 GH 5
Alvord Lake 150-151 D 4
Älvsborgs län 130-131 E 8-9
Älvsbyn 130-131 J 5
Alwar 180-181 M 5
Alys = Kızılırmak 180-181 D 3
Alytus 130-131 L 10
Alytus 138-139 E 6
Alzada, MT 152-153 D 3
Alzamaj 178-179 S 6
Alžir = Al-Jazā'ir 166-167 E 1
Alžirsko 166-167 D-F 3
Alžírská Kólpos 136-137 DF 3
AlallCourt House, VA 148-149 E 7
Aljaska 152-153 K5
Alzira 134-135 G 9
Almada 146-147 F 3
Am Dam 133 D-F 2-4
Amandalupgai 184-185 H 2
Allen, OK 154-155 G 3
Allendale, SC 148-149 G 8
Allison, IL 152-153 K 4
Al
Amabele 174-175 G 7
Amadeus, Lake - 194-195 F 4
Amâdi 166-167 L 7
'Āmādīyah, Al- 182-183 K 4
Amadjuak Lake 144-155 W 4-5
Amagasaki 188-189 K 5
Amahai 186-187 J 7
Amakusa nada 188-189 G 6
Amakusa-rettō 184-185 O 5
Amakusa syotō = Amakusa-rettō 184-185 O 5
Amál 130-131 E 8
Amalfi 136-137 F 5
Amaliás 136-137 J 7
Amalner 180-181 L 6
Amambaí 160-161 E 5
Amambaí, Rio - 160-161 E 5
Amambaí, Serra de - 160-161 E 5
Amambay 160-161 DE 5
Amami-guntō 184-185 O 6
Amami-ō-shima 184-185 O 6
Amami-Ō sima = Amami-ō-shima 184-185 O 6
Amandola 136-137 E 4
Amangel'dy 178-179 M 7-8
Amanos Dağları = Nur Dağları 182-183 G 4
Amantea 136-137 F 6
Amanu 192-193 NO 6
Amapá [BR, Amapá ●] 158-159 J 4
Amapá [BR , Amapá ●] 158-159 J 4
Amará 166-167 M 7
'Amārah, Al- 180-181 F 4
Amaramba, Lagoa = Lagoa Chiuta 168-169 J 5
Amarante [BR] 158-159 L 6
Amarawati = Amravati 180-181 M 6
Amargo, CA 150-151 E 8
Amargosa Desert 150-151 E 7-8
Amargosa Range 150-151 E 7-8
Amarillo, TX 146-147 F 4
'Amarinah, Tell - = Tall al- 'Amārinah 170 D 4
'Amārinah, Tell al- = Tall al- 'Amārinah 170 D 4
Amaro Leite 158-159 JK 7

Amarume 188-189 M 3
Amarúsion 136-137 KL 6-7
Amasa 152-153 M 2
Amasra 182-183 E 2
Amasya 180-181 D 2
Amatignak Island 120 D 36
Amatique, Bahia de - 146-147 J 8
Amatonga 174-175 K 2
Amauā, Lago - 158-159 G 5
Amazon = Amazonas
Amazonas [BR] 158-159 F-H 5
Amazonas, Estuário do Rio - 158-159 JK 4
Amazonas, Plataforma continental do - 124-125 G 5-6
Amazonas, Plataforma del - 124-125 G 5-6
Amazonas, Rio - [BR] 158-159 HJ 5
Amazonas, Rio - [PE] 158-159 E 5
Amazonasschelf 124-125 G 5-6
Amazone, Plateau Continental de l' 124-125 G 5-6
Amazzoni, Conoide delle - 124-125 G 5-6
Amazonka = Rio Amazonas 158-159 HJ 5
Amazon Shelf 124-125 G 5-6
Amba Alagê 166-167 MN 6
Amba Alaji = Amba Alagê 166-167 MN6
Ambajogai 180-181 M 7
Ambala 180-181 M 4
Ambalavao 168-169 L 7
Ambam 166-167 G 8
Ambanja 168-169 L 5
Ambarčik 178-179 fg 4
Ambaro, Baie d' 168-169 L 5
Ambato 158-159 C 5
Ambatoboeny 168-169 L 6
Ambatolampy 168-169 L 6
Ambatondrazaka 168-169 L 6
Ambatosoratra 168-169 L 6
Ambelau, Pulau - 186-187 J 7
Amber, WA 150-151 E 2
Ambergris Cay 146-147 J 8
Ambidédi 172-173 C 2
Ambikapur 180-181 N 6
Ambilobe 168-169 LM 5
Ambodifotra 168-169 LM 6
Ambohibe 168-169 K 7
Ambohimahasoa 168-169 L 7
Amboina = Pulau Ambon 186-187 J 7
Amboise 134-135 H 5
Amboland = Ovamboland 168-169 DE 6
Ambon 186-187 J 7
Ambon, Pulau - 186-187 J 7
Amboositra 168-169 L 7
Ambovombe 168-169 L 8
Amboy, CA 150-151 F 8
Amboy, IL 152-153 M 5
Amboy Cay 186-187 F 5
Ambrakikós Kólpos 136-137 J 6
Ambre, Cap d' 168-169 LM 5
Ambre, Montagne d' 168-169 L 5
Ambridge, PA 148-149 CD 4
Ambrim 194-195 N 3
Ambriz 168-169 C 4
Ambrizete = N'Zeto 168-169 D 4
Ambrolauri 140-141 L 5
Ambrósio, Serra do 160-161 L 8
Amburgo = Hamburg 133 E 2
Amchitka Island 120 D 1
Am Dam 166-167 J 6
Amderma 178-179 L 4
Amdo 184-185 F 5
Ameca 146-147 F 7
Amedabad = Ahmadabad 180-181 K 6
Amelia, NE 152-153 G 4
Amelia Court House, VA 148-149 DE 6
Amémas, In - 'Ayn Umannâs 166-167 G 3
Amenia, NY 148-149 G 4
Amer, Lac - = Al-Buhayrat al-Murrat al-Kubrâ 170 E 2
Amerasia Basin 120 A
Amer. Samoa [USA] 122-123 A 5
América del Norte 124-125 DE 3
América del Norte, Cuenca de 124-125 FG 6
América del Norte, Dorsal de 124-125 DE 3
América do Sul 124-125 FG 6
América Meridionale 124-125 FG 6
América, Meseta de - = American Highland 121 B 9
América Settentrionale 124-125 DE 3
American Falls, ID 150-151 G 4
American Falls Reservoir 150-151 G 4
American Fork, UT 150-151 H 5
American Highland 121 B 8
American River North Fork 150-151 C 6
American. Samoa [USA] 122-123 A 6
Americus, GA 146-147 K 5
Amerikaans Samoa 122-123 A 6
Amerik. Samoa [V.S.] 122-123 A 6
Amerikanisch Samoa 122-123 A 6
Amerikai Egyesült Államok 146-147 DF 4
Amerikai-magasföld = American Highland 121 B 8
Amerikanisches Hochland = American Highland 121 B 8
Amerikan-Ő sima = Amami-ō-shima 184-185 O 6
Amersfoort [ZA] 174-175 HJ 4
Amersfoort 134-135 K 2
Amery, WI 152-153 K3
Amery Ice Shelf 121 BC 7-8
Amethi 180-181 N 5
Amfíklia 136-137 K 6
Amfissa 136-137 K 6
Amga [SU, -] 178-179 X 6
Amga [SU, -] 178-179 Z 6
Amgar, Al- 182-183 L 8
Am Gēréda 166-167 J 6
Amgu 178-179 a 8
Amguéma 178-179 h 4
Amgun' [SU, -] 178-179 a 7
Amgun' [SU, ●] 178-179 a 7
Amhara = 166-167 M 6

Amherst 144-145 XY 8
Amherst, MA 148-149 G 3
Amherstburg 152-153 P 4
Amherst Junction, WI 152-153 M 3
Amhurst, Mount - 194-195 E 3
Ami, Mont - 171 B 2
Amidon, ND 152-153 E 2
Amiens 134-135 J 4
'Amij, Wādī - 182-183 J 6
Amik Gölü 182-183 G 4
Amindivi Islands 180-181 L 8
Amine 168-189 K 5
Aminuis 168-169 E 7
Aminuis-Reserve 174-175 C 2
Amirantes 168-169 LM 3
Amiraute, Îles de l' = Admiralty Islands 186-187 MN 7
Âmirîyah, Al- 170 CD 2
Amisós = Samsun 180-181 D 2
Amistad, NM 154-155 D 3
Amite, LA 154-155 K 5
Amity, AR 154-155 J 3
Amizade, Ponte da - 160-161 E 6
Amla Island 120 D 36
Amman 180-181 D 4
Ammarfjället 130-131 FG 4
Ammersee 133 E 5
Amnok-kang 184-185 O 3
Amnyemachhen Gangri 184-185 H J 5
Amol 160-161 J 5
Amolar 160-161 D 3
Amores, Los - 162 DE 3
Amorgós 136-137 LM 7
Amory, MS 154-155 L 3-4
Amos 144-145 V 8
Amos, CA 150-151 F 9
'Amoudâ = 'Amudâ 182-183 J 4
Amoy = Xiamen 184-185 M 7
Ampanihy 168-169 K 7
Amparo 160-161 J 5
Ampasindava, Baie d' 168-169 L 5
Ampato, Nevado de - 158-159 E 8
Amphipolis 136-137 K 5
Amposta 134-135 H 8
Ampurias 134-135 J 7
Amqui 144-145 X 8
Amrâm = Amravati 180-181 M 6
Amrâvati 180-181 M 6
Amreli 180-181 K 6
Amritsar 180-181 LM 4
Amroha 180-181 M 5
Amsid, An- 182-183 J 4
Amstel 134-135 K 2
Amsterdam [ZA] 174-175 J 4
Amsterdam, NY 148-149 FG 3
Amsterdam, Platea di - 124-125 NO 8
Amsterdam, Plateau d' 124-125 NO 8
Amsterdamdrempel 124-125 NO 8
Amsterdamplateau 124-125 NO 8
Amstetten 133 G 4
Amt'ae-do 188-189 EF 5
Am Timan 166-167 J 6
'Āmūdâ 182-183 J 4
Amudarja 180-181 J 2
Amund Ringnes Island 144-145 RS 2
Amundsen Bay 121 C 9
Amundsen Glacier 121 A 23-20
Amundsen Gulf 144-145 L-N 3
Amundsen havet 121 BC 25-26
Amundsen-Scott 121 A
Amur = Heilong Jiang 184-185 P 2
'Āmūr, 'Ayn - 170 CD 5
Amurang 186-187 H 6
Amurskij zaliv 188-189 H 1
Amvrosíjevka 140-141 HJ 3
Anaa 192-193 N 6
Anabar 178-179 V 3
Anabuki 188-189 K 5-6
Anaco 158-159 G 2
Anaconda 150-151 G 2-3
Anacortes, WA 150-151 B 1
Anadarko, OK 154-155 FG 3
Anadolu 180-181 CD 3
Anadyr' [SU, ~] 178-179 hj 5
Anadyr' [SU, ●] 178-179 j 5
Anadyrskaja nizmennost' 178-179 h 4
Anadyrskoje ploskogorje 178-179 h 4
Anáfé 136-137 LM 7
Anagni 136-137 E 5
'Anah 182-183 JK 5
Anaheim, CA 150-151 DE 9
Anahuac, TX 154-155 H 6
Anáhuac, Mesa de - 146-147 FG 7-8
Anaiza, Jebel = Jabal Unayzah 180-181 DE 4
Anájás 158-159 JK 5
Anak 188-189 E 3
Anakapalle 180-181 N 7
Anakāpalli = Anakapalle 180-181 N 7
Anak Krakatau, Pulau - 186-187 DE 8
Analalava 168-169 L 5
Anamã 158-159 G 5
Anambas, Kepulauan - 186-187 E 6
Anambra 166-167 F 7
Anamba River -172-173 G 4
Anamoose, ND 152-153 FG 2
Anamosa, IA 152-153 L 4
Anamur 180-181 C 3
Anamur Burnu 180-181 C 3
Anan 188-189 K 6
Ananjev 140-141 EF 2
Ananjev 136-137 NO 2
Anand 180-181 L 6
Anandpur 180-181 O 6
Anantag 180-181 M 4
Anantapur 180-181 M 8
Anápolis 158-159 K 8
Anár 180-181 G 4
Anárak 180-181 G 4
Añasco 158-159 N 2
Anastasia Island 148-149 c 2
Anatahan 192-193 F 3
Anatolia 180-181 CD 3
Anatolië 180-181 CD 3
Anatólia-magasföld 180-181 C 3
Anatolien 180-181 CD 3
Anatone, WA 150-151 E 2

Andrejevka [SU, Ukrainskaja SSR] 140-141 H 3
Andrelândia 160-161 KL 4
Andrews, NC 154-155 O 3
Andrews, OR 150-151 D 4
Andrews, SC 148-149 D 8
Andrews, TN 148-149 B 7
Andrews, TX 154-155 D 4
Ándria 136-137 FG 5
Andriba 168-169 L 6
Andringitra 168-169 L 7
Androka 168-169 K 8
Andronovskoje = Vinnicy 138-139 X 3
Ándros 136-137 L 7
Androscoggin River 148-149 H 2
Andros Island 146-147 L 7
Androth Island 180-181 L 8
Andrušëvka 140-141 D 1
Andr'uškino 178-179 f 4
Andsfjord 130-131 G 3
Andújar 134-135 EF 9
Andulo 168-169 E 5
Andy = Cordillera de los Andes 158-159 E 3-F 9
Anefis 172-173 F 1
Anegada 146-147 O 8
Anegada Passage 146-147 O 8
Aneho 166-167 E 7
Aneityum 194-195 N 4
Añelo 162 C 5
Anenous 174-175 B 5
Anes Baraka = Agnes Baraka 172-173 G 1
Aneta, ND 152-153 GH 2
Aneto, Pico de - 134-135 H 7
Aney 166-167 G 5
Anfeng 190-191 H 5
Anfu 190-191 H 5
An-fu = Linli 184-185 L 6
Angamos, Punta - 162 B 2
Ang-ang-ch'i = Ang'angxi 184-185 N 2
Ang'angxi 184-185 N 2
Angara 178-179 S 6
Angarsk 178-179 T 7
Angarskij kr'až 178-179 S-U 6
Angatau 192-193 NO 6
Angatuba 160-161 H 7
Ånge 130-131 F 6
Angechakot 140-141 M 7
Angel, Salto del - 158-159 G 3
Ángel de la Guarda, Isla - 146-147 D 6
Ángeles, Los - [RCH] 162 B 5
Angelholm 130-131 E 9
Ángermanälven 130-131 GH 5
Angermünde 133 FG 2
Angers 134-135 G 5
Angesån 130-131 K 4
Angka, Doi - = Doi Inthanon 186-187 C 3
Angkor 186-187 D 4
Anglesey 132 E 5
Angleton, TX 154-155 H 6
Anglia 132 E-G 5
Anglie 132 E-G 5
Angmagssalik = Angmagssaliq 144-145 de 4
Angmagssaliq 144-145 de 4
Ango 168-169 G 2
Angoche 168-169 JK 6
Angoche, Ilhas - 168-169 JK 6
Angol 162 B 5
Angola 168-169 EF 5
Angola, IN 152-153 O 5
Angola, NY 148-149 D 3
Angola Basin 168-169 BC 6
Angolabecken 168-169 BC 5-6
Angola, Bacia de - 168 CD 4-5
Angola, Bacino d' 168-169 BC 5-6
Angola, Bassin de l' 168-169 BC 5-6
Angola, Cuenca de - 168-169 BC 5-6
Angola Basin 168-169 BC 5-6
Angolabekken 168-169 BC 5-6
Angolai-medence 168-169 BC 5-6
Angolská pánev 168-169 BC 5-6
Angolski, Basen - 168-169 BC 5-6
Angora = Ankara 180-181 C 3
Angostura = Ciudad Bolívar 158-159 G 3
Angostura I, Salto de - 158-159 E 4
Angostura II, Salto de - 158-159 E 4
Angostura Reservoir 152-153 E 4
Angoulême 134-135 H 6
Angoumois 134-135 GH 6
Angrapa 133 KL 1
Angra Pequena = Lüderitzbaai 168-169 DE 8
Angra dos Reis 160-161 K 5
Angren 180-181 KL 2
Angrenšáchtstroj = Angren 180-181 KL 2
Anguila = Anguilla 146-147 O 8
Anguilla 146-147 O 8
Angumu 168-169 G 3
Anguo 190-191 G 2
Anhandui-Guaçu, Rio - 160-161 EF 4
Anhanduizinho, Rio - 160-161 EF 4
Anholt 130-131 D 9
An-hsi = Anxi 184-185 H 3
An-hsiang = Anxiang 190-191 D 7
Anhua 190-191 C 7
Anhuei = Anhui 184-185 M 5
Anhui 184-185 M 5
Anhumas 158-159 HJ 8
Ani 188-189 N 2-3
An-i = Anyi [TJ, Jiangxi] 190-191 E 6
An-i = Anyi [TJ, Shanxi]190-191 C 4
Aniai = Ani 188-189 N 2-3
Anicuns 160-161 GH 2
Anie 172-173 F 4
Anie, Pic d' 134-135 G 7
Anikovo 139-139 P 4
Animas, Las - 154-155 D 7
Animas Peak 150-151 J 10
Anina 136-137 J 3
Anipemza 140-141 LM 6
Anita, AO 150-151 G 8
Anita, IA 152-153 J 5
Anitápolis 160-161 H 7
Aniva, mys - 178-179 b 8
Aniva, zaliv - 178-179 b 8
Anjar 180-181 KL 6
An-jên = Anren 190-191 D 8
Anji 190-191 G 6
Anjou 134-135 G 5

…jou, ostrova - = ostrova
…žu 120 B 4-5
…jouan = Ndzuwani 168-169 KL 5
…ju 184-185 O 4
…judin 138-139 W 2
…ka 172-173 G 2
…kang 190-191 B 5
…kara 180-181 C 3
…kara Cayı 182-183 DE 3
…karatra 168-169 L 6
…kazoabo 168-169 K 7
… Khe 186-187 E 4
…ki = Anxi 190-191 G 9
…kiu = Anqiu 190-191 G 3
…klam 133 F 2
…kober 166-167 MN 7
…kūr, Jabal - 170 FG 7
…kwe, River - 172-173 H 3
…long 184-185 JK 6
…lu 190-191 D 6
…-lu = Zhongxiang 190-191 D 6
…lung = Anlong 184-185 JK 6
…ma-do 188-189 E 5
…n, Cape - 148-149 H 3
…na 140-141 K 1
…na, IL 152-153 M 7
…naba = 'Annābah 166-167 F 1
…nābah 166-167 F 1
…nai 158-159 H 4
…nam = Trung Bô 186-187 D 3-E 4
…na Maria Key 148-149 b 3
…nan 132 E 4
…nandale, MN 152-153 J 3
…napolis, MD 146-147 L 4
…napolis,MO 152-153 L 7
…napolis Royal 144-145 XY 9
…n Arbor, MI 146-147 K 3
…necy 134-135 L 6
…nenskij Most 138-139 L 3
… Nho'n 186-187 E 4
…niston, AL 146-147 JK 5
…nu 172-173 H 3
…oka, MN 152-153 K 3
…ou Mellene 172-173 F 1
…ou Tagueï 172-173 H 1
…-pien-pao = Anbianbu 190-191 AB 3
…ping 190-191 E 2
…pu 190-191 C 11
…pu Gang 190-191 B 11
…qing 184-185 M 5
…qui 190-191 G 3
…ren 190-191 D 8
…ṣāb 180-181 F 8
…ṣāb = Niṣāb 180-181 EF 5
…sai 190-191 B 3
…ṣārīyah, Jabal al- 182-183 G 5
…sbach 133 E 4
…se, L', MI 152-153 M 2
…sekūla 138-139 D 4
…sekūll = Ansekūla 138-139 D 4
…selmo, NE 152-153 FG 5
…shan 190-191 G 2
…shun 184-185 K 6
…siang = Anxiang 190-191 D 7
…sley, NE 152-153 G 5
…só 134-135 G 7
…son, TX 154-155 EF 4
…son Bay 194-195 EF 2
…songo 188-189 F 4
…songo 166-167 E 5
…sonia, CT 148-149 G 4
…sted, WV 148-149 C 5
…ta [PE] 158-159 E 7
…-ta = Anda 184-185 NO 2
…tabamba 158-159 E 7
…tâkya 166-167 M 1
…takya 166-167 M 1
…takya = Hatay 180-181 D 3
…talaha 168-169 M 5
…tâlia = Antalya 180-181 C 3
…talya 180-181 C 3
…talya Körfezi 180-181 C 3
…tananarivo = Tananarive 168-169 L 6
…tarctica 121 B 28-9
…tarctic Peninsula 121 BC 130-131
…tarctic Sound 121 C 31
…tarctida 121 B 28-9
…tarctique 121 B 28-9
…tarktika 121 B 28-9
…tarktis 121 B 28-9
…tarktisz 121 B 128-129
…tarktyda 121 B 28-9
…tártida 121 B 28-9
…tartide 121 B 28-9
…tas, Rio das - [BR, Santa Catarina] 160-161 F 7
…telope, OR 150-151 C 3
…telope Hills 150-151 J 4
…telope Island 150-151 G 5
…telope Range 150-151 E 6
…tequera 134-135 E 10
…tero Reservoir 152-153 CD 6
…thony, KS 154-155 FG 2
…thony, NM 154-155 B 5
…thony Lagoon 194-195 FG 3
…ti-Atlas = Al-Aṭlas aṣ-Ṣaghir 166-167 C 2-3
…ti Atlas = Al-Aṭlas aṣ-Ṣaghir 166-167 C 2-3
…tiatlas = Al-Aṭlas aṣ-Ṣaghir 166-167 C 2-3
…ti-Atlasz = Al-Aṭlas aṣ-Ṣaghir 166-167 C 2-3
…tibes 134-135 L 7
…ticosti, Île d' 144-145 Y 8
…tigo, WI 152-153 M 3
…tigua 146-147 O 8
…tigua a Barbuda 146-147 OP 8
…tigua and Barbuda 146-147 OP 8
…tigua e Barbuda 146-147 OP 8
…tigua en Barbuda 146-147 OP 8
…tigua és Barbuda 146-147 OP 8
…tigua et Barbuda 146-147 OP 8
…tigua Guatemala 146-147 H 9
…tigua i Barbuda 146-147 OP 8
…tigua und Barbuda 146-147 OP 8
…tigua y Barbuda 146-147 OP 8
…tikýthēra 136-137 K 8
…ti Lebanon = Jabal Lubnān ash-Sharqī 182-183 G 5-6
…tilhas 146-147 L-O 7
…ti Liban = Jabal Lubnān ash-Sharqī 182-183 G 5-6
…tilibano = Jabal Lubnān ash-Sharqī 182-183 G 5-6
…tilibanon = Jabal Lubnān ash-Sharqī 182-183 G 5-6
…tilla-tenger = Karib-tenger 146-147 K-N 8
…tille, Mare delle - 146-147 K-N 8
…tille Australe, Bacino dell' 124-125 G 8
…tilles, Mer des - 146-147 K-N 8
Antilles du Sud, Bassin des - 124-125 G 8
Antillas 146-147 LM 7
Antimēlos 136-137 KL 7
Antimony, UT 150-151 H 6
Antinopolis 170 D 4
Antioch, CA 150-151 C 6-7
Antioch, IL 152-153 M 4
Antióchеia = Antakya 182-183 FG 4
Antiokia = Antakya 182-183 FG 4
Antioquia [CO, ●] 158-159 D 4
Antiparos 136-137 L 7
Antipino 138-139 J 6
Antipodeninseln = Antipodes Islands 198-199 HJ 7
Antipodes Islands 198-199 HJ 7
Antitauro = Güneydoğu Toroslar 180-181 DE 3
Anti Taurus = Güneydoğu Toroslar 180-181 DE 3
Antiqua e Barbuda 146-147 OP 8
Antler, ND 152-153 F 1
Antlers, OK 154-155 H 3
Antofagasta [RCH, ●] 162 B 2
Antofagasta de la Sierra 162 C 3
Anton, CO 152-153 E 6
Anton, TX 154-155 D 4
Anton Chico, NM 154-155 C 3
Antongila, Helodrano - 168-169 LM 6
Antonibe 168-169 L 5-6
Antonina 160-161 H 6
António Carlos 160-161 L 4
Antônio Dias 160-161 L 3
António João 160-161 E 5
Antonito, CO 152-153 CD 7
Antrim 132 C 4
Antrim Mountains 132 CD 4
Antropovo 138-139 O 4
Antsalova 168-169 K 6
Antseh = Anze 190-191 D 3
Antsirabé 168-169 L 6
Antsiranana 168-169 LM 5
Antsla 130-131 M 9
Antsla 138-139 F 5
Antsohihy 168-169 L 5
An Tuc = An Khe 186-187 E 4
Antuerpia = Antwerpen 126-127JK 5
Antung = Dandong 184-185 N 3
An-tung = Lianshui 190-191 G 5
An-tung-wei = Andongwei 190-191 G 4
Antuševo 138-139 L 4
Antwerpen 134-135 J 3
Antyatlas = Al-Aṭlas aṣ-Ṣaghir 166-167 C 2-3
Antyliban = Jabal Lubnān ash-Sharqī 180-181 G 5-6
Anūi 188-189 F 5
An'ujsk 178-179 f 4
An'ujskij chrebet 178-179 fg 4
Anuradhapura = Anuradhapuraya 180-181 MN 9
Anuradhapuraya 180-181 MN 9
Anvers = Antwerpen 134-135 J 3
Anvers, Île - 121 C 30
Anxi [TJ, Fujian] 190-191 G 9
Anxi [TJ, Gansu] 184-185 H 3
Anxiang 190-191 D 7
Anxious Bay 194-195 F 6
Anyang [ROK] 188-189 F 4
Anyang [TJ] 184-185 LM 4
Anyi [TJ, Jiangxi] 190-191 E 7
Anyi [TJ, Shanxi] 190-191 C 4
Anyuan 190-191 E 9
Anzá [CO] 158-159 D 3
Anzarān, Bi'r - 166-167 B 4
'Anz ar-Ruhaymāwi 182-183 K 7
Anze 190-191 D 3
Anzen = Antsla 138-139 F 5
Anžero-Sudžensk 178-179 PQ 6
Ànzio 136-137 E 5
Anžu, ostrova - 178-179 a-d 2
Añatuya 162 D 3
Añelo 162 C 5
Aoba = Oba 194-195 N 3
Aoga-shima 184-185 Q 5
Aoga sima = Aoga-shima 184-185 Q 5
Aoji 188-189 H 1
Aojiang 190-191 H 8
Äolische Inseln = Ìsole Eòlie 136-137 F 6
Aomen = Macau 184-185 L 7
Aomori 184-185 QR 3
Aonae 188-189 a 2
Aosta 136-137 B 3
Aouguéssés 172-173 G 1
Aouk, Bahr - 166-167 HJ 7
Aouker = Āwkār 166-167 BC 5
Aourou 172-173 C 2
Aoya 188-189 JK 5
Aozou 166-167 H 4
Apa, Rio - 162 E 2
Apache, AZ 150-151 J 10
Apache, OK 154-155 F 3
Apache Mountains 154-155 C 5
Apalachee Bay 146-147 K 6
Apalachicola, FL 154-155 N 6
Apalachicola Bay 154-155 N 6
Apalachicola River 154-155 N 5
Apaporis, Rio - 158-159 EF 5
Aparado, Salto do - 160-161 G 6
Aparecida 160-161 K 5
Aparecida do Taboado 160-161 G 4
Aparri 186-187 H 3
Apat 144-145 ab 4
Apatity 178-179 EF 4
Apatzingan de la Constitución 146-147 F 8
Ape 138-139 F 5
Apeldoorn 134-135 KL 2
Apeninos 128-129 K 7-M 8
Apeninos 128-129 K 7-M 8
Apeniny 136-137 C 3-G 5
Apennine 128-129 K 7-M 8
Apenninen 128-129 K 7-M 8
Apennins 128-129 K 7-M 8
Apennijnen 128-129 K 7-M 8
Apenrade = Åbenrå 130-131 C 10
Apex, NC 148-149 D 7
Api [ZRE] 168-169 G 2
Apia 186-187 c 1
Apiacás, Serra dos - 158-159 H 6-7
Apiai 162 G 3
Apiai, Rio - 160-161 H 5
Apiaú, Serra do - 158-159 G 4
Apishapa River 152-153 D 7
Apiūna 160-161 H 7
Apo, Mount - 186-187 HJ 5
Apodi, Chapada do - 158-159 M 6
Apolda 133 E 3
Apolinario Saravia 162 D 2
Apollo Bay 196 F 7
Apollonia = Sūsah 166-167 J 2
Apolo 158-159 F 7
Apolyont Gölü = Uluabat Gölü 182-183 C 2
Apopka, FL 148-149 c 2
Aporé, Rio - 158-159 J 8
Apostle Islands 146-147 HJ 2
Apóstoles 162 E 3
Apoteri 158-159 H 4
Appalache-hegység = Appalachian Mountains 146-147 K 5-N 2
Appalachen = Appalachian Mountains 146-147 K 5-N 2
Appalaches = Appalachian Mountains 146-147 K 5-N 2
Appalachia, VA 148-149 B 6
Appalachian Mountains 146-147 K 5-N 2
Appalachy = Appalachian Mountains 146-147 K 5-N 2
Appalačské pohoří = Appalachian Mountains 146-147 K 5-N 2
Appennini 136-137 C3-G 5
Appennino Abruzzese 136-137 E 4-F 5
Appennino Toscano 136-137 D 3-4
Appennino Umbro-Marchigiano 136-137 E 4 '
Appleton, MN 152-153 HJ 3
Appleton, WI 146-147 J 3
Appleton City, MO 152-153 JK 6
Appomattox, VA 148-149 D 6
Apposai 180-181 K 4
Apscheron, Halbinsel - = Apšeronskij poluostrov
Apšeronskij poluostrov 140-141 OP 6
Apšeronsk 140-141 JK 4
Apšeronskij poluostrov 140-141 OP 6
Apsley Strait 194-195 EF 2
Apucarana 162 F 2
Apucarana, Serra de - 162 F 2
Apulien = Pùglia 136-137 FG 5
Apure, Rio - 158-159 F 3
Apurimac, Rio - 158-159 E 7
'Aqabah, Al- [IRQ] 182-183 KL 7
'Aqabah, Al- [JOR] 180-181 CD 5
'Aqabah, Khalīj al- 180-181 C 5
'Aqabah, Wādī al- 170 EF 2-3
'Aqabat aṣ-Ṣaghīrah, Al- 170 E 5
Aqā Jarī = Āghā Jarī 180-181 FG 4
Aqchalar 182-183 L 5
Aq Chāy 182-183 L 3
Aqdogh Mish, Rūd-e - 182-183 M 4
'Aqeila, el - = Al-'Uqaylah 166-167 H2
Aq Chāy 182-183 L 3
'Aqiq 166-167 M 5
Aqjawajat 166-167 B 5
'Aqrah 182-183 K 4
Aqshār 166-167 B 4
Āq Sū [IRQ] 182-183 L 5
Aqsu [TJ] 184-185 E 3
Aq Tagh altai = Mongol Altajn Nuruu 184-185 F-H 2
Aquarius Plateau 150-151 H 6-7
Äquatorialguinea 166-167 FG 8
Aquidabán-mi, Rio - 160-161 D 5
Aquidauana 158-159 H 9
Aquidauana, Rio - 160-161 D 3
Aquila, L' 136-137 E 4
Aquiles Serdán 154-155 C 6
Ārā = Arrah 180-181 N 5
Arab 180-181 G 6
'Arab, Bahr al- 166-167 K 6-7
'Arab, Khalīj al- 170 C 2
'Arab, Shaṭṭ al- 180-181 F 4
'Arabah, Wādī - 170 E 3
'Arabah, Wādī al- 182-183 F 7
Araban 182-183 G 4
Arabatskaja Strelka, kosa - 140-141 G 3-4
Arab Emirségek 180-181 G 6-H 5
'Arabestān = Khūzestān 180-181 F 4
Arabi, GA 148-149 B 9
'Arabī, Al-Khalīj al- 182-183 N 8
Arabia 124-125 LM 4
Arábia 124-125 LM 4
Arábia, Mar da 124-125 N 5
Arábia Saudita 180-181 D 5-F 6
Arabia Saudita 180-181 D 5-F 6
Arabian Basin 124-125 N 5
Arabian Desert 166-167 L 3-4
Arabian Sea 180-181 JK 7
Arabia Saudí 180-181 D 5-F 6
Arabia Saudyjska 180-181 D 5-F 6
Arabië 124-125 LM 4
Arabie 124-125 LM 4
Arabie, Bassin d' 124-125 N 5
Arabie, Mer d' 180-181 JK 7
Arabien 124-125 LM 4
Arabie Saoudite 180-181 D 5-F 6
Arabisch Bekken 124-125 N 5
Arabisches Becken 124-125 N 5
Arabisches Meer 180-181 JK 7
Arabische Woestijn 166-167 L 3-4
Arabische Wüste 166-167 L 3-4
Arabische Zee 180-181 JK 7
Arabistan = Khūzestān 180-181 F 4
Arab-sivatag 166-167 L 3-4
Arab-sivatag = Ar-Rub' al-Khālī 180-181 F 7-G 6
Arabska, Pustynia - 166-167 L 3-4
Arabské moře 180-181 JK 7
Arabskie, Morze - 180-181 JK 7
Arab-tenger 180-181 JK 7
Araç 182-183 E 2
Aracaju 158-159 M 7
Aracatuba 158-159 JK 9
Araceli = Dumaran Island 186-187 GH 4
Aracena, Sierra de - 134-135 D 10
Arachthós 136-137 J 6
Araçuai 158-159 L 8
Araçuai, Rio - 160-161 L 2
Arad 136-137 J 2
Arada 166-167 J 5-6
Arafura, Mar de - 194-195 FG 2
Arafura, Mar de - 186-187 KL 8
Arafura, Mare di - 186-187 KL 8
Arafura, Mer d' 194-195 FG 2
Arafura, Morze - 194-195 FG 2
Arafura Sea 194-195 FG 2
Arafurasee 194-195 FG 2
Arafura-tenger 194-195 FG 2
Arafurazee 194-195 FG 2
Arafurské moře 194-195 FG 2
Aragac 140-141 L 6
Aragac, gora - 140-141 M 6
Arago, Cape - 150-151 A 4
Aragón 134-135 G 7-8
Aragón, Rio - 134-135 G 7
Aragonien = Aragón 134-135 G 7-8
Araguacema 158-159 K 6
Aragua de Barcelona 158-159 G 3
Araguaia, Parque Nacional do - 158-159 JK 7
Araguaia, Rio - 158-159 J 7
Araguaiana 160-161 FG 1
Araguari 158-159 K 8
Araguari, Rio - [BR, Amapá] 160-161 H 3
Araguari, Rio - [BR, Minas Gerais] 160-161 H 3
Araguatins 158-159 K 6
Arahoab = Aranos 174-175 C 3
Arai 188-189 M 4
'Araïch, el - = Al-'Arā'ish 166-167 C1
Araioses 158-159 L 5
'Arā'ish, Al- 166-167 C 1
Araito = ostrov Altasova 178-179 de 7
'Araiwiḍa, Bir - = Bi'r 'Urayyiḍah 170 DE 3
'Araj, Al- 170 B 3
Arak [DZ] 166-167 E 3
Arāk [IR] 180-181 F 4
Arakan = Ragaing Pyinnei 186-187 B 2
Arakawa 188-189 M 3
Araklı 182-183 HJ 2
Araks 140-141 O 7
Araks = Rūd-e Aras 182-183 L 3
Aral 178-179 L 8
Aral, Mar de - = Aral'skoje more 178-179 KL 8-9
Aralda 140-141 P 4
Aral', Mer de - = Aral'skoje more 178-179 KL 8-9
Aralık 182-183 L 3
Aralmeer = Aral teņizi 178-179 KL 8-9
Aral Sea = Aral teņizi 178-179 KL 8-9
Aralsee = Aral teņizi 178-179 KL 8-9
Aralské jezero = Aral teņizi 178-179 KL 8-9
Aralskie, Jezioro - = Aral teņizi more 178-179 KL 8-9
Aralsor, ozero - 140-141 NO 2
Aralsul'fat 178-179 L 8
Aral teņizi 177 JK 5
Aral-tó = Aral teņizi 178-179 KL 89
Aramac 194-195 HJ 4
'Aramah, Al- 180-181 F 5-6
Aran 132 B 4
Aranda de Duero 134-135 F 8
Arandis 174-175 A 2
Arandjelovac 136-137 J 3
Aran Islands 132 AB 5
Aranjuez 134-135 F 8-9
Aranos 174-175 C 3
Aransas Pass, TX 154-155 G 7
Arantes, Rio - 160-161 GH 3
Arany-part 166-167 DE 8
Arao 188-189 H 6
Araouane 166-167 D 5
Arapahoe, NE 152-153 G 5
Arapey 162 E 4
Arapkir 182-183 H 3
Araponga 162 F 2
Arapoti 160-161 GH 6
Arapuá 160-161 F 4
Arapuá 160-161 F 4
'Ar'ar 182-183 J 7
'Ar'ar' Wādī - 182-183 J 7
Araranguá 162 G 3
Arapira 160-161 HJ 6
Araraquara 158-159 K 9
Araraquara, Serra de - 160-161 HJ 4
Araras [BR, Pará] 158-159 J 6
Araras [BR, São Paulo] 158-159 K 9
Araras, Monte das - 160-161 J 4
Araras, Serra das - [BR, Mato Grosso] 158-159 J 8
Araras, Serra das - [BR, Paraná] 162 F 2-3
Ararat [AUS] 194-195 H 7
Ararat [SU] 140-141 M 7
Ararat = Büyük Ağrı Dağı 180-181 E 2-3
Arari, Cachoeira do - 158-159 K 5
Araripe, Chapada do 158-159 LM 6
Arariúna = Cachoeira do Arari 158-159 K 5
Araruama 160-161 L 5
Araruama, Lagoa de - 160-161 L 5
Araruna [BR, Paraná] 160-161 G 5
Aras, Rūd-e - 182-183 L 3
Ārāsanj 182-183 O 5
Aras Nehri 180-181 E 2
Arato = Shirataka 188-189 MN 3
Arauan = Araouane 166-167 D 5
Arauca [CO, ●] 158-159 E 3
Arauca, Rio - 158-159 F 3
Araucо 162 B 5
Aravaipa Valley 150-151 H 9
Arāvala Parvata = Aravalli Range 180-181 L 6-M 5
Aravalli Range 180-181 L 6-M 5
Arawa 186-187 j 6
Araxá 158-159 K 8
Araxes = Rūd-e Aras 182-183 L 3
Arba Jahan 171 D 2
Arbaj Cheere = Arvajcheer 184-185 J 2
Arba Minch = Arba Minty 166-167 M 7
Arba Minty 166-167 M 7
Arbat 182-183 L 5
Arbaž 138-139 R 5
Arbil 180-181 E 3
Arboga 130-131 F 8
Arbon, ID 150-151 G 4
Arbroath 132 E 3
Arbuckle, CA 150-151 B 6
Arbuckle Mountains 154-155 G 3
Arcachon 134-135 G 6
Arcadia, FL 148-149 c 3
Arcadia, IN 152-153 N 5
Arcadia, KS 152-153 J 7
Arcadia, NE 152-153 G 5
Arcadia, TX 154-155 J 4
Arcadia, WI 152-153 L 3
Arcadie = Arkadía 136-137 JK 7
Arcata, CA 150-151 A 5
Arc Dome 150-151 E 6
Archangaj = 7 ◁ 184-185 J 2
Archangel'sk 178-179 G 5
Archangel'skoje [SU, Stavropol'] 140-141 M 4
Archangel'skoje [SU, Voronež] 140-141 K 1
Archenú, Gebel - = Jabal Arkanū 166-167 J 4
Archer City, TX 154-155 F 4
Archer River 194-195 H 2
Arches National Monument 150-151 J 6
Arch Henda 172-173 DE 1
Arcipelago Malese 124-125 O 5-Q 6
Archip. Jardines de la Raina 146-147 L 7
Arciz 136-137 N 3
Arciz 140-141 D 4
Arckaringa 194-195 FG 5
Arckaringa Creek 196 B 1-2
Arco 136-137 D 3
Arco, ID 150-151 G 4
Arcola, IL 152-153 M 6
Arctic Bay 144-145 TU 3
Arctic Institute Range 121 B 16
Arctic Ocean 120 C 19-B 17
Arctic Ocean 120 AB 32-5
Ártico Central, Bacio do - 120 A
Arctic Red River [CDN, ~] 144-145 K 4
Arctic Red River [CDN, ●] 144-145 K 4
Archipiélago Malayo 124-125 O 5-Q 6
Arḍ, Rā's al- 182-183 N 8
Arda 136-137 L 5
Ardabil 180-181 F 3
Ardahan 182-183 K 2
Ardakān 180-181 G 4
Ardakān = Ardekān 180-181 GH 4
Årdalstangen 130-131 BC 7
Ardanuç 182-183 K 2
Ardar Gwagwa, Jabal - 170 F 6
Ardasa = Torul 182-183 H 2
Ardatov [SU, Mordovskaja ASSR] 138-139 PQ 6
Ardatov [SU, Nižnij Novgorod] 138-139 O 6
Ardebil = Ardabil 180-181 F 3
Ardèche 134-135 K 6
Ardekān 180-181 GH 4
Arden, NV 150-151 F 7
Ardennes 134-135 K 4-L 3
Ardennes, Canal des - 134-135 K 4
Ardeşen 182-183 J 2
Ardestān 180-181 G 4
Ardila 134-135 D 9
Ardlethan 196 H 5
Ardmore, OK 146-147 G 5
Ardmore, SD 152-153 E 4
Ardoch, ND 152-153 H 1
Ards Peninsula 132 D 4
Ardud 136-137 K 2
Åre 130-131 E 6
Areado 160-161 J 4
Areal 160-161 L 5
Arecibo 146-147 N 8
Arefino 138-139 M 4
Aregua 160-161 D 6
Areia Branca 158-159 M 5-6
Areia, Rio da - 160-161 F 5-6
Arena, Point - 150-151 AB 6
Arenales, Cerro - 162 B 7
Arenas, Punta de - 162 C 8
Arendal 130-131 C 8
Arensburg = Kingisepp 138-139 D 4
Arequipa [PE, ●] 158-159 E 8
Arere 158-159 J 5
Åreskutan 130-131 E 6
Arévalo 134-135 E 8
Arezzo 136-137 DE 4
Arfayyāt, Al- 182-183 K 8
Arğa = Akçadağ 182-183 GH 3
Argachtach 178-179 d 4
Arga-Muora-Sise, ostrov - 178-179 XY 3
Argel = Al-Jazā'ir 166-167 E 1
Argel = Al-Jazā'ir 166-167 E 1
Argelès-sur-Mer 134-135 J 7
Argelia 166-167 D-F 3
Argélia 122-123 JK 4
Argenta 136-137 D 3
Argentan 134-135 GH 4
Argenteuil 134-135 J 4
Argentia 144-145 Za 8
Argentina 162 C 7-D 3
Argentina 162 C 7-D 3
Argentina [RA Estado] 162 C 7-D 3
Argentina, Bacia 124-125 GH 7-8
Argentine 162 C 7-D 3
Argentine, Bassin d' 124-125 GH 7-8
Argentine Basin 124-125 GH 7-8
Argentine Islands 121 C 30
Argentinia 156 BC 8-6
Argentinië 162 C 7-D 3
Argentinien 162 C 7-D 3
Argentinisches Becken 124-125 GH 7-8
Argentyna 162 C 7-D 3
Argentijns Bekken 124-125 GH 7-8
Argeş 136-137 M 3
Arghandāb Rōd 180-181 K 4
Argolikòs Kòlpos 136-137 K 7
Argonne 134-135 K 4
Argonne, WI 152-153 M 3
Argos 136-137 K 7
Argos, IN 152-153 N 5
Argostólion 136-137 J 6
Arguello, Point - 150-151 C 8
Argun [SU, ●] 140-141 MN 5
Argun' [SU, ~ ◁ Amur] 178-179 WX 7
Argun [SU, ~ ◁ Terek] 140-141 M 5
Argungu 166-167 EF 6
Argut 178-179 Q 8
Arguvan 182-183 H 3
Argyle, MN 152-153 H 1
Arhavi 182-183 J 2
Århus 130-131 D 9
Ariake kai = Ariakeno-umi 188-189 H 6
Ariakeno-umi 188-189 H 6
Ariake-wan = Shibushi-wan 188-189 H 7
Ariamsvlei 174-175 C 5
Ariano Irpino 136-137 F 5
Aribinda 166-167 D 6
Arica [CO] 158-159 E 5
Arica [RCH] 162 B 1
'Arīḍ, Al- 180-181 F 6-7
Arid, Cape - 194-195 D 6
Aridea 136-137 J 5
Ariel, WA 150-151 B 3
Ariha 182-183 F 5
Arikaree River 152-153 E 6
Arikawa 188-189 G 6
Arimā [BR] 158-159 G 6
Arinos, ID 150-151 GH 4
Arinos 158-159 K 8
Arinos, Rio - 158-159 H 7
Arion, IA 152-153 J 5
Aripuanã, Rio - 158-159 G 6
Ariquemes 158-159 G 6
Ariranha, Ribeiro - 160-161 F 2
Ariranha, Salto - 160-161 G 6
Aris [Namibia] 174-175 B 2
'Arish, Al- 166-167 L 2
'Arish, Wādī al- 170 E 2-3
Arismendi 158-159 F 3
Arita 188-189 K 5
Ariton, AL 154-155 N 5
Arivaca, AZ 150-151 H 10
Ariza 134-135 FG 8
Arízaro, Salar de - 162 C 2
Arizona [RA] 162 C 5
Arizona [USA] 146-147 D 5
Ärjäng 130-131 E 8
Arjeplog 130-131 GH 4
Arjona [CO] 158-159 D 2
Arka 178-179 b 5
Arkabutla Lake 154-155 KL 3
Arkadak 138-139 O 8
Arkadelphia, AR 154-155 J 3
Arkadía 136-137 JK 7
Arkadien = Arkadía 136-137 JK 7
Arkalyk 178-179 M 7
Arkansas 146-147 H 4
Arkansas City, AR 154-155 K 4
Arkansas City, KS 154-155 G 2
Arkansas River 146-147 F 4
Arkanū, Jabal - 166-167 J 4
Arkenu, Jebel - = Jabal Arkanū 166-167 J 4
Arklow 132 CD 5
Arkoma, OK 154-155 H 3
Arkona, Kap - 133 F 1
Arktičeskogo Instituta, ostrova - 178-179 OP 2
Arktyczne, Morze - 120 AB 32-5
Arkul' 138-139 S 5
Arlanzón 134-135 EF 7
Arlberg 133 E 5
Arlee, MT 150-151 F 2
Arles 134-135 K 7
Arlington, 174-175 GH 4
Arlington, CO 152-153 E 6
Arlington, GA 154-155 N 5
Arlington, OR 150-151 CD 3
Arlington, SD 152-153 H 3
Arlington, TN 154-155 L 3
Arlington, TX 154-155 G 4
Arlington, VA 146-147 L 4
Arlington, WA 150-151 BC 1
Arlington Heights, IL 152-153 M 4
Arlit 166-167 F 5
Arlon 134-135 K 4
Armadale 194-195 C 6
Armagh 132 C 4
Armagnac 134-135 GH 7
Armand, Rivière - 144-145 W 6
Arm'anskaja Sovetskaja Socialističeskaja Respublika = Armenien 140-141 LM 6
Armant 170 E 5
Armavir 140-141 K 4
Armawir = Armavir 140-141 K 4
Armenia 126-127 RS 7
Armenia 140-141 LM 6
Arménia 140-141 LM 6
Arménie 140-141 LM 6
Armenië 140-141 LM 6
Armenien 140-141 LM 6
Armentières 134-135 J 3
Armero 158-159 E 4
Armevistēs, Akrōtērion - 136-137 M 7
Armidale 194-195 K 6
Arminto, WY 152-153 C 4
Armour, SD 152-153 G 4
Armstead, MT 150-151 G 3
Armstrong, IA 152-153 J 4
Armstrong, TX 154-155 FG 7
Armuña, La - 134-135 DE 8
Arnarfjördhur 130-131 ab 2
Arnarvatn 130-131 cd 2
Arnávtē, Akrōtērion - 182-183 DE 5
Årnes 130-131 cd 2
Arnett, OK 154-155 F 2
Arnheim = Arnhem 134-135 K 2-3
Arnhem 134-135 KL 2-3
Arnhem, Cape - 194-195 G 2
Arnhem Bay 194-195 G 2
Arnhem Land 194-195 FG 2
Arniston 174-175 D 8
Arno 136-137 D 4
Arno Bay 196 C 4
Arno, TX 154-155 D 5
Arnold, NE 152-153 FG 5
Arnold, PA 148-149 D 4
Arnøy 130-131 J 2
Arnsberg 133 D 3
Arnstadt 133 E 3
Arnswalde = Choszczno 133 GH 2
Aroab 168-169 E 8
Arocha 154-155 D 7
Aroeira [BR, Mato Grosso do Sul] 160-161 E 4
Arõmā = Arũmā 166-167 M 5
Aroostook River 144-145 X 8
Arorae 186-187 H 3
Arourou = Aourou 172-173 C 2
Arpaçaj 140-141 M 7
Arpaçay 182-183 K 2
Arpa Çayı 182-183 K 2
Arpoador, Ponta do - [BR, São Paulo] 160-161 J 6
Arqa tagh 184-185 FG 4
'Arqūb, Al- 166-167 AB 4
Arquipélago Malaio 124-125 O 5-Q 6
Arrah [CI] 172-173 DE 4
Arrah [IND] 180-181 N 5
Arraias 158-159 K 7
Arraijān 146-147 b 3
Arran 132 D 4
Arras 134-135 J 3
Arrecife 166-167 B 3
Arrecifes, Gran Barrera de - = Great Barrier Reef 194-195 H 1-K 4
Arrée, Monts d' 134-135 EF 4
Arrey, NM 154-155 B 4
Arriaga 146-147 H 8
Ar-Rijad = Ar-Riyāḍ 180-181 F 6
Arriola, CO 150-151 J 7
Arroyo Grande, CA 150-151 CD 8
Arroyo Seco [USA] 150-151 F 9
Arroyos y Esteros 160-161 D 6
Arša Nuur = Chagan nuur 184-185 L 3
Arsenjev 178-179 Z 9
Arsenjeo 138-139 L 7
Arsincevo 140-141 H 4
Arsk 138-139 RS 5
Arsuz = Uluçlnar 182-183 F 4
Årta 136-137 J 6
Artaki = Erdek 182-183 B 2
Artašat 140-141 M 7
Artāwiyah, Al - 180-181 EF 5
Artemivs'k 140-141 HJ 2
Artesia 174-175 FG 3
Artesia, CO 150-151 J 5
Artesia, MS 154-155 L 4
Artesia, NM 146-147 EF 5
Artesian, SD 152-153 GH 3-4
Artesia Wells, TX 154-155 F 6
Arthur 148-149 C 3
Arthur, NE 152-153 F 5
Arthur City, TX 154-155 H 4
Arthur River 196 b 2
Arthur's Pass 194-195 O 8
Ártico Central, Cuenca del - 120 A
Artigas [ROU, ●] 162 E 4
Artik 140-141 LM 6
Artjärvi 130-131 LM 7
Artois 134-135 J 3
Art'om 178-179 Z 9
Artomovka 140-141 G 2
Art'omovsk [SU, Rossijskaja SFSR] 178-179 R 7
Art'omovsk [SU, Ukrainskaja SSR] 140-141 HJ 2
Art'omovskij [SU ↗ Bodajbo] 178-179 VW 6
Art'omovskij [SU ↗ Sverdiovsk] 178-179 L 6
Artova 182-183 G 2
Artur de Paiva = Capelongo 168-169 E 5
Arturo Prat 121 C 30-31
Artvin 180-181 E 2
Aru 168-169 H 2
Aru, Kepulauan - 186-187 KL 8
Arua 168-169 H 2
Aruab 168-169 E 8
Aruanã 158-159 J 7
Aruba 146-147 N 9
Arumã [BR] 158-159 G 5
Arũmā [Sudan] 166-167 M 5
Arumbi 168-169 G 2
Arumpo 196 F 4
Arun 180-181 O 5
Arunachal Pradesh 180-181 P 5
Arundel [ZA] 174-175 F 6
Arunta Desert = Simpson Desert 194-195 G 4-5
Arusha 168-169 J 3
Aruwimi 168-169 G 2
Arvada, CO 152-153 D 6
Arvada, WY 152-153 CD 3
Arvajcheer 184-185 J 2
Arvidsjaur 130-131 H 5
Arvika 130-131 E 8
Arvin, CA 150-151 D 8
Arvoredo, Ilha do - 160-161 HJ 7
Arys' 178-179 M 9
Arzamas 178-179 GH 6
Arzgir 140-141 M 4
Åsa [S] 130-131 E 9
Asab 174-175 B 3
Asaba 172-173 G 4
Asābah, Al- 172-173 BC 1
Asadābād [AFG] 180-181 L 4
Asadābād [IR] 182-183 MN 5
Aşağıçigil 182-183 DE 3
Aşağı Pınarbaşı 182-183 E 3
Asahi 188-189 N 5
Asahi dake [J, Hokkaidō] 184-185 R 3
Asahi dake [J, Yamagata] 188-189 M 3
Asahigava = Asahikawa 184-185 R 3
Asahi gawa 188-189 J 5
Asahikawa 184-185 R 3
Asalē [ETH, ●] 166-167 MN 6
Asalē [ETH, ≈] 166-167 N 6
Asam 180-181 P 5
Asamankese 172-173 E 4
Asángaro = Azangaro 158-159 EF 7
Asansol 180-181 O 6
Asante = Ashanti 166-167 D 7
Åsarna 130-131 F 6
'Asayr 180-181 G 8
Asayta 166-167 N 6
Asben = Azbine 166-167 F 5
Asbesberge 174-175 E 5
Asbest 178-179 L 6
Asbestberge = Asbesberge 174-175 E 5
Asbestos Mountains = Asbesberge 174-175 E 5
Asbe Teferi 166-167 N 7
Asbury Park, NJ 148-149 FG 4
Ascensión [BOL] 158-159 G 8
Ascension [GB] 165 E 9
Ascensión, Bahía de la - 146-147 J 8
Aschabad 180-181 HJ 3
Aschaffenburg 133 D 4
Àscoli-Piceno 136-137 E 4
Aščyozek 140-141 N 2
Aseb 166-167 N 6
Asekejevoje 138-139 T 7
Asela 166-167 M 7
Åsele 130-131 G 5
Aselle = Asela 166-167 M 7
Asenovgrad 136-137 L 4-5
Aserbaidschan 140-141 NO 6
Asfal'titovyj Rudnik 138-139 U 2
Aṣfi = Ṣāfī 166-167 C 2
Asfūn 170 E 5
Ashanti 166-167 D 7
Ashāqif, Tulūl al- 182-183 G 6
'Asharah, Al- 182-183 J 5
Ashburn, GA 148-149 B 9
Ashburton 194-195 O 8
Ashburton River 194-195 C 4
Ashdōd 182-183 F 7
Ashdown, AR 154-155 H 4
Asheboro, NC 148-149 CD 7
Asherton, TX 154-155 EF 6
Asheville, NC 146-147 K 4
Ashe Yōma 186-187 C 3
Ashford 132 G 6
Ashford [AUS] 196 K 2
Ashford, AL 154-155 N 5
Ashford, WA 150-151 BC 2
Ash Fork, AZ 150-151 G 8
Ash Giove, MO 154-155 J 2
Ashibetsu 188-189 c 2
Ashikaga 188-189 M 4
Ashizuri-zaki 188-189 J 6
Ashkelon = Ashqĕlōn 182-183 F 7
Ashkum, IL 152-153 MN 5
Ashland, AL 154-155 MN 4
Ashland, IL 152-153 L 6
Ashland, KS 154-155 EF 2
Ashland, KY 146-147 K 4
Ashland, ME 148-149 J 1
Ashland, MT 152-153 CD 3
Ashland, NE 152-153 H 5
Ashland, OH 148-149 BC 4
Ashland, OR 150-151 B 4
Ashland, VA 148-149 E 6
Ashland, WI 146-147 H 2
Ashland, Mount - 150-151 B 4
Ashland City 154-155 M 2
Ashley, IL 152-153 M 6
Ashley, MI 152-153 O 4
Ashley, ND 152-153 G 2
Ashmūn 170 D 2
Ashmūnayn, Al- 170 D 4
Ashqĕlōn 182-183 F 7
Ashshur = Assur 180-181 E 3
Ashtabula, OH 148-149 C 3-4
Ashtabula, Lake - = Baldhill Reservoir 152-153 GH 2
Ashton, 174-175 CD 7
Ashton, ID 150-151 H 3
Ashton, IL 152-153 M 5
Ashuanipi Lake 144-145 X 7
'Ashūrīyah, Al- 182-183 K 7
'Āṣī, Al- 182-183 K 4
'Āṣī, Nahr al- 182-183 G 5
Ásia 124-125 N-P 3
Asia 124-125 N-P 3
Asia 124-125 N-P 3
Asia, Kepulauan - 186-187 K 6
Asie 124-125 N-P 3
Asiекре 172-173 F 4
Asien 124-125 N-P 3
Asike 186-187 LM 8
Asinara 136-137 BC 5
Asinara, Golfo dell' 136-137 C 5
Asi Nehri 182-183 G 4
Asino 178-179 PQ 6
'Asīr 180-181 E 7
Asiut = Asyūt 166-167 L 3
Aşkale 182-183 J 3
Askalon = Ashqĕlōn 182-183 F 7
Askanija-Nova 140-141 FG 3
Asker 130-131 D 8
Askersund 130-131 F 8
Askam 174-175 D 4
Aski Muşil 182-183 K 4
Askiz 178-179 R 7
Askja 130-131 e 2
Askol'd, ostrov - 188-189 J 1
Åsljándúz 182-183 M 3
Asmaca = Feke 182-183 F 4
Asmara = Asmera 166-167 M 5
Asmera 166-167 M 5
Asnām, Al- = Shiliif 166-167 E 1
Asosa 166-167 LM 6
Asotin, WA 150-151 E 2
Asow = Azov 140-141 J 3
Asowsches Meer = Azovskoje more 140-141 GH 3-4
Aso zan 188-189 H 6
Aspen, CO 152-153 C 6
Aspen Hill, MD 148-149 E 5
Aspermont, TX 154-155 E 4
Aspindza 140-141 L 6
Aspiring, Mount - 194-195 N 8
Aspromonte 136-137 FG 6
'Aṣr, Jabal al- 170 D 6
Assa 140-141 M 5
Assab = Aseb 166-167 N 6
Assad, Buhayrat al- 180-181 D 3
Assaitta = Asaita 166-167 N 6
Assal, Lac - = Asalē 166-167 N 6
Assale = Asalē 166-167 MN 6
Assam = Asam 180-181 P 5
Assam Hills 180-181 P 5
Assam Himālaya 180-181 OP 5
Assaouas 172-173 G 1
Assateague Island 148-149 F 5
Assegai = Mkondo 174-175 J 4
Assen 134-135 L 2
Assens 130-131 CD 10
Assiniboine, Mount - 144-145 NO 7
Assiniboine River 144-145 Q 7
Assis 158-159 J 9
Assis Chateaubriand 160-161 F 6
Assisi 136-137 E 4
Assiut = Asyūt 166-167 L 3
Assuan = Aswān 166-167 L 4
Assumption, IL 152-153 M 6
Assumption Island 168-169 L 4
Assunção = Asunción 162 E 3
Assur 180-181 E3
Asszuán = Aswān 166-167 L 4
Astakós 136-137 J 6
Astana 178-179 MN 7
Āstāneh 182-183 N 4
Āstārā [IR] 182-183 N 3
Astara [SU] 140-141 O 7
Aštarak 140-141 M 6
Astin tagh = Altin tagh 184-185 EF 4
Astorga 134-135 DE 7
Astorga [BR] 160-161 G 5
Astoria, OR 146-147 B 2
Astoria, SD 152-153 H 3
Astove Island 168-169 L 5
Astra 162 C 7
Astrachan' 140-141 O 3
Astrachan Bazar = Džalilabad 140-141 O 7
Astrachanskij zapovednik 140-141 O 3
Astrida 168-169 G 3
Astrolabe Bay 186-187 N 7-8
Asturias 134-135 DE 7
Astypálaia 136-137 LM 7
Asunción [PY] 162 E 3
Asunción, La - 158-159 G 2
Asūtarībah, Jabal - 170 G 7
Aswa 168-169 H 2
Aswān 166-167 L 4
'Aswān, Sad el - = Sadd al-'Āli 166-167 L 3
Asyūṭ 166-167 L 3
Asyūṭī, Wādī al- 170 D 4
Aszjút = Asyūṭ 166-167 L 3
Ata 192-193 K 7
Atacama [RA] 162 BC 3
Atacama, Desierto de 162 B 3-C 2
Atacama, Fosa de - 124-125 F 6-7
Atacama, Fossa de - 124-125 F 6-7
Atacama, Fossa di - 124-125 F 6-7
Atacama, Fosse d' 124-125 FG 7
Atacama, Salar de - 162 C 2
Atacamagraben 124-125 F 6-7
Atacamagraben 198-199 O 5-6
Atacama Trench 124-125 F 6-7
Atacamatrog 124-125 F 6-7
Atakor = Atākūr 166-167 F 4
Atakora 172-173 F 3
Atakora, Chaîne de l' 166-167 E 6-7
Atakpamé 166-167 E 7
Atākūr 166-167 F 4
Atalaya [PE, ●] 158-159 E 7
Ataleia 158-159 L 8
Atami 188-189 M 5
Ataniya = Adana 180-181 D 3
Ataouat, Day Nui - 186-187 E 3
Atapupu 186-187 H 8
'Atāqah, Jabal - 170 E 2-3
Atâr 166-167 B 4
Atarque, NM 150-151 J 8
Atascadero, CA 150-151 C 8
At'aševo 138-139 PQ 6
Atasu 178-179 N 8
Atatürk Barajı 182-183 H 4

tic Sea 130-131 G 10-J 8
tijsk 133 J 1
tijskoje more 138-139
B 6-C 4
tijsko-Ladožskij ustup
138-139 E-J 4
tim 170 D 2
timore 174-175 H 2
timore [GB] 132 B 6
timore, MD 146-147 L 4
tisches Meer = Ostsee
138-139 B 5-C 4
tischport = Paldiski
138-139 DE 4
tistān 180-181 M 3-4
tit 180-181 L 3
ti-tenger 130-131 G 10-J 8
tské moře 130-131 G 10-J 8
tyckie, Morze - 130-131
G 10-J 8
lūchistān 180-181 J 5-K 4
vi 130-131 M 9
vi 138-139 F 5
win Aboriginal Reserve
194-195 E 3-4
ya 182-183 B 3
yanā, Al- 166-167 L 3
ygyčan 178-179 d 5
ykši 140-141 PQ 3
m 180-181 H 5
ma 166-167 G 6
maco = Bamako 166-167 C 6
mako 166-167 C 6
mba [EAK] 171 D 3
mba [ZRE] 168-169 E 4
mbara Maoundé 172-173 E 2
mbari 166-167 J 7
mberg 133 E 4
mberg, SC 148-149 C 8
mbesa 168-169 G 2
mbinga 168-169 E 3
mboesbaai 174-175 BC 6
mboi 172-173 E 3
mbouk 166 B 6
mboulos, Mount -
172-173 H 4
mbui 158-159 K 8-9
menda 166-167 G 7
menda Highlands 172-173 H 4
mingui 166-167 HJ 7
mingui, Parc national de la -
166-167 HJ7
mingui-Bangoran 166-167
HJ 7
miyān 180-181 K 4
mpūr, Rūd-e 180-181 HJ 5
mTsho 184-185 G 5
mum = Foumban 166-167 G 7
mungu 171 B 2
na [MW] 171 C 6
ña, Punta de la - 134-135 H 8
naadir [SP, ≡] 166-167 ab 3
naadir [SP, ⁎] = 2 ◁
166-167 O 8
nāder va Jazāyer-e Bahr-e
'Ommān = 6 ◁ 180-181 H 5
nāder va Jazāyer-e Khalij-e
rs = 5◁ 180-181 G 5
nadia 158-159 E 3
nagi 171 C 3
nalia 168-169 FG 2
namana, Lago - 174-175 KL 2
namba 172-173 D 2
nāmichi 150-151 H 10
nana 168-169 D 4
nanal 166-167 F 7
nana Islands 172-173 B 3
nanal 160-161 K 5
nanal, Ilha do - 158-159 J 7
naneiras 158-159 M 6
nat 136-137 J 3
natului, Munții - 136-137 JK 3
naz 182-183 C 3
naz Çayı 182-183 C 3
nbury 132 F 5
nco, El - 158-159 E 3
ncroft 148-149 E 2
ncroft, ID 150-151 H 4
nda = Sainte-Marie 168-169
D 3
nda, Bacia Meridional de -
186-187 J 8
nda, Bacia Setenrional de
186-187 HJ 7
nda, Bacino Meridionale delle
- 186-187 J 8
nda, Bacino Settentrionale
delle - 186-187 HJ 7
nda, Cuenca Meridional de -
186-187 J 8
nda, Cuenca Septentrional
de - 186-187 HJ 7
nda, Kepulauan - 186-187 J 7
nda, La - 162 D 3
nda, Mar de - 186-187 JK 8
nda, Mare di - 186-187 JK 8
nda, Mer de - 186-187 JK 8
nda, Morze - 186-187 JK 8
nda, Punta - 146-147 C 5
nda Aceh 186-187 BC 5
ndama 166-167 CD 7
ndama Blanc 172-173 D3
ndama Rouge 172-173 D 4
nda Méridional, Bassin de -
186-187 J 8
ndar= Machilipatnam
180-181 N 7
ndāra = Machilipatnam
180-181 N 7
ndar Banhā = Banhā 170 D 2
ndarbeyla 166-167 c 2
ndar-e 'Abbās 180-181 H 5
ndar-e Anzali 180-181 FG 3
ndar-e Būshehr 180-181 G 5
ndar-e Chāh Bahār 180-181
HJ 5
ndar-e Khomeyni 180-181
FG 4
ndar-e Lengeh 180-181 GH 5
ndar-e Māhshar 182-183 N 7
ndar-e Shāh 180-181 G 3
ndar Lampung 186-187 DE 8
ndar Maharani = Muar
186-187 D 6
ndar Murcaayo 166-167 bc 1
ndar Penggaram = Batu Pahat
186-187 D 6
ndar Seri Begawan
186-187 FG 5-6
nda Sea 186-187 JK 8
ndasee 186-187 JK 8
nda Septentrional, Bassin de
- 186-187 HJ 7
nda-tenger 186-187 JK 8
ndawe 168-169 H 5
ndazee 186-187 JK 8
nd Bābā, Kuh-i- 180-181 J 4
ndeira, Pico da - 158-159 L 9
ndeirante 158-159 JK 7
ndeirantes 160-161 GH 5
ndelierkop 174-175 H 2
ndelier National Monument
154-155 B 3
ndera, TX 154-155 F 6
Banderas 154-155 C 5
Band-e Qir 182-183 N 7
Bandera 162 D 3
Banderas, Bahia de - 146-147
E 7
Bänd-e Turkestān = Selselae-i-
Band-i-Turkestān 180-181
JK 3
Bandiagara 166-167 D 6
Bandırma 180-181 B 2
Band-i-Turkestān, Selselae-i-
180-181 JK 3
Bandjarmasin = Banjarmasin
186-187 F 7
Bandon 132 B 6
Bandon, OR 150-151 A 4
B'andovan 140-141 O 7
Bāndra, Bombay- 180-181 L 7
Bandské moře 186-187 JK 8
Bandundu [ZRE, ●] 168-169 E 3
Bandundu [ZRE, ⁎] 168-169
E 3-4
Bandung 186-187 E 8
Bāneh 182-183 L 4-5
Banes 146-147 L 7
Bañeza, La - 134-135 DE 7
Banff [CDN] 144-145 NO 7
Banff [GB] 132 E 3
Banff National Park 144-145
NO 7
Banfora 166-167 D 6
Banga = River Bunga 172-173
H 3
Bangāl Khāri = Bay of Bengal
180-181 N-P 7
Bangalore 180-181 M 8
Bangangté 172-173 H 4
Bangassou 166-167 J 8
Bangassu = Bangassou
166-167 J 8
Bangfou = Bengbu 184-185 M 5
Banggai 186-187 H 7
Banggai, Kepulauan -
186-187 H 7
Banggai, Pulau - 186-187 H 7
Banggala Au = Bay of Bengal
180-181 N-P 7
Banggi,Pulau - 186-187 G 5
Banghāzi 166-167 HJ 2
Bangka, Pulau - 186-187 E 7
Bangka, Selat - 186-187 E 7
Bangkinang 186-187 D 6
Bangko 186-187 D 7
Bangkok = Krung Thep
186-187 D 4
Banglades 180-181 OP 6
Bangladesh 180-181 OP 6
Bangladesh 180-181 OP 6
Bangladesz 180-181 OP 6
Bangladéš 180-181 OP 6
Bangolo 172-173 D 4
Bangor 132 DE 5
Bangor, ME 146-147 N 3
Bangor, MI 152-153 N 4
Bangor, PA 148-149 F 4
Bangs, TX 154-155 F 5
Bangu, Rio de Janeiro -
160-161 L 5
Banguecouque = Krung Thep
186-187 D 8
Bangui [RCA] 166-167 H 8
Bangui [RP] 186-187 GH 3
Bangweulu, Lake - 189-169 GH 5
Banhā 170 D 2
Bani = Dani 172-173 E 2
Bani [DOM] 146-147 M 8
Bani [RMM] 166-167 C 6
Bani, Jabal - 166-167 C 2-3
Bani 'Abbās 166-167 D 2
Banias 186-187 NO 8
Banilouli 172-173 F 2
Bani Mallilah 166-167 C 2
Bani Mazār 166-167 L 3
Bani Sa 'd 182-183 L 6
Bani Shuqayr 170 D 4
Bani Suwayf 166-167 L 3
Bani Wanif 166-167 D 2
Bāniyās [SYR, Al-Lādhiqiyah]
180-181 D3
Bāniyās [SYR, Dimashq]
182-183 FG 6
Banjak, Kepulauan - 186-187 C 6
Banja Luka 136-137 G 3
Banjar 186-187 E 8
Banjarmasin 186-187 F 7
Banjermassin = Banjarmasin
186-187 F 7
Banjo = Banyo 166-167 G 7
Banjul 166-167 A 6
Banjuwangi = Banyuwangi
186-187 F 8
Bank 140-141 O 7
Banka = Pulau Bangka 186-187
E 7
Bankas 172-173 E 2
Banko 172-173 D 2
Bankoto 172-173 F 3
Banks, ID 150-151 E 3
Banks, OR 150-151 B 3
Banks Island [CDN, British
Columbia] 144-145 KL 7
Banks Island [CDN, District of
Inuvik] 144-145 MN 3
Banks Islands 194-195 N 2
Banks Lake 150-151 D 2
Banks Peninsula 194-195 O 8
Banks Strait 194-195 J 8
Banks Strait = MacClure Strait
144-145 MN 2-3
Banmau 186-187 C 2
Ban Me Thuôt 186-187 E 4
Ban Muang = Pong 186-187 CD 3
Bannack, MT 150-151 G 3
Banner, WY 152-153 C 3
Banning, CA 150-151 E 9
Banningville = Bandundu
168-169 E 3
Bannockburn [CDN] 148-149
DE 2
Bannockburn [ZW] 168-169
GH 7
Bannock Range 150-151 G 4
Bannū 180-181 KL 4
Baños, Los - [MEX] 154-155 B 7
Ban Phai 186-187 D 3
Banská Bystrica 133 J 4
Banská Štiavnica 133 J 4
Banta Eng 186-187 GH 8
Bantam = Banten 186-187 E 8
Banten 186-187 E 8
Bantry 132 B 6
Bantry Bay 132 AB 6
Bantyū 166-167 KL 7
Banyak, Pulau-pulau -
Kepulauan Banjak 186-187 C 6
Banyo 166-167 G 7
Banyuwangi 186-187 F 8
Banzaburō-dake 188-189 M 5
Banzare Land 121 C 13
Banzystad = Yasanyama
168-169 F 2
Banzyville = Yasanyama
168-169 F 2
Banzyville, Collines des -
168-169 F 2
Bao'an [TJ, Guangdong] 190-191
DE 10
Bao'an [TJ, Shaanxi] 190-191
BC 4
Baode 190-191 L 4
Baodi 190-191 F2
Baoding 184-185 LM 4
Baofeng 190-191 D 5
Baohu Jiao 190-191 C 11
Baoji 184-185 K 5
Baojidun = Badajia 190-191 H 5
Baojing 184-185 K 6
Baokang 190-191 C 6
Baoqing 184-185 P 2
Baoshan [TJ, Shanghai] 190-191
H 6
Baoshan [TJ, Yunnan] 184-185
HJ 6
Baotou 184-185 KL 3
Baoulé 166-167 C 6
Baoying 184-185 M 5
Baptai 138-139 DE 6
Baptiste 148-149 DE 2
Bāqir, Jabal - 182-183 F 8
Baqqah 172-173 B 1
Ba'qūbah 180-181 EF 4
Baquedano 162 BC 2
Baquiria, República Autónoma da -
7 ◁ 178-179 K 7
Bar 136-137 H 4
Bar [SU] 140-141 C 2
Bara [WAN] 172-173 H 3
Baraawe 166-167 N 8
Barabinsk 178-179 OP 6
Barabinskaja nizmennost'
178-179 O 6-7
Baraboo, WI 152-153 M 4
Baracaldo 134-135 F 7
Baraga, MI 152-153 M 2
Bārāganul 136-137 M 3
Barage Sansanding 172 D 2
Bārah 166-167 L 6
Barahi = Barhi 180-181 0 6
Barahona [DOM] 146-147 M 8
Barāij, Al- 182-183 G 5
Barak = Karkamış 182-183 G 4
Baraka 166-167 M 5
Baraki [AFG] 180-181 K 4
Baralaba 194-195 JK 4
Bārāmūlā 180-181 L 4
Baranavičy 130-131 M 11
Barā Nikōbār = Great Nicobar
180-181 P 9
Baranof Island 144-145 JK 6
Baranoviči 138-139 EF 7
Baranovitschi = Baranoviči
138-139 EF 7
Barão de Cocais 160-161 L 3-4
Barão de Grajaú 158-159 L 6
Barão de Melgaço [BR, ●]
160-161 E 2
Barataria Bay 154-155 KL 6
Bar'atino 138-139 K 6
Barbacena 158-159 L 9
Barbade 146-147 OP 9
Barbados 146-147 OP 9
Barbar 166-167 L 5
Barbastro 134-135 GH 7
Barberspan 174-175 F 4
Barberton 168-169 H 8
Barberton, OH 148-149 C 4
Barborá = Berbera 166-167 O 6
Barbosa [CO, Boyacá]
158-159 E 3
Barbosa Ferraz 160-161 F 6
Barbourville, KY 152-153 P 7
Barca = Al-Marj 166-167 J 2
Barcaldine 194-195 HJ 4
Barcellona = Barcelona
134-135 J 8
Barcellona Pozzo di Gotto
136-137 F 6
Barcelona [E] 134-135 J 8
Barcelona [YV] 158-159 G 2
Barcelone = Barcelona
134-135 J 8
Barcelonnette 134-135 L 6
Barcelos [BR] 158-159 G 5
Barchama Guda 171 D 2
Barchöl Choto = Bar köl
184-185 G 3
Barcoo River 194-195 H 4-5
Barda [SU, Azerbajdžanskaja
SSR] 140-141 N 6
Barda [SU, Rossijskaja SFSR]
138-139 U 5
Bardai 166-167 H 4
Bardarash 182-183 K 4
Bardawil, Sabkhat al- 170 E 2
Barddhmān = Burdwan
180-181 O 6
Bardejov 133 K 4
Bárdharbunga 130-131 e 2
Bardis 170 D 4
Bardiyah 166-167 K 2
Bardiz = Gaziler 182-183 K 2
Bardstown, KY 152-153 O 7
Barduba 146-147 O 8
Bardwell, KY 154-155 L 2
Bare' 172-173 E 2
Bareilly 180-181 MN 5
Barēli = Bareilly 180-181 MN 5
Bäreninsel 120 B 16-17
Barents, Mar de - 120 D 14-15
Barents, Mer de -19 B 14-15
Barents, Mar di - 120 B 14-15
Barents, Mer de -19 B 14-15
Barentsa, Morze - 120 B 14-15
Barentsburg 130-131 jk 5
Barentsovo moře 120 B 14 15
Barentsøya 130-131 1 5
Barents Sea 120 B 14-15
Barentssee 120 B 14-15
Barents-tenger 120 B 14-15
Barentszzee 120 B 14-15
Barentu 166-167 M 5
Barfleur, Pointe de - 134-135
G 4
Barga [TJ] 184-185 M 2
Barguzin 178-179 UV 7
Barguzinskij chrebet
178-179 U 7-V 6
Barhampura = Berhampur
180-181 NO 7
Bar Harbor ME 148-149 J 2
Barhi [IND, Bihar] 180-181 O 6
Bari [I] 136-137 G 5
Bari [SP] 166-167 bc 1
Baricho 171 DE 3
Barim 180-181 E 8
Barinas [YV, ●] 158-159 EF 3
Baring, Cape - 144-145 MN 3
Baring, IA 152-153 K 5
Baringo, Lake - 171 D 2
Bariri 160-161 H 5
Bāris 170 D 5
Barisal 180-181 OP 6
Barit, Al- 182-183 K 7
Barito, Sungai - 186-187 F 7
Barkā' 180-181 H 6
Barka = Al-Marj 166-167 J 2
Barka = Baraka 166-167 M 5
Barkaîna = Barkeyna 172-173
E 1
Barkan, Rās-e - = Ra's-e Bahrgān
182-183 N 7-8
Barkeyna 172-173 E 1
Barkley, Lake - 154-155 LM 2
Barkly East = Barkly-Oos
174-175 G 6
Barkly-Oos 174-175 G 6
Barkly-Pas 174-175 G 6
Barkly Pass = Barkly-Pas
174-175 G 6
Barkly Tableland 194-195 F G 3
Barkly-Wes 174-175 F5
Barkly West = Barkly-Wes
174-175 F 5
Bar Köl [TJ, ●] 184-185 G 3
Bar köl [TJ, ≈] 184-185 G 3
Bark Point 152-153 L2
Bârlad [●] 136-137 MN 2
Bârlad [~] 136-137 M 3-2
Barla Dağı 182-183 D 3-4
Bar-le-Duc 134-135 K4
Barlee, Lake - 194-195 C 5
Barletta 136-137 G 5
Barlovento, Islas de - 146-147
OP 8-9
Barma 186-187 BC 2
Barmer 180-181 L 5
Barmera 194-195 H 6
Barnabus, WV 148-149 BC 6
Barnard, KS 152-153 GH 6
Barnato 196 G 3
Barnaul 178-179 P 7
Barnegat Bay 148-149 FG 5
Barne Glacier 121 A 17-18
Barnesville, GA 154-155 NO 4
Barnesville, MN 152-153 H2
Barnesville, OH 148-149 C 4-5
Barney Top 150-151 GH 7
Barnhart, TX 154-155 E 5
Barnsdall, OK 154-155 GH 2
Barnstable, MA 148-149 H 4
Barnstaple 132 D 6
Barnwell, SC 148-149 C 8
Baro 166-167 F 7
Baroda 174-175 F 7
Baroda = Vadodara 180-181 L 6
Baroe 174-175 F 7
Barôngā Kyûnmya 186-187 B 3
Barpeta 180-181 P 5
Barqa = Al-Marj 166-167 J 2
Barqah [LAR] 166-167 J 2
Barqah, Jabal al- 170 E 5
Barquisimeto 158-159 EF 2-3
Barra 132 C 3
Barra Bonita 160-161 H 5
Barra Bonita, Represa de -
160-161 HJ 5
Barra Falsa, Ponta da -
174-175 L 2
Barra, Ponta da - 174-175 L 2
Barra [BR, Bahia] 158-159 L 7
Barra 194-195 K 6
Barracão [BR, Santa Catarina]
160-161 F 7
Barracão do Barreto 158-159
H 6
Barra de São João 160-161
LM 5
Barra do Bugres 158-159 H 7-8
Barra do Corda 158-159 KL 6
Barra do Garças 158-159 J 8
Barra do Piraí 160-161 KL 5
Barra do São Manuel 158-159
H 6
Barrage 166-167 C 6
Barrage de 3 gorges 190-191 C 6
Barragem de 3 Barrancos
190-191 C 6
Barra Head 132 BC 3
Barra Islands 132 C 3
Barranca [PE] 158-159 D 5
Barrancabermeja 158-159 E 3
Barrancas [YV, Monagas]
158-159 G 3
Barra Longa 160-161 L 4
Barra Mansa 160-161 KL 5
Barranco Branco 160-161 D 4
Barranqueras 162 DE 3
Barranquilla 158-159 DE 2
Barra Velha 162 G 3
Barre, VT 148-149 G 2
Barreal, El - [MEX] 154-155 B 5
Barreiras 158-159 KL 7
Bárreirinha 158-159 H 5
Barreirinhas 158-159 L 5
Barreiro 134-135 C 9
Barreiros 158-159 MN 6
Barren Grounds 144-145
O 4-S 5
Barrenland = Barren Grounds
144-145 O 4-S 5
Barren Sage Plains 150-151 E 4
Barretos 158-159 K 9
Barrie 144-145 UV 9
Barrier Range 194-195 H 6
Barrington, IL 152-153 M 4
Barrington Tops 194-195 K 6
Barro [Guiné Bissau] 172-173
B 2
Barro Colorado, Isla -
146-147 b 2
Barron, WI 152-153 KL 3
Barros, Tierra de - 134-135 D 9
Barroso 160-161 KL 4
Barroterán 154-155 E 7
Barrow [IRL] 132 C 5
Barrow, AK 144-145 E 3
Barrow, Point - 144-145 EF 3
Barrow Creek 194-195 FG 4
Barrow in Furness 132 E 4
Barrow Island 194-195 BC 4
Barrow Strait 144-145 RS 3
Barrydale 174-175 D 7
Barșā' 182-183 H 4
Barsakel mes, ostrov -
178-179 KL 8
Barsaloi 168-169 J 2
Barșatas 178-179 O 8
Barshi = Barsi 180-181 M 7
Barsi 180-181 M 7
Barstow, CA 146-147 C 4-5
Barstow, TX 154-155 D 5
Bar-sur-Aube 134-135 K 4
Barșatas 178-179 O 8
Bārta [SU, ●] 138-139 C 5
Barṭallah 182-183 K 4
Bartau = Bārta 138-139 C 5
Bartenstein = Bartoszyce 133
K 1
Bartica 158-159 H 3
Bartın [TR] 182-183 E 2
Bartın çayı = Koca ırmak
182-183 E 2
Bartle, CA 150-151 C 5
Bartlesville, OK 146-147 G 4
Bartlett, NE 152-153 G 5
Bartlett, TX 154-155 G 5
Bartolomeu Dias 168-169 J 7
Barton, ND 152-153 FG 1
Bartoszyce 133 K 1
Bartow, FL 148-149 bc 3
Barú, Volcán - 146-147 K 10
Barun-Šabartuj, gora -
178-179 UV 8
Baruun Urt 184-185 L 2
Barvenkovo 140-141 H 2
Barwon River 194-195 J 5
Barwon River = Darling River
194-195 H 6
Barykova, mys - 178-179 jk 5
Barylas 178-179 Z 4
Baryš [~] 138-139 Q 6
Baryš [●] 138-139 Q 7
Barysaŭ 126-127 O 5
Barzanja = Barzinjah 182-183
L 5
Barzas 178-179 Q 6
Barzinjah 182-183 L 5
Başaliyat Qibli, Al- 170 E 5
Basankusu 168-169 EF 2
Bašanta = Gorodovikovsk
140-141 K 3
Baschkirische Autonome
Republik = 7 ◁ 165-67 K 7
Basco 184-185 N 7
Bas-Congo 168 DE 4
Basel 133 C 5
Basharri 182-183 G 5
Basheerivier 174-175 H 7
Bashi Haixia = Pashih Haihsia
184-185 N 7
Bāshim = Bāsim 180-181 M 5
Bashkir Autonomous Republic =
7 ◁ 178-179 K 7 Bashkiria,
República Autónoma de - = 7 ◁
178-179 K 7
Bash Kurghan = Bash Qurghan
184-185 G 4
Bash Malghun 184-185 F 4
Bash Qurghan 184-185 G 4
Bashshār 166-167 D 2
Ba Shui 190-191 E 6
Basiano 186-187 H 7
Basilan Island 186-187 H 5
Basilan Strait 186-187 H 5
Basileia = Basel 126-127 K 6
Basilicata 136-137 FG 5
Basilio 162 F 4
Basim 180-181 M 6
Basin, MT 150-151 G 2
Basin, WY 152-153 BC 3
Basingstoke 132 F 6
Basit, Rā's al- 182-183 F 5
Basjkiren. Autonome Republiek -
=7◁ 178-179 K 7 Başkale
182-183 KL 3
Baskil 182-183 H 3
Baskir Autonóm Köztársaság
178-179 K 7
Baskiria, Repubblica Autonoma
della 7◁ 178-179 K 7
Bas-Kongo 168 DE 4
Başköy = Aralık 182-183 L 3
Baskunčak, ozero - 140-141 N 2
Bašmakovo 138-139 O 7
Bāsmenj 182-183 M 4
Basoko [ZRE, Haute Zaïre]
168-169 F 2
Basquiria, República Autónoma da -
= 7 ◁ 126-127 U 5
Başrah, Al- 180-181 F 4
Bass, Détroit de - = Bass Strait
194-195 HJ 7
Bass, Stretto di - 196 bc 1
Bassa, Cieśnina - = Bass Strait
194-195 HJ 7
Bassac = Champasak 186-187
DE 4
Bassa California 143 K 6-7
Bassala 172-173 D 2
Bassar 172-173 F 3
Bassano del Grappa 136-137
D 3
Basse Californie 150-151 F 10
Basse-Guinée 124-125 K 5-6
Basse-Inn = Puthein 186-187 a 3
Basse Kotto 166-167 J 7-8
Basse Santa Su 172-173 B 2
Basseterre [Saint Kitts und Nevis]
146-147 O 8
Basse-Terre [Guadeloupe, ●]
146-147 O 8
Bassett, NE 152-153 G 4
Bassett, VA 148-149 C 6
Bassin Algéroprovençal
128-129 J 8-K 7
Bassin Antarctico-Indien
124-125 O-Q 8
Bassin Arctique Central 120 A
Bassin Atlantique Indien
Antarctique 124-125 J-M 9
Bassin Australien Méridional
124-125 PQ 8
Bassin Australien Occidental
124-125 P 7
Bassin Australien Oriental
124-125 RS 8
Bassin Australien Septentrional
194-195 C 2
Bassin Brésilien 124-125 H 6
Bassin Canadien 120 AB 132-33
Bassin Caraïbe 146-147 MN 8
Bassin Central Indienne
124-125 NO 6
Bassin Chinois Méridional
186-187 FG 3-4
Bassin Corallien 194-195 K 2
Bassin Chinois Méridional
186-187 FG 3-4
Bassin Eurasiatique 120 A
Bassin Ibérique 124-125 HJ 3
Bassin Ionien 136-137 GH 7
Bassin Ionien 138-139 B 10
Bassin Islandais 128-129 CD 4
Bassin Norvégien 124-125 JK 2
Bassin Océanique japonais
188-189 J-L 2
Bassin Rouge = Sichuan Pendi
184-185 JK 5-6
Bass Islands 152-153 P 5
Bass Strait 194-195 HJ 7
Bass-Straße = Bass Strait
194-195 HJ 7
Bass-szoros = Bass Strait
194-195 HJ 7
Bassův průliv = Bass Strait
194-195 HJ 7
Basswood Lake 152-153 L 1
Bastia 136-137 C 4
Bastianøyane 130-131 l 5
Bastogne 134-135 KL 3-4
Bastos 160-161 G 4
Bastrop, LA 146-147 H 5
Bastrop, TX 154-155 G 5
Bastutråsk 130-131 HJ 5
Bāsūr, Bi'r al- 170 AB 3
Basutoland = Lesotho 168-169 G 8
Basutos 168-169 G 6
Basyurt Tepesi 182-183 D 3
Baszkirska Autonomiczna
Republika = 7 ◁ 178-179 K 7
Baškirskaja Avtonomnaja
Sovetskaja Socialističeskaja
Respublika = Baschkirische
Autonome Republik = 7 ◁
178-179 K 7
Baškortostān = 7 ◁ 178-179 K 7
Baszra = Al-Basrah 180-181 F 4
Bata 166-167 F 8
Batabanó, Golfo de - 146-147
K 7
Batac 186-187 GH 3
Batagaj 178-179 Za 4
Batagaj-Alyta 178-179 YZ 4
Bataguaçu 160-161 F 4
Bataiporã 160-161 F 5
Batajsk 140-141 JK 3
Batala 180-181 M 4
Batalha 134-135 C 9
Batam, Pulau - 186-187 D 6
Batamaj 178-179 YZ 5
Batan 190-191 GH 4
Batang [TJ] 184-185 H 6
Batanga 172-173 H 6
Batangafo 166-167 H 7
Batangan, Mui - 186-187 EF 3
Batangas 186-187 H 4
Batan Island 184-185 N 7
Batan Islands 184-185 N 7
Batanta, Pulau - 186-187 JK 7
Batao = Batan 190-191 GH 4
Bâtâs 182-183 L 4
Batatais 160-161 J 4
Batatchatu = Chulaq Aqqan Su
184-185 G 4
Batavia, NY 148-149 DE 3
Batavia = Jakarta 186-187 E 8
Batavia, OH 152-153 OP 6
Batbakkara = Amangel'dy
178-179 M 7
Bateckij 138-139 H 4
Batemans Bay 196 K 5
Batesburg, SC 148-149 C 8
Batesville, AR 154-155 K 3
Batesville, IN 152-153 O 6
Batesville, MS 154-155 L 3
Batesville, OH 148-149 A 5
Batesville, TX 154-155 F 6
Bath 132 E 6
Bath, ME 148-149 J 3
Bath, NY 148-149 E 3
Batha 166-167 H 6
Batha, Al- 182-183 L 7
B'athar Zajū, Jabal - 170 E 7
Bathurst [AUS] 194-195 JK 6
Bathurst [CDN] 144-145 XY 8
Bathurst [ZA] 174-175 G 7
Bathurst = Banjul 166-167 A 6
Bathurst, Cape - 144-145 KL 3
Bathurst Inlet [CDN, ◡] 144-145
P 4
Bathurst Inlet [CDN, ●] 144-145
P 4
Bathurst Island [AUS] 194-195
EF 2
Bathurst Island [CDN]
144-145 R 2
Bathurst [ZA] 174-175 G 7
Batié 166-167 D 6-7
Bāṭin, Al- [IRQ ↙ As-Salmān]
182-183 K 7-L 8
Bāṭin, Al- [IRQ ↘ As-Salmān]
182-183 M 8
Bāṭin, Humrat al- 182-183 KL 8
Bāṭin, Wādi al- 180-181 F 5
Bāṭinah, Al - 180-181 H 6
Batlow 196 HJ 5
Batman 180-181 E 3
Batna = Batnah 166-167 F 1
Batnah 166-167 F 1
Batoche 144-145 PQ 7
Baton Rouge, LA 146-147 H 5
Batouri 166-167 G 8
Batovi 160-161 F 1
Batrā, Jabal al- 182-183 F 8
Batrūn, Al- 182-183 F 5
Battambang 186-187 D 4
Batterbee Range 121 BC 30
Batticaloa = Maḍakalapūwa
180-181 N 9
Battle Creek, MI 146-147 J 3
Battle Creek [USA ◁ Milk River]
152-153 B 1
Battle Creek [USA ◁ Owyhee River]
150-151 E 4
Battle Harbour 144-145 Za 7
Battle Mountain, NV 150-151 E 5
Battle River 144-145 OP 7
Battonya 133 K 5
Batu 166-167 M 7
Batu, Kepulauan 186-187 C 7
Batu Arang 186-187 D 6
Batūfah 182-183 K 4
Batumi 140-141 K 6
Batu Pahat 186-187 D 6
Baturaja 186-187 D 7
Baturi = Batouri 166-167 G 8
Baturino 178-179 Q 6
Baturité 158-159 M 5
Batutinggi = Kasongan
186-187 F 7
Batvand 182-183 N 6-7
Baú, Pico - 160-161 K 5
Baubau 186-187 H 8
Bauchi [WAN, ●] 166-167 FG 6
Bauchi [WAN, ⁎] 172-173 H 3
Baudette, MN 152-153 J 1
Baudh 180-181 N 6
Baudouinville = Moba 168-169
G 4
Baudwin 186-187 C 2
Bauhinia 194-195 J 4
Baukau 186-187 J 8
Baúl, El - 158-159 F 3
Bauld, Cape - 144-145 Za 7
Baule-Escoublac, la -
134-135 F 5
Baumann, Pic - 172-173 F 4
Bā'ūrah, Sabkhat 182-183 J 5
Baures 158-159 G 7
Bauru 158-159 K 9
Baús 160-161 F 3
Baús, Serra dos - 160-161 F 2-3
Bauska 130-131 L 9
Bauska 138-139 E 5
Bauske = Bauska 138-139 E 5
Bautino 140-141 OP 4
Bautzen 133 G 3
Bauxite, AR 154-155 J 3
Bauya 166-167 B 7
Bavispe, Rio de - 150-151 J 10
Bavly 138-139 T 6
Bawean, Pulau 186-187 F 8
Ba Xian 190-191 F 2
Baxten Springs 154-155 H 2
Būwīti, Al- 166-167 K 3
Bawku 166-167 D 6
Bawlagé 186-187 C 3
Baxter State Park 148-149 J 1-2
Bay 166-167 a 3
Bayāḍ, Al- [DZ] 166-167 E 2
Bayāḍ, Al- [Saudi-Arabien]
180-181 F 6
Bayāḍiyah, Al- 170 E 5
Bay al-Kabir, Wādi - 166-167
GH 2
Bayamo 146-147 L 7
Bayard, NE 152-153 E 5
Bayat [TR, Afyon] 182-183 D 3
Bayat [TR, Çorum] 182-183 F 2
Baybay 186-187 HJ 4
Bayboro, NC 148-149 E 7
Baybū 182-183 KL 4
Bayburt 180-181 E 2
Bay City, MI 146-147 K 3
Bay City, TX 154-155 GH 6
Baydā', Al- [LAR] 166-167 J 2
Baydā', Al- [Y] 180-181 EF 8
Baydā', 'Ayn al- 182-183 GH 7
Baydā', Barqat al- 166-167
HJ 2-3
Baydā', Bi'r - 170 FG 4
Baydā', Jabal - 170 F 6
Baydāh, 'Ayn al- 182-183 GH 5
Baydhabo 166-167 a 3
Bayerischer Wald 133 F 4
Bayern 133 E 4
Bayeux 134-135 G 4
Bayfield, WI 152-153 L 2
Bayhān al-Qaṣab 180-181 F 8
Bay Hasan 182-183 L 5
Bayiji 190-191 F 4
Bayındır 182-183 B 3
Bayingolin Monggol Zizhizhou
184-185 FG 4
Baykan 182-183 J 3
Bay Minette, AL 154-155 M 5
Bay Mountains 148-149 B 6
Bayonne 134-135 G 7
Bay Port, MI 152-153 P 4
Bayraktar = Karayazı 182-183
JK 3
Bayramiç 182-183 B 3
Bayreuth 133 E 4
Bayrūt 180-181 CD 4
Bay Saint Louis, LA 154-155 L 5
Bays, Lake of - 148-149 D 2
Bays Mountains 154-155 O 2
Bay Shore, NY 148-149 G 4
Bay Springs, MS 154-155 L 4-5
Bayt al-Faqih 180-181 E 8
Bayt Laḥm 182-183 F 7
Baytown, TX 146-147 GH 6
Bayyūḍ, Bi'r al- 182-183 H 5
Bayyūdah, Ṣahrā' - 166-167 L 5
Bayzah, Wādi - 170 E 5
Baza 134-135 F 10
Bazai 190-191 E 9
Bazarčulan 140-141 PQ 2
Bazar Dere 184-185 D 4
Bazard'uz'u, gora - 140-141 N 6
Bāzargān 182-183 L 3
Bazarnyje Mataki 138-139 RS 6
Bazarnyj Karabulak 138-139 Q 7
Bazarnyj Syzgan 138-139 Q 7
Bazartobe 140-141 PQ 2
Bazaruto, Ilha do - 168-169 J 7
Bazas 134-135 G 6
Bāzdar 180-181 JK 5
Bazhao Dao = Pa-chao Tao
190-191 G 10
Bazias 136-137 J 3
Bazine, KS 152-153 G 6
Baziya 174-175 H 6
Beach, ND 152-153 DE 2
Beachport 194-195 G 7
Beacon, NY 148-149 G 4
Beagle, Canal 162 C 8
Beagle Bay 194-195 D 3
Bealanana 168-169 L 5
Beals Creek 154-155 E 4
Beara 186-187 MN 8
Bearcreek, MT 150-151 J 3
Bearden, AR 154-155 J 4
Beardmore Glacier 121 A 20-18
Beardmore Reservoir 196 HJ 1
Beardsley, AZ 150-151 G 9
Beardstown , IL 152-153 LM 5
Bear Hill 152-153 F 5
Bear Island [Arctica] 120 B 16-17
Bear Island [Antarctica] 121 B 26
Bear Lake [USA] 146-147 D 3
Bear Lodge Mountains
152-153 D 3
Béarn 134-135 G 7
Bearpaw Mountain 150-151 J 1
Bear River [USA] 146-147 D 3
Bear River Bay 150-151 G 5
Beata, Isla - 146-147 M 8
Beatrice 168-169 H 6
Beatrice, AL 154-155 M 5
Beatrice, NE 146-147 G 3
Beatrice, Cape - 194-195 G 2
Beatty, NV 150-151 E 7
Beattyville, KY 152-153 P 7
Beaucaire 134-135 K 7
Beauce 134-135 H 4
Beauchene Island 162 E 8
Beaudesert 196 L 1
Beaufort [AUS] 196 F 6
Beaufort, NC 148-149 E 7
Beaufort, SC 148-149 C 8
Beaufort, Mar de - 120 B 32-33
Beaufort, Mar de - 120 B 32-33
Beaufort, Mar di - 120 B 32-33
Beaufort, Mer de - 120 B 32-33
Beauforta, Morze 120 B 32-33
Beaufort Inlet 148-149 E 7
Beaufortovo moře 120 B 32-33
Beaufort Sea 120 B 32-33
Beaufortsee 120 B 32-33
Beaufort-tenger 120 B 32-33
Beaufort-Wes 168-169 F 9
Beaufort West = Beaufort-Wes
168-169 F 9
Beaufortzee 120 B 32-33
Beauharnois 148-149 FG 2
Beaujolais 134-135 K 5
Beauly 132 D 3
Beaumont, CA 150-151 E 9
Beaumont, MS 154-155 L 5
Beaumont, TX 146-147 GH 5
Beaune 134-135 K 5
Beauty 174-175 GH 2
Beauvais 134-135 HJ 4
Beaver, KS 152-153 G 6
Beaver, UT 150-151 G 6
Beaver Bay, MN 152-153 L 2
Beaver City, NE 152-153 FG 5
Beaver City, OK 154-155 E 2
Beaver Creek [USA ◁ Cheyenne
River] 152-153 D 4
Beaver Creek [USA ◁ Little
Missouri River] 152-153 DE 2
Beaver Creek [USA ◁ Milk River]
150-151 J 1-K 2
Beaver Creek [USA ◁ Missouri
River] 152-153 F 2
Beaver Creek [USA ◁ Republican
River] 152-153 F 6
Beaver Creek [USA ◁ South
Platte River] 152-153 E 5-6
Beaver Creek Mountain
154-155 M 4
Beaver Dam, WI 152-153 M 4
Beaverdam, VA 148-149 DE 6
Beaver Falls, PA 148-149 C 4
Beaverhead Range 150-151 G 3
Beaverhead River 150-151 G 3
Beaver Lake 154-155 HJ 2
Beaver River 144-145 P 7
Beaverton 148-149 D 2
Beawar 180-181 LM 5
Beazley 162 C 4
Bebedouro 158-159 K 9
Bebeji 172-173 H 3
Bebra 133 D 3
Beccles 132 G 5
Bečej 136-137 HJ 3
Bečevinka 138-139 LM 4
Béchar = Bashshār 166-167 D 2
Becharof Lake 144-145 EF 6
Bechtery 136-137 P 2
Beckley, WV 146-147 K 4
Beclean 136-137 KL 2
Beczuana = Botswana 168-169
F 8
Bečuánsko = Botswana
168-169 F 8
Bécs 133 H 4
Becsuánaföld = Botswana
168-169 FG 7
Beda 166-167 M 7
Beddington, ME 148-149 JK 2
Bedelē 166-167 M 7
Bedestadpan 174-175 D 4
Bedford 132 F 5
Bedford [CDN, Quebec]
148-149 G 2
Bedford [ZA] 174-175 FG 7
Bedford, IA 152-153 J 5
Bedforf, IN 152-153 N 6
Bedford, KY 152-153 O 6
Bedford PA 148-149 D 4
Bedford, VA 148-149 D 6
Bedirli 182-183 G 3
Bednodemjanovsk 138-139 OP 7
Bēdja = Bājah 166-167 F 1
Bedourie 194-195 GH 4
Beebe, AR 154-155 JK 3
Beech Creeks OR 150-151 D 3
Beechworth 196 H 6
Beegum, CA 150-151 B 5
Beeler, KS 152-153 FG 6
Beerenberg 120 B 19
Be'ēr-Mĕnūha 182-183 F 7
Beersheba = Bĕ'er-Sheva'
180-181 C 4
Bĕ'er-Sheva' 180-181 C 4
Beers Mine, De - 174-175 F 5
Beeshoek 174-175 E 5
Beestekraal 174-175 G 3
Beeville, TX 146-147 G 6
Befale 168-169 F 2
Befandriana-atsimo 168-169 K 7
Befandriana-avaratva 168-169 L 6
Bega [AUS] 194-195 JK 7
Bega, Canal - 136-137 J 3
Beggs, OK 154-155 G 3
Begičeva - ostrov - = ostrov
Boľšoj Begičev 178-179 VW 3
Begna 130-131 C 7
Begoml' 138-139 FG 6
Begorītis, Limnē - 136-137 JK 5
Behagle, De - = Laï 166-167 H 7
Behágue' Pointe 158-159 J 3-4
Behara 168-169 L 7
Behbahān 180-181 G 4
Behn, Mount - 194-195 E 3
Behnen = Bĕne 138-139 D 5
Bei'an 184-185 O 2
Beibei 184-185 K 6
Beibu Wan 184-185 K 7-8
Beichuan He 190-191 C 3
Beiḍa, Bir - = Bi'r Bayḍā' 170 EF 4
Beidachi 190-191 A 2-3
Beida', El - = Al-Bayḍā'
166-167 J 2
Beida, Gebel - = Jabal Bayḍā'
170 F 6
Beifei He 190-191 F 5
Beihai [TJ, Guangxi Zhuangzu
Zizhiqu] 184-185 K 7
Bei Jiang 190-191 D 10
Beijing = Pei-kang 190-191 H 10
Beijing 184-185 LM 3-4
Beijingzi 188-189 DE 3
Beiji Shan 190-191 H 8
Beiliu 190-191 C 10
Beiliu Jiang 190-191 C 10
Beipa'a 186-187 N 8
Beipiao 188-189 C 2
Beira 168-169 HJ 6
Beira [P] 134-135 CD 8
Beiroet = Bayrūt 180-181 CD 4
Beiroût = Bayrūt 180-181 CD 4
Beirut = Bayrūt 180-181 CD 4
Beirute = Bayrūt 180-181 CD 4
Beiru He 190-191 D 4
Beisan = Bēt Shĕan 180-181 F 6
Bei Shan 184-185 GH 3
Beishanchengzhen = Caoshi
188-189 E 1
Beitbridge 168-169 GH 7
Beit Lahm = Bayt Laḥm 182-183
F 7
Beit She'an 180-181 F 6
Beizah, Wādi - = Wādi Bayzah
170 E 5
Beizhen [TJ, Liaoning] 188-189
C 2
Beizhen [TJ, Shandong] 190-191
FG 3
Beja 134-135 D 9-10
Béja = Bājah 166-167 F 1
Bejaïa = Bijāyah 166-167 EF 1
Béjar 134-135 E 8
Bejestān 180-181 H 4
Bejlagan 140-141 N 7
Bejrut = Bayrūt 180-181 CD 4
Bejrút = Bayrūt 180-181 CD 4
Bejsug 140-141 J 4
Bekabad 180-181 KL 2
Bekasi 186-187 E 8
Bek-Budi = Karši 180-181 K 3
Bekdaš 180-181 G 2
Békés 133 K 5
Békéscsaba 133 K 5
Beketovka, Volgograd-
140-141 M 2
Bekily 168-169 L 7
Bekovo 138-139 O 7
Bekwai 172-173 E 4
Belā [PAK] 180-181 K 5
Bela Crkva 136-137 J 3
Belaga 186-187 F 6
Belagām = Belgaum 180-181 LM 7
Belaia = Beleye 166-167 b 2-3
Bel Air 134-135 F 4
Bel Air, MD 148-149 E 5
Belaja [SU, ~] 178-179 J 6
Belaja [SU, ●] 140-141 GH 1
Belaja Ber'ozka 138-139 JK 7
Belaja Cerkov' 140-141 E 2
Belaja Cholunica 138-139 S 4
Belaja Glina 140-141 K 3
Belaja Kalitva 140-141 K 2
Belaja Zemľa, ostrova -
178-179 L-N 1
Bel'ajevka 136-137 O 2

Bel'ajevka 140-141 E 3
Bela Lorena 160-161 KM 1
Belang 186-187 HJ 6
Bela Palanka 136-137 K 4
Belau = Palau 186-187 KL 5
Bela Vista [BR, Mato Grosso do Sul] 158-159 H 9
Bela Vista [Moçambique] 168-169 H 8
Bela Vista, Cachoeira - 158-159 J 5
Bela Vista de Goiás 158-159 K 8
Bela Vista do Paraíso 160-161 G 5
Belawan 186-187 C 6
Belbird 196 K 4
Belcher Channel 144-145 RS 2
Belcher Islands 144-145 U 6
Belchite 134-135 G 8
Belcik = Yavi 182-183 G 3
Belcher Channel 144-145 RS 2
Belden, CA 150-151 C 5
Belding, MI 152-153 O 4
Belebej 178-179 J 7
Belebelka 138-139 G 6
Belebweyne 166-167 O 8
Beléehédé 172-173 E 2
Bélehrad = Beograd 136-137 J 3
Belékou 172-173 D 2
Belém [BR, Pará] 158-159 K 4
Belém [Moçambique] 171 CD 6
Belén [PY] 160-161 D 5
Belen, NM 146-147 E 5
Belep, Îles - 194-195 M 3
Beleye 166-167 M 6
Belfair, WA 150-151 B 2
Belfast 132 CD 4
Belfast, ME 148-149 J 2
Belfast [ZA] 174-175 HJ 3
Belfield, ND 152-153 E 2
Bélfoyo 166-167 LM 6
Belfort 134-135 L 5
Belfry, MT 152-153 B 3
Bělgány = Belgaum 180-181 LM 7
Belgaon = Belgaum 180-181 LM 7
Belgard (Persante) = Białogard 133 GH 1-2
Belgaum 180-181 LM 7
Belgia 134-135 JK 3
Bélgica 126-127 JK 3
Bélgica 134-135 JK 3
Bélgica 133 AB 3
Belgica Mountains 121 B 3-4
Belgii 134-135 JK 3
Belgien 134-135 JK 3
Belgien 134-135 JK 3
Belgio 134-135 JK 3
Belgique 134-135 JK 3
Belgium 134-135 JK 3
Belgorod 140-141 H 1
Belgorod-Dnestrovskij 140-141 DE 3
Belgrad = Beograd 136-137 J 3
Bělgrad = Beograd 136-137 J 3
Belgrade, MT 150-151 H 3
Belgrade, MN 152-153 J 3
Belgrade = Beograd 136-137 J 3
Belgrade = Beograd 136-137 J 3
Belgrado = Beograd 136-137 J 3
Belgrado = Beograd 128-129 N 7
Belhaven, NC 148-149 E 7
Beli = Gorouol 172-173 EF 2
Belice 156 A 2
Beli Hill 172-173 H 4
Belīkh, Nahr - = Nahr Balīh 182-183 H 4
Beliki 140-141 FG 2
Beli Lom 136-137 LM 4
Belinskij 138-139 O 7
Beli Timok 136-137 K 4
Belitung, Pulau 186-187 E 7
Belize [BH, ●] 146-147 J 8
Belize [BH, ★] 146-147 J 8
Bel'kovskij, ostrov - 178-179 Za 2
Bell, FL 148-149 b 2
Bella, Laguna la - 160-161 B 6
Bella Coola 144-145 L 7
Bellaire, MI 152-153 O 3
Bellaire, OH 148-149 C 4-5
Bellaire, TX 154-155 H 6
Bellary 180-181 M 7
Bellata 196 J 2
Bella Unión 162 E 4
Bella Vista [BOL] 158-159 G 8
Bella Vista [PY] 160-161 D 5
Bella Vista [RA, Corrientes] 162 E 3
Bell Bay 196 c 2
Belle, MO 152-153 L 6
Bellefontaine, OH 152-153 P 5
Bellefonte, PA 148-149 DE 4
Belle Fourche, SD 152-153 DE 3
Belle Fourche Reservoir 152-153 E 3
Belle Fourche River 152-153 E 3
Belle Glade, FL 148-149 c 3
Belle Île 134-135 F 5
Belle Isle 144-145 Za 7
Belle Isle, Strait of - 144-145 Z 7
Belle Plaine, IA 152-153 K 5
Belle Plaine, KS 152-153 H 7
Belle Plaine, MN 152-153 J 3
Bellemont, AZ 150-151 GH 8
Belleville, IL 152-153 M 6
Belleville, KS 152-153 H 6
Belleville, IA 152-153 L4
Bellevue, MT 152-153 O 3
Bellevue, OH 152-153 P 5
Bellevue, TX 154-155 F 4
Belle Yella 172-173 C 4
Bellin [CDN] 144-145 WX 5
Bellingham, WA 150-151 BC 2
Bellingshausen Sea 121 BC 28
Bellinzona 133 D 5
Bell Island = Wabana 144-145 a 8
Bello [CO] 158-159 DE 3
Bello Horizonte = Belo Horizonte 158-159 L 8
Bellona 186-187 j 7
Bellota, CA 150-151 C 6
Bellows Falls, VT 148-149 G 3
Bell Peninsula 144-145 U 5
Bells, TN 154-155 L 3
Belluno 136-137 DE 2
Bell Ville [RA] 162 D 4
Bellville [ZA] 174-175 C 7
Bellville, TX 154-155 G 6
Bellvue, CO 152-153 D 5
Belmez 134-135 E 9
Belmond, IA 152-153 K 4
Belmont, NY 148-149 DE 3
Belmont [ZA] 174-175 L 1
Belmonte [BR] 158-159 M 8
Belmopan 146-147 J 8
Belogorsk [SU, Krym']
140-141 FG 6
Belogorsk [SU, Rossijskaja SFSR] 178-179 YZ 7
Belogorsk [SU, Ukrainskaja SSR] 140-141 G 4

Belo Horizonte [BR, Minas Gerais] 158-159 L 8
Beloit, KS 152-153 GH 6
Beloit, WI 146-147 J 3
Beloje, ozero - 178-179 F 5
Belokuricha 178-179 PQ 7
Belomorsko-Baltijskij kanal 138-139 K 4
Belomut 138-139 M 6
Belopolje 140-141 G I
Belopula 136-137 K 7
Beloreck 178-179 L 7
Beloreček 140-141 J 4
Bělören 182-183 E 4
Belorusko 138-139 E-H 6-7
Belorussia 138-139 L 2
Belorusskaja gr'ada 138-139 E7-G6
Belorusskaja Sovetskaja Socialistíčeskaja Respublika = Weißrußland 138-139 E-H 6-7
Belorussija 138-139 E-H 6-7
Belo Tairibhina 168-169 K 6
Bel'ov 138-139 L 7
Belo Vale 160-161 K 4
Belovodsk 140-141 J 2
Beloz'orsk 178-179 F 5-6
Belpre 138-139 K 7
Belpre, KS 152-153 G 7
Belpre, OH 148-149 C 5
Belsund 130-131 j 6
Belt, MT 150-151 H 2
Belted Range 150-151 E 7
Belton, SC 148-149 B 7
Belton, TX 154-155 G 6
Beluchia = Balúčhistán 180-181 J 5-K 4
Beluchistan = Balúčhistán 180-181 J 5-K 4
Belumut, Gunung - 186-187 D 6
Beluša Guba 178-179 HJ 3
Belvidere, IL 152-153 M 4
Belvidere, NJ 152-153 NO 4
Belvidere, SD 152-153 F 4
Belyj, ostrov - 178-179 MN 3
Belyj Jar 178-179 Q 6
Belyj 138-139 K 6
Belyje Berega 138-139 K 7
Belyje gory 138-139 GH 7
Belyj Gorodok 138-139 L 5
Belyničí 138-139 G 6-7
Belzoni, MS 154-155 K 5
Bemaraha 168-169 KL 6
Bembe 168-169 E 4
Bembéréké 166-167 E 6
Bembou = Bimbou 172-173 C 2
Bembou Sambayabé 172-173 B 3
Bement, IL 152-153 M 6
Bemidji, MN 146-147 GH 2
Bemis, TN 154-155 L 3
Benàb = Bonàb 182-183 M 4
Bena, MN 152-153 JK 2
Bena-Dibele 168-169 F 3
Benadir = Banaadir 166-167 ab 3
Benalla 194-195 J 7
Ber'ozovo 178-179 LM 5
Benares = Varanasi 180-181 N 5
Benas, Ras - = Râ's Banâs 166-167 M 4
Benatky = Venedig 136-137 E 3
Benavente 134-135 DE 7
Benavides [MEX] 154-155 D 8
Benavides, TX 154-155 FG 7
Benbecula 132 BC 3
Bend, OR 146-147 B 3
Bendaja 172-173 C 4
Bender Abas = Bandar 'Abbàs 180-181 H 5
Bender Bayla = Bandarbeyla 166-167 c 2
Bendigo 194-195 HJ 7
Bène 138-139 D 5
Beneden Egypte = As-Sa'íd 166-167 L 3-4
Beneden Trajanuswal = Nižnij Trajanov val 136-137 N 3
Benešov 136-137 F 5
Benfica [BR, Minas Gerais] 160-161 L 4
Benga 168-169 H 6
Bengal, Bay of - 180-181 N-P 7
Bengala, Crista de - 124-125 O 5-6
Bengala, Dorsal de - 124-125 O 5-6
Bengala, Golfo de - 180-181 N-P 7
Bengala, Golfo de - 180-181 N-P 7
Bengala, Golfo del - 180-181 N-P 7
Bengale, Dorsale du - 124-125 O 5-6
Bengale, Golfe du - 180-181 N-P 7
Bengalen, Golf van - 180-181 N-P 7
Bengalen, Golf von - 180-181 N-P 7
Bengalischer Rücken 124-125 O 5-6
Bengalore = Bangalore 180-181 M 8
Bengal Ridge 124-125 O 5-6
Bengalska, Zatoka - 180-181 N-P 7
Bengálský záliv 180-181 N-P 7
Bengaluru = Bangalore 180-181 M 8
Ben Gania, Bir - = Bi'r Bin Ganiyah 166-167 J 2
Bengasi = Banghazî 166-167 HJ 2
Benga 184-185 M 5
Benge, WA 150-151 D 2
Benghazi = Banghazî 166-167 HJ 2
Beng He 190-191 G 4
Bengkalis, Pulau - 186-187 D 6
Bengkayang 186-187 EF 6
Bengkulu [RI, ●] 186-187 D 7
Bengkulu [RI, ★] 186-187 D 7
Benguela 168-169 D 5
'Ben Guerir = Bin Gharir 166-167 C 2
Benguérua, Ilha - 174-175 L 1
Beni, Rio - 158-159 F 7
Beni-Abbès = Bani 'Abbàs 166-167 D 2
Benicia, CA 150-151 BC 6
Beni Mazâr = Banî Mazâr 166-167 L 3
Beni Mellal = Banî Malilíah 166-167 C 2
Benin 166-167 E 7-8

Bénin, Baie de - 166-167 E 7-8
Benin, Bight of - 166-167 E 7-8
Benin City 166-167 F 7
Beni Shiqeir = Bani Shuqayr 170 D 4
Beni Suêf = Bani Suwayf 166-167 L 3
Beni Suêf = Bani Suwayf 166-167 L 3
Benito Juarez 162 DE 5
Benjamin, TX 154-155 EF 4
Benjamin Aceval 160-161 D 5
Benjamim Constant 158-159 EF 5
Benkelman, NE 152-153 F5
Benkulen = Bengkulu 186-187 D 7
Benkzee 168-169 G 8
Bennett, CO 152-153 D 6
Bennett, WI 152-153 L 2
Bennett, Lake - 194-195 EF 4
Bennetta, ostrov - 178-179 cd 2
Bennettsville, SC 148-149 B 7
Bennington, VT 148-149 G 3
Benoni 174-175 H 4
Benonivo 174-175 H 1
Berkot 172-173 H 1
Benowa = Berxi 184-185 N 3
Bensheim 133 D 4
Benson, AZ 150-151 H 10
Benson, MN 152-153 J 3
Benti 172-173 B 4
Bentinck Island 194-195 GH 3
Bentiú = Bantyú 166-167 KL 7
Bent Jebail = Bint Jubayl 182-183 F 6
Bento Gomes, Rio - 160-161 D 2
Benton, AK 154-155 M 4
Benton, AR 154-155 J 3
Benton, CA 150-151 D 7
Benton, IL 152-153 M 6-7
Benton, LA 154-155 J 4
Benton, WI 152-153 L 4
Benton City, WA 150-151 D 2
Benton Harbor, MI 152-153 N 4
Bentonia, MS 154-155 K 5
Bentonville, AR 154-155 H 2
Benty = Benti 172-173 B 4
Benué - River Benue 166-167 F 7
Benue, River - 166-167 F 7
Benue Plateau 166-167 F 7
Benxi 184-185 N 3
Beograd 136-137 J 3
Béoumi 172-173 D 4
Beppu 188-189 H 6
Beqâ', El- = Al-Biqâ' 182-183 FG 5-6
Beraldje = Al-Baràdi 182-183 G 5
Beraisolé 166-167 M 6
Berat 136-137 H 5
Berau, Teluk - 186-187 K 7
Berber = Barbar 166-167 L 5
Berbera 166-167 b 1
Berbérati 166-167 a 1
Berch 184-185 L 2
Berchtesgaden 133 F 5
Berck 134-135 H 3
Berd'ansk 140-141 H 3
Berd'anskaja kosa 140-141 H 3
Berd'anskij zaliv 140-141 H 3
Berdičev 140-141 E 2
Berdigest'ach 178-179 XY 5
Berditschew = Berdičev 140-141 E 2
Ber'ozovo 178-179 LM 5
Berdjansk = Berd'ansk 140-141 H 3
Berea, KY 152-153 O 7
Berea, NE 152-153 D 6
Berea, OH 148-149 C 4
Béréba 172-173 E 3
Béréby = Mani 172-173 D 4
Bereg [SU, Vologda] 138-139 LM 4
Beregomet 140-141 B 2
Beregovo 133 L 4
Bereku 171 CD 4
Beren, liman - 140-141 M 3
Berenda, CA 150-151 CD 7
Berendejevo 138-139 M 5
Bereneiland [ZR] B 16-17
Berenike 166-167 LM 4
Berens River [CDN, ~] 144-145 R 7
Berens River [CDN, ○] 144-145 R 7
Berent = Kościerzyna 133 HJ 1
Beresford 196 C 2
Beresford SD 152-153 H 4
Beresina = Berezina 138-139 G 6-7
Beresniki = Bereznikí 178-179 JK 6
Beretàu = Barsàl 182-183 H 4
Berezina [SU, Perm'] 178-179 JK 6
Berežany [SU, ●] 138-139 JK 4-5
Berežany 140-141 B 2
Berezina 138-139 G 6-7
Bergama 180-181 B 3
Bergamo 136-137 CD 3
Bergbadachschanen, Autonome Oblast der - 180-181 L 3
Bergen [N] 130-131 A 7
Bergen, ND 152-153 F 1-2
Bergerac 134-135 H 6
Bergkarabachen, Autonome Oblast der - 140-141 N 6-7
Bessaz gora 178-179 M 9
Bergland, MI 152-153 M 2
Bergland [Namibia] 174-175 B 2
Bergen 182-183 J 5
Berghampore = Baharampur 180-181 O 6
Berhampur 180-181 NO 7
Berhampur = Baharampur 180-181 O 6
Berilo 160-161 L 2
Bering, Détroit de - 144-145 B 5-C 4
Bering, Estrecho de - 144-145 B 5-C 4
Bering, Estreito de - 144-145 B 5-C 4
Bering, Mar de - 120 D 35-1
Bering, Mar de - 120 D 35-1
Bering, Mār di - 120 D 35-1
Bering, mys - 178-179 k 5
Bering, Straat van - 144-145 B 5-C 4
Bethal 168-169 G 8

Bethanié = Bethanien 168-169 E 8
Bethanien 168-169 E 8
Bethany, MO 152-153 JK 5
Bethel, AK 144-145 D 5
Bethel, ME 148-149 H 2
Bethel, MN 152-153 JK 3
Bethel, NC 148-149 E 7
Bethel, OH 152-153 OP 6
Bethel, OK 154-155 H 3
Bethel, VT 148-149 G 3
Bethlehem 168-169 G 8
Bethlehem, PA 148-149 F 4
Beth Shaan = Beit She'àn 180-181 D 2
Bethulie 168-169 G 9
Béthune 134-135 J 3
Betim 166-167 L 6
Beticky 168-169 K 7
Berkeley, CA 146-147 B 4
Berkner Island [B 31-32
Berkot 172-173 H 1
Berkovica 136-137 K 4
Berkvåg 130-131 N 2
Berlejem = Baytlahm 182-183 F 7
Betlem = Bayt Lahm 182-183 F 7
Berlin = Berlin 128-129 L 5
Berlin [D] 133 FG 2
Berlin, [ZA] 174-175 G 7
Berlin, ND 148-149 F 5
Berlin, ND 152-153 G 2
Berlin, NH 146-147 M 3
Berlin, WI 152-153 M 4
Berlin, Mount - 121 B 23
Berlin = Berlin 133 FG 2
Berlino = Berlin 133 FG 2
Berlijn = Berlin 133 FG 2
Bermejo [BOL] 158-159 G 9
Bermejo [RA] 162 C 2
Bermejo, Rio - [RA ← Rio Paraguay] 162 D 2
Bermeo 134-135 FG 7
Bermuda Islands 146-147 NO 5
Bern 133 C 5
Berna = Bern 126-127 K 6
Bernalillo, NM 146-147 E 4
Bernardino de Campos 160-161 H 5
Bernburg 133 F 3
Berne, IN 152-153 O 5
Berne, WA 150-151 C 2
Berne = Bern 133 C 5
Bern Alpen 133 C 5
Bernhardina 174-175 H 4
Bernice, LA 154-155 J 4
Bernier Bay 144-145 ST 3
Bernier Island 194-195 B 4
Bernina 133 D 5
Béroiha 136-137 JK 5
Beroroha 168-169 KL 7
Beroun 133 FG 4
Beroroha = Bèr She'àn 180-181 D 2
Berthold, ND 152-153 EF 1
Bertioga 160-161 J 5
Bertiskos 136-137 K 5
Bertolinia 158-159 L 6
Bertoua 166-167 J 8
Bertram, TX 154-155 FG 5
Bertua = Bertoua 166-167 G 8
Beru 192-193 J 5
Berunda 171 B 2
Beruni 178-179 L 9
Beruri 158-159 G 5
Berwick, LA 154-155 K 6
Berwick, PA 148-149 E 4
Berwick-upon-Tweed 132 EF 4
Beryn, IL 152-153 MN 5
Beryl, UT 150-151 G 7
Berytus = Bayrut 180-181 CD 4
Besalampy 168-169 K 6
Besançon 134-135 L 5
Besarabeasca 140-141 D3
Besarabie = Bessarabija 140-141 C 2-D 3
Besaràbie = Bessarabija 140-141 C 2-D 3
Besed' 138-139 H 7
Besenkovici 138-139 G 6
Besirê, El- = Busayrah 182-183 J 5
Beşiri 182-183 J 4
Beskiden = Beskidy 133 JK 4
Beskidy 133 JK 4
Beskonak 182-183 D 4
Beslan 140-141 M 5
Besna Kobila 136-137 K 4
Besni 180-181 D 3
Beşparmak Daği 182-183 BC 4
Bessa 168-169 D 4
Bessarabia = Bessarabija 140-141 C2-D 3
Bessarabie = Bessarabija 140-141 C2-D 3
Bessarabien = Bessarabija 140-141 C2-D 3
Bessaz gora 178-179 M 9
Bessels, Kapp - 130-131 lm 5
Bessemer, AL 146-147 J 5
Bessemer City, NC 148-149 C 7
Beshi 188-189 d 6
Bessóky, Ozero - 178-179 N 9
Bickleton, WA 150-151 CD 2-3
Bicknell, IN 152-153 N 6
Bidar = Bidar 180-181 M 6
Bid', AL - 170 F 3
Bida 166-167 F 7
Bidar = Bidar 180-181 M 7
Biddeford, ME 146-147 MN 3
Biddle, MT 152-153 D 3
Bidele Depression = Djourab 166-167 H 5
Bié = Kuito 168-169 E 5
Bié = Bié - 170 C 4
Biebrza 171 CD 6
Bieber, CA 150-151 C 5

Biebrza 133 L 2
Biegun północny 120 A
Biegun południowy 121 A
Biel 133 C 5
Bielawa 133 H 3
Bielefeld 133 D 2
Bieler Karpaty 133 HJ 4
Bielitz-Biala = Bielsko-Biała 133 J 4
Bielo-Russia [BY, Minsk] 138-139 E-H 6-7
Bielo-Rùssia 126-127 O 5
Bielorrùssia 138-139 E-H 6-7
Bielorùssia, República da - 138-139 E-H 6-7
Bielorussia 138-139 E-H 6-7
Bielsko-Biała 133 J 4
Bielsk Podlaski 133 L 2
Bienne = Biel 133 C 5
Bienville, LA 154-155 J 4
Biesiesfontein 174-175 B 6
Biesiespoort = Biesiespoort 174-175 E 6
Bifuka 188-189 c 1
Biga 182-183 B 3
Bigadiç 182-183 C 3
Big Arm, MT 150-151 FG 2
Big Baldy 150-151 F 4
Big Bay, MI 152-153 N 2
Big Bell 194-195 C 5
Big Belt Mountains 150-151 H 2-3
Big Bend, CA 150-151 C 5
Big Bend, CO 152-153 E 6
Big Bend National Park 146-147 F 6
Bigbyhill 132 DE 2
Betvâ = Betwa 180-181 M 6
Beulah, MI 152-153 N 3
Beulah, ND 152-153 EF 2
Beulah, ND 152-153 FG 6
Beulah, WY 152-153 D 3
Beurkot = Beurkot 172-173 H 1
Beuthen = Bytom 133 J 3
Beverley 132 F 5
Beverly, MA 148-149 H 3
Beverly, WA 150-151 CD 2
Bexley, OH 152-153 P-6
Beyâbân, Kûh- e- = 180-181 H 5
Beyce = Orhaneli 182-183 C 3
Bey Daği 182-183 D 4
Beydili 182-183 D 2
Beykoz, İstanbul- 182-183 C 2
Beyla 166-167 C 7
Beylikova 182-183 D 3
Beypazarı 182-183 DE 2
Beypinari 182-183 G 3
Beyrouth = Bayrut 180-181 CD 4
Beyşehir 182-183 DE 4
Beyşehir Gölü 180-181 C 3
Beyt = Okhâ 180-181 K 6
Beytişebap = Elki 182-183 K 4
Beyt - Okhâ 180-181 K 6
Bezhta 180-181 N 7
Bhadrak 180-181 O 6
Bhagalpur 180-181 O 5-6
Bhairab Bazar 180-181 P 6
Bhamo = Banmau 186-187 C 2
Bhandâra 180-181 MN 6
Bharatpur [IND, Rajasthan] 180-181 M 5
Bharuch 180-181 L 6
Bhâtgaon = Bhâtgaon 180-181 O 5
Bhatgaon 180-181 O 5
Bhatinda 180-181 L 4
Bhâtpara 180-181 O 6
Bhavnagar = Bhavnagar 180-181 L 6
Bhavnagar 180-181 L 6
Bhawanipatna = Bhawanipatna 180-181 N 7
Bhelsâ = Vidisha 180-181 M 6
Bhilai 180-181 N 6
Bhilsa = Vidisha 180-181 M 6
Bhima 180-181 M 7
Bhir = Bir 180-181 M 7
Bhivâni = Bhiwani 180-181 M 5
Bhiwani 180-181 M 5
Bhopal 180-181 L 7
Bhor 180-181 L 7
Bhubaneshwar = Bhubaneswar 180-181 O 6
Bhubaneswar 180-181 O 6
Bhuj 180-181 KL 6
Bhusâval = Bhusawal 180-181 M 6
Bhusawal 180-181 M 6
Bhutan 180-181 OP 5
Bhûtan 180-181 OP 5
Bhutan 180-181 OP 5
Biâblân, Kûh-e - = Kûh-e Beyâbân 180-181 H 5
Bia 172-173 E 4
Biafra 166-167 F 7
Biak, Pulau - 186-187 L 7
Biala Podlaska 133 L 2-3
Białobrzegi 133 K 2
Białogard 133 GH 1-2
Białystok 133 L 2
Biale, Morze - 178-179 FG 4
Biał̃orus 138-139 E-H 6-7
Biankouma 172-173 CD 4
Biar = Bihar 180-181 NO 6
Biaro, Pulau - 186-187 J 6
Biarritz 134-135 G 7
Bias Fortes 160-161 KL 4
Biasso = Bissau 166-167 A 6
Bibà 170 F 3
Bibai 188-189 bc 2
Bibala 168-169 D 5
Biberach 133 D 4
Bibiani 172-173 D 4
Bibi=O'r 176-173 F 5
Bibür 166-167 L 7
Bicaner = Bikaner 180-181 L 5
Bicas 160-161 L 4
Bichi 172-173 H 2
Bickerton Island 194-195 G 2
Bickerton, WA 150-151 CD 2-3
Bicknell, IN 152-153 N 6
Bicknell, UT 150-151 H 6
Bid = Bir 180-181 M 7
Bid', AL - 170 F 3
Bida 166-167 F 7
Bidar = Bidar 180-181 M 7
Biddeford, ME 146-147 MN 3
Biddle, MT 152-153 D 3
Bidele Depression = Djourab 166-167 H 5
Bié = Kuito 168-169 E 5
Bié = Bié - 170 C 4
Biebrza 171 CD 6

Bill, WY 152-153 D 4
Billefjord 130-131 k 5
Billings, MT 146-147 E 2
Billiton = Pulau Belitung 186-187 E 7
Bill Williams River 150-151 FG 8
Bilma 166-167 G 5
Bilo gora 136-137 G 2-3
BMS, MS 146-147 J 5
Biloela 194-195 K 4
Biloxi, MS 146-147 J 5
Bilqâs 170 D 2
Bilqas Qism Auwal = Bilqâs 170 D 2
Bilugyn = Bilü Kyûn 186-187 C 2
Bilü Kyûn 186-187 C 2
Bilü Kyûn 186-187 C 2
Bimbéréké = Bembéréké 166-167 E6
Bimbila 172-173 F 3
Bimbo 166-167 H 8
Bimlipatam 180-181 M 7
Binalbagan 186-187 H 4
Binboğa 182-183 G 3
Binbou 172-173 C 2
Bindloe = Isla Marchena 158-159 a 1
Bin Ganiyah, Bi'r - 166-167 J 2
Bingara 196 K 2
Bingen 133 D 4
Binger, OK 154-155 F 3
Bingerville 166-167 D 7
Binggöta 182-183 G 3
Bingham, MT 150-151 FG 2
Bingham, ME 148-149 J 2
Bingham, NE 152-153 EF 4
Bingham, NY 146-147 LM 3
Bingham Canyon, UT 150-151 GH 5
Binghamton, NY 146-147 M 3
Bin Gharir = Bin Jarir 166-167 M 3
Binghui = Tianchang 190-191 G 5
Bingo Bay = Hiuchi-nada 188-189 J 5
Bingöl 182-183 J 3
Bingöl Daglari 182-183 J 3
Binhai 190-191 GH 4-5
Binjai 186-187 C 6
Bin Jarir 166-167 M 3
Bin Jiang 190-191 D 9-10
Binnaway 194-195 J 6
Binnen-Mongolie 184-185 K 3-M 2
Binnenzee = Seto-naikai 184-185 P 5
Bint Jubayl 182-183 F 6
Bintan, Pulau - 186-187 DE 6
Bintuan 186-187 D 7
Bintulu 186-187 F 6
Bin Xian [CDN] 144-145 P 7
Bin Xian [TJ, Shaanxi] 190-191 AB 4
Bin Xian [TJ, Shandong] 190-191 FG 3
Binzart 166-167 FG 1
Binzart = Binzart 166-167 FG 1
Bio Bio, Rio - 162 B 5
Biograd 136-137 F 4
Bioko 166-167 F 8
Bioko, CA 150-151 CD 7
Bionga 171 AB 3
Biqâ', Al - 4 = 182-183 G 6
Biqâ', Al - RL [≡] 182-183 FG 5-6
Biqâ', Al = Sahl al-Biqâ' 182-183 FG 5-6
Bir 180-181 M 7
Bir Anzarane 166-167 B 3
Birâk 166-167 G 3
Bir'akovo 138-139 N 4
Bi'r al-Abd 170 E 2
Bi'r 'Ali 180-181 F 8
Birao 166-167 J 6
Birchip 196 F 5
Birch Lake [USA]152-153 L 2
Birch Mountains 144-145 O 6
Bird City, KS 152-153 F 6
Bird Island, MN 152-153 J 3
Bird Island = Vo*eiland 174-175 G 7
Birdsville 194-195 G 5
Birecik 182-183 GH 4
Birền Terara 166-167 M 6
Birgui 158-159 J 9
Biri'ussy = Novobiri'ussy 178-179 QR 6
Birimşe = Sincik 182-183 H 3
Birjand 180-181 H 4
Birkenhead 132 E 5
Birket Fatimé 166-167 HJ 6
Birkim 182-183 L 4
Birma 186-187 BC 2
Birma = Mianma 186-187 BC 2
Birmania = Myanmar 186-187 BC 2
Birmingham [GB] 132 EF 5
Birmingham, AL 146-147 J 5
Birney, MT 152-153 C 3
Birnie 192-193 K 5
Birnin Gwari 172-173 G 3
Birnin Kudu 172-173 H 3
Birnin Kebbi 166-167 EF 6
Birni N'konni 166-167 F 6
Birobidžan 178-179 Z 8
Birrie River 196 H 2
Birrindudu 194-195 EF 3
Birsche = Biržai 138-139 E 5
Birsen = Biržai 138-139 E 5
Birsk 178-179 K 6
Biržai = Obluč'e 178-179 Z 8
Birtavarre 130-131 J 3
Bi'r'učij ostrov, kosa - 140-141 G 3
Bi'r'ulovo, Moskva- 138-139 LM 6
Bi'r Umm Qarayn 166-167 B 3
Biruni = Beruni 178-179 L 9
Bir'usa 170 D 1
Biržai 130-131 L 9
Biržai 138-139 E 5
Bisa, Pulau - 186-187 J 7
Bisalíya, El - = Al-Başaliyat Qibli 170 E 5
Bisbee, AZ 150-151 HJ 10
Bisbee, ND 152-153 FG 1
Biscaglia, Golfo di - 134-135 EF 6
Biscaia, Golfo da 128-129 GH 6
Biscaje, Golf van - 134-135 EF 6
Biscay, Bay of - 134-135 EF 6
Biscay , Golf von - 134-135 EF 6
Biscayne Bay 148-149 c 4
Biscéglie 136-137 G 5
Bischofshofen 133 F 5
Biscoe Islands 121 C 30
Bisese = Biskrah 166-167 F 2
Bisert' 138-139 T 4
Biserovo 138-139 T 4
Bisevo 136-137 F 4
Bishah, Wâdi - 180-181 E 6
Bisheh, İstgah-e - 182-183 N 6
Bishenpur 180-181 P 6
Bishop, CA 150-151 D 7
Bishop, TX 154-155 F 7
Bishopville, SC 148-149 C 7
Bishri, Jabal al- 182-183 H 5
Bisina, Lake - 168-169 HJ 2
Biskajska, Zatoka - 134-135 EF 6
Biskajský zaliv 134-135 EF 6
Biskayerhuken 130-131 hj 5

Biškek 178-179 NO 9
Biskrah 166-167 F 2
Bisling 186-187 J 5
Bismarck, MO 152-153 L 7
Bismarck, ND 146-147 F 2
Bismarck, Archipel - 186-187 NO 7
Bismarck, Arcipelago di - 186-187 NO 7
Bismarck, Arcipélago de - 186-187 NO 7
Bismarck, Arquipélago de - 186-187 NO 7
Bismarck, Arquip de Bismarck 186-187 NO 7
Bismarck, Mare di - 186-187 gh 5
Bismarck, Mar de - 186-187 NO 7
Bismarck, Mer de - 186-187 NO 7
Bismarcka, Archipelag 186-187 NO 7
Bismarckarchipel 186-187 NO 7
Bismarck Archipel 186-187 NO 7
Bismarckburg = Kasanga 168-169 H 4
Bismarckovo moře 186-187 NO 7
Bismarckovo souostroví 186-187 NO 7
Bismarck Range 186-187 M 7-N 8
Bismarck Sea 186-187 NO 7
Bismarck-szigetek 186-187 NO 7
Bismarck-tenger 186-187 NO 7
Bismarckzee 186-187 NO 7
Bismil 182-183 J 4
Bison, SD 152-153 E 3
Bisoftin 182-183 M 5
Bissau 166-167 A 6
Bissau-Guinea 166-167 AB 6
Bistchio Lake 144-145 N 6
Bistineau, Lake - 154-155 J 4
Bistonis, Limné - 136-137 L 5
Bistrija [R, ↓] 136-137 M 2
Bistrija [R, ↑] 136-137 L 2
Bitam 168-169 D 2
Bitely 140-141 P 1
Bitis 180-181 E 3
Bitlis Dağları 182-183 JK 3
Bitola 136-137 J 5
Bitonto 136-137 G 5
Bitter Creek 150-151 J 5
Bitter Creek, WY 152-153 B 5
Bitterfeld 133 F 3
Bitterfontein 168-169 E 9
Bitterwater = Al-Buhayrat al- Murrat al-Kubrâ 170 E 2
Bitterroot Range 146-147 C 2-D 3
Bitterroot River 152-153 J 1
Bittou 172-173 F 3
Bit'ug 140-141 K 1
Bitung 186-187 J 6
Bituruna 160-161 G 7
Biu 166-167 G 6
Biu Plateau 172-173 H 3
Bivirala 186-187 M 8
Biwa-ko 184-185 Q 4
Biyad, Al - Al-Bayâd 180-181 F 6
Biyala 170 D 2
Biyang 190-191 D 5
Bižbul'ak 139-1
Bizerta = Binzart 166-167 FG 1
Bizerte = Binzart 166-167 FG 1
Bjargtangar 130-131 a 2
Bjelovar 136-137 G 3
Bjelovo = Belovo 178-179 Q 7
Bjelucha - gora Belucha 178-179 Q 8
Björkholmen 130-131 H 4
Björko = Bol'šoj Ber'ozovyj ostrov 138-139 FG 3
Björko = Primorsk 138-139 G 3
Björna 130-131 H 6
Björneborg - Pori 130-131 J 7
Bjuröklubb 130-131 JK 5
Bla 172-173 D 2
Blaauwberg = Blouberg 174-175 H 2
Blaauwpan 174-175 D 4
Blaauwkop = Bloukop 174-175 H 4
Blacall 194-195 HJ 4
Black Bell 146-147 J 5
Blackburn 132 EF 5
Blackburn,Mount - 144-145 H 5
Black Butte 152-153 E 2
Black Canyon 150-151 F 4
Black Canyon of the Gunnison National Monument 152-153 C 6
Black Diamond, WA 150-151 BC 2
Black Duck 144-145 ST 6
Blackfeet Indian Reservation 150-151 G 1
Blackfoot, ID 150-151 GH 4
Blackfoot, MT 150-151 G 1
Blackfoot Reservoir 150-151 H 4
Blackfoot River 150-151 G 2
Black Hills 146-147 F 3
Black Lake [USA, Michigan] 152-153 OP 3
Blackleaf, MT 150-151 G 1
Black Mountain 174-175 J 4
Black Mountain [USA] 148-149 A 7
Black Mountain, NC 148-149 BC 7
Black Mountains [USA] 146-147 D 4-5
Black Nossob = Swart Nossob 174-175 C 2
Black Pine Peak 150-151 G 4
Blackpool 132 E 5
Black Range 154-155 B 4
Black Sea 126-127 M 6
Black River, MI 152-153 P 3
Black River [USA ← Henderson Bay] 148-149 F 3
Black River [USA ← Mississippi River] 152-153 L 3
Black River [USA ← Saint Clear River] 152-153 P 4
Black River [USA ← Salt River] 150-151 HJ 9
Black River [USA ← White River] 154-155 J 3
Black River Falls, WI 152-153 L 3
Black Rock 162 B 7
Black Rock, AR 154-155 K 2
Black Sea 146-147 K 5
Black Rock Desert 146-147 C 3
Blacksburg, VA 148-149 BC 6
Black Springs, NM 152-153 J 7
Black Squirrel Creek 152-153 D 6
Blackstone, VA 148-149 DE 6
Blackville, SC 148-149 C 8
Black Umfolozi = Swart Umfolozi 174-175 J 4-5
Blackville, SC 148-149 C 8
Black Volta 166-167 D 7
Black Waxy Prairie 146-147 G 5

Bristol, VA 146-147 K 4
Bristol Bay 144-145 DE 6
Bristol Channel 132 DE 6
Bristol Lake 150-151 EF 8
Bristow, OK 154-155 G 3
Britannia Range 121 AB 15-16
Brit Columbia = British Columbia 144-145 L 6-N 7
Britische Inseln 128-129 F 5-G 4
Britisch-Kolumbien = British Columbia 144-145 L 6-N 7
British Columbia 144-145 L 6-N 7
British Isles 128-129 F 5-G 4
British Mountains 144-145 HJ 4
Brits 174-175 G 3
Britse Eilanden 128-129 F 5-G 4
Britská Kolumbie = British Columbia 144-145 L 6-N 7
Britstown 168-169 F 9
Britt, IA 152-153 K 4
Britton, SD 152-153 GH 3
Britvino 138-139 OP 3
Brive-la-Gaillarde 134-135 H 6
Brixen = Bressanone 136-137 DE 2
Brixham 132 E 6
Brjansk = Br'ansk [SU] 138-139 JK 7
Brno 133 H 4
Broach = Bharuch 180-181 L 6
Broadford 132 CD 3
Broad Law 132 E 4
Broad River 148-149 C 7
Broad Sound 194-195 JK 4
Broadus, MT 152-153 D 3
Broadview, MT 152-153 B 2
Broadwater, NE 152-153 E 5
Broceni 138-139 D 5
Brochet 144-145 Q 6
Brocken 133 E 3
Brock Island 144-145 N 2
Brockman, Mount - 194-195 C 4
Brockport, NY 148-149 DE 3
Brockton, MA 148-149 H 3
Brockton, MT 152-153 D 1
Brockville 144-145 V 9
Brockway, PA 148-149 D 4
Brockway, MT 152-153 D 2
Brodeur Peninsula 144-145 T 3
Brodhead, WI 152-153 M 4
Brodnax, VA 148-149 DE 6
Brodnica 133 J 2
Brodósqui 160-161 J 4
Brody [SU, Ukrainskaja SSR] 140-141 B 1
Brogan, OR 150-151 E 3
Brokaw, WI 152-153 M 3
Broken, Dorsale di - 124-125 O 7
Broken Arrow, OK 154-155 H 2
Broken Bow, NE 152-153 G 5
Broken Bow, OK 154-155 H 3-4
Broken Hill 194-195 H 6
Broken Hill = Kabwe 168-169 G 5
Brokopondo 158-159 HJ 3
Bromberg = Bydgoszcz 133 HJ 2
Brønderslev 130-131 CD 9
Bronevskaja 138-139 M 3
Brong-Ahafo 172-173 E 4
Bronkhorstspruit 174-175 H 3
Brønnøysund 130-131 DE 5
Bronson, FL 148-149 b 2
Bronson, MI 152-153 O 5
Bronson, TX 154-155 H 5
Bronte 136-137 F 7
Bronte, TX 154-155 E 5
Bronte Park 194-195 J 8
Broodsnyersplaas 174-175 H 4
Brookeland, TX 154-155 HJ 5
Brookfield, MO 152-153 K 6
Brookhaven, MS 154-155 K 5
Brookings, OR 150-151 A 4
Brookings, SD 146-147 G 3
Brookline, MA 148-149 H 3
Brooklyn, IA 152-153 K 5
Brooklyn, MS 154-155 L 5
Brooklyn Park, MN 152-153 K 3
Brookneal, VA 148-149 D 6
Brooks Range 144-145 E-H 4
Brookston, IN 152-153 N 5
Brookston, MN 152-153 K 2
Brooksville, FL 148-149 b 2
Brooksville, KY 152-153 OP 6
Brookville, IN 152-153 O 6
Brookton 194-195 C 6
Brookville, OH 148-149 A 5
Brookville, PA 148-149 D 4
Broome 194-195 D 3
Brotas 160-161 H 5
Brotas de Macaúbas 158-159 L 7
Brothers, OR 150-151 C 4
Brothers, The - = Jazā'ir al-Ikhwān 170 F 4
Brothers, The - = Samhah, Darsah 180-181 G 8
Brotzen = Broceni 138-139 D 5
Brovary 140-141 E 1
Brovio 172-173 C 4
Brovki 140-141 D 2
Brown, Mount - 121 BC 9
Brown, Point - 196 A 4
Brownfield, TX 154-155 DE 4
Browning, MT 150-151 G 1
Brownlee, NE 152-153 F 4
Brownsville, OR 150-151 B 3
Brownsville, PA 148-149 CD 4-5
Brownsville, TX 146-147 G 6
Brownsweg 158-159 H 3-4
Brownstown, IN 152-153 NO 6
Browns Valley, MN 152-153 H 3
Brownsville, TN 154-155 L 3
Brownville Junction, ME 148-149 J 2
Brownwood, TX 146-147 G 5
Broxton, GA 148-149 B 9
Bruay-en-Artois 134-135 J 3
Bruce Crossing, MI 152-153 M 2
Bruce, Mount - 194-195 C 4
Bruce, MS 154-155 L 3-4
Bruce Peninsula 152-153 Q 3
Bruce Rock 194-195 C 6
Bruceton, TN 154-155 L 2
Bruce, WI 152-153 L 3
Br'uchoveckaja 140-141 J 4
Br'uchovo 138-139 U 5
Bruchsal 133 D 4
Bruck an der Leitha 133 H 4
Bruck an der Mur 133 G 5
Brug, De - 174-175 F 5
Bruges = Brugge 134-135 J 3
Brugge 134-135 J 3
Bruin Peak 150-151 H 6
Bruja, Cerro - 146-147 b 2
Brukkaros, Mount - = Groot Brukkaros 168-169 E 8
Bruksel = Bruxelles 134-135 JK 3
Brule, NE 152-153 F 5
Brule, WI 152-153 L 2
Brule Lake 152-153 L 2
Brumadinho 160-161 K 4
Brumado 158-159 L 7
Brundidge, AL 154-155 MN 5
Bruneau, ID 150-151 F 4
Bruneau River 150-151 F 4
Brunei 186-187 F 6
Brunei = Bandar Seri Begawan 186-187 FG 5-6
Brunej 186-187 F 6
Bruni, TX 154-155 F 7
Brünn = Brno 133 J 4
Brunsvique = Braunschweig 126-127 L 5
Brunswick, GA 146-147 K 5
Brunswick, MD 148-149 E 5
Brunswick, MO 152-153 K 6
Brunswick, ME 148-149 HJ 3
Brunswick, Peninsula - 162 B 8
Brunswick Bay 194-195 D 3
Brunswick Heads 196 LM 2
Bruny Island 194-195 J 8
Bruselas = Bruxelles 134-135 JK 3
Brusel = Bruxelles 134-135 JK 3
Brusenec 138-139 OP 3
Brush, CO 152-153 E 5
Brushy Mountains 148-149 C 6-7
Brusovo 138-139 K 5
Brusque 162 G 3
Brussel 134-135 JK 3
Brüssel = Bruxelles 134-135 JK 3
Brüssel = Bruxelles 134-135 JK 3
Brussel = Bruxelles 134-135 JK 3
Brussels 174-175 F 4
Brussels = Bruxelles 134-135 JK 3
Brüx = Most 133 F 3
Bruxelas = Bruxelles 134-135 JK 3
Bruxelles 128-129 J 5
Bruxelles 134-135 JK 3
Bruyns Hill 174-175 J 5
Brüsszel = Bruxelles 134-135 JK 3
Bryan, OH 152-153 O 5
Bryan, TX 146-147 G 5
Bryan, WY 150-151 J 5
Bryant, SD 152-153 H 3
Bryce Canyon National Park 150-151 GH 7
Bryson, TX 154-155 F 4
Bryson City, NC 154-155 O 3
Bryson City, TN 148-149 B 7
Brzeg 133 H 3
Bsaiya, Al- = Al-Busaiyah 180-181 EF 4
Bsharri = Basharri 182-183 G 5
Btaymān, Bi'r - 182-183 H 4
Bua 171 C 6
Buake = Bouaké 166-167 CD 7
Buala 186-187 jk 6
Bu'Amrān 182-183 HJ 5
Bu'ayrat al-Hsūn 166-167 H 2
Būbiyan, Jazīrat - 180-181 FG 5
Bubu 171 C 4
Bucaale 166-167 N 8
Bućač 140-141 B 2
Bucak 182-183 D 4
Bucakkışla 182-183 E 4
Bucaramanga 158-159 E 3
Bucarest = București 136-137 L 3
Bucarest = București 136-137 LM 3
Bucarest = București 136-137 LM 3
Bucareste = București 128-129 O 7
Bucatunna, MS 154-155 L 5
Buccaneer Archipelago 194-195 D 3
Buchan [AUS] 196 J 6
Buchanan [LB] 166-167 B 7
Buchanan, MI 152-153 N 5
Buchanan, NM 154-155 C 3
Buchanan, VA 148-149 CD 6
Buchanan Lake 154-155 F 5
Buchans 144-145 Z 8
Buchara 180-181 JK 3
Buchardo 162 D 4
Bucharest = București 136-137 LM 3
Bucharevo 138-139 S 5
Buchon, Point - 150-151 C 8
Buchtarma 178-179 Q 8
Buchtarminskoje vodochranilišče 178-179 PQ 8
Buchyn Mangnaj uul 184-185 EF 4-5
Buckeye, AZ 150-151 G 9
Buckhannon, WV 148-149 C 5
Buckhaven 132 E 3
Buckhorn Lake 148-149 D 2
Buckie 132 E 3
Buckland Tableland 194-195 J 4-5
Buckleboo 194-195 G 6
Buckle Island 121 C 16-17
Buckley, WA 150-151 BC 2
Buckley Bay 121 C 15-16
Bucklin, KS 152-153 G 7
Bucklin, MO 152-153 K 6
Bucksport, ME 148-149 J 2
Bucovina 136-137 LM 2
Buco Zau 168-169 D 3
București 136-137 LM 3
Bucyrus OH 152-153 P 5
Buda, TX 154-155 FG 5
Budai = Pu-tai 190-191 GH 10
Buda-Košelevo 138-139 H 7
Budakskij liman 136-137 O 3
Budakskij liman 140-141 E 4
Budapest 133 J 5
Budapeszt = Budapest 133 HJ 5
Budapešť 133 J 5
Budapeste = Budapest 128-129 M 6
Budarino 140-141 P 1
Budaun 180-181 M 5
Budayr, Al- 182-183 L 7
Budd Land 121 C 12
Bude, MS 154-155 K 5
Budennovka 138-139 T 8
Budennovsk 140-141 LM 4
Bude-Stratton 132 D 6
Būdhardalur 130-131 c 2
Būdhiyah, Jabal - 170 E 3
Budjala 168-169 EF 2
Budogošč' 138-139 J 4
Bud'onnovskaja 140-141 KL 3
Budva 136-137 H 4
Budweis = České Budějovice 133 G 4
Budyšin = Bautzen 133 G 3
Budua 172-173 H 2
Buea 166-167 F 8
Buena Esperanza, Cabo de - 168-169 E 9
Buenaventura [CO] 158-159 D 4
Buenaventura, Bahia de - 158-159 D 4
Buena Vista, GA 154-155 N 4
Buena Vista [MEX] 150-151 E 10
Buena Vista [PY] 160-161 E 6
Buena Vista, VA 148-149 D 6
Buena Vista Lake Bed 150-151 D 8
Buenolândia 160-161 GH 1
Buenópolis 160-161 KL 2
Buenos Aires [PA] 146-147 b 2
Buenos Aires [RA, ●] 162 E 4
Buenos Aires [RA, ⋆] 162 DE 5
Buenos Aires, Lago - 162 B 7
Buen Retiro 146-147 b 3
Bueyeros, NM 154-155 D 2-3
Buffalo, MN 152-153 K 3
Buffalo, MO 152-153 K 7
Buffalo, ND 152-153 H 2
Buffalo, NY 146-147 L 3
Buffalo, OK 154-155 F 2
Buffalo, SD 152-153 E 3
Buffalo, TX 154-155 GH 5
Buffalo, WV 148-149 C 5
Buffalo, WY 152-153 C 3
Buffalo Bill Reservoir 152-153 B 3
Buffalo Hump 150-151 F 3
Buffalo Lake 144-145 NO 5
Buffalo River = Bloedrivier 174-175 J 4-5
Buffalorivier = Buffelsrivier 174-175 J 4
Buffelsrivier [ZA, Drakensberge] 174-175 J 4
Buffelsrivier [ZA, Groot Karoo] 174-175 D 7
Buffelsrivier [ZA, Namakwaland] 174-175 C 6
Buford, GA 154-155 NO 3
Buford, ND 152-153 E 1-2
Buford, WY 152-153 D 5
Buford Reservoir = Lake Sidney Lanier 154-155 NO 3
Bug 133 L 2
Bug = Južnyi Bug 140-141 E 2
Bug-Dnepr-Kanal = Dneprovsko-Bugskij kanal 138-139 E 7
Buga 158-159 D 4
Bugant 184-185 K 2
Bugária 136-137 K-M 4
Bugiri 171 C 2
Bugorkan 178-179 U 5
Bugrino 178-179 H 4
Bugt 184-185 N 2
Bugul'ma 178-179 J 7
Bugul'minsko-Belebejevskaja vozvyšennost' 138-139 TU 6
Buguruslan 178-179 J 7
Buhăeşti 136-137 M 2
Buheirat 166-167 KL 7
Buhemba 171 C 3
Buhl, ID 150-151 F 4
Buhl, MN 152-153 K 2
Buhoro 171 B 4
Bui Dam 172-173 E 3
Buin [PNG] 186-187 j 6
Bū'īn-e Zahrā', 182-183 O 5
Buinsk [SU, Čuvašskaja ASSR] 138-139 Q 6
Buinsk [SU, Tatarskaja ASSR] 138-139 R 6
Buir Nur 184-185 M 2
Buitenzorg = Bogor 186-187 E 8
Buj 178-179 G 6
Bujalance 134-135 EF 10
Bū Jaydūr, Rā's - 166-167 AB 3
Buji 186-187 M 8
Bujnaksk 140-141 N 5
Bujumbura 168-169 G 3
Bukačača 178-179 W 7
Buka Island 186-187 hj 6
Bukama 168-169 G 4
Bükān 182-183 LM 4
Bukarest = București 136-137 LM 3
Bukareszt = București 136-137 L 3
Bukavu 168-169 G 3
Bukene 168-169 H 3
Bukit Besi 186-187 D 6
Bukit Betong 186-187 D 6
Bukittinggi 186-187 CD 7
Bükk 133 K 4-5
Bukoba 168-169 H 3
Bukurešt = București 136-137 L 3
Bukuru 172-173 H 3
Bū Kutub 166-167 E 2
Bula [RI] 186-187 K 7
Bula [SU] 138-139 R 6
Bulagan = Bulgan 184-185 J 2
Bulan 186-187 H 4
Bulancak 182-183 GH 2
Bulangu 172-173 H 2
Bulanık 182-183 K 3
Bülāq 170 D 5
Bulawayo 168-169 G 7
Bulaydah 166-167 E 1
Buldan 182-183 C 3
Bulgan [MVR, ● Bulgan] 184-185 J 2
Bulgan [MVR, ● Chovd] 184-185 G 2
Bulgan [MVR, ⋆ = 9 ◁] 184-185 J 2
Bulgária 136-137 K-M 4
Bulgaria 136-137 K-M 4
Bulgarie 136-137 K-M 4
Bulgarien 136-137 K-M 4
Bulgarije 136-137 K-M 4
Bulharsko 136-137 K-M 4
Buli = Pu-li 190-191 H10
Buli, Teluk - 186-187 J 6
Bulki 166-167 M 7
Bulla, ostrov - 140-141 O 6
Bullard, TX 154-155 H 4
Bullaxaar 166-167 a 1
Buller, Mount - 196 H 6
Bullfinch 194-195 C 6
Bull Mountains 152-153 B2
Bulloo Downs 194-195 H 5
Bulloo River 194-195 H 5
Bulls Bay 148-149 D 8
Bull Shoals Lake 154-155 J 2
Bullfontein 174-175 FG 5
Bulu 186-187 J 6
Buluan 186-187 H 5
Bulucan = Emirhan 182-183 GH 3
Bulukumba 186-187 GH 8
Bulungan 186-187 G 6
Buluntou Hai = Ojorong nuur 184-185 F 2
Bulu Rantekombola 186-187 GH 7
Bulwater 174-175 D 7
Bulwer 174-175 H 5
Bumba [ZRE, Bandundu] 168-169 E 4
Bumba [ZRE, Équateur] 168-169 F 2
Bumba = Boumba 166-167 H 8
Bumbeni 174-175 K 4
Buna [EAK] 168-169 J 2
Buna [PNG] 186-187 N 8
Buna, TX 154-155 J 5
Bunbah, Khalij al- 166-167 J 2
Bunbury 194-195 BC 6
Bundaberg 194-195 K 4
Bundelkhand 180-181 MN 6
Bundi 180-181 M 5
Bundooma 194-195 FG 4
Bundoran 132 B 4
Bunga 172-173 H 4
Bunga, River - 172-173 H 3
Bunge, zemľa - 178-179 b 2-3
Bungendore 196 JK 5
Bunger Oasis 121 C 11
Bungo-suidō 184-185 P 5
Bungotakada 188-189 H 6
Bunguran, Pulau - = Pulau Natuna Besar 186-187 E 6
Buni 172-173 HJ 3
Bunia 168-169 GH 2
Bunji 180-181 M 4
Bunkeya 168-169 G 5
Bunkie, LA 154-155 JK 5
Bunnell, FL 148-149 c 2
Bunsuru, River - 172-173 G 2
Bunta 186-187 H 7
Buntok 186-187 FG 7
Bunya = Buya 172-173 EF 3
Bünyan 182-183 F 3
Bunyu, Pulau - 186-187 G 6
Bunzlau = Bolesławiec 133 GH 3
Buol 186-187 H 6
Buolkalach 178-179 W 3
Buona Speranza, Capo di 168-169 E 9
Buôn Ma Thuôt = Ban Mê Thuôt 186-187 E 4
Buor-Chaja, guba - 178-179 Z 3
Buor-Chaja, mys - 178-179 Z 3
Buqaliq tagh 184-185 G 4
Buqian = Puqian 190-191 C 11
Buquq 184-185 E 3
Būr 166-167 L 7
Bura 168-169 JK 3
Bur Acaba = Buur Hakkaba 166-167 N 8
Buram 166-167 K 6
Burao = Bur'o 166-167 O 7
Bur'atskaja Avtonomnaja Sovetskaja Socialističeskaja Respublika = Burjatische Autonome Republik 178-179 T 7-V 6
Burajevo 138-139 U 6
Buras, LA 154-155 L 6
Būr Atyan = Nawādhibu 166-167 A4
Buraydah 180-181 E 5
Buraymi, Al- 180-181 H 6
Burbank, CA 150-151 DE 8
Burbank, OK 154-155 G 2
Burchanbuudaj 184-185 H 2
Burcher 196 H 4
Burchun 184-185 F 2
Burco 166-167 b 2
Burdeau = Mahdiyah 166-167 E 1
Burdekin River 194-195 J 4
Burdett, KS 152-153 G 6
Burdur 180-181 BC 3
Burdur Gölü 182-183 CD 4
Burdwan 180-181 O 6
Burdwood, Banc de - 162 DE 8
Burdwood, Banco de - 162 DE 8
Burdwood, Banco de - 162 DE 8
Burdwood, Banco di - 162 DE 8
Burdwoodbank 162 DE 8
Burdwood Bank 162 DE 8
Burdwood-pad 162 DE 8
Burê [ETH, Gojam] 166-167 M 6
Burē [ETH, Īlubabor] 166-167 M 7
Bureå 130-131 J 5
Büreen = Büren 184-185 K 2
Burejnskij chrebet 178-179 Z 7-8
Bureja 178-179 Z 7
Büren [MVR] 184-185 K 2
Burenchaan [MVR, Chentij] 184-185 L 2
Burenchaan [MVR, Chövsgöl] 184-185 H 2
Bürencogt 184-185 L 2
Būr Fu'ād = Būr Sādāt 170 E 2
Burg 133 EF 2
Būr Gābo = Buur Gaabo 168-169 K 3
Bur Gao = Buur Gaabo 168-169 K 3
Burgas 136-137 M 4
Burgaski zaliv 136-137 MN 4
Burgaw, NC 148-149 DE 7
Burg el-'Arab = Burj al-'Arab 182-183 C 7
Burgenland 133 H 5
Burgersdorp 168-169 G 9
Burgersfort 174-175 J3
Burgerville 174-175 F 6
Burgfjället 130-131 F 5
Burghersdorp = Burgersdrop 168-169 G 9
Bùrgio 136-137 E 7
Burgos 134-135 F 7
Burgsvik 130-131 H 9
Burgund = Bourgogne 134-135 K 5-6
Burhaniye 182-183 B 3
Burhanpur 180-181 M 6
Buri 160-161 H 5
Buriacka Autonomiczna Republika 178-179 T 7-V 6
Burias Island 186-187 H 4
Buriatas de Aguinskí, Circunscrição Nacional dos - = 11 ◁ 178-179 V 7
Buriatas de Ust-Ordynski, Circunscrição Nacional de - = 10 ◁ 178-179 T 7
Buriati, Repubblica Autonoma dei - 180-181 T 7-V 6
Buriatos, República Autónoma de los - 178-179 T 7-V 6
Buriatos, República Autônoma dos - 178-179 T 7-V 6
Buriatos de Aguinsk, Circunscripción Nacional de los - 178-179 V 7
Buriatos de Ust-Orda, Circunscripción Nacional de los - = 11 ◁ 178-179 T 7
Burica, Punta - 146-147 K 10
Burin Peninsula 144-145 Z 8
Buri Ram 186-187 D 3-4
Buriti Alegre 160-161 H 3
Buriti Bravo 158-159 L 6
Buriti [BR, Maranhão] 158-159 L 5
Buriti [BR, Minas Gerais] 160-161 HJ 3
Buriti dos Lopes 158-159 L 5
Buritis 160-161 J 1
Buritizeiro 160-161 K 2
Buri Ye-Midir Selatê 166-167 M 5
Burj al-'Arab 170 C 2
Burj al-Haṭṭabah 166-167 F 2
Burját Autonóm Köztársaság 178-179 T 7-V 6
Burjatische Autonome Republik 178-179 T 7-V 6
Burjatská autonomní republika 178-179 T 7-V 6
Burj Ban Būl'īd = Qal'at Makmāhūn 166-167 E 3
Burjing = Burchun 184-185 F 2
Burj Luṭfī 166-167 F 3-4
Burj 'Umar Idris = 166-167 EF 3
Burkburnett, TX 154-155 F 3
Burke, SD 152-153 G 4
Burkesville, KY 154-155 N 2
Burketown 194-195 GH 3
Burkeville, VA 148-149 DE 6
Burkina 166-167 DE 6
Burleson, TX 154-155 G 4
Burley, ID 150-151 G 4
Burlin 138-139 T 8
Burlingame, CA 150-151 B 7
Burlingame, KS 152-153 HJ 6
Burlington 148-149 D 3
Burlington, CO 152-153 E 6
Burlington, IA 146-147 H 3
Burlington, KS 152-153 HJ 6
Burlington, NC 148-149 D 6
Burlington, VT 146-147 M 3
Burlington, WA 150-151 BC 1
Burlington, WI 152-153 M 4
Burlington Junction, MO 152-153 J 5
Burma 186-187 BC 2
Burma = Myanmar 186-187 BC 2
Burnet, TX 154-155 F 5
Burney, CA 150-151 C 5
Burnie 194-195 HJ 8
Burns, CO 152-153 C 6
Burns, KS 152-153 H 6
Burns, OR 150-151 D 4
Burns Flat, OK 154-155 F 3
Burnside, KY 152-153 O 7
Burns Lake 144-145 LM 7
Burnsville, MS 154-155 L 3
Burnsville , WV 148-149 C 5
Burnt Creek 144-145 X 6-7
Burntop 174-175 J 4
Burnt River 150-151 DE 3
Burnt River Mountains 150-151 DE 3
Buron [SU] 140-141 M 5
Burqah, Khahrat - 182-183 GH 6
Burqān 182-183 M 8
Burra 194-195 G 6
Burrendong Reservoir 196 J 4
Burren Junction 196 J 3
Burrinjuck Reservoir 194-195 J 7
Burro, El - 154-155 E 6
Burro, Serranias del - 146-147 F 6
Burrton, KS 152-153 H 6
Burruyacú 162 CD 3
Burrwood, LA 154-155 L 6
Bursa 180-181 B 2-3
Būr Sādāt 170 E 2
Būr Safāga = Safājah 166-167 L 3
Būr Sa'īd 166-167 L 2
Burštyn 140-141 B 2
Būr Sūdān 166-167 M 5
Burt, IA 152-153 J 4
Būr Tawfīg 170 E 3
Burt Lake 152-153 O 3
Buru, Pulau - 186-187 J 7
Burullus, Buhayrat al- 170 D 2
Burūm 180-181 F 8
Burundi 168-169 GH 3
Burun-Šibertuj, gora - = gora Burun-Šabartuj 178-179 UV 8
Bururi 168-169 G 3
Burutu 172-173 G 4
Burwell, NE 152-153 G 5
Buryat Autonomous Region 178-179 T 7-V 6
Burye = Burē 166-167 M 6
Buryn' 140-141 F 1
Burynšik 140-141 P 4
Bury Saint Edmunds 132 G 5
Buṣaiyah, Al- 180-181 EF 4
Buṣayrah 182-183 J 5
Busayṭā, Al- 182-183 G 7-H 8
Būs Cagaan Nuur = Böön Cagaan nuur 184-185 HJ 2
Būsh 170 D 3
Bushehr 180-181 G 5
Bushire = Būshehr 180-181 G 5
Bushland, TX 154-155 DE 3
Bushnell, IL 152-153 L 5
Bushnell, NE 152-153 E 5
Busia 171 C 2
Businga 168-169 F 2
Busira 168-169 E 2-3
Buskerud 130-131 C 7-D 8
Buṣrat ash-Shām 182-183 G 6
Bussa 172-173 G 3
Busselton 194-195 BC 6
Bustamente 154-155 E 7
Busto Arsìzio 136-137 C 3
Busuanga Island 186-187 G 4
Busuluk = Buzuluk 178-179 J 7
Buta 168-169 F 2
Butān 180-181 OP 5
Butão 180-181 OP 5
Butare 171 B 3
Butembo 171 B 2
Butere 171 C 2
Butha Qi 184-185 N 2
Butha Buthe 174-175 H 5
Butiaba 168-169 H 2
Bū Tilimit 166-167 B 5
Butler, AL 154-155 L 4
Butler, GA 154-155 N 4
Butler, IN 152-153 O 5
Butler, MO 152-153 J 6
Butler, OK 154-155 F 3
Butler, PA 148-149 D 4
Butmah 182-183 K 4
Buton, Pulau - 186-187 H 7-8
Butre 138-139 K 7
Butsha 171 B 2
Butsikáki 136-137 J 6
Butte, ND 152-153 F 2
Butte, NE 152-153 G 4
Butte Creek, MT 152-153 C 2
Butte Meadows, CA 150-151 BC 5
Butterworth 186-187 D 5
Butterworth = Gcuwa 168-169 G 9
Butte-Silver Bow, MT 146-147 D 2
Butuan 186-187 HJ 5
Buturlinovka 140-141 K 1
Buulobarde 166-167 b 3
Buur Gabo 168-169 K 3
Buurhakaba 166-167 N 8
Buur Hakkaba 168-169 K 2
Buwārah, Jabal - 170 F 3
Buxton [ZA] 174-175 F 4
Buxton, ND 152-153 H 2
Buya 172-173 EF 3
Buyo 172-173 D 4
Buyo, Lake du - 172-173 D 4
Büyükada, İstanbul- 182-183 C 2
Büyük Ağrı Dağı 180-181 E 2-3
Büyük Köhne 182-183 F 3
Büyük Mahya 182-183 B 2
Büyük Menderes Nehri 180-181 B 3
Buzači, poluostrov - 180-181 G 1-2
Buzău [R, ~] 136-137 M 3
Buzău [R, ●] 136-137 M 3
Buzaymah 166-167 J 4
Buzd'ak 138-139 U 6
Buzi 190-191 G 5
Buzi = Po-tzu 190-191 H 10
Búzios, Cabo dos - 160-161 M 5
Búzios, Ilha dos - 160-161 K 5
Bužory 136-137 N 2
Buzuluk 178-179 J 7
Bužory 140-141 D 3
Buzovna 140-141 P 6
Buzzards Bay 148-149 H 4
Byam Martin Channel 144-145 PQ 2
Byam Martin Island 144-145 Q 2-3
Byāvar = Beawar 180-181 LM 5
Byawar = Beawar 180-181 LM 5
Býblos = Jubayl 182-183 F 5
Bychawa 133 L 3
Bychov 138-139 GH 7
Bydgoszcz 133 HJ 2
Bydhošť = Bydgoszcz 133 H 2
Bygdin 130-131 C 7
Bygland 130-131 BC 8
Byhalia, MS 154-155 L 3
Byk 140-141 D 3
Bykov [SU, Volgograd] 140-141 M 2
Bylot Island 144-145 V 3
Byoritsu = Miaoli 190-191 H 9
Byrd 121 AB 25
Byrd, Cape - 121 C 29
Byrd Land 121 AB 23-22
Byrock 194-195 J 6
Byron, CA 150-151 C 7
Byron, Cape - 194-195 K 5
Byron, IL 152-153 M 4
Byron Bay 196 LM 2
Byrranga , gory - 178-179 Q 3-V 2
Byske 130-131 J 5
Byssa 178-179 Z 7
Bystrica 138-139 R 4
Bystryj Tanyk 138-139 U 6
Bytom 133 J 3
Bytoš 138-139 JK 7
Bytów 133 H 1
Bzémā = Buzaymah 166-167 J 4
Bzura 133 J 2
Bzyp' 140-141 K 5

C

Caacupé 162 E 3
Čaadajevka 138-139 P 7
Caaguazú [PY, ●] 162 EF 3
Caaguazú [PY, ⋆] 160-161 DE 6
Caaguazú, Cordillera de - 162 E 3
Caála 168-169 DE 5
Caapucú 162 E 3
Caarapó 160-161 E 5
Caatinga 158-159 K 8
Caatinga, Rio - 160-161 JK 2
Caatingas 158-159 L 7-M 6
Caazapá [PY, ●] 162 E 3
Caazapá [PY, ⋆] 160-161 DE 7
Cabaçal, Rio - 160-161 CD 1
Caballeria, Cabo de - 134-135 K 8
Caballero 160-161 D 6
Caballococha 158-159 E 5
Caballo Reservoir 154-155 B 4
Caballo Reservoire 154-155 B 4
Caballos Mesteños, Llanos de los - 154-155 CD 6
Cabanatuan 186-187 H 3
Cabardini - Balcari, RA dei 140-141 L 5
Cabardini-Balcari, Repubblica Autonoma di 11 ◁ 126-127 R 7
Cabardini-Balcari, Rep. Aut. dei - 140-141 L 5
Cabardinose Balcares, República Autónoma dos - = 11 ◁ 126-127 R 7
Cabardinos e Balcares, República Autónoma dos - 140-141 LM 2
Cabecão 160-161 L 5
Cabeceira do Apa 160-161 E 4-5
Cabedelo 158-159 N 6
Cabeza del Buey 134-135 E 9
Cabezas 158-159 G 8
Cabezon, NM 154-155 B 3
Cabimas 158-159 E 2
Cabinda [Angola, ●] 168-169 D 4
Cabinda [Angola, ⋆] 168-169 D 4
Cabinet Mountains 150-151 E 1-F 2
Cable WI 152-153 L 2
Cabo, Bacia do - 124-125 K 7
Cabo, Cuenca del - 124-125 K 7
Cabo, Patamar do - 124-125 K 8
Cabo, Ramal del - 124-125 K 8
Cabo Alto = Cape Dolphin 162 E 8
Cabo Blanco [CR] 146-147 J 10
Cabo Blanco [RA] 162 CD 7
Cabo Branco 158-159 N 6
Cabo Delgado [Moçambique, ∧] 168-169 K 5
Cabo Delgado [Moçambique, ⋆] 168-169 JK 5
Cabo Falso [MEX] 146-147 D 7
Cabo Frio [BR, ∧] 158-159 L 9
Cabo Frio [BR, ●] 158-159 L 9
Cabo Johnson, Fossa do - 186-187 J 4
Cabool, MO 154-155 JK 2
Caboolture 196 L 1
Cabo Pantoja = Pantoja 158-159 DE 5
Cabo Pasado 158-159 C 5
Cabora Bassa 168-169 H 6
Cabo Raso [RA, ●] 162 CD 6
Cabo Raso = Cabo Norte 158-159 K 4
Caborca Heroica 146-147 D 5
Cabo Rojo [MEX] 146-147 G 7
Cabot Strait 144-145 YZ 8
Cabot, AR 154-155 JK 3
Cabot Head 152-153 Q 3
Cabo Verde, Bacia de - 124-125 GH 4-5
Cabo Verde, Cuenca de - 124-125 GH 4-5
Cabo Verde, Islas - 124-125 H 5
Cabo Verde, Patamar de - 124-125 H 4-5
Cabo Verde, Umbral de - 124-125 H 4-5
Cabra 134-135 E 10
Cabra, Monte - 146-147 b 3
Cabral, Serra do - 160-161 K 2
Cabras [BR] 160-161 J 5
Cabrera, Isla - 134-135 J 9
Cabriel 134-135 G 9
Cabrillo, Point - 150-151 AB 6
Cabul = Kābul 180-181 K 4
Cabullona 150-151 J 10
Caca 140-141 M 2
Caçador 162 F 3
Čačak 136-137 J 4
Caçapava 160-161 K 5
Caçapava do Sul 162 F 4
Cacássia, Região Autónoma de - = 9 ◁ 178-179 R 7
Càccia, Capo - 136-137 BC 5
Cacequi 162 F 3
Cáceres [BR] 158-159 H 8
Cáceres [CO] 158-159 D 3
Cáceres [E] 134-135 D 9
Cachar [TJ] 184-185 M 3
Chace, OK 154-155 F 3
Cachegar = Qāshqār 184-185 CD 4
Cachemira = Kashmir 180-181 LM 4
Cachemire = Kashmir 180-181 LM 4
Cache Peak 150-151 G 4
Cacheu 166-167 A 6
Cacheu, Rio - 172-173 B 2
Cachi 162 C 3
Cachi, Nevado de - 162 C 2
Cachimbo, Serra do - 158-159 HJ 6
Cachimo 168-169 F 4
Cachoeira Alta [BR, Paraná 160-161 G 3
Cachoeira [BR ↓ Feira de Santana] 158-159 M 7
Cachoeira do Sul 162 F 3-4
Cachoeiro de Itapemirim 158-159 LM 9
Cachoeiras de Macacu 160-161 LM 5
Cachoeira Paulista 160-161 K 5
Cachos, Punta 162 B 3
Cáchy = Aachen 133 C 3
Cacine 172-173 B 3
Caçiporé , Cabo - 158-159 JK 4
Caçiporé, Rio - 158-159 J 4
Çaçmak 182-183 F 3
Cacolo 168-169 E 4-5
Caconda 168-169 DE 5
Cactus, TX 154-155 F 7
Cactus Range 150-151 E 7
Caçu 160-161 G 3
Caculé 158-159 L 7
Cacuso 168-169 E 4
Cadale 166-167 b 3
Čadan 178-179 R 7
Caddabde, Raas - 166-167 b 1
Caddo, OK 154-155 G 3
Caddo Lake 154-155 HJ 4
Cadena, La - 154-155 C 8
Cadena Costera = Coast Mountains, Coast Range 144-145 K 6-M 9
Cadibarrawirracanna, Lake 196 AB 2
Cadice = Cadiz 134-135 D 10
Cadillac, MI 152-153 O 3
Cádiz 134-135 D 10
Cadiz, CA 150-151 F 8
Cádiz, KY 154-155 LM 2
Cádiz, Golfo de - 134-135 D 10
Čadobec [SU, ~] 178-179 S 6
Čadobec [SU, ●] 178-179 S 6
Čadyr-Lunga 140-141 D 3
Caen 134-135 G 4
Caernarfon 132 D 5
Caesarea 182-183 F 6
Caesarea = Kayseri 180-181 D 3
Caesarea Philippi = Bāniyās 182-183 FG 6
Caeté 160-161 L 3
Caetité 158-159 L 7
Cafayate 162 C 3
Cafta = Kafta 166-167 M 6
Cafelândia 160-161 H 4
Cagaan Cherem = Wanli Changcheng 184-185 K 4
Cagayan de Oro 186-187 HJ 5
Cagayan Islands 186-187 H 5
Cagayan Sulu Island 186-187 GH 5
Čagda 178-179 Z 6
Cageri 140-141 L 5
Caggan nuur 184-185 FG 2
Càgliari 136-137 C 6
Càgliari, Golfo di - 136-137 C 6
Čagoda 178-179 EF 6
Čagodošča 138-139 K 4
Çağrankaya-İkizdere 182-183 J 2
Cag Sum = Dzag 184-185 H 2
Caguán, Rio - 158-159 E 4
Caguas 146-147 N 8
Cahama 168-169 DE 6
Cahirciveen 132 AB 6
Cahors 134-135 H 6
Cahuapanas 158-159 D 6
Cahuilla Indian Reservation 150-151 E 9
Cahul 140-141 D 4
Cahungula = Caungula 168-169 E 4
Caia [Moçambique] 168-169 J 6
Caiabis, Serra dos - 158-159 H 7
Caiambé 158-159 FG 5
Caiapó Serra do - 160-161 FG 2
Caiapônia 160-161 FG 2
Cai Ban, Đao - 186-187 E 2
Caibarién 146-147 L 7
Caicara [W] 158-159 F 3
Caicos Islands 146-147 M 7
Caicos Passage 146-147 M 7
Caillou Bay 154-155 K 6
Caillou Lake 154-155 K 6
Caiman, Fossa das - 146-147 KL 8
Caimito 146-147 b 3
Caimito, Rio - 146-147 b 3
Cain Creek 152-153 G 3
Cainsville, MO 152-153 K 5
Cairari 158-159 K 5
Caird Land 121 B 33-34
Caire, le - = Al-Qāhirah 166-167 KL 2
Cairns 194-195 J 3
Cairo, GA 154-155 N 5
Cairo, Il - = Al-Qāhira 166-167 KL 2
Cairo, IL 146-147 J 4
Cairo, NE 152-153 G 5
Cairo = Al-Qahira 166-167 KL 2
Cairo, El - = Al-Qihira 166-167 KL 2
Caiundo 168-169 E 6
Caizi Hu 190-191 F 6
Cajabamba 158-159 D 6
Cajamar 160-161 J 5
Cajamarca [PE, ●] 158-159 D 6
Cajapió 158-159 KL 5
Cajatambo 158-159 D 7
Cajdam nuur 184-185 M 2
Cajdamyn nuur, Ich - 184-185 GH 4
Čajek 180-181 L 2
Čajkovskij 138-139 U 5
Cajon Pass 150-151 E 8
Cajuás, Ponta dos - 158-159 M 5
Cajuru 160-161 J 4
Çakırlan 182-183 F 2
Čakva 140-141 K 6
Cal 182-183 C 3
Çal = Demirciköy 182-183 C 3
Cala [ZA] 174-175 G 6
Calabar 166-167 F 7-8
Calabogie 148-149 E 2
Calabozo 158-159 F 3
Calabre = Calàbria 136-137 FG 6
Calàbria 136-137 FG 6
Calada, CA 150-151 F 8
Calafat 136-137 K 3-4
Calafate 162 B 8
Calagua Islands 186-187 H 4
Calahari = Kalahari Desert 168-169 EF 7
Calahorra 134-135 G 7
Calais 134-135 H 3
Calais, Pas de - 134-135 HJ 3
Calalaste, Sierra de - 162 C 2-3
Calama [BR] 158-159 G 6
Calama [RCH] 162 C 2
Calamar [CO ↘ Bogotá] 158-159 E 4
Calamian Group 186-187 G 4
Calamus River 152-153 G 4
Calang 186-187 C 6
Calapan 186-187 H 4
Călăraşi 136-137 M 3
Călăraşi [SU] 140-141 D 3
Cala Road = Calaweg 174-175 G 6
Calatayud 134-135 G 8
Calate = Qalāt 180-181 K 5
Călăţele 136-137 K 2
Calaweg 174-175 G 6
Calayan Island 186-187 H 3
Calbayog 186-187 HJ 4
Calca 158-159 E 7
Calcanhar, Ponta do 158-159 M 6-N 5
Calcasieu Lake 154-155 J 6
Calcasieu River 154-155 J 5
Calçoene 158-159 J 4
Calcuta = Calcutta 180-181 O 6
Calcutta 180-181 O 6
Caldas [BR] 160-161 J 4
Caldas da Rainha 134-135 C 9
Caldas Novas 160-161 H 2
Caldera 162 B 3
Çaldıran 182-183 K 3
Caldwell, ID 150-151 E 4
Caldwell KS 154-155 G 2
Caldwell, OH 148-149 C 5
Caldwell, TX 154-155 G 5
Calecute = Calicut 180-181 LM 8
Caledon 166-167 EF 9
Caledon Bay 194-195 G 2
Caledonia [CDN, Ontario] 148-149 D 3
Caledonia, MN 152-153 L 4
Caledonian Canal 132 D 3
Caledonrivier 168-169 G 8-9
Calera, AL 154-155 M 4
Calera, La - [MEX] 154-155 C 6
Caleta de Vique 146-147 b 3
Caleta Olivia 162 C 7
Caleufú 162 D 5
Calexico, CA 150-151 F 9
Çalgan 182-183 H 4
Calgary 144-145 O 7
Calhan, CO 152-153 D 6
Calhoun, GA 154-155 N 3
Calhoun, LA 154-155 J 4
Calhoun, TN 148-149 A 7
Calhoun, City, MS 154-155 L 4
Calhoun Falls, SC 148-149 B 7
Cali 158-159 D 4
Calico Rock, AR 154-155 JK 2
Calicut = Kozhikote 180-181 LM 8
Caliente, CA 150-151 D 8
Caliente, NV 146-147 CD 4
California [BR] 160-161 G 6
California [USA] 146-147 B 3-C 5
California [USA] 146-147 B 3-C 5
California = California 146-147 B 3-C 5
California, MO 152-153 K 6
California, Golfo da - 146-147 D 5-E 7
California, Golfo de 146-147 D 5-E 7
California, Golfo di - 146-147 D 5-E 7
California, Gulf of 146-147 D 5-E 7
Californie = California 146-147 B 3-C 5
Californie, Golfe de 146-147 D 5-E 7
Californië, Golf van 146-147 D 5-E 7
Căliman, Munţii - 136-137 L 2
Calimere, Point - 180-181 MN 8
Călineşti 136-137 L 3
Calingasta 162 BC 4
Calion, AR 154-155 J 4
Calipatria, CA 150-151 F 9
Calipso, Fossa de - 128-129 N 8
Calispell Peak 150-151 E 1
Calistoga, CA 150-151 B 6
Calitzdorp 174-175 D 7
Calka 140-141 M 6
Calkini 146-147 H 7
Callabonna, Lake - 194-195 G 5
Callabonna Creek 196 E 2
Callahan, FL 148-149 c 1
Callahan, Mount - 150-151 E 6
Callao 158-159 D 7
Callaway, NE 152-153 FG 5
Calmar, IA 152-153 KL 4
Calmon 160-161 G 7
Calmucchi, Rep. Aut. dei - 140-141 MN 3
Calmucchi, Repubblica Autonoma dei - 8 ◁ 126-127 S 6
Calmuchia, Rebubblica Autonoma di 140-141 MN 3
Calmucos, República Autónoma de los - 140-141 MN 3
Calmucos, República Autónoma dos - = 8 ◁ 126-127 S 6
Calmucos, Re, Aut. dos - 140-141 MN 3
Calna 138-139 JK 3
Calobre 160-161 GH 5
Caloosahatchee River 148-149 c 3
Caltagirone 136-137 F 7
Caltanissetta 136-137 EF 7
Calulo 168-169 DE 4-5

210

Chicoa 168-169 H 6
Chicoana 162 CD 3
Chicoma Peak = Tschicoma Peak 154-155 BC 2-3
Chicomo 174-175 KL 3
Chiconomo 171 CD 6
Chicopee, MA 148-149 G 3
Chicoutimi 144-145 WX 8
Chicualacuala 168-169 H 7
Chicualacuala 174-175 JK 2
Chidenguele 174-175 L 3
Chidester, AR 154-155 J 4
Chidley, Cape - 144-145 Y 5
Chi-do 188-189 EF 5
Chiefland, FL 148-149 b 2
Chiefs Point 152-153 Q 3
Chieh-hsiu = Jiexiu 190-191 CD 3
Chiehmo = Chärchän 184-185 F 4
Chieh-shih = Jieshi 190-191 E 10
Chieh-shih Wan = Jieshi Wan 190-191 E 10
Chieh-shou = Jieshou 190-191 E 5
Chieh-yang = Jieyang 190-191 F 10
Chiemsee 133 F 5
Ch'i en-an = Qian'an 190-191 G 1
Chien-ch'ang = Nancheng 190-191 F 8
Chien-ch'ang = Jianchang [TJ → Benxi] 188-189 E 2
Chien-ch'ang = Jianchang [TJ ↙ Jinzhou] 188-189 B 2
Chien-ch'ang-ying = Jianchangying 190-191 G 1
Chien-chi = Qianji 190-191 G 4-5
Ch'ien-chiang = Qianjiang [TJ, Guanxi Zhuangzu Zizhiqu] 190-191 B 10
Ch'ien-chiang = Qianjiang [TJ, Hubei] 184-185 L5
Ch'ien-chiang = Qianjiang [TJ, Sichuan] 190-191 B 7
Chiengi 168-169 G 4
Chiengmai = Chiang Mai 186-187 C 3
Chien-Ho = Jian He [TJ, ~] 188-189 D 2
Chien-ho = Jianhe [TJ, ●] 190-191 B 8
Ch'ien-hsi = Qianxi 190-191 G 1
Ch'ien-hsien = Qian Xian 190-191 B 4
Chien-ko = Jiange 184-185 JK 5
Chien-li = Jianli 190-191 D 7
Chien-ning = Jianning 190-191 F 8
Chien-ning = Jian'ou 184-185 M 6
Chien-ou = Jian'ou 184-185 M 6
Chien-p'ing = Jianping 188-189 B 2
Chien-p'ing = Langxi 190-191 G 6
Ch'ien-shan = Qianshan 190-191 F 6
Chien-shui = Jianshui 184-185 J 7
Chien-tê = Jiande 190-191 G 7
Ch'ien-wei = Qianwei 188-189 C 2
Chien-yang = Jianyang [TJ, Fujian] 190-191 FG 8
Chien-yang = Jianyang [TJ, Sichuan] 184-185 JK 5
Ch'ien-yang = Qianyang 190-191 C 8
Ch'ien-yu Ho = Qianyou He 190-191 B 5
Chieti 136-137 F 4
Chifeng 184-185 M 3
Chifre, Serra do - 158-159 L 8
Chignik, AK 144-145 E 6
Chigubo 174-175 K 2
Chigyŏng 188-189 F 3
Ch'ih-ch'i = Chixi 190-191 D 10-11
Chih-chiang = Zhijiang [TJ, Hubei] 190-191 C 6
Chih-chiang = Zhijiang [TJ, Hunan] 184-185 KL 6
Ch'ih-fêng = Chifeng 184-185 M 3
Chih-fu = Yantai 184-185 N 4
Chihe 190-191 FG 5
Ch'ih-ho = Chihe 190-191 FG 5
Ch'ih-k'an = Chikan 190-191 C 11
Chih-kiang = Zhijiang 184-185 KL 6
Chih-li Wan = Bo Hai 184-185 M 4
Chi-hsi = Jixi 184-185 P 2
Chi-hsien = Ji Xian [TJ, Henan] 190-191 E 4
Chi-hsien = Ji Xian [TJ, Shanxi] 190-191 C 3
Chi-hsien = Ji Xian [TJ, Hebei → Beijing] 190-191 F 1
Chi-hsien = Ji Xian [TJ, Hebei ↘ Shijiazhuang] 190-191 E 3
Ch'i-hsien = Qi Xian [TJ, Shanxi] 190-191 D 3
Ch'i-hsien = Qi Xian [TJ, Henan ↘ Kaifeng] 190-191 E 4
Ch'i-hsien = Qi Xian [TJ, Henan ↗ Xinxiang] 190-191 DE 4
Chihtan = Zhidan 190-191 B 3
Chihuahua 146-147 E 6
Chi-hu 190-191 H 9-10
Ch'i-i = Qiyi 190-191 D 5
Chii-san = Chiri-san 188-189 F 5
Chikan 190-191 C 11
Chike = Xunke 184-185 O 2
Chikkai = Chixi 190-191 D 10-11
Chikugo 188-189 H 6
Chikwawa 168-169 HJ 6
Chilapa de Alvarez 146-147 G 8
Chilās 180-181 L 3
Chilca 158-159 D 7
Chilcoot, CA 150-151 CD 6
Childersburg, AL 154-155 M 4
Childress, TX 154-155 EF 3
Chile 162 B 5-C 2
Chile, Bacia do - 124-125 E 7-F 6
Chile Basin 124-125 EF 6-7
Chilebecken 124-125 EF 6-7
Chilebecken 198-199 O 5-6
Chilecito [RA, La Rioja] 162 C 3
Chilhowee, MO 152-153 K 6
Chilete 158-159 D 6
Chili 162 B 5-C 2
Chili, Bassin du - 124-125 E 7-F 6
Chilia, Braţul - 136-137 N 3
Chilibekken 124-125 EF 6-7
Chilibre 146-147 b 2
Ch'i-li-chên = Qilizhen 190-191 B 4
Chilicote 154-155 C 6
Ch'i-lien Shan = Qilian Shan 184-185 HJ 4
Chilika Hrada = Chilka Lake 180-181 NO 7
Chililabombwe 168-169 G 5
Chi-lin = Jilin [TJ, ●] 184-185 O 3
Chi-lin = Jilin [TJ, ⁎] 184-185 N 2-O 3
Chilivani 136-137 C 5
Chilka Lake 180-181 NO 7
Chilko Lake 144-145 M 7
Chillán 162 B 5
Chill Chainnigh = Kilkenny 132 C 5
Chillicothe, IL 152-153 M 5
Chillicothe, MO 146-147 H 3-4
Chillicothe, OH 146-147 K 4
Chillicothe, TX 154-155 F 3
Chilly 140-141 O 7
Chilly, ID 150-151 FG 3
Chiloé, Isla de - 162 AB 6
Chilok 178-179 UV 7
Chilonga 171 B 5-6
Chilongozi 171 BC 6
Chiloquin, OR 150-151 C 4
Chilpancingo de los Bravos 146-147 G 8
Chiltern Hills 132 F 6
Chilton, WI 152-153 M 3
Chilung = Kee-lung 184-185 N 6
Chilwa, Lake - 168-169 J 6
Chiman tagh 184-185 FG 4
Chimborazo [EC, ▲] 158-159 D 5
Chimbote 158-159 D 6
Chimei Hsü = Ta-Yü 190-191 G 10
Ch'i-mên = Qimen 190-191 F 7
Chi-ming-ho = Jiminghe 190-191 E 6
Chimney Peak = One Tree Peak 154-155 C 4
Chi-mo = Jimo 190-191 H 3
Chimoio 168-169 H 6
Chimpay 162 C 5
Chimpembe 171 B 5
China 184-185 E-K 5
China Meridional, Bacia da - 186-187 FG 3-4
China Meridional, Mar da - 186-187 E 5-G 2
China Oriental, Mar da - 184-185 N 6-O 5
China, Republiek - 184-185 N 7
China Lake, CA 150-151 E 8
Chinan 188-189 F 5
Chinan = Jinan 184-185 M 4
Ch'in-an - Qin,an 184-185 K 5
Chinandega 146-147 J 9
Chinapa 150-151 HJ 10
China Point 150-151 D 9
Chinati Peak 154-155 C 6
Chinbo 188-189 G 4
Chincha Alta 158-159 D 7
Chin-ch'êng = Jincheng 184-185 L 4
Chin-Ch'i = Jin Xi [TJ, ~] 190-191 F 8
Chin-ch'i = Jinxi [TJ, ●] 190-191 F 8
Chin Chiang = Jin Jiang 190-191 E 7
Chinchilla 194-195 K 5
Chinchilla de Monte-Aragón 134-135 G 9
Chin-ching = Jinjing 190-191 D 7
Chinchorro, Banco - 146-147 J 8
Chinchow = Jinzhou 184-185 N 3
Chincoteague, VA 148-149 F 6
Chincoteague Bay 148-149 F 5
Chinde 168-169 J 6
Chin-do [ROK, ⊙] 188-189 EF 5
Chindo [ROK, ●] 188-189 F5
Chindwin Myit 186-187 C 1-2
Chine 184-185 E-K 5
Chine Méridionale, Mer de - 186-187 E 5-G 3
Chine Orientale, Mer de - 184-185 N 6-O 5
Chinese muur 184-185 K 4
Ching-an = Jing'an 190-191 E 7
Ch'ing-chang Ho = Qingzhang Dongyuan 190-191 D 3
Ching-chi = Jingzhi 190-191 G 3
Ching-chiang = Jingjiang 190-191 H 5-6
Ch'ing Chiang = Qing Jiang 190-191 C 6
Ch'ing-chien = Qingjian 190-191 C 3
Ching-ch'uan = Yinchuan 184-185 JK 4
Ch'ing-fêng = Qingfeng 190-191 E 4
Ch'ing Hai = Chöch nuur 184-185 H 4
Ching-hai = Jinghai 190-191 F 2
Chinghai = Qinghai 184-185 GH 4
Ching-Ho = Jing He [TJ , ~] 190-191 B 4
Ching-ho = Jinghe [TJ , ●] 184-185 E 3
Ch'ing-ho = Qinghe 190-191 E 3
Ch'ing-ho-ch'ên = Qinghezhen 190-191 F 3
Ch'ing-ho-ch'êng = Qinghecheng 188-189 E 2
Ch'ing-ho-mêng = Qinghemen 188-189 C 2
Ching-hsien = Jing Xian [TJ, Anhui] 190-191 G 6
Ching-hsien = Jing Xian [TJ, Hunan] 190-191 B 6
Ching-hsing = Jingxing 190-191 DE 2
Ching-ku = Jinggu 184-185 J 7
Ch'ing-lien = Qinglian 190-191 D 9
Ch'ing-liu = Qingliu 190-191 F 8
Ching-lo = Jingle 190-191 CD 2
Ching-mên = Jingmen 190-191 CD 6
Ching-ning = Jingning 184-185 K 4
Chingola 168-169 G 5
Chingombe 171 B 6
Chingovo, Rio - 174-175 K 2
Ching-pien = Jingbian 190-191 B 3
Ching-po Hu = Jingbo Hu 184-185 O 3
Ch'ing-p'u = Qingpu 190-191 H 6
Ching Shan = Jing Shan [TJ, ▲▲] 190-191 C 6
Ching-shan = Jingshan [TJ, ●] 190-191 D 6
Ch'ing-shui Ho = Qingshui He [TJ, ~] 190-191 B 2
Ch'ing-shui-ho = Qingshuihe [TJ, ●] 190-191 C 2
Ching-t'ai = Jingtai 184-185 J 4
Ch'ing-tao = Qingdao 184-185 N 4
Ching-tê = Jingde 190-191 G 6
Ch'ing-t'ien = Qingtian 190-191 H 7
Ch'ing-tui-tzŭ = Qingduizi 188-189 D 3
Ching-tung = Jingdong 184-185 J 7
Ching-tzŭ-kuan = Jingziguan 190-191 C 5
Ching-yang = Jingyang 190-191 B 4
Ch'ing-yang = Qingyang [TJ, Anhui] 190-191 FG 6
Ch'ing-yang = Qingyang [TJ, Gansu] 184-185 K 4
Ching-yüan = Jingyuan 184-185 JK 4
Ch'ing-yüan = Qingyuan [TJ, Fujian] 190-191 G 8
Ch'ing-yüan = Qingyuan [TJ, Guangdong] 190-191 D 10
Ch'ing-yüan = Qingyuan [TJ, Liaoning] 188-189 E 1
Ch'ing-yün = Qingyun 190-191 F3
Chinhae 188-189 G 5
Chinhae-man 188-189 G 5
Ch'in Ho = Qin He 190-191 D 4
Chinhoyi 168-169 GH 6
Chin-hsiang = Jinxiang [TJ, Shandong] 190-191 EF 4
Chin-hsiang = Jinxiang [TJ, Zhejiang] 190-191 H 8
Chin-hsien = Jinxian [TJ, Hebei] 190-191 E 2
Chin-hsien = Jinxian [TJ, Jiangxi] 190-191 F 7
Chin-hsien = Jin Xian [TJ, Liaoning ↗ Jinzhou] 188-189 C 2
Chin-hsien = Jin Xian [TJ, Liaoning ↑ Lüda] 184-185 N 4
Chinhsien = Jinzhou 184-185 N 3
Chinhsien = Qin Xian 190-191 D 3
Chin-hua = Jinhua 184-185 MN 6
Ch'in-huang-tao = Qinhuangdao 184-185 MN 3-4
Chi-ning = Jining [TJ, Nei Monggol Zizhiqu] 184-185 L 3
Chi-ning = Jining [TJ, Shandong] 184-185 M 4
Chinju 184-185 O 4
Chinko 166-167 J 7
Chin-k'ou = Jinkou 190-191 E 6
Chinle, AZ 150-151 J 7
Chinle Valley 150-151 J 7
Ch'in Ling = Qin Ling 184-185 KL 5
Chin-mên Tao 184-185 M 7
Chinnamp'o= Nampo 184-185 NO 4
Chin-niu = Jinniu 190-191 E 6-7
Chinon 134-135 H 5
Chinook, MT 152-153 B 1
Chino Valley, AZ 150-151 G 8
Chin-p'ing = Jinping 190-191 B 8
Chinquião = Zhenjiang 184-185 M 5
Chinsali 168-169 H 5
Chin-sha Chiang = Jinsha Jiang 184-185 J 6
Chin-shan = Jinshan 190-191 H 6
Ch'in Shui = Qingshui Jiang 190-191 B 8
Ch'in-shui = Qinshui 190-191 D 4
Chinsiang = Jinxiang 190-191 EF 4
Chinsura 180-181 O 6
Chin-t'an = Jintan 190-191 G 6
Chinwangtao = Qinhuangdao 184-185 MN 3-4
Chinwithetha Pyinnei 186-187 B 2
Chiny 184-185 E-K 5
Chin-yang = Qinyang 184-185 L 4
Chinyŏng 188-189 G 5
Chin-yüan = Jinyuan 190-191 D 3
Chinyuan = Qinyuan 190-191 D 3
Ch'in-yüan = Qinyuan 190-191 D 3
Chin-yün = Jinyun 190-191 H 7
Chióco 168-169 H 6
Chióggia 136-137 E 3
Chios [GR, ⊙] 136-137 L 6
Chios [GR, ●] 136-137 M 6
Chipata 168-169 H 5
Chipili 171 B 5
Chipinge 168-169 H 7
Chipley, FL 154-155 N 5
Chipley, GA 154-155 N 4
Chipoka 171 C 6
Chiporiro 168-169 H 6
Chippewa Falls, WI 152-153 L 3
Chippewa Flowage 152-153 L3
Chippewa Reservoir = Chippewa Flowage 152-153 L 3
Chippewa River [USA, Michigan] 152-153 O 4
Chippewa River [USA, Wisconsin] 152-153 KL 3
Chipre 180-181 C 4
Chiputneticook Lakes 148-149 JK 2
Chiquimula 146-147 HJ 9
Chiquitos, Llanos de - 158-159 G 8
Chira 171 D 2
Chira Bazar 184-185 DE 4
Chiraz = Shīrāz 180-181 G 5
Chiredzi 168-169 H 7
Chirfa 166-167 G 4
Chiricahua National Monument 150-151 J 9-10
Chiricahua Peak 150-151 J 10
Chirikof Island 144-145 EF 6
Chiriqui, Golfo de - 146-147 K 10
Chiriqui, Laguna de - 146-147 K 9-10
Chiri-san 188-189 F 5
Chiromo 168-169 J 6
Chirripo Grande, Cerro - 146-147 K 10
Chirundu 168-169 G 6
Ch'i-shan 190-191 H 10
Chisamba 168-169 G 5-6
Chisel Lake 144-145 QR 7
Chi-shih Shan = Amnyemachhen Shan 184-185 HJ 5
Chi-shui = Jishui 190-191 E 8
Chishtian Mandi = Chishtiyān Maṇḍī 180-181 L 5
Chishtiyān Maṇḍī 180-181 L 5
Chisimaio = Kismaayo 168-169 K 3
Chişinău 140-141 D 3
Chişlavičl 138-139 HJ 6
Chisos Mountains 154-155 D 6
Chitado 168-169 D 6
Chita-hantō 188-189 L 5
Ch'i-t'ai = Qitai 184-185 FG 3
Chitambo 171 B 6
Chitembo 168-169 E 5
Chitogarh = Chittaurgarh 180-181 L 6
Chitose 188-189 b 2
Chitradurga 180-181 M 8
Chitrāl 180-181 L 3
Chitré 146-147 K 10
Chi-tsê = Jize 190-191 E 3
Chittagong 180-181 P 6
Chittaldurga = Chitradurga 180-181 M 8
Chittaorgarh = Chittaurgarh 180-181 L 6
Chittaurgarh 180-181 L 6
Chittoor 180-181 M 8
Chittor = Chittoor 180-181 M 8
Ch'i-tung = Qidong [TJ, Jiangsu] 190-191 H 6
Ch'i-tung = Qidong [TJ, Shanndong] 190-191 F 3
Chiu-chiang = Jiujiang 190-191 D 10
Chiuchuan = Jiuquan 184-185 H 4
Chiu-ho-hsü = Jiuhe 190-191 E 10
Chiu-hsien = Qiu Xian 190-191 E 3
Chiulezi, Rio - 171 D 5-6
Chiu-ling Shan = Jiuling Shan 190-191 E 7
Chiu-lung Ch'i = Jiulong Xi 190-191 F 8
Chiu-lung Chiang = Jiulong Jiang 190-191 F 9
Chiu-lung Shan = Jiulong Shan 190-191 G 7
Chiuma, ostrov - = Hiiuma 138-139 CD 4
Chiumbe, Rio - 168-169 F 4
Chiume 168-169 F 5-6
Ch'iung-chou Hai-hsia = Qiongzhou Haixia 184-185 KL 7
Chiungshan = Qiongshan 184-185 L 8
Ch'iung-tung = Qionghai 184-185 L 8
Chiu-shan Lieh-tao = Jiushan Liedao 190-191 J 7
Chiuta, Lagoa - 168-169 J 5
Chiu-tao-liang = Jiudaoliang 190-191 J 7
Chiva [SU] 178-179 L 9
Chivasso 136-137 B 3
Chivay 158-159 E 8
Chivilcoy 162 DE 4
Chivu 168-169 H 6
Chiwanda 168-169 HJ 5
Chiwefwe 171 B 6
Chiweta 168-169 H 5
Chixi 190-191 D 10-11
Chixoy, Rio - 146-147 H 8
Chi-yang = Jiyang [TJ, Fujian] 190-191 FG 8
Chi-yang = Jiyang [TJ, Shandong] 190-191 F3
Ch'i-yang = Qiyang 190-191 CD 8
Chi-yüan = Jiyuan 190-191 D 4
Chjargas 184-185 G 2
Chjargas nuur 184-185 GH 2
Chlevnoje 138-139 M 7
Chloride, AZ 150-151 F 8
Chmeiṭīyē = Shmayṭīyah 182-183 H 5
Chmelevoje 140-141 E 2
Chmel'nyc'kyi 140-141 C 2
Chobe 168-169 F 6
Chobe National Park 168-169 FG 6
Chocaya 158-159 F 9
Chocca 158-159 D 7
Cho-chang Ho = Zhuozhang He 190-191 D 3
Chochiang = Charqiliq 184-185 F 4
Choch'iwŏn 188-189 F 4
Chöch nuur 184-185 H 4
Chochol'skij 140-141 J 1
Choch Šili 184-185 G 4
Choch Šili uul 184-185 FG 4
Chociebuż = Cottbus 133 G 3
Chocolate Mountains 150-151 F 9
Choconta 158-159 E 3
Choctaw, AL 154-155 L 4
Choctawhatchee Bay 154-155 M 5
Choctawhatchee River 154-155 MN 5
Ch'o-do [Nordkorea] 188-189 E 3-4
Ch'o-do [ROK] 188-189 F 5
Chodorov 140-141 B 2
Chodžambas 180-181 JK 3
Chodžejli 178-179 K 9
Chodżent = Leninabad 180-181 KL 2-3
Chodzież 133 F1 2
Choele-Choel 162 CD 5
Chohsien = Zhuo Xian 190-191 E 2
Choibalsan = Čojbalsan 184-185 L 2
Choiseul 186-187 j 6
Chojna 133 G 2
Chojnice 133 HJ 2
Chojniki 138-139 G 8
Chōkai-zan 188-189 MN 3
Cholamandala = Coromandel Coast 180-181 N 7-8
Cholame, CA 150-151 CD 8
Chold = Chuld 184-185 K 2-3
Cholet 134-135 G 5
Cholgwan 188-189 E 3
Chŏlla-namdo 188-189 F 5
Chŏlla-pukto 188-189 F 5
Cholm 138-139 H 5
Cholmogorskaja 138-139 N 2
Cholmogory 178-179 G 5
Cholmsk 178-179 b 8
Cholm-Žirkovskij 138-139 JK 6
Cholopeniči 138-139 G 6
Cholos nuur 184-185 H 4
Ch'ŏlsan 188-189 E 3
Choluteca 146-147 J 9
Cho-lu = Zhuolu 190-191 E 1
Choma 168-169 G 6
Chomba 171 D 5
Chomutovka 138-139 K 8
Ch'ŏnan 188-189 F 4
Chon Buri 186-187 D 4
Chŏnch'ŏn 188-189 F 2
Chone 158-159 CD 5
Chong'an 190-191 F 8
Ch'ŏng'chŏn-gang 188-189 EF 2-3
Chongde 190-191 H 6
Chongdjin = Ch'ŏngjin 184-185 OP 3
Chŏnggŏ-dong 188-189 E 3
Ch'ŏngha 188-189 G 4
Ch'ŏngjin 184-185 OP 3
Chongjin—Ch'ŏngjin 184-185 OP 3
Chŏngju 184-185 O 4
Chongling Shui 190-191 D8-9
Chongming 184-185 N 5
Chongming Dao 190-191 HJ 6
Chongoene 174-175 KL 3
Chongor 184-185 L 2
Chongor = Bajan Adraga 184-185 KL 2
Chongor Oboo Sum = Bajandalaj 184-185 J 3
Chongor Tagh = Qungur tagh 184-185 D 4
Ch'ŏngp'yŏngch'ŏn 188-189 FG 4
Chongqing 184-185 K 6
Chongren 190-191 EF 8
Ch'ŏngsan-do 188-189 F 5
Chongshan = Chongzuo 184-185 K 7
Chongshanpai = Jitan 190-191 E 9
Ch'ongsŏktu-ri 188-189 EF 3
Chongsŏng 188-189 GH 1
Chŏngŭp 188-189 F 5
Chŏnju 184-185 O 4
Chonwu 190-191 G 9
Ch'ŏngyang [ROK] 188-189 F 4
Chongyang [TJ] 190-191 E 7
Chongyang = Zhongyang 190-191 C 3
Chongyang Xi 190-191 FG 8
Chongyi 190-191 E 9
Chongzuo 184-185 K 7
Chŏnju 184-185 O 4
Chonos, Archipiélago de los - 162 AB 6-7
Chonuu 178-179 b 4
Chooloj Gov' 184-185 H 3
Chopim, Rio - 160-161 F 6-7
Chopinzinho 160-161 F 6
Chop'or 138-139 P 7
Chor 178-179 Za 8
Chorasan = Khorāsān 180-181 H 3-4
Chŏra Sfakion 136-137 L 8
Chordogoj 178-179 W 5
Chor He 184-185 N 2
Chorinsk 178-179 U 7
Chorlovo 138-139 M 6
Chorog 180-181 L 3
Chorol 140-141 F 2
Chorrera, La - [PA] 146-147 b 3
Chorsabad = Khorsabad 182-183 K 4
Chorwacja 136-137 F-H 3
Chŏrwŏn 188-189 F 3
Chŏryŏng-do = Yŏng-do 188-189 G 5
Chorzele 133 K 2
Chorzów 133 J 3
Chŏsen-kaikyō 184-185 O 5
Chōshi 188-189 N 5
Cho-shui Hsi 190-191 H 10
Chos-Malal 162 BC 5
Chosŏn-man = Tonghan-man 184-185 O 4
Choszczno 133 GH 2
Chota 158-159 D 6
Chota Nāgpur 180-181 NO 6
Choteau, MT 150-151 G 2
Chotimsk 138-139 J 7
Chotin 140-141 C 2
Chotynek 138-139 K 7
Chou-chih = Zhouzhi 190-191 AB 4
Chou-k'ou-tien = Fangshan 190-191 E 2
Chou-ning = Zhouning 190-191 G 8
Chou Shan = Zhoushan Dao 184-185 N 5-6
Chou-shan Ch'ün-tao = Zhoushan Qundao 184-185 N 5
Chou-tang-p'an = Zhoudangfang 190-191 E 6
Chouteau, OK 154-155 H 2
Chou-ts'un = Zhoucun 190-191 FG 3
Chovd [MVR , ●] 184-185 G 2
Chovd [MVR, ⁎ = 3 ◁] 184-185 G 2
Chovd gol 184-185 G 2
Chövsgöl [MVR, ●] 184-185 KL 3
Chövsgöl [MVR, ⁎ = 6 ◁] 184-185 J 1
Chövsgöl nuur 184-185 J 1
Chowan River 148-149 E 6
Chowchilla, CA 150-151 C 7
Chozapini, ozero - 140-141 L 6
Chrapovickaja Dača = Peredel 138-139 N 6
Chrenovoje 140-141 K 1
Chrisman, IL 152-153 N 6
Chrissiesmeer 174-175 J 4
Christchurch [NZ] 194-195 OP 8
Christiana 174-175 F 4
Christian Island 148-149 C 2
Christiansburg, VA 148-149 CD 6
Christianshåb = Qasigiánguit 144-145 ab 4
Christie Bay 144-145 O 5
Christina MT 152-153 B 2
Christinovka 140-141 DE 2
Christmas Creek 194-195 E 3
Christmas Island [AUS] 186-187 E 9
Christoforovo 138-139 QR 3
Christoval TX 154-155 E 5
Chromo, CO 152-153 C 7
Chromtau 178-179 K 7
Chrudim 133 GH 4
Chrysê 136-137 LM 8
Chrysochûs, Kólpos - 182-183 E 5
Chuali, Lagoa - 174-175 K 3
Chuambo 174-175 L 1
Chuanchang He 190-191 GH 5
Ch'üan-ch'i = Quanxishi 190-191 D 8
Ch'üan-chiao = Qaunjiao 190-191 FG 5
Ch'üan-chou Chiang = Quanzhou Gang 190-191 G 9
Chuang-ho = Zhuanghe 188-189 D 3
Chuansha 190-191 HJ 6
Chubb Crater = New Quebec Crater 144-145 VW 5
Chubbuck, CA 150-151 F 8
Chubisgalt = Chövsgöl 184-185 KL 3
Chubsugul = Chövsgöl nuur 184-185 J 1
Chübu 188-189 LM 4-5
Chubut 162 BC 6
Chubut, Rio - 162 C 6
Chucheng = Zhucheng 184-185 MN 4
Chu-chi = Zhuji 184-185 N 6
Chu-ch'i = Zhuxi 190-191 BC 5
Chu-chia Chien = Zhujia Jian 190-191 J 7
Chu-ch'iao = Zhuqiao 190-191 GH 3
Ch'ü-chieh = Qujie 190-191 C 11
Ch'ü-ching = Qujing 184-185 J 6
Ch'ü-chou = Quzhou 190-191 E 3
Ch'ü-chou = Qu Xian 184-185 M 6
Chu-chou = Zhuzhou 184-185 L 6
Chuchow = Zhuzhou 184-185 L 6
Chuchwa 174-175 D 3
Chučni 140-141 N 6
Chudat 140-141 O 6
Ch'üeh-shan = Queshan 184-185 L 5
Ch'ü-fou = Qufu 190-191 F 4
Chugach Mountains 144-145 GH 5
Chugoku 188-189 HJ 5
Chūgoku-sammyaku 188-189 JK 5
Chuguchak 184-185 E 2
Chūgūchak = Tarbagataj 184-185 EF 2
Chugwater , WY 152-153 D 5
Chuhsien = Chu Xian 190-191 FG 5
Chuhsien = Ju Xian 190-191 G 4
Chü-hsien = Ju Xian 190-191 G 4
Chuhsien = Qu Xian 184-185 M 6
Ch'ü-hsiung = Chuxiong 184-185 J 7
Chü-hua Tao = Juhua Dao 188-189 C 2
Ch'uja-do 188-189 F 6
Chü-jung =Jurong 190-191 G 6
Chukchi Plateau 120 B 35
Chukchi Sea 120 BC 35-36
Chukchos, Circunscrição Nacional dos - 178-179 g-k 4
Chukchos, Mar de - 120 BC 35-36
Chukchos, Patamar de - 120 B 35
Chuki–Zhuji 184-185 N 6
Chukot Autonomous Area 178-179 g-j 4
Chü-k'ou-p'u = Jukoupu 190-191 C 8
Chu-kuang Shan = Zhuguang Shan 190-191 DE 8-9
Chukudu Kraal 168-169 F 7
Chül, Gardaneh-ye - 182-183 MN 6
Chulaq Aqqan Su 184-185 G 4
Chula Vista, CA 146-147 C 5
Chulchuta 140-141 N 3
Chuld 184-185 K 2-3
Chü-liu-ho = Juliuhe 188-189 D 1
Chulp'o 188-189 F 5
Ch'ü-lu = Julu 190-191 E 3
Chulucanas 158-159 CD 6
Chulumani 158-159 F 8
Chu-lung Ho = Zhulong He 190-191 E 2
Chu-ma-tien = Zhumadian 190-191 DE 5
Chumbicha 162 C 3
Chum Phae 186-187 D 3
Chumphon 186-187 CD 4
Chumsaeng 186-187 D 3
Chumunjin 188-189 G 4
Chun'an 190-191 G 7
Ch'unch'ŏn 184-185 O 4
Chungam-ni 188-189 G 5
Chungan = Chong'an 190-191 F 8
Ch'ung Ch'i = Chongyang Xi 190-191 FG 8
Ch'ungch'ŏng-namdo 188-189 F 4
Ch'ungch'ŏng-pukto 188-189 FG 4
Chüngges 184-185 E 3
Chung-hsiang = Zhongxiang 190-191 D 6
Chung-hsin-hsü = Zhongxin 190-191 E 9
Chunghwa 188-189 EF 3
Ch'ung-i = Chongyi 190-191 E 9
Ch'ung-jên = Chongren 190-191 EF 8
Ch'ungju 188-189 FG 4
Chungking = Chongqing 184-185 K 6
Chungking = Chongqing 184-185 K 6
Chung-li 190-191 H 9
Ch'ung-ming = Chongming 184-185 N 5
Ch'ung-ming Tao = Chongming Dao 190-191 HJ 6
Chung-mou = Zhongmou 190-191 DE 4
Ch'ungmu 188-189 G 5
Chung-pu = Huangling 190-191 B 4
Chŭngsan 188-189 E 3
Chungshan = Zhongshan 184-185 L 7
Chungsiang = Zhongxiang 190-191 D 6
Chung-t'iao Shan = Zhongtiao Shan 190-191 CD 4
Chung-tien—Zhongdian 184-185 HJ 6
Chung-tu = Zhongdu 190-191 B 9
Chŭngŭij pyŏl 184-185 GH 2
Chung-wei = Zhongwei 184-185 JK 4
Ch'ung-wu = Chongwu 190-191 G 9
Chungyang = Chongyang 190-191 E 7
Chün-hsien = Jun Xian 190-191 C 5
Chunhua 190-191 B 4
Chunya 168-169 H 4
Chunzach 140-141 N 5
Chupadera, Mesa - 154-155 B 3-4
Ch'ü-qu = Quwo 190-191 C 4
Chuquibamba 158-159 E 8
Chuquicamata 162 C 2
Chuquisaca = Sucre 158-159 FG 8
Chur 133 D 5
Churchill [CDN] 144-145 RS 6
Churchill, ID 150-151 FG 4
Churchill, Cape - 144-145 S 6
Churchill Falls 144-145 XY 7
Churchill Peak 144-145 LM 6
Churchill River [CDN, Manitoba] 144-145 RS 6
Churchill River [CDN ◁ Hamilton Inlet] 144-145 Y 7
Church Point, LA 154-155 JK 5
Churchs Ferry ND 152-153 G 1
Churu 180-181 LM 5
Chusei-hokudō = Ch'ungch'ŏngpukto 188-189 FG 4
Chusei-nandō = Ch'ungch'ŏngnamdo 188-189 F 4
Ch'ü Shan = Daqu Shan 190-191 J 6
Chu-shan = Zhushan 184-185 KL 5
Chusistan = Khūzestān 180-181 F 4
Chuska Mountains 150-151 J 7-8
Chust 140-141 A 2
Chutag 184-185 J 2
Chu-t'an = Zhutan 190-191 E 7
Chuučnar 184-185 G 5
Chu-t'ing = Zhuting 190-191 D 8
Chutorskoj 140-141 L 3
Chu-tung 190-191 H 9
Ch'ü-tzŭ-chen = Quzi 190-191 A 3
Chuŭronjang 188-189 GH 2
Chuvacos, República Autónoma dos - = 4 ◁ 178-179 H 6
Chuvash Autonomous Republic = 4 ◁ 178-179 H 6
Chuvashi, Republica Autónoma dos - = 4 ◁ 178-179 H 6
Chuwārtah 182-183 L 5
Chu Xian 190-191 FG 5
Chuxiong 184-185 J 7
Chuxiong Yizu Zizhizhou 184-185 J 6
Chuy 162 F 4
Ch'ü-yang = Quyang [TJ, Hebei] 190-191 E 2
Ch'ü-yang = Quyang [TJ, Jiangxi] 190-191 E 8
Chu Yang Sin 186-187 E 4
Chü-yeh = Juye 190-191 F 4
Chužand 180-181 K 2-L 3
Chužir 178-179 U 7
Chvalynsk 138-139 QR 7
Chvatovka 138-139 Q 7
Chvojnaja 138-139 K 4
Chwansha = Chuansha 190-191 HJ 6
Chwārta = Chuwārtah 182-183 L 5
Chypre 180-181 C 3
Cianorte 160-161 F 5
Ciad 166-167 HJ 5
Čiatura 140-141 L 5
Čibit 178-179 Q 7
Čibju = Uchta 138-139 T 2
Cibola, AZ 150-151 F 9
Cibulev 140-141 DE 2
Cibuta 150-151 H 1 0
Çiçekbaba Tepesi 182-183 C 4
Çiçekdağı 182-183 F 3
Cicero, IL 152-153 N 5
Cicero Dantas 158-159 M 7
Čichač'ovo 138-139 GH 5
Čičikleja 140-141 E 3
Cicladas 136-137 L 7
Ciclades 128-129 NO 8
Cicladi 136-137 L 6
Cidade do Cabo = Kaapstad 168 E 9
Cidade do Vaticano 136-137 KL 7
Cide 182-183 E 2
Ciechanów 133 K 2
Ciego de Ávila 146-147 L 7
Ciénaga 158-159 DE 2
Cienega, NM 154-155 C 4
Cienfuegos 146-147 K 7
Cieza 134-135 G 9
Çifteler 182-183 D 3
Çiftlik = Camlibel 182-183 G 2
Çiftlik = Kelkit 182-183 H 2
Cifuentes 134-135 F 8
Čiganak 178-179 N 8-9
Çiğli 182-183 K 4
Cihanbeyli 182-183 E 3
Cihanbeyli Yaylâsı 182-183 E 3
Čili 178-179 M 9
Cijara, Embalse de - 134-135 E 9
Cikola 140-141 L 5
Cilacap 186-187 E 8
Çıldır 182-183 K 2
Çıldır Gölü 182-183 K 2
Cile 162 B 5-C 2
Cile, Bacino del - 124-125 EF 6-7
Cili 190-191 C 7
Cilli = Celje 136-137 F 2
Cilo dağı 182-183 KL 4
Cima, CA 150-151 F 8
Cimaltepec 146-147 G 8
Cimarron KS 152-153 FG 7
Cimarron NM 154-155 C 2
Čimbaj 178-179 KL 9
Ciml'ansk 140-141 KL 3
Ciml'anskoje vodochranilišče 140-141 L 2-3
Cimarron River 146-147 F 4
Cimone, Monte - 136-137 D 3
Cina 184-185 E-K 5
Cina Meridionale, Bacino della - 186-187 FG 3-4
Cinandali 140-141 M 6
Çınar 182-183 J 4
Cinca 134-135 H 8
Cincinnati, OH 146-147 K 4
Çine 182-183 BC 4
Cingaly 178-179 MN 5
Cinnabar Mountain 150-151 E 4
Cinta, Serra da - 158-159 K 6
Cinto, Mont - 136-137 C 4
Cintra = Sintra [BR] 158-159 G 6
Ciotat, la - 134-135 K 7
Čiovo 136-137 G 4
Cipikan 178-179 V 7
Cipó 158-159 M 7
Cipó, Rio - 160-161 L 3
Cipó, Serra do - 160-161 L 3
Cipro 180-181 C 3
Ciprus 180-181 C 3
Čir 140-141 L 2
Čiragidzor 140-141 N 6
Circassi Karačaj, Provincia Autonoma del - = 10 ◁ 126-127 R 7
Circeo, Monte - 136-137 E 5
Čirčik 178-179 M 9
Circle, AK 144-145 H 4
Circle, MT 152-153 D 2
Circle Cliffs 150-151 H 7
Circleville,OH 152-153 P 6
Circleville, UT 150-151 G 6
Cirebon 186-187 E 8
Cirenaica = Barqah 166-167 J 2
Cirenaica = Barqah 166-167 J 2
Cirene = Shahhāt 166-167 J 2
Ciri, Rio - 146-147 a 3
Cirò Marina 136-137 G 6
Čirpan 136-137 L 4
Cisa, Passo della - 136-137 CD 3
Cisco, TX 154-155 F 4
Cisco, UT 150-151 J 6
Ciskei = 7 ◁ 174-175 G 7
Cisne,IL 152-153 M 6
Cisne, Ilhas del - = Swan Islands 146-147 K 8
Cisneros 158-159 DE 3
Čisťakovo = Thorez 140-141 J 2-3
Cisterna di Latina 136-137 E 5
Cisternino 136-137 G 5
Čistopol' 178-179 HJ 6
Čita 178-179 V 7
Čitajevo 138-139 R 3
Citlaltépetl 146-147 G 8
Citra, FL 148-149 bc 2
Citronelle, AL 154-155 L 5
Citrusdal 168-169 EF 9
Citrus Heights, CA 146-147 B 4
Città del Capo = Kaapstad 168-169 E 9
Città di Agugli = Agulhas 174 D 8
Città di Messico 124-125 DE 5
Città di Buona Speranza 174 BC 8
Cittanova 136-137 FG 6
Ciucaş 136-137 LM 3
Ciudad Bolivar 158-159 G 3
Ciudad Bolivia 158-159 E 3
Ciudad Camargo 154-155 F 7
Ciudad Camargo = Camargo 146-147 E 6
Ciudad del Carmen 146-147 H 8
Ciudad del Este 162 EF 3
Ciudad Delicias = Delicias 146-147 E 6
Ciudadela 134-135 J 8-9
Ciudad Guayana 158-159 G 3
Ciudad Guzmán 146-147 F 8
Ciudad Juárez = Juárez 146-147 E 5
Ciudad Lerdo 146-147 EF 6
Ciudad Linares = Linares 146-147 G 7
Ciudad Madero 146-147 G 7
Ciudad Mante 146-147 G 7
Ciudad Obregón 146-147 DE 6
Ciudad Ojeda 158-159 E 2-3
Ciudad Piar 158-159 G 3
Ciudad Real 134-135 EF 9
Ciudad-Rodrigo 134-135 DE 8
Ciudad Trujillo = Santo Domingo 146-147 MN 8
Ciudad Valles 146-147 G 7
Ciudad Victoria 146-147 G 7
Ciuvasci, Repubblica Autonoma dei - = 4 ◁ 178-179 H 6
Civa Burnu 182-183 G 2
Civil'sk 138-139 Q 6
Civita Castellana 136-137 E 4
Civitanova Marche 136-137 EF 4
Civitavècchia 136-137 D 4
Çivril 182-183 C 3
Cixi 190-191 H 6
Ci Xian 190-191 E 3
Čiža 178-179 G 4
Čiža dvaja 140-141 OP 1
Cizre 180-181 E 3
Čkalov = Orenburg 178-179 JK 7
Čkalovsk 138-139 O 5
Clacton on Sea 132 G 6
Clain 134-135 H 5
Claire, Lake - 144-145 O 6
Clairemont, TX 154-155 E 4
Clairton, PA 148-149 CD 4
Clamecy 134-135 J 5
Clan Alpine Mountains 150-151 DE 6
Clanton, AL 154-155 M 4
Clanwilliam 168-169 E 9
Clanwilliamdam 174-175 C 7
Clapham, NM 154-155 D 2
Clara River 194-195 H 3
Clara City, MN 152-153 J 3
Clare [AUS] 194-195 G 6
Clare, MI 152-153 O 4
Claremont, NH 148-149 GH 3
Claremont, SD 152-153 GH 3
Claremore, OK 154-155 H 2
Claremorris 132 B 5
Clarence, Cape - 144-145 S 3
Clarence, Isla - 162 B 8
Clarence Island 121 C 31
Clarence Strait [AUS] 194-195 F 2
Clarendon, AR 154-155 K 3
Clarendon, TX 154-155 E 3
Clarinda, IA 152-153 J 5
Clarion, IA 152-153 JK 4
Clarion, PA 148-149 D 4
Clarión-Bruchzone 198-199 KL 4
Clarion, Fosse - 124-125 B-D 5
Clarión, Fractura de - 124-125 B-D 5
Clarionbreukzone 124-125 B-D 5
Clarión-Bruchzone 124-125 B-D 5
Clarión, Fractura de - 124-125 B-D 5
Clarión Fracture Zone 124-125 B-D 5
Clarión, Frattura di - 124-125 B-D 5
Clark, CO 152-153 C 5
Clark, SD 152-153 H 3
Clarkdale, AZ 150-151 G 8
Clarkebury 174-175 H 6
Clarke City 144-145 X 7
Clarke Island 194-195 J 8
Clarkfield, MN 152-153 HJ 3
Clark Fork, ID 150-151 E 1
Clark Fork River 146-147 CD 2
Clark Hill Lake 148-149 B 8
Clarkia, ID 150-151 EF 2
Clark Mountain 150-151 F 8
Clark Point 152-153 PQ 3
Clarks, NE 152-153 GH 5
Clarksburg, WV 146-147 K 4
Clarksdale, MS 146-147 HJ 5
Clarks Fork 152-153 B 3
Clarks Fork Yellowstone River 152-153 B 3
Clarkson 174-175 F 8
Clarkston, WA 150-151 E 2
Clarksville, AR 154-155 J 3
Clarksville, IA 152-153 K 4
Clarksville, TN 146-147 J 4
Clarksville, TX 154-155 H 4
Clarksville, VA 148-149 D 6
Claude, TX 154-155 E 3
Cláudio 160-161 K 4
Claunch, NM 154-155 BC 3
Claxton, GA 148-149 BC 8
Clay, KY 152-153 N 7
Clay, WV 148-149 C 5
Clay Belt 144-145 T-V 7
Clay Center, KS 152-153 H 6
Clay Center, NE 152-153 GH 5
Claymont, DE 148-149 F 5
Claypool, AZ 150-151 H 9
Clayton, AL 154-155 N 5
Clayton, GA 148-149 B 7
Clayton, ID 150-151 F 3
Clayton, IL 152-153 L 5
Clayton, MO 152-153 L 6
Clayton, NC 148-149 D 7
Clayton, NM 154-155 D 2
Clayton, NY 148-149 EF 2
Clayton, OK 154-155 H 3

Clearbrook, MN 152-153 J 2
Clearcreek, UT 150-151 H 6
Clearfield, PA 148-149 D 4
Clearfield, UT 150-151 GH 5
Clear Fork Brazos River 154-155 F 4
Clear Hills 144-145 N 6
Clear Lake 150-151 B 6
Clear Lake, IA 152-153 K 4
Clear Lake, MN 152-153 K 3
Clear Lake, SD 152-153 H 3
Clear Lake, WI 152-153 KL 3
Clear Lake Reservoir 150-151 C 5
Clearmont, WY 152-153 C 3
Clearwater, FL 146-147 C 6
Clearwater Lake 154-155 K 2
Clearwater Mountains 150-151 F 2-3
Clearwater River [USA] 150-151 E 2
Cleburne, TX 146-147 G 3
Cle Elum, WA 150-151 C 2
Clendenin, WV 148-149 C 5
Clermont [AUS] 194-195 J 4
Clermont, FL 148-149 bc 2
Clermont-Ferrand 134-135 J 6
Cleve 196 C 4
Cleveland, OH 146-147 K 3
Cleveland, TN 146-147 K 4
Cleveland, Mount - 146-147 D 2
Cleveland, MS 154-155 K 4
Cleveland, MT 152-153 B 1
Cleveland, OK 154-155 G 2
Cleveland, TX 154-155 H 5
Cleveland, WI 152-153 N 4
Cleveland Heights, OH 148-149 C 4
Clevelândia 160-161 F 7
Clewiston, FL 148-149 c 3
Clifden 132 A 5
Cliff, NM 150-151 J 9
Cliff Lake, MT 150-151 H 3
Cliffs, ID 150-151 E 4
Clifton 194-195 K 5
Clifton, AZ 150-151 J 9
Clifton, KS 152-153 H 6
Clifton, NJ 148-149 F 4
Clifton Forge, VA 148-149 D 6
Clifton Hills 194-195 G 5
Clifton, TX 154-155 G 5
Clifton, WY 152-153 D 4
Climax, CO 152-153 C 6
Climax, GA 154-155 N 5
Climax, MI 152-153 O 4
Climax, MN 152-153 H 2
Clinch Mountain 154-155 O 2
Clinchco, VA 148-149 B 6
Clinch Mountains 148-149 B 6
Clinch River 148-149 B 6
Cline, TX 154-155 E 6
Clint, TX 154-155 B 5
Clinton, AR 154-155 J 3
Clinton [CDN, Ontario] 148-149 C 3
Clinton, IA 146-147 H 3
Clinton, IL 152-153 M 5
Clinton, IN 152-153 N 6
Clinton, KY 154-155 L 2
Clinton, LA 154-155 K 5
Clinton, MI 152-153 O 4
Clinton, MO 152-153 K 6
Clinton, MS 154-155 K 4
Clinton, MT 150-151 G 2
Clinton, NC 148-149 D 7
Clinton, OK 154-155 F 3
Clinton, SC 148-149 C 7
Clinton, TN 154-155 NO 2
Clinton, WI 152-153 M 4
Clinton, Cape - 194-195 K 4
Clintonville, WI 152-153 M 3
Clio, AL 154-155 N 5
Clio, MI 152-153 P 4
Clipperton, Fosse de - 124-125 CD 5
Clipperton, Fractura de - 124-125 CD 5
Clipperton, Fractura de - 124-125 CD 5
Clipperton, Frattura di - 124-125 CD 5
Clipperton, Île - 146-147 E 9
Clippertonbreukzone 124-125 CD 5
Clipperton-Bruchzone 198-199 LM 4
Clipperton Fracture Zone 124-125 CD 5
Clisham 132 C 3
Cloates, Point - 194-195 B 4
Clocolan 174-175 G 5
Clonakilty 132 B 6
Cloncurry 194-195 H 4
Cloncurry River 194-195 H 3
Clonmel 132 BC 5
Cloppenburg 133 CD 2
Cloquet, MN 152-153 KL 2
Cloquet, River 152-153 KL 2
Cloucester, VA 148-149 E 6
Cloudcroft, NM 154-155 C 4
Cloud Peak 146-147 E 3
Clover, VA 148-149 D 6
Cloverdale, CA 150-151 B 6
Cloverdale, NM 150-151 J 10
Cloverport, KY 116-117 N 7
Clovis, CA 150-151 D 7
Clovis, NM 146-147 F 5
Cluj-Napoca 136-137 KL 2
Cluny 134-135 K 5
Clutha River 194-195 N 9
Clyde 144-145 X 3
Clyde, Firth of - 132 D 4
Clyde, KS 152-153 H 6
Clyde, ND 152-153 G 1
Clyde, OH 152-153 P 5
Clyde Park, MT 150-151 H 3
Clyde, TX 154-155 F 4
Clydesdale 174-175 GH 4
Clyo, GA 148-149 C 8
Cna [SU ◁ Mokša] 138-139 O 6
Cna [SU ◁ Prip'at'] 138-139 F 7
Cnori 140-141 MN 6
Coa 134-135 D 8
Coachella , CA 150-151 E 9
Coachella Canal 150-151 EF 9
Coahoma, TX 154-155 E 4
Coahuila 146-147 F 6
Coalbrook 174-175 GH 4
Coaldale, NV 150-151 E 6
Coalgate, OK 154-155 G 3
Coalinga, CA 150-151 C 7
Coalmont, CO 152-152 C5
Coalville, UT 150-151 H 5
Coari 158-159 G 5
Coari , Rio - 158-159 G 5-6
Coast Mountains 144-145 K 6-M 7
Coast Range 146-147 B 2-C 5
Coatá, Cachoeira do - 158-159 G 6
Coatepec 146-147 G 8
Coatesville, PA 148-149 EF 4-5
Coaticook 148-149 GH 2
Coats Island 144-145 U 5
Coats Land 121 B 33-34
Coatzacoalcos 146-147 H 8
Cobán 146-147 H 8
Çobandede 182-183 JK 3
Cobar 194-195 J 6
Cobargo 196 JK 6
Cobbo = Kobo 166-167 MN 6
Cobe = Köbe 184-185 PQ 5
Cobh 132 B 6
Cobija 158-159 F 7
Coblença = Koblenz 126-127 K 5
Cobleskill, NY 148-149 F 3
Coboconk 148-149 D 2
Cobourg 148-149 DE 3
Cobourg Peninsula 194-195 F 2
Cobre, NV 150-151 F 5
Cobre, Rio do - 160-161 FG 6
Cobue 171 C 6
Coburg 133 E 3
Coburg, OR 150-151 B 3
Coburg Island 144-145 V 2
Coca 134-135 E 8
Cocalzinho, Serra do - 160-161 H 1
Cocanada = Kakinada 180-181 N 7
Cochabamba [BOL, ●] 158-159 F 8
Cochem 133 C 3
Cochi = Kōchi 184-185 P 5
Cochim = Cochin 180-181 M 9
Cochin 180-181 M 9
Cochinchina = Nam Bô 180-181 DE 5
Cochise, AZ 150-151 J 9
Cochran , GA 148-149 B 8
Cochrane [CDN, Ontario] 144-145 U8
Cochrane River 144-145 Q 6
Cockburn, Canal - 162 B 8
Cockburn Land 144-145 UV 3
Cockeysville , MD 148-149 E 5
Coco, El - 146-147 b 3
Coco, Isla del - 158-159 B 3
Coco, Rio - 146-147 K 9
Cocoa, FL 148-149 c 2
Coco Channel 186-187 B 4
Cocodrie, LA 154-155 K 6
Coco Island 168-169 NO 6
Cocolalla, ID 150-151 E 1
Coconino Plateau 150-151 G 7-8
Cocos [AUS] 124-125 O 6
Cocos = Isla del Coco 158-159 B 3
Cocos, Bacino di - 124-125 OP 6
Coco Solo 146-147 b 2
Cocos Rise 124-125 E 5
Cocuy , El - 158-159 E 3
Cod, Cape - 146-147 N 3
Codajás 158-159 G 5
Codera, Cabo - 158-159 F 2
Codihue 162 BC 5
Codó 158-159 L 5
Cody, NE 152-153 F 4
Cody, WY 152-153 B 3
Coen 194-195 H 2
Coerney, 174-175 F 7
Coesfeld 133 C 3
Coetivy Island 168-169 N 4
Coeur d'Alene, ID 146-147 C 2
Coeur d'Alene Indian Reservation 150-151 E 2
Coeur d'Alene Lake 150-151 E 2
Coffee Bay 174-175 H 6
Coffeeville, MS 154-155 KL 4
Coffeyville, KS 146-147 G 4
Coffin Bay 194-195 FG 6
Coffin Bay Peninsula 194-195 FG 6
Coffs Harbour 194-195 K 6
Cofimvaba 174-175 G 7
Cofrentes 134-135 G 9
Cofu = Kōfu 184-185 Q 4
Cogealac 136-137 N 3
Cognac 134-135 G 6
Çogujev 140-141 H 2
Çoğun 182-183 F 3
Coguno 174-175 L 3
Cohagen, MT 152-153 C 2
Cohoes, NY 148-149 G 3
Cohuna 194-195 HJ 7
Cohutta Mountain 154-155 N 3
Coi, Sông - = Sông Nhi Ha 186-187 D 2
Coiba, Isla - 146-147 K 10
Coihaique 162 B 7
Coimbatore 180-181 M 8
Coimbra 134-135 C 8
Coimbra [BR] 160-161 L 4
Coin 134-135 E 10
Coin, IA 152-153 J 5
Coipasa, Salar de - 158-159 F 8
Čojbalsan = 18 184-185 L 2
Čojbalsangijn Ajmag = Dornod = 18 ◁ 184-185 LM 2
Cojimies 158-159 C 4
Cojudo Blanco, Cerro - 162 BC 7
Çokak 182-183 G 4
Cokato, MN 152-153 J 3
Cokeville, WY 150-151 H 4
Čokurdach 178-179 cd 3
Colac 194-195 H 7
Colapur = Kolhapur 180-181 L 7
Cólar = Kolar Gold Fields 180-181 M 8
Colares 134-135 C 9
Colbeck, Cape - 121 B 20-21
Colbert, OK 154-155 G 4
Colbert, WA 150-151 E 2
Colbinabbin 196 G 6
Colby, KS 152-153 F 6
Colca, Rio - 158-159 E 8
Colchester 132 G 6
Colchester [ZA] 174-175 FG 7
Cold Spring, MN 152-153 J 3
Coldspring, TX 154-155 H 5
Coldstream [ZA] 174-175 E 7-8
Coldwater 148-149 D 2
Coldwater, KS 154-155 F 2
Coldwater, MI 152-153 O 5
Coldwater, OH 152-153 O 5
Colebrook, NH 148-149 H 2
Cole Camp, MO 152-153 K 6
Colégio = Porto Real do Colégio 158-159 M 6-7
Coleman, MI 152-153 O 4
Coleman River 194-195 H 2-3
Coleman, TX 154-155 F 5
Çölemerik = Hakkâri 182-183 K 4
Colenso 174-175 H 5
Coleraine 132 C 4
Coleraine [AUS] 196 EF 6
Coles, Punta de - 158-159 E 8
Colesburg 168-169 FG 9
Colesville, CA 150-151 D 6
Colfax, CA 150-151 C 6
Colfax, IA 152-153 K 5
Colfax, LA 154-155 J 5
Colfax, WA 150-151 E 2
Colfax, WI 152-153 L 3
Colhué Huapí, Lago - 162 C 7
Coligny 174-175 G 4
Colima 146-147 F 8
Colima, Nevado de - 146-147 EF 8
Colina [BR] 160-161 H 4
Colinas 158-159 L 6
Coll 132 C 3
Collaguasi 162 C 2
Collarenebri 196 HJ 2
College, AK 144-145 G 4-5
College Park, GA 154-155 NO 4
College Station,TX 154-155 G 5
Collie 194-195 C 6
Collier Bay 194-195 D 3
Collierville, TN 154-155 L 3
Collingwood [CDN] 148-149 CD 2
Collins, IA 152-153 K 5
Collins, MS 154-155 L 5
Collins, MT 150-151 H 2
Collinson Peninsula 144-145 Q 3-4
Collinston, LA 154-155 K 4
Collinsville 194-195 J 4
Collinsville, Al 154-155 MN 3
Collinsville,IL 152-153 M 6
Collinsville, OK 154-155 H 2
Colmar 134-135 L 4
Colmor, NM 154-155 C 2
Colomor,NM 154-155 C 2
Colnett, Bahia - 150-151 E 10
Cologne = Köln 133 C 3
Cololo, Nevado - 158-159 F 7
Colomb-Béchar = Bashshār 166-167 D 2
Colombia 158-159 D-F 4
Colômbia [BR] 158-159 K 9
Colômbia [COL] 158-159 D-F 4
Colombia [MEX] 154-155 EF 7
Colombia 158-159 EF 4
Colombie 158-159 D-F 4
Colombine, Kaap - 174-175 B 7
Colombo 160-161 H 6
Colombo = Kolamba 180-181 M 9
Colome, SD 152-153 G 4
Colón [C] 146-147 K 7
Colón [PA, ●] 146-147 b 2
Colón [PA, ☆] 146-147 ab 2
Colón, Archipiélago de - 158-159 AB 5
Colona 194-195 F 6
Colona, CO 152-153 C 6
Colonia = Köln 133 C 3
Colônia = Köln 127 K 5
Colonia Benjamin Aceval = Benjamin Aceval 160-161 D 6
Colonia del Sacramento 162 E 4
Colonia 25 de Mayo 162 C 5
Colonia Fernando de Trejo y Sanabria 160-161 E 6
Colonia Fram 160-161 DE 7
Colonia Las Heras = Las Heras 162 C 7
Colonial Beach, VA 148-149 E 5
Colonial Heights, VA 148-149 E 6
Colonia Mennonita 160-161 C 5
Colonia Morelos 150-151 J 1 0
Colonia Yacubó 160-161 DE 7
Colonne, Capo delle - 136-137 G 6
Colonsay 132 C 3
Colorado [USA] 146-147 EF 4
Colorado, Rio - [MEX] 146-147 CD 5
Colorado, Rio - [RA, La Pampa] 162 C 5
Colorado, Rio - [RA, Neuquén] 162 D 5
Colorado, Rio - [RA, Rio Negro] 162 CD 5
Colorado Desert 150-151 EF 9
Colorado National Monument 150-151 J 6
Colorado Plateau 146-147 DE 4
Colorado River [USA, Colorado] 146-147 E 4
Colorado River [USA, Texas] 146-147 G 5
Colorado River Aqueduct 150-151 F 8
Colorado River Indian Reservation 150-151 F 9
Colorados, Cerros - [RA] 162 C 6
Colorados, Cerros - [RCH] 162 C 3
Colorado Springs, CO 146-147 F 4
Colo River 196 K 4
Colquitt, GA 154-155 N 5
Colstrip, MT 152-153 C 3
Colton, SD 152-153 H 4
Colton, UT 150-151 H 6
Columbia, KY 152-153 O 7
Columbia, LA 154-155 JK 4
Columbia, MD 148-149 E 5
Columbia, MO 146-147 H 4
Columbia, MD 148-149 E 5
Columbia, MS 154-155 L 5
Columbia, PA 148-149 E 4
Columbia, SC 146-147 K 5
Columbia, SD 152-153 GH 3
Columbia, TN 154-155 M 3
Columbia, Cape - 120 A 25-26
Columbia, District of - 148-149 E 5
Columbia, Mount - 144-145 N 7
Columbia Basin 150-151 D 2
Columbia Britânica = British Columbia 144-145 L 6-N 7
Columbia City, IN 152-153 O 5
Columbia Falls, MT 150-151 FG 1
Columbiana, AL 154-155 M 4
Columbia Plateau 146-147 C 2-3
Columbia River 146-147 BC 2
Columbia River, WA 150-151 C 2
Columbien 158-159 D-F 4
Columbine, WY 152-153 C 4
Columbretes, Islas - 134-135 H 9
Columbus, GA 146-147 K 5
Columbus, IN 152-153 O 6
Columbus, KS 154-155 H 2
Columbus, MS 146-147 J 5
Columbus, MT 152-153 B 3
Columbus, ND 152-153 E 1
Columbus, NE 146-147 G 3
Columbus, NM 154-155 B 5
Columbus, OH 146-147 K 3-4
Columbus, TX 154-155 G 6
Columbus, WI 152-153 M 4
Columbus Junction, IA 152-153 L 5
Čolun Chamur 140-141 M 4
Colusa, CA 150-151 BC 6
Colville, WA 150-151 E 1
Colville Indian Reservation 150-151 D 1
Colville River 144-145 EF 4
Comàcchio 136-137 E 3
Comàcchio, Valli di - 136-137 E 3
Comales, Los - 154-155 F 7
Comana 136-137 LM 3
Comanche, OK 154-155 G 3
Comanche, TX 154-155 F 5
Comayagua 146-147 J 9
Comber 152-153 P 4
Combomune 174-175 K 2
Combourg 134-135 G 4
Comboussouggou 172-173 E 3
Combs, KY 152-153 P 7
Comeau, Baie - 144-145 X 8
Come By Chance 196 J 3
Comendador, Ilha de - 178-179 f 6-j 7
Comer, GA 148-149 B 7
Comercinho 160-161 M 2
Cometela 174-175 L 1
Comfort, TX 154-155 F 5-6
Comilla = Komillā 180-181 P 6
Comino, Capo - 136-137 CD 5
Comiso 136-137 F 7
Comitán de Domínguez 146-147 H 8
Commadagga = Kommadagga 174-175 F 7
Commerce, GA 148-149 B 7
Commerce, TX 154-155 GH 4
Commissionerssoutpan 174-175 C 6
Committee Bay 144-145 T 4
Commonwealth Range 121 A
Commonwealth Territory 194-195 K 7
Como 136-137 C 3
Como, Lago di - 136-137 C 2-3
Comodoro Rivadavia 162 C 7
Comoé = Komoe 166-167 D 7
Comore 168-169 KL 5
Comore, Bacino delle - 168-169 L 5
Comore-medence 168-169 L 5
Comoren 168-169 KL 5
Comores 169 KL 5
Comores 168 HJ 4
Comores, Archipel des - 168-169 KL 5
Comores, Bassin des - 168-169 L 5
Comores, Crista das - 169 L 5
Comores, Cuenca de - 168-169 L 5
Comore-szigetek 168-169 KL 5
Comorin, Cape - 180-181 M 9
Comoros 168-169 KL 5
Compiègne 134-135 J 4
Comprida, Cachoeira - = Treze Quedas 158-159 H 4
Comprida, Ilha - [BR, São Paulo] 162 G 2-3
Comprida, Ilha - [BR, Rio Paraná] 160-161 G 4
Comprida, Lago - = Lagoa Nova 158-159 J 4
Compton, CA 150-151 DE 9
Comrat = Komrat 140-141 D 3
Comstock, TX 154-155 E 6
Čona 178-179 V 5
Conakry 166-167 B 7
Conata, SD 152-153 E 4
Conca = Cuenca 158-159 D 5
Concarneau 134-135 EF 5
Conceição [BR, Mato Grosso] 158-159 H 6
Conceição da Barra 158-159 M 8
Conceição das Alagoas 160-161 HJ 3
Conceição do Araguaia 158-159 JK 6
Conceição do Castelo 160-161 M 4
Conceição do Mato Dentro 160-161 L 3
Conceição do Rio Verde 160-161 K 4
Concelho = Inhambane 168-169 J 7
Concepción [BOL] 158-159 G 8
Concepción [CO, Putumayo] 158-159 DE 4
Concepción [RA, Tucumán] 162 C 3
Concepción [RCH] 162 AB 5
Concepcion, CA 150-151 C 8
Concepción [PY, ●] 162 E 2
Concepción [PY, ☆] 160-161 D 5
Concepción, Canal - 162 AB 8
Concepción, La - 158-159 E 2
Concepción, Rio - 150-151 G 1 0
Concepción del Oro 146-147 F 7
Concepción del Uruguay 162 E 4
Conception, Point - 146-147 B 5
Conceptionbaai 174-175 A 2
Conception Bay = Conceptionbaai 174-175 A 2
Conchas 160-161 J 5
Conchas Dam, NM 154-155 C 3
Conchas Lake 154-155 C 3
Conchi [RCH, Antofagasta] 162 C 2
Concho 154-155 C 7
Concho, AZ 150-151 J 8
Concho River 154-155 EF 5
Conchos, Rio - 146-147 EF 6
Concord, CA 150-151 BC 7
Concord, NC 148-149 C 7
Concord, NH 146-147 M 3
Concórdia [BR, Santa Catarina] 160-161 FG 7
Concordia [RA] 162 E 4
Concordia [ZA] 174-175 BC 5
Concordia, KS 152-153 GH 6
Concordia,MO 152-153 K 6
Côn Đao 186-187 E 5
Conde 158-159 M 7
Conde, SD 152-153 GH 3
Conde de Araruama 160-161 M 5
Condobolin 194-195 J 6
Condon, OR 150-151 C 3
Conecuh River 154-155 M 5
Conejera, Isla - 134-135 J 9
Conejos 154-155 D 7
Conejos, CO 152-153 C 7
Conejos River 152-153 C 7
Confusion Range 150-151 G 6
Conghua 190-191 D 10
Congjiang 190-191 B 9
Congo 168-169 D 3-F 2
Congo 168-169 D3-E 2
Congo 168-169 D 3-E 2
Congo, Rep. Dem. del 167 JK 8
Congo, Rep. Dem. do 167 JK 8
Congo, Democratic Republic of the - 168-169 EF 3
Congo (Dem. Republiek) 168-169 EF 3
Congo, República Dem. de - 168-169 EF 3
Congo, République Dém. du - 168-169 EF 3
Congo = Zaïre [Estado] 168 F 3
Congonhas 160-161 L 4
Congress, AZ 150-151 G 8
Cónia = Konya 180-181 C 3
Conjeeveram = Kanchipuram 180-181 MN 8
Conlen, TX 154-155 D 2
Connaught 132 B 4-5
Conneaut, OH 148-149 C 3-4
Connecticut 146-147 M 3
Connecticut River 148-149 G 3-4
Connell, WA 150-151 D 2
Connellsville, PA 148-149 D 4
Conner, MT 150-151 FG 3
Conner, Mount - 194-195 F 5
Connersville, IN 152-153 O 6
Connersville, OH 148-149 A 5
Connors Pass 150-151 F 6
Conover, WI 152-153 M 2
Conquista [BR] 160-161 J 3
Conrad, MT 150-151 H 1
Conroe, TX 154-155 H 5
Conselheiro Lafaiete 158-159 L 9
Conselheiro Pena 160-161 M 3
Constable = Konstabel 174-175 CD 7
Constança = Constanţa 128-129 O 7
Constância dos Baetas 158-159 G 6
Constanţa 136-137 M 3
Constantina = Qusţanţīn 166-167 F 1
Constantina = Qunstantinah 126-127 K 8
Constantine, Cape - 144-145 DE 6
Constantinople = İstanbul 180-181 BC 2
Constanza = Constanţa 136-137 N 3
Constitución 162 B 5
Contact, NV 150-151 F 5
Contagem 160-161 K 3
Contamana 158-159 DE 6
Contas, Rio de - 158-159 L 7
Continental, AZ 150-151 H 10
Continental, OH 174-175 O 5
Contratación 158-159 E 3
Contreras, Isla - 162 AB 8
Contria 160-161 K 3
Contwoyto Lake 144-145 OP 4
Converse, LA 154-155 J 5
Conway, AR 154-155 J 5
Conway, ND 152-153 H 1
Conway, NH 148-149 H 3
Conway, SC 148-149 D 8
Conway, TX 154-155 E 3
Conyers, GA 154-155 NO 4
Coober Pedy 194-195 F 5
Cook 194-195 F 6
Cook, MN 152-153 K 2
Cook, NE 152-153 H 5
Cook, Bahia - 162 B 9
Cook, Mount - [NZ] 194-195 NO 8
Cook Bay 121 C 16
Cooke City, MT 150-151 J 3
Cookeville, TN 154-155 N 2
Cookhouse = Kookhuis 174-175 FG 7
Cook Inlet 144-145 F 5-6
Cook Islands 198-199 K 6
Cooks, MI 152-153 N 3
Cook Strait 194-195 O 8
Cooktown 194-195 HJ 3
Coolabah 196 H 3
Coolah 196 J 3
Coolamon 196 H 5
Coolgardie 194-195 CD 6
Coolidge, AZ 150-151 H 9
Coolidge, KS 152-153 EF 6
Coolidge Dam 150-151 H 9
Coolin, ID 150-151 E 1
Cooma 194-195 J 7
Coonabarabran 194-195 JK 6
Coonamble 194-195 J 6
Coonana 194-195 D 6
Coonbah 196 EF 4
Coondambo 196 BC 3
Coondapoor 180-181 L 8
Coongoola 194-195 HJ 5
Coon Rapids, IA 152-153 J 5
Cooper 174-175 DE 8
Cooper, TX 154-155 H 4
Cooper Creek 194-195 G 5
Cooper Lake 152-153 CD 5
Cooperstown, ND 152-153 GH 2
Cooperstown, NY 148-149 F 3
Coorong, The - 194-195 G 7
Coosa River 154-155 N 3
Coos Bay 150-151 A 4
Coos Bay, OR 146-147 AB 3
Cootamundra 194-195 J 6
Čop 140-141 A 2
Copahue, Paso - 162 BC 5
Copán 146-147 J 9
Copano Bay 154-155 G 6
Copco, CA 150-151 B 4-5
Cope, CO 152-153 E 6
Copeland, KS 152-153 F 7
Copenhaga = København 128-129 L 4
Copenhagen = København 130-131 DE 10
Copenhagen = København 130-131 DE 10
Copenhague = København 130-131 DE 10
Copiapó 162 BC 3
Čopoviči 140-141 D 1
Copparo 136-137 DE 3
Copperas Cove, TX 154-155 FG 5
Copperbelt 168-169 G 5
Copper Center, AK 144-145 G 5
Copper Harbor, MI 152-153 N 2
Coppermine 144-145 N 4
Coppermine Point 152-153 O 2
Coppermine River 144-145 NO 4
Copper River 144-145 GH 5
Copşa Mică 136-137 L 2
Coquilhatville = Mbandaka 168-169 E 2-3
Coquille, OR 150-151 AB 4
Coquille River 150-151 AB 4
Coquimbo [RCH, ●] 162 B 2
Corabia 136-137 L 4
Coração de Jesus 160-161 K 2
Coracora 158-159 E 7-8
Corail, Grande Barrière de - 194-195 H 2-K 4
Corail, Mer de - 194-195 K-M 3
Corais, Ilhas dos - 160-161 HJ 6
Coral, Bacia de - 194-195 K 2
Coral, Cuenca del - 194-195 K 2
Coral, Mar de 192-193 G 6
Coral, Mar de 194-195 K-M 3
Coral, Mar del - 194-195 K-M 3
Coral Gables, FL 146-147 KL 6
Coral Harbour 144-145 U 5
Coralli, Mare di 194-195 K-M 3
Coral Sea 194-195 K-M 3
Coral Sea Basin 194-195 K 2
Coral Sea Islands Territory 194-195 JK 3
Coral Springs, FL 194-195 c 3
Corantijn 158-159 H 4
Corato 136-137 G 5
Corbeil-Essonnes 134-135 J 4
Corbélia 160-161 F 6
Corbières 134-135 J 7
Corbin, KY 146-147 K 4
Corcaigh = Cork 132 B 6
Córcega = Corse 136-137 C 4
Corcoran, CA 150-151 D 7
Corcovado, Volcán - 162 B 6
Corcubión 134-135 C 7
Cordeiro 160-161 L 4-5
Cordele, GA 148-149 AB 8
Cordell, OK 154-155 F 3
Cordigliera Alta 120 A
Cordillera 160-161 D 6
Cordillera Azul 158-159 D 6
Cordillera Blanca 158-159 D 6
Cordillera Central [BOL] 158-159 F 8-G 9
Cordillera Central [CO] 158-159 D 4-E 3
Cordillera Central [DOM] 146-147 M 8
Cordillera Central [PE] 158-159 D 6
Cordillera Central [RP] 186-187 H 3
Cordillera Iberica 134-135 F 7-G 8
Cordillera Negra 158-159 D 6
Cordillera Occidental [CO] 158-159 D 3-4
Cordillera Occidental [PE] 158-159 D 6-E 8
Cordillera Oriental [BOL] 158-159 FG 8
Cordillera Oriental [CO] 158-159 D 4-E 3
Cordillera Oriental [DOM] 146-147 N 8
Cordillera Oriental [PE] 158-159 D 5-E 7
Cordillera Penibética 134-135 E 9-G 8
Cordillera Real [EC] 158-159 D 5
Cordillère Bétique = Cordillera Penibética 134-135 E 9-G 8
Cordisburgo 160-161 KL 3
Córdoba [E] 134-135 E 10
Córdoba [MEX, Durango] 154-155 D 7
Córdoba [MEX, Veracruz] 146-147 G 8
Cordoba [RA] 162 D 4
Córdoba, Sierra de - [RA] 162 C 4-D 3
Córdova 158-159 DE 7
Córdova = Córdoba 134-135 E 10
Cordova, AK 144-145 G 5
Cordova, AL 154-155 M 4
Corea del Norte 184-185 O 3-4
Corea del Norte 184-185 O 3-4
Corea del Sud 184-185 OP 4
Corea del Sur 184-185 OP 4
Corée du Nord 184-185 O 3-4
Corée du Sud 184-185 OP 4
Core Sound 148-149 E 7
Coreia do Norte 184-185 O 3-4
Coreia do Sul 184-185 OP 4
Corfield 194-195 H 4
Corfou = Kérkyra 136-137 H 6
Corfu = Kérkyra 136-137 H 6
Corguinho 160-161 E 4
Coria 134-135 D 8-9
Coriachi, Circolo Nazionale dei - 178-179 g 5-e 6
Coria del Rio 134-135 D 10
Coringa Islands 194-195 K 3
Corinne, UT 150-151 G 5
Corinth, MS 154-155 L 3
Corinth = Kórinthos 136-137 K 7
Corinthe = Kórinthos 136-137 K 7
Corinto [BR] 158-159 KL 8
Corinto [NIC] 146-147 J 9
Corinto = Kórinthos 136 K 7
Corinto = Kórinthos 136-137 K 7
Corinto = Kórinthos 136-137 K 7
Corisco, Isla de - 166-167 F 8
Corixão 160-161 D 3
Cork 132 B 6
Corleone 136-137 E 7
Corleto Perticara 136-137 FG 5
Çorlu 182-183 B 2
Çorlusuyu Deresi 182-183 B 2
Cormoranes, Rocas - = Shag Rocks 162 H 8
Č'ormoz 138-139 UV 4
Čornaja [SU, Tajmyrskaja AO] 178-179 Q 3
Č'ornaja Cholunica 138-139 ST 4
Č'ornaja Sloboda = Ignatovo 138-139 LM 3
Cornelia 174-175 H 4
Cornelia, GA 154-155 O 3
Cornélio Procópio 162 FG 2
Cornell, WI 152-153 L 3
Corner Brook 144-145 Z 8
Corner Inlet 196 H 7
Corning, AR 154-155 K 2
Corning, CA 150-151 B 6
Corning, IA 152-153 J 5
Corning, KS 152-153 HJ 6
Corning, NY 148-149 E 3
Č'ornomorskoje 140-141 F 4
Cornouaille 134-135 EF 4
Č'ornovskoje 138-139 QR 4
Cornudas Mountains 154-155 C 4-5
Cornwall [GB] 132 D 6
Cornwall [CDN] 144-145 VW 8
Cornwallis Island 144-145 RS 2-3
Cornwall Island 144-145 RS 2
Č'ornyje zemli 140-141 N 3-4
Č'ornyj Jar 140-141 MN 2
Corny Point 196 C 5
Coro 158-159 EF 2
Coroaci 160-161 L 3
Coroados 160-161 G 4
Coroatá 158-159 L 5
Corocoro 158-159 F 8
Coroico 158-159 F 8
Coromandel 160-161 J 3
Coromandel, Côte de - = Coromandel Coast 180-181 N 7-8
Coromandelküste = Coromandel Coast 180-181 N 7-8
Coromandel-part = Coromandel Coast 180-181 N 7-8
Corona, CA 150-151 E 9
Corona, NM 154-155 C 3
Coronado, CA 150-151 E 9
Coronado, Bahía de - 146-147 K 10
Coronados, Islas de - 150-151 E 9
Coronation Gulf 144-145 OP 4
Coronation Island [South Orkneys] 121 CD 132
Coronation Islands 194-195 D 2
Coronel Dorrego 162 DE 5
Coronel Eugenio Garay 160-161 DE 6
Coronel Fabriciano 158-159 L 8
Coronel Francisco Sosa 162 CD 5-6
Coronel Galvão = Rio Verde de Mato Grosso 158-159 HJ 8
Coronel Murta 160-161 L 2
Coronel Oviedo 158-159 E 2-3
Coronel Ponce 160-161 E 1
Coronel Pringles 162 D 5
Coronel Rosales 162 D 5
Coronel Suárez 162 D 5
Coronel Vivida 160-161 F 6-7
Coropuna, Nudo - 158-159 E 8
Corowa 196 H 5-6
Corozal [BH] 146-147 J 8
Corpus Christi, TX 146-147 G 6
Corpus Christi Bay 154-155 G 7
Corpus Christi Pass 154-155 G 7
Corque 158-159 F 8
Corral [RCH] 162 B 5
Correctionsville, IA 152-153 HJ 4
Corregidor Island 186-187 GH 4
Corrente 158-159 KL 7
Corrente, Rio - [BR, Bahia] 158-159 L 7
Correntes [BR, Mato Grosso] 158-159 HJ 8
Correntes, Rio - [BR, Goiás] 160-161 G 3
Correntes, Rio - [BR, Mato Grosso] 160-161 E 2
Correntina 158-159 KL 7
Correo, NM 154-155 B 3
Corrib, Lough - 132 B 5
Corrientes, Cabo - [CO] 158-159 D 3
Corrientes, Cabo - [MEX] 146-147 E 7
Corrientes, Cabo - [RA] 162 E 5
Corrigan, TX 154-155 H 5
Corrigin 194-195 C 6
Corry, PA 148-149 D 4
Corse 136-137 C 4
Corse, Cap - 136-137 C 4
Corséga 126-127 K 7
Corsica = Corse 136-137 C 4
Corsicana, TX 146-147 G 5
Č'orskogo, chrebet - 178-179 a 4-c 5
Corte 136-137 C 4
Cortez, CO 150-151 J 7
Cortez Mountains 150-151 E 5
Cortina d'Ampezzo 136-137 E 2
Čortkov 140-141 BC 2
Cortland, NE 152-153 H 5
Cortland, NY 148-149 EF 3
Cortona 136-137 D 4
Corubal, Rio - 172-173 B 3
Çoruh = Artvin 180-181 E 2
Çoruh Nehri 182-183 J 2
Çorum 180-181 CD 2
Corumbá 158-159 H 8
Corumbá, Rio - 158-159 K 8
Corumbá de Goiás 160-161 H 1
Corumbaíba 160-161 H 3
Corumbataí, Rio - 160-161 G 6
Corundum 174-175 J 3
Corunha = Acoruña 126-127 FG 7
Corunna, MI 152-153 O 4
Coruña, La - 134-135 C 7
Coruña, La - = A Coruña 134-135 C 7
Corupá 160-161 H 7
Corvallis, MT 150-151 FG 2
Corvallis, OR 146-147 B 3
Corwin Springs, MT 150-151 H 3
Corydon, IA 152-153 K 5
Corydon, IN 152-153 NO 6
Cosenza 136-137 FG 6
Coshocton, OH 148-149 BC 4
Cosigüina, Punta - 146-147 J 9
Cosigüina, Volcán - 146-147 J 9
Cosmoledo Islands 168-169 L 4
Cosmópolis 160-161 J 5
Cosmopolis, WA 150-151 B 2
Cosmos, MN 152-153 J 3
Cosmos Newberry Aboriginal Reserve 194-195 D 5
Č'ošskaja guba 178-179 H 4
Costa, Cordillera de la - [RCH] 162 B 2-3
Costa, Cordillera de la - [YV] 158-159 FG 3
Costa Brava 134-135 J 8
Costa d'Avorio [★] 172 D 3
Costa d'Avorio [∪] 172 D 4
Costa degli Schiavi 173 F 4
Costa de Marfil [★] 166-167 CD 7
Costa d'Oro 173 EF 4
Costa del Pepe 172 C 4
Costa Grande 146-147 F 8
Costa Machado 160-161 FG 5
Costanza = Constanţ a 136-137 N 3
Costa Rica [CR] 146-147 JK 9-10
Costa Smeralda 121 B 3
Costermansville = Bukavu 168-169 G 3
Costilla, NM 154-155 C 2
Cotabato 186-187 H 5
Cotagaita [BOL] 158-159 F 9
Cotahuasi 158-159 E 8
Cotati, CA 150-151 B 6
Coteau des Prairies, Plateau du - 146-147 G 2-3
Coteau du Missouri, Plateau du - 146-147 FG 2
Côteau-Station 148-149 F 2
Cote Blanche Bay 154-155 K 6
Côte d'Azur 134-135 L 7
Côte d'Ivoire [★] 1 166-167 CD 7
Côte Française = French Shore 144-145 Z 7-8
Cotentin 134-135 G 4
Cotia 160-161 J 5
Cotonou 166-167 E 7
Cotonu = Cotonou 166-167 E 7
Cotopaxi, CO 152-153 D 6
Cotopaxi [EC, ▲] 158-159 D 5
Cotswold Hills 132 EF 6
Cottage Grove, OR 150-151 B 4
Cottageville, SC 148-149 C 8
Cottbus 133 G 3
Cotter, AR 154-155 J 2
Cottica 158-159 J 4
Cottondale, FL 154-155 N 5
Cotton Valley, LA 154-155 J 4
Cottonwood, AZ 150-151 GH 8
Cottonwood, CA 150-151 B 5
Cottonwood, ID 150-151 E 2
Cottonwood, SD 152-153 F 4
Cottonwood Creek 150-151 B 5
Cottonwood Falls, KS 152-153 H 6
Cottonwood River 152-153 J 3
Cottonwood Wash 150-151 HJ 8
Coudersport, PA 148-149 DE 4
Cotulla, TX 154-155 F 6
Coulee, ND 152-153 EF 1
Coulee City, WA 150-151 D 2
Coulee Dam, WA 150-151 D 1-2
Coulman Island 121 B 18
Coulterville, IL 152-153 M 6
Council, ID 150-151 E 3
Council Bluffs, IA 146-147 GH 3
Council Grove, KS 152-153 H 6
Council Mountain 150-151 E 3
Courlande 138-139 CD 5
Courtenay [CDN] 144-145 LM 8
Courtrai = Kortrijk 134-135 J 3
Coushatta, LA 154-155 J 4
Coutances 134-135 G 4
Couves, Ilha das - 160-161 K 5
Cove, AR 154-155 H 3
Coveñas 158-159 D 3
Coventry 132 F 5
Coveñas 158-159 D 3
Covilhã 134-135 D 8
Covington, GA 154-155 O 4
Covington, IN 152-153 N 5
Covington, KY 146-147 JK 4
Covington, LA 154-155 K 5
Covington, MI 152-153 M 2
Covington, OH 152-153 O 5
Covington, OK 154-155 G 2
Covington, TN 154-155 L 3
Covington, VA 148-149 CD 6
Cowal, Lake - 194-195 J 6
Cowan, TN 154-155 MN 3
Cowan, Lake - 194-195 D 6
Cowansville 148-149 G 2
Coward Springs 194-195 G 5
Cowarie 194-195 G 5
Cowden, IL 152-153 M 6
Cowdrey, CO 152-153 C 5
Cowell 196 C 4
Cowen, Mount - 150-151 H 3
Cowlitz River 150-151 B 2
Cowra 194-195 J 6
Coxilha Grande 162 F 3
Coxilha Rica 160-161 G 7
Coxim 158-159 J 8
Coxim, Rio - 160-161 E 3
Coxipó do Ouro 160-161 D 1
Coxipó Ponte 160-161 DE 1
Cox River 194-195 FG 3
Cox's Bazar = Koks Bāzār 180-181 P 6
Coyote, NM 154-155 C 4
Coyote, Arroyo el - 150-151 G 10
Coyotes Indian Reservation, Los - 150-151 E 9
Cozad, NE 152-153 G 5
Cozumel 146-147 J 7
Cozumel, Isla de - 146-147 J 7
Crab Creek 150-151 D 2
Cracovia 128-139 M 5-6
Cracovia = Kraków 133 JK 3
Cradock 168-169 G 9
Craig, CO 152-153 C 5
Craig, MT 150-151 GH 2
Craig Harbour 144-145 UV 2
Craigmont, ID 150-151 E 2
Craiova 136-137 K 3
Crampel = Ra's al-Mā' 166-167 D 2
Cranbrook 144-145 NO 8
Crandon, WI 152-153 M 3
Crane, MO 154-155 J 2
Crane, OR 150-151 D 4
Crane, TX 154-155 D 5
Crane Lake, MN 152-153 KL 1
Crane Mountain 150-151 CD 4
Cranston, RI 148-149 H 4
Crary Mountains 121 B 25
Crasna [R, ~] 136-137 K 2
Crasna [R, ●] 136-137 M 2
Crater Lake 146-147 B 3
Crater Lake, OR 150-151 BC 4
Crater Lake National Park 150-151 BC 4
Crateús 158-159 LM 6
Crato [BR] 158-159 M 6
Crau 134-135 K 7
Crauford, Cape - 144-145 TU 3
Cravinhos 160-161 J 4
Cravo Norte 158-159 EF 3
Crawford, GA 148-149 B 8
Crawford, NE 152-153 E 4
Crawfordsville, IN 152-153 N 5
Crawfordville, FL 148-149 AB 8
Crazy Mountains 150-151 H 2-3
Crazy Peak 150-151 HJ 3
Crazy Woman Creek 152-153 C 3
Creede, CO 152-153 C 7
Creedmoor, NC 148-149 D 6
Cree Lake [CDN, ≈] 144-145 P 6
Creighton, NE 152-153 GH 4
Creil 134-135 J 4
Crema 136-137 C 3
Cremona 136-137 CD 3
Crenshaw, MS 154-155 K 3
Cres [YU, ⊙] 136-137 F 3
Cres [YU , ●] 136-137 F 3
Crescent, OK 154-155 G 2-3
Crescent, OR 150-151 C 4
Crescent, La - , MN 152-153 L 4
Crescent, Lake - 150-151 B 1
Crescent City, CA 150-151 A 5
Crescent City, FL 148-149 c 2
Crescent Junction, UT 150-151 J 6
Crescent Lake, OR 150-151 C 4
Cresco, IA 152-153 KL 4
Cressy 196 F 7
Crested Butte, CO 152-153 C 6
Crestline, NV 150-151 F 7
Creston, IA 152-153 J 5
Creston, WY 152-153 BC 5
Crestview, FL 154-155 M 5
Creswell, OR 150-151 B 4
Creta = Krētē 136-137 L 8
Crete, NE 152-153 H 5
Creus, Cabo - 134-135 J 7
Creuse 134-135 H 5
Creusot, le - 134-135 K 5
Creve Coeur, IL 152-153 M 5
Crewe 132 E 5
Crewe, VA 148-149 D 6
Cribi = Kribi 166-167 F 8
Crib Point 196 G 7
Crichna = Krishna 180-181 M 7
Crikvenica 136-137 F 3
Crillon, mys - = mys Kriljon 178-179 b 8
Crimea = Krym 140-141 FG 4
Crimée = Krym 140-141 FG 4
Crimeia = Krym 140-141 FG 4
Crimeia, Oblast de - 140-141 FG 4
Cripple Creek, CO 152-153 D 6
Crişana 136-137 JK 2
Crisfield, MD 148-149 F 5-6
Crista Índico-Atlântica 124-125 J-L
Cristais, Serra dos - 160-161 J 2
Cristalina 160-161 J 2
Cristina 160-161 K 5
Cristobal 146-147 b 2
Crişul Alb 136-137 JK 2
Crişul Negru 136-137 JK 2
Crivitz, WI 152-153 MN 3
Crna Gora 136-137 H 4
Crna Reka 136-137 J 5
Croacia 136-137 F-H 3
Croácia 136-137 FG 3
Croatia 136-137 F-H 3
Croatie 136-137 F-H 3
Croazia 136-137 F-H 3
Crocker, MO 152-153 K 7
Crocker, Banjaran - 152-153 L 3-M 2
Crockett, TX 154-155 H 5

Crocodile Islands 194-195 FG 2
Crofton, KY 154-155 M 2
Crofton, NE 152-153 H 4
Croker Island 194-195 F 2
Cromer 132 G 5
Cromwell 194-195 NO 8-9
Cromwell, MN 152-153 K 2
Crook, CO 152-153 E 5
Crooked Creek 150-151 DE 4
Crooked Island 146-147 M 7
Crooked Island Passage 146-147 LM 7
Crooked River [USA] 150-151 C 3
Crookston, MN 152-153 H 2
Crookston, NE 152-153 F 4
Crooksville, OH 148-149 B 5
Crookwell 196 J 5
Crosby, MN 152-153 JK 2
Crosby, MS 154-155 K 5
Crosby, ND 152-153 E 1
Crosbyton, TX 154-155 E 4
Cross 172-173 H 4
Cross, Cape - = Kaap Kruis 168-169 D 7
Cross City, FL 148-149 b 2
Crossen (Oder) = Krosno Odrzańskie 133 G 2-3
Crossett, AR 154-155 K 4
Crossman Peak 150-151 FG 8
Cross Plains, TX 154-155 F 4
Cross River 166-167 F 7-8
Cross Sound 144-145 J 6
Crossville, TN 154-155 N 3
Croswell, MI 152-153 P 4
Crotone 136-137 G 6
Crow Agency, MT 152-153 C 3
Crow Creek 152-153 D 5
Crow Creek Indian Reservation 152-153 G 3
Crowder, OK 154-155 GH 3
Crowell, TX 154-155 F 4
Crowie Creek 196 H 4
Crow Indian Reservation 152-153 BC 3
Crowley, LA 146-147 H 5-6
Crowley, Lake - 150-151 D 7
Crowleys Ridge 154-155 K 2-3
Crown King, AZ 150-151 G 8
Crown Point, IN 152-153 N 5
Crownpoint, NM 150-151 JK 8
Crows Nest 196 L 1
Croydon 194-195 H 3
Croydon, London- 132 FG 7
Crozet 124-125 M 8
Crozet, Bacino delle - 124-125 MN 7
Crozet, Dorsal de - 124-125 M 8
Crozet, Dorsale delle - 124-125 M 8
Crozet, Patamar de - 124-125 M 8
Crozet, Seuil des - 124-125 M 8
Crozetdrempel 124-125 M 8
Crozet Ridge 124-125 M 8
Crozetschwelle 124-125 M 8
Crucero,CA 150-151 EF 8
Cruces, Las - 146-147 b 2
Cruz, Cabo - 146-147 L 8
Cruz, La - [MEX] 154-155 C 7
Cruz Alta [BR] 162 F 3
Cruz del Eje 162 CD 4
Cruzeiro 158-159 L 9
Cruzeiro do Oeste 160-161 F 5
Cruzeiro do Sul 158-159 E 6
Cruzen Island 121 B 124-125
Cruzilia 160-161 K 4
Cruz Machado 160-161 G 6
Crystal, ND 152-153 H 1
Crystal Bay 148-149 b 2
Crystal Brook 196 CD 4
Crystal City, MO 152-153 L 6
Crystal City, TX 154-155 F 6
Crystal Falls, MI 152-153 M 2-3
Crystal Lake 152-153 NO 3
Crystal Lake, IL 152-153 MN 4
Crystal River, FL 148-149 b 2
Crystal Springs, MS 154-155 K 4-5
Csongrád 133 K 5
Ctesiphon = Ktesiphon 182-183 L 6
Cu 178-179 N 9
Cuamba 168-169 J 5
Cuando, Rio - 168-169 F 6
Cuando-Cubango 168-169 E 5-F 6
Cuangar 168-169 E 6
Cuango 168-169 E 4
Cuango, Rio - 168-169 E 6
Cuan Long 186-187 DE 5
Cuanza Norte 168-169 DE 4-5
Cuanza Sul 168-169 D 4-5
Cu'a Rao 186-187 DE 3
Cuarepoti, Arroyo - 160-161 D 6
Cuauhtémoc 146-147 C 6
Cuba 146-147 KL 7
Cuba 146-147 KL 7
Cuba [C] 146-147 KL 7
Cuba, KS 152-153 H 6
Cuba, MO 152-153 L 6
Cuba, NM 154-155 B 2
Cubabi, Cerro - 150-151 G 10
Cubal 168-169 D 5
Cubango, Rio - 168-169 E 6
Cubartau = Baršatas 178-179 O 8
Cubatão 160-161 J 5
Cubero, NM 154-155 B 3
Cubo 174-175 K 2
Cubuk 182-183 E 2
Cuchi, Rio - 168-169 E 5-6
Cuchilla Grande [ROU] 162 EF 4
Cuchillo Parado 154-155 C 6
Cuchloma 138-139 O 4
Cucui 158-159 F 4
Cucumbi 168-169 E 5
Cucunor = Chöch nuur 184-185 H 4
Cucurpe 150-151 H 10
Cúcuta 158-159 E 3
Cudahy, WI 152-153 N 4
Cuddalore 180-181 MN 8
Cuddapah 180-181 M 8
Cudgewa 196 HJ 6
Cudi Daği 182-183 K 4
Cudovo 178-179 E 6
Cudskoje ozero 178-179 O 6
Cue 194-195 C 5
Cuenca [E] 134-135 FG 8
Cuenca [EC] 158-159 D 5
Cuenca, Serrania de - 134-135 F 8-G 9
Cuenca Arábiga 124-125 N 5
Cuenca Argelinoprovenzal 128-129 J 8-K 7
Cuenca Argentina 124-125 GH 7-8
Cuenca Atlántico-Índico Antártica 124-125 J-M 9
Cuenca Brasileña 124-125 H 6
Cuenca Canadiense 120 AB 132-33
Cuenca Euroasiática 120 A
Cuenca Ibérica 124-125 HJ 3
Cuenca Índico-Antártica 124-125 O-Q 8
Cuenca Jónica 136-137 GH 7
Cuenca Levantina 180-181 BC 4
Cuenca Mexicana 146-147 HJ 6
Cuenca Norteamericana 124-125 FG 4
Cuenca Pacifico-Antártica 124-125 B-E 8-9
Cuenlum = Kunlun Shan 184-185 D-H 4
Cuernavaca 146-147 FG 8
Cuero, TX 154-155 G 6
Cuervo, NM 154-155 C 3
Cuervo Grande, El - 154-155 C 5
Cuesta Pass 150-151 C 8
Cuevas del Almanzora 134-135 G 10
Cufra, Wáhât el - = Wāḥāt al-Kufrah 166-167 J 4
Cuiabá [BR, Amazonas] 158-159 H 6
Cuiabá [BR, Mato Grosso] 158-159 H 8
Cuiabá, Rio - 158-159 H 8
Cuieté, Rio - 160-161 M 3
Cuillin Sound 132 C 3
Cuilo, Rio - 168-169 E 4
Cuima 168-169 E 5
Cuipo 146-147 a 2
Cuito, Rio - 168-169 EF 6
Cuito Cuanavale 168-169 EF 6
Čukči, Circolo Nazionale dei - 178-179 g-k 4
Čukči, Mare dei - 120 BC 35-36
Čukči, Platea dei - 120 B 35
Čukotskij, mys - 178-179 l 5
Čukotskij poluostrov 178-179 kl 4
Çukurca 182-183 K 4
Culbertson, MT 152-153 D 1
Culbertson, NE 152-153 F 5
Culcairn 194-195 J 7
Culebra [PA] 146-147 b 2
Culgoa River 194-195 J 5
Culiacán 146-147 E 6-7
Culiacán Rosales = Culiacán 146-147 E 6-7
Culion Island 186-187 G 4
Čulkovo 178-179 Q 5
Cúllar de Baza 134-135 F 10
Cullera 134-135 GH 9
Cullinan 174-175 H 3
Cullman, AL 154-155 M 3
Čul'man 178-179 XY 6
Culpeper, VA 148-149 DE 5
Culuene, Rio - 158-159 J 7
Čuluut gol 184-185 J 2
Culver, Point - 194-195 DE 6
Čulym [SU, ~] 178-179 Q 6
Čulym [SU, ●] 178-179 P 6
Cum = Qom 180-181 G 4
Cumae 136-137 EF 5
Cumamoto = Kumamoto 184-185 P 5
Cumaná 158-159 G 2
Cumari 160-161 HJ 3
Cumassia = Kumasi 166-167 D 7
Cumberland, IA 152-153 J 5
Cumberland, KY 148-149 B 6
Cumberland, MD 146-147 L 4
Cumberland, VA 148-149 DE 6
Cumberland, WI 152-153 KL 3
Cumberland, Cape - 194-195 N 2
Cumberland, City, TN 154-155 M 2
Cumberland, Lake - 148-149 A 6
Cumberland Island 148-149 C 9
Cumberland Islands 194-195 JK 4
Cumberland Peninsula 144-145 XY 4
Cumberland Plateau 146-147 J 5-K 4
Cumberland Point 152-153 M 2
Cumberland River 146-147 J 4
Cumberland Sound [CDN] 144-145 X 4-Y 5
Cumberland Sound [USA] 148-149 c 1
Cumborah 196 H 2
Cumbre, Paso de la - 162 BC 4
Cumbres Pass 152-153 C 7
Cumbria 132 F 4
Cumbrian Mountains 132 E 4
Čumikan 178-179 Za 7
Cuminá, Rio - 158-159 H 5
Cummings, CA 150-151 B 6
Cummins 194-195 G 6
Cumpas 150-151 J 10
Çumra 182-183 E 4
Čuna [SU ◁ Angara] 178-179 S 6
Čun'a [SU ◁ Podkamennaja Tunguska] 178-179 ST 5
Cunani 158-159 J 4
Cunco 162 B 5
Cunene 168-169 E 6
Cunene, Rio - 168-169 D 6
Cùneo 136-137 B 3
Cuney, TX 154-155 H 4
Çüngüş 182-183 H 3
Cunha 160-161 K 5
Čunnamulla 194-195 HJ 5
Cunningham, WA 150-151 D 2
Čuokkarašša 130-131 KL 2
Cupica, Golfo de - 158-159 D 3
Cuprum, ID 150-151 E 3
Čur 138-139 T 5
Curaçá [BR, Amazonas] 158-159 G 6
Curaçá [BR, Bahia] 158-159 LM 6
Curaçao 146-147 N 9
Curacautin 162 B 5
Curanilahue 162 B 5
Čurapča 178-179 Z 5
Curaray, Rio - 158-159 D 5
Curdistan = Kordestān 180-181 F 3
Curdistão 182-183 M 5
Curiapo 158-159 G 3
Curicó 162 B 4
Curilhas 184-185 S 3-T 2
Curilhas, Fossa das - 120 D 2-E 3
Curili 184-185 S 3-T 2
Curili, Fossa delle - 120 D 2-E 3
Curitiba 162 G 3
Curitibanos 160-161 G 7
Curiúva 160-161 G 6
Curlandia 130-131 JK 9
Curlândia 138-139 CD 5
Curlandia 138-139 CD 5
Curlew, WA 150-151 D 1
Curnamona 194-195 GH 6
Currais Novos 158-159 M 6
Currant, NV 150-151 F 6
Current River 154-155 K 2
Currie 194-195 H 7-8
Currie, MN 152-153 J 3
Currie, NV 150-151 F 5
Currituck Sound 148-149 F 6
Curtea-de-Argeș 136-137 L 3
Curtin Springs 194-195 F 5
Curtis, NE 152-153 F 5
Curtis Island [AUS] 194-195 K 4
Curtis Island [NZ] 194-195 Q 6
Curuá, Rio - [BR ◁ Rio Iriri] 158-159 J 6
Curuai 158-159 H 5
Curuçá 158-159 K 5
Curuguaty 160-161 E 6
Curup 186-187 D 7
Curupai, Rio - 160-161 EF 5
Čurupinsk 136-137 P 2
C'urupinsk 140-141 F 3
Cururú 158-159 G 8
Cururupu 158-159 L 5
Curuzú Cuatiá 162 E 3
Curva Grande 158-159 K 5
Curvelo 158-159 L 8
Curych = Zürich 133 C 5
Čuševicy 138-139 N 3
Cushing, OK 154-155 G 3
Cushing, TX 154-155 H 5
Cushman, AR 154-155 K 3
Cusihuiriachic 154-155 B 6
Cusino, MI 152-153 N 2
Cusseta Pass 150-151 C 8
Čusovoj 178-179 K 6
Čusovskoj 138-139 V 3
Cusseta, GA 154-155 N 4
Čust 180-181 L 2
Custer, SD 152-153 E 4
Cut Bank, MT 150-151 GH 1
Cutch = Kutch 180-181 K 6
Cutervo 158-159 D 6
Cuthbert, GA 154-155 N 5
Cutler, CA 150-151 D 7
Cuttaburra Creek 196 G 2
Cuttack 180-181 NO 6
Cu'u Long, Cu'a Sông - 186-187 E 5
Cuvelai 168-169 E 6
Cuvier, Cape - 194-195 B 4
Cuvo, Rio - 168-169D5
Cuxhaven 133 D 2
Cuy, El - 162 C 5
Cuyahoga Falls, OH 148-149 C 4
Cuyama River 150-151 C 8
Cuyo Islands 186-187 H 4
Cuyuni River 158-159 G 3
Cuzco [PE, ●] 158-159 E 7
Cuzistão 183-184 N 6-8
C.W. MacConaughy, Lake 152-153 E 5
Cyangugu 171 B 3
Cyclades 136-137 L 7
Cyklady 136-137 L 7
Cynthiana, KY 152-153 OP 6
Cyphergat = Syfergat 174-175 G 6
Cyp-Navolok 130-131 PQ 3
Cypr 180-181 C 3
Cypress, LA 154-155 J 5
Cypress, TX 154-155 GH 6
Cypress Hills 144-145 OP 8
Cyprus 180-181 C 3
Cyrenaica = Barqah 166-167 J 2
Cyrénaïque = Barqah 166-167 J 2
Cyrenajka = Barqah 166-167 J 2
Czad 166-167 HJ 5
Czad, Jezioro - = Lac Tchad 166-167 G6
Czarne, Morze - 140-141 D-K 5
Czarne, Morze - 136-137 N 4-P 3
Czarnogóra 136-137 H 4
Czech Republic 133 F-H 4
Czeczeńsk Autonomiczna Republika 140-141 MN 5
Czeluskin, Przylądek - = mys Čel'uskin 178-179 UV 2
Czernowitz = Černovcy 140-141 B 2
Czersk 133 J 2
Czerwone, Morze - 180-181 D 5-7
Czeska, Republika - 178-179 B-E 7
Czeska, Republika - 133 FH 4
Częstochowa 133 JK 3
Czingis-chana, Wały - 184-185 LM 2
Czomolungma 184-185 F 6
Czukockie, Morze - 120 BC 35-36
Czukockie, Wzniesienie - 120 B 35
Czukocki Okręg Autonomiczny 178-179 g-j 4
Czuwaska Autonomiczna Republika = 4 ◁ 178-179 H 6

Ch

Chaaltyn gol 184-185 GH 4
Cha-am [T] 186-187 CD 4
Chaapsalu = Haapsalu 138-139 D 4
Chaba 184-185 F 2
Chabarovo 178-179 L 4
Chabarovsk 178-179 a 8
Chablis 134-135 J 5
Chačmas 140-141 O 6
Chaco 162 D 3
Chaco Austral 162 DE 3
Chaco Boreal 162 DE 2
Chaco Canyon National Monument 154-155 AB 2-3
Chaco Central 162 D 2-E 3
Chaco River 150-151 J 7
Chachapoyas 158-159 D 6
Chācharān 146-147 K 4
Ch'a-chên = Chazhen 190-191 B 5
Cha-chiang = Zhajiang 190-191 D 8
Cha-ching = Zhajin 190-191 E 7
Chachoengsao 186-187 D 4
Chad 166-167 HJ 5
Chadasan 184-185 J 2
Chadchal = Chatgal 184-185 HJ 1
Chadron, NE 152-153 E 4
Chadum 168-169 F 6
Chadwick, IL 152-153 M 4
Chadzaar 184-185 G 4
Chaeryŏng 188-189 EF 3
Chaffee, MO 154-155 KL 2
Chagang-do 188-189 EF 2
Chagan nuur 184-185 L 3
Chagos 160-161 H 1
Chageri = Hageri 138-139 E 4
Chaghcharān 180-181 K 4
Chagny 134-135 K 5
Chagos 124-125 N 6
Chagres [PA, ~] 146-147 ab 2
Chagres [PA, ●] 146-147 b 2
Chagres, Brazo del - 146-147 b 2
Chagres, Rio - 146-147 bc 2
Chagres Arm = Brazo del Chagres 146-147 b 2
Chahār Burjak 180-181 J 4
Chahār Burjak = Chahār Burjak 180-181 J 4
Chahār Maḥāl-e Bakhteyārī = 3 ◁ 180-181 G 4
Chahbā = Shahbā' 182-183 G 6
Chāh Bāhār = Bandar-e Chāh Bahār 180-181 HJ 5
Ch'aho 188-189 G 2
Chaidamu Pendi = Tsaidam 184-185 GH 4
Ch'ail-bong 188-189 F 2
Chai Nat 186-187 D 3
Chain Butte 152-153 B 2
Chaîne Pontique 180-181 C-E 2
Chaine Rocheuse = Rocky Mountains 144-145 L 5-P 9
Chaiqiao 190-191 HJ 7
Chaiya 186-187 C 5
Chajari 162 E 4
Chajdag gol 184-185 EF 3
Chajian 190-191 G 5
Chajlar 184-185 M 2
Chajlar = Hailar 184-185 M 2
Chajlar gol = Hailar He 184-185 MN 2
Chajrchan 184-185 J 2
Chajr'uzovo 178-179 e 6
Chaka Nor = Chöch nuur 184-185 H 4
Chakassien, AR = 9 ◁ 178-179 Q 7
Chake Chake 171 DE 4
Chakassia, Prov. Aut. della = 9 ◁ 178-179 R 7
Chāl = Shāl 182-183 N 5
Chala 158-159 E 8
Chalab, gora - 140-141 M 6
Chalabesa 171 B 5
Cha-lan-tun = Yalu 184-185 N 2
Chalawa, River - 172-173 G 3
Chalbi Desert 171 D 2
Chalchyn gol 184-185 M 2
Chaleur Bay 144-145 XY 8
Chalhuanca 158-159 E 7
Chaling 190-191 D 8
Cha-ling Hu = Kyaring Tsho 184-185 H 5
Chálkē 136-137 M 7
Chalkidikē 136-137 K 3
Chalkis 136-137 K 6
Challawa = River Chalawa 172-173 G 3
Chal'mer-Ju 178-179 L 4
Chalmer-Sede = Tazovskij 178-179 OP 4
Châlons-en-Champagne 134-135 JK 4
Chalon-sur-Saône 134-135 K 5
Chalosse 134-135 G 7
Chalturin 178-179 H 6
Challapata 158-159 F 8
Challis, ID 150-151 F 3
Cham 133 F 4
Chama 172-173 E 3
Chama, NM 152-153 C 7
Chama, Rio - 154-155 B 2
Chaman 180-181 K 4
Chamaites 174-175 B 4
Chamba [EAT] 171 D 5
Chamba [IND] 180-181 M 4
Chambal [IND ◁ Kali Sindh] 180-181 M 5-6
Chambal [IND ◁ Yamuna] 180-181 M 5-6
Chamberlain, SD 152-153 G 4
Chamberlain Lake 148-149 J 1
Chamberlain River 194-195 E 3
Chambersburg, PA 148-149 DE 4-5
Chambers Island 152-153 N 3
Chambéry 134-135 K 6
Chambeshi 168-169 H 5
Chambres Pass = Cumbres Pass 152-153 C 7
Chamchamāl 182-183 L 5
Chamdo = Chhamdo 184-185 H 5
Chami Choto = Hami 184-185 G 3
Chamo, Lake - = Tyamo 166-167 M 7
Champa [IND] 180-181 N 6
Champa [SU] 178-179 X 5
Champagne 134-135 J 5-K 4
Champagne Castle 174-175 H 5
Champagny Islands 194-195 D 3
Champaign, IL 146-147 J 3-4
Champāran = Motihari 180-181 N0 5
Champasak 186-187 DE 4
Champlain, Lake - 146-147 LM 3
Champotón 146-147 H 8
Chanāb = Chenab 180-181 M 4
Chan Bogd 184-185 K 3
Chancay 158-159 D 7
Chanch 184-185 J 1
Chan-chiang = Zhanjiang 184-185 L 7
Chanchoengsao 186-187 D 4
Chânda = Chandrapur 180-181 M 7
Chandalar River 144-145 G 4
Chandeleur Islands 146-147 J 6
Chandeleur Sound 154-155 L 5-6
Chandigarh 180-181 LM 4
Chandler 144-145 Y 8
Chandler, OK 154-155 G 3
Chandler, AZ 150-151 H 9
Chandlers Falls 171 D 2
Chandpur 180-181 OP 6
Chandrapur 180-181 M 7
Chandyga 178-179 a 5
Chang, Ko- [T → Krung Thep] 186-187 D 4
Changai = Shanghai 184-185 N 5
Changaj 184-185 H 2
Changajn nuruu 184-185 HJ 2
Changalane 174-175 K 4
Chang'an 190-191 B 4
Ch'ang-an = Xi'an 184-185 K 5
Changane, Rio - 168-169 H 7
Chang'ankou = Laopukou 190-191 B 9
Chang'anzhen = Rong'an 190-191 B 9
Changara 168-169 H 6
Changbai 188-189 FG 2
Changbai Shan 184-185 O 3
Chang-chia-k'ou = Zhangjiakou 184-185 L 3
Ch'ang Chiang = Chang Jiang 190-191 F 7
Chang-chia-p'ang = Zhangjiapang 190-191 E 6
Changchih = Changzhi 184-185 L 4
Ch'ang-chih = Changzhi 184-185 L 4
Ch'ang-ch'ing = Changqing 190-191 F 3
Chang-ch'iu = Zhangqiu 190-191 F 3
Changchun 184-185 NO 3
Changcun 188-189 F 5
Changde 184-185 L 6
Changdu = Chhamdo 184-185 H 5
Changfeng = 190-191 F 5
Changge 190-191 D 4
Chang-hai = Shanghai 184-185 N 5
Changhang 188-189 F 4-5
Chang Ho = Zhang He 190-191 E 3
Changhowŏn 188-189 F 4
Ch'ang-hsing = Changxing 190-191 G 6
Ch'ang-hsing Tao = Changxing Dao 188-189 C 3
Chang Hu 190-191 D 6
Chang-hua [RC] 190-191 H 9
Chang-hua [TJ] 190-191 G 6
Chang-huang = Zhanghuang 190-191 B 10
Changhŭng 188-189 F 5
Changhŭng-ni 188-189 FG 2
Changhwa = Chang-hua 190-191 H 9
Ch'ang-i = Changyi 190-191 G 3
Chang Jiang [TJ, ~ ◁ Dong Hai] 184-185 K 5-6
Chang Jiang [TJ, ~ ◁ Poyang Hu] 190-191 F 7
Changji Huizu Zizhizhou 184-185 FG 3
Changjin 188-189 F 2
Changjin-gang 188-189 F 2
Changjin-ho 188-189 F 2
Changjŏn 188-189 G 3
Changkiakow= Zhangjiakou 184-185 L 3
Changkou = Zhangqiu 190-191 F 3
Chang-kuang-ts'ai Ling = Zhangguangcai Ling 184-185 O 2-3
Changkung = Cheng-kung 190-191 H 10
Changle [TJ, Fujian] 190-191 G 9
Changle [TJ, Guangdong] 190-191 B 11
Changle [TJ, Shandong] 190-191 G 3
Changli 190-191 G 2
Ch'ang-lo = Changle [TJ, Guangdong] 190-191 B 11
Ch'ang-lo = Changle [TJ, Shandong] 190-191 G 3
Changluo = Changle 190-191 G 9
Changnim-ni 188-189 F 3
Changning 190-191 D 8
Ch'angnyŏng 188-189 G 5
Ch'ang-pai = Changbai 188-189 FG 2
Ch'ang-pai Shan = Changbai Shan 184-185 O 3
Changping 190-191 F 1
Changping = Zhangping 190-191 F 9
Changpu = Zhangpu 190-191 F 9
Chang-p'u = Zhangpu 190-191 F 9
Changqing 190-191 F 3
Chang-san-ying = Zhangsanying 188-189 AB 2
Changsha 184-185 L 6
Changshan 190-191 G 7
Changshan Dao = Miao Dao 190-191 H3
Changsheng 190-191 EF 8
Changshu 184-185 N 5
Changshui 190-191 C 4
Chang Shui = Zhang Shui 190-191 E9
Ch'angsŏng = Chongsŏng 188-189 GH 1
Changtai 190-191 F 9
Chang Tang = Jang Thang 184-185 E-G 5
Ch'ang-tê = Anyang 184-185 LM 4
Ch'ang-tê = Changde 184-185 L 6
Changteh = Changde 184-185 L 6
Changting 184-185 M 6
Changtsing = Changqing 190-191 F 3
Ch'ang-tu = Chhamdo 184-185 H 5
Changtutsung = Chhamdo 184-185 H 5
Chang-tzŭ = Zhangzi 190-191 D 3
Ch'angwŏn 188-189 G 5
Changxing 190-191 G 6
Changxing Dao [TJ, Dong Hai] 190-191 HJ 6
Changxing Dao [TJ, Liaodong Wan] 188-189 C 3
Changyang 190-191 C 6
Changyeh = Zhangye 184-185 J 4
Changyi 190-191 G3
Changyŏn 184-185 NO 4
Changyuan 190-191 E 4
Changzhi 184-185 L 4
Changzhou 184-185 M 5
Chan-hua = Zhanhua 190-191 FG 3
Chania 136-137 KL 8
Chaniōn, Kolpos - 136-137 KL 8
Chanka, ozero - 178-179 Z 9
Chankiang—Zhanjiang 184-185 L 7
Channāb = Chenab 180-181 M 4
Channel Islands [GB] 132 E 7
Channel Islands [USA] 150-151 CD 9
Channel Islands National Park = Anacapa Island, Santa Barbara Island 150-151 D 9
Channel-Port-aux-Basques 144-145 Z8
Channing, MI 152-153 MN 2
Channing, TX 154-155 DE 3
Chansi = Shanxi 184-185 L 4
Chanskoje, ozero - 140-141 J 3
Chantaburi = Chanthaburi 186-187 D 4
Chantada 134-135 CD 7
Chantajka 178-179 PQ 4
Chantajskoje, ozero - 178-179 QR 4
Chanten en Mansen, Nationaal Gebied der - 178-179 L-P 5
Chan Tengri, pik - 180-181 MN 2
Chanthaburi 186-187 D 4
Chantong = Shandong 184-185 M 4
Chantrey Inlet 144-145 RS 4
Chantye dos Mansi, Circun- Scrição Nacional dos - 126-127 V-X 3
Chanty-Mansijsk 178-179 M 5
Chanty y los Mansi, Circunscripción Nacional de los - 178-179 L-P 5
Chañar 162 C 4
Chañaral [RCH ↖ Copiapó] 162 B 3
Chañaral, Isla - 162 B 3
Chanute, KS 152-153 J 7
Chao-an = Zhao'an 190-191 F 10
Chao-an Wan = Zhao'an Wan 190-191 F 10
Chao-ch'êng = Jiaocheng 190-191 CD 3
Chaochow = Chao'an 184-185 M 7
Chaohsien = Zhao Xian 190-191 E 3
Chao-hsien = Zhaoxian 190-191 G 4
Chao Hu 184-185 M 5
Chao-i = Chaoyi 190-191 BC 4
Chao Phraya, Mae Nam - 186-187 CD 3-4
Chaoping = Zhaoping 190-191 C 9
Chaor He 184-185 N 2
Chaotung = Zhaotong 184-185 J 6
Chao-t'ung = Zhaotong 184-185 J 6
Chao Xian 190-191 FG 6
Chaoyang [TJ, Guangdong] 184-185 M 7
Chaoyang [TJ, Liaoning] 184-185 MN 3
Ch'ao-yang-chên = Huinan 184-185 O 3
Chaoyi 190-191 BC 4
Chao-yüan = Zhaoyuan 190-191 H 3
Chaozhou 184-185 M 7
Chapada da Veadeiros, Parque Nacional dos - 158-159 K 7
Chapada Diamantina 158-159 L 7
Chapada dos Guimarães 160-161 E 1
Chapadinha 158-159 L 5
Chapala, Lago de - 146-147 F 7
Chapčeranga 178-179 V 8
Chapel Hill, NC 148-149 D 7
Chapel Hill, TN 154-155 M 3
Chaperito, NM 154-155 C 3
Chapman, MT 152-153 BC 1
Cha-p'o = Zhapo 190-191 C 11
Chappell, NE 152-153 E 5
Chapra 180-181 N 5
Chaqui 158-159 F 8
Chá'r, Jebel - = Jabal Shā'r 182-183 GH 5
Charabali 140-141 N 3
Charadai 162 E 3
Charagua 158-159 G 8
Charagua, Cordillera de - 158-159 G 8-9
Char Ajrag 184-185 KL 2
Charaña 158-159 F 8
Charbin = Harbin 184-185 O 2
Chār Burjak 180-181 J 4
Charcas 146-147 F 7
Charco, El - 154-155 BC 6
Charcos de Figueroa 154-155 DE 7
Charcos de Risa 154-155 D 7
Charcot, Île - 121 C 29
Chārchān 184-185 F 4
Chārchān Darya 184-185 F 4
Char Chorin 184-185 J 2
Char Choto 184-185 J 3
Chardāvol 182-183 M 6
Chardon, OH 148-149 C 4
Charente 134-135 G 6
Chargla = Hargla 138-139 F 5
Char Gov' 184-185 GH 3
Chari 166-167 H 6
Chārikār 180-181 K 3-4
Char Irčis 184-185 F 2
Chariton, IA 152-153 K 5
Charitona Lapteva, bereg 178-179 Q 3-R 2
Chariton River 152-153 K 5-6
Charity 158-159 H 3
Charkiv 120 D 13-14
Charleroi 134-135 K 3
Charles, Cape - 146-147 LM 4
Charles City, IA 152-153 K 4
Charles Island 144-145 VW 5
Charleston, IL 152-153 MN 6
Charleston, MO 154-155 L 2
Charleston, MS 154-155 KL 3-4
Charleston, SC 146-147 KL 5
Charleston, TN 154-155 N 3
Charleston, WV 146-147 K 4
Charleston Peak 150-151 F 7
Charlestown 146-147 O 8
Charlestown [ZA] 174-175 HJ 4
Charlestown, IN 152-153 O 6
Charlesville 168-169 F 4
Charleville [AUS] 194-195 J 5
Charleville-Mézières 134-135 K 4
Charlevoix, MI 152-153 O 3
Charlevoix, Lake - 152-153 O 3
Charlotte, MI 152-153 O 4
Charlotte, NC 146-147 KL 4-5
Charlotte, TN 154-155 M 2
Charlotte, TX 154-155 F 6
Charlotte Amalie 146-147 O 8
Charlotte Harbor 146-147 K 6
Charlottenberg 130-131 E 8
Charlottesville, VA 146-147 L 4
Charlottetown 144-145 Y 8
Charlottetown = Roseau 146-147 O 8
Charlton 196 F 6
Charlton Island 144-145 UV 7
Charlu 138-139 H 3
Char Narijn uul 184-185 K 3
Char nuur [MVR] 184-185 G 2
Char nuur [TJ] 184-185 H 4
Charolais, Monts du - 134-135 K 5
Charovsk 178-179 G 6
Charqi, Jebel ech- = Jabal ar-Ruwāq 182-183 G 5-6
Charqiliq 184-185 F 4
Charters Towers 194-195 J 3-4
Chartres 134-135 H 4
Char us nuur 184-185 G 2
Chasan 188-189 H 1
Chasav'urt 140-141 N 5
Chascomús 162 E 5
Chase City, VA 148-149 D 6
Chasŏng 188-189 F 2
Chassahowitzka Bay 148-149 b 2
Chašuri 140-141 L 5-6
Chatanga 178-179 TU 3
Chatan gol 184-185 K 3
Chatangskij zaliv 178-179 UV 3
Châteaubriant 134-135 G 5
Château-du-Loir 134-135 H 5
Châteaudun 134-135 H 4
Châteaulin 134-135 EF 4
Châteauroux 134-135 H 5
Château-Thierry 134-135 J 4
Châtellerault 134-135 H 5
Chatfield, MN 152-153 K 4
Chatgal 184-185 HJ 1
Chatham [CDN, New Brunswick] 144-145 XY 8
Chatham [CDN, Ontario] 144-145 U 9
Chatham, LA 154-155 J 4
Chatham, NY 148-149 G 3
Chatham, VA 148-149 D 6
Chatham = Isla San Cristóbal 158-159 B 5
Chatham, Îles - 194-195 Q 8
Chatham, Isla - 162 B 8
Chatham Islands 194-195 Q 8
Chatham Strait 144-145 K 6
Châtillon 136-137 B 3
Châtillon-sur-Seine 134-135 K 5
Chatom, AL 154-155 L 5
Chatsworth 148-149 C 2
Chatsworth, GA 154-155 N 3
Chattahoochee, FL 154-155 N 5
Chattahoochee River 146-147 JK 5
Chattanooga, TN 146-147 J 4
Chattarpur = Chhatarpur 180-181 M 6
Châu Đôc = Châu Phu 186-187 E 4
Chaumont 134-135 K 4
Chaŭn-do 188-189 EF 5
Châu Phu 186-187 E 4
Chautauqua Lake 148-149 D 3
Chautavara 138-139 J 2
Chaux-de-Fonds, La - 133 C 5
Chavast 180-181 K 2
Chaves 134-135 D 8
Chaves [BR] 158-159 K 5
Chaves, NM 154-155 C 4
Chaves, Isla - = Isla Santa Cruz 158-159 AB 5
Chavib Deh 182-183 N 7
Chaviva 158-159 E 4
Chaya - Drayā 184-185 H 5
Ch'a-yü = Dsayul 184-185 H 6
Chazhen 190-191 B 5
Chazón 162 D 4
Cheat Mountain 148-149 CD 5
Cheat River 148-149 D 5
Cheb 133 F 3
Chebāyesh, Al- = Al-Jaza'ir 182-183 M 7
Chebir, Uáu el - = Wādī Bay al Kabīr 166-167 GH 2
Cheboygan, MI 146-147 K 2
Chech, Erg - = 'Irq ash-Shaykh 166-167 D 3-4
Chechaouène = Shifshāwn 166-167 CD 1
Chechenes e Ingush, República Autónoma de los - 140-141 MN 5
Checheng = Zhecheng 190-191 E 4
Checheno-Ingush Autonomous Republic 140-141 MN 5
Chech'on 188-189 G 4
Checotha, OK 154-155 H 3
Checoslováquia 133 FK 4
Chedâdi, El- = Ash-Shiddādī 182-183 J 4
Cheektowaga, NY 148-149 DE 3
Cheepie 194-195 HJ 5
Cheesman Lake 152-153 D 6
Chefoo = Yantai 184-185 N 4
Chefu = Yantai 184-185 N 4
Chegga = Ash-Shaqqāt 166-167 C3
Chegutu 168-169 GH 6
Chehalis, WA 150-151 B 2
Chehalis River 150-151 B 2
Chehel-e Chashmeh, Kūhhā-ye - 182-183 M 5
Cheikh Ahmed = Shaykh Ahmad 182-183 J 4
Cheikh Hilâl = Shaykh Hilāl 182-183 G 5
Cheikh Salâh = Shaykh Salāh 182-183 J 4
Cheikh Zerâfa = Zilāf 182-183 G 6
Cheju 184-185 O 5
Cheju-do 184-185 NO 5
Cheju-haehyŏp 184-185 O 5
Chê-jung = Zherong 190-191 GH 4
Chekiang = Zhejiang 184-185 MN 6
Chekkā, Rās - = Rā's ash-Shikk'ah 182-183 F 5
Chela, Serra da - 168-169 D 6
Chelan, WA 150-151 CD 2
Chelan, Lake - 150-151 C 1
Chê-lang Chiao = Zhelang Jiao 190-191 E 10
Chélia, Djebel - = Jabal Shilyah 166-167 F1
Cheline 174-175 L 2
Chê-ling Kuan = Zheling Guan 184-185 L 6
Chelm 133 L 3
Chelmińskre , Pojezierze - 133 J 2
Chełmża 133 J 2
Chelsea, MI 152-153 OP 4
Chelsea, OK 154-155 H 2
Chelsea, VT 148-149 G 2-3
Cheltenham 132 EF 6
Cheltenham, PA 148-149 F 4
Chelyuskin, Cape - = mys Čel'uskin 178-179 UV 2
Chelleh Khāneh, Kūh-e - 182-183 N 4
Chemawa, OR 150-151 B 3
Chemba 168-169 H 6
Chemehuevi Valley Indian Reservation 150-151 F 8
Chemnitz 133 F 3
Chemulpo = Inch'ŏn 184-185 O 4
Chemult, OR 150-151 C 4
Chenab 180-181 M 4
Chên-an = Zhen'an 190-191 B 5
Ch'ên-ch'i = Chenxi 184-185 L 6
Ch'ên-chia-chiang = Chenjiajiang 190-191 GH 4
Chên-chiang = Zhenjiang 184-185 M 5
Ch'ên-chou = Yuanling 184-185 L 6
Cheney, KS 152-153 H 7
Cheney, WA 150-151 E 2
Chên-fan = Minqin 184-185 J 4
Chengbu 190-191 C 8
Chêng-chia-i = Zhengjiayi 190-191 C 7
Ch'êng-chiang = Chengjiang 184-185 J 7
Chengde 184-185 M 3
Chengdong Hu 190-191 F 5
Chengdu 184-185 J 5
Chenghai 190-191 F 10
Chengjiang 184-185 J 7
Chengkiang = Chengjiang 184-185 J 7
Chengkou 184-185 K 5
Cheng-kung 190-191 H 10
Chengmai 184-185 KL 8
Chêng-ning = Zhengning 190-191 B 4
Chêng-pu = Chengbu 190-191 C 8
Ch'êng-shan Chiao = Chengshan Jiao 190-191 J 3
Chengshan Jiao 190-191 J 3
Chengteh = Chengde 184-185 M 3
Chengting = Zhengding 190-191 E 2
Chengtu = Chengdu 184-185 J 5
Chengwu 190-191 E 4
Cheng-Xian = Sheng Xian 184-185 N 6
Chengxi Hu 190-191 EF 5
Chengyang 190-191 GH 7
Chengyang = Zhengyang 190-191 E 5
Chêng-yang-kuan = Zhengyangguan 190-191 F 5
Chengzitan 188-189 D 3
Chenhai = Zhenhai 190-191 H 6-7
Chenjiajiang 190-191 GH 4
Chenjiazhuang 190-191 G 3
Chên-hsi = Bar Köl 184-185 G 3
Chenkiang = Zhenjiang 184-185 M 5
Chennapattanam = Madras 180-181 N 8
Chênng-ho = Zhenghe 190-191 G 8
Chenoa, IL 152-153 M 5
Chenping = Zhenping 190-191 D 5
Chensi = Bar Köl 184-185 G 3
Chensi = Shanxi 184-185 L 4
Chentiin nuruu 184-185 K 2
Chentij = 15 ◁ 184-185 L 2
Chên-t'ung = Zhentong 190-191 GH 5
Chenxi 184-185 L 6
Chen Xian 184-185 L 6
Chenyang = Shenyang 184-185 NO 3
Chenyuan = Zhenyuan [TJ, Guizhou] 190-191 B 8
Chenyuan = Zhenyuan [TJ, Yunnan] 184-185 J 7
Chên-yüan = Zhenyuan [TJ, Yunnan] 184-185 J 7
Chepan 190-191 FG 8
Chepes 162 C 4
Chequamegon Bay 152-153 L 2
Cher 134-135 J 5
Cherangani 171 C 2
Cheraw, CO 152-153 E 6
Cheraw, SC 148-149 CD 7
Cherbourg 134-135 G 4
Cherchen = Chārchān 184-185 F 4
Cheren = Keren 166-167 M 5
Cherepon 172-173 EF 3
Chergui, Chott ech - = Ash-Shaṭṭ ash-Sharqi 166-167 DE 2
Cherkassi = Čerkassy 140-141 EF 2
Cherlen gol 184-185 KL 2
Cherlen gol = Herlen He 184-185 M 2
Chernovtsy = Černovcy 140-141 B 2
Cherokee, IA 152-153 J 4
Cherokee, OK 154-155 F 2
Cherokee, TX 154-155 F 5
Cherokee Lake 154-155 O 2
Cherrapunj = Cherrapunjee 180-181 P 5
Cherrapunjee 180-181 P 5
Cherry 194-195 N 2
Cherry Creek 152-153 E 3
Cherry Creek, NV 150-151 F 6
Cherry Creek, SD 152-153 F 3
Cherrypatch Ridge 152-153 B 1
Cherryvale, ks 154-155 H 2
Cherson [SU] 140-141 F 3
Chersones, mys - 140-141 F 4
Chesaning, MI 152-153 OP 4
Chesapeake, VA 146-147 LM 4
Chesapeake Bay 146-147 L 4
Cheshire, OR 150-151 B 3
Chesley 148-149 C 2
Chester 132 E 5
Chester, CA 150-151 C 5
Chester, IL 152-153 M 7
Chester, MT 150-151 H 1
Chester, NE 152-153 H 5
Chester, PA 148-149 F 5
Chester, SC 148-149 C 7
Chesterfield 132 F 5
Chesterfield, Île - 168-169 K 6
Chesterfield, Îles - 194-195 L 3
Chesterfield Inlet [CDN, ∪] 144-145 ST 5
Chesterfield Inlet [CDN, ●] 144-145 ST 5
Chestertown, MD 148-149 EF 5
Chesuncook Lake 148-149 HJ 1-2
Cheta [SU, ~] 178-179 S 3
Cheta [SU, ●] 178-179 S 3
Chetek, WI 152-153 L 3
Chetlat Island 180-181 L 8
Chetopa, KS 154-155 H 2
Chetumal 146-147 J 8
Chetumal, Bahia de - 146-147 J 8
Cheviot, The - 132 EF 4
Cheviot Hills 132 E 4
Chewelah, WA 150-151 DE 1
Chê-yang = Zherong 190-191 GH 8
Cheyenne, OK 154-155 F 3
Cheyenne, TX 154-155 D 5
Cheyenne, WY 146-147 F 3
Cheyenne Pass 152-153 D 5
Cheyenne River 146-147 F 3
Cheyenne River Indian Reservation 152-153 F 3
Cheyenne Wells, CO 152-153 E 6
Chhamdo 184-185 H 5
Chhaprā = Chapra 180-181 N 5
Chhārikār = Chārikār 180-181 K 3-4
Chhatarpur [IND, Madhya Pradesh] 180-181 M 6
Chhattisgarh 180-181 N 6
Chhergundo 184-185 H 5
Chhergundo Zhou = Yushu Zangzu Zizhizhou 184-185 GH 5
Chhibchang Tsho 184-185 G 5
Chhindwāra = Chhindwara [IND ← Seoni] 180-181 M 6
Chhindwara [IND ← Seoni] 180-181 M 6
Chhōṭā Andamān = Little Andaman 180-181 P 8
Chhōṭā Nikōbār = Little Nicobar 180-181 P 9
Chhumar 184-185 G 4-5
Chhushul 184-185 FG 6
Chia-ho = Jiahe 190-191 D 9
Chia-hsien = Jia Xian [TJ, Heran] 190-191 D 5
Chia-hsien = Jia Xian [TJ, Shanxi] 190-191 C 2
Chia-hsing = Jiaxing 184-185 N 5
Chia-i = Jiayi 184-185 MN 7
Chia-li 190-191 GH 10
Chia-li = Lharugö 184-185 G 5
Chia-li-chuang = Chia-li 190-191 GH 10
Chia-ling Chiang = Jialing Jiang 184-185 K 5
Chia-lu Ho = Jialu He 190-191 E 4
Chia-mu-szŭ = Jiamusi 184-185 P 2
Chi-an = Ji'an [TJ, Jiangxi] 184-185 LM 6
Chi-an = Ji'an [TJ, Jilin] 188-189 EF 2
Chiang-chou = Xinjiang 184-185 L 4
Chiang Dao 186-187 CD 3
Chiange 168-169 D 6
Chiang-hsi = Jiangxi 184-185 LM 6
Chiang-hung = Jianghong 190-191 B 11
Chiang Khan 186-187 D 3
Chiang-k'ou = Jiangkou [TJ, Guangxi Zhuangzu Zizhiqu] 190-191 C 10
Chiang-k'ou = Jiangkou [TJ, Guizhou] 190-191 B 8
Chiang-ling = Jiangling 184-185 L 5
Chiang-lo = Jiangle 190-191 F 8
Chiang Mai 186-187 C 3
Chiang-mên = Xinhui 190-191 D 10
Chiang-ning-chên = Jiangning 190-191 G 6
Chiang-p'u = Jiangpu 190-191 G 5
Chiang Rai 186-187 CD 3
Chiang-shan = Jiangshan 190-191 G 7
Chiang-su = Jiangsu 184-185 MN 5
Chiang-yin = Jiangyin 190-191 H 5
Chiao-chou Wan = Jiaozhou Wan 190-191 H 3-4
Chiao-ho-k'ou = Jiaohekou 190-191 B 4
Chiao-ling = Jiaoling 190-191 EF 9
Chiapa, Rio - = Rio Grande 146-147 H 8
Chiapas 146-147 H 8
Chiari 136-137 CD 3
Chia-shan = Jiashan [TJ, Anhui] 190-191 G 5
Chia-shan = Jiashan [TJ, Zhejiang] 190-191 H 6
Chia-ting = Jiading 190-191 H 6
Chiau 174-175 K 3
Chi-an Ho = Jiyun He 190-191 F 2
Chiavari 136-137 C 3
Chiavenna 136-137 C 2
Chia -yü = Jiayu 190-191 D 6-7
Chiba 188-189 N 5
Chibabava 168-169 H 7
Chibemba 168-169 DE 6
Chibia 168-169 D 6

Chibinogorsk = Kirovsk 178-179 EF 4
Chibougamau 144-145 VW 7-8
Chiburi-jima 188-189 J 5
Chicacole = Shrikakulam 180-181 N 7
Chicago, IL 146-147 J 3
Chicago Heights, IL 152-153 N 5
Chicapa, Rio - 168-169 F 4
Chic-Chocs, Monts - 144-145 X 8
Chickamauga, GA 154-155 LM 5
Chickamauga Lake 154-155 N 3
Chickasaw, AL 154-155 LM 5
Chiclayo 158-159 CD 6
Chico, CA 146-147 B 4
Chico, Rio - [RA, Chubut] 162 C 6
Chico, Rio - [RA, Chubut] 162 C 6
Chico, Rio - [YV] 158-159 F 2
Chico, Rio - [RA, Santa Cruz ⊲ Bahia Grande] 162 C 7
Chico, Rio - [RA, Santa Cruz ⊲ Rio Gallegos] 162 C 7
Chico, TX 154-155 G 4
Chicoa 168-169 H 6
Chicoana 162 CD 3
Chicoma Peak = Tschicoma Peak 154-155 BC 2-3
Chiconomo 171 CD 6
Chicopee, MA 148-149 G 3
Chicoutimi 144-145 WX 8
Chicualacuala 174-175 JK 2
Chicualacuala 168-169 H 7
Ch'i-ch = Qiqihar 184-185 N 2
Chichagof Island 144-145 J 6
Chichén Itzá 146-147 J 7
Chichester 132 F 6
Chi-ch'i ⊲Jixi 190-191 Q 3
Chichocane 174-175 L 2
Chidenguele 174-175 L 2
Chidley, Cape - 144-145 Y 5
Chi-do 188-189 EF 5
Chiefland, FL 148-149 b 2
Chiefs Point 152-153 G 3
Chieh-hsiu = Jiexiu 190-191 CD 3
Chiehmo = Chärchän 184-185 F 4
Chieh-shih-shih = Jieshi 190-191 E 10
Chieh-shih Wan = Jieshi Wan 190-191 E 10
Chieh-yang = Jieyang 190-11 F 10
Chiemsee 133 F 5
Ch'i-en-an = Qian'an 190-191 G 1
Chien-ch'ang = Jianchang [TJ → Benxi] 188-189 D 2
Chien-ch'ang = Jianchang [TJ ⊲ Jinzhou] 188-189 B 2
Chien-ch'ang = Nancheng 190-191 F 8
Chien-ch'ang-ying = Jianchangying 190-191 G 1
Ch'ien-chi = Qianji 190-191 G 4-5
Ch'ien-chiang = Qianjiang [TJ, Guangxi Zhuangzu Zizhiqu] 190-191 B 10
Ch'ien-chiang = Qianjiang [TJ, Hubei] 184-185 L 5
Ch'ien-chiang = Qianjiang [TJ, Sichuan] 190-191 B 7
Chiengi 168-169 G 4
Chiengmai = Chiang Mai 186-187 C 3
Chien-Ho = Jianhe [TJ, ~] 188-189 D2
Chien-ho = Jianhe [TJ, ●] 190-191 B 8
Ch'ien-ho = Qian Xian 190-191 B 4
Chien-hsien = Qian Xian 190-191 B 4
Chien-li = Jianli 190-191 D 7
Chien-ning = Jianning 190-191 E 8
Chien-ou = Jian'ou 184-185 M 6
Chien-ou = Jian'ou 184-185 M 6
Chien-p'ing = Jianping 188-189 B 2
Chien-p'ing = Langxi 190-191 G 6
Chien-shan = Qianshan 190-191 F 6
Chien-shui = Jianshui 184-185 J 7
Chien-tê = Jiande 190-191 G 6
Chien-wei = Qianwei 188-189 C 2
Chien-yang = Jianyang [TJ, Fujian] 190-191 FG 8
Chien-yang = Jianyang [TJ, Sichuan] 184-185 JK 5
Ch'ien-yang = Qianyang 190-191 C 8
Chien-yu Ho = Qianyou He 190-191 B 5
Chieti 136-137 F 4
Chifeng 184-185 M 3
Chifre, Serra do - 158-159 L 8
Chignik, AK 144-145 E 6
Chigyong 188-189 J 3
Ch'ih-ch'i = Chixi 190-191 D 10-11
Chih-chiang = Zhijiang [TJ, Hubei] 190-191 C 6
Chih-chiang = Zhijiang [TJ, Hunan] 184-185 KL 6
Chihe 190-191 FG 5
Ch'ih-fêng = Chifeng 184-185 M 3
Ch'ih-ho = Chihe 190-191FG 5
Chih-ho = Chihe 190-191 E 4
Chihkiang = Zhijiang 184-185 KL 6
Chih-li Wan = Bo Hai 184-185 M 4
Chi-hsi = Jixi 184-185 P 2
Chi-hsien = Ji Xian [TJ, Henan] 190-191 E 4
Chi-hsien = Ji Xian [TJ, Shanxi] 190-191 D 3
Chi-hsien = Ji Xian [TJ, Hebei = Beijing] 190-191 F 1
Chi-hsien = Ji Xian [TJ, Hebei ⊲ Shijiazhuang] 190-191 E 2
Ch'i-hsien = Qi Xian [TJ, Shanxi] 190-191 D 3
Ch'i-hsien = Qi Xian [TJ, Henan ⊲ Kaifeng] 190-191 E 4
Ch'i-hsien = Qi Xian [TJ, Henan ⊲ Xinxiang] 190-191 DE 4
Chihtan = Zhidan 190-191 C 3
Chi-hu 190-191 H 9-10
Chihuahua 146-147 E 6
Ch'i-i = Qiyi 190-191 D 5
Chii-san = Chiri-san 188-189 F 5
Chike = Chixi 190-191 D 10-11
Chikugo 188-189 H 6
Chikwawa 168-169 HJ 6
Chilapa de Alvarez 146-147 G 8
Chilas 180-181 L 3
Chilcoot, CA 146-147 J 7
Chilcoot, CA 146-147 J 7
Childersburg, AL 154-155 M 4
Childress, TX 154-155 F 3
Chile, Cuenca de - 124-125 E 7-F 6
Chile, Bacia do - 124-125 E 7-F 6

Chile Basin 124-125 EF 6-7
Chilebecken 198-199 O 5-6
Chilecito [RA, La Rioja] 162 C 3
Chilete 158-159 D 6
Chilhowee, MO 152-153 K 6
Chili 162 B 5-C 2
Chili, Bassin du - 124-125 E 7-F 6
Chilia, Bratul - 136-137 N 3
Chilibekken 124-125 EF 6-7
Chilibre 146-147 b 2
Chilicote 154-155 C 6
Ch'i-lien-chên = Qilizhen 190-191 B 4
Ch'i-lien Shan = Qilian Shan 184-185 HJ 4
Chilika Hrada = Chilka Lake 180-181 NO 7
Chilka Lake 180-181 NO 7
Chilko Lake 144-145 M 7
Chilkoot, Isla de - 162 AB 4
Chilok 178-179 UV 7
Chilonga 171 B 5-6
Chilongozi 171 B 5
Chiloquin, OR 150-151 C 4
Chilpancingo de los Bravos 146-147 G 8
Chiltern Hills 132 F 6
Chilton, WI 152-153 M 3
Chilung = Kee-lung 184-185 N 6
Chilwa, Lake - 168-169 J 6
Chillán 162 B 5
Chill Chainnigh = Kilkenny 132 C 5
Chillicothe, IL 152-153 M 5
Chillicothe, MO 146-147 H 3-4
Chillicothe, OH 146-147 K 4
Chillicothe, TX 154-155 F 3
Chilly 140-141 Q 7
Chilly, ID 150-151 FG 3
Chiman tagh 184-185 FG 4
Chimanimani [EC, ▲] 158-159 D 5
Chimbote 158-159 C 6
Chimei Hsü = Ta-Yü 190-191 G 10
Chimkent 132 D 3
Chimki 138-139 L 5-6
Chimney Peak = One Tree Peak 171 B 6
Chi-mo = Jimo 190-191 H 3
Chimoio 168-169 H 6
Chimpay 162 C 5
Chimpembe 171 B 5
China, Republik - 184-185 N 7
China, Meridional, Bacia da - 186-187 FG 3-4
China Lake, CA 150-151 E 8
China Meridional, Cuenca de - 186-187 FG 3-4
China Meridional, Mar da - 186-187 E 5-G 2
China Meridional, Mar de - 186-187 E 5-G 3
Chinan = Jinan 184-185 M 4
China Oriental, Mar da - 186-187 E 5-G 2
China Oriental, Mar de - 184-185 N 6-O 5
Chinapa 150-151 HJ 10
China Point 150-151 C 9
Chinati Peak 154-155 C 6
Chinbo 188-189 G 4
Chincoteague, VA 148-149 F 6
Chincoteague Bay 154-155 D 7
Chincha Alta 158-159 D 7
Chin-ch'êng = Jincheng 184-185 L 4
Chin Ch'i = Jin Xi [TJ, ~] 184-185 L 6
Chin-ch'i = Jinxi [TJ, ●] 190-191 F 8
Chinchilla 194-195 K 5
Chinchilla de Monte-Aragón 134-135 G 9
Chinchorro, Banco - 146-147 J 8
Chinchow = Jinzhou 184-185 N 3
Chinde 168-169 J 6
Chin-do [ROK, ⊙] 188-189 EF 5
Chindo [ROK, ●] 188-189 F 5
Chine 184-185 E-K 5
Chine Méridionale, Mer de - 186-187 E 5-G 3
Chine Orientale, Mer de - 184-185 N 6-O 5
Chinese music 184-185 K 4
Chingan = Jing'an 190-191 E 7
Ching-chang Ho = Qingzhang Dongyuan 190-191 D 3
Ching-chi = Jingzhi 190-191 GH 3
Ching-chiang = Jingjiang 190-191 H 5-6
Ching Chiang = Qing Jiang 190-191 C 6
Ch'ing-chien = Qingjian 190-191 D 3
Ching-ch'uan = Yinchuan 184-185 K 4
Ch'ing-fêng = Qingfeng 190-191 E 4
Ch'ing Hai = Chöch nuur 184-185 H 4
Ching-hai = Jinghai 190-191 F 2
Ch'ing-hai = Qinghai 184-185 GH 4
Ching-ho = Jinghe [TJ, ●] 184-185 D 3
Ching-ho = Jing He [TJ, ~] 190-191 B 4
Ch'ing-ho = Qinghe 190-191 E 3
Ch'ing-ho chên = Qinghezhen 190-191 F 3
Ch'ing-ho-mêng = Qinghemen 188-189 C 2
Ch'ing-ho-mêng = Qinghemen 188-189 C 2
Ching-hsien = Jing Xian [TJ, Anhui] 190-191 G 6
Ching-hsien = Jing Xian [TJ, Hunan] 190-191 B 8
Ching-hsing = Jingxing 190-191 DE 2
Ching-jang = Jingyang 184-185 J 7
Ching-lu = Qinglian 190-191 D 9
Ch'ing-lou = Qinglu 190-191 F 8
Ching-lo = Jingle 190-191 CD 2
Ching-mên = Jingmen 190-191 D 6
Ching-ning = Jingning 184-185 K 4
Ching-po Hu = Jingbo Hu 190-191 H 6
Ch'ing-p'u = Qingpu 190-191 H 6

Ching Shan = Jing Shan [TJ, ▲▲] 190-191 C 6
Ching-shan = Jingshan [TJ, ●] 190-191 D 6
Chis-tsê = Jize 190-191 E 2
Chittagong = Châṭṭagām 180-181 P 6
Chittadurga = Chitradurga 180-181 M 8
Chittoor = Chittor 180-181 M 8
Chittaurgarrh = Chittaurgarh 180-181 L 6
Chittoor = Chittor 180-181 M 8
Chittoor = Chittor 180-181 M 8
Ch'i-tung = Qidong [TJ, Jiangsu] 190-191 H 6
Ch'i-tung = Qidong [TJ, Hunan] 190-191 D 8
Ching-tzŭ-kuan = Jingziguan 190-191 C 5
Ching-yang = Jingyang 190-191 B 4
Ching-yang = Qingyang [TJ, Anhui] 190-191 FG 6
Ching-yang = Qingyang [TJ, Gansu] 184-185 K 4
Ch'ing-yüan = Jingyuan 184-185 JK 4
Ch'ing-yüan = Qingyuan [TJ, Fujian] 190-191 G 8
Ch'ing-yüan = Qingyuan [TJ, Liaoning] 188-189 E 1
Chinhae 188-189 G 5
Chinhae-man 188-189 G 5
Chin In Ho = Qin He 190-191 D 4
Chinhoyi 168-169 GH 6
Chin-hsiang = Jinxiang [TJ, Shandong] 190-191 EF 4
Chin-hsiang = Jinxiang [TJ, Zhejiang] 190-191 H 8
Chin-hsien = Jinxian [TJ, Hebei] 190-191 E 2
Chin-hsien = Jinxian [TJ, Jiangxi] 190-191 F 7
Chin-hsien = Jin Xian [TJ, Liaoning ↗ Jinzhou] 188-189 C 2
Chin-hsien = Jin Xian [TJ, Liaoning ↓ Lüda] 184-185 N 4
Chin-hsien = Jinzhou 184-185 N 3
Chinhsien = Jin Xian 188-189 C 2
Chin-hua = Jinhua 184-185 MN 6
Ch'in-huang-tao = Qinhuangdao 184-185 MN 3-4
Chinju 184-185 O 4
Chinko 166-167 J 7
Chin-k'ou = Jinkou 190-191 D 6
Chinle, AZ 150-151 J 7
Chinle Valley 150-151 J 7
Chin Ling = Qin Ling 184-185 KL 5
Chin-mên Tao 184-185 M 7
Chinnamp'o = Nampo 184-185 NO 4
Chin-niu = Jinniu 190-191 E 6-7
Chinon 134-135 H 5
Chinook, MT 152-153 B 1
Ch'in-an = Qin'an 184-185 K 5
Chinandega 146-147 J 9
Chinqualão = Zhenjiang 184-185 N 5
Chinsali 168-169 H 5
Chin-sha Chiang = Jinsha Jiang 184-185 J 6
Chin-shan = Jinshan 190-191 H 6
Ch'in Shui = Qingshui Jiang 190-191 B 8
Ch'in-shui = Qinshui 190-191 D 4
Chinsiang = Jinxiang 190-191 EF 4
Chinsura 180-181 O 6
Chin-t'an = Jintan 190-191 G 6
Chinwangtao = Qinhuangdao 184-185 MN 3-4
Chinwhetha Pyinnei 186-187 B 2
Ch'in-yang = Qinyang 184-185 L 4
Chinyŏng 188-189 G 5
Chin-yüan = Jinyuan 190-191 D 3
Chin-yüan = Qinyuan 190-191 D 3
Chin-yüan = Qinyuan 190-191 D 3
Chioco 168-169 H 6
Chiòggia 136-137 E 3
Chios [GR, ⊙] 136-137 L 6
Chios [GR, ●] 136-137 M 6
Chipata 168-169 H 5
Chipili 171 B 5
Chipinge 168-169 H 7
Chipley, FL 154-155 N 7
Chipley, GA 154-155 N 4
Chipoka 171 C 6
Chiporiro 168-169 H 6
Chippewa Falls, WI 152-153 L 3
Chippewa Flowage 152-153 L 3
Chippewa Reservoir = Chippewa Flowage 152-153 L 3
Chippewa River [USA, Michigan] 152-153 KL 3
Chippewa River [USA, Wisconsin] 152-153 KL 3
Chipre 180-181 C 3
Chipre 180-181 C 3
Chiputneticook Lakes 148-149 JK 2
Chiquimula 146-147 HJ 9
Chiquitos, Llanos de - 158-159 G 8
Chira 171 D 2
Chira Bazar 181-181 DE 4
Chiraz = Shīrāz 180-181 GJ 5
Chiredzi 168-169 H 7
Chirfa 166-167 G 4
Chiricahua National Monument 150-151 J 9-10
Chiricahua Peak 150-151 J 10
Chirikof Island 144-145 EF 6
Chiriquí, Golfo de - 146-147 K 10
Chiriquí, Laguna de - 146-147 K 9-10
Chiromo 168-169 J 6
Chirripó Grande, Cerro - 146-147 K 10
Chirundu 168-169 G 6
Chisamba 168-169 G 5-6
Chisel Lake 144-145 QR 7
Chishtian Mandi = Chishtiyān Mandi 180-181 L 5
Chishtiyān Mandi 180-181 L 5
Chishui = Jishui 190-191 E 8
Chisimaio = Kismaayo 168-169 K 3
Chisinău 140-141 D 3
Chislaviči 138-139 K 6
Chisos Mountains 154-155 D 6
Chitado 168-169 C 5
Chita-hantō 188-189 L 5
Ch'i-t'ai = Qitai 184-185 FG 3
Chitambo 171 B 6
Chitembo 168-169 E 5
Ch'i-t'ou-chên = Qitouzhen 190-191 H 6
Chitipa 168-169 H 4
Chitose 188-189 b 2

Chitradurga 180-181 M 8
Chitrāl 180-181 L 3
Chitré 146-147 K 10
Chittagong = Châṭṭagām 180-181 P 6
Chittagong = Châṭṭagām 180-181 M 8
Chittaurgarrh = Chittaurgarh 180-181 L 6
Chittoor = Chittor 180-181 M 8
Chittor 180-181 M 8
Chi'i-tung = Qidong [TJ, Jiangsu] 190-191 H 6
Ch'i-tung = Qidong [TJ, Hunan] 190-191 D 8
Chiuchuan = Jiuquan 184-185 H 4
Chiu-ho-hsü = Jiuhe 190-191 E 10
Chiu-hsien = Qiu Xian 190-191 E 2
Chiuling Shan = Jiuling Shan 190-191 E 7
Chiu-lung Ch'i = Jiulong Xi 190-191 F 8
Chiu-lung Chiang = Jiulong Jiang 190-191 F 9
Chiu-lung Shan = Jiulong Shan 190-191 G 7
Chiuma, ostrov – Hiiumaa 138-139 CD 4
Ch'iu-p'u = Zhouzhi 190-191 AB 4
Chiu-shan Ch'ün-tao = Zhoushan Qundao 184-185 N 5-6
Chiu-shan Ch'ün-tao = Zhoushan Qundao 184-185 N 5
Chiuta, Lagoa - 168-169 J 6
Chiu-tao-liang = Jiudaoliang 190-191 BC 6
Chiu-tu Hsi 190-191 H 10
Chivasso 136-137 B 3
Chivay 158-159 E 8
Civilcoz 162 DE 4
Chivu 168-169 H 6
Chiwanda 168-169 HJ 5
Chiwefwe 171 B 6
Chiweta 168-169 H 5
Chixi 190-191 D 10-11
Chixoy, Rio - 146-147 H 8-9
Chi-yang = Jiyang [TJ, Fujian] 190-191 F 8
Chi-yang = Jiyang [TJ, Shandong] 190-191 F 3
Chi-yüan = Jiyuan 190-191 D 4
Ch'i-yüan = Qiyuan 190-191 D 4
Chizha 178-179 NO 4
Chloride, AZ 150-151 E 7
Chmeitiyé = Shmaytiyah 182-183 H 5
Chmelevoje 140-141 E 2
Chmel'nickij 140-141 C 2
Chmel'nik 140-141 CD 2
Chobe 168-169 F 6
Chobe National Park 168-169 FG 6
Chocaya 158-159 D 7
Chocca 158-159 D 7
Chocolate Mountains 150-151 F 9
Choconta 158-159 E 3
Chod-chiang = Chargilig 184-185 F 4
Chochi'wŏn 188-189 F 4
Chŏch Shili 184-185 G 4
Chŏch Shili uul 184-185 FG 4
Chodzamba 180-181 JK 3
Chodžeili 178-179 K 9
Chodžent = Leninabad 180-181 KL 2-3
Chodziez 133 H 2
Choele-Choel 162 CD 5
Chohsien = Zhuo Xian 190-191 E 2
Choibalsan = Čojbalsan 184-185 L 2
Chojna 133 FG 2
Chojnice 133 H 2
Chojnik 138-139 G 8
Chōkai-zan 188-189 MN 3
Chŏlamaṇḍala = Coromandel Coast 180-181 N 7-8
Cholame, CA 150-151 CD 8
Cho'ld = Chuld 184-185 K 2-3
Cholet 134-135 G 5
Cholgwan 188-189 G 3
Cholm 138-139 H 5
Cholmogorskaja 138-139 N 2
Cholmogory 178-179 O 5
Cholmsk 178-179 b 8
Cholm-Žirkovskij 138-139 JK 6
Cholopeniči 138-139 G 6
Cholos nuur 184-185 H 3
Ch'ŏlsan 188-189 E 3
Cho-lu = Zhuolu 190-191 E 1
Choluteca 146-147 J 9
Chŏlla-namdo 188-189 F 5
Chŏlla-pukto 188-189 F 5
Choma 168-169 G 6
Chomchon 134-135 W 9-10
Chomutovka 138-139 K 8
Chŏnan 188-189 F 4
Chonburi = Chon Buri 186-187 D 4
Chŏnch'ŏn 188-189 F 3
Chone 158-159 CD 5
Chong'an 190-191 F 8
Chŏngjin = Ch'ŏngjin 184-185 OP 3
Ch'ŏngjin 184-185 OP 3
Chongju = Ch'ŏngju 188-189 G 4
Chŏngju 184-185 O 4
Chŏngju 184-185 O 4
Chongli = Ch'ongjin 184-185 OP 3
Chongming Shui 190-191 B 8-9
Chongming 184-185 N 5
Chongoene 174-175 KL 3
Chongor 184-185 L 2
Chongqin-shi = Bajan Adraga 184-185 KL 2
Chongor Oboo Sum = Bajandalaj 184-185 J 2
Chongor Tagh = Qungur tagh 184-185 EF 2
Ch'ŏngp'yŏngch'ŏn 188-189 FG 4

Chongqing 184-185 K 6
Chongren 190-191 EF 8
Chŏngsan-do 188-189 F 5
Chongshanpai = Jitan 190-191 D 10
Chongsŏng 188-189 GH 1
Chongwu 190-191 G 9
Ch'ongyang [ROK] 188-189 F 4
Chongyang [TJ] 190-191 E 7
Chongyang = Zhongyang 190-191 D 3
Chongyang Xi 190-191 F 8
Chongyi 190-191 E 9
Chongzuo 184-185 K 7
Chonju 184-185 O 4
Chonouu 178-179 Za 8
Choolooj Gov' 184-185 H 3
Chopim, Rio - 160-161 F 6-7
Chopinzinho 160-161 F 6
Chop'or 178-179 U 7
Chor 178-179 Za 8
Chorasan = Khorāsān 180-181 H 3-4
Chöra Sfakion 136-137 L 8
Chordoğoj 178-179 W 5
Chor He 184-185 N 2
Chorlovo 138-139 M 6
Chorol 140-141 F 2
Chorrera, La - Chorrera [PA] 146-147 b 3
Chorsabad = Khorsabad 182-183 K 4
Chŏrwŏn 188-189 F 3
Chŏryŏng-do = Yŏng-do 188-189 G 5
Chorzele 133 K 2
Chorzów 133 J 3
Chŏsen-kakyŏ 184-185 O 5
Chos- shu Hsi 190-191 H 10
Chos-Malal 30 BC 5
Chosŏn-man = Tonghan-man 184-185 O 4
Choszczno 133 GH 2
Chota 158-159 GH 2
Chota Nāgpur 180-181 NO 6
Choteau, MT 150-151 G 2
Chotimsk 138-139 J 7
Chotin 140-141 C 2
Chotynec 138-139 K 7
Chou-chih = Zhouzhi 190-191 AB 4
Chou-k'ou-tien = Fangshan 190-191 E 1
Chou-kou = Zhouning 190-191 G 8
Chou Shan = Zhoushan Dao 184-185 N 5-6
Chou-shan Ch'ün-tao = Zhoushan Qundao 184-185 N 5
Chou-tang-p'an = Zhoudangfan 190-191 C 6
Chouteau, OK 154-155 H 2
Chou-ts'un = Zhoucun 190-191 FG 3
Chovd [MVR, ●] 184-185 G 2
Chovd [MVR, ✳ ⊲ 3 ⊲] 184-185 G 2
Chovd gol 184-185 G 2
Chövsgöl [MVR, ●] 184-185 KL 3
Chövsgöl [MVR, ✳] 184-185 J 1
Chövsgöl nuur 184-185 J 1
Chowan River 148-149 F 6
Chowan River = Zhouning 190-191 G 8
Chowchilla , CA 150-151 C 7
Chozapini, ozero - 140-141 L 6
Chrapovickaja Dača = Peredel 138-139 N 6
Chrenovoje 140-141 K 1
Chrisman, TX 152-153 N 4
Chrissiesmeer 174-175 J 4
Christchurch 194-195 OP 8
Christiana 174-175 F 4
Christian Island 148-149 C 2
Christiansburg, VA 148-149 CD 6
Christiansdorp = Qasigiangnuit 144-145 ba 3
Christie Bay 144-145 O 5
Christina, MT 152-153 B 2
Christinovka 140-141 DE 2
Christmas Creek 194-195 G 3
Christmas Island [AUS] 186-187 DE 9
Christoforovo 138-139 QR 3
Christoval, TX 154-155 E 5
Chromo, CO 152-153 C 7
Chromtau 178-179 K 7
Chrudim 133 H 4
Chryse 136-137 LM 8
Chrysochŏús, Kólpos - 182-183 E 5
Chuali, Lagoa - 174-175 K 3
Chuambo 171 D 5
Chuanchang He 190-191 GH 5
Ch'üan-ch'i = Quanxishi 190-191 F 8
Ch'uan-chiao = Quanjiao 190-191 G 9
Ch'üan-chou Chiang = Quanzhou Gang 190-191 G 9
Chuang-ho = Zhuanghe 188-189 D 2
Chuansha 190-191 HJ 6
Chubb Crater = New Quebec Crater 144-145 XY 5
Chubbuck, CA 150-151 F 8
Chubisgalt = Chövsgöl 184-185 KL 3
Chubsugul = Chövsgöl nuur 184-185 J 1
Chübu 188-189 LM 4-5
Chubut 188-189 LM 4-5
Chubut, Rio - 162 C 6
Chuchi 140-141 N 6
Chucheng = Zhucheng 184-185 MN 4
Chu-chi = Zhuji 184-185 N 6
Chu-ch'i = Zhuxi 190-191 BC 5
Chu-chia Chien = Zhujia Jian 190-191 J 6
Ch'u-ch'iao = Zhuqiao 190-191 GH 3
Ch'ü-chieh = Qujie 190-191 C 11
Ch'ü-chou = Qu Xian 184-185 M 6
Ch'ü-chou = Quzhou 190-191 F 8
Chuchow = Zhuzhou 184-185 L 6
Chuchwa 190-191 D 5
Chudat 140-141 O 6
Chü-fou = Qufu 190-191 F 3
Chugach Mountains 144-145 GH 5
Chugoku 188-189 HJ 5
Chu-hai = Zhuhai 190-191 E 10
Chu-i-chi = Zhuji 184-185 N 6
Chujsk aja dolina = Čujsk 140-141 N 5
Chuja 140-141 N 5
Chu-ki = Zhuji 184-185 N 6
Chuju = Qujing 184-185 J 6
Chu Yang Sin 186-187 E 4
Ch'ü-yeh = Juye 190-191 F 3
Chukuvacos, República Autónoma - 4 ⊲ 178-179 H 6
Chugwater, WY 152-153 D 5

Chuhsien = Chu Xian 190-191 FG 5
Chuhsien = Ju Xian 190-191 G 4
Chü-hsien = Ju Xian 190-191 G 4
Chuhsien = Qu Xian 184-185 M 6
Ch'u-hsiung = Chuxiong 184-185 J 7
Chu'jung = Jurong 190-191 G 6
Chukchi Plateau 52 BC 35
Chukchi Sea 120 BC 35-36
Chukchi Sea 120 B 35
Chukchos, Circunscripção Nacional dos - 178-179 g-k 4
Chukchos, Circunscripcion Nacional de los - 178-179 g-j 4
Chukchos, Dorsal de - 120 B 35
Chukchos, Archipiélago de los - 162 AB 6-7
Chonuu 178-179 b 4
Choolooj Gov' 184-185 H 3
Chukot Autonomous Area 178-179 g-j 4
Ch'ü-wu = Quwu 190-191 C 4
Chu'wu = Quwu 190-191 C 4
Chuku-kraal 184-185 O 4
Chukudu Kraal 168-169 F 7
Chul, Gardaneh-ye - 182-183 MN 6
Chula Aqqan su 184-185 G 4
Chula Vista, CA 146-147 C 5
Chulchuta 140-141 N 4
Chüliu-ho = Juliuhe 188-189 D 1
Chulp'o 188-189 F 5
Chu'lu = Julu 190-191 E 3
Chulucanas 158-159 CD 6
Chulumani 158-159 F 8
Chu-lung Ho = Zhulong He 190-191 E 2
Chumikcha 162 C 3 `
Chum Phae 186-187 D 3
Chumsaeng 186-187 D 3
Chumunjin 188-189 G 4
Chun'an 190-191 G 6
Chunghwa 188-189 EF 3
Ch'ungju 188-189 G 4
Chungking = Chongqing 184-185 K 6
Chung-li 190-191 H 9
Chung-ming = Chongming 184-185 N 5
Chung-ming Tao = Chongming Dao 184-185 N 5
Chungmou = Zhongmou 190-191 DE 4
Ch'ungmu 188-189 G 5
Chung-pu = Huangling 190-191 B 4
Ch'üngsan 188-189 E 3
Chungsiang = Zhongxiang 184-185 L 7
Chungsiang = Zhongxiang 190-191 D 6
Chung-tien = Zhongdian 184-185 HJ 6
Chung-tu = Chongdu 184-185 HJ 6
Chung-tu = Zhongdian 184-185 HJ 6
Chungu = Zhongwei 190-191 D 8
Chung-wei = Zhongwei 184-185 JK 4
Ch'ung-wu = Chongwu 190-191 G 9
Chungyang = Chongyang 190-191 E 7
Ch'u-ng-yang = Chongyang 190-191 E 7
Chunhua 190-191 B 4
Chunya = Zhutan 190-191 E 7
Chunzach 140-141 N 5
Chupadera, Mesa - 154-155 B 3-4
Ch'ü-qu = Quwo 190-191 C 4
Chuquibamba 158-159 E 8
Chuquicamata 162 C 2
Chuquisaca = Sucre 158-159 FG 8
Chur 133 D 5
Ch'üranjie 188-189 GH 2
Church [CDN] 144-145 RS 6
Churchill, ID 150-151 FG 4
Churchill, Cape - 144-145 XY 7
Churchill Falls 144-145 XY 7
Churchill Peak 144-145 LM 6
Churchill River [CDN, Manitoba] 144-145 RS 6
Churchill River [CDN ⊲ Hamilton Inlet] 144-145 Y 7
Church Point, LA 154-155 JK 5
Churchs Ferry, ND 152-153 G 1
Churu 180-181 LM 5
Chusei-hokudō = Ch'ungch'ŏngbuk-to 188-189 FG 4
Chusei-nandō = Ch'ungch'ŏngnam-do 188-189 FG 4
Ch'ü Shan = Daqu Shan 190-191 J 5
Chu-shan = Zhushan 184-185 KL 5
Chusistan = Khuzestān 180-181 FG 4
Chuska Mountains 150-151 J 7-8
Chust 140-141 LM 4
Chutag 184-185 J 2
Chu-t'an = Zhutan 190-191 E 7
Ch'u-t'ing = Zhuting 190-191 D 8
Chutovo 140-141 G 2
Ch'u-tzŭ-chên = Quzi 190-191 A 3
Chuuçnar 184-185 G 5
Chuy = Zhuhai 190-191 E 10
Chu Yang Sin 186-187 E 4
Dai Xian 190-191 D 2
Dai Xian = Taishan Liedao 190-191 H 8
Daisy, WA 150-151 D E 1
Đa Nẵng 186-187 E 3

Chužir 178-179 U 7
Chvalynsk 138-139 QR 7
Chvatovka 138-139 Q 7
Chvojnaja 138-139 N 4
Chwansha 190-191 HJ 6
Chu'ja-do 188-189 F 6
Chwärta = Chuwārtah 182-183 L 5
Chypre 180-181 C 3 = S

D

Đa, Sông - 186-187 D 2
Da'an 190-191 C10
Đạb'ah 182-183 G 7
Đab'ah, Ad- 166-167 K 2
Đạb'ah, Rā's ad- 170 C 2
Dabaidi 190-191 C10
Dabbah, Ad- 166-167 K 3
Dabbūsah, Ad- 182-183 J 7
Dabie Shan [TJ, ▲▲] 184-185 M 5
Dabie Shan [TJ, ✳] 190-191 EF 6
Dabola 166-167 B 66
Daboya 166-167 b 2
Daboya 172-173 E 3
Dabuxun Hu = Dabas nuur 184-185 H 4
Dacar = Dakar 166-167 A 6
Dacca = Ḍhāka 180-181 OP 6
Dachaidan = Tagalgan 184-185 H 4
Dachangshan Dao 188-189 D 3
Dachau 133 E 4
Dachen Dao 190-191 HJ 7
Dacheng = Daicheng 190-191 F 2
Dachovskaja 140-141 JK 4
Dachstein 133 F 5
Đắc Lắc, Cao Nguyên = 186-187 E 4
Dachovskaja 140-141 JK 4
Dadache, Rio - 174-175 K 2
Dadaituan = Shentuan 190-191 G 4
Daday 182-183 E 2
Dade City, FL 148-149 b 2
Dadeville, AL 154-155 MN 4
Dadian [TJ, Anhui] 190-191 F 5
Dadian [TJ, Shaanxi] 190-191 B 4
Dadinskoje, ozero - 140-141 M 4
Dalian 177 PQ 6
Dadukou 184-185 N 4
Dalias 134-135 F 10
Daet 186-187 H 4
Dafan 190-191 E 7
Dafdaf, Jabal - 170 C 3
Dafeng 190-191 H 5
Dafeng Shan = Shinaibeidong 190-191 E 8
Dagana 166-167 A 5
Dagana 166-167 A 5
Dagangtou 190-191 G 7
Đagash = Dāghāsh 182-183 H 4
Dagda 138-139 F 5
Dagestan, Autonome Republiek - 140-141 N 5
Dagestan, Autonomous Republic - 140-141 MN 5
Dagestanskaja Avtonomnaja Sovetskaja Socialističeskaja Respublika = Autonome Republik Dagestan 140-141 MN 5
Dagestanskije Ogni 140-141 O 5
Dagestanti Autonóm Köztársaság 140-141 MN 5
Daggett, CA 150-151 E 8
Dagu He 184-185 MN 4
Dagu Shui 190-191 D 6
Dagabur = Degeh Bur 166-167 N 7
Dagana 166-167 A 5
Dagangtou 190-191 G 7
Dagh'gharah, Ad- 182-183 L 6
Daglica 182-183 KL 4
Dago = Hiiumaa 138-139 CD 4
Dagomba 166-167 D 7
Dagomys, Soči - 140-141 J 5
Dagu 190-191 F 2
Dagua [PNG] 186-187 M 7
Daguan 184-185 J 6
Daguestán, República Autónoma de - 140-141 MN 5
Daguestán, República Autónoma del - = 15 ⊲ 126-127 S 7
Daguestão, República Autónoma do - = 15 ⊲ 166-167 T 5
Daguila 188-189 E 1
Dagu He 190-191 D 2
Daguenthe, R. A. del 140-141 N 5
Dàhānu 180-181 L 6
Dahangweri 130-131 b 2
Daheishan Dao 190-191 HJ 3
Dahl, Nafūd ad- 180-181 EF 6
Dahongcheng 190-191 CD 1
Dahlak = Dehalak Desēt 166-167 N 5
Dahná', Ad- 180-181 E 5-F 6
Dahomey = Benin 166-167 E 6-7
Đahrah 166-167 F 1
Ḍahr Walātah 166-167 C 5
Dahshūr = Minshāt Dahshūr 170 D 3
Dahuk 182-183 K 4
Dahushan = Dapeng Wan 190-191 E 10
Daimiel 134-135 F 9
Daingerfield, TX154-155 H 4
Daiō zaki 188-189 L 5
Daipingdian = Taipingshao 190-191 D 2
Dai Xian 190-191 D 2
Dairen = Dalian 184-185 N 4
Đairū'= Dayrūt 166-167 L 3
Dai-sen 188-189 J 5
Daisy, WA 150-151 D E 1
Đa Nẵng 186-187 E 3
Danbury, CT 148-149 G 4

Daitō sima = Daitō-shima 184-185 P 5-6
Dai Xian 190-191 D 2
Daijangou = Jiangkou 190-191 C 8
Dajiangou = Dagangtou 190-191 G 7
Dajarra 194-195 G 4
Dajin [TJ, Guangdong] 190-191 C10
Dajin [TJ, Zhejiang]190-191 H 7
Daka 172-173 E 3
Dakar 166-167 A 6
Dakawa 171 D 4
Dakaye 172-173 E 3
Daketa Shet 166-167 N 7
Đakhan = Deccan 180-181 M 6-8
Đakhilah, Wāḥat ad- 166-167 K 3
Dakhlah, Ad- 166-167 A 4
Dakhla Oasis = Wāḥāt ad-Dākhilah 166-167 K 3
Dakka = Ḍhāka 180-181 OP 6
Dakoro 172-173 G 2
Dakota Północna = North Dakota 146-147 FG 2
Dakota Południowa = South Dakota 146-147 FG 3
Dakshin Andamān = South Andamān 180-181 P 8
Dakshin Pāthār = Deccan 180-181 M 6-8
Dala 130-131 D 4
Dalaba 166-167 B 6
Dalafi 177-73 E 3
Dalai 184-185 N 2
Dalai Lama Gangri 184-185 GH 5
Dalai Nur 184-185 M 2
Dalaj Nuur = Hulun Nur 184-185 M 2
Dalāk, Kūh-e - 182-183 N 4
Dalaman Nehri 182-183 C 4
Dalandzadgad 184-185 JK 3
Dalanzadgad 184-185 JK 3
Dalarna 130-131 EF 7
Da Lat 186-187 E 4
Dalavakasir = Oyalï 182-183 J 4
Đālbandin 180-181 J 5
Dalby [AUS] 194-195 K 5
Dale, OR 150-151 D 3
Dale, PA 148-149 D 4
Dale Hollow Lake 154-155 N 2
Dalen 130-131 C 8
Daleville, AL 154-155 N 5
Dalhart, TX 154-155 D 2
Dalhousie, Cape - 144-145 KL 3
Dali [TJ, Shaanxi] 190-191 B 4
Dali [TJ, Yunnan] 184-185 HJ 6
Dalies, NM 154-155 B 3
Dalian 177 PQ 6
Dalian 184-185 N 4
Dalias 134-135 F 10
Dali Baizu Zizhizhou 184-185 HJ 6
Dali He 190-191 C 3
Daling He 188-189 C 2
Daljā' 170 D 4
Ḍalkūt = Kharītūt 180-181 G 7
Ḍāllah, 'Ayn - 170 B 4
Dallas, GA 154-155 N 4
Dallas, IA 152-153 K 5
Dallas, OR 150-151 B 3
Dall Island 144-145 K 6
Dallol Bosso 166-167 E 5-6
Dalmacia = Dalmacija 136-137 F 3-H 4
Dalmacija 136-137 F 3-H 4
Dalmaj, Hawr - 182-183 L 6
Dalmatia = Dalmacija 136-137 F 3-H 4
Dalmatie = Dalmacija 136-137 F 3-H 4
Dalmatien = Dalmacija 136-137 F 3-H 4
Daľnegorsk 178-179 a 9
Daľnereченsk 178-179 Za 8
Daľ'negorsk 178-179 a 9
Dalnje = Lüda-Dalian 184-185 N 4
Dalrymple, Mount - 194-195 J 4
Dalton, GA 144-147 JK 5
Dalton, MA 148-149 G 3
Dalton, NE 152-153 E 5
Dalton Ice Tongue 121 C 12-13
Dalton in Furness 132 E 4
Dalvik 130-131 d 2
Dalwhinnie 132 DE 3
Daly City, CA 150-151 B 7
Daly River 194-195 F 2
Daly Waters 194-195 F 3
Damakania 172-173 B 3
Damā, Wadi - 170 FG 4
Daman 180-181 L 6
Dāmān 180-181 L 6
Đamanhūr 166-167 L 2
Damaq 182-183 N 5
Damar, Pulau - 186-187 J 8
Damara 166-167 H 8
Damaraland 168-169 B 7
Damas = Dimashq 180-181 D 4
Damasco = Dimashq 180-181 D 4
Damascus = Dimashq 180-181 D 4
Damascus, VA 148-149 C 6
Damaskus = Dimashq 180-181 D 4
Damaszek = Dimashq 180-181 D 4
Damaturu 166-167 G 6
Damāvand, Kūh-e - 180-181 G 3
Damāzin = Ad- 166-167 LM 6
Dāmāzīn, Ad- 166-167 LM 6
Damboa 172-173 G 3
Damboa 172-173 G 3
Dambulla 184-185 S 3-T 2
Dam Dam = South Dum Dum 180-181 O 6
Damđān, Bīr - 170 BC 2
Ḍamghān 180-181 GH 3
Damghaan = Rongshui 190-191 B 9
Damietta = Dumyāt 166-167 L 2
Damietta Mouth = Maṣabb Dumyāt 170 DE 2
Đāmir, Ad- 166-167 L 5
Đāmir Qābū 182-183 JK 4
Dammam, Ad- 180-181 FG 5
Damodar 180-181 NO 6
Damongo 172-173 E 3
Damot 166-167 b 2
Dampier 194-195 C 4
Dampier, Détroit de - 186-187 K 7
Dampier Downs OC 194-195 D 3
Dampier Land 194-195 D 3
Dampier Archipelago 194-195 C 4
Dai-sen 188-189 J 5
Daisy, WA 150-151 DE 1
Đa Nẵng 186-187 E 3
Danbury, CT 148-149 G 4

anbury, WI 152-153 K 2-3
anby Lake 150-151 F 8
ancharia 134-135 G 7
andarah 170 E 4
andong 184-185 N 3
änemark 130-131 C-E 10
anemark 130-131 C-E 10
anemark, Détroit du - 120 C 20-22
änemarkstraße 120 C 22-20
anfeng 190-191 C 5
anforth, ME 148-149 JK 2
anfu 186-187 h 5
angan Liedao 190-191 E 10-11
ange, Rio - 168-169 D 4
ang Raek, Phanom -
186-187 DE 4
angraek, Phnom - = Phanom
Dang Raek 186-187 DE 4
angshan 190-191 F 4
angtu 190-191 G 6
an Gulbi 172-173 G 3
an Guno 166-167 F 6-7
angyang 190-191 CD 6
anhao Dao 190-191 DE 10
an He 190-191 D 4
ani 172-173 E 2
ania 130-131 CD 10
ánia 130-131 CD 10
ánia-szoros 120 C 22-20
ánia-szoros 130-131 ab 1
aniel, WY 150-151 H 4
anilov 178-179 G 6
anilovka 138-139 P 7
anilovo 138-139 KL 2
animarca 130-131 CD 10
animarca, Stretto di - 120 C 22-20
aning 190-191 C 3
anişment 182-183 GH 3
anissa 171 E 2
an Jiang 190-191 C 5
anjo-shotō 188-189 G 6
ank 180-181 H 6
ankama 172-173 GH 2
anli 146-147 J 9
annemora, NY 148-149 FG 2
annevirke 194-195 P 8
annhauser 174-175 HJ 4-5
ankov 138-139 M 7
an River 148-149 CD 6
anshui 190-191 E 10
anshui He = Tanshui Chiang
190-191 H 9
anshui = Tan-shui 184-185 N 6
ansia 158-159 H 4
ánsko 130-131 CD 10
ánský průliv 120 C 22-20
ánský pruliv 130-131 ab 1
ans, Monts des - 172-173 CD 4
ansville , NY 148-149 E 3
ante, VA 148-149 B 6
ante = Xaafuun 166-167 c 1
anube = Dunărea 136-137 M 3
anubio = Duna 136-137 H 2
anubio = Dunărea 136-137 M 3
anúbio = Dunărea 133 J 5
anushkodi 180-181 MN 9
anville, AR 154-155 J 3
anville, IL 146-147 J 3
anville, IN 152-153 N 6
anville, KY 152-153 O 7
anville, ME 148-149 H 2-3
anville, VA 146-147 L 4
an Xian 184-185 K 8
anyang 190-191 G 3
anzica = Gdansk 120 D 17
anzig = Gdańsk 133 J 1
anziger Bucht = Zatoka
Gdańska 133 J 1
aoli 190-191 H 3
ao Shui 190-191 E 6
ao-Timni 166-167 G 4
aou, Eḍ- = Aḍ-Ḍaw 182-183 G 5
ao Xian 190-191 C 9
apaong 172-173 F 3
apchi 172-173 H 2
apeng 190-191 E 10
apeng Wan 190-191 E 10
apodi = Dabaidi 190-191 E 8
apsang = K 2 180-181 M 3
apu = Dabu 190-191 F 9
apupan 186-187 GH 3
aqi = Ta-chi 190-191 H 9
aqi = Ta-hsi 190-191 H 10
aqiao 190-191 E 7
aqing Shan 184-185 L 3
aqmā', Ad- 180-181 FG 6
aquan 184-185 H 3
aqu Shan 190-191 J 6
ar'ā 182-183 G 6
arā, Jazireh - 182-183 N 7
ārāb 180-181 E 4
arabani 136-137 M 1
arad = Dardistān 180-181 L 3
arag = Legaspi 186-187 H 4
aragh 166-167 G 2
ar al-Bayḍ' ā', Ad- 166-167 BC 2
arašun = Veršino-Darasunskij
178-179 VW 7
arau = Darāw 170 E 5
arāw 170 E 5
arb, Ad- 180-181 E 7
ar Bādām 182-183 M 6
arband, Kūh-e - 180-181 H 4
arbandi Khan, Sadd ad-
182-183 L 5
arbanga = Darbhanga
180-181 O 5
arbėnai 138-139 C 5
arbhanga 180-181 O 5
arbi = Darvi 184-185 G 2
arby, MT 150-151 FG 2
archan 184-185 K 2
ardanele–Çanakkale Boğazı
180-181 B 2-3
ardanele = Çanakkale Boğazı
136-137 M 5
ardanellák = Çanakkale Boğazi
180-181 B 2-3
ardanellen = Çanakkale Bogazı
180-181 B 2-3
ardanelles = Çanakkale Bogazı
180-181 B 2-3
ardanelli = Çanakkale boğazi
180-181 B 2-3
ardanelos = Çanakkale Bogazı
180-181 B 2-3
ardanelos = Çanakkale boğazı
180-181 B 2-3
ār Dishah 182-183 J 5
ardo = Kangding 184-185 J 5-6
ār el Beiḍā', ed - = Ad-Dār al-
Bayḍā, 166-167 BC 2
arende 182-183 G 3
ar es Salaam 168-169 JK 4
ārfūr 166-167 J 6
argagā, Jebel ed - = Jabal
Ardar Gwagwa 170 F 6
argan-Ata 180-181 J 2
argaville 194-195 O 7
argo 196 H 6
argol 172-173 F 2
ar Hu = Dalaj Nur 184-185 M 3
Darien, GA 148-149 C 9
Darién [PA, ≅] 146-147 L 10
Darien [PA, ●] 146-147 b 2
Darien = Dalian 184-185 N 4
Darién, Golfo del - 158-159 D 3
Dārigah 182-183 K 5
Dariganga 184-185 L 2
Darjeeling 180-181 O 5
Dārjiling = Darjeeling 180-181 O 5
Darjinskoje 138-139 S 8
Darkhazineh 182-183 N 7
Darling 174-175 C 7
Darling Downs 194-195 JK 5
Darling, Lake - 152-153 F 1
Darling Range 194-195 C 6
Darling River 194-195 H 6
Darlington 132 EF 4
Darlington, SC 148-149 CD 7
Darlington, WI 152-153 LM 4
Darlowo 133 H 1
Darmstadt 133 D 4
Darnah 166-167 J 2
Darnall 174-175 J 5
Darnick 194-195 H 6
Darnley, Cape - 121 C 7-8
Daroca 134-135 G 8
Darovskoj 138-139 Q 4
Darrington, WA 150-151 C 1
Darsah 180-181 G 8
Dart, Cape - 121 B 24
Dartmoor Forest 132 E 6
Dartmouth [CDN] 144-145 Y 9
Dartuch, Cabo - 134-135 J 9
Daru 186-187 M 8
Darūdāb 166-167 M 5
Daruvar 136-137 G 3
Darvaza 180-181 H 2
Darvi 184-185 G 2
Darvinskij zapovednik 138-139
LM 4
Darwešān 180-181 JK 4
Darwin [AUS] 194-195 F 2
Darwin , CA 150-151 E 7
Darwin, Bahia - 162 AB 7
Darwin zapovednik = Darvinskij
zapovednik 138-139 LM 4
Dās 180-181 G 5
Dašava 140-141 AB 2
Dašev 140-141 D 2
Dasha He 190-191 E 2
Dashen Terara , Ras - 166-167 M 6
Dashiqiao 188-189 D 2
Dasht 180-181 J 5
Dasht-e Āzādegān 182-183 N 7
Dashtiārī = Polān 180-181 J 5
Daškesan 140-141 MN 6
Dassa-Zoumé 172-173 F 4
Dassel, MN 152-153 J 3
Dasseneiland 174-175 BC 7
Datang 190-191 B 9
Dataran Tinggi Cameron = Tanah
Tinggi Cameron 186-187 D 6
Datça = Reşadiye 182-183 B 4
Date 188-189 b 2
Datia 180-181 M 5
Datian 190-191 F 9
Datil, NM 154-155 B 3
Datiyā = Datia 180-181 M 5
D'atkovo 138-139 K 7
D'atlovo 138-139 E 7
Datong [TJ, Anhui] 190-191 F 6
Datong [TJ, Shanxi] 184-185 L 3
Datong He 184-185 J 4
Datori-Tiokossi 172-173 F 3
Datu, Tanjung - 186-187 E 6
Datu, Teluk - 186-187 EF 6
Datu Piang 186-187 H 5
Dau'an = Al-Hurayba 180-181 F 7
Daudmannsodden 130-131 hj 5
Daugava 138-139 E 5
Daugava = Severnaja Dvina
138-139 M 3
Daugavpils 138-139 EF 6
Daulagiri = Dhaulāgiri 180-181 N 5
Daule, Rio - 158-159 CD 5
Dauna Parma = Dawa
166-167 M 7-8
Dauphin 144-145 QR 7
Dauphin Lake 144-145 KL 6
Dauphin Island 154-155 LM 5
Daura 172-173 GH 2
Daurskij chrebet = chrebet
Čerskogo 178-179 V 7
Dautlatābād = Malāyer 180-181 F 4
Davalguiri = Dhaulagiri 180-181 N 5
Davalinskogo = Ararat 140-141 M 7
Davao 186-187 J 5
Davao Gulf 186-187 J 5
Davel 174-175 H 4
Davenport, IA 146-147 H 3
Davenport, NE 152-153 H 5
Davenport, ND 152-153 H 2
Davenport, WA 150-151 D 2
Davenport Downs 194-195 H 4
Davenport Range 194-195 FG 4
Davey, Port - 194-195 HJ 8
David 146-147 K 10
David City, NE 152-153 H 5
David-Gorodok 138-139 FG 4
Davidson Mountains 144-145 H 4
Davidson, OK 154-155 F 3
Daviesville 174-175 HJ 2
Davignab 174-175 C 4
Davis, CA 150-151 BC 6
Davis, IL 152-153 M 4
Davis, OK 154-155 G 3
Davis, WV 148-149 D 5
Davis , Détroit de - 144-145 Z 4-5
Davis, Estrecho de - 144-145 Z 4-5
Davis, Estreito de - 144-145 Z 4-5
Davis, Straat - 144-145 Z 4-5
Davis, Stretto di - 144-145 Z 4-5
Davisa, Cieśnina = 144-145 Z 4-5
Davis Bay 121 C 14
Davis Creek, CA 150-151 C 5
Davis Dam, AZ 150-151 F 8
Davis Mountains 154-155 CD 5
Davis Sea 121 C 10
Davis Strait 144-145 Z 4-5
Davisstraße 144-145 Z 4-5
Davis-szoros 144-145 Z 4-5
Davisův průliv 144-145 Z 4-5
Davlekanovo 178-179 JK 7
Davo 172-173 D 4
Davos 133 DE 5
Davydovka 140-141 J 1
Dawadawa 172-173 E 3
Dawan 190-191 B 10
Ḍaw, Aḍ - 182-183 G 5
Dawādimā, Ad- 180-181 EF 6
Dawangjia Dao 188-189 D 3
Dawanle = Dewelē 166-167 N 6
Dawāsir, Wādī ad- 180-181 EF 6
Dawa Weniz 166-167 M 7-8
Dawenkou 190-191 F 3-4
Dawhah, Ad- 180-181 G 5
Dawingnab = Davignab
174-175 C 4
Dawr, Ad- 182-183 KL 5
Dawrah, Baghdād- 182-183 L 6
Dawson, GA 154-155 N 5
Dawson, ND 152-153 G 2
Dawson 144-145 J 5
Dawson, Isla - 162 BC 8
Dawson Creek 144-145 M 6
Dawson-Lambton Glacier
121 B 133-34
Dawson Range 144-145 J 5
Dawson Springs, KY 152-153 MN 7
Dawu = Ta-wu 190-191 H 10
Dawwah 180-181 H 6
Dawwāya = Jamā'at al-Ma'yuf
182-183 M 7
Dax 134-135 G 7
Da Xi 190-191 G 7-8
Da Xi = Longquan Xi 190-191 G 7-8
Da Xian 184-185 K 5
Daxindian 190-191 H 3
Daxing 190-191 F 2
Daxue Shan 184-185 J 5-6
Day, FL 148-149 b 1
Dayang Bunting, Pulau -
186-187 C 5
Dayang He 188-189 D 2
Daya Wan 190-191 E 10
Daye 190-191 E 6
Daylesford 196 G 6
Daym Zubayr 166-167 K 7
Dayong 184-185 L 6
Dayr, Ad- 170 E 5
Dayr as-Suryānī 170 CD 2
Dayr az-Zawr 180-181 DE 3
Dayr Ḥāfir 182-183 G 4
Dayr Katrinah 170 E 3
Dayr Māghar 182-183 H 4
Dayr Mawās 170 D 4
Dayr Samū'il 170 D 3
Dayrūṭ 166-167 L 3
Dayton, NM 154-155 C 4
Dayton, NV 150-151 D 6
Dayton, OH 146-147 K 4
Dayton, TN 154-155 N 3
Dayton, TX 154-155 H 5
Dayton, WA 150-151 E 2
Dayton, WY 152-153 C 3
Daytona Beach, FL 146-147 KL 6
Dayu 184-185 L 6
Dayu Ling 190-191 DE 9
Da Yunhe [TJ, Jiangsu]
184-185 M 5
Da Yunhe [TJ, Shanddong]
190-191 EF 3
Dayu Shan 190-191 H 6
Dayville, OR 150-151 D 3
Dazhang Xi 190-191 G 9
Dazkırı 182-183 CD 4
Dead Indian Peak 150-151 HJ 3
Deadman Bay 148-149 b 2
Dead Lake 152-153 HJ 2
Dead Sea = Bahr al-Mayyit
180-181 D 4
Deadwood Reservoir 150-151 F 3
Deadwood, SD 152-153 E 3
Dealesville 174-175 F 5
Deal Island 196 cd 1
De'an 190-191 EF 7
Deán Funes 162 D 4
Dean River 144-145 L 7
Dearborn, MI 152-153 P 4
Dearg, Beinn - 132 D 3
Deary, ID 150-151 E 2
Dease Arm 144-145 MN 4
Dease Lake 144-145 KL 6
Dease Strait 144-145 P 4
Death Valley 146-147 C 4
Death Valley, CA 150-151 E 7
Death Valley National Park
150-151 E 7-8
Deauville 134-135 GH 4
Deaver, WY 152-153 B 3
Debal'cevo 140-141 J 2
Debar 136-137 J 5
Debark 166-167 M 6
Debeeti 174-175 G 2
De Beque, CO 152-153 BC 6
Debesy 138-139 T 5
Debica 133 K 3-4
Deblin 133 KL 3
Děbo, Lac - 166-167 D 5
De Borgia, MT 150-151 F 2
Debre Birhan 166-167 MN 7
Debrecen 133 K 5
Debrecin = Debrecen 133 K 5
Debre Markos 166-167 M 6
Debre Tabor 166-167 M 6
Decamere = Dekemharē
166-167 M 5
Decatur, AL 146-147 J 5
Decatur, GA 146-147 K 5
Decatur, IL 146-147 HJ 3-4
Decatur, IN 152-153 O 5
Decatur, MI 152-153 NO 4
Decatur, NE 152-153 H 5
Decatur, TX 154-155 G 4
Decazeville 134-135 J 6
Decepción, Cabo - = Cape
Disappointment 162 J 8-9
Deception 121 C 30
Decherd, TN 154-155 MN 3
Děčín 133 G 3
Decker, MT 152-153 C 3
Declo, ID 150-151 G 4
Decorah, IA 152-153 L 4
Decoplis-Ckaro 140-141 MN 6
Dedoviči 138-139 GH 5
Dedovsk 138-139 L 6
Dedougou 166-167 D 6
Dedza 168-169 H 5
Dee [GB, Cambrian Mts.] 132 E 5
Dec [GB, Cambrian Mts.] 132 E 3
Deelfontein 174-175 E 6
Deep Creek Range 150-151 G 5-6
Deep River [USA] 148-149 D 7
Deepwater 196 K 2
Deepwater, MO 152-153 K 6
Deer, AR 154-155 J 3
Deerfield Beach, FL 148-149 cd 3
Deering, Mount - 194-195 E 5
Deering, ND 152-153 F 1
Deer Lodge, MT 150-151 G 2
Deer Lodge Mountains 150-151 G 2
Deer Lodge Pass 150-151 G 3
Deer Park, AL 154-155 L 5
Deer Park, WA 150-151 E 2
Deer River, MN 152-153 JK 2
Deerton, MI 152-153 N 2
Deer Trail, CO 152-153 DE 6
Deerwood, MN 152-153 K 2
Deeth, NV 150-151 F 5
Deffa, ed - = Aḍ- Ḍiffah
166-167 J 2
Defiance, OH 152-153 O 5
De Funiak Springs, FL 154-155
MN 5
Dêge 184-185 H 5
Degeh Bur 166-167 N 7
Deggendorf 133 F 4
De Grey 194-195 CD 4
De Grey River 194-195 CD 4
Degt'anka 138-139 N 7
Dehalak Desēt 166-167 N 5
Dehgolān 182-183 M 5
Dehkhwāreqan = Āzar Shahr
182-183 LM 4
Dehlorān 180-181 F 4
Dehna = Ad Dahnā, 180-181
E 5-F 6
Dehna, Ed- = Ad-Dahnā'
180-181 E 5-F 6
Dehōk–Dahūk 182-183 K 4
Dehong Daizu Zizhizhou = D ◁
184-185 H 6-7
Dehra Dun 180-181 M 4
Dehu 184-185 H 4
Dehua 190-191 G 9
Deir, Ed - = Ad-Dayr 170 E 5
Deir es-Suryânî = Dayr as-
Suryānī 170 CD 2
Deir ez Zōr = Dayr az-Zawr
180-181 DE 3
Deir Hafir = Dayr Hāfir 182-183 G 4
Deir Katerina = Dayr Katrinah
170 E 3
Deir Mâghar = Dayr Māghar
182-183 H 4
Deir Mawâs = Dayr Mawās 170 D 4
Deir Samweil = Dayr Samū'il
170 D 3
Dej 136-137 K 2
Dejnev, Cap - = mys Dežneva
178-179 lm 4
De Jongs, Tanjung - 186-187 L 8
De Kalb, IL 152-153 M 5
De Kalb, MS 154-155 L 4
De Kalb, TX 154-155 H 4
De-Kastri 178-179 ab 7
Dekemhare 166-167 M 5
Dekese 168-169 F 3
Dekoûa, Tell - = Tall adh-
Dhakwah 182-183 G 6
Dél-Afrika 168-169 F-H 8
Delagua, CO 152-153 D 7
Delaimiya, Ad- = Ad-Dulaymiyah
182-183 K 6
De Land, FL 148-149 c 2
Delano, CA 150-151 D 8
Delano, MN 152-153 JK 3
Delano Peak 146-147 D 4
Delareyville 174-175 F 4
Delavan, IL 152-153 M 5
Delavan, WI 152-153 M 4
Delaware 146-147 LM 4
Delaware, OH 152-153 P 5
Delaware Bay 146-147 LM 4
Delaware Lake 152-153 P 5
Delaware Reservoir 148-149 B 4
Delaware River 148-149 F 5
Delcambre, LA 154-155 JK 6
Delčevo 136-137 K 4-5
Delegate 196 J 6
De Leon, TX 154-155 F 4
Delfi = Delphoi 136-137 K 6
Delfim Moreira 160-161 K 5
Delfinópolis 160-161 J 4
Delfijl 134-135 L 2
Delgerchet 184-185 L 2
Delger mörön 184-185 H 1-2
Delgo = Delqū 166-167 L 4-5
Delhi [CDN] 148-149 C 3
Delhi, CO 152-153 DE 7
Delhi, LA 154-155 K 4
Delhi [IND] 180-181 M 5
Delhi, NY 148-149 F 3
Delhi = Dili 186-187 J 8
Deli, Pulau - 186-187 DE 8
Déli-Banda-medence 186-187 J 8
Delice 182-183 E 3
Delicermak 182-183 F 3
Délices 158-159 J 4
Delicias 146-147 E 6
Déli-Fidzsi-medence 194-195
OP 4-5
Déli-Georgia = South Georgia
162 J 8
Déli-Georgia-hát 121 D 33-E 34
Delijān 182-183 O 5-6
Delingde 178-179 WW 4
Déli-Sandwich-árok 121 D 34
Dél-kínai-medence 186-187 FG 3-4
Dél-kínai-tenger 186-187 E 5-G 2
Dél-Korea 184-185 OP 4
Dell, MT 150-151 G 3
Delle, UT 150-151 G 5
Delmar, IA 152-153 L 4-5
Del Mar, CA 150-151 E 9
Delmas 174-175 H 4
Delmenhorst 133 CD 2
Del Norte, CO 152-153 C 7
Dél-Oszét Autonóm Terület
140-141 LM 5
Délnyugat-Afrika = Namibia
168-169 E 7
Dényugat - csendesóceáni -
medence 121 D 21-19
de Long, proliv - = proliv Longa
178-179 j 3-4
De Longa, ostrova - 178-179 c-e 2
De Long Mountains 144-145 D 4
Deloraine 196 c 2
Dēlos 136-137 L 7
Delphi, IN 152-153 N 5
Delphoi 136-137 K 6
Delphos, OH 152-153 O 5
Delportshoop 174-175 EF 5
Delray Beach, FL 148-149 cd 3
Del Rio 150-151 H 10
Del Riol TX 146-147 F 6
Delta, CO 152-153 B 6
Delta, UT 150-151 G 6
Delta Mendota Canal 150-151 C 7
Delta [WAN, ☆] 172-173 G 4
Delvinë 136-137 HJ 6
Delwin, TX 154-155 E 4
Demachi = Tonami 188-189 L 4
Dem'ansk 138-139 J 5
Demavend = Kūh-e Damāvānd
180-181 G 3
Demba 168-169 F 4
Dembi Dolo 166-167 LM 7
Demchhog 184-185 D 5
Demer = Ḍumayr 182-183 G 6
Déméké 172-173 C 2
Demidov 138-139 H 6
Deming, WA 150-151 BC 1
Demini, Rio - 158-159 G 4-5
Demirci 182-183 C 3
Demirciköy = Çal 182-183 C 3
Demirkent 182-183 JK 2
Demirköprü Barajı 182-183 C 3
Demirköy 182-183 BC 2
Demir Qâboû = Damir Qābū
182-183 JK 4
Demjanka 178-179 N 6
Demjanovo 138-139 N 4
Demjanovskaja 138-139 P 3
Demjanskoje 178-179 MN 6
Demmin 133 F 2
Demopolis, AL 154-155 LM 4
Dempo, Gunung - 186-187 D 7
Demta 186-187 M 7
Denakil 166-167 N 6
Denan 166-167 N 7
Denau 180-181 K 3
Denbigh [CDN] 148-149 E 2
Dendang 186-187 E 7
Denemarken 130-131 C-E 10
Denemarken, Straat - 120 C 20-22
Dengkou = Bajan Gol 184-185 K 3
Denglou Jiao = Kami Jiao
190-191 B 11
Deng Xian 190-191 D 5
Den Haag = 's-Gravenhage
134-135 JK 2
Denham 194-195 B 5
Denham Springs, LA 154-155 K 5
Denia 134-135 H 9
Denial Bay 196 A 4
Denikil = Denakil 166-167 N 6
Deniliquin 194-195 HJ 7
Denio, OR 150-151 D 5
Denison, TX 146-147 G 5
Denison, IA 152-153 J 4-5
Denisovskaja = Šelota
138-139 NO 3
Denizli 180-181 B 3
Denman 196 K 4
Denman Glacier 121 BC 10-11
Denmark 130-131 C-E 10
Denmark 194-195 C 6
Denmark, SC 148-149 C 8
Denmark Strait 120 C 20-22
Denmark, WI 152-153 N 3
Denndoudi 172-173 B 2
Denpasar 186-187 FG 8
Dent, ID 150-151E2
Denton, MD 148-149 EF 5
Denton, MT 152-153 B 2
Denton, NC 148-149 CD 7
Denton, TX 146-147 G 5
d'Entrecasteaux Islands
186-187 h 6
Denver, CO 146-147 EF 4
Denver City, TX 154-155 D 4
Deoghar 180-181 O 6
Depew, OK 154-155 G 3
Deping 190-191 F 3
Deqen 184-185 H 6
Dêqên Zangzu Zizhizhou = B ◁
184-185 H 6
Değirmenlik 182-183 E 5
Deqing [TJ, Guangdong]
190-191 C 10
Deqing [TJ, Zhejiang] 190-191 GH 6
De Queen, AR 154-155 H 3
De Quincy, LA 154-155 J 5
Der'ā = Dar'ā 182-183 G 6
Dera, Lak- 168-169 K 2
Ḍerah Ghāzi Khān 180-181 L 4
Ḍerah Ismā'īl Khān 180-181 L 4
Derażn'a 140-141 C 2
Derbent 140-141 O 5
Derbesiye = Şenyurt 182-183 J 4
Derbeškinskij 138-139 T 6
Derby 132 F 5
Derby [ZA] 174-175 G 3
Derby [AUS] 194-195 D 3
Derdepcort 174-175 G 3
Dereköy = Şerefiye 182-183 G 2
Dereli 182-183 H 2
Dergači [SU, Rossijskaja SFSR]
138-139 R 8
Dergači [SU, Ukrainskaja SSR]
140-141 H 1
Derg' = Daraj 166-167 G 2
Derg, Lough - 132 BC 5
De Ridder, LA 154-155 J 5
Derik 182-183 J 4
Derinkuyu 182-183 F 3
Derkali 171 E 2
Derm 174-175 C 2
Dermott, AR 154-155 K 4
Derna = Darnah 166-167 J 2
Derry, NH 148-149 H 3
Derūdēb = Darudāb 166-167 M 5
Derventa 136-137 G 3
Derwent 174-175 H 3
Derwent River 196 c 3
Deržavino 138-139 T 7
Deržavinsk 178-179 M 7
Desaguadero, Rio - [BOL]
158-159 F 8
Des Arc, AR 154-155 K 3
Des Arc, MO 154-155 K 2
Descalvado 160-161 D 2
Descanso 160-161 F 7
Deschutes River 150-151 C 3
Desdemona, TX 154-155 F4
Desē 166-167 MN 6
Deseado = Puerto Deseado
162 CD 7
Deseado 160-161 EF 6
Deseado, Cabo - 162 AB 8
Deseado, Rio - 162 BC 7
Desenzano del Garda 136-137 D 3
Deseret Peak 150-151 G 5
Deseronto 148-149 E 2
Désert Arabique 166-167 L 3-4
Desertas, Ilhas - 166-167 A 2
Desert Center, CA 150-151 F 9
Desierto Arábico 166-167 L 3-4
Deserto Arabico 166-167 L 3-4
Deserto da Libia 170 BC 4-6
Deserto Libico 166-167 J 3-L 4
Deserto Nubiano 166-167 LM 4
Deserto Salato = Dasht-e Kavir
180-181 GH 4
Deserto Siriaco 180-181 DE 4
Deserto Sirio 183-184 HJ 6
Desful = Dezfūl 180-181 F 4
Deshler, OH 152-153 P 5
Desierto Arábigo 166-167 L 3-4
Desierto Líbico 166-167 J 3-L 4
Desierto Sirio 180-181 DE 4
Des Moines, IA 146-147 GH 3
Des Moines, NM 154-155 D 2
Des Moines River 146-147 GH 3
Desna 138-139 K 7
Desolación, Isla - 162 AB 8
Desolation Canyon 150-151 J 6
Despatch 174–175 F 7
Despeñaperros, Puerto de -
134-135 F 9
Des Plaines, IL 152-153 MN 4
Desroches, Isle - 168-169 MN 4
De Soto, MO 152-153 L 6
De Soto, WI 152-153 L 4
Dessau 133 F 3
D' Estrees Bay 196 CD 5-6
Destruction Island 150-151 A 2
Desventurados 157 BC 5
Detčino 138-139 KL 6
Dete 168-169 G 6
Detmold 133 D 3
De Tour, MI 152-153 OP 2-3
Detrital Valley 150-151 F 7-8
Detroit Harbor, WI 152-153 N 3
Detroit Lake 150-151 B 3
Detroit Lakes, MN 152-153 HJ 2
Detroit, MI 146-147 K 3
Detroit River 152-153 P 4-5
Detroit, TX 154-155 H 4
Dettitoss 130-131 e 2
Deutsche Bucht 133 C 1
Deutsch Krone = Wałcz 133 H 2
Deutschland 133 D-F 2-4
Deva 136-137 K 3
De Valls Bluff, AR 154-155 K 3
Dévaványa 133 K 5
Deveci Dağları 182-183 FG 2
Develi [TR, Kayseri] 182-183 F 3
Deventer 134-135 L 2
Devils Gate 150-151 D 6
Devil's Hole 132 G 3
Devil's Hole 132 G 3
Devils Lake 152-153 G 1
Devils Lake, ND 152-153 G 1
Devils Playground 150-151 EF 8
Devils Tower 152-153 D 3
Devils Tower National Monument
152-153 D 3
Devin 136-137 L 5
Devine, TX 154-155 F 6
Devoll 136-137 J 5
Devon [GB] 132 DE 6
Devon, MT 150-151 H 1
Devon Island 144-145 S-U 2
Devonport [AUS] 194-195 J 8
Devonport [NZ] 194-195 O 7
Devrek 182-183 DE 2
Devrekâni 182-183 EF 2
Devrez Çayı 182-183 EF 2
de Vries, proliv - 184-185 S 2
Dewelē 166-167 N 6
Dewetsdorp 174-175 G 5
Dewey Lake 148-149 B 6
Dewey, OK 154-155 GH 2
Dewey, SD 152-153 DE 4
De Witt, AR 154-155 K 3
De Witt, IA 152-153 L 5
De Witt, NE 152-153 H 5
Dewundara Tuḍuwa 180-181 N 9
Dexian = Dezhou 184-185 M 4
Dexing 190-191 F 7
Dexter, ME 148-149 J 2
Dexter, MO 154-155 KL 2
Dexter, NM 154-155 C 4
Deyālā = Diyālā 180-181 EF 4
Dey-Dey, Lake - 194-195 F 5
Deylamān 182-183 NO 4
Dez, Rūd-e - 182-183 N 6
Dezfūl 180-181 F 4
Dezhnev, Cape - = mys
Dežneva 178-179 lm 4
Dezhou 184-185 M 4
Dezh Shāhpur = Marivān
182-183 M 5
Dezinga 171 D 6
Dežneva, mys - 178-179 lm 4
Dhahab 170 F 3
Dhahran = Az-Zahrān 180-181 FG 5
Dhakwah, Tall adh- 182-183 G 6
Dhamār 180-181 EF 8
Dhamtari 180-181 N 6
Dhankuta 180-181 O 5
Dhanushkodi 180-181 MN 9
Dhanushkōṭi = Dhanushkodi
180-181 MN 9
Dhaolāgiri = Daulāgiri 180-181 N 5
Dhar 180-181 M 6
Dharamsala 180-181 M 4
Dhāravāda = Dharwar 180-181
LM 7
Dharmsala = Dharamsala
180-181 M 4
Dharmshala = Dharamsala
180-181 M 4
Dharoor 166-167 c 1
Ḍhār Walātah 166-167 C 5
Dhāt al-Hājj = Hājj 170 FG 3
Dhaulāgiri 180-181 N 5
Dhāvan'gerē = Davangere
180-181 M 8
Dhiinsoor = Diinsor 166-167 N 8
Dhikār, Bi'r adh- 166-167 J 3
Dhi-Oâr 182-183 LM 7
Dhond 180-181 L 7
Dhoraji 180-181 L 6
Dhubari = Dhubri 180-181 OP 5
Dhubri 180-181 OP 5
Dhufar = Ẓufār 180-181 G 7
Dhule 180-181 L 6
Dhūliyā = Dhulia 180-181 L 6
Dhūlja = Dhule 180-181 L 6
Dhuusamaareeb 166-167 E 2
Dia 136-137 L 8
Diable, Île du - 158-159 J 3
Diablo Heights 146-147 b 3
Diablo Range 146-147 BC 4
Diablo, Sierra - 154-155 C 5
Diabo, Serra do - 160-161 F 5
Diaca 171 DE 5
Diadema 160-161 J 5
Diagbe 171 AB 1
Diagonal, IA 152-153 JK 5
Dialafara 172-173 C 2
Dialloubé 172-173 DE 2
Diamant, Fosse du - 124-125 P 7
Diamante [RA] 162 DE 4
Diamantina 158-159 L 8
Diamantina, Fosa - 124-125 P 7
Diamantina, Fossa - 124-125 P 7
Diamantina, Fossa di Frattura -
124-125 P 7
Diamantinadiep 124-125 P 7
Diamantina River 194-195 H 4
Diamantinatiefe 124-125 P 7
Diamantino [BR ↖ Cuiabá]
158-159 H 7
Diamantino [BR ↗ Alto Garças]
160-161 F 2
Diamantino, Rio - 160-161 F 2
Diamond, OR 150-151 D 4
Diamond Lake 150-151 B 4
Diamond Peak 150-151 EF 6
Diamondville, WY 150-151 H 5
Diamou 172-173 C 2
Dianbai 190-191 C 11
Diancheng 184-185 L 7
Dian Chi 184-185 J 7
Dianfou = Feidong 190-191 F 6
Dianópolis 158-159 K 7
Dianra 172-173 D 3
Diaocha Hu 190-191 D 6
Diapaga 166-167 E 6
Diari 172-173 E 3
Diavolo, Buca del 128-129 HJ 4
Diavolo, Isola del - = Île du Diable
158-159 J 3
Diaz [MEX] 154-155 C 7
Dibaga = Dībagah 182-183 KL 5
Dibagah 182-183 KL 5
Dibaya 168-169 F 4
Dibbāgh, Jabal - 170 F 4
Dibble Ice Tongue 121 C 14
Dibdibah, Ad- 182-183 M 8
Dibella 166-167 G 5
Dibeng 174-175 E 4
Dibis, Bi'r - 166-167 K 4
Diboll, TX 154-155 H 5
Dibrugarh 180-181 PQ 5
Dibsah 182-183 GH 5
Dibulla 158-159 E 2
Dickens, TX 154-155 E 4
Dickey, ND 152-153 G 2
Dickinson, ND 146-147 F 2
Dickinson, TX 154-155 H 6
Dick's Head = Raas Jumbo
168-169 K 3
Dickson = Dikson 178-179 P 3
Dickson, TN 154-155 M 2-3
Dickson City, PA 148-149 EF 4
Dickson Harbour =
P'asinskij zaliv 178-179 PQ 3
Dickson, TN 154-155 M2-3
Dicle [TR, Diyarbakır] 182-183 J 3
Dicle [TR, Mardin] 182-183 JK 4
Dicle Nehri 182-183 J 4
Didi-Abuli, gora 140-141 LM 6
Didiéni 166-167 C 6
Didymóteichon 136-137 LM 5
Diébougou 172-173 E 3
Diedenhofen = Thionville
134-135 KL 4
Diéma 172-173 C 2
Diego de Amagro, Isla - 162 A 8
Diego Garcia 124-125 N 6
Diego Ramirez, Islas - 162 C 9
Diégo-Suarez = Antsiranana
168-169 LM 5
Dieme's Land, Van - =
Tasmania 194-195 HJ 8
Điện Biên Phu 186-187 D 2
Diepholz 133 D 2
Dieppe 134-135 H 4
Dierks, AR 154-155 HJ 3
Dietrich, ID 150-151 F 4
Diêu, Mui - 186-187 EF 4
Dieżniewa, Przylądek - = mys
Dezneva 178-179 lm 4
Dif 168-169 K 2
Diffa 166-167 G 6
Ḍiffah, Aḍ- 166-167 J-2
Difícil, El - 158-159 E 3
Diga di 3 gole 190-191 C 6
Dighton, KS 152-153 F 6
Digne 134-135 L 6
Digoin 134-135 JK 5
Digor 182-183 K 2
Digos 186-187 J 5
Digul, Sungai - 186-187 M 8
Digya National Park 172-173 E 4
Dih 182-183 K 4
Dihang 180-181 PQ 5
Dihua = Ürümqi 184-185 F 3
Di'ib, Wādī - 170 FG 6-7
Diinsor 166-167 N 8
Dijlah, Nahr - 180-181 E 3
Dijlah, Shaṭṭ- 180-181 F 4
Dijon 134-135 K 5
Dikabi 174-175 G 2
Dikākah, Ad- 180-181 G 7
Dikanās 130-131 F 5
Dikhil 166-167 N 6
Dikili 182-183 B 3
Dikimďa 178-179 X 6
Dikoa = Dikwa 166-167 G 6
Dikson 178-179 P 3
Diktē Oros 136-137 L 8
Dikwa 166-167 G 6
Dila 166-167 M 7
Dilam, Ad- 180-181 F 6
Dili 186-187 J 8
Di Linh 186-187 E 4
Dilinjāt, Ad- 170 D 2
Diližan 140-141 M 6
Dill City, OK 154-155 F 3
Dilley, TX 154-155 F 6
Dilli - Delhi 180-181 M 5
Dillia 166-167 G 5-6
Dillingham, AK 144-145 DE 6
Dillinj, Ad- 166-167 KL 6
Dillman = Shāhpūr 182-183 L 3
Dillon, CO 152-153 C 6
Dillon, MT 150-151 G 3
Dillon, SC 148-149 D 7
Dillwyn, VA 148-149 D 6
Dilolo 168-169 F 5
Dima, Lak - 171 E 2
Dimashq 180-181 D 4
Dimbokro 166-167 D 7
Dimboola 196 EF 6
Dimitrijevskoje = Talas 180-181 L 2
Dimitrov 140-141 H 2
Dimitrovgrad [BG] 136-137 LM 4
Dimitrovgrad [SU] 178-179 HJ 7
Dimlang 172-173 HJ 3
Dimmitt, TX 154-155 D 3
Dimōna 182-183 F 7
Dimpo 174-175 D 3
Dinagat Island 186-187 J 4
Dinamarca 122-123 GH 2
Dinamarca 130-131 C-E 10
Dinamarca, Estrecho de -
120 C 20-22
Dinamarca, Estreito da -
120 C 22-20
Dinan 134-135 F 4
Dinant 134-135 K 3
Dinar 182-183 CD 3
Dinār, Kūh-e - 180-181 G 4
Dinara 136-137 G 3-4
Dinard 134-135 F 4
Dinarisches Gebirge = Dinara
136-137 G 3-4
Dindigul 180-181 M 8
Dindukkal = Dindigul 180-181 M 8
Ding 184-185 M 4
Dingbian 190-191 A 3
Dinghai 190-191 J 6-7
Dingjiang = Qingjiang 190-191 E 7
Dingle 132 A 5
Dingle Bay 132 A 5
Dingnan 190-191 E 9
Dingqiang = Dingxiang 190-191 D 2
Dingshan = Qingshuzhen
190-191 G 6
Dingshuzhen 190-191 G 6
Dingtao 190-191 E 4
Dinguiraye 166-167 BC 6
Dingwall 132 D 3
Dingxi 184-185 J 4
Ding Xian 190-191 E 2
Dingxiang 190-191 D 2
Dingxin 184-185 H 3
Dingyuan 190-191 F 5
Dingzi Gang 190-191 H 3
Dingzi Wan = Dingzi Gang
190-191 H 3
Dinh, Mui - 186-187 E 4
Dinkimo 172-173 G 2
Dinnebito Wash 150-151 H 8
Dinosaur National Monument
150-151 J 5
Dinuba, CA 150-151 D 7
Diogo Island 190-191 H 11
Dioïla 166-167 C 6
Dioka 172-173 C 2
Diomida, ostrova - 144-145 C 4-5
Dionisio Cerqueira 160-161 F 7
Diosig 136-137 JK 2
Diouloulou 166-167 A 6
Diourbel 166-167 A 6
Dioungani 172-173 E 2
Dioura 172-173 D 2
Dipfaryas = Dipkarpaz
182-183 EF 5
Dipkarpaz 182-183 EF 5
Dipolog 186-187 H 5
Dir 180-181 L 3
Diradawa = Dirē Dawa 166-167 N 7
Dirē [ETH] 166-167 M 6
Diré [RMM] 166-167 D 5
Dirē Dawa 166-167 N 7
Direkli 182-183 G 3
Dirfys 136-137 KL 6
Dirico 168-169 F 6
Dirk Hartog Island 194-195 B 5
Dirkiesdorp 174-175 J 4
Dirkou 166-167 G 5
Dirranbandi 194-195 J 5
Dirschau = Tczew 133 J 1
Dirty Devil River 150-151 H 6-7
Disappointment, Cape -
[Falkland Islands] 162 J 8-9
Disappointment, Cape - [USA]
150-151 A 2
Disappointment, Lake -
194-195 DE 4
Discovery Bay 194-195 GH 7
Discovery Well 194-195 D 4
Dishnā 170 E 4
Disko 144-145 a 4
Disko Bugt 144-145 a 4
Diskobukta 130-131 l 6
Dismal River 152-153 F 5
Dismal Swamp 148-149 E 6
Disna 130-131 N 10
Disna [SU,~] 138-139 FG 6
Disna [SU,●] 138-139 G 6
Disston, OR 150-151 B 4
Distrito Federal [BR] 158-159 K 8
Distrito Federal [RA] 162 E 4
Disūq 170 D 2
Diu 180-181 L 6
Divāndarreh 182-183 M 5
Divāngiri 180-181 P 5
Divejevo 138-139 O 6
Diviči 140-141 O 6
Divide, MT 150-151 G 3
Divino 160-161 L 4
Divinópolis 158-159 KL 9
Divisa, Monte da - 160-161 J 4
Divisa Nova 160-161 J 4
Divisões, Serra das - 158-159 JK 8
Divisor, Sierra de - 158-159 E 6
Divrigi 182-183 GH 3
Divnoje 140-141 L 4
Divo 172-173 D 4
Diwānganj 180-181 OP 5
Diwāniyah, Ad- 180-181 EF 4
Diweir, Ed - = Ad-Duwayr 170 D 4
Dixfield, ME 148-149 H 2
Dixie, ID 150-151 F 3
Dixie, WA 150-151 DE 2
Dixon, CA 150-151 C 6
Dixon, IL 152-153 M 5
Dixon, MO 152-153 KL 6-7
Dixon, MT 150-151 F 2
Dixon, NM 154-155 C 2
Dixon Entrance 144-145 K 7
Diyadin 182-183 K 3
Diyālā 180-181 EF 4
Diyāla, Nahr - 180-181 EF 4
Diyālá, Sadd ad- 182-183 L 5
Diyarbakır 180-181 DE 3
Diyarbakır havzası 182-183 J 3
Dizābād 182-183 N 5
Dize = Yüksekova 182-183 L 4
Dizful = Dezfūl 180-181 F 4
Dja 166-167 G 8
Djado 166-167 G 4
Djado, Plateau du - 166-167 G 4
Djafou, Hassi - = Hāssī Jafū
166-167 E 2
Djakarta = Jakarta 186-187 E 8
Djakovica 136-137 J 4
Djakovo 136-137 H 3
Djala 136-137 J 2
Djalon 166-167 B 6
Djambala 168-169 DE 3
Djelfa = Jilfah 166-167 E 2
Djema 166-167 K 7
Djénné 166-167 D 6
Djérém 166-167 G 7
Djerid, Chott el - = Shaṭṭ al-
Jarīd 166-167 F 2
Djibhalanta–Uliastaj 184-185 H 2
Djibo 166-167 D 6
Djibouti [●] 166-167 N 6
Djibouti [★] 166-167 N 6
Djibuti 166-167 N 6
Djidda = Jiddah 180-181 D 6
Djidjelli = Jījlī 166-167 F 1
Djiguina 172-173 G 2
Djilolo = Halmahera 186-187 J 6
Djingiz Chanwal 184-185 LM 2
Djirgalanta = Chovd 184-185 G 2
Djokjakarta = Yogyakarta
186-187 EF 8
Djolu 168-169 F 2
Djouah 168-169 D 2
Djougou 166-167 E 7
Djoungarie = Junggariya
184-185 EF 2
Djourab 166-167 H 5
Djuba = Webi Ganaane
166-167 N 8
Djugu 168-169 GH 2
Djúpavík 130-131 c 2
Djúpivogur 130-131 fg 2
Djurdjura = Jurjurah 166-167 EF 1
Dmitrija Lapteva, proliv -
178-179 a-c 3
Dmitrijevka = Dmitrevka 140-141 F 1
Dmitrijev-L'govskij 138-139 KL 7
Dmitrijevka = Talas 180-181 L 2
Dmitrov 178-179 F 6
Dmitrovka 140-141 F 1
Dmitrovsk-Orlovskij 138-139 KL 7
Dnepr-Bug-Kanal = Dneprovsko-
Bugskij kanal 138-139 E 7
Dneprodzeržinsk 140-141 FG 2
Dneprodzeržinskoje vodochranilišče
140-141 F 2
Dnepropetrovsk = Dnipropetrovs'k
149-141 GH 2
Dneprorudnoje 140-141 G 3
Dneprovskij liman 140-141 DE 3
Dneprovsko-Bugshij Kanal
138-139 E 7
Dneprovskoje 138-139 JK 6
Dnestr 140-141 D 2-3
Dnestrovskij liman 140-141 DE 3
Dnipro 180-181 H 7
Dnipro (Dnjepr) 180-181 E 1-3
Dnipropetrovs'k 140-141 GH 2
Dnjeprodserschinsk =
Dneprodzeržinsk 140-141 FG 2
Dnjeprpetrowsk = Dnepropetrovsk
140-141 GH 2
Dnjestr = Dnestr 140-141 D 2-3
Dno 138-139 G 5
Doab 180-181 MN 5
Doba 166-167 H 7
Dobbiaco 136-137 E 2
Dobbin, TX 154-155 H 5
Dobbyn 194-195 G 3
Dobele 138-139 D 5
Doblas 162 D 5
Doblen = Dobele 138-139 D 5
Dobo 186-187 K 8
Doboj 136-137 GH 3
Dobovka 140-141 M 2
Dobr'anka [SU, Rossijskaja SFSR]
138-139 V 4

Dobŕanka [SU, Ukrainskaja SSR] 138-139 H 7
Dobrej Nadziei, Przylądek - 168-169 E 9
Dobré nadeje, mys - 168-169 E 9
Dobreta Turnu Severin 136-137 K 3
Dobrić 136-137 MN 4
Dobrinka [SU] 138-139 N 7
Dobrodsja 136-137 M 4-N 3
Doboje 136-137 M 7
Doboje [SU, Rossijskaja SFSR] 138-139 MN 7
Doboje [SU, Ukrainskaja SSR] 140-141 F 7
Dobropolje [SU] 140-141 H 2
Dobroudja 136-137 M 4-N 3
Dobrudža 136-137 M 4-N 3
Dobrudža 136-137 M 4-N 3
Dobrudzsa 136-137 M 4-N 3
Dobrugia 136-137 M 4-N 3
Dobruja 136-137 M 4-N 3
Dobruš 138-139 H 7
Doč' 140-141 F 1
Doctor Gumersindo Sayago 160-161 B 5
Doctor Luis de Gásperi 160-161 B 5
Doctor Pedro P. Peña 162 D 2
Doda Betta 180-181 M 8
Doddecanese = Dödekánēsos 136-137 M 7-8
Dodécanese = Dödekánēsos 136-137 M 7-8
Dodekanes = Dödekánēsos 136-137 M 7-8
Dödekánēsos 136-137 M 7-8
Dode Zee = Bahr al-Mayyit 180-181 D 2
Dodge Center, MN 152-153 K 3-4
Dodge City, KS 146-147 FG 4
Dodgeville, WI 152-153 LM 4
Dodoma 168-169 J 4
Dodson, MT 152-153 BC 1
Dodson, TX 154-155 EF 3
Dodson Peninsula 121 B 30-31
Dodurga 182-183 C 3
Doerun, GA 148-149 B 9
Dofar = Zufār 180-181 G 7
Dogai Tshoring 184-185 F 5
Doğanhisar 182-183 D 3
Doğankent 182-183 G 3
Doğanşehir 182-183 G 3
Doğantepe 182-183 F 2
Dogden Buttes 152-153 F 2
Dogger, Banco de - 132 H 4
Dogger, Banco de - 132 H 4
Dogger, Bank 132 H 4
Dogger, Ławica - 132 H 4
Doggerbank 132 H 4
Dogger Bank 132 H 4
Doggersbank 132 H 4
Doggerská lavice 132 H 4
Doggerbank 132 H 4
Dogo 184-185 P 4
Dogondoutchi 166-167 E 6
Dogoni 172-173 C 4
Dōgo yama 188-189 J 5
Doğubayazit 182-183 KL 3
Dogué 172-173 F 3
Doha = Ad-Dawhah 180-181 G 5
Dohlen = Doln 138-139 D 5
Dois Córregos 160-161 HJ 5
Dois Irmãos' Serra - 158-159 L 6
Dois Vizinhos 160-161 F 6
Dukán 182-183 L 4-5
Dokan, Sad ad- = Sadd ad-Dukán 182-183 L 4-5
Dokan Tofa 172-173 H 3
Dokka 130-131 D 7
Dokos 136-137 K 6
Dokšicy 138-139 FG 6
Doland, SD 152-153 GH 3
Dolbeau 144-145 W 8
Dôle 134-135 L 5
Dolgaja, kosa - 140-141 HJ 3
Dolganen en Nentsen, Tajmyr-Nationaal Gebied der - 178-179 P-U 3
Dolganen und Nenzen, Tajmyr-Nationalkreis der - 178-179 P-U 3
Dolgano-Nenets Autonomous Area 178-179 P-U 3
Dolgellau 132 DE 5
Dolgij, ostrov - 178-179 K 4
Dolgij ostrov [SU, Azovskoje more] 140-141 HJ 3
Dolgij ostrov [SU, Č'ornoje more] 140-141 J 3
Dolginovo 130-131 MN 10
Dolgoje 138-139 F 6
Dolgoje [SU, Rossijskaja SFSR Or'ol] 138-139 G 5
Dolgorukovo 138-139 H 5
Dolgyj, ostrov - 136-137 O 2
Dolhasca 136-137 M 2
Dolina 140-141 AB 2
Dolinsk 178-179 b 8
Dolinskaja 140-141 F 2
Dolinskoje 140-141 DE 3
Dolleman Island 121 B 130-131
Dolomites = Dolomiti 136-137 DE 2
Dolomites = Dolomiti 136-137 DE 2
Dolomiti 136-137 DE 2
Dolo Odo 166-167 N 8
Doloon Choolojn Gobi = Zaaltajn Gov' 184-185 H 3
Doloon Nuur 184-185 LM 3
Dolores, TX 154-155 F 7
Dolores [RA] 162 E 5
Dolores [ROU] 162 E 4
Dolores, CO 150-151 J 7
Dolores River 146-147 E 4
Doloroso, MS 154-155 K 5
Dolphin, Cape - 162 E 8
Dolphin and Union Strait 144-145 NO 4
Doğarinsko-Nieniecki Okręg Autonomiczny 178-179 P-U 3
Dolžanskaja 140-141 HJ 3
D'oma [SU] 138-139 U 7
Doma [WAN] 172-173 H 3
Domačevo 138-139 DE 8
Domanevka 140-141 EF 3
Dom Aquino 160-161 E 1
Domažlice 133 F 4
Dombaj-Uel'gen, gora - 140-141 KL 5
Dombarovskij 178-179 K 7
Dombás 132-133 C 6
Dombe Grande 168-169 D 5
Dombóvár 133 HJ 4
Dome, AZ 150-151 F 9
Dôme, Puy de - 134-135 J 6
Dömel = Mužaffarābād 180-181 LM 4
Dome Rock Mountains 150-151 F 9
Domesnäs = Kolkasrags 138-139 D 5

Domesnäs, Meerenge von - = Irbeni väin 138-139 CD 5
Domeyko, Cordillera - 162 C 2-3
Dominica 146-147 O 8
Dominicaanse Republiek 146-147 MN 7-8
Dominican Republic 146-147 MN 7-8
Dominicana 146-147 MN 7-8
Dominikana 146-147 MN 7-8
Dominikanische Republik 146-147 MN 7-8
Dominikánská republika 146-147 MN 7-8
Dominion Range 121 A 18-19
Dom Joaquim 160-161 L 3
Domodedovo 138-139 G 5
Domodòssola 136-137 C 2
Dom Pedrito 162 F 4
Dom Silverio 160-161 L 4
Domsjö 130-131 J 6
Domuyo, Volcán - 162 BC 3
Don [GB] 132 E 4
Don [SU] 138-139 M 7
Donald 194-195 H 7
Donaldson, AR 154-155 J 3
Donaldsonville, LA 154-155 K 5
Donalsonville, GA 154-155 N 5
Doña Maria, Punta - 158-159 D 7
Donau 133 H 3
Donaueschingen 133 D 5
Donauwörth 133 E 4
Don Benito 134-135 E 9
Donbei 190-191 D 9
Doncaster 132 F 5
Dondangen = Dundaga 138-139 D 5
Dondo [Angola] 168-169 D 4
Dondo [Moçambique] 168-169 HJ 6
Dondra Head = Dewundara Tuḍuwa 180-181 N 9
Donec 140-141 J 2
Doneck 140-141 H 2-3
Doneckij kr'až 140-141 H-K 2
Donegal 132 B 4
Donegal Bay 132 B 4
Donetsk = Doneck 140-141 H 2-3
Donez = Donec 140-141 J 2
Donezplatte = Doneckij kr'až 140-141 H-K 2
Dong'a = Dong'ezhen 190-191 F 9
Dong'an 190-191 C 8
Dongara 194-195 B 5
Dongbei 190-191 D 9
Dongbei = Xinfeng 190-191 EF 8
Dongbi = Dongbei 190-191 D 9
Dongbo = Dongbei 190-191 D9
Dongchuan 184-185 J 6
Dong'ezhen 190-191 F 3
Dongfang 184-185 K8
Donggala 188-189 DE 3
Donggou 184-185 LM 7
Dongguan 190-191 F 3
Donghai 190-191 J 4
Dong He 190-191 A 3
Dòng Ho'i 186-187 E 3
Dong Hu = Chengdong Hu 190-191 F 5
Dong Jiang 190-191 DE 10
Dongjian = Congjiang 190-191 B 9
Dongjiang = Tung Kang 190-191 H 10
Dong Jiang = Xu Jiang 190-191 C 7
Dongjin = Dongjiang 190-191 BC 10
Dongjing Wan = Beibu Wan 184-185 K 7-8
Dongjingping = Zou'an 190-191 E 4
Dongkalale 186-187 GH 6
Dongkou 190-191 C 8
Dongliu 190-191 F 6
Dongming 190-191 E 4
Dongo 168-169 E 2
Dong Phaya Yen 186-187 D 3
Dongping 190-191 F 4
Dongping = Anhua 190-191 C 7
Dongping Hu 190-191 F 3-4
Dongshan 190-191 F 10
Dongshan Dao 190-191 F 10
Dongshannei Ao 190-191 F 10
Dongsha Qundao 184-185 LM 7
Dongsheng 184-185 KL 4
Dongtai 184-185 N 5
Dongting Hu 184-185 L 6
Dongtou Shan 190-191 H 8
Donguztau 178-179 K 8
Dòng Voi Mẹp 186-187 E 3
Dongxiang 190-191 F 7
Dongxi Lian Dao 190-191 GH 4
Dongxing 184-185 K 7
Dòng Xoai 186-187 E 4
Dongyang 190-191 H 7
Dong Yunhe = Chuanchang He 190-191 GH 5
Dongzhen = Xinyi 190-191 C 10
Dongzhi 190-191 F 6
Doniphan, MO 154-155 K 2
Donji Vakuf 136-137 G 3
Donkerpoort 174-175 F 6
Don Martin 154-155 E 7
Dønna 130-131 DE 4
Donnelly, ID 150-151 EF 3
Donner Pass 146-147 B 4
Donnybrook 174-175 H 5
Donskoj 138-139 M 7
Donsol 186-187 H 4
Donūša 136-137 LM 7
Donuzlav, ozero - 140-141 F 4
Donyztau = Donguztau 178-179 K 8
Donžère 184-185 K 6
Doña Maria, Punta - 158-159 D 7
Doonerak, Mount - 144-145 EG 4
Doornbosch = Doringbos 174-175 C 6
Doornriver = Doringrivier 174-175 C 6
Doorns, De - 174-175 CD 7
Door Peninsula 152-153 N 3
Dör, Ad- = Ad-Dawr 182-183 K L 5
Dora, NM 154-155 D 4
Dòra, Baghdad = Baghdad-Dawrah 182-183 L 6
Dora, Lake - 194-195 D 4
Dora Baltea - 136-137 B 3
Dorada = La-158-159 E 3
Dorado 184-185 F 3
Dorbjany = Darbénai 138-139 C 5
Dörböt Daban 184-185 FG 2
Dorchester 132 E 6
Dorchester, NE 152-153 H 5
Dorchester, Cape - 144-145 V 4
Dordábis 168-169 E 7
Dordogne 134-135 H 6
Dordrecht 134-135 JK 3
Dore 134-135 J 6
Dores [ZA] 174-175 G 6
Dores, Mont - 134-135 J 6
Dores do Indaiá 160-161 K 3

Dorey 172-173 E 2
Dorgali 136-137 C 5
Dori 166-167 DE 6
Doringberge 174-175 E 5
Doringbos 174-175 C 6
Doringriver 174-175 C 6
Dornoch 132 D 3
Dornoch Firth 132 D 3
Dornod = 18 ◁ 184-185 LM 2
Dornogov' = 16 ◁ 184-185 K 3
Doro 172-173 E 1
Dorochovo 138-139 L 2
Dorofejevskaja 178-179 P 3
Dorogobuž 138-139 J 6
Dorohoi 136-137 M 2
Dorotea 130-131 G 5
Dörööö nuur 184-185 GH 2
Dorpat = Tartu 130-131 M 8
Dorpat = Tartu 138-139 F 4
Dorre Island 194-195 B 5
Dorris, CA 150-151 C 5
Dorsale Atlantico-Indiana 124-125 J-L 8
Dorsale Atlantique-Indienne 124-125 J-L 8
Dorsale Centrale Indienne 124-125 N 5-7
Dorsale della Liberia 172 B 5
Dorsale Indiana-Sudorientale 124-125 OP 8
Dorsale Medioatlantica 124-125 H 3-J 8
Dorsale Medio-Indiana 124-125 N 5-7
Dorsale Nord-Atlantique 124-125 H 5-J 5
Dorsale Pacifico-Antarctica 121 D 22-C 20
Dorsale Pacifico-Orientale 124-125 D 6-7
Dorsale Sud-Atlantique 124-125 J-L 8
Dorsal Índico-Atlántico 124-125 J-L 8
Dortmund 133 CD 3
Dortmund-Ems-Kanal 133 C 2-3
Dörtyol 182-183 G 4
Dorüd 182-183 N 6
Doruma 168-169 G 2
Dörvöldžin 184-185 GH 2
Dorya, Ganale - = Genale 166-167 N 7
Dorylaeum = Eskişehir 180-181 C 2
Dos Bahias, Cabo - 162 CD 7
Dos de Mayo 158-159 DE 6
Dösemealti 182-183 D 4
Dos Pozos 162 CD 6
Dos Rios, CA 150-151 B 6
Doswell, VA 148-149 H 6
Dothan, AL 146-147 J 5
Dothan, OR 150-151 B 4
Dotsero, CO 152-153 C 6
Doty, WY 150-151 D 9
Douai 134-135 J 3
Douala = Douala 166-167 FG 8
Douarnenez 134-135 C 4
Double Mountain Fork 154-155 E 4
Double Springs, AL 154-155 M 3-4
Doubs 134-135 L 5
Doudaogoumen = Yayuan 188-189 F 2
Douentza 166-167 D 6
Dougherty, OK 154-155 G 3
Dougherty, TX 154-155 E 4
Dougherty Plain 154-155 NO 5
Douglas 132 D 4
Douglas [ZA] 168-169 F 8
Douglas, AZ 146-147 F 5
Douglas, GA 148-149 B 9
Douglas, WA 150-151 CD 2
Douglas, WY 152-153 D 4
Douglas Lake [USA] 154-155 O 2-3
Douglas Point 152-153 PQ 3
Douglas Range 121 BC 29-30
Dougou 190-191 F 5
Douhudi = Gong'an 190-191 D 6-7
Doúma = Dûmâ 182-183 G 6
Doumé 166-167 G 8
Douna [HV] 172-173 D 2
Douna [RMM] 172-173 E 2
Dounan = Tou-nan 190-191 H 10
Dourada, Cachoeira - 160-161 H 3
Dourada, Serra - 158-159 K 7
Douradina 160-161 E 4
Dourado 160-161 H 5
Dourados [BR ↖ Corumbá] 160-161 D 3
Dourados [BR ↘ Ponta Porã] 158-159 J 9
Dourados, Rio - [BR, Mato Grosso do Sul] 160-161 E 3
Dourados, Rio - [BR, Minas Gerais] 160-161 J 3
Dourados, Serra dos - 162 F 2
Douro 134-135 D 8
Dou Rüd = Dorüd 182-183 N 6
Dou Sar = Dow Sar 182-183 N 5
Dovey's 140-141 L 1
Dove Creek, CO 150-151 J 7
Dover [GB] 132 G 7
Dover [ZA] 174-175 G 4
Dover, DE 146-147 L 4
Dover, GA 148-149 C 8
Dover, NE 148-149 E 5
Dover, NH 148-149 H 3
Dover, NJ 148-149 F 4
Dover, OH 148-149 C 4
Dover, OK 154-155 FG 2-3
Dover, Strait of - 132 GH 6
Dover, Straße von - = Strait of Dover 132 GH 6
Dover-Foxcroft, ME 148-149 J 2
Doveyrich, Rüd-e - 182-183 M 6
Dovrefjell 130-131 C 6
Dovsk 138-139 H 7
Dow, Lake - 168-169 F 6
Dowa 168-169 H 5
Dowagiac, MI 152-153 NO 4-5
Dowlatábád = Malayer 180-181 F 4
Downey, ID 150-151 G 4
Downieville, CA 150-151 C 6
Downpatrik 132 D 4
Downs, IA 152-153 K 4
Dow Sar 182-183 N 5
Doyle, CA 150-151 C 5
Doylesville 150-151 C 6
Dözen 184-185 P 4
Dra, Hamáda du - = Hammádat Dra 166-167 CD 3
Drã, Ouèd ed - = Wâdi Drã 166-167 BC 3
Drã', Wâdi - 166-167 BC 3
Dracena 160-161 G 4

Drăgănești-Vlașca 136-137 L 3
Drăgășani 136-137 L 3
Dragerton, UT 150-151 H 6
Draghoender 174-175 E 5
Dragonera, Isla - 134-135 HJ 9
Dragoon, AZ 150-151 HJ 9
Draguignan 134-135 L 7
Drain, OR 150-151 B 4
Drake, AZ 150-151 G 8
Drake, ND 152-153 F 2
Drake, Détroit de - 162 B-D 9
Drake, Estrecho de - 162 B-D 9
Drake, Estreito de - 162 C 9
Drake, Straat - 162 B-D 9
Drake'a, Cieśnina - 162 B-D 9
Drake-átjáró 162 B-D 9
Drakensberge 168-169 G 9-H 8
Drakes Bay 150-151 B 6
Drake Strait 162 B-D 9
Drakestraße 162 B-D 9
Drakeův průliv 162 B-D 9
Dráma 136-137 KL 5
Dramburg = Drawsko Pomorskie 133 GH 2
Drammen 130-131 CD 8
Dranda = Babušara 140-141 K 5
Drangajökull 130-131 bc 1
Drangsnes 130-131 G 2
Draper, NC 148-149 G 6
Drau 133 F 4
Drava 133 H 6
Drawa 133 G 2
Drawsko Pomorskie 133 GH 2
Drayá 184-185 H 5
Drayton Plains, MI 152-153 P 4
Drenthe, ND 152-153 F 2
Dresden [CDN] 152-153 P 4
Dresden 133 FG 3
Dresden, TN 154-155 L 2
Dresv'anka 138-139 R 3
Dreunberg 174-175 FG 6
Dreux 134-135 H 4
Drew, MS 154-155 K 4
Drewsey, OR 150-151 D 4
Drexel MO 152-153 J 6
Drezno = Dresden 133 G 3
Dribin 138-139 H 6
Drifton, FL 148-149 ab 1
Driggs, ID 150-151 H 4
Drin 136-137 J 4
Drin 136-137 H 3
Drini i Bardhë 136-137 J 4
Drini i Zi 136-137 J 5
Drinit, Gjiri i - 136-137 H 5
Drinkwater Pass 150-151 D 4
Drissa 138-139 H 6
Dröback 130-131 D 8
Drogheda 132 CD 5
Drohobyč 140-141 AB 2
Droichead Átha = Drogheda 132 CD 5
Drôme 134-135 K 6
Dronne 134-135 H 6
Dronning Maud fjellkjede 121 A
Dronning Maud land 121 B 36-4
Droupolé, Monts de - = Monts des Dans 172-173 CD 4
Druja 138-139 F 6
Drumheller 144-145 O 7
Drummond, MI 152-153 P 2
Drummond, MT 150-151 H 2
Drummond, WI 152-153 L 2
Drummond Island 152-153 OP 3
Drummondea 174-175 H 3
Drummondville 144-145 W 8
Drummochter Pass 132 D 3
Druskienniki = Druskininkai 138-139 DE 8
Druskienniki = Druskininkai 130-131 L10
Druskininkai 130-131 L 10-11
Druskininkai 138-139 DE 6-7
Druskininkaj = Druskininkai 138-139 DE 6-7
Druso, Gebel - = Jabal ad-Durūz 180-181 D 4
Družba [SU] Kazachskaja SSR] 178-179 P 8
Družba [SU, Ukrainskaja SSR] 138-139 J 7
Družina 178-179 bc 4
Drvar 136-137 G 3
Dry Creek 152-153 C 2
Dryden 144-145 K 1
Dryden, TX 154-155 D 5-6
Drygalski Glacier 121 B 17-18
Drygalskiinsel 121 C 10
Dry Lake, NV 150-151 F 7
Dry Tortugas 148-149 b 4
Dsaudschikau = Ordžonikidze 140-141 M 5
Dsayul 184-185 H 6
Dschang 166-167 G 7
Dschibuti 166-167 N 6
Dsungarei = Junggharia 184-185 EF 2
Dua 168-169 F 2
Duala = Douala 166-167 FG 8
Du'an 184-185 K 7
Duanshi 190-191 D 4
Duarte, Pico - 146-147 M 8
Duartina 160-161 H 5
Duas Igrejas 134-135 DE 8
Duas Onças, Ilha das - 160-161 F 3
Du'ayn, Ad- 166-167 K 6
Dubā 170 F 4
Dubach, LA 154-155 J 4
Dubawnt Lake 144-145 Q 5
Dubawnt River 144-145 Q 5
Dubay 180-181 GH 5
Dubbo 194-195 J 6
Dubie 171 B 5
Dubin 132 CD 5
Dublin, GA 146-147 K 5
Dublin, MI 152-153 NO 3
Dublin, TX 154-155 F 4
Dublje 136-137 N 2
Dubno 140-141 C 2
Dubois, ID 150-151 G 3
Du Bois, PA 148-149 D 4
Dubois, WY 150-151 J 4
Dubosari 140-141 E 3
Dubossary 136-137 N 2
Dubovka 140-141 J 2
Dubovoje 140-141 LM 2
Dubovskoje 140-141 L 3
Dubovyj Umet 138-139 R 7
Dubrajpur 140-141 J 6
Dubreka 166-167 B 7
Dubrovica 138-139 EF 8

Dubrovka [SU, Br'ansk] 138-139 JK 7
Dubrovka [SU, St. Peterburg] 138-139 H 4
Dubrovnik 136-137 GH 4
Dubrovno 138-139 H 6
Dubuque, IA 146-147 H 3
Dubysa 138-139 D 5
Duchang 190-191 F 7
Duchcov, UT 150-151 H 5
Duchess [AUS] 194-195 G 4
Duchovnickoje 138-139 R 7
Duchovščina 138-139 J 6
Ducie [GH] 154-155 LM 3
Ducie [Pitcairn] 198-199 L 6
Duck Hill, MS 154-155 N 3
Duck River 154-155 M 2-3
Ducktown, TN 154-155 N 3
Duckwater Peak 150-151 F 6
Ducor, CA 150-151 D 8
Dudinka 178-179 PQ 4
Dudorovskij 138-139 K 7
Duékoué 172-173 D 4
Duero 134-135 F 8
Dufayt, Wādi - 170 F 6
Duff Islands 186-187 I 6
Dufur, OR 150-151 C 3
Duga-Zapadnaja, mys - Dugdown Mountain 154-155 N 3-4
Dugi Otok 136-137 F 4
Dugna 138-139 L 6
Dugo Selo 136-137 G 3
Du He 190-191 C 5
Duğur = Posof 182-183 K 2
Duḫuk 182-183 K 4
Duisburg 133 C 3
Duitse Bocht 133 C 1
Duitsland 133 D-F 2-4
Duivelskloof = Duiwelskloof 174-175 J 2
Dujail = Ad-Dujayl 182-183 KL 6
Dujayl, Ad- 182-183 KL 6
Dujiawobu = Ningcheng 188-189 B 2
Dükán 182-183 L 4-5
Dukat 178-179 de 5
Dukds, OK 154-155 F 3
Duk Ayod = Ayod 166-167 L 7
Dūk Fayil 166-167 L 7
Dukhān 180-181 G 5
Dukielska, Przelęcz - 133 KL 4
Dukkülāh 166-167 C 2
Dukou 184-185 J 6
Dükštas 138-139 EF 6
Duku 172-173 H 3
Duku 190-191 J 3
Dulaanchaan 184-185 H 4
Dulac, LA 154-155 K 6
Dulawan = Datu Piang 186-187 H 5
Dulaymiyah, Ad- 182-183 K 6
Dulce, OK 150-151 J 6
Dulce, Rio - 162 D 3-4
Dulgalach 178-179 Z 4
Dulia Jiang 190-191 B 9
Dull Center, WY 152-153 D 4
Dullstroom 174-175 J 3
Dulovo 136-137 M 4
Duluth, MN 146-147 H 2
Dümä 182-183 G 6
Dumanjiang 138-139 D 5
Dumaran Island 186-187 GH 4
Dumas [ZA] 168-169 F 8
Dumaran Island 186-187 GH 4
Dumas, AR 154-155 J 3
Dumas TX 154-155 D 2
Dumbar, Mount - 182-183 C 3
Dumbarton 132 D 3
Dumbéa 198-199 J 6
Dume=Doumé 166-167 G 8
Dumfries 132 E 4
Dumga, Ad- 166-167 L 6
Dumjor 182-183 C 3
Dumka, OK 154-155 G H 3
Dumlu 182-183 J 2
Dumlupinar 182-183 CD 3
Dumyät 182-183 F 2
Dumyät, Masabb - 170 DE 2
Duna 133 J 5
Düna = Daugava 138-139 EF 6
Dünaburg = Daugavpils 138-139 EF 6
Dunaföldvár 133 J 5
Dunaj [SU] 188-189 J 1
Dunaj, ostrova - 178-179 XY 3
Dunaj = Donau 133 J 5
Dunaj = Duna 133 J 5
Dunajevcy 140-141 C 2
Dunărea 136-137 M 3
Dunarii, Delta - 136-137 N 3
Dunaújváros 133 J 5
Dunav 178-179 bc 4
Dunav = Duna 133 J 5
Duna-Völgyi-focsatorna 178-179 G 10
Dunbar, OK 154-155 H 3
Dunbar, PA 148-149 D 4
Dunblane 132 DE 3
Duncan, AZ 150-151 J 9
Duncan, OK 146-147 G 5
Duncan, WY 150-151 J 3
Duncan Passage 180-181 P 8
Dundalk 132 CD 4-5
Dundalk 148-149 D 5
Dundalk, MD 148-149 E 5
Dundas, Lake - 194-195 D 6
Dundas Peninsula 144-145 O 2-3
Dundas Strait 194-195 F 2
Dün Dealgan = Dundalk 132 CD 4-5
Dundee 132 E 3
Dundee [ZA] 168-169 H 8
Dundee, MI 152-153 P 5
Dundee, NY 148-149 E 3
Dundoo 196 K 4
Dundgov' = 13 ◁ 184-185 K 2
Dundwa Range 184-185 J 5
Dunedin 194-195 O 9
Dunedin, FL 148-149 b 2
Dunedoo 196 K 4
Dunfermline 132 DE 3
Dún [SU] – Biškek] 178-179 MN 9
Dunga [ZRE] – Gurjev] 140-141 J 3
Dungarvan 132 C 5
Dungas 166-167 G 6
Dungeness 132 G 6
Dungu [ZRE] - 171 B 2
Dungu [ZRE, ●] 168-169 G 2
Dungujľa'n = Tongji 178-179 L 8
Dżankoj 140-141 G 4
Dzanybek 140-141 J 2
Dzaoudzi 168-169 L 5
Džarkurgan 178-179 K 10
Džardžan 178-179 X 4
Dżargalant 184-185 LM 2
Dżaratdas = Chovd 184-185 G 2
Džarkent = Panfilov 178-179 OP 9
Džarma Dabas nuur 184-185 H 3
Dżarylgač, ostrov 140-141 F 4
Dzasag = Xinjie 190-191 C 8
Dzaudžikau = Ordžonikidze 140-141 M 5
Dżava 140-141 LM 5

Dubrovka [SU, Br'ansk] 138-139 JK 7
Dubrovka [SU, St. Peterburg] 138-139 H 4
Dubrovnik 136-137 GH 4
Dubrovno 138-139 H 6
Dubuque, IA 146-147 H 3
Dubysa 138-139 D 5
Duchang 190-191 F 7
Duchcov, UT 150-151 H 5
Duchess [AUS] 194-195 G 4
Duchovnickoje 138-139 R 7
Duchovščina 138-139 J 6
Ducie [GH] 154-155 LM 3
Ducie [Pitcairn] 198-199 L 6
Duck Hill, MS 154-155 N 3
Duck River 154-155 M 2-3
Ducktown, TN 154-155 N 3
Duckwater Peak 150-151 F 6
Ducor, CA 150-151 D 8
Dudinka 178-179 PQ 4
Dudorovskij 138-139 K 7
Duékoué 172-173 D 4
Duero 134-135 F 8
Dufayt, Wādi - 170 F 6
Duff Islands 186-187 I 6
Dufur, OR 150-151 C 3
Duga-Zapadnaja, mys - Dugdown Mountain 154-155 N 3-4
Dugi Otok 136-137 F 4
Dugna 138-139 L 6
Dugo Selo 136-137 G 3
Du He 190-191 C 5
Duğur = Posof 182-183 K 2
Duḫuk 182-183 K 4
Duisburg 133 C 3
Duitse Bocht 133 C 1
Duitsland 133 D-F 2-4
Duivelskloof = Duiwelskloof 174-175 J 2
Dujail = Ad-Dujayl 182-183 KL 6
Dujayl, Ad- 182-183 KL 6
Dujiawobu = Ningcheng 188-189 B 2
Dükán 182-183 L 4-5
Dukat 178-179 de 5
Dukds, OK 154-155 F 3
Duk Ayod = Ayod 166-167 L 7
Dūk Fayil 166-167 L 7
Dukhān 180-181 G 5
Dukielska, Przelęcz - 133 KL 4
Dukkülāh 166-167 C 2
Dukou 184-185 J 6
Dükštas 138-139 EF 6
Duku 172-173 H 3
Duku 190-191 J 3
Dulaanchaan 184-185 H 4
Dulac, LA 154-155 K 6
Dulawan = Datu Piang 186-187 H 5
Dulaymiyah, Ad- 182-183 K 6
Dulce, OK 150-151 J 6
Dulce, Rio - 162 D 3-4
Dulgalach 178-179 Z 4
Dulia Jiang 190-191 B 9
Dull Center, WY 152-153 D 4
Dullstroom 174-175 J 3
Dulovo 136-137 M 4
Duluth, MN 146-147 H 2
Dümä 182-183 G 6
Dumanjiang 138-139 D 5
Dumaran Island 186-187 GH 4
Dumas [ZA] 168-169 F 8
Dumaran Island 186-187 GH 4
Dumas, AR 154-155 J 3
Dumas TX 154-155 D 2
Dumbar, Mount - 182-183 C 3
Dumbarton 132 D 3
Dumbéa 198-199 J 6
Dume=Doumé 166-167 G 8
Dumfries 132 DE 4

Dunnellon, FL 148-149 b 2
Dunning NE 152-153 FG 5
Dunnolly 196 F 6
Dunphy, NV 150-151 E 5
Dunqul 170 D 6
Dunqulah 166-167 KL 5
Dunqulah 166-167 M 4
Duns 132 E 4
Dunseith ND 152-153 F 1
Duńska, Cieśnina - 120 C 22-20
Dunsmuir, CA 150-151 B 5
Duolun = Doloon Nuur 184-185 LM 3
Duo Qi = Ting Jiang 190-191 F 9
Duozhu 190-191 D 10
Dupang Ling 190-191 C 9
Dupont IN 152-153 O 6
Dupree SD 152-153 F 3
Dupuyer, MT 150-151 G 1
Duque de Bragança 168-169 E 4
Duque de Caxias 158-159 L 9
Duque de York, Isla - 162 A 8
Duquesne, PA 148-149 D 4
Durack Range 194-195 E 3
Durağan 182-183 F 2
Durand MI 152-153 P 4
Durand, WI 152-153 L 3
Durango [MEX] 146-147 GH 6
Durango, CO 146-147 E 4
Durant, OK 146-147 G 5
Duranzo [ROU, ●] 162 E 4
Durazno [ROU, ●] 162 E 4
Durban 168-169 H 8
Durban, Capo - 175-175 C 7
Durbanville 174-175 C 7
Durbe 138-139 C 5
Durbin, WY 152-153 D 4
Durdano = Durbe 138-139 C 5
Durdurmitor 136-137 H 4
Durness 132 D 2
Durrës 182-183 C 3
Dursunbey 182-183 C 3
D'urt'uli 138-139 U 6
Duru [ZRE] - 171 B 1
Duru [ZRE, ●] 171 B 1
Duruz, Jabal ad- 180-181 D 4
Durüz, Jabal ad- 180-181 D 4
Dušanbe 180-181 K 3
Dušeti 140-141 M 5
Düsh 170 D 5
Du Shan [TJ, ▲] 188-189 B 2
Du Shan = Lu Shan 190-191 FG 3
Dusheng 190-191 F 2
Du Shui = Du He 190-191 C 5
Dussin Gol 190-191 A 2
Dustin,OK 154-155 GH 3
Dutch Habor 120 D 35
Dutch John, UT 150-151 J 5
Dutou 190-191 D 9
Dutse 172-173 H 3
Dutsen Wai 172-173 H 3
Dutton, MT 150-151 H 2
Dutton, Mount - [USA] 150-151 G 6-7
Duvan 178-179 K 6
Duvefjord 130-131 l 4
Duwah, Jabal ad- 180-181 E 5
Duwaym, Ad- 166-167 L 6
Duway, Ad- 170 D 4
Duxun 190-191 F 10
Duyfken Point 194-195 H 2
Duyun 184-185 J 6
Duyürah, Qatṭārat ad- 170 C 2
Dúzce 182-183 D 3
Düziçi 182-183 G 4
Dvina Occidental = Daugava 130-131 M 9
Dvina Occidental = Daugava 130-131 E 5
Dvinsk = Daugavpils 138-139 EF 6
Dvorecznaja 140-141 H 2
Dvůr Králové nad Labem 133 GH 3
Dwangwa 171 C 6
Dwarsberg 174-175 G 3
Dwarsrand 174-175 H 4
Dwarsrivier 174-175 H 2
Dwight, AL 152-153 P 5
Dworshak Reservoir 150-151 F 2
Dwyka 174-175 D 7
Dyaul Island 186-187 gh 5
Dychtau, gora - 140-141 L 5
Dyer, Cape - 144-145 YZ 4
Dyereiland 174-175 D 8
Dyer Island = Dyereiland 174-175 D 8
Dyer Plateau 121 BC 30
Dyers Bay 152-153 O 3
Dyersburg, TN 146-147 J 4
Dyersville, IA 152-153 L 4
Dyje 133 H 4
Dylewska Gora 133 JK 2
Dymer 140-141 E 2
Dyrhólaey 130-131 d 3
Dyrnesvägen 130-131 B 6
Dysselsdorp 174-175 E 7
Dzaanhushuu 184-185 H 4
Dzadzgay 174-175 G 6
Dzag 184-185 H 2
Dżagdy, chrebet - 178-179 YZ 7
Dza Chhu 184-185 H 5
Dżalal-Abad 180-181 L 2
Dżalal-Abad 180-181 L 2
Dzalalabad,KS 152-153 O 7
Dżalinda 178-179 XY 7
Dżambajskij, ostrov - 140-141 OP 3
Dżambul [SU] – Biškek] 178-179 MN 9
Dżankoj 140-141 G 4
Dzanybek 140-141 J 2

Eaton, CO 152-153 D 5
Eaton Rapids, MI 152-153 O 4
Eatonton, GA 148-149 B 8
Eatonville, WA 150-151 BC 2
Eau Claire, WI 146-147 H 3
Eau Claire, Lac à l' 144-145 VW 6
Eauripik 186-187 M 5
Ebbw Vale 132 E 6
Ebbw Junction, MI 152-153 N 2
Eber Gölü 182-183 D 3
Eberswalde-Finow 133 F 2
Ebi nuur 184-185 E 3
Eboli 136-137 F 5
Ebolowa 168-169 D 3
Ebony 168-169 D 7
Ebrähimäbad [IR ↗ Aräk] 182-183 N 5
Ebrähimäbad [IR ↘ Qazvin] 182-183 N 5
Ebro 134-135 G 8
Ebro, Delta del - 134-135 H 8
Ebuţţäbäd 180-181 L 4
Ecbatana = Hamadän 180-181 F 3-4
Eceabat 182-183 AB 2
Echeng 190-191 E 6
Echeta, WY 152-153 CD 3
Echigo sammyaku 188-189 M 4-N 5
Echo, OR 150-151 D 3
Echo, UT 150-151 H 5
Echo, UT 150-151 H 5
Echo, Lake - 196 c 3
Echo Bank 144-145 P 7
Echobank 144-145 P 7
Echo Cliffs 150-151 H 7
Echo-pad 146-147 P 7
Echuca 194-195 H 7
Êd [ETH] 166-167 N 6
Ed Damur = Ad-Dämür 182-183 F 6
Eddy, MT 150-151 F 2
Eddy, TX 154-155 G 5
Eddystone Point 196 d 2
Eddyville, KY 154-155 LM 2
Eddyville, NE 152-153 G 5
Ede [WAN] 172-173 G 4
Edéa 166-167 G 8
Edeen 194-195 JK 7
Eden, MT 150-151 H 2
Eden, NC 148-149 D 6
Eden, NC 148-149 D 6
Eden River [USA] 152-153 D 4
Eden River, WI 152-153 M 2
Eden River, WI 152-153 M 3
Eden,WY 150-151 J 4
Edenburg [ZA, Oranje-Vrystaat] 174-175 FG 5
Edendale [ZA, Kwazulu] 174-175 HJ 5
Edenton, NC 148-149 H 6
Edenville 174-175 G 4
Eder 133-E 3
Edessa 136-137 JK 5
Edgar, NE 152-153 H 5
Edgar, WI 152-153 LM 3
Edgard, LA 154-155 K 5-6
Edgartown, MA 148-149 H 4
Edgefield, SC 148-149 BC 8
Edgeley, ND 152-153 G 2
Edgell Island 144-145 Y 5
Edgemont, SD 152-153 E 4
Edgeøya 130-131 l 5-6
Edgerton, MN 152-153 HJ 4
Edgerton, WI 152-153 M 4
Edgewood, IL 152-153 M 6
Edina, MO 152-153 KL 5
Edina, MO 152-153 O 6
Edina, MO 152-153 O 6
Edinburg, IN 152-153 O 6
Edinburg, MS 154-155 L 4
Edinburg, TX 146-147 GH 6
Edineţ 140-141 C 2
Edirne 182-183 AB 2
Edison, GA 154-155 N 5
Edison, NJ 148-149 F 4
Edisto Island, SC 148-149 CD 8
Edisto River 148-149 C 8
Edithburgh 196 C 5
Edjelé = 'Ajilah 166-167 F 3
Edmond, OK 154-155 G 3
Edmonds, WA 150-151 BC 2
Edmonton 144-145 NO 7
Edmore, MI 152-153 O 4
Edmore, ND 152-153 G 1
Edmundston 144-145 X 8
Edna, TX 154-155 G 6
Edo [WAN, ●] 172-173 G 4
Edo = Tökyö 184-185 QR 4
Edremit 180-181 B 3
Edri = Adri 166-167 G 3
Edsbyn 130-131 F 7
Edsel Ford Range 121 B 124-125
Eduardo Castex 162 D 5
Eduardsee = Rutanzige 168-169 G 3
Edward, Jezioro - = Rutanzige 168-169 G 3
Edwardovo jezero = Rutanzige 168-169 G 3
Edward River Aboriginal Reserve 194-195 H 2
Edwards, CA 150-151 D 8
Edwards, MS 154-155 K 4
Edwards Creek 194-195 G 5
Edwards Plateau 146-147 FG 5
Edward-tó = Rutanzige 168-169 G 3
Edward VII Peninsula 121 B 21-22
Edynburg = Edinburgh 132 E 4
'Eelbuur = Ceel Buur 166-167 b 3
Eel River, CA 150-151 B 6
Eel River [USA, Indiana] 152-153 NO 5
Eel Xamurre = Ceel Xamure 166-167 bc 2

ensaamheidpan = Eenzamheidpan 174-175 D 4
enzamheidpan 174-175 D 4
esti = Estnische Republik 138-139 EF 4
fate 194-195 N 3
fes 182-183 B 4
feso = Efes 182-183 B 4
ffingham, IL 146-147 F 4
flâni 182-183 E 2
frichu = Evrýchu 182-183 E 5
fu = Idfu 166-167 L 3
gadi, Isole - 136-137 DE 6
gbe [WAN, Kwara] 172-173 G 3
gbert, WY 152-153 D 5
ge denizi 180-181 A 2-B 3
gedesminde = Auslait 144-145 Za 4
geische Zee 136-137 L 5-M 7
gejské moře 136-137 L 5-M 7
gejskie, Morze - 136-137 L 5-M 7
geland, ND 152-153 G 1
ger 133 K 5
ger = Cheb 133 F 3
ggers Ø 144-145 bc 6
gg Harbor City, NJ 148-149 F 5
gg Lake [CDN, Quebec] 144-145 W 7
gijin gol 184-185 J 1-2
gil 182-183 HJ 3
gilsstadhir 130-131 f 2
gipt 166-167 KL 3
gipto 166-167 KL 3
gipto 166-167 KL 3
girdir 180-181 C 3
girdir Gölü 182-183 D 4
gitto 166-167 KL 3
glab, El - = Aghlâb 166-167 CD 3
glinton Island 144-145 MN 2
gmont, Mount - 194-195 O 7
goji, Kelay - = Afrēra Ye-Tyew Hayik 166-167 N 6
gošinskaja 138-139 QR 3
gret = İhsaniye 182-183 D 3
grigöz Dağı 182-183 C 3
gumenitsa 136-137 J 6
gypt 166-167 KL 3
gypte 166-167 KL 3
gypte 166-167 KL 3
gyenlitői-Guinea 166-167 FG 8
gyiptom 166-167 KL 3
ha Amufu 172-173 G 4
hime 188-189 J 6
cheng 190-191 E 6
cheta, WY 152-153 CD 3
iao 192-193 N 5
ichstätt 133 E 4
id 130-131 AB 7
idfjord 130-131 B 7
idsvåg 130-131 BC 6
idsvoll 130-131 D 7
idsvollfjellet 130-131 j 5
ifel 133 C 3
ige, Carn - 132 D 3
igersund 130-131 A 8
igg 132 C 3
ights Coast 121 B 27-28
ighty Mile Beach 194-195 D 3
ilat 180-181 C 5
ildon, Lake - 194-195 J 7
ilerts de Haan Gebergte 158-159 H 4
il Roba 168-169 JK 2
inasleigh 194-195 HJ 3
inasleigh River 194-195 H 3
indhoven 134-135 K 3
indpaal 174-175 C 3
in-Hazēva 182-183 F 7
in-Yahav 182-183 F 7
iriksjökull 130-131 cd 2
iriksstadhir 130-131 f 2
irunepé 158-159 EF 6
iseb 168-169 E 7
isenach 133 E 3
isenerz 133 G 5
isenhüttenstadt 133 FG 2
isenstadt 133 H 5
išiškės 138-139 E 6
isleben 133 E 3
iwugen = Saint Lawrence Island 144-145 BC 5
jeda 168-169 K 7
jer Bavnehøj 130-131 C 9-10
jin Horo Qi 190-191 BC 2
jura 172-173 E 4
kalaka, MT 152-153 D 3
kang 172-173 H 4
kbatana = Hamadān 180-181 F 3-4
kece = Liz 182-183 JK 3
kecek Dağı 182-183 EF 3
kenäs 130-131 K 7-8
kenie 172-173 G 4
ket 172-173 G 4
kiatapskij chrebet 178-179 jk 4
kibastuz 178-179 NO 7
kimčan 178-179 Z 7
konda 178-179 TU 4
ksjö 130-131 F 9
ktagh Altai = Mongol Altajn Nuruu 184-185 F-H 2
kvádor 158-159 CD 5
kvador 158-159 CD 5
kwan River 144-145 U 7
lafonēsu, Stenón - 136-137 K 7
la Medo = Ēl Medo 166-167 N 7
lands Height 174-175 H 6
landshoek 174-175 J 3
landsrivier [ZA, ◁ Krokodilrivier] 174-175 G 3
landsrivier [ZA, ◁ Olifantsrivier] 174-175 H 3
landsvlai 174-175 C 7
langa 174-175 H 6
lassŏn 136-137 K 6
lat = Eilat 180-181 C 5
lâto 186-187 N 5
lâziğ 180-181 D 3
lba 136-137 D 4
lba, AL 154-155 MN 5
lba, ID 150-151 G 4
lba, NE 152-153 G 5
lbasan 136-137 HJ 5
lbaşı 182-183 FG 3
lbe 133 DE 1-2
lbert, Mount - 146-147 E 4
lberton, GA 148-149 B 7
lbeuf 134-135 H 4
lbing = Elbląg 133 J 1
lbistan 182-183 G 3
lbląg 133 J 1
lboers 180-181 G 3
lborz 180-181 G 3
lbourz 180-181 G 3
lbow Lake, MN 152-153 HJ 2-3
l'brus, gora - 140-141 L 5
lburgon 171 C 3
lburs 180-181 G 3
lburs 180-181 G 3
lburz = Reshteh Kūhhā-ye Alborz 180-181 G 3
lburz Mountains 180-181 G 3
l Cabo, Ciudad de - = Kaapstad 168-169 E 9
El Cajon, CA 150-151 E 9
El Campo, TX 154-155 G 6
El Centro, CA 146-147 CD 5
Elche 134-135 G 9
Elcho Island 194-195 G 2
Elda 134-135 G 9
Ël'dikan 178-179 a 5
Eldon, IA 152-153 KL 5
Eldon, MO 152-153 K 6
Eldon, WA 150-151 B 2
Eldora, IA 152-153 K 4
El Dorado, AR 146-147 H 5
El Dorado [CO] 158-159 E 4
El Dorado [YV] 158-159 G 3
Eldorado [BR] 160-161 HJ 6
Eldorâdo [RA] 162 EF 3
Eldorado, IL 152-153 M 7
El Dorado, KS 152-153 H 7
Eldorado, OK 154-155 F 3
Eldorado, TX 154-155 E 5
Eldorado Mountains 150-151 F 8
Eldorado Springs, MO 152-153 JK 7
Eldoret 168-169 J 2
Electra, TX 154-155 F 3
Electric Mills, MS 154-155 L 4
Electric Peak 150-151 H 3
Eléfantcsont-part [Cl, ≅] 166-167 CD 8
Elefántcsontpart [Cl, ★] 166-167 CD 7
Elefantes, Rio dos - 174-175 K 2-3
Elefantina = Elephantine 166-167 L 4
Éléfants, Réserve aux - 168-169 G 2
Elei, Wâdi - = Wādi llay 170 F 7
Ëlekmonar 178-179 Q 7
Ëlektrostal' 138-139 M 5-6
Elephant Butte Reservoir 154-155 B 4
Elephantine 166-167 L 4
Elephant Island 121 CD 31
Eleşkirt = Zidikân 182-183 K 3
Elets = Jelec 138-139 M 7
Eleuthera Island 146-147 LM 6
Elevi = Görele 182-183 H 2
Elfenbeinküste [Cl, ≅] 166-167 CD 8
Elfenbeinküste [Cl, ★] 166-167 CD 7
Elghena = Algēna 166-167 M 5
Elgin [GB] 132 E 3
Elgin, IL 146-147 J 3
Elgin, ND 152-153 F 2
Elgin, NE 152-153 G 5
Elgin, NV 150-151 F 7
Elgin, OR 150-151 E 3
Elgin, TX 154-155 G 5
Elgon, Mount - 168-169 H 2
Elhovo 136-137 M 4
Eli, NE 152-153 F 4
Eliasville, TX 154-155 F 4
Elida, NM 154-155 D 4
Éliki, Vallée d' 166-167 F 6
Elila 168-169 G 3
Elim [ZA] 174-175 C 8
Eling Hu = Ngoring Tsho 184-185 H 4-5
Elisabethbaai 174-175 A 4
Elisabethbucht = Elisabethbaai 174-175 A 4
Elisabeth Reef 194-195 L 5
Elisabethville = Lubumbashi 168-169 G 5
Ëlisenvaara 138-139 GH 3
Ëlista 140-141 M 3
Elizabeth, IL 152-153 LM 4
Elizabeth, LA 154-155 J 5
Elizabeth, NJ 148-149 F 4
Elizabeth, Adelaide- 194-195 G 6
Elizabeth , Cape - 148-149 HJ 3
Elizabeth , Cape - = Cape Pillar 194-195 J 8
Elizabeth Bay = Elisabethbaai 174-175 A 4
Elizabeth City, NC 148-149 E 6
Elizabethton, TN 148-149 BC 6
Elizabethtown, KY 152-153 O 7
Elizabethtown, NC 148-149 D 7
Elizabethtown, NY 148-149 FG 2
Elk 133 L 2
Elk, CA 150-151 B 6
Elk, WA 150-151 E 1
Elkader, IA 152-153 L 4
Elk City, ID 150-151 F 3
Elk City, OK 154-155 F 3
Elk Creek, CA 150-151 B 6
Elkedra 194-195 G 4
Elk Grove, CA 150-151 C 6
Elkhart, IN 152-153 NO 5
Elkhart, KS 154-155 E 2
Elkhart, TX 154-155 H 5
Elkhead Mountains 152-153 C 5
El Khenâchich, 'Oglat - = El Khnâchich 166-167 D 4
Elkhorn, WI 152-153 K 4
Elkhorn Peak 150-151 H 2
Elkhorn Peaks 150-151 H 4
Elkhorn River 152-153 G 4
Elki 182-183 K 4
Elkin, NC 148-149 C 6
Elkins, NM 154-155 CD 4
Elkins, WV 148-149 CD 5
Elk Mountain 152-153 C 5
Elko, NV 146-147 C 3
Elkol, WY 150-151 H 5
Elk Point, SD 152-153 H 4
Elk Rapids, MI 152-153 O 3
Elk Ridge 150-151 J 7
Elk River, ID 150-151 EF 2
Elk River, MN 152-153 K 3
Elk Springs, CO 152-153 BC 5
Elkton, KY 154-155 M 2
Elkton, MD 148-149 EF 5
Elkton, OR 150-151 B 4
Elkton, SD 152-153 H 3
Ellaville, GA 154-155 N 4
Ellef Ringnes Island 144-145 Q 2
Ellen, Mount - 150-151 H 6
Ellendale, ND 152-153 G 2-3
Ellensburg, WA 150-151 C 2
Ellenville, NY 148-149 F 4
Ellerbe, NC 148-149 D 7
Ellesmere Island 120 B 27-A 26
Elliotdale = Xhora 174-175 H 6
Ellijay, GA 154-155 N 3
Ellikine 172-173 H 2
Ellinwood, KS 152-153 G 6
Elliot 168-169 G 9
Ellice Island 198-199 H 5
Elliot Lake [CDN, ●] 144-145 U 8
Elliott 194-195 F 3
Elliott Knob 148-149 D 5
Ellis, ID 150-151 F 3
Ellis, KS 152-153 G 6
Elliston [AUS] 194-195 F 6
Ellisville, MS 154-155 L 5
Ellon 132 E 3
Ellore = Eluru 180-181 N 7
Elloree, SC 148-149 C 8
Ellsinore, MO 154-155 K 2
Ellsworth, KS 152-153 G 6
Ellsworth, ME 148-149 J 2
Ellsworth, WI 152-153 K 3
Ellsworth Highland 121 B 28-25
Ellwood City, PA 148-149 C 4
Elma, IA 152-153 K 4
Elma, WA 150-151 B 2
Elmadağ 182-183 E 3
Elma Dağı 182-183 E 3
Elmalı 182-183 CD 4
Elmalı Dağı 182-183 CD 4
El Mamoun 152-153 E 1
Elm Creek, NE 152-153 G 5
El Medo 166-167 N 7
Elmer, MO 152-153 K 6
Elmhurst, IL 152-153 MN 5
Elmira [CDN, Ontario] 148-149 C 3
Elmira, CA 150-151 C 6
Elmira, ID 150-151 E 1
Elmira, MI 152-153 O 3
Elmira, NY 146-147 L 3
Elm Lake 152-153 G 3
Elmore 196 G 6
Elmshorn 133 DE 2
Elmvale 148-149 D 2
Elmwood, IL 152-153 LM 5
Elmwood, OK 154-155 E 2
Elne 134-135 J 7
El Nevado, Cerro - 158-159 E 4
Elói Mendes 160-161 K 4
Elorza 158-159 F 3
Eloy, AZ 150-151 H 9
El Paso, IL 152-153 M 5
El Paso, TX 146-147 E 5
El Portal, CA 150-151 CD 7
El Reno, OK 146-147 G 4
Elroy, WI 152-153 L 4
El Salvador [ES] 146-147 J 9
Elsaß 134-135 L 4-5
Elsberry, MO 152-153 L 6
Elsinore, CA 150-151 E 9
Elsmore, KS 152-153 J 7
Ël'ton [SU] 140-141 N 2
Elton, LA 154-155 J 5
Ël'ton, ozero - 140-141 N 2
Eltopia, WA 150-151 D 2
Eluan Bi = O-luan-pi 190-191 H 11
Eluru 180-181 N 7
Elva 130-131 M 8
Elva [SU] 138-139 F 4
Elvanlar = Eşme 182-183 C 3
Elvas 134-135 D 9
Elverum 130-131 DE 7
Elvesis 136-137 K 6
Elvira 158-159 E 6
Elvira, Cape - 144-145 P 3
Elwa = Elva 138-139 F 4
Elwell Lake 150-151 H 1
Elwood, IN 152-153 O 5
Elwood, NE 152-153 FG 5
Ely 132 G 5
Ely, MN 152-153 KL 2
Ely, NV 146-147 D 4
Elyria, OH 148-149 B 4
Elzas 134-135 L 4-5
Elzasz 134-135 L 4-5
Elk 133 L 2
Ellef Ringnes Island 144-145 Q 2
Ellen, Mount - 150-151 H 6
Ellensburg, WA 150-151 C 2
Ellenville, NY 148-149 F 4
Ellerbe, NC 148-149 D 7
Ellesmere Island 120 B 27-A 26
Ellikine 172-173 H 2
Ellinwood, KS 152-153 G 6
Elliot 168-169 G 9
Elliot Lake [CDN, ●] 144-145 U 8
Elliott 194-195 F 3
Elliott Knob 148-149 D 5
Ellis, ID 150-151 F 3
Elliston [AUS] 194-195 F 6
Ellon 132 E 3
Ellore = Eluru 180-181 N 7
Elloree, SC 148-149 C 4
Ellsworth Highland 121 B 28-25
Ellwood City, PA 148-149 C 4
Emagusheni = Magusheni 174-175 H 6
Ema jõgi 138-139 F 4
Ema joki 130-131 M 8
Emāmzādeh 'Abbās 182-183 MN 6
Emån 130-131 F 9
Emas, Parque Nacional dos - 158-159 J 8
Ëmba [SU, ●] 178-179 K 8
Embach = Ema jõgi 138-139 F 4
Embarcación 162 D 2
Embarrass, MN 152-153 K 2
Embarrass River 152-153 MN 6
Embenčime 178-179 ST 4
Embetsu 188-189 b 1
Ëmbi [SU, ~] 178-179 K 8
Emblem, WY 152-153 B 3
Emboscada, 160-161 D 6
Embu 168-169 J 3
Embuguaçu 160-161 J 5
Emden 133 C 2
Emden, Abisso di - 186-187 J 5
Emden, Abysse d' 186-187 J 5
Emden, Fosa de - 186-187 J 5
Emden, Fosse de - 186-187 J 5
Emden-mélység 186-187 J 5
Emdentiefe 186-187 J 5
Emei Shan 184-185 J 6
Emel gol 184-185 E 2
Emerald 194-195 J 4
Emerson, AR 154-155 J 4
Emerson, MI 152-153 O 2
Emery, UT 150-151 H 6
Emesa = Homs 180-181 D 4
Emet 182-183 C 3
Emi 178-179 S 7
Emigrant, MT 150-151 H 3
Emigrant Gap, CA 150-151 C 6
Emigrant Pass 150-151 E 5
Emigrant Peak 150-151 H 3
Emigrant Valley 150-151 F 7
Emi Koussi 166-167 H 5
Emi Kusi = Emi Koussi 166-167 H 5
Emiliano Martinez 154-155 C 8
Emilia-Romagna 136-137 C-E 3
Emine, nos - 136-137 MN 4
Eminence, KY 152-153 O 6
Eminence, MO 154-155 K 2
Emiratos Árabes Unidos 180-181 GH 6
Emirati Arabi Uniti 180-181 GH 6
Emiratos Árabes Unidos 180-181 G 6-H 5
Émirats Arabes Unis 180-181 G 6-H 5
Emirdağ 182-183 D 3
Emita 194-195 J 7-8
Emjanyana = Mjanyana 174-175 GH 6
Emmast = Emmaste 138-139 D 4
Emmaste 138-139 D 4
Emmen 134-135 L 2
Emmet 194-195 HJ 4
Emmet, ID 150-151 E 4
Emmetsburg, IA 152-153 J 4
Emory, TX 154-155 H 4
Emory Peak 154-155 D 6
Empalme 146-147 DE 6
Empangeni 168-169 H 8
Empedrado [RA] 162 E 3
Empfängnisbucht = Conceptionbaai 174-175 A 2
Empire 146-147 b 2
Ëmpoli 136-137 D 4
Emporia , KS 146-147 G 4
Emporia, VA 148-149 E 6
Emporium, PA 148-149 D 4
Ems 133 C 2
Emumägi 138-139 F 4
Emu Park 194-195 K 4
Ena 188-189 L 5
Enare = Inari 130-131 M 3
Encampment, WY 152-153 C 5
Encantada, Sierra de la - 154-155 D 6
Encarnación 162 E 3
Encheng 190-191 EF 3
Enchi 166-167 D 7
Encinal, TX 154-155 F 6
Encinillas 154-155 B 6
Encinillas, Laguna de - 154-155 B 6
Encinitas, CA 150-151 E 9
Encino, NM 154-155 C 3
Encino, TX 154-155 F 7
Encontrados 158-159 E 3
Endako 144-145 LM 7
Endau 171 D 3
Endau = Padang Endau 186-187 D 6
Endeh 186-187 H 8
Enderby Land 121 C 5-6
Endere Langar 184-185 E 4
Enderlin, ND 152-153 H 2
Enders Reservoir 152-153 F 5
Endevour Strait 194-195 H 2
Endicott, NE 152-153 H 5
Endicott, NY 148-149 E 3
Endicott Mountains 144-145 F 4
Ene, Rio - 158-159 E 7
Energia 162 E 5
Enez 182-183 B 2
Enfer, Portes de l' 168-169 G 4
Enfield, CT 148-149 G 4
Enfield, IL 152-153 M 6
Enfield, NC 148-149 E 6
Engabeni = Ngabeni 174-175 J 6
Engadin 133 DE 5
Engano = Pulau Enggano 186-187 D 8
Engaru 188-189 c 1
Engcobo 174-175 GH 6
Engeland 132 E-G 5
Engelhard, NC 148-149 EF 7
Ëngel's 138-139 Q 8
Engelwood, CO 152-153 D 6
Engenheiro Beltrao 160-161 F 5
Enggano, Pulau - 186-187 D 8
Engizek Dağı 182-183 G 4
England 132 E-G 5
England, AR 154-155 K 3
Engle, NM 154-155 B 4
Englewood, KS 154-155 EF 2
English, IN 152-153 N 6
English Channel 132 E 7-F 6
English Coast 121 B 29-30
English Company's Islands, The - 194-195 G 2
English Channel 132 E 7-F 6
Ëng-Tëng = Yongding 190-191 F 9
'Ën-Hazeva = 'Ein-Hazëva 182-183 F 7
Enid, OK 146-147 G 4
Enid, Mount - 194-195 C 4
Enid Lake 154-155 L 3
Enid Reservoir = Enid Lake 154-155 L 3
Eniwa 188-189 b 2
Enkeldoorn = Chivu 168-169 H 6
Enken, mys - 178-179 b 6
Enköping 130-131 G 8
Ënmelen 178-179 kl 4
Enna 136-137 F 7
Ennadai Lake 144-145 Q 5
Ennedi 166-167 J 5
Ennersdale 174-175 H 5
Enngonia 194-195 HJ 5
Ennis 132 B 5
Ennis, MT 150-151 H 3
Ennis, TX 154-155 G 4
Enniscorthy 132 C 5
Enniskillen 132 C 4
Ennistimon 132 B 5
Enns 133 G 5
Eno 130-131 O 6
Enontekiö 130-131 K 3
Enos = Enez 182-183 B 2
Enping 190-191 D 10
Enrique Lage = Imbituba 160-161 H 8
Enschede 134-135 L 2
Ensenada [MEX] 146-147 C 5
Ensenada Ferrocarril 154-155 G 8
Enshi 184-185 K 5
Enshih = Enshi 184-185 K 5
Enshū nada 188-189 LM 5
Ensign, KS 152-153 F 7
Enso = Svetogorsk 138-139 G 3
Entebbe 168-169 H 2
Entenbühl 133 F 4
Enterprise, AL 154-155 N 5
Enterprise, MS 154-155 L 4
Enterprise, OR 150-151 E 3
Enterprise, UT 150-151 G 7
Entiat, WA 150-151 C 2
Entiat Mountains 150-151 C 1-2
Entiat River 150-151 C 1-2
Entinas, Punta de las - 134-135 F 10
Entrecasteaux, Point d' 194-195 BC 6
Entrecasteaux, Récife d' 194-195 M 3
Entre Rios [BOL] 158-159 G 9
Entre Rios [BR, Bahia] 158-159 M 7
Entre Rios [RA] 162 E 4
Entre-Rios = Malema 168-169 J 5
Entre Rios, Cordillera - 146-147 J 9
Entre Rios de Minas 160-161 K 4
Entro, AZ 150-151 G 8
Entroncamento 134-135 CD 9
Enugu 166-167 F 7
Enumclaw, WA 150-151 C 2
Ënurmino 178-179 l 4
Envira 158-159 EF 6
Enxian = Encheng 190-191 EF 3
'Ën-Yahav = 'Ein-Yahav 182-183 F 7
Enyellé 168-169 E 2
Enz 133 D 4
Enzan 188-189 M 5
Enzeli = Bandare-e Anzalī 180-181 FG 3
Eólie o Lipari, Isole - 136-137 F 6
Epe [NAM] 172-173 FG 4
Ëpeiros 136-137 J 6
Epéna 168-169 E 2
Epernay 134-135 J 4
Ephesos = Efes 182-183 B 4
Ephraim, UT 150-151 H 6
Ephrata, PA 148-149 E 4
Ephrata, WA 150-151 D 2
Epi 194-195 N 3
Epidauros 136-137 K 7
Epifania = Hamāh 180-181 D 3
Epinal 134-135 L 4
Epiphania = Hamāh 180-181 D 3
Epiphanie, l' 148-149 G 2
Epira 158-159 H 3
Epire = Ëpeiros 136-137 J 6
Epiro = Ëpeiros 136-137 J 6
Epirus = Ëpeiros 136-137 J 6
Episkopēs, Kólpos - 182-183 E 5
Epping, ND 152-153 E 1
Epulu 171 B 2
Equador 158-159 CD 5
Équateur [★] 158-159 CD 5
Équateur [≅] 168-169 EF 2
Equatore 172 A-D 6
Equatoriaal Guinea 166-167 FG 8
Equatorial Guinea 166-167 FG 8
Erakchiouene 172-173 E 1
Eraclea = Ereğli 180-181 C 2
Ërakleia 136-137 L 7
Ërakleion 136-137 L 8
Erāwadī Myit 186-187 C 2
Erāwadī Myitwanyā 186-187 BC 3
Erāwadī Taing 186-187 B 3
Erbaa 182-183 G 2
Erçek 182-183 K 3
Erçek Gölü 182-183 K 3
Erciş 182-183 K 3
Erciyas Dağı 180-181 D 3
Erd 133 J 5
Erdek 182-183 B 2
Erdek Körfezi 182-183 B 2
Erdély 136-137 K-M 2
Erdemli 182-183 F 4
Erdenecagaan 184-185 LM 2
Erdenet 184-185 JK 2
Erde Plateau = Erdi 166-167 J 5
Erdi 166-167 J 5
Erê, Campos - 160-161 F 6
Erebus, Mount - 121 B 17-18
Erebus and Terror Gulf 121 C 31
Ereencav 184-185 M 2
Ereen Chabarg 184-185 EF 3
Ereğli [TR, Konya] 182-183 EF 4
Ereğli [TR, Zonguldak] 180-181 C 2
Erego 168-169 J 6
Erenhot = Erlian 184-185 L 3
Erentepe 182-183 K 3
Erepecu, Lago de - 158-159 H 5
Eresós 136-137 L 6
Erevanz = Jerevan 140-141 M 6
Erewań = Jerevan 140-141 M 6
Erewan = Jerevan 140-141 M 6
Erexim 162 F 3
Erfelek 182-183 F 2
Erfenisdam 174-175 G 5
Erfurt 133 E 3
'Erg, el - = Al-'Irq 166-167 J 3
Ergani 182-183 H 3
Erge-Muora-Sisse, ostrov - = ostrov Arga-Muora-Sise 178-179 XY 3
Ergene Nehri 182-183 B 2
Ergh, El - = Al-'Irq 166-167 J 3
Ergli 138-139 E 5
Er Hai 184-185 J 6
Ërh-ch'iang = Charqiliq 184-185 F 4
Ërh-lien = Erlian 184-185 L 3
Ërh-lin 190-191 H 10
Ërice 136-137 E 6
Erick, OK 154-155 F 3
Erie, CO 152-153 D 5-6
Erie, IL 152-153 LM 5
Erie, KS 152-153 J 7
Erie, ND 152-153 H 2
Erie, PA 146-147 K 3
Erie, Jezioro - = Lake Erie 146-147 KL 3
Erie, Lake - 146-147 KL 3
Erieau 148-149 C 3
Erie Canal 148-149 D 3
Eriesee = Lake Erie 146-147 KL 3
Erie-tó = Lake Erie 146-147 KL 3
'Erigaabo = Cerrigaabo 166-167 b 1
Erijské jezero = Lake Erie 146-147 KL 3
Erik Eriksenstredet 130-131 m-o 5
Erimo misaki = Erimo-saki 184-185 RS 3
Erimo-saki 184-185 RS 3
Erin, TN 154-155 M 2
Erin Dzab = Ereencav 184-185 M 2
Erin Tal 184-185 L 3
Eritrea 166-167 M 5-N 6
Ëritrea 166-167 MN 6
Eritrea 167 M 5- N 6
Eritrea 166-167 M 5-N 6
Erivan 140-141 M 6
Erivan = Jerevan 126-127 RS 7
Eriwan = Jerevan 140-141 M 6
Erizkan = Ahlat 182-183 K 3
Erlangen 133 E 4
Erlau = Ergli 138-139 E 5
Erldunda 194-195 F 5
Erlian 184-185 L 3
Erlin = Ërh-lin 190-191 H 10
Ermelo [ZA] 168-169 GH 8
Ermenak 182-183 E 4
Ërmo = Gediz Nehri 182-183 C 3
Ermúpolis 136-137 L 7
Erode 180-181 M 8
Eromanga [AUS] 194-195 H 5
Eromanga [Vanuatu] 194-195 NO 3
Erongo 168-169 E 7
Erqiang = Charqiliq 184-185 F 4
Errigal 132 BC 4
Erris Head 132 AB 4
Errol, NH 148-149 H 2
Errol Island 154-155 L 6
Ersekë 136-137 J 5
Erskine, MN 152-153 HJ 2
Ërtil'138-139 N 8
Ërtil' MN 152-153 N 8
Ërtira 166-167 M 5-N 6
Ertis 177 L 4
Ertvågøy 130-131 BC 6
Eruh = Dih 182-183 K 4
Erwin, NC 148-149 D 7
Erwin, TN 148-149 B 6
Erýmanthos 136-137 JK 7
Erythrea = Ërtira 166-167 M 5-N 6
Érythrée 177 GH 8
Erzerum = Erzurum 180-181 E 2-3
Erzgebirge 133 F 3
Ërzin 178-179 S 7
Erzincan 180-181 D 3
Erzurum 180-181 E 2-3
Esan-saki 188-189 b 3
Esashi [J ↑ Asahikawa] 188-189 c 1
Esashi [J ← Hakodate] 188-189 ab 3
Esbjerg 130-131 C 10
Esbo = Espoo 130-131 L 7
Escalante, UT 150-151 H 7
Escalante Desert 150-151 G 6-7
Escalante River 150-151 H 7
Escalvos, Costa de los - 166-167 E 7
Escanaba, MI 146-147 J 2
Escanaba River 152-153 N 2-3
Escandinávia 128-129 K 4-N 1
Escandinnavia 128-129 K 4-N 1
Eschwege 133 DE 3
Escalves, Côte des - 166-167 E 7
Escalves, Grand Lac des - 144-145 NO 5
Esclaves, Rivière des - 144-145 O 5-6
Esclavo, Gran Lago de - 144-145 NO 5
Esclavo, Pequeño Lago del - 144-145 O 6
Esclavo , Rio del - 144-145 O 5-6
Escobal 146-147 ab 2
Escocia 132 D 3-E 4
Escócia 128-129 GH 4
Escócia 126-127 H 4
Escócia, Crista da - 124-125 G 8
Escondido, CA 150-151 E 9
Escorial, El - 134-135 EF 8
Escravo, Grande Lago do - 144-145 NO 5
Escravo, Pequeno Lago do - 144-145 O 6
Escravo, Rio do - 144-145 O 5-6
Escravos, Costa dos - 166-167 E 7
Escuinapa de Hidalgo 146-147 E 7
Escuintla 146-147 H 9
Escutári = İstanbul-Üsküdar 180-181 BC 2
Eséka 172-173 H 5
Eşen [TR] 182-183 C 4
Eşen Cayı 182-183 C 4
Esendere 182-183 L 4
Esenli = Aybastı 182-183 G 2
Eşfahān 180-181 G 4
Eshowe 168-169 H 8
Eshtehārd 182-183 O 5
Esim 126-127 W 6
Eskifjördhur 130-131 g 2
Eskilstuna 130-131 G 8
Eskimo Lakes 144-145 K 4
Eskimo Point 144-145 S 5
Eskipazar 182-183 E 2
Eskişehir 180-181 C 2-3
Esla 134-135 E 8
Eslāmābād 180-181 F 4
Eslāmshahr 182-183 O 5
Eslöv 130-131 E 10
Eslovaquia 133 JK 4
Eslováquia 133 J 7-L 7
Eslováquia 126-127 MN 6
Eslováquia 140-141 A 2
Eslovénia 133 J 7-L 7
Eslovenia 136-137 F 3-G 2
Eslovénia 133 GH 6
Eşme 182-183 C 3
Esmeralda [MEX] 154-155 D 7
Esmeralda, La - [PY] 162 D 2
Esmeraldas [EC, ●] 158-159 CD 4
Esmeraldas, Rio - 158-159 D 4
Esmirna = İzmir 180-181 B 3
Esmirna = İzmir 180-181 B 3
Esmond, ND 152-153 G 1
Esna = Isnā 166-167 L 3
Espagne 134-135 D 7-G 9
Espanha 122-123 JK 3-J 4
Española, Isla - 158-159 B 5
España 134-135 D 7-G 9
Espanola, NM 154-155 BC 3
Española, Isla - 158-159 B 5
Esparança 171 D 6
Esparta = Spártē 136 K 7
Esparta = Spártē 136-137 K 7
Esparto, CA 150-151 BC 6
Espera Feliz 160-161 M 4
Esperança , Serra da 160-161 G 6-7
Esperance 194-195 D 6
Esperance Bay 194-195 D 6
Esperanza [RA, Santa Cruz] 162 B 8
Esperanza [RA, Santa Fé] 162 D 4
Esperanzas, Las - 154-155 E 7
Espichel, Cabo de - 134-135 C 9
Espigão, Serra do - 160-161 G 7
Espinal 158-159 DE 4
Espinazo 154-155 E 7
Espinhaço, Serra do - 158-159 L 8
Espinilho 162 E 2
Espirito Santo 158-159 L 9-M 8
Espiritu Santo 194-195 N 3
Espiye 182-183 H 2
Esplanada 158-159 M 7
Espoo 130-131 L 7
Espóradas 136-137 M 6-8
Espóradas de la Polinesia Central 192-193 L 4-M 5
Espórades 128-129 O 8
Espungabera 168-169 H 7
Esquel 162 B 6
Esquimalt 144-145 M 8
Essaouira = Aş-Şawirah 166-167 BC 2
Essé [RFC] 172-173 J 4
Esseg = Osijek 136-137 H 3
Essen 133 C 3
Essendon, Mount - 194-195 D 4
Essequibo River 158-159 H 4
Essex, CA 150-151 F 8
Essex, MT 150-151 G 1
Essex, VT 148-149 G 2
Essex Junction, VT 148-149 G 2
Esslingen 133 D 4
Ësso 178-179 e 6
Estaca de Bares, Punta de la - 134-135 D 6-7
Estación Pichi Ciego = Pichi Ciego 162 C 4
Estados, Isla de los - 162 D 8
Estados Unidos 146-147 D-K 4
Estados Unidos 146-147 C-K 4
Estambul = İstanbul 180-181 BC 2
Estância 158-159 M 7
Estancia, NM 154-155 BC 3
Estancia Ocampo-cué 160-161 D 5
Estcourt 174-175 HJ 5
Este 136-137 D 3
Esteli 146-147 J 9
Estella 134-135 F 7
Estelline, TX 154-155 E 3
Estepona 134-135 E 10
Esterhazy 144-145 Q 7
Estero, FL 148-149 c 3
Estero Bay 150-151 C 8
Esteros 160-161 B 5
Estes Park, CO 152-153 D 5
Estevan 144-145 Q 8
Estherville, IA 152-153 J 4
Estill, SC 148-149 C 8
Estland 130-131 LM 8
Estland 138-139 EF 4
Estocolmo = Stockholm 130-131 GH 8
Estocolomo = Stockholm 128-129 M 4
Estonia 138-139 LM 8
Estonia 130-131 LM 8
Estónia 126-127 NO 4
Estónia, República 138-139 D-F 4
Estonie 138-139 LM 8
Estonskaja Sovetskaja Socialističeskaja Respublika = Estland 138-139 EF 4
Estonsko 138-139 EF 4
Estrada, La - 134-135 C 7
Estrasburgo = Strasbourg 134-135 L 4
Estrasburgo = Strasbourg 128-129 K 6
Estreito, Represa do - 160-161 J 4
Estrela, Serra da - 134-135 CD 8
Estrela do Sul 160-161 J 3
Estrella, AZ 150-151 G 9
Estremadura 134-135 C 9
Estremoz 134-135 D 9
Estrondo, Serra do - 158-159 K 6
Esztergom 133 J 5
Észak-ausztráliai-medence 194-195 C 2
Észak-Borneó = Sabah 186-187 G 5
Északi-Banda-medence 186-187 HJ 7
Északi-Fidzsi-medence 194-195 O 3
Észak-Írország 132 C 4
Északi-tenger 132 F-J 3
Észak-Korea 184-185 O 3-4
Északnyugati terület = Northwest Territories 144-145 M -U 4
Észak-Oszét Autonóm Köztársaság 140-141 LM 5
Észak-Rhodézia = Zambia 168-169 G 6-J 5
Eszék = Osijek 136-137 FI 3
Észtország 138-139 EF 4
Észtország 130-131 LM 9
Etadunna 194-195 G 5
Etah 144-145 W 2
Etah = Etawah 180-181 M 5
Étampes 134-135 HJ 4
États-Unis 146-147 D-K 4
Eterikan, proliv - 178-179 ab 3
Eternity Range 121 BC 30
Ethan, SD 152-153 GH 4
Ethel, MS 154-155 L 4
Ethiopië = Ethiopië 166-167 MN 7
Ethiopie = Ethiopië 166-167 MN 7
Etiópia = Ethiopië 166-167 MN 7
Etiopia = Ethiopië 166-167 MN 7
Etiopia = Ethiopië 166-167 MN 7
Etiopia = Ethiopië 166-167 MN 7
Etiopia = Ethiopië 166-167 MN 7
Etiopia = Ethiopië 166-167 MN 7
Etiopië 177 GH 9
Etna, CA 150-151 B 5
Etna, Monte - 136-137 F 7
Etnesjøen 130-131 AB 8
Etobikoke 148-149 D 3
Étoile du Congo 168-169 G 5
Etolin Strait 144-145 C 5-6
Eton [AUS] 194-195 J 4
Etorofu = ostrov Iturup 178-179 c 9
Etosha Game Park 168-169 E 6
Etosha Pan 168-169 E 6
Etowah, TN 154-155 N 3
Etri, Jebel - = Jabal Itrī 170 F 7
Etter, TX 154-155 DE 2
Euabalong 196 GH 4
Eubank, KY 152-153 O 7
Eubea = Kai Évboia 136-137 K 6-L 7
Eubée = Kai Évboia 136-137 K 6-L 7
Eubóa = Kai Évboia 136-137 K 6-L 7
Euboea = Kai Évboia 136-137 K 6-L 7
Euclid, OH 148-149 C 4
Euclides da Cunha 158-159 M 7
Eucumbene, Lake - 196 J 6
Eudora, AR 154-155 K 4
Eufaula, AL 154-155 N 5
Eufaula, OK 154-155 H 3
Eufaula Reservoir 154-155 H 3
Eufraat = Nahr al-Furāt 180-181 E 4
Eufrat = Nahr al-Furāt 180-181 E 4
Éufrates = Nahr al-Furāt 180-181 E 4
Éufrates = Nahr al-Furāt 180-181 E 4
Eufrates = Nahr al-Furāt 180-181 E 4
Eufrátesz = Nahr al-Furāt 180-181 E 4
Eugene, OR 146-147 B 3
Eugenia, Punta - 146-147 C 6
Eugênio Penzo 160-161 E 5
Euice, NM 154-155 D 4
Eulo 194-195 J 5
Eunice, LA 154-155 J 5
Eupen 134-135 KL 3
Euphrat—Nahr al-Furāt 180-181 E 4
Euphrate = Nahr al-Furāt 180-181 E 4
Eupora, MS 154-155 L 4
Eurajoki 130-131 J 7
Eurasia Basin 120 A
Eurasisches Becken 120 A
Euraziatisch Bekken 120 A
Eurázsiai-medence 120 A
Eure 134-135 Fl 4
Eureka [CDN] 144-145 T 1
Eureka [ZA] 174-175 J 3
Eureka, CA 146-147 AB 3
Eureka, IL 152-153 M 5
Eureka, KS 152-153 H 7
Eureka, MT 150-151 F 1
Eureka, NV 150-151 EF 6
Eureka, SD 152-153 G 3
Eureka , UT 150-151 G 5-6
Eureka, WA 150-151 D 2
Eureka Sound 144-145 TU 2
Eureka Springs, AR 154-155 J 2
Euroa 196 G 6
Euroazjatycki, Basen - 120 A
Europa 124-125 K-M 3
Europa, Île - 168-169 K 7
Europa Occidentale, Bacino dell' 124-125 HJ 3
Europa Occidental, Bacia da - 124-125 HJ 3
Europa, Picos de - 134-135 E 7
Europa, Point - 134-135 E 10
Europa [região] 124-125 K-M 3
Europäisches Nordmeer 120 C 19-B 17
Europa Occidental Cuenca de - 124-125 HJ 3
Europe 124-125 K-M 3
Euskadi 134-135 F 7
Eustis, FL 148-149 c 2
Eustis, NE 152-153 FG 5
Eutaw, AL 154-155 M 4
Eva, OK 154-155 DE 2
Evans, Mount - [USA, Colorado] 152-153 D 6
Evans, Mount - [USA, Montana] 150-151 G 2
Evans Head 194-195 K 5
Evans Strait 144-145 U 5
Evanston, IL 152-153 N 4
Evanston, WY 150-151 H 5
Evansville, IL 152-153 M 6
Evansville, IN 146-147 J 4
Evansville, WI 152-153 M4
Evant, TX 154-155 FG 5
Evart, MI 152-153 O 4
Evaton 174-175 G 4
Évboia, Kai - 136-137 K 6-L 7
Evboïkòs Kólpos 136-137 KL 6
Eveleth, MN 152-153 K 2
Evencký autonomni okruh 178-179 R-T 7
Evenki Autonóm Körzet 178-179 R-T 5
Evenki Autonomous Area 178-179 R-T 5
Evenki, Circolo Nazionale degli - 178-179 R-T 5
Evenkis, District National des - 178-179 R-T 5
Evenkos, Circunscrição Nacional dos - 178-179 R-T 5
Evenkos, Circunscripción Nacional de los - 178-179 R-T 5
Évensk 178-179 e 5
Everard, Cape - 194-195 JK 7
Everard, Lake - 194-195 F 6
Everard Park 194-195 F 5
Everard Ranges 194-195 F 5
Everest, Mount - = Sagarmatha 184-185 F 6
Everett, GA 148-149 C 9
Everett, WA 146-147 B 2
Everett, Mount - 148-149 G 3
Everglades 146-147 K 6
Everglades, FL 148-149 c 4
Everglades National Park 146-147 K 6
Evergreen, AL 154-155 M 5
Evinayong 166-167 G 8
Evje 130-131 BC 8
Évora 134-135 CD 9
Évreux 134-135 H 4
Evrýchu 182-183 E 5
Evrykhou = Evrýchu 182-183 E 5
Ewan, WA 150-151 E 2
Ewenken, Nationaal Gebied der - 178-179 R-T 5
Ewenken, Nationalkreis der - 178-179 R-T 5
Ewenkijski Okręg Autonomiczny 178-179 R-T 7
Ewing, KY 152-153 P 6
Ewing, MO 152-153 L 5-6
Ewing, NE 152-153 G 4
Ewing, VA 154-155 O 2
Ewo 168-169 DE 3
Exaltación [BOL] 158-159 F 7
Excelsior 174-175 G 5
Excelsior Mountains 150-151 D 6
Excelsior Springs, MO 152-153 JK 6
Exe 132 E 6
Executive Committee Range 121 B 121
Exeland, WI 152-153 L 3
Exeter 132 E 6
Exeter [CDN] 152-153 Q 4
Exeter, CA 150-151 D 7
Exeter, MO 154-155 J 2
Exeter, NE 152-153 H 5
Exeter, NH 148-149 H 3
Exira, IA 152-153 J 5
Exmoor Forest 132 E 6
Exmore, VA 148-149 EF 6
Exmouth 132 E 6
Exmouth Gulf [AUS, ◡] 194-195 B 4
Exmouth Gulf [AUS, ●] 194-195 B 4
Expedition Range 194-195 J 4
Extrema 160-161 JK 5
Extremadura 134-135 D 9-E 8
Exuma Sound 146-147 L 7
Eyasi, Lake - 168-169 HJ 3
Eyjafjardhar 130-131 d 2
Eyjafjördhur 130-131 d 1
Eyl 166-167 b 2
Eynihal = Kale 182-183 CD 4
Eyota, MN 152-153 K 3-4
Eyrarbakki 130-131 c 3
Eyre, Lake - 194-195 G 5
Eyre, Seno - 162 B 7
Eyre Creek 194-195 G 5
Eyre North, Lake - 196 C 2
Eyre Peninsula 194-195 G 6
Eyre South, Lake - 196 C 2
Ezine 182-183 B 3
Ezinepazar = Zigala 182-183 G 2
Ezraa = Izra' 182-183 G 6
Ežva 138-139 S 3

F

Fabens, TX 154-155 BC 5
Fabriano 136-137 E 4
Fachi 166-167 G 5
Fada 166-167 J 5
Fada-Ngourma 166-167 DE 6
Faddeja, zaliv - 178-179 UV 2
Fadejevskij, ostrov - 178-179 b-d 2
Fadghāmi 182-183 J 5
Fadu N'Gurma = Fada-Ngourma 166-167 DE 6
Faenza 136-137 D 3
Færingehavn 144-145 a 5
Fær Øer, Banco delle - 128-129 FG 3
Faeroe Iceland Ridge 128-129 FG 3
Fafa 172-173 F 2
Fafan = Fafen 166-167 N 7
Fafanlap 186-187 K 7
Fafen Shet' 166-167 N 7
Faga 172-173 F 2
Făgăraş 136-137 L 3
Fagatogo 187 c 1
Fagernes 130-131 C 7
Fagersta 130-131 FG 7-8
Faguibine, Lac - 166-167 CD 5
Fagundes [BR, Pará] 158-159 H 6
Fāhna = Vääna 138-139 E 4
Fahraj 180-181 H 5
Fa'īd 170 E 2
Faiḍ'āt = Fayḍāt 182-183 HJ 5
Faijum, El - = Al-Fayyūm 166-167 KL 3
Fairbank, AZ 150-151 H 10
Fairbanks, AK 144-145 G 5
Fairburn, GA 154-155 N 4
Fairburn, SD 152-153 E 4
Fairbury, IL 152-153 M 5
Fairbury, NE 146-147 G 3
Fairchild, WI 152-153 L 3
Fairfax, AL 154-155 N 4
Fairfax, MN 152-153 J 3
Fairfax, MO 152-153 J 5
Fairfax, OK 154-155 G 2
Fairfax, SC 148-149 C 8
Fairfax, SD 152-153 G 4
Fairfield, AL 154-155 M 5
Fairfield, CA 150-151 BC 6
Fairfield, IA 152-153 L 5
Fairfield, ID 150-151 F 4
Fairfield, IL 152-153 M 6
Fairfield, ME 148-149 J 2

Georgetown [AUS, Queensland] 194-195 H 3
George Town [AUS, Tasmania] 194-195 J 8
Georgetown [CDN, Ontario] 148-149 D 3
Georgetown [GUY] 158-159 H 3
George Town [MAL] 186-187 CD 5
Georgetown, [WAG] 172-173 B 2
Georgetown, CA 150-151 C 6
Georgetown, DE 148-149 F 5
Georgetown, GA 154-155 N 5
Georgetown, ID 150-151 H 4
Georgetown, IL 152-153 N 6
Georgetown, KY 152-153 O 6
Georgetown, OH 152-153 N 6
Georgetown, SC 148-149 D
Georgetown, TX 154-155 G 5
George Washington Birthplace National Monument 148-149 E 5
George West, TX 154-155 F 6
Georgia 140-141 LM 6
Geórgia 158-159 R 7
Georgia [≈] 146-147 K 5
Geórgia, República da – 140-141 LM 6
Georgia [US] 126-127 RS 7
Georgia, Strait of – 144-145 M 8
Georgia Australe, Platea della – 121 D 133-E 34
Georgia del Sur = South Georgia 162 J 8
Georgia del Sur, Dorsal de – 121 D 133-E 34
Geórgias do Sul, Crista das – 121 D 133-E 34
Georgiana, AL 154-155 N 5
Georgian Bay 144-145 U 8-9
Georgias Południowa = South Georgia 162 J 8
Georgias del Sur, Islas –= South Georgia 162 J 8
Géorgie 140-141 LM 6
Géorgie 140-141 LM 6
Géorgie du Sud = South Georgia 162 J 8
Géorgie du Sud, Seuil de – 121 D 133-E 34
Georgien 140-141 LM 6
Georgijevka 178-179 P 8
Georgijevsk 140-141 LM 4
Georgijevskoje 138-139 P 4
Georgina River 194-195 G 4
Georg von Neumayer 121 B 36
Gera 133 EF 3
Gerais, Campos – 160-161 GH 6
Gerais, Chapada dos – 158-159 K 8
Geraldine, MT 150-151 HJ 2
Geraldton [AUS] 194-195 B 5
Geraldton [CDN] 144-145 T 8
Gerasimovka 178-179 N 6
Gerçüş 182-183 J 4
Gerdảänehbälä 182-183 M 5
Gerdine, Mount – 144-145 F 5
Gerede 182-183 E 2
Gerede = Beydili 182-183 D 2
Gerede Çayı 182-183 E 2
Géres 158-159 JK 8
Gergebil 140-141 N 5
Gerger 182-183 H 3
Gering, NE 152-153 E 4
Geriş 182-183 D 4
Gerlach, NV 150-151 D 5
Gerlachovský štít 133 JK 4
Gêrlogubê = Gedlegubê 166-167 NO 7
Germania 133 D 4-F 2
Germantown, TN 154-155 L 3
Germany 133 D-F 2-4
Germencik 182-183 B 4
Germi 182-183 N 3
Germiston 168-169 G 8
Ger'nsy = Goris 140-141 N 7
Gerona 134-135 J 3
Gers 134-135 H 7
Gerusalemme = Yěrûshâlayim 180-181 CD 4
Gerze 182-183 F 2
Gesellschaftsinseln 198-199 K 5-6
Gestro Weniz, Wabê – 166-167 N 7
Gettysburg, PA 148-149 E 5
Gettysburg, SD 152-153 G 3
Getulina 160-161 GH 4
Getz Ice Shelf 121 B 23-24
Geuda Springs, KS 154-155 G 2
Gevar ovasi 182-183 K 3
Gevaş, 182-183 K 3
Gevgelija 136-137 K 5
Gewanê 166-167 N 6
Geyang = Guoyang 190-191 F 5
Geyik Dağları 182-183 E 4
Geyser, MT 150-151 H 2
Geyser, Banc du – 168-169 L 5
Geysir 130-131 c 2
Geyve 182-183 D 2
Gezira 166-167 L 6
Ghâb, Al- 182-183 G 5
Ghâb, El- = Al-Ghâb 182-183 G 5
Ghâb, Jabal - 182-183 H 3
Ghadai = Ghaday 182-183 M 8
Ghadâmes = Ghadâmis 166-167 FG 2-3
Ghaday 182-183 M 8
Ghadûn, Wâdî - 180-181 G 7
Ghaghara 180-181 N 5
Ghallah, Bi'r - 170 E 3
Ghana 166-167 DE 7
Ghânim, Jazirat - 170 E 4
Ghanzi 168-169 F 7
Gharaq as-Sultâni, Al- 170 CD 3
Gharbi, Jabal - 182-183 H 5
Gharbiyah, Al- 170 C 3
Ghardaqah, Al- 166-167 L 3
Ghardâyah 166-167 E 2
Ghârib, Jabal - 166-167 L 3
Gharqâbâd 182-183 NO 5
Gharyân 166-167 G 2
Ghat 166-167 G 4
Ghâtâ', Al- 182-183 J 5
Ghawdex 136-137 F 7
Ghaydah, Al- [Y ≈ Sayhût] 180-181 FG 7-8
Ghaydah , Al- [Y ≈ ≈ Sayhût] 180-181 G 7
Ghazâl, 'Ayn al- [ET] 170 E 5
Ghazâl, Bahr al- [Sudan, ~] 166-167 KL7
Ghazâl, Bahr al- [Sudan, ≈] 166-167 JK7
Ghazawât, Al- 166-167 D 1
Ghazir = Jazir 182-183 F 5
Ghaz köl 184-185 G 4
Ghazni 180-181 K 4
Ghazzah 180-181 C 4
Ghedo = Gêdo 166-167 M 7
Gheorghe Gheorghiu-Dej 136-137 M 2
Gheorgheni 136-137 LM 2
Gherla 136-137 KL 2
Gherlogubí = Gerlogubi 166-167 NO 7
Ghiedo = Gêdo 166-167 M 7

Ghigner = Ginir 166-167 N 7
Ghimbi = Gimbi 166-167 M 7
Ghinah, Wâdi al- 182-183 F 7
Ghôr, El- = Al-Ghûr 182-183 F 7
Ghuja 184-185 E 3
Ghûr, Al- 182-183 F 7
Ghurdaqa, El - = Al-Ghardaqah 166-167 L 3
Ghuryân 180-181 J 4
Giamaica 146-147 L 8
Giannina = Ioánnina 194-195 J 6
Giannitsá 136-137 K 5
Giannuti 136-137 D 4
Giappone 184-185 Q 5-R 3
Giappone, Bacino del - 188-189 J-L 2
Giappone, Fossa del - 124-125 R 4
Giappone, Mar del 188-189 P 4-Q 3
Giant Mounments 133 GH 3
Giant's Castle 174-175 H 5
Giant's Castle National Park 174-175 H 5
Gia Nai 186-187 E 5
Giarre 136-137 F 7
Giava, Mar di - 186-187 EF 8
Gibbon, NE 152-153 G 5
Gibbon, OR 150-151 D 3
Gibbonsville, ID 150-151 G 3
Gibbs City,MI 152-153 M 2
Gibeil = Juhail 170 E 3
Gibeon [Namibia, •] 168-169 E 8
Gibeon [Namibia, ≈] 174-175 C 3
Gibilterra, Stretto di - 134-135 D 11
Gibilterra = Gibraltar 128-129 E 9
Gibilterra, Estreito de - 128-129 G 8
Gibilterra, Détroit de - 134-135 D 11-E 10
Gibilterra, Estrecho de 134-135 D 11-E 10
Gibraltar, Straat van 134-135 D 11-E 10
Gibraltar, Strait of - 134-135 D 11-E 10
Gibraltar, Straße von 134-135 D 11-E 10
Gibraltári-szoros 134-135 DE 11
Gibraltarska, Cieśn. 134-135 DE 11
Gibraltarský průliv 134-135 DE 11
Gibsland, LA 154-155 J 4
Gibson City, IL 152-153 M 5
Gibson Desert 194-195 DE 4
Gibuti 166-167 N 6
Gidajevo 138-139 ST 4
Giddings, TX 154-155 G 5
Gideon, MO 154-155 KL 2
Gidole 166-167 M 7
Gien 134-135 J 5
Gießen 133 D 3
Gifu 182-183 N 3
Gigant 140-141 K 3
Giganta, Sierra de la 146-147 D 6-7
Gigantes Mtes 133 GH 3
Giglio 136-137 D 4
Gigüela 134-135 F 9
Gíhán, Râs - = Râ's al-Bálâ'im 170 E 3
Giheina = Juhaynah 170 D 4
Gihu = Gifu 184-185 Q 4
Gijón 134-135 E 7
Gila Bend, AZ 150-151 G 9
Gila Cliff 150-151 J 9
Gila Cliff Dwellings National Monument 150-151 J 9
Gila Desert 146-147 D 5
Gila Mountains 150-151 J 9
Gilān 180-181 FG 3
Gilān, Sārâb-e - 182-183 LM 5
Gilān-e Gharb 182-183 LM 5
Gila River 146-147 D 5
Gila River Indian Reservation 150-151 GH 9
Gilbertown, AL 154-155 L 5
Gilbert River [AUS, →] 194-195 H 3
Gilbert River [AUS, ~] 194-195 H 3
Gilbués 158-159 K 6
Gilby, ND 152-153 H 1
Gilford, MT 152-153 A 1
Gilead 174-175 H 2
Gilf Kebir Plateau = Haqbat al-Jilf al-Kabir 166-167 K 4
Gilgandra 194-195 J 6
Gilgat = Gilgit 180-181 L 3
Gilgil 171 CD 3
Gilgit 180-181 L 3
Gill, CO 152-153 D 5
Gillam 144-145 S 6
Gillen, Lake - 194-195 D 5
Gilles, Lake - 196 C 4
Gillespie, IL 152-153 LM 6
Gillet, AR 154-155 K 3
Gillet, WY 152-153 D 3
Gillette, WY 152-153 D 3
Gilman, IA 152-153 K 5
Gilman, IL 152-153 MN 5
Gilman, WI 152-153 L 3
Gilman, MT 150-151 H 4
Gilmore, ID 150-151 G 3
Gilroy, CA 150-151 C 7
Giluwe, Mount - 186-187 M 8
Gimbala, Jebel - = Jabal Marrah 166-167 JK 6
Gimbi 166-167 M 7
Gimma = Jima 166-167 M 7
Gimpu 186-187 GH 7
Ginebra = Genève 133 C 5
Gineifa = Junayfah 170 E 3
Ginevra = Genève 133 C 5
Ginevrabotnen 130-131 kl 5
Gingiova 136-137 KL 4
Gin'gir = Ginir 166-167 N 7
Giôba del Colle 136-137 G 5
Giordania 180-181 D 4
Giovi, Passo dei - 136-137 C 3
Gippsland 194-195 J 7
Girard, IL 152-153 M 6
Girard, KS 152-153 J 7
Girard, OH 148-149 D 4
Girard, PA 148-149 C 3-4
Girard, TX 154-155 D 4
Girardot 158-159 E 4
Giren = Jirin 166-167 M 7
Giresun 180-181 D 2
Giresun Dağları 182-183 H 2
Girga = Jirjā 166-167 L 3
Giri 166-169 E 2
Giridih 180-181 O 6
Girilambone 196 H 3
Girishk 180-181 J 4
Girne 182-183 E 5
Gironde 134-135 G 6
Gironde 134-135 G 6
Girovo 138-139 RS 4
Girvan 130-131 O 4
Girvas [SU, Karel'skaja ASSR] 138-139 F 3
Girvas 130-131 O 4
Girvas, vodopad - 138-139 J 2
Girvin, TX 154-155 D 5

Gisborne 194-195 P 7
Gisenyi 168-169 G 3
Gislaved 130-131 E 9
Gisr ash-Shughur 182-183 G 5
Gitega 168-169 GH 3
Giulianova 136-137 EF 4
Giumbo—Jumbo 168-169 K 3
Giůra 136-137 L 6
Giurgiu 136-137 L 4
Givet 134-135 K 3
Giyani 174-175 J 2
Gizeh = Al-Jizah 166-167 KL 3
Giżiga 178-179 f 5
Giżiginskaja guba 178-179 e 5
Gizmel 182-183 M 5
Gizo 186-187 j 6
Giżycko 133 KL 1
Gizzar = Guna 180-181 M 6
Gjøbel 182-183 J 4
Gjirokastër 136-137 J 6
Gjøa Haven 144-145 ST 4
Gjögurta 130-131 d 1
Gjøvik 130-131 D 7
Gjuhes, Kepi i - 136-137 H 5
Gjumri 172-173 K 2
Glace Bay 144-145 YZ 8
Glacier Bay National Monument 144-145 J 6
Glacier National Park [USA] 146-147 CD 2
Glacier Peak 150-151 C 1
Gladbrook, IA 152-153 K 4
Glade Park, CO 150-151 J 6
Gladstone, MI 152-153 O 4
Gladwin, MI 152-153 O 4
Gladstone [AUS, Queensland] 194-195 K 4
Gladstone [AUS, South Australia] 194-195 G 6
Glasgow, KY 152-153 O 7
Glasgow, MO 152-153 K 6
Glasgow, MT 152-153 K 1
Glasco, KS 152-153 G 6
Glasgow 130-131 O 4
Glassboro, NJ 148-149 F 5
Glass Mountains 154-155 D 5
Glatz = Kłodzko 133 H 3
Glauchau 133 F 3
Glazier, TX 154-155 D 4
Glazok 138-139 N 7
Glazov 138-139 U 5
Gleeson, AZ 150-151 J 10
Gleisdorf 133 GH 5
Gleiwitz = Gliwice 133 J 3
Glen 134-135 J 5
Glen, NE 152-153 E 4
Glen Canyon 150-151 H 7
Glencoe [CDN] 148-149 C 3
Glencoe [ZA] 174-175 HJ 5
Glencoe,MN 152-153 K 3
Glendale, AZ 146-147 D 5
Glendale, CA 146-147 C 5
Glendale, OR 150-151 B 4
Glendevey, CO 152-153 D 5
Glendive, MT 152-153 D 2
Glendo, IL 152-153 L 5
Golden City, MO 152-153 J 7
Goldendale, WA 150-151 C 2
Golden Gate 146-147 B 4
Golden Meadow, LA 154-155 K 6
Golden Vale 132 BC 5
Goldfield, NV 150-151 E 7
Gold Hill, UT 152-153 E 4
Goldingen = Kuldiga 138-139 CD 5
Goldküste 166-167 D 8-E 7
Gold Point, NV 150-151 E 7
Goldsboro, NC 146-147 L 4-5
Goldsmith, TX 154-155 D 4-5
Goldthwaite, TX 154-155 F 5
Gölcük 182-183 K 2
Golconda, IL 152-153 M 7
Golconda, NV 150-151 E 5-6
Gölcük [TR, Kocaeli] 182-183 CD 2
Gôtdap 133 L 1
Gold Beach, OR 150-151 A 4
Goldburg, ID 150-151 G 3
Gold Butte, MT 150-151 H 1
Gold Coast [AUS, ≈] 166-167 D 8-E 7
Gold Coast [≈] 166-167 D 8-E 7
Gold Coast-Southport 196 LM 1
Golden, ID 150-151 F 3
Golden, IL 152-153 L 5

Goba [ETH] 166-167 N 7
Goba [Moçambique] 174-175 K 4
Gobabis 168-169 E 7
Gobas 174-175 C 4
Gobernador Gregores 162 BC 7
Gobi 184-185 H-L 3
Gobô 188-189 K 6
Gochas 174-175 C 3
Godavari 180-181 N 7
Godavari Delta 180-181 N 7
Goddard, KS 152-153 G 6
Godech 136-137 L 4
Godfrey Tank 194-195 E 4
Godhavn = Qeqertarssuq 144-145 Za 4
Gods Lake [CDN, •] 144-145 S 7
Gods Lake [CDN, ≈] 144-145 S 7
Godthåb = Nûk 144-145 a 5
Godwin Austen, Mount - = K 2 180-181 M 3
Goede Hoop, Kaap de - 168-169 E 9
Goélands, Lac aux - 144-145 Y 6
Goeree 134-135 J 3
Goffs, CA 150-151 F 8
Gogebic, Lake - 152-153 M 2
Gogebic Range 152-153 LM 2
Gogland, ostrov - 130-131 M 7
Gogra = Ghaghara 180-181 N 5
Gogrial = Qûqriyâl 166-167 K 7
Goiana 158-159 MN 6
Goiandira 158-159 K 8
Goianésia 158-159 K 8
Goiânia 158-159 JK 8
Goiás [BR, •] 158-159 JK 8
Goiás [BR, ≈] 158-159 K 7
Goiás, Serra Geral de - 158-159 K 7
Goio-Erê 160-161 F 6
Goiaxim 160-161 FG 6
Gojjam = Gojam 166-167 M 6
Gôkbel 182-183 C 4
Gokova Körfezi 182-183 BC 4
Gôkova, Gulf of - 182-183 B 4
Göksu [TR, ~] 182-183 FG 4
Göksu [TR, •] 182-183 K 3
Göksun 182-183 G 3
Göksu Nehri 180-181 C 3
Gök Tepe [TR, •] 182-183 E 4
Göktepe [TR, ≈] 182-183 E 4
Gokwe 168-169 G 5
Gol 130-131 C 7
Golaja Pristan' 140-141 F 3
Golan 182-183 F 6
Gôlâshkerd 180-181 H 5
Gôlbaşi [TR, Adiyaman] 182-183 G 4
Gölbaşi [TR, Ankara] 182 G 4
Golconda, IL 152-153 M 7
Golconda, NV 150-151 E 5-6
Gölcük [TR, Kocaeli] 182-183 CD 2
Gôldap 133 L 1
Gold Beach, OR 150-151 A 4
Goldburg, ID 150-151 G 3
Goldsboro, NC 146-147 L 4-5

Gonbad-e Qâbus 180-181 H 3
Gondar = Gonder 166-167 M 6
Gonder [ETH, •] 166-167 M 6
Gonder [ETH, ≈] 166-167 M 6
Gönen 182-183 B 2
Gong'an 190-191 D 6-7
Gongcheng 190-191 DE 7
Gongga Shan 184-185 J 6
Gongdu = Guangdu 190-191 DE 7
Gongguan 190-191 B 11
Gonghui 190-191 O 3
Gongjiatun = Gangtun 188-189 C 2
Gonglaio 172-173 C 4
Gongliao = Kungliao 190-191 HJ 9
Gongoji, Serra do - 158-159 LM 7-8
Gongola 166-167 G 7
Gongolgon 194-195 J 5
Gongshan 184-185 J 6
Gonhagawara 188-189 MN 2
Goshute Indian Reservation 150-151 F 5
Goslar 133 DE 3
Göspic 136-137 F 3
Gosport 132 F 6
Goss, MS 154-155 KL 5
Gossas 172-173 A 2
Gostini 138-139 EF 5
Gostynin 133 J 2
Gostyn 133 H 2-3
Göta älv 130-131 D 9-E 8
Göta kanal 130-131 EF 8
Götaland 130-131 E-G 9
Göteborg 130-131 D 8
Göteborg och Bohus 130-131 D 8
Gotha 133 DE 3
Gothenburg, NE 152-153 FG 5
Gotland 130-131 H 9
Gotland [S, •] 130-131 H 9
Gotland [S, ≈] 130-131 H 9
Gotlanddiep 130-131 HJ 9
Gotlands-Fossa de - 130-131 HJ 9
Gotland, Fossa di - 130-131 HJ 9
Gotland, Fosse de - 130-131 HJ 9
Gotland-melyseg 130-131 HJ 9
Gotlandzka, Gtebia - 130-131 HJ 9
Gotô-rettô 184-185 D 5
Gotska Sandön 130-131 HJ 8
Göttingen 133 DE 3
Gottsche = Kočevje 136-137 F 3
Goubangzi 188-189 CD 2
Goubéré 166-167 K 7
Gouda [ZA] 174-175 C 7
Goudiry 166-167 B 6
Goudkust 166-167 D 8-E 7
Gough, GA 154-155 B 8
Gouin, Réservoir - 144-145 VW 8
Goulbin Kaba 172-173 G 2
Goulburn Islands 194-195 F 2
Goulburn River 194-195 J 3
Gould, AR 154-155 K 4
Gould, CO 152-153 CD 5
Goulimím = Julímínâ 166-167 BC 3
Goulumbo 172-173 B 2
Goundi 172-173 H 1
Goundam 166-167 D 5
Goungo 172-173 F 2
Gouph, De - = Die Koup 174-175 D 7
Gouré 166-167 G 6
Gourits 174-175 D 8
Gouritz River = Gourits 174-175 D 8
Gourma 166-167 E 6
Gourma Rharous 166-167 D 5
Gourock 130-131 O 4
Gouverneur, NY 148-149 F 2
Governador, NM 154-155 B 2
Governor, NY 148-149 F 2
Gôvê = Goa 180-181 L 7
Gov'altaj = 5 ◁ 184-185 H 3
Gov'altaj nuruu 184-185 H 2-J 3
Govena, 178-179 g 6
Goverla 136-137 L 1
Governador Valadares 158-159 L 8
Gowanda, NY 148-149 D 3
Gower Peninsula 132 DE 6
Gowrie, IA 152-153 J 4
Goya 162 E 3
Goyder, TX 154-155 D 4
Göynücek 182-183 F 2
Göynük [TR, Bingöl] 182-183 J 3
Göynük [TR, Bolu] 182-183 D 2
Goze Delčev 136-137 KL 5
Gozha Tsho 184-185 E 4
Görögország 136-137 J 7-L 5
Goz Beida 166-167 J 6
Graaf-Reinet 168-169 FG 9
Grabo [CI] 172-173 D 4
Grabow 133 E 2

Grady, AR 154-155 K 3
Grady, NM 154-155 D 3
Graetlinger, IA 152-153 J 4
Grafton, IL 152-153 L 6
Grafton, ND 152-153 H 1
Grafton, WV 148-149 D 5
Graham, NC 148-149 D 6-7
Graham, TX 154-155 FG 4
Graham, Mount - 146-147 DE 5
Graham Bell, ostrov - ostrov 178-179 MN 1
Graham Moore, Cape - 144-145 V-X 3
Grahamstad = Grahamstown 168-169 G 9
Grain Coast 166-167 B 7 C 8
Graines, Côte des - 166-167 B 7-C 8
Grajfield, KS 152-153 F 6
Grajau 158-159 K 6
Grajau , Rio - [BR, Maranhão] 158-159 K 5-6
Grajewo 133 L 2
Grajvoron 140-141 G 1
Grambuša, Akötérion - 136-137 K 8
Grammos 136-137 J 5
Grampian Mountains 132 DE 3
Gran = Esztergom 133 J 5
Granada [NIC] 146-147 JK 9
Granada [NIC] 146-147 JK 9
Granada [US, Colorado] 152-153 E 6-7
Granada [Estado] 146-147 O 9
Granada, CO 152-153 CD 6
Grana Atlas 166-167 CD 2
Gran Bahia Australiana = Great Australia Bight 194-195 E 6-G 7
Gran Bajo [RA, Santa Cruz] 162 F-H 4-5
Granbury, TX 154-155 FG 4
Granby 144-145 W 8
Granby, CO 152-153 CD 5
Granby, Lake - 152-153 D 5
Gran Canaria 166-167 AB 3
Gran Chaco 162 D 3-E 2
Gran Desierto 146-147 C 5
Grand, MT 150-151 G 3
Grand Ballon 133-134 L 5
Grand Bassa = Buchanan 166-167 B7
Grand-Bassam 166-167 D 7-8
Grand-Bourg 146-147 OP 8
Grand Canyon 146-147 D 4
Grand Canyon, AZ 150-151 GH 7
Grand Canyon National Monument 150-151 G 7
Grand Canyon National Park 146-147 D 4
Grand Cape Mount 172-173 C 4
Grand Cayman 146-147 KL 8
Grand Chenier, LA 154-155 J 6
Grand Coulee [USA] 150-151 D 2
Grand Coulee, WA 150-151 D 2
Grand Coulee Dam 146-147 BC 2
Grand Deep 130-131 HJ 9
Grande Antillas 156 A-C 1-2
Grande Atlas 166-167 CD 2
Grande Chingâo 184-185 M 3-N 1
Grande Comore = Ngazidja 168-169 K 5
Grande Dépression Centrale 168-169 EF 3
Grande Khingan 184-185 M 3-N 1
Grandes Antillas 146-147 K 7-N 8
Grandes Antillas 146-147 K 7-N 8
Grande Muraglia 184-185 K 4
Grande Muraille 184-185 K 4
Grande Muralha 184-185 K 4
Grande Prairie 144-145 N 6-7
Grandfalls, TX 154-155 D 5
Grand Falls [CDN] 144-145 Za 8
Grand Falls [EAK] 171 D 3
Grand Falls [USA] 150-151 H 8
Grand Falls = Churchill Falls 144-145 XY 7
Grandfather Mountain 148-149 C 6-7
Grandfield, OK 154-155 F 3
Grand Forks, ND 146-147 G 2
Grand Gedeh = Grand Jide 172-173 CD 4
Grand Haven, MI 152-153 N 4
Grandi Antille 146-147 K 7-N 8
Grandioznyj, pik - 178-179 RS 7
Grand Island [USA, Louisiana] 154-155 L 5
Grand Island [USA, Michigan] 152-153 N 2
Grand Island [USA, New York] 148-149 D 3
Grand Isle, LA 154-155 K 6
Grand Jide 172-173 CD 4
Grand Junction, CO 146-147 DE 4
Grand Junction, IA 152-153 J 4
Grand Khingan 184-185 M 3-W 1
Grand-Lahou 166-167 CD 7-8
Grand Lake [USA, Louisiana] 154-155 K 6
Grand Lake [USA, Maine] 148-149 K 2
Grand Lake [USA, Michigan] 152-153 P 3
Grand Lake [USA, Ohio] 152-153 O 5

Grand Prairie, TX 154-155 G 4
Grand Rapids, MI 146-147 J 3
Grand Rapids, MN 152-153 J 2
Grand River [CDN] 148-149 CD 3
Grand River [USA, Michigan] 152-153 NO 4
Grand River [USA, Missouri] 152-153 K 6
Grand River [USA, South Dakota] 146-147 F 2
Grand River Valley 150-151 J 6
Grand Saline, TX 154-155 H 4
Grand Teton National Park 150-151 H 3-4
Grand Teton Peak 146-147 D 3
Grand Traverse Bay 152-153 NO 3
Grand Trunk Pacific Railway = Canadian National Railways 144-145 PQ 7
Grand View, ID 150-151 F 4
Grandview, MA 150-151 D 2
Grandview, WA 150-151 D 2
Grand Wash Cliffs 150-151 G 7-8
Gran Erg Occidental = Al-'Irq al-Kabir al-Gharbi 166-167 F 2-3
Grand Erg Oriental = Al 'Irq al-Kabir ash-Sharqi 166-167 F 2-3
Granger, TX 154-155 G 5
Granger, WA 150-151 CD 2
Granger, WV 150-151 J 3
Grängesberg 130-131 F 7
Grangeville, ID 150-151 EF 3
Granite, OK 154-155 F 3
Granite, OK 154-155 F 3
Granite City, IL 152-153 LM 6
Granite Downs 194-195 F 5
Granite Falls, MN 152-153 J 3
Granite Island [USA, Michigan] 152-153 N 2
Granite Peak [USA, Montana] 146-147 E 2
Granite Peak [USA, Utah] 150-151 G 5
Granite Range [USA, Nevada] 150-151 D 5
Granite Springs Valley 150-151 D 5-6
Graniteville, SC 148-149 C 8
Granja 158-159 L 5
Gran Jingân 184-185 M 3-N 1
Granki = Golynki 138-139 H 6
Gran Lago Salado = Great Salt Lake 146-147 D 3
Gran Malvina = West Falkland 162 D 8
Gran Pampa Pelada 158-159 F 9
Gran Sabana, La - 158-159 H 3
Gran San Bernardo 136-137 B 3
Gran Sasso 136-137 E 4
Grant, FL 148-149 c 3
Grant, MT 150-151 G 3
Grant, Mount - [USA, Clan Alpine Mountains] 150-151 DE 6
Grant, Mount - [USA, Wassuk Range] 150-151 D 6
Grant, NE 152-153 F 5
Grant City, MO 152-153 J 4
Grant Land 120 A 25-27
Grants, NM 146-147 E 4
Grantsburg, WI 152-153 K 3
Grants Pass, OR 150-151 B 4
Grantsville, UT 150-151 G 5
Grantsville , WV 148-149 C 5
Granville 134-135 G 4
Grão-Mogol 160-161 L 2
Grapeland, TX 154-155 H 5
Graskop 174-175 J 3
Grasse 134-135 L 7
Grass Creek, WY 152-153 B 4
Grass Lake, CA 150-151 B 5
Grass Range, MT 152-153 B 2
Grassridge Dam 174-175 F 6
Grass Valley, CA 150-151 C 6
Grass Valley, OR 150-151 C 3
Grassy 194-195 H 7-8
Grassy Knob 150-151 A 4
Gratangen 130-131 GH 3
Graudenz = Grudziądz 133 J 2
Gravatá 158-159 M 6
Gravenhage, 's- 134-135 JK 2
Gravenhurst 148-149 D 2
Grave Peak 150-151 F 2
Gravesend 196 JK 2
Gravette, AR 154-155 H 2
Gravina di Púglia 136-137 G 5
Grawn, MI 152-153 NO 3
Gray, GA 148-149 B 8
Gray, OK 154-155 E 2
Grayling, MI 152-153 O 3
Grayson, KY 152-153 P 6
Grayson, IL 152-153 MN 6
Graz 133 G 5
Gr'azi 133 MN 4
Gr'aznoje 138-139 M 6-7
Gr'azovec 138-139 MN 4
Grdelica 136-137 JK 4
Great Abaco Island 146-147 L 6
Great Artesian Basin 194-195 GH 4
Great Australian Bight 194-195 E 6-G 7
Great Bahama Bank 146-147 L 6-7
Great Bak River = Groot-Brakrivier 174-175 E 8
Great Barrier Island 194-195 P 7
Great Barrier Reef 194-195 H 2-K 4
Great Basin 146-147 CD 3-4
Great Bay 148-149 F 5
Great Bear Lake 144-145 MN 4
Great Bear River 144-145 LM 4-5
Great Berg River = Groot Bergrivier 174-175 C 7
Great Bitter Lake = Al-Buhayrat al-Murrat al-Kubrá 170 E 2
Great Dividing Range 194-195 H-K 3-7
Great Driffield 132 FG 4-5
Greater Antilles 146-147 K 7-N 8
Greater Leech Lake Indian Reservation 152-153 J 2
Greater Sunda Islands 186-187 E-H 7-8
Great Exuma Island 146-147 L 7
Great Falls 154-155 K 6
Great Falls, MT 146-147 DE 2
Greater Sunda Islands 186-187 E-H 7-8
Great Fish River = Groot Visrivier 174-175 G 7
Great Fish River = Groot Visrivier [Namibia] 174-175 B 4

Halbstadt = Moloćansk 140-141 GH 3
Halden 130-131 D 8
Haldensleben 133 E 2
Hale, Mount - 194-195 C 5
Haleakala Crater 186-187 ef 3
Haleb = Halab 180-181 D 3
Hale Center, TX 154-155 DE 3
Haleyville, AL 154-155 M 3
Half Assini 172-173 E 4
Halfanäa, Al- 182-183 M 7
Halfeti 182-183 GH 4
Halfin, Wādī - 180-181 H 6
Hal Flood Range 121 B 23
Halī = Khay' 180-181 E 7
Haliburton 148-149 D 2
Halicarnassus = Bodrum 182-183 B 4
Hālidah, Bī'r - 170 B 2
Halifax [CDN] 144-145 Y 9
Halifax, VA 148-149 D 6
Halifax Bay 194-195 J 3
Halīl, Al- 182-183 J 7
Halī Rūd 180-181 H 5
Hall, MT 150-151 G 2
Hall = A 133 E 5
Hall, ostrov -- ostrov Gall'a 178-179 KL 1
Halland 130-131 E 9
Hallandale, FL 148-149 c 4
Halla-san 188-189 F 6
Halle 133 EF 3
Halleck, NV 150-151 F 5
Hällefors 130-131 F 8
Hallein 133 F 5
Hallettsville, TX 154-155 G 6
Halley Bay 121 B 133-34
Halliday, ND 152-153 E 2
Hallingdal 130-131 C 7
Hallingskarvet 130-131 BC 7
Hall Lake 144-145 U 4
Hällnäs 130-131 H 5
Hallock, MN 152-153 H 1
Hallowell, ME 148-149 J 2
Hall Peninsula 144-145 X 5
Hallsberg 130-131 F 8
Halls Creek 194-195 E 3
Hallstavik 130-131 H 7-8
Halmahera 186-187 J 6
Halmahera, Laut - 186-187 J 7
Halmeu 136-137 K 2
Halmstad 130-131 E 9
Hälsingland 130-131 F 7-G 6
Halsey, NE 152-153 F 5
Haltdalen 130-131 D 6
Haltiatunturi 130-131 J 3
Halvmåneøya 130-131 lm 6
Halyć = Galić 140-141 B 2
Hálys = Kızılırmak 180-181 D 3
Ham [Namibia] 174-175 C 5
Hama = Hamáā 182-183 G 3
Hamáb = Hamrivier 174-175 C 5
Hamād, Al- 182-183 H 6-J 7
Hamada 188-189 H 5
Hamáh 180-181 D 3
Hamadán 180-181 F 3-4
Hamáh 180-181 D 3
Hamamatsu 188-189 L 5
Hamamatu = Hamamatsu 184-185 Q 5
Haman = Sankaya 182-183 F 3
Hamanaka 188-189 d 2
Hamana ko 188-189 L 5
Hamar 130-131 D 7
Hamar, ND 152-153 G 2
Hamár, 182-183 M 8
Hamár, Dār - 166-167 K 6
Hamár, Wādī - 182-183 H 4
Hamas = Hamáā 180-181 D 3
Hamasaka 188-189 K 5
Hamátah, Jabal - 166-167 LM 4
Hama-Tombetsu = Hama-Tombetsu 189 de 1
Hamatombetu = Hama-Tombetsu 189 de 1
Hambergbreen 130-131 k 6
Hamber Provincial Park 144-145 N 7
Hambourg = Hamburg 133 E 2
Hamburg 133 E 2
Hamburg, [ZA] 174-175 G 6
Hamburg, AR 154-155 JK 4
Hamburg, CA 150-151 B 5
Hamburg, IA 152-153 HJ 5
Hamburg, NY 148-149 D 3
Hamburg, PA 148-149 EF 4
Hamburgo = Hamburg 133 E 2
Hamburgo = Hamburg 130-131 CD 11
Hamch'ang 188-189 G 4
Ham-ch'uan = Hanchuan 190-191 DE 6
Hamḍ, Wādī al- 180-181 D 5
Hamḍah 180-181 E 7
Hamdániyah, Al- 182-183 G 5
Hämeen lääni 130-131 KL 7
Hamelin Pool 194-195 B 5
Hameln 133 D 2
Hamersley Range 194-195 C 4
Ham-gang = Namhan-gang 188-189 F4
Hamgyŏng-namdo 188-189 FG 2-3
Hamgyŏng-pukto 188-189 G 2-H 1
Hamhŭng 184-185 O 3-4
Hami 184-185 G 3
Hamidiyah 182-183 F 5
Hamilton [AUS] 194-195 H 7
Hamilton [Bermuda Islands] 146-147 O 5
Hamilton [CDN] 144-145 V 9
Hamilton [NZ] 194-195 OP 7
Hamilton, AL 154-155 LM 3
Hamilton, KS 152-153 H 6-7
Hamilton, MI 152-153 NO 4
Hamilton, MO 152-153 JK 6
Hamilton, MT 150-151 F 2
Hamilton, NY 148-149 F 3
Hamilton, OH 146-147 K 4
Hamilton, TX 154-155 FG 5
Hamilton, WA 150-151 C 1
Hamilton, The - 194-195 GH 4
Hamilton City, CA 150-151 BC 6
Hamilton Inlet 144-145 Z 7
Hamilton, Mount - 150-151 F 6
Hamilton River 194-195 FG 5
Hamilton River = Churchill River 144-145 Y 7
Hamilton Square, NJ 148-149 F 4
Hamina 130-131 M 7
Hamir, Wādī - [IRQ] 182-183 JK 7
Hamir, Wadi - [Saudi-Arabien] 182-183 J 7
Hamitabad = Ísparta 180-181 C 3
Hamlet, NC 148-149 D 7
Hamlin, TX 154-155 E 5
Hamm 133 CD 3
Hammál, Wādī al- = Wādī 'Ajaj 182-183 J 5
Hammám = Makhfir al-Hammám 182-183 H 5
Hammám, Al- 170 C 2
Hammám, Khalīj al- 166-167 G 1

Hammanskraal 174-175 H 3
Hammár, Hawr al- 180-181 F 4
Hammerdal 130-131 F 6
Hammerfest 130-131 KL 2
Hammon, OK 154-155 F 3
Hammond, IN 146-147 J 3
Hammond, LA 154-155 K 5
Hammond, MT 152-153 D 3
Hammond, OR 150-151 AB 2
Hammond Bay 152-153 OP 3
Hampton, AR 154-155 J 4
Hampton, FL 148-149 bc 2
Hampton, IA 152-153 K 4
Hampton, NH 148-149 H 3
Hampton, OR 150-151 C 4
Hampton, SC 148-149 C 8
Hampton, VA 148-149 E 6
Hampton Tableland 194-195 E 6
Hamrá', Al- [Saudi-Arabien] 180-181 D 5
Hamrá', Al- [SYR] 182-183 G 5
Hamrá' Al-Hammádat al- 166-167 G 2-3
Hamrin, Jabal - 182-183 KL 5
Hamrivier 174-175 C 5
Hamsah, Bī'r al- = Bī'r al-Khamsah 166-167 K 2
Hams Fork 150-151 H 4-5
Hámûl, Al- 170 D 2
Hamun = Daryácheh Sistán 180-181 HJ 4
Hamur 182-183 K 3
Hamza, Al- = Qawám al-Hamzah 182-183 L 7
Hanak = Ortahanak 182-183 K 2
Hanákiyah, Al- 180-181 E 6
Hanamaki 188-189 N 3
Hanamatsi 174-175 B 3
Hanam Plateau = Hanamiplato 174-175 B 3
Hanang 168-169 J 3
Hanazura-oki = Sukumo wan 188-189 J 6
Hancheng 190-191 C 4
Hancheu = Hangzhou 184-185 NN 5
Han Chiang = Han Jiang 190-191 F 9-10
Hanchuan 190-191 DE 6
Han-chuang = Hanzhuang 190-191 F 4
Hancock, MT 152-153 M 2
Hancock, NY 148-149 F 3-4
Handa 188-189 L 5
Handae-ri 188-189 FG 2
Handan 184-185 LM 4
Handaq, Al- = Al-Khandaq 166-167 KL 5
Handeni 168-169 J 4
Handrän 182-183 L 4
Hanford, CA 150-151 D 7
Hanford Works United States Atomic Energy Commission Reservation 150-151 D 2
Hangai = Changajn Nuruu 184-185 HJ 2
Hang-chou Wan = Hangzhou Wan 190-191 H 6
Hangchow= Hangzhou 184-185 NN 5
Hangcsou = Hangzhou 184-185 NN 5
Hanggin Qi 190-191 B 2
Hang-hsien = Hangzhou 184-185 NN 5
Hanging Rock 196 H 5
Hangjinqi = Hanggin Qi 190-191 B 2
Hangklip, Cape - = Kaap Hangklip 174-175 C 8
Hangklip, Kaap - 174-175 C 8
Hängö 130-131 K 8
Hangu 184-185 M 4
Hanguang 190-191 D 9
Hangzhou 184-185 NN 5
Hangzhou Wan 190-191 H 6
Hani 182-183 J 3
Hanifah, Wādī - 180-181 F 6
Haniyah, Al- 182-183 LM 8
Han Jiang 190-191 F 9-10
Hank, Al- 166-167 C-3 4
Hankewicze = Gancevići 138-139 EF 7
Hankey 174-175 F 7
Hankinson, ND 152-153 H 2-3
Hanko = Hangö 130-131 K 8
Hankou, Wuhan- 184-185 LM 5
Hankow = Wuhan-Hankou 184-185 LM 5
Hanksville, UT 150-151 H 6
Hanley Falls, MN 152-153 H 3
Hanku = Hangu 184-185 M 4
Hann, Mount - 194-195 E 3
Hanna, WY 152-153 C 5
Hannaford, ND 152-153 GH 2
Hannah, ND 152-153 G 1
Han-Negev 182-183 G 2
Hannibal, MO 146-147 H 3-4
Hannô 188-189 M 5
Hannover 133 D 2
Hanöbukten 130-131 F 1 0
Ha Nôi 186-187 DE 2
Hanoi = Ha Nôi 186-187 DE 2
Hanočt Yóna = Khân Yûnus 182-183 EF 7
Hanover [CDN] 148-149 C 2
Hanover [ZA] 174-175 F 6
Hanover, KS 152-153 H 6
Hanover, MT 152-153 F 3
Hanover, NH 148-149 GH 3
Hanover, PA 148-149 E 5
Hanover, VA 148-149 E 6
Hanover, Isla - 162 AB 8
Hanover Road = Hanoverweg 174-175 F 6
Hanoverweg 174-175 F 6
Hansboro, ND 152-153 G 1
Hansenfjella 121 B 26
Hanshan 190-191 G 6
Han Shui 184-185 K 5
Hanson River 194-195 F 4
Hanti-Manszi Autonóm Körzet 178-179 LP 5
Hanyang, Wuhan- 184-185 L 5
Hanyin 190-191 B 5
Hanzhuang 190-191 F 4
Haocheng 190-191 F 4
Haofeng = Hefeng 190-191 BC 7
Haoli = Hegang 184-185 OP 2
Haora 180-181 O 6
Haouach, Ouadi - 166-167 J 5
Haoxue 190-191 D 6
Haparanda 130-131 KL 5
Hapch'ôn 188-189 FG 5
Happy, TX 154-155 D 3
Happy Camp, CA 150-151
Happy, Haapsalu 138-139 D 4
Haql 180-181 CD 5

Haqûniyah' Al- 166-167 B 3
Harad 180-181 F 6
Haramachi 188-189 N 4
Haram Dågh 182-183 M 4
Haranomachi = Haramachi 188-189 N 4
Hara nur = Char nuur 184-185 G 2
Harare = Xarardeere 166-167 b3
Harare 168-169 H 6
Haräsis, Jiddat al- 180-181 H 6-7
Harawa = Harewa 166-167 N 6-7
Harbel 172-173 C 4
Harbin 184-185 O 2
Harbor Beach, MI 152-153 P 4
Harbor Springs, MI 152-153 O 3
Hardangerfjord 130-131 A 8-B 7
Hardangervidda 130-131 B 7
Hardee, MS 154-155 K 4
Hardeeville, SC 148-149 C 8
Hardesty, OK 154-155 E 2
Hardeveld 174-175 C 6
Hardey River 194-195 C 4
Hardin, IL 152-153 L 6
Hardin, MO 152-153 K 5
Harding 168-169 GH 9
Hardinsburg, KY 152-153 NO 7
Hardvár = Hardwar 180-181 M 4
Hardwár = Hardwar 180-181 M 4
Hardwar 180-181 M 4
Hardwick, VT 148-149 G 2
Hardy, AR 154-155 J 3
Hardy, Peninsula - 162 BC 9
Hardy, Rio - 150-151 F 9
Hareidlandet 130-131 A 6
Harelbeke 128-129 C 3
Harem = Harim 182-183 G 3
Harer 166-167 N 7
Harewa 166-167 N 6-7
Hargeisa = Hargeysa 166-167 a 2
Hargill, TX 154-155 FG 7
Hargla 138-139 F 5
Hari, Batang - 186-187 D 7
Haribes 174-175 B 3
Haribongo, Lac - 172-173 E 1
Haridwar = Hardwar 180-181 M 4
Harim 182-183 G 3
Harima nada 188-189 K 5
Harimgwe 188-189 G 4
Harírôd 180-181 J 4
Haris 174-175 B 2
Häritah, Al- 182-183 M 7
Härjerälen 130-131 E 6-F 7
Harj = Hargla 138-139 F 5
Harkov = Char'kov 140-141 H 1-2
Harlan, IA [ET] 170 C 3
Harlan, TX 152-153 J 5
Harlan County Lake 152-153 G 5-6
Härläu 130-131 M 2
Harlem, GA 148-149 B 8
Harlem 152-153 B 1
Harlingen 134-135 K 2
Harlingen, TX 146-147 G 6
Harlowton, MT 152-153 B 2
Harlu = Charlu 138-139 H 3
Harmal, Al- 182-183 G 5
Harmancık = Çardı 182-183 C 3
Harmanli 136-137 LM 5
Harmatan [TR] 182-183 GH 4
Harmonia 160-161 G 6
Harmony, ME 148-149 J 2
Harmony, MN 152-153 K 4
Harney Basin 146-147 BC 3
Harney Lake 150-151 D 4
Harney Peak 152-153 E 4
Härnösand 130-131 H 6
Haro, Cabo - 147 D 6
Harold Byrd Range 121 A 25-22
Haro Strait 150-151 B 1
Harper [GB] 132 E 6
Harper, KS 154-155 FG 2
Harper, OR 150-151 E 4
Harper, TX 154-155 F 5
Harpers Ferry, WV 148-149 DE 5
Harpster, ID 150-151 E 3
Harquahala Mountains 150-151 G 9
Harquahala Plains 150-151 G 9
Harrah, Al- [ET] 170 C 3
Harrah, Al- [Saudi-Arabien] 180-181 D 4
Harran [TR] 182-183 H 4
Harrar = Harer 166-167 N 7
Harrawa = Harawa 166-167 N 6-7
Harrell, AR 154-155 J 4
Harricana , Rivière - 144-145 V 7-8
Harriman, TN 154-155 N 3
Harrington, DE 148-149 F 5
Harrington Harbour 144-145 Z 7
Harris 132 C 3
Harris, Dorsal de - Dorsal de Lomonosov 120 A
Harris, Lake - 196 B 3
Harrisburg, IL 152-153 M 7
Harrisburg, NE 152-153 E 5
Harrisburg, OR 150-151 B 3
Harrisburg, PA 146-147 L 3
Harrismith 168-169 G 8
Harrison 186-187 N 5
Harrison, AR 154-155 J 2
Harrison, ID 150-151 E 2
Harrison, MI 152-153 O 3
Harrison, MT 150-151 H 3
Harrison, NE 152-153 E 5
Harrison, Cape - 144-145 Z 7
Harrisonburg, VA 148-149 D 5
Harrismville, MO 152-153 J 6
Harris Ridge = Lomonosov Ridge 120 A
Harrisrücken = Lomonosowrücken 120 A
Harrisrug = Lomonosovrug 120 A
Harriston 148-149 C 3
Harriston, MS 154-155 K 5
Harrisville, MI 148-149 C 3
Harrisville, WV 148-149 C 5
Harrodsburg, KY 152-153 O 7
Harrogate 132 F 4-5
Harrold, SD 152-153 G 3
Harrow, London- 132 F 6
Harry Strunk Lake 152-153 FG 5
Harsin 182-183 M 5
Harsit Deresi 182-183 HJ 3
Harstad 130-131 FG 3
Harsvik 130-131 CD 5
Hart, MI 152-153 N 4
Hart, TX 154-155 DE 3
Hart, Cape - 196 D 5-6
Harteigen = As-Sa'id 166-167 L 3
Hartbeesfontein, 174-175 G 4
Hartbeespoort 174-175 GH 3
Hartbeesrivier, 174-175 D 5
Hartebeespoort Dam = Hartbeespoortdam 174-175 GH 3
Hartenggole He = Chaaltyn gol 184-185 GH 4
Hartford, AL 154-155 N 5
Hartford, CT 146-147 M 3
Hartford, KY 152-153 N 6
Hartford, MI 152-153 N 4-5
Hartford, WI 152-153 M 4

Hartford City, IN 152-153 O 5
Hartington,NE 152-153 H 4
Hartlepool 132 F 4
Hartley, IA 152-153 J 4
Hartley, TX 154-155 D 3
Hartley = Chegutu 168-169 GH 6
Hartline, WA 150-151 D 2
Hartman, AAR 154-155 J 3
Hart Mountain 150-151 D 4
Hartselle, AL 154-155 M 3
Harts Range 194-195 FG 4
Hartsville, SC 148-149 CD 7
Havelock, TN 154-155 MN 2
Hartwell, GA 148-149 B 7
Hartwell Lake 148-149 B 7
Harüj al-Aswad, Al- 166-167 H 3
Härünäbäd [IR] 182-183 N 4
Härüt Röd 180-181 J 4
Harvard, CT 152-153 M 4
Harvard, IL 152-153 M 4
Harvard, NE 152-153 GH 5
Harvard, Mount - 152-153 C 8
Harvey, ND 152-153 FG 2
Harvey, IL 152-153 N 5
Harvey, MI 152-153 D 2
Harwell 132 F 6
Harwich 132 G 6
Harwich, MA 148-149 HJ 4
Harwood, TX 154-155 G 6
Haryana 180-181 M 5
Harz 133 E 2
Häs, Jabal al- 182-183 G 5
'Hasä, Al- 180-181 D 3
Hasä, Wādī al- [JOR, Al-Karak] 182-183 F 7
Hasä, Wādī al- [JOR, Ma'än] 182-183 G 7
Hasäheisa, El - Al-Husayhisah 166-167 L 6
Hasakah, Al- 180-181 D 3
Häsana = Hassan 180-181 M 8
Hasançelebi 182-183 GH 3
Hasan Dağı 182-183 EF 3
Hasankale = Pasinler 182-183 J 2-3
Hasb, Sha'ib - 180-181 K 4
Hasb, Sha'ib - 180-181 K 4
Hasenpot = Aizpute 138-139 C 5
Hasedtche, Al- = Al-Hasakah 180-181 D 3
Hashemiya, Al- = Al-Häshimiyah 182-183 L 6
Häshimiyah, Al- 182-183 L 6
Hashimoto 188-189 K 5
Hashir 182-183 K 4
Hashtpar 182-183 N 4
Hashtrüd 182-183 M 4
Hashun Shamo = Gaśuun Gov' 184-185 J 3
Hasi, Sha'ib - = Sha'ib Hasb 180-181 K 4
Hasilpur = Pasilpur 180-181 L 4
Haskell, OK 154-155 H 3
Haskell, TX 154-155 F 4
Haskovo 136-137 L 5
Hasmat 'Umar, Bi'r - 170 EF 7
Hassa 182-183 G 4
Hassan 180-181 M 8
Hassayampa River 150-151 G 9
Hassell, NM 154-155 J 3
Hassel Sound 144-145 R 2
Hasselt 134-135 K 3
Hassi ar-Raml 166-167 E 2
Hassi-Inifel = Hässi İnifil 166-167 E 2-3
Hässi İnifil = Hässi İnifil 166-167 E 2-3
Hässi Mas'üd 166-167 F 2
Hassi-Messaoud = Hässi Mas' üd 166-167 F 2
Hassi-R'Mel = Hässi ar-Raml 166-167 E 2
Hässleholm 130-131 EF 9
Hastings [GB] 132 G 6
Hastings [NZ] 194-195 P 7
Hastings, FL 148-149 c 2
Hastings, MI 152-153 O 4
Hastings, MN 152-153 K 3
Hastings, NE 146-147 G 3
Hasuur = Hazuur 174-175 C 4
Hasvik 182-183 JK 2
Haswell, CO 152-153 E 6
Hatab, Wādī al- 170 E 7
Hate'ae-do 188-189 E 5
Hätätibah, Al- 170 D 2
Hatch, NM 154-155 B 4
Hatch, UT 150-151 G 7
Hatchie River 154-155 L 3
Hateg 136-137 K 3
Hatfield [AUS] 196 F 4
Hathaway, MT 152-153 CD 2
Hathras 180-181 M 5
Hatinohe = Hachinohe 184-185 R 3
Hatip 182-183 E 4
Hatizyö zima = Hachijö-jima 184-185 Q 5
Ha-tongsan-ni 188-189 F 3
Hatteras, NC 148-149 F 7
Hatteras, Cape - 146-147 LM 4
Hatteras Island 146-147 LM 4
Hattfjelldal 130-131 F 5
Hattiesburg, MS 146-147 J 5
Hattingspruit 174-175 HJ 5
Hattiyah 182-183 F 5
Hatton 144-145 P 7
Hatton, ND 152-153 H 2
Hatvan 133 JK 5
Hat Yai 186-187 D 5
Hatzfeld = Jimbolia 136-137 J 3
Hauchab 174-175 B 3
Haud 166-167 NO 7
Haugesund 130-131 A 8
Haukadalur 130-131 c 2
Haukeligrend 130-131 B 8
Haukipudas 130-131 M 5
Haukivesi 130-131 N 6-7
Haukivuori 130-131 M 6-7
Häurä = Haora 180-181 O 6
Hauula = Al-Hawrah 180-181 H 8
Hauraki Gulf 194-195 OP 7
Hausah = Hawsah 182-183 G 6
Hausruck 133 F 4
Haut-Atlas 166-167 CD 2
Hautavaara = Chautavara 138-139 J 2
Haut-Congo 166-167 K 8
Haut-Kongo 167 K 8
Haute Egypte = As-Sa'id 166-167 L 3
Haute-Guinée 124-125 JK 5
Haute-Kotto 166-167 J 7
Haute-Sangha 166-167 H 8
Hautes Plateaux = Nijäd al-'Alí 166-167 D 2-E 1
Haut-Kongo 168-169 G 2
Haut Plateau d'Amérique = American Highland 121 A 3
Havai, Crista das - 124-125 AB 4
Havaí, Ilhas = Hawaiian Islands 186-187 d 3-e 4

Havajské ostrovy = Hawaiian Islands 186-187 d 3-e 4
Havajský hřbet 198-199 AB 4
Havana, FL 154-155 N 5
Havana, ND 152-153 H 3
Havana = La Habana 146-147 K 7
Havana = La Habana 146-147 K 7
Havana = La Habana 146-147 K 7
Havanna = La Habana 146-147 K 7
Havasu Lake 150-151 F 8
Havel 133 F 2
Havelock 148-149 DE 2
Havelock, NC 154-155 FF 7
Havelock, TN 154-155 MN 2
Haverfordwest 132 D 6
Haverhill, NH 148-149 GH 3
Haverhill, NH 148-149 GH 3
Haverstraw, NY 148-149 F 3-4
Havlíčkův Brod 133 G 4
Havøysund 130-131 L 2
Havre, MT 146-147 DE 2
Havre de Grace , MD 148-149 EF 5
Havre-Saint-Pierre 144-145 Y 7
Havsa 182-183 B 2
Havza 182-183 F 2
Hawai = Hawaii 186-187 ef 4
Hawaii, Dorsal de las - 124-125 AB 4
Hawai, Islas - = Hawaiian Islands 186-187 d 3-e 4
Hawaii, Dorsale delle - 124-125 AB 4
Hawaii, Dorsale des - 124-125 AB 4
Hawaii, Îles - =Hawaiian Islands 186-187 d 3-e 4
Hawaiian Ridge 124-125 AB 4
Hawaii-Inseln = Hawaiian Islands 186-187 d 3-e 4
Hawaiirücken 124-125 AB 4
Hawaiiryg 124-125 AB 4
Hawaii-szigetek = Hawaiian Islands 186-187 d 3-e 4
Hawal, River - 172-173 J 3
Hawana = La Habana 146-147 K 7
Hawarden, IA 152-153 H 4
Hawashiyah, Wādī - 170 E 3
Hawâtah, Al- 166-167 LM 6
Hawd = Haud 166-167 NO 7
Hawd, Al- [RIM] 166-167 C 5
Hawd al Gharbi, Al- 172-173 C 1
Hawd ash-Sharqi, Al- 172-173 D 1
Hawera 194-195 OP 7
Hawesville, KY 152-153 N 7
Hawick 132 E 4
Hawizah, Hawr al- 182-183 M 7
Hawke, Cape - 194-195 K 6
Hawke Bay 194-195 P 7
Hawker 194-195 G 6
Hawkes, Mount - 121 A 132-33
Hawkinsville, GA 148-149 B 8
Hawkins, WI 152-153 L 3
Hawks, MI 152-153 P 3
Hawk Springs, WY 152-153 D 5
Hawley, MN 152-153 HJ 2
Hawley, TX 154-155 F 4
Hawrah, Al- 180-181 H 8
Hawrán, Wādī - 180-181 E 4
Haw River 148-149 D 7
Hawsah 182-183 G 6
Hawsh 'İsä 170 D 2
Hawston 174-175 C 8
Hawtah, Al- = Al-Hillah 180-181 F 6
Hawthorn, FL 148-149 bc 2
Hawthorne, NV 150-151 D 6
Haxby, MT 152-153 D 2
Haxtun, CO 152-153 E 5
Hay [AUS] 194-195 HJ 6
Haya, La - = 's-Gravenhage 134-135 JK 2
Haydar Daği 182-183 DE 4
Hayden, AZ 150-151 H 9
Hayden, CO 152-153 L 6
Haye, La - = 's-Gravenhage 134-135 JK 2
Hayes, LA 154-155 J 5
Hayes, SD 152-153 F 3
Hayes, Mount - 144-145 G 5
Hays Center, NE 152-153 F 5
Hayes Halvø = 144-145 XY 2
Hayfield, MN 152-153 K 4
Hayfork, CA 150-151 B 5
Hay Lake = Habay 144-145 N 6
Haylow, GA 148-149 B 9
Haymana 182-183 E 3
Haymana Yaylâsi 182-183 E 3
Haymür, Abar - 170 EF 6
Haymür, Wādī - 170 E 6
Haynesville, LA 154-155 J 4
Hayneville, AL 154-155 M 4
Hayrabolu 182-183 B 2
Hay River [AUS] 194-195 G 4
Hay River [CDN, ~] 144-145 N 6
Hay River [CDN, •] 144-145 NO 5
Hays 180-181 F 7
Hays, KS 146-147 G 4
Hays, MT 152-153 B 2
Hayshán, Jabal - 170 C 4
Haysi, Bī'r al- 170 F 3
Hay Springs, NE 152-153 E 4
Haystack Mountain 148-149 G 3
Haystack Peak 150-151 G 6
Hayti, MO 154-155 L 2
Hayti, SD 152-153 H 3
Hayton's Falls 171 CD 3
Hayward, CA 150-151 BC 7
Hayward, WI 152-153 L 3
Hayy, Al- 182-183 M 6
Hayyä 166-167 M 5
Hayy Alläh, Jabal - 170 B 4
Hayy, Al- 170 C 3-4
Hazar = İdil 182-183 J 4
Hazárän 180-181 H 5
Hazard, KY 146-147 K 4
Hazawzā' 182-183 GH 7
Hazebrouck 128-129 J 3
Hazelton, AR 154-155 J 3
Hazen, AR 154-155 J 3
Hazen, ND 152-153 E 2
Hazen, NV 150-151 D 6
Hazen, NM 154-155 OP 2
Hazím, Al- 182-183 G 7
Hazím, Wādī al- 182-183 J 6
Hazlehurst, GA 148-149 B 8
Hazlehurst, MS 154-155 K 5
Hazleton, PA 148-149 F 4
Hazlett, Lake - 194-195 E 4
Hazm, Al- 170 G 2
Hazo = Kozluk 182-183 J 3
Hazro 182-183 J 3
Hazul, Al- = Al-Huzul 182-183 K 8
Hazuur 174-175 C 4
Headland, AL 154-155 N 5
Headquarters, ID 150-151 F 2
Heads , The - 150-151 A 4

Healdsburg, CA 150-151 B 6
Healdton, OK 154-155 G 3
Healesville 196 GH 6
Healy, KS 152-153 F 6
Heard 124-125 N 8
Hearne, TX 154-155 G 5
Hearst 144-145 U 8
Hearst Island 121 BC 130-131
Heart Butte 152-153 EF 2
Heart Butte Reservoir = Lake Tschida 152-153 EF 2
Heart River 152-153 F 2
Heavener, OK 154-155 H 3
Hebbronville, TX 154-155 F 7
Hebei 184-185 LM 4
Heber, UT 150-151 H 5
Heber Springs, AR 154-155 J 3
Hebgen Lake 150-151 H 3
Hebi 190-191 D 4
Hebo, OR 150-151 AB 3
Hebrides, Sea of the - 132 C 3
Hebron [CDN] 144-145 Y 6
Hebron [ZA] 174-175 F 8
Hebron, ND 152-153 EF 2
Hebron–Al-Halil 182-183 F 7
Hecate Strait 144-145 K 7
Heceta Head 150-151 A 3
Hecheng 190-191 D 10
Hechuan 184-185 JK 5
Hecla, SD 152-153 GH 3
Hecla and Griper Bay 144-145 O 2
Hectorspruit 174-175 JK 3
Hede 130-131 E 6
He Devil Mountain 150-151 E 3
Hedien = Khotan 184-185 DE 4
Hedjas = Al-Hijäz 180-181 D 5-6
Hedjaz 180-181 D 5-6
Hedley, TX 154-155 E 3
Hedmark 130-131 D 6-E 7
Hedrick, IA 152-153 K 5
Hedzsáz 180-181 D 5-6
Hefa 180-181 D 3
Hefei 184-185 M 5
Hefeng 190-191 BC 7
Heflin, AL 154-155 N 4
Hegang 184-185 OP 2
Heho = Jiexi 190-191 E 10
Hei-ho = Aihui 184-185 O 1
Heian-hokudo = Pyŏngan-pukto 188-189 E 2-3
Heian-nandö= Pyŏngan-namdo 188-189 EF 3
Heidarābād = Heydarābād 182-183 L 4
Heide 133 D 1
Heide [Namibia] 174-175 B 2
Heidekruiz = Šilutė 138-139 C 6
Heidelberg 133 D 4
Heidelberg [ZA, Kaapland] 174-175 D 8
Heidelberg [ZA, Transvaal] 174-175 GH 4
Heidenheim, MG 154-155 L 5
Heihe 184-185 O 1
Heijing 190-191 C 4
Heilan = Chajlar gol 184-185 N 1-2
Heilbron 174-175 GH 4
Heilbronn 133 D 4
Heiligenbeil = Mamonovo 133 JK 1
Heilong Jiang [TJ, ~] 184-185 O 1
Heilongjiang [TJ, *] 184-185 M-P 2
Hei-lung Chiang = Heilong Jiang 184-185 O 1
Heilung Kiang = Heilong Jiang 184-185 O 1
Heimaey 130-131 c 3
Heinola 130-131 M 7
Heinsee, WI 152-153 N 4
Heishan 188-189 CD 2
Heisi, Bi'r al- = Bi'r al-Haysi 170 F 3
Hejian 190-191 EF 2
Hejiang [TJ, •] 190-191 C 11
Hejie 190-191 G 4
Hejin 190-191 C 4
Hekimdaği 182-183 D 3
Hekimhan 182-183 G 3
Hekla 130-131 d 2
Hekou = Hekouji 190-191 F 5
Hekouji 190-191 F 5
Hekpoort 174-175 G 3
Helagsfjället 130-131 E 6
Helder, Den - 134-135 K 2
Helen, Mount - 150-151 E 7
Helen, AR 146-147 H 5
Helendale, CA 150-151 E 8
Helen Reef 186-187 K 6
Heleysund 130-131 m 5
Helgeland 130-131 E 5-F 4
Helgoland 133 C 1
Helgoland, Golfo di - 133 C 1
Helikön 130-131 K 5
Heliopolis = Al-Qahirah-Misr al-Jadidah 170 DE 2
Heliqi = Helixi 190-191 G 6
Helixi 190-191 G 6
Helix, OR 150-151 D 3
Helixi190-191 G 6
Hella 130-131 c 3
Helleland 130-131 B 8
Hellepoort = Portes de l'Enfer 168-169 G 4
Hellin 134-135 G 9
Hell-Ville 168-169 L 5
Hezärän 180-181 H 5
Helmand Röd 180-181 K 4
Helmeringhausen 174-175 B 3-4
Helmond 134-135 KL 3
Helmsdale 132 E 2
Helmstedt 133 E 2
Helmville, MT 150-151 G 2
Helong 184-185 O 3
Helpekaar 174-175 HJ 5
Helpmekaar 174-175 HJ 5
Helsingborg 130-131 E 9
Helsingfors = Helsinki 130-131 L 7
Helsingör 130-131 E 9
Helsinki 130-131 L 7
Helsinki = Helsinki 130-131 L 7
Helsingya = Helsinki 126-127 NO 4
Helska, Mierzeja - 133 J 1
Helvetia 174-175 F 7
Helwân = Hulwân 166-167 L 3
Hemel, el- = Al-Harmal 182-183 G 5
Hemet, CA 150-151 E 9
Hemingford, NE 152-153 E 4
Hemphill, TX 154-155 J 5
Hempstead, NY 148-149 G 4

Hempstead, TX 154-155 G 5
Henan 184-185 L 5
Henares 134-135 F 8
Henashi-saki 188-189 M 2
Henchow = Hengyang 184-185 L 6
Hendawashi 171 C 3
Hendaye 134-135 G 7
Henderson 182-183 D 2
Henderson [GB] 192-193 P 7
Henderson, KY 146-147 J 4
Henderson, NC 148-149 D 6
Henderson, NV 150-151 F 7
Henderson, TX 154-155 H 4
Henderson, TN 154-155 L 3
Henderson Bay 148-149 E 2-3
Hendersonville, NC 148-149 B 7
Hendersonville, TN 154-155 M 2
Hendrik Verwoerd Dam 174-175 FG 6
Hendrina 174-175 HJ 4
Heng'ang = Hengyang 184-185 L 6
Heng-chan = Hengyang 184-185 L 6
Heng-chou = Heng Xian 184-185 K 7
Heng-chun 190-191 H 10
Hengdong 190-191 D 8
Hengduan Shan 184-185 H 6
Hengelo 134-135 L 2
Hengfeng 190-191 F 7
Henghsien = Heng Xian 184-185 K 7
Heng Sha = South Henik Lake 144-145 R 5
Hengshan [TJ, Shaanxi] 190-191 B 3
Heng Shan [TJ, Shabxi] 190-191 D 2
Hengshan = Hengyang 184-185 L 6
Hengshui 184-185 LM 4
Heng Xian 184-185 K 7
Hengyang 184-185 L 6
Hengyang [TJ, Shandong] 190-191 G 4
Henik Lake = South Henik Lake 144-145 R 5
Henlopen, Cape - 148-149 F 5
Henly, TX 154-155 F 5
Hennebont 134-135 F 5
Hennenman 174-175 G 4
Hennessey, OK 154-155 G 3
Hennesberget 130-131 E 4
Henrietta, TX 154-155 F 4
Henrietta Maria, Cape - 144-145 U 6
Henriette, ostrov -- ostrov Genrietty 178-179 ef 2
Henrique de Carvalho = Saurimo 168-169 F 4
Henry, IL 152-153 M 5
Henry, SD 152-153 H 3
Henry, Cape - 148-149 F 6
Henry, Mount - 150-151 F 1
Henryetta, OK 154-155 GH 3
Henry Kater Peninsula 144-145 XY 5
Henry Mountains 150-151 H 6
Henrys Fork 150-151 H 3-4
Hensall 152-153 C 3
Henty 196 H 5
Henzada = Hinthada 186-187 BC 3
Heping 190-191 E 9
Hepo = Jiexi 190-191 E 10
Heppner Junction, OR 150-151 D 3
Hepu 184-185 K 7
Hequ 190-191 C 2
Hepworth 152-153 Q 3
Heraclea = Ereğli 180-181 C 2
Héradhsflói 130-131 f 2
Héradhsvötn 130-131 d 2
Heräkleia = Ereğli 180-181 C 2
Herald, ostrov - 120 B 36
Heras, Las - [RA, Santa Cruz] 162 C 7
Herät 180-181 J 4
Herbertsdale 174-175 DE 8
Hercegnovi 136-137 H 4
Hercílio, Rio 160-161 G 7
Hereford 132 E, TX 154-155 D 3
Herefoss 130-131 C 8
Hérèhérètué 192-193 N 6
Herero 174-175 C 2
Hereroland 168-169 EF 7
Herford 133 D 2
Heri Rud–Harī Rūd 180-181 J 4
Herington, KS 152-153 H 6
Heris 182-183 M 3
Heritage Range 121 B 28-A 29
Herkimer, NY 148-149 F 3
Herlen He 184-185 M 2
Herman, MN 152-153 HJ 3
Hermann, MO 152-153 L 6
Hermannsburg [AUS] 194-195 F 4
Hermansfjord 130-131 EF 6
Hermannstadt = Sibiu 136-137 KL 3
Hermansverk 130-131 B 7
Hermansville, MI 152-153 N 3
Hermanus 174-175 C 8
Hermel, el- = Al-Harmal 182-183 G 5
Hermes, Cape - = Kaap Hermes 174-175 H 6
Hermes, Kaap - 174-175 H 6
Hermiston, OR 150-151 D 3
Hermitage, AR 154-155 J 4
Hermite, Isla - 162 C 9
Hermit Islands 186-187 N 7
Hermleigh, TX 154-155 E 4
Hermón = Jabal as-Saykh 182-183 FG 6
Hérmon = Gediz çayı 182-183 C 3
Hermosa, SD 152-153 EF 4
Hermosillo 146-147 D 6
Hernandarias 162 F 3
Hernando, MS 154-155 L 3
Herndon, KS 152-153 F 6
Herning 130-131 C 9
Heroica Alvarado = Alvarado 146-147 H 8
Heroica Guaymas 146-147 D 6
Heroica Matamoros = Matamoros 146-147 G 6
Heroica Puebla de Zaragoza = Puebla de Zaragoza 146-147 G 8
Heroica Veracruz = Veracruz 146-147 GH 8
Heron, MT 150-151 F 1
Heron Lake 152-153 J 4
Heros, SD 152-153 FG 3
Herreid, SD 152-153 F 3
Herrera 134-135 F 7
Herrera de Duque 134-135 E 9
Herrera de Pisuerga 134-135 EF 7
Herreras, Los - 154-155 K 5
Herrick 194-195 J 8
Herrin, IL 152-153 M 7
Herrington Island 148-149 AB 5-6

Herrington, Lake 152-153 O 7
Herschel [ZA] 174-175 G 6
Herschel Island 144-145 J 4
Herson = Cherson 140-141 F 3
Hertford 132 FG 6
Hertford, NC 148-149 E 6
Hertogenbosch, 's- 134-135 KL 3
Hervey 192-193 M 6
Hervey Bay [AUS, ~] 194-195 K 4-5
Hervey Bay [AUS, •] 194-195 K 5
Herzogenbusch = 's-Hertogenbosch 134-135 KL 3
Hertzogville 174-175 F 5
Herzberg 133 F 2
Herzog-Ernst-Bucht 121 B 132-33
Heshjin 190-191 D 3
Heshui [TJ, Gansu] 190-191 B 4
Heshui [TJ, Guangdong] 190-191 CD 10
Heshun 190-191 D 3
Hesperia, CA 150-151 E 8
Hesperus, CO 152-153 BC 7
Hestøyri 130-131 b 1
Hetian [TJ, Fujian] 190-191 F 9
Hetian [TJ, Guangdong] 190-191 E 10
Hetou 190-191 B 11
Hettinger, ND 152-153 E 2-3
Heuglin, Kapp - 130-131 lm 5
Heuningspruit 174-175 G 4
Heuningvleisoutpan 174-175 E 4
Heves 133 K 5
He Xian [TJ, Guangxi Zhuangzu Zizhiqu] 184-185 L 7
He Xian [TJ, Anhui] 190-191 G 6
Hexigten Qi 184-185 M 3
Hexrivier 174-175 C 7
Hexrivierberge 174-175 C 7
Hext, TX 154-155 F 5
Hexue = Haoxue 190-191 D 6
Heyang [TJ, Shaanxi] 190-191 C 4
Heyang [TJ, Shandong] 190-191 G 4
Heyburn, ID 150-151 G 4
Heydarābād 182-183 L 4
Heyuan 190-191 E 10
Heywood [AUS] 196 EF 7
Hezárán, Küh-e - 180-181 H 5
Heze 184-185 M 4
Hezelton 144-145 L 6
Hialeah, FL 148-149 c 4
Hiawatha. KS 152-153 H 6
Hiawatha, UT 150-151 H 6
Hibbing, MN 146-147 H 2
Hibbs, Point - 196 b 3
Hichiro-wan = zaliv Terpenija 178-179 b 8
Hickman, KY 154-155 L 2
Hickman, SD 152-153 DE 4-5
Hickman, NM 154-155 AB 3
Hickory, NC 148-149 C 7
Hickory, Lake - 148-149 C 7
Hicksville, OH 152-153 O 5
Hico, TX 154-155 FG 4-5
Hidaka 188-189 c 2
Hidaka-sammyaku 188-189 c 2
Hidalgo [MEX, Coahuila] 154-155 EF 7
Hidalgo [MEX, Hidalgo] 146-147 G 7
Hidalgo del Parral 146-147 EF 6
Hida sammyaku 188-189 L 4-5
Hiddensee 133 F 1
Hidrolândia 160-161 H 2
Hidzaz, Al- = Al-Hijäz 180-181 D 5-6
Hidžáz = Al-Hijäz 180-181 D 5-6
Hidžäzah 170 E 5
Hienghène 194-195 MN 4
Hierisós 136-137 KL 5
Hieropolis = Manbij 182-183 GH 4
Hierro 166-167 A 3
Higashii-suido 188-189 KL 5
Higbee, MO 152-153 K 6
Higgins, TX 154-155 E 2
Higgins Lake 152-153 NO 3
High Atlas 166-167 CD 2
Highflats 174-175 J 6
High Island 152-153 NO 3
High Island, TX 154-155 HJ 6
Highland, IL 152-153 M 6
Highland Park, IL 152-153 N 4
Highland Park, MI 152-153 P 4
Highland Peak 150-151 F 7
Highmore, SD 152-153 G 3
High Point, NC 146-147 KL 4
High Prairie 144-145 NO 6
Highwood, MT 150-151 H 2
Higiaz = Al-Hijäz 180-181 D 5-6
Hiidenma = Hiiumaa 138-139 D 4
Hiiraan 166-167 ab 3
Hiiumaa 130-131 JK 8
Hiiumaa 138-139 D 4
Hijärah, Şahrä' al- [IRQ] 182-183 L 7
Hijärah, Şahrä' al- [Saudi-Arabien] 182-183 J 7
Hijäz, Al- 180-181 D 5-6
Hijäz, Al- 180-181 D 5-6
Hijäzah 170 E 5
Hijo = Tagum 186-187 J 5
Hikari 188-189 H 6
Hiko, NV 150-151 F 7
Hikone 188-189 L 5
Hiko-san 188-189 H 6
Hikueru 192-193 N 6
Hikurangi 192-193 P 7
Hildäl, Wādī al- 182-183 J 7
Hilbert, WI 152-153 MN 3
Hildesheim 133 DE 2
Hilger, MT 152-153 B 2
Hill, MT 150-151 H 1
Hillah, Al- [Saudi-Arabien] 180-181 F 6
Hill City, ID 150-151 F 4
Hill City, KS 152-153 G 6
Hill City, NM 152-153 K 2
Hill City, SD 152-153 E 3-4
Hillerød 130-131 DE 10
Hillman, MN 152-153 H 4
Hillsboro, GA 148-149 B 8
Hillsboro, IL 152-153 M 6
Hillsboro, ND 152-153 H 2
Hillsboro, NH 148-149 H 3
Hillsboro, NM 154-155 B 4
Hillsboro, OH 152-153 O 6
Hillsboro, TX 154-155 G 4
Hillsboro Canal 148-149 c 3
Hillsborough 152-153 O 5
Hillsdale, MI 152-153 O 5
Hillside, AZ 150-151 G 8
Hillston 194-195 HJ 6
Hillsville, VA 148-149 C 6
Hilltop 174-175 H 5

ronwood, MI 146-147 HJ 2
roquois, SD 152-153 H 3
roquois Falls 144-145 U 8
rország 132 BC 5
rō saki 188-189 M 5
rpen' [SU, ~] 140-141 DE 1
rpen' [SU, ●] 140-141 E 1
lrq, Al- 166-167 J 3
lrqah 180-181 F 8
lrq al-Gharbi al-Kabir, Al-
166-167 D 3-E 2
lrq ash-Sharqī al-Kabir, Al
166-167 F 2-3
rrawaddy = Erāwadi Myit
186-187 C 2
rša 140-141 D 1
ršava 140-141 A 2
rské moře 132 D 5
rsko 132 BC 5
r-tenger 132 D 5
rtyš = Ertis 178-179 N 6
rtyšskoje 178-179 NO 7
rumu 168-169 G 2
rūn 134-135 G 7
ruya 162 CD 2
rvine, KY 152-153 P 7
rving, TX 154-155 G 4
rvington, KY 152-153 N 7
rwin, ID 150-151 H 4
rwin, NE 152-153 EF 4
wōl-san 188-189 G 4
s,Jabal - 170 F 6
sa 172-173 G 2
sabel, SD 152-153 F 3
sabela 186-187 H 5
sabela, Isla - 158-159 A 5
sabela, CA 150-151 D 8
sabella, MN 152-153 L 2
sabella, Cordillera - 146-147 J 9
sabella Lake 150-151 D 8
sachsen 144-145 Q 2
sachsen, Cape - 144-145 OP 2
safjardhardjúp 130-131 b 1
safjördhur 130-131 b 1
sahara = Isahaya 188-189 GH 6
sahaya 188-189 GH 6
sakly 138-139 S 6
sakogorka, Archangel'sk-
138-139 MN 1
sangi 168-169 F 2
sar 133 F 4
sāwiyah, Al- 180-181 D 4
sāwuwan, 'Irq - 166-167 F 3
schia 136-137 E 5
se [J] 188-189 L 5
sejevka 138-139 QR 6
seo 136-137 D 3
sère 134-135 K 6
sère, Pointe - 158-159 J 3
serim, gora - 178-179 K 5
sērnia 136-137 F 5
set' 178-179 L 6
se-wan 188-189 L 5
seyin 166-167 E 7
sezaki 188-189 M 4
sfahan = Eşfahān 180-181 G 4
sfjorden 130-131 j 5
shan = Yishan 184-185 K 7
shibashi 188-189 N 3
shigaki-shima 184-185 NO 7
shikari 188-189 b 2
shikari gawa 188-189 b 2
shikari-wan 188-189 b 2
shikawa 188-189 L 4
shinomaki 188-189 N 3
shinomaki wan 188-189 N 3
shioka 188-189 N 4
shizuchino san 188-189 J 6
shpeming, MI 152-153 N 2
shui = Yishui 190-191 G 4
sigaki sima = Ishigaki-shima
184-185 NO 7
signy-sur-Mer 134-135 G 4
sik Daği 182-183 E 2
sil'kul' 178-179 N 7
sim [SU, ~] 178-179 M 7
sim [SU, ●] 178-179 M 6
simbaj 178-179 K 7
simbira 171 BC 4
simskaja ravnina 178-179 N 6-7
siolo 168-169 J 2
sipingo Beach 174-175 J 5-6
siro 168-169 G 2
sisford 194-195 H 4
sispynten 130-131 mn 5
skandar 178-179 M 9
skandariyah, Al- 166-167 KL 2
skar 136-137 L 4
skardū = Skardū 180-181 M 3
skejevo 138-139 S 6
skele = Karataş 182-183 F 4
skenderun 180-181 D 3
skenderun Körfezi 182-183 F 4
skilip 182-183 F 2
skitim 178-179 P 7
skorost' = Korosten' 140-141 D 1
skushuban 166-167 bc 1
sla Alta 160-161 D 7
sla-Cristina 134-135 D 10
slāhiye 182-183 G 4
slāmābād 180-181 L 4
slāmābād = Anantnag 180-181 M 4
slamorada, FL 148-149 c 4
sland 130-131 c-f 2
slandia 130-131 cd 2
slandbecken 128-129 CD 4
sland City, OR 150-151 E 3
slande 130-131 c-f 2
sland Falls, ME 148-149 J 1-2
slanda - Fær øer, Dorsale -
128-129 FG 3
slandia 130-131 c-f 2
slândia 130-131 c-f 2
slândia, Bacia da - 128-129 CD 4
slandia, Cuenca de - 128-129 CD 4
sland-Jan-Mayen-Rücken
128-129 F 2
sland Lagoon 194-195 G 6
sland Lake [CDN ≈]
144-145 RS 7
sland Mountain, CA 150-151 B 5
sland Park, ID 150-151 H 3
sland Park Reservoir 150-151 H 3
sland Pond, VT 148-149 GH 2
slands, Bay of - [NZ] 194-195 OP 7
la Nueva 162 C 9
las Anglo-Normandas =
Channel Islands 132 E 7
las Británicas 128-129 F 5-G 4
las Jónicas 136-137 H 6-J 7
lay 132 C 4
le 134-135 H 6
le au Haut 148-149 J 2-3
le Royale 146-147 J 2
le Royale National Park
152-153 M 2
les Dernieres 154-155 K 6
leta, NM 154-155 B 3
leton, CA 150-151 C 6
ma'īliyah, Al- 166-167 D 2
mailly 140-141 O 6
may, MT 152-153 D 2
metpaşa = Yeşilyurt 182-183 H 3
Isnā 166-167 L 3
Isohama = Ōarai 188-189 N 4
Isoka 168-169 H 5
Isole Britanniche 128-129 F 6-G 4
Isole Ioniche 136-137 H 6-J 7
Ispahan = Eşfahān 180-181 G 4
Isparta 180-181 C 3
Isperih 136-137 M 4
İspir 182-183 J 2
Israel 180-181 CD 4
Israël 180-181 CD 4
Israele 180-181 CD 4
Israelite Bay 194-195 DE 6
Issa 138-139 P 7
Issano 158-159 G 3
Issati 172-173 F 3
Issaouane, Erg - = 'Irq Isāwuwan
166-167 F 3
Issia 172-173 D 4
Issoudun 134-135 HJ 5
Issyk-Kul' 180-181 M 2
Issyk-Kul', ozero - 184-185 M 3
Istabl, Bi'r - 170 B 2
Istāda-Moqur, Ab-e - 180-181 K 4
Istambul = İstanbul 180-181 BC 2
İstanbul 180-181 BC 2
Istanbul 180-181 BC 2
Istiaia 136-137 K 6
Istisu 140-141 MN 7
Istmina 158-159 D 3
Istra [SU] 138-139 L 6
Istria 136-137 EF 3
Istria = Istra 136-137 EF 3
Istrie = Istra 136-137 EF 3
Istrien = Istria 136-137 EF 3
Išerim, gora - 178-179 K 5
Išim [SU, ●] 178-179 M 6
Išimbaj 178-179 K 7
Išimskaja ravnina 178-179 N 6-7
Itabaianinha 158-159 M 7
Itabaina 158-159 M 6
Itabapoana 160-161 M 4
Itabapoana, Rio - 160-161 M 4
Itaberá 160-161 H 5
Itaberaba 158-159 L 7
Itaberaí 158-159 JK 8
Itabira 160-161 L 3
Itabirito 160-161 L 4
Itaboraí 160-161 L 5
Itabuna 158-159 M 7
Itacaiúnas, Rio - 158-159 JK 6
Itacambiruçu, Rio - 160-161 L 2
Itacaré 158-159 M 7
Itacoatiara 158-159 H 5
Itacolomi, Ilhas - 160-161 H 6
Itacolomi, Pico - 158-159 L 9
Itacurubí del Rosario 160-161 D 6
Itaetê 158-159 L 7
Itaguai 160-161 KL 5
Itaguara 160-161 K 4
Itaguatins 158-159 K 6
Itaguyry 160-161 E 6
Itai 162 G 9
Itaimbey, Rio - 160-161 E 6
Itaiópolis 160-161 H 7
Itaipava, Cachoeira - [BR, Rio
Araguaia] 158-159 K 6 Itaipava,
Cachoeira - [BR, Rio Xingu]
158-159 J 5
Itaipu, Ponta - 160-161 J 6
Itaipú, Presa de - 160-161 EF 6
Itaipú, Represa de - 160-161 EF 6
Itaituba 158-159 H 5
Itajaí 162 G 3
Itajaí, Rio - 160-161 H 7
Itajaí do Sul, Rio - 160-161 H 7
Itajaí-Mirim, Rio - 160-161 H 7
Itajubá 158-159 K 9
Itajuípe 158-159 LM 7
Itaka 178-179 W 7
Italia 122-123 K 3-4
Itália 136-137 C 3-F 5
Italia 136-137 C 3-F 5
Itálica 134-135 DE 10
Italie 136-137 C 3-F 5
Italië 136-137 C 3-F 5
Italie 136-137 C 3-F 5
Italien 136-137 C 3-F 5
Italy 136-137 C 3-F 5
Italy, TX 154-155 G 4
Itamarandiba 160-161 L 2
Itambacuri 160-161 M 3
Itambacuri, Rio - 160-161 M 3
Itambé 158-159 L 8
Itambé, Pico de - 160-161 L 3
Itambira, Pico - 160-161 L 2
Itamoji 160-161 J 4
Itanhaém 160-161 J 6
Itanhandu 160-161 K 5
Itanhomi 160-161 M 3
Itany 158-159 J 4
Itaocara 158-159 L 9
Itapaci 158-159 JK 7
Itapajé 158-159 LM 5
Itapé [PY] 160-161 D 6
Itapebi 158-159 M 8
Itapemirim 158-159 LM 9
Itapercerica 160-161 K 4
Itaperuna 160-161 LM 4
Itapetinga 158-159 LM 8
Itapetininga 162 G 2
Itapeva 162 G 2
Itapicuru, Rio - [BR, Bahia]
158-159 M 7
Itapicuru, Rio - [BR, Maranhão]
158-159 L 5
Itapicuru, Serra - 158-159 KL 6
Itapicurumirim 158-159 L 5
Itapipoca 158-159 M 5
Itapira 158-159 K 9
Itapiranga 160-16 F 7
Itapirapuã, Pico - 160-161 H 6
Itápolis 160-161 H 4
Itapora 160-161 E 4-5
Itaporanga [BR, São Paulo]
160-161 H 5
Itapúa [PY] 160-161 DE 7
Itapuí 160-161 H 1
Itapuranga 160-161 H 1
Itaqui 162 E 3
Itararé 160-161 H 6
Itararé, Rio - 160-161 H 5
Itairi 160-161 J 6
Itarsi 180-181 M 6
Itarumã 160-161 G 3
Itasca, TX 154-155 G 4
Itasca, Lake - 146-147 G 2
Itaiba 160-161 J 5
Itatina, Serra dos - 160-161 J 6
Itatinga 160-161 H 5
Itatuba 158-159 G 6
Itaúçuk 160-161 H 2
Itaúna 160-161 K 4
Itawa = Etawah 180-181 M 5
Itbayat Island 190-191 H 11
Itebero 171 AB 3
Itende 171 C 4
Ithaca, MI 152-153 O 4
Ithaca, NY 146-147 L 3
Ithákē 136-137 J 6
Ithrā = Itrah 182-183 G 7
Itigi 168-169 H 4
Itimbiri 168-169 F 2
Itinga [BR, Minas Gerias]
160-161 M 2
Itinoseki = Ichinoseki 184-185 QR 4
Itiquira 158-159 J 8
Itiquira, Rio - 158-159 H 8
Itirapina 160-161 J 5
Itiruçu 158-159 L 7
Itiúba 158-159 M 7
'Itmāniya, El- = Al-'Uthmāniyah
170 DE 4
Itō 188-189 M 5
Itoigawa 188-189 L 4
Itoikawa = Itoigawa 188-189 L 4
Itrah 182-183 G 7
Itri, Jabal - 170 F 7
Itsā 170 D 3
Itsjang = Yichang 184-185 L 5
I-tu [WAN] 172-173 G 4
I-tu = Yidu [TJ, Hubei] 190-191 C 6
I-tu = Yidu [TJ, Shandong]
184-185 M 4
Iucatão = Yucatán 146-147 J 7
Iucatão, Bacia do - 146-147 JK 8
Iucatão, Canal do - = Canal de
Yucatán 146-147 J 7
Ituaçu 158-159 L 7
Itueta 160-161 M 3
Ituí, Rio - 158-159 E 6
Ituiutaba 160-161 H 3
Itula 168-169 G 3
Itumbiara 158-159 K 8
Itumbiara, Represa de -
160-161 H 3
Itumirim 160-161 K 4
Ituni Township 158-159 H 3
Itupiranga 158-159 JK 6
Ituporanga 160-161 H 7
Iturama 160-161 GH 3
Ituri 168-169 G 2
Iturup, ostrov - 178-179 c 8
Ituverava 160-161 J 4
Ituxi, Rio - 158-159 F 6
Itzawisis 174-175 C 4
Itzehoe 133 D 1-2
Iugoslavia 136-137 F 3-J 5
Iuka, MS 154-155 L 3
Iva, SC 148-149 B 7
Icaceviči 138-138 E 7
Ivai, Rio - 162 F 2
Ivaiporã 160-161 G 6
Ivajlovgrad 136-137 M 5
Ivalo 130-131 M 3
Ivalojoki 130-131 M 3
Ivan, AR 154-155 J 4
Ivancevo 138-139 S 4
Ivančino 138-139 TU 3
Ivangorod 130-131 N 8
Ivangorod 138-139 G 4
Ivanhoe 194-195 H 6
Ivanhoe, MN 152-153 HJ 3
Ivaniči 140-141 B 1
Ivankov 140-141 DE 1
Ivan'kovo [SU, Tver'] 138-139 L 5
Ivanovka 136-137 O 2
Ivano-Frankivs'k 140-141 B 2
Ivano-Frankivs'k Cernivci
126-127 NO 6
Ivano-Frankovo 140-141 B 2
Ivanovo 140-141 D 2
Ivanovka [SU, Rossijskaja SFSR]
138-139 T 7
Ivanovka [SU, Ukrainskaja SSR]
140-141 E 3
Ivanovo [SU, Belorusskaja SSR]
138-139 E 7
Ivanovo [SU, Rossijskaja SFSR
Ivanovo] 178-179 FG 6
Ivanovskaja 138-139 UV 3
Ivantejevka [SU, Saratov]
138-139 R 7
Ivanuškova = Koršunovo
178-179 UV 6
Ivaščenkovo = Čapajevsk
178-179 HJ 7
Ivatuba 160-161 FG 5
Ivdel' 178-179 L 5
Ivenec 130-131 M 11
Ivenec 138-139 F 7
Iversen, Banc d' 178-179 EF 3
Iversen, Banco 178-179 EF 3
Iversen, Banco de - 178-179 EF 3
Iversen, Banco de - 178-179 EF 3
Iversenbank 178-179 EF 3
Iversen-pad 178-179 EF 3
Ivigtût 144-145 b 5
Ivindo 168-169 D 2
Ivinheima 160-161 F 5
Ivinheima, Rio - 158-159 J 9
Ivje 138-139 E 7
Ivnica 140-141 D 1
Ivohibe 168-169 L 7
Ivoire, Côte d' [≅] 166-167 CD 8
Ivoorkust [≅] 166-167 CD 8
Ivoorkust [★] 166-167 CD 7
Ivory-Coast [★] 172-173 D 3
Ivory-Coast [∪] 172-173 DE 4
Ivot 138-139 K 7
Ivrea 136-137 B 3
Ivrindi 182-183 B 3
Ivuna 171 C 5
Iwadate 188-189 MN 2
Iwaizumi 188-189 NO 3
Iwaki 188-189 N 4
Iwaki yama 188-189 N 3
Iwakuni 188-189 J 5
Iwamizawa 184-185 R 3
Iwanai 188-189 b 2
Iwanowo = Ivanovo 178-179 FG 6
Iwanuma 188-189 N 3
Iwata 188-189 LM 5
Iwate [J, ●] 188-189 N 3
Iwate [J, ☆] 188-189 N 2-3
Iwate-yama 188-189 N 3
Iwo 166-167 E 7
Iwō-jima = Iō-jima 188-189 H 7
Iwōn 188-189 G 2
Iwopin 172-173 G 4
Iwu = Yiwu 190-191 GH 4
Ixiamas 158-159 F 7
Ixopo 168-169 GH 9
Ixtepec 146-147 G 8
I-yang = Yiyang [TJ, Hunan]
184-185 L 6
Iyang = Yiyang [TJ, Jiangxi]
190-191 F 7
Iyo 188-189 J 6
Iyomishima 188-189 J 6
Iyonada 188-189 HJ 6
I-yüan = Yiyuan 190-191 G 3
Iž 138-139 T 5
Izabal, Lago de - 146-147 HJ 8
Izalco 146-147 H 9
Izashiki = Sata 188-189 H 7
Iz'aslav 140-141 C 1
Izbat ash-Shaykh 170 C 5
Izberbaš 140-141 NO 5
Izborsk 138-139 FG5
Izdeškovo 138-139 JK 6
Iževsk 178-179 J 6
Izjum 140-141 H 2
Izki 180-181 H 6
Izland 130-131 c-f 2
Izland 130-131 cd 2
Ižma [SU, ≅] 178-179 J 5
Ižma [SU, ●] 178-179 J 4
Izmajil 140-141 D 4
Izmajlovo 138-139 Q 7
Izmalkovo 138-139 LM 7
İzmir 180-181 B 3
İmir Körfezi 182-183 B 3
İzmit = Kocaeli 180-181 BC 2
İzmit Körfezi 182-183 C 2
İznik 182-183 C 2
İznik Gölü 182-183 C 2
Izobil'nyj 140-141 KL 4
Izoplit 138-139 KL 5
Izozog, Bañados de - 158-159 G 8
Izra' 182-183 G 6
Izrael 180-181 CD 4
Izu hantō 188-189 M 5
Izuhara 188-189 G 5
Izumi 188-189 H 6
Izumo 188-189 J 5
Izu-shotō 184-185 QR 5
Izu syotō = Izu-shotō 184-185 QR 5
Izvestij CIK, ostrova - 178-179 OP 2

J

Ja = Dja 166-167 G 8
Jaagupi 138-139 E 4
Jāb, Tall - 182-183 G 6
Jabal, Bahr al- 166-167 L 7
Jabalayn, Al- 166-167 L 6
Jabal Lubnān = 2 [RL, ☆ ◁]
182-183 F 6
Jabalón 134-135 F 9
Jabalpur 180-181 MN 6
Jabal Lubnān = 2◁ 182-183 F 6
Jabiru 194-195 F 2
Jabjabah, Wādī - 170 E 7
Jablah 182-183 F 5
Jablanica [AL] 136-137 J 5
Jablanica [BG] 136-137 L 4
Jablanica [YU] 136-137 G 4
Jablunkovský průsmyk 133 J 4
Jabung, Tanjung - 186-187 DE 7
Jaboticabal 158-159 K 9
Jaboticatubas 160-161 L 3
Jaca 134-135 G 7
Jacaré, Rio - [BR, Bahia]
158-159 L 6-7
Jacaré, Rio - [BR, Minas Gerais]
160-161 K 4
Jacarei 158-159 K 9
Jacarèzinho 160-161 H 5
Jáchal = San José de Jáchal
162 C 4
Jachhen 184-185 E 5
Jachroma 138-139 L 5
Jáchymov 133 F 3
Jaciara 160-161 E 1
Jaciparaná 158-159 G 6
Jackman Station, ME 148-149 H 2
Jacksboro, TX 154-155 FG 4
Jackson, AL 154-155 M 5
Jackson, CA 150-151 C 6
Jackson, GA 154-155 NO 4
Jackson, KY 152-153 P 7
Jackson, LA 154-155 K 5
Jackson, MI 146-147 JK 3
Jackson, MN 152-153 J 4
Jackson, MO 152-153 M 7
Jackson, MS 146-147 HJ 5
Jackson, MT 150-151 G 3
Jackson, OH 148-149 B 5
Jackson, TN 146-147 J 4
Jackson, WY 150-151 H 4
Jackson, ostrov - = ostrov
Džeksona 178-179 H-K 1
Jackson Head 194-195 N 8
Jackson Lake 150-151 H 4
Jackson Mountains 150-151 D 5
Jackson Prairie 154-155 L 4
Jacksonville, AL 154-155 MN 4
Jacksonville, FL 146-147 KL 5
Jacksonville, IL 152-153 LM 6
Jacksonville, NC 148-149 E 7
Jacksonville, OR 150-151 B 4
Jacksonville, TX 154-155 H 4-5
Jacksonville Beach,
FL 148-149 C 9
Jäckvik 130-131 G 4
Jacmel 146-147 M 8
Jacobina 158-159 L 7
Jacob Lake, AZ 150-151 GH 7
Jacobsdal 174-175 F 5
Jacobstadt = Jēkabpils 138-139 E 5
Jacques Cortier, Détroit de -
144-145 Y 7-8
Jacuí [BR, Minas Gerais]
160-161 J 4
Jacuípe, Rio - 158-159 LM 7
Jacumba, CA 150-151 EF 9
Jacundá 158-159 K 5
Jacupiranga 160-161 HJ 6
Jacutinga 160-161 J 5
Jacuzia, Repubblica Autónoma della
178-179 U-b 4
Jadā, Sha'ib - = Sha'ib al-Judā'
182-183 LM 7-8
Jadaf, Wādī al- 180-181 E 4
Jadaf al-Jadaf 182-183 J 6
Jaddī, Wādī - 166-167 E 2
Jade 133 D 2
Jaderské moře 136-137 E 3-H 5
Jadida, el - = Al-Jadidah
166-167 C2
Jadidah, Al- [ET] 170 C 5
Jadīdah, Al- [MA] 166-167 G 2
Jadīd Rā's al-Fīl 166-167 K 6
Jadotville = Likasi 168-169 G 5
Jadrin 138-139 Q 6
Jādū 166-167 G 2
Jaén 134-135 F 10
Jæren 130-131 A 8
Jaesalmēr= Jaisalmer
180-181 KL 5
Jafa, Tel Avive - = Tel-Aviv-Yafō
180-181 C 4
Ja'farābād [IR] 180-181 F 3
Jaffa, Cape - 196 D 6
Jaffatin = Jazā'ir Jiftūn 170 EF 4
Jaffna = Yāpanaya 180-181 MN 9
Jafr, Al- [JOR, ≅] 182-183 G 7
Jafr, Al- [JOR, ●] 180-181 D 4
Jafr, El- = Al-Jafr 180-181 D 4
Jafū, Hāssī - 166-167 E 2
Jagdalpur 180-181 N 7
Jägerndorf = Krnov 133 HJ 3
Jagersfontein 174-175 F 5
Jaghbūb, Al- 166-167 J 3
Jaghiagh, Wādī - 182-183 J 4
Jaghjagh, Ouâdî - = Wādī
Jaghiagh 182-183 J 4
Jagl'ajarvi 138-139 H 2
Jagodnoje 178-179 cd 5
Jagog Tsho 184-185 F 5
Jagotin 140-141 E 1
Jagst 133 DE 4
Jagtial 180-181 M 7
Jagua, La - 158-159 E 3
Jaguara, Represa de -
160-161 J 3-4
Jaguarão 162 F 4
Jaguarari 158-159 LM 7
Jaguaribe, Rio - 158-159 M 6
Jagüé, Rio del - 162 C 3
Jaguariaíva 160-161 H 6
Jaguaruna 160-161 H 8
Jahotyn = Jagotin 140-141 E 1
Jahrah, Al- 180-181 F 5
Jahrom 180-181 G 5
Jaicós 158-159 L 6
Jailagebirge = Krymskije gory
140-141 FG 4
Jailolo 186-187 J 6
Jaipur 180-181 M 5
Jaisalmer 180-181 KL 5
Jaja 178-179 Q 6
Jajah, Al- 170 D 5
Jājarm 180-181 H 3
Jajce 136-137 G 3
Jajva [SU, ~] 138-139 V 4
Jajva [SU, ●] 138-139 V 4
Jakan, mys - 178-179 j 4
Jakarta 186-187 E 8
Jakasia, República Autónoma de -
=10 ◁ 178-179 R 7
Jakima = Lachdenpochja
138-139 GH 3
Jakkalawater 174-175 A 2
Jakobsdal = Jacobsdal 174-175 F 5
Jakobshavn = Jlullssat
144-145 ab 4
Jakobstad 130-131 JK 6
Jakobstadt = Jēkabpils 138-139 E 5
Jakoeten Autonome Republiek
178-179 U-b 4
Jakovlevo 140-141 H 1
Jakovo 138-139 T 3
Jakša 178-179 K 5
Jakšanga 138-139 PQ 4
Jakšur-Bodja 138-139 T 5
Jakuck = Jakutsk 178-179 Y 5
Jakucka Autonomiczna Republika
178-179 U-b 4
Jakut Autonóm Köztársaság
178-179 U-b 4
Jakutische Autonome Republik
178-179 U-b 4
Jakutsk 178-179 Y 5
Jakutská autonomní republika
178-179 U-b 4
Jakutskaja Avtonomnaja Sovetskaja
Socialističeskaja Respublika =
Jakutische Autonome Republik
178-179 U-b 4
Jal, NM 154-155 D 4
Jalādah, Al- 180-181 F 7
Jalālābād 180-181 KL 4
Jalālat al-Bahriyah,
Jabal al- 170 DE 3
Jalālat al-Qibliyah,
Jabal al- 170 E 3
Jalāl Kōt = Jalālābād 180-181 KL 4
Jalama 140-141 O 6
Jalāmīd, Al- 182-183 HJ 7
Ja'lan 180-181 H6
Jalandar = Jullundur 180-181 LM 4
Jalandhar 180-181 LM 4
Jalapa 146-147 G 8
Jalawlā' 182-183 L 5
Jales 160-161 G 4
Jalgāriv = Jālgaon [IND ← Bhusawal]
180-181 M 6
Jālgaon [IND ← Bhusawal]
180-181 M 6
Jalhāk, Al- 166-167 L 6
Jalib, Maqarr al- 182-183 J 6
Jalibah 182-183 M 7
Jalib Shahab 182-183 M 7
Jalingo 166-167 G 7
Jalisco 146-147 EF 7
Jallekān 182-183 N 6
Jālna 180-181 M 7
Jalon, Rio - 134-135 G 8
Jalo Oasis = Wāhāt
Jālū 166-167 J 3
Jalpug 140-141 D 3-4
Jalpug, ozero - 140-141 D 4
Jalta 140-141 G 4
Jaltuškov 140-141 C 2
Jalu = Yalu Jiang 188-189 EF 2
Jālū, Wāhāt - 166-167 J 3
Jamaame 166-167 N 8
Jamaare 172-173 H 3
Jamaat 184-185 E 2
Jam'āt al-Ma'yuf 182-183 M 7
Jamaica 146-147 L 8
Jamaica 146-147 L 8
Jamaica Channel 146-147 L 8
Jamaika 146-147 L 8
Jamaïque 146-147 L 8
Jamajka 146-147 L 8
Jamakhaṇḍi = Jamkhandi
180-181 LM 7
Jamal, poluostrov - 178-179 MN 3
Jamal-Nenets, Circunscrição
Nacional de - 178-179 M-P 4
Jamal-Nenets, Circunscripción
Nacional de los
178-179 M-O 4-5
Jamal-Nenets, Nacional de
126-127 WW 2
Jamal-Nentsen, Nationaal Gebied der
- 178-179 M-O 4-5
Jamal-Nenzen, Nationalkreis der
- 178-179 M-O 4
Jamal-Nyenyec Autonóm Körzet
178-179 M-P 4
Jamalo-Nemec, Circolo Nazionale -
178-179 M-P 4
Jamalsko-něnecký autonomní okruh
178-179 M-P 4-5
Jamalsko-Nieniecki Okręg
Autonomiczny 178-179 M-P 4-5
Jamantau, gora - 178-179 K 7
Jamanxim, Rio - 158-159 H 6
Jamari, Rio - 158-159 G 6
Jamāši = Zainsk 138-139 S 6
Jambi [RI, ●] 186-187 D 7
Jambi [RI, ☆ = 5 ◁] 186-187 D 7
Jambol 136-137 M 4
Jambongan, Pulau - 186-187 G 5
Jambūr 182-183 L 5
Jamburg = Kingisepp 138-139 D 4
Jamdena, Pulau - = Pulau Yamdena
186-187 K 8
James, Baie - 144-145 UV 7
James Bay 144-145 UV 7
James Ranges 194-195 F 4
James River [USA ◁ Chesapeake
Bay] 146-147 L 4
James River [USA ◁ Missouri
River] 146-147 G 2
Jamestown [AUS] 196 D 4
Jamestown [ZA] 174-175 G 6
Jamestown, KS 152-153 H 6
Jamestown, KY 152-153 O 7
Jamestown, ND 146-147 G 2
Jamestown, NY 146-147 L 3
Jamestown, OH 152-153 P 6
Jamestown, TN 154-155 N 2
Jamestown Reservoir 152-153 G 2
Jamkhandi 180-181 LM 7
Jamm 138-139 G 4
Jammerbugt 130-131 C 9
Jammerdrif 174-175 G 5
Jammu 180-181 LM 4
Jammu and Kashmir 180-181
LM 3-4
Jamnā = Yamuna 180-181 MN 5
Jāmnagar 180-181 L 6
Jampol' [SU, Chmel'nickij]
140-141 C 2
Jampol' [SU, Vinnica] 140-141 D 2
Jāmpūr 180-181 KL 5
Jamsah 170 E 4
Jämsänkoski 130-131 L 7
Jamshedpur 180-181 NO 6
Jamsk 178-179 de 6
Jämtland 130-131 E-G 6
Jämtlands Sikås 130-131 F 6
Jamursba, Tanjung = Tanjung
Yamursba 186-187 K 7
Jana 178-179 Z 4
Janaperi, Rio - 158-159 G 4
Janaúba 158-159 L 8
Janaucu, Ilha - 158-159 JK 4
Janaul 178-179 JK 6
Jandaia 160-161 GH 2
Jandaia do Sul 160-161 G 5
Jandaq 180-181 GH 4
Jandiatuba, Rio - 158-159 F 5-6
Jandowae 194-195 K 5
Janesville, CA 150-151 C 5
Janesville, WI 152-153 M 4
Jangada 160-161 G 7
Jangamo 174-175 L 3
Jangarej 178-179 L 4
Jangce = Chang Jiang
184-185 K 5-6
Jangcy = Chang Jiang
184-185 K 5-6
Jangijul' 178-179 M 9
Jango 160-161 E 4
Jangory 138-139 LM 2
Jang Thang 184-185 E-G 5
Jangtsekiang = Chang Jiang
184-185 K 5-6
Jang-tse-tjiang = Chang Jiang
184-185 K 5-6
Jāni Beyglū 182-183 M 3
Janin 182-183 F 6
Janina = Iōannina 136-137 J 6
Jánina = Iōánnina 136-137 J 6
Janischki = Joniškis 138-139 DE 5
Janisjarvi, ozero - 138-139 H 3
Jan Kemp 174-175 F 4
Jan Mayen 120 B 19-20
Jan Mayen, Dorsal de -
128-129 F 2
Jan Mayen, Dorsale de -
128-129 F 2
Jan Mayen, Dorsale Meridionale -
128-129 F 2
Jan Mayen, Patamar de -
128-129 F 2
Jan Mayen, Plataforma de -
128-129 H 1-2
Jan Mayen, Platea - 128-129 H 1-2
Jan Mayen, Seuil de -
128-129 H 1-2
Jan-Mayendrempel 128-129 H 1-2
Jan Mayen Ridge 128-129 H 1-2
Jan-Mayen-Schwelle 128-129 H 1-2
Jannah 166-167 FG 4
Jano-Indigirskaja nizmennost'
178-179 Z-c 3
Janos 150-151 J 10
Jánoshalma 133 J 5
Janov = Gënova 136-137 C 3
Janoviči 138-139 H 6
Janovka = Ivanovka 140-141 E 3
Janow = Jonava 138-139 E 6
Janowo = Jonava 138-139 E 6
Janquara, Serra - 160-161 D 1
Jansenville 174-175 F 7
Janskij 178-179 Za 4
Janskij zaliv 178-179 Za 3
Jantarnyj 133 J 1
Jantra 136-137 M 4
Januária 158-159 KL 8
Jao-ho = Raohe 184-185 P 2
Jaonpur = Jaunpur 180-181 N 5
Jaoping = Raoping 190-191 F 10
Jaoyang = Raoyang 190-191 EF 2
Jao-yang Ho = Raoyang He
188-189 D 2
Japán 184-185 Q 5-R 3
Japan 184-185 Q 5-R 3
Japan Basin 188-189 J-L 2
Japangraben 198-199 G 3
Japanisches Becken 188-189 J-L 2
Japanisches Meer 184-185 P 4-Q 3
Japán-medence 188-189 J-L 2
Japans Bekken 188-189 J-L 2
Japan Sea 184-185 P 4-Q 3
Japanse Zee 184-185 P 4-Q 3
Japán-tenger 184-185 P 4-Q 3
Japan Trench 124-125 R 4
Japantrog 124-125 R 4
Japão 184-185 Q 5-R 3
Japão, Bacia do - 188-189 J-L 2
Japão, Fossa do - 124-125 R 4
Japão, Mar do - 184-185 P 4-Q 3
Japón 184-185 P 5-Q 3
Japon 184-185 P 5-Q 3
Japón, Cuenca del - 188-189 J-L 2
Japón, Fosa del - 124-125 R 4
Japon, Fosse du - 124-125 R 4
Japón, Mar de - 184-185 P 4-Q 3
Japon, Mer du - 184-185 P 4-Q 3
Japonia 184-185 Q 5-R 3
Japonské moře 184-185 P 4-Q 3
Japonskie, Morze -
184-185 P 4-Q 3
Japonsko 184-185 Q 5-R 3
Japurá, Rio - 158-159 F 5
Jar 138-139 T 4
Jara, La - 134-135 E 9
Jara, La -, CO 152-153 CD 7
Jarābulus 182-183 GH 4
Jarādah 166-167 D 2
Jaraguá 160-161 H 1
Jaraguá, Serra do - 160-161 H 7
Jaraguá do Sul 160-161 H 7
Jaraguari 158-159 HJ 8-9
Jaralito, El - 154-155 C 7
Jaransk 178-179 H 6
Jararaca, Cachoeira - 160-161 G 6
Jarārah, Wādī - 170 F 6
Jarāwī, Al- 182-183 H 7
Jarbah, Jazīrat - 166-167 G 2
Jarbidge, NV 150-151 F 5
Jarcevo [SU, Jenisej] 178-179 R 5
Jarcevo [SU, Smolensk]
138-139 J 6
Jardim [BR, Mato Grosso do Sul]
160-161 D 4
Jardinésia 160-161 H 3
Jardinópolis 160-161 J 4
Jarega 138-139 TU 2
Jarenga [SU, ~] 138-139 R 2
Jarenga [SU, ●] 138-139 R 4
Jarensk 178-179 H 5
Jares'ki 140-141 FG 2
Jari, Rio - 158-159 J 5
Jarid, Shaṭṭ al- 166-167 F 2
Jarir, Wādī - 180-181 E 5-6
Jarkand = Yarkand 184-185 D 4
Jarkov = Char'kov 140-141 H 1-2
Jarkovo 178-179 M 6
Jarmashin, 'Ayn - 170 CD 5
Jarnema 138-139 MN 2
Jarny 134-135 K 4
Jarocin 133 H 2-3
Jarok, ostrov - 178-179 a 3
Jaroslavl' 178-179 FG 6
Jarosław 133 L 3-4
Jaroso, CO 152-153 D 7
Jarotschin = Jarocin 133 H 2-3
Järpen 130-131 E 6
Jarrāhī, Rūd-e - 182-183 N 7
Jar-Sale 178-179 MN 4
Jartum–Al-Kharṭūm 166-167 L 5
Jaru 158-159 G 7
Järva-Jaani 138-139 EF 4
Järvenpää 130-131 L 7
Jarvis 198-199 K 5
Jarygino 138-139 K 6
Jasel'da 138-139 E 7
Jasenskaja kosa 140-141 HJ 3
Jasikan 172-173 F 4
Jasinovataja 140-141 H 2
Jāsk 180-181 H 5
Jaškino 138-139 T 7
Jaškul' 140-141 M 3
Jasnogorsk 138-139 LM 6
Jasnyj 178-179 Y 7
Jasonhalvøy 121 C 130-131
Jason Islands 162 D 8
Jasonville, IN 152-153 N 6
Jasper [CDN, Alberta] 144-145 N 7
Jasper [CDN, Ontario] 148-149 F 2
Jasper, AL 154-155 M 4
Jasper, AR 154-155 J 2-3
Jasper, FL 148-149 b 1
Jasper, GA 154-155 N 3
Jasper, IN 152-153 N 6
Jasper, MN 152-153 H 4
Jasper, MO 154-155 H2
Jasper, TX 154-155 HJ 5
Jasper National Park 144-145 N 7
Jaşşān 182-183 L 6
Jastrebac 136-137 J 4
Jastrebovka 140-141 H 1
Jászberény 133 JK 5
Jász-Nagykun-Szolnok 178-179 H 9
Jatai [BR ✓ Rio Verde] 158-159 J 8
Jatapu, Rio - 158-159 H 5
Jatei 160-161 E 5
Játiva 134-135 G 9
Jatobá 158-159 JK 5
Jat Poti = Kārēz 180-181 K 4
Jaú 158-159 K 9
Jaú, Rio - 158-159 G 5
Jau'aliyat, Jebel el- = Jabal al-
Aḍ iriyāt 182-183 G 7
Jauer = Jawor 133 H 3
Jauf, Al- = Al-Jawf 180-181 DE 5
Jauf, El - = Al-Jawf 166-167 J 4
Jauja 158-159 DE 7
Jaunde = Yaoundé 166-167 G 8
Jaunjelgava 138-139 E 5
Jaunpiebalga 138-139 F 5
Jaunpur 180-181 N 5
Jauru 160-161 E 3
Jauru, Rio - [BR ◁ Rio Coxim]
160-161 EF 3
Jauru, Rio - [BR ◁ Rio Paraguai]
160-161 CD 2
Jāva 186-187 EF 8
Java [R I] 186-187 EF 8
Java, Fosse de - 124-125 P 6
Java, Mar de - 186-187 EF 8
Java, Mer de - 186-187 EF 8
Java Head = Tanjung Layar
186-187 DE 8
Javaj, poluostrov - 178-179 NO 3
Javalambre 134-135 G 8
Javari, Rio - 158-159 E 6
Java Sea 186-187 EF 8
Javasee 186-187 EF 8
Java-tenger 186-187 EF 8
Javatrog 124-125 P 6
Javazee 186-187 EF 8
Javhār = Jawhār 180-181 L 7
Javlenka 178-179 M 7
Javor 136-137 HJ 4
Javorov 140-141 A 2
Javské moře 186-187 EF 8
Jawa 186-187 EF 8
Jawa = Java 186-187 EF 8
Jawa Barat = 11 ◁ 186-187 E 8
Jawajskie, Morze - 186-187 EF 8
Jaw'aliyat, Jabal al- 182-183 G 7
Jawa Tengah = 12 ◁ 186-187 E 8
Jawa Timur = 14 ◁ 186-187 F 8
Jawf, Al- [LAR] 166-167 J 4
Jawf, Al- [Saudi-Arabien]
180-181 DE 5
Jawf, Al- [Y] 180-181 EF 7
Jawhār 180-181 L 7
Jawhar [ETH] 166-167 ab 3
Jawhariyal, Al - 170 D 5
Jawor 133 H 3
Jaxartes = Syrdarja 180-181 K 2
Jay, OK 154-155 H 2
Jaya, Gunung - 186-187 L 7
Jayapura 186-187 M 7
Jayawijaya, Pegunungan
186-187 LM 7
Jay Em, WY 152-153 D 4
Jāyid 182-183 J 6
Jaypur = Jaipur 180-181 M 5
Jaypura = Jeypore 180-181 N 7
Jayton, TX 154-155 E 4
Jaza'ir, Al- [DZ] 166-167 E 1
Jaza'ir, Al- [IRQ] 182-183 M 7
Jazir 182-183 F 5
Jazira, Al- = Arḍ al-Jazirah 180-181
E 3-F 4
Jazirah, Al- [IRQ] 182-183 J 5
Jazirah, Arḍ al- 180-181 E 3-F 4
Jāz Mūreyān, Hāmūn-e
180-181 H 5
Jaz'va 138-139 V 3
Jazykovo [SU, Baškirskaja ASSR]
138-139 U 6
Jazykovo [SU, Uljanov] 138-139 Q 6
Jazzin 182-183 F 6
Jean , NV 150-151 F 8
Jeanerette, LA 154-155 K 6
Jeanette, ostrov - = ostrov
Žanetty 178-179 ef 2
Jebail = Jubayl 182-183 F 5
Jebba 166-167 E 7
Jebel, Bahr el - = Bahr al-Jabal
166-167 L7
Jebelein, El- = Al-Jabalayn
166-167 L6
Jeblé = Jablah 182-183 F 5
Jechegnadzor 140-141 M 7
Jécori 150-151 J 1
Jeddah = Jiddah 180-181 D 6
Jeďma 138-139 O 3
Jędrzejów 133 K 3
Jeffers, MN 152-153 J 3
Jefferson, CO 152-153 D 6
Jefferson, GA 154-155 O 3
Jefferson, IA 152-153 J 4-5
Jefferson, MT 150-151 G H 2
Jefferson, OH 148-149 C 4
Jefferson, OR 150-151 B 3
Jefferson, TX 154-155 H 4
Jefferson , WI 152-153 M 4
Jefferson, Mount - [USA,
Nevada] 150-151 E 6
Jefferson, Mount - [USA,
Oregon] 150-151 C 3
Jefferson City, MO 146-147 H 4
Jefferson City, TN 154-155 O 2
Jeffersonville , GA 148-149 B 8
Jeffersonville , IN 152-153 O 6
Jeffrey, Abysse de - 194-195 F 7
Jeffrey, Fosa - 194-195 F 7
Jeffrey, Fossa - 194-195 F 7
Jeffrey Fossa di - 194-195 F 7
Jeffrey Depth 194-195 F 7
Jeffreydiep 194-195 F 7
Jeffrey-mélység 194-195 F 7
Jeffreytiefe 194-195 F 7
Jefremov 138-139 LM 7
Jega 172-173 G 2
Jeges-tenger 120 AB 132-5
Jegorjevsk 178-179 FG 6
Jegorlyk 140-141 K 4
Jegorlykskaja 140-141 K 3
Jegyrjach 178-179 M 5
Jehlam = Jihlam 180-181 L 4
Jehlum = Jihlam 180-181 L 4
Jehol = Chengde 184-185 M 3
Jeja 140-141 J 3
Jejsk 140-141 J 3
Jejuí Guazú, Rio - 160-161 DE 6
Jēkabpils 138-139 E 5
Jekatarinburg 178-179 L 6
Jekaterinburg 178-179 L 7
Jekaterinfel'd = Bolnisi 140-141 M 6
Jekaterinodar = Krasnodar
140-141 J 4
Jekaterinoslav = Dnepropetrovsk
140-141 GH 2
Jekaterinovka [SU, Primorskij Kraj]
188-189 J 1
Jekaterinovka [SU, Saratov]
138-139 OP 7
Jekaterinštadt = Marks
138-139 Q 8
Jekimoviči 138-139 J 6
Jekubābād 180-181 K 5
Jelan' [SU, ~] 140-141 L 1
Jelan' [SU, ●] 140-141 L 1
Jelanec 140-141 E 3
Jelan '-Kolenovskij 140-141 K 1
Jelchovka 138-139 S 7
Jelec 138-139 M 7
Jelenia Góra 133 GH 3
Jelenovka = Sevan 140-141 M 6
Jelenskij 138-139 K 7
Jelets = Jelec 138-139 M 7
Jelfa = Jilfah 166-167 E 2
Jelgava 138-139 DE 5
Jelgavkrasti 138-139 DE 5
Jelgava 130-131 KL 9
Jelgawa = Jelgava 138-139 DE 5
Jelizavetgrad = Kirovograd
140-141 EF 2
Jelizavetpol' = Kirovabad
140-141 N 6
Jelizavety, mys - 178-179 b 7
Jelizovo [SU, Belorusskaja SSR]
138-139 G 7
Jelizovo [SU, Rossijskaja SFSR]
178-179 e 7
Jellico, TN 154-155 N 2
Jel'na 138-139 J 6
Jeloga 138-139 T 4
Jelovo 138-139 U 5
Jelpačicha 138-139 UV 5
Jelšanka 138-139 Q 8
Jel'sk 138-139 G 8
Jelva 138-139 S 2
Jema = Djema 166-167 K 7
Jemaja, Pulau - 186-187 DE 6
Jembiani 171 DE 4
Jemca [SU, ~] 138-139 N 2
Jemca [SU, ●] 138-139 N 2
Jemeck 178-179 G 5
Jemeljanovka 138-139 H 2
Jemeljanovo 138-139 K 5
Jemen 180-181 E 7-8
Jemez Pueblo, NM 154-155 B 3
Jemn 167 N 5-6
Jena 133 E 3
Jena, LA 154-155 JK 5
Jenakijeve 140-141 J 2
Jenakijevo 140-141 J 2
Jenašimskij Polkan, gora -
178-179 RS 6
Jeneponto 186-187 G 8
Jên Ho = Ren He 190-191 B 5
Jenhsien = Ren Xian 190-191 E 3
Jên- hua = Renhua 190-191 D 9
Jenisej 178-179 Q 4
Jenisejsk 178-179 R 6
Jenisejskij kr'až 178-179 R 5-6
Jenisejskij zaliv 178-179 OP 3
Jenkins, KY 148-149 B 6
Jenkiu = Renqiu 184-185 M 4
Jenner, CA 150-151 B 6
Jennings, KS 152-153 F 6
Jennings, LA 154-155 J 5
Jennings, MT 150-151 F 1
Jenny Lind Island 144-145 Q 4
Jenotajevka 140-141 N 3
Jensen, UT 150-151 J 5
Jensen Beach, FL 148-149 cd 3
Jens Munk Island 144-145 UV 4
Jens Munks Ø 144-145 cd 5
Jenud = Gorē 166-167 M 7
Jen'uka 178-179 X 6
Jeol = Chengde 184-185 M 3
Jepara 186-187 F 8
Jequeri 160-161 L 4
Jequié 158-159 L 7
Jequitaí 158-159 L 8
Jequitai, Rio - 160-161 K 2
Jequitinhonha, Rio - 158-159 L 8
Jerābulus = Jarābulus
182-183 GH 4
Jerachtur 138-139 N 6
Jerāda = Jarādah 166-167 D 2
Jerantut 186-187 D 6
Jerba = Jazirat Jarbah 166-167 G 2
Jerbogač'on 178-179 U 5
Jerčevo 138-139 MN 3
Jeremejevo [SU, Komi ASSR]
138-139 V 2
Jérémie 146-147 M 8
Jeremoabo 158-159 M 6-7
Jerevan 140-141 M 6
Jerevan = Jerevan 140-141 M 6
Jerez de Garcia Salinas
146-147 F 7
Jerez de la Frontera 134-135 DE 10
Jerez de los Caballeros
134-135 D 9
Jergeni 140-141 M 2-3
Jericho [AUS] 194-195 J 4
Jericho [ZA] 174-175 GH 3
Jericho = Ariha 182-183 F 7
Jerilderie 196 G 5
Jerik = Ilovatka 140-141 MN 1

Jermak 178-179 O 7
Jermakovskoje 178-179 R 7
Jermentau 178-179 N 7
Jermi 182-183 L 4
Jerofej Pavlovič 178-179 X 7
Jerome, AZ 150-151 G 8
Jerome, ID 150-151 F 4
Jeropol 178-179 g 4
Jerozolima = Yěrūshālayim 180-181 CD 4
Jersey 132 E 7
Jersey City, NJ 146-147 M 3-4
Jersey Shore, PA 148-149 E 4
Jerseyville, IL 152-153 L 6
Jeršiči 138-139 J 7
Jerumenha 158-159 L 6
Jerusalem = Yěrūshālayim 180-181 CD 4
Jerusalém = Yěrūshālayim 180-181CD 4
Jérusalem = Yěrūshālayim 180-181 CD 4
Jerusalén = Yěrūshālayim 180-181 CD 4
Jeruzalém = Yěrūshālayim 180-181 CD 4
Jeruzalem = Yěrūshālayim 180-181 CD 4
Jeruzsálem = Yěrūshālayim 180-181 CD 4
Jervis Bay 194-195 K 7
Jervois Range 194-195 G 4
Jerzovka 140-141 M 2
Jesenice 136-137 EF 2
Jesenik 133 H 3
Jesil' 178-179 M 7
Jessalange 171 D 5
Jessaur = Jessore 180-181 O 6
Jessej 178-179 T 4
Jessentuki 140-141 L 4
Jesselton = Kota Kinabalu 186-187 FG 5
Jesso = Hokkaidō 184-185 RS 3
Jessore 180-181 O 6
Jestro, Webi - = Weyb 166-167 N7
Jesup, GA 148-149 BC 9
Jesup, IA 152-153 KL 4
Jesús 160-161 E 7
Jesús Maria [RA] 162 D 4
Jet, OK 154-155 F 2
Jetmore, KS 152-153 FG 6
Jevdino 138-139 S 2
Jevgora 138-139 J 2
Jevlach 140-141 N 6
Jevlaševo 138-139 Q 7
Jevpatorija 140-141 F 4
Jewell, IA 152-153 K 4
Jewell, KS 152-153 GH 6
Jewish Autonomous Region 178-179 Z 8
Jewpatorija = Jevpatorija 140-141 F 4
Jeypore 180-181 N 7
Ježicha 138-139 Q 4
Jez'ovo [SU, Udmurtskaja ASSR] 138-139 T 4
Jezovo [SU, Vologda] 138-139 M 3
Jez'ovo-Čerkessk=Čerkessk 140-141 L 4
Jezzīn = Jazzīn 182-183 F 6
Jhang Maghiana = Jhang-Maghiyānh 180-181 L 4
Jhang-Maghiyānh 180-181 L 4
Jhānsi 180-181 M 5
Jharsuguda 180-181 NO 6
Jharsugura = Jharsuguda 180-181 N0 6
Jhelum = Jihlam 180-181 L 4
Jiading 190-191 H 6
Jiahe 190-191 D 9
Jiali = Lharugö 184-185 G 5
Jiali = Qionghai 184-185 L 8
Jialing Jiang 184-185 K 5
Jialu He 190-191 E 4
Jiamusi 184-185 P 2
Ji'an [TJ, Jiangxi] 184-185 LM 6
Ji'an [TJ, Jilin] 188-189 EF 2
Jianchang [TJ → Benxi] 188-189 E 2
Jianchang [TJ ← Jinzhou] 188-189 B2
Jianchangying 190-191 G 1
Jiande 190-191 G 7
Jiangcun 190-191 D 2
Jiangdu 190-191 G 5
Jiangdu = Yangzhou 184-185 M 5
Jiange 184-185 JK 5
Jianghong 190-191 B 11
Jianghua 190-191 C 9
Jiangkou [TJ, Guangxi Zhuangzu Zizhiqu] 190-191 C 10
Jiangkou [TJ, Guizhou] 190-191 B 8
Jiankou [TJ, Hubei] 190-191 C 6
Jiangkou [TJ, Hunan] 190-191 C 8
Jiangle 190-191 F 8
Jiangling 184-185 L 5
Jiangmen 184-185 L 7
Jiangnan = Shankou 190-191 C 7
Jiangning 190-191 G 6
Jiangpu 190-191 G 5
Jiangshan 190-191 G 7
Jiangsu 184-185 MN 5
Jiangxi 184-185 LM 6
Jiang Xian 190-191 CD 4
Jiangyin 190-191 H 6
Jiangyong 190-191 C 9
Jian He [TJ, ~] 188-189 D 2
Jianhe [TJ, ●] 190-191 B 8
Jianhu 190-191 G 5
Jianli 190-191 D 7
Jianning 190-191 F 8
Jian'ou 184-185 M 6
Jianping 188-189 B 2
Jianqian He 190-191 BC 5
Jianshi 190-191 B 6
Jianshui 184-185 J 7
Jianyang [TJ, Fujian] 184-185 M 6
Jianyang [TJ, Sichuan] 184-185 JK 5
Jiaocheng 190-191 CD 3
Jiaohekou 190-191 B 4
Jiaokou 190-191 C 3
Jiaoling 190-191 EF 9
Jiaonan 190-191 G 4
Jiao Xi 190-191 G 8
Jiao Xian 184-185 M 4
Jiaozhou Wan 190-191 OH 3- 4
Jiaozou 184-185 L 4
Jia Qi = Jiao Xi 190-191 G 8
Jia Qi = Xiao Xi 190-191 GH 7- 8
Jiaqian = Jia Xian 190-191 C 2
Jiashan [TJ, Anhui] 190-191 G 5
Jiashan [TJ, Zhejiang] 190-191 H 6
Jia Xian [TJ, Henan] 190-191 D 5
Jia Xian [TJ, Shanxi] 190-191 C 2
Jiaxing 184-185 N 5
Jiayi = Chiayi 184-185 MN 7
Jiayu 190-191 D 6-7
Jiayuguan 184-185 H 4
Jiazi 190-191 F 10
Jibhalanta = Uliastaj 184-185 H 2
Jibiya 172-173 G 2
Jibou 136-137 K 2
Jicarilla Apache Indian Reservation 154-155 B 2
Jičin 133 G 3
Jidaidat Hāmir = Judayyiat Ḥāmir 182-183 J 7
Jiḍāmī, B'ir al- 170 E 4
Jiddah 180-181 D 6
Jiddī, Jabal al- 170 E 2
Jido 180-181 P 5
Jidole = Gīdolē 166-167 M 7
Jiekkevarre 130-131 H 3
Jie Shan = Wudang Shan 190-191 C 5
Jieshi 190-191 E 10
Jieshi Wan 190-191 E 10
Jieshou [TJ, Anhui] 190-191 E 5
Jieshou [TJ, Guangxi Zhuangzu Zizhiqu] 190-191 C 9
Jieshou [TJ, Jiangsi] 190-191 G 5
Ješjavrre 130-131 L 3
Jiexi 190-191 E 10
Jiexiu 190-191 CD 3
Jieyang 190-191 F 10
Jiftūn, Jazā'ir - 170 EF 4
Jiggithai Tsho 184-185 F 4
Jih-chao = Rizhao 190-191 G 4
Jihlam [PAK, ~] 180-181 L 4
Jihlam [PAK, ●] 180-181 L 4
Jihlava 133 G 4
Jihočínská pánev 186-187 FG 3-4
Jihočínské moře 186-187 E 5-G 2
Jihofidžijská pánev 194-195 OP 4-5
Jihoosetinská autonomni oblast 140-141 LM 5
Jihopacifický práh 121 D 22-C 20
Jihopolární plošina 121 A 31-6
Jihosandwichský příkop 121 D 34
Jihozápadní Afrika = Namibie 168-169 E 7
Jihozapadní pacifická pánev 121 D 21-19
Jijiga 166-167 N 7
Jijili 166-167 F 1
Jil, Al- 182-183 KL 7
Jilava, București- 136-137 M 5
Jilemutu 184-185 N 1
Jilfah, Al- 166-167 E 2
Jilf al-Kabīr, Haḍbat al- 166-167 K 4
Jilib 166-167 N 8
Jilīb Bākūr = Qalīb Bākūr 182-183 L 8
Jilidah, Al- = Al-Jaladah 180-181 F 6-7
Jilin [TJ, ●] 184-185 O 3
Jilin [TJ, ⭑] 184-185 N 2-O 3
Jiljila, Hōr al- = Hawr al-Jiljilah 182-183 L 6
Jiljilah, Hawr al- 182-183 L 6
Jill, Al- = Al-Jil 182-183 KL 7
Jilong = Chilung 184-185 N 6
Jīma 166-167 M 7
Jimaja = Pulau Jemaja 186-187 DE 6
Jimāl, Wādī - 170 F 5
Jimbolia 136-137 J 3
Jiménez [MEX, Chihuahua] 146-147 F 6
Jiménez [MEX, Coahuila] 154-155 E 6
Jimeta 172-173 J 3
Jiminghe 190-191 E 6
Jimma = Jīma 166-167 M 7
Jimo 190-191 H 3
Jinaḥ 170 D 5
Jinan 184-185 M 4
Jincheng 184-185 L 4
Jindabyne 196 J 6
Jing'an 190-191 E 7
Jing'anji 190-191 F 4
Jingbian 190-191 B 3
Jingbo Hu 184-185 O 3
Jingchuan 184-185 K 4
Jingde 190-191 G 6
Jingdezhen 184-185 M 6
Jingdong 184-185 J 7
Jinggu 184-185 J 7
Jinghai 190-191 F 2
Jing He [TJ,~] 190-191 B 4
Jinghe [TJ, ●] 184-185 E 3
Jinghong 184-185 J 7
Jingji = Jingzhi 190-191 G 3
Jingjiang 190-191 H 5-6
Jingjiang = Tongguan 190-191 D 7
Jingle 190-191 CD 2
Jingmen 190-191 CD 6
Jingning 184-185 K 4
Jing Shan [TJ, ▲▲] 190-191 C 6
Jingshan [TJ, ●] 190-191 D 6
Jingshi = Jinshi 184-185 L 6
Jingtai 184-185 J 4
Jingtian 190-191 E 8
Jing Xian [TJ, Anhui] 190-191 G 6
Jing Xian [TJ, Hebei] 190-191 EF 3
Jing Xian [TJ, Hunan] 190-191 B 8
Jingxing 190-191 DE 2
Jingyang 190-191 B 4
Jingyu 188-189 F 1
Jingyuan 184-185 JK 4
Jingzhen = Xinchengbu 184-185 K 4
Jingzheng = Jiyiz 190-191 C 4
Jingzhi 190-191 G 3
Jingziguan 190-191 C 5
Jinhua 184-185 MN 6
Jiniiang = Quanzhou 184-185 MN 6-7
Jining [TJ, Nei Monggol Zizhiqu] 184-185 L 3
Jining [TJ, Shandong] 184-185 M 4
Jinja 168-169 H 2
Jin Jiang [TJ◁Gang Jiang] 190-191 E 7
Jin Jiang [TJ◁Quanzhou Gang] 190-191 FG 9
Jinjing 190-191 D 7
Jinjing He = Jinqian He 190-191 BC 5
Jinkou 190-191 E 6
Jinlanshi = Jinlansi 190-191 D 8
Jinlansi 190-191 D 8
Jinmen = Kinmen Dao 184-185 M 7
Jinmu Jiao = Jintu Jiao 184-185 KL 8
Jinniu 190-191 E 6-7
Jinotega 146-147 J 9
Jinping 190-191 B 8
Jin Qi = Jin Xi [TJ, Fujian] 190-191 F 8
Jinqi = Jinxi [TJ, Jiangsi] 190-191 F 8
Jinsen = Inch'ŏn 184-185 O 4
Jinsha Jiang 184-185 J 6
Jinshan 190-191 H 6
Jinshi 184-185 L 6
Jinshi = Jianshi 190-191 B 6
Jintan 190-191 G 6
Jintian 190-191 E 8
Jintu Jiao 184-185 KL 8
Jing Xi [TJ, Fujian] 190-191 F 8
Jinxi [TJ, Jiangsi] 190-191 F 8
Jinxi [TJ, Liaoning] 188-189 C 2
Jin Xian [TJ, Hebei] 190-191 E 2
Jinxian [TJ, Jiangxi] 190-191 F 7
Jin Xian [TJ, Liaoning ↑ Dalian] 184-185 N 4
Jin Xian [TJ, Liaoning ↗ Jinzhou] 188-189 C 2
Jingxian [TJ, Shandong] 190-191 EF 4
Jingxian [TJ, Zhejiang] 190-191 H 8
Jinxiu 190-191 C 9
Jinyuan 190-191 D 3
Jinyun 190-191 H 7
Jinzhai 190-191 E 6
Jinzhou 184-185 N 3
Jiparaná, Rio - 158-159 G 6-7
Jipijapa 158-159 C 5
Jiqi = Jixi 190-191 G 6
Jirays, Jabal - 170 F 7
Jiren = Jīma 166-167 M 7
Jirgalanta = Chovd 184-185 G 2
Jiriid = Kiridh 166-167 b 2
Jirjā 166-167 L 3
Jīroft 180-181 H 5
Jirwān 180-181 G 6
Jishar 190-191 C 4
Jishi Shan = Amnyemachhen Gangri 184-185 HJ 5
Jishou 190-191 B 7
Jishui 190-191 E 8
Jisr ech Chaghoûr = Gisr ash-Shughūr 182-183 G 5
Jitan 190-191 E 9
Jiu 136-137 K 3
Jiuchaoxian = Chao Xian 190-191 FG 6
Jiudaoliang 190-191 BC 6
Jiufeng Shan 190-191 G 8
Jiugong'an = Nanping 190-191 D 7
Jiugou = Jiukou 190-191 D 6
Jiuhe 190-191 E 10
Jiujiang [TJ, Guangdong] 190-191 D 10
Jiujiang [TJ, Jiangxi] 184-185 M 6
Jiukou 190-191 D 6
Jiuling Shan 190-191 E 7
Jiuling Jiang 190-191 F 9
Jiulong Shan 190-191 G 7
Jiulong Xi 190-191 F 8
Jiunantian = Nantian 190-191 HJ 7
Jiuquan 184-185 H 4
Jiurongcheng 190-191 J 3
Jiushan Liedao 190-191 J 7
Jiusiyang = Siyang 190-191 G 5
Jiuxian 190-191 D 5
Jiuxiangcheng 190-191 E 5
Jiuxian He 190-191 F 9
Jiuyuhang 190-191 GH 6
Jiwā', Al- 180-181 G 6
Jiwānī 180-181 J 5-6
Jixi [TJ, Anhui] 190-191 G 6
Jixi [TJ, Heilongjiang] 184-185 P 2
Ji Xian [TJ, Henan] 190-191 E 4
Ji Xian [TJ, Shanxi] 190-191 C 3
Ji Xian [TJ, Hebei → Beijing] 190-191 F 1
Ji Xian [TJ, Hebei ↘ Shijiazhuang] 190-191 E 3
Jiyang [TJ, Fujian] 190-191 F G 8
Jiyang [TJ, Shandong] 190-191 F 3
Jiyi 190-191 C 4
Jiyizhen = Jiyi 190-191 C 4
Jiyuan He 190 191 F 2
Jiyun He 190-191 F 2
Jīzah, Al- [ET] 166-167 KL 3
Jīzah, Al- [JOR] 182-183 FG 7
Jīzah, El- = Al-Jīzah 182-183 FG 7
Jīzān 180-181 E 7
Jize 190-191 E 3
Jizerské hory 133 G 3
Jizl, Wādī al- 180-181 D 5
Jižni Afrika 168-169 F-H 8
Jižni Georgie = South Georgia 162 J 8
jižní pól 121 A
Jlaiba = Jalībah 182-183 M 7
Jllovo Beach 174-175 J 6
Jlullssat 144-145 ab 4
Joaçaba 162 F 3
Joachimsthal = Jáchymov 133 F 3
Joal-Fadioth 172-173 A 2
Joana Peres 158-159 JK 5
Joanesburgo = Johannesburg 168 G 8
Joanna Spring 194-195 DE 4
João 158-159 J 5
João de Almeida = Chibia 168-169 D 6
João Monlevale 160-161 L 3
João Pessoa 158-159 N 6
João Pinheiro 160-161 JK 2
Joaquim Felício 158-159 KL 8
Joaquim Murtinho 160-161 GH 6
Joaquim Távora 160-161 GH 5
Joaquín V. González 162 D 3
Jobal Island = Jazā'ir Qaysūm 170 EF 4
Job Peak 150-151 D 6
Jo-ch'iang = Charqiliq 184-185 F 4
Jocolí 162 C 4
Joden, Autonome Oblast der - 178-179 Z 8
Jodhpur 180-181 L 5
Jodpur = Jodhpur 180-181 L 5
Joegoslavië 136-137 H 4-J 5
Joensuu 130-131 NO 6
Joerg Plateau 121 B 29-30
Joes, CO 152-153 E 6
Jõesuu, Narva-138-139 FG 4
Jofane 168-169 H 7
Jofra Oasis, el - = Wāḥāt al-Jufrah 166-167 GH 3
Joganischkelje = Joniškėlis 138-139 DE 5-6
Jõgeva 138-139 F 4
Jögödseer Chijd = Erdenecagaan 184-185 LM 2
Jogyakarta = Yogyakarta 186-187 EF 8
Jōhana 188-189 L 4
Johanna Island = Ndzuwani 168-169 KL5
Johannes = Sovetskij 138-139 G 3
Johannesburg 168-169 G 8
Johannisburg = Pisz 133 K 2
Johi [GUY] 158-159 H 4
John Day, OR 150-151 D 3
John Day River 150-151 C 3
John Martin Reservoir 152-153 E 6-7
Johnson, KS 152-153 F 7
Johnsonburg, PA 148-149 D 4
Johnson City, NY 148-149 F 3
Johnson City, TN 146-147 K 4
Johnson City, TX 154-155 F 5
Johnsonville, SC 148-149 D 8
Johnston, SC 148-149 C 8
Johnston, Lakes - 194-195 D 6
Johnstown, NY 148-149 FG 3
Johnstown, PA 146-147 L 3-4
Johor Baharu 186-187 DE 6
Jõhvi 138-139 F 4
Joinvile 162 G 3
Joinville, Île - 121 C 31
Jōkāu = Jūkāw 166-167 L 7
Jokkmokk 130-131 HJ 4
Joko = Yoko 166-167 G 7
Jokohama = Yokohama 184-185 QR 4
Jökulsa á Brú 130-131 f 2
Jökulsá á Fjöllum 130-131 ef 2
Jolfā 180-181 F 3
Joliet, IL 146-147 J 3
Joliette 144-145 W 8
Joliette, ND 152-153 H 1
Joló 186-187 H 5
Joló Island 186-187 H 5
Jomotsering 180-181 O 5
Jomu 171 C 3
Jomuro 172-173 E 4
Jonava 138-139 E 6
Jonesboro,GA 154-155 N 4
Jonesboro,IL 152-153 M 7
Jonesboro,LA 154-155 J 4
Jonesboro, AR 146-147 H 4
Jonesport, ME 148-149 K 2
Jones Sound 144-145 TU 2
Jonesville,LA 154-155 JK 5
Jonesville,MI 152-153 O 4-5
Jongkha 184-185 F 6
Jonglei 166-167 L 7
Joniškėlis 138-139 DE 5-6
Joniškis 138-139 DE 5
Jonkersberg 174-175 DE 7
Jonköping 130-131 EF 9
Jönköpings län 130-131 EF 9
Jón-medence 166-167 HJ 1-2
Jonquière 144-145 WX 8
Jónské moře 136-137 GH 7
Jónské ostrovy 136-137 H 6-J 7
Jońskie, Morze - 136-137 GH 7
Jońskie, Wyspy - 136-137 H 6-J 7
Jón-szigetek 136-137 H 6-J 7
Jonzac 134-135 G 6
Joontoy 168-169 K 3
Joowhar = Jawhar 166-167 ab 3
Joplin, MO 146-147 H 4
Joplin, MT 150-151 H 1
Jordan 180-181 D 4
Jordan,MN 152-153 K 3
Jordan, MT 152-153 C 2
Jordan = Nahr ash-Sharī'ah 182-183 F 6-7
Jordan Creek 150-151 E 4
Jordánia 180-181 D 4
Jordania 180-181 D 4
Jordânia [JOR] 180-181 D 4
Jordanië 180-181 D 4
Jordanie 180-181 D 4
Jordanien 180-181 D 4
Jordánsko 180-181 D 4
Jordan Valley, OR 150-151 E 4
Jordão, Rio - 160-161 G 6
Jörden = Juuru 138-139 E 4
Jóreménység foka 168-169 E 9
Jorhat 180-181 PQ 5
Jörn 130-131 J 5
Jornada del Muerto 154-155 B 4
Jortom 138-139 Q 2
Jos 166-167 F 7
José de San Martín 162 BC 6
José Bonifácio [BR, São Paulo] 160-161 H 4
José La Haye 160-161 D 6
Joselândia [BR, Mato Grosso] 160-161 DE 2
José Pedro, Rio - 160-161 M 3-4
Joseph, OR 150-151 E 3
Joseph, Lac - 144-145 XY 7
Joseph, Lake - 148-149 D 2
Joseph Bonaparte Gulf 194-195 E 2
Joseph City, AZ 150-151 H 8
Joshua Tree, CA 150-151 E 8
Joshua Tree National Park 146-147 CD 5
Joškar-Ola 178-179 H 6
Joson Bulag = Altaj 184-185 H 2
Jos Plateau 166-167 E 6-7
Josselin 134-135 F 5
Jostedalsbreen 130-131 B 7
Joškar-Ola 178-179 H 6
Jotunheimen 130-131 BC 7
Joubertina 174-175 EF 7
Joûniyé = Jūnīyah 182-183 F 6
Jourdanton, TX 154-155 F 6
Joutsa 130-131 LM 7
Jow Kār 182-183 N 5
Joya, La - [MEX] 154-155 B 7
Juan Aldama 146-147 F 7
Juan A. Pradere 162 D 5
Juancheng 190-191 E 4
Juan de Fuca, Strait of 144-145 LM 8
Juan de Mena 160-161 D 6
Juan de Nova 168-169 K 6
Juan Diaz 146-147 c 2
Juan Fernández 157 BC 6
Juan Fernández, Dorsal de las islas - 124-125 E 7
Juan Fernández, Dorsale - 124-125 E 7
Juan Fernández, Seuil de 124-125 E 7
Juan Fernández Ridge 124-125 E 7
Juan Fernández-Rücken 198-199 N 6
Juan Fernandezrug 124-125 E 7
Juan Gallegos, Isla - 146-147 b 2
Juan José Castelli 162 DE 3
Juanjiang 190-191 D7
Juanjuí 158-159 D 6
Juankoski 130-131 N 6
Juan Stuven, Isla - 162 A 7
Juárez [MEX ↑ Chihuahua] 146-147 E 5
Juárez, Sierra de - 146-147 C 5
Juarzon = Juazhon 172-173 C 4
Juatinga, Ponta do - 158-159 L 9
Juazeiro 158-159 L 6
Juazeiro do Norte 158-159 M 6
Juazohn 172-173 C 4
Jūbā 166-167 L 8
Juba, Webi - 166-167 N 8
Jubab, Qar'at - 182-183 J 5
Jubail, Al- = Al-Jubayl al-Baḥrī 180-181 FG 5
Jubal, Madiq - = Jazīrat Shadwan 166-167 LM 3
Jubayl [ET] 170 E 3
Jubayl [RL] 182-183 F 5
Jubayl al-Baḥrī, Al- 180-181 FG 5
Jubayt 166-167 M 4
Jubba = Jubbah 182-183 K 6
Jubba, Jasiiradha - 168-169 K 3
Jubbada Hoose = 4 ◁ 166-167 N 8
Jubbade Dhexe 166-167 N 8
Jubbah 182-183 K 6
Jubbulpore = Jabalpur 180-181 MN 6
Jubeil = Jubayl 182-183 F 5
Jubilee Lake 194-195 E 5
Júcar 134-135 G 9
Juçara [BR, Goiás] 160-161 G 1
Juçara [BR, Paraná] 160-161 F 5
Jucás 158-159 LM 6
Juchitán de Zaragoza 146-147 GH 8
Juchmači 138-139 RS 6
Juchnov, 138-139 K 6
Judā', Sha'ib al- 182-183 L 8-M 7
Judayyidat-Ar'ar 180-181 DE 4
Judayyidat Ḥāmir 182-183 J 7
Judea 174-175 BC 2
Juden, Autonome Oblast der - 178-179 Z 8
Judenburg 133 G 5
Judeus, Região Autónoma dos - = 12 ◁ 178-179 Z 8
Judino, Kazan' - 138-139 R 6
Judino = Petuchovo 178-179 M 6
Judith, Point - 148-149 H 4
Judith Basin 152-153 AB 2
Judith Bassin 150-151 HJ 2
Judith Gap, MT 152-153 B 2
Judith Mountains 152-153 B 2
Judoma 178-179 a 6
Juejiang = Rudong 190-191 H 5
Jufrah, Wāḥāt al- 166-167 GH 3
Jug [SU, ~] 138-139 Q 3
Jug [SU, ●] 138-139 V 5
Juggernaut = Puri 180-181 O 7
Jugiong 196 J 5
Jugo-Kamnskij 138-139 UV 5
Jugo-Osetinskaja Avtonomnaja Oblast' = Südossetische Autonome Oblast 140-141 LM 5
Jugorskij poluostrov 178-179 L 4
Jugorskij Šar, proliv - 178-179 L 4-M 3
Jugoslavia 136-137 H 4-K 3
Jugoslávia 122-123 K 3
Jugoslávie 136-137 F 3-J 5
Jugoslawien 136-137 H 4-5
Jugosławia 136-137 F 3-J 5
Jugoszlávia 136-137 F 3-J 5
Jugydtydor 138-139 T 2
Juhaym 182-183 L 8
Juhaynah 170 D 4
Ju He = Ju Shui 190-191 C 6
Juhua Dao 188-189 C 2
Juian = Rui'an 190-191 H 8
Juichang = Ruichang 190-191 E 7
Juifs, Province des - 178-179 Z'8
Juikin = Ruijin 184-185 M 6
Jui-sui 190-191 H 10
Juiz de Fora 158-159 KL 9
Jujuy 162 C 2
Jujuy = San Salvador de Jujuy 162 CD 2
Jukagirskoje ploskogorje 178-179 de 4
Jukamenskoje 138-139 T 5
Jukao = Rugao 184-185 N 5
Jukatański, Basen - 146-147 JK 8
Jūkāw 166-167 L 7
Jukoupu 190-191 C 8
Juksejevo 138-139 TU 4
Jukta 178-179 TU 5
Jula 138-139 P 2
Julaca 158-159 F 9
Julesburg, CO 152-153 EF 5
Juli 158-159 F 8
Juliaca 158-159 E 8
Julia Creek 194-195 H 4
Júliai-Alpok 136-137 EF 2
Julian, CA 150-151 E 9
Julian Alps 136-137 EF 2
Julianehåb = Qaqortoq 144-145 b 5
Jülich 133 C 3
Julijskie, Alpi - 136-137 EF 2
Julimes 154-155 C 6
Julische Alpen 136-137 EF 2
Juliuhe 188-189 D 1
Jullundur = Jalandhar 180-181 LM 4
Jūlmīnā [MA, Aghādīr] 166-167 BC 3
Julské Alpy 136-137 EF 2
Julu 190-191 E 3
Julundur = Jalandhar 180-181 LM 4
Jumaima, Al- = Al-Jumaymah 182-183 KL 8
Jumaymah, Al- 182-183 KL 8
Jumbe Salim's 171 D 5
Jumbilla 158-159 D 6
Jumbo 168-169 K 3
Jumbo, Raas - 168-169 K 3
Jumilla 134-135 G 9
Jumna = Yamuna 180-181 MN 5
Jun = Jun Xian 190-191 C 5
Junagadh 180-181 KL 6
Junagarh = Junagadh 180-181 KL 6
Junan 190-191 G 4
Junayfah 170 E 2
Junaynah 166-167 J 6
Junction, TX 154-155 F 5
Junction, UT 150-151 G 6
Junction City, AR 154-155 J 4
Junction City, KS 146-147 G 4
Jundah 194-195 H 4
Jundiai 160-161 J 5
Jundtion City, OR 150-151 B 3
Juneau, WI 152-153 M 4
Juneau, AK 144-145 K 6
Junee 196 H 5
June Lake, CA 150-151 D 7
Jungar Qi 190-191 C 2
Jungcheng = Rongcheng 190-191 EF 2
Jungferninseln 146-147 NO 8
Junggharíyä 184-185 EF 2
Jung-hsien = Rong Xian 190-191 C 10
Jungo, NV 150-151 D 5
Jun-ho-chi = Runheji 190-191 F 5
Juniata River 148-149 E 4
Junín [RA, Buenos Aires] 162 D 4
Junín [PE, ●] 158-159 D 7
Junín de los Andes 162 BC 5
Juniper Mountains 150-151 G 8
Jūnīyah 182-183 F 6
Juniye = Jūnīyah 182-183 F 6
Juno, TX 154-155 E 5
Junsele 130-131 G 6
Junten = Sunch'ŏn 184-185 O 4-5
Juntura, OR 150-151 DE 4
Junxian = Xun Xian 190-191 E 4
Jupiá, Represa de - 158-159 J 9
Jūr, Nahr - 166-167 K 7
Jūr, Nahr el - = Nahr Jūr 166-167 K7
Jura [CH] 133 BC 5
Jura [GB] 132 D 3-4
Jura, Sound of - 132 D 4
Juratiški 138-139 EF 6
Jurab = Djourab 166-167 H 5
Juraiba, Al- = Al-Juraybah 182-183 KL 8
Juraybah, Al- 182-183 KL 8
Jurbarkas 138-139 D 6
Jurborg = Jurbarkas 138-139 D 6
Juréia, Praia da - 160-161 J 6
Jurdī, Wādī - 170 E 4
Jurf ad-Darāwish 182-183 FG 7
Jurf ed Darāwīsh = Jurf ad-Darāwish 182-183 FG 7
Jurga 178-179 P 6
Jurien Bay 194-195 B 6
Juries, Los - 162 D 3
Jurino 138-139 PQ 5
Jurja 138-139 R 4
Jurjevec 178-179 G 6
Jurjev-Pol'skij 138-139 MN 5
Jurjurah 166-167 EF 1
Jurla 138-139 U 4
Jurlovka 138-139 N 7
Jurmala 138-139 DE 5
Jurmala 130-131 K 9
Jurong 190-191 G 6
Jūrqāy, Jabal - 166-167 JK 6
Juruá, Rio - 158-159 F 6
Juruena 158-159 H 7
Juruena, Rio - 158-159 H 6-7
Jur'ung-Chaja 178-179 VW 3
Jushan = Rushan 190-191 H 3
Ju Shui 190-191 C 6
Juškozero 178-179 E 5
Jussey 134-135 K 5
Juškozero 178-179 E 5
Justa 140-141 N 3
Justiceburg, TX 154-155 E 4
Justo Daract 162 CD 4
Jus'va 138-139 U 4
Jutaí, Rio - 158-159 F 5
Jutaza 138-139 T 6
Jüterbog 133 F 2-3
Jūṭhī Antarīp = False Point 180-181 O 6
Juti 160-161 E 5
Jutiapa 146-147 HJ 9
Juticalpa 146-147 J 9
Jütland 130-131 C 10-D 9
Jutland 130-131 C 10-D 9
Jutlandia 130-131 C 9-10
Jutlândia 130-131 C 9-10
Jutlandia 130-131 C 10-D 9
Jutský pol. 130-131 C 9-10
Jutský poloostrov 130-131 C 9-10
Ju-tung = Rudong 190-191 C 11
Juuka 130-131 N 6
Juuru 138-139 E 4
Juva 130-131 MN 7
Juventud, Isla de la - 146-147 K 7
Juwārah, Al- 180-181 H 7
Ju Xian 184-185 M 4
Juye 190-191 F 4
Ju-yüan = Ruyuan 190-191 D 9
Juža 138-139 O 5
Jūzān 182-183 N 5
Južnaja Kel'tma 138-139 U 3
Južna Morava 136-137 JK 4
Južno-Kuril'sk 178-179 c 9
Južno-Sachalinsk 178-179 bc 8
Južnyj, mys - 178-179 e 6
Južnyj An'ujskij chrebet = An'ujskij chrebet 178-179 fg 4
Južnyj Bug 140-141 E 2
Južnyj Ural 178-179 K 7-L 6
Juzovka = Doneck 140-141 H 2-3
Južsib 178-179 L 7
Južno-Kuril'sk 178-179 c 9
Južno-Sachalinsk 178-179 bc 8
Južnyj, mys - 178-179 e 6
Južnyj An'ujskij chrebet = An'ujskij chrebet 178-179 fg 4
Južnyj Ural 178-179 K 7-L 6
Južsib 178-179 L 7
Jyekunde = Chhergundo 184-185 H 5
Jylland 130-131 C 9-10
Jyväskylä 130-131 L 6

K

K 2 180-181 M 3
K XVIII, Dorsal - 124-125 O 7
K XVIII, Dorsale - 124-125 O 7
K XVIII Ridge 124-125 O 7
K XVIII-Rug 124-125 O 7
Kaain Veld = Kaiingveld 174-175 D 6-E 5
Kaalkaroo 174-175 C 6
Kaamanen 130-131 M 3
Kaapmuiden 174-175 J 3
Kaapbekken 124-125 K 7
Kaapdrempel 124-125 K 8
Kaapplato 168-169 F 8
Kaapprovinsie = Kaapland 168-169 FG 9
Kaapstad 168-169 E 9
Kaap Verdebekken 124-125 GH 4-5
Kaap Verdedrempel 124-125 H 4-5
Kaaschka 180-181 HJ 3
Kaba = Little Scarcies 172-173 B 3
Kabaena, Pulau - 186-187 H 8
Kabahaydar 182-183 H 4
Kabála [GR] 136-137 L 5
Kabala [WAL] 166-167 B 7
Kabale 168-169 GH 3
Kabalo 168-169 G 4
Kabambare 168-169 G 3
Kabango 171 B 5
Kabansk 178-179 U 7
Kabara 172-173 E 1
Kabardin-Balkar Autonóm Köztársaság 140-141 LM 2
Kabardiner und Balkaren, Autonome Republik der- 140-141 LM 2
Kabardino-Balkar Autonomous Republic 140-141 LM 2
Kabardino-Balkarische Autonome Republiek 140-141 LM 2
Kabardino-Balkars, République Autonome des - 140-141 LM 2
Kabardino-Balkarskaja Avtonomnaja Sovetskaja Socialističeskaja Respublika = Autonome Republik der Kabardiner und Balkaren 140-141 LM 5
Kabardinos y Balkares, República Autónoma de los - 140-141 LM 2
Kabardinsko-balkarská autonomni republika 140-141 L 5
Kabardyńsko- Balkarska Autonomiczna Republika 140-141 L 5
Kabare [RCB] 168-169 G 3
Kabarei 186-187 K 7
Kabarnet 171 CD 2
Kabba 166-167 F 7
Kåbdalis 130-131 J 4
Kabelega Falls 168-169 H 2
Kabelega Falls National Park 168-169 H 2
Kaberamaido 171 C 2
Kabetogama Lake 152-153 K 1
Kab-hegy 178-179 E 9
Kabia, Pulau - = Pulau Selayar 186-187 H 8
Kabin Buri 186-187 D 4
Kabinda 168-169 FG 4
Kabinda = Cabinda 168-169 D 4
Kabīr, Wāw al- 166-167 H 3
Kabīr, Zāb al- 182-183 K 4
Kabīr Kūh 180-181 F 4
Kabkābīyah 166-167 J 6
Kabo 166-167 H 7
Kabobo 171 B 4
Kaboel = Kabul 180-181 K 4
Kabompo 168-169 F 5
Kabongo 168-169 FG 4
Kaboul = Kabul 180-181 K 4
Kaboža 138-139 K 4
Kabudārāhang 182-183 N 5
Kābul 180-181 K 4
Kábul = Kābul 180-181 K 4
Kabul = Kābul 180-181 K 4
Kabunda 171 B 6
Kaburuan, Pulau - 186-187 J 6
Kābuwītā 166-167 L 8
Kabwe 168-169 G 5
Kača 140-141 F 4
Kačalinskaja 140-141 M 2
Kačanovo 138-139 FG 5
K'achana = Kafan 140-141 N 7
Kachchh = Kutch 180-181 K 6
Kacheliba 171 C 2
Ka-Chem = Malyj Jenisej 178-179 RS 7
Kachgar = Qäshqär 184-185 CD 4
Kachi 140-141 N 6
Kachia 172-173 G 3
Kachin Pyinnei 186-187 C 1-2
Kachovka 140-141 F 3
Kachovskoje vodochranolišče 140-141 F 3
K'achta 178-179 U 7
K XVIII-Rücken 124-125 O 7
Kaçkar Dağı 182-183 J 2
Kačug 178-179 U 7
Ka-Chem = Malyj Jenisej 178-179 RS 7
Kadada 138-139 Q 7
Kadaingdi 186-187 C 3
Kadaingti = Kadaingdi 186-187 C 3
Kadan Kyûn 186-187 C 4
Kaḍappa = Cuddapah 180-181 M 8
Kade [GH] 166-167 D 7
Kade = Kadié 172-173 B 2
Kadéï 166-167 H 8
Kadgoron = Ardon 140-141 M 5
Kadhdhāb, Sinn al- 170 DE 6
Kadié 172-173 B 2
Kadijewka = Stachanov 140-141 J 2
Kadıköy, İstanbul- 182-183 C 2
Kadiköy Deresi 182-183 B 2-3
Kadina 196 CD 4-5
Kadınhanı 182-183 E 3
Kadiolo 172-173 D 3
Kadirli 182-183 FG 4
Kadmat Island 180-181 L 8
Kadnikov 138-139 N 4
Ka-do 188-189 E 3
Kadoka, SD 152-153 F 4
Kadoma 168-169 G 6
Kadugli = Kāduqlī 166-167 KL 6
Kaduj 138-139 L 4
Kaduna [WAN, ●] 166-167 F 6
Kaduna [WAN, ⭑] 172-173 G 3
Kaduna, River - 172-173 G 3
Kāduqlī 166-167 KL 6
Kadyi 138-139 O 5
Kadykčan 178-179 C 5
Kadyks = Cádiz 134-135 D 10
Kadžaran N 7
Kaech'i-ri 188-189 G 2
Kaesŏng 184-185 O 4
Kāf 180-181 D 4
Kāf, Al- 166-167 F 1
Kafan 140-141 N 7
Kafanchan 166-167 F 7
Kafērévs, Akrōtḗrion - 136-137 L 6
Kafferrivier 174-175 FG 5
Kaffrine 166-167 AB 6
Kafr ash-Shaykh 170 D 2
Kafr az-Zayyāt 170 D 2
Kafta = Ḳeftiya 166-167 M 6
Kafu 168-169 H 2
Kafue [Z, ~] 168-169 G 6
Kafue [Z, ●] 168-169 G 6
Kafue Flats 168-169 G 6
Kafue National Park 168-169 G 5-6
Kafulwa 171 B 5
Kaga 188-189 L 4
Kaga Bandoro 166-167 HJ 7
Kagan 180-181 J 3
Kaganovič = Popasnaja 140-141 J 2
Kagarlyk 140-141 E 2
Kagawa 188-189 JK 5
Kagera 168-169 H 3
Kagera, Parc national de la - 168-169 H 3
Kagera Magharibi 168-169 H 3
Kagi = Chiayi 184-185 MN 7
Kağızman 182-183 K 2
Kagmār = Kajmār 166-167 L 6
Kagoro 166-167 F 7
Kagoshima 184-185 OP 5
Kagoshima wan 188-189 H 7
Kagosima = Kagoshima 184-185 OP 5
Kahama 168-169 H 3
Kahayan, Sungai - 186-187 F 7
Kahemba 168-169 E 4
Kahia 168-169 G 4
Káhira = Al-Qāhirah 166-167 KL 2
Kahlā [IR] 182-183 N 5
Kahler Asten 133 D 3
Kahlotus, WA 150-151 D 2
Kahoga, MO 152-153 KL 5
Kahoku-gata 188-189 L 4
Kahoolawe 186-187 e 3
Kahramanmaraş 180-181 D 3
Kâhta 182-183 H 4
Kai, Kepulauan - 186-187 K 8
Kaiama 166-167 E 7
Kaibab Indian Reservation 150-151 G 7
Kaibab Plateau 150-151 G 7
K'ai-chien = Nanfeng 190-191 C 10
Kaidong = Tongyu 184-185 N 3
Kaieteur Falls 158-159 GH 3
Kaifeng 184-185 LM 5
K'ai-fong = Kaifeng 184-185 LM 5
Kaihsien = Kai Xian 190-191 B 6
Kaihua 190-191 G 7
Kaihwa = Wenshan 184-185 JK 7
Kaiingveld 174-175 D 6-E 5
Kaijian = Nanfeng 190-191 C 10
Kai Kecil 186-187 K 8
Kaikohe 194-195 O 7
Kaikoura 194-195 O 8
Kailahun 172-173 C 3
Kailas Gangri = Kailash Gangri 184-185 E 5
Kailash Gangri 184-185 E 5
Kailu 184-185 N 3
Kaimana 186-187 K 7
Kaimon-dake 188-189 H 7
Kainan 188-189 K 5
Kainantu 186-187 N 8
Kainji Dam 166-167 EF 6-7
Kainji Lake 172-173 G 3
Kainsk = Kujbyšev 178-179 O 6
Kaipara Harbour 194-195 O 7
Kaiparowits Plateau 150-151 H 7
Kaiping [TJ, Guangdong] 190-191 D 10
Kaiping [TJ, Hebei] 190-191 G 2
Kair = Al-Qāhirah 166-167 KL 2
Kairiru 186-187 M 7
Kairó = Al-Qāhirah 166-167 KL 2
Kaïrouan = Al-Qayrawān 166-167 FG 1
Kairuku 186-187 N 8
Kaisariyah = Caesarea 182-183 F 6
Kaiserkanal = Da Yunhe 190-191 G 6
Kaiser Peak 150-151 D 7
Kaiserslautern 133 CD 4
Kaiser-Wilhelm II.-Land 121 C 9-10
Kaishū = Haeju 184-185 O 4
Kaitaia 194-195 O 7
Kaitangata 194-195 NO 9
Kaitum älv 130-131 HJ 4
Kai Xian 190-191 B 6
Kaizanchin = Hyesanjin 184-185 O 3
Kaj 138-139 T 4
Kajaani 130-131 MN 5
Kajabbi 194-195 H 4
Kajakent 140-141 N 5
Kajakī 180-181 JK 4
Kajang [RI] 186-187 H 8
Kajasula 140-141 M 4
Kajiado 168-169 J 3
Kajmán-árok 146-147 KL 8
Kajmański, Rów - 146-147 KL 8
Kajmanský příkop 146-147 KL 8
Kajmār 166-167 L 6
Kajnar [SU, Kazachskaja SSR] 178-179 O 8
Kajsajmas 140-141 P 1
Kākā 166-167 L 6
Kakamas 168-169 F 8
Kakamega 168-169 HJ 2
Kakarka = Sovetsk 178-179 H 6
Kakata 166-167 B 7
Kakbil = Karaoğlan 182-183 H 3
Kake 188-189 J 5
Kakegawa 188-189 LM 5
Kakelwe 171 B 4
Kakhea = Kakia 174-175 E 3
Kakia 168-169 F 7-8
Kakinada 180-181 N 7
Käkisalmi = Prioz'orsk 178-179 DE 5
Kakogawa 188-189 K 5
Kakonko 171 B 3
Kakpin 172-173 E 3
Kakšaal-Too, chrebet - 180-181 M 2
Kakuda 188-189 N 4
Kakulu 171 AB 4
Kakuma 168-169 HJ 2
Kakunodate 188-189 N 3
Kala 171 B 5
Kala, El - = Al-Qal'ah 166-167 F 1
Kalabahi 186-187 H 8
Kalabo 168-169 F 6
Kalabrien = Calàbria 136-137 FG 6
Kalábryta 136-137 K 6
Kalābsha 166-167 L 4
Kalač 140-141 K 1
Kalač-na-Donu 140-141 L 2
Kaladar 148-149 E 2
Ka Lae 186-187 e 4
Kalahari = Kalahari Desert 168-169 EF 7
Kalahari Desert 168-169 EF 7
Kalahari Gemsbok National Park 168-169 F 8
Kalakan 178-179 W 6
Kalama, WA 150-151 B 2-3
Kalamáta 136-137 JK 7
Kalamazoo, MI 146-147 J 3
Kalamazoo River 152-153 O 4
Kalambo Falls 168-169 H 4
Kalamitskij zaliv 140-141 F 4
Kalampáka 136-137 JK 6
Kalana 172-173 CD 3
Kalan = Tunceli 180-181 DE 3
Kalančak 136-137 P 2
Kalančak 140-141 F 3
Kalangali 171 C 4
Kalankpa, Mount - 172-173 F 3
Kalannie 194-195 C 6
Kalanshiyu, Sarīr - = Sarīr Qalanshū 166-167 J 3
Kalaotao, Pulau - 186-187 H 8
Kalar 178-179 W 6
Kalaraš 136-137 N 2
Kalasin [RI] 186-187 F 6
Kalasin [T] 186-187 D 3
Kalašnikovo 138-139 K 5
Kalat = Qalāt 180-181 K 5
Kalāt, Jabal - 170 F 6
Kalâtdlit nunât 144-145 b 2-c 5
Kalāt-i Ghilzay = Qalāt 180-181 K 4
Kalatrava 172-173 H 5
Kalaus 140-141 L 4
Kal'azin 138-139 LM 5
Kale [TR, Antalya] 182-183 CD 4
Kale [TR, Denizli] 182-183 C 4
Kale [TR, Gümüşane] 182-183 H 2
Kalecik 182-183 E 2
Kalecik = Kabahaydar 182-183 H 4
Kalehe 168-169 G 3
Kalemie 168-169 G 4
Kalemma 171 CD 3
Kalenyj 140-141 P 2
Kale Sultanie = Çanakkale 180-181 B 2
Kaletwa 186-187 B 2
Kaleva, MI 152-153 NO 3
Kalevala 178-179 E 4
Kalewa 186-187 BC 2
Kaleybar 182-183 M 3
Kálfafell 130-131 de 2-3
Kálfafellstadhur 130-131 f 2
Kalgačicha 138-139 L 2
Kalgan = Zhangjiakou 184-185 L 3
Kalgary, TX 154-155 E 4
Kalgoorlie 194-195 D 6
Kalhāt 180-181 H 6
Kali [Guinée] 172-173 C 2
Kali = Sangha 168-169 E 2-3
Kaliakra, nos - 136-137 N 4
Kalibo 186-187 H 4
Kalifornia = California 146-147 B 3-C 5
Kaliforniai-öböl 146-147 D 5-E 7
Kalifornie = California 146-147 B 3-C 5
Kalifornien = California 146-147 B 3-C 5
Kalifornien, Golf von 146-147 D 5-E 7
Kalifornijska, Zatoka 146-147 D 5-E 7
Kalifornský záliv 146-147 D 5-E 7
Kalikata = Calcutta 180-181 O 6
Kalima 168-169 G 3
Kalimantan 186-187 F 7-G 6
Kalimantan Barat = 7 ◁ 186-187 F 7
Kalimantan Selatan = 9 ◁ 186-187 G 7
Kalimantan Tengah = 8 ◁ 186-187 F 7
Kalimantan Timur= 10 ◁ 186-187 G 6
Kalinin = Tver' 178-179 EF 6
Kalinindorf = Kalininskoje 140-141 F 3
Kaliningrad 133 K 1

alinino [SU, Rossijskaja SFSR Perm] 138-139 UV 5
alinkoviči 138-139 G 7
alininsk [SU, Rossijskaja SFSR] 138-139 P 8
alininsk [SU, Rossijskaja SFSR DV 5
alinovka 140-141 O 2
alinju 171 C 5
alininskoje 140-141 F 3
alinovka 140-141 D 2
alisch = Kalisz 133 J 3
alisizo 171 D 5
alispell, MT 146-147 CD 2
alisz 133 J 3
alisz Pomorski 133 GH 2
alitva 140-141 K 2
aliua 168-169 H 3-4
alix äIv 130-131 JK 4
alkaska, MI 152-153 O 3
alkfeld 168-169 E 7
alkfontein 174-175 D 2
alkfontein = Karasburg 168-169 E 8
alkfonteindam 174-175 F 5
alkhochebene = Kalkplato 174-175 C 3
alk Plateau = Kalkplato 174-175 C 3
alkplato 174-175 C 3
alkrand 168-169 E 7
alkuta = Calcutta 180-181 O 6
alkutta = Calcutta 180-181 O 6
allafo = Kelafo 166-167 N 7
allaste 138-139 F 4
allipolis = Gelibolu 180-181 B 2
allsjön 130-131 E 6
almar 130-131 G 9
almarjaut 130-131 FG 9
almarsund 130-131 G 9
al'mius 140-141 MN 3
almouks, République Autonome des - 140-141 MN 3
almucka Autonomica Republika 140-141 MN 3
almükische Autonome Republik 140-141 MN 3
lmukken Autonome Republiek 140-141 MN 3
lmük Autonóm Köztársaság 140-141 MN 3
lmyckaja autonomni republika 140-141 MN 3
lmyckaja avtonomnaja Sovetskaja Socialistitčeskaja Respublika = Kalmükische Autonome Republik 140-141 MN 3
lmyckij Bazar = Privolžskij 140-141 NO 3
lmyk Autonomous Republic 140-141 MN 3
lmykovo 178-179 J 8
lnciems 138-139 D 5
lnibolotskaja 140-141 JK 3
lnzeem = Kalnciems 138-139 D 5
loko 168-169 G 4
lola 171 B 5
lomo 168-169 G 6
lomža 171 B 6
lperi Island 180-181 L 8
ltasy 180-181 F 5
luga 138-139 KL 6
luga = Kaluga 138-139 KL 6
lulaui = Kahoolawe 186-187 e 3
lundborg 130-131 D 10
lundu 171 B 3
lungwishi 171 B 3
luš 140-141 B 2
lutara 180-181 MN 9
lvarija 138-139 D 6
lymnos 136-137 M 7
m [WAN] 172-173 H 3
ma [RCB] 168-169 G 5
ma [SU, -] 178-173 J 6
ma [SU, •] 138-139 TU 5
mae 188-189 HJ 6
maeura = Kamae 188-189 HJ 6
maggas Mountains = Komaggasberge 174-175 B 5-6
maishi 184-185 R 4
maishi wan 188-189 NO 3
maiwi 172-173 BC 3
malampakea 171 B 4
man [TR] 182-183 E 3
marän 180-181 F 1
mar'u = Artašat 140-141 M 7
mba [WAN] 172-173 FG 3
mba [ZRE] 168-169 F 3
mbalnaja Sopka, vulkan - 178-179 e 7
mbaria 138-139 U 5
mbia 166-167 B 7
mbing, Pulau - = Pulau Atauro 186-187 J 4
mbja 138-139 F 4
mbodža 186-187 DE 4
mbodscha 186-187 DE 4
mbodža 186-187 DE 4
mbodža 186-187 DE 4
mbodzsa 186-187 DE 4
mboe 168-169 G 5
mbrisches Gebirge = Cambrian Mountains 132 D 5-E 6
mćatka, poluostrov - 178-179 e 6-7
mčatskij 178-179 fg 6
mčatskij zaliv 178-179 f 6
mčija 138-139 M 4
mčija 136-137 M 4
mčatka, Peninsula de - 178-179 e 6-7
mcsatka-félsziget = poluostrov Kamčatka 178-179 e 6-7
mele, OR 150-151 D 3
mčugskij 138-139 D 7
menec 138-139 D 7
menjak, Rt - 136-137 E 3
menka [SU, Rossijskaja SFSR Mezenskaja guba] 178-179 g 4
menka [SU, Rossijskaja SFSR Penza] 138-139 OP 7
menka [SU, Rossijskaja SFSR Voronež] 140-141 J 1
menka-Bugskaja 140-141 B 1
menka-Dneprovskaja 140-141 G 3
men'-na-Obi 178-179 OP 7
mennogorsk 138-139 GH 3
mennomostskij 140-141 K 4
mennyj Jar 140-141 M 2
mennyj 140-141 MN 1
menskoje 178-179 fg 5

Kamenskoje = Dneprodzeržinsk 140-141 FG 2
Kamensk-Sachtinskij 140-141 K 2
Kamensk-Schachtinskij = Kamensk-Šachtinskij 140-141 K 2
Kamensk-Ural'skij 178-179 LM 6
Kamenz 133 FG 3
Kameoka 188-189 K 5
Kameroen 166-167 G 7-8
Kamerun 166-167 G 7-8
Kameshli = Al-Qāmishliyah 180-181 E 3
Kameškovo 138-139 N 5
Kámět 180-181 M 4
Kamiah, ID 150-151 EF 2
Kamians'ke = Dneprodzeržinsk 140-141 FG 2
Kamień Pomorski 133 G 2
Kamiesberge 174-175 BC 6
Kamieskroon 174-175 B 6
Kamiiso 188-189 b 3
Kami Jiao 190-191 B 11
Kamikawa 188-189 c 2
Kami-Koshiki-shima 188-189 G 7
Kámil, Al- 180-181 N 6
Kamilin, Al- 166-167 L 5
Kamina 168-169 FG 4
Kaminokuni 188-189 ab 3
Kaminoshima 188-189 E 6
Kaminoyama 188-189 N 3
Kami-Sihoro 188-189 c 2
Kamissar 172-173 B 3
Kamit, Jabal - 170 B 6
Kamitsushima 188-189 G 5
Kamiyaku 188-189 H 7
Kam'janec'-Podil's'kyi 140-141 C 2
Kämlin, El- = Al-Kamilin 166-167 L 5
Kamloops 144-145 MN 7
Kammanassieriver 174-175 E 7
Kammenik, gora - 138-139 HJ 5
Kammuri yama 188-189 H 5
Kamnasie River = Kammanassieriver 174-175 E 7
Kamniokan 178-179 V 6
Kamo [J] 188-189 M 4
Kamo [SU] 140-141 M 6
Kamoenai 188-189 b 2
Kamortá Drip = Camorta Island 180-181 P 9
Kamp 133 G 4
Kampala 168-169 H 2
Kampanien = Campánia 136-137 F 5
Kampar 186-187 D 6
Kamparkalns 138-139 D 5
Kampemha 171 AB 5
Kampe, River - 172-173 G 3
Kamp'o 188-189 G 5
Kampo = Campo 166-167 F 8
Kampolombo, Lake - 168-169 G 5
Kampot 186-187 D 4
Kampuchea = Kambodscha 186-187 DE 4
Kampuchea = Kambodzsa 186-187 DE 4
Kampulu 171 B 5
Kampung Pasir Besar 186-187 D 6
Kamsar = Kamissar 172-173 B 3
Kamskoje Ustje 138-139 R 6
Kamskoje vodochranilišče 178-179 K 9
Kamtchatka, Presqu'île de - = Kamčatka 178-179 e 6-7
Kamtchatka Peninsula = Kamčatka 178-179 e 6-7
Kamtschatka, Halbinsel - = poluostrov Kamčatka 178-179 e 6-7
Kamtsjatka = Kamčatka 178-179 e 6-7
Kamudi [EAK] 171 D 3
Kamui-misaki 188-189 ab 3
Kamunars'ke = Kommunarsk 140-141 J 2
Kämyārān 182-183 M 5
Kamýsin 140-141 M 1
Kamyšlov 178-179 M 7
Kamyš-Zar'a 140-141 H 3
Kamyz'ak 140-141 O 3
Kan [SU] 178-179 S 6-7
Kanaal, Het - 132 T 7-F 6
Kanaal-Eilanden = Channel Islands 132 E 7
Kanab, UT 150-151 G 7
Kanab Creek 150-151 G 7
Kanada 144-145 M 5-W 7
Kanadai-medence 120 AB 132-33
Kanadej 138-139 Q 7
Kanadisches Becken 120 AB 132-33
Kanadská pánev 120 AB 132-33
Kanadyjski, Basen - 120 AB 22-33
Kanagawa 188-189 M 5
Kana'is, Ra's al- 170 BC 2
Kanal, Der - 132 F 7-6
Kanala = Canala 194-195 N 4
Kanalinseln = Channel Islands 132 E 7
Kan'an 182-183 L 6
Kananga 168-169 F 4
Kanarenschwelle 124-125 HJ 4
Kanarische Inseln = Islas Canarias 166-167 A 3
Kanari-szigetek = Islas Canarias 166-167 A 3
Kanarraville, UT 150-151 G 7
Kanárské ostrovy = Islas Canarias 166-167 A 3
Kanaryjskie, Wyspy - = Islas Canarias 166-167 A 3
Kanaš 178-179 H 6
Kanawha River 148-149 BC 5
Kanazawa 184-185 Q 4
Kanchanaburi 186-187 C 4
Kancheepuram = Kanchepuram 180-181 MN 8
Kanchenjunga = Gangchhendsönga 180-181 O 5
Kan Chiang = Gan Jiang 190-191 N 5
Kanchhibia 171 B 5
Kánchipuram = Kanchepuram 180-181 MN 8
Kanchow = Zhangye 184-185 J 4
Kanchuan = Ganquan 190-191 B 3
Kanda 138-139 M 1
Kandahár = Qandahár 180-181 K 4
Kandalakša 178-179 EF 4
Kandalakšskij zaliv 178-179 EF 4
Kandangan 186-187 FG 7
Kandau = Kandava 138-139 D 5
Kandava 138-139 D 5
Kandé = Kanté 172-173 F 3
Kandi [DY] 166-167 F 6
Kandika 172-173 B 2
Kandira 182-183 CD 2
Kandla 180-181 L 6

Kandos 194-195 JK 6
Kandreho 172-173 J 4
Kandüleh 182-183 M 5
Kandulu 171 D 5
Kandy = Maha Nuwara 180-181 N 9
Kane, PA 148-149 WX 2
Kane Basin 144-145 WX 2
Kanem 166-167 H 6
Kanev 140-141 G 2
Kanevskaja 140-141 J 3
Kaneyama 188-189 M 4
Kang 168-169 F 7
Kangal 182-183 G 3
Kangar 186-187 D 5
Kangaroo Island 194-195 G 7
Kangâvar 182-183 M 5
Kangding 184-185 J 5
Kangean, Pulau - 186-187 G 8
Kangdong 188-189 F 3
Kangean, Pulau - 186-187 G 8
Kanggye 184-185 O 3
Kanggyŏng 188-189 F 4
Kanghwa 188-189 EF 4
Kanghwa-do 188-189 EF 4
Kanghwa-man 188-189 E 4
Kangjin 188-189 F 5
Kang-liao 190-191 HJ 9
Kangnüng 184-185 OP 4
Kango 168-169 F 2
Kang-shan 190-191 GH 10
Kangsŏ 188-189 E 3
Kangwane = 11 ◁ 174-175 J 4
Kangwŏn-do [Nordkorea]
Kangwŏn-do [ROK] 188-189 G 4
Kan Ho = Gan He 184-185 N 1
Kani [RB] 174-175 D 3
Kaniama 168-169 FG 4
Kaniapiskau Lake 144-145 W 7
Kaniet Islands 186-187 N 7
Kâni Masi 182-183 K 4
Kani, poluostrov - 178-179 GH 4
Kanin Nos, mys - 178-179 G 4
Kanirep = Karlowa 182-183 J 3
Kanita 188-189 N 2
Kankakee, IL 146-147 J 3
Kankabeaul 180-181 JK 3
Kankan 166-167 C 6
Kankõ = Hamhüng 184-185 O 3-4
Kankõ = Hamhüng 184-185 O 4
Kankossa = Kanküssah 166-167 B 5
Kan-kou-chên = Gango 188-189 B 2
Kanküssah 166-167 B 5
Kankwi 174-175 D 3
Kankyõ-hokudõ = Hamgyŏng-pukto 188-189 G 2-H 1
Kankyõ-nandõ = Hamgyŏngnamdo 188-189 FG 2-3
Kannnanur = Cannanore 180-181 LM 8
Kannapolis, NC 148-149 C 7
Kannus 130-131 K 6
Kano [WAN, •] 166-167 F 6
Kano [WAN, ✩] 172-173 H 3
Kano, River - 172-173 H 3
Kanoji 188-189 J 5
Kanoma Hill 172-173 G 2
Kanona 171 B 6
Kanopolis Lake 152-153 H 6
Kanorado, KS 152-153 EF 6
Kanosh, UT 150-151 G 6
Kanouri 166-167 G 6
Kanoya 188-189 H 7
Kanpur 180-181 MN 5
Kansas 146-147 FG 4
Kansas, OK 154-155 H 7
Kansas City, KS 146-147 GH 4
Kansas City, MO 146-147 H 4
Kansas River 146-147 G 4
Kansk 178-179 S 6
Kansŏng 188-189 G 3
Kansu = Gansu 184-185 G 3-J 4
Kantabrisches Gebirge = Cordillera Cantábrica 134-135 D-F 7
Kan-t'ang = Gantang 190-191 B 10
Kantalahti = Kandalakša 178-179 EF 4
Kantani = Centane 174-175 H 7
Kantara = Al-Qantarah 170 E 2
Kantchari 166-167 E 6
Kanté 172-173 F 3
Kantemirovka 140-141 JK 2
Kantõ 188-189 MN 4
Kantõ sammyaku 188-189 M 4-5
Kanukov = Privolžskij 140-141 NO 3
Kanuma 188-189 M 4
Kanuri = Kanouri 166-167 G 6
Kanus 174-175 C 4
Kanyakumári Antarip = Cape Comorin 180-181 M 9
Kanyama 171 B 2
Kanye 168-169 FG 7
Kanyu = Ganyu 190-191 G 4
Kan-yü = Ganyu 190-191 G 4
Kanzanli 180-181 B 4
Kao-an = Gao'an 184-185 LM 6
Kao-chia-fang = Gaojiafang 190-191 D 7
Kao-hsiung 184-185 MN 7
Kao-i = Gaoyi 190-191 B 4
Kao-lan Tao = Gaolan Dao 190-191 D 11
Kaoling = Gaoling 190-191 B 4
Kaokoveld 168-169 D 6-7
Kaolack 166-167 A 6
Kao-li-kung Shan = Gaoligong Shan 184-185 H 6
Kaomi = Gaomi 190-191 G 4
Kaoping = Gaoping 190-191 D 4
Kao-p'ing Hsi 190-191 H 10
Kao-sha = Gaosha 190-191 C 8
Kaosiung = Kao-hsiung 184-185 MN 7
Kaotai = Gaotai 184-185 H 4
Kaotang = Gaotang 190-191 F 3
Kao-tien-tzü = Gaodianzi 190-191 BC 4
Kaotsu-hsien = Gaocun 190-191 D 6
Kaotwe 174-175 E 2
Kaouar 166-167 G 5
Kaoyang = Gaoyang 190-191 E 2
Kaoyou = Gaoyou 190-191 G 4
Kao-yüan = Gaoyuan 190-191 F 3
Kao-yu Hu = Gaoyou Hu 190-191 G 5
Kap'a-do 188-189 F 6
Kapagere 186-187 N 8-9
Kapanga 168-169 F 4
Kapatu 171 B 5
Kapbecken 124-125 K 7
Kapčagajskoje vodochranilišče 178-179 O 9

Kapenguria 171 C 2
Kapfenberg 133 G 4
Kapidağı Yarımadası 182-183 BC 2
Kapiolani 196 B 5
Kapiri Mposhi 168-169 G 5
Kapit 186-187 F 6
Kaplan, LA 154-155 J 5-6
Kaplanova = Babajurt 140-141 N 5
Kapona 168-169 G 4
Kapongolo 171 AB 4
Kaporo 172-173 B 3
Kapos 133 J 5
Kaposvár 133 HJ 5
K'appese'ga 138-139 JK 2
Kapsan 188-189 G 2
Kapschwelle 124-125 K 8
Kapské Mêsto = Kaapstad 168-169 B 9
Kapsowar 171 CD 2
Kapstadt = Kaapstad 168-169 E 9
Kapsukas 130-131 K 10
Kapuas, Sungai - [RI, Kalimantan Barat] 186-187 E 7
Kapunda 196 D 5
Kapuskasing 144-145 U 8
Kaputar, Mount - 194-195 JK 3
Kaputdžuch, gora - 140-141 MN 7
Kaputir 171 C 2
Kapverde 122-123 H 5
Kapverdenschwelle 124-125 H 4-5
Kap Verde Gipon 124-125 H 4-5
Kapverdisches Becken 124-125 GH 4-5
Kapýdžik, gora - = gora Kaputdžuch 140-141 MN 7
Kara 172-173 F 3
Kara = Ust'-Kara 178-179 LM 4
Kara, Mar de - 178-179 K 3-R 2
Kara, Mar di - 178-179 L 3-Q 2
Kara, Mar di - 178-179 L 3-Q 2
Kara, Mer de - 178-179 K 3-Q 2
Karaali 182-183 E 4
Karababa Dağı 182-183 FG 3
Karabah-hegyvidéki Autonóm Terület 140-141 MN 7
Karabanovo 138-139 M 5
Karabekaul 180-181 JK 3
Karabiga 182-183 B 2
Kara-Bogaz-Gol, zaliv 180-181 G 2
Karabük 180-181 C 2
Karaburun [TR] 182-183 B 3
Karabutak 178-179 L 8
Karaca = Şiran 182-183 H 2
Karacabey 182-183 C 2
Karaca Dağ [TR, Ankara] 182-183 E 3
Karacadağ [TR, Konya] 182-183 E 4
Karacadağ [TR, Şanlı Urfa ▲▲] 182-183 H 4
Karacadağ [TR, Şanlı Urfa •] 182-183 H 4
Karáčaj-Circassi, Rep. Aut. dei 140-141 KL 5
Karáčaj-Circassi, RA dei 140-141 KL 5
Karac, River - 172-173 H 3
Karacsaj-Cserkeszka Avtonomnaja Respublika 140-141 KL 5
Karačajevsko-Čerkeská autonomni republika 140-141 KL 5
Karačajevsk 140-141 KL 5
Karacaköy 182-183 C 2
Karačala 140-141 O 7
Karacasu 182-183 C 4
Karačev 138-139 K 7
Karachai e Cherkeses, Oblast Autónoma dos - 139-140 KL 5
Karachaie Cherkeses, República Autónoma dos - 10 ◁ 126-127 ...
Karachai y Cherkeses, República de los - 140-141 KL 5
Karachayevo-Cherkess Autonomous Region 140-141 KL 5
Karachi 180-181 K 6
Kárachi 180-181 K 6
Karáčí = Karáchi 180-181 K 6
Karacsáj-Cserkesz Autonóm Terület 140-141 KL 5
Karáčí = Karáchi 180-181 K 6
Karadağ = Kibrisak
Karadağ 182-183 D 4
Karadeniz Boğazı = Boğazici 180-181 BC 2
Karadeniz Boğazı = Boğazici 180-181 BC 2
Karafuto = Sachalin 178-179 b 7-8
Karagaj 138-139 U 4
Karagajly 178-179 NO 8
Karagan 140-141 P 4
Kara'ağıno = Fizuli 140-141 N 7
Karaginskij, ostrov - 178-179 fg 6
Karaginskij zaliv 178-179 fg 6
Karagoua 166-167 G 6
Karahalli 180-181 C 3
Karahasanli 182-183 F 3
Karaibskie, Morze - 146-147 KN 8
Kárai'kkál = Karajkal 180-181 MN 8
Karaisali = Çeceli 182-183 F 4
Karaj 180-181 G 3
Karajkal 180-181 MN 8
Karakaar 166-167 b 2
Karakar Island 186-187 N 7
Karakax = Moyu 180-181 MN 3
Karakecili = Özalp 182-183 K 3
Kárakëlong, Pulau - 186-187 J 6
Kárakli's = Kirovakan 140-141 LM 6
Karakoram 180-181 L 3-M 4
Karakoram Pass = Qaramurun davan 180-181 M 3
Kara Körë 166-167 MN 6
Karakorum = Char Chorin 184-185 J 2
Karaköse = Ağrı 180-181 E 3
Karakubstroj = Komsomol'skoje 140-141 HJ 3
Karakumskij kanal 180-181 J 3
Karakumy 180-181 H 3
Kárákürü, Nahr al- 172-173 C 1-2
Karalat 140-141 NO 3
Karam = Karin 166-167 O 6
Karaman 180-181 D 4
Karaman-Maras 129 Q 8
Karamanmaras 182-183 G 4

Karmøy 130-131 A 8
Karnøy, Al- 170 E 5
Karnak, IL 152-153 M 7
Karnal 180-181 M 5
Karnes City, TX 154-155 FG 6
Karnī-Alpok 133 F 5
Karnijiskie, Alpi - 133 F 5
Karnijiskie, Alpi - 136-137 E 2
Karnische Alpen 136-137 E 2
Karnobat 136-137 M 4
Karnsche Alpy 133 E 2
Karoi 168-169 G 6
Karokobe = Kurukubi 171 B 2
Karokobe = Kurukubi 171 B 2
Karonga 168-169 H 4
Karoonda 196 DE 5
Kárõra = Kárúrah 166-167 M 5
Karosa 186-187 G 7
Karpapa 182-183 E 3
Karpaten = Carpazi 136-137 L 2-3
Karpathos [GR, ◦] 136-137 M 8
Kárpathos [GPs, ☆] 136-137 M 8
Karpaty 136-137 L 2-M 3
Karpedo 171 D 2
Karpenêsion 136-137 JK 6
Karpentaria, Zatoka - = Gulf of Carpentaria 194-195 G 2
Karpinsk= Krasnoturjinsk 178-179 L 5-6
Karpogory 138-139 P 1
Karrats Fjord 144-145 Za 3
Karree = Karee 174-175 G 5
Kars 180-181 E 2
Karsakpaj 178-179 M 8
Kársava 138-139 F 5
Karsiaka 136-137 M 6
Karsi 180-181 K 3
Karsiyaka, İzmir- 182-183 B 3
Kárún, Rüd-e - 180-181 FG 4
Karungi 130-131 K 4-5
Karungu 171 C 3
Kárúrah 166-167 M 5
Karviná 133 J 4
Karwar 180-181L8
Karyai 136-137 KL 5
Karymkary 178-179 M 5
Kás 180-181 BC 3
Kasa = Ui-do 188-189 E 5
Kasaba 171 AB 5
Kasaba = Kiği 182-183 J 3
Kasaba = Turgutlu 182-183 BC 3
Kasache 171 C 6
Kasachstan 178-179 J-P 8
Kasai [ZRE] 168-169 F 3
Kasai-Occidental 168-169 EF 3-4
Kasai-Oriental 168-169 FG 3-4
Kasaji 168-169 F 5
Kasama 168-169 H 5
Kasan = Kazan' 178-179 HJ 6
Kasana 171 BC 2
Kasane 168-169 FG 6
Kasanga 168-169 GH 4
Kasaoka 188-189 J 5
Kasari 171 J 2
Kasassa = Kościerzyna 133 HJ 2
Kasba Lake 144-145 Q 5
Kaschau = Kośice 133 K 4
Kaseda 188-189 H 7
Kasempa 168-169 G 5
Kasenga 168-169 G 5
Kasenyi 168-169 GH 2
Kasese 168-169 GH 2
Kashan = Káshán 180-181 G 4
Kashgar = Kashi 180-181 L 4
Kashi 184-185 D 4
Kashiba 188-189 G 5
Kashihara 188-189 K 5
Kashima [J, Ibaraki] 188-189 N 4
Kashima [J, Saga] 188-189 G 6
Kashin 138-139 L 5
Kashiwa 188-189 MN 5
Kashiwazaki 188-189 M 4
Kashk = K 333 K 4
Kashmar 180-181 H 3
Kashmir 180-181 LM 4
Kashmir 180-181 LM 4
Kashmir 180-181 LM 4
Kashi = Qáshqár 184-185 CD 4
Kashmor 180-181 K 6
Kashmund Ghar 180-181 L 4
Kasi = Qáshqár 184-185 CD 4
Kásifa 182-183 L 5
Kasia 188-189 A 4
Kasima 188-189 GH 6
Kasira 138-139 L 6
Kasirota = Pulau Kasiruta 186-187 J 7
Kasiruta, Pulau - 186-187 J 7
Kasivobara = Severo-Kuril'sk 178-179 de 7
Kaskaskia River 152-153 M 6
Kaskinen = Kaskö 130-131 J 6
Kaskö 130-131 J 6
Kasli 178-179 L 6
Kasimov 178-179 G 7
Kašin 138-139 L 5
Kašira 138-139 L 6
Kašira 138-139 L 6
Kasirskaja River 152-153 M 6
Kaslo 144-145 N 8
Kaso 130-131 J 6
Kasongan 186-187 F 7
Kasongo 168-169 G 3
Kasongo-Lunda 168-169 E 4
Kásos 136-137 M 8
Kaspicke more 180-181 F 1-G 3
Kaspijskij, Morze - 180-181 F 1-G 3
Kaspiroyka, Syzran'- 138-139 R 7
Kaspische Senke = Prikaspijskaja nizmennost' 140-141 MN 4-Q 2
Kaspisches Meer 180-181 F 1-G 3
Kaspische Zee 180-181 F 1-G 3
Kaspl'a 138-139 J 6
Kassnik = Kirkgeçit 182-183 K 3
Kassa = Kaşi 168-169 J 3
Kassa = Kośice 133 K 4
Kassa = K 333 K 4
Kassala 166-167 M 5

186-187 D 3
Kawthaung 186-187 C 4
Kaya [HV] 166-167 D 6
Kaya [J] 188-189 K 5
Kaya [RI] 186-187 J 6
Kayadirısı = Salmanli 182-183 F 3
Kayak Island 144-145 H 6
Kayambi 168-169 H 4
Kayâ Pyinnei 186-187 C 3
Kayar 172-173 A 2
Kaya-san 188-189 G 5
Kaycee, WY 152-153 C 4
Kayenta, AZ 150-151 H 7
Kayes 166-167 B 6
Kayhaydi 166-167 B 5
Kaymas 182-183 D 2
Kaynar 182-183 Q 3
Kaynaslı 182-183 D 2
Kayoa, Pulau - 186-187 J 6
Kaypak 182-183 G 4
Kayseri 180-181 D 3
Kaysville, UT 150-151 GH 5
Kayu, Teluk - 186-187 J 6
Kayumbi 168-169 H 4
Kayâ Pyinnei 186-187 C 3
Kazach 140-141 M 6
Kazachskij melkosopočnik 178-179 M-P 7-8
Kazachstan 178-179 J-P 8
Kazachstán 178-179 J-P 8
Kazahsztán = Aksaj 178-179 J 7
Kazak 140-141 M 6
Kazakh 140-141 M 6
Kazaki 178-179 UV 6
Kazáčinskoje [SU, Jenisej] 178-179 R 6
Kazáčinskoje [SU, Kirenga] 178-179 U 6
Kazáčje 178-179 a 3
Kazáčinskoje [SU, Jenisej] 178-179 R 6
Kazáčinskoje [SU, Kirenga] 178-179 U 6
Kazáčje 178-179 a 3
Kazah-hátság = Kazachskij Melkosopočnik 178-179 M-P 7-8
Kazahsztán 178-179 J-P 8
Kazachskij melkosopočnik 178-179 M-P 7-8
Kazachstán 178-179 J-P 8
Kazajstán 178-179 J-P 8
Kazakhie, Steppe de - = Kazachskij Melkosopočnik 178-179 M-P 7-8
Kazakhstan 178-179 J-P 8
Kazakistan 141-140 N-Q 2
Kazamoto = Katsumoto
Kazan [SU, Tatarskaja ASSR] 178-179 HJ 6
Kazan' [SU, Vjatka] 138-139 RS 4
Kazan [TR] 182-183 E 2
Kazandağ 182-183 K 3
Kazandžik 180-181 GH 2
Kazanka [SU, Rossijskaja SFSR] 138-139 R 6
Kazanka [SU, Ukrainskaja SSR] 140-141 F 3
Kazanlak 136-137 L 4
Kazanovka 138-139 M 7
Kazan River 144-145 Q 5
Kazanskaja 140-141 K 2
Kazan [SU, Zapadno-Sibirskaja nizmennost'] 178-179 M 6
Kazantip, mys - 140-141 G 4
Kazaskie, Pogórze - = Kazachskij Melkosopočnik 178-179 M-P 7-9
Kazašská plošina = Kazachskij Melkosopočnik 178-179 M-P 7-9
Kazatin 140-141 D 2
Kazaure 172-173 GH 2
Kazbegi 140-141 M 5
Kazbek, gora - 140-141 M 5
Kazerün 180-181 G 5
Kažım = Kažym 138-139 ST 3
Kazi-Magomed 140-141 O 6
Kázimíyah, Baghdad-Al- 182-183 L 6
Kazimoto 171 D 5
Kazincbarcika 133 K 4
Kazlu Rüda 138-139 DE 6
Kaztalovka 140-141 O 2
Kazumba 168-169 F 4
Kazungula 168-169 G 6
Kazvin = Qazvin 180-181 FG 3
Kažym [SU, Chanty-Mansijskaja AO] 178-179 K 6
Kažym [SU, Komi ASSR] 138-139 ST 3
Kbaisa = Kubaysah 182-183 K 6
Kea 136-137 L 7
Kearns Canyon, AZ 150-151 H 8
Kearney, NE 146-147 G 3
Keban 182-183 H 3
Keban Baraji 182-183 H 3
Kebäng 180-181 PQ 5
Kebbi 172-173 FG 2
Kébémèr 166-167 A 5
Kebkábiya = Kabkábiyah 166-167 J 6
Kebnekajse 130-131 H 4
Kebumen 186-187 E 8
Keçiborlu 182-183 CD 3
Kecskemét 133 J 5
Keda 140-141 K 6
Kedabek 140-141 M 6
Kedainiai 138-139 DE 6
Keddie, CA 150-151 C 5-6
Kedia d'Idjil = Kidyat Ijjíl 166-167 B 4
Kédiri 186-187 F 8
Kédougou 166-167 B 6
Keele Peak 144-145 KL 5
Keeler, CA 150-151 E 7
Keele River 144-145 L 5
Keeling, Bacia de - 124-125 OP 6
Keeling, Bassin de - 124-125 OP 6
Keeling, Cuenca de - 124-125 OP 6
Keeling Basin 124-125 OP 6
Keelingbecken 124-125 OP 6
Keelingbekken 124-125 OP 6
Kee-lung 184-185 N 6
Keene, NH 148-149 G 3
Keesevielle, NY 148-149 G 2
Keetmanshoop 168-169 E 7
Keewatin, District of 144-145 RS 4-5
Kefa 166-167 M 7
Kefallénía 136-137 J 6
Kéfalos 136-137 M 7
Kefamenanu 186-187 HJ 8
Kefar Ata = Qiryat-Ata' 182-183 F 6
Keferdiz 182-183 G 4
Keffi 172-173 G 3
Kéfira = Kebira 166-167 JK 5
Kéfisiá 182-183 L 5
Kefkén1 Adasi 182-183 D 2
Keftiya 166-167 M 6
Kegel = Keila 138-139 E 4
Kegeun Terbi 166-167 H 4
Kegulta 140-141 M 3
Kehl 133 CD 4
Kei 171 B 2

Keiki-dō = Kyŏnggi-do 188-189 F 4
Keila 138-139 E 4
Keimoes 174-175 D 5
Kei Mouth 174-175 H 7
Keishō-hokudō = Kyŏngsangpukto 188-189 G 4
Keishō-nandō = Kyŏngsangnamdo 188-189 FG 5
Keiskamahoek = Keiskammahoek 174-175 G 7
Keiskammahoek 174-175 G 7
Keiskammarivier 174-175 G 7
Keitele 130-131 LM 6
Keith 132 E 3
Keith [AUS] 194-195 GH 7
Keith Arm 144-145 M 4
Keithsburg, IL 152-153 L 5
Keithville, LA 154-155 HJ 4
Keitsaub 174-175 C 2
Keitū = Keytū 182-183 N 5
Kék-Nílus = Abay 166-167 M 6
Kela 172-173 C 3
Kelafo 166-167 N 7
Kelan 190-191 C 2
Keles 182-183 C 3
Keleti-Erg = Al-'Irq al-Kabīr ash-Sharqī 166-167 F 2-3
Kelet-szibériai-hát 120 B 36-1
Kelet-szibériai-tenger 178-179 d-h 3
Kelford, NC 148-149 E 6
Kelifely, Causse du - 168-169 KL 6
Kelil'vun, gora - 178-179 g 4
Kelkit 182-183 H 2
Kelkit Çayı 182-183 G 2
Kellė 168-169 D 2-3
Keller Lake 144-145 M 5
Kellett, Cape - 144-145 L 3
Kelleys Island 152-153 P 5
Kelleys Islands 148-149 B 4
Kelliher, MN 152-153 J 1-2
Kellogg, ID 150-151 EF 2
Kelloselkä 130-131 N 4
Kelm = Kelmė 138-139 D 6
Kelmė 138-139 D 6
Kélo 166-167 H 7
Kelowna 144-145 N 7-8
Kelso [ZA] 168-169 H 9
Kelso, CA 150-151 F 8
Kelso, WA 150-151 B 2
Kelta-tenger 132 C 6
Keltische See 132 C 6
Keltische Zee 132 C 6
Kelton Pass 150-151 G 5
Kelu 190-191 C 11
Kelulun He = Herlen He 184-185 M 2
Kelushi = Kelu 190-191 C 11
Kelvin, AZ 150-151 H 9
Kem' [SU, ●] 178-179 E 4
Kemä 184-185 H 6
Ké Macina 166-167 C 6
Kemah 182-183 H 3
Kemaliye 182-183 H 3
Kemaliye = Vakfıbekir 182-183 H 2
Kemalpaşa [TR, Artvin] 182-183 J 2
Kemalpaşa [TR, İzmir] 182-183 B 3
Kemanai = Towada 188-189 N 2
Kembalpur 180-181 L 4
Kembolcha 166-167 MN 6
Kemer [TR, Antalya] 182-183 D 4
Kemer [TR, Burdur] 182-183 D 4
Kemer [TR, Muğla] 182-183 C 4
Kemer = Eskiköy 182-183 D 4
Kemerovo 178-179 PQ 6
Kemi 130-131 L 5
Kemijärvi [SF, ●] 130-131 M 4
Kemijärvi [SF, ~] 130-131 MN 4
Kemijoki 130-131 L 4-5
Kemijoki = Kem' 178-179 E 4
Kemľa 138-139 P 6
Kemmerer, WY 150-151 H 5
Kémo-Ibingui 166-167 H 7
Kemparana 172-173 D 2
Kemp, TX 154-155 G 4
Kemp Land 121 C 6
Kemp, Lake - 154-155 F 4
Kemp Peninsula 121 B 31
Kempsey 194-195 K 6
Kempten 133 E 5
Kemptville 148-149 EF 2
Kena 138-139 M 2
Keňa 168-169 JK 2
Kena = Qinā 166-167 L 3
Kenai, AK 144-145 F 5
Kenai Mountains 144-145 F 6-G 5
Kenai Peninsula 144-145 FG 5
Kenamo 144-145 L 7
Kenansville, FL 148-149 c 3
Kenbridge, VA 148-149 DE 6
Kendal 132 E 4
Kendal [ZA] 174-175 H 4
Kendall, KS 152-153 F 7
Kendallville, IN 152-153 O 5
Kendari 186-187 H 7
Kendawangan 186-187 F 7
Kēndrāpaḍā = Kendrapara 180-181 O 6
Kendrāpāra 180-181 O 6
Kendrew 174-175 F 7
Kendrick, ID 150-151 E 2
Kendu 171 C 3
Kenedy, TX 154-155 FG 6
Kenega = Kenegha 174-175 H 6
Kenegha 174-175 H 6
Kenema 166-167 B 7
Kenesaw, NE 152-153 G 5
Kenge 168-169 D 3
Kengtung = Kyöngdôn 186-187 CD 2
Kenhardt 168-169 F 8
Kenia 168-169 JK 2
Kéniéba 166-167 B 6
Kenitra = Al-Q'nitrah 166-167 C 2
Kenli 190-191 G 3
Kenmare, ND 152-153 EF 1
Kenmare [IRL, ~] 132 A 6
Kenmare [IRL, ●] 132 B 6
Kenmore, NY 148-149 D 3
Kenna, NM 154-155 CD 4
Kennebec, SC 152-153 FG 4
Kennebec River 148-149 HJ 2
Kennebunk, ME 148-149 H 3
Kennedy, Mount - 144-145 J 5
Kennedy Channel 144-145 WX 1-2
Kenner, LA 154-155 K 5-6
Kennett, MO 154-155 KL 2
Kennewick, WA 150-151 D 2
Kenney Dam 144-145 M 7
Keno Hill 144-145 JK 5
Kenora 144-145 S 8
Kenosha, WI 146-147 J 3
Kenova, WV 148-149 B 5
Kenozero 138-139 M 2
Kensal, ND 152-153 G 2
Kensett, AR 154-155 K 3
Kent 132 G 6
Kent, MN 152-153 H 2
Kent, OH 148-149 C 4
Kent, OR 150-151 C 3
Kent, TX 154-155 C 5
Kent, WA 150-151 B 2
Kentau 178-179 M 9
Kent Group 196 cd 1
Kentland, IN 152-153 N 5
Kenton, OH 152-153 P 5
Kenton, OK 154-155 D 2
Kent Peninsula 144-145 P 4
Kentucky 146-147 JK 4
Kentucky Lake 146-147 J 4
Kentucky River 152-153 O 6
Kentwood, LA 154-155 K 5
Kenya 168-169 JK 2
Kenya 168-169 JK 2
Kenya, Mount - 168-169 J 2-3
Keokuk, IA 146-147 H 3
Keosauqua, IA 152-153 L 5
Kepce Dağları 182-183 K 4
Kępno 133 J 3
Keppel Bay 194-195 K 4
Kepsut 182-183 C 3
Kepulauan Banjak 186 C 6
Kerala 180-181 M 8-9
Kerang 194-195 H 7
Kerasus = Giresun 180-181 D 2
Kerava 130-131 L 7
Kerbi = Poliny-Osipenko 178-179 a 7
Kerby, OR 150-151 B 4
Kerč' 140-141 H 4
Kerčenskij poluostrov 140-141 GH 4
Kerčenskij proliv 140-141 H 4
Kerčevskij 138-139 UV 4
Kerčomja 138-139 T 3
Kerema 186-187 N 8
Kerempe Burnu 182-183 E 1
Keren 166-167 M 5
Kerens, TX 154-155 G 4
Kerewan 172-173 A 2
Kerga 138-139 PQ 2
Kerguelen 124-125 N 8
Kerguelen 124-125 N 8
Kerguelen, Grande Dorsale des - 124-125 N 8-J 9
Kerguelen, Plataforma das - 124-125 N 8-O 9
Kerguelen, Plataforma de las - 124-125 N 8-J 9
Kerguelen e Gaussberg, Platea di 124-125 N 8-O 9
Kerguelen-Gaussberg Ridge 124-125 N 8-J 9
Kerguelen-Gaußberg-Rücken 124-125 N 8-O 9
Kerguelen-Gaussbergrug 124-125 N 8-J 9
Kericho 171 C 3
Kerinci, Gunung - 186-187 D 7
Kerio 171 D 2
Keriske 178-179 Z 4
Keriya 184-185 E 4
Keriya Darya 184-185 E 4
Kerkenna, Îles - = Arkhbīl Qarqannah 166-167 G 2
Kerkhoven, MN 152-153 J 3
Kerki 180-181 K 3
Kérkyra [GR, ⊙] 136-137 H 6
Kérkyra [GR , ●] 136-137 H 6
Kerling 130-131 de 2
Kerlingarfjöll 130-131 d 2
Kerma = Karmah 166-167 L 5
Kermadec, Fossa de - 194-195 Q 6-7
Kermadec, Fossa di - 194-195 Q 6-7
Kermadec, Fosse des - 194-195 Q 6-7
Kermadec, Îles - 194-195 PQ 6
Kermadec-árok 194-195 Q 6-7
Kermadecgraben 194-195 Q 6-7
Kermadec Islands 194-195 PQ 6
Kermadec-Tonga, Fossa - 124-125 T 6-7
Kermadec-Tonga, Fossa de - 124-125 T 6-7
Kermadecký příkop 194-195 Q 6-7
Kermadec-Tonga, Fosa de - 194-195 Q 6-7
Kermadec-Tonga, Fosse de - 124-125 T 6-7
Kermadec-Tonga-Graben 198-199 J 5-6
Kermadec Tonga Trench 124-125 T 6-7
Kermadec Tongatrog 124-125 T 6-7
Kermadec Trench 194-195 Q 6-7
Kermadectrog 194-195 Q 6-7
Kerman 180-181 H 4
Kerman, CA 150-151 CD 7
Kermānshāh = Bākhtarān 180-181 F 4
Kermānshāhān = 1 ◃ 180-181 F 4
Kerme Körfezi 182-183 B 4
Kermit, TX 154-155 D 5
Kernaka = Kornaka 172-173 G 2
Kern River 150-151 D 8
Kernville, CA 150-151 D 8
Kérouané 166-167 C 7
Kerrick, TX 154-155 D 2
Kerrville, TX 154-155 F 5
Kershaw, SC 148-149 C 7
Kertel = Kärdla 138-139 D 4
Kertsch = Kerč' 140-141 H 4
Kerulen = Cherlen gol 184-185 L 2
Keržencc 138-139 P 5
Keşan 182-183 B 2
Kesánē = Keşan 182-183 B 2
Keşap 182-183 H 2
Kesennuma 188-189 NO 3
Keserü-tavak = Al-Buḥayrat al-Murrat al-Kubrá 170 E 2
Keshan 184-185 O 2
Keshvar, Īstgāh-e - 182-183 N 6
Keskin 182-183 E 3
Keski-Suomen lääni 130-131 L 6
Kes'ma 138-139 L 4
Kestell 174-175 H 5
Kestenga 130-131 OP 5
Kesten'ga 178-179 E 4
Keszthely 133 H 5
Keť 178-179 P 6
Keta 166-167 E 7
Keta, ozero - 178-179 QR 4
Ketapang [RI, Kalimantan] 186-187 EF 7
Ketchikan, AK 144-145 K 6
Ketchum, ID 150-151 F 4
Kete Krachi 166-167 DE 7
Kętrzyn 133 K 1-2
Kettharin Kyûn 186-187 C 4
Kettle Falls, WA 150-151 DE 1
Kettle River Range 150-151 D 1
Ketou 172-173 F 4
Kettle Point 152-153 PQ 4
Kettle River 152+153 K 2
Ketumbaine 171 D 3
Keulen = Köln 133 C 3
Kevin, MT 150-151 H 1
Kevir = Dasht-e Kavīr 180-181 GH 4
Kewanee, IL 152-153 M 5
Kewaunee, WI 152-153 N 3
Keweenaw Bay 152-153 MN 2
Keweenaw Peninsula 146-147 J 2
Keweenaw Point 152-153 N 2
Kewir = Dasht-e Kavīr 180-181 GH 4
Kexholm = Prioz'orsk 178-179 DE 5
Keya Paha River 152-153 FG 4
Keyes, OK 154-155 D 2
Keyhole Reservoir 152-153 D 3
Key Largo 148-149 cd 4
Key Largo, FL 148-149 c 4
Keyser, WV 148-149 D 5
Keystone, SD 152-153 E 4
Keysville, VA 148-149 D 6
Keytū 182-183 N 5
Key West, FL 146-147 K 7
Kez 138-139 T 5
Kgokgole 174-175 E 4
Kgokgolelaagte = Kgokgole 174-175 E 4
Khaanzuur, Raas - = Raas Khansiir 166-167 ab 1
Khabīr, Zāb al = Zāb al-Kabīr 182-183 K 4
Khabra Najid = Habrat Najid 182-183 K 7
Khābūr, Nahr al- 180-181 E 3
Khābūrah, Al- 180-181 H 6
Khādim, Shūshat al- 170 B 3
Khāf , Rūd - = Khvāf 180-181 J 4
Khaibar = Shurayf 180-181 D 5
Khairabad 180-181 N 5
Khakass Autonomous Republic = 10 ◃ 178-179 R 7
Khalafābād 182-183 N 7
Khâlda, Bîr - = Bi'r Hālidah 182-183 B 7
Khalīj as-Sīntirā', Al- 166-167 A 4
Khalīj -e Fārs , Banāder va Jazāyere - = 5 ◃ 180-181 G 5
Khalil, El- = Al-Halil 182-183 F 7
Khaliq tau 184-185 E 3
Khāliṣ, Al- 182-183 L 6
Khalkhāl 182-183 N 4
Khalūf, Al- 180-181 H 6
Kham 184-185 H 5
Khamāsin, Al- 180-181 EF 6
Khambat = Khambhat 180-181 L 6
Khambhat 180-181 L 6
Khambhāt nī Khāḍī = Gulf of Cambay 180-181 L 6
Khamir 180-181 E 7
Khāmis, Al-Jandal al- 166-167 L 5
Khampa Dsong 184-185 F 6
Khamsa, Bîr el- = Bi'r al-Khamsah 166-167 K 2
Khamsah, Bi'r al- 166-167 K 2
Khan 174-175 A 2
Khān al-Baghdādī 182-183 K 6
Khānaqīn = Khāniqīn 182-183 L 5
Khān az-Zabīb 182-183 G 7
Khandaq, Al- 166-167 KL 5
Khandaq, El- = Al-Khandaq 166-167 KL 5
Khaṅḍavā = Khandwa 180-181 M 6
Khandwa 180-181 M 6
Khan ez Zābib = Khān az-Zabīb 182-183 G 7
Khangai = Changajn nuruu 184-185 HJ 2
Khāniqīn 180-181 F 4
Khānpūr [PAK, Sindh] 180-181 KL 5
Khanshalah 166-167 F 1
Khansiir, Raas - 166-167 ab 1
Khantan = Kuantan 186-187 D 6
Khanty-Mansi Autonomous Area 178-179 L-P 5
Khanty-Mansis, District National des - 178-179 L-P 5
Khān Yūnūs 170 EF 2
Khanzi 168-169 F 7
Khanzi = Ghanzi 168-169 F 7
Khānzūr, Ras - = Raas Khaanzuur 166-167 ab 1
Kharāb, Al- 180-181 EF 7
Kharagpur [IND, West Bengal] 180-181 O 6
Kharan Kalat = Khārān Qalāt 180-181 K 5
Khārān Qalāt 180-181 K 5
Kharaz, Jabal - 180-181 E 8
Kharbin = Harbin 184-185 O 2
Khârga, El- = Al-Khārījah 166-167 L 3
Khârga, Wâḥât el- = Al-Wāḥāt al-Khārījah 166-167 KL 3-4
Kharīfūt 180-181 G 7
Khārijah, Al- 166-167 L 3
Khārijah, Al-Wāḥāt al- 166-167 KL 3-4
Kharīṭ, Wādī al- 170 EF 5
Kharîṭ, Wâdî el- = Wādī al-Kharīṭ 170 EF 5
Kharj, Al- 180-181 F 6
Khārk, Jazīreh-ye - 180-181 FG 5
Kharkassie, Région Autonome des - = 10 ◃ 178-179 R 7
Kharkheh, Rūd-e - 182-183 M 6
Kharkov = Char'kov 140-141 H 1-2
Khar Rūd 182-183 N 5
Khartoem = Al-Khartūm 166-167 L 5
Khartoum = Al-Khartūm 166-167 L 5
Khartúm = Al-Khartūm 166-167 L 5
Khartúm, Al- 166-167 L 5
Khartum = Al-Khartūm 166-167 L 5
Khartūm Baḥrī, Al- 166-167 L 5
Khartûm Baḥrī, El- = Al-Khartūm Baḥrī 166-167 L 5
Khaṣab, Al- 180-181 H 5
Khashm al-Qirbah 166-167 LM 6
Khāsh Rōd 180-181 J 4
Khaṭâṭba, El- = Al-Haṭāṭibah 170 D 2
Khaṭṭ, Wād al- 166-167 B 3
Khawr al-Amaīyah 182-183 N 8
Khawr al-Fakkān 180-181 H 5
Khawr Rūrī 180-181 G 7
Khay' 180-181 E 7
Khaybar, Ḥarrat - 180-181 DE 5
Khāybar, Kotal - 180-181 L 4
Khayrpūr [PAK, Punjab] 180-181 K 5
Khazhung Tsho 184-185 F 5
Khāzir, Nahr al- 182-183 K 4
Khazir Su = Nahr al-Khāzir 182-183 K 4
Khechmâ = Al-Bogham 182-183 J 5
Khedir, Al- = Khiḍr Dardash 182-183 L 7
Khemarat 186-187 DE 3
Khem Belder = Kyzyl 178-179 R 7
Khenachich, El - 166-167 D 4
Khenchela = Khanshalah 166-167 F 1
Khentei Nuruu = Chentijn Nuruu 184-185 K 2
Kherson = Cherson 140-141 F 3
Khiḍr Dardash 182-183 L 7
Khiehshow = Jieshou 190-191 E 5
Khīrābād = Khairabad 180-181 N 5
Khirr, Wādī al- 180-181 E 4
Khmel'nyc'kij = Chmel'nickij 140-141 C 2
Khnâchich, El - 166-167 D 4
Khobdo = Chovd 184-185 G 2
Khobso Gol = Chövsgöl nuur 184-185 J 1
Khökh Nuur = Chöch nuur 184-185 H 4
Khökh Schili uul = Chöch Šili uul 184-185 FG 4
Khomām 182-183 NO 4
Khomas Highland = Khomasplato 168-169 E 7
Khomeyn 182-183 NO 6
Khomodimo 174-175 EF 2
Khondāb 182-183 N 5
Khong, Mae Nam - 186-187 D 3
Khong Sedone = Muang Khôngxédon 186-187 E 3
Khon Kaen 186-187 D 3
Khorāsān 180-181 H 3-4
Khorāsān, Kavīre - = Dasht-e Kavīr 180-181 GH 4
Khore 174-175 E 2
Khorat = Nakhon Ratchasima 186-187 D 3-4
Khōrmāl = Hūrmāl 182-183 LM 5
Khorramābād [IR, Lorestān] 180-181 FG 4
Khorramābād [IR, Māzandarān] 182-183 O 4
Khorramshahr 180-181 F 4
Khorsabad 182-183 K 4
Khosrovī 182-183 L 5
Khosrowābād [IR, Hamadān] 182-183 N 5
Khosrowābād [IR, Kordestan] 182-183 M 5
Khotan 184-185 DE 4
Khotan darya 184-185 E 3-4
Khoti 174-175 E 3
Khourībga = Khurībqah 166-167 C 2
Khowst 180-181 KL 4
Khūḍdar 180-181 K 5
Khuff 180-181 E 6
Khuis 174-175 D 4
Khükhe Noor = Chöch nuur 184-185 H 4
Khums, Al- 166-167 GH 2
Khurasan = Khorāsān 180-181 H 3-4
Khurayṣ 180-181 F 5
Khurībqah 166-167 C 2
Khūrīyā Mūrīyā, Jazā'ir - 180-181 H 7
Khurmah, Al- 180-181 E 6
Khūrmāl 182-183 LM 5
Khurr, Wādī al- = Wādī al-Khirr 182-183 K 7
Khushāb 180-181 L 4
Khūzestān 180-181 F 4
Khvāf 180-181 J 4
Khvoy 180-181 EF 3
Khwāf = Khvāf 180-181 J 4
Khyber Pass = Kotal Khāybar 180-181 L 4
Khyetentshering 184-185 G 5
Kiabakari 171 C 3
Kiama 196 K 5
Kiambi 168-169 G 4
Kiamichi Mountains 154-155 H 3
Kiamichi River 154-155 H 3-4
Kiamusze = Jiamusi 184-185 P 2
Kian = Ji'an 184-185 LM 6
Kiangling = Jiangling 190-191 CD 6
Kiangning = Nanjing 184-185 M 5
Kiangshan = Jiangshan 190-191 G 7
Kiangsi = Jiangxi 184-185 LM 6
Kiangsu = Jiangsu 184-185 MN 5
Kiangtu = Jiangdu 190-191 G 5
Kiangyin = Jiangyin 190-191 H 6
Kiantajärvi 130-131 N 5
Kiaohsien = Jiao Xian 184-185 M 4
Kiating = Jiading 190-191 H 6
Kiautschoubucht = Jiazhou Wan 190-191 H 3-4
Kiawah Island 148-149 CD 8
Kiayu = Jiayu 190-191 D 6-7
Kiayukwan = Jiuquan 184-185 H 4
Kibaha = Bagamoyo 168-169 J 4
Kibale 171 B 2
Kibali 168-169 GH 2
Kibamba 168-169 G 3
Kibangou 168-169 D 3
Kibarty = Kybartai 138-139 D 6
Kibau 168-169 HJ 4
Kibaya 168-169 J 4
Kiberashi 171 D 4
Kiberege 168-169 J 4
Kibiti 171 D 4
Kiboko 171 D 3
Kibombo 168-169 G 3
Kibondo 168-169 H 3
Kıbrıscık 182-183 DE 2
Kibungu 168-169 H 3
Kibuye 171 AB 5
Kibwezi 168-169 J 3
Kičevo 136-137 J 5
Kichčik 178-179 de 7
Kichinev = Kišin'ov 140-141 D 3
Kicking Horse Pass 144-145 NO 7
Kičmengskij Gorodok 138-139 P 3
Kidal 166-167 E 5
Kidaroupérou 172-173 F 3
Kidatu 168-169 J 4
Kidd's Beach 174-175 GH 7
Kidepo National Park 168-169 H 2
Kidete 171 D 4
Kidira 166-167 B 6
Kidjaboun 172-173 EF 3
Kidston 194-195 H 3
Kiel 133 E 1
Kiel, WI 152-153 M 4
Kielce 133 K 3
Kieler Bucht 133 E 1
Kienan = Qian'an 190-191 G 1
Kiến Hung = Go Quao 186-187 DE 5
Kienkiang = Qianjiang 190-191 B 7
Kienli = Jianli 190-191 D 7
Kienning = Jian'ou 184-185 M 6
Kienshih = Jianshi 190-191 B 6
Kienshui = Jianshui 184-185 J 7
Kienteh = Jiande 190-191 G 7
Kierunavaara 130-131 J 4
Kiestinki = Kesten'ga 178-179 E 4
Kieta 186-187 j 6
Kiev = Kijev 140-141 DE 1
Kiëv = Kijev 140-141 DE 1
Kiew = Kijev 140-141 DE 1
Kiewietskuil 174-175 E 7
Kifah 166-167 B 5
Kifaya 172-173 B 2
Kiffa = Kifah 166-167 B 5
Kifl, Al- 182-183 L 6
Kifrī 182-183 L 5
Kigali 168-169 GH 3
Kiganga 171 C 4
Kiği 182-183 J 3
Kigoma 168-169 G 3
Kigosi 171 B 3
Kıgzı = Gürpinar 182-183 K 3
Kiha = Kwiha 166-167 MN 6
Kihelkonna 138-139 D 4
Kihindi 171 D 5
Kihnu 138-139 D 4
Kihowera 171 D 5
Kihsien = Qi Xian [TJ, Henan] 190-191 E 4
Kihsien = Qi Xian [TJ, Shanxi] 190-191 D 3
Kihti = Skiftet 130-131 J 7
Kihurio 171 D 4
Kichčik 178-179 de 7
Kii hantō 184-185 Q 5
Kiik-Atlama, mys - 140-141 GH 4
Kii sammyaku 188-189 KL 5-6
Kii-suidō 184-185 PQ 5
Kijang 188-189 G 5
Kijevka [SU, Kazachskaja SSSR] 178-179 N 7
Kijevka [SU, Rossijskaja SFSR] 188-189 J 1
Kijevskoje vodochranilišče 140-141 E 1
Kijów = Kyyiv 38-39 F 5
Kijów = Kijev 140-141 DE 1
Kikerino 138-139 G 4
Kikinda 136-137 J 3
Kikládok 136-137 L 6
Kiknur 138-139 Q 5
Kikombo 171 CD 4
Kikonai 188-189 B 3
Kikori 186-187 M 8
Kikus = Boľšoje Kikus 138-139 V 3
Kikwit 168-169 E 4
Kil 130-131 E 8
Kilange, River - 172-173 J 3
Kilauea Crater 186-187 ef 4
Kil'azi 140-141 O 6
Kilbuck Mountains 144-145 E 5-D 6
Kilchu 188-189 G 2
Kilcoy 194-195 K 5
Kildinstroj 130-131 PQ 3
Kildonan 168-169 H 6
Kilemary 138-139 Q 5
Kilembe 171 B 2
Kilemon 174-175 D 2
Kilgore, ID 150-151 GH 3
Kilgore, TX 154-155 H 4
Kili 192-193 H 4
Kilifi 168-169 JK 3
Kilija 140-141 D 4
Kilimanjaro [EAT, ▲] 168-169 J 3
Kilimanjaro [EAT, ⭑] 168-169 J 3
Kilimatinde 168-169 HJ 4
Kilin = Jilin 184-185 N 2-O 3
Kilingi-Nõmme 138-139 E 4
Kilis 182-183 G 4
Kilkee 132 AB 5
Kilkenny 132 C 5
Kilkis 136-137 K 5
Killarney [IRL] 132 B 5
Killarney [AUS] 196 L 2
Killdeer, ND 152-153 E 2
Killdeer Mountains 152-153 E 2
Killeen, TX 154-155 G 5
Killiecrankie Pass 132 E 3
Killin 132 D 3
Killinek Island 144-145 Y 5
Killington Peak 148-149 G 3
Killybegs 132 B 4
Kilmarnock 132 DE 4
Kil'mez' [SU, ~] 138-139 S 5
Kil'mez' [SU, ● Udmurtskaja ASSR] 138-139 S 5
Kil'mez' [SU, ● Vjatka] 138-139 S 5
Kilmichael, MS 154-155 L 4
Kilmore 196 G 6
Kilo 171 B 2
Kilombero 168-169 J 4
Ki-long = Chilung 184-185 N 6
Kilonia = Kiel 133 E 1
Kilosa 168-169 J 4
Kilossa = Kilosa 168-169 J 4
Kilpisjärvi 130-131 J 3
Kilrea 132 C 4
Kilrush 132 B 5
Kiltān Island 180-181 L 8
Kilwa 168-169 G 4
Kilwa, Khirbat - 182-183 G 8
Kilwa Kisiwani 168-169 JK 4
Kilwa-Kissiwni = Kilwa Kisiwani 168-169 JK 4
Kilwa Kivinje 168-169 JK 4
Kilwa-Kiwindje = Kilwa Kivinje 168-169 JK 4
Kim 172-173 H 4
Kim, CO 152-153 E 7
Kimaam 186-187 L 8
Kimali 171 C 3
Kimama, ID 150-151 G 4
Kimasozero 130-131 O 5
Kimba 196 C 4
Kimball, MN 152-153 J 3
Kimball, NE 152-153 E 5
Kimball, SD 152-153 G 4
Kimbe 186-187 gh 6
Kimbe Bay 186-187 h 6
Kimberley [AUS] 194-195 E 3
Kimberley [CDN] 150-151 EF 1
Kimberley [ZA] 168-169 FG 8
Kimberly, NV 150-151 F 6
Kimchaek 184-185 OP 3
Kimch'ŏn 184-185 O 4
Kimen = Qimen 190-191 F 7
Kimhandu 171 D 4
Kimje 188-189 F 5
Kimkang = Chengmai 184-185 KL 8
Kimōlos 136-137 L 7
Kimparana = Kemparana 172-173 D 2
Kimpoku san 188-189 LM 3
Kimry 178-179 F 6
Kimuenza 168-169 E 3
Kina 184-185 E-K 5
Kinabalu, Gunung - 186-187 G 5
Kincaid, KS 152-153 J 6
Kincardine [CDN] 152-153 Q 3
Kinchinjunga = Gangchhendsönga 180-181 O 5
Kinder, LA 154-155 J 5
Kindersley 144-145 P 7
Kindia 166-167 B 6
Kindu 168-169 G 3
Kinel' 178-179 J 7
Kinel'skije jary 138-139 ST 7
Kinešma 178-179 G 6
King and Queen Court House, VA 148-149 E 6
Kingchow = Jiangling 184-185 L 5
Kingchwan = Jingchuan 184-185 K 4
King City, CA 150-151 C 7
King City, MO 152-153 J 5
King Edward VIIIth Gulf 121 C 6-7
Kingfisher, OK 154-155 G 3
King George V[th] Land 121 BC 15-16
King George VIth Sound 121 B 29-30
King George Island 121 CD 130-131
King George Sound 194-195 CD 7
King Hill, ID 150-151 F 4
Kinghsien = Jing Xian 190-191 G 6
Kingisepp 138-139 G 4
Kingisepp [SU, Luga] 130-131 N 8
Kingisepp [SU, Saaremaa] 130-131 K 8
King Island [AUS] 194-195 H 7
Kingku = Jinggu 184-185 J 7
King Lear 150-151 D 5
King Leopold Ranges 194-195 DE 3
Kingman, AZ 150-151 FG 8
Kingman, KS 152-153 GH 7
Kingmen = Jingmen 190-191 CD 6
King Mountain [USA, Oregon] 150-151 D 4
King Mountain [USA, Texas] 154-155 D 5
Kingoonya 194-195 G 6
King Oscar Land 144-145 TU 2
Kings Canyon National Park 150-151 D 7
Kingscote 194-195 G 7
Kingscourt 132 C 5
Kingsland, GA 148-149 C 9
Kingsland, TX 154-155 F 5
Kingsley 174-175 J 4
Kingsley, IA 152-153 HJ 4
King's Lynn 132 FG 5
Kings Mountain, NC 148-149 C 7
King Sound 194-195 D 3
Kings Peaks 146-147 DE 3
Kingsport, TN 148-149 B 6
Kings River 150-151 CD 7
Kingston [CDN] 144-145 Y 9
Kingston [JA] 146-147 L 8
Kingston [NZ] 194-195 N 9
Kingston, MO 152-153 J 6
Kingston, NY 148-149 FG 4
Kingston, OK 154-155 G 3-4
Kingston, PA 148-149 EF 4
Kingston, WA 150-151 B 2
Kingston Peak 150-151 EF 8
Kingston SE 194-195 G 7
Kingston upon Hull 132 FG 5
Kingstown [WV] 146-147 O 9
Kingstown [IRL] 132 CD 5
Kingstree, SC 148-149 D 8
Kingsville, TX 146-147 G 6
Kingswood 174-175 F 4
King William Island 144-145 R 4
King William's Town 168-169 G 9
Kingwood, WV 148-149 D 5
Kingyang = Qingyang 184-185 K 4
Kingyuan = Yishan 184-185 K 7
Kingyun = Qingyun 190-191 F 3
Kinhwa = Jinhua 184-185 MN 6
Kınık 182-183 B 3
Kinkala 168-169 D 3
Kinkazan tō 188-189 NO 3
Kinmen 190-191 G 9
Kinmen Dao = Chin-mên Tao 184-185 M 7
Kinmount 148-149 D 2
Kinmundy, IL 152-153 M 6
Kinnaird's Head 132 F 3
Kinneret, Yam - 180-181 D 4
Kino kawa 188-189 K 5
Kinomoto = Kumano 188-189 L 6
Kinosaki 188-189 K 5
Kinross 132 E 3
Kinsale 132 B 6
Kinsey, MT 152-153 D 2
Kinshan = Jinshan 190-191 H 6
Kinshasa 168-169 E 3
Kinsien = Jin Xian 184-185 N 4
Kinsley, KS 152-153 G 7
Kinston, NC 146-147 L 4
Kintampo 166-167 D 7
Kintan = Jintan 190-191 G 6
Kin-tcheou = Jinzhou 184-185 N 3
Kintinian 172-173 C 3
Kintinku 171 C 4
Kintop 186-187 G 7
Kintyre 132 D 4
Kinyangiri 171 C 4
Kinyati 171 C 1
Kioesjoedrempel 184-185 P 6-Q 7
Kios = Gemlik 182-183 C 2
Kioshan = Queshan 184-185 L 5
Kioto = Kyōto 184-185 PQ 4
Kiowa, CO 152-153 D 6
Kiowa, KS 154-155 F 2
Kiowa, OK 154-155 GH 3
Kiowa Creek 152-153 D 5-6
Kipembawe 168-169 H 4
Kipengere 171 C 5
Kipeta 171 B 5
Kipili 168-169 H 4
Kipini 168-169 K 3
Kiptopeke, VA 148-149 F 6
Kipushi 168-169 G 5
Kir'a 138-139 Q 6
Kirakira 186-187 k 7
Kiraz 182-183 C 3
Kırbaşı 182-183 DE 2-3
Kirbyville, TX 154-155 HJ 5
Kirenaika = Barqah 166-167 J 2
Kirenga 178-179 U 6
Kirensk 178-179 U 6
Kirghizistan 184-185 CD 3
Kirghizistan 180-181 LM 2
Kirghizistan 178-179 N 9
Kirgisensteppe = Kazachskij Melkosopočnik 178-179 M-P 7-8
Kirgis Nor = Chjargas nuur 184-185 GH 2
Kirgisistan 184-185 CD 3
Kirgiz Kizilsu Zizhizhou 184-185 CD 3-4
Kirgizistan 184-185 CD 3
Kirgizskij chrebet 180-181 LM 2
Kirguizistán 180-181 LM 2
Kiri 168-169 E 3
Kiribati 122-123 S 6
Kiridh 166-167 b 2
Kiries East = Kiries-Oos 174-175 C 4
Kiries-Oos 174-175 C 4
Kiries Wes = Kiries West 174-175 C 4
Kiries West 174-175 C 4
Kırık 182-183 J 2
Kırıkhan 182-183 G 4
Kırıkkale 180-181 C 2-3
Kirillov 178-179 F 6
Kirillovka 140-141 G 3
Kirin = Jilin [TJ, ●] 184-185 O 3
Kirin = Jilin [TJ, ⭑] 184-185 N 2-O 3
Kirin-do 188-189 E 4
Kirishima-yama 188-189 H 7
Kiriši 138-139 J 4
Kiris-Ost = Kiries-Oos 174-175 C 4
Kiris-West = Kiries West 174-175 C 4
Kirit = Jiriid 166-167 O 7
Kiriwina Islands = Trobriand Islands 186-187 h 6
Kırka 182-183 D 3
Kırkağaç 182-183 BC 3
Kirkcaldy 132 E 3
Kirkcudbright 132 DE 4
Kirkenes 130-131 O 3
Kırkgeçit = Kasrık 182-183 K 3
Kirkjuból 130-131 g 2
Kirkland, TX 154-155 E 3
Kirkland, WA 150-151 BC 2
Kirkland Lake 144-145 U 8
Kırklareli 180-181 B 2
Kirksville, MO 146-147 H 3
Kirkūk 180-181 EF 3
Kirkwall 132 E 2
Kirkwood 168-169 FG 9
Kirkwood, MO 152-153 L 6
Kirman–Kermān 180-181 H 4
Kirmir Çayı 182-183 E 2
Kırobası 182-183 EF 4
Kirongwe 171 DE 4
Kirov 138-139 K 6
Kirov 178-179 HJ 6
Kirova, zaliv - 140-141 O 7
Kirova, zapovednik - = Kyzylagačskij zapovednik 140-141 O 7
Kirovakan 140-141 LM 6
Kirovo-Čepeck 138-139 S 4
Kirovograd = Kirovohrad 140-141 EF 2
Kirovohrad 140-141 EF 2
Kirovsk [SU, Azerbajdžanskaja SSR] 140-141 O 7
Kirovsk [SU, Rossijskaja SFSR Murmansk] 178-179 EF 4
Kirovsk [SU, Rossijskaja SFSR St. Peterburg] 138-139 H 4
Kirovskij [SU, Kazachskaja SSR] 178-179 O 9
Kirovskij [SU, Rossijskaja SFSR ↓ Astrachan'] 140-141 O 4
Kirovskij [SU, Rossijskaja SFSR ↖ Petropaviovsk-Kamčatskij] 178-179 de 7
Kirow = Kirov 138-139 K 6
Kirowabad = Kirovabad 140-141 N 6
Kirowograd = Kirovograd 140-141 EF 2
Kirpil'skij liman 140-141 HJ 4
Kirs 178-179 J 6
Kirsanov 138-139 O 7
Kırşehir 180-181 C 3
Kirstonia 174-175 E 3
Kīrthar, Koh - 180-181 K 5
Kirthar Range = Koh Kīrthar 180-181 K 5
Kirtland, NM 150-151 J 7
Kiruna 130-131 HJ 4
Kiruru 186-187 KL 7
Kirwin, KS 152-153 G 6
Kirwin Reservoir 152-153 G 6
Kiryū 188-189 M 4
Kiržač 138-139 M 5
Kisa 130-131 F 8-9
Kisabi 171 B 4-5
Kisakata 188-189 M 3
Kisaki 171 D 4
Kisale, Lac - 168-169 G 4
Kisangani 168-169 G 2
Kisangire 168-169 J 4
Kis-Antillák 146-147 N 9-O 8
Kisar, Pulau - 186-187 J 8
Kisarawe 168-169 J 4
Kisarazu 188-189 MN 5
Kisel'ovsk 178-179 Q 7
Kisen = Hŭich'ŏn 184-185 O 3
Kisengwa 168-169 G 4
Kišen'ki 140-141 G 2
Kisenyi = Gisenyi 168-169 G 3
Kish 182-183 L 6
Kish, Jazīreh-ye - 180-181 G 5
Kishan = Ch'i-shan 190-191 H 10
Kishb, Ḥarrat al- 180-181 E 6
Kishi 172-173 F 3
Kishiwada 50-5 1 K 5
Kishm = Qeshm [IR, ≅] 180-181 H 5
Kishm = Qeshm [IR, ●] 180-181 H 5
Kishui = Jishui 190-191 E 8
Kisigo 171 C 4
Kisii 168-169 H 3
Kisiju 171 D 4
Kısır Dağı 182-183 K 2
Kiska Island 120 D 1
Kiskunfélegyháza 133 JK 5
Kiskunhalas 133 J 5
Kislovodsk 140-141 L 5
Kislowodsk = Kislovodsk 140-141 L 5
Kismaanyo 168-169 K 3
Kismayu = Kismaayo 168-169 K 3
Kismet, KS 154-155 E 2
Kis-Nefud-sivatag = Ad-Dahnā 180-181 E 5-F 6
Kiso gawa 188-189 L 5
Kiso sammyaku 188-189 L 5
Kis-Rabszolga-tó 144-145 NO 6
Kisreka 130-131 O 5
Kissangire = Kisangire 168-169 J 4
Kissaraing Island = Kettharin Kyûn 186-187 C 4
Kissenje = Gisenyi 168-169 G 3
Kissenji = Gisenyi 168-169 G 3
Kisserawe = Kisarawe 168-169 J 4
Kissidougou 166-167 BC 7
Kissimmee, FL 148-149 c 2
Kissimmee, Lake - 148-149 c 2-3
Kissimmee River 148-149 c 3
Kis-Szunda-szigetek 186-187 GH 8
Kistna = Krishna 180-181 M 7
Kistufell 130-131 f 2
Kisumu 168-169 HJ 3
Kisvárda 133 KL 4
Kiswere 171 D 5
Kita 166-167 C 6
Kita Daitō-jima 184-185 P 6
Kita-Daitō zima = Kita-Daitō-jima 184-185 P 6
Kitagō 188-189 H 7
Kitai = Qitai 184-185 FG 3
Kita-Ibaraki 188-189 N 4
Kitakami 188-189 N 3
Kitakami gawa 184-185 R 4
Kitakami kōti 188-189 N 2-3
Kitakata 188-189 MN 4
Kita-Kyūshū 184-185 OP 5
Kita-Kyūsyū = Kita-Kyūshū 184-185 OP 5
Kitale 168-169 J 2
Kitami 184-185 R 3
Kita ura 188-189 N 4
Kitčan 178-179 Y 5
Kit Carson, CO 152-153 E 6
Kitchioh = Jieshi 190-191 E 10
Kitchioh Wan = Jieshi Wan 190-191 E 10
Kitchener 144-145 U 9
Kitee 130-131 O 6
Kitega = Gitega 168-169 GH 3
Kitendwe 171 B 4
Kitengela Game Reserve 171 D 3
Kitgum 168-169 H 2
Kitimat 144-145 L 7
Kitimeot, District of - 144-145 M-S 4
Kitinen 130-131 LM 3
Kitsansara 138-139 GH 3
Kitseh = Jize 190-191 E 3
Kitsuki 188-189 H 6
Kittanning, PA 148-149 D 4
Kittery, ME 148-149 H 3
Kitthareng = Kettharin Kyûn 186-187 C 4
Kittilä 130-131 L 4
Kitty Hawk, NC 148-149 F 6
Kitu 171 A 4
Kitui 168-169 J 3
Kituku 171 B 4
Kitumbini 171 DE 5
Kitunda 168-169 H 4
Kitwe 168-169 G 5
Kityang = Jieyang 190-191 F 10
Kitzbühel 133 EF 5
Kitzingen 133 E 4
Kiuchuan = Jiuquan 184-185 H 4
Kiuhsien = Qiu Xian 190-191 E 3
Kiukiang = Jiujiang 184-185 M 6
Kiulong Kiang = Jiulong Jiang 190-191 F 9
Kiunga 186-187 M 8
Kiung-chow = Qiongshan 184-185 L 8
Kiungchow Hai-hsia = Qiongzhou Haixia 184-185 KL 7
Kiuruvesi 130-131 M 6
Kiushiu = Kyūshū 184-185 P 5
Kiu-Shu, Dorsal de - 184-185 P 6-Q 7
Kiu-Shu, Patamar de 184-185 P 6-Q 7
Kiusiu, Grzbiet - 184-185 P 6-Q 7
Kivač, vodopad - 138-139 J 2
Kivalo 130-131 L 5-M 4
Kivercy 140-141 B 1
Kiveriči 138-139 L 5
Kivu 168-169 G 3
Kivu, Lac - 168-169 G 3
Kiyang = Qiyang 190-191 CD 8
Kiyāt = Khay' 180-181 E 7
Kıyıköy 182-183 C 2
Kizel 178-179 K 6
Kizema 138-139 P 3
Kiziba 171 C 2
Kızılcahamam 182-183 E 2
Kızılçakcak = Akkaya 182-183 K 2
Kızılırmak [TR, ~] 180-181 D 3
Kızılırmak [TR, ●] 182-183 EF 2
Kızılkoca = Şefaatli 182-183 F 3
Kizilsu Kirgiz Zizhizhou 184-185 C 4-D 3
Kızıltepe 182-183 J 4
Kizil'urt 140-141 N 5
Kızılveran = Uğurludağ 182-183 F
Kızılyaka 182-183 E 4
Kizľar 140-141 N 5
Kizľarskij zaliv 140-141 N 4
Kizner 138-139 S 5
Kızören 182-183 E 3
Kizyl-Arvat 180-181 H 3
Kizyl-Atrek 180-181 G 3
Kjækan 130-131 K 3
Kjerringøy 130-131 EF 4
Kjøllefjord 130-131 MN 2
Kjøpsvik 130-131 G 3
Klaarstroom 174-175 E 7
Kladno 133 FG 3
Kladovo 136-137 K 3
Klagenfurt 133 G 5
Klaipėda 130-131 J 10
Klaipėda 138-139 C 6
Kłajpeda = Klaipėda 138-139 C 6
Klajpeda = Klaipėda 138-139 C 6
Klamath, CA 150-151 A 5
Klamath Falls, OR 146-147 B 3
Klamath Mountains 146-147 B 3
Klamath River 146-147 B 3
Klamono 186-187 K 7
Klapper = Pulau Deli 186-187 DE 8
Klarälven 130-131 E 7
Kl'asticy 138-139 G 6
Klatovy 133 F 4
Klattau = Klatovy 133 F 4
Klausenburg = Cluj-Napoca 136-137 KL 2
Klaver = Klawer 168-169 E 9
Kl'avlino 138-139 ST 6
Klawer 168-169 E 9
Klay = Bomi Hills 166-167 B 7
Kl'az'ma 138-139 N 5
Kleck 138-139 F 7
Kleinbegin 174-175 D 5
Klein Bosmanland 174-175 C 5
Klein-Buschmannland = Klein Bosmanland 174-175 D 5
Kleine Antillen 146-147 N 9-O 8
Kleine Nefud = Ad-Dahnā' 180-181 E 5-F 6
Kleine Paternosterinseln = Kepulauan Balabalangan 186-187 G 7
Kleiner Khingan = Xiao Hinggan Lin 184-185 O 1-2
Kleiner Sklavensee 144-145 NO 6
Kleine Sunda-Eilanden 186-187 GH 8
Kleine Sundainseln 186-187 GH 8
Klein-Irben = Mazirbe 138-139 CD 5
Klein-Karas 174-175 C 4
Klein Karasberge 174-175 C 4
Klein-Karoo 168-169 F 9
Klein-Karras = Klein-Karas 174-175 C 4
Klein Letaba 174-175 J 2
Klein Namakwaland 174-175 B 5
Kleinpoort 174-175 F 7
Klein Rietrivier 174-175 D 6-7
Klein Roggeveld 174-175 D 7
Kleinsee 174-175 B 5
Klein Swartberge 174-175 D 7
Kléla 172-173 D 3
Klerksdorp 168-169 G 8
Kleščevo 138-139 M 2
Klesov 138-139 F 8
Kletn'a 138-139 J 7
Klēts kalns 138-139 F 5
Kletskij 140-141 L 2
Klevan' 140-141 BC 1
Kleve 133 BC 3
Kleven' 140-141 F 1
Kličev 138-139 G 7
Klickitat, WA 150-151 C 3
Klickitat River 150-151 C 2-3
Klimoviči 138-139 HJ 7
Klimovo 138-139 J 7
Klimovsk 138-139 L 6
Klin 178-179 F 6
Klincovka 138-139 R 8
Klincy 138-139 J 7
Klinovec 133 F 3
Klintehamn 130-131 GH 9
Klipdale 174-175 C 8
Klipdam 174-175 C 4
Klipkrans 174-175 E 7
Klippan 130-131 E 9
Klipplaat 174-175 F 7
Kliprivier [ZA, Drakensberge] 174-175 H 4
Kliprugberg 174-175 C 6
Kliprug Kop = Kliprugberg 174-175 C 6
Kłodzko 133 H 3
Klondike 144-145 HJ 5
Klong, Mae - = Mae Nam Khong 186-187 D 3
Klosterneuburg 133 GH 4
Kluane Lake 144-145 J 5

229

Krotoszyn 133 H 3
Krotovka 138-139 S 7
Krottingen = Kretinga 138-139 C 6
Krotz Springs, LA 154-155 K 5
Kruger National Park 168-169 H 7-8
Krugers 174-175 F 5
Krugersdorp 168-169 G 8
Krugloje 138-139 G 6
Kruglyži 138-139 QR 4
Krui 186-187 D 8
Kruidfontein 174-175 D 7
Kruis, Kaap - 168-169 D 7
Krujë 136-137 HJ 5
Kruleвščina 138-139 FG 6
Krung Thep 186-187 D 4
Krupki 138-139 G 6
Kruševac 136-137 J 4
Kruševo 136-137 J 5
Krušné hory 133 F 3
Krutaja 138-139 U 2
Krutec 138-139 M 3
Krylovskaja = Tichoreck 140-141 JK 3
Krym 140-141 FG 4
Krymsk 140-141 HJ 4
Krymskije gory 140-141 FG 4
Krymskij zapovednik 140-141 G 4
Krynica 133 K 4
Kryvyi Rih 140-141 F 3
Krzyż 133 H 2
Ksar-el-Boukhari = Qaṣr al-Bukhari 166-167 E 1
Ksar el Kebir = Al-Qṣar al-Kabir 166-167 C 1
Ksar es Seghir = Al-Qaṣr as-Ṣaghir 166-167 D 2
Ksar es Souk = Al-Qaṣr as-Sūq 166-167 K2
Ksenjevka 178-179 WX 7
Kstovo 138-139 P 5
Ksyl-Orda = Kzyl-Orda 178-179 M 8-9
Ktesiphon 182-183 L 6
Kuai He 190-191 F 5
Kuaji Shan = Guiji Shan 190-191 H 7
Kuala Belait 186-187 F 6
Kuala Berang 186-187 D 5-6
Kuala Kangsar 186-187 CD 6
Kualakapuas 186-187 F 7
Kuala Kerai 186-187 D 5
Kualalangsa 186-187 C 6
Kuala Lumpur 186-187 D 6
Kuala Merang 186-187 D 5
Kuala Perlis 186-187 CD 5
Kuala Selangor 186-187 D 6
Kuala Trengganu 186-187 DE 5
Kuan = Gu'an 190-191 F 2
Kuancheng 188-189 B 2
Kuan Chiang = Guan Jiang 190-191 C 9
Kuandian 188-189 E 2
Kuang-an = Guang'an 184-185 K 5
Kuang-ch'ang = Guangchang 184-185 M 6
Kuangchou = Guangzhou 184-185 L 7
Kuang-chou Wan = Zhanjiang Gang 184-185 L 7
Kuang-fêng = Guangfeng 190-191 G 7
Kuang-hai = Guanghai 184-185 L 7
Kuang-hsi = Guangxi Zhuangzu Zizhiqu 184-185 KL 7
Kuang-hsin = Shangrao 184-185 M 6
Kuang-jao = Guangrao 190-191 G 3
Kuang-ling = Guangling 190-191 E 2
Kuang-lu Tao = Guanglu Dao 188-189 D 3
Kuang-nan = Guangnan 184-185 JK 7
Kuang-ning = Guangning 190-191 D 10
Kuango = Kwango 168-169 E 3-4
Kuang p'ing = Guangping 190-191 E 3
Kuang-shan = Guangshan 190-191 E 5
Kuang-shui = Guangshui 190-191 E 6
Kuangsi = Guangxi Zhuangzu Zizhiqu 184-185 KL 7
Kuang-tê = Guangde 190-191 G 6
Kuang-tsê = Guangze 190-191 F 8
Kuangtung = Guangdong 184-185 L 7
Kuang-yüan = Guangyuan 184-185 K 5
Kuanhsien = Guan Xian 190-191 E 3
Kuan-shan 190-191 H 10
Kuantan 186-187 D 6
Kuantan, Batang - = Sungai Inderagiri 186-187 D 7
Kuan-t'ao = Guantao 190-191 E 3
K'uan-tien = Kuandian 188-189 E 2
Kuan-tung Pan-tao = Guandong Bandao 188-189 C 3
Kuan-yang = Guanyang 190-191 C 9
Kuan-yin-t'ang = Guanyintang 190-191 CD 4
Kuan-yün = Guanyun 184-185 MN 5
Kub [SU] 138-139 V 4
Kub [ZA] 174-175 B 3
Kuba [C] 146-147 KL 7
Kuba [SU] 140-141 O 6
Kuban' 140-141 J 4
Kubango = Rio Cubango 168-169 E 6
Kubaysah 182-183 K 6
Kubbar, Jazirat - 182-183 N 8
Kubbum 166-167 J 6
Kubena 138-139 N 3
Kubenskoje 138-139 M 4
Kubenskoje, ozero - 138-139 M 4
Kuberle 140-141 KL 3
Kubiskowberge 174-175 C 6
Kubli Hill 172-173 FG 3
Kubn'a 138-139 Q 6
Kubokawa 188-189 J 6
Kubolta 140-141 C 2
Kuboos = Richtersveld 174-175 B 5
Kučevo 136-137 J 3
Kucha 184-185 E 3
Ku-chang = Guzhang 190-191 BC 7
Kuche = Kucha 184-185 E 3
Ku-chên = Guzhen 190-191 F 5
Ku-ch'êng = Gucheng [TJ, Hebei] 190-191 EF 3
Kucheng = Gucheng [TJ, Hubei] 190-191 C 5
Kuchengtze = Qitai 184-185 FG 3
Ku-chiang = Gujiang 190-191 E 8
Kuching 186-187 F 6
Kuchinoerabu-jima 188-189 GH 7
Kuchino-shima 188-189 G 7
Kuchow = Quzhou 190-191 E 3
Ku-chu = Guzhu 190-191 E 10
Kuçovë 136-137 HJ 5
Küçük Ağrı Dağı 182-183 L 3
Küçüksu = Kotum 182-183 K 3
Küçükyozgat = Elma Dağı 182-183 E 3
Kudamatsu 188-189 H 5-6
Kudat 186-187 G 5
Kuddla = Kandla 180-181 L 6
Kudever' 138-139 G 5
Kudirkos Naumiestis 130-131 K 10
Kudō = Taisei 188-189 ab 2
Kudük 166-167 L 6-7
Kudumalapshwe 174-175 F 2
Kudymkar 178-179 JK 6
Kuei-ch'i = Guixi 190-191 F 7
Kuei Chiang = Gui Jiang 190-191 C 9-10
Kuei-ch'ih = Guichi 184-185 M 5
Kueichou = Guizhou 184-185 JK 6
Kuei-chou = Zigui 190-191 C 6
Kuei-p'ing = Guiping 184-185 KL 7
Kuei-t'an = Kuitan 190-191 E 10
Kuei-tê = Guide 184-185 J 4
Kuei-ting = Guiding 184-185 K 6
Kuei-tung = Guidong 190-191 D 8
Kuei-yang = Guiyang [TJ, Guizhou] 184-185 K 6
Kuei-yang = Guiyang [TJ, Hunan] 184-185 L 6
Kūfah, Al- 182-183 L 6
Kufra = Wāḥāt al-Kufrah 166-167 J 4
Kufra, Al- = Wāḥāt al-Kufrah 166-167 J 4
Kufra, Oasis de - = Wāḥāt al-Kufrah 166-167 J 4
Kufra, oaza - = Wāḥāt al-Kufrah 166-167 J 4
Kufrah, Wāḥāt al- 166-167 J 4
Kufraoasen = Wāḥāt al-Kufrah 166-167 J 4
Kufra Oasis = Wāḥāt al-Kufrah 166-167 J 4
Kufra-oázis = Wāḥāt al-Kufrah 166-167 J 4
Küfre = Sirvan 182-183 K 3
Kufstein 133 F 5
Kūh, Pish-e - 182-183 M 6
Kūhak 180-181 J 5
Kuh dağı = Kazandağ 182-183 K 3
Kūhdasht 182-183 M 6
Kühin 182-183 N 4
Kuhmo 130-131 NO 5
Kuibis = Guibes 174-175 B 4
Kuiepan 174-175 DE 4
Kuis 174-175 B 3
Kuiseb 174-175 B 2
Kuitan 190-191 E 10
Kuito 168-169 E 5
Kuitozero 130-131 O 5
Kuiu Island 144-145 K 6
Kuivaniemi 130-131 L 5
Kuja 178-179 G 4
Kujal'nickij liman 140-141 E 3
Kujang-dong 188-189 EF 3
Kujawy 133 J 2
Kujbyšev 178-179 O 6
Kujbyšev = Samara 178-179 HJ 7
Kujbyševka-Vostočnaja = Belogorsk 178-179 YZ 7
Kujbyševo 140-141 J 3
Kujbyševskoje vodochranilišče 178-179 HJ 7
Kujbyšev 178-179 O 6
Kujbyšev = Samara 178-179 HJ 7
Kujbyševka-Vostočnaja = Belogorsk 178-179 YZ 7
Kujeda 138-139 U 5
Kujgenkol' 140-141 NO 2
Kuji 184-185 R 3
Kujto, ozero - 178-179 E 5
Kujumba 178-179 S 5
Kujū-san 188-189 H 6
Kukami 174-175 E 3
Kukarka = Sovetsk 178-179 H 6
Kukawa 166-167 G 6
Kuke 168-169 F 7
Kukiang = Qujiang 190-191 D 9
Kukkus = Privolžskoje 140-141 MN 1
Kukmor 138-139 S 5
Kukong 174-175 E 3
Kukumane Kraal 174-175 F 2
Kuku Noor = Chöch nuur 184-185 H 4
Kula [BG] 136-137 K 4
Kula [TR] 182-183 C 3
Kula [YU] 136-137 H 3
Kul'ab 180-181 K 3
Kulagino 140-141 P 2
Kulal 171 D 2
Kulaly, ostrov 140-141 O 4
Kulambangra = Kolombangara 186-187 j 6
Kulanjin 182-183 N 5
Kular, chrebet - 178-179 Z 4
Kulaura 180-181 P 6
Kuldiga 130-131 J 9
Kuldiga 138-139 CD 5
Kulebaki 138-139 O 6
Kulfo 172-173 G 3
Kulgera 194-195 F 5
Kulha Gangri 184-185 G 6
Kulhakangri = Kulha Gangri 184-185 G 6
Kuliga 138-139 T 4
Kulikoro = Koulikoro 166-167 C 6
Kulikovka 140-141 E 1
Kulikovo Pole = Kurkino 138-139 LM 7
Kulja = Ghulja 184-185 E 3
Kullen 130-131 E 9
Küllük = Güllük 182-183 B 4
Kulm, ND 152-153 G 2
Kulmbach 133 E 3
Kulmsee = Chełmża 133 J 2
Kuloj [SU, ~] 138-139 O 3
Kuloj [SU, ●] 138-139 O 3
Kulotino 138-139 J 4
Kulp 182-183 J 3
Kulpawn 172-173 E 3
Kul'sary 178-179 J 8
Kultuk 178-179 T 7
Kulu 182-183 E 3
Kulu = Julu 190-191 E 3
Kulumadau 186-187 h 6
Kulunda 178-179 OP 7
Kulundinskaja ravnina 178-179 O 7
Kulwin 196 F 5
Kum = Qom 180-181 G 4
Kuma [J] 188-189 J 6
Kuma [SU] 140-141 N 4
Kumagaya 188-189 M 4
Kumai, Teluk - 186-187 F 7
Kumaishi 188-189 ab 2
Kumalar Dağı 182-183 D 3
Kumamba, Kepulauan - 186-187 LM 7
Kumamoto 184-185 P 5
Kumano 188-189 L 6
Kumano-nada 188-189 L 5-6
Kumanovo 136-137 JK 4
Kumasi 166-167 D 7
Kumaun 180-181 M 4
Kumayt, Al- 182-183 M 6
Kumba 166-167 F 8
Kumbakale 186-187 j 6
Kumbakonam 180-181 MN 8
Kumbe 186-187 LM 8
Kŭmch'on 188-189 F 3
Kŭmch'ŏn = Kimch'ŏn 184-185 O 4
Kumeny 138-139 RS 4
Kumertau 178-179 K 7
Kŭm-gang 188-189 F 4
Kŭmgang-san 188-189 FG 3
Kŭmhwa 188-189 F 3
Kumini-dake 188-189 H 6
Kŭmje = Kimje 188-189 F 5
Kumla 130-131 F 8
Kumluca 182-183 D 4
Kŭmnyŏng 188-189 F 6
Kumo 172-173 H 3
Kŭmo-do 188-189 FG 5
Kumo-Manyčskaja vpadina 140-141 K 3-M 4
Kumon Range = Kŭmûn Taungdan 186-187 C 1
Kumphawapi 186-187 D 3
Kŭmsan 188-189 F 4
Kumuch 140-141 N 5
Kumul = Hami 184-185 G 3
Kŭmûn Taungdan 186-187 C 1
K'um'urk'oj, gora - 140-141 O 7
Kunašir, ostrov - 178-179 c 9
Kunatata Hill 172-173 H 4
Kunayt, Al- 182-183 M 6
Kuncevo, Moskva - 138-139 L 6
Kunda 130-131 M 8
Kunda [SU] 138-139 F 4
Kundabwika Falls 171 B 5
Kuṅḍāpura = Condapoor 180-181 L 8
Kundelungu 168-169 G 4-5
Kundelungu, Parc National de - 171 AB 5
Kundiawa 186-187 M 8
Kunduk = ozero Sasyk 140-141 DE 4
Kundur, Pulau - 186-187 D 6
Kunduz 180-181 K 3
Kunene 168-169 DE 6
Kung-ch'êng = Gongcheng 190-191 C 9
K'ung-ch'êng = Kongcheng 190-191 F 6
Kung-hsien = Gong Xian 190-191 D 4
Kung-hui = Gonghui 190-191 C 9
Kung-kuan = Gongguan 190-191 B 11
Kungliao = Kang-liao 190-191 HJ 9
K'ung'o-Ala-Too, chrebet - 178-179 O 9
Kungrad 178-179 K 9
Kungsbacka 130-131 DE 9
Kung Shui = Gong Shui 190-191 E 9
Kungu 168-169 E 2
Kungur 178-179 K 6
Kung-ying-tsŭ = Gongyingzi 188-189 BC 2
Kunie = Île des Pins 194-195 N 4
Kunja 138-139 H 5
Kunjirap Daban 184-185 D 4
Kunkür 166-167 L 7
Künlön 186-187 C 2
Kunlun Shan 184-185 D-H 4
Kunming 184-185 J 6
Kunsan 184-185 O 4
Kunsan-man 188-189 F 5
Kunshan 190-191 H 6
Kuntillā, Al- 170 F 3
K'ŭnyŏnp'yŏng-do = Taeyŏnp'yŏng-do 188-189 E 4
Kunyu Shan 190-191 H 3
Kuocang Shan 190-191 H 7
Kuo Ho = Guo He 190-191 F 5
Kuo-hsien = Yuanping 190-191 D 2
Kuolisma 138-139 HJ 2
Kuopio 130-131 M 6
Kupa 136-137 FG 3
Kupang 186-187 H 9
Kup'ansk 140-141 H 2
Kupanskoje 138-139 M 5
Kup'ansk- Uzlovoj 140-141 HJ 2
Kupčin 140-141 C 2
Kupino 178-179 O 7
Kupischki = Kupiškis 138-139 E 6
Kupiškis 138-139 E 6
Kupreanof Island 144-145 K 6
Kura [SU ◁ Kaspisches Meer] 140-141 MN 6
Kura [SU ◁ Nogajskaja step'] 140-141 M 4
Kura-Araksinskaj nizmennost' = Širvanskaja ravnina 140-141 NO 6-7
Kurahashi-jima 188-189 J 5
Kurashiki 188-189 J 5
Kuratovo 138-139 R 3
Kuraymah 166-167 L 5
Kurayoshi 188-189 JK 5
Kurchahan Hu = Chagan nuur 184-185 L 3
K'urdamir 140-141 O 6
Kurdikos Naumiestis 138-139 D 6
Kurdistan = Kordestān 180-181 F 3
Kure [J] 184-185 P 5
Kure [USA] 192-193 K 2
Küre [TR] 182-183 E 2
Kurejka [SU, ~] 178-179 QR 4
Kurejka [SU, ●] 178-179 PQ 4
Kuremäe 138-139 F 4
Kurgan 178-179 M 6
Kurganinsk 140-141 K 4
Kurganovka 138-139 U 4
Kurgan-T'ube 180-181 KL 3
Kuria 192-193 J 4
Kuria Muria Island = Jazā'ir Khūrīyā Mūrīyā 180-181 H 7
Kurikka 130-131 JK 6
Kurikoma yama 188-189 N 3
Kuril-arok 120 D 2-E 3
Kurilen 184-185 S 3-T 2
Kurilengraben 198-199 GH 2
Kuriles 184-185 S 3-T 2
Kuriles, Fosa de las - 120 D 2-E 3
Kuril Islands 184-185 S 3-T 2
Kurilovka 140-141 O 1
Kuril'sk 178-179 c 8
Kuril'skije ostrova 184-185 S 3-T 2
Kurilský příkop 198-199 GH 2
Kuril-szigetek 184-185 S 3-T 2
Kuril Trench 120 D 2-E 3
Kurily 120 E 3-4
Kurinskaja kosa 140-141 O 7
Kurinskaja Kosa = Kurkosa 140-141 O 7
Kurja 138-139 V 3
Kürkcü = Sarıkavak 182-183 E 4
Kurkosa 140-141 O 7
Kurkur 170 E 6
Kurland 138-139 CD 5
Kurland 130-131 JK 9
Kurländische Aa = Lielupe 138-139 D 5
Kurlandzkie, Wzn. - 130-131 JK 9
Kurle = Korla 184-185 F 3
Kurleja 178-179 WX 7
Kurlovskij 138-139 N 6
Kurmanajevka 138-139 ST 7
Kurman-Kamel'či = Krasnogvardejskoje 140-141 G 4
Kurmuk 166-167 L 6
Kurnool 180-181 M 7
Kurobe 188-189 L 4
Kuroishi 188-189 N 2
Kuromatsunai 188-189 b 2
Kuronsko 138-139 CD 5
Kurosawajiri = Kitakami 188-189 N 3
Kuro-shima 188-189 G 7
Kurovskoje 138-139 M 6
Kursavka 140-141 L 4
Kurschany = Kuršėnai 138-139 D 5
Kuršėnai 138-139 D 5
Kursi 182-183 J 4
Kursk 138-139 KL 8
Kurskaja kosa 133 K 1
Kurskij zaliv 133 K 1
Kursū, Wādī - 170 E 6
Kuršumlija 136-137 J 4
Kurşunlu [TR, Çankırı] 182-183 E 2
Kuršumlija 136-137 J 4
Kurtalan 182-183 J 4
Kurthasanlı 182-183 E 3
Kürti 166-167 L 5
Kurtoğlu Burnu 182-183 C 4
Kurucaşile 182-183 E 2
Kuruçay 182-183 H 3
Kuruman 168-169 F 8
Kuruman Heuvels 174-175 E 4
Kurume [J, Kyūshū] 188-189 H 6
Kurumkan 178-179 V 7
Kurunẹgala 180-181 MN 9
Kurupukari 158-159 H 4
Kurusku, Wādī - 170 E 6
Kuryle 120 E 3-4
Kurylsko-Kamczacki, Rów - 198-199 GH 2
Kuryongp'o 188-189 G 5
Kurzeme 138-139 CD 5
Kuşadası 182-183 B 4
Kuşadası Körfezi 182-183 B 4
Kusakaki-shima 188-189 G 7
Kusatsu 188-189 KL 5
Kusayban, Bi'r - 166-167 K 4
Kuş Gölü 182-183 BC 2
Kusal = Kuusalu 138-139 E 4
Kusary 140-141 O 6
Kuščinskij 140-141 N 6
Kuščovskaja 140-141 JK 3
Ku-shan = Gushan 188-189 D 3
Kusheriki 172-173 G 3
Kushih = Gushi 184-185 M 5
Kushikino 188-189 GH 7
Kushima 188-189 H 7
Kushimoto 188-189 K 6
Kushiro 184-185 RS 3
Kūshkak 182-183 NO 5
Kushui 184-185 G 3
Kusiro = Kushiro 184-185 RS 3
Kuška 180-181 J 3
Kuskokwim Bay 144-145 D 6
Kuskokwim Mountains 144-145 EF 5
Kuskokwim River 144-145 DE 5
Kuşluyan = Gölköy 182-183 G 2
Kušmurun 178-179 LM 7
Kušnarenkovo 138-139 U 6
Kusnezk = Kuzneck 178-179 H 7
Kusŏng 188-189 E 2-3
Kustanaj = Kostanaj 126-127 V 7
Küstendil 136-137 K 4
Küstenkanal 133 CD 2
Küstri 166-167L6
Küstrin = Kostrzyn 133 G 2
Kusu 188-189 H 6
Kušum 140-141 P 1
Kus'ur 178-179 Y 3
Kus'va 178-179 K 6
Kūt, Al- 180-181 F 4
Kut, Ko - 186-187 D 4
Kut 'Abdollāh 182-183 N 7
Kütahya 180-181 BC 3
Kutai 186-187 G 6
Kutais 140-141 J 4
Kutaisi 140-141 L 5
Kut-al-Imara = Al-Kūt 180-181 F 4
Kutaradja = Banda Aceh 186-187 BC 5
Kutch 180-181 K 6
Kutch, Gulf of - 180-181 KL 6
Kutch, Rann of - 180-181 KL 6
Kutchan 188-189 b 2
Kutcharo-ko 188-189 d 2
Kutchi Hill 172-173 H 3
Kutien = Gutian 190-191 G 8
Kutina 136-137 G 3
Kutno 133 J 2
Kutsing = Qujing 184-185 J 6
Kutu 168-169 E 3
Kutum 166-167 J 6
Kutunbul, Jabal - 180-181 E 7
Kuusalu 138-139 E 4
Kuusamo 130-131 N 5
Kuusankoski 130-131 M 7
Kuvandyk 178-179 K 7
Kuvšinovo 138-139 K 5
Kuwait 180-181 F 5
Kuwana 188-189 L 5
Kuwayt, Al- 180-181 F 5
Kuwejt 180-181 F 5
Kuwo = Quwo 190-191 C 4
Kuyang = Quyang 190-191 E 2
Kuyeh = Juye 190-191 F 4
Kuye He 190-191 C 2
K'u-yeh Ho = Kuye He 190-191 C 2
Küysanjaq 182-183 L 4
Kuyucak 182-183 C 4
Kuyung = Jurong 190-191 G 6
Kuz'movka 178-179 QR 5
Kuzenkino 138-139 J 5
Kuzneck 178-179 H 7
Kuzneckij Alatau 178-179 Q 6-7
Kuzneck-Sibirskij = Novokuzneck 178-179 Q 7
Kuznetsk = Kuzneck 178-179 H 7
Kuzomen' 178-179 F 4
Kuzucubelen 182-183 EF 4
Kvænangen 130-131 J 2
Kvaløy 130-131 KL 2
Kvalsund 130-131 KL 2
Kvalvågen 130-131 k 6
Kvareli 140-141 MN 6
Kvarken 130-131 J 6
Kvarner 136-137 F 3
Kvarnerić 136-137 F 3
Kverkfjöll 130-131 ef 2
Kvigtind 130-131 EF 5
Kvikne 130-131 D 6
Kvirily = Zestafoni 140-141 L 5
Kvitøya 130-131 no 4
Kwa 168-169 E 3
Kwabhaca 174-175 H 6
Kwaggablad 174-175 EF 4
Kwai 174-175 D 3
Kwair, Al- = Al-Quwayr 182-183 K 4
Kwakhanai 168-169 F 7
Kwale 171 D 4
Kwa Mbonambi 174-175 K 5
Kwambonambi = Kwa Mbonambi 174-175 K 5
Kwamouth 168-169 E 3
Kwa Mtoro 171 CD 4
Kwandang 186-187 H 6
Kwangan = Guang'an 184-185 K 5
Kwangando 171 D 3
Kwangchang = Guangchang 184-185 M 6
Kwangch'on 188-189 F 4
Kwangchow= Guangzhou 184-185 L 7
Kwangjao = Guangrao 190-191 G 3
Kwangju 184-185 O 4
Kwango 168-169 E 3-4
Kwangsi = Guangxi Zhuangzu Zizhiqu 184-185 KL 7
Kwangteh = Guangde 190-191 G 6
Kwangtseh = Guangze 190-191 F 8
Kwangtung = Guangdong 184-185 L 7
Kwangyuan = Guangyuan 184-185 K 5
Kwania, Lake - 171 C 2
Kwankwasa 172-173 GH 3
Kwanmo-bong 188-189 G 2
Kwanto = Kantō 188-189 MN 4
Kwanyun = Guanyun 184-185 MN 5
Kwanza, Rio - 168-169 E 4-5
Kwara 172-173 G 3
Kwatta 180-181 K 4
Kwazulu-Natal 168-169 H 8
Kwazulu [ZA, ~] 168-169 H 8
Kwazulu [ZA, ⌖ = 12-20 ◁] 174-175 H-K 4-6
Kwedia 174-175 F 3
Kweiang = Guiyang 184-185 K 6
Kweichih = Guichi 184-185 M 5
Kweichow - Fengjie 184-185 K 5
Kweichow = Guizhou 184-185 JK 6
Kweichu = Guiyang 184-185 K 6
Kweilin = Guilin 184-185 KL 6
Kweiping = Guiping 184-185 KL 7
Kweiteh = Shangqiu 184-185 LM 5
Kweiyang = Guiyang 184-185 K 6
Kwekwe 168-169 G 6
Kwenge 168-169 E 4
Kwenlun = Kunlun Shan 184-185 D-H 4
Kwesang-bong 188-189 G 2
Kwethluk, AK 144-145 DE 5
Kwidzyn 133 J 2
Kwigillingok, AK 144-145 D 6
Kwiha 166-167 MN 6
Kwilu 168-169 E 3
Kwinana 194-195 BC 6
Kwohsien = Juanping 190-191 D 2
Kwona 172-173 G 3
Kwonghoi = Guanghai 184-185 L 7
K XVIII, Cresta de 124-125 O 7
Kyaiktô 186-187 C 3
Kyaka 171 B 3
Kyancutta 194-195 G 6
Kyaring Tsho [TJ, Qinghai] 184-185 H 5
Kyaring Tsho [TJ, Xizang Zizhiqu] 184-185 F 5
Kyaukhsi 186-187 C 2
Kyaukse = Kyaukhsi 186-187 C 2
Kybartei 138-139 D 6
Kydöniai = Ayvacık 182-183 B 3
Kyebang-san 188-189 G 4
Kyezimanzan 186-187 C 2
Kyjiv = Kiev 140-141 DE 1
Kyjiv 140-141 DE 1
Kykladen 136-137 L 7
Kyklades 136-137 L 7
Kykládes Nēsoi 136-137 L 7
Kylady 136-137 L 6
Kyle of Lochalsh 132 D 3
Kyllênê 136-137 J 7
Kymé 136-137 L 6
Kymen lääni 130-131 MN 7
Kymijoki 130-131 M 7
Kynö = Kihnu 138-139 D 4
Kynuna 194-195 H 4
Kyoga, Lake - 168-169 H 2
Kyōga-saki 188-189 K 5
Kyogle 196 L 2
Kyŏmip'o = Songnim 184-185 O 4
Kyŏngan-ni 188-189 F 4
Kyŏngdŏn 186-187 CD 2
Kyŏnggi-do 188-189 F 4
Kyŏnghŭng 188-189 H 1
Kyŏngju 184-185 OP 4
Kyŏngnyŏlbi-yŏlto 188-189 E 4
Kyŏngsan 188-189 G 5
Kyŏngsang-pukto 188-189 G 4
Kyŏngsang-namdo 188-189 FG 5
Kyŏngsŏng 188-189 GH 2
Kyŏngsŏng = Sŏul 184-185 O 4
Kyŏngwŏn 188-189 H 1
Kyōto 184-185 PQ 4
Kyparissia 136-137 J 7
Kyparissiakòs Kólpos 136-137 J 7
Kypr 180-181 C 3
Kyrá Panagia 136-137 KL 6
Kyrgyzstan 184-185 CD 3
Kyrgyzstan 180-181 LM 2
Kyrkanda 138-139 P 3
Kyrksæterøra 130-131 C 6
Kyrkslätt 130-131 L 7
Kyrönjoki 130-131 K 6
Kyštovka 178-179 O 6
Kyštym 178-179 L 6
Kysykkamys 140-141 P 2
Kythēra 136-137 K 7
Kythêron, Stenôn - 136-137 K 7-8
Kythnos 136-137 L 7
Kytyl-Žura 178-179 Y 5
Kyūgŏk 186-187 C 2
Kyuschuschwelle 184-185 P 6-Q 7
Kyūshū 184-185 P 5
Kyushu, Dorsale - 184-185 P 6-Q 7
Kyushu, Seuil des - 184-185 P 6-Q 7
Kyūshū-hátság 184-185 P 6-Q 7
Kyushu Ridge 184-185 P 6-Q 7
Kyūshū sammyaku 188-189 H 6
Kyūsyū = Kyūshū 184-185 P 5
Kyyiv = Kiev 140-141 DE 1
Kywong 196 H S
Kyzyl 178-179 R 7
Kyzyl-Kija 180-181 L 2-3
Kyzylagačskij zapovednik 140-141 O 7
Kyzylkum 178-179 LM 9
Kyzyl-Mažalyk 178-179 QR 7
Kyzyl-Orda 180-181 B 2-3
Kyzyl-Suu 180-181 L 3

L

Laa 133 H 4
La'ā', Al- = Al-Lu'ā'ah 182-183 L 7
Laascaanood 166-167 b 2
Laasqoray 166-167 b 1
Laas Warwar 166-167 bc 2
Laba 172-173 G 2
La Barge, WY 150-151 HJ 4
Labbezanga 166-167 E 5-6
Labe 133 G 3
Labé [Guinea] 166-167 B 6
La Belle, FL 148-149 c 3
La Belle, MO 152-153 KL 5
Labiau = Polessk 133 K 1
Labin 136-137 F 3
Labinsk 140-141 K 4
Labis 186-187 D 6
La Blanquilla, Isla - 158-159 G 2
Laboulaye 162 D 4
Labrador, Bacia do - 124-125 G 3
Labrador, Bacino del - 124-125 G 3
Labrador, Bassin du - 124-125 G 3
Labrador, Coast of - 144-145 YZ 6-7
Labrador, Cuenca del - 124-125 G 3
Labrador, Mar del - 144-145 Y-a 5-6
Labrador, Mar do - 144-145 Za 5-6
Labrador, Mare del - 144-145 Y-a 5-6
Labrador, Mer du - 144-145 Y-a 5-6
Labrador Basin 124-125 G 3
Labradorbecken 124-125 G 3
Labradorbekken 124-125 G 3
Labrador City 144-145 X 7
Labrador Peninsula 144-145 V 6-Y 7
Labrador Sea 144-145 Y-a 5-6
Labradorsee 144-145 Y-a 5-6
Labradorskie, Morze - 144-145 Y-a 5-6
Labrador-tenger 144-145 Y-a 5-6
Labradorzee 144-145 Y-a 5-6
Lábrea 158-159 G 6
Labuan 186-187 FG 5
Labuan, Pulau - 186-187 FG 5
Labuha 186-187 J 7
Labuhan 186-187 E 8
Labuhanbajo 186-187 GH 8
Labuhanbilik 186-187 CD 6
Labytnangi 178-179 M 4
Laća, ozero - 138-139 M 3
Laccadive Islands 180-181 L 9
Lac Courte Oreilles Indian Reservation 152-153 L 3
Lac du Flambeau Indian Reservation 152-153 L 2-3
Lacepede Islands 194-195 D 3
Lacey, WA 150-151 B 2
Lachdenpochja 138-139 GH 3
Lachlan River 194-195 HJ 6
L'achoviči 138-139 EF 7
Lačin 140-141 N 7
Lacio = Latium 136-137 E 4-5
Lackawanna, NY 148-149 D 3
Lacolle 148-149 G 2
Lacombe 144-145 O 7
Laconia, NH 148-149 H 3
Lacoochee, FL 148-149 b 2
La Coruña 134-135 C 7
Lacq 134-135 G 7
Lac qui Parle 152-153 H 3
La Crosse, KS 152-153 G 6
Lacrosse, WA 150-151 E 2
La Crosse, WI 146-147 H 3
Lac Superior = Lake Superior 146-147 HJ 2
Ladakh 180-181 M 4
Ladakh Range 180-181 M 3-4
Ladan 140-141 F 1
Ladder Creek 152-153 F 6
Laddonia, MO 152-153 L 6
Lādhiqiyah, Al- 180-181 CD 3
La Digue Island 168-169 N 3
Lādik 182-183 FG 2
Ladiqiya, El- = Al-Lādhiqiyah 180-181 CD 3
Ladismith 168-169 F 9
Ladoga, IN 152-153 N 6
Ladožskoje ozero 178-179 E 5
Ladronen = Mariana Islands 198-199 G 3-4
Ladrones Peak 154-155 B 3
Ladron Mountains 154-155 B 3
L'ady 130-131 N 8
L'ady [SU, Nižnij Novgorod] 138-139 P 5
L'ady [SU, Pskov] 138-139 G 4
Ladybrand 168-169 G 8
Lady Franklinfjord 130-131 k 4
Lady Frere 174-175 G 6
Lady Grey 174-175 G 6
Lady Newnes Ice Shelf 121 B 18-17
Ladysmith, WI 152-153 L 3
Ladysmith [ZA] 168-169 G 8
Lae 186-187 N 8
La Encantada, Cerro de - 146-147 C 5
Lærdalsøyri 130-131 BC 7
Læsø 130-131 D 9
La Española 156 BC 2
Lafagu 172-173 G 3
Lafayette, AL 154-155 N 4
La Fayette, GA 154-155 N 3
Lafayette, IN 146-147 J 3
Lafayette, LA 146-147 H 5-6
Lafayette, TN 154-155 MN 2
Lafia 166-167 F 7
Lafiagi 166-167 EF 7
La Follette, TN 154-155 N 2
Lagan 130-131 E 9
Lagan' [SU] 140-141 N 4
Lagan' = Kaspijskij 140-141 N 4
Lagarfljót 130-131 f 2
Lagarterito 146-147 b 2
Lagarto = Palmas Bellas 146-147 a 2
Lagbar 172-173 B 2
Lageadinho 160-161 G 7
Lågen 130-131 CD 7
Laghouat = Al-Aghwāṭ 166-167 E 2
Lagič 140-141 O 6
Lågneset 130-131 j 6
Lago Argentino 162 B 8
Lagoa Bonita 160-161 EF 5
Lagoa da Prata 160-161 K 4
Lagoa Santa 160-161 L 3
Lagodechi 140-141 MN 6
Lagodei, El- = Qardho 180-181 F 9
Lagolândia 160-161 H 1
Lago Maggiore 136-137 C 2-3
Lagonegro 136-137 FG 5
Lago Novo 158-159 J 4
Lagos [P] 134-135 C 10
Lagos [WAN] 166-167 E 7
Lagosa 168-169 GH 4
Lagos Amorgas = Al-Buḥayrat al-Murrat al-Kubrā 170 E 2
Lagos de Moreno 146-147 F 7
Lago Superior = Lake Superior 146-147 HJ 2
Lagowa, El - = Al-Laqawah 166-167 K6
Lågøya 130-131 k 4
La Grande, OR 150-151 D 3
Lagrange 194-195 D 3
Lagrange, IN 152-153 O 5
La Grange, GA 146-147 JK 5
La Grange, KY 152-153 O 6
La Grange, NC 148-149 E 7
La Grange, TX 154-155 G 5-6
Lagrange, WY 152-153 D 5
Laguna [BR] 162 G 3
Laguna, La - [PA ↑ Panamá] 146-147 b 2
Laguna, La - [PA ← Panamá] 146-147 b 3
Laguna, NM 154-155 B 3
Laguna Beach, CA 150-151 DE 9
Laguna Dam 150-151 FG 9
Laguna Mountains 150-151 E 9
Lagunas [PE] 158-159 DE 6
Lagunas [RCH] 162 BC 2
Laguna de Jaco 154-155 D 7
Laguna Superior 146-147 H 8
Laguna Yema 162 D 2
Laguneninsel = Ellice Islands 189-199 H 5
Lahad Datu 186-187 G 5-6
Laham [RI] 186-187 G 6
Laham [RN] 172-173 G 2
Lahat 186-187 D 7
Lahewa 186-187 C 6
Lahij 180-181 EF 8
Lāhījān 180-181 FG 3
Lahn 133 D 3
Laholm 130-131 E 9
Laholms bukten 130-131 E 9
Lahontan Reservoir 150-151 D 6
Lahore 180-181 L 4
Lahti 130-131 LM 7
Laï 166-167 H 7
Lai'an 190-191 G 5
Laibach = Ljubljana 136-137 F 2
Laibin 190-191 B 10
Lai-chou Wan = Laizhou Wan 190-191 G 3
Lai Châu 186-187 D 2
Laidley 196 L 1
Laifeng 190-191 B 7
Lai HKa = Lechā 186-187 C 2
Lailā = Laylā 180-181 F 6
Lailān = Laylān 182-183 L 5
Lainé 172-173 C 3
Laingsburg 168-169 EF 9
Lai-pin = Laibin 190-191 B 10
Laipo = Lipu 184-185 KL 7
Laird, CO 152-153 E 5
Laisamis 171 D 2
Laiševo 138-139 RS 6
Laishui 190-191 E 2
Laiwu 190-191 F 3
Laixi 190-191 H 3
Laiyang 190-191 H 3
Laiyuan 184-185 LM 4
Lai-yüan = Laiyuan 184-185 LM 4
Laizhou Wan 190-191 G 3
Lajā', Al- 182-183 G 6
Lajes [BR, Rio Grande do Norte] 158-159 M 6
Lajes [BR, Santa Catarina] 162 F 3
Lajinha 160-161 M 4
Lajkovac 136-137 HJ 3
La Jolla, CA 150-151 E 9
La Joya, NM 154-155 B 3
Lajtamak 178-179 M 6
La Junta, CO 146-147 F 4
Lake, WY 150-151 H 3
Lake Andes, SD 152-153 G 4
Lake Arthur, LA 154-155 J 5
Lake Arthur, NM 154-155 C 4
Lake Benton, MN 152-153 HJ 3
Lake Bolac 196 F 6
Lake Butler, FL 148-149 b 1
Lake Cargelligo 194-195 J 6
Lake Charles, LA 146-147 H 5
Lake Chrissie = Chrissiesmeer 174-175 J 4
Lake City, CO 152-153 C 6
Lake City, FL 148-149 b 1
Lake City, IA 152-153 J 4
Lake City, MI 152-153 O 3
Lake City, MN 152-153 K 3
Lake City, SC 148-149 D 8
Lake City, SD 152-153 H 3
Lake Cormorant, MS 154-155 KL 3
Lake Crystal, MN 152-153 J 3
Lake Charles, LA 146-147 H 5
Lakefield [AUS] 194-195 H 2-3
Lakefield, MN 152-153 J 4
Lake Geneva, WI 152-153 M 4
Lake George, NY 148-149 FG 3
Lake Grace 194-195 C 6
Lake Harbour 144-145 WX 5
Lake Havasu City, AZ 150-151 F-G 8
Lake Jackson, TX 154-155 H 6
Lake King 194-195 CD 6
Lakeland, FL 146-147 K 6
Lakeland, GA 148-149 B 9
Lake Livingstone 154-155 H 5
Lake Mead National Recreation Area 150-151 FG 7-8
Lake Mills, IA 152-153 K 4
Lake Mills, WI 152-153 M 4
Lake Odessa, MI 152-153 O 4
Lake Oswego, OR 150-151 B 3
Lake Park, IA 152-153 J 4
Lake Placid, FL 148-149 c 3
Lake Placid, NY 146-147 M 3
Lake Pleasant, NY 148-149 F 3
Lakeport, CA 150-151 B 6
Lake Preston, SD 152-153 H 3
Lake Providence, LA 154-155 K 4
Lake Range 150-151 D 5
Lakes Entrance 196 HJ 6
Lakeside, AZ 150-151 J 8
Lakeside, NE 152-153 E 4
Lakeside, OR 150-151 A 4
Lakeside, UT 150-151 G 5
Lakeside, VA 148-149 E 6
Lake Toxaway, NC 148-149 B 7
Lake Victor, TX 154-155 F 5
Lakeview, MI 148-149 A 3
Lakeview, OR 150-151 C 4
Lake Village, AR 154-155 K 4
Lake Wales, FL 148-149 c 3
Lakewood, CO 152-153 D 6
Lakewood, NJ 148-149 F 4
Lakewood, NM 154-155 C 4
Lakewood, NY 148-149 D 3
Lakewood, OH 148-149 BC 4
Lake Worth, FL 146-147 KL 6
Lakhadsweep 180-181 L 8
Lakhnaū = Lucknow 180-181 MN 5
Lakin, KS 152-153 F 7
Lakinsk 138-139 M 5
Lakōnikòs Kólpos 136-137 K 7
Lakota 172-173 D 4
Lakota, IA 152-153 J 4
Lakota, ND 152-153 G 1
Laksefjord 130-131 M 2
Laksely 130-131 L 2
Lakshadvip = Lakshadweep 180-181 L 8
Lālāpaşa 182-183 B 2
La Lara 172-173 H 5
Lalaua 168-169 J 5
Lālī 182-183 N 6
Lalibela 166-167 M 6
Lal'sk 138-139 QR 3
La Luz, NM 154-155 BC 4
Lamadrid 154-155 E 7
Lama-Kara = Kara 172-173 F 3
La Manche, průliv - 132 E 7-F 6
Lamar, CO 152-153 E 6
Lamar, MO 152-153 J 7
La Marque, TX 154-155 H 6
Lambaréné 168-169 D 3
Lambasa 186-187 a 2
Lambayeque [PE, ●] 158-159 CD 6
Lambert, MS 154-155 KL 3
Lambert, MT 152-153 D 2
Lambert Glacier 121 B 8
Lambertsbaai 174-175 BC 7
Lamberts Bay = Lambertsbaai 174-175 BC 7
Lambi Kyûn 186-187 C 4
Lambourti 172-173 F 3
Lambton, Cape - 144-145 M 3
L'amca 138-139 L 1
Lāmding = Lumding 180-181 P 5
Lamé 166-167 G 7
Lame Deer, MT 152-153 C 3
Lamego 134-135 D 8
La Mesa, CA 150-151 E 9
La Mesa, NM 154-155 B 4
Lamesa, TX 154-155 E 4
Lamézia Terme 136-137 FG 6
Lamia 136-137 K 6
L'amin 178-179 N 5
Lamo = Lamu 168-169 K 3
Lamoille, NV 150-151 F 5
La Moine, CA 150-151 B 5
Lamona, WA 150-151 D 2
Lamon Bay 186-187 H 4
Lamoni, IA 152-153 JK 5
Lamont, CA 150-151 D 8
Lamont, ID 150-151 H 3-4
Lamont, WY 152-153 C 4
Lamotrek 186-187 N 5
Lampa [PE] 158-159 EF 8
Lampang 186-187 C 3
Lampasas, TX 154-155 F 5
Lampedusa 136-137 E 8
Lampedusa, Isola - 166-167 G 1
Lampi Island = Lambi Kyûn 186-187 C 4
Lampung 186-187 DE 7
Lamskoje = Lomskoje 138-139 LM 7
Lamu [EAK] 168-169 K 3
Lamy, NM 154-155 C 3
Lan' 138-139 F 7
Lanai 186-187 e 3
Lanao, Lake - 186-187 HJ 5
Lancang Jiang 184-185 HJ 7
Lancaster 132 E 4
Lancaster, CA 150-151 DE 8
Lancaster, IA 152-153 K 5
Lancaster, KY 152-153 O 7
Lancaster, MN 152-153 H 1
Lancaster, NH 148-149 H 2
Lancaster, OH 152-153 P 6
Lancaster, PA 148-149 EF 4
Lancaster, SC 148-149 C 7
Lancaster, WI 152-153 L 4
Lancaster Sound 144-145 TU 3
Lančchuti 140-141 K 5
Lancheu = Lanzhou 184-185 JK 4
Lan-ch'i = Lanxi [TJ, Hubei] 190-191 E 6
Lan-ch'i = Lanxi [TJ, Zhejiang] 190-191 G 7
Lanchou = Lanzhou 184-185 JK 4
Lanchow = Lanzhou 184-185 JK 4
Lancian = Lan Xian 190-191 C 2
Lanciano 136-137 F 4
Lancun 184-185 N 4
Landa, ND 152-153 F 1
Lan Dao = Danhao Dao 190-191 DE 10
Landau 133 D 4
Landeck 133 E 5
Landego 130-131 EF 4
Lander, WY 152-153 B 4
Landerneau 134-135 E 4
Lander River 194-195 F 4
Landi 172-173 C 3
Landrum, SC 148-149 B 7
Landsberg am Lech 133 E 4
Landsberg (Warthe) = Gorzów Wielkopolski 133 GH 2
Land's End 132 CD 6
Land's End [CDN] 144-145 LM 2
Landshut 133 F 4
Landskrona 130-131 E 10
Landsort, Fosa de - 130-131 H 8
Landsort, Fossa de 128-129 M 4
Landsort, Fosse du - 130-131 H 8
Landsort, Głębia - 130-131 H 8
Landsortdiep 130-131 H 8
Landsortsdjupet 130-131 H 8
Landsorttief 130-131 H 8
Landwarowo = Lentvaris 138-139 E 6
Lanett, AL 154-155 N 4
Lanfeng = Lankao 190-191 E 4
Langao 190-191 B 5
L'angasovo 138-139 RS 4
Langberge 174-175 E 4-5
Langchhen Khamba 184-185 DE 5
Lang-ch'i = Langxi 190-191 G 6
Langchung = Langzhong 184-185 JK 5
Langdon, ND 152-153 G 1
Langebaan 174-175 BC 7
Langeberge [ZA ← Hoë Karro] 174-175 C 6
Langeberge [ZA ↙ Klein Karro] 174-175 CD 7
Langeland 130-131 D 10
Langen = Langao 190-191 B 5
Langerüd 182-183 O 4
Langford, SD 152-153 H 3
Langjökull 130-131 cd 2
Langkawi, Pulau - 186-187 C 5
Langklip 174-175 D 5
Langkrans 174-175 J 4
Langlois, OR 150-151 A 4
Langon 134-135 G 6
Langøy 130-131 F 3
Langping 190-191 C 6
Langres 134-135 K 5
Langres, Plateau de - 134-135 K 5
Langsa 186-187 C 6
Lang Shan = Char Narijn uul 184-185 K 3
Lang So'n 186-187 E 2
Langtans udde 121 C 31
Langtry, TX 154-155 E 6
Languedoc 134-135 J 7-K 6
Langtry, TX 154-155 E 6
Langxi 190-191 G 6
Langzhong 184-185 JK 5
Lanín, Volcán - 162 B 5
Lankao 190-191 E 4
Lankou 190-191 E 10
Lannion 134-135 F 4
Lansdale, PA 148-149 F 4
L'Anse, MI 152-153 M 2
Lansford, ND 152-153 F 1
Lanshan 190-191 D 9
Lansing, IA 152-153 L 4
Lansing, MI 146-147 K 3
Lan Tao = Danhao Dao 190-191 DE 10

ntian 190-191 B 4
ntian = Lianyuan 190-191 C 8
n-t'ien = Lantian 190-191 B 4
n-ts'ang Chiang = Lancang
Jiang 184-185 HJ 7
n-ts'un = Lancun 184-185 N 4
nusei 136-137 C 6
nxi [TJ, Hubei] 190-191 E 6
nxi [TJ, Zhejiang] 190-191 G 7
n Xian 190-191 C 2
n Yü 184-185 N 7
nzarote 166-167 B 3
nzhou 184-185 JK 4
oag 186-187 GH 3
o-chung-chi = Laozhong
190-191 E 5
odicea = Al-Lādhiqīyah
180-181 CD 3
oha He 188-189 B 2
o-ha Ho = Laoha He 188-189 B 2
ohekou = Guanghua 184-185 L 5
o-hu-k'ou = Hu-kou 190-191 H 9
ohushan 188-189 BC 2
o Kay 186-187 D 2
olong = Longchuan 190-191 E 9
on 134-135 J 4
ona, WI 152-153 M 3
epukou 190-191 B 9
ora 186-187 H 7
os 186-187 D 2-3
oshan 184-185 N 4
oshan Wan 190-191 H 3
osz 186-187 D 2-E 3
o-t'ieh-shan-hsi Chiao =
Laotieshanxi Jiao 188-189 C 3
otieshanxi Jiao 190-191 H 2
ozhong 190-191 E 5
oa 162 FG 3
oa, Campos de - 160-161 GH 6
Panza Range 150-151 CD 8
Paz, Bahía de - 146-147 DE 7
eer, MI 152-153 P 4
eeruza, proliv - 178-179 b 8
oéthos = Lapta 182-183 E 5
oine, OR 150-151 C 4
oin lääni 130-131 L-N 4
oinlahti 130-131 MN 6
olace, LA 154-155 K 5
oland 130-131 F 5-N 3
olandskij zapovednik
130-131 OP 4
Plant, ND 152-153 F 3
Plant, SD 152-153 F 3
Plata, IA 152-153 K 5
Plata, MD 148-149 E 5
Plata, MO 152-153 K 5
oónia 130-131 F 5-N 3
oonia 130-131 F 5-N 3
oónia 130-131 F 5-N 3
oonsko 130-131 F 5-N 3
Porte, IN 152-153 N 5
oorte, PA 148-149 E 4
Porte, TX 154-155 H 6
oovo 136-137 J 3
opajärvi 130-131 KL 6
opeenranta 130-131 N 7
opföld 130-131 F 5-N 3
opi 130-131 L 5
opland 130-131 F 3-N 5
oponia 130-131 F 5-N 3
orida [RA, Buenos Aires] 162 D 5
Pryor, TX 154-155 EF 6
oseki 182-183 B 2
ota 182-183 E 5
otev, Mar de - 178-179 V 2-Z 3
otev, Mar de - 178-179 V 2-a 3
otev, Mar di - 178-179 V 2-Z 3
otev, Mer du - 178-179 V 2-a 3
otev Sea 178-179 V 2-a 3
otévů moře - 178-179 V 2-Z 3
otevzee 178-179 V 2-a 3
otewsee 178-179 V 2-a 3
otiewów, Morze- 178-179 V 2-Z 3
otyev-tenger 178-179 V 2-Z 3
ua 130-131 K 6
ush, WA 150-151 A 2
ry 133 L 2
jawah, Al- 166-167 K 6
jiyat 166-167 K 4
[IR] 180-181 G 5
ache = Al-Ar'ā'ish 166-167 C 1
amie, WY 146-147 EF 3
amie Peak 152-153 D 4
amie Plains 152-153 D 4-5
amie Range 146-147 E 3
amie River 152-153 D 4-5
anjal Paulista 160-161 HJ 5
anjeiras do Sul 162 F 3
antuka 186-187 H 8
at, Pulau - 186-187 K 8
bro 130-131 H 9
e 171 D 2
edo, IA 152-153 K 4-5
edo, TX 146-147 G 6
estān 180-181 G H 5
geau = Faya-Largeau
166-167 H 5
go, FL 148-149 b 3
go Remo, Isla - 146-147 b 2
go Remo Island 146-147 b 2
iang 186-187 G 7
imore, ND 152-153 GH 2
ino 136-137 F 5
isa 136-137 K 6
istan = Lārestān 180-181 GH 5
jak 178-179 OP 5
kānah 180-181 K 5
kspur, CO 152-153 D 6
naca = Lárnax 180-181 C 4
nax 180-181 C 4
ned, KS 152-153 G 6
ne 132 D 4
rey Point 194-195 C 3
rimah 194-195 F 3
s Christensen land 121 BC 7
sen is-shelf 121 C 130-131
slan, MT 152-153 CD 1
teh 172-173 EF 4
vik 130-131 D 8
sa = Lhasa 184-185 G 6
Sal, UT 150-151 J 6
s Aves, Islas - 158-159 F 2
car, CO 152-153 D 7
s Cruces, NM 146-147 E 5
gird = Lāsjerd 180-181 G 3
he lowayn 180-181 J 4
hio = Lāshō 186-187 C 2
hkar = Gwalior 180-181 M 5
hkar Gāh 180-181 JK 4
hkar Satma 184-185 F 4
hō 186-187 C 2
Silveta, Cerro - 162 B 8
ithion 136-137 L 8
jerd 180-181 G 3
skel'a 138-139 H 3
ma 138-139 N 6
Minas, Bahia - 146-147 b 2
solo, Teluk - 186-187 H 7
Palomas, NM 154-155 B 4
sance 158-159 KL 8
sen Peak 146-147 B 3
sen Volcanic National Park
150-151 C 5
Last Chance, CO 152-153 DE 6
Lastoursville 168-169 D 3
Lastovo 136-137 G 4
Las Vegas, NM 146-147 EF 4
Las Vegas, NV 146-147 C 4
Las Vegas Bombing and Gunnery
Range 150-151 EF 7
Latacunga 158-159 D 5
Latady Island 121 BC 29
Latakia = Al-Lādhiqīyah
180-181 CD 3
Late 186-187 c 2
Latina 136-137 E 5
Latium = Làzio 136-137 E 4-5
La Tortuga, Isla - 158-159 FG 2
Latrobe 196 c 2
Latrobe, PA 148-149 D 4
Latvia 130-131 K-M 9
Latvia 138-139 D-F 5
Latvija = Lettland 138-139 D-F 5
Latvijskaja Sovetskaja
Socialističeskaja Respublika =
Lettland 138-139 D-F 5
Lau 172-173 H 3
Lauban = Lubań 133 G 3
Lauderdale 196 c 3
Lauderdale, MS 154-155 L 4
Lauenburg/Elbe 133 E 2
Lauenburg in Pommern =
Lębork 133 H 1
Laughing Fish Point 152-153 N 2
Laughlan Islands 186-187 h 6
Laughlin Peak 154-155 CD 2
Lau Group 186-187 b 2
Launceston [AUS] 194-195 J 8
Launceston [GB] 132 D 6
Laura 194-195 H 3
Laura = Lavry 138-139 F 5
Laurel, DE 148-149 F 5
Laurel, IN 152-153 O 6
Laurel, MD 148-149 E 5
Laurel, MS 146-147 J 5
Laurel, MT 152-153 B 3
Laurel, NE 152-153 H 4
Laurel, OH 148-149 A 5
Laurel Hill 148-149 D 4-5
Laureles [PY] 160-161 D 7
Laurel Hill, FL 154-155 M 5
Laurens, IA 152-153 J 4
Laurens, SC 148-149 BC 7
Laurentides, Parc provincial des
- 144-145 W 8
Laurie Island 121 C 32
Laurinburg, NC 148-149 D 7
Lauritsala 130-131 N 7
Laurium, MI 152-153 M2
Lauro Müller 160-161 H 8
Lausanne 133 C 5
Lausitzer Gebirge 133 G 3
Laut, Pulau - [RI, Kepulauan
Natuna] 186-187 E 6
Laut, Pulau - [RI, Selat Makasar]
186-187 G 7
Laut Kecil, Kepulauan -
186-187 G 7-8
Lautoka 186-187 a 2
Lauwater 174-175 C 2
Lava, NM 154-155 B 4
Lava Bads 150-151 JK 8
Lava Beds [USA, Oregon ↘
Cedar Mountains] 150-151 E 4
Lava Beds [USA, Oregon ←
Harney Basin] 150-151 C 4
Lava Beds [USA, Oregon ↘
Steens Mountain] 150-151 D 4
Lava Beds [USA, New Mexico ←
Oscura Peak] 154-155 B 4
Lava Beds [USA, New Mexico ↑
Tularosa Basin] 154-155 BC 4
Lava Beds [USA, New Mexico ←
United Pueblos Indian Reservation]
154-155 AB 3
Lava Beds National Monument
150-151 C 5
Laval [CDN] 144-145 VW 8
Laval [F] 134-135 G 4
L'Avana = La Habana 156 A 1
Lavansaari = ostrov Moščnyj
138-139 FG 4
Lavapié, Punta - 162 AB 5
Laveaga Peak 150-151 C 7
Lavelanet 134-135 HJ 7
La Verkin, UT 150-151 G 7
Laverne, OK 154-155 EF 2
La Vernia, TX 154-155 FG 6
Laverton 194-195 D 5
Lavina, MT 152-153 B 2
Lavinia 160-161 G 4
Lavongai = New Hanover
186-187 gh 5
Lavonia, GA 148-149 B 7
Lavrador = Labrador Peninsula
144-145 V 6-Y 7
Lavras 158-159 L 9
Lávrion 136-137 KL 7
Lavry 138-139 F 5
Lawa 158-159 J 4
La Ward, TX 154-155 G 6
Lawen, OR 150-151 D 4
Lawers, Ben - 132 DE 3
Lawit, Gunung - [RI] 186-187 F 6
Lawn, TX 154-155 F 4
Lawowa 186-187 H 7
Lawqah 182-183 K 8
Lawra 166-167 D 6
Lawrence, KS 152-153 J 6
Lawrence, MA 148-149 H 3
Lawrence, NE 152-153 GH 5
Lawrence, NY 148-149 G 4
Lawrenceburg, IN 152-153 O 6
Lawrenceburg, KY 152-153 O 6-7
Lawrenceburg, OH 148-149 A 5
Lawrenceburg, TN 154-155 M 3
Lawrenceville, VA 148-149 E 6
Lawrenceville, GA 154-155 NO 4
Lawrenceville, IL 152-153 N 6
Laws, CA 150-151 D 7
Lawson, CO 152-153 CD 6
Lawton, OK 146-147 G 5
Lawz, Jabal al- 180-181 D 5
Laxå 130-131 F 8
Lay, CO 152-153 C 5
Laya 172-173 B 3
Lāyalpūr = Faisalābād 180-181 L 4
Layar, Tanjung - 186-187 DE 8
Laylā 180-181 F 6
Laylān 182-183 L 5
Layton, UT 150-151 G 5
Laž 138-139 R 5
Lazarev 178-179 ab 7
Lazarevskoje, Soči- 140-141 J 5
Lazdijai 138-139 D 6
Làzio 136-137 E 4-5
Lazurnoje [SU, Cherson]
140-141 G 3
Lbiščensk = Čapajevo 140-141 P 1
Leach Island 152-153 O 2
Leachville, AR 154-155 K 3
Lead, SD 146-147 F 3
Leadore, ID 150-151 G 3
Leadville, CO 152-153 C 6
Leakesville, MS 154-155 L 5
Leakey, TX 154-155 F 6
Leaksville, NC 148-149 D 6
Leal = Lihula 138-139 DE 4
Leamington 152-153 P 4-5
Leamington, UT 150-151 GH 6
Le'an 190-191 E 8
Leander, TX 154-155 FG 5
Le'an Jiang 190-191 F 7
Leavenworth, KS 152-153 J 6
Leavenworth, WA 150-151 C 2
Leavitt Peak 150-151 D 6
Łeba 133 H 1
Lebādeia 136-137 K 6
Lebam, WA 150-151 B 2
Lebanon 184-185 D 4
Lebanon, IN 152-153 N 5
Lebanon, KS 152-153 G 6
Lebanon, KY 152-153 O 7
Lebanon, MO 152-153 K 7
Lebanon, NE 152-153 F 5
Lebanon, NH 148-149 GH 3
Lebanon, OH 152-153 O 6
Lebanon, OR 150-151 B 3
Lebanon, PA 148-149 E 4
Lebanon, SD 152-153 FG 3
Lebanon, TN 154-155 MN 2
Lebanon Junction, KY 152-153 O 7
Leb'ažje [SU, Rossijskaja SFSR]
178-179 M 6
Leb'ažje [SU, Kazachskaja SSR]
178-179 O 7
Lebed'an' 138-139 M 7
Lebedin 140-141 G 1
Lebesby 130-131 M 2
Lébithia 136-137 M 7
Lebo 168-169 F 2
Lebo, KS 152-153 HJ 6
Lebomboberge 174-175 JK 2-4
Lèbòn 186-187 B 2
Lebon Regis 160-161 G 7
Lębork 133 H 1
Lebowa = 21-27 ◁ 174-175 H-J 2-3
Lebowa-Kgomo 174-175 H 3
Lebrija 134-135 DE 10
Lebú 162 B 5
Lecce 136-137 H 5
Lecco 136-137 C 3
Lech 133 E 4
Lechā 186-187 C 2
Lechang 190-191 D 9
Lecompte, LA 154-155 J 5
Lectoure 134-135 H 7
Ledao Sha = Xinliao Dao
190-191 C 11
Ledong = Lo-tung 190-191 HJ 9
Leduc 144-145 O 7
Lee, MA 148-149 G 3
Leech Lake 152-153 J 2
Leedey, OK 154-155 F 3
Leeds 132 F 5
Leeds, AL 154-155 M 4
Leeds, ND 152-153 G 1
Leer 133 C 2
Leesburg, FL 148-149 bc 2
Leesburg, ID 150-151 FG 3
Leesburg, VA 148-149 E 5
Leesville, LA 154-155 J 5
Leeton 194-195 J 6
Leeudoringstad 174-175 G 4
Leeu Gamka 174-175 D 7
Leeupoort 174-175 G 3
Leeuwarden 134-135 KL 2
Leeuwin, Cape - 194-195 B 6
Leeuwin, Dorsal de -
194-195 A 8-B 7
Leeuwin, Dorsale di -
194-195 A 8-B 7
Leeuwin, Patamar de -
194-195 A 8-B 7
Leeuwin, Seuil - 194-195 A 8-B 7
Leeuwindrempel 194-195 A 8-B 7
Leeuwin-hát 194-195 A 8-B 7
Leeuwin Rise 194-195 A 8-B 7
Leeuwinschwelle 194-195 A 8-B 7
Leeuwpoort = Leeupoort
174-175 G 3
Lee Vining, CA 150-151 D 7
Leeward Islands 146-147 O 8
Lefini 168-169 E 3
Lefka 182-183 E 5
Lefors, TX 154-155 E 3
Lefroy, Lake - 194-195 D 6
Legaspi 186-187 H 4
Legaupi = Legaspi 186-187 H 4
Leghorn = Livorno 136-137 CD 4
Legnica 133 GH 3
Le Grand, Cape - 194-195 D 6
Leh 180-181 M 4
Lehi, UT 150-151 GH 5
Lehliu 136-137 M 3
Lehrte 133 DE 2
Lehua 190-191 EF 7
Lehututu 168-169 F 7
Leiah = Leya 180-181 L 4
Leibnitz 133 G 5
Leicester 132 F 5
Leichhardt Range 194-195 J 4
Leichhardt River 194-195 GH 3
Lei-chou Pan-tao = Leizhou
Bandao 184-185 L 7
Lei-chou Wan = Leizhou Wan
190-191 C 11
Leiden 134-135 K 2
Leie 134-135 J 3
Leigh Creek 194-195 G 6
Leighton, AL 154-155 M 3
Leikanger 130-131 A 6
Leine 133 D 3
Leinster 132 C 5
Leipsic, OH 152-153 OP 5
Leipsoi 136-137 M 7
Leipzig 133 F 3
Leipzig = Bessarabka 140-141 D 3
Leiranger 130-131 F 4
Leiria 134-135 C 9
Lei Shui 190-191 D 8-9
Leisler, Mount - 194-195 EF 4
Leitchfield, KY 152-153 NO 7
Leiter, WY 152-153 C 3
Leitha 133 H 5
Leith Harbour 162 J 8
Leitměřitz = Litoměřice 133 G 3
Leiyang 184-185 L 6
Leizhou Bandao 184-185 L 7
Leizhou Wan 190-191 C 11
Lejāā, El- = Al-Lajā' 182-183 G 6
Lejasciems 138-139 F 5
Lek 134-135 K 3
Leka 130-131 D 5
Lekef = Al-Kāf 166-167 F 1
Lekemti = Nekemtē 166-167 M 7
Leksand 130-131 F 7
Leksozero 130-131 O 6
Leksozero, ozero - 138-139 H 2
Leksula 186-187 J 7
Lekuru 174-175 E 3
Lel = Lēh 180-181 M 4
Lela, TX 154-155 E 3
Leland, MI 152-153 NO 3
Leland, MS 154-155 K 4
Leland Elk Rapids, MI 148-149 A 2
Lel'čicy 138-139 FG 8
Lelekovka 140-141 EF 2
Leleque 162 B 6
Leling 190-191 F3
Lelingluang 186-187 K 8
Lemahabang 186-187 E 8
Léman 133 C 5
Le Marie, Estrecho de -
162 C 9-D 8
Lembale 171 BC 4
Lemberg = L'vov 140-141 AB 2
Lemesós 180-181 C 4
Lemhi, ID 150-151 G 3
Lemhi Range 150-151 G 3
Lemhi River 150-151 G 3
Leming, TX 154-155 F6
Lemitar, NM 154-155 B3
Lemland 130-131 J 8
Lemmenjoen kansallispuisto
130-131 LM 3
Lemmon, SD 152-153 E3
Lemmon, Mount - 150-151 H 9
Lēmnos 136-137 L 6
Lemoore, CA 150-151 CD 7
Lemoyne, NE 152-153 F5
Lemsal = Limbaži 138-139 E5
Lemvig 130-131 C 9
Lena [SU] 178-179 W 5-6
Lena, LA 154-155 J 5
Lena, MS 154-155 L 4
Lena, OR 150-151 D 3
Lençóis 158-159 L 7
Lençóis Paulista 160-161 H 5
Lenda 171 B 2
Lendery 178-179 E 5
Lenger 178-179 MN 9
Lengerskij = Georgijevka
178-179 P 8
Lengshuijiang 190-191 C 8
Lengshuitan 190-191 C 8
Lengua de Vaca, Punta - 162 B 4
Lengyelország 133 H-L 3
Lenina, pik - 180-181 L 3
Leninabad 180-181 KL 2-3
Leninakan = Kumajiri 140-141 LM 6
Leningrad = Sankt-Peterburg
178-179 E 5-6
Leningradskaja 140-141 J 3
Lenino 140-141 G 4
Lenino = Leninsk-Kuzneckij
178-179 Q 6-7
Leninsk 140-141 M 2
Leninsk-Kuzneckij 178-179 Q 6-7
Leninskaja Sloboda 138-139 P 5-6
Leninskij [SU Marijskaja ASSR]
138-139 P 5
Leninskoje 138-139 Q 4
Lenkoran' 140-141 O 7
Lennep, MT 150-151 H 2
Lennewarden = Lielvārde
138-139 E 5
Lennox, SD 152-153 H 4
Lennox, Isla - 162 C 9
Lenoir, NC 148-149 C 7
Lenoir City, TN 154-155 N3
Lenora, KS 152-153 FG 6
Lenorah, TX 154-155 DE 4
Lenox, IA 152-153 J 5
Lens 134-135 J 3
Lensk 178-179 V 5
Lentini 136-137 F 7
Lentvaris 138-139 E 6
Lèo 166-167 D 6
Leoben 133 G 5
Leola, AR 154-155 J3
Leola, SD 152-153 G 3
Leoma, TN 154-155 M 3
Leominster, MA 148-149 GH 3
León [MEX] 146-147 F 7
León [NIC] 146-147 J 9
Leon, IA 152-153 K5
León [E, ≅] 134-135 E 7-8
León [E, ●] 134-135 E 7
León, Cerro - 160-161 B 4
León, Cerro del - 146-147 G 8
León, Montes de - 134-135 D 7
Léon, Pays de - 134-135 E 4
Leonardtown, MD 148-149 E 5
Leonardville 168-169 E 7
Leona River 154-155 F 6
Leongatha 196 G 7
Leoni 160-161 E 7
Leonidion 136-137 K 7
Leonora 194-195 D 5
Leon River 154-155 F 5
Léopold II, Lac - = Mai Ndombe
168-169 E 3
Leopoldina 160-161 L 4
Leopoldo de Bulhões 160-161 H 2
Léopoldville = Kinshasa
168-169 E 3
Leopoli = L'viv 126-127 NO 6
Leoti, KS 152-153 F6
Leova 140-141 D 3
Leovo 136-137 MN 2
Lepanto, AR 154-155 K 3
Lepel' 138-139 G 6
Lepar, Pulau - 186-187 E 7
Leper Colony = Balboa Heights
146-147 b 3
Lephepe 168-169 FG 7
Lépi = Caála 168-169 DE 5
Leping 184-185 M 6
Lepl'avo 140-141 E 2
Lepsy 178-179 O 8
Leptis magna 166-167 GH 2
Lequeitio 134-135 F 7
Lêr = Lir 166-167 KL 7
Léraba 172-173 D 3
Léré [RMM] 172-173 D 2
Léré [Tschad] 166-167 G 7
Lere [WAN] 172-173 H 3
Leribe 174-175 H 5
Lérida 134-135 H 8
Lérida [CO, Vaupés] 158-159 E 4
Lerik 140-141 O 7
Lerma 134-135 F 7-8
Lermontov 140-141 L 4
Léros 136-137 M 7
Le Roy, IL 152-153 M 5
Le Roy, MI 148-149 A 2
Le Roy, MN 152-153 K 4
Le Roy, NY 148-149 DE 3
Le Roy, WY 150-151 H 5
Lerwick 132 F 1
Lésbos 136-137 L 6
Leščevo = Charovsk 178-179 G 6
Leshan 184-185 J 6
Lesistyje Karpaty 133 KL 4
Leskhimstroj 140-141 H 2
Lesken 140-141 L 5
Leskovac 136-137 J 4
Leslie 174-175 H 4
Leslie, AD 154-155 J 3
Leslie, ID 150-151 G 4
Leslie, MI 152-153 O 4
Lesnoj [SU, Vjatka] 178-179 J 6
Lesnoj = Umba 178-179 J 6
Lesnoje [SU, Rossijskaja SFSR]
138-139 K 4
Lesnoj Umba 178-179 EF 4
Lesobeng 174-175 H 5
Lesosibirsk 178-179 R 6
Lesotho 168-169 G 8
Lesozavodsk 178-179 Za 8
Lesozavodskij 130-131 P 4
Lesser Antilles 146-147 N 9-O 8
Lesser Sunda Islands
186-187 GH 8
Lester, IA 152-153 H 4
Lešukonskoje 178-179 H 5
Leszno 133 H 3
Letaba [ZA, ~] 168-169 H 7
Letaba [ZA, ● Drakensberge]
174-175 J 2
Letaba [ZA, ● Kruger National Park]
174-175 J 2
Letcher, SD 152-153 G 4
Lethbridge 144-145 O 8
Lethem 158-159 H 4
Leti, Kepulauan - 186-187 J 8
Letiahau 168-169 F 7
Letičev 140-141 C 2
Leticia 158-159 EF 5
Leting 190-191 G 2
Letjesbosch = Letjesbos
174-175 DE 7
Letjesbos 174-175 DE 7
Letka [SU, ~] 138-139 R 4
Letka [SU, ●] 138-139 R 4
Letland 138-139 D-F 5
Letn'aja Stavka 140-141 L 4
Letnerečenskij 138-139 JK 1
Letohatchee, AL 154-155 M 4
Letonia 138-139 D-F 5
Letónia 138-139 D-F 5
Letpadan = Letpandan 186-187 C 3
Letpandan 186-187 C 3
Lettland 138-139 D-F 5
Lettonia 130-131 D-F 5
Lettonie 138-139 D-F 5
Lettország 138-139 D-F 5
Leucite Hills 152-153 B 5
Leuser, Gunung - 186-187 C 6
Leuven 134-135 K 3
Levan, UT 150-151 H 6
Levanger 130-131 D 6
Levant, Bassin du - 180-181 BC 4
Levante, Bacia do - 180-181 BC 4
Levante, Bacino del - 180-181 BC 4
Levantei-medence 180-181 BC 4
Levantine Basin 180-181 BC 4
Levantisches Becken 180-181 BC 4
Levantské moře 182-183 C 5
Levantské moře 136-137 NO 8
Levantijns Bekken 180-181 BC 4
Lèvanzo 136-137 DE 6
Levelland, TX 154-155 D 4
Levent 182-183 G 3
Leveque, Cape - 194-195 D 3
Leverett Glacier 121 A 24-22
Leverger = San Antônio do Leverger
160-161 DE 1
Leverkusen 133 C 3
Levice 133 J 4
Levick, Mount - 121 B 16-17
Levin 194-195 P 8
Levinópolis 160-161 K 1
Lévis 144-145 W 8
Levittown, PA 148-149 F 4
Lévka = Lefka 182-183 E 5
Levká Óre 136-137 KL 8
Levkás [GR, ≅] 136-137 J 6
Levkás [GR, ●] 136-137 J 6
Levkōsia 180-181 C 3
Levokumskoje 140-141 M 4
Levski 136-137 L 4
Levskigrad 136-137 L 4
Lev Tolstoj 138-139 M 7
Levubu 174-175 J 2
Lewantyński, Basen -
138-139 D-F 5
Lewellen, NE 152-153 EF 5
Lewes, DE 148-149 F 5
Lewis and Clark Lake 152-153 H 4
Lewis, Butt of - 132 C 2
Lewis, Isle of - 132 C 2
Lewisburg, KY 154-155 M 2
Lewisburg, PA 148-149 E 4
Lewisburg, TN 154-155 M 3
Lewisburg, WV 148-149 C 6
Lewis Pass 194-195 O 8
Lewis Range 146-147 D 2
Lewis River 150-151 BC 2
Lewiston, ID 146-147 C 2
Lewiston, ME 146-147 MN 3
Lewiston, MI 152-153 OP 3
Lewiston, UT 150-151 H 5
Lewistown, IL 152-153 LM 5
Lewistown, MT 152-153 B 2
Lewistown, PA 148-149 DE 4
Lewisville, AR 154-155 J 4
Lewisville, TX 154-155 G 4
Lexington, KY 146-147 K 4
Lexington, MO 152-153 K 6
Lexington, MS 154-155 KL 4
Lexington, NC 148-149 CD 7
Lexington, NE 152-153 G 5
Lexington, OR 150-151 D 3
Lexington, TN 154-155 L 3
Lexington, TX 154-155 G 5
Lexington, VA 148-149 D 6
Lexūrion 136-137 J 6
Leyah 180-181 L 4
Leydsdorp 168-169 H 7
Leyte 186-187 J 4
Leža [SU, ●] 138-139 N 4
Ležajsk 133 L 3
Ležnē 136-137 H 5
Ležnevo 138-139 N 5
L'gov 138-139 K 8
Lha Ri 184-185 E 5
Lharugö 184-185 G 5
Lhasa 184-185 G 6
Lhatse Dsong 184-185 F 6
Lhokkruet 186-187 BC 6
Lhokseumawe 186-187 C 5
Lhunpo Gangri 184-185 EF 5-6
Liancheng 190-191 F 9
Liangcheng 190-191 GH 4
Liang-ch'iu = Liangqiu
190-191 FG 4
Lianggezhuang 190-191 E 2
Lianghekou 190-191 B 7
Liang-ho-k'ou = Lianghekou
190-191 B 7
Liangjiadian 188-189 CD 3
Liang-ko-chuang =
Lianggezhuang 190-191 E 2
Liangqiu 190-191 FG 4
Liangshan 190-191 EF 4
Liangshan Yizu Zizhizhou
184-185 J 6
Liangshan Zizhizhou 184-185 J 6
Liangtian [TJ, Guangxi Zhuangzu
Zizhiqu] 190-191 BC 10
Liangtian [TJ, Hunan] 190-191 D 9
Liang-t'ien = Liangtian 190-191 D 9
Liang Xiang 184-185 LM 4
Liangxiangzhen 184-185 LM 4
Liangyuan 190-191 F 5
Liangzi Hu 190-191 E 6
Lianhua 184-185 L 6
Lianhua Shan 190-191 E 10
Lianjiang [TJ, ● Fujian]
190-191 G 8
Lianjiang [TJ, ● Guangdong]
184-185 KL 7
Lian Jiang [TJ, ~ ◁Bei Jiang]
190-191 D 9
Lian Jiang [TJ, ~ ◁Gan Jiang]
190-191 E 9
Lian Jiang = Ping Jiang 190-191 E 8
Liannan 190-191 D 9
Lianping 184-185 LM 7
Lianshan 190-191 CD 9
Lianshanguan 188-189 D 2
Lian Shui [TJ, ~] 190-191 CD 8
Lianshui [TJ, ●] 190-191 G 5
Liantang 190-191 E 7
Lian Xian 190-191 D 9
Lianyuan 190-191 C 8
Lianyungang 184-185 MN 5
Lianyun Shan 190-191 D 7
Lianzhen 190-191 F 3
Liaocheng 184-185 LM 4
Liao-chung = Liaozhong
188-189 D 2
Liaodong Bandao 184-185 N 4
Liaodong Wan 184-185 MN 3-4
Liao He 188-189 D 1
Liao Ho = Liao He 188-189 D 1
Liaoning 184-185 MN 3
Liaosi = Liaoxi 184-185 N 3
Liaotung = Liaodong Bandao
184-185 N 4
Liaoxi 184-185 N 3
Liaoyang 184-185 N 3
Liaoyuan 184-185 NO 3
Liaoyuan = Shuangliao 184-185 N 3
Liard River 144-145 M 5
Liaunim = Liaoning 184-185 MN 3
Liban 184-185 D 4
Liban 180-181 D 4
Libano 180-181 D 4
Libano 184-185 D 4
Libano [RL] 180-181 D 4
Libanon 184-185 D 4
Libao 190-191 H 5
Libau = Liepāja 138-139 C 5
Libby, MT 150-151 F 1
Libby Reservoir 150-151 F 1
Libebe = Andara 168-169 F 6
Libenge 168-169 E 2
Liberal, KS 146-147 F 4
Liberata 160-161 G 7
Liberec 133 G 3
Libéria 166-167 BC 7
Libéria 166-167 BC 7
Libéria [LB] 166-167 BC 7
Libéria, Dorsale della - 124-125 J 5
Libéria, Patamar da - 124-125 J 5
Libéria, Ramal de - 124-125 J 5
Libéria, Seuil du - 124-125 J 5
Libéria, Umbral da 172-173 BC 5
Liberia Basin 124-125 J 5
Liberiadrempel 124-125 J 5
Liberiaschwelle 124-125 J 5
Libérie 166-167 BC 7
Libertador General San Martín
[RA, Misiones] 160-161 E 7
Libertas 174-175 G 5
Liberty, IN 152-153 O 6
Liberty, KY 152-153 O 7
Liberty, MO 152-153 J 6
Liberty, NY 148-149 F 4
Liberty, OH 148-149 A 5
Liberty, TX 154-155 H 5-6
Liberty, WA 150-151 C 2
Libia 166-167 G-J 3
Líbia 166-167 G-J 3
Libia, Deserto de - 166-167 J 3-L 4
Libiai-sivatag 166-167 J 3-L 4
Libië 166-167 G-J 3
Libijska, Pustynia - 166-167 J 3-L 4
Libische Woestijn 166-167 J 3-L 4
Libourne 134-135 GH 6
Libreville 168-169 CD 2
Libya 166-167 G-J 3
Libyan Desert 166-167 J 3-L 4
Libye 166-167 G-J 3
Libye, Désert de - 166-167 J 3-L 4
Libyen 166-167 G-J 3
Libyjská poušť' 166-167 J 3-L 4
Libysche Wüste 166-167 J 3-L 4
Licantén 162 B 4
Licata 136-137 E 7
Lice 182-183 J 3
Lichangshan Liedao 188-189 D 3
Li-ch'ang-shan Lieh-tao =
Lichangshan Liedao 188-189 D 3
Licheng 190-191 D 3
Li- ch'i = Lixi 190-191 E 7
Li-chia-chuang = Lijiazhuang
190-191 G 4
Li-chiang = Lijiang 184-185 J 6
Li-chia-tu = Lijiadu 190-191 F 7
Li-chin = Lijin 190-191 G 3
Lichinga 168-169 J 5
Lichoslavl' 138-139 K 5
Lichovskoj 140-141 JK 2
Lichtenburg 168-169 FG 8
Lichtenštejnsko 133 D 5
Lichuan [TJ, Hubei] 190-191 B 6
Lichuan [TJ, Jiangxi] 190-191 F 8
Licking, MO 152-153 L 7
Licosa, Punta - 136-137 F 5
Lida 138-139 E 7
Lida, NV 150-151 E 7
Lidām, Al- = Al-Khamāsīn
180-181 EF 6
Lidfontein 174-175 C 3
Lidgerwood, ND 152-153 H 2
Lidingö 130-131 H 8
Lidinon, Akrōtérion - 136-137 L 8
Lidköping 130-131 E 8
Lido di Òstia, Roma- 136-137 DE 5
Liebenbergsvleirivier 174-175 H 4-5
Liechtenstein 133 D 5
Liedao 190-191 J 6
Liège 134-135 K 3
Liége = Liège 134-135 L 3
Liegnitz = Legnica 133 GH 3
Lieja = Liège 134-135 K 3
Lieksa 130-131 NO 6
Lielupe 138-139 D 5
Lielvārde 138-139 E 5
Lienartville 168-169 G 2
Lien-chên = Lianzhen 190-191 F 3
Lien-ch'êng = Liancheng
190-191 F 9
Lien-chiang = Lianjiang [TJ, Fujian]
190-191 G 8
Lien-chiang = Lianjiang [TJ,
Guangdong] 184-185 KL 7
Lien Chiang = Ping Jiang
190-191 E 8
Lien-hsien = Lian Xian 190-191 D 9
Lien-hua = Lianhua 184-185 L 6
Lienhwa = Lianhua 184-185 L 6
Lienkong = Lianjiang 190-191 G 8
Lienping = Lianping 190-191 E 9
Lien-shan-kuan = Lianshanguan
188-189 D 2
Lien Shui = Lian Shui [TJ, ~]
190-191 CD 8
Lienshui = Lianshui [TJ, ●]
190-191 G 5
Lien-t'ang = Liantang 190-191 E 7
Lienyunkang = Lianyungang
184-185 MN 5
Lien-yün Shan = Lianyun Shan
190-191 D 7
Lienz 133 F 5
Liepāja 138-139 C 5
Liepna 138-139 F 5
Lietuva = Litauen 138-139 DE 6
Lievenhof = Livāni 138-139 F 5
Liezen 133 FG 5
Lifi Mahuida 162 C 6
Lifīyah, Al- 182-183 K 7
Lifou, Île - 194-195 N 4
Lifu = Île Lifou 194-195 N 4
Lifubu 171 B 5
Liganga 171 C 5
Ligat = Ligatne 138-139 E 5
Ligatne 138-139 E 5
Light, Cape - 121 B 130-131
Lightning Ridge 196 HJ 2
Ligonha, Rio - 168-169 J 6
Ligua, La - 162 B 4
Ligúria 136-137 B 4-C 3
Liguria, Mar da - 128-129 K 7
Liguria, Mar de - 136-137 BC 4
Ligurian Sea 136-137 BC 4
Ligurie = Ligùria 136-137 B 4-C 3
Ligurien = Ligùria 136-137 B 4-C 3
Ligurisches Meer 136-137 BC 4
Ligurische Zee 136-137 BC 4
Ligurské moře 136-137 C 4
Liguryjskie, Morze - 136-137 C 4
Li He 190-191 D 5
Lihir Group 186-187 h 5
Li Ho = Li He 190-191 D 5
Lihua = Litang 184-185 J 5
Lihula 130-131 K 8
Lihsien = Li Xian [TJ, Hebei]
190-191 E 2
Lihsien = Li Xian [TJ, Hunan]
190-191 C 7
Lihuang = Jinzhai 190-191 E 6
Lihula 138-139 DE 4
Lijiadu 190-191 F 7
Lijiaping 190-191 CD 8
Lijiazhuang 190-191 G 4
Lijin 190-191 G 3
Lijepaja = Liepāja 130-131 J 9
Lijiang 184-185 J 6
Likasi 168-169 G 5
Likati 168-169 F 2
Likely, CA 150-151 C 5
Likiang = Lijiang 184-185 J 6
Likiep 192-193 H 3
Likino-Dulevo 138-139 M 6
Likoma Island 168-169 HJ 5
Likoto 168-169 F 3
Likouala [RCB ◁ Sangha]
168-169 E 2
Likouala [RCB ◁ Zaïre] 168-169 E 2
Likuala = Likouala [RCB ◁
Sangha] 168-169 E 2
Likuala = Likouala [RCB ◁ Zaïre]
168-169 E 2
Likupang 186-187 J 6
Liland 130-131 G 3
Lilbourn, MO 154-155 L 2
Liling 190-191 D 8
Lille 134-135 J 3
Lille Bælt 130-131 CD 10
Lille-Ballangen 130-131 G 3
Lillehammer 130-131 D 7
Lillesand 130-131 C 8
Lillestrøm 130-131 D 7-8
Lilliput 174-175 H 2
Lilongwe [MW, ~] 171 C 6
Lilongwe [MW, ●] 168-169 H 5
Lilung 190-191 H 10
Lilydale 196 c 2
Lim 136-137 H 4
Lima [P] 134-135 C 8
Lima [PY] 160-161 D 5
Lima, MT 150-151 G 3
Lima, OH 146-147 K 3
Lima [PE, ●] 158-159 D 7
Lima = Dsayul 184-185 H 6
Lima Duarte 160-161 L 4
Limão, Cachoeira do - 158-159 J 6
Lima Qundao = Dangan Liedao
190-191 E 10-11
Lima Reservoir 150-151 GH 3
Limassol = Lemesós 180-181 C 4
Limay, Río - 162 C 5
Limay Mahuida 162 C 5
Limbang 186-187 FG 6
Limbaži 138-139 E 5
Limbe 166-167 F 8
Limburg 133 D 3
Limchow = Hepu 184-185 K 7
Limeira 158-159 K 9
Limerick 132 B 5
Limfjorden 130-131 D 9
Limia 134-135 C 7
Li Miao Zhou = Hainan Zangzu
Zizhizhou 184-185 K 8
Limietskop 174-175 D 6
Liminka 130-131 L 5
Limkong = Lianjiang 184-185 KL 7
Limmen Bight 194-195 G 2
Límnē 136-137 K 6
Limoges 134-135 H 6
Limoges [CDN] 148-149 F 2
Limón 146-147 K 9-10
Limon, Co 152-153 E 6
Limón, Bahía - 146-147 b 2
Limon Bay 146-147 ab 2
Limousin 134-135 HJ 6
Limoux 134-135 J 7
Limpia, Laguna - [RA ↖
Resistencia] 162 DE 3
Limpopo 168-169 G 7
Limpopo, Represa do - 174-175 K 3
Limpopo - Rio - 174-175 K 3
Limpoporivier 174-175 H 2
Limpopo-Staudamm = Represa
do Limpopo 174-175 K 3
Limu 190-191 C 9
Lin 136-137 J 5
Lin'an 190-191 G 6
Linan = Jianshui 184-185 J 7
Linares [CO] 158-159 D 4
Linares [E] 134-135 F 9
Linares [MEX] 146-147 G 7
Linares [RCH] 162 B 5
Lincang 184-185 HJ 7
Lincheng 190-191 E 3
Lincheng = Xuecheng 190-191 F 4
Lin-ch'i = Linqi 190-191 D 4
Lin-chiang = Linjiang [TJ, Fujian]
190-191 G 8
Lin-chiang = Linjiang [TJ, Jilin]
184-185 O 3
Lin-ch'ing = Linqing 184-185 M 4
Linchow = Hepu 184-185 K 7
Linchu = Linqu 190-191 G 3
Linchuan = Fuzhou 184-185 MN 6
Lin-ch'üan = Linquan 190-191 E 5
Lincoln [GB] 132 F 5
Lincoln [RA] 162 D 4
Lincoln, CA 150-151 C 6
Lincoln, IL 152-153 M 5
Lincoln, KS 152-153 G 6
Lincoln, ME 148-149 J 2
Lincoln, NE 146-147 G 3
Lincoln, NH 148-149 GH 2
Lincoln, NM 154-155 C 4
Lincoln, Mount - 152-153 CD 6
Lincoln City, IN 152-153 N 6
Lincoln Park, MI 152-153 P 4
Lincoln Sea 120A 121-25
Lincolnton, NC 148-149 C 7
Lind, WA 150-151 D 2
Linda [SU] 138-139 P 5
Lindale, GA 154-155 N 3
Lindale, TX 154-155 H 4
Lindau 133 D 5
Linde [SU] 178-179 X 4
Linden, AL 154-155 M 4
Linden, IN 152-153 N 5
Linden, TN 154-155 M 3
Linden, TX 154-155 H 4
Lindesberg 130-131 F 8
Lindesnes 130-131 B 9
Lindi [EAT] 168-169 J 4-5
Lindi [ZRE] 168-169 G 2
Lindian 184-185 NO 2
Lindley 174-175 GH 4
Lindos 136-137 N 7
Lindozero 138-139 J 2
Lindsay 148-149 D 2
Lindsay, CA 150-151 D 7
Lindsay, MT 152-153 D 2
Lindsay, OK 154-155 G 3
Lindsborg, KS 152-153 H 6
Linea, La - 134-135 E 10
Linec = Linz 133 EF 4
Lineville, AL 154-155 N 4
Lineville, IA 152-153 K 5
Linfen 184-185 L 4
Lingao 184-185 K 8
Lingayen Gulf 186-187 GH 3
Lingbao 190-191 C 4
Lingbi 190-191 F 5
Ling Chiang = Ling Jiang
190-191 H 7
Lingchuan 190-191 BC 9
Lingding Yang = Zhujiang Kou
190-191 D 10
Linge [BUR] 186-187 C 2
Lingeh = Bandar-e Lengeh
180-181 GH 5
Lingen 133 C 2
Lingga, Kepulauan - 186-187 DE 7
Lingga, Pulau - 186-187 DE 7
Ling-hsien = Ling Xian
190-191 DE 8
Lingle, WY 152-153 D 4
Lingling 184-185 L 6
Lingmar 184-185 F 5
Lingpao = Lingbao 190-191 C 4
Lingpi = Lingbi 190-191 F 5
Lingqiu 190-191 E 2
Lingschantau = Lingshan Dao
190-191 H 4
Lingshan 190-191 B 10
Lingshan Dao 190-191 H 4
Lingshanwei 190-191 H 4
Lingshi 190-191 C 3
Lingshih = Lingshi 190-191 C 3
Lingshou 190-191 E 2
Linguère 166-167 AB 5
Ling Xian [TJ, Hunan] 190-191 DE 8
Ling Xian [TJ, Shandong]
190-191 F 3
Lingyan 190-191 F 6
Lingyuan 188-189 B 2
Ling-yüan = Lingyuan 188-189 B 2
Lingyun 184-185 K 7
Linhai 184-185 N 6
Linhares 158-159 LM 8
Linh Cam 186-187 E 3
Linhe 184-185 K 3
Lin-ho = Linhe 184-185 K 3
Linhong Kou 190-191 G 4
Lin-hsi = Linxi 184-185 M 3
Lin-hsia = Linxia 184-185 J 4
Lin-hsien = Lin Xian [TJ, Henan]
190-191 DE 3
Linhsien = Lin Xian [TJ, Shanxi]
190-191 C 3
Linhuaiguan 190-191 FG 5
Lin-huai-kuan = Linhuaiguan 190-
191 FG 5
Linhuan-chi = Linhuanji
190-191 F 5
Linhuanji 190-191 F 5
Lin-i = Linyi [TJ ↑ Jinan]
190-191 F 3
Lini = Linyi [TJ ↗ Xuzhou]
184-185 M 4
Linieninseln = Gilbert Islands
198-199 H 4-5
Linjiang [TJ, Fujian] 190-191 G 8
Linjiang [TJ, Jilin] 184-185 O 3
Linju = Linru 190-191 D 4
Linkiang = Linjiang 190-191 G 8
Linköping 130-131 FG 8
Linkou 184-185 OP 2
Linkow = Linkou 184-185 OP 2
Linkowo = Linkuva 138-139 D 5
Linkuva 138-139 D 5
Linli 184-185 L 6
Linn, KS 152-153 H 6
Linn, MO 152-153 K 6
Linn, TX 154-155 F 7
Linn, Mount - 150-151 B 5
Linné, Kapp - 130-131 j 5
Linnhe, Loch - 132 D 3
Linosa 136-137 E 8
Linosa, Ìsola - 166-167 G 1
Linqi 190-191 D 4
Linqing 184-185 M 4
Linqu 190-191 G 3
Linquan 190-191 E 5
Linru 190-191 D 4
Lins 158-159 JK 9
Linshan = Zhouxiang 190-191 H 6
Linshu 190-191 G 4
Linsia = Linxia 184-185 J 4
Linsin = Linxia 184-185 J 4
Lintan 184-185 J 5
Lintao 184-185 J 4
Lintien = Lindian 184-185 NO 2
Linton, IN 152-153 N 6
Linton, ND 152-153 FG 2
Lintong 190-191 B 4
Lintsing = Linqing 184-185 M 4
Lintung = Lintong 190-191 B 4
Linwu 190-191 D 9
Linxi 184-185 M 3
Linxia 184-185 J 4
Linxia Huizu Zizhizhou =
A ◁ 184-185 J 4
Lin Xian [TJ, Henan]
190-191 DE 3
Lin Xian [TJ, Shanxi] 190-191 C 3
Linxiang 190-191 D 7
Linyanti 168-169 F 6
Linyi [TJ, Shanxi] 190-191 C 4
Linyi [TJ, Shandong ↑ Jinan]
190-191 F 3
Linyi [TJ, Shandong ↗ Xuzhou]
184-185 M 4
Linying 190-191 D 5
Linyou 190-191 AB 4
Linyu = Linyou 190-191 AB 4
Linyu = Shanhaiguan 188-189 BC 2
Linz 133 FG 4
Lion, Golf du - 134-135 JK 7
Lione = Lyon 134-135 K 6

Lion River = Löwenrivier
174-175 C 4
Lions Head 152-153 Q 3
Liorne 136-137 D 4
Liouesso 168-169 DE 2
Liozno 138-139 H 6
Li-pao = Libao 190-191 H 5
Lipari 136-137 F 6
Lipawa = Liepāja 138-139 C 5
Lipeck 138-139 M 7
Lipetsk = Lipeck 138-139 M 7
Lipez, Cordillera de - 158-159 F 9
Lipin Bor 138-139 LM 3
Liping 184-185 K 6
Lipkany 140-141 C 2
Lipljan 136-137 J 4
Lipno 133 J 2
Lipova 136-137 J 2
Lippe 133 C 3
Lippstadt 133 D 3
Lipscomb, TX 154-155 E 2
Lipsk = Leipzig 133 F 3
Lipsko = Leipzig 133 F 3
Lipu 184-185 KL 7
Lir 166-167 KL 7
Lira 168-169 H 2
Liranga 168-169 E 3
Lisabon = Lisboa 134-135 C 9
Lisala 168-169 F 2
Lisār 182-183 N 3
Lisboa 134-135 C 9
Lisboa 134-135 C 9
Lisbon, ND 152-153 H 2
Lisbon, OH 148-149 C 4
Lisbon = Lisboa 134-135 C 9
Lisbona = Lisboa 134-135 C 9
Lisbonne = Lisboa 134-135 C 9
Lisburn 132 CD 4
Lisburne, Cape - 144-145 C 4
Lishan 190-191 D 6
Lishi 184-185 L 4
Lishih = Lishi 184-185 L 4
Li Shui [TJ, Hunan] 190-191 C 7
Lishui [TJ, Jiangsu] 190-191 G 6
Lishui [TJ, Zhejiang] 184-185 MN 6
Lishui = Limu 190-191 C 9
Lisianski 192-193 K 2
Lisieux 134-135 H 4
Liski 140-141 JK 1
Lisle, NY 148-149 EF 3
Lismore [AUS] 194-195 K 5
Lismore [IRL] 132 C 5
Lissa = Leszno 133 H 3
Lissabon = Lisboa 134-135 C 9
Lista 130-131 B 8
Lister, Mount - 121 B 17
Listowel 148-149 C 3
Listowel 132 B 5
Litan 184-185 J 5
Litang 184-185 K 7
Liṭānī, Nahr al- 182-183 F 6
Litauen 138-139 DE 6
Litchfield, CA 150-151 CD 5
Litchfield, IL 152-153 M 6
Litchfield, MN 152-153 J 3
Litchfield, NE 152-153 G 5
Litchville, ND152-153 G 2
Lith, Al- 180-181 E 6
Lithgow 194-195 JK 6
Lithuania 138-139 DE 6
Litin 140-141 D 2
Litke 178-179 ab 7
Litóchōron 136-137 K 5
Litoměřice 133 G 3
Litomyšl 133 GH 4
Litouwen 130-131 KL 10
Litouwen 138-139 DE 6
Litovkaja Sovetskaja
Socialističeskaja Respublika =
Litauen 138-139 DE 6
Litovko 178-179 Za 8
Litsin = Lijin 190-191 G 3
Little Andaman 180-181 P 8
Little Bay de Noc 152-153 N 3
Little Belt Mountains 150-151 H 2
Little Bighorn River 152-153 C 3
Little Blue River 152-153 G 5
Little Cayman 146-147 KL 8
Little Colorado River 146-147 DE 5
Little Desert, The - 196 E 6
Little Falls, MN 152-153 J 2-3
Little Falls, NY 148-149 F 3
Littlefield, AZ 150-151 G 7
Littlefield, TX 154-155 DE 4
Littlefork, MN 152-153 K 1
Little Fork River 152-153 K 1
Little Gombi 172-173 J 3
Little Humboldt River 150-151 E 5
Little Karas Mountains = Klein
Karasberge 174-175 C 4
Little Lake, CA 150-151 E 8
Little Mecatina River 144-145 YZ 7
Little Minch 132 C 3
Little Missouri River 152-153 E 2
Little Namaqua Land = Klein
Namakwaland 174-175 B 5
Little Nicobar 180-181 P 9
Little Osage River 152-153 J 7
Little Pee Dee River 148-149 D 7-8
Little Powder River 152-153 D 3
Little River, KS 152-153 GH 6
Little Rock, AR 146-147 H 5
Littlerock, CA 150-151 DE 8
Little Rock, WA 150-151 B 2
Little Rock Mountains
150-151 J 1 -2
Little Rocky Mountains
152-153 B 1
Little Ruaha 171 C 4-5
Little Sable Point 152-153 N 4
Little Sanke River 152-153 B 5
Little Scarcies 172-173 B 3
Little Sioux River 152-153 J 4
Little Smoky Valley 150-151 F 6
Little Snake River 150-151 J 5
Littleton, CO 152-153 D 6
Littleton, NC 148-149 DE 6
Littleton, NH 148-149 H 2
Little Traverse Bay 152-153 O 3
Little Valley, NY 148-149 D 3
Little Wood River 150-151 FG 4
Lituania 130-131 KL 10
Lituania 130-131 K-M 10
Lituânia 126-127 NO 4
Lituânia, Republica da -
138-139 C-E 6
Lituanie 138-139 DE 6
Litunde 171 CD 6
Litva 138-139 DE 6
Litvánia 138-139 DE 6
Litwa 138-139 DE 6
Liucheng 190-191 B 9
Liu-chia-tzŭ = Liujiazi 188-189 C 2
Liuchow = Liuzhou 184-185 K 7
Liu-ch'üan = Liuquan 190-191 F 4
Liu-chuang = Liuzhuang
190-191 GH 5
Liuhe [TJ, Henan] 190-191 E 4
Liuhe [TJ, Jiangsu] 190-191H 6
Liuhe [TJ, Jilin] 188-189 E 1
Liu-he = Liuhe 190-191 G 5
Liuheng Dao 190-191 J 7
Liu-hêng Tao = Liuheng Dao
190-191 J 7
Liu-ho = Liuhe [TJ, Henan]
190-191 E 4
Liu-ho = Liuhe [TJ, Jiangsu]
190-191 H 6
Liu-ho = Liuhe [TJ, Jilin]
188-189 E 1
Liu-ho = Luhe 190-191 G 5
Liulihezhen 190-191 EF 2
Liu-li-ho = Liulihezhen 190-191 EF 2
Liujiazi 188-189 C 2
Liuquan 190-191 F 4
Liurbao 188-189 D 2
Liushouying 190-191 G 2
Liuwa Plain 168-169 F 5
Liuyang 190-191 D 7
Liuzhou 184-185 K 7
Liuzhuang 190-191 GH 5
Livāni 138-139 F 5
Live Oak, FL 148-149 b 1
Livermore, CA 150-151 C 7
Livermore, IA 152-153 JK 4
Livermore, KY 152-153 N 7
Livermore, Mount - 146-147 F 5
Livermore Falls, ME 148-149 HJ 2
Liverpool 132 E 5
Liverpool Bay [CDN] 144-145 L 3-4
Liverpool Range 194-195 JK 6
Livingston, AL 154-155 LM 4
Livingston, KY 152-153 OP 7
Livingston, MT 150-151 H 3
Livingston, TN 154-155 N 2
Livingston, TX 154-155 H 5
Livingstone 168-169 G 6
Livingstone Memorial 168-169 GH 5
Livingstone Mountains
168-169 H 4-5
Livingstonia 171 C 5
Livingstonia = Chiweta 168-169 H 5
Livingston Island 121 CD 30
Livland 130-131 L 9-M 8
Livländische Aa = Gauja
138-139 EF 5
Livno 136-137 G 4
Livny 138-139 L 7
Livónia 130-131 L 9-M 8
Livonia 130-131 L 9-M 8
Livonia, MI 152-153 P 4
Livonie 130-131 L 9-M 8
Livonsko 130-131 L 9-M 8
Livorno 136-137 CD 4
Livourne = Livorno 136-137 CD 4
Liwale 168-169 J 4
Liwenhof = Livāni 138-139 F 5
Lixi 190-191 E 7
Li Xian [TJ, Hebei] 190-191 E 2
Li Xian [TJ, Hunan] 190-191 C 7
Lixin 190-191 F 5
Liyang 190-191 G 6
Lī Yūbū 166-167 K 7
Lizarda 158-159 K 6
Lizard Head Peak 150-151 J 4
Lizard Point 132 D 7
Lizerorta 138-139 C 5
Ljubljana 136-137 F 2
Ljungan 130-131 G 6
Ljungby 130-131 E 9
Ljusdal 130-131 FG 7
Ljusnan 130-131 F 6-7
Ljusne 130-131 G 7
Llamellin 158-159 D 6
Llandrindod Wells 132 E 5
Llanes 134-135 E 7
Llangefni 132 D 5
Llano 150-151 H 10
Llano, TX 154-155 F 5
Llano Estacado 146-147 F 5
Llano Estacado, Bluffs of -
154-155 D 3
Llano River 154-155 F 5
Llanquihue, Lago - 162 B 6
Llata 158-159 D 6
Llerena 134-135 DE 9
Lleyn Peninsula 132 D 5
Llobregat 134-135 H 7-8
Llorena, Punta - = Punta San
Pedro 146-147 K 10
Lloyd Bay 194-195 H 2
Lloydminster 144-145 OP 7
Llullaillaco, Volcán - 162 C 2-3
Loa, UT 150-151 H 6
Loa, Rio - 162 BC 2
Loange 168-169 F 3-4
Loango 168-169 D 3
Loan = Le'an 190-191 E 8
Loban' 138-139 S 5
Lobata 186-187 H 7
Lobatse 168-169 FG 8
Lobaye 166-167 H 8
Loberia [RA, Buenos Aires] 162 E 5
Lobito 168-169 D 5
Lob nuur 184-185 G 3
Lobo 172-173 D 4
Lobstick Lake 144-145 Y 7
Locate, MT 152-153 D 2
Loche, La - 144-145 P 6
Lo-ch'êng = Luocheng 190-191 B 9
Loch Garman = Wexford 132 C 5
Lochgilphead 132 D 3
Lochiel 174-175 J 4
Lo-ching = Yueqing 184-185 N 6
Lo-ch'ing Ho = Luoqing Jiang
190-191 B 9
Lo-ch'ing Wan = Yueqing Wan
190-191 H 7-8
Lochnagar 132 E 3
Lochsa River 150-151 F 2
Lo-ch'uan = Luochuan 190-191 B 4
Lochvica 140-141 F 1
Lock 196 BC 4
Lockes, NV 150-151 F 6
Lockesburg, AR 154-155 HJ 4
Lockhart 196 H 5
Lockhart, AL 154-155 M 5
Lockhart, TX 154-155 G 6
Lockhart River Aboriginal
Reserve 194-195 H 2
Lock Haven, PA 148-149 E 4
Lockney, TX 154-155 E 3
Lockport, LA 154-155 K 6
Lockport, NY 148-149 D 3
Lockwood, MO 154-155 HJ 2
Locust Creek 152-153 K 5
Lôc Ninh 186-187 E 4
Locri 136-137 G 6
Lod 182-183 F 7
Lodejnoje Pole 138-139 JK 3
Lodge Creek 152-153 B 1
Lodge Grass, MT 152-153 C 3
Lodgepole, NE 152-153 E 5
Lodgepole Creek 152-153 D 5
Lodi 136-137 C 3
Lodi, CA 150-151 C 6
Lodi, WI 152-153 M 4
Lodi = Ayni 182-183 JK 4
Loding = Luoding 190-191 C 10
Lødingen 130-131 F 3
Lodja 168-169 F 3
Lodsch = Łódź 133 J 3
Lodwar 168-169 J 2
Łódź 133 J 3
Loei 186-187 D 3
Loeriesfontein 174-175 C 6
Lofa 172-173 C 4
Lo-fang = Luofang 190-191 E 8
Lofa River 166-167 B 7
Lofocki, Basen - 130-131 A-C 2
Lofotbecken 128-129 JK 1
Lofoten 130-131 E 3-4
Lofoten, Bacia das - 128-129 JK 1
Lofoten, Bacino delle -
128-129 JK 1
Lofoten, Bassin des - 128-129 JK 1
Lofoten, Cuenca de las -
128-129 JK 1
Lofoten Basin 128-129 JK 1
Lofotenbekken 128-129 JK 1
Lofthus 130-131 B 7
Lofty Range, Mount - 194-195 G 6
Lofusa = Lufusā 171 C 2
Log 140-141 LM 2
Loga [RN] 172-173 F 2
Logan, IA 152-153 HJ 5
Logan, KS 152-153 G 6
Logan, NE 152-153 F 5
Logan, NM 154-155 D 3
Logan, OH 148-149 B 5
Logan, UT 146-147 D 3
Logan, WV 148-149 BC 6
Logan, Mount - [CDN, Yukon
Territory] 144-145 HJ 5
Logandale, NV 150-151 F 7
Logan Mountains 144-145 L 5
Logansport, IN 146-147 J 3
Logansport, LA 154-155 J 5
Loge, Rio - 168-169 D 4
Loginjag 138-139 T 3
Logojsk 130-131 M 10
Logojsk 138-139 FG 6
Logone 166-167 H 7
Logroño 134-135 F 7
Løgstør 130-131 C 9
Lohardaga 180-181 N 6
Lōhārdaggā = Lohardaga
180-181 N 6
Lōhit = Luhit 180-181 Q 5
Lohja 130-131 KL 7
Lo Ho = Luo He [TJ ◁Huang He]
190-191 CD 4
Lo Ho = Luo He [TJ ◁Wei He]
190-191 B 4
Lohtaja 130-131 K 5
Lo-hua = Lehua 190-191 EF 7
Lohumbo 171 C 3
Lohusuu 138-139 F 4
Loibl 133 G 5
Loikaw = Lûykau 186-187 C 3
Loimaa 130-131 K 7
Loir 134-135 G 5
Loire 134-135 H 5
Loiya 171 C 2
Loja [E] 134-135 E 10
Loja [EC, ●] 158-159 D 5
Loji 186-187 J 7
Lojno 138-139 T 4
Lo-jung = Luorong 184-185 K 7
Loka = Lūkā 171 B 1
Lokan tekojärvi 130-131 MN 3
Lokbatan 140-141 O 6
Lokčim 138-139 ST 3
Lokichoggio 171 C 1
Lokila = Lukilā 171 C 1
Lokitaung 168-169 HJ 2
Lokka 130-131 MN 4
Lokn'a 138-139 H 5
Lokoja 166-167 F 7
Loko 172-173 G 3-4
Lokolo 168-169 EF 3
Loko Mountains 172-173 C 3
Lokossa 172-173 F 4
Lokot' 138-139 K 7
Lo-k'ou = Luokou 190-191 E 8
Loksa 138-139 E 4
Loks Land 144-145 Y 5
Lokwabe 174-175 DE 3
Lōl, Nahr - = Nahr Lul 166-167 K 7
Lola, Mount - 150-151 C 6
Loleta, CA 150-151 A 5
Lolgorien 171 C 3
Loliondo 171 C 3
Loling = Leling 190-191 F 3
Lol Laikumaiki 171 D 4
Lolland 130-131 D 10
Lolmuryoi 171 D 4
Lolo 168-169 D 2
Lolo, MT 150-151 F 2
Lolobau 186-187 h 5
Loloda 186-187 J 6
Lolodorf 172-173 H 5
Lolui 171 C 3
Lom [BG] 136-137 K 4
Lom [RFC] 166-167 G 7
Loma, MT 150-151 H 1-2
Loma, ND 152-153 G 1
Loma = Lomai 172-173 C 4
Lomadi 186-187 C 3
Lomai 172-173 C 4
Lomami 168-169 FG 3
Loma Mountains 166-167 B 7
Lomas [PE] 158-159 E 8
Lomas de Vallejos 160-161 D 7
Lomax, IL 152-153 L 5
Lombard, MT 150-151 H 2
Lombarda, Serra - 158-159 J 4
Lombardei = Lombardia
136-137 C 3-D 2
Lombardia 136-137 C 3-D 2
Lombardie = Lombardia
136-137 C 3-D 2
Lomblem = Pulau Lomblen
186-187 H 8
Lomblen, Pulau - 186-187 H 8
Lombok, Pulau - 186-187 G 8
Lombok, Selat - 186-187 G 8
Lomé 166-167 E 7
Lomela [ZRE, ~] 168-169 F 3
Lomela [ZRE, ●] 168-169 F 3
Lometa, TX 154-155 F 5
Lomié 166-167 G 8
Lomitas, Las - 162 D 2
Lomond, Ben - [AUS] 196 cd 2
Lomond, Loch - 132 D 3
Lomonosov 138-139 G 4
Lomonosov, Crista de - 120 A
Lomonosov, Dorsal de - 120 A
Lomonosov, Dorsale di - 120 A
Lomonosov Ridge 120 A
Lomonosova 178-179 M 7
Lomonosovrug 120 A
Lomonosovův hřbet 120 A
Lomonosowrücken 120 A
Lomonossov, Crête de - 120 A
Lomonoszov-hátság 120 A
Lompoc, CA 150-151 C 8
Lompoul 172-173 A 2
Lom Sak 186-187 D 3
Lomskoje 138-139 LM 7
Łomża 133 L 2
Lonan = Luonen 190-191 C 4
Loncoche 162 B 5
Londen = London 132 G 6
Londiani 171 C 3
London [CDN] 144-145 UV 9
London [GB] 132 G 6
London, KY 152-153 OP 7
London, OH 152-153 P 6
London, TX 154-155 F 5
Londonderry 132 C 4
Londonderry, Cape - 194-195 E 2
Londonderry, Islas - 162 B 9
Londra = London 132 G 4
Londres = London 132 G 6
Londres = London 128-129 H 35
Londrina 162 FG 2
Londýn = London 132 G 4
Londyn = London 132 G 4
Lone Mountain 150-151 E 7
Lone Pine, CA 150-151 DE 7
Lone Oak, TX 154-155 GH 4
Lonerock, OR 150-151 D 3
Lone Rock, WI 152-153 LM 4
Lonetree, WY 150-151 H 5
Lone Wolf, OK 154-155 F 3
Longa [Angola] 168-169 E 5
Longa, proliv - 178-179 j 3-4
Long Bay 146-147 L 5
Long Beach, CA 146-147 BC 5
Longboat Key 148-149 b 3
Long Branch, NJ 148-149 FG 4
Longchuan [TJ, Dehong Daizu
Zizhizhou] 184-185 H 7
Longchuan [TJ, Guangdong]
190-191 E 9
Long Creek, OR 150-151 D 3
Longdor, gora - 178-179 W 6
Long Eddy, NY 148-149 F 4
Longfellow, TX 154-155 D 5
Longford 194-195 J 8
Longford 132 BC 5
Longgang 190-191 GH 5
Longhai 190-191 FG 9
Long Hu 190-191 F 7
Longhua 184-185 M 3
Longhui 190-191 C 8
Longido 171 D 3
Longiram 186-187 G 6-7
Long Island [BS] 146-147 LM 7
Long Island [CDN] 144-145 UV 7
Long Island [PNG] 186-187 N 7-8
Long Island [USA] 146-147 M 3-4
Long Island, KS 152-153 G 6
Long Island Sound 148-149 G 4
Long Jiang 190-191 B 9
Longjing 188-189 G 1
Longkou 190-191 GH 3
Longkou Wan 190-191 GH 3
Long Lake [USA, Michigan]
152-153 P 3
Long Lake [USA, North Dakota]
152-153 G 2
Long Lake, WI 152-153 M 3
Longleaf, LA 154-155 J 5
Longling 184-185 H 7
Longmalinau 186-187 G 6
Longmen [TJ ↗ Guangzhou]
190-191 E 10
Longmire, WA 150-151 C 2
Longmont, CO 152-153 D 5
Longnan 184-185 LM 7
Longnawan 186-187 FG 6
Longonot 171 D 3
Long Pine, NE 152-153 G 4
Longping = Longyao 190-191 E 3
Long Point [CDN, Ontario]
148-149 CD 3
Long Point Bay 148-149 CD 3
Long Prairie, MN 152-153 J 2-3
Longqi = Zhangzhou 184-185 M 7
Longquan 184-185 M 6
Longquan Xi 190-191 G 7-8
Long Range Mountains
144-145 Z 7-8
Longreach 194-195 H 4
Longshan 190-191 B7
Longsheng [TJ ↖ Guilin]
190-191 BC 9
Longsheng [TJ ↙ Wuzhou]
190-191 C 10
Longs Peak 146-147 E 3
Longtan [TJ, Hunan] 190-191 C 8
Longtan [TJ, Jiangsu] 190-191 G 5
Longtian 190-191 G 9
Longton, KS 154-155 GH 2
Long Valley [USA, California]
150-151 D 7
Long Valley [USA, Nevada]
150-151 D 5
Longvalley, SD 152-153 F 4
Longview, TX 146-147 GH 5
Longview, WA 146-147 B 2
Longxi 184-185 J 4-5
Long Xuyên 186-187 DE 4
Longyan 190-191 F 9
Longyao 190-191 E 3
Longyearbyen 130-131 jk 5
Longyou 184-185 M 6
Longzhen 184-185 O 2
Lo-ning = Luoning 190-191 C 4
Lonja 136-137 G 3
Lonoke, AR 154-155 JK 3
Lønsdal 130-131 F 4
Lons-le-Saunier 134-135 K 5
Lontra, Rio - 160-161 F 4
Loogootee, IN 152-153 N 6
Lookout, Cape - [USA, North
Carolina] 146-147 L 5
Lookout, Cape - [USA, Oregon]
150-151 A 3
Lookout Mountain 150-151 E 3
Lookout Mountains [USA,
Alabama] 154-155 N 3
Lookout Mountains [USA,
Washington] 150-151 BC 2-3
Lookout Pass 150-151 F 2
Loolmalasin 171 CD 3
Loongana 194-195 E 6
Loop Head 132 A 5
Lopandino 138-139 K 7
Lopatin 140-141 NO 5
Lopatina, gora - 178-179 b 7
Lopatino, 138-139 PQ 7
Lopatino = Volžsk 178-179 H 6
Lopatka, mys - 120 D 3
Lop Buri 186-187 D 4
Loperot 171 C 2
Lopez, Cap - 168-169 C 3
López Collada 150-151 FG 10
Loping = Leping 184-185 M 6
Lo-p'ing = Xiyang 190-191 D 3
Lop Noor = Lob nuur 184-185 G 3
Lopori 168-169 F 2
Lopphavet 130-131 JK 2
Lopt'uga 138-139 QR 2
Lopydino 138-139 ST 3
Lōra, Hāmūn-e - 180-181 JK 5
Lora Creek 194-195 FG 5
Lora del Rio 134-135 E 10
Lorain, OH 146-147 K 3
Loralai = Lorālāy 180-181 K 4
Lorālāy 180-181 K 4
Lorca 134-135 G 10
lorda Howea, práh - 194-195 M 5-7
Lord Howe, Dorsale di -
194-195 M 5-7
Lord Howe Island 194-195 LM 6
Lord Howe Islands = Ontong
Java Islands 186-187 j 6
Lord Howe Rise 194-195 M 5-7
Lord Mayor Bay 144-145 ST 4
Lordsburg, NM 150-151 J 9
Lorena 158-159 KL 9
Lorena 134-135 KL 4
Lorena 133 BC 4
Lorengau 186-187 N 7
Lorestān 180-181 F 4
Loreto [BOL] 158-159 G 8
Loreto [BR, Maranhão] 158-159 K 6
Loreto [CO] 158-159 E F 5
Loreto [MEX, Baja California
Norte] 146-147 D 6
Loreto [PY] 160-161 D 5
Lorian Swamp 168-169 JK 2
Lorica 158-159 D 3
Lon dere 182-183 HJ 2
Lorient 134-135 F 5
Lorimor, IA 152-153 J 5
Loring, MT 152-153 C 1
Loris, SC 148-149 D 7
Lorne, Firth of - 132 CD 3
Loro 158-159 F 4
Loros, Los - 162 BC 3
Lörrach 133 C 5
Lorraine 134-135 KL 4
Lorugumu 171 C 2
Los Alamos, CA 150-151 C 8
Los Alamos, NM 146-147 E 4
Los Angeles, CA 146-147 BC 5
Los Angeles, TX 154-155 F 6
Los Angeles Aqueduct
150-151 DE 8
Los Banos, CA 150-151 C 7
Los Gatos, CA 150-151 C 7
Lošinj 136-137 F 3
Losevo 138-139 H 5
Lo-shan = Luoshan 190-191 E 5
Los, Îles de - 172-173 B 3
Los Lunas, NM 154-155 B3
Los Molinos, CA 150-151 BC 5
Los Monjes, Islas - 158-159 EF 2
Los Roques, Islas - 158-159 F 2
Lossiemouth 132 E 3
Lost Creek 152-153 B 4
Los Testigos, Islas - 158-159 G 2
Lost Hills, CA 150-151 D 8
Lost River Range 150-151 FG 3-4
Lost Springs, WY 152-153 D 4
Lost Trail Pass 150-151 G 3
Lot 134-135 H 6
Lota 162 B 5
Lotagipi Swamp 168-169 HJ 2
Lotaryngia 134-135 KL 4
Lothair 174-175 J 4
Lothair, MT 150-151 H 1
Lotharingen 134-135 KL 4
Lotharingia 134-135 KL 4
Lothringen 134-135 KL 4
Lo-t'ien = Luotian 190-191 E 6
Loting = Leting 190-191 G 2
Loting = Luoding 190-191 C 10
Lotlake 174-175 E 2
Lotmozero 130-131 NO 3
Lotošino 138-139 K 5
Lotrinsko 134-135 KL 4
Lotsani 174-175 G 2
Lott, TX 154-155 G 5
Lo-tung 190-191 HJ 9
Lotyšsko 138-139 D-F 5
Lötzen = Giżycko 133 KL 1
Louang Namtha 186-187 D 2
Louangphrabang 186-187 D 3
Loubad 174-175 H 3
Loubnān, Jabal - = Jabal
Lubnān [RL, ▲▲]
182-183 FG 5-6
Loubomo 168-169 D 3
Louchi 178-179 E 4
Loudéac 134-135 F 4
Loudi 190-191 C 8
Loudonville, OH 148-149 BC 4
Louellen, KY 152-153 P 7
Loufan 190-191 C 2
Louga 166-167 A 5
Lougheed Island 144-145 PQ 2
Louisa, VA 148-149 DE 5
Louisbourg 144-145 Z 8
Louisburg, NC 148-149 D 6
Louise, TX 154-155 G 6
Louisiade, Archipel de -
186-187 h 7
Louisiade Archipelago 186-187 h 7
Louisiana 146-147 H 5
Louisiana, MO 152-153 L 6
Louisiana Point 154-155 HJ 6
Louis Trichardt 168-169 GH 7
Louisville, CO 152-153 D 6
Louisville, GA 148-149 B 8
Louisville, IL 152-153 M 6
Louisville, KY 146-147 JK 4
Louisville, MS 154-155 L 4
Louisville, NE 152-153 H 5
Loulan = Loulanyiyi 184-185 F 3
Loulanyiyi 184-185 F 3
Loulé 134-135 C 10
Loup City, NE 152-153 G 5
Loup River 146-147 G 3
Louqsor = Al Uqsur 170-5
Lourdes 134-135 G 7
Lourenço Marques = Maputo
168-169 H 8
Lourenço Marques, Baia de - =
Baia do Maputo 168-169 H 8
Lousia, KY 148-149 B 5
Louth 132 FG 5
Louth [AUS] 194-195 HJ 6
Lou Shui 190-191 C 7
Lou-ti = Loudi 190-191 C 8
Louvain = Leuven 134-135 K 3
Louviers 134-135 H 4
Louviers, CO 152-153 D 6
Louwsburg 174-175 J 4
Lovat' 138-139 H 5
Lovászi 133 H 5
Loveč 136-137 L 4
Lovelady, TX 154-155 H 5
Loveland, CO 152-153 D 5
Loveland, OH 152-153 O 6
Lovell, WY 152-153 B 3
Lovelock, NV 150-151 D 5
Lovenia, Mount - 150-151 H 5
Loviisa = Lovisa 130-131 M 7
Lovilia, IA 152-153 K 5
Loving, NM 154-155 CD 4
Lovingston, VA 148-149 D 6
Lovington, IL 152-153 M 6
Lovington , NM 154-155 CD 4
Lovisa 130-131 M 7
Lovľa 138-139 R 4
Lövskär = ostrov Moščnyj 138-139
FG 4
Lóvua 168-169 F 5
Low, Cape - 144-145T5
Lowa 168-169 G 3
Lowell, ID 150-151 F 2
Lowell, IN 152-153 N 5
Lowell, MA 146-147 M 3
Lowell, MI 152-153 O 4
Lowell, OR 150-151 B 4
Löwenfluß = Löwenrivier
174-175 C 4
Löwenrivier 174-175 C 4
Lower Adamson 174-175 G 6
Lower Brule Indian Reservation
152-153 F 3
Lower California 150-151 F 10
Lower Guinea 124-125 K 5-6
Lower Hutt 194-195 OP 8
Lower Lake 150-151 CD 5
Lower Lake, CA 150-151 B 6
Lower Lough Erne 132 BC 4
Lower Peninsula 146-147 JK 3
Lower Red Lake 152-153 J 2
Lower Woolgar 194-195 H 3
Lowestoft 132 GH 5
Łowicz 133 J 2
Lowlands 132 D 4-E 3
Lowman , ID 150-151 F 3
Low Rocky Point 196 b 3
Lowville, NY 148-149 F 3
Loxton 196 E 5
Loyalton, CA 150-151 C 6
Loyalton, SD 152-153 G 3
Loyang = Luoyang 184-185 L 5
Loyauté, Îles - 194-195 N 4
Loyuan = Luoyuan 190-191 G 8
Lo-yüan = Luoyuan 190-191 G 8
Lozanna = Lausanne 133 C 5
Lozère 134-135 J 6
Loznica 136-137 H 3
Lozowa 140-141 H 2
Lozym 138-139 S 3
Lu'ā'ah, Al- 182-183 L 7
Luacano 168-169 F 5
Luachimo 168-169 F 4
Luala 168-169 G 4
Lualaba 168-169 G 4
Luama 168-169 G 3
Luambe 171 C 6
Lu'an 184-185 M 5
Luancheng [TJ, Guangxi Zhuangzu
Zizhiqu] 190-191 B 10
Luancheng [TJ, Hebei] 190-191 E 2
Luanchuan 190-191 C 5
Luanda 168-169 D 4
Luando, Rio - 168-169 E 5
Luang, Khao - [T ← Nakhon Si
Thammarat] 186-187 CD 5
Luang, Thale - 186-187 D 5
Luanginga, Rio - 168-169 F 5
Luangue, Rio - 168-169 E 4
Luangwa 168-169 H 5
Luan He 190-191 G 2
Luan Ho = Luan He 190-191 G 2
Luan-hsien = Luan Xian
190-191 G 2
Luannan 190-191 G 2
Luanping 184-185 M 3
Luanshya 168-169 G 5
Luan Xian 184-185 M 4
Luapula 168-169 G 5
Luarca 134-135 D 7
Luatizi, Rio - 171 D 6
Luau 168-169 F 5
Luba 172-173 H 5
L'uban' [SU, Belorusskaja SSR]
138-139 G 7
L'uban' [SU, Rossijskaja SFSR]
138-139 H 4
Luban 133 G 3
Lubāna 138-139 F 5
Lubānas ezers 138-139 F 5
Lubandaye 171 B 4
Lubang Islands 186-187 G 4
Lubango 168-169 D 5
Lubansee = Lubānas ezers
138-139 F 5
Lub'any 138-139 S 5
L'ubar 140-141 C 2
L'ubaševka 140-141 E 3
L'ubča 138-139 F 7
Lubbock, TX 146-147 F 5
L'ubča 138-139 F 7
L'ubeč 138-139 H 8
Lübeck 133 E 2
Lubefu [ZRE, ~] 168-169 F 3
Lubefu [ZRE, ●] 168-169 F 3
Lubeka = Lübeck 133 E 2
L'ubercy 138-139 LM 6
L'ubešov 138-139 E 8
Lubero 168-169 G 3
Lubiana = Ljubljana 136-137 F 2
Lubika 171 B 4
Lubilash 168-169 F 4
L'ubim 138-139 N 4
L'ubimovka [SU, Kursk] 140-141 G 1
Lubin 133 H 3
L'ubinskij 178-179 N 6
Lublana = Ljubljana 136-137 F 3
Lublaň = Ljubljana 136-137 F 3
Lublin 133 L 3
Lubliniec 133 J 3
Lublinitz = Lubliniec 133 J 3
Lubnān al - Janūbi 182-183 =
3 ◁ 182-183 F 6
Lubnān, Jabal - 182-183 FG 5-6
Lubnān al-Janubī =
◁ 3 182-183 F 6
Lubnān ash-Sharqi, Jabal -
182-183 G 5-6
Lubnān ash-Shimālī =
1 ◁ 182-183 G 5
Lubnān ash-Shimālī = 182-183
1 ◁ FG 5
Lubny 140-141 F 1-2
L'ubochna 138-139 K 7
L'uboml' 138-139 DE 8
Lubosalma 138-139 HJ 2
L'ubotin 140-141 GH 2
Lubu 190-191 D 10
Lubudi [ZRE, ~] 168-169 FG 4
Lubudi [ZRE, ●] 168-169 G 4
Lubuklinggau 186-187 D 7
Lubuksikaping 186-187 CD 6
Lubumbashi 168-169 G 5
Lubutu 168-169 G 3
Lubwe 171 B 5
L'ubytino 138-139 J 4
Lucania, Mount - 144-145 HJ 5
Lucas, IA 152-153 K 5
Lucas, KS 152-153 G 6
Lucas, Punta - = Cape
Meredith 162 D 8
Lucas Channel = Main Channel
152-153 Q 3
Lucca 136-137 D 4
Lucedale, MS 154-155 L 5
Lucélia 160-161 G 4
Lucemburk = Luxembourg
134-135 KL 4
Lucembursko 134-135 KL 4
Lucena [E] 134-135 E 10
Lucena [RP] 186-187 H 4
Lučenec 133 J 4
Lucera 136-137 F 5
Lucerne, IA 152-153 K 5
Lucerne Lake 150-151 E 8
Lucerne Valley, CA 150-151 E 8
Lucero 154-155 B 5
Lucero, EL - [MEX] 154-155 D 8
Luch [SU, ~] 138-139 O 5
Lu-chai = Luzhai 190-191 B 9
Lucheng 190-191 D 3
Lucheringo 171 CD 6
Lu-ch'i = Luxi 190-191 C 7
Lu-chiang = Lujiang 190-191 F 6
Lu-chou = Hefei 184-185 M 5
Luchow = Lu Xian 184-185 K 6
Luchuan 184-185 KL 7
Luchwan = Luchuan 184-185 KL 7
Lucia, CA 150-151 C 7
Lucin, UT 150-151 G 5
Lucipara, Kepulauan - 186-187 J 8
Lucira 168-169 D 5
Luck [SU] 140-141 B 1
Luck, WI 152-153 K 3
Luckenwalde 133 F 2
Luckhoff 174-175 F 5
Lucknow [CDN] 152-153 Q 4
Lucknow [IND] 180-181 MN 5
Lučenec 133 J 4
Lucy, NM 154-155 C 3
Luda 138-139 M 1
Ludden, ND 152-153 G 2
Ludell, KS 152-153 F 6
Lüderitz [Namibia] 168-169 DE 8
Lüderitzbaai 168-169 DE 8
Ludhiana 180-181 M 4
Ludhiyānā = Ludhiana 180-181 M 4
Ludington, MI 152-153 N 4
L'udinovo 138-139 K 7
Ludlow, CA 150-151 EF 8
Ludlow, CO 152-153 D 7
Ludlow, SD 152-153 E 3
Ludogorie 136-137 M 4
Ludowici, GA 148-149 C 9
Ludsen = Ludza 138-139 F 5
Luduș 136-137 KL 2
Ludvika 130-131 F 7
Ludwigsburg 133 D 4
Ludwigshafen 133 CD 4
Ludwigslust 133 E 2
Ludza 138-139 F 5
Luebo 168-169 F 4
Lueders, TX 154-155 F 4
Luele, Rio - 168-169 F 4
Luemba 171 B 3
Luembe, Rio - 168-169 F 4
Luena 168-169 F 5
Luena, Rio - 168-169 F 5
Luena Flats 168-169 F 5
Lufeng 184-185 M 7
Lufira 168-169 G 4-5
Lufkin, TX 146-147 H 5
Lufusā 171 C 2
Luga [SU, ~] 178-179 D 6
Luga [SU, ●] 178-179 D 6
Lugano 133 D 5
Luganville 194-195 N 3
Lugard's Falls 171 D 3
Lugela 168-169 J 6
Lugenda, Rio - 168-169 J 5
Lugh Ferrandi = Luuq 166-167 N 8
Luginino 138-139 K 5
Lugo [E] 134-135 D 7
Lugo [I] 136-137 D 3
Lugoj 136-137 JK 3
Luhans'k 140-141 JK 2
Luhayyah, Al- 180-181 E 7
Luhe [TJ] 190-191 G 5
Luhit 180-181 Q 5
Luhsien = Lu Xian 184-185 K 6
Lu Hu 190-191 E 6
Lu-i = Luyi 190-191 E 5
Luiana, Rio - 168-169 F 6
Luichow = Haikang 184-185 KL 7
Luik = Li ge 134-135 K 3
Luilaka 168-169 F 3
Luimneach–Limerick 132 B 5
Luirojoki 130-131 M 4
Luis Alves 160-161 H 7
Luis Alves 160-161 G 4
Luis Correira 158-159 L 5
Luishia 168-169 G 5
Luisiāna 160-161 G 4
Luisiāna 160-161 G 4
Luiza 168-169 F 4
Luizhou Jiang = Leizhou Wan
190-191 C 11
Luizjana = Louisiana 146-147 H 5
Luján [RA, Buenos Aires] 162 E 4
Lujenda = Rio Lugenda
168-169 J 5
Lujiang 190-191 F 6
Lujiang = Lu-kang 190-191 H 9
Lujiapuzi 188-189 D 2
Lūkā 171B1
Lu-kang 190-191 H 9
Lukanga Swamp 168-169 G 5
Lukašek 178-179 Z 7
Lukenie 168-169 E 3
Lukenie Supérieure, Plateau de la -
168-169 F 3
Lukiang = Lujiang 190-191 F 6
Lukilā 171 C 1
Lukimwa 171 D 5
Lukino 138-139 L 7
Lukojanov 138-139 P 6
Lukolela 168-169 E 3
Lukou 190-191 D 8
Lukovit 136-137 L 4
Lukovnikovo 138-139 K 5
Łuków 133 L 3
Luksemburg = Luxembourg
134-135 KL 4
L'uksemburg-Gruzinskij = Bolnisi
140-141 M 6
L'ukšudja 138-139 T 5
Lukuga 168-169 G 4
Lukuledi 171 D 5
Lukull, mys - 140-141 F 4
Lukulu 171 B 6
Lukusashi 171 B 6
Lūl, Nahr - 166-167 K 7
Lula, MS 154-155 K 3
Luleå 130-131 JK 5
Lule älv 130-131 J 4-5
Lulebargas = Lüleburgaz
182-183 B 2
Lüleburgaz 182-183 B 2
Luling, TX 154-155 G 6
Lulong 190-191 G 2
Lulonga 168-169 E 2
Lulua 168-169 F 4
Luluabourg = Kananga 168-169 F 4
Lulung = Lulong 190-191 G 2
Luma 171 D 6
Lumbala 168-169 F 5
Lumber River 148-149 D 7
Lumberton, MS 154-155 L 5
Lumberton, NC 146-147 L 5
Lumberton, NM 152-153 C 7
Lumbo 168-169 K 5-6
Lumding 180-181 P 5
Lumege = Cameia 168-169 F 5
Lumeje 168-169 F 5
Lumpkin, GA 154-155 N 4
Lumu 186-187 G 7
Lumut 186-187 D 5
Lün 184-185 K 2
Luna, NM 150-151 J 9
Lund 130-131 E 10
Lund, NV 150-151 F 6
Lund, UT 150-151 G 6-7
Lunda 168-169 EF 4
Lundazi [Z, ~] 171 C 6
Lundazi [Z, ●] 168-169 H 5
Lundenburg = Břeclav 133 H 4
Lundi [ZW, ~] 168-169 H 7
Lundi [ZW, ●] 168-169 H 7
Lundy 132 D 6
Lüneburg 133 E 2
Lüneburger Heide 133 DE 2
Lunenburg 144-145 Y 9
Lunéville 134-135 L 4
Lung Chiang = Long Jiang
190-191 B 9
Lungchuan = Longquan
190-191 G 7
Lunga [Z] 168-169 G 5
Lunga Game Reserve
168-169 FG 5
Lungala N'Guimbo 168-169 EF 5
Lung-chên = Longzhen
184-185 O 2
Lung-chiang = Qiqihar 184-185
Lung-ching-ts'un = Longjing
188-189 G 1
Lung-chuan = Suichuan
184-185 L 6
Lung-hui = Longhui 190-191 C 8
Lung-hsi = Longxi 184-185 J 4-5
Lung-hua = Longhua 188-189 AE
Lungi 172-173 B 3
Lung-k'ou = Longkou 190-191 G
Lung-kuan Hu = Long Hu
190-191 F 7
Lunglē = Lungleh 180-181 P 6
Lungleh 180-181 P 6
Lungling = Longling 184-185 H 7
Lungmen = Longmen 190-191 E
Lung-nan = Longnan 184-185 LM
Lungshan = Longshan 190-191 E
Lung-shêng = Longsheng [TJ ↖
Guilin] 190-191 BC 9
Lung-shêng = Longsheng [TJ ↙
Wuzhou] 190-191 C 10
Lung-shih = Ninggang
190-191 DE 8
Lungsi = Longxi 184-185 J 4-5
Lung-t'an = Longtan 190-191 C 8
Lung-t'ien = Longtian 190-191 G
Lungué-Bungo, Rio - 168-169 F
Lung-yen = Longyan 190-191 F
Lungyu = Longyou 184-185 M 6
Luni [IND, ~] 180-181 L 5
Luninec 138-139 F 7
Lunino 138-139 P 7
Lunjevka 138-139 V 4
Lunno 138-139 E 7
Lunsar 172 B 3
Lunsemfwa 168-169 GH 5
Lunsklip 174-175 H 3
Luntai = Buquq 184-185 E 3
Luochang = Lechang 190-191 D
Luocheng 190-191 B 9
Luochuan 190-191 B 4
Luoding 190-191 C 10
Luoding Jiang 190-191 C 10
Luofang 190-191 E 8
Luofu 171 B 3
Luohe [TJ, ●] 190-191 E 5
Luo He [TJ, ~ ◁ Huang He]
190-191 CD 4
Luo He [TJ, ~ ◁ Wei He]
190-191 B4
Luokou 190-191 E 8
Luombwa 171 B 6
Luonan 190-191 C 4
Luongo 171 B 5
Luoning 190-191 C4
Luoqing 190-191 BC 9
Luorong 184-185 K 7
Luoshan 190-191 E 5
Luotian 190-191 E 6
Luoyang 184-185 L 5
Luoyuan 190-191 G 8
Luozi 168-169 D 3
Lupa 171 C 5
Lupilichi 171 C 5
Łupkowska , Przełęcz - 133 L 4
Lupolovo, Mogil'ov- 138-139 H 7
Lu-pu = Lubu 190-191 D 10
Luputa 168-169 F 4
Luque [PY] 160-161 D 6
Luray, VA 148-149 D 5
Lurio 171 E 6
Lúrio, Rio - 168-169 JK 5
Luristan = Lorestān 180-181 F 4
Lusaca = Lusaka 168 G 6
Lusaka 168-169 G 6
Lusambo 168-169 F 3
Lusenga Flats 168-169 G 4
Lushan [TJ, Henan] 190-191 D 5
Lu Shan [TJ, Jiangxi] 184-185 M 6
Lu Shan [TJ, Shandong]
190-191 FG 3
Lu Shan = Yi Shan 190-191 G 3
Lushi 190-191 C 4
Lu-shih = Lushi 190-191 C 4
Lushnjë 136-137 H 5
Lushoto 168-169 J 3
Lüshun 184-185 MN 4
Lüsi 190-191 H 5
Lusien = Lu Xian 184-185 K 6
Lusikisiki 174-175 H 6
Lusk, WY 152-153 D 4
Luso = Moxico 168-169 EF 5
Lussemburgo 134-135 KL 4
Lustre, MT 152-153 D 1
Lü-szŭ = Lüsi 190-191 H 5
Lü-Tao = Huo-shao Tao
190-191 H 10
Lutcher, LA 154-155 K 5-6
Lūṭ, Dasht-e - 180-181 H 4
Lutembwe 171 C 6
Luther, MI 152-153 O 3
Luther, OK 154-155 G 3
Lutie, TX 154-155 E 3
Lutlhe 174-175 E 2
Luton 132 F 6
Lutong 186-187 F 6
Lüttich = Liège 134-135 K 3
Luttig 174-175 E 7
Lutunguru 171 B 3
Lutych = Liège 134-135 K 3
Lützow-Holm bukt 121 C 4-5
Lutzputs 174-175 D 5
Luuq 166-167 N 8
Luverne, AL 154-155 M 5
Luverne, IA 152-153 JK 4
Luverne, MN 152-153 H 4
Luvua 168-169 G 4
Luwegu 168-169 J 4
Luwingu 168-169 GH 5
Luwu 186-187 GH 7
Luwuk 186-187 H 7
Luxembourg [L] 133 C 4
Luxembourg [L, ●] 134-135 KL 4
Luxembourg [★] 134-135 KL 4
Luxemburg 134-135 KL 4
Luxemburgo [★] 134-135 KL 4
Luxemburgo = Luxembourg
133 BC 4
Luxi [TJ, Hunan] 190-191 C7
Lu Xian 184-185 K 6
Luxora, AR 154-155 KL 3
Luxor = Al-Uqsur 166-167 L 3
Luya Shan 190-191 CD 2
Lüyang 188-189 C 2

May Point, Cape - 148-149 F 5
Mayrhofen 133 EF 5
Maysarī, Al- 182-183 H 7
Maysville, KY 152-153 P 6
Maysville, MO 152-153 J 6
Maysville, NC 148-149 E 7
Mayu, Pulau - 186-187 J 6
Mayunga 168-169 G 3
Mayville, ND 152-153 H2
Mayville, NY 148-149 D 3
Maywood, NE 152-153 F 5
Mayyit, Bahr al- 180-181 D 4
Mazabuka 168-169 G 6
Mazagan = Al-Jadīdah 166-167 C 2
Mazagão 158-159 J 5
Mazaka = Kayseri 180-181 D 3
Mazalet = Mazelet 172-173 H 1
Mazamet 134-135 J 7
Mazan = Villa Mazán 162 C 3
Māzandarān 180-181 GH 3
Mazār, Al- 182-183 F 7
Mazara del Vallo 136-137 DE 7
Mazār-i-Sharīf 180-181 K 3
Mazarrón 134-135 G 10
Mazarrón, Golfo de - 134-135 G 10
Mazar tagh 184-185 D 4
Mazatenango 146-147 H 9
Mazatlán 146-147 E 7
Mazatzal Peak 150-151 H 8
Mazedonien 136-137 JK 5
Mažeikiai 138-139 D 5
Mazelet 172-173 H 1
Mazeppabaai 174-175 H 7
Mazeppa Bay = Mazeppabaai 174-175 H 7
Mazgirt 182-183 H 3
Mazhafah, Jabal - = Jabal Buwārah 170 F 3
Mazhan 190-191 G 3
Mazıdağı 182-183 J 4
Mazimchopes, Rio - 174-175 K 3
Mazirbe 138-139 CD 5
Mazoco 171 C 5
Mazomanie, WI 152-153 M 4
Mazr'a, Al- 182-183 F 7
Mazsalaca 138-139 E 5
Mazū 182-183 N 6
Mazurskie, Pojezierze - 133 K 2-L 1
Mažeikiai 130-131 K 9
Mazyr 138-139 G 7
Mbabane 168-169 H 8
Mbacké 172-173 B 2
Mbaiki 166-167 H 8
Mbala 168-169 H 4
Mbalabala 168-169 GH 7
Mbale 168-169 H 2
M'Balmayo 166-167 G 8
Mbam 172-173 H 4
Mbam, Massif - 172-173 H 4
Mbamba Bay 171 C 5
Mbandaka 168-169 E 2-3
Mbanga 166-167 FG 8
Mbanza Congo 168-169 D 4
Mbanza Ngungu 168-169 D 3-4
Mbaracayú, Cordillera de - 160-161 E 5-6
Mbarangandu [EAT, ~] 171 D 5
Mbarangandu [EAT, ●] 171 D 5
Mbarara 168-169 H 3
Mbari 166-167 J 7
M'Bé 168-169 E 3
Mbemkuru 168-169 JK 4
Mbenkuru 171 D 5
Mbeya [EAT, ▲] 171 C 5
Mbeya [EAT, ●] 168-169 H 4
M'Bigou 168-169 D 3
Mbin 166-167 F 8
M'Binda 168-169 D 3
Mbindera 171 D 5
Mbinga 171 C 5
Mbini [Guinea Ecuatorial, ~] 172-173 H 5
Mbini 166-167 G 8
Mbizi 168-169 H 7
Mbogo's 171 C 4
Mbomou 166-167 J 7-8
Mbonge 172-173 H 4
M'Boro 171 AB 2
Mbour 166-167 A 6
Mbozi 171 C 5
Mbud 166-167 B 5
Mbuji-Mayi 168-169 F 4
Mbulu 171 C 3
Mburu 171 C 5
Mburucuyá 162 E 3
Mbuyapey 160-161 D 7
Mccheta 140-141 M 6
Mcensk 138-139 L 7
Mchinga 168-169 JK 4
Mchinji 168-169 H 5
Mdaina, Al- = Al-Madīnah 182-183 M 7
Mdandu 171 C 5
Meacham, OR 150-151 D 3
Mead, WA 150-151 E 2
Mead, Lake - 146-147 D 4
Meade, KS 152-153 F 7
Meade Peak 150-151 H 4
Meadow, TX 154-155 DE 4
Meadow Lake 144-145 P 7
Meadow Valley Range 150-151 F 7
Meadow Valley Wash 150-151 F 7
Meadville, PA 148-149 CD 4
Meaford 148-149 C 2
Mealy Mountains 144-145 Z 7
Meandro = Büyük Menderes Nehri 182-183 B 4
Mearim, Rio - 158-159 L 5
Meaux 134-135 J 4
Mebote 168-169 H 7
Mebreije, Rio - = Rio
Mebridege 168-169 D 4
Mebridege, Rio - 168-169 D 4
Meca = Makkah 180-181 DE 6
Meca = Makkah 180-181 DE 6
Meca, La - = Makkah 180-181 DE 6
Mecca, CA 150-151 EF 9
Mecca, La - = Makkah 180-181 DE 6
Mecca=Makkah 180-181 DE 6
Mechanicsburg, PA 148-149 E 4
Mechanicville, NY 148-149 G 3
Meched = Mashhad 180-181 HJ 3
Mechelen 134-135 K 3
Mechren'ga 138-139 N 2
Mechéria = Mishriyah 166-167 DE 2
Mecidiye 182-183 B 3
Mecitözü 182-183 F 2
Mecklenburg 133 EF 2
Mecklenburger Bucht 133 EF 1
Mecque, la - = Makkah 180-181 DE 6
Mecsek 133 J 5
Mecúfi 168-169 K 5
Mecula 168-169 J 5
Medan 186-187 C 6
Médanos [RA, Buenos Aires ●] 162 D 5
Medanosa, Punta - 162 CD 7
Medaryville, IN 152-153 N 5
Medea 180-181 C 3
Medellín [CO] 158-159 D 3
Medellín [RA] 162 D 3
Medelpad 130-131 GH 6
Medenin = Madaniyīn 166-167 FG 2
Medford, OK 154-155 G 2
Medford, OR 146-147 B 3
Medford, WI 152-153 LM 3
Medgidia 136-137 N 3
Médiadilet 172-173 E 1
Mediano 134-135 H 7
Mediapolis, IA 152153 L 5
Mediaș 136-137 L 2
Medical Lake, WA 150-151 DE 2
Medicine Bow, WY 152-153 C 5
Medicine Bow Mountains 152-153 CD 5
Medicanceli 134-135 F 8
Medicine Bow Peak 146-147 EF 3
Medicine Bow River 152-153 CD 5
Medicine Hat 144-145 O 7
Medicine Lake 152-153 DE 1
Medicine Lake, MT 152-153 D 1
Medicine Lodge, KS154-155 FG 2
Medicine Mound, TX 154-155 F 3
Medina [BR] 160-161 DE 1
Medina [WAG] 172-173 B 2
Medina, ND 152-153 G 2
Medina, OH 148-149 BC 4
Medina, TX 154-155 F 6
Medina = Al-Madīnah 180-181 DE 6
Medina = Al-Madīnah 180-181 DE 6
Medina del Campo 134-135 E 8
Medina de Rioseco 134-135 E 8
Medina-Sidonia 134-135 DE 10
Medina River 154-155 F 6
Médine = Al-Madīnah 180-181 DE 6
Medinilla, Farallon de - 192-193 FG 3
Medininkai 138-139 E 6
Medinipur 180-181 O 6
Mediolan = Milano 136-137 C 3
Mediterranean Sea 128-129 J 8-O 9
Medjdel, El = Ashqĕlōn 182-183 F 7
Mednogorsk 178-179 K 7
Mednoje 138-139 K 5
Mednyi, ostrov - 120 D 2
Médoc 134-135 G 6
Medvedi ostrov 120 B 16-17
Medora, KS 152-153 H 6
Medora, ND 152-153 E 2
Medvedica [SU ◁ Don] 138-139 P 7
Medvedok 138-139 S 5
Medvedovskaja 140-141 J 4
Medve-sziget 120 B 16-17
Medvežij ostrova 178-179 f 3
Medvežjegorsk 178-179 EF 5
Medyn' 138-139 KL 6
Medyna = Al-Madīnah 180-181 DE 6
Medżiboż 140-141 C 2
Meekatharra 194-195 C 5
Meeker, CO 152-153 C 5
Meeker, OK 154-155 G 3
Meerut 180-181 M 5
Mēga [ETH] 166-167 M 8
Mega [RI] 186-187 K 7
Megalē Prespa, Limnē - 136-137 J 5
Megalópolis 136-137 JK 7
Megalo Sofráno 136-137 M 7
Meganom, mys - 140-141 G 4
Megantic 148-149 H 2
Mégara 136-137 K 6-7
Meghalaya 180-181 P 5
Megion 178-179 O 5
Megísté 182-183 C 4
Megler, WA 150-151 B 2
Megrega 178-179 E 5
Mehadia 136-137 K 3
Mehdia = Mahdīyah 166-167 E 1
Meherrin River 148-149 E 6
Mehétia 192-193 N 6
Mehrabān 182-183 M 3-4
Mehrān 182-183 M 6
Mehšāna 180-181 L 6
Meia Ponte, Rio - 158-159 K 8
Meicheng 190-191 G 7
Mei-ch'i = Meixi 190-191 G 6
Mei-chou Wan = Meizhou Wan 190-191 G 9
Meighen Island 144-145 RS 1
Meihekou = Shanchengzhen 188-189 EF 1
Meihsien = Mei Xian 190-191 EF 9
Meiktilā 186-187 BC 2
Meiktila = Meiktilā 186-187 BC 2
Meiling Guan = Xiaomei Guan 184-185 LM 6
Meilin Jiang = Lian Jiang 190-191 E 9
Meilong 190-191 E 10
Meiningen 133 E 3
Meiqi = Meixi 190-191 G 6
Meißen 133 F 3
Meitene = Meitene 138-139 DE 5
Meitene 138-139 DE 5
Meixi 190-191 G 6
Mei Xian 184-185 M 7
Meizhou Wan 190-191 G 9
Mejicana, Cumbre de - 162 C 3
Mejillones 162 B 2
Mejnypil'gyno 178-179 j 5
Meka Galla 171 D 2
Mekambo 168-169 D 2
Mekelē 166-167 M 6
Mekerrhane, Sebkra - = Sabkhat Mukrān 166-167 E 3
Mekka = Makkah 180-181 DE 6
Meknès = Miknās 166-167 C 2
Mekong = Lancang Jiang 184-185 HJ 7
Mekran = Mokrān 180-181 HJ 5
Mékrou 166-167 E 6
Meksyk 146-147 E 6-G 8
Meksykańska, Zatoka - 146-147 G-J 7
Meksykański, Basen - 146-147 HJ 6
Mel, Ilha do - 160-161 H 6
Melagénai 138-139 F 6
Melah, Yam ham - 182-183 F 7
Melaka [MAL, ●] 186-187 D 6
Melaka, Selat - 186-187 CD 6
Melanesia 180-181 DE 6
Melanesia 124-125 Q 5-S 6
Melanésia 124-125 Q 5-S 6
Melanésie 124-125 Q 5-S 6
Melanesië 124-125 Q 5-S 6
Melanesien 124-125 Q 5-S 6
Melanesien 198-199 F 4-H 5
Melanieskop 174-175 H 5
Mēlas 136-137 L 7
Melayu 186-187 D 6
Melba, ID 150-151 E 4
Melbourne [AUS] 194-195 H 7
Melbourne, AR 154-155 K 2-3
Melbourne, FL 148-149 c 2
Melbu 130-131 F 3
Melchers, Kapp - 130-131 m 6
Melchor, Isla - 162 AB 7
Melchor Múzquiz 146-147 F 6
Meldrim, GA 148-149 G 8
Melekgon 174-175 D 4
Melendiz Dağları 182-183 F 3
Melenki 138-139 N 6
Mélèzes, Riviere aux - 144-145 W 6
Melfi 136-137 F 5
Melfi [Tschad] 166-167 H 6
Melfort 144-145 Q 7
Melik, Wadi el - = Wādī al-Malik 166-167 KL5
Melili 171 CD 6
Melilla = Melilla 166-167 D 1
Melilla 166-167 D 1
Melimoyu, Monte - 162 B 6
Melinde = Malindi 168-169 K 3
Melipilla 162 B 4
Melitene = Malatya 180-181 D 3
Melito di Porto Salvo 136-137 FG 7
Melitopol' 140-141 G 3
Melk 133 G 4
Melkbosch Point = Melkbospunt 174-175 B 5
Melkbospunt 174-175 B 5
Mellen, WI 152-153 L 2
Mellerud 130-131 E 8
Mellette, SD 152-153 G 3
Mellit = Mallit 166-167 K 6
Mellizo Sur, Cerro - 162 B 7
Mellwood, AR 154-155 K 3
Melmoth 174-175 J 5
Mel'nica- Podol'skaja 140-141 C 2
Mělník 133 G 3
Mel'nikovo [SU ← Tomsk] 178-179 P 6
Melo [ROU] 162 F 4
Meloco 171 D 6
Melovoje 140-141 JK 2
Melovoj Syrt 138-139 T 7
Melovskaja, gora - 138-139 NO 2
Melrhir, Chott - = Shaṭṭ Malghīr 166-167 F2
Melrose, MN 152-153 J 3
Melrose, MT 150-151 G 3
Melrose, NM 154-155 D 3
Melsetter = Mandidzudzure 168-169 H 6-7
Melstone, MT 152-153 BC 2
Meltaus 130-131 L 4
Melton Mowbray 132 F 5
Meluco 171 D 6
Melun 134-135 J 4
Melunga 168-169 E 6
Melut = Malut 166-167 L 6
Melville, LA 154-155 K 5
Melville, MT 150-151 HJ 2
Melville, Cape - 194-195 HJ 2
Melville, Lake - 144-145 YZ 7
Melville Bay 194-195 G 2
Melville Bugt 144-145 X-Z 2
Melville Hills 144-145 M 4
Melville Island [AUS] 194-195 F 2
Melville Island [CDN] 144-145 N-P 2
Melville Peninsula 144-145 U 4
Melville Sound = Viscount Melville Sound 144-145 O-Q 3
Memala 186-187 F 7
Memba 168-169 K 5
Memboro 186-187 G 8
Memel 174-175 H 4
Memel = Klaipėda 138-139 C 6
Memel = Neman 138-139 D 6
Memmingen 133 DE 5
Memphis 166-167 L 3
Memphis, IA 152-153 K 5
Memphis, TN 146-147 HJ 4
Memphis, TX 154-155 E 3
Memphremagog, Lac - 148-149 GH 2
Memuro 188-189 c 2
Memyō 186-187 C 2
Mena 140-141 F 1
Mena, AR 154-155 H 3
Menado = Manado 186-187 H 6
Ménaka 166-167 E 5
Menam = Mae Nam Chao Phraya 186-187 CD 3-4
Menan Khong 186-187 D 3
Menarandra 168-169 KL 7-8
Menard, MT 150-151 H 3
Menard, TX 154-155 EF 5
Menasha, WI 152-153 M 3
Menbij = Manbij 182-183 G 4
Mende 134-135 J 6
Mendelejevsk 138-139 T 6
Mendenhall, MS 154-155 L 4-5
Mendez [EC] 158-159 D 5
Mendi [ETH] 166-167 M 7
Mendi [PNG] 186-187 M 8
Mendocino, CA 150-151 AB 6
Mendocino, Cape - 146-147 AB 3
Mendocino, Fractura de - 124-125 BC 4
Mendocino, Fractura de - 124-125 BC 4
Mendocino, Frattura - 124-125 BC 4
Mendocino, Gradin de - 124-125 BC 4
Mendocino Fracture Zone 124-125 BC 4
Mendocino Range 150-151 AB 5
Mendocinostufe 198-199 KL 3
Mendocinotrap 124-125 BC 4
Mendol, Pulau - 186-187 D 6
Mendong Gonpa 184-185 F 5
Mendota, CA 150-151 C 7
Mendota, IL 152-153 M 5
Mendoza [PA] 146-147 b 2
Mendoza [RA, ●] 162 C 4
Mēnē 168-169 E 2
Mene de Mauroa 158-159 E 2
Menemen 182-183 B 3
Mengcheng 190-191 F 5
Mêng-chia-lou = Mengjialou 190-191 CD 5
Mengen [TR] 182-183 E 2
Mengene Dağı 182-183 KL 3
Menggala 186-187 E 7
Menggongshi 190-191 C 8
Mengguda 190-191 B 2
Mengjialou 190-191 CD 5
Mengjiang 190-191 C 10
Mengjin 190-191 D 4
Mengkoka, Gunung - = Pulau Penyeler 186-187 H 7
Mêng-kung-shih = Menggongshi 190-191 C 8
Meng Shan [TJ, ▲▲] 190-191 FG 4
Mengshan [TJ, ●] 190-191 C 9
Mengtze = Mengzi 184-185 J 7
Mengulek, gora - 178-179 Q 7
Mengyin 190-191 FG 4
Mengzi 184-185 J 7
Menindee 194-195 H 6
Menindee Lake 196 EF 4
Menlo, KS 152-153 F 6
Menno, SD 152-153 H 4
Menominee, MI 152-153 N 3
Menominee Indian Reservation 152-153 M 3
Menominee River 152-153 MN 3
Menomonee Falls, WI 152-153 M 4
Menomonie, WI 152-153 KL 3
Menongue 168-169 E 5
Menorca 134-135 K 8
Men'šikova' mys - 178-179 KL 3
Mentakab 186-187 D 6
Mentawai, Kepulauan - 186-187 CD 7
Mentès 172-173 G 1
Mentok 186-187 DE 7
Menton 134-135 L 7
Mentougou 190-191 E 2
Mên-t'ou-kou = Mentougou 190-191 E 2
Mentzdam 174-175 F 7
Menzelinsk 138-139 T 6
Menzies 194-195 D 5
Menzies, Mount - 121 B 6-7
Meobbaai 174-175 A 3
Meob Bay = Meobbaai 174-175 A 3
Meoqui 146-147 E 6
Mepiskaro, gora - 140-141 L 6
Meponda 171 C 6
Meppel 134-135 KL 2
Meppen 133 C 2
Meqdādiya' Al- = Al-Miqdādīyah 182-183 L 6
Mequinenza 134-135 GH 8
Mer Adriatique 136-137 E 3-H 5
Meramangye, Lake - 194-195 F 5
Merano 136-137 D 2
Merapoh 186-187 D 6
Mérath = Meerut 180-181 M 5
Meratus, Pegunungan - 186-187 G 7
Merauke 186-187 LM 8
Mer Baltique 130-131 G 10-J 8
Merbein 196 EF 5
Mer Blanche 178-179 FG 4
Merca = Marka 168-169 KL 2
Mercan Dağları 182-183 H 3
Mercara 180-181 M 8
Mer Caspienne 180-181 F 2-G 3
Merced, CA 146-147 BC 4
Mercedario, Cerro - 162 BC 4
Mercedes [RA, Buenos Aires] 162 DE 4
Mercedes [RA, Corrientes] 162 E 3
Mercedes [RA, San Luis] 162 C 4
Mercedes [ROU] 162 E 4
Mercedes, TX 154-155 FG 7
Merced, Las - 158-159 F 3
Merced River 150-151 C 7
Mer Celtique 132 C 6
Mercer, WI 152-153 LM 2
Mercimekkale 182-183 J 3
Mercy, Cape - 144-145 Y 5
Merdenik = Göle 182-183 K 2
Meredit, Cabo - = Cape Meredith 162 D 8
Meredith, Cape - 162 D 8
Meredosia, IL 152-153 L 6
Mereeg 166-167 b 3
Merefa 140-141 H 2
Mer Egee 136-137 L 5-M 7
Meregh = Mareeg 168-169 L 2
Meregh = Mereeg 166-167 b 3
Merena = Santo 194-195 MN 3
Merga = Nukhaylah 166-167 K 5
Mergenevo 140-141 P 2
Mergui = Myeik 186-187 C 4
Mergui, Archipelag - = Myeik Kyûnzu 186-187 C 4
Mergui, Archipel de - = Myeik Kyunzu 186-187 C 4
Mergui, Arcipelago di - = Myeik Kyûnzu 186-187 C 4
Mergui, Archipiélago de - = Myeik Kyûnzu 186-187 C 4
Mergui, Arquipélago - = Myeik Kyûnzu 186-187 C 4
Mergui-Archipel = Myeik Kyûnzu 186-187 C 4
Mergui-szigetek = Myeik Kyûnzu 186-187 C 4
Mergujské souostroví = Myeik Kyûnzu 186-187 C 4
Meriç = Büyük Doğanca 182-183 B 2
Meriç Nehri 182-183 B 2
Mérida [E] 134-135 D 9
Mérida [MEX] 146-147 J 7
Mérida [YV] 158-159 E 3
Mérida, Cordillera de - 158-159 EF 3
Meriden, CT 148-149 G 4
Meriden, WY 152-153 D 5
Meridian, ID 150-151 E 4
Meridian, MS 146-147 J 5
Meridian, TX 154-155 G 5
Meridith, Lake - 154-155 E 3
Merimbula 196 JK 6
Meringur 194-195 H 6
Mer Intérieure = Seto-naikai 184-185 P 5
Mer Ionienne 136-137 GH 7
Merir 186-187 K 6
Mer Jaune 184-185 N 4
Merke [SU] 178-179 N 9
Merkel, TX 154-155 E4
Merket Bazar = Marqat Bazar 184-185 D 4
Merla 140-141 G 1-2
Mer Ligurienne 136-137 BC 4
Merlin, OR 150-151 B 4
Merluna 194-195 H 2
Mer Méditeranée 128-129 J 8-O 9
Mermer 182-183 J 3
Mer Morte = Bahr al-Mayyit 180-181 D 4
Merna, NE 152-153 G 5
Merna, WY 150-151 H 4
Méroua = Koré Mayroua 172-173 F 2
Merowë = Marawi 166-167 L 5
Merq, el- = Al-Marj 166-167 J 2
Merredin 194-195 C 6
Merrick 132 D 4
Merrill, IA 152-153 H 4
Merrill, MS 154-155 L 5
Merrill, OR 150-151 C 4
Merrill, WI 152-153 M 3
Merrillan, WI 152-153 L 3
Merrimack River 148-149 H 3
Merriman 174-175 E 6
Merriman, NE 152-153 EF 4
Merrit 144-145 M 7
Merriwa 196 JK 4
Mer Rouge 180-181 D 5-7
Mer Rouge, LA 154-155 K 4
Merryville, LA 154-155 J 5
Mērsrags 138-139 D 5
Merseburg 133 EF 3
Mersey 132 E 5
Mersin = İçel 180-181
Mersing 186-187 D 6
Mers-les-Bains 134-135 H 3
Merthyr Tydfil 132 DE 6
Merti 171 D 2
Mer Tyrrhénienne 136-137 D-F 6
Mertz Glacier 121 C 15
Mertzon, TX 154-155 E 5
Meru [EAK] 168-169 J 2-3
Meru [EAT] 168-169 J 3
Meru National Park 171 D 2
Mervy 180-181 J 3
Merv = Mary 180-181 J 3
Merwar = Marwar 180-181 L 5
Merzifon 182-183 F 2
Mesa, AZ 146-147 D 5
Mesa, NM 154-155 C 3-4
Mesabi Range 146-147 H 2
Mesa Central = Mesa de Anáhuac 146-147 FG 7-8
Mesagne 136-137 GH 5
Mesarya 182-183 E 5
Mesa Verde National Park 150-151 J 7
Mescalero, NM 154-155 C 4
Mescalero Apache Indian Reservation 154-155 C 4
Mescalero Ridge 154-155 CD 4
Mescalero Valley 154-155 CD 4
Mešč'orskaja nizina 138-139 MN 6
Meščovsk 138-139 K 6
Meščura 138-139 S 2
Mescit Dağı 182-183 J 2
Mescit Dağları 182-183 J 2
Mescitli = Söylemez 182-183 JK 3
Meseta del Norte 146-147 F 6
Meshed = Mashhad 180-181 HJ 3
Meshkīn Shar 182-183 M 3
Meshra' er Req = Mashrā' ar-Raqq 166-167 K 7
Mesick, MI 152-153 O 3
Mesilla, NM 154-155 B 4
Mesin 166-167 LM 1
Meskene = Maskanah 182-183 GH 4-5
Meškovskaja 140-141 K 2
Mesmiyé = Al-Mismiyah 182-183 G 6
Mesolóngion 136-137 J 6
Mesopotamia 180-181 E 3-F 4
Mesopotamia 180-181 E 3-F 4
Mesopotâmia [IRQ] 180-181 E 3-F 4
Mesopotamia [RA] 162 E 3-4
Mesopotamie 180-181 E 3-F 4
Mesopotamië 180-181 E 3-F 4
Mesopotamien 180-181 E 3-F 4
Mesquite, NV 150-151 F 7
Mesquite, TX 154-155 G 4
Messalo, Rio - 168-169 J 5
Messēnē [GR, ●] 136-137 JK 7
Messēnē [GR, Ø] 136-137 J 7
Messēniakos Kólpos 136-137 JK 7
Messico 146-147 E 6-G 8
Messico, Golfo del - 146-147 G-J 7
Messina 136-137 F 6
Messina [ZA] 168-169 GH 7
Messina, Stretto di - 136-137 F 6-7
Messinge 171 C 5
Messojacha 178-179 O 4
Messeñas, Las - 154-155 C 6
Mestia 140-141 L 5
Mestre, Venèzia- 136-137 E 3
Mesudiye 182-183 G 2
Meta, Rio - 158-159 E 3
Meta Incognita Peninsula 144-145 X 5
Metairie, LA 146-147 H 6
Metalici, Munții - 136-137 K 2
Metaline Falls, WA 150-151 E 1
Metán 162 D 3
Metangula 168-169 HJ 5
Metaponto 136-137 G 5
Metarica 171 D 6
Metechi 140-141 M 6
Metema 166-167 M 6
Meteor, Abisso - 124-125 HJ 8
Meteor, Abysse - 124-125 HJ 8
Meteor, Banco del - 124-125 H 4
Meteor, Fosa de - 124-125 HJ 8
Metéōra 136-137 J 6
Meteorbank 124-125 H 4
Meteor Crater 150-151 H 8
Meteor Depth 124-125 HJ 8
Meteordiep 124-125 HJ 8
Meteoro, Banco do - 124-125 H 4
Meteoro, Cume do - 124-125 HJ 8
Meteortiefe 124-125 HJ 8
Methow River 150-151 CD 1
Mê Thuôt = Ban Me Thuôt 186-187 E 4
Méthymna 136-137 LM 6
Metinic Island 148-149 J 3
Metković 136-137 GH 4
Metlakatla, AK 144-145 KL 6
Metlaoui, El - = Al-Mitlawi 166-167 F 2
Metolius, OR 150-151 C 3
Metropolis, IL 152-153 M 7
Metorica 171 D 6
Metsobon 136-137 J 6
Metter, GA 148-149 B 8
Mettur Kulam = Stanley Reservoir 180-181 M 8
Metuge 171 E 6
Metulla 182-183 F 6
Metundo 171 E S
Metz 134-135 L 4
Meulaboh 186-187 C 6
Meureudu 186-187 C 5
Meuse 134-135 K 4
Mevume 174-175 L 2
Mexcala, Rio - = Rio Balsas 146-147 F 8
Mexia, TX 154-155 G 5
Mexicaans Bekken 146-147 HJ 6
Mexicali 146-147 C 5
Mexican Hat, UT 150-151 J 7
Mexická pánev 146-147 HJ 6
Mexický záliv 146-147 G-J 7
Mexico 146-147 E 6-G 8
Mexico 146-147 E 6-G 8
Mexico, MO 152-153 KL 6
México [MEX, Estado] 146-147 E 6-G 8
México [MEX, localidade] 146-147 G 8
México [MEX, ●] 146-147 HJ 6
México, Fosa de - 124-125 DE 5
Mexico, Fossa do - 124-125 DE 5
México, Golfo de - 146-147 HJ 7
México, Golfo do - 146-147 G-J 7
Mexico, Gulf of - 146-147 HJ 7
Mexico Basin 146-147 HJ 6
Mexico Bay 148-149 E 3
México City = México 146-147 G 8
Mexico City = México 146-147 G 8
Mexikograben 198-199 MN 4
Mexikóvölgy 146-147 HJ 7
Mexikanisches Becken 146-147 HJ 6
Mexikó 146-147 E 6-G 8
Mexiko 146-147 E 6-G 8
Mexiko, Golf von - 146-147 G-J 7
Mexikograben 124-125 DE 5
Mexikói-medence 146-147 HJ 6
Mexikói-öböl 146-147 J 7
Mexique 146-147 E 6-G 8
Mexique, Bassin du - 146-147 HJ 6
Mexique, Golfe du - 146-147 HJ 7
Meyādīn = Mayādīn 182-183 J 5
Meyāndowab = Miāndowāb 182-183 M 4
Meyāneh 180-181 F 3
Meyāneh, Kūreh-ye - 182-183 M 5
Meydān Dāgh 182-183 MN 4
Meydān-e Naftūn 182-183 N 7
Meyersdale, PA 148-149 D 5
Mezdra 136-137 KL 4
Meždurečenskij 178-179 MN 6
Meždušarskij, ostrov - 178-179 HJ 3
Mezen' [SU, ~] 178-179 H 5
Mezen' [SU, ●] 178-179 G H 4
Mézenc, Mont - 134-135 JK 6
Mezenskaja guba 178-179 G 4
Mežgorje 140-141 A 2
Mežirečje 140-141 B 2
Mezőkövesd 133 K 5
Mezopotámia 180-181 E 3-F 4
Mezopotamia 180-181 E 3-F 4
Mezopotámie 180-181 E 3-F 4
Meždurečenskij 178-179 MN 6
Meždušarskij, ostrov - 178-179 HJ 3
Mežirečje 140-141 B 2
Mežpjanje 138-139 P 6
Mezquite 154-155 B 5
Mfongosi = Mfongozi 174-175 J 5
Mfongozi 174-175 J 5
Mfūlū 166-167 KL 7
Mfwanganu 171 C 3
Mga 138-139 H 4
Mglin 138-139 J 7
Mhlatuze 174-175 J 5
Mia, Wed - = Wādī Miyāh 166-167 EF 2
Miagas, Pulau - 186-187 J 5
Miajadas 134-135 E 9
Miajlar 180-181 KL 5
Miali = Miao-li 190-191 H 9
Miami, AZ 150-151 H 9
Miami, FL 146-147 K 6
Miami, OK 154-155 H 2
Miami, TX 154-155 E 3
Miami Beach, FL 146-147 KL 6
Miami Canal 146-147 K 6
Miamisburg, OH 152-153 O 6
Miami Shores, FL 148-149 cd 4
Mianchi 190-191 CD 4
Miāndou Āb = Miāndowāb 182-183 M 4
Miandrivazo 168-169 L 6
Mianma 186-187 BC 2
Mianwali = Miyānwālī 180-181 L 4
Mian Xian 184-185 K 5
Mianyang [TJ, Hubei] 190-191 D 6
Mianyang [TJ, Sichuan] 184-185 J 5
Miao Dao 190-191 H 3
Miaodao Qundao 184-185 N 4
Miao-li 190-191 H 9
Miao Liedao = Miaodao Qundao 184-185 N 4
Miao-tzŭ = Miaozi 190-191 CD 5
Miaozi 190-191 CD 5
Miass [SU, ●] 178-179 L 7
Miastko 133 H 1-2
Miasto Ho Chi Minha = Thàn Phô Ho Chi Minh 186-187 E 4
Miaws, Bi'r - 170 F 6
Mica 174-175 J 3
Micay 158-159 D 4
Michaia Ivanoviča Kalinina 138-139 P 4-5
Michajliki 138-139 K 5
Michajlov 138-139 M 6
Michajlovka [SU, Rossijskaja SFSR Astrachan] 140-141 N 3
Michajlovka [SU, Rossijskaja SFSR Kursk] 138-139 KL 7
Michajlovka [SU, Rossijskaja SFSR Volgograd] 140-141 L 1
Michajlovka [SU, Ukrainskaja SSR] 140-141 G 3
Michajlovskaja 138-139 PQ 3
Michajlovskij 178-179 OP 7
Michalitsion = Karacabey 182-183 C 2
Michalovce 133 KL 4
Michelson, Mount - 144-145 GH 4
Michigamme Reservoir 152-153 MN 2
Michigan 146-147 J 2-K 3
Michigan, ND 152-153 G 1-2
Michigan City, IN 152-153 N 5
Michigan, Jezioro - = Lake Michigan 146-147 J 2-3
Michigan, Lake - 146-147 J 2-3
Michigansee = Lake Michigan 146-147 J 2-3
Michigan-tó = Lake Michigan 146-147 J 2-3
Michipicoten Island 144-145 T 8
Michnevo 138-139 LM 6
Michoacán 146-147 F 8
Micronesia [○] 124-125 R-T 5
Micronesia [Estado] 122-123 RS 5
Micronésia [região] 124-125 R-T 5
Micronesia [regione] 124-125 RS 5
Micronesia [Stato] 122-123 RS 5
Micronesia [★] 186-187 MN 5
Micronesia, estados federados de 198-199 GH 4
Micronesia, estados federados da 198-199 GH 4
Micronesia, federale Staten van 198-199 GH 4
Micronesia, federated states of 198-199 GH 4
Micronésie [○] 124-125 R-T 5
Micronésie [○] 124-125 R-T 5
Micronesië [★] 186-187 MN 5
Micronésie [★] 186-187 MN 5
Micronésie, états fédérés de 198-199 GH 4
Mičurin 136-137 MN 4
Mičurinsk 138-139 N 7
Mida 171 DE 3
Midāeion = Eskişehir 180-181 C 2-3
Midai, Pulau - 186-187 E 6
Midas, NV 150-151 E 5
Mid Atlantic Ridge 124-125 H 5-3
Middelburg [ZA, Kaapland] 168-169 FG 9
Middelburg [ZA, Transvaal] 168-169 GH 8
Middelfart 130-131 CD 1 0
Middellandse Zee 128-129 J 8-O 9
Middelpos 174-175 D 6
Middelpost = Middelpos 174-175 D 6
Middel Roggeveld 174-175 D 7
Middelveld [ZA, Kaapland] 174-175 E 5
Middelveld [ZA, Transvaal] 174-175 FG 4
Middelwit 174-175 G 3
Midden Atlas = Al-Aṭlas al-Mutawassiṭ 166-167 CD 2
Midden Siberisch Bergland 178-179 R-W 4-5
Middle Alkali Lake 150-151 CD 5
Middle America Trench 124-125 DE 5
Middle Andaman 180-181 P 8
Middle Atlas = Al-Aṭlas al-Mutawassiṭ 166-167 CD 2
Middlebury, VT 148-149 G 2
Middle Concho River 154-155 E 5
Middle East, The - 124-125 NO 4
Middle Fork John Day River 150-151 D 3
Middle Fork Salmon River 150-151 F 3
Middle Loup River 152-153 G 5
Middleport, OH 148-149 B 5
Middle River, MN 152-153 HJ 1
Middlesboro, KY 146-147 JK 4
Middlesbrough 132 F 4
Middleton, ID 150-151 E 4
Middleton, TN 154-155 L 3
Middleton Island 144-145 GH 6
Middleton Reef 194-195 L 5
Middleton [ZA] 174-175 F 7
Middletown, NY 148-149 F 4
Middletown, NJ 148-149 F 4
Middletown, OH 152-153 OP 6
Middle Water, TX 154-155 D 3
Middle West 146-147 F-J 3
Midhdharidhrah, Al- 166-167 A 5
Midhsandur 130-131 c 2
Midia = Midye 182-183 C 2
Mid-Illovo 174-175 J 5-6
Mid Indian Basin 124-125 NO 6
Midland 148-149 CD 2
Midland, CA 150-151 F 9
Midland, MI 152-153 O 4
Midland, SD 152-153 F 3
Midland, TX 146-147 F 5
Midlothian, TX 154-155 G 4
Midnapore = Medinipur 180-181 O 6
Midnapur = Medinipur 180-181 O 6
Midongy-atsimo 168-169 L 7
Midsayap 186-187 HJ 5
Midvale, ID 150-151 E 3
Midvale, UT 150-151 H 5
Midville, GA 148-149 B 8
Midway 198-199 J 3
Midwest, WY 152-153 CD 4
Midwest City, OK 154-155 G 3
Midyān II 170 F 3
Midyat 182-183 J 4
Midžor 136-137 K 4
Mie 188-189 L 5
Międzyrec Podlaski 133 L 3
Mielec 133 K 3
Mien-ch'ih = Mianchi 190-191 CD 4
Mienhsien = Mian Xian 184-185 K 5
Mienyang = Mianyang [TJ, Hubei] 190-191 D 6
Mien-yang = Mianyang [TJ,Sichuan] 184-185 J 5
Miercurea-Ciuc 136-137 L 2
Mieres 134-135 DE 7
Miēso 166-167 N 7
Mifflintown, PA 148-149 E 4
Migamuwa 180-181 M 9
Migdal Ashqĕlōn = Ashqĕlōn 182-183 F 7
Migdal Gad = Ashqĕlōn 182-183 F 7
Mighān, Kavīr-e - 182-183 N 5
Migole 171 CD 4
Miguel Alves 158-159 L 5
Miguel Calmon 158-159 LM 7
Migulinskaja 140-141 K 2
Mihajlovgrad 136-137 K 4
Mihalgazi 182-183 D 2
Mihalıççık 182-183 D 3
Mihara 188-189 J 5
Mi He 190-191 G 3
Mi He = Ming He 190-191 E 3
Mi Ho = Mi He 190-191 G 3
Miho wan 188-189 J 5
Mi-hsien = Mi Xian 190-191 D 4
Michiganské jezero = Lake Michigan 146-147 J 2-3
Mito = Moyto 166-167 H 6
Mijares 134-135 G 8-9
Mijriyyah, Al- 166-167 B 5
Mikaševiči 138-139 F 7
Mikata 188-189 K 5
Mikawa wan 188-189 L 5
Miki 188-189 K 5
Mikindani 168-169 K 5
Mikkaichi = Kurobe 188-189 L 4
Mikkeli 130-131 M 7
Miknās 166-167 C 2
Mikojan-Šachar = Karačajevsk 140-141 KL 5
Mikronesien, Förderieste Staaten von 198-199 GH 4
Mikronesien, ≡ 124-125 R-T 5
Mikronesien, ★ 186-187 MN 5
Mikumi 171 D 4
Mikumi National Park 171 D 4
Mikun' 178-179 HJ 5
Mikuni 188-189 KL 4
Mila = Milah 166-167 F 1
Milaan = Milano 136-137 C 3
Milaca, MN 152-153 K 3
Milagro, El - 162 C 4
Milah 166-167F1
Milāhah, Wādī - 170 E 4
Milājerd 182-183 N 5
Milan, IA 152-153 K 5
Milan, MI 152-153 P 4
Milan, TN 154-155 L 3
Milan, WA 150-151 E 2
Milan = Milano 136-137 C 3
Milán = Milano 136-137 C 3
Milano 136-137 C 3
Miláno = Milano 136-137 C 3
Milano, TX 154-155 G 5
Milão = Milano 128-129 K 4
Milas 182-183 B 4
Milazzo 136-137 F 6
Milbank, SD 152-153 H 3
Milbridge, ME 148-149 K 2
Mildred, MT 152-153 D 2
Mildura 194-195 H 6
Mileh, Küh-e - 182-183 M 6
Milepa 171 D 5
Miles 194-195 JK 5
Miles, TX 154-155 EF 5
Milesville, SD 152-153 EF 3
Miles, WA 150-151 D 2
Miles City, MT 146-147 E 2
Milet 182-183 B 4
Miletos = Milet 180-181 B 3
Miletus = Milet 180-181 B 3
Milford, CA 150-151 C 5
Milford, DE 148-149 F 5
Milford, MA 148-149 H 3
Milford, NE 152-153 H5
Milford, NH 148-149 H 3
Milford, PA 148-149 F 4
Milford, UT 150-151 G 6
Milford Lake 152-153 H 6
Milford Sound [NZ, ◡] 194-195 N 8
Milgis 171 D 2
Milh, Qurayyāt al- 182-183 G 7
Milicz 133 H 3
Miling 194-195 C 6
Militsch = Milicz 133 H 3
Milk, Wādī el - = Wādī al-Malik 166-167 KL 5
Mil'kovo 178-179 ef 7
Milk River 146-147 E 2
Millau 134-135 J 6
Mill City, OR 150-151 B 3
Milledgeville, GA 148-149 B 8
Millegan, MT 150-151 H 2
Mille Lacs Lake 146-147 H 2
Millen, GA 148-149 C 8
Miller 174-175 E 7
Miller, MO 154-155 HJ 2
Miller, NE 152-153 G 5
Miller, SD 152-153 G 3
Millerovo 140-141 K 2
Miller Peak 150-151 H 10
Millersburg, OH 148-149 BC 4
Millersburg, PA 148-149 E 4
Millerton Lake 150-151 D 7
Millevaches, Plateau de - 134-135 HJ 6
Millican, OR 150-151 C 4
Millicent 194-195 GH 7
Millington, TN 154-155 L 3
Millinocket, ME 148-149 J 2
Mill Island 121 C 11
Millmerran 194-195 K 5
Millport, AL 154-155 LM 4
Millry, AL 154-155 L 5
Mills, NM 154-155 C 2
Millston, WI 152-153 L 3
Millwood Lake 154-155 H 4
Millville, NJ 148-149 F 5
Milne Bay 186-187 h 7
Milnesand, NM 154-155 D 4
Milnor, ND 152-153 H 2
Milo [Guinea] 166-167 C 7
Milo, IA 152-153 K 5
Milo, ME 148-149 J 2
Milo, OR 150-151 B 4
Milton, FL 154-155 M 5
Milton, ND 152-153 GH 1
Milton, OR 150-151 D 3
Milton, PA 148-149 E 4
Milton, WI 152-153 M 4
Milton, WW 148-149 B 5
Miltonvale, KS 152-153 H 6
Miluo 184-185 L 6
Milou Jiang 190-191 D 7
Mil'utinskaja 140-141 KL 2
Miluza = Mulhouse 134-135 L 5
Milverton 148-149 C 3
Milwaukee, WI 146-147 J 3
Milwaukee, Abisso - 146-147 N 8
Milwaukee, Abysse de - 146-147 N 8
Milwaukee, Fossa de - 146-147 N 8
Milwaukee, Głębia - 146-147 N 8
Milwaukee Depth 146-147 N 8
Milwaukeediep 146-147 N 8
Milwaukee-mélység 146-147 N 8
Milwaukeetiefe 146-147 N 8
Milwaukie, OR 150-151 B 3
Mim 172-173 E 4
Mimitsu 188-189 H 6
Mimongo 168-169 D 3
Mimoso do Sul 160-161 M 4
Mina 154-155 E 7
Mina, NV 150-151 DE 6
Mina, SD 152-153 G 3
Minā' al-Aḥmadī 182-183 N 8
Min' 'Abd Allāh 182-183 N 8
Mina de São Domingos 134-135 D 10
Minahasa 186-187 H 6
Minakami 188-189 M 4
Minam, OR 150-151 E 3
Minamata 184-185 P 5
Minami Tori 198-199 H 3
Minami Daitō-jima 184-185 P 6
Minami-Daitō zima = Minami-Daitō-jima 184-185 P 6
Minamitane 188-189 H 7
Minas 162 EF 4
Minas, Serra de - 160-161 L 3
Minas Cué 162 E 2
Minas de Riotinto 134-135 DE 10
Minas Gerais 158-159 KL 8-9
Minas Novas 160-161 L 2
Minatare, NE 152-153 E 5
Minatitlán 146-147 H 8
Minato = Nakaminato 188-189 N 4
Min Chiang = Min Jiang [TJ, Fujian] 190-191 G 8
Min Chiang = Min Jiang [TJ, Sichuan] 184-185 J 5-6
Min-ch'in = Minqin 184-185 J 4
Min-ch'ing = Minqing 190-191 G 8
Min-ch'üan = Minquan 190-191 E 4
Minco, OK 154-155 FG 3
Mindanao 186-187 J 5
Mindanao Sea 186-187 HJ 5
Mindanau = Mindanao 186-187 J 5
Minden, IA 152-153 J 5
Minden, LA 154-155 J 4
Minden, NE 152-153 G 5
Minden 133 D 2
Minden, NV 150-151 D 6
Minderoo 194-195 C 4
Mindoro 186-187 GH 4
Mindoro Strait 186-187 GH 4
Mindra, Virful - 136-137 KL 3
Mindživan 140-141 N 7
Mine 188-189 H 5
Mineiga, Bir - = Bi'r Munayjah 170 F 6
Mineola, NY 148-149 G 4
Mineola, TX 154-155 H 4
Miner, MT 150-151 H 3
Mineral, CA 150-151 C 5
Mineral, WA 150-151 B 2
Mineral Mountains 150-151 G 6
Mineral'nyje Vody 140-141 L 4
Mineral Point, WI 152-153 LM 4
Mineral Wells, TX 154-155 FG 4
Minersville, UT 150-151 G 6
Minerva, OH 148-149 C 4
Minervino Murge 136-137 FG 5
Mingan Passage = Jacques Cartier Passage 144-145 Y 7-8
Mingary 196 E 4
Mingečaur 140-141 N 6
Mingecaurskoje vodochranilišče 140-141 N 6
Mingenew 194-195 C 5
Mingfeng = Niya Bazar 184-185 E 4
Minggang 190-191 E 5
Ming He 190-191 E 3
Mingjiang = Minggang 190-191 E 5
Mingo Junction, OH 148-149 C 4
Mingoya 171 D 5
Mingxi 190-191 F 8
Minho [P, ~] 134-135 C 7
Minho [P, ≡] 134-135 C 8
Minhou 190-191 G 8
Minhow = Fuzhou 184-185 MN 6
Min-hsien = Min Xian 184-185 J 5
Minicoy Island 180-181 L 9
Minidoka, ID 150-151 G 4
Minier, IL 152-153 M 5
Mingwal, Lake - 194-195 D 5
Minikköy Dvip = Minicoy Island 180-181 L 9
Minilya River 194-195 BC 4
Ministro João Alberto 158-159 J 7
Min Jiang [TJ, Fujian] 184-185 M 6
Min Jiang [TJ, Sichuan] 184-185 J 5-6
Minkébé 168-169 D 2
Min'kovo 138-139 O 4

Minle 184-185 J 4
Min-lo = Minle 184-185 J 4
Minna 166-167 F 7
Minneapolis,KS 152-153 H 6
Minneapolis, MN 146-147 GH 2-3
Minnekahta, SD 152-153 E 4
Minneola, KS 152-153 FG 4
Minneota, MN 152-153 HJ 3
Minnesota 146-147 H 2-3
Minnesota River 146-147 H 3
Minnewaska, Lake - 152-153 J 3
Minnewaukan, ND 152-153 G 1
Minnipa 196 B 4
Miño 134-135 D 7
Mino 188-189 L 5
Mino-Kamo 188-189 L 5
Minong, WI 152-153 KL 2
Minonk, IL 152-153 M 5
Minot, ND 146-147 F 2
Minqin 184-185 J 4
Minqing 190-191 G 8
Minquan 190-191 E 4
Min Shan 184-185 J 5
Minshāt Dahshūr 170 D 3
Minsk 138-139 FG 7
Minster, OH 152-153 O 5
Minto, Lac - 144-145 V 5
Minto Inlet 144-145 N 3
Minturn, CO 152-153 C 6
Minūf 170 D 2
Minusinsk 178-179 R 7
Min Xian 184-185 J 5
Minyā, Al- 166-167 KL 3
Mio, MI 152-153 O 3
Miqdādiyah, Al- 182-183 L 6
Mir 138-139 F 7
Mira 136-137 DE 3
Mirā', Wādī al- 182-183 HJ 7
Miracatu 160-161 J 6
Miracema 160-161 LM 4
Miracema do Norte 158-159 K 6
Mirador [BR] 158-159 KL 6
Miradouro 160-161 L 4
Miraflores [PA] 146-147 b 2
Miraflores, Esclusas de
146-147 b 3
Miraflores Locks = Esclusas de Miraflores 146-147 b 3
Miramar 162 E 5
Mirai 160-161 L 4
Miralta 160-161 KL 2
Miramar, Isla - 150-151 F 10
Mirampéllu, Kólpos - 136-137 LM 8
Miranda [BR] 158-159 H 9
Miranda, Rio - 158-159 H 9
Miranda de Ebro 134-135 F 7
Miranda do Douro 134-135 D 8
Mirande 134-135 H 7
Mirandela 134-135 D 8
Mirando City, TX 154-155 F 7
Mirândola 136-137 D 3
Mirante, Serra do - 160-161 GH 5
Mirante do Paranapanema
160-161 FG 5
Mirapinima 158-159 G 5
Mirassol 160-161 H 4
Mirbāṭ 180-181 GH 7
Mirĕar, Geziret - = Jazīrat Mirgorod 140-141 FG 1-2
Marir 170 FG 6
Miri 186-187 F 6
Mirim, Lagoa - 162 F 4
Miriti 158-159 H 6
Mirjāveh 180-181 J 5
Mirnyj [Antarktika] 121 C 10
Mirnyj [SU] 178-179 V 5
Mironovka 140-141 E 2
Mirslavl' 138-139 MN 5
Mirtaĝ = Mutki 182-183 J 3
Miryang 188-189 G 5
Mirzaani 140-141 N 6
Mirzapur 180-181 N 5-6
Misāhah, Bi'r - 166-167 K 4
Misān 182-183 M 6
Misau 172-173 H 3
Misau, River - 172-173 H 3
Misgund 174-175 E 7
Mish'āb, Al- 180-181 F 5
Mishāb, Kūh-e - 182-183 L 3
Mishan 184-185 P 2
Mishawaka, IN 152-153 NO 5
Mishbih, Jabal - 166-167 L 4
Mi-shima 188-189 H 5
Mi Shui 190-191 D 8
Misima 186-187 h 7
Misión del Divino Salvador
160-161 E 6
Misión, La - 150-151 E 9
Misiones [PY] 160-161 D 7
Misiones [RA] 162 EF 3
Misiones, Sierra de
160-161 EF 7
Miskito, Cayos - 146-147 K 9
Miskolc 133 K 4
Misli = Gölcük 182-183 F 3
Mismāh, Tall al- 182-183 G 6
Mismār 166-167 M 5
Mismiyah, Al- 182-183 G 6
Misool, Pulau - 186-187 K 7
Misore = Mysore 180-181 M 8
Miṣr, Al- 166-167 KL 3
Miṣr al-Jadīdah, Al-Qāhirah
170 DE 2
Misrātah 166-167 H 2
Miṣr Bahrī 170 DE 2
Miṣr el-Gedida = Al-Qāhirah-Miṣr al-Jadīdah 170 DE 2
Misriç = Kurtalan 182-183 J 4
Missale 171 C 6
Missinaibi River 144-145 U 7
Mission, SD 152-153 F 4
Mission, TX 154-155 F 7
Missippinewa Lake 152-153 NO 5
Mississauga 148-149 D 3
Mississippi 146-147 J 5
Mississippi River 146-147 H 3
Mississippi River Delta 146-147 J 6
Mississippi Sound 154-155 L 5
Missoula , MT 146-147 D 2
Missouri 146-147 H 3-4
Missouri River 146-147 G 3
Missouri Valley, IA 152-153 HJ 5
Mistassini , Lac - 144-145 W 7
Mistelbach 133 H 4
Misumi 188-189 H 6
Misurața = Misrātah 166-167 H 2
Mita, Punta de - 146-147 E 7
Mitai 188-189 H 6
Mitau = Jelgava 138-139 DE 5
Mitchell [AUS] 194-195 J 5
Mitchell [CDN] 148-149 C 3
Mitchell, IN 152-153 N 6
Mitchell, NE 152-153 E 5
Mitchell, OR 150-151 CD 3
Mitchell, SD 146-147 G 3
Mitchell Lake 154-155 M 4
Mitchell, Mount - 146-147 K 4
Mitchell River [AUS, ~]
194-195 H 3
Mitchell River [AUS, ●]
194-195 H 3
Miteja 171 D 5
Mithrāw 180-181 KL 5
Mi'tiq, Gebel - = Jabal Mu'tiq
170 E 4
Mit Jamr 170 D 2
Mitlawi, Al- 166-167 F 2
Mito 184-185 R 4
Mitowa 171 D 5
Mitra, Monte de la - 172-173 H 5
Mitre 194-195 O 2
Mitre, Peninsula - 162 CD 8
Mitrofanovka 140-141 JK 2
Mitschurinsk = Mičurinsk
138-139 N 7
Mitsinjo 168-169 L 6
Mitsio, Nosy - 168-169 L 5
Mitsiwa 166-167 MN 5
Mitsuke 188-189 M 4
Mitsumata 188-189 c 2
Mitsushima 188-189 G 5
Mittelfeld = Middelveld
174-175 FG 4
Mittelländisches Meer
128-129 J 8-O 9
Mittellandkanal 133 CD 2
Mittelrussischer Landrücken = Sredne-Russkaja vozvyšennost
138-139 L 6-8
Mittelsibirisches Bergland
178-179 R-W 4-5
Mittlerer Atlas = Al-Aṭlas al-Mutawassiṭ 166-167 CD 2
Mittlerer Westen = Middle West
146-147 F-J 3
Mitú 158-159 EF 4
m-i Tubkaragan 140-141 OP 4
Mitumba, Chaîne des -
168-169 G 4-5
Mitumba, Monts - 168-169 G 3
Mitwaba 168-169 G 4
Mityana 171 BC 2
Mitzic 168-169 D 2
Mitzusawa 184-185 QR 4
Mi Xian 190-191 D 4
Miyagi 188-189 N 3
Miyāh, Wādī - 166-167 EF 2
Miyāh, Wadi al- 170 E 5
Miyāh, Wādī al- = Wādī Jarir
180-181 E 5-6
Miya kāwa 188-189 L 5
Miyake-jima 184-185 QR 5
Miyake zima = Miyake-jima
184-185 QR 5
Miyako 188-189 N 3
Miyako-jima 184-185 O 7
Miyakonojō 184-185 P 5
Miyakonozyô= Miyakonojō
184-185 P 5
Miyako wan 188-189 NO 3
Miyako zima = Miyako-jima
184-185 O 7
Miyāneh = Meyāneh 180-181 F 3
Miyanoura = Kamiyaku 188-189 H 7
Miyānwālī 180-181 L 4
Miyazaki 184-185 P 5
Miyazu 188-189 K 5
Miyet, Bahr el- = Bahr al-Mayyit
180-181 D 4
Miyoshi 188-189 J 5
Mizar = Karakeçi 182-183 H 4
Mizdah 166-167 G 2
Mizen Head 132 AB 6
Mizhi 190-191 C 3
Mizil 136-137 M 3
Mizoč 140-141 BC 1
Mizoram 180-181 P 6
Mizpah, MN 152-153 JK 2
Mizpah, MT 152-153 D 2
Mizque 158-159 FG 8
Mizur = Buron 140-141 M 5
Mizusawa 184-185 QR 4
Mjanyana 174-175 GH 6
Mjölby 130-131 F 8
Mjøsa 130-131 D 7
Mkambati 174-175 HJ 6
Mkata 171 D 4
Mkhili = Al-Makīlī 166-167 J 2
Mkobela 171 D 5
Mkokotoni 171 D 4
Mkondo 174-175 J 4
Mkondoa 171 D 4
Mkonga 171 CD 4
Mkulwe 171 C 5
Mkuranga 171 D 4
Mkushi 171 B 6
Mkusi = Mkuze 174-175 K 4
Mkuze [ZA,~] 174-175 K 4
Mkuze [ZA,●] 174-175 JK 4
Mkuze Game Reserve 174-175 K 4
Mkuzi = Mkuze 174-175 JK 4
Mladá Boleslav 133 G 3
Mladenovac 136-137 J 3
Mlangali 171 C 5
Mława 133 K 2
Mlayhān, Bi'r - 182-183 H 4
Mlcusi Bay = Kosibaai 174-175 K 4
Mligaži 171 D 4
Mljet 136-137 G 4
Mmabatho = Mafikeng
168-169 FG 8
Mnichov = München 133 EF 4
Moa [WAL] 172-173 C 4
Moa, Pulau - 186-187 J 8
Moab, UT 150-151 J 6
Mōāb, Jabal - 182-183 F 7
Moa Island 194-195 H 2
Moala 186-187 a 2
Moamba 168-169 H 8
Moapa, NV 150-151 F 7
Moba [ZRE] 168-169 G 4
Mobaye 166-167 J 8
Mobeetie, TX 154-155 E 3
Moberly, MO 146-147 H 4
Mobile, AL 146-147 J 5
Mobile Bay 146-147 J 5
Mobridge, SD 152-153 FG 3
Mobutu-Sese-Seko, Lac -
168-169 H 2
Moca = Al-Mukhā 180-181 E 8
Mocajuba 158-159 K 5
Moćališče 138-139 N 5
Moçambique [★] 171 D 6
Moçambique 168-169 H 7-J 5
Moçambique [Moçambique, Estado]
168-169 H 7-J 5
Moçambique [Moçambique, ●]
168-169 K 6-7
Moçambique, Canal de -
168-169 K 6-7
Moçambique, Straße von -
168-169 K 7-5
Moçambiquebecken 168-169 K 5
Moçâmedes = Namibe 168-169 D 6
Moccasin, MT 152-153 AB 2
Mocha = Al-Mukhā 180-181 E 8
Mocha, Isla - 162 B 5
Mochis, Los - 146-147 E 6
Möch Sar'dag uul 184-185 HJ 1
Mochudi 168-169 G 7
Mocimboa da Praia 168-169 JK 5
Mocksville, NC 148-149 C 7
Moclips, WA 150-151 A 2
Mocoa 158-159 D 4
Mococa 160-161 J 4
Mocoduene 174-175 L 2
Moçoró 158-159 M 6
Moctezuma [MEX, Chihuahua]
154-155 B 5
Mocuba 168-169 J 6
Moçul = Al-Mūṣil 180-181 E 3
Modane 134-135 L 6
Modderpoort 174-175 G 5
Modderrivier [ZA,~] 174-175 F 5
Modderrivier [ZA,●] 174-175 F 5
Moddi Kwara 172-173 F 2
Model, CO 152-153 DE 7
Mòdena 136-137 D 3
Modena, UT 150-151 FG 7
Modesto, CA 146-147 BC 4
Mòdica 136-137 F 7
Modjamboli 168-169 F 2
Modoc Lava Bed 150-151 C 5
Modriča 136-137 H 3
Modrý Nil = Abay 166-167 M 6
Moeda, Serra da - 160-161 KL 4
Moedig 174-175 J 3
Moengo 158-159 J 3
Moenkopi Wash 150-151 H 7
Moermanskdrempel 178-179 EF 2
Moe-Yallourn 194-195 J 7
Moffat, CO 152-153 D 6-7
Moffen 130-131 j 4
Moffit, ND 152-153 F 2
Mogadischu = Muqdiisho
168-169 O8
Mogadisho = Muqdiisho
168-169 L 2
Mogadishu = Muqdisho
166-167 O8
Mogadiszu = Muqdisho
166-167 O 8
Mogadišo = Muqdisho
166-167 O 8
Mogador = Aṣ-Ṣawīrah
166-167 BC 2
Mogalakwenarivier 168-169 G 7
Mogami gawa 188-189 MN 3
Mogdy 178-179 Z 7
Moghān, Dasht-e - 180-181 F 3
Mogila Bel'mak, gora - 140-141 H 3
Mogilew = Mogil'ov 138-139 GH 7
Mogiljow = Mogil'ov 138-139 GH 7
Mogil'ov = Mahilëŭ 138-139 GH 7
Mogil'ov Podd'skij 140-141 CD 2
Mogincual 168-169 K 6
Mogoča [SU, ●] 178-179 WX 7
Mogočin 178-179 P 6
Mogol 174-175 G 2
Mogollon Mountains 150-151 J 9
Mogollon Rim 150-151 H 8
Mogororo = Mongororo
166-167 J 6
Moguer 134-135 D 10
Mogúncia = Mainz 126-127 K 6
Mogzon 178-179 V 7
Mohács 133 J 6
Mohājerān 182-183 N 5
Mohaleshoek 174-175 G 6
Mohall, ND 152-153 F 1
Mohammadia = Muhammadiyah
166-167 DE 1
Mohammed, Ras - = Rā's
Muhammad 166-167 LM 4
Mohammerah = Khorramshar
180-181 F 4
Mohawk, AZ 150-151 G 9
Mohawk, MI 152-153 MN 2
Mohawk River 148-149 F 3
Mohe 184-185 N 1
Mohéli = Mwali 168-169 K 5
Mohican, Cape - 144-145 C 5
Mohilla = Mwali 168-169 K 5
Mohine 174-175 K 3
Mohn, Kapp - 130-131 m 5
Mo-ho = Mohe 184-185 N 1
Mohon Peak 150-151 G 8
Mohoro 168-169 J 4
Mohuč = Mainz 133 C 4
Mointy = Mojynty 178-179 N 8
Mo i Rana 130-131 F 4
Moira River 148-149 E 2
Möisaküla 138-139 E 4
Moisekull = Möisekula 138-139 E 4
Moisie, Rivière - 144-145 X 7
Moissac 134-135 H 6
Moissala 166-167 H 7
Mojave, CA 150-151 DE 8
Mojave Desert 146-147 C 4
Mojave River 150-151 E 8
Mojero 178-179 T 4
Moji das Cruzes 158-159 KL 9
Mojiguaçu 160-161 J 5
Mojiguaçu, Rio - 160-161 HJ 4
Mojimirim 160-161 J 5
Mojo, Pulau - = Pulau Moyo
186-187 G 8
Mojokerto 186-187 F 8
Mojynkum, peski - 178-179 MN 9
Mojynty 178-179 N 8
Mōka 188-189 MN 4
Mokai 194-195 P 7
Mokambo 168-169 G 5
Mokane, MO 152-153 KL 6
Mokatani 174-175 F 2
Mokeetsi = Mooketsi 174-175 J 2
Mokelumne Aqueduct River
150-151 C 6-7
Mokhotlong 174-175 H 5
Mokil 192-193 G 4
Mokka = Al-Mukhā 180-181 E 8
Mokolo 166-167 G 6
Mokp'o 184-185 O 5
Mokraja Ol'chovka 140-141 M 1
Mokrān 180-181 HJ 5
Mokrous 138-139 Q 8
Mokša 138-139 P 7
Mokšan 138-139 P 7
Möktama 186-187 C 3
Möktama Kwe 186-187 C 3
Moktok-to= Kyŏngnyŏlbi-yŏlto
188-189 E4
Mola di Bari 136-137 G 5
Molalla, OR 150-151 B 3
Molat 136-137 F 3
Moldary = Konečnaja 178-179 O 7
Moldau [≅] 136-137 M 2-3
Moldava 140-141 CD 3
Moldávia 128-129 O 6
Moldavia [≅] 136-137 M 2-3
Moldavia [★] 140-141 CD 3
Moldávia 140-141 CD 3
Moldávie 140-141 CD 3
Moldavië [≅] 136-137 M 2-3
Moldavië [≅] 136-137 M 2-3
Moldavië [★] 140-141 CD 3
Moldavië [★] 140-141 CD 3
Moldavskaja Sovetskaja Socialističeskaja Respublika = Moldawien 140-141 CD 3
Moldavsko 136-137 M 2-3
Mołdawia [★] 140-141 CD 3
Moldawien 140-141 CD 3
Moldava = Vltava 133 G 4
Moldavia [R] 136-137 M 2-3
Moldavia [SU] 126-127 O 6
Molde 130-131 B 6
Moldova 136-137 M 2
Moldoviţa 136-137 L 2
Moldva 136-137 M 2-3
Mole Creek 196 bc 2
Mole National Park 172-173 E 3
Molepolole 168-169 FG 7
Molfetta 136-137 G 5
Molina de Segura 134-135 G 9
Moline, IL 146-147 HJ 3
Moline, KS 154-155 G 2
Molino, FL 154-155 M 5
Moliro 168-169 GH 4
Molise 136-137 F 5
Mollakendi 182-183 H 3
Mollālar 182-183 M 4
Mollendo 158-159 E 8
Mollera, zaliv - 178-179 HJ 3
Mölndal 130-131 DE 9
Moločansk 140-141 GH 3
Moločnoje 138-139 M 4
Moločnyj, liman - 140-141 G 3
Moločue 168-169 J 6
Molodečno = Maladzečna
138-139 F 6
Molodežnaja 121 C 5
Molodogvardejskoje 178-179 N 7
Molodoj Tud 138-139 JK 5
Mologa 138-139 L 5
Molokai 186-187 e 3
Molokovo 138-139 L 4
Moloma 138-139 P 4
Molong 194-195 J 6
Molopo 168-169 F 8
Molotovsk = Nolinsk 178-179 HJ 6
Molotovsk = Severodvinsk
178-179 FG 5
Moloundou 166-167 H 8
Molucas 192-193 E 3-4
Malucas, Mar das 192-193 D 5
Molucche 186-187 J 6-8
Molucche, Mare delle -
186-187 HJ 7
Molsgat 174-175 H 3
Molt, MT 152-153 B 3
Molteno [ZA] 174-175 G 6
Molu, Pulau - 186-187 K 8
Molucas, Mar de las -
186-187 HJ 6-7
Moluccas 186-187 J 6-8
Molucca Sea 186-187 HJ 6-7
Molucké moře 186-187 HJ 7
Moluckie, Morze - 186-187 HJ 7
Moluki 186-187 J 6-8
Molukken 186-187 J 6-8
Molukkensee 186-187 HJ 7
Molukkenzee 186-187 HJ 7
Moluky 186-187 J 6-8
Molundu = Moloundou 166-167 H 8
Moluques 186-187 J 6-8
Moluques, Mer des -
186-187 HJ 6-7
Molvoticy 138-139 HJ 5
Moma [Moçambique] 168-169 J 6
Moma [SU] 178-179 bc 4
Momba 171 C 5
Mombasa 168-169 JK 3
Mombetsu 184-185 R 3
Mombongo 168-169 F 2
Momboyo 168-169 E 3
Mombuca, Serra da -
160-161 FG 3
Momčilgrad 136-137 L 5
Momence, IL 152-153 N 5
Mōminābād = Ambajogai
180-181 M 7
Momskij chrebet 178-179 b 4-c 5
Møn 130-131 E 10
Mona 146-147 N 8
Mona, UT 150-151 GH 6
Mona, Canal de la - 146-147 N 8
Monachium = München 133 EF 4
Mónaco 134-135 L 7
Mónaco [MC, Estado] 134-135 L 7
Monaco [MC, localidade]
134-135 L 7
Monaco [MC, ●] 134-135 L 7
Monaco [MC, ●] 134-135L7
Mónaco = München 133 EF 4
Monaghan 132 C 4
Monahans, TX 146-147 F 5
Monako 134-135 J 6
Monango, ND 152-153 G 2
Monapo 168-169 K 5-6
Monarch, MT 150-151 H 2
Monashee Mountains 144-145 N 7
Monastyrščina [SU, Smolensk]
138-139 HJ 6
Monbetsu 188-189 bc 2
Monča Guba = Mončegorsk
178-179 DE 4
Monção [BR] 158-159 K 5
Mončegorsk 178-179 DE 4
Mönchchaan 184-185 L 2
Mönch Chajrchan uul 184-185 FG 2
Mönchengladbach 133 BC 3
Monchique, Serra de -
134-135 C 10
Moncks Corner, SC 148-149 CD 8
Monclova 146-147 F 6
Moncton 144-145 XY 8
Mondai 160-161 F 7
Mondamin, IA 152-153 HJ 5
Monday, Rio - 160-161 E 6
Mond, Rūd-e - 180-181 G 5
Mondego 134-135 CD 8
Mondego, Cabo - 134-135 C 8
Mondo 171 CD 4
Mondoñedo 134-135 D 7
Mondovi 136-137 BC 3
Mondovi, WI 152-153 L 3
Mondragon 134-135 K 6
Moné Lávras 136-137 L 5
Monemvasia 136-137 K 7
Moneron, ostrov - 178-179 b 8
Monessen , PA 148-149 D 4
Moneta, VA 148-149 D 6
Moneta, WY 152-153 C 4
Monett, MO 154-155 J 2
Monfalcone 136-137 E 3
Monforte de Lemos 134-135 D 7
Monga [EAT] 171 D 5
Monga [ZRE] 168-169 F 2
Mongala 168-169 EF 2
Mongalla = Manqalah 166-167 L 7
Mongbwalu 171 B 2
Möngbyat 186-187 CD 2
Möngdön 186-187 C 2
Mongers Lake 194-195 C 5
Monggŭmp'o-ri 188-189 E 3
Monghyr = Munger 180-181 O 5
Mongo [Tchad] 166-167 H 6
Mongol-Altaj = Mongol Altajn Nuruu
184-185 F-H 2
Mongol Altajn Nuruu 182-183 F-H 2
Mongolei 182-183 H-L 2
Mongólia 184-185 H-L 2
Mongolia 182-183 H-L 2
Mongolia 184-185 H-L 2
Mongólia, Republica Popular da -
184-185 H-L 2
Mongólia Interior, Região Autónoma
da - 184-185 K 3-M 2
Mongolia interrior, Région Autónoma
de - 184-185 K 3-M 2
Mongolia Interna 184-185 K 3-M 2
Mongolia Wewnętrzna
184-185 K 3-M 2
Mongolië 182-183 H-L 2
Mongolie 182-183 H-L 2
Mongolischer Altai = Mongol
Altajn Nuruu 182-183 F-H 2
Mongolsko 184-185 H-L 2
Mongolský Altaj = Mongol Altajn
Nuruu 184-185 F-H 2
Mongoroгo 166-167 J 6
Möng Tun = Möngdön 186-187 C 2
Mongu 168-169 F 6
Monhegan Island 148-149 J 3
Monico, WI 152-153 M 3
Monida Pass 150-151 GH 3
Monino 138-139 M 6
Monitor Range 150-151 E 6
Monkoto 168-169 F 3
Monmouth, IL 152-153 L 5
Monmouth, OR 150-151 B 3
Mono 166-167 E 7
Mono Island 186-187 j 6
Mono Lake 146-147 C 4
Monmouth, IL 152-153 L 5
Monomoy Point 148-149 J 4
Monon, IN 152-153 N 5
Monópoli 136-137 G 5
Monor 133 J 5
Mon Pyinnei 186-187 C 3
Mŏnqalla = Manqalah 166-167 L 7
Monreale 136-137 E 6
Monroe, GA 154-155 NO 4
Monroe, LA 146-147 H 5
Monroe, MI 152-153 P 4-5
Monroe, NC 148-149 C 7
Monroe, OR 150-151 B 3
Monroe, UT 150-151 GH 6
Monroe, VA 148-149 D 6
Monroe, WA 150-151 C 2
Monroe, WI 152-153 M 4
Monroe City, MO 152-153 KL 6
Monroeville, AL 154-155 M 5
Monroeville, IN 152-153 O 5
Monrovia 166-167 B 7
Mons 134-135 J 3
Monsélice 136-137 DE 3
Mönsterås 130-131 FG 9
Montagnana 136-137 D 3
Montagne Tremblante, Parc
provincial de la - 144-145 VW 8
Montagu 174-175 D 7
Montague, CA 150-151 B 5
Montague, MI 152-153 N 4
Montague, TX 154-155 FG 4
Montague, Isla - 150-151 F 10
Montague Island 144-145 G 6
Montain View, WY 150-151 HJ 5
Montana 146-147 DE 2
Montaña, La - 134-135 DE 7
Montaña, La - [PE] 158-159 E 5-6
Montañas Rocosas = Rocky
Mountains 144-145 L 5-P 9
Montargis 134-135 J 5
Montauban 134-135 H 6
Montauk, NY 148-149 H 4
Montauk Point 148-149 H 4
Montbard 134-135 K 5
Montbéliard 134-135 L 5
Mont Blanc 134-135 L 6
Montbrison 134-135 K 6
Montceau-les-Mines 134-135 K 5
Mont Cenis, Col du - 134-135 L 6
Mont-de-Marsan 134-135 GH 7
Monteagudo [RA] 162 F 3
Monte Albán 146-147 G 8
Monte Alegre [BR, Pará]
158-159 J 5
Monte Alegre de Minas
160-161 H 3
Monte Alto [BR] 160-161 H 4
Monte Aprazível 160-161 GH 4
Monte Azul 158-159 L 8
Monte Azul Paulista 160-161 H 4
Monte Bello Islands 194-195 BC 4
Monte Belo 160-161 J 4
Monte Belo Padre 160-161 M 2
Montebu = Mombetsu 184-185 R 3
Montecarlo [RA] 160-161 E 7
Monte Carmelo 160-161 J 3
Monte Caseros 162 E 4
Montecatini Terme 136-137 D 4
Monte Comán 162 C 4
Montecristo 136-137 D 4
Monte do Ponto 182-183 EJ 2
Montefiascone 136-137 DE 4
Montego Bay 146-147 L 8
Montegut, LA 154-155 K 6
Montejinni 194-195 F 3
Montélimar 134-135 K 6
Monte Lindo, Rio - 160-161 CD 5
Monte Lirio 146-147 b 2
Montell, TX 154-155 E 6
Montello, NV 150-151 F 5
Montello, WI 152-153 M 4
Montemayor, Meseta de -80 C 6-7
Montemorelos 146-147 G 6
Montenegro 136-137 H 4
Montenégro 136-137 H 4
Montepuez [Moçambique, ~]
171 D 6
Montepuez [Moçambique, ●]
168-169 JK 5
Montepulciano 136-137 D 4
Monte Quemado 162 D 3
Monterey, CA 146-147 B 4
Monterey, TN 154-155 N 2
Monterey, VA 148-149 D 5
Monterey Bay 146-147 B 4
Monteria 158-159 D 3
Montero 158-159 G 8
Monte Rosa 136-137 BC 2-3
Monterrey 146-147 FG 6
Montesano, WA 150-151 B 2
Monte Sant'Àngelo 136-137 FG 5
Monte Santo 158-159 M 7
Monte Santo de Minas 160-161 J 4
Montes Cambricos = Cambrian
Mountains 132 D 6-E 5
Montes Claros 158-159 KL 8
Monte Sião 160-161 J 5
Monte Tristo 162 D 4
Montevideo 162 EF 4-5
Montevideo, MN 152-153 HJ 3
Montevideu = Montevideo
162 EF 4-5
Montevidiu 160-161 G 2
Monte Vista, CO 152-153 C 7
Montewideo = Montevideo
162 EF 4-5
Montezuma 160-161 L 1
Montezuma, GA 154-155 NO 4
Montezuma, IA 152-153 K 5
Montezuma, IN 152-153 N 6
Montezuma, KS 152-153 F 7
Montezuma Castle National
Monument 150-151 H 8
Montfort 134-135 FG 4
Montfort, WI 152-153 L 4
Montgomery, AL 146-147 J 5
Montgomery, LA 154-155 J 5
Montgomery, MN 152-153 K 3
Montgomery, WV 148-149 C 5
Montgomery = Sāhīwāl 180-181 L 4
Montgomery City,
MO 152-153 L 6
Montgomery Pass 150-151 D 6
Monticello, AR 154-155 K 4
Monticello, FL 148-149 b 1
Monticello, GA 148-149 B 8
Monticello,IA 152-153 L 4
Monticello,, IL 152-153 M 5
Monticello, IN 152-153 N 5
Monticello, KY 154-155 N 2
Monticello, MS 154-155 KL 5
Monticello, NM 154-155 B 4
Monticello, NY 148-149 F 4
Monticello, UT 146-147 DE 4
Monticello Reservoir = Lake
Berryessa 150-151 B 6
Montijo 134-135 D 9
Montilla 134-135 E 1 0
Mont-Laurier 144-145 V 8
Montluçon 134-135 J 5
Montmorillon 134-135 H 5
Monto 194-195 K 4
Montoro 134-135 E 9
Montosa, Mesa - 154-155 C 3
Montoya, NM 154-155 C 3
Montpelier, ID 150-151 H 4
Montpelier, OH 152-153 O 5
Montpelier, VT 146-147 M 3
Montpellier 134-135 JK 7
Montréal [CDN] 144-145 VW 8
Montreal Island 152-153 O 2
Montreuil [F - Berck] 134-135 H 3
Montreuil [F - Paris] 134-135 J 4
Montreux 133 C 5
Montrose 132 EF 3
Montrose, AR 154-155 K 4
Montrose, CO 146-147 E 4
Montrose, PA 148-149 F 4
Montross, VA 148-149 E 5
Mont-Saint-Michel, le -
134-135 FG 4
Monts Cantabriques = Cordillera
Cantabrica 134-135 D-F 7
Montseny 134-135 J 8
Monserrado 172-173 C 4
Montserrat 134-135 H 8
Montserrat [West Indies]
146-147 O 8
Monts Ibériques = Cordillera
Iberica 134-135 F 7-G 9
Montsinéry 158-159 J 4
Monts Mandingues 172 C 2-3
Mont Tremblant Provincial Park
= Parc provincial de la
Montagne Tremblante
144-145 VW 8
Mont Wright 144-145 X 7
Monument, CO 152-153 D 6
Monument, NM 154-155 D 4
Monument, OR 150-151 D 3
Monumental Hill 152-153 D 3
Monument Valley 150-151 H 7
Monza 136-137 C 3
Monze 168-169 G 6
Monzon 134-135 H 8
Moody, TX 154-155 G 5
Mooi River = Mooirivier
174-175 HJ 5
Mooirivier [ZA,~] 174-175 J 5
Mooirivier [ZA,●] 174-175 HJ 5
Mookane 174-175 G 2
Mooketsi 174-175 J 2
Mookhorn 148-149 F 6
Moolman 174-175 J 4
Moolawatana 196 DE 2-3
Moon = Muhu [SU, ◎] 138-139 D 4
Moonaree 196 B 3
Moonda Lake 194-195 H 5
Moonie 196 K 1
Moonie River 196 J 1
Moon National Monument,
Craters of the - 150-151 G 4
Moonsund = Suur väin 138-139 D 4
Moonta 194-195 G 6
Moora 194-195 C 6
Moorcroft, WY 152-153 D 3
Moore, ID 150-151 G 4
Moore, MT 152-153 B 2
Moore, OK 154-155 G 3
Moore, TX 154-155 F 6
Moore, Cape - 121 BC 17
Moore, Lake - 194-195 C 5
Mooréa 192-193 M 6
Mooreland, OK 154-155 F 2
Mooresville, IN 152-153 N 6
Mooresville, NC 148-149 C 7
Moorhead, MN 146-147 G 2
Moorhead, MS 154-155 K 4
Moorhead, MT 152-153 CD 3
Mooreesburg 174-175 C 7
Moose, WY 150-151 H 4
Moosehead Lake 148-149 J 2
Moose Jaw 144-145 P7
Moose Lake, MN 152-153 K 2
Moose Lake [CDN, ≅]
144-145 R 7
Mooselookmeguntic Lake
148-149 H 2
Moose River [CDN, ~] 144-145 U 7
Moosonee 144-145 U 7
Moosrivier = Mosesrivier
174-175 H 3
Mopane 174-175 HJ 2
Mopani = Mopane 174-175 HJ 2
Mopeia 168-169 J 6
Mopelia 192-193 M 6
Mopipi 168-169 FG 7
Moppo = Mokp'o 184-185 O 5
Mopti 166-167 D 6
Moquegua [PE, ●] 158-159 E 8
Moqur 180-181 K 4
Mora [E] 134-135 EF 9
Mora [RFC] 166-167 G 6
Mora [S] 130-131 F 7
Mora, MN 152-153 K 3
Mora, NM 154-155 C 3
Moraća 136-137 H 4
Moradabad 180-181 MN 5
Morafenobe 168-169 K 6
Moraleda, Canal de - 162 B 6-7
Moral, El - 154-155 E 6
Moramanga 168-169 L 6
Moran,KS 152-153 J 7
Moran, MI 152-153 O 2-3
Moran, TX 154-155 F 4
Moran, WY 150-151 H 4
Morane 192-193 O 7
Morant Cays 146-147 L 8
Moras, Punta de - 134-135 D 6-7
Moratalla 134-135 FG 9
Morava [CS] 133 H 4
Morava [YU] 136-137 J 3
Moravia = Morava 133 G -J 4
Moravia = Morava 133 G -J 4
Moravie = Morava 133 G -J 4
Morawa 194-195 C 5
Morawhanna 158-159 H 3
Moray Firth 132 DE 3
Morcenx 134-135 G 6
Mordāb = Mordāb-e Pahlavi
182-183 N 4
Mordāb-e Pahlavī 182-183 N 4
Mordāgī 182-183 L 4
Mordino 138-139 S 3
Mordovian Autonomous Republic
= 5 ◁ 178-179 H 7
Mordovo 138-139 N 7
Mordovskaja Avtonomnaja
Sovetskaja Socialističeskaja
Respublika = Mordwinische
Autonome Republik =
5 ◁ 178-179 H 7
Mordovskij zapovednik 138-139 O 6
Mordvanos, República Autónoma de
los ~ = 5 ◁ 178-179 H 7
Mordves, République Autonome
des - = 5 ◁ 178-179 H 7
Mordvin Autonóm Köztársaság
178-179 H 7
Mordvinen Autonome Republiek =
5 ◁ 178-179 H 7
Mordvini, Repubblica Autonoma
dei - = 5 ◁ 178-179 H 7
Mordvinska autonomni republika =
5 ◁ 178-179 H 7
Mordwini, Rep. Auton. dei
138-139 OP 6
Mordwinische Autonome Republik =
5 ◁ 178-179 H 7
Mordwińska Autonomiczna
Republika = 5 ◁ 178-179 H7
More, Ben - [GB, Mull] 132 C 3
More, Ben - [GB, Outer Hebrides]
132 C 3
More Assynt, Ben - 132 DE 2
Moreau River 152-153 F 3
Morecambe Bay 132 E 4-5
Moree 194-195 J 5
Morehead, KY 152-153 P 6
Morehead City, NC 148-149 E 7
Morehouse, MO 154-155 L 2
Moreland, ID 150-151 G 4
Morelia 146-147 F 8
Morella 134-135 GH 8
Morella [AUS] 194-195 H 4
Morelos [MEX, ● Coahuila]
154-155 E 6
Morelos [MEX, ◎] 146-147 G 8
Morenci, AZ 150-151 J 9
Morenci, MI 152-153 OP 5
Moreno [BR] 158-159 M 6
Møre og Romsdal 130-131 BC 6
Moresby Island 144-145 K 7
Moreton Bay 196 L 1
Moreton Island 194-195 K 5
Morgan 194-195 GH 6
Morgan, TX 154-155 G 4
Morgan City, LA 154-155 K 6
Morganfield, KY 152-153 N 7
Morgan Hill, CA 150-151 C 7
Morganton, NC 148-149 C 7
Morgantown, IN 152-153 N 6
Morgantown, KY 152-153 N 7
Morgantown, WV 148-149 CD 5
Morgat 134-135 E 4
Morgenzon 174-175 HJ 4
Mori [J] 188-189 b 2
Mori [RI] 186-187 H 7
Mori = Kusu 188-189 H 6
Moriah, Mount - 150-151 FG 6
Moriarty, NM 154-155 BC 3
Moribaya 172-173 C 3
Morija 174-175 G 5
Moriki 172-173 G 3
Morioka 184-185 R 4
Morisset 196 K 4
Morita, La - 154-155 C 6
Morizane = Yamakuni 188-189 H 6
Morjärv 130-131 K 4
Morkoko 178-179 V 4
Morlaix 134-135 F 4
Morland, KS 152-153 FG 6
Mormon Range 150-151 F 7
Mornington, Isla - 162 A 7
Mornington Island 194-195 G 3
Morno 172-173 E 3
Moro, OR 150-151 C 3
Morobe 186-187 N 8
Morocco 166-167 C 3-D 2
Morogoro 168-169 J 4
Moro Gulf 186-187 H 5
Morokwen = Morokweng
168-169 F 8
Morokweng 168-169 F 8
Morombe 168-169 K 7
Morón [C] 146-147 L 7
Mörön [MVR] 184-185 J 2
Morón [RA] 162 E 4
Morona, Rio - 158-159 D 5
Morondava 168-169 K 7
Morón de la Frontera 134-135 E 10
Moroni 168-169 K 5
Moroni, UT 150-151 H 6
Mörön Us He = Ulaan Mörön
190-191 BC 2
Mörönus 184-185 G 5
Morotai , Pulau - 186-187 J 6
Moroto [EAU, ▲] 171 C 2
Moroto [EAU, ●] 168-169 H 2
Morovanos, República Autónoma
dos - = 5 ◁ 126-127 R 5
Morovanos, República Autónoma
dos - = 5 ◁ 178-179 H 7
Morozovsk 140-141 KL 2
Morpeth 132 F 4
Morphou = Mórfu 182-183 E 5
Morretes 160-161 H 6
Morrilton, AR 154-155 J 3
Morrinsville 194-195 OP 7
Morris, IL 152-153 M 5
Morris, MN 152-153 H 3
Morrisburg 148-149 F 2
Morris Jesup, Kap - 120 A 19-23
Morrison, IL 152-153 LM 5
Morristown, SD 152-153 EF 3
Morristown, TN 146-147 K 4
Morro Agudo 160-161 HJ 4
Morro, Punta - 162 B 3
Morro Grande 158-159 HJ 5
Morros [BR, Maranhão]
158-159 L 5
Morrosquillo, Golfo de -
158-159 D 2-3
Morrumbala 168-169 J 6
Morrumbene 168-169 J 7
Mors 130-131 C 9
Moršansk 138-139 NO 7
Morse, TX 154-155 E 2
Mortara 136-137 C 3
Morteros 162 D 4
Mortes, Rio das - 160-161 K 4
Mortimer 174-175 F 7
Mortlake 196 F 7
Morton, MN 152-153 J 3
Morton, TX 154-155 D 4
Morundah 196 GH 5
Moruya 194-195 K 7
Morvan 134-135 K 5
Morven 194-195 J 5
Morwell 194-195 J 7
Moržovec, ostrov - 178-179 GH 4
Moša 138-139 N 2-3
Mosal'sk 138-139 K 6
Mosambický průliv 168-169 K 7-5
Mosambik 168-169 H 7-J 5
Mosby, MT 152-153 C 2
Mosca = Moskva 178-179 F 6
Mośćnyj,ostrov - 138-139 FG 4
Mośćnyj, ozero - 130-131 MN 8
Moscou e Moskva 178-179 F 6
Moscovo = Moskva 178-179 F 6
Moscow, ID 146-147 C 2
Moscow, KS 152-153 F 7
Moscow = Moskva 178-179 F 6
Moscú = Moskva 178-179 F 6
Mosèdis 138-139 CD 5
Mosel 133 C 4
Moselle 134-135 L 4
Mošenskoje 138-139 K 4
Mosera = Jazirat al-Masirah
180-181 H 6
Moses, NM 154-155 D 2
Moses Lake 150-151 D 2
Moses Lake, WA 150-151 D 2
Mosesriver 174-175 H 3
Moshi [EAT] 168-169 J 3
Moshi River - 172-173 G 3
Mosimane 174-175 D 3
Mosinee, WI 152-153 M 3
Mosi-Oa-Toenja 168-169 FG 6
Mosjøen 130-131 E 5
Moskal'vo 178-179 b 7
Moskau = Moskva 178-179 F 6
Moskenesøy 130-131 EF 4
Moskou = Moskva 178-179 F 6
Moskovo = Moskva 126-127 Q 4
Moskovskaja vozvyšennost
138-139 K-M 5-6
Moskva [SU, ~] 138-139 K 6
Moskva [SU, ●] 178-179 F 6
Moskvy, kanal - 138-139 L 5
Mosolovo 138-139 N 6
Mosonmagyaróvár 133 HJ 5
Mospino 140-141 HJ 3
Mosquera 158-159 D 4
Mosquero, NM 154-155 CD 3
Mosquitia 146-147 K 8
Mosquito, Rio - 160-161 M 1-2
Mosquito Lagoon 148-149 c 2
Mosquitos, Costa de - 146-147 K 9
Mosquitos, Golfe de los -
146-147 K 10
Moss 130-131 D 8
Mossaka 168-169 E 3
Mossâmedes 160-161 GH 2
Mosselbaai 168-169 F 9
Mossendjo 168-169 D 3
Mossi 166-167 D 6
Mossman 194-195 HJ 3
Moss Point, MS 154-155 L 5
Mossul = Al-Mūṣil 180-181 E 3
Mossul = Al-Mūṣil 180-181 E 3
Moss Vale 194-195 JK 6
Most 133 F 3
Mostaganem = Mustaghānam
166-167 DE 1
Mostar 136-137 GH 4
Mostardas 162 D 4
Mostiska 140-141 A 2
Mostva 138-139 F 8
Mosty 138-139 E 7
Mosūlp'o 188-189 EF 6
Moszkva = Moskva 178-179 F 6
Moszul = Al-Mūṣil 180-181 E 3
Mota 166-167 M 6
Motaba 168-169 E 2
Motala 130-131 F 8
Motalerivier 174-175 J 2
Motherwell and Wishaw 132 DE 4
Motīhāri 180-181 NO 5
Motley, MN 152-153 J 2
Motoichiba = Fuji 188-189 M 5
Motol' 138-139 E 7
Motomiya 188-189 N 4
Motovskij zaliv 130-131 PQ 3
Motril 134-135F10
Mott, ND 152-153 E 2
Mottinger, WA 150-151 D 2-3
Motul de Felipe Carillo Puerto
146-147 J 7
Motygino 178-179 RS 6
Motyklejka 178-179 c 6
Mouila 168-169 D 3
Mouka 166-167 J 7
Moulamein 194-195 HJ 6-7
Moulamein Creek 194-195 HJ 7
Mould Bay 144-145 MN 2
Moulins 134-135 J 5
Moulmein = Maulamyaing
186-187 C 3
Moulouÿa, Ouêd - = Wādī al-Mulūyah 166-167 D 2
Moulton, AL 154-155 M 3
Moulton, IA 152-153 K 5
Moultrie, GA 146-147 K 5
Moultrie, Lake - 148-149 C 8
Mound City, IL 152-153 M 7
Mound City, KS 152-153 J 6
Mound City, MO 152-153 J 5
Mound City, SD 152-153 FG 3
Moundou 166-167 H 7
Moundsville, WV 148-149 C 5
Moundville, AL154-155 M 4
Moung 186-187 D 4
Mount, Cape - = Grand Cape Mount
172-173 C 4
Mountain, WI 152-153 M 3
Mountainair, NM 154-155 B 3
Mountain City, NV 150-151 F 5
Mountain City, TN 148-149 BC 6
Mountain Grove, MO 154-155 J 2
Mountain Home, AR 154-155 J 3
Mountain Home, ID 150-151 F 4
Mountain Park, OK 154-155 F 3
Mountain Pine, AR 154-155 J 3
Mountains, Gates of the -
150-151 H 2
Mountain View, AR 154-155 JK 3
Mountain View, MO 154-155 K 2
Mountain View, OK 154-155 F 3
Mountain Village, AK 144-145 D 5
Mount Airy, NC 148-149 C 6
Mount Alida 174-175 J 5
Mount Ayliff = Maxesibeni
174-175 H 6
Mount Ayr, IA 152-153 JK 5
Mount Barker 194-195 C 6
Mount Cambriens = Cambrian
Mountains 132 D 6-E 5
Mount Carmel, IL 152-153 MN 6
Mount Carmel, PA 148-149 E 4
Mount Carmel, UT 150-151 G 7
Mount Caroll, IL 152-153 LM 4
Mount Darwin 168-169 H 6
Mount Desert Island 148-149 JK 2
Mount Dora, FL 148-149 c 2
Mount Dora, NM 154-155 D 2
Mount Dutton [AUS] 196 BC 1
Mount Elliot = Selwyn
194-195 H 4
Mount Fletcher 174-175 H 6
Mount Forest 148-149 C 2-3
Mount Frere = Kwabhaca
174-175 H 6
Mount Gambier 194-195 GH 7
Mount Garnet 194-195 HJ 3
Mount Gilead, OH 152-153 P 5
Mount Hagen 186-187 M 8
Mount Hebron, CA 150-151 BC 5
Mount Holly, NJ 148-149 F 4-5

ount Hope [AUS, New South Wales] 196 GH 4
ount Hope [AUS, South Australia] 194-195 FG 6
ount Hope, WV 148-149 C 6
ount Horeb, WI 152-153 M 4
ount Isa 194-195 G 4
ount Kenya National Park 171 D 3
ount Kilimanjaro National Park 171- D 3
ount MacKinley National Park 144-145 FG5
ount Magnet 194-195 C 5
ount Manara 194-195 HJ 6
ount Morgan 194-195 K 4
ount Morris, MI 152-153 OP 4
ount Morris, NY 148-149 E 3
ount Olive, NC 148-149 D 7
ount Perry 194-195 K 5
ount Pleasant, IA 152-153 L 5
ount Pleasant, MI 152-153 O 4
ount Pleasant, TN 154-155 M 3
ount Pleasant, TX 154-155 H 4
ount Pleasant, UT 150-151 H 6
ount Rainier National Park 150-151 C 2
ount Riley, NM 154-155 B 5
ount Shasta, CA 150-151 B 5
ount Sterling, IL 152-153 L 6
ount Swan 194-195 G 4
ount Union, PA 148-149 E 4
ount Vernon, GA 148-149 B 8
ount Vernon, IA 152-153 L 5
ount Vernon, IL 146-147 J 4
ount Vernon, IN 152-153 MN 7
ount Vernon, KY 152-153 O 7
ount Vernon, NY 148-149 G 4
ount Vernon, OH 152-153 P 5
ount Vernon, OR 150-151 D 3
ount Vernon, TX 154-155 H 4
ount Vernon, WA 150-151 BC 1
ount Victory, OH 152-153 P 5
ount Willoughby 194-195 F 5
ouping = Muping 190-191 H 3
oura 134-135 D 9
oura [AUS] 194-195 JK 4
oura [BR] 158-159 G 5
ourão 134-135 D 9
ourdi, Dépression du - 166-167 J 5
ourdiah 166-167 C 6
oure, La -, ND 152-153 GH 2
ourmansk, Seuil de - 178-179 EF 2
ouslimiyé = Muslimiyah 182-183 G 4
oussoro 166-167 H 6
outiers 134-135 L 6
outohora 194-195 P 7
outong 186-187 H 6
outsamoudou = Mutsamudu 168-169 KL 5
ovano 154-155 D 7
oville, IA 152-153 HJ 4
oweaqua, IL 152-153 M 6
owich, OR 150-151 BC 4
owming = Maoming 184-185 L 7
ozico 168-169 EF 5
oyale 168-169 J 2
oyamba 166-167 B 7
o-yang Chiang = Moyang Jiang 190-191 C 10-11
oyang Jiang 190-191 C 10-11
oye Dao 190-191 J 3
o-yeh Tao = Moye Dao 190-191 J 3
oyen Atlas = Al-Aṭlas al-Mutawassit 166-167 CD 2
oyie Springs, ID 150-151 E 1
oyo [EAU] 171 B 2
oyo = Pulau Moyo 186-187 G 8
oyo, Pulau - 186-187 G 8
oyobamba 158-159 D 6
oyock, NC 148-149 EF 6
oyowosi 171 B 3-4
øysalen 130-131 FG 3
oyto 166-167 H 6
'oža [SU ◁ Unža] 138-139 P 4
'oža [SU ◁ Zapadnaja Dvina] 138-139 J 5-6
ožajsk 138-139 KL 6
ozambicki, Basen - 168-169 K 5
ozambicki, Kanał = 168-169 K 7-5
ozambik 168-169 H 7-J 5
ozambiki-csatorna 168-169 K 7-5
ozambiki-medence 168-169 K 5
ozambico 168-169 H 7-J 5
ozambico, Canala di - 168-169 K 7-5
ozambico, Platea di - 168-169 J 8-9
ozambique 168-169 H 7-J 5
ozambique = Moçambique [Moçambique, ●] 168-169 K 5-6
ozambique, Bassin de - 168-169 K 5
ozambique, Canal de - 168-169 K 7-5
ozambique, Cuenca de - 168-169 K 5
ozambique, Estrecho de - 168-169 K 7-5
ozambique, Straat - 168-169 K 7-5
ozambique Basin 168-169 K 5
ozambiquebekken 168-169 K 5
ozambique Channel 168-169 K 7-5
ožary = Boľšije Možary 138-139 N 7
ozdok 140-141 M 5
ožga 178-179 J 6
ozuli 138-139 G 5
ozyr' 138-139 G 7
pampáeski = Babaeski 182-183 B 2
panda 168-169 H 4
pepo 168-169 H 5
pika 168-169 H 5
poroko so 168-169 GH 4
'Pouya 168-169 E 3
pulungu 168-169 H 4
pumalanga 174-175 HJ 3
purakasese 168-169 J 5
pwapwa 171 D 4
r'râïti, Al- 166-167 C 4
rayyah, Al- 166-167 C 5
rreïti, El - = Al-M'râïti 166-167 C4
rtvé moře = Bahr al-Mayyit 180-181 D 4
sagali 168-169 J 4
sai'ida = Musā'idah 182-183 M 7
sasa 171 B 3
seleni 174-175 K 4
sta [SU, ~] 178-179 E 6
sta [SU, ●] 138-139 HJ 6
stinskij Most 138-139 J 4
stislavl' 138-139 HJ 6
swega 171 D 5
takuja 168-169 H 4
tama 171 D 5
tatarivier 174-175 H 6
Mtimbo 171 D 5
Mtito Andei 171 D 3
Mtowabaga 171 C 3
Mtubatuba 174-175 K 5
Mtwalume 174-175 J 6
Mtwara 168-169 K 5
Mualama 168-169 J 6
Muan 188-189 F 5
Muang Khammouan 186-187 E 3
Muang Không 186-187 E 4
Muang Khôngxêdon 186-187 E 3
Muang Paksé 186-187 DE 3-4
Muang Pakxan 186-187 D 3
Muang Xaignabouri 186-187 D 3
Muar 186-187 D 6
Muaraaman 186-187 D 7
Muaraancalong 186-187 G 6
Muaraenim 186-187 D 7
Muaralesan 186-187 G 6
Muarasiberut 186-187 C 7
Muaratebo 186-187 D 7
Muaratembesi 186-187 D 7
Muaratewe 186-187 FG 7
Mu'askar, Al- 166-167 E 1
Mubārak, Jabal - 182-183 F 8
Mubende 168-169 H 2
Mubi 166-167 G 6
Mucajaí, Rio - 158-159 G 4
Mucajaí, Serra do - 158-159 G 4
Muchinga Mountains 171 BC 5
Muchino 138-139 S 4
Muchorskij 140-141 P 2
Muchtolovo 138-139 O 6
Mučkapskij 138-139 O 8
Mucojo 168-169 K 5
Muconda 168-169 F 5
Mucoque 174-175 L 1
Mucuburi, Rio - 171 D 6
Mucur 182-183 F 3
Mucuri 158-159 M 8
Mucuri, Rio - 158-159 L 8
Mucuripe, Ponta de - 158-159 M 5
Mucusso 168-169 F 6
Mudanjiang 184-185 OP 3
Mudanya 182-183 C 2
Mudawwarah, Al- 180-181 D 5
Mudaysisāt, Jabal - 182-183 G 7
Mud Butte, SD 152-153 E 3
Muddo Gashi = Mado Gashi 168-169 J 2
Muddus-nationalpark 130-131 J 4
Muddy Creek 150-151 H 6
Muddy Gap 152-153 C 4
Muddy Gap, WY 150-151 K 4
Muddy Peak 150-151 F 7
Mudgee 194-195 JK 6
Mudīrīyat esh Shimālīya = Ash-Shimālīyah 166-167 KL 5
Mudjuga 138-139 M 2
Mud Lake 150-151 E 7
Mudôn 186-187 C 3
Műdros 136-137 L 6
Mudug 166-167 b 2
Mudurnu 182-183 D 2
Muecate 168-169 J 5
Mueda 168-169 J 5
Muendaze 171 E 6
Mufulira 168-169 G 5
Mufu Shan 190-191 E 7
Muganskaja ravnina 140-141 O 7
Mughayrā', Al- 182-183 G 8
Mugi 188-189 K 6
Mugila, Monts - 168-169 G 4
Muğla 180-181 B 3
Mugodžary, gory - 178-179 K 8
Muqayshit 180-181 G 6
Mugombazi 171 B 4
Mugrejevskij 138-139 O 5
Muhammad, Rā's - 166-167 LM 4
Muhammadī, Wādī - 182-183 K 6
Muḥammad Tulayb 170 D 5
Muhammed, Ras - = Rā's Muhammad 166-167 LM 4
Muhārī, Al- 182-183 L 7
Muhārī, Sha'īb al- 182-183 KL 7
Muhembo 168-169 F 6
Muhinga = Muyinga 168-169 GH 3
Mühlbach = Sebeş 136-137 K 2-3
Mühldorf 133 F 4
Mühlhausen 133 E 3
Mühlig-Hoffmann-Gebirge 121 B 1-2
Muhu 138-139 D 4
Muhuwesi 171 D 5
Muirite 171 D 6
Muizenberg 174-175 BC 8
Muja = Ust'-Muja 178-179 W 6
Mujezerskij 178-179 E 5
Mujlad, Al- 166-167 K 6
Mujnak 178-179 K 9
Muju 188-189 F 4-5
Mujunkum = peski Mojynkum 178-179 MN 9
Muka = Mouka 166-167 J 7
Mukačeve 140-141 A 2
Mukah 186-187 F 6
Mukallā, Al- 180-181 FG 8
Mukatschjowo = Mukačevo 140-141 A 2
Mukawa 188-189 b 2
Mukawwa', Jazirat - 170 FG 6
Mukdahan 186-187 D 3
Mukden = Shenyang 184-185 NO 3
Mukebo 171 AB 4
Mukhā, Al- 180-181 E 8
Mukhalid = Netanya 182-183 F 6
Mukinbudin 194-195 C 6
Mukoko 171 BC 3
Mukomuko 186-187 D 7
Mukrān, Sabkhat - 166-167 E 3
Mukry 180-181K 3
Mukumbi = Makumbi 168-169 F 4
Mula, LA - 154-155 C 6
Mulainagiri 180-181 LM 8
Mulan 184-185 O 2
Mulanje 168-169 J 6
Mulanje, Mount - 168-169 J 6
Mūlayit Taung 186-187 C 3
Mulberry, KS 152-153 J 7
Muldoon, ID 150-151 G 4
Muldrow, OK 154-155 H 3
Muleba 171 BC 3
Mule Creek, NM 150-151 J 9
Mule Creek, WY 152-153 D 4
Muleshoe, TX 154-155 D 3
Mulgubi 188-189 G 2
Mulhacén 134-135 F 10
Mulhall, OK 154-155 G 2
Mülhausen = Mulhouse 134-135 L 5
Mulhouse 134-135 L 5
Muli = Vysokogornyj 178-179 ab 7
Mulka 196 D 2
Mull 132 CD 3
Mullan, ID 150-151 EF 2
Mullan Pass 146-147 D 2
Mullen, NE 152-153 F 4
Mullens, WV 148-149 C 6
Muller, Pegunungan - 186-187 F 6
Müllerberg 130-131 I 6
Mullet Lake 152-153 O 3
Mullewa 194-195 C 5
Mullin, TX 154-155 F 5
Mullingar 132 C 5
Mullins, SC 148-149 D 7
Mulobezi 168-169 FG 6
Multān 180-181 L 4
Mulu, Gunung - 186-187 FG 6
Mulucas 186-187 J 6-8
Mulula, Wed - = Wādī al-Mūlūyah 166-167 D 2
Mulūṣī, Bi'r al- 182-183 J 6
Mulūṣī, Shādir al- 182-183 HJ 6
Mūlūyah, Wādī al- 166-167 D 2
Muluzia 171 B 5
Mulvane, KS 152-153 H 7
Mulymja 178-179 LM 5
Mumbai = Bombay 180-181 L 7
Mumbwa 168-169 G 6
Mumeng 186-187 N 8
Mumford, TX 154-155 G 5
Mumpu, Mount - 171 B 6
Mumra 140-141 N 4
Mun, Mae Nam - 186-187 D 3
Muna [SU] 178-179 W 4
Muna, Pulau - 186-187 H 8
Munasarowar Lake = Mapham Tsho 184-185 E 5
Munayjah, Bi'r - 170 F 6
München 133 EF 4
Munch'ŏn 188-189 F 3
Muncie, IN 146-147 JK 3
Munday, TX 154-155 F 4
Münden 133 D 3
Mundiwindi 194-195 CD 4
Mundo, Rio - 134-135 F 9
Mundo Novo [BR, Mato Grosso do Sul] 160-161 E 5
Mundrabilla 194-195 E 6
Mundubbera 194-195 JK 5
Munfordville, KY 152-153 O 7
Mungallala Creek 194-195 J 5
Mungana 194-195 H 3
Mungari 168-169 H 6
Mungbere 168-169 G 2
Munger 180-181 O 5
Mungindi 194-195 J 5
Munhango 168-169 E 5
Munich = München 133 EF 4
Munique = München 133 E 4
Munising, MI 152-153 N 2
Muniz Freire 160-161 M 4
Munkács = Mukacevo 133 L 4
Munkfors 130-131 EF 8
Munksund 130-131 JK 5
Munnik 174-175 HJ 2
Muñoz Gamero, Peninsula - 162 B 8
Munsan 188-189 F 4
Munsfjället 130-131 F 5
Münster [D] 133 C 2-3
Münster [IRL] 132 B 5
Munte 186-187 G 6
Muntok = Mentok 186-187 DE 7
Muñoz Gamero, Peninsula - 162 B 8
Munyu 174-175 H 6
Muodoslompolo 130-131 K 4
Mu'o'ng Khoua 186-187 D 2
Mu'o'ng Pak Beng 186-187 D 2-3
Muong Plateau = Cao Nguyên Trung Phân 186-187 E 4
Mu'o'ng Sen, Đeo - 186-187 DE 3
Muonio 130-131 KL 4
Muonio älv 130-131 K 4
Mupa Upare Hill 172-173 GH 3
Muping 190-191 H 3
Mupvŏng-ni = Chŏnch,ŏn 188-189 F 2
Muqayshit 180-181 G 6
Muqayyar, Al- = Ur 180-181 F 4
Muqdisho = Mogadishu 166-167 0 8
Muqsim, Jabal - 170 EF 6
Muqui 160-161 M 4
Muqur = Moqur 180-181 K 4
Mur 133 FG 5
Mura 136-137 FG 2
Murādābād = Moradabad 180-181 MN 5
Muradiye [TR, Manisa] 182-183 B 3
Muradiye [TR, Van] 182-183 KL 3
Murafa 140-141 CD 2
Murakami 188-189 M 3
Murallón, Cerro - 162 B 7
Murān [IR] 182-183 N 7
Muranga 168-169 J 3
Mur'anyo = Bandar Murcaayo 166-167 bc 1
Muraši 178-179 H 6
Murat Dağı 180-181 B 3
Murat Dağları = Şierafettin Dağları 182-183 J 3
Murathüyügü = Musabeyli 182-183 G 4
Murat Nehri 180-181 E 3
Muravera 136-137 CD 6
Muravl'anka [SU → Ražsk] 138-139 N 7
Murawjewo = Mažeikiai 138-139 D 5
Murayama 188-189 N 3
Muraywad, Al- 182-183 L 8
Murchison, Cape - 144-145 S 3
Murchisonberge 174-175 J 2
Murchison Falls = Kabelega Falls 168-169 H 2
Murchison Falls National Park = Kabelega Falls National Park 168-169 H 2
Murchisonfjord 130-131 k 4-5
Murchisonfjorden 130-131 kl 4
Murchison River 194-195 C 5
Murcia [E, ≅] 134-135 G 9- 0
Murcia [E, ●] 134-135 G 9- 10
Murdo, SD 152-153 F 4
Murdochville 144-145 XY 8
Murdock, FL 148-149 b 3
Mureş 136-137 K 2-3
Murfreesboro, AR 154-155 J 3
Murfreesboro, NC 148-149 E 6
Murfreesboro, TN 146-147 J 4
Murgab [SU, ~] 180-181 J 3
Murgab [SU, ●] 180-181 L 3
Murge 136-137 G 5
Murghāb Rōd 180-181 JK 3-4
Murgon 194-195 K 5
Muriaé 158-159 L 9
Muriaé, Rio - 160-161 M 4
Murilo 192-193 G 4
Müritz 133 F 2
Murmansk 178-179 EF 4
Murmansk, Dorsale di 178-179 EF 2
Murmansk, Patmar de 178-179 EF 2
Murmansk, Plataforma de - 178-179 EF 2
Murmansk Rise 178-179 EF 2
Murmanskschwelle 178-179 EF 2
Murmaši 178-179 E 4
Murom 178-179 G 6
Muromcevo 178-179 O 6
Muroran 184-185 R 3
Muros 134-135 C 7
Muroto 188-189 JK 6
Muroto zaki 188-189 K 6
Murphy, ID 150-151 E 4
Murphy, NC 154-155 N 3
Murphy, TN 148-149 A 7
Murphysboro, IL 152-153 M 7
Murr, Bi'r - 170 D 6
Murrat al-Kubrā, Al-Buhayrat al- 170 E 2
Murrat el-Kubrâ, Buheiret el - = Al-Buhayrat al-Murrat al-Kubrā 170 E 2
Murray, Bacino di - 180-181 H 7-J 6
Murray, KY 154-155 L 2
Murray, Fosse de - 124-125 BC 4
Murray, Fractura de - 124-125 BC 4
Murray, Fractura de 124-125 BC 4
Murray, Frattura di - 124-125 BC 4
Murray, Lake - [PNG] 186-187 M 8
Murray, Lake - [USA] 148-149 C 7
Murraybreukzone 124-125 BC 4
Murray Bridge 196 D 5
Murray-Bruchzone 198-199 KL 3
Murray Fracture Zone 124-125 BC 4
Murray River [AUS] 194-195 H 6-7
Murraysburg 174-175 E 6
Murrumbidgee River 194-195 HJ 6
Murrumburrah 196 J 5
Mursala, Pulau - 186-187 C 6
Murtafi'at Tāsili 166-167 F 3
Murtoa 196 F 6
Murumush 174-175 E 3
Murundu 160-161 M 4
Murupara 194-195 P 7
Murupu 158-159 G 4
Mururoa 192-193 O 7
Murvārā = Murwara 180-181 N 6
Murwara 180-181 N 6
Murwillumbah 194-195 K 5
Murygino 138-139 R 4
Murzūq = Marzūq 166-167 G 3
Murzūq, Edeien el- = Sahrā' Marzūq 166-167 G 3-4
Mürzzuschlag 133 G 5
Muş 180-181 E 3
Mūsā, Khūr-e - 182-183 N 7-8
Musa Ali Terara 166-167 N 6
Musabeyli 182-183 G 4
Musā'idah 182-183 M 7
Musala 136-137 K 4
Musan 184-185 OP 3
Musā Qal'a 180-181 JK 4
Musay'īd 180-181 G 5-6
Musayyib, Al- 182-183 L 6
Musazade = Arhavi 182-183 J 2
Muscat = Masqaṭ 180-181 H 6
Muscatine, IA 152-153 L 5
Muscoda, WI 152-153 L 4
Muscongus Bay 148-149 J 3
Musgrave 194-195 H 2
Musgrave Ranges 194-195 F 5
Mūshā 170 D 4
Mushāsh, Bi'r – 182-183 G 7
Mushie 168-169 E 3
Mushin 172-173 F 4
Mushkābād = Ebrāhimābād 182-183 O 5
Mushora = Mushūrah 182-183 K 4
Mushūrah 182-183 K 4
Musi, Air - 186-187 D 7
Musi, Al- 180-181 E 3
Musinia Peak 150-151 H 6
Musisi 171 C 4
Musiyān 182-183 M 6
Muskat = Masqaṭ 180-181 H 6
Muskegon, MI 146-147 J 3
Muskegon Heights, MI 152-153 N 4
Muskegon River 152-153 NO 4
Muskingum River 148-149 BC 5
Muskogee, OK 146-147 GH 4
Muskoka, Lake - 148-149 D 2
Muslimiyah 182-183 G 4
Musl'umovo 138-139 T 6
Musmār = Mismār 166-167 M 5
Musoma 168-169 H 3
Musoshi 171 AB 5
Muş ovasi 182-183 J 3
Mussali, Mount - = Musa Ali 166-167 N6
Mussanāt, Al- 182-183 M 8
Mussau 186-187 N 7
Musselburgh 132 E 4
Musselshell River 146-147 E 2
Mussende 168-169 E 5
Mussuma 168-169 F 5
Mustafa Kemalpaşa 182-183 C 2-3
Mustaghānam 166-167 DE 1
Mustajevo 138-139 T 8
Mustang, OK 154-155 FG 3
Mustang Island 154-155 G 7
Musters, Lago - 162 BC 7
Mustla 138-139 EF 4
Mustvee 138-139 F 4
Mustwee=Mustvee 138-139 F 4
Mustvee 130-131 M 8
Musu-dan 188-189 GH 2
Muswellbrook 194-195 K 6
Mût [ET] 166-167 K 3
Mut [TR] 182-183 E 4
Muta 171 A 3
Mutankiang = Mudanjiang 184-185 OP 3
Mutare 168-169 H 6
Muthanna, Al- 182-183 L 7
Mu'tiq, Jabal - 170 E 4
Mutis, Gunung - 186-187 H 8
Mutki 182-183 J 3
Mutlah = Al-Maṭlā' 182-183 M 8
Mutsamudu 168-169 KL 5
Mutshatsha 168-169 F 5
Mutsu 188-189 N 2
Mutsu-wan 188-189 N 2
Muttra = Mathurā 180-181 M 5
Mutum Biyu 172-173 H 3
Muwaffaqiyah, Al- 182-183 L 6
Muwayh, Al- 180-181 E 6
Muwaylih, Al- 170 F 4
Muxima 168-169 D 4
Muyinga 168-169 GH 3
Muyumba 168-169 G 4
Muzaffarābād 180-181 LM 4
Muẓaffargarh 180-181 L 4-5
Muzaffarnagar 180-181 M 5
Muzaffarpur 180-181 NO 5
Muzambinho 160-161 J 4
Muži 178-179 L 4
Muz tagh 184-185 E 4
Muz tagh ata 184-185 D 4
Mvōlō = Mvūlū 166-167 KL 7
Mvuma 168-169 GH 6
Mwali 168-169 K 5
Mwambwa 171 C 5
Mwanamundia 171 DE 3
Mwanza [EAT] 168-169 H 3
Mwanza [ZRE] 168-169 G 4
Mwatate 171 D 3
Mwaya 168-169 H 4
Mwazya 171 BC 5
Mweka 168-169 F 3
Mwene-Ditu 168-169 F 4
Mwenga 168-169 G 3
Mwenzo 171 C 5
Mweru, Lake - 168-169 G 4
Mweru Swamp 168-169 G 4
Mwingi 171 D 3
Mwinilunga 168-169 FG 5
Mwitikira 171 C 4
Myan'aung 186-187 BC 3
Myanmar 184-185 GH 7
Myanmar = Birmania 186-187 BC 2
Myeik 186-187 C 4
Myeik Kyūnzū 186-187 C 4
Myingyan 186-187 BC 2
Myjeldino 138-139 U 3
Myitkyinā 186-187 C 1
Mykénai 136-137 K 7
Mykolajiv 136-137 OP 2
Mýkonos 136-137 L 7
Mymensingh = Maimansingh 180-181 OP 6
Mynämäki 130-131 JK 7
Mynaral 178-179 N 8
Mynfontein 174-175 EF 6
Myntobe 140-141 O 3
Myohyang-sanmaek 188-189 E 3-F 2
Myökö-zan 188-189 LM 4
Myŏngch'ŏn 188-189 GH 2
Myra 130-131 c 2
Myrdal 130-131 B 7
Mýrdalsjökull 130-131 d 3
Mýrdalssandur 130-131 d 3
Myre 130-131 F 3
Mýrina 136-137 L 6
Myrthle 148-149 D 2
Myrtle Beach, SC 148-149 D 8
Myrtle Creek, OR 150-151 B 4
Myrtleford 196 H 6
Myrtle Point, OR 150-151 AB 4
Myšega 138-139 L 6
Mysen 130-131 D 8
Myškin 138-139 LM 5
mys Kriljon 178-179 b 8
Myślenice 133 JK 4
Mysovsk = Babuškin 178-179 U 7
Mystic, IA 152-153 K 5
Mystic, SD 152-153 E 3
Mys Vchodnoj 178-179 QR 3
Mysy 138-139 TU 3
Mys Želanija 178-179 MN 2
My Tho 186-187 E 4
Mytilēnē 136-137 M 6
Mytischtschi = Mytišči 138-139 L 6-M 5
Mytišči 138-139 L 6-M 5
Myton, UT 150-151 HJ 5
Mývatn 130-131 e 2
Mziha 168-169 J 4
Mzimba 168-169 H 5
Mzuzu 171 C 5

N

Naab 133 F 4
Na'āg, Gebel - = Jabal Nī'āj 170 E 6
Na'ām, Bi'r an- 182-183 G 7
Na'ām, Maqarr an- 182-183 HJ 7
Na'am Zarqat 170 F 6
Naantali 130-131 JK 7
Naas 132 C 5
Näätämöjoki 130-131 MN 3
Naauwpoort = Noupoort 168-169 FG 9
Nauwte, De - 174-175 DE 6
Nababeep = Nababiep 174-175 B 5
Nababiep 174-175 B 5
Nābah, Bi'r - 170 E 7
Nabc 184-185 G 4
Naberežnyje Čelny 138-139 T 6
Nābeul = Nābul 166-167 G 1
Nabiac 196 L 4
Nabilatuk 171 C 2
Nabileque Pantanal de - 160-161 D 3-4
Nabileque, Rio 160-161 D 4
Nabire 186-187 L 7
Nabisar 180-181 KL 5-6
Nabk, An- [Saudi-Arabien] 182-183 G 7
Nabk, An- [SYR] 180-181 D 4
Nāblus = Nābulus 182-183 F 6
Nabolo 172-173 E 3
Naboomspruit 174-175 H 3
Nabordo 172-173 H 3
Nabou 172-173 C 3
Nabq 170 F 3
Nābul 166-167 G 1
Nābulus 182-183 F 6
Nacaca 171 D 5
Naçala 168-169 K 5
Nacfa = Nakfa 166-167 M 5
Naches, WA 150-151
Nachicevan, Republica Autónoma de - = 18 ◁ 126-127 S 8
Nachicevan, Republica Autonoma - 140-141 MN 7
Nachiczewańska Autonomiczna Republika 140-141 M 7
Nachingwea 168-169 J 5
Nachičevan' 140-141 M 7
Nachičevan [Azerbaigian] = 1 ◁ 141 M 7
Nachičevan, Autonome Republik - 140-141 MN 7
Nachičevan, República Autónoma de 140-141 M 7
Nachičevan, Rep. Aut. di - 140-141 M 7
Nachičevanská autonomní republika 140-141 MN 7
Nachičevanskaja Avtonomnaja Sovetskaja Socialističeskaja Respublika = Autonome Republik Nachičevan 140-141 MN 7
Nachičevan, Repubblica Autonoma di- = 18 ◁ 126-127 S 8
Nachitsjevan Autonome Republiek 140-141 MN 7
Nachodka 178-179 Z 9
Nachraci = Kondirskoje 178-179 M 6
Nachtigal Falls 172-173 HJ 4
Nacimiento Mountains 154-155 B 2-3
Nacka 130-131 H 8
Naco, AZ 150-151 HJ 10
Nacogdoches, TX 154-155 H 5
Nacololo 171 D 6
Nacozari de Gracia 146-147 DE 5
Ñacunday 160-161 E 7
Ñacunday, Rio - 160-161 E 6
Nadadores 154-155 E 7
Nadelkap 168-169 F 9
Nådendal = Naantali 130-131 JK 7
Nadeždinsk = Serov 178-179 L 6
Nadhatah, An- 182-183 J 6
Nadiād 180-181 L 6
Nadjaf, An- = An-Najaf 180-181 E 4
Nadjd = Najd 180-181 E 5-6
Nădlac 136-137 J 2
Nadoa = Dan Xian 184-185 K 8
Nadqān 180-181 G 6
Nadvoicy 138-139 K 2
Nadvornaja 140-141 B 2
Næstved 130-131 DE 10
Nafada 166-167 G 6
Nafishah 170 DE 2
Naftalan 140-141 N 6
Naft, Āb i - 182-183 L
Naft-e Sefid 182-183 N
Naft-e Shāh 182-183 L 5-6
Naft Hānah 182-183 L 5
Naft Khāna = Naft Hānah 182-183 L 5
Nafūd, An- 180-181 E 5
Nafusah, Jabal - 166-167 G 2
Naga 186-187 H 4
Nagahama [J, Ehime] 188-189 J 6
Nagahama [J, Shiga] 188-189 L 5
Nagai 188-189 MN 3
Nagaland 180-181 P 5
Nagano 184-185 Q 4
Naganohara 188-189 M 4
Nagaoka 184-185 Q 4
Nāgaor = Nagaur 180-181 L 5
Nagapattinam 180-181 MN 8
Naga Pradesh = Nagaland 180-181 P 5
Nagara gawa 188-189 L 5
Nagar Āveli = Dadra and Nagar Haveli 180-181 L 6
Nāgarkoyil = Nāgercoil 180-181 M 9
Nagar Pārkar 180-181 KL 6
Nagasaki 184-185 O 5
Naga-shima [J, ◌] 188-189 GH 6
Nagashima [J, ●] 188-189 L 5
Nagato 188-189 H 5
Nagaur 180-181 L 5
Nag Chhu 184-185 G 5
Nagchhu Dsong 184-185 G 5
Nagchhukha = Nagchhu Dsong 184-185 G 5
Nag Chhu 184-185 G 5
Nāgercoil 180-181 M 9
Nāgishōt = Nāqishut 166-167 L 8
Nagorje 138-139 M 5
Nagorno Karabach, OA di 140-141 N 6-7
Nagorno-Karabach, Obl. Aut. de - 140-141 N 6
Nagorno-Karabag, Oblast Autónoma de - 140-141 N 6
Nagorno-Karabagh, Region Autonome de - 140-141 N 6-7
Nagorno-Karabagh Autonome Oblast 140-141 N 6-7
Nagorno-Karabah Autonomous Region 140-141 N 6-7
Nagorno-Karabah, Provincia Autonoma di - = 120 ◁ 126-127 S 7
Nagorno-Karabaj, Oblast Autónoma de - 184-185 N 6
Nagornyj 178-179 Y 6
Nagorsk 138-139 S 4
Nagoudé = Nguél Daoudi 172-173 H 2
Nagoya 184-185 Q 4
Nāgpur 180-181 M 6
Nagura, Ras en - = Rā's an-Naqurah 182-183 F 6
Naguun Mörön 184-185 NO 1-2
Nagykanizsa 133 H 5
Nagykőrös 133 JK 5
Nagyvárad = Oradea 136-137 JK 2
Nagy-Antillák 146-147 K 7-N 8
Nagy-Ausztráliai-öböl = Great Australian Bight 194-195 E 6-G 7
Nagy-Bahama-pad 146-147 L 6-7
Nagy-Britannia és Észak-Írország 132 F-H 4-5
Nagy Fal 184-185 K 4
Nagy-Hingan 184-185 M 3-N 1
Nagy-korallzátony = Great Barrier Reef 194-195 H 2-K 4
Nagy-Medve-tó 144-145 MN 4
Nagy-Rabszolga-tó 144-145 NO 5
Nagy-Sóstó = Great Salt Lake 146-147 D 3
Nagyszeben = Sibiu 136-137 L 3
Nagy-Szunda-szigetek 186-187 GH 8
Naha 184-185 O 6
Nahanni National Park 144-145 LM 5
Nahari 188-189 JK 6
Nahariya = Nahariyya 182-183 F 6
Nahariyya 182-183 F 6
Nahāvand 182-183 N 5
Nahicsevani Autonóm Köztársaság 140-141 M 7
Nāhid, Bi'r - 170 C 2
Nahorní Karabašská autonomní oblast 140-141 N 6
Nahuel Huapi, Lago - 162 B 6
Nahungo 171 D 5
Nahunta, GA 148-149 BC 9
Naica 154-155 C 7
Nain [CDN] 144-145 Y 6
Nā'īn [IR] 180-181 G 4
Naindi 186-187 a 2
Naini Tal 180-181 M 5
Nain Singh Range = Nganglong Gangri 184-185 E 5
Nairn 132 E 3
Nairobi 168-169 J 3
Naissaar 138-139 E 4
Naivasha 168-169 J 3
Najaf, An- 180-181 E 4
Najafābād 180-181 G 4
Najd 180-181 E 5-6
Naj' Hammādī 170 DE 4-5
Najin 184-185 P 3
Najran 180-181 E 7
Najstenjarvi 138-139 J 2
Naju 188-189 F5
Nakadōri-shima 188-189 G 6
Naka gawa 188-189 K 6
Nakajō 188-189 M 3
Nakaminato 188-189 N 4
Nakamura 188-189 J 6
Nakamura = Sōma 188-189 N 4
Nakano 188-189 M 4
Nakano-shima 188-189 J 4
Nakano-umi 188-189 J 5
Nakasato 188-189 N 2
Naka-Shibetsu 188-189 d 2
Nakasongola 171 C 2
Nakatane 188-189 H 7
Nakatsu 188-189 H 6
Nakatsukawa 188-189 L 5
Nakatsukawa = Nakatsugawa 50-5 1 L 5
Nakatu 188-189 H 6
Nakel = Nakto nad Notecią 133 H 2
Nakfa 166-167 M 5
Nakhīlī, Bi'r - 182-183 K 5
Nakhl 170 E 3
Nakhlāy, Bi'r - 170 D 6
Nakhon Lampang = Lampang 186-187 C 3
Nakhon Pathom 186-187 CD 4
Nakhon Phanom 186-187 D 3
Nakhon Ratchasima 186-187 D 3-4
Nakhon Sawan 186-187 CD 3
Nakhon Si Thammarat 186-187 CD 5
Nakhichevan, République Autonome de - 140-141 MN 7
Nakhichevan Autonomous Republic 140-141 M 7
Nakina 144-145 T 7
Nakop 174-175 CD 5
Nakou 190-191 F 8
Nakpanduri 172-173 EF 3
Nakło nad Notecią 133 H 2
Naknek, AK 144-145 E 6
Nakonde 171 C 5
Nakskov 130-131 D 10
Naktong-gang 188-189 G 5
Nakuru 168-169 J 3
Nakwaby 172-173 E 3
Nāl 180-181 K 5
Nalajch 184-185 K 2
Nalazi 174-175 K 3
Nal'čik 140-141 L 5
Nallıhan 182-183 D 2
Naltschik = Nal'čik 140-141 L 5
Nālūt 166-167 G 2
Nama 174-175 BC 3
Namacurra 168-169 J 6
Na'mah, An- 166-167 C 5
Namak, Daryācheh - 180-181 G 4
Namak-e Mighan, Kavire 180-181 H 4
Namakwaland 168-169 E 8
Namakwaland = Klein Namakwaland 174-175 B 5
Namakzār-e Khwāf 180-181 HJ 4
Namaland 168-169 E 8
Na'mān, Jazirat an - = Jazirat an-Nu'mān 170 F 4
Namanga 168-169 J 3
Namangan 180-181 L 2
Na'māniyah, An- 182-183 L 6
Namanyere 168-169 H 4
Namapa 168-169 JK 5
Namarrói 168-169 J 6
Namasagali 168-169 H 2
Namasakata 171 D 5
Namatanai 186-187 h 5
Namatele 171 D 5
Nambane 171 D 5
Nam Bô 186-187 DE 5
Nambour 194-195 K 5
Nằm Cǎn 186-187 D 5
Nam Choed Yai = Kra Buri 186-187 C 4
Namch'ŏnjŏm 188-189 F 3
Namcy 178-179 Y 5
Nam Choed Yai = Kra Buri 186-187 C 4
Nam Định 186-187 E 2-3
Namerikawa 188-189 L 4
Nametil 168-169 JK 6
Nam-gang 188-189 F 3
Namhae-do 188-189 G 5
Namhan-gang 188-189 F 4
Namhoi = Foshan 184-185 L 7
Namib = Namibwoestyn 168-169 D 6-E 8
Namib Desert = Namibwoestyn 168-169 D 6-E 8
Namibia 168-169 E 7
Namibie 168-169 E 7
Namib-Naukluft Park 168-169 DE 7
Namib-sivatag = Namib woestijn 168-169 D 6-E 8
Namibwoestyn 168-169 D 6-E 8
Namies 174-175 C 5
Namiziz 174-175 B 4
Namjabarba Ri 184-185 H 6
Namlea 186-187 J 7
Namling Dsong 184-185 FG 6
Namoa = Nan'ao 190-191 F 10
Namoa = Nan'ao Dao 190-191 F 10
Namoi River 194-195 J 6
Namonuito 192-193 F 4
Namorik 192-193 H 4
Namous, Oued en - = Wādī an-Namru He = Ru He 190-191 E 5
Nāmus 166-167 D 2
Nampa, ID 146-147 C 3
Nampala 166-167 C 5
Nampo 184-185 NO 4
Namp'ot'ae-san 188-189 G 2
Nampula 168-169 JK 6
Namru He = Ru He 190-191 E 5
Namsen 130-131 E 5
Namsi 188-189 E 3
Namsos 130-131 DE 5
Nam Tsho 184-185 G 5
Namuli, Serra - 168-169 J 6
Namuling Zong = Namling Dsong 184-185 FG 6
Namulo 171 D 6
Namuno 171 D 6
Namur 134-135 K 3
Nāmūs, Wādī an- 166-167 D 2
Namus, Wau en - = Wāw an Nāmūs 166-167 H 4
Nāmūs, Waw an- 166-167 H 4
Namutoni 168-169 E 6
Namwala 168-169 G 6
Namwŏn 188-189 F 5
Nan 186-187 D 3
Nan, Mae Nam - 186-187 D 3
Nana Candungo 168-169 F 5
Nanae 188-189 b 3
Nanafalia, AL 154-155 M 4
Nanaimo 144-145 M 8
N'an'ajol' 138-139 S 2
Nanam 188-189 GH 2
Nana-Mambéré 166-167 GH 7
Nan'an 190-191 G 9
Nananib Plateau = Nananibplato 174-175 B 3
Nananibplato 174-175 B 3
Nanango 194-195 K 5
Nanao [J] 188-189 L 4
Nan-ao [RC] 190-191 H 9
Nan'ao [TJ] 190-191 F 10
Nan'ao Dao 190-191 F 10
Nan-ao Tao = Nan'ao Dao 190-191 F 10
Nanao wan 188-189 L4
Nanau 171 E 1
Nanay, Rio - 158-159 E 5
Nancha 184-185 O 2
Nanchang 184-185 LM 6
Nanchang = Nanchong 184-185 JK 5
Nan-chang = Nanzhang 190-191 CD 6
Nancheng 184-185 M 6
Nancho = Nanzhao 190-191 D 5
Nancheng 184-185 M 6
Nan-ch'iao = Fengxian 190-191 H 6
Nan-ching = Nanjing [TJ, Fujian] 190-191 F 9
Nan-ching = Nanjing[TJ, Jiangsu] 184-185 M 5
Nanchino = Nanjing 184-185 M 5
Nan-chi Shan = Nanji Shan 190-191 H 8
Nanchong 184-185 JK 5
Nanchung = Nanchong 184-185 JK 5
Nancy 134-135 L 4
Nanda Devi 180-181 MN 4
Nandan 188-189 K 5
Nanded 180-181 M 7
Nandeir = Nanded 180-181 M 7
Nandi 186-187 a 2
N'andoma 178-179 G 5
Nandurbār 180-181 L 6
Nandyal 180-181 M 7
Nanfeng [TJ, Guangdong] 190-191 C 10
Nanfeng [TJ, Jiangxi] 190-191 F 8
Nangade 171 DE 5
Nanga Eboko 166-167 G 8
Nangah Pinoh 186-187 F 7
Nan-gang = Nam-gang 188-189 F 3
Nānga Parbat 180-181 LM 3-4
Nangatayap 186-187 F 7
Nang-ch'ien = Nangqian 184-185 H 5
Nangnim-sanmaek 188-189 F 2
Nangong 190-191 E 3
Nangqian 184-185 H 5
Nangsin Sum = Menggudai 190-191 B 2
Nanguan 190-191 D 3
Nan Hai 184-185 L 8-M 7
Nanhai = Foshan 184-185 L 7
Nan He [TJ, ~] 190-191 C 5
Nanhe [TJ, ●] 190-191 E 3
Nan Ho = Nan He [TJ, ~] 190-191 C 5
Nan-ho = Nanhe [TJ, ●] 190-191 E 3
Nanhsien = Nan Xian 190-191 D 7
Nan-hsiung = Nanxiong 184-185 LM 6
Nanhuatang 190-191 C 5
Nanhui 190-191 HJ 6
Nanjiangqiao 190-191 DE 7
Nanjih Tao = Nanri Qundao 190-191 G 9
Nanjing [TJ, Fujian] 190-191 F 9
Nanjing [TJ, Jiangsu] 184-185 M 5
Nanji Shan 190-191 H 8
Nankang [TJ, Guangdong] 190-191 B 11
Nankang [TJ, Jiangxi] 190-191 E 9
Nan-kang = Xingzi 190-191 F 7
Nankhu 184-185 G 3
Nankin = Nanjing 184-185 M 5
Nanking = Nanjing 184-185 M 5
Nankoku 188-189 JK 6
Nan-kuan = Nanguan 190-191 D 3
Nankung = Nangong 190-191 E 3
Nanlaoye Ling 188-189 E 2-F 1
Nanle 190-191 E 3-4
Nan Ling [TJ, ▲▲] 184-185 L 6-7
Nanling [TJ, ●] 184-185 M 5
Nan-liu Chiang = Nanliu Jiang 190-191 B 10-11
Nanliu Jiang 190-191 B 10-11
Nan-lo = Nanle 190-191 E 3-4
Nanma 190-191 H 7
Nanning 184-185 K 7
Nannup 194-195 C 6
Nanpan Jiang 184-185 JK 7
Nanpi 190-191 F 2
Nanping [TJ, Fujian] 184-185 M 6
Nanping [TJ, Hubei] 184-185 L 6
Nan-p'u Ch'i = Nanpu Xi 190-191 G 8
Nanpu Xi 190-191 G 8
Nanqi = Youxikou 190-191 G 8
Nanripo 171 D 6
Nanri Qundao 190-191 G 9
Nansei-shotō 184-185 NO 6-7
Nansei syotō = Nansei-shotō 184-185 NO 6-7
Nansen Sound 144-145 ST 1
Nan Shan 184-185 HJ 4
Nansio 168-169 H 3
Nantai-san 188-189 M 4
Nan-tch'ang = Nanchang 184-185 LM 6
Nan-tch'eng = Nancheng 184-185 M 6
Nan-tch'ong = Nanchong 184-185 JK 5
Nantes 134-135 G 5
Nantian 190-191 HJ 7
Nantian Dao 190-191 HJ 7
Nanticoke, PA 148-149 EF 4
Nantong 184-185 N 5
Nan-tou [RC] 190-191 H 10
Nantou [TJ] 190-191 D 10
Nantsang = Nanchang 184-185 LM 6
Nantucket, MA 148-149 HJ 4
Nantucket Island 146-147 N 3
Nantucket Sound 148-149 H 4
Nantung = Nantong 184-185 N 5
Nanty Glo, PA 148-149 D 4
Nanumanga 192-193 J 5
Nanuque 158-159 LM 8
Nanusa, Kepulauan - 186-187 J 6
Nan Xian 190-191 D 7
Nanxiong 184-185 LM 6
Nanyang Hu 190-191 F 4
Nanyang 184-185 L 5
Nanyi = Nancha 184-185 O 2
Nanyuki 168-169 J 2
Nanzhang 190-191 CD 6
Nanzhao 190-191 D 5
Nanzheng = Hanzhong 184-185 K 5
Nao, Cabo de la - 134-135 H 9
Naoconane Lake 144-145 W 7
Naoetsu 188-189 LM 4
Naǧgata = Nõgata 188-189 H 6
Naoli He 184-185 P 2
Nao-li Ho = Naoli He 184-185 P
Naos 174-175 B 2
Naos, Isla - 146-147 bc 3
Naoua = Nawā 182-183 FG 6
Naozhou Dao 190-191 C 11
Napa, CA 150-151 B 6
Napaku 186-187 G 6
Napanee 148-149 E 2
Napanwainami 186-187 L 7
Napas 178-179 P 6
Nape 186-187 DE 3
Napels = Nápoli 136-137 EF 5
Napier [NZ] 194-195 P 7
Napier [ZA] 174-175 C 8
Napier, Mount - 194-195 EF 3
Napier Mountains 121 C 6
Naples, FL 146-147 K 6
Naples, NY 148-149 E 3
Naples = Nápoli 136-137 EF 5
Napo, Rio - 158-159 E 5
Napoleon, ND 152-153 G 2
Napoleon, OH 152-153 OP 5
Napoleonville, LA 154-155 K 5-6
Nápoles = Nápoli 136-137 EF 5
Napoles = Napoli 128-129 L 7
Napoli 136-137 E 5
Napoli, Golfo di - 136-137 EF 5
Nápoly = Nápoli 136-137 EF 5
Nappanee, IN 152-153 NO 5
Napuka 192-193 N 6
Naqāda = Naqādah 170 E 5
Naqādah 170 E 5
Naqadeh 182-183 L 4
Nāqishūt 166-167 L 8

Naque 160-161 L 3
Naqūrah, Ra's an- 182-183 F 6
Nara [J] 188-189 KL 5
Nārā [PAK] 180-181 K 5
Nara [RMM] 166-167 C 5
Naracoorte 194-195 GH 7
Naradham 196 GH 4
Naranjas, Punta - 158-159 C 3
Narathiwat 186-187 DE 5
Nara Visa, NM 154-155 D 3
Narāyanganj 180-181 OP 6
Narbadā = Narmada 180-181 LM 6
Narbonne 134-135 J 7
Nardò 136-137 GH 5
Narembeen 194-195 C 6
Naréna 172-173 C 2
Narew 133 K 2
Nargen = Naissaar 138-139 E 4
Narib 174-175 B 3
Narimanabad 140-141 O 7
Nāri 180-181 K 5
Narin 190-191 C 2
Narinda, Helodranon'i - 168-169 L 5
Narin Nur 190-191 AB 2
Narjan-Mar 178-179 JK 4
Narli 182-183 G 4
Narmada 180-181 LM 6
Narman 182-183 JK 2
Naroč' 138-139 F 6
Narodnaja, gora - 178-179 L 5
Naro Fominsk 138-139 KL 6
Narok 168-169 J 3
Narooma 194-195 JK 7
Narop 174-175 B 3
Narovl'a 138-139 G 8
Narrabri 194-195 JK 6
Narragansett Bay 148-149 H 4
Narrandera 194-195 J 6
Narran Lake 196 H 2
Narran River 196 H 2
Narrogin 194-195 C 6
Narromine 194-195 J 6
Narrows, OR 150-151 D 4
Narrows, VA 148-149 C 6
Narssaq 144-145 bc 5
Narssarssuaq 144-145 bc 5
Nartkala 140-141 LM 5
Narubis 174-175 C 4
Narugas 174-175 C 5
Narugo 188-189 N 3
Narungombe 171 D 5
Naru-shima 188-189 G 6
Naruto 188-189 K 5
Narva [SU, ●] 178-179 D 6
Narva [SU, ~] 138-139 F 4
Narva laht 138-139 F 4
Narvik 130-131 G 3
Narvskoje vodochranilišče 138-139 G 4
Narwa = Narva 178-179 D 6
Narym 178-179 P 6
Naryn [SU, Kirgizskaja SSR ~] 180-181 L 2
Naryn [SU, Kirgizska ja SSR ●] 180-181 M 2
Naryn [SU, Rossijskaja SFSR] 178-179 S 7
Naryn = Taš-Kumyr 180-181 L 2
Narynkol 180-181 MN 2
Naryškino 138-139 K 7
Nasafjell 130-131 F 4
Nasarawa [WAN, Gongola] 172-173 J 3
Nasarawa [WAN, Plateau] 166-167 F 7
Nasaret = Nazērat 182-183 F 6
Nāsāud 136-137 L 2
Naschitti, NM 150-151 J 7
Nāshik = Nasik 180-181 L 6-7
Nashua, MT 152-153 C 1
Nashua, NH 148-149 H 3
Nashville, AR 154-155 HJ 3-4
Nashville, GA 148-149 B 9
Nashville, IL 152-153 M 6
Nashville, KS 152-153 G 7
Nashville, MI 152-153 O 4
Nashville, TN 146-147 J 4
Nashville Basin 154-155 M 2
Nashwauk, MN 152-153 K 2
Nasia 172-173 E 3
Našice 136-137 H 3
Nāsijārvi 130-131 KL 7
Nasik 180-181 L 6-7
Nāşir, An- 166-167 L 7
Nasir, Jabal an- 166-167 F 4
Nāsiriyah [IRQ] 180-181 F 4
Nasiyah, Jabal - 170 E 6
Nas Nas Point = Melkbospunt 174-175 B 5
Nasondoye 168-169 FG 5
Naşr 170 D 2
Naşr, An- 170 E 5
Naşr, Khazzan an- 166-167 L 4
Nāşriyah 182-183 G 6
Nassarawa = Nasarawa 166-167 F 7
Nassau [◌] 198-199 J 5
Nassau [BS] 146-147 L 6
Nassau, Bahia - 162 C 9
Nassau Sound 148-149 c 1
Nässjö 130-131 F 9
Nass River 144-145 L 6-7
Nastapoka Islands 144-145 V 6
Nasva 138-139 GH 5
Našice 136-137 H 3
Nata 168-169 G 7
Na-ta = Dan Xian 184-185 K 8
Natagaima 158-159 DE 4
Natal [BR, Rio Grande do Norte] 158-159 MN 6
Natal [RI] 186-187 C 6
Natal [ZA] 168-169 GH 8
Natal, Bacia do - 124-125 LM 7
Natal, Patamá do - 168-169 J 9
Natal, Bacino di 124-125 LM 7
Natal, Bassin de - 124-125 LM 7
Natal, Cuenca de - 124-125 LM 7
Natal, Ramal de - 168-169 J 9
Natal, Seuil de - 168-169 J 9
Natal Basin 124-125 LM 7
Natalbecken 124-125 LM 7
Natalbekken 124-125 LM 7
Nataldrempel 168-169 J 9
Natalia, TX 154-155 F 6
Natali-hátság 168-169 J 8-9
Natal Ridge 168-169 J 9
Natalschwelle 168-169 J 8-9
Natanya = Nētanya 182-183 F 6
Natash, Wādī - 170 EF 5
Natashquan River 144-145 Y 7
Natchez, MS 146-147 H 5
Natchitoches, LA 146-147 H 5
Nathorst land 130-131 jk 6
Nathrop, CO 152-153 C 6
National City, CA 150-151 E 9
National City, MI 152-153 OP 3
National Park 148-149 B 7
National Reactor Testing Station 150-151 G 4
Natitingou 166-167 E 6
Natividade 158-159 K 7
Natoma, KS 152-153 G 6
Nätong Dsong 184-185 G 6
Natron, Lake - 168-169 J 3
Natrūn, Wādī an- 170 CD 2
Natrun Lakes = Wādī an-Natrun 170 CD 2
Natuna, Kepulauan - 186-187 E 6
Natuna Besar, Pulau - 186-187 E 6
Natural Bridges National Monument 150-151 HJ 7
Naturaliste, Cape - 194-195 B 6
Naturita, CO 150-151 J 6
Nauchas = Naukhas 174-175 B 2
Nauja Vileika, Vilnius- 138-139 EF 6
Naukhas 174-175 B 2
Naukluftgebirge = Noukloofberge 174-175 AB 3
Naukurr 194-195 FG 2
Naulavaraa 130-131 N 6
Naulila 168-169 DE 6
Nā'ūr 182-183 F 7
Nauru 198-199 H 5
Nâusa 136-137 JK 5
Nauški 178-179 U 7
Nauta 158-159 E 5
Nauvo 130-131 JK 7
Nava [MEX] 154-155 E 6
Nava de Ricomalillo, La - 134-135 E 9
Navajo, AZ 150-151 J 8
Navajo Indian Reservation 150-151 HJ 7-8
Navajo Mountain 150-151 H 7
Navajo Reservoir 152-153 C 7
Navan 132 C 5
Navangar = Jāmnagar 180-181 L 6
Navarin, mys - 178-179 jk 5
Navarino, Isla - 162 C 9
Navarra 134-135 G 7
Navašino 138-139 O 6
Navasota, TX 154-155 GH 5
Navasota River 154-155 G 5
Navassa Island 146-147 LM 8
Naver 132 D 2
Navia 134-135 D 7
Navirai 160-161 E 5
Nav'la 138-139 K 7
Navoi 178-179 M 9
Navojoa 146-147 E 6
Navolato 146-147 E 7
Navoloki 138-139 NO 5
Návpaktos 136-137 JK 6
Návplion 136-137 K 7
Navrongo 166-167 D 6
Navşar = Şemdinli 182-183 L 4
Navy Board Inlet 144-145 U 3
Nawā 182-183 FG 6
Nawa = Naha 184-185 O 6
Nawābshāh 180-181 K 5
Nawādhibu 166-167 A 4
Nawākshūt 166-167 A 5
Nawari = Nahari 188-189 JK 6
Nawāşif, Harrat - 180-181 E 6
Nawfalīyah, An- 166-167 H 2
Naws, Rā's - 180-181 H 7
Naxos [I] 136-137 F 7
Náxos [GR, ◌] 136-137 L 7
Náxos [GR, ●] 136-137 L 7
Nayarit 146-147 EF 7
Nāy Band [IR, Banāder va Jazāyer-e Khalij-e Fārs] 180-181 G 5
Nāy Band [IR, Khorāsān] 180-181 H 4
Nāy Band, Ra's-e - 180-181 G 5
Naylor, MO 154-155 K 2
Nayoro 188-189 c 1
Nayoro = Gornozavodsk 178-179 b 8
Nazaré 134-135 C 9
Nazaré [BR, Amazonas] 158-159 F 4
Nazaré [BR, Bahia] 158-159 M 7
Nazaré = Nazērat 182-183 F 6
Nazareth = Nazērat 182-183 F 6
Nazareth Banco = Nazareth Bank 168-169 O 5
Nazareth Bank 168-169 O 5
Nazarovka 138-139 N 6
Nazca 158-159 DE 7
Nazca, Cresta de - 124-125 E 7-F 6
Nazca, Dorsal de - 124-125 E 7-F 6
Nazca, Dorsale - 124-125 E 7-F 6
Nazca, Seuil de - 124-125 E 7-F 6
Nazca Ridge 124-125 F 7-E 6
Nazcarug 124-125 E 7-F 6
Nazcaschwelle 198-199 N 6-O5
Nazērat 182-183 F 6
Nazija 138-139 HJ 4
Nazilli 182-183 C 4
Nazimiye 182-183 HJ 3
Nazimovo = Novonazimovo 178-179 QR 6
Nazino 178-179 OP 5-6
Nāzlū Rūd 182-183 L 4
Nazombe 171 D 5
Nazrēt 166-167 M 7
Nazwā 180-181 H 6
Nazyvajevsk 178-179 N 6
Nazzah 170 D 4
Nchanga 171 AB 6
Nchelenge 171 B 5
Ndabala 171 B 6
N'daghāmshah, Sabkhat - 166-167 AB 5
Ndai 186-187 k 6
Ndala 171 C 4
Ndalatando 168-169 DE 4
Ndali 166-167 E 7
Ndande 172-173 A 2
Ndélé 166-167 J 7
N'Dendé 168-169 D 3
Ndeni 186-187 17
Ndikiniméki 172-173 H 4
Ndioum 172-173 B 1
N'djamena 166-167 GH 6
Ndjolé [Cameroun] 172-173 H 4
N'Djolé [Gabun] 168-169 CD 3
Ndola 168-169 G 5
Ndumu Game Reserve 174-175 K 4
Nduye 171 B 2
Ndwedwe 174-175 J 5
Ndye 171 B 2
Ndzuwani 168-169 KL 5
Neagh, Lough - 132 C 4
Neah Bay, WA 150-151 A 1
Neale, Lake - 194-195 F 4
Neales, The - 194-195 G 5
Neapel = Nápoli 136-137 EF 5
Neápolis [GR, Grámmos] 136-137 J 5
Neápolis [GR, Pelopónnēsos] 136-137 K 7
Neapol = Nápoli 136-137 EF 5
Near Islands 120 D 1
Nebbou 172-173 E 3
Nebek, En- = An-Nabk 180-181 D 4
Nebine Creek 194-195 J 5
Nebit-Dag 180-181 GH 3
Neblina, Pico da - 158-159 FG 4
Nebbou 172-173 E 3
Nebolči 138-139 J 4
Nebo, Mount - 150-151 H 6
Nebov = Nebbov 172-173 E 3
Nebraska 146-147 FG 3
Nebraska City, NE 152-153 HJ 5
Nebrodie, Monti - 136-137 F 7
Necadah, WI 152-153 L 3
Nechako Plateau 144-145 L 7
Nechvorošča 140-141 G 2
Neckar 133 D 4
Neches, TX 154-155 H 5
Neches River 154-155 H 5
Necochea 162 E 5
Neder-Californië 150-151 F 10
Neder-Guinee 124-125 K 5-6
Nederland 134-135 K 3-L 2
Nederland, TX 154-155 H 6
Neebish Island 152-153 O 2
Needle Peak 150-151 E 8
Needles, CA 150-151 F 8
Ñeembucú 160-161 CD 7
Neenah, WI 152-153 M 3
Neepawa 144-145 R 7
Nefousa, Djebel - = Jabal
Neftečala = 26 Bakinskij Komissarov 140-141 OP 7
Neftegorsk 140-141 J 4
Neftejugansk 178-179 NO 5
Neftekamsk 138-139 U 5
Neftekumsk 140-141 M 4
Nefud = An-Nafūd 180-181 E 5
Nefud, En- = An-Nafūd 180-181 E 5
Negade = Naqādah 170 E 5
Néganzi 172-173 F 3
Negapatam = Nagapattinam 180-181 MN 8
Negara 186-187 FG 8
Negaunee, MI 152-153 N 2
Negeb = Han-Negev 182-183 F 7
Negēlē 166-167 MN 7
Negerpynten 130-131 16
Neggio = Nejo 166-167 M 7
Neghilli = Negēlē 166-167 MN 7
Negoiu 136-137 L 3
Negomane 171 D 5
Negombo = Migamuwa 180-181 M 9
Negoreloje 138-139 F 7
Negotin 136-137 K 3
Negribreen 130-131 k 5
Negros 186-187 H 5
Negru Vodă 136-137 N 4
Negueve = Han-Negev 182-183 F 7
Nehalem, OR 150-151 B 3
Nehbandān 180-181 HJ 4
Nehe 184-185 NO 2
Neiafu 186-187 c 2
Nei-chiang = Neijiang 184-185 JK 6
Nei-ch'iu = Neiqiu 190-191 E 3
Neihart, MT 150-151 H 2
Nei-hsiang = Neixiang 190-191 C 5
Neihuang 190-191 E 4
Neijiang 184-185 JK 6
Nei-kiang = Neijiang 184-185 JK 6
Neilersdrif 174-175 D 5
Neillsville, WI 152-153 L 3
Nei Menggu = Nei Monggol Zizhiqu 184-185 K 3-M 2
Neimenggu, Région Autonome - 184-185 K 3-M 2
Neineva 182-183 JK 5
Neiqiu 190-191 E 3
Neiße 133 G 3
Neisse = Nysa 133 H 3
Neiva 158-159 DE 4
Neixiang 190-191 C 5
Neja 178-179 G 6
Nejd = Najd 180-181 E 5-6
Nejo 166-167 M 7
Nékaounié 172-173 D 4
Nekemtē 166-167 M 7
Nekl'udovo [SU, Nižni Novgorod] 138-139 O 5
Nekoosa, WI 152-153 M 3
Nekrasovskoje 138-139 N 5
Nekropolis 170 E 5
Neksø 130-131 F 10
Nelidovo 138-139 J 5
Neligh, NE 152-153 GH 4
Nel'kan 178-179 Za 6
Nellore 180-181 MN 8
Nellūru = Nellore 180-181 MN 8
Nel'ma 178-179 ab 8
Nelson [CDN] 144-145 N 8
Nelson, NE 152-153 G 5
Nelson [NZ] 194-195 O 8
Nelson [RA] 162 DE 4
Nelson, AZ 150-151 G 8
Nelson, CA 150-151 C 6
Nelson, WI 152-153 L 3
Nelson, Estrecho - 162 AB 8
Nelson Forks 144-145 M 6
Nelson Island 144-145 C 5
Nelson Reservoir 152-153 BC 1
Nelson River 144-145 RS 6
Nelsonville, OH 148-149 B 5
Nelspoort 174-175 E 7
Nelspruit 168-169 H 8
Nem 138-139 U 3
Nema 138-139 S 5
Nemah, WA 150-151 B 2
Neman 130-131 J 10
Neman [SU] 138-139 E 7
Ne'māniya, An- = An-Na'māniyah 182-183 L 6
Německo 133 C-F 2-4
Nemenčine 138-139 E 6
Nemira, Muntele - 136-137 M 2
Nemirov [SU, Vinnica] 140-141 D 2
Nemours = Ghazawat 166-167 D 1
Nemrut Daği 182-183 JK 3
Nemunas 130-131 K 10
Nemunas = Neman 138-139 E 7
Nemuro 184-185 S 3
Nemuro-kaikyō 188-189 d 1-2
Nemuro wan 188-189 d 2
Nenagh 132 BC 5
Nenana, AK 144-145 FG 5
Nenec, Circolo Nazionale dei - 178-179 J-L 4
Něnecký autonomni okruh 178-179 J-L 4
Nenets, Circunscrição Nacional dos - 178-179 J-L 4
Nenets, Circunscripción Nacional de los - 178-179 J-L 4
Nenets, Circunscrição Nacional dos - Nenets, District National des - 178-179 J-L 4
Nenets, Nacional dos 126-127 S-U 2
Nenets Autonomous Area 178-179 J-L 4
Nengonego 192-193 N 6
Nen Jiang [TJ, ~] 184-185 N 2
Nenjiang [TJ, ●] 184-185 O 2
Nen Jiang = Naguun Mörön 184-185 NO 1-2
Nentsen, Nationaal Gebied der - 178-179 J-L 4
Nenzen, Nationalkreis der - 178-179 J-L 4
Neodesha, KS 152-153 HJ 7
Neoga, IL 152-153 M 6
Neola, UT 150-151 H 5
Neopit, WI 152-153 M 3
Neosho, MO 154-155 H 2
Neosho River 146-147 G 4
Nepa 178-179 U 6
Nepāl 180-181 NO 5
Nepal 180-181 NO 5
Nephi, UT 150-151 GH 6
Nephin 132 B 4
Nepoko 168-169 G 2
Nepomuceno 160-161 K 4
Nérac 134-135 H 6
Nerbudda = Narmada 180-181 LM 6
Nerča 178-179 W 7
Nerčinsk 178-179 W 7
Nerčinskij Zavod 178-179 W 7
Nerdva 138-139 U 4
Nerechta 138-139 N 5
Nereta 138-139 E 5
Neretva 136-137 H 4
Neringa 138-139 C 6
Neriquinha = N'Riquinha 168-169 F 6
Neris 130-131 L 10
Neris 138-139 E 6
Nerl' [SU, ● Tver'] 138-139 LM 5
Nerl' [SU, ~◁ Volga] 138-139 LM 5
Ñermete, Punta - 158-159 C 6
Nero, ozero - 138-139 M 5
Nerojka, gora - 178-179 KL 5
Nerópolis 160-161 H 2
Nerskoje ploskogorje 178-179 c 5
Ner'ungri 178-179 XY 6
Nesebăr 136-137 MN 4
Neskaupstadhur 130-131 fg 2
Nesna 130-131 E 4
Ness City, KS 152-153 FG 6
Ness, Loch - 132 D 3
Nesterov [SU, Lvov] 140-141 AB 1
Nestoria, MI 152-153 MN 2
Néstos 136-137 L 5
Nesttun, Bergen- 130-131 AB 7
Nesviž 138-139 F 7
Nētanya 182-183 F 7
Nethanya = Nētanya 182-183 F 7
Netherdale 194-195 J 4
Netherlands 134-135 K 3-L 2
Nettilling Lake 144-145 W 4
Nett Lake 152-153 K 1
Nett Lake Indian Reservation 152-153 K 1-2
Nettleton, MS 154-155 L 3
Neubad = Saulkrasti 138-139 DE 5
Neubrandenburg 133 F 2
Neubraunschweig = New Brunswick 144-145 X 8
Neuchâtel 133 C 5
Neuchâtel, Lac de - 133 C 5
Neue Hebriden = Vanuatu 194-195 N 2-O 3
Neuengland = New England 146-147 M 3-N 2
Neufchâteau [B] 134-135 K 4
Neufchâteau [F] 134-135 KL 4
Neufchâtel-en-Bray 134-135 H 4
Neufundland = Newfoundland 144-145 Za 8
Neufundlandbank 124-125 G 3
Neufundlandbecken 124-125 GH 3
Neufundlandschwelle 124-125 G 3-H 4
Neuguinea 186-187 L 7-M 8
Neuguineaschwelle 186-187 M 5-6
Neuhebridenbecken 194-195 MN 3
Neuhebridengraben 194-195 N 3-4
Neu-Heusis 174-175 B 2
Neukaledonien 196-59 MN 3
Neukastilien = Castilla la Nueva 134-135 E 8-F 7
Neumarkt 133 E 4
Neumiestis = Kurdikos Naumiestis 138-139 D 6
Neumünster 133 DE 1
Neunkirchen [A] 133 H 5
Neunkirchen [D] 133 C 4
Neu-Pebalga = Jaunpiebalga 138-139 F 5
Neupommern-Bougainville-Graben 186-187 h 6
Neuquén [RA, ●] 162 C 5
Neuruppin 133 F 2
Neusatz = Novi Sad 136-137 HJ 3
Neuschottland = Nova Scotia 144-145 X 9-Y 8
Neuschwabenland 121 B 36-2
Neuseeland 194-195 N 8-O 7
Neuseelandschwelle 194-195 M 5-7
Neuse River 148-149 E 7
Neusibirische Inseln = Novosibirskije ostrova 178-179 Z-f 2
Neusiedler See 133 H 5
Neustettin = Szczecinek 133 H 2
Neustrelitz 133 F 2
Neu-Ulm 133 E 4
Neuwied 133 CD 3
Neva [SU] 138-139 H 4
Nevada 146-147 CD 4
Nevada, IA 152-153 K 4-5
Nevada, MO 152-153 J 7
Nevada City, CA 150-151 C 6
Nevado, Cerro el - 162 C 5
Nevado, Sierra del - 162 C 5
Nevel' 138-139 G 5
Never 178-179 XY 7
Nevers 134-135 J 5
Nevinnomyssk 140-141 KL 4
Nevis 146-147 O 8
Nevis, Ben - 132 D 3
Nevis, MN 152-153 J 2
Nevjansk 178-179 KL 6
Nevşehir 180-181 C 3
Newala 168-169 J 5
New Albany, IN 146-147 J 4
New Albany, MS 154-155 L 3
New Amalfi 174-175 H 6
New Amsterdam 158-159 H 3
New Athens, IL 152-153 M 6
Newark [GB] 132 F 5
Newark, DE 148-149 F 5
Newark, NJ 146-147 M 3
Newark, NY 148-149 E 3
Newark, OH 148-149 B 4
Newaygo, MI 152-153 O 4
New Bedford, MA 146-147 MN 3
Newberg, OR 150-151 B 3
New Bern, NC 146-147 L 4
Newbern, TN 154-155 L 2
Newberry, CA 150-151 E 8
Newberry, MI 152-153 O 2
Newberry, SC 148-149 C 7
New Bethesda = Niev-Bethesda 174-175 F 6
New Boston, IL 152-153 L 5
New Boston, OH 148-149 B 5
New Boston, OH 152-153 P 6
New Boston, TX 154-155 H 4
New Braunfels, TX 146-147 G 6
New Britain 186-187 gh 6
New Britain, CT 148-149 G 4
New Britain Bougainville Trench 186-187 h 6
New Brunswick 144-145 X 8
New Brunswick, NJ 148-149 F 4
New Buffalo, MI 152-153 N 5
Newburg, MO 152-153 L 7
Newburgh [CDN] 148-149 E 2
Newburgh, NY 148-149 F 4
Newbury 132 F 6
Newburyport, MA 148-149 H 3
New Caledonie 194-195 MN 3
Newcastel Creek 194-195 F 3
New Castile = Castilla la Nueva 134-135 E 9-F 8
Newcastle [AUS] 194-195 K 6
Newcastle [GB] 132 D 4
New Castle, CO 152-153 C 6
New Castle, IN 152-153 O 5-6
Newcastle, TX 154-155 F 4
Newcastle, WY 152-153 D 4
Newcastle [ZA] 168-169 GH 8
New Castle, OH 148-149 A 5
New Castle, PA 148-149 C 4
Newcastle, VA 148-149 C 6
Newcastle Bay 194-195 H 2
Newcastle upon Tyne 132 EF 4
Newcastle Waters 194-195 F 3
Newcomb, NM 150-151 J 7
Newcomerstown, OH 148-149 C 4
Newdale, ID 150-151 H 4
Newdegate 194-195 CD 6
New Delhi 180-181 M 5
Newell, SD 152-153 E 3
Newellton, LA 154-155 K 4
New England, ND 152-153 E 2
New England [USA] 146-147 M 3-N 2
New England [ZA] 174-175 G 6
New England Range 194-195 K 5-6
Newenham, Cape - 144-145 D 6
Newfane, VT 148-149 G 3
Newfolden, MN 152-153 HJ 1
Newfoundland Basin 124-125 GH 3
Newfoundland [CDN, ◌] 144-145 Za 8
Newfoundland[CDN, ⋆] 144-145 Y 6-Z 8
Newfoundland Bank 124-125 G 3
Newfoundlandbekken 124-125 GH 3
Newfoundlanddrempel 124-125 G 3-H 4
Newfoundland-Ondiepte 124-125 G 3
Newfoundland Ridge 124-125 G 3-H 4
New Georgia 186-187 j 6
New Georgia Group 186-187 j 6
New Georgia Sound = The Slot 186-187 j 6
New Glasgow 144-145 Y 8
New Guinea 186-187 L 7-M 8
New Guinea Rise 186-187 M 5-6
Newgulf, TX 154-155 H 6
Newhalem, WA 150-151 C 1
Newhall, CA 150-151 D 8
New Hampshire 146-147 M 3
New Hampton, IA 152-153 KL 4
New Hanover [PNG] 186-187 gh 5
New Hanover [ZA] 174-175 J 5
New Harmony, IN 152-153 N 6
Newhaven [GB] 132 G 6
New Haven, CT 146-147 M 3
New Haven, IN 152-153 O 5
New Haven, KY 152-153 O 7
New Hebrides 194-195 N 2-O 3
New Hebrides Basin 194-195 MN 3
New Hebrides Trench 194-195 N 3-4
New Iberia, LA 146-147 H 5-6
Newington 174-175 J 3
New Ireland 186-187 h 5
New Jersey 146-147 M 3
New Kensington, PA 148-149 D 4
Newkirk, OK 154-155 G 2
New Kowloon 184-185 LM 7
New Lexington, OH 148-149 BC 5
Newlin, TX 154-155 E 3
New Liskeard 144-145 UV 8
New London, CT 148-149 GH 4
New London, IA 152-153 L 5
New London, MN 152-153 J 3
New London, MO 152-153 L 6
New London, WI 152-153 M 3
New Madrid, MO 154-155 L 2
Newman, CA 150-151 C 7
Newman, NM 154-155 BC 4
Newman Grove, NE 152-153 GH 5
Newmarket [CDN] 148-149 D 2
New Martinsville, WV 148-149 C 5
New Meadows, ID 150-151 E 3
New Mexico 146-147 EF 5
Newnan, GA 154-155 N 4
New Norfolk 194-195 J 8
New Orleans, LA 146-147 HJ 5-6
New Philadelphia, OH 148-149 C 4
New Pine Creek, OR 150-151 C 4
New Plymouth 194-195 O 7
Newport [GB, I. of Wight] 132 F 6
Newport [GB, Severn] 132 E 6
Newport, AR 154-155 K 3
Newport, KY 146-147 K 4
Newport, ME 148-149 J 2
Newport, NH 148-149 GH 3
Newport, OR 150-151 A 3
Newport, RI 148-149 H 4
Newport, TN 148-149 B 6-7
Newport, TX 154-155 FG 4
Newport, VT 148-149 GH 2
Newport, WA 150-151 E 1
Newport News, VA 146-147 L 4
New Providence Island 146-147 L 6-7
Newquay 132 D 6
New Raymer, CO 152-153 E 5
New Richmond, WI 152-153 KL 3
New Roads, LA 154-155 K 5
New Rochelle, NY 148-149 G 4
New Rockford, ND 152-153 G 2
Newry 132 CD 4
New Salem, ND 152-153 F 2
New Sharon, IA 152-153 K 5
New Siberian Islands = Novosibirskije ostrova 178-179 Z-f 2
New Smyrna Beach, FL 148-149 c 2
New South Wales 194-195 H-K 6
Newton, AL 154-155 N 5
Newton, IA 152-153 K 5
Newton, IL 152-153 M 6
Newton, KS 146-147 G 4
Newton, MA 148-149 H 3
Newton, MS 154-155 L 4
Newton, NC 148-149 C 7
Newton, NJ 148-149 F 4
Newton, TX 154-155 J 5
Newton Falls, NY 148-149 F 2
Newtontoppen 130-131 k 5
New Town, ND 152-153 E 1-2
Newtownards 132 D 4
New Ulm, MN 152-153 J 3
New Ulm, TX 154-155 G 6
New Underwood, SD 152-153 E 3
New Westminster 144-145 MN 8
New York 146-147 LM 3
New York, NY 146-147 M 3-4
New York Mountains 150-151 F 8
New Zealand 194-195 N 8-O 7
Neyed = Najd 180-181 E 5-6
Nežin 140-141 E 1
Neyrīz 180-181 G 5
Neyshābūr 180-181 H 3
Nezametnyj = Aldan 178-179 XY 6
Nezlobnaja 140-141 L 4
Nezperce, ID 150-151 EF 2
Nez Perce Indian Reservation 150-151 EF 2
Ngabang 186-187 EF 6
Ngambé [RFC ⇢ Douala] 172-173 H 4
N'Gambe [RFC ⇢ Foumban] 172-173 H 4
Ngamdo Tsonag Tsho 184-185 G 5
Ngami, Lake - 168-169 F 7
Nganghoueí = Anhui 184-185 M 5
Nganglaring Tso = Ngangiha Ringtsho 184-185 EF 5
Nganglong Gangri 184-185 EF 5
Ngangtha Ringtsho 184-185 EF 5
Ngangtse Tsho 184-185 F 5
Ngan-yang = Anyang 184-185 LM 4
Ngao 186-187 CD 3
Ngaoundéré 166-167 G 7
Ngara 171 B 3
Ngatik 192-193 G 4
Ngau 186-187 a 2
Ngaumdere = Ngaoundéré 166-167 G7
Ngaundere = Ngaoundéré 166-167 G7
Ngazidja 168-169 K 5
Ngerengere 171 D 4
Ngiro, Ewaso - 168-169 J 3
Ngiva 168-169 E 6
Ngoc Linh 186-187 E 3
Ngoko 168-169 E 2
Ngomba 171 C 5
Ngome 174-175 J 4
Ngong 168-169 J 3
Ngoring Tsho 184-185 H 4-5
Ngorongoro Crater 168-169 HJ 3
Ngouma 172-173 E 2
N'Gounié 168-169 D 3
Ngoura 166-167 H 6
Ngouri 166-167 H 6
Ngourti 166-167 G 5
Ngoywa 168-169 H 4
Ngozi 171 B 3
Ngqeleni 174-175 H 6
Nguèl Daoudi 172-173 H 2
Nguigmi 166-167 G 6
Ngulu 186-187 L 5
Ngumu 172-173 H 4
Nguna 168-169 D 5
N'Guri = Ngouri 166-167 H 6
Nguru 166-167 G 6
Nguti 172-173 H 4
Ngwanedzi 174-175 J 2
Nhachengue 174-175 L 2
Nha Trang 186-187 EF 4
Nhecolândia 158-159 H 8
Nhi Ha, Sông - 186-187 D 2
Nhill 194-195 H 7
Niafounké 166-167 D 5
Niagara Falls 146-147 KL 3
Niagara Falls, NY 146-147 L 3
Niagara River 148-149 D 3
Niagassola 172-173 C 2
Niagué 172-173 D 4
Niah 186-187 F 6
Ni'āj, Jabal - 170 E 6
Niamey 166-167 E 6
Niamina = Nyamina 172-173 D 2
Niamtougou 172-173 F 3
Niandan Koro 172-173 C 3
Niangara 168-169 G 2
Niangay, Lac - 172-173 E 2
Niangua River 152-153 K 7
Nia-Nia 168-169 G 2
Nianqingtanggula Shan = Nyanchhenthanglha 184-185 G 5-6
Nias, Pulau - 186-187 C 6
Niassa 168-169 J 5
Niassa = Malawi 168-169 HJ 5
Nibāk 180-181 G 6
Nibe 130-131 C 9
Niblinto 162 B 5
Nicaragua 146-147 JK 9
Nicaragua, Lago de - 146-147 JK 9
Nicaro 146-147 L 7
Nice 134-135 L 7
Nice 128-129 K 7
Nicea = Nice 134-135 L 7
Niceville, FL 154-155 M 5
Nicgale 138-139 F 5
Nichinan 188-189 H 7
Nicholasville, KY 152-153 O 7
Nicholson [AUS] 194-195 E 3
Nicholson River 194-195 G 3
Nickel = Nikel' 178-179 E 4
Nickol Bay 194-195 C 4
Nicobar Islands 180-181 P 9
Nicolás, Canal - 146-147 KL 7
Nicomedia = İzmit 180-181 BC 2
Nico Pérez 162 EF 4
Nicosia 136-137 F 7
Nicosia = Levkōsia 180-181 C 3
Nicosia = Levkōsia 180-181 C 3
Nicósia = Levkōsia 180-181 C 3
Nicosie = Levkōsia 180-181 C 3
Nicoya 146-147 J 9
Nicoya, Golfo de - 146-147 J 9
Nicoya, Peninsula de - 146-147 J 9-10
Nida 133 K 3
Ni Dilli = New Delhi 180-181 M 5
Nido,El - 186-187 G 4
Niebüll 133 D 1
Niedere Tauern 133 FG 5
Niederguinea 124-125 K 5-6
Niederkalifornien 143 K 6-7
Niederlande 134-135 K 3-L 2
Niederösterreich 133 GH 4
Niedersachsen 133 C-E 2
Niedźwiedzia, Wyspa - 120 B 16-17
Niekerkshoop 174-175 E 5
Niekerkshope = Niekerkshoop 174-175 E 5
Niélé 172-173 D 3
Niemba [ZRE, ~] 171 B 4
Niemba [ZRE, ●] 171 B 4
Niemcy 133 C-F 2-4
Niemen = Neman 138-139 E 7
Niéna 172-173 D 3
Nienburg 133 D 2
Nienchentangla = Nyanchhent-hanglha 184-185 F 6-G 5
Nieniecki Okręg Autonomiczny 178-179 J-L 4
Nietverdiend 174-175 G 3
Nieu-Bethesda 174-175 F 6
Nieuw Amsterdam [SME] 158-159 HJ 3
Nieuw-Antwerpen = Nouvelle-Anvers 168-169 EF 2
Nieuw-Caledonië 194-195 MN 3
Nieuw-Castilië = Castilla la Nueva 134-135 E 9-F 8
Nieuwe Hebriden 194-195 N 2-O 3
Nieuwe Hebriden Bekken 194-195 MN 3
Nieuwe Hebridentrog 194-195 N 3-4
Nieuwerust = Nuwerus 174-175 C 6
Nieuw-Guinea 186-187 L 7-M 8
Nieuw Guineadrempel 186-187 M 5-6
Nieuw Nickerie 158-159 H 3
Nieuwoudtville 168-169 E 9
Nieuwsiberische Eilanden = Novosibirskije ostrova 178-179 Z-f 2
Nieuwveld Range = Nuweveldberge 174-175 DE 7
Nieuw-Zeeland 194-195 N 8-O 7
Nieuw-Zeelandrug 194-195 M 5-7
Nieves, Las - 154-155 C 7
Nieves = Nevis 146-147 O 8
Niewa = Neva 138-139 H 4
Niewolnicza, Rzeka - 144-145 O 5-6
Niewolnicze, Wybrzeże - 166-167 E7
Niffur = Nippur 182-183 L 6
Nifisha = Nafishah 170 DE 2
Niğde 180-181 CD 3
Nigel 174-175 H 4
Niger [RN, ⋆] 166-167 FG 5
Niger [RN, ⋆] 166-167 F 7
Niger, Bouches du - 166-167 F 8
Niger, Mouths of the - 166-167 F 7-8
Niger, River - 166-167 E 6
Nigéria 166-167 E-G 7
Nigérie 166-167 E-G 7
Nighthawk, WA 150-151 D 1
Nigrita 136-137 K 5
Nihah 182-183 J 2
Nihommatsu = Nihonmatsu 188-189 N 4
Niigata 184-185 Q 4
Niihama 188-189 J 5-6
Niihau 186-187 de 3
Niimi 188-189 J 5
Nii-shima 188-189 M 5
Niitsu 188-189 M 4
Nijād al-'Alī 166-167 D 2-E 1
Nijamābād = Nizamabad 180-181 M 7
Nijmegen 134-135 KL 3
Nikaragua 146-147 JK 9
Nikeľ 178-179 E 4
Nikēphorion = Ar-Raqqah 180-181 DE 3
Nikhaib, An- = Nukhayb 180-181 E 4
Nikheila, En - = An Nuhaylah 170 D 4
Nikito-Ivdel'skoje = Ivdel' 178-179 L 5
Nikki 166-167 E 6-7
Nikolajev 140-141 EF 3
Nikolajevka [SU, Rossijskaja SFSR] 138-139 Q 7
Nikolajevka [SU, Ukrainskaja SSR Dnepropetrovsk] 140-141 F 3
Nikolajevo 138-139 G 4
Nikolajevsk 140-141 MN 1
Nikolajevsk = Pugač'ov 178-179 HJ 7
Nikolajevsk-na-Amure 178-179 b 7
Nikolajevskoje = Bautino 140-141 OP 4
Nikolajew = Nikolajev 140-141 EF 3
Nikolo-Berezovka 138-139 U 5
Nikol'sk [SU, Severnyje uvaly] 178-179 H 6
Nikol'sk [SU, Penza] 138-139 PQ 7
Nikol'skij 178-179 M 8
Nikol'skoje [SU, Komandorskije ostrova] 178-179 fg 6
Nikol'skoje [SU, Volgograd] 140-141 MN 3
Nikomēdeia = İzmit 180-181 BC 2
Nikonga 171 B 3-4
Nikopol 136-137 L 4
Nikopol' [SU] 140-141 G 3
Nikosia = Levkōsia 180-181 C 3
Nikósie = Levkōsia 180-181 C 3
Nikozja = Levkōsia 180-181 C 3
Nik Pey 182-183 N 4
Niksar 182-183 G 2
Nikšić 136-137 H 4
Nikulino [SU, Perm']138-139 V 4
Nil = Bahr an-Nil 166-167 L 3-4
Nil, Bahr an- 166-167 L 3-4
Nila, Pulau - 186-187 JK 8
Nilagiri = Nilgiri Hills 180-181 M 8
Nil al-Abyaḍ, An- 166-167 L 6
Nil al-Azraq, An- 166-167 L 6
Niland, CA 150-151 F 9
Nil Błękitny = Abay 166-167 M 6
Nile = Bahr an-Nil 166-167 L 3-4
Nile Bleu = Abay 166-167 M 6
Niles, MI 152-153 N 5
Niles, OH 148-149 C 4
Nilo = Bahr an-Nil 166-167 L 3-4
Nilo = Bahr an-Nil 166-167 L 3-4
Nilus = Bahr an-Nil 166-167 L 3-4
Nimba, Mont - 166-167 C 7
Nimba 172-173 C 4
Nimega = Nijmegen 134-135 KL 3
Nimega = Nijmegen 134-135 L 3
Nimega = Nijmegen 133 C 3
Nimègue = Nijmegen 134-135 KL 3
Nîmes 134-135 JK 7
Nimmitabel 196 J 6
Nimnyrskij = Malyj Nimnyr 178-179 Y 6
Nimrod, MT 150-151 G 2
Nimūlī 166-167 L 8
Nimwegen = Nijmegen 134-135 KL 3
Ninawā 182-183 JK 5
Ninawā = Ninive 182-183 K 4
Nindigully 196 J 2
Nine Degree Channel 180-181 L 9
Nineve = Ninive 180-181 E 3
Ninfas, Punta - 162 D 6
Ning'an 184-185 OP 3
Ningbo 184-185 N 6
Ningcheng 188-189 B 2
Ning-chin = Ningjin [TJ ↗ Dezhou] 190-191 F 3
Ning-chin = Ningjin [TJ ↘ Shijiazhuang] 190-191 E 3
Ningde 184-185 M 6
Ningdu 184-185 M 6
Ninggang 190-191 DE 8
Ningguo 184-185 M 5
Ninghai 190-191 H 7
Ninghe 190-191 FG 2
Ning-ho = Ninghe 190-191 FG 2
Ninghsia 184-185 K 3-4
Ninghsia, Autonomes Gebiet 184-185 H 3-K 4
Ning-hsiang = Ningxiang 184-185 L 6
Ninghsien = Ning Xian 184-185 K 4
Ninghszia-Huj 184-185 JK 3-4
Ninghua 184-185 M 6
Ninghwa = Ninghua 184-185 M 6
Ningjin [TJ ↗ Dezhou] 190-191 F 3
Ningjin [TJ ↘ Shijiazhuang] 190-191 E 3
Ning-kang = Ninggang 190-191 DE 8
Ningling 190-191 E 4
Ning-po = Ningbo 184-185 N 6
Ningshan 190-191 B 5
Ningsia, Autonomes Gebiet - 184-185 JK 3-4
Ningsia Autonomous Region 184-185 JK 3-4
Ningsia Hui 184-185 K 4
Ningteh = Ningde 184-185 M 6
Ningtsin = Ningjin 190-191 E 3
Ningtsing = Ningjin 190-191 F 3
Ninguta = Ning'an 184-185 OP 3
Ningwu 190-191 D 2
Ningxia 184-185 H 3-K 4
Ningxia, Región Autónoma de - 184-185 JK 3-4
Ningxiahui, Région Autonome - 184-185 JK 3-4
Ningxiahui, Region autonomiczny - 184-185 JK 3-4
Ningxia Huizu Zizhiqu 184-185 JK 3-4
Ningxia Huizu Zizhiqu 184-185 JK 3-4
Ning Xian 184-185 K 4
Ningxiang 184-185 L 6
Ningyuan 190-191 CD 9
Ninh Giang 186-187 E 2
Ninh Hoa [VN ↑ Nha Trang] 186-187 EF 4
Ninigo Group 186-187 M 7
Ninive 180-181 E 3
Ninjintangla Shan = Nyanchhenthanglha 184-185 G 5-6
Ninnis Glacier 121 C 16-15
Ninua = Ninive 180-181 E 3
Nioaque 160-161 E 4
Niobe, ND 152-153 E 1
Niobrara, NE 152-153 GH 4
Niobrara River 146-147 F 3
Niokolo Koba, Parc national du - 166-167 B6
Niono 172-173 D 2
Nioro du Rip 166-167 A 6
Nioro du Sahel 166-167 C 5
Niort 134-135 G 5
Niou = Nyou 172-173 E 2
Nipawin 144-145 Q 7
Nipepe 171 D 6
Nipigon 144-145 T 8
Nipigon, Lake - 144-145 ST 8
Nipissing, Lake - 144-145 UV 8
Nippur 182-183 L 6
Nipton, CA 150-151 F 8
Niquelândia 158-159 K 7
Nir 182-183 N 3
Nirasaki 188-189 M 5
Niriz, Daryacheh i - = Daryācheh Bakhtegān 180-181 G 5
Nirka 138-139 J 3
Niš 136-137 JK 4
Nişāb 180-181 E 5
Nişāb, An - = Ansāb 180-181 F 8
Nišava 136-137 K 4
Niscemi 136-137 F 7
Nisch = Niš 136-137 JK 4
Nishinomiya 188-189 K 5
Nishinoomote 188-189 H 7
Nishino shima 188-189 J 4
Nishio 188-189 L 5
Nishisonoki hantō 188-189 G 6
Nishiyama 188-189 M 4
Nishtawn 180-181 G 7
Nishtūn = Nishtawn 180-181 G 7
Nisia Floresta 158-159 MN 6
Nisibin = Nusaybin 180-181 E 3
Nisibis = Nusaybin 180-181 E 3
Nisko 133 KL 3
Nisland, SD 152-153 E 3
Nissan 130-131 E 9
Nisser 130-131 C 8
Nistru 140-141 DE 3
Nisutlin Plateau 144-145 K 5
Nisyros 136-137 M 7
Nisz = Niš 136-137 JK 4
Nitau = Nītaure 138-139 E 5
Nitaure 138-139 E 5
Niterói 158-159 L 9
Nitra 133 J 4
Nitro, WV 148-149 C 5
Nitzgal = Nicgale 138-139 F 5
Niuafo'ou 186-187 b 2
Niuatoputapu 186-187 c 2
Niue 198-199 J 5
Niutou Shan = Nantian Dao 190-191 HJ 7
Niva 130-131 P 4
Nivernais 134-135 J 5
Nivšera [SU, ~] 138-139 T 2
Nivšera [SU, ●] 138-139 T 2
Nivskij 178-179 E 4
Nixon, TX 154-155 G 6
Niya Bazar 184-185 E 4
Niyut, Gunung - 186-187 E 6
Niza = Nice 134-135 L 7
Nizamabad 180-181 M 7
Nizamghāt, 180-181 Q 5
Nizam Sagar 180-181 M 7
Nižankoviči 140-141 A 2
Nizgal = Nicgale 138-139 F 5
Nizip 182-183 G 4
Nizke Tatry 133 JK 4
Nizkij, mys - 178-179 hj 5
Nižn'aja Omra 138-139 U 2
Nižn'aja Palomica 138-139 Q 4
Nižn'aja Peša 178-179 H 4
Nižn'aja Tojma 138-139 P 2
Nižn'aja Tunguska 178-179 TU 5
Nižn'aja Tura 178-179 K 6
Nižn'aja Voč 138-139 TU 3
Nižneangarsk 178-179 UV 6
Nižne Čir 140-141 L 2
Nižnegorskij 140-141 G 4
Nižneilimsk 178-179 T 6
Nižneimbatskoje 178-179 QR 5
Nižneje Sančelejevo 138-139 RS 7
Nižnekamsk 178-179 J 7
Nižneleninskoje 178-179 Z 8
Nižnetroickij 138-139 TU 6
Nižneudinsk 178-179 S 7
Nižnevartovsk 178-179 O 5
Nižnevolžsk 140-141 N 3
Nižnij Baskunčak 140-141 N 2
Nižnije Serogozy 140-141 G 3
Nižnij Jenangsk 138-139 Q 4
Nižnij Karanlug = Martuni 140-141 M 6
Nižnij Lomov 138-139 OP 7
Nižnij Novgorod 178-179 GH 6
Nižnij Oseredok, ostrov- 140-141 O 4
Nižnij Tagil 178-179 KL 6
Nižnij Trajanov val 136-137 N 3
Nizovaja 140-141 O 6
Nizozemsko 134-135 J 3-L 2
Nizy 140-141 G 1
Nizza = Nice 134-135 L 7
Njala = Mono 166-167 E7
Njardhvik 130-131 b 3

assa = Lake Malawi 168-169 H 5
eleli 174-175 J 2
emen = Neman 138-139 E 7
ementschyn = Nemenčine
138-139 E 6
ombe [EAT, ~] 168-169 H 4
ombe [EAT, ●] 168-169 HJ 4
andhla = Nkandla 174-175 J 5
andla 174-175 J 5
ata Bay = Nkhata Bay
168-169 H 5
awkaw 172-173 E 4
hata Bay 168-169 H 5
ōna 136-137 K 6
ongsamba 166-167 FG 8
Kogo 172-173 H 6
réko, Ákra - = Akrōtērion
Grēko 182-183 F 5
ululu 171 C 4
walini 174-175 J 5
netország 133 C-F 2-4
achabeb 174-175 C 4
anama 158-159 D 4
atak, AK 144-145 D 4
atak River 144-145 DE 4
beoka 184-185 P 5
blesfontein 174-175 E 6
blesville, IN 152-153 NO 5
c, Big Bay de - 152-153 N 3
ckatunga 196 F 1
daway River 152-153 J 5
el, MO 154-155 H 2
filia, en - = An-Nawfaliyah
166-167 H 2
gajsk = Primorskoje 140-141 H 3
gajskaja step' 140-141 MN 4
gal = Nugal 180-181 F 9
gales [MEX] 150-151 J 10
gales, AZ 146-147 D 5
gales Heroica 146-147 D 5
gat 133 J 1
gata 188-189 H 6
ginsk 138-139 M 5-6
goyá 162 DE 4
heji 188-189 N 2
ir, Isla - 162 B 8
irmoutier, Île de - 134-135 F 5
jima-saki 188-189 MN 5
jon 184-185 J 3
kia 130-131 K 7
k Kundi 180-181 J 5
komis, IL 152-153 M 6
la [RCA] 166-167 H 8
linsk 178-179 HJ 6
mamisaki 188-189 GH 7
mbre de Dios 154-155 B 6
me, AK 144-145 C 5
-min Ho = Nuomin He
184-185 N 2
mme, Reval- = Tallinn-Nõmme
138-139 E 4
mme, Tallinn- 138-139 E 4
mo-saki 188-189 G 6
mtsas 174-175 B 3
muka 192-193 K 7
ndweni 174-175 J 5
ng'an 184-185 NO 3
ng Khai 186-187 D 3
ngoma 168-169 H 8
nni = Nen Jiang 184-185 O 1-2
nouti 192-193 J 5
nsan 188-189 F 4
ord-Amerika 124-125 DE 3
oordamerikaans Bekken
124-125 FG 4
oordatlantische Rug
124-125 H 5-3
oordaustralisch Bekken
194-195 C 2
oordbandabekken 186-187 HJ 7
oordelijke IJszee 120 AB 132-5
oord-Ierland 132 CD 4
oord-Korea 184-185 O 3-4
oordossetische Autonome
Republiek 140-141 LM 5
oordpacifisch Bekken
124-125 AB 3-4
oordwestaustralisch Bekken
124-125 OP 6
oordwestpacifisch Rug
124-125 S 3-4
oordzee 132 F-J 3
oordzeekanal 134-135 K 2
oormarkku 130-131 JK 7
oors Bekken 124-125 JK 2
oorse Geul 130-131 A 8-C 9
oorvik, AK 144-145 DE 4
oorweegse Zee 120 C 19-B 17
oorwegen 130-131 C 7-L 2
ootka Island 144-145 L 8
oqui 168-169 D 4
ora 130-131 F 8
orah 166-167 MN 5
orašen = Iljič'ovsk 140-141 M 7
orcatur, KS 152-153 F 6
órcia 136-137 E 4
orcross, GA 154-155 N 4
ord, Cap del - 132 CD 4
ord, Mare del - 128-129 J 4
ord, Mer du - 132 F-J 3
ordalbanische Alpen = Alpet e
ngipërisë 136-137 HJ 4
ordamerika 124-125 DE 3
ordamerikanisches Becken
124-125 FG 4
ordatlantischer Rücken
124-125 H 5-3
ordaustlandet 130-131 k-m 5
ordaustralisches Becken
194-195 C 2
ordbandabecken 186-187 HJ 7
ordborneo = Sabah 186-187 G 5
ordcross, GA 148-149 A 8
orden 133 C 2
ordenšel'da, archipelag -
178-179 RS 2
ordenšel'da, zaliv - 178-179 JK 2
ordenskiøldbukta 130-131 14
ordenskiøld land 130-131 jk 6
ord-Fidschibecken 194-195 O 3
ordfjord 130-131 AB 7
ordfjorden 130-131 j 5
ordfriesische Inseln 133 D 1
ordhausen 133 E 3
ordhorn 133 C 2
ordhur-Ísafjardhar 130-131 b 1-2
ordhur-Múla 130-131 f 2
Nordhur-Thingeyjar 130-131 ef 1-2
Nordirland 132 CD 4
Nordkanal = North Channel
132 CD 4
Nordkapp [N] 130-131 LM 2
Nordkapp [Svalbard] 130-131 k 4
Nordkinn 130-131 MN 2
Nordkjosbotn 130-131 HJ 3
Nordkorea 184-185 O 3-4
Nordland 130-131 E 5-G 3
Nördliche Dwina = Severnaja
Dvina 178-179 G 5
Nördlicher Ural = Severnyj Ural
178-179 K 5-6
Nördlingen 133 E 4
Nord-Marianen 122-123 RS 5
Nordos Çayı 182-183 K 3
Nordossetische Autonome Republik
140-141 LM 5
Nordostrundingen 120 A 18-20
Nord-Ostsee-Kanal 133 D 1-2
Nord-Ouest, Territoire du - =
Northwest Territories
144-145 M-U 4
Nord-Ouest Australien, Bassin du
- 124-125 OP 6
Nord-Ouest Indien, Dorsale du -
124-125 N 5-6
Nordpazifisches Becken
124-125 AB 3-4
Nordpolarmeer 120 AB 32-5
Nordre Kvaløy 130-131 H 2
Nordre Strømfjord 144-145 a 4
Nordrhein-Westfalen 133 CD 3
Nordrhodesien = Sambia
168-169 G 6-J 5
Nordsee 132 F-J 3
Nord-Trøndelag 130-131 DE 5
Nordvik 178-179 V 3
Nordwestaustralisches Becken
124-125 OP 6
Nordwestindischer Rücken
124-125 N 5-6
Nordwestindische Rug
124-125 N 5-6
Nordwestpazifischer Rücken
124-125 S 3-4
Nordwestpazifischer Rücken
198-199 H 2-3
Nordwestpazifisches Becken
198-199 GH 3
Nordwest-Territorien =
Northwest Territories
144-145 M-U 4
Nore 130-131 C7
Norfolk, NE 146-147 G 3
Norfolk, VA 146-147 LM 4
Norfolk, Dorsal de - 194-195 N 6-7
Norfolk, Dorsale di - 194-195 N 6-7
Norfolk, Grzbiet - 194-195 C 2
Norfolk, Palamar de -
194-195 N 6-7
Norfolk, Seuil - 194-195 N 6-7
Norfolkdrempel 194-195 N 6-7
Norfolk-hátság 194-195 N 6-7
Norfolk Island 194-195 N 5
Norfolk Lake 154-155 JK 2
Norfolk Ridge 194-195 N 6-7
Norfolkschwelle 194-195 N 6-7
Norheimsund 130-131 AB 7
Nori 178-179 N 4
Norias, TX 154-155 G 7
Norias, Las - 154-155 D 6
Norikura dake 188-189 L 4
Noril'sk 178-179 Q 4
Norische Alpen 133 FG 5
Norlina, NC 148-149 D 6
Normal, IL 152-153 M 5
Norman, AR 154-155 J 3
Norman, OK 146-147 G 4
Normanby 132 F 4
Normanby Island 186-187 h 7
Normandie 134-135 GH 4
Normangee, TX 154-155 G 5
Normannische Inseln = Channel
Islands 132 E 7
Norman River 194-195 H 3
Normanton [AUS] 194-195 H 3
Norman Wells 144-145 KL 4
Noroeste, Territorios del - =
Northwest Territories
144-145 M-U 4
Norquinco 162 B 6
Norra Bergnäs 130-131 H 4
Norra Storfjället 130-131 FG 5
Norrbotten [S, ≡] 130-131 J 5-K 4
Norrbotten [S, ⬧] 130-131 G-K 4
Nørresundby, Ålborg- 130-131 CD 9
Norris, MT 150-151 H 3
Norris City, IL 152-153 M 7
Norris Lake 154-155 NO 2
Norristown, PA 148-149 F 4
Nörrköping 130-131 G 8
Norrland 130-131 F-J 5
Norrtälje 130-131 H 8
Norseman 194-195 D 6
Norsk 178-179 Y 7
Norské moře 120 C 19-B 17
Norsko 130-131 C 8-L 2
Norský příkop 130-131 A 8-C 9
Nortbruk, ostrov - 178-179 GH 2
Norte, Cabo - 158-159 K 4
Norte, Canal del - = North
Channel [GB] 132 CD 4
Norte, Canal do - 158-159 JK 4
Norte, Mar do 122-123 K 3
Norte, Punta - 162 D 6
Norte, Serra do - 158-159 H 7
North [GH] 172-173 E 3
North [WAL] 172-173 BC 3
North, SC 148-149 C 8
North, Cape - [CDN, Nova
Scotia] 144-145 YZ 8
North Adams, MA 148-149 G 3
Northallerton 132 F 4
Northam [AUS] 194-195 C 6
Northam [ZA] 168-169 G 8
North America 124-125 DE 3
North American Basin
124-125 FG 4
Northampton 132 FG 5
Northampton [AUS] 194-195 B 5
Northampton, MA 148-149 G 3
North Andaman 180-181 P 8
North Arm 144-145 NO 5
North Augusta, SC 148-149 BC 8
North Australian Basin 194-195 C 2
North Baltimore, OH 152-153 P 5
North Banda Basin 186-187 HJ 7
North Battleford 144-145 P 7
North Bay 144-145 UV 8
North Belcher Islands 144-145 U 6
North Bend, NE 152-153 H 5
North Bend, OR 150-151 A 4
North Bend, WA 150-151 C 2
Northbrook, ostrov - = ostrov
Nortbruk 178-179 GH 2
North Bruny Island 196 cd 3
North Canadian River 146-147 FG 4
North Cape [NZ] 194-195 O 6
North Caribou Lake 144-145 ST 7
North Carolina 146-147 KL 4
North Cascades National Park
150-151 C 1
North Channel 132 CD 4
North Channel [CDN] 144-145 U 8
North Charleston, SC 148-149 D 8
North Chicago, IL 152-153 N 4
Northcliffe 194-195 C 6
North Creek, NY 148-149 FG 3
North Dakota 146-147 FG 2
North East, PA 148-149 CD 3
North East Carry, ME 148-149 HJ 2
North Eastern 168-169 K 2-3
Northeast Providence Channel
146-147 L 6
Northeim 133 DE 3
Northern [MW] 171 C 5-6
Northern [Z] 168-169 H 4
Northern Bahr al-Ghazzal
166-167 K 7
Northern Cape 174-175 CE 5
Northern Cheyenne Indian
Reservation 152-153 C 3
Northern Darfur 166-167 JK 5
Northern Ireland 132 CD 4
Northern Kordofan 166-167 KL 5-6
Northern Pacific Railway
146-147 EF 2
Northern State 166-167 KL 5
Northern Territory 194-195 FG 3-4
Northfield, MN 152-153 K 3
Northfield, VT 148-149 G 2
North Fiji Basin 194-195 O 3
North Foreland 132 GH 6
North Fork, CA 150-151 D 7
North Fork, ID 150-151 FG 3
North Fork Cimarron River
154-155 E 2
North Fork Clearwater River
150-151 F 2
North Fork Feather River
150-151 C 5-6
North Fork Grand River
152-153 E 3
North Fork Humboldt River
150-151 F 5
North Fork John Day River
150-151 D 3
North Fork Moreau River
152-153 E 3
North Fork Mountain 148-149 D 5
North Fork Powder River
152-153 C 4
North Fork Red River 154-155 F 3
North Fork Smoky Hill River
152-153 EF 6
North Fork Solomon River
152-153 FG 6
North Fox Island 152-153 O 3
North Fork Payette River
150-151 E 3
North Horr 168-169 J 2
North Channel 132 CD 4
North Channel [CDN] 144-145 U 8
North Charleston, SC 148-149 D 8
North Chicago, IL 152-153 N 4
North Island [NZ] 194-195 P 7
North Island [USA] 148-149 D 8
North Islands 154-155 L 6
North Judson, IN 152-153 N 5
North Korea 184-185 O 3-4
Northland, MI 152-153 N 2
Northland Mountains 144-145 WX 8
North Laramie River 152-153 D 4
North Las Vegas, NV 150-151 F 7
North Little Rock, AR
146-147 H 4-5
North Loup, NE 152-153 G 5
North Loup River 152-153 G 5
North Luangwa National Park
171 BC 5-6
North Manchester, IN 152-153 O 5
North Miami, FL 148-149 cd 4
North Minch 132 C 3-D 2
North New River Canal 148-149 c 3
North Ossetian Autonomous
Republic 140-141 LM 5
North Pacific Basin 124-125 AB 3-4
North Palisade 146-147 C 4
North Pass 146-147 J 6
North Pease River 154-155 E 3
North Platte, NE 146-147 F 3
North Platte River 146-147 F 3
North Point 152-153 P 3
Northport, AL 154-155 M 4
Northport, MI 152-153 O 3
Northport, NE 152-153 E 5
Northport, WA 150-151 E 1
North Powder, OR 150-151 DE 3
North Range 152-153 KL 2
North Rona 132 D 2
North Ronaldsay 132 EF 2
North Santiam River 150-151 B 3
North Saskatchewan River
144-145 OP 7
North Sea 132 F-J 3
North Shore Range 152-153 L 1-2
North Stradbroke Island
194-195 K 5
North Stratford, NH 148-149 H 2
North Taranaki Bight 194-195 O 7
North Tonawanda, NY 148-149 D 3
North Truchas Peak 146-147 E 4
North Uist 132 BC 3
Northumberland Islands
194-195 JK 4
Northumberland Strait 144-145 Y 8
North Umpqua River 150-151 B 4
North Vernon, IN 152-153 O 6
Northwest Australian Basin
124-125 OP 6
North West Cape 194-195 B 4
North Western 168-169 FG 5
North-West-Frontier 180-181 L 3-4
Northwest Highlands 132 D 2-3
Northwest Indian Ridge
124-125 N 5-6
Northwest Pacific Basin
124-125 ST 3-4
Northwest Pacific Ridge
124-125 S 3-4
Northwest Passage 144-145 J-L 3
Northwest Territories
144-145 K-O 4-5
North Wilkesboro, NC 148-149 C 6
Northwood, IA 152-153 K 4
Northwood, ND 152-153 H 2
North York 148-149 D 3
Norton, KS 152-153 G 6
Norton, VA 148-149 B 6
Norton Sound 144-145 D 5
Nortonville, ND 152-153 G 2
Noruega 130-131 C 7-L 2
Noruega 130-131 C 8-L 2
Noruega, Bacia da - 124-125 JK 2
Noruega, Canal de - 132 J 1-2
Noruega, Cuenca de -
124-125 JK 2
Noruega, Mar da 126-127 F-K 2
Noruega, Mar de - 120 C 19-B 17
Noruega, Mar de - 120 C 19-B 17
Norvège 130-131 C 7-L 2
Norvège, Mer de - 120 C 19-B 17
Norvegia 130-131 C 8-L 2
Norvegia 130-131 C 8-L 2
Norvegia, Bacino di - 124-125 JK 2
Norvegia, Fossa di -
130-131 A 8-C 9
Norvegia, Kapp - 121 B 134-135
Norvegia, Mare di - 120 C 19-B 17
Norvég-tenger 120 C 19-B 17
Norvég-tenger 130-131 B 5-J 2
Norwalk, CT 148-149 G 4
Norwalk, MI 152-153 NO 3
Norwalk, OH 152-153 P 5
Norway 130-131 C7-L2
Norway, IA 152-153 KL 5
Norway, ME 148-149 H2
Norway, MI 152-153 N 3
Norway House 144-145 R 7
Norwegen 130-131 C 7-L 2
Norwegia 130-131 C 8-L 2
Norwegian Basin 124-125 JK 2
Norwegian Bay 144-145 ST 2
Norwegian Trench 130-131 A 8-C 9
Norwegische Rinne
130-131 A 8-C 9
Norwegisches Becken
124-125 JK 2
Norweska, Rynna -
130-131 A 8-C 9
Norweskie, Morze - 120C 19-B 17
Norweskie, Morze -
130-131 B 5-J 2
Norwich 132 G 5
Norwich [CDN] 148-149 C 3
Norwich, CT 148-149 GH
Norwich, NY 148-149 F 3
Norwood, MN 152-153 JK 3
Norwood, NC 148-149 C 7
Norwood, NY 148-149 F 2
Norwood, OH 152-153 O 6
Noshiro 184-185 QR 3
Nosiro = Noshiro 184-185 QR 3
Nosovka 140-141 EF 1
Nosovščina 138-139 L2
Nossa Senhora do Livramento
160-161 D 1
Nossob 168-169 E 7
Nossombougou 172-173 D 2
Nošul' 138-139 R 3
Nosy-Be 168-169 L 5
Nosy-Varika 168-169 L 7
Notch Peak 150-151 G 6
Noteć 133 G 2
Noto 136-137 F 7
Noto [J] 188-189 L 4
Notodden 130-131 C 8
Noto hantō 184-185 Q 4
Noto-jima 188-189 L 4
Notoro-ko 188-189 d 1
Notre Dame, Monts - 144-145 WX 8
Notre Dame Bay 144-145 Z 8-a 7
Notsé 172-173 F 4
Nottawasaga Bay 148-149 C 2
Nottaway, Rivière - 144-145 V 7
Nottingham 132 F 5
Nottingham Island 144-145 VW 5
Nottinghamroad 174-175 HJ 5
Nottoway River 148-149 E 6
Notwani 174-175 FG 3
Nouadhibou = Nawādhibu
166-167 A4
Nouakchott = Nawākshūt
166-167 A5
Noukloofberge 174-175 AB 3
Noukloof Mountains = Noukloof-
berge 174-175 AB 3
Nouméa 194-195 N 4
Noun 172-173 H 4
Noupoort 168-169 FG 9
Nous 174-175 C 5
Nous West = Nous 174-175 C 5
Nouveau Brunswick = New
Brunswick 144-145 X 8
Nouveau-Québec 144-145 V-X 6
Nouveau-Québec, Cratère du -
144-145 VW 5
Nouvelle Amsterdam 124-125 NO 7
Nouvelle Angleterre = New
England 146-147 M 3-N 2
Nouvelle-Anvers 168-169 EF 2
Nouvelle-Calédonie 194-195 MN 3
Nouvelle-Castille = Castilla la Nueva
134-135 E 9-F 8
Nouvelle-Ecosse = Nova Scotia
144-145 X 9-Y 8
Nouvelle-Guinée 186-187 L 7-M 8
Nouvelle-Guinée, Seuil de
- 186-187 M 5-6
Nouvelle-Hébrides, Bassin de
- 194-195 MN 3
Nouvelle-Hébrides, Fosse des
- 194-195 N 3-4
Nouvelles-Hébrides
194-195 N 2-O 3
Nouvelle Sibérie, Îles - =
Novosibirskije ostrova
178-179 Z-f 2
Nouvelle-Zélande 194-195 N 8-O 7
Nouvelle-Zemble, Gouttière de la -
178-179 K 3-L 2
Nova Andradina 160-161 F 5
Nová Anglie = New England
146-147 M 3-N 2
Novabad 180-181 L 3
Nova Bretanha-Bougainville, Fossa
da - 186-187 h 6
Nova Caledónia 194-195 MN 3
Nova Chaves = Muconda
168-169 F 5
Nova Cruz 158-159 MN 6
Nova Chaves = Muconda
168-169 F 5
Nova Era 160-161 L 3
Nova Esperança 160-161 FG 5
Nova Europa 160-161 H 4
Nova Freixo = Cuamba 168-169 J 5
Nova Friburgo 160-161 L 5
Nova Gaia 168-169 E 4-5
Nova Gradiška 136-137 GH 3
Nova Granada 160-161 H 4
Nova Guiné 186-187 L 7-M 8
Nova Guiné 186-187 L 7-M 8
Nova Chaves = Muconda
168-169 F 5
Nova Iguaçu 158-159 L 9
Nova Iorque = New York, NY
146-147 M 3-4
Novaja Basan' 140-141 E 1
Novaja Buchara = Kagan
180-181 J 3
Novaja Kachovka 140-141 F 3
Novaja Kalitva 140-141 K 1
Novaja Kazanka 140-141 O 2
Novaja Ladoga 138-139 HJ 3
Novaja Odessa 140-141 EF 3
Novaja Pis'm'anka =
Leninogorsk 178-179 J 7
Novaja Sibir', ostrov - 178-179 de 3
Novaja Usman' 140-141 J 1
Novaja Zemľa 178-179 J 3-L 2
Novaja Zemlja-hasadék
178-179 K 3-L 2
Novaja Zemlja, Fossa Orientale della
- 178-179 K 3-L 2
Nová Kaledonie 194-195 MN 3
Nova Lamego = Gabú 166-167 B 6
Nova Lima 158-159 L 8-9
Nova Lisboa = Huambo
168-169 E 5
Nova Londrina 160-161 F 5
Nova Lusitânia 168-169 H 6
Nova Mambone 168-169 J 7
Novanta Est, Dorsale -
124-125 O 5-6
Nova Ponte 160-161 J 3
Novara 136-137 C 3
Nova Scotia 144-145 X 9-Y 8
Novas Hébridas = Vanuatu
194-195 N 2-O 3
Novas Hébridas, Bacia das -
194-195 MN 3
Novas Hébridas, Fossa das -
194-195 N 2-3
Nova Sibéria, Arquipélago da - =
Novosibirskije ostrova
178-179 Z-f 2
Nova Sofala 168-169 HJ 7
Novato, CA 150-151 B 6
Nova Trento 160-161 H 7
Novaya Zemlya Trough
178-179 K 3-L 2
Nova Zagora 136-137 LM 4
Nova Zelândia 194-195 N 8-O 7
Nova Zembla, Canal da -
178-179 K 3-L 2
Nova Zemblageul 178-179 K 3-L 2
Nové Hebridy = Vanuatu
194-195 N 2-O 3
Nové Skotsko = Nova Scotia
144-145 X 9-Y 8
Nové Zámky 133 J 4
Novgorod 178-179 E 6
Novgorod-Severskij 138-139 J 8
Novi Bečej 136-137 J 3
Novigrad 136-137 E 3
Novije Basy 140-141 G 1
Novije Belokoroviči 140-141 C 1
Novinka [SU ↓ Leningrad]
138-139 H 4
Novi Pazar [BG] 136-137 M 4
Novi Pazar [YU] 136-137 M 4
Novi Sad 136-137 HJ 3
Novoagansk 178-179 O 5
Novoajdar 140-141 J 2
Novoaleksandrovsk 140-141 K 4
Novoaleksejevka = Lazurnoje
140-141 G 3
Novoaltajsk 178-179 PQ 7
Novoanninskij 140-141 L 1
Novoazovskoje 140-141 HJ 3
Novobelica, Gomel'-138-139 H 7
Novobiril'ussy 178-179 QR 6
Novobogatinskoje 140-141 P 3
Novočeremšansk 138-139 RS 6
Novočerkassk 140-141 K 3
Novochop'orskij 140-141 K1
Novo Cruzeiro 160-161 M 2
Novodugino 138-139 K 6
Novodvinsk 138-139 N 1
Novoekonomičeskoje = Dimitrov
140-141 H 2
Novograd-Volynskij 140-141 CD 1
Novogrigorovka 140-141 G 3
Novogrudok 138-139 EF 7
Novo Hamburgo 162 FG 3
Novo Horizonte 160-161 H 4
Novoje'n'a 138-139 EF 7
Novojerudinskij 178-179 RS 6
Novokazalinsk 178-179 L 8
Novokubansk 140-141 K 4
Novokujbyševsk 138-139 RS 7
Novokuzneck 178-179 Q 7
Novoladožskij kanal
138-139 H 4-J 3
Novolazarevskaja 121 B 1
Novo-Mariinsk = Anadyr'
178-179 j 5
Novo Mesto 136-137 F 3
Novomirgorod 140-141 EF 2
Novomoskovsk [SU, Rossijskaja
SFSR] 138-139 M 6
Novomoskovsk [SU, Ukrainskaja
SSR] 140-141 GH 2
Novonazimovo 178-179 QR 6
Novonikolajevsk = Novosibirsk
178-179 P 6-7
Novo-Nikolajevskaja 140-141 L 1
Novonikolajevskij 140-141 L 1
Novopiscovo 138-139 NO 5
Novopokrovka = Liski 140-141 J 1
Novopokrovskaja 140-141 K 4
Novopolock 138-139 G 6
Novopskov 140-141 J 2
Novor'azsk 138-139 N 7
Novo Redondo = N'Gunza
Kabolo 168-169 D 5
Novorepnoje 140-141 O 1
Novorossijsk 140-141 HJ 4
Novoržev 138-139 G 5
Novošachtinsk 140-141 J 3
Novoselje 138-139 G 4
Novosergijevka 138-139 T 7
Novosibirsk 178-179 P 6-7
Novosibirskije ostrova 178-179 Z-f 2
Novosibiřské ostrovy =
Novosibirskije ostrova 178-179 Z-f 2
Novosil' 138-139 L 7
Novosokol'niki 138-139 GH 5
Novos'olovo 178-179 R 6
Novotroick 178-179 K 7
Novo-Troickij Promysel = Balej
178-179 W 7
Novotroickoje [SU, Cherson]
140-141 FG 3
Novotroickoje [SU, Vjatka]
138-139 Q 4
Novotulka 140-141 NO 1
Novotul'skij 138-139 LM 6
Novoukrainka 140-141 EF 2
Novo-Urgenč = Urgenč 178-179 L 9
Novouzensk 140-141 O 1
Novovasilevka 140-141 GH 3
Novov'atsk, V'atka 138-139 RS 4
Novov'azniki 138-139 NO 5
Novovoronež 140-141 JK 2
Novozavidovskij 138-139 L 5
Novozybkov 138-139 HJ 7
Novska 136-137 G 3
Nový Brunšvik = New Brunswick
70-7 1 X 8
Novyj Bug 140-141 F 3
Novyj Buran 138-139 RS 7
Novyje Burasy 138-139 PQ 7
Novyje Karymkary 178-179 MN 5
Novyje Sanžary 140-141 FG 2
Novyj Karymkary = Karymkary
178-179 M 5
Novyj Margelan = Fergana
180-181 L 2-3
Novyj Nekouz 138-139 LM 4-5
Novyj Oskol 140-141 HJ 1
Novyj Port 178-179 MN 4
Novyj Terek 140-141 N 5
Novyj Tevriz 178-179 O 6
Novyj Uštagan = Uštagan
140-141 O 3
Novyj Zaj 138-139 ST 6
Nový Zéland 194-195 N 8-O 7
Nowa Anglia = New England
146-147 M 3-N 2
Nowa Fundlandia =
Newfoundland 144-145 Za 8
Nowa Gwinea 186-187 L 7-M 8
Nowaja-Semlja-Rinne
178-179 K 3-L 2
Nowa Kaledonia 194-195 MN 3
Nowa Sól 133 G 3
Nowa Szkocja = Nova Scotia
144-145 X 9-Y 8
Nowata, OK 154-155 H 2
Nowa Zelandia 194-195 N 8-O 7
Nowbarān 182-183 N 5
Nowe 133 J 2
Nowe Hebrydy = Vanuatu
194-195 N 2-O 3
Nowgorod = Novgorod 178-179 E 6
Nowkash 182-183 MN 6
Nowlin, SD 152-153 F 3-4
Nowogródek = Novogrudok
138-139 EF 7
Nowogwinejski, Rów -
186-187 M 5-6
Nowogwinejskie, Morze -
186-187 NO 7
Nowohebrydzki, Basen -
194-195 MN 3
Nowohebrydzki, Rów -
194-195 N 3-4
Nowojelnia = Novojel'n'a
138-139 EF 7
Nowood Creek 152-153 C 3-4
Noworossijsk = Novorossijsk
140-141 HJ 4
Nowoschachtinsk = Novošachtinsk
140-141 J 3
Nowosyberyjskie, Wyspy - =
Novosibirskije ostrova
178-179 Z-f 2
Nowotscherkassk = Novočerkassk
140-141 K 3
Nowozelandzki, Grzbiet -
194-195 M 5-6
Nowra 194-195 K 6
Nowy Brunszwik = New
Brunswick 144-145 X 8
Nowy Jork = New York, NY
146-147 M 3-4
Nowy Korczyn 133 K 3
Nowy Sącz 133 K 4
Nowy Targ 133 K 4
Noxon, MT 150-151 F 1-2
Noya 134-135 C 7
Noyon 134-135 J 4
Nqabeni 174-175 J 6
Nqutu 174-175 J 5
N'Riquinha = Lumbala 168-169 F 6
Nsanje 168-169 J 6
Nsawam 172-173 E 4
Nsefu 171 BC 6
Nsukka 166-167 F 7
Ntcheu 168-169 HJ 5
Ntywenka 174-175 H 6
Nuanetsi = Mwenezi 168-169 GH 7
Nuanetzi, Rio - 174-175 J 2
Nuatja = Notsé 172-173 F 4
Nūbah, An- 166-167 K-M 4-5
Nūbah, Jibāl an- 166-167 KL 6
Núbia, Desierto de - 166-167 LM 4
Núbiai-sivatag 166-167 LM 4
Nubie, Désert de - 166-167 LM 4
Nubieber, CA 150-151 C 5
Nubijska, Pustynia - 166-167 LM 4
Nubijská poušť 166-167 LM 4
Nubische Woestijn 166-167 LM 4
Nubische Wüste 166-167 LM 4
Nūbiya = An-Nubah
166-167 K-M 4-5
Nucha = Sheki 140-141 N 6
N'uchča 138-139 Q 2
Nu Chiang = Nag Chhu
184-185 G 5
N'učpas 138-139 S 3
Nueces River 146-147 G 6
Nueltin Lake 144-145 R 5
Nueva Antioquia 158-159 EF 3
Nueva Asunción 160-161 B 4
Nueva Bretaña-Bougainville, Fosa
de - 186-187 h 6
Nueva Caledonia 194-195 MN 3
Nueva Casas Grandes 146-147 E 5
Nueva Delhi = New Delhi
180-181 M 5
Nueva Escocia = Nova Scotia
144-145 X 9-Y 8
Nueva Germania 162 E 2
Nueva Guinea 186-187 L 7-M 8
Nueva Guinea, Dorsal de
186-187 M 5-6
Nueva Inglaterra = New England
146-147 M 3-N 2
Nueva Providencia 146-147 b 2
Nueva Rosita 146-147 F 6
Nueva San Salvador 146-147 HJ 9
Nuevas Hébridas, Cuenca de 194-
195 MN 3
Nuevas Hébridas, Fosa de
194-195 N 3-4
Nueva Siberia, Islas de - = Novosi-
birskije ostrova 178-179 Z-f 2
Nueva York = New York, NY
146-147 M 3-4
Nueva Zelanda 194-195 N 8-O 7
Nueva Zelanda, Dorsal de
194-195 M 5-7
Nueva Zembla, Dorsal de
178-179 K 3-L 2
Nueve de Julio [RA, Buenos Aires]
162 D 5
Nuevo Chagres 146-147 ab 2
Nuevo Emperador 146-147 b 2
Nuevo Laredo 146-147 FG 6
Nuevo León 146-147 F 7-G 6
Nuevo Rocafuerte 158-159 D 5
Nuevo San Juan 146-147 b 2
Nuffar = Nippur 182-183 L 6
Nugaal 166-167 b 2
Nugruş, Gebel - = Jabal Nuqruş
170 F 5
Nûgssuaq 144-145 YZ 3
Nûgssuaq Halvø 144-145 a 3
Nuguria Islands 186-187 hj 5
Nuhaylah, An- 170 D 4
Nuhu Cut 186-187 K 8
Nuhūd, An- 166-167 K 6
Nuhurowa = Kai Kecil 186-187 K 8
Nuhu Rowa = Kai Kecil
186-187 K 8
Nuhu Tjut = Nuhu Cut 186-187 K 8
Nuhu Yut = Nuhu Cut 186-187 K 8
Nu Chiang–Nag Chhu 184-185 G 5
Nui Đeo 186-187 E 2
N'uja [SU, ~] 178-179 V 5
N'uja [SU, ●] 178-179 W 5
Nu Jiang = Nag Chhu 184-185 G 5
Nujiang Lisuzu Zizhizhou =
C ◁ 184-185 H 6
Nûk 144-145 a5
Nukey Bluff 196 BC 4
Nukhayb 180-181 E 4
Nukhaylah 166-167 K 5
Nukheila, Bir - = Nukhaylah
166-167 K5
N'uksenica 138-139 P 3
Nuku'alofa 198-199 HJ 6
Nukufetau 192-193 J 5
Nuku Hiva 192-193 N 5
Nukumanu Islands 186-187 jk 5
Nukunau 192-193 J 5
Nukunono 192-193 K 5
Nukus 178-179 KL 9
N'ukža 178-179 X 6-7
Nulato, AK 144-145 E 5
Nullagine 194-195 D 4
Nullarbor 194-195 EF 6
Nullarbor Plain 194-195 ES 6
Num, Meos - 186-187 KL 7
Numakunai = Iwate 188-189 N 3
Numan 166-167 G 7
Nu'mân, Jazirat an- 170 F 4
Numancia 134-135 F 8
Numata [J, Gunma] 188-189 M 4
Numata [J, Hokkaidō] 188-189 bc 2
Numazu 188-189 M 5
Numedal 130-131 C 7-8
Numeia = Nouméa 194-195 N 4
Numero 1 Station = Mahattat 1
170 D 7
Numero 2 Station = Mahattat 2
170 DE 7
Numero 3 Station = Mahattat 3
170 DE 7
Numero 4 Station = Mahattat 4
170 E 7
Numfoor, Pulau - 186-187 KL 7
Numto 178-179 MN 5
Numurkah 196 G 6
Nunavut Territory 144-145 O-U 4
Nun Chiang = Nen Jiang
184-185 O 1-2
Nundle 196 K 3
Nungan = Nong'an 184-185 NO 3
Nungo 168-169 J 5
Nunica, MI 152-153 NO 4
Nunivak Island 144-145 C 6
Nunn, CO 152-153 D 5
Nuomin He 184-185 N 2
Nuoro 136-137 C 5
Nuova Caledonia 194-195 MN 3-4
Nuova Guinea 186-187 L 7-M 8
Nuova Pomerania-Bougainville,
Fossa - 186-187 h 6
Nuova Siberia, Isole della - = Novo-
sibirskije ostrova 178-179 Z-f 2
Nuova Zelanda 194-195 N 8-O 7
Nuove Ebridi = Vanuatu
194-195 N 2-O 3
Nuove Ebridi, Bacino delle -
194-195 MN 3
Nuove Ebridi, Fossa delle -
194-195 N 3-4
Nuqrat as-Salmān = As-Salmān
182-183 L 7
Nuqruş, Jabal - 170 F 5
Nura 178-179 N 7
Nuratau, chrebet - 178-179 M 9
N'urba 178-179 W 5
Nur Dağları 182-183 G 4
Nuremberga = Nürnberg
126-127 L 6
Nūrestān 180-181 KL 3-4
Nurhak Dağı 182-183 G 3
Nurlat 138-139 S 6
Nurlaty 138-139 R 6
Nurmes 130-131 N 6
Nürnberg 133 E 4
Nusa Tenggara Barat =
16 ◁ 186-187 G 8
Nusa Tenggara Timur =
17 ◁ 186-187 H 8
Nusaybin 180-181 E 3
Nusf, Bi'r an- 170 B 2
Nushagak River 144-145 E 5-6
Nu Shan 184-185 H 6
Nūshki 180-181 K 5
Nutak 144-145 Y 6
Nutrias = Puerto de Nutrias
158-159 EF 3
Nutt, NM 154-155 B 4
Nutzotin Mountains 144-145 H 5
N'uvčim 138-139 S 3
Nuwara Eliya 180-181 N 9
Nuwaybi, al-Muzayyinah 170 F 3
Nuweiba' = Nuwaybi' al-
Muzayyinah 170 F 3
Nuwerus 174-175 C 6
Nuweveld 174-175 DE 6
Nuweveldberge 174-175 DE 7
Nuweveldrecks = Nuweveldberge
174-175 DE 7
Nuyts Archipelago 194-195 F 6
Nwa 172-173 H 4
Nwatle 174-175 D 2
Nxai Pan National Park
168-169 FG 6
Nyaake 166-167 C 8
Nya Chhu = Yalong Jiang
184-185 HJ 5
Nyahanga 168-169 H 3
Nyakahanga 168-169 H 3
Nyālā 166-167 J 6
Ny Ålesund 130-131 hj 5
Nyalikungu 171 C 3
Nyamandhlovu 168-169 G 6
Nyamasane 174-175 J 3
Nyambiti 168-169 H 3
Nyamina 172-173 D 2
Nyāmlil 166-167 K 7
Nyamtam 172-173 H 4
Nyamtumbu 168-169 J 5
Nyanchhenthanglha[TJ, ▲▲]
184-185 F 6-G 5
Nyanchhenthanglha [TJ, ⌿]
184-185 G 5
Nyanga 168-169 D 3
Nyanji 171 BC 6
Nyanza [EAK] 168-169 H 2-3
Nyanza [RU] 171 B 4
Nyanza [RWA] 171 B 3
Nyasa = Lake Malawi 168-169 H 5
Nyaunglebin 186-187 C 3
Nyawalu 171 AB 3
Nyborg 130-131 D 10
Nybro 130-131 F 9
Nyda 178-179 N 4
Nyenasi 172-173 E 4
Nyenchentanglha = Nyanchhent-
hanglha 184-185 F 6-G 5
Nyeri [EAK] 168-169 J 3
Nyeri [EAU] 171 B 2
Nyeweni 174-175 H 6
Ny Friesland 130-131 k 5
Nyika Plateau 168-169 H 4-5
Nyinahin 172-173 E 4
Nyira Gonga 171 B 3
Nyirbátor 133 KL 5
Nyiregyháza 133 K 5
Nyiri Desert 171 D 3
Nyiro, Uaso - = Ewaso Ngiro
168-169 J 3
Nyiru, Mount - 168-169 J 2
Nyitra = Nitra 133 J 4
Nykarleby 130-131 K 6
Nykøbing Falster 130-131 DE 10
Nykøbing Mors 130-131 C 9
Nykøbing Sjælland 130-131 D 9-10
Nyköping 130-131 G 8
Nijl = Bahr an-Nil 166-167 L 3-4
Nyland = Uusimaa 130-131 KL 7
Nylrivier 174-175 H 3
Nylstroom 168-169 G 7
Nymagee 196 H 4
Nymboida 196 L 2
Nymburk 133 G 3
Nynäshamn 130-131 GH 8
Nyngan 194-195 J 6
Nyong 166-167 G 8
Nyonga 168-169 H 4
Nyou 172-173 E 2
Nyrob 138-139 V 3
Nyrud 130-131 N 3
Nysa 133 H 3
Nysa Kłodzka 133 H 3
Nysa Łużycka 133 F 3
Nyslott = Savonlinna 130-131 N 7
Nyssa, OR 150-151 E 4
Nystad = Uusikaupunki 130-131 J 7
Nytva 178-179 JK 6
Nyūdō-saki 188-189 M 2
Nyunzu 168-169 G 4
Nzébéla 172-173 C 3-4
Nzega 168-169 H 3
N'Zérékoré 166-167 C 7
N'Zeto 168-169 D 4
Nzheledam 174-175 HJ 2
Nzi 172-173 D 4
Nzo 172-173 D 4
Nzoia 171 C 2
Nzoro 171 B 2

O

Oahe, Lake - 146-147 F 2
Oahu 186-187 e 3
Oakbank 194-195 H 6
Oak City, UT 150-151 G 6
Oak Creek, CO 152-153 C 5
Oakdale, CA 150-151 C 7
Oakdale, LA 154-155 J 5
Oakdale, NE 152-153 GH 4
Oakes, ND 152-153 G 2
Oakey 194-195 K 5
Oak Grove, LA 154-155 K 4
Oakharbor, OH 152-153 P 5
Oak Harbor, WA 150-151 B 1
Oak Hill, FL 148-149 c 2
Oak Hill, WV 148-149 C 5-6
Oakhurst, TX 154-155 H 5
Oak Island 152-153 L 2
Oakland, CA 146-147 B 4
Oakland, IA 152-153 J 5
Oakland, MD 148-149 D 5
Oakland, NE 152-153 H 5
Oakland, OR 150-151 B 4
Oakland City, IN 152-153 N 6
Oaklands 196 GH 5
Oak Lawn, IL 152-153 MN 5
Oakley, ID 150-151 FG 4
Oakley, KS 152-153 F 6
Oakover River 194-195 D 4
Oak Park, IL 152-153 N 5
Oakridge, OR 150-151 B 4
Oak Ridge, TN 146-147 K 4
Oakville 148-149 D 3
Oakwood, OK 154-155 F 3
Oakwood, TX 154-155 GH 5
Oamaru 194-195 O 9
Ōarai 188-189 N 4
Oas 174-175 C 2
Oasis, CA 150-151 DE 7
Oasis, NV 150-151 F 5
Oates Land 121 B 16-17
Oatlands [AUS] 196 cd 3
Oatlands [ZA] 174-175 F 7
Oatman, AZ 150-151 F 8
Oaxaca 146-147 G 8
Oaxaca de Juárez 146-147 GH 8
Ob' 178-179 NO 5
Oba [Vanuatu] 194-195 N 3
Obama 188-189 K 5
Oban 132 D 3
Oban [NZ] 194-195 N 9
Oban Hills 172-173 H 4
Obara = Ōchi 188-189 J 5
Obasi 182-183 F 4
Obdorsk = Salechard 178-179 M 4
Obeidh, El- = Al-Ubayyid
166-167 KL 6
Oberá 162 E 3
Oberägypten = As-Sa'id
166-167 L 3-4
Oberer See = Lake Superior
146-147 HJ 2
Oberer Trajanswall = Verchnij
Trajanov val 136-137 N 2
Obere Tunguska = Angara
178-179 S 6
Oberguinea 124-125 JK 5
Oberhausen 133 C 3
Oberlin, KS 152-153 F 6
Oberlin, LA 154-155 J 5
Oberon, ND 152-153 G 2
Oberösterreich 133 F-i 1 4
Oberpahlen = Põltsamaa
138-139 EF 4
Oberpfälzer Wald 133 F 4
Oberstdorf 133 E 5
Obetz, OH 152-153 P 6
Obi, Pulau - 186-187 J 7
Obiaruku 172-173 G 4
Óbidos [BR] 158-159 HJ 5
Obihiro 184-185 R 3
Obil'noje 140-141 M 3
Obion, TN 154-155 L 2
Obirgbene = Obrigbene
172-173 G 4
Obitočnaja kosa 140-141 H 3
Obitočnyj zaliv 140-141 GH 3
Objačevo 178-179 H 5
Obkeik, Jebel - = Jabal
'Ubkayk 166-167 M 4
Oblačnaja, gora - 178-179 Za 9
Oblivskaja 140-141 L 2
Oblučje 178-179 Z 8
Obninsk 138-139 L 6
Obo 166-167 K 7
Oboa 171 C 2
Obobogorap 174-175 D 4
Obock 166-167 N 6
Obojan' 140-141 H 1
Obok = Obock 166-167 N 6
Obol' 138-139 G 6
Obonai = Tazawako 188-189 N 3
Oboz'orskij 138-139 N 2
Obra 133 G 2
Obrenovac 136-137 HJ 3
Obrian Peak = Trident Peak
150-151 D 5
Obrigbene 172-173 G 4
Obrovac 136-137 F 3
Obruk = Kizören 182-183 E 3
Obruk Yaylâsı 182-183 E 3
Obščij Syrt 178-179 H-K 7
Obskaja guba 178-179 N 3-4
Obuasi 166-167 D 7
Obuchi = Rokkasho 188-189 N 2
Obuchov 140-141 E 1
Obva 138-139 U 4
Očakov 136-137 O 2
Ocala, FL 146-147 K 6
Očamčira 140-141 K 5
Ocaña [CO] 158-159 E 3
Ocaña [E] 134-135 F 9
Ocauçu 160-161 H 5
Océan Arctique 120 AB 132-5
Océan Atlantique 124-125 G 4-J 7
Ocean City, MD 148-149 F 5
Ocean City, NJ 148-149 F 5
Ocean Falls 144-145 L 7
Oceanlake, OR 150-151 AB 3
Océano Atlántico 124-125 G 4-J 7
Oceano Atlantico 124-125 G 4-J 7
Oceano Atlântico 124-125 G 4-J 7
Océano Glacial Ártico
120 AB 32-5

Payette River 150-151 E 3-4
Payne, OH 152-153 O 5
Payne, Lac - 144-145 W 6
Payne Bay = Bellin 144-145 WX 5
Paynes Creek, CA 150-151 BC 5
Paynesville 172-173 C 4
Paynesville, MN 152-153 J 3
Paysandú [ROU, ●] 162 E 4
Pays-Bas 134-135 K 3-L 2
Payson, AZ 150-151 H 8
Payson, UT 150-151 GH 5
Payún, Cerro - 162 BC 5
Paz, La - [MEX, Baja California Sur] 146-147 DE 7
Paz, La - [RA, Entre Ríos] 162 DE 4
Paz, La - [RA, Mendoza] 162 C 4
Paz, La - [BOL, ●] 158-159 F 8
Pazar 182-183 J 2
Pazar = Şorba 182-183 E 2
Pazarbası Burnu 182-183 D 2
Pazarcık 182-183 G 4
Pazarcık = Pazaryeri 182-183 C 2-3
Pazardžik 136-137 KL 4
Pazaryeri [TR, Bilecik] 182-183 C 2-3
Pazifischer Ozean 198-199 G-L 4-6
Pčinja 136-137 J 4-5
Peabody, KS 152-153 H 6
Peace River [CDN, ~] 144-145 MN 6
Peace River [CDN, ●] 144-145 N 6
Peach Springs, AZ 150-151 G 8
Peacock Bay 121 B 126-127
Peake Creek 196 B 1-2
Peak Hill [AUS, New South Wales] 196 J 4
Peak Hill [AUS, Western Australia] 194-195 C 5
Peale, Mount - 146-147 DE 4
Pearce, AZ 150-151 J 10
Pearl Harbor 186-187 e 3
Pearl River 146-147 H 5
Pearl River, LA 154-155 KL 5
Pearsall, TX 154-155 F 6
Pearson, GA 148-149 B 9
Pearston 174-175 F 7
Peary Channel 144-145 R 2
Peary Land 120 A 21-23
Pebane 168-169 J 6
Pebas 158-159 E 5
Peć 136-137 J 4
Peçanha 160-161 L 3
Pecan Island, LA 154-155 J 6
Peças, Ilha das - 162 G 3
Pecatonica River 152-153 M 4
Pečenežin 140-141 B 2
Pečenga [SU, ●] 178-179 E 4
Pechabun = Phetchabun 186-187 CD 3
Pechawar = Pashāwar 180-181 KL 4
Pêcheurs, Presqu'île des - = poluostrov Rybačij 178-179 EF 4
Pechino = Beijing 184-185 LM 3-4
Pečora [SU, ~] 178-179 K 5
Pečora [SU, ●] 178-179 K 4
Pecoraro, Monte - 136-137 FG 6
Pečoro-Ilyčskij zapovednik 138-139 VW 2
Pečorskaja guba 178-179 JK 4
Pečorskaja magistral' 178-179 JK 5
Pečory 138-139 FG 5
Pecos, TX 146-147 F 5
Pecos River 146-147 F 5
Pécs 133 HJ 5
Pecs = Pécs 133 HJ 5
Pečenga [SU, ●] 178-179 E 4
Pedder, Lake - 196 bc 3
Peddie 174-175 G 7
Pedee, OR 150-151 B 3
Pedernal [PY] 160-161 D 5
Pedernal, NM 154-155 C 3
Pedernales [EC] 158-159 CD 4
Pedernales [YV] 158-159 G 3
Pederneira, Cachoeira 158-159 FG 6
Pederneiras 160-161 H 5
Pedra Azul 158-159 L 8
Pedra Corrida 160-161 L 3
Pedras de Maria da Cruz 160-161 K 1
Pedras Negras 158-159 G 7
Pedregal [PA] 146-147 c 2
Pedregulho 160-161 J 4
Pedreira 160-161 J 5
Pedreiras 158-159 KL 5
Pedrera, La - 158-159 EF 5
Pedro, Point - = Pēduru Tuḍuwa 180-181 N 9
Pedro Alonso 157 F 3
Pedro Cays 146-147 L 8
Pedro de Valdivia 162 BC 2
Pedro Gomes 160-161 E 3
Pedro Gonzáles 160-161 CD 7
Pedro II 158-159 L 5
Pedro Juan Caballero 162 E 2
Pedro Leopoldo 160-161 K 3
Pedro Lustosa 160-161 FG 6
Pedro Miguel 146-147 b 2
Pedro Miguel, Esclusas de 146-147 b 2
Pedro Miguel Locks = Esclusas de Pedro Miguel 146-147 b 2
Pedro R. Fernández 162 E 3
Pedro Versiani 160-161 M 2
Pēduru Tuḍuwa [CL, ^] 180-181 N 9
Peebinga 194-195 H 6
Peebles 132 E 4
Peebles, OH 152-153 P 6
Pee Dee River 146-147 L 5
Peekskill, NY 148-149 G 4
Peel River 144-145 JK 4
Peel Sound 144-145 R 3
Peene 133 F 2
Peera Peera Poolanna Lake 194-195 G 5
Peerless, MT 152-153 D 1
Peetz, CO 152-153 E 5
Pegasus Bay 194-195 O 8
Pegram, ID 150-151 H 4
Pègū 186-187 C 3
Pehpei = Beipei 184-185 K 6
Pehuajó 162 D 5
Peian = Bei'an 184-185 O 2
Pei-chên = Beizhen 188-189 C 2
Peicheng 190-191 FG 4
Pei Chiang = Bei Jiang 190-191 D 10
Peichiang = Pei-kang 190-191 H 10
Pei-ch'uan Ho = Beichuan He 190-191 C 3
Pei-fei Ho = Beifei He 190-191 F 5
Peighambār Dāgh = Peyghambar Dāgh 182-183 N 4
Pei-hai = Beihai 184-185 K 7
P'ei-hsien = Pei Xian 184-185 M 5
Pei-kang 190-191 H 10
Pei-kan-t'ang Tao 190-191 H 8
Pei-liu = Beiliu 190-191 C 10
Peine 133 E 2
Pei-ngan = Bei'an 184-185 O 2
Peipei = Beipei 184-185 K 6
Pei-p'iao = Beipiao 188-189 C 2
Peiping = Beijing 184-185 LM 3-4
Peiraiévs 136-137 K 7
Pei Shan = Bei Shan 184-185 GH 3
Peita-wu Shan 190-191 H 10
Peixe 158-159 K 7
Peixe, Rio do - [BR, Goiás] 160-161 F 2
Peixe, Rio do - [BR, Santa Catarina] 160-161 G 7
Peixe, Rio do - [BR, São Paulo] 160-161 G 4
Peixe, Rio do - [BR, Minas Gerais ◁ Rio Preto] 160-161 L 4
Peixe, Rio do - [BR, Minas Gerais ◁ Rio Santo António] 160-161 L 3
Pei Xian [TJ ↖ Xuzhou] 184-185 M 5
Pei Xian [TJ → Xuzhou] 190-191 FG 4
Peixoto, Represa do - 160-161 J 4
Pejpus, Jezioro - = Cudskoje ozero 178-179 O 6
Pekalongan 186-187 EF 8
Pekan 186-187 D 6
Pekanbaru 186-187 D 6
Pe Kiang = Bei Jiang 190-191 D 10
Pekin, IL 152-153 M 5
Pekin, IN 152-153 NO 6
Pekin, ND 152-153 G 2
Pekin = Beijing 184-185 LM 3-4
Pekín = Beijing 184-185 LM 3-4
Pékin = Beijing 184-185 LM 3-4
Peking = Beijing 184-185 LM 3-4
Pektubajevo 138-139 R 5
Pekul'nej, chrebet - 178-179 hj 4
Pelahatchie, MS 154-155 L 4
Peleaga 136-137 K 3
Peleduj 178-179 V 6
Pelée, Montagne - 146-147 O 8
Pelee Island 152-153 P 5
Pelee Point 152-153 P 5
Pelēnaion 136-137 LM 6
Peleng, Pulau - 186-187 H 7
Pelgrimsrus 174-175 J 3
Pelham, GA 154-155 N 5
Pelican Lake, WI 152-153 M 3
Pelikan Lake 152-153 K 1
Pelikan Rapids, MN 152-153 H 2
Pēlion 136-137 K 6
Pelješac 136-137 G 4
Pelkosenniemi 130-131 MN 4
Pella [ZA] 174-175 C 5
Pella, IA 152-153 K 5
Pell City, AL 154-155 MN 4
Pello 130-131 L 4
Pellston, MI 152-153 O 3
Pelly Bay 144-145 S 4
Pelly Mountains 144-145 K 5
Pelly River 144-145 K 5
Peloncillo Mountains 150-151 J 9
Pelopónnēsos 136-137 JK 7
Peloritani, Monti - 136-137 F 6-7
Pelotas 162 F 4
Pelotas, Rio - 162 F 3
Pelusium 170 E 2
Pelusium, Bay of - = Khallj aṭ-Ṭinah 170 E 2
Pelvoux 134-135 L 6
Pelym [SU, ~] 178-179 L 5
Pelym [SU, ●] 178-179 L 6
Pemadumcook Lake 148-149 J 2
Pemalang 186-187 EF 8
Pemangkat 186-187 E 6
Pematangsiantar 186-187 C 6
Pemba [EAT] 168-169 JK 4
Pemba [Moçambique] 168-169 K 5
Pemba [Z] 168-169 G 6
Pemberton [AUS] 194-195 C 6
Pembina 144-145 NO 7
Pembina River [USA] 152-153 G 1
Pembine, WI 152-153 MN 3
Pembroke 132 D 6
Pembroke [CDN] 146-147 L 2
Pembroke, GA 148-149 C 8
Peña, Sierra de la - 134-135 G 7
Peñafiel 134-135 EF 8
Peñagolosa 134-135 G 8
Peña Negra, Punta - 158-159 C 5
Peña Nevada, Cerro 146-147 FG 7
Penang = George Town 186-187 CD 5
Penápolis 160-161 GH 4
Peñarroya 134-135 G 8
Peñarroya-Pueblonuevo 134-135 E 9
Peñas, Cabo de - 134-135 E 7
Peñas, Golfo de - 162 AB 7
Peñas, Punta - 158-159 G 2
Penawawa, WA 150-151 E 2
Penck, Cape - 121 C 9
Pendembu 166-167 B 7
Pender, NE 152-153 H 4
Pender Bay 194-195 D 3
Pendjab = Punjab [IND] 180-181 LM 4
Pendjab = Punjab [PAK] 180-181 L 4
Pendjari 172-173 F 3
Pendleton, OR 146-147 C 2
Pend Oreille Lake 150-151 E 1-2
Pend Oreille River 150-151 E 1
Pendroy, MT 150-151 GH 1
Pendžikent 180-181 K 3
Peneiós 136-137 K 6
Penetanguishene 148-149 CD 2
Penganga 180-181 M 7
Peng-chia Yü 190-191 HJ 9
Penge [ZA] 174-175 J 3
Penge [ZRE, Haut-Zaïre] 171 AB 2
Penge [ZRE, Kasai-Oriental] 168-169 FG 4
Peng-hu 190-191 G 10
Penghu Dao = P'êng-hu Tao 190-191 G 10
Penghu Liedao = Penghu Lieh-tao 184-185 M 7
Penghu Lieh-tao 184-185 M 7
P'êng-hu Shui-tao 190-191 GH 10
P'êng-hu Tao 190-191 G 10
Pengjia Xu = Pêng-chia Yü 190-191 HJ 9
Pengkou 190-191 F 9
Penglai 184-185 N 4
Pengra Pass 150-151 BC 4
Penguin Eilanden 174-175 A 3-5
Penguin Island = Penguin Eilanden 174-175 A 3-5
Pengze 184-185 M 6
Penha, São Paulo- 160-161 J 5
Penida, Nusa - 186-187 FG 8
Peninga 138-139 HJ 2
Peninsula Malaya 186-187 C 5-D 6
Peñíscola 134-135 H 8
Penitente, Serra do - 158-159 K 6
Penki = Benxi 184-185 N 3
Penmarch, Pointe de - 134-135 E 5
Penne 136-137 EF 4
Penn Hills, PA 148-149 D 4
Pennine Chain 132 E 4-F 5
Pennsylvania 146-147 KL 3
Penn Yan, NY 148-149 E 3
Penny Highland 144-145 X 4
Penny Strait 144-145 R 2
Peno 138-139 J 5
Penobscot Bay 148-149 J 2
Penobscot River 148-149 J 2
Penong 194-195 F 6
Penrhyn 192-193 M 5
Penrith 132 E 4
Pensa = Penza 178-179 GH 7
Pensacola, FL 146-147 J 5
Pensacola Bay 154-155 M 5
Pensacola Mountains 121 A 33-34
Pentecost Island 194-195 N 3
Penticton 144-145 N 8
Pentland Firth 132 E 2
Pentwater, MI 152-153 N 4
Penwell, TX 154-155 D 5
Penyu, Kepulauan - 186-187 J 8
Penza 178-179 GH 7
Penzance 132 CD 6
Penžina 178-179 g 5
Penžinskaja guba 178-179 f 5
Peoples Creek 152-153 B 1
Peoria, AZ 150-151 G 9
Peoria, IL 146-147 HJ 3
Peotone, IL 152-153 N 5
Pepani 174-175 E 3
Pepe, Costa del - 166-167 B 7-C 8
Pepel 166-167 B 7
Peperiguaçu, Rio - 160-161 F 7
Peperkust 166-167 B 7-C 8
Pepin, WI 152-153 K 3
Pepřonosné pobřeží 166-167 B 7-C 8
Pequeni, Rio - 146-147 bc 2
Pequenas Antilhas 146-147 N 9-O 8
Pequeñas Antillas 146-147 N 9-O 8
Pequi 160-161 K 3
Pequim = Beijing 184-185 LM 3-4
Pequiri, Rio - 160-161 E 2
Pequop Mountains 150-151 F 5
Pequot Lakes, MN 152-153 J 2
Perälä 130-131 JK 6
Perche 134-135 H 4
Percival Lakes 194-195 DE 4
Perdekop 174-175 H 4
Perdido Bay 154-155 M 5
Perdido, Monte - 134-135 GH 7
Perdizes 160-161 J 3
Perdões 160-161 K 4
Peredel [SU ↘ Vladimir] 138-139 N 6
Pereguete, Rio - 146-147 b 3
Pereira 158-159 D 4
Pereira, Cachoeira - 158-159 H 5
Pereira Barreto 160-161 G 4
Pereira d'Eça = N'Giva 168-169 E 6
Perejaslav-Chmel'nickij 140-141 EF 1
Perekop 140-141 F 3
Perelazovskij 140-141 L 2
Perelik 136-137 L 5
Perel'ub 138-139 S 8
Peremul Par 180-181 L 8
Peremyšl' 138-139 L 6
Pereslavl'-Zalesskij 138-139 M 5
Perevoz [SU ↗ Arzamas] 138-139 P 6
Perevoz [SU ↗ Bodajbo] 178-179 W 6
Pergamino 162 D 4
Pergamon 182-183 B 3
Pergamos = Pergamon 182-183 B 3
Perham, MN 152-153 J 2
Perhonjoki 130-131 KL 6
Péribonca, Rivière - 144-145 W 7-8
Perico 162 CD 2
Perico, TX 154-155 D 2
Périgord 134-135 H 6
Perigoso, Canal - 158-159 K 4
Périgueux 134-135 H 6
Perija, Sierra de - 158-159 E 2-3
Perim Island = Barim 180-181 E 8
Perin = Colonia Perin 160-161 BC 6
Periquito, Cachoeira do 158-159 G 6
Peri Suyu 182-183 J 3
Perito Moreno 162 BC 7
Perkins, OK 154-155 G 2-3
Perlas, Archipiélago de las 146-147 KL 10
Perlas, Punta de - 146-147 K 9
Perly, MN 152-153 H 2
Perm' 178-179 K 6
Permas 138-139 P 4
Permskoje = Komsomol'sk-na-Amure 178-179 a 7
Pernambuco 158-159 LM 6
Pernambuco = Recife 158-159 N 6
Pernau = Pärnu 138-139 E 4
Pernigel = Liepupe 138-139 DE 5
Pernik 136-137 K 4
Péronne 134-135 J 4
Peron Peninsula 194-195 B 5
Pérou 158-159 D 5-E 7
Pérou, Bassin du - 124-125 E 6
Perouse, proliv la - = proliv Laperuza 178-179 b 8
Perovo, Moskva 138-139 LM 6
Perovsk = Kzyl-Orda 178-179 M 9
Perpignan 134-135 J 7
Perpignano = Perpignan 134-135 J 7
Perpinhão = Perpignan 126-127 J 7
Perrégaux = Muḥammadiyah 166-167 DE 1
Perrin, TX 154-155 FG 4
Perrine, FL 148-149 c 4
Perris, CA 150-151 E 9
Perry, FL 148-149 b 1
Perry, GA 154-155 O 4
Perry, IA 152-153 JK 5
Perry, NY 148-149 DE 3
Perry, OK 154-155 G 2
Perrysburg, OH 152-153 P 5
Perryton, TX 154-155 E 2
Perryville, AR 154-155 J 3
Perryville, MO 152-153 LM 7
Perse = Iran 180-181 F-H 4
Perşembe 182-183 G 2
Persepolis 180-181 G 5
Perseverancia 158-159 G 7
Persia = Iran 180-181 F-H 4
Persian Gulf 180-181 FG 5
Persie = Írán 180-181 F-H 4
Persien = Iran 180-181 F-H 4
Peršinskaja 138-139 N 3
Persip 174-175 C 3
Persischer Golf 180-181 FG 5
Persja = Iran 180-181 F-H 4
Perska, Zatoka - 180-181 FG 5
Perský záliv 180-181 FG 5
Pertek 182-183 H 3
Perth [AUS, Tasmania] 196 c 2
Perth [AUS, Western Australia] 194-195 BC 6
Perth [CDN] 148-149 E 2
Perth [GB] 132 E 3
Perth Amboy, NJ 148-149 F 4
Pertominsk 138-139 LM 1
Peru [PE] 158-159 D 5-E 7
Perù 158-159 D 5-E 7
Perú 158-159 D 5-E 7
Perú [RA] 162 D 5
Peru, IL 152-153 M 5
Peru, IN 152-153 NO 5
Peru, Bacia do - 124-125 E 6
Perú, Cuenca del - 124-125 E 6
Perú, Fosa del - 158-159 C 6-D 7
Peru, Fossa do - 158-159 C 6-D 7
Peru, Rów - 158-159 C 6-D 7
Peru Basin 124-125 E 6
Perubecken 198-199 N 5
Perubekken 124-125 E 6
Perù-Chile, Fossa - 158-159 C 6-D 7
Peru Chile Trench 158-159 C 6-D 7
Perùgia 136-137 E 4
Perugraben 158-159 C 6-D 7
Perui-árok 158-159 C 6-D 7
Peruibe 162 G 2
Perutrog 158-159 C 6-D 7
Pervari = Hashır 182-183 K 4
Perveri 182-183 GH 4
Pervomajsk [SU, Rossijskaja SFSR] 138-139 OP 6
Pervomajsk [SU, Ukrainskaja SSR] 140-141 E 2
Pervomajskaja 138-139 T 3
Pervomajskij [SU Tambov] 138-139 N 7
Pervomajskij = Novodvinsk 138-139 N 1
Pervoural'sk 178-179 KL 6
Pervyj Kuril'skij proliv 178-179 de 7
Perzië = Iran 180-181 F-H 4
Perzische Golf 180-181 FG 5
Perzsa-öböl 180-181 FG 5
Perzsia = Irán 180-181 F-H 4
Pèsaro 136-137 E 4
Pescadero, CA 150-151 B 7
Pescadores Channel = P'êng-hu Shui-tao 190-191 GH 10
Pescadores = Penghu Lieh-tao 184-185 M 7
Pesčanaja 140-141 D 2
Pesčanoje 138-139 KL 2
Pesčanyj, mys - 140-141 P 5
Pesčanyj, ostrov - 178-179 WX 3
Pescara 136-137 F 4
Pèschici 136-137 FG 5
Peshawar = Pashāwar 180-181 KL 4
Peshtigo, WI 152-153 N 3
Peshtigo River 152-153 M 3
Peshwar = Pashāwar 180-181 KL 4
Peski [SU, Rossijskaja SFSR Moskva] 138-139 M 6
Peski [SU, Rossijskaja SFSR Voronež] 140-141 L 1
Peski [SU, Ukrainskaja SSR] 140-141 F 1
Peskovka [SU, Rossijskaja SFSR] 138-139 ST 4
Peskovka [SU, Ukrainskaja SSR] 140-141 DE 1
Pešnoj, poluostrov - 140-141 P 3
Peštera 136-137 KL 4
Pesočnoje 138-139 M 5
Pesqueria, Rio - 154-155 F 8
Pessene 174-175 K 3
Pestovo 138-139 K 4
Pestravka 138-139 R 7
Petah Tiqua = Pētaḥ Tiqwa 182-183 F 6
Pētaḥ Tiqwa 182-183 F 6
Petaliõn, Kólpos - 136-137 L 7
Petaluma, CA 150-151 B 6
Petauke 168-169 H 5
Petén, El - 146-147 H 8
Petenwell Lake 152-153 M 3
Petenwell Reservoir = Petenwell Lake 152-153 M 3
Peterborough 132 FG 5
Peterborough [AUS, South Australia] 194-195 GH 6
Peterborough [AUS, Victoria] 196 F 7
Peterborough [CDN] 144-145 V 9
Peterborough, NH 148-149 GH 3
Peterhead 132 F 3
Peterhof = Petrodvorec 138-139 G 4
Petermann Ranges 194-195 E 4-F 5
Peter Pond Lake 144-145 P 6
Petersburg, AK 144-145 K 6
Petersburg, IL 152-153 M 5
Petersburg, IN 152-153 N 6
Petersburg, TN 154-155 M 3
Petersburg, TX 154-155 E 4
Petersburg, VA 146-147 L 4
Petersburg, WV 148-149 D 5
Petersburg = Sankt-Peterburg 178-179 E 5-6
Pētikostell = Pécs 133 HJ 5
Petilia Policastro 136-137 G 6
Petites Antilles 146-147 N 9-O 8
Petitjean = Sidi Qāsim 166-167 CD 2
Petit Bois Island 154-155 L 5-6
Petit Manan Point 148-149 K 2
Petitot River 144-145 M 5-6
Peto 146-147 J 7
Petorca 162 B 4
Petoskey, MI 152-153 O 3
Petra [JOR] 182-183 F 7
Petra, ostrova - 178-179 VW 2
Petra I, ostrov - 121 C 27
Petra Velikogo, zaliv - 178-179 Z 9
Petre, Point - 148-149 E 3
Petrič 136-137 K 5
Petrified Forest National Monument 150-151 J 8
Petrikov 138-139 G 7
Petrikovka 140-141 G 2
Pétriou = Chachoengsao 186-187 D 4
Petriščevo 138-139 KL 6
Petroaleksandrovsk = Turtkuľ 178-179 L 9
Petrodvorec 138-139 G 4
Petrohrad = Sankt-Peterburg 178-179 E 5-6
Petrolândia 158-159 M 6
Petrólea 158-159 E 3
Petroleum,TX 154-155 F 7
Petrolia 152-153 P 4
Petrolia, CA 150-151 A 5
Petrolina [BR, Pernambuco] 158-159 L 6
Petrolina de Goiás 160-161 H 2
Petropavlovka 178-179 TU 7
Petropavlovsk 178-179 MN 7
Petropavlovsk-Kamčatskij 178-179 ef 7
Petropavlavskoje = Sabirabad 140-141 O 6-7
Petropavlovskij = Achtubinsk 140-141 MN 2
Petrópolis 158-159 L 9
Petros, TN 154-155 N 2
Petroşeni 136-137 K 3
Petroskoi = Petrozavodsk 178-179 EF 5
Petrovaradin 136-137 HJ 3
Petrovka [SU, Samara] 138-139 ST 7
Petrovka [SU, Vladivostok] 188-189 J 1
Petrovsk 138-139 P 7
Petrovskaja 140-141 HJ 4
Petrovskij Jam 138-139 KL 2
Petrovskij Zavod = Petrovsk-Zabajkal'skij 178-179 U 7
Petrovskoje [SU, Jaroslavl'] 138-139 M 5
Petrovskoje [SU, Tambov] 138-139 N 7
Petrovskoje = Balabino 140-141 G 3
Petrovsk-Port = Machačkala 140-141 NO 5
Petrovsk-Zabajkal'skij 178-179 U 7
Petrov Val 140-141 M 1
Petrozavodsk 178-179 EF 5
Petrusburg 174-175 F 5
Petrus Steyn 174-175 H 4
Petrusville 174-175 F 6
Petseri = Pečory 138-139 FG 5
Pettau = Ptuj 136-137 FG 2
Pettibone, ND 152-153 G 2
Pettigrew, AR 154-155 J 3
Pettus, TX 154-155 FG 6
Petuchovo 178-179 M 6
Peude = Pöide 138-139 D 4
Peumo 162 B 4
Pevek 178-179 gh 4
Peyghambar Dāgh 182-183 N 4
Peyton, CO 152-153 D 6
Pézenas 134-135 J 7
Pežma 138-139 N 3
Pezmog 138-139 ST 3
Pfaffenhofen 133 E 4
Pfarrkirchen 133 F 4
Pfefferküste 166-167 B 7-C 8
Pforzheim 133 D 4
Phalaborwa 174-175 J 2
Phalodi 180-181 L 5
Phaltan 180-181 LM 7
Phangan, Ko - 186-187 CD 5
Phanggong Tsho 184-185 DE 5
Phan Rang 186-187 EF 4
Phan Thiet 186-187 E 4
Pharr, TX 154-155 F 7
Phatthalung 186-187 D 5
Phaykkhaphum Phisai 186-187 D 3
Phelps, WI 152-153 M 2-3
Phelps Lake 148-149 E 7
Phenix City, AL 146-147 J 5
Phenjan = P'yŏngyang 184-185 NO 4
Phetchabun 186-187 CD 3
Phetchaburi 186-187 CD 4
Philadelphia [ET] 170 D 3
Philadelphia [ZA] 174-175 C 7
Philadelphia, MS 154-155 L 4
Philadelphia, PA 146-147 LM 3-4
Philip, SD 152-153 F 3
Philip Island 194-195 N 5
Philipp, MS 154-155 KL 4
Philippe-Thomas = Al-Mittawi 166-167 F2
Philippeville 134-135 K 3
Philippeville = Sakikdah 166-167 F 1
Philippi, WV 148-149 CD 5
Philippine Basin 124-125 Q 5
Philippinen 186-187 H 3-J 5
Philippinenbecken 198-199 F 4
Philippinengraben 198-199 F 4
Philippines 186-187 H 3-J 5
Philippines, Bassin des - 124-125 Q 5
Philippines, Fosse des - 124-125 Q 5
Philippine Trench 124-125 Q 5
Philippolis 174-175 F 6
Philipsburg, MT 150-151 G 2
Philipsburg, PA 148-149 D 4
Philip Smith Mountains 144-145 GH 4
Philipstown 174-175 F 6
Phillipi, Lake - 194-195 G 4
Phillip Island 196 G 7
Phillippines 186-187 H 3-J 5
Phillips, ME 148-149 H 2
Phillips,WI 152-153 L 3
Phillipsburg, KS 152-153 G 6
Phillipsburg, MO 152-153 K 7
Phillipsburg, NJ 148-149 F 4
Phillips Mountains 121 B 124-125
Philo, CA 150-151 B 6
Phippsøya 130-131 kl 4
Phitsanulok 186-187 D 3
Phnom Penh 186-187 D 4
Phnum Pénh = Phnom Penh 186-187 D 4
Pho, Laem - 186-187 D 5
Phoenix, AZ 146-147 D 5
Phoenix, Fosse des - 124-125 AB 6
Phoenixgraben 198-199 J 5
Phoenix Islands 198-199 J 5
Phoenix Trench 124-125 AB 6
Phoenixtrog 124-125 AB 6
Phoenixville, PA 148-149 EF 4
Phôngsaly 186-187 D 2
Phosphate Hill 194-195 GH 4
Phra Chedi Sam Ong 186-187 C 3-4
Phra Nakhon Si Ayutthaya 186-187 D 4
Phu Diễn Châu 186-187 E 3
Phuket 186-187 C 5
Phuket, Ko - 186-187 C 5
Phu Ly 186-187 E 2
Phum Rovieng 186-187 E 4
Phunakha 180-181 OP 5
Phu Quốc, Dao - 186-187 D 4
Phu Tho 186-187 DE 2
Phutha-Ditjhaba 174-175 H 5
Piacá 158-159 K 6
Piacenza 136-137 C 3
Piangil 194-195 H 7
Pianguan 190-191 C 2
Pianosa, Ìsola - 136-137 D 4
Piaseczno 133 K 2
Piatra 136-137 L 3
Piatra-Neamţ 136-137 M 2
Piattaforma Patagonica 124-125 FG 8
Piaui 158-159 L 6
Piaui, Rio - 158-159 L 6
Piave 136-137 E 2
Piazza Armerina 136-137 F 7
Picabo, ID 150-151 F 4
Picacho, AZ 150-151 H 9
Picacho, CA 150-151 F 9
Picacho, NM 154-155 C 4
Pičajevo 138-139 O 7
Picayune, MS 154-155 L 5
Pibōr = Bibūr 166-167 L 7
Pibōr, Nahr - = Nahr Bibūr 166-167 L7
Picardie 134-135 HJ 4
Piccole Antille 146-147 N 9-O 8
Pichanal 162 CD 2
Picher, OK 154-155 H 2
Pichi Ciego 162 C 4
Pichieh = Bijie 184-185 K 6
Pichilemú 162 B 4
Pichtovka 178-179 P 6
Pickens, MS 154-155 KL 4
Pickens, SC 148-149 B 7
Pickle Crow 144-145 ST 7
Pico, El - 158-159 G 8
Picola 196 G 5
Picos 158-159 L 6
Pico Truncado 162 C 7
Picton [CDN] 148-149 E 2-3
Picton [NZ] 194-195 O 8
Picton, Mount - 196 bc 3
Picui 158-159 M 6
Picún Leufú 162 BC 5
Picunda, mys - 140-141 K 5
Pidurutalāgala 180-181 N 9
Piedade, Pico da - 160-161 L 3
Pie de Palo 162 C 4
Piedade do Rio Grande 160-161 KL 4
Piedmont 146-147 K 5-L 4
Piedmont, AL 154-155 N 4
Piedmont, SC 148-149 B 7
Piedmont, SD 152-153 E 3
Piedmont, WV 148-149 D 5
Piedra del Águila 162 BC 6
Piedras 158-159 CD 5
Piedras, Rio - [PA] 146-147 b 2
Piedras, Rio de las - 158-159 E 7
Piedras Negras 146-147 F 6
Pieksämäki 130-131 M 6
Pielinen 130-131 N 6
Piemonte 136-137 BC 3
Pienaarsriver 174-175 GH 3
P'ien-kuan = Pianguan 190-191 C 2
Pieprzowe, Wybrzeże - 166-167 B 7-C 8
Pierce, ID 150-151 F 2
Pierce, NE 152-153 H 4
Pierce City, MO 154-155 HJ 2
Pierceville, KS 152-153 F 7
Piercy, CA 150-151 B 6
Pierre, SD 146-147 F 3
Pierson, FL 148-149 c 2
Piešťany 133 HJ 4
Pietarsaari = Jakobstad 130-131 JK 6
Pietermaritzburg 168-169 H 8
Pietersburg 168-169 G 7
Pietrasanta 136-137 CD 4
Piet Retief 174-175 J 4
Pietrosul [R ↙ Borşa] 136-137 L 2
Pietrosul [R ↙ Vatra Dornei] 136-137 L 2
Pigailoe 186-187 N 5
Pigeon, MI 152-153 P 4
Pigeon Bay 152-153 P 5
Pigeon Point 150-151 B 7
Piggott, AR 154-155 K 2
Pigg's Bay 152-153 J 3
Pigg's Peak 174-175 J 3
Pigūm-do 188-189 E 5
Pi He 190-191 F 6
Pihsien = Pei Xian 190-191 FG 4
Pihtipudas 130-131 LM 6
Pi-hu = Bihu 190-191 G 7
Pihyŏn 188-189 E 2
Piippola 130-131 LM 5
Pija, Sierra de - 146-147 J 8
Pikal'ovo 138-139 JK 4
Pikelot 186-187 N 5
Pikes Peak 146-147 F 4
Piketberg 168-169 E 9
Piketberge 174-175 C 7
Piketon, OH 152-153 P 6
Pikeville, KY 148-149 B 6
Pikeville, TN 154-155 N 3
Pikkenwynrots 174-175 B 5
Pikou 188-189 D 3
Piła 133 H 2
Pilane 174-175 FG 3
Pilanesberg 174-175 G 3
Pilão Arcado 158-159 L 7
Pilar [PY] 162 E 3
Pilar do Sul 160-161 J 5
Pilares de Nacozari 150-151 J 10
Pilas Group 186-187 H 5
Pilawa 133 K 3
Pilcaniyeu 162 BC 6
Pilcomayo, Rio - [BR] 162 D 2
Pilcomayo, Rio - [PY] 160-161 C 6
Pil'gyn 178-179 jk 4
Pilica 133 K 3
Pillar, Cape - 194-195 J 8
Pillau = Baltijsk 133 J 1
Pilões, Chapada dos - 160-161 J 2-3
Pilot Mountain, NC 148-149 C 6
Pilot Peak [USA, Absaroka Range] 150-151 HJ 3
Pilot Peak [USA, Gabbs Valley Range] 150-151 E 6
Pilot Peak [USA, Toano Range] 150-151 FG 5
Pilot Point, TX 154-155 G 4
Pilot Rock, OR 150-151 D 3
Pilottown, LA 154-155 L 6
Pilsen = Plzeň 133 F 4
Pilten = Piltene 138-139 C 5
Piltene 138-139 C 5
Piltene 130-131 JK 9
Pilzno = Plzen 133 F 4
Pim 178-179 N 5
Pimba 194-195 G 6
Pimenta, Costa da - 166-167 B 7-C 8
Pimenta Bueno 158-159 G 7
Pimienta, Costa de la - 166-167 B 7-C 8
Piña [PA] 146-147 a 2
Pina [SU] 138-139 E 7
Pinaki 192-193 O 6
Pinaleno Mountains 150-151 HJ 9
Pinamelayan 186-187 H 4
Pinang = George Town 186-187 CD 5
Pınar = Ören 182-183 BC 4
Pınarbaşı 182-183 G 3
Pinar del Rio 146-147 K 7
Pinaré 160-161 G 6
Pınarhisar 182-183 B 2
Pin Chiang = Bin Jiang 190-191 D 9-10
Pinckneyville, IL 152-153 M 6
Pinconning, MI 152-153 OP 4
Pindamonhangaba 160-161 K 5
Pindaré, Rio - 158-159 K 5
Pindorama 160-161 H 4
Pindos Óros 136-137 J 5-6
Pine, ID 150-151 F 4
Pinduši 138-139 K 2
Pine Bluff, AR 146-147 H 5
Pine City, WA 150-151 E 2
Pine Apple, AL 154-155 M 5
Pine Bluffs, WY 152-153 D 5
Pine City, MN 152-153 K 3
Pine Creek [AUS] 194-195 F 2
Pine Creek [USA] 150-151 E 5
Pinedale, WY 150-151 J 4
Pine Forest Mountains 150-151 D 5
Pinega 178-179 G 5
Pine Hills 146-147 J 5
Pine Island 148-149 b 3
Pine Island, MN 152-153 K 3
Pine Island Bay 121 B 26
Pine Islands 148-149 c 4
Pineland, TX 154-155 HJ 5
Pine Mountain [USA, Georgia] 154-155 N 4
Pine Mountain [USA, Kentucky] 154-155 NO 2
Pine Point 144-145 O 5
Pine Ridge 152-153 C 2-3
Pine Ridge, SD 152-153 E 4
Pine Ridge Indian Reservation 152-153 EF 4
Pine River, MN 152-153 JK 2
Pinerolo 136-137 B 3
Pinetown 174-175 J 5
Pine Valley Mountains 150-151 G 7
Pineville, KY 152-153 P 7
Pineville, LA 154-155 J 5
Piney Buttes 152-153 C 2
Ping, Mae Nam - 186-187 C 3
P'ing-chiang = Pingjiang 190-191 D 7
P'ing-ch'üan = Pingquan 188-189 B 2
Pingding 190-191 DE 3
Pingdingshan 190-191 D 5
Pingdong = Ping-tung 184-185 N 7
Pingdu 190-191 G 3
Pinggu 190-191 F 1
Pinghai 190-191 E 10
P'ing-hai = Pinghai 190-191 G 9
Pinghe 190-191 F 9
P'ing-ho = Pinghe 190-191 F 9
P'ing-hsiang = Pingxiang 184-185 L 6
P'ing-hsien = Pingxiang 184-185 K 7
Pinghu 190-191 H 6
Pingi 190-191 F 4
Ping Jiang [TJ, ~] 190-191 E 8
Ping Jiang [TJ, ●] 190-191 D 7
Pingkiang = Pingjiang 190-191 D 7
P'ing-ku = Pinggu 190-191 F 1
Pingli 190-191 B 5
Pingle [TJ] 184-185 L 7
P'ing-leang = Pingliang 184-185 K 4
Pingliang 184-185 K 4
Pingliang = Pingtung 184-185 N 7
Pinglo = Pingle 184-185 L 7
P'ing-lo = Pingluo 184-185 K 4
Pinglu [TJ, Henan] 190-191 C 4
Pinglu [TJ, Shanxi] 190-191 D 2
Pinglucheng 190-191 CD 2
Pingluo 184-185 K 4
Pingnan [TJ, Fujian] 190-191 G 8
Pingnan [TJ, Guangxi Zhuangzu Zizhiqu] 190-191 C 10
Pingquan 188-189 B 2
Pingree, ID 150-151 G 4
Pingree, ND 152-153 G 2
Pingrup 194-195 C 6
Pingshan 190-191 DE 2
Pingshan = Huidong 190-191 E 10
Pingshi [TJ, Guangdong] 190-191 D 9
Pingshi [TJ, Henan] 190-191 D 5
Pingshun 190-191 D 3
Pingsiang = Pingxiang 184-185 L 6
Pingtan 190-191 GH 9
Pingtan Dao 184-185 MN 6
Pingting = Pingding 190-191 DE 3
P'ing-ting-shan = Pingdingshan 190-191 D 5
Ping-tung 184-185 N 7
Pinguininseln = Penguin Elanden 174-175 A 3-4
Pingwu 184-185 J 5
Pingxiang [TJ, Guangxi Zhuangzu Zizhiqu] 184-185 K7
Pingxiang [TJ, Jiangxi] 184-185 L 6
Pingyang 190-191 H 8
Pingyao 190-191 D 3
Pingyi 190-191 F 4
Pingyin 190-191 F 3
Pingyuan [TJ, Guangdong] 190-191 EF 9
Pingyuan [TJ, Shandong] 190-191 F 3
P'ing-yüan = Pingyuan 190-191 F 3
Pingyuan = Renju 190-191 E 9
Pinhal 158-159 K 9
Pinhão 160-161 G 6
Pinheiro 158-159 KL 5
Pinheiro, Ponta do - 160-161 H 7
Pinhsien = Bin Xian [TJ, Shaanxi] 190-191 AB 4
Pinhsien = Bin Xian [TJ, Shandong] 190-191 FG 3
Pini, Pulau - 186-187 C 6
Pinjarra 194-195 C 6
Pinkiang = Harbin 184-185 O 2
Pinkwan = Pianguan 190-191 C 2
Pinnacles National Monument 150-151 C 7
Pinnaroo 194-195 H 7
Pinon, CO 152-153 D 6
Pinon, NM 154-155 C 4
Pinón, Monte - 146-147 b 2
Pinos, Mount - 150-151 D 8
Pinos, Point - 150-151 BC 7
Pinrang 186-187 G 7
Pins, Îles de - 194-195 N 4
Pins, Pointe aux - 148-149 C 3
Pinsk 138-139 F 7
Pińsk = Pinsk 138-139 F 7
Pinta, Isla - 158-159 A 4
Pintada [BR, Rio Grande do Sul] 162 F 4
Pintados 162 BC 2
Pintas, Sierra de - 150-151 F 10
Pinto [RA] 162 D 3
Pin'ug 138-139 QR 3
Pioche, NV 150-151 F 7
Piombino 136-137 D 4
Pioneer Mountains 150-151 G 3
Pioner, ostrov - 178-179 QR 2
Pionki 133 K 3
Piorini, Lago - 158-159 G 5
Piorini, Rio - 158-159 G 5
Piotrków Trybunalski 133 J 3
Pipérion 136-137 L 6
Pipestone, MN 152-153 HJ 3-4
Pipinas 162 E 5
Piqua, KS 152-153 J 7
Piqua, OH 152-153 O 5
Piquetberg = Piketberg 168-169 E 9
Piquetberge = Piketberge 174-175 C 7
Piquête 160-161 K 5
Piquiri, Rio - 162 F 2
Pira 172-173 F 3
Pirabeiraba 160-161 H 7
Piracaia160-161 J 5
Piracanjuba 158-159 JK 8
Piracanjuba, Rio - 160-161 H 2
Piracicaba 160-161 HJ 5
Piracicaba, Rio - [BR, Minas Gerais] 160-161 L 4
Piracicaba, Rio - [BR, São Paulo] 160-161 J 5
Piraçununga 158-159 K 9
Piracuruca 158-159 L 5
Piraeus = Peiraiévs 136-137 K 7
Pirai do Sul 162 G 2
Piraju 160-161 H 5
Pirajui 158-159 K 9
Pir 'Ali Emāmzādeh 182-183 N 6
Piran 136-137 E 3
Piran = Dicle 182-183 J 3
Pirané 162 E 3
Piranga 160-161 L 4
Piranhas 158-159 M 6
Piranhas, Rio - [BR, Rio Grande do Norte] 158-159 M 6
Piranhas, Rio - [BR, Goiás ◁ Rio Caiapo] 160-161 G 2
Pirapetinga 160-161 L 4
Pirapó, Arroyo - 160-161 E 4
Pirapó, Rio - [BR] 160-161 F 5
Pirapó, Rio - [PY] 160-161 D 7
Pirapora 158-159 L 8
Pirapòzinho 160-161 G 5
Piraputangas 160-161 D 3
Piraquara 160-161 H 6
Pir'atin 140-141 F 1
Piratininga 160-161 H 5
Piratuba 162 F 3
Piray Guazú, Arroyo - 160-161 E 7
Pirayú 160-161 D 6
Pirčevan = Mindživan 140-141 N 7
Piräus = Peiraiévs 136-137 K 7
Pirée, le - = Peiraiévs 136-137 K 7
Pirenei 134-135 G-J 7
Pireneje 134-135 G-J 7
Pirenéus 135 GJ 7
Pireneus, Serra dos - 160-161 HJ 1
Pireneusok 134-135 G-J 7
Pirenópolis 160-161 H 1
Pireo = Peiraiévs 136-137 K 7
Pireo, El - = Peiraiévs 136-137 K 7
Pires do Rio 160-161 HJ 2
Pireu = Peiraiévs 128-129 N 8
Pireus = Peiraiévs 136-137 K 7
Pireusz = Peiraievs 136-137 K 7
Pirin 136-137 K 5
Pirinçlik 182-183 H 4
Pirineos 134-135 G-J 7
Piripiri 158-159 L 5
Pirizal 160-161 D 2
Pirmasens 133 C 4
Pirna 133 F 3
Piro-bong 188-189 G 3
Pirogovka 138-139 J 8
Pirot 136-137 K 4
Pirpintos, Los - 162 D 3
Pirtleville, AZ 150-151 J 10
Pirsagat 140-141 O 7
Piru 186-187 J 7
Pisa 136-137 D 4
Pisagua 162 B 1
Pisco 158-159 D 7
Pisco, Bahia de - 158-159 D 7
Písek 133 G 4
Pisgah, Mount - 150-151 C 3
Pishan = Guma Bazar 184-185 D 4
P'i-shan = Guma Bazar 184-185 D 4
Pisticci 136-137 G 5
Pistòia 136-137 D 3-4
Pistol River, OR 150-151 A 4
Pisuerga 134-135 E 7
Pisz 133 K 2
Pita 166-167 B 6
Pitanga 160-161 G 6
Pitanga, Serra da - 160-161 G 6
Pitangui 160-161 K 3
Pitcairn 198-199 L 6
Piteå 130-131 J 5
Pite älv 130-131 HJ 5
Piterka 140-141 N 1
Piteşati 136-137 L 3
Pit-Gorodok 178-179 RS 6
Pithara 194-195 C 6
Piti, Cerro - 162 C 2
Piti, Lagoa - 174-175 K 4
Pitigliano 136-137 D 4
Pitiquito 150-151 G 10
Pitk'ajarvi 130-131 NO 3
Pitk'aranta 138-139 HJ 3
Pitkin, LA 154-155 J 5
Pit River 150-151 BC 5
Pitsani 174-175 F 3
Pitssville, WI 152-153 LM 3
Pitt Island [CDN] 144-145 KL 7
Pitt Island [NZ] 194-195 Q 8
Pittsboro, NC 148-149 D 7
Pittsburg, CA 150-151 C 6
Pittsburg, KS 146-147 H 4
Pittsburg, KY 152-153 O 7
Pittsburg, TX 154-155 H 4
Pittsburgh, PA 146-147 KL 3
Pittsfield, IL 152-153 L 6
Pittsfield, MA 148-149 G 3
Pittsfield, ME 148-149 J 2
Pittston, PA 148-149 F 4
Pittsworth 196 K 1
P'i-tzŭ-wo = Pikou 188-189 D 3
Piui 160-161 K 4
Piuka = Bifuka 188-189 c 1
Piura [PE, ●] 158-159 CD 6
Piute Peak 150-151 D 8
Piva 136-137 H 4
Pivka 136-137 F 3
Pi-yang = Biyang 190-191 D 5
Pižma [SU,~] 138-139 QR 5
Pižma [SU,●] 138-139 Q 5
Pizzo 136-137 FG 6
Pjagina, poluostrov - 178-179 de 6
Pjana 138-139 P 6
P.K. le Roux Dam 174-175 F 6
Placentia Bay 144-145 Za 8
Placerville, CA 150-151 C 6
Placerville, CO 152-153 B 6-7
Placetas 146-147 L 7
Plácido de Castro 158-159 F 7
Plain City, OH 152-153 P 5
Plains, GA 154-155 N 4-5
Plains, KS 154-155 E 2
Plains, MT 150-151 F 2
Plains, TX 154-155 D 4
Plainview, MN 152-153 KL 3
Plainview, NE 152-153 GH 4
Plainview, TX 146-147 F 5
Plainville, KS 152-153 G 6
Plainwell, MI 152-153 O 4
Planada, CA 150-151 CD 7
Planaltina 158-159 K 8
Planalto Brasileiro 158-159 KL 8
Plankinton, SD 152-153 G 4
Plano, TX 154-155 G 4
Plantation, FL 148-149 c 3
Plant City, FL 148-149 b 2-3
Plaquemine, LA 154-155 K 5
Plasencia 134-135 D 8
Plast 178-179 L 7
Plaster City, CA 150-151 EF 9
Plaston 174-175 J 3
Plastun 178-179 a 9
Plata, Isla de la - 158-159 C 5
Plata, La - [CO] 158-159 D 4
Plata, La - [RA] 162 E 5
Plata, Rio de la - 162 EF 5
Plateau 166-167 F 7
Plateau Central = Cao Nguyên Trung Phân 186-187 E 4

Plateau Continental Patagonien 124-125 FG 8
Plateaux 172-173 F 4
Platen, Kapp - 130-131 lm 4
Platero 160-161 D 7
Platinum, AK 144-145 D 6
Platovskaja = Bud'onnovskaja 140-141 KL 3
Platrand 174-175 H 4
Platte, SD 152-153 G 4
Platte City, MO 152-153 J 6
Platte Island 168-169 N 4
Plattensee = Balaton 133 HJ 5
Platte River [USA, Missouri, Iowa] 152-153 J 5
Platte River [USA, Nebraska] 146-147 FG 3
Platteville, CO 152-153 D 5
Platteville, WI 152-153 L 4
Platt National Park 154-155 G 3
Plattsburg, MO 152-153 J 6
Plattsburgh, NY 146-147 LM 3
Plattsmouth, NE 152-153 HJ 5
Plauen 133 F 3
Plaviņas 138-139 EF 5
Plavno = Plauen 133 F 3
Plavsk 138-139 L 7
Playas 158-159 C 5
Plaza, ND 152-153 F 1
Plaza Huincul 162 BC 5
Pleasant, Mount - 148-149 D 6
Pleasant Grove, UT 150-151 H 5
Pleasant Hill, MO 152-153 J 6
Pleasanton, KS 152-153 J 6
Pleasanton, TX 154-155 F 6
Pleasant Valley, OR 150-151 E 3
Pleasant View, WA 150-151 DE 2
Pleasantville, NJ 148-149 FG 5
Pleihari 186-187 F 7
Pleiku 186-187 E 4
Pleniţa 136-137 K 3
Plenty, Bay of - [NZ, ◡] 194-195 P 7
Plentywood, MT 152-153 D 1
Pleščenicy 138-139 FG 6
Pleseck 178-179 G 5
Pleskau = Pskov 138-139 G 5
Pleskauer See = Pskovskoje ozero 138-139 FG 4-5
Pleß = Pszczyna 133 J 3-4
Pleszew 133 HJ 3
Plettenbergbaai 174-175 E 8
Plettenberg Bay = Plettenbergbaai 174-175 E 8
Plevna, MT 152-153 D 2
Pleven 136-137 L 4
Plitvice 136-137 F 3
Plitvička Jezera 136-137 FG 3
Pljevlja 136-137 H 4
Płock 133 JK 2
Ploieşti 136-137 LM 3
Plomo, El - 150-151 GH 10
Pl'os 138-139 N 5
Ploskoje [SU, Rossijskaja SFSR] 138-139 M 7
Ploskoš 138-139 H 5
Plovdiv 136-137 L 4
Plumas, Las - 162 C 6
Plummer, ID 150-151 E 2
Plummer, MN 152-153 HJ 2
Plumtree 168-169 G 7
Plungė 138-139 CD 6
Plungė 130-131 J 10
Plush, OR 150-151 D 4
Pl'ussa [SU,~] 138-139 G 4
Pl'ussa [SU,●] 138-139 G 4
Plymouth 132 DE 6
Plymouth, CA 150-151 C 6
Plymouth, IN 152-153 NO 5
Plymouth, MA 148-149 H 4
Plymouth, NC 148-149 E 7
Plymouth, NH 148-149 GH 3
Plymouth, PA 148-149 EF 4
Plymouth, WI 152-153 MN 4
Plzeň 133 F 4
Po 136-137 D 3
Pô [HV] 166-167 D 6
Pobè 166-167 E 7
Pobeda, gora - 178-179 c 4
Pobedino 178-179 b 8
Pobedy, pik - 180-181 MN 2
Poblacion 160-161 C 4
Pobohe = Pohe 190-191 E 6
Pobřeží Slonoviny 166-167 CD 8
Pobřeží Slonoviny = Côte d'Ivoire 166-167 CD 7
Pocahontas, AR 154-155 K 2
Pocahontas, IA 152-153 J 4
Pocatello, ID 146-147 D 3
Počep 138-139 J 7
Poch'ŏn 188-189 F 4
Pochvistnevo 138-139 ST 7
Pochval'nyj 178-179 cd 4
Počinki 138-139 P 6
Počinok [SU, Smolensk] 138-139 J 6
Pocklington Reef 186-187 j 7
Poções 158-159 LM 7
Pocomoke City, MD 148-149 F 5
Pocomoke Sound 148-149 EF 6
Poconé 158-159 H 8
Poços de Caldas 158-159 K 9
Poczdam = Potsdam 133 F 2
Podberezje 138-139 H 5
Podborovje 138-139 K 4
Podčinnyj 140-141 M 1
Poddorje 138-139 H 5
Podgorenskij 140-141 J 1
Podgorica 136-137 H 4
Podgornoje 178-179 P 6
Podgorodnoje 140-141 G 2
Podkamennaja Tunguska 178-179 R 5
Podkova 136-137 L 5
Podlesien = Polesje 138-139 E 8-H 7
Podol'sk 138-139 L 6
Podol'skaja vozvyšennost' 140-141 B 2-D 3
Podor 166-167 AB 5
Podosinovec 138-139 Q 3
Podporožje 178-179 EF 5
Podravska Slatina 136-137 GH 3
Podsosenje 138-139 NO 2
Podsvilje 138-139 FG 6
Podtesovo 178-179 R 6
Pod'uga 138-139 N 3
Podvološčisk 140-141 BC 2
Po-êrh-t'a-la Chou = Bortala Monggol Zizhizhou 184-185 E 2
Poelela, Lagoa - 174-175 L 3
Pofadder 168-169 EF 8
Pogar 138-139 J 7
Pogegen = Pagėgiai 138-139 CD 6
Poggibonsi 136-137 D 4 P
Pogibi 178-179 b 7
Pogoreloje 138-139 K 5
Pogrebišče 140-141 D 2
Pogyndeno 178-179 fg 4
P'oha-dong 188-189 G H 2
Po Hai = Bo Hai 184-185 M 4
Po-hai Hai-hsia = Bohai Haixia 184-185 N 4
Po-hai Wan = Bohai Wan 190-191 FG 2
P'ohang 184-185 OP 4
Pohe 190-191 E 6
Pohjanmaa 130-131 K 6-M 5
Pohjois-Karjalan lääni 130-131 N 6
Pohsien = Bo Xian 184-185 LM 5
Pöide 138-139 D 4
Poinsett, Lake - 152-153 H 3
Point Abbaye 152-153 MN 2
Point Arena, CA 150-151 AB 6
Point Detour 152-153 N 3
Pointe, La -, WI 152-153 L 2
Pointe a la Hache, LA 154-155 L 6
Pointe-à-Pitre 146-147 O 8
Pointe Aux Barques 152-153 P 3
Pointe-Noire 168-169 D 3
Point Harbor, NC 148-149 F 6
Point Lake 144-145 O 4
Point Marion PA 148-149 D 5
Point of Rocks, WY 152-153 B 5
Point Pleasant, NJ 148-149 FG 4-5
Point Pleasant, WV 148-149 BC 5
Point Roberts, WA 150-151 B 1
Poitevin, Marais - 134-135 G 5
Poitiers 134-135 H 5
Poitou 134-135 GH 5
Poivre, Côte du - = Malabar Coast 180-181 L 8-M 9
Poix 134-135 HJ 4
Pojarkovo 178-179 Y 8
Pokataroo 196 J 2
Pokča 138-139 V 2
Pokegama Lake 152-153 JK 2
Pokhara 180-181 N 5
Poko 168-169 G 2
Pokrovka [SU, ↘ Abdulino] 138-139 T 7
Pokrovka [SU, ↘ Buzuluk] 138-139 T 8
Pokrovsk 178-179 Y 5
Pokrovsk = Engels 138-139 Q 8
Pokrovskoje [SU, Archangel'sk] 138-139 M 1
Pokrovsk-Ural'skij 178-179 K 5
Pokšen'ga 138-139 O 2
Pola [SU, ●] 138-139 H 5
Pola [SU, ~ ◁ ozero Il'men] 138-139 J 5
Polacca Wash 150-151 H 8
Polack 138-139 G 6
Pola de Siero 134-135 E 7
Polān [IR] 180-181 J 5
Poland 133 H-L 3
Polangen = Palanga 138-139 C 6
Pol'arnoje 178-179 c 3
Polarny, Płaskowyż - 121 A 31-6
Pol'arnyj Ural 178-179 LM 4
Polar Plateau 121 A 31-6
Polathane = Akçaabat 182-183 H 2
Polatlı 180-181 C 3
Polcirkeln 130-131 J 4
Poldarsa 138-139 PQ 3
Polen 133 H-L 3
Polesie = Polesje 138-139 E 8-H 7
Polesje 138-139 E 8-H 7
Polessk 133 K 1
Pŏlgyo 188-189 F 5
Poli 166-167 G 7
Poli = Boli 184-185 P 2
Policastro, Golfo di - 136-137 F 5-6
Polillo Islands 186-187 H 3-4
Polinesia 124-125 A 5-6
Polinesia 124-125 A 5-6
Polinésia 124-125 A 6-7
Poliny Osipenko 178-179 a 7
Pólis 182-183 E 5
Polist' 138-139 H 5
Polk, PA 148-149 CD 4
Pollensa 134-135 J 9
Pollino 136-137 G 5-6
Pollock, ID 150-151 E 3
Pollock, LA 154-155 J 5
Pollock, SD 152-153 FG 3
Polmak 130-131 N 2
Polna [SU] 138-139 G 4
Polnovo 138-139 J 5
Polo, IL 152-153 M 5
Polo = Boluo 190-191 E 10
Polo Nord 120 A
Polo Norte 120 A
Pólo Norte Magnético 144-145 Q 3
Polo Sud 121 A
Polock 138-139 G 6
Pologi 140-141 H 3
Pologne 133 H-L 3
Polonezköy 182-183 C 2
Polonia 133 H-L 3
Polonia 133 H-L 3
Polónia 122-123 KL 3
Polônia 126-127 MN 5
Polonio, Cabo - 162 F 4
Polonnoje 140-141 C 1
Polotn'anyj Zavod 138-139 KL 6
Polousnyj kr'až 178-179 bc 4
Polovinki 138-139 S 2
Polovo 138-139 J 5
Polska 133 H-L 3
Polsko 133 H-L 3
Polson, MT 150-151 FG 2
Poltava 140-141 G 2
Poltavskaja = Krasnoarmejskaja 140-141 J 4
Poltawa = Poltava 140-141 G 2
Poltorack = Aschabad 180-181 HJ 3
Põltsamaa 138-139 EF 4
Pol'udov Kamen' 138-139 V 3
Pol'udov kr'až 138-139 V 3
Põltsamaa 130-131 LM 8
Poluj 178-179 M 4
Poluj = Pospolnj 178-179 MN 4
Polunočnoje 178-179 L 5
Põlva 138-139 F 4
Pölwe = Põlva 138-139 F 4
Polyaigos 136-137 L 7
Polýchnitos 136-137 LM 6
Polýgyros 136-137 K 5
Polynesia 124-125 A 5-6
Polynésia 124-125 A 6-7
Polynésie 124-125 A 5-6
Polynesien 124-125 A 6-7
Północne, Morze - 132 F-J 3
Północnoaustralijski, Basen 194-195 C 2
Północnofidżyjski, Basen 194-195 O 3
Północnofryzyjskie, W-y - 130-131 C 10
Północnofryzyjskie, W-y - = Nordfriesische Inseln 133 D 1
Północnoosetyńska Autonomiczna Republika 140-141 LM 5
Południowej Afryki Republika 168-169 F-H 8
Południowej Georgii, Wzniesienie - 121 D 33-34
Południowochiński, Basen 186-187 FG 3-4
Południowochińskie, Morze 186-187 E 5-G 2
Południowofidżyjski, Basen 194-195 OP 4-5
Południowoosetyński Obwód Autonomiczny 140-141 LM 5
Południowopacyficzny, Basen 121 D 21-19
Południowopacyficzny, Grzbiet 121 D 22-C 20
Poma, La - 162 C 2
Pomarão 134-135 D 10
Pomasi, Cerro de - 158-159 E 8
Pomba, Rio - 160-161 L 4
Pombal 134-135 C 9
Pombal [BR] 158-159 M 6
Pombetsu = Honbetsu 188-189 cd 2
Pomerania 133 G 2-H 1
Pomerania 133 G 2-H 1
Pomerânia 130-131 F 11-G 10
Poméranie 133 G 2-H 1
Pomeroy, OH 148-149 BC 5
Pomeroy, WA 150-151 E 2
Pomfret 174-175 E 3
Pomme de Terre River 152-153 J2-3
Pommeren 133 G 2-H 1
Pommern 133 G 2-H 1
Pommersche Bucht 133 FG 1
Pomořanská záliv 130-131 EF 10
Pomona, CA 150-151 E 8-9
Pomona, KS 152-153 J 6
Pomona, MO 154-155 K 2
Pomona [Namibia] 174-175 A 4
Pomorie 136-137 MN 4
Pomorska, Zatoka - 130-131 F 11
Pomorska, Zatoka - 133 G 1
Pomorze 130-131 F 11 -G 10
Pomořanská záliv 130-131 EF 10
Pomořanská zátoka = Pommersche Bucht 133 G 1
Pomořansko 130-131 F 11-G 10
Pomořansko 133 G 2-H 1
Pomorskij bereg 138-139 K 1-L 2
Pomošnaja 140-141 E 2
Pomozdino 138-139 U 2
Pompano Beach, FL 148-149 cd 3
Pompeia 160-161 G 5
Pompeji 136-137 F 5
Pompéu 160-161 K 3
Pompeys Pillar, MT 150-151 JK 2
Ponazyrevo 138-139 Q 4
Ponca, NE 152-153 H 4
Ponca City, OK 146-147 G 4
Ponca Creek 152-153 G 4
Ponce 146-147 N 8
Ponce de Leon, FL 154-155 MN 5
Ponce de Leon Bay 148-149 c 4
Poncha Springs, CO 152-153 C 6
Ponchatoula, LA 154-155 K 5
Pond Creek 152-153 E 6
Pond Creek, OK 154-155 G 2
Pondicheri = Pondicherry 180-181 MN 8
Pondicherry 180-181 MN 8
Pond Inlet [CDN, ◡] 144-145 VW 3
Pond Inlet [CDN, ●] 144-145 V 3
Pondo Dsong 184-185 G 5
Pondoland 174-175 H 6
Pondosa, CA 150-151 C 5
Pondosa, OR 150-151 E 3
Ponedjel = Pandėlys 138-139 E 5
Ponferrada 134-135 D 7
Pong 186-187 CD 3
Pongnim-ni = Pŏlgyo 188-189 F 5
Pongola [ZA, ~] 168-169 H 8
Pongola [ZA, ●] 174-175 J 4
Pongolapoortdam 174-175 JK 4
Poniewiesh = Panevėžys 138-139 E 6
Ponizovje [SU, Smolensk] 138-139 H 6
Ponoj [SU, ●] 178-179 FG 4
Ponomar'ovka 138-139 TU 7
Ponta Albina 168-169 D 6
Ponta de Pedras 158-159 JK 5
Ponta Grossa [BR, Amapá] 158-159 K 4
Ponta Grossa [BR, Paraná] 162 F 3
Pontal 160-161 HJ 4
Pontalina 160-161 H 2
Ponta Porã 158-159 HJ 9
Pontarlier 134-135 KL 5
Pontchartrain, Lake - 146-147 HJ 5
Ponte Firme 160-161 JK 3
Ponte de Itabapoana 160-161 M 4
Ponte de Pedra [BR ↖ Diamantino] 158-159 H 7
Ponte de Pedra [BR ↘ Cuiabá] 160-161 E 2
Ponte-Leccia 136-137 C 4
Ponte Nova 158-159 L 9
Pontes-e-Lacerda 158-159 H 8
Pontevedra 134-135 C 7
Ponthierville = Ubundu 168-169 FG 3
Ponti, Monti del - 140-141 F-J 6
Pontiac, IL 152-153 M 5
Pontiac, MI 146-147 K 3
Pontianak 186-187 E 7
Pontiac, IL 152-153 M 5
Pontic Mountains 180-181 C-E 2
Pontisches Gebirge 180-181 C-E 2
Pontisch Gebergte 180-181 C-E 2
Pontivy 134-135 F 4
Ponto, Monti del 180-181 C-E 2
Ponto, Montes del - 180-181 C-E 2
Ponto, Montes do - 180-181 C-E 2
Pontoise 134-135 HJ 4
Pontotoc, MS 154-155 L 3
Pontrèmoli 136-137 CD 3
Pontské pohoří 180-181 C-E 2
Pontuszi-hegység 180-181 C-E 2
Pontyjskie, Góry - 180-181 C-E 2
Pony, MT 150-151 GH 3
Ponza 136-137 E 5
Ponziane, Isole - 136-137 E 5
Poochera 196 B 4
Poole 132 E 6
Poona = Pune 180-181 L 7
Pooncarie 194-195 H 6
Poopó 158-159 F 8
Poopó, Lago de - 158-159 F 8
Poortje = Poortjie 174-175 E 6
Poortjie 174-175 E 6
Pöösaspea 138-139 DE 4
Popa = Pulau Kofiau 186-187 JK 7
Po-pai = Bobai 190-191 BC 10
Popasnaja 140-141 J 2
Popayán 158-159 D 4
Popeljany = Papilė 138-139 D 5
Popeys Pillar, MT 152-153 BC 2-3
Popigaj 178-179 UV 3
Popihe = Pohe 190-191 E 6
Popilta Lake 196 E 4
Po-p'ing = Boping 190-191 F 3
Poplar, MT 152-153 D 1
Poplar, WI 152-153 L 2
Poplar Bluff, MO 146-147 H 4
Poplar River [USA] 152-153 D1
Poplarville, MS 154-155 L 5
Popocatépetl 146-147 G 8
Popokabaka 168-169 E 4
Popondetta 186-187 N 8
Popovo 136-137 M 4
Poprad [CS, ~] 133 K 4
Poprad [CS, ●] 133 K 4
Pŏpsŏngp'o 188-189 F 5
Porāli 180-181 K 5
Porangatu 158-159 K 7
Porbandar 180-181 K 6
Porbunder = Porbandar 180-181 K 6
Porchov 138-139 G 5
Porciúncula 160-161 LM 4
Porcos, Ilha dos 160-161 K 5
Porcupine Creek 152-153 C 1
Porcupine Mountain 144-145 Q 7
Porcupine River 144-145 H 4
Pordenone 136-137 E 2-3
Pore 158-159 E 3
Porecatu 160-161 G 5
Poreče [SU, Belorusskaja SSR] 138-139 E 7
Porez 138-139 S 5
Pori 130-131 J 7
Porjus 130-131 HJ 4
Porlamar 158-159 G 2
Pornic 134-135 F 5
Poronajsk 178-179 b 8
Poroshiri-dake 188-189 c 2
Porosozero 138-139 J 2
Porpoise Bay 121 C 13
Porsangerfjord 130-131 LM 2
Porsangerhalvøya 130-131 L 2
Porsgrunn 130-131 CD 8
Porsuk Çayı 182-183 D 3
Portachuelo 158-159 G 8
Portadown 132 C 4
Portage, UT 150-151 G 5
Portage, WI 152-153 M 4
Portage-la-Prairie 146-147 R 8
Portal, ND 152-153 E 1
Port Alberni 144-145 LM 8
Port Albert [AUS] 196 H 7
Port Albert [CDN] 152-153 PQ 4
Portalegre 134-135 D 9
Portales, NM 146-147 F 5
Port Alfred 168-169 G 9
Port Allegany, PA 148-149 DE 4
Port Allen, LA 154-155 K 5
Port Angeles, WA 150-151 B 1
Port Antonio 146-147 L 8
Port Arthur 196 cd 3
Port Arthur, TX 146-147 H 6
Port Arthur = Lüshun 184-185 MN 4
Port Augusta 194-195 G 6
Port-au-Prince 146-147 M 8
Port Austin, MI 152-153 P 3
Port-Bergé 168-169 L 6
Port Blair 180-181 P 8
Port-Bou 134-135 J 7
Port-Bouët 172-173 DE 4
Port Brega = Marsā al-Burayqah 166-167 H2
Port Burwell [CDN, Ontario] 148-149 C 3
Port Burwell [CDN, Quebec] 144-145 XY 5
Port Cartier 144-145 X 7
Port Chalmers 194-195 O 9
Port Colborne 148-149 D 3
Port Curtis 194-195 K 4
Port Chalmers 194-195 O 9
Port Clinton, OH 152-153 P 5
Port Darwin 162 E 8
Port Dunford = Buur Gaabo 168-169 K 3
Portel [BR] 158-159 J 5
Port Eads, LA 154-155 L 6
Porte City, IA 152-153 KL 4
Porte des Morts 152-153 N 3
Port Edward [ZA] 174-175 J 6
Porteirinha 160-161 L 1
Portela 160-161 M 3
Port Elgin [CDN, Ontario] 152-153 Q3
Port Elizabeth 168-169 G 9
Porterdale, GA 154-155 NO 4
Port Erin 132 D 4
Porterville 168-169 EF 9
Porterville, CA 150-151 D 7-8
Port Essington 144-145 KL 7
Port-Étienne = Nawādhibu 166-167 A4
Port Fairy 194-195 H 7
Port-Francqui = Ilebo 168-169 F 3
Port Fu'ad = Būr Sādāt 170 E 2
Port-Gentil 168-169 C 3
Port Gibson, MS 154-155 K 5
Port Harcourt 166-167 F 8
Port Hardy 144-145 L 7
Port Harrison = Inoucdjouac 144-145 V 6
Port Hedland 194-195 C 4
Port Henry, NY 148-149 G 2-3
Port Herald = Nsanje 168-169 J 6
Porthill, ID 150-151 E 1
Port Hope 148-149 D 2-3
Port Hope, MI 152-153 P 4
Port Hudson, LA 154-155 K 5
Port Hueneme, CA 150-151 D 8
Port Huron, MI 146-147 K 3
Port-Iljič 140-141 O 7
Port Chalmers 194-195 O 9
Portimão 134-135 C 10
Port Isabel, TX 154-155 G 7
Port Jefferson, NY 148-149 G 4
Port Jervis, NY 148-149 F 4
Port Keats 194-195 EF 2
Port Kembla, Wollongong- 194-195 K 6
Port Kenney 194-195 F 6
Port Lairge = Waterford 132 C 5
Portland [AUS, New South Wales] 196 JK 4
Portland [AUS, Victoria] 194-195 H 7
Portland [CDN] 148-149 EF 2
Portland, IN 152-153 O 5
Portland, ME 146-147 MN 3
Portland, MI 152-153 O 4
Portland, OR 146-147 B 2
Portland, TN 154-155 M 2
Portland, TX 154-155 G 7
Portland = Dyrhólaey 130-131 d 3
Portland, Bill of - 132 EF 6
Portland, Cape - 196 c 2
Portland Promontory 144-145 UV 6
Port Laoise 132 C 5
Port Lavaca, TX 154-155 G 6
Port Lincoln 194-195 FG 6
Port Loko 166-167 B 7
Port Louis 168-169 N 7
Port-Lyautey = Al-Q'nitrah 166-167 C2
Port Macdonnell 196 DE 7
Port Macquarie 196 L 3
Port Mathurin 168-169 O 6
Port Mayaca, FL 148-149 c 3
Port Moresby 186-187 N 8
Port Musgrave 194-195 H 2
Port Natal = Durban 168-169 H 8
Port Neches, TX 154-155 J 6
Port Neill 196 C 5
Port Nelson [CDN, ◡] 144-145 S 6
Port Nelson [CDN, ●] 144-145 S 6
Port Nolloth 168-169 E 8
Port Norris, NJ 148-149 F 5
Porto 134-135 C 8
Porto Acre 158-159 F 6
Porto Alegre [BR, Rio Grando do Sul] 162 FG 4
Porto Alegre do Sul 160-161 F 4
Porto Alexandre 168-169 D 6
Porto Alexandre, Parque National de - 168-169 D 6
Porto Amazonas 160-161 GH 6
Porto Amboim 168-169 D 5
Porto Amélia = Pemba 168-169 K 5
Porto Artur 158-159 HJ 7
Porto Barra do Ivinheima 160-161 EF 5
Portobelo [PA] 146-147 b 1
Porto Belo [BR] 160-161 H 7
Porto Britânia 160-161 EF 6
Porto Camargo 160-161 F 5
Porto Caneco 158-159 HJ 7
Porto Conceição 158-159 H 8
Porto das Caixas 160-161 L 5
Porto de Más 158-159 H 8
Porto de Mós [BR] 158-159 J 5
Porto 15 de Novembro 160-161 F 4
Porto Empèdocle 136-137 E 7
Porto Esperança [BR, Mato Grosso do Sul] 160-161 D 3
Porto Feliz 160-161 J 5
Portoferràio 136-137 CD 4
Porto Ferreira 160-161 J 4
Porto Franco 158-159 K 6
Porto Guarei 160-161 F 5
Port of Spain 146-147 O 9
Portogallo 134-135 C 10-D 8
Portogruaro 136-137 E 3
Porto Guaíra 162 F 2
Portola, CA 150-151 C 6
Pörtom 130-131 J 6
Porto Mendes 162 F 2
Porto Murtinho 160-161 D 4
Porto Nacional 158-159 K 7
Porto-Novo [DY] 166-167 E 7
Port Orchard, WA 150-151 B 2
Porto Real do Colégio 158-159 M 6-7
Port Orford, OR 150-151 A 4
Porto Rico, Fossa do - 124-125 FG 4
Porto Rico, Fosse de 124-125 FG 4
Portoriko = Puerto Rico 146-147 N 8
Porto Santana 158-159 J 5
Porto Santo 166-167 AB 2
Porto São José 162F2
Porto Seguro 158-159 M 8
Porto Tolle 136-137 E 3
Porto Tòrres 136-137 C 5
Porto União 162 F 3
Porto-Vecchio 136-137 C 5
Porto Velho 158-159 G 6
Portoviejo 158-159 C 5
Porto Walter 158-159 E 6
Portpatrik 132 D 4
Port Phillip Bay 194-195 H 7
Port Pirie 194-195 G 6
Port Radium 144-145 NO 4
Port Rowan 148-149 C 3
Port Royal = Annapolis Royal 144-145 XY 9
Port Royal Sound 148-149 C 8
Port Safâga = Safājah 166-167 L 3
Port Said = Būr Sa'īd 166-167 L 2
Port Saint Joe, FL 154-155 N 6
Port Shepstone 168-169 H 9
Portsmouth [GB] 132 F 6
Portsmouth, NH 146-147 MN 3
Portsmouth, OH 146-147 K 4
Portsmouth, VA 146-147 L 4
Port Stanley 148-149 C 3
Port Stanley = Stanley 162 E 8
Port Sūdān = Būr Sūdān 166-167 M5
Port Sulphur, LA 154-155 L 6
Port Talbot 132 DE 6
Port Tewfik = Būr Tawfīq 170 E 3
Porttipahdan tekojärvi 130-131 LM 3-4
Port Townsend, WA 150-151 B 1
Portugal 134-135 C 10-D 8
Portugalete 134-135 F 7
Portugalia 134-135 C 10-D 8
Portugalia 134-135 C 10-D 8
Portugália = Luachimo 168-169 F 4
Portugalsko 134-135 C 10-D 8
Portugues, El - 158-159 D 6
Portuguesa, Rio - 158-159 F 3
Port-Vendres 134-135 J 7
Port Victoria [AUS] 196 C 5
Port Victoria [EUA] 168-169 H 2-3
Port Vila 192-193 H 6
Port Wakefield 196 CD 5
Port Washington, WI 152-153 N 4
Port Weld 186-187 CD 6
Port Wing, WI 152-153 L 2
Porvenir, EL - [MEX] 154-155 BC 5
Porvoo = Borgå 130-131 LM 7
Posadas [RA] 162 E 3
Posad-Pokrovskoje 140-141 F 3
Pošechonje-Volodarsk 138-139 MN 4
Posen = Poznań 133 H 2
Posen, MI 152-153 P 3
Poshan = Boshan 184-185 M 4
Posio 130-131 N 4
Posjet 178-179 Z 9
Poso 186-187 H 7
Posof 182-183 K 2
Posŏng 184-185 O 5
Pospoluj 178-179 MN 4
Posse 158-159 K 7
Possession Island = Possessions Eiland 174-175 A 4
Possessions Eiland 174-175 A 4
Possum Kingdom Reservoir 154-155 F 4
Post, OR 150-151 C 3
Post, TX 154-155 E 4
Postavy 138-139 F 6
Post Falls, ID 150-151 E 2
Postmasburg 168-169 F 8
Postojna 136-137 F 3
Poston, AZ 150-151 F 8
Postupim = Potsdam 133 F 3
Postville, IA 152-153 L 4
Poswol = Pasvalys 138-139 E 5
Potawatomi Indian Reservation 152-153 HJ 6
Potchefstroom 168-169 G 8
Potčurk, gora - 138-139 T 2
Poté 160-161 M 2
Poteau, OK 154-155 H 3
Poteet, TX 154-155 F 6
Potenza 136-137 F 5
Potfontein 174-175 F 6
Potgietersrus 168-169 G 7
Potholes Reservoir 150-151 D 2
Potiskum 166-167 G 6
Poti [SU] 140-141 K 5
Potlatch, ID 150-151 E 2
Potloer 174-175 D 6
Pot Mountain 150-151 F 2
Potomac River 148-149 E 5
Potosi, MO 152-153 L 7
Potosí [BOL, ●] 158-159 F 8
Potrerillos [RCH] 162 C 3
Potrero, EL - 154-155 C 6
Potsdam 133 F 2
Potsdam, NY 148-149 F 2
Potter, NE 152-153 E 5
Potts Camps, MS 154-155 L 3
Pottstown, PA 148-149 F 4
Pottsville, PA 148-149 E 4
Pottuvil = Potuvil 180-181 N 7
Pötürge 182-183 H 3
Potuvil 180-181 N 7
Po-tzu 190-191 H 10
Poughkeepsie, NY 146-147 LM 3
Pouilles = Púglia 136-137 FG 5
Poŭn 188-189 F4
Poupan 174-175 EF 6
Pouso Alegre [BR, Mato Grosso] 158-159 H 7
Pouso Alegre [BR, Minas Gerais] 158-159 K 9
Pouté 172-173 B 2
Povenec 138-139 K 2
Poveneckij zaliv 138-139 K 2
Poventsa = Povenec 138-139 K 2
Póvoa de Varzim 134-135 C 8
Povorino 140-141 L 1
Povraz adası = Alibey Adası 182-183 B 3
Povungnituk 144-145 V 6
Powder River, WY 152-153 C 4
Powder River Pass 152-153 C 3
Powder River [USA, Montana] 146-147 E 2
Powder River [USA, Oregon] 150-151 E 3
Powderville, MT 152-153 D 3
Powell, WY 152-153 B 3
Powell, Lake - 146-147 D 4
Powell Butte, OR 150-151 C 3
Powell River 144-145 M 8
Powell, WY 152-153 B 3
Power, MT 150-151 H 2
Powers, MI 152-153 N 3
Powers, OR 150-151 AB 4
Powers Lake, ND 152-153 E 1
Powhatan, LA 154-155 J 5
Poxoréu 158-159 J 8
Poyang = Boyang 190-191 F 7
Poyang Hu 184-185 M 6
Poygan, Lake - 152-153 M 3
Pozantı 182-183 F 4
Požarevac 136-137 J 3
Poza Rica 146-147 G 7
Požeg 138-139 U 3
Poževrevicy 138-139 G 5
Poznań 133 H 2
Pozo Almonte 162 C 2
Pozo Anta 160-161 B 5
Pozoblanco 134-135 E 9
Pozo Colorado 162 E 2
Pozo Hondo [RA] 162 D 3
Pozony = Bratislava 133 H 4
Pozva 138-139 UV 4
Pozzallo 136-137 F 7
Pozzuoli 136-137 EF 5
Pra [WG] 166-167 D 7
Praag = Praha 133 G 3
Prachuap Khiri Khan 186-187 CD 4
Praděd 133 H 3
Prades 134-135 J 7
Prado [BR] 158-159 M 8
Prag = Praha 133 G 3
Praga = Praha 128-129 LM 5-6
Praga = Praha 133 G 3
Prága = Praha 133 G 3
Praga = Praha 133 G 3
Prague, NE 152-153 H 6
Prague, OK 154-155 G 3
Prague = Praha 133 G 3
Praha 133 G3
Praia de Leste 160-161 H 6
Praia Grande 160-161 J 6
Praião, Cachoeira do - 158-159 K 8
Praia Redonda 160-161 H 8
Prainha [BR, Amazonas] 158-159 G 6
Prainha [BR, Pará] 158-159 J 5
Prairie, ID 150-151 F 4
Prairie City, OR 150-151 D 3
Prairie Dog Creek 152-153 F 6
Prairie Dog Town Fork 154-155 EF 3
Prairie du Chien, WI 152-153 L 4
Prairies 144-145 Q 7-R 9
Pran Buri 186-187 CD 4
Prangli 138-139 E 4
Pranhita 180-181 MN 7
Praskoveja 140-141 M 4
Praslin Island 168-169 N 3
Prasonēsion, Akrōtērion - 136-137 MN 8
Prata [BR, Pará] 158-159 K 5
Prata [BR, Minas Gerais] 160-161 H 3
Prata, Rio da - [BR ◁ Rio Paracatu] 160-161 J 2
Prata, Rio da - [BR ◁ Rio Paranaíba] 160-161 H 3
Pratápolis 160-161 J 4
Pratas = Dongsha Qundao 184-185 LM 7
Pratinha 160-161 J 3
Prato 136-137 D 4
Pratt, KS 152-153 G 7
Prattville, AL 154-155 M 4
Pravdinsk [SU, Volga] 138-139 O 5
Prawle, Point - 132 E 6
Pr'aža 138-139 JK 3
Prébeza 136-137 J 6
Prečistoje [SU, Jaroslavl'] 138-139 MN 4
Precordillera 162 C 3-4
Predeal, Pasul - 136-137 L 3
Predivinsk 178-179 R 6
Pregradnaja 140-141 K 5
Pregol'a 133 K 1
Preiļi 138-139 F 5
Prekuln = Priekulė 138-139 C 6
Premier Mine 174-175 H 3
Premont, TX 154-155 FG 7
Premuda 136-137 F 3
Prentice, WI 152-153 LM 3
Prentiss, MS 154-155 L 5
Prenzlau 133 FG 2
Přerov 133 H 4
Presa alimentada por tres quebradas 190-191 C 6
Presa Lázaro Cárdenas 154-155 C 8
Prescott 148-149 F 2
Prescott, AR 154-155 J 4
Prescott, AZ 146-147 D 5
Prescott, WI 152-153 K 3
Presho, SD 152-153 FG 4
Presidencia Roque Saenz Peña 162 D 3
Presidente Alves 160-161 GH 5
Presidente Bernardes 160-161 G 4-5
Presidente Dutra 158-159 L 6
Presidente Epitácio 158-159 J 9
Presidente Hayes 160-161 CD 5
Presidente Hermes 158-159 G 7
Presidente Murtinho 160-161 F 1
Presidente Olegário 160-161 J 3
Presidente Prudente 158-159 J 9
Presidente Venceslau 160-161 FG 4
Presidio, TX 146-147 F 6
Prešov 133 K 4
Prespansko Ezero 136-137 J 5
Presque Isle, ME 146-147 N 2
Presque Isle Point 152-153 N 2
Preßburg = Bratislava 133 H 4
Prestea 166-167 D 7
Preston 132 E 5
Preston, CA 150-151 B 6
Preston, ID 150-151 H 4
Preston, MN 152-153 KL 4
Preston, MO 152-153 K 7
Prestonsburg, KY 148-149 B 6
Prestwick 132 DE 4
Prešov 133 K 4
Preto, Rio - [BR ◁ Rio Grande] 158-159 K 7
Preto, Rio - [BR ◁ Rio Paracatu] 158-159 K 8
Preto, Rio - [BR ◁ Rio Paraíba] 160-161 L 5
Preto, Rio - [BR ◁ Rio Paranaíba] 160-161 G 3
Pretoria 168-169 G 8
Pretoriuskop 174-175 J 3
Pretty Prairie, KS 152-153 GH 7
Preußisch Eylau = Bagrationovsk 133 K 1
Preußisch Stargard = Starogard Gdański 133 HJ 2
Prey Veng 186-187 E 4
Priargunsk 178-179 WX 7
Pribilof Islands 120 D 35-36
Příbram 133 G 4
Pribrežnyj chrebet 178-179 Za 6
Price, UT 146-147 D 4
Price River 150-151 H 6
Prichard, AL 146-147 J 5
Prichard, ID 150-151 EF 2
Prič'ornomorskaja nizmennost' 140-141 E-G 2-3
Pridneprovskaja nizmennost' 140-141 E-G 1-2
Pridneprovskaja vozvyšennost' 140-141 D-G 2
Priego de Córdoba 134-135 E 10
Priekulė 138-139 C 6
Prienai 138-139 DE 6
Prieska 168-169 F 8
Priest Lake 150-151 E 1
Priest Rapids Reservoir 150-151 CD 2
Priest River, ID 150-151 E 1
Prijedor 136-137 G 3
Prijutnoje 140-141 L 3
Prijutovo 138-139 T 7
Prikaspijskaja nizmennost' 140-141 M 4-Q 2
Prikolotnoje 140-141 H 1
Prikubanskaja nizmennost' 140-141 J 4
Prikumsk = Budennovsk 140-141 LM 4
Prilep 136-137 J 5
Primeiro de Maio 160-161 G 5
Primghar, IA 152-153 J 4
Primorsk 130-131 N 7
Primorsk [SU, Azerbajdžanskaja SSR] 140-141 O 6
Primorsk [SU, Rossijskaja SFSR Karjala] 138-139 G 3
Primorsk [SU, Ukrainskaja SSR] 140-141 H 3
Primorsko-Achtarsk 140-141 HJ 3
Primorskoje 138-139 FG 3
Primorskij chrebet 178-179 TU 7
Prince Albert 144-145 P 7
Prince Albert Mountains 121 B 16-17
Prince Albert National Park 144-145 P 7
Prince Albert Peninsula 144-145 NO 3
Prince Albert Road = Prins Albertweg 174-175 D 7
Prince Albert Sound 144-145 NO 3
Prince Alfred, Cape - 144-145 KL 3
Prince Alfred's Hamlet = Prins Alfred Hamlet 174-175 CD 7
Prince Charles Island 144-145 V 4
Prince Charles Range 121 B 7
Prince Edward Bay 148-149 E 2-3
Prince Edward Island 144-145 Y 8
Prince Edward Islands 121 E 4
Prince Edward Peninsula 148-149 E 2-3
Prince Frederick, MD 148-149 E 5
Prince George 144-145 M 7
Prince Gustaf Adolf Sea 144-145 P 2
Prince Charles Island 144-145 V 4
Prince Charles Range 121 B 7
Prince Island = Pulau Panaitan 186-187 DE 8
Prince of Wales, Cape - 144-145 C 4-5
Prince of Wales Island [AUS] 194-195 H 2
Prince of Wales Island [CDN] 144-145 QR 3
Prince of Wales Island [USA] 144-145 JK 6
Prince of Wales Island = Wales Island 144-145 T 4
Prince of Wales Strait 144-145 N 3
Prince Patrick Island 144-145 M 2
Prince Regent Inlet 144-145 ST 3
Prince Rupert 144-145 KL 7
Princess Anne, MD 148-149 F 5
Princess Charlotte Bay 194-195 H 2
Princess Elizabeth Land 121 BC 8-9
Princess Charlotte Bay 194-195 H 2
Princess Royal Island 144-145 L 7
Princeton, CA 150-151 BC 6
Princeton, IA 152-153 K 5
Princeton, IL 152-153 M 5
Princeton, IN 152-153 N 6
Princeton, KY 154-155 M 2
Princeton, MI 152-153 N 2
Princeton, MN 152-153 K 3
Princeton, NJ 148-149 F 4
Princeton, WI 152-153 M 4
Princeton, WV 148-149 C 6
Prince William Sound 144-145 G 5
Príncipe, Ilha do - 166-167 F 8
Príncipe da Baira 158-159 G 7
Prineville, OR 150-151 C 3
Pringle, SD 152-153 E 4
Prins Albert 174-175 E 7
Prins Albertweg 174-175 D 7
Prins Alfred Hamlet 174-175 CD 7
Prins Christian Sund 144-145 c 5-d 6
Prinsesse Astrid land 121 B 1-2
Prinsesse Ragnhild land 121 B 3
Prins Harald land 121 B 4-C 5
Prins Christian Sund 144-145 c 5-d 6
Prinzregent-Luitpold-Land 121 B 33-34
Priokskij 138-139 M 6
Prior, Cabo - 134-135 C 7
Priozersk = Prioz'orsk 178-179 DE 5
Prioz'orsk 178-179 DE 5
Prip'at' 138-139 G 8
Pripet = Prip'at' 138-139 G 8
Pripjetsümpfe = Polesje 138-139 E 8-H 7
Pripol'arnyj Ural 178-179 KL 4-5
Prišib 140-141 O 7
Prišib = Leninsk 140-141 M 2
Pristen' 140-141 H 1
Priština 136-137 J 4
Pritchett, CO 152-153 E 7
Privas 134-135 K 6
Priverno 136-137 E 5
Privetnoje 140-141 G 4
Prividencia, Isla de - 158-159 C 2
Privodino 138-139 PQ 3
Privol'noje 140-141 EF 3
Privolžje 138-139 R 7
Privolžskaja vozvyšennost' 138-139 P 8-Q 6
Privolžskij 140-141 NO 3
Privolžskoje 140-141 MN 1
Privolžsk 138-139 N 5
Prizren 136-137 J 4
Probolinggo 186-187 F 8
Prochladnyj 140-141 LM 5
Proctor, TX 154-155 F 4-5
Proddattūru = Proddatur 180-181 M 8
Proddatur 180-181 M 8
Professor Dr. Ir. W. J. van Blommesteinmeer 158-159 H 4
Progreso [MEX, Yucatán] 146-147 J 7
Progreso [MEX, Coahuila] 154-155 E 7
Progreso [RA] 162 D 4
Progreso, El - [Honduras] 146-147 J 8
Projeto Carajás 158-159 JK 6
Prokopjevsk 178-179 Q 7
Prōkuls = Priekulė 138-139 C 6
Prokuplje 136-137 J 4
Proletarij 138-139 H 4
Proletarsk 140-141 KL 3
Proletarskij [SU, Belgorod] 140-141 GH 1
Proletarskij [SU, Moskva] 138-139 L 6
Prome = Pyin 186-187 C 3
Promissão 160-161 H 4
Promissao, Represa de - 160-161 H 4
Promyslovka 188-189 J 1
Pron'a [SU, ~ ◁ Oka] 138-139 N 6
Pron'a [SU, ~ ◁ Sož] 138-139 H 7
Prončiščeva, bereg - 178-179 UV 2-3
Pronsk 138-139 M 6
Propriá 158-159 M 7
Propriano 136-137 C 5
Pros'anaja 140-141 H 2
Proserpine 194-195 J 4
Proskurov = Chmel'nickij 140-141 C 2
Prosna 133 J 3
Prospect, OR 150-151 B 4
Prosser, WA 150-151 D 2
Prostějov 133 H 4
Protection, KS 154-155 F 2
Protem 174-175 D 8
Protva 138-139 L 6
Provadija 136-137 M 4
Provence 134-135 K 7-L 6
Providence, KY 152-153 N 7
Providence, RI 146-147 MN 3
Providence, Cape - [NZ] 194-195 MN 9
Providence Island 168-169 M 4
Providence Mountains 150-151 F 8
Providencia 146-147 KL 9
Providenija 144-145 B 5
Provincetown, MA 148-149 HJ 3
Provins 134-135 J 4
Provo, SD 152-153 E 4
Provo, UT 146-147 D 3
Provost 144-145 O 7
Pru 172-173 D 7
Prudentópolis 160-161 G 6
Prudenville, MI 152-153 O 3
Prudhoe Bay [CDN, ●] 144-145 G 3
Prudhoe Land 144-145 XY 2
Prüm 133 C 3
Průsa = Bursa 180-181 B 2-3
Pruszków 133 K 2
Prut [SU, ~] 140-141 C 3
Prut [SU, ●] 140-141 D 3
Pruth 136-137 N 3
Pruth = Prut 140-141 C 2
Pružany 138-139 E 7
Pryluki 140-141 F 1
Pryor, OK 154-155 H 2
Pryor Creek 152-153 B 3
Pryor Mountains 152-153 B 3
Prypeć = Prip'at 138-139 G 8
Przemyśl 133 L 4
Przeworsk 133 L 3
Prževal'sk 180-181 M 2
Prževal'skoje 138-139 HJ 6
Psará 136-137 L 6
Psérimos 136-137 M 7
Psiol = Ps'ol 140-141 F 2
Pskov 138-139 G 5
Pskovskoje ozero 138-139 FG 4-5
Pskow = Pskov 138-139 G 5
Ps'ol 140-141 F 2
Pszczyna 133 J 3-4
Ptič' 138-139 FG 7
Ptolemaïs 136-137 J 5
Ptuj 136-137 FG 2
Pubei 190-191 B 10
Pucallpa 158-159 E 6
Pucarani 158-159 F 8
Pučež 138-139 O 5
Puchang Hai = Lob nuur 184-185 G 3
Pucheng [TJ, Fujian] 184-185 M 6
Pucheng [TJ, Shaanxi] 184-185 KL 4-5
Pucheng [TJ, Shandong] 190-191 E 4
Puchi = Puqi 184-185 L 6
P'u-chiang = Pujiang 190-191 G 7
Puck 133 J 1
Pūdāō 186-187 C 1
Pudasjärvi 130-131 M 5
Pudem 138-139 T 4
Pudimoe 174-175 F 4
Pudino 178-179 OP 6
Pudož 178-179 F 5
Puebla [MEX, ●] 146-147 G 8
Puebla, La - 134-135 J 9
Puebla de Sanabria 134-135 D 7
Puebla de Zaragoza 146-147 G 8
Pueblo, CO 146-147 F 4
Pueblo Bonito, NM 154-155 AB 2-3

atka, Wādī ar- = Wādī ar-Ratqah 182-183 J 5-6
atlam 180-181 LM 6
atnagiri [IND, Maharashtra] 180-181 L 7
atno 138-139 E 8
atō = Lo-tung 190-191 HJ 9
aton, NM 146-147 F 4
atqah, Wād ar- 182-183 J 5-6
attlesnake Creek 152-153 G 7
attlesnake Range 152-153 C 4
ättvik 130-131 F 7
atyzbona = Regensburg 133 EF 4
aualpindi = Rāwalpinḍi 180-181 L 4
auch 162 E 5
audhamelur 130-131 bc 2
audhatayn 182-183 M 8
aufarhöfn 130-131 f 1
aul Soares 160-161 L 4
auma 130-131 J 7
aumo = Rauma 130-131 J 7
aurkela = Rourkela 180-181 NO 6
ausu 188-189 d 1-2
avalli, MT 150-151 F 2
avalpindi = Rāwalpinḍi 180-181 L 4
avānsar 182-183 M 5
āvar 180-181 H 4
ava-Russkaja 140-141 AB 1
avena = Ravenna 136-137 E 3
avena = Raven... 136-137 E 3
avendale, CA 150-151 CD 5
avenna, NE 152-153 G ...
avenna, OH 148-149 C 4
avenne = Ravenna 136-137 E 3
avensburg 133 D 5
avenshoe 194-195 HJ 3
avensthorpe 194-195 D 6
avenswood, WV 148-149 C 5
āvi 180-181 L 4
āwah 182-183 JK 5
āwalpinḍi 180-181 L 4
awa Mazowiecka 133 K 3
awāndūz 182-183 L 4
awḍah, Ar- 170 D 4
awenna = Ravenna 136-137 E 3
aw Hide Butte 152-153 D 4
awi, 'Irq ar- 166-167 D 3
awicz 133 H 3
awitsch = Rawicz 133 H 3
awlinna 194-195 E 6
awlins, WY 146-147 E 3
awlinson Range 194-195 E 4-5
awson [RA, Chubut] 162 CD 6
awwāfah, Ar- 170 G 4
ay, MN 152-153 H 1
ay, ND 152-153 E 1
ay, Cape - 144-145 Z 8
aya, Bukit - 186-187 F 7
ayachuru = Raichur 180-181 M 7
ayāq 182-183 G 6
āyāt 182-183 L 4
ayāytt, Wādī - 170 F 6
āy Barēlī = Rae Bareli 180-181 N 5
aydat aṣ-Ṣay'ar 180-181 F 7
āygarh = Raigarh 180-181 N 6
aymond, CA 150-151 D 7
aymond, IL 152-153 M 6
aymond, MS 154-155 K 4
aymond, MT 152-153 D 1
aymond, WA 150-151 B 2
aymond Terrace 196 KL 4
aymondville, TX 146-147 G 6
ay Mountains 144-145 F 4
ayne, LA 154-155 J 5
aynesford, MT 150-151 H 2
ayong 186-187 D 4
āypur = Raipur [IND, Madhya Pradesh] 180-181 N 6
ayton 174-175 H 3
ayville, LA 154-155 JK 4
az, Pointe du - 134-135 E 4
āzān [IR, Bākhtarān] 182-183 N 5
azan [IR, Lorestān] 182-183 N 6
'azan' [SU] 138-139 M 6
'azancevo 138-139 M 5
azazah, Hawr ar- 182-183 KL 6
azdan 140-141 M 6
azdel'naja 140-141 E 3
azdolinsk 178-179 R 6
azdol'noje 140-141 F 4
azeh 182-183 N 6
azelm, Lacul - 136-137 N 3
azgrad 136-137 M 4
'ažsk 138-139 N 7
'dayif, Ar- = Ar-Rudayyif 166-167 F2
é, Île de - 134-135 G 5
eading [GB] 132 F 6
eading, PA 146-147 L 3
ead Island 144-145 O 4
eal del Castillo 150-151 E 9-10
ealengo, Rio de Janeiro- 160-161 L 5
ealeza 160-161 L 4
ealicó 162 CD 4-5
ealitos, TX 154-155 F 7
éam 186-187 D 4
éao 192-193 O 6
eata 154-155 E 7
ebbenesøy 130-131 GH 2
ebbo 172-173 C 4
ebeca, Lagoa da - 160-161 BC 1
ebecca, Lake - 194-195 D 6
ebia, Umm er - = Nahr Umm ar-abī' 166-167 C 2
ebiāna = Ribyānah 166-167 J 4
eboledo 162 EF 4
eboly 138-139 H 2
ebouças 160-161 G 6
ebun-jima 184-185 QR 2
ecalde 162 D 5
echerche, Archipelago of the 194-195 D 6
echerche, Archipel de la 194-195 D 6
echō Taung 186-187 C 4
echt = Rasht 180-181 FG 3
ečica 138-139 H 7
ecife 158-159 N 6
ecife, Cape - = Kaap Recife 174-175 FG 8
ecife, Kaap - 174-174 FG 8
econquista 162 DE 3
ecreio 160-161 L 4
ecreo [RA, La Rioja] 162 CD 3
ector, AR 154-155 K 2
ečyra 138-139 GH 7
edā'iyeh = Orūmiyeh 180-181 EF 3
edā'iyeh, Daryācheh - = Urmia 180-181 F 3
ed Bank, NJ 148-149 F 4
ed Bay, TN 154-155 LM 3
ed Bluff, CA 146-147 B 3
ed Bluff Lake 154-155 CD 5
ed Bluff Reservoir = Red Bluff Lake 154-155 CD 5
ed Bud, IL 152-153 LM 6
ed Butte 150-151 GH 8
Redby, MN 152-153 J 2
Redcliffe, Brisbane- 194-195 K 5
Red Cliffs 196 F 5
Red Cloud, NE 152-153 G 5
Redd City, MI 152-153 O 4
Red Deer 144-145 O 7
Red Deer River [CDN, Alberta] 144-145 07
Reddersburg 174-175 G 5
Red Desert 152-153 B 4-5
Reddick, FL 148-149 b 2
Redding, CA 146-147 B 3
Reddit 152-153 J 1
Redd Peak 152-153 D 4
Redelinghuis = Redelinghuys 174-175 C 7
Redelinghuys 174-175 C 7
Redenção da Serra 160-161 K 5
Redeyef, Er - = Ar-R'dayif 166-167 F2
Redfield, AR 154-155 J 3
Redfield, SD 152-153 G 3
Red Hill 194-195 HJ 7
Red Hills [USA, Alabama] 146-147 J 5
Red Hills [USA, Kansas] 152-153 G 7
Red House, NV 150-151 E 5
Redig, SD 152-153 E 3
Red Lake [USA] 146-147 G 2
Red Lake [CDN, ●] 144-145 S 7
Red Lake Falls, MN 152-153 HJ 2
Red Lake Indian Reservation 152-153 J 1-2
Red Lake River 152-153 H 1-2
Redlands, CA 150-151 E 8-9
Red Lion, PA 148-149 E 5
Red Lodge, MT 152-153 B 3
Redmond, OR 150-151 C 3
Red Mountain [USA, California] 150-151 B 5
Red Mountain [USA, Montana] 150-151 G 2
Red Mountain, CA 150-151 E 8
Rednitz 133 E 4
Red Oak, IA 152-153 J 5
Redon 134-135 F 5
Redonda, Ponta - 158-159 M 5
Redondela 134-135 C 7
Redondo Beach, CA 150-151 D 9
Red River 146-147 H 5
Red River of the North 146-147 G 2
Redrock, AZ 150-151 H 9
Redrock, NM 150-151 J 9
Red Rock, OK 154-155 G 2
Red Rocks Point 194-195 E 6
Red Sea [≈] 180-181 D 5-7
Red Sea [≈] 166-167 LM 5
Red Springs, NC 148-149 D 7
Redstone, MT 152-153 D 1
Red Tank 146-147 b 2
Redvandeh 182-183 N 4
Red Volta 172-173 E 3
Redwater Creek 152-153 D 2
Red Willow Creek 152-153 F 5
Red Wing, MN 152-153 K 3
Redwood City, CA 150-151 B 7
Redwood Falls, MN 152-153 J 3
Redwood National Park 150-151 A 5
Redwood Valley, CA 150-151 B 6
Ree, Lough - 132 C 5
Reece, KS 152-153 H 7
Reed City, MI 148-149 A 3
Reeder, ND 152-153 E 2
Reedley, CA 150-151 D 7
Reedpoint, MT 152-153 B 3
Reedsburg, WI 152-153 LM 4
Reedsport, OR 150-151 AB 4
Reefton 194-195 O 8
Reese, MI 152-153 P 4
Reese River 150-151 E 6
Refā'ī, Ar- = Ar-Rifā'ī 182-183 M 7
Refaniye 182-183 H 3
Reform, AL 154-155 LM 4
Refugio, TX 154-155 G 6
Regen 133 F 4
Regência 158-159 M 8
Regência, Ponta de - 158-159 M 8
Regensburg 133 EF 4
Regent, ND 152-153 E 2
Regente Feijó 160-161 G 5
Reggane = Rijān 166-167 E 3
Règgio di Calàbria 136-137 FG 6
Règgio nell'Emilia 136-137 D 3
Regina [CDN] 144-145 Q 7
Regina Elisabetta, Ìsole - 144-145 N-V 2
Régina [Französisch-Guyana] 158-159 J 4
Regina, MT 152-153 C 2
Registan = Rīgestān 180-181 JK 4
Registro 162 G 2
Registro do Araguaia 160-161 FG 1-2
Regresso, Cachoeira 158-159 HJ 5
Reguengos de Monsaraz 134-135 D 9
Reh 184-185 M 3
Rehoboth 168-169 E 7
Rehoboth Beach, DE 148-149 F 5
Rehovot 182-183 F 7
Rei = Rey 182-183 O 5
Reichenberg = Liberec 133 G 3
Reichle, MT 150-151 G 3
Reid 194-195 E 6
Reidsville, NC 148-149 D 6
Reigate 132 FG 6
Reihoku 188-189 GH 6
Reims 134-135 JK 4
Reina Adelaida, Archipiélago 162 AB 8
Reina Isabel, Islas de la 144-145 N-U 2
Reina Maud, Banco de la 121 C 1
Reinbeck, IA 152-153 K 4
Reindeer Lake 144-145 Q 6
Reine Elizabeth, Îles de la - 144-145 N-U 2
Reinosa 134-135 E 7
Reino Unido da Grã Bretanha e Irlanda do Norte 126-127 F-H 4
Reino Unido de Gran Bretaña e Irlanda del Norte 132 F-H 4-5
Reinøy 130-131 H 2-3
Reiquejavique = Reykjavik 126-127 DE 3
Reisa 130-131 J 3
Reitz 174-175 H 4
Rejaf = Rijāf 171 B 1
Relem, Cerro - 162 B 5
Reliance, SD 152-153 G 4
Reliance, WY 150-151 J 5
Rélizane = Ghālizān 166-167 E 1
Rellano 154-155 C 7
Remansão 158-159 JK 5
Remanso 158-159 L 6
Remarkable, Mount - 194-195 G 6
Rembate = Lielvārde 138-139 E 5
Remédios [BR, Fernando de Noronha] 158-159 N 5
Remer, MN 152-153 K 2
Remeshk 180-181 H 5
Remington, IN 152-153 N 5
Remington, VA 148-149 E 5
Rémire 158-159 J 3-4
Remiremont 134-135 KL 4
Remontnaja = Dubovskoje 140-141 L 3
Remontnoje 140-141 L 3
Remote, OR 150-151 B 4
Rems 133 D 4
Remscheid 133 C 3
Remsen, NY 148-149 F 3
Remus, MI 152-153 O 4
Rena 130-131 D 7
Renas, Lago das - 144-145 Q 6
Renascença 158-159 F 6
Rendova Island 186-187 j 6
Rendsburg 133 DE 1
Rënëia 136-137 L 7
Rengat 186-187 D 7
Ren He 190-191 B 5
Renhua 190-191 D 9
Reni 140-141 D 4
Reniferowe, Jezioro - 144-145 Q 6
Renju 190-191 E 9
Renk = Al-Rank 166-167 L 6
Renmark 194-195 H 6
Renne, Lago delle - 144-145 Q 6
Rennell Island 186-187 k 7
Rennes 134-135 G 4
Rennick Glacier 121 C 16-17
Reno [I] 136-137 DE 3
Reno, ID 150-151 G 3
Reno, NV 146-147 C 4
Renohill, WY 152-153 C 4
Renos, Lago de los - 144-145 Q 6
Renosterkop [ZA, ▲] 174-175 H 3
Renosterkop [ZA, ●] 174-175 E 7
Renosterrivier [ZA, ~ ◁ Groot Visrivier] 174-175 D 6
Renosterrivier [ZA, ~ ◁ Vaalrivier] 174-175 G 4
Renoville, CA 150-151 EF 8
Renovo, PA 148-149 E 4
Renqiu 184-185 M 4
Rensselaer, IN 152-153 N 5
Rensselaer, NY 148-149 FG 3
Renszarvas-tó 144-145 Q 6
Rentiersee 144-145 Q 6
Renton, WA 150-151 B 2
Renville, MN 152-153 J 3
Ren Xian 190-191 E 3
Reo 186-187 H 8
Repjevka 140-141 J 1
Repki 138-139 H 8
Repola = Reboly 138-139 H 2
Repubblica Centrafricana 166-167 HJ 7
Repubblica Dominicana 146-147 MN 7-8
Republic, MI 152-153 N 2
Republic, MO 154-155 J 2
Republic, WA 150-151 D 1
República Centroafricana 166-167 HJ 7
República Centro-Africana 166-167 HJ 7
Republica Ceca 126-127 LM 6
Republika Ceka 133 F-H 4
Republika Cheka 133 F-H 4
República Dominicana 146-147 MN 7-8
Republican River 146-147 G 3
République Centrafricaine 166-167 HJ7
République Dominicaine 146-147 MN 7-8
République Tchèque 133 F-H 4
Repulse Bay [AUS] 194-195 JK 4
Repulse Bay [CDN, ◡] 144-145 T 4
Repulse Bay [CDN, ●] 144-145 TU 4
Repunshiri = Rebun-jima 188-189 b 1
Reqi = Ruoxi 190-191 E 7
Requena [PE] 158-159 E 6
Requena 134-135 G 9
Reşadiye [TR, Bitlis] 182-183 K 3
Reşadiye [TR, Muğla] 182-183 B 4
Reşadiye [TR, Tokat] 182-183 G 2
Reşadiye Yarimadasi 182-183 BC 4
Reşâfe, Er- = Risāfah 182-183 H 5
Resa'iya = Orūmiyeh 180-181 EF 3
Reschenpaß 133 E 5
Resende [BR] 160-161 K 5
Resende Costa 160-161 K 4
Reserva 160-161 G 6
Reserve, NM 150-151 J 9
Rešetilovka 140-141 FG 2
Rešety 138-139 G 5
Resht = Rasht 180-181 FG 3
Resistencia 162 DE 3
Reşiţa 136-137 J 3
Resolute 144-145 S 3
Resolution Island 144-145 Y 5
Resplendor 160-161 M 3
Rethel 134-135 K 4
Réthymnon 136-137 L 8
Retowo = Rietavas 138-139 C 6
Reunion 168-169 N 7
Réunion 168-169 N 7
Reunião 165 M 11
Reus 134-135 H 8
Reuss 133 D 5
Reut 140-141 D 3
Reutersbron 174-175 A 3
Reutersbrunn = Reutersbron 174-175 A 3
Reut 136-137 N 2
Reutlingen 133 D 4
Reva, SD 152-153 E 3
Revā = Narmada 180-181 LM 6
Reval = Tallinn 178-179 CD 5
Revda [SU, Srednij Ural] 178-179 KL 6
Revelstoke 144-145 N 7
Revillagigedo, Islas de - 146-147 D 8
Revillagigedo Island 144-145 KL 6
Revillo, SD 152-153 H 3
Révivim 182-183 F 7
Revoil-Beni-Ounif = Bani Wanif 166-167 D 2
Rewā = Narmada 180-181 LM 6
Rewda = Revda 178-179 KL 6
Rex, Mount - 121 B 29
Rexburg, ID 150-151 H 4
Rexford, MT 150-151 F 1
Rexford, ID 152-153 O 2
Rexton, MI 152-153 O 2
Rey, Isla del - 146-147 L 10
Reydon, OK 154-155 F 3
Reyes, Point - 150-151 B 6-7
Reyhanli 182-183 G 4
Reykhólar 130-131 b 2
Reykholt 130-131 c 2
Reykjanes 130-131 b 3
Reykjanes, Crista de - 124-125 M 2-3
Reykjanes, Dorsal de - 124-125 H 2-3
Reykjanes, Dorsale - 124-125 H 2-3
Reykjanes, Seuil de - 124-125 H 2-3
Reykjanes Ridge 124-125 H 2-3
Reykjanesrücken 124-125 H 2-3
Reykjanesrug 124-125 H 2-3
Reykjavík 130-131 bc 2
Reynolds, ID 150-151 E 4
Reynolds, IN 152-153 N 5
Reynolds Range 194-195 F 4
Reynoldsville, PA 148-149 D 4
Reynosa 146-147 G 6
Rezā'iyeh = Orūmiyeh 180-181 EF 3
Rēzekne 138-139 F 6
Rezina 140-141 D 3
Rhein 133 C 3
Rheine 133 C 2
Rheinland-Pfalz 133 CD 3-4
Rhenosterkop = Renosterkop 174-175 E 7
Rhenoster River = Renosterrivier 174-175 D 6
Rhin = Rhein 133 C 3
Rhinelander, WI 152-153 M 3
Rhine = Rhein 133 C 3
Rhino Camp 168-169 H 2
Rhode Island [USA, ☉] 148-149 H 4
Rhode Island [USA, ✲] 146-147 MN 3
Rhodes 174-175 G 6
Rhodesdrif 174-175 H 2
Rhodopē 136-137 KL 5
Rhodope 136-137 KL 5
Rhodope Mountains 136-137 KL 5
Rhodopen 136-137 KL 5
Rhön 133 DE 3
Rhondda 132 E 6
Rhone [CH] 133 C 5
Rhône [F] 134-135 K 6
Rhône au Rhin, Canal du - 134-135 L 4-5
Riaad = Ar-Riyāḍ 180-181 F 6
Riachão 158-159 K 6
Riad = Ar-Riyāḍ 180-181 F 6
Riad, Er- = Ar-Riyāḍ 180-181 F 6
Riade = Ar-Riyāḍ 180-181 F 6
Riang 180-181 P 5
Riau = 4 ◁ 186-187 D6
Riau, Kepulauan - 186-187 DE 6
Ribacsij-félsziget = poluostrov Rybačij 178-179 EF 4
Ribadeo 134-135 D 7
Ribas do Rio Pardo 158-159 J 9
Ribāṭ, Ar- 166-167 C 2
Ribatejo 134-135 C 9
Ribauè 168-169 J 5-6
Ribe 130-131 C 10
Ribeira 134-135 C 7
Ribeira [BR] 160-161 H 6
Ribeira do Iguape, Rio - 160-161 H 6
Ribeirão [BR, Pernambuco] 158-159 MN 6
Ribeirão [BR, Rondônia] 158-159 FG 7
Ribeirão Bonito 160-161 HJ 5
Ribeirão Branco 160-161 H 6
Ribeirão Claro 160-161 H 5
Ribeirão do Pinhal 160-161 G 5
Ribeirão Preto 158-159 K 9
Ribeirão Vermelho 160-161 K 4
Ribeirinha, Rio - 160-161 H 6
Ribeiro Gonçalves 158-159 KL 6
Riberalta 158-159 F 7
Rib Lake, WI 152-153 LM 3
Ribyānah 166-167 J 4
Ribyānah, Ṣaḥrā' - 166-167 J 4
Riccione 136-137 E 3-4
Rice, CA 150-151 F 8
Riceboro, GA 148-149 C 9
Rice Lake 148-149 DE 2
Rice Lake, WI 152-153 L 3
Richardsbaai 174-175 K 5
Richard's Bay 168-169 H 8
Richards Bay = Richardsbaai 174-175 K 5
Richardson Mountains 144-145 J 4
Richardton, ND 152-153 EF 2
Richey, MT 152-153 D 2
Richfield, ID 150-151 FG 4
Richfield, KS 152-153 F 7
Richfield, MN 152-153 K 3
Richfield, UT 150-151 GH 6
Richford, VT 148-149 G 2
Richgrove, CA 150-151 D 8
Rich Hill, MO 152-153 J 6
Richland, GA 154-155 N 4
Richland, MO 152-153 K 7
Richland, MT 152-153 C 1
Richland, WA 146-147 C 2
Richland Balsam 148-149 B 7
Richland Center, WI 152-153 LM 4
Richlands, VA 148-149 C 6
Richland Springs, TX 154-155 F 5
Richmond [AUS] 194-195 H 4
Richmond [ZA, Kaapland] 168-169 F 9
Richmond [ZA, Natal] 168-169 G 9-H 8
Richmond, CA 146-147 B 4
Richmond, IN 146-147 JK 3-4
Richmond, KS 152-153 J 6
Richmond, KY 152-153 O 7
Richmond, MO 152-153 JK 6
Richmond, TX 154-155 GH 6
Richmond, VA 146-147 L 4
Richmond Gulf 144-145 V 6
Richmond Hill, GA 148-149 C 9
Rich Mountain 154-155 H 3
Richtberg 174-175 B 4
Richtersveld 174-175 B 5
Richton, MS 154-155 L 5
Richwood, OH 152-153 P 5
Richwood, WV 148-149 C 5
Rico, CO 152-153 BC 7
Ridder = Leninogorsk 178-179 P 7
Riddle, ID 150-151 EF 4
Riddle, OR 150-151 B 4
Rideau Lake 148-149 E 2
Ridgecrest, CA 150-151 E 8
Ridgeland, SC 148-149 C 8
Ridgely, TN 154-155 L 2
Ridgetown 148-149 C 3
Ridgeway, SC 148-149 C 7
Ridgway, CO 152-153 BC 6
Ridgway, PA 148-149 D 4
Riding Mountain National Park 70-71 Q 7
Ridisiya, Er- = Ar-Radisiyat Bahri 170 E 5
Ridvan = Alenz 182-183 J 4
Riebeek-Wes 174-175 C 7
Riebeek West = Riebeek-Wes 174-175 C 7
Riekertsdam 174-175 G 3
Riesa 33 F 3
Riesco, Isla - 162 B 8
Riesengebirge 133 GH 3
Riesi 136-137 F 7
Rietavas 138-139 C 6
Rietbron 174-175 E 7
Rietfontein 168-169 F 8
Rieth, OR 150-151 D 3
Rieti 136-137 E 4
Rietkuil 174-175 H 4
Rietrivier 174-175 F 5
Rif = Ar-Rif 166-167 CD 1-2
Rif, Ar- 166-167 CD 1-2
Rif, er - = Ar-Rif 166-167 CD 1-2
Rifā'ī, Ar- 182-183 M 7
Rifle, CO 152-153 C 6
Rifstangi 130-131 ef 1
Rift Valley 168-169 J 2
Riga 130-131 KL 9
Riga 138-139 E 5
Riga, Golfe d' = Rigas Jūŗas Licis 130-131 KL 9
Riga, Golfe de - = Rigas Jūŗas Licis 138-139 DE 5
Riga, Golfo de - = Rigas Jūŗas Licis 138-139 DE 5
Riga, Golf van - = Rigas Jūŗas Licis 138-139 DE 5
Riga, Gulf of - = Rigas Jūŗas Licis 138-139 DE 5
Rigaer Bucht = Rigas Jūŗas Licis 138-139 DE 5
Rigaer Meerbusen = Rigas Jūŗas Licis 138-139 DE 5
Rigai-öböl = Rigas Jūŗas Licis 138-139 DE 5
Rigas Jūŗas Licis 138-139 DE 5
Rigby, ID 150-151 H 4
Rigestān 180-181 JK 4
Riggins, ID 150-151 E 3
Rigo 186-187 N 8
Rigolet 144-145 Z 7
Rihāb, Ar- 182-183 L 7
Riihimäki 130-131 L 7
Riiser-Larsen halvøy 121 C 4-5
Rijād = Ar-Riyāḍ 180-181 F 6
Rijadh = Ar-Riyāḍ 180-181 F 6
Rijāf 171 B 1
Rijān 166-167 E 3
Rijeka 136-137 F 3
Rijpfjord 130-131 l 4
Rikeze = Zhigatse 184-185 F 6
Rikorda, ostrov - 188-189 H 1
Riksgränsen 130-131 GH 3
Rikubetsu 188-189 c 2
Rikuzen-Takada 188-189 NO 3
Rila 136-137 K 4-5
Rilay, KS 152-153 H 6
Riley, KS 152-153 H 6
Rim, Bi'r - 170 B 2
Rimah, Wādī ar- 180-181 E 5
Rimāl, Ar- = Ar-Rub, al-Khālī 180-181 F 7-G 6
Rimatara 192-193 M 7
Rimini 136-137 E 3
Rimouski 144-145 X 8
Rim Rocky Mountains 150-151 C 4
Rim = Roma 136-137 E 4
Rin = Rhein 133 C 3
Rinca, Pulau - 186-187 G 8
Rincão 160-161 HJ 4
Rincon, NM 154-155 B 4
Rinconada 162 C 2
Rincon Peak 154-155 C 3
Rin'gang = Riāng 180-181 P 5
Ringerike-Hønefoss 130-131 CD 7
Ringgold, LA 154-155 J 4
Ringgold, TX 154-155 G 4
Ringim 172-173 H 2
Ringkøbing 130-131 BC 9
Ringling, MT 150-151 H 2
Ringling, OK 154-155 G 3
Ringold, OK 154-155 H 3
Ringvassøy 130-131 H 3
Ringwood, OK 154-155 F 2
Riñihue [RCH, ●] 162 B 5-6
Rinjani, Gunung - 186-187 G 8
Rio Abajo 146-147 bc 2
Rio Acima 160-161 L 4
Rio Alegre [BE, ~] 160-161 C 1
Rio Alegre [BE, ●] 160-161 D 2
Rio Azul [BR, Paraná] 160-161 G 6
Riobamba 158-159 D 5
Rio Blanco [BR] 158-159 G 7
Rio Bonito 160-161 L 5
Rio Branco [BR, Amazonas] 158-159 F 6
Rio Branco [BR, Mato Grosso do Sul] 160-161 D 4
Rio Branco [BR, Rio Branco] 158-159 G 4-5
Rio Branco do Sul 160-161 H 6
Rio Bravo 154-155 E 6
Rio Bravo del Norte 146-147 E 5-F 6
Rio Casca 160-161 L 4
Rio Chico [RA, Santa Cruz ●] 162 C7
Rio Claro [BR, Mato Grosso] 160-161 D 2
Rio Claro [BR, São Paulo] 160-161 J 5
Rio Claro [TT] 146-147 O 9
Rio Claro [BR, Goiás ◁ Rio Araguaia] 158-159 J 8
Rio Claro [BR, Goiás ◁ Rio Paranaíba] 158-159 J 8
Rio Claro, Serra do - 160-161 G 2
Rio Cuarto [RA, ●] 162 D 4
Rio Chico [RA, Santa Cruz ●] 162 C 7
Rio das Antas [BR, ●] 160-161 G 7
Rio das Pedras [Moçambique] 174-175 L 2
Rio das Pedras [BR, ●] 160-161 J 5
Rio de Janeiro [BR, ●] 158-159 L 9
Rio de Janeiro [BR, ✲] 158-159 LM 9
Rio do Sul 162 G 3
Rioekioetreog 184-185 O 7-P 6
Rio Grande [BR, Minas Gerais] 158-159 K 8-9
Rio Grande [BR, Rio Grande do Sul] 162 F 4
Rio Grande [BOL, ~] 158-159 G 8
Rio Grande [MEX] 146-147 H 8
Rio Grande [NIC, ~] 146-147 JK 9
Rio Grande [RA, Tierra del Fuego ●] 162 C 8
Rio Grande [USA, Colorado] 154-155 BC 2
Rio Grande [USA, Texas] 146-147 FG 6
Rio Grande, Dorsale di - 124-125 GH 7
Rio Grande, Patamar do - 124-125 GH 7
Rio Grande, Ramal de - 124-125 GH 7
Rio Grande, Represa do - 160-161 J 5
Rio Grande, Seuil du - 124-125 GH 7
Rio Grande City, TX 154-155 F 7
Rio Grande de Santiago 146-147 F 7
Rio Grande do Norte 158-159 M 6
Rio Grande do Norte = Natal 158-159 MN 6
Rio Grande do Sul 162 F 3-4
Rio Grandedrempel 124-125 GH 7
Rio Grande Rise 124-125 GH 7
Rio-Grande-Schwelle 124-125 GH 7
Riohacha 158-159 E 2
Rioja [PE] 158-159 D 6
Rioja, La - [E] 134-135 F 7
Rioja, La - [RA, ●] 162 C 3
Rio Largo 158-159 MN 6
Rio Mayo [RA, ●] 162 BC 7
Rio Mulatos 158-159 F 8
Rio Muni = Mbini 166-167 G 8
Rio Negrinho 160-161 H 7
Rio Negro [BR, Amazonas] 158-159 G 5
Rio Negro [BR, Mato Grosso] 158-159 H 8
Rio Negro [BR, Mato Grosso do Sul] 160-161 D 3
Rio Negro [BR, Paraná ●] 162 F 3
Rio Negro [BR, Paraná ~] 160-161 H 7
Rio Negro [BR, Rio de Janeiro] 160-161 L 4
Rio Negro [PY] 160-161 D 6
Rio Negro [RA, Rio Negro ~] 162 D 5-6
Rio Negro [RA, Rio Negro ✲] 162 C 6
Rio Negro [ROU, ~] 162 EF 4
Rio Negro, Embalse del - 162 E 4
Rio Negro, Pantanal do 158-159 H 8
Rioni 140-141 KL 5
Rio Novo [BR, Minas Gerais] 160-161 L 4
Rio Pardo de Minas 158-159 L 8
Rio Perdido [BR, Mato Grosso do Sul] 160-161 D 4
Rio Preto, Serra do - 160-161 J 2
Rio Primero [RA, ●] 162 D 4
Rio Real 158-159 M 7
Rio Sonora 146-147 D 6
Riosucio [CO, ●] 158-159 D 3
Rio Tercero [RA, ●] 162 D 4
Riou-Kiou, Fosse des 184-185 O 7-P 6
Riouw Archipel = Kepulauan Riau 186-187 DE 6
Rio Verde [BR, Goiás ●] 158-159 J 8
Rio Verde [MEX, Oaxaca] 146-147 G 8
Rio Verde [PY] 162 E 2
Rio Verde [RCH] 162 B 8
Rio Verde [BR, Goiás ◁ Chapada dos Pilões] 160-161 J 2
Rio Verde [BR, Minas Gerais ◁ Represa de Furnas] 160-161 K 4
Rio Verde [BR, Goiás ◁ Represa de São Simão] 158-159 J 8
Rio Verde [BR, Minas Gerais ◁ Rio Grande] 160-161 H 3
Rio Verde [BR, Goiás ◁ Rio Maranhão] 160-161 H 1
Rio Verde [BR, Mato Grosso ◁ Rio Paraná] 158-159 J 9
Rio Verde [BR, Goiás ◁ Rio Paranaíba] 160-161 J 2-3
Rio Verde [BR, Mato Grosso ◁ Rio Teles Pires] 158-159 H 7
Rio Verde [BR, Goiás ◁ Serra do Verdinho] 160-161 G 3
Rio Verde de Mato Grosso 158-159 HJ 8
Rio Verde do Sul 160-161 E 5
Rio Vermelho [BR, Minas Gerais] 160-161 L 3
Riparia, WA 150-151 DE 2
Ripley, CA 150-151 F 9
Ripley, MS 154-155 L 3
Ripley, NY 148-149 D 3
Ripley, TN 154-155 L 3
Ripley, WV 148-149 C 5
Ripoll 134-135 J 7
Ripon, WI 152-153 M 4
Risāfah 182-183 H 5
Risām' Anayzah 170 E 2
Risāni, Ar- 166-167 D 2
Risasi 168-169 G 3
Rishiri suidō 188-189 b 1
Rishiri tō 184-185 QR 2
Ri'shōn Lèẕiyyōn 182-183 F 7
Rising Star, TX 154-155 F 4
Rising Sun, IN 152-153 O 6
Rising Sun, OH 148-149 A 5
Risiri 188-189 b 1
Risle 134-135 H 4
Rison, AR 154-155 JK 4
Risør 130-131 C 8
Risso, Colonia - 160-161 D 5
Ristikent 130-131 O 3
Ristna neem 138-139 CD 4
Rito Gaviel, Mesa del - 154-155 D 4
Ritscherhochland 121 B 36
Ritter, Mount - 146-147 C 4
Rittman, OH 148-149 BC 4
Ritzville, WA 150-151 D 2
Riukiu = Ryūkyū 184-185 N 7-O 6
Riu-Kiu, Fosa de - 184-185 O 7-P 6
Riu-Kiu, Fossa de - 184-185 O 7-P 6
Riukiu, Rów - 184-185 O 7-P 6
Riunione 168-169 N 7
Riva 136-137 D 3
Rivadavia [RA, Buenos Aires] 162 D 5
Rivadavia [RA, Salta] 162 D 2
Rivadavia [RCH] 162 B 3
Rivalensundet 130-131 mn 5
Riva Palacio 154-155 B 6
Rivera [RA] 162 D 5
Rivera [ROU, ●] 162 E 4
Riverbank, CA 150-151 C 7
River Cess 166-167 BC 7
Riverdale, CA 150-151 D 7
River Falls, WI 152-153 K 3
Riverhead, NY 148-149 G 4
Riverina 194-195 HJ 6-7
Rivers 166-167 F 7-8
Riversdal 168-169 F 9
Riversdale = Riversdal 168-169 F 9
Riverside, CA 146-147 C 5
Riverside, OR 150-151 DE 4
Riverton [AUS] 194-195 G 6
Riverton, WY 152-153 B 4
Riviera, TX 154-155 FG 7
Riviera Beach, FL 148-149 cd 3
Rivière-du-Loup 144-145 WX 8
Riviersonderend 174-175 CD 8
Rivne 126-127 O 5
Rivoli 136-137 B 3
Rivungo 168-169 F 6
Riyad = Ar-Riyāḍ 180-181 F 6
Riyāḍ, Ar- 180-181 F 6
Riyadh = Ar-Riyāḍ 180-181 F 6
Rize 180-181 E 2
Rize Dağları 182-183 J 2
Rizhao 190-191 G 4
Rizzuto, Capo - 136-137 G 6
Rīžsky záliv = Rigas Jūŗas Licis 138-139 DE 5
Rjasan = R'azan' 138-139 M 6
Rjeschiza = Rēzekne 138-139 F 5
Rjukan 130-131 C 8
R'kiz, Ar- 166-167 AB 5
R'kiz, Lac - = Ar-R'kiz 166-167 AB 5
Roachdale, IN 152-153 N 6
Roan Cliffs 150-151 J 6
Roan Creek 152-153 B 6
Roanne 134-135 K 5
Roanoke, AL 154-155 N 4
Roanoke, VA 146-147 KL 4
Roanoke Island 148-149 F 7
Roanoke Rapids, NC 148-149 E 6
Roanoke River 146-147 L 4
Roan Plateau 152-153 B 6
Roaring Fork 152-153 C 6
Roaring Springs, TX 154-155 E 4
Roatán, Isla de - 146-147 J 8
Robāṭ 182-183 M 5
Robbeneiland 174-175 BC 7
Robben Island = Robbeneiland 174-175 BC 7
Robberson, TX 154-155 F 7
Robbinsdale, MN 152-153 K 3
Robbins Island 196 b 2
Robe [NZ] 196 D 6
Robe, Mount - 196 E 3
Robeline, LA 154-155 J 5
Roberta, GA 154-155 NO 4
Robert Lee, TX 154-155 E 5
Roberts, ID 150-151 GH 4
Roberts Creek Mountain 150-151 E 6
Robertsfors 130-131 J 5
Robertson 174-175 C 7
Robertson, WY 150-151 HJ 5
Robertson Bay 121 BC 17-18
Robertsons øy 121 C 31
Robertsport 166-167 B 7
Robertstown 196 D 4
Roberval 144-145 W 8
Robinette, OR 150-151 E 3
Robinson, IL 152-153 N 6
Robinson, TX 154-155 G 5
Robinson Crusoe 157 C 6
Robinson Island 121 C 30
Robinson Range 194-195 C 5
Robinson River 194-195 G 3
Robinvale 194-195 H 6
Robla, La - 134-135 E 7
Robson, Mount - [CDN, ▲] 144-145 N 7
Robstown, TX 154-155 G 7
Roby, TX 154-155 E 4
Roca, Cabo da - 134-135 C 9
Roçadas = Xangongo 168-169 E 6
Roçalgate = Rās al-Hadd 180-181 HJ 6
Rocamadour 134-135 HJ 6
Rocas, Atol das - 158-159 N 5
Rocas Negras = Black Rock 162 H 8
Roċegda 138-139 O 2
Rocha [ROU, ●] 162 F 4
Rochedo 160-161 E 3
Rochefort 134-135 G 5-6
Rochelle, IL 152-153 M 5
Rochelle, LA 154-155 J 5
Rochelle, TX 154-155 F 5
Rochelle, la - 134-135 G 7
Rocheport, MO 152-153 K 6
Rochester, IN 152-153 NO 5
Rochester, MI 152-153 P 4
Rochester, MN 146-147 H 3
Rochester, NH 148-149 H 3
Rochester, NY 146-147 L 3
Roche-sur-Yon, la - 134-135 G 5
Rock, MI 152-153 N 2
Rock, The - 196 H 5
Rockall 128-129 EF 4
Rockall, Banco de - 128-129 E 4
Rockall, Ramal de - 128-129 E 4
Rockall, Rialzo di - 128-129 E 4
Rockall Plateau 128-129 E 4
Rockallplateau 128-129 E 4
Rock Creek, OR 150-151 CD 3
Rock Creek [USA ◁ Clark Fork River] 150-151 G 2
Rock Creek [USA ◁ Milk River] 152-153 C 1
Rockdale, TX 154-155 G 5
Rockefeller Plateau 121 AB 23-24
Rock Falls, IL 152-153 M 5
Rockford, IA 152-153 K 4
Rockford, IL 146-147 HJ 3
Rockford, OH 152-153 O 5
Rockham, SD 152-153 G 3
Rockhampton 194-195 JK 4
Rock Harbor, MI 152-153 MN 1
Rock Hill, SC 146-147 K 4-5
Rockingham [AUS] 194-195 BC 6
Rockingham, NC 148-149 CD 7
Rockingham Bay 194-195 J 3
Rock Island, IL 146-147 HJ 3
Rock Island, WA 150-151 CD 2
Rock Lake 150-151 E 2
Rockland, ID 150-151 G 4
Rockland, ME 148-149 J 2-3
Rocklands Reservoir 194-195 H 7
Rockmart, GA 154-155 N 3
Rockport, IN 152-153 N 7
Rockport, MO 152-153 J 5
Rockport, TX 154-155 G 6
Rockport, WA 150-151 C 1
Rock Rapids, IA 152-153 HJ 4
Rock River [USA, Illinois] 152-153 M 4-5
Rock River [USA, Minnesota] 152-153 H 4
Rock River, WY 152-153 CD 5
Rock Springs, AZ 150-151 GH 8
Rocksprings, MT 152-153 CD 2
Rocksprings, TX 154-155 E 5
Rock Springs, WY 146-147 E 3
Rockstone 158-159 H 3
Rockton, IL 152-153 M 4
Rock Valley, IA 152-153 HJ 4
Rockville, IN 152-153 N 6
Rockville, MD 148-149 E 5
Rockville, OR 150-151 E 4
Rockwall, TX 154-155 G 4
Rockwell City, IA 152-153 J 4
Rockwood, PA 148-149 D 5
Rockwood, TN 154-155 N 3
Rocky Boys Indian Reservation 152-153 B 1
Rocky Ford, CO 152-153 DE 6
Rockyford, SD 152-153 E 4
Rocky Mount, NC 148-149 E 6-7
Rocky Mount, VA 148-149 D 6
Rocky Mountain 150-151 G 2
Rocky Mountain National Park 146-147 EF 3
Rocky Mountains 144-145 L 5-P 9
Rocky Mountain Trench 144-145 L 6-N 7
Rocky Point [USA, California] 150-151 A 5
Rōḍa, Er- = Ar-Rawḍah 170 D 4
Roda, La - 134-135 F 9
Rodalquilar 134-135 FG 10
Rødberg 130-131 C 7
Rødby Havn 130-131 D 10
Rode 174-175 H 6
Rode Bekken = Sichuan Pendi 184-185 JK 5-6
Rodeio 160-161 H 7
Rodenpois = Ropaži 138-139 E 5
Rodeo 162 BC 4
Rodeo, NM 150-151 J 10
Rodez 134-135 J 6
Rode Zee 180-181 D 5-7
Rodezja i Niasa = Zambia 168-169 G 6-H 5
Rodney 148-149 C 3
Rodniki 138-139 NO 5
Rodopes 136-137 KL 5
Ródopes 128-129 NO 7
Rodopi 136-137 KL 5
Rodopy 136-137 KL 5
Ródos [GR, ☉] 136-137 N 7
Ródos [GR, ●] 136-137 N 7
Rodosto = Tekirdağ 182-183 B 2
Rodosto = Tekirdağ 180-181 B 2
Rodrigues [Mascarene Islands] 124-125 N 6-7
Rodrigues [MS] 168-169 O 6
Rodriguez 154-155 E 7
Roebourne 194-195 C 4
Roebuck Bay 194-195 D 3
Roedtan 174-175 H 3
Roelofskamp 174-175 F 4
Roemelië = Rumelija 136-137 LM 4
Roemenië 136-137 K-M 2
Roermond 134-135 K 3
Roeselare 134-135 J 3
Roe's Welcome Sound 144-145 T 4-5
Rogač'ov 138-139 H 7
Rogagua, Lago - 158-159 F 7
Rogaland 130-131 B 8
Rogers, AR 154-155 HJ 2
Rogers, ND 152-153 G 2
Rogers, TX 154-155 G 5
Rogers City, MI 152-153 P 3
Rogerson, ID 150-151 F 4
Rogersville, TN 148-149 B 6
Roggeveldberge 174-175 C 6-D 7
Roggeveld Mountains = Roggeveldberge 174-175 C 6-D 7
Rognan 130-131 F 4
Rogoaguado, Lago - 158-159 F 7
Rogowo = Raguva 138-139 E 6
Rogue River 150-151 A 4
Rogue River Mountains 150-151 AB 4
Roha-Lalibela = Lalibela 166-167 M6
Rohan 134-135 F 4
Rohri 180-181 K 5
Rohtak 180-181 M 5
Roja 138-139 D 5
Rojas 162 D 4
Rojen = Roja 138-139 D 5
Rokel 172-173 B 3
Rokitnoje 138-139 F 8
Rokitnosümpfe = Polesje 138-139 E 8-H 7
Rokkasho 188-189 N 2
Rokugō-saki = Suzu misaki 188-189 L 4
Roland, AR 154-155 J 3
Rolândia 160-161 G 5
Rolette, ND 152-153 FG 1
Rolfe, IA 152-153 J 4
Rolla 130-131 G 3
Rolla, KS 154-155 E 2
Rolla, MO 146-147 H 4
Rolla, ND 152-153 G 1
Rolleston 194-195 J 4
Rolling Fork, MS 154-155 K 4
Rolvsøy 130-131 K 2
Rom 130-131 B 8
Rom [EAU] 171 C 2
Rom = Roma 136-137 E 5
Roma 136-137 E 5
Roma [AUS] 194-195 J 5
Roma [LS] 174-175 G 5
Romain, Cape - 148-149 D 8
Romaine, Rivière - 144-145 Y 7
Roma-Los Saenz, TX 154-155 F 7
Roman 136-137 M 2
Romana, La - 146-147 J 8
Román Arreola 154-155 C 7
Romanche Deep 124-125 J 6
Romanchediep 124-125 J 6
Romancherinne 124-125 J 6
Romanche, Zona di Frattura di - 124-125 J 6
Romang, Pulau - 186-187 J 8
Romāni = Rummānah 170 E 2
Romania 136-137 K-M 2
Romania 136-137 K-M 2
Románia 136-137 K-M 2
Roman-Koš, gora - 140-141 FG 4
Romano, Cape - 148-149 bc 4
Romano, Cayo - 146-147 L 7
Romanov = Dzeržinsk 140-141 CD 1
Romanovka [SU, Bur'atskaja ASSR] 178-179 V 7
Romanovka [SU, Saratov] 138-139 O 8
Romanovka = Bessarabka 140-141 D 3
Romanovskij = Kropotkin 140-141 K 4
Romans-sur-Isère 134-135 K 6
Romanvloer 174-175 D 6
Roman Wall 132 E 4
Romanzof, Cape - 144-145 C 5
Róma = Roma 136-137 E 5
Romblon 186-187 H 4
Rome, GA 146-147 J 5
Rome, NY 146-147 LM 3
Rome, OR 150-151 E 4
Rome = Roma 136-137 E 5
Romen = Romny 140-141 F 1
Roménia 126-127 NO 6
Roménia 136-137 K-M 2
Romeo, MI 152-153 P 4
Romero, TX 154-155 D 3
Romilly-sur-Seine 134-135 J 4
Romney, WV 148-149 D 5
Romny 140-141 F 1
Rømø 130-131 C 10
Romodan 140-141 F 1
Romodanovo 138-139 P 6
Romsdal 130-131 BC 6
Romsdalfjord 130-131 B 6
Ronan, MT 150-151 FG 2
Roncador 160-161 F 6
Roncador, Serra do - 158-159 J 7
Roncador Reef 186-187 j 6
Roncesvalles 134-135 G 7
Ronceverte, WV 148-149 C 6
Ronda 134-135 E 10
Ronda das Salinas 160-161 BC 1
Rondane 130-131 C 7
Rondon 160-161 F 5
Rondón = Puerto Rondón 158-159 E 3
Rondônia [BR, ●] 158-159 G 7
Rondônia [BR, ✲] 158-159 G 7
Rondonópolis 158-159 HJ 8
Rong'an 190-191 B 9
Rongcheng [TJ, Hebei] 190-191 EF 2

Rongcheng [TJ, Shandong] 190-191 J 3
Rongcheng = Jiurongcheng 190-191 J 3
Ronge, la - 144-145 P 6
Ronge, Lac la - 144-145 Q 6
Rongerik 192-193 H 3
Rong Jian [TJ, ~] 190-191 B 9
Rong Jian [TJ, ●] 190-191 B 9
Rongshui 190-191 B 9
Rongui 171 E 5
Rong Xian 190-191 C 10
Rongxu = Cangwu 190-191 C 10
Ron Ma, Mui - 186-187 E 3
Rønne 130-131 F 10
Ronne Bay 121 B 29
Ronneby 130-131 F 9
Roodebank 174-175 H 4
Roodehoogte = Rooihoogte 174-175 F 6
Roodepoort 174-175 G 4
Roodhouse, IL 152-153 LM 6
Roof Butte 150-151 J 7
Rooiberg [ZA, Kaapland] 174-175 C 6
Rooiberg [ZA, Transvaal ▲] 174-175 H 2
Rooiberg [ZA, Transvaal ●] 174-175 G 3
Rooiberge 174-175 H 5
Rooihoogte 174-175 F 6
Rooiwal 174-175 G 4
Roosendaal en Nispen 134-135 K 3
Roosevelt, MN 152-153 J 1
Roosevelt, OK 154-155 F 3
Roosevelt, Tx 154-155 EF 5
Roosevelt, UT 150-151 HJ 5
Roosevelt, WA 150-151 C 3
Roosevelt, Rio - 158-159 G 6-7
Roosevelt Island 121 AB 122-123
Roossenekal 174-175 H 3
Root River 152-153 KL 4
Ropaži 138-139 E 5
Roper River 194-195 F 2
Roper Valley 194-195 F 2-3
Ropi 130-131 J 3
Roquefort-sur-Soulzon 134-135 J 7
Roraima 158-159 GH 4
Roraima, Mount - 158-159 G 3
Rorke's Drift 174-175 J 5
Røros 130-131 D 6
Rørvik 130-131 D 5
Ros' 140-141 E 2
Rosa 168-169 H 4
Rošal' 138-139 MN 6
Rosales [MEX] 154-155 C 6
Rosalia, WA 150-151
Rosamond, CA 150-151 D 8
Rosamond Lake 150-151 DE 8
Rosário [BR] 158-159 L 5
Rosairo [MEX, Coahuila] 154-155 D 7
Rosario [PY] 160-161 D 6
Rosario [RA, Santa Fe] 162 DE 4
Rosario, Rio del - 150-151 F 10
Rosario de la Frontera 162 D 3
Rosario del Tala 162 E 4
Rosário do Sul 162 EF 4
Rosário Oeste 158-159 HJ 7
Rosarito [MEX, Baja California Norte ↓ Tijuana] 150-151 E 9
Rosas 134-135 J 7
Roščino 138-139 G 3
Roscoe, NY 148-149 F 4
Roscoe, SD 152-153 G 3
Roscoe, TX 154-155 E 4
Roscoff 134-135 EF 4
Roscommon 132 BC 5
Roscommon, MI 152-153 O 3
Rose 192-193 L 6
Rose, NE 152-153 G 4
Roseau 146-147 O 8
Roseau, MN 152-153 HJ 1
Roseau River 152-153 HJ 1
Rosebery 194-195 HJ 8
Roseboro, NC 148-149 D 7
Rosebud, TX 154-155 G 5
Rosebud Creek 152-153 C 3
Rosebud Indian Reservation 152-153 F 4
Rosebud Mountains 152-153 C 3
Roseburg, OR 150-151 B 4
Rosedale, NM 154-155 B 4
Roșeires, Er- = Ar-Rușayriș 166-167 LM 6
Rosenberg, TX 154-155 GH 6
Rosengarten 120 C 19-20
Rosenheim 133 EF 5
Rose River 190-195 G 2
Rosetown 144-145 P 7
Rosetta = Rashid 170 D 2
Rosetta Mouth = Maşabb Rashid 170 D 2
Rosette = Rashid 170 D 2
Roseville, IL 152-153 L 5
Roseville, MI 152-153 P 4
Rose Wood 196 L 1
Rosholt, SD 152-153 H 3
Rosholt, WI 152-153 M 3
Rosiclare, IL 152-153 M 7
Rosignano Marittimo 136-137 CD 4
Rosignol 158-159 H 3
Roşiori-de-Vede 136-137 L 3-4
Rositten = Rēzekne 138-139 F 5
Rosja 178-179 L-g 4
Roskilde 130-131 E 10
Rosl'atino 138-139 P 4
Roslavl' 138-139 J 7
Roslyn, WA 150-151 C 2
Rosmead 174-175 F 6
Ross 194-195 O 8
Ross, WY 152-153 D 4
Ross, Mar de - = Ross Sea 121 B 20-18
Ross, Mer de - = Ross Sea 121 B 20-18
Rossa, Morze - = Ross Sea 121 B 20-18
Rossano 136-137 G 6
Rossel Island 186-187 hi 7
Ross Ice Shelf 121 AB 20-17
Rossieny = Raseiniai 138-139 D 6
Rossijskaja Sovetskaja Federativnaja Socialističeskaja Respublika = Rußland 178-179 L-g 4
Rössing [Namibia] 174-175 A 2
Ross Island [Antarktika, Ross Sea] 121 B 17-18
Ross Island [Antarktika, Weddell Sea] 121 C 31
Ross Island [CDN] 144-145 R 7
Rosslare 132 CD 5
Rosslyn 174-175 GH 3
Rossmeer = Ross Sea 121 B 20-18
Rosso 166-167 A 5
Rossoš' 140-141 J 1
Rossouw 174-175 G 6
Rossovo more = Ross Sea 121 B 20-18
Ross River 144-145 K 5
Ross Sea 121 B 20-18
Ross-Schelfeis = Ross Ice Shelf 121 AB 20-1 7
Ross-tenger = Ross Sea 121 B 20-18
Rosston, OK 154-155 F 2
Røssvatn 130-131 E 5
Røssvik 130-131 FG 4
Rossville 194-195 HJ 3
Rossville, GA 154-155 N 3
Rossville, IL 152-153 N 5
Rostock 133 F 1
Rostov 178-179 FG 6
Rostov-na-Donu 140-141 J 3
Rostow am Don = Rostov-na-Donu 140-141 J 3
Roswell, NM 146-147 F 5
Rota 134-135 D 10
Rota [Guam] 192-193 F 3
Rotan, TX 154-155 E 4
Rote, Pulau - 186-187 H 9
Rotes Becken = Sichuan Pendi 184-185 JK 5-6
Rotes Meer 180-181 D 5-E 7
Rothaargebirge 133 D 3
Rothbury 132 EF 4
Rothenburg 133 DE 4
Rothesay 132 D 4
Rothsay, MN 152-153 HJ 2
Roto 194-195 J 6
Rotondo, Mont - 136-137 C 4
Rotorua 194-195 P 7
Rotterdam 134-135 JK 3
Rotti = Pulau Rote 186-187 H 9
Roubaix 134-135 J 3
Rouen 134-135 H 4
Roukkula = Rovkuly 138-139 H 1
Roulers = Roeselare 134-135 J 3
Roumanie 136-137 K-M 2
Roumélie = Rumelija 136-137 LM 4
Round Island 168-169 N 6
Round Mountain 194-195 K 6
Round Mountain, NV 150-151 E 6
Round Mountain, TX 154-155 F 5
Round Rock, TX 154-155 G 5
Round Spring, MO 154-155 K 2
Roundup, MT 152-153 B 2
Round Valley Indian Reservation 150-151 B 6
Rounga , Dar - 166-167 J 6-7
Rourkela 180-181 NO 5
Rousay 132 E 2
Rouses Point, NY 148-149 G 2
Roussillon 134-135 J 7
Routbé, El- = Ar-Ruṭbah 182-183 G 6
Rouxville 174-175 G 6
Rouyn 144-145 V 8
Rovaniemi 130-131 L 4
Rovdino 138-139 O 3
Roven'ki 140-141 J 2
Rovereto 136-137 D 3
Rovigo 136-137 D 3
Rovinj 136-137 E 3
Rovkuly 138-139 H 1
Rovniková Guinea 166-167 FG 8
Rovno = Rivne 126-127 O 5
Rovuma, Rio - 168-169 J 5
Rowe, NM 154-155 C 3
Rowley Island 144-145 UV 4
Rowley Shoals 194-195 C 3
Rowuma = Rio Rovuma 168-169 J 5
Rox, NV 150-151 F 7
Roxas 186-187 H 4
Roxboro, NC 148-149 D 6
Roxburgh [NZ] 194-195 N 9
Roxie, MS 154-155 K 5
Roy, MT 152-153 B 2
Roy, NM 154-155 C 3
Roy, UT 150-151 G 5
Royal Canal 132 C 5
Royal Center, IN 152-153 N 5
Royal Natal National Park 174-175 H 5
Royal Society Range 121 B 15-16
Royalton, MN 152-153 JK 3
Royan 134-135 G 6
Royaume-Uni 132 F-H 4-5
Røykenvik 130-131 D 7
Royse City, TX 154-155 G 4
Royston, GA 148-149 B 7
Roždestveno [SU, Tver'] 138-139 L 5
Roždestvenskoje 138-139 P 4
Rozel, KS 152-153 G 6
Rozet, WY 152-153 D 3
Rozewie, Przylądek - 133 J 1
Rožišče 140-141 B 1
Rožňava 133 K 4
Roztocze 133 L 3
Roztoky = Rostock 133 F
Rschew = Ržev 138-139 K 5
Rtiščevo 138-139 O 7
Ruacana Falls 168-169 DE 6
Ruaha National Park 171 C 4
Ruanda = Rwanda 168-169 GH 3
Ruanda = Rwanda 168 EF 2
Ruapehu 194-195 P 7
Rubā'i, Ash-Shallāl ar- = Al-Jandal ar-Rāb'i 166-167 L 5
Rub al Chali, Pustynia - = Ar-Rub'al-Khāli 180-181 F 7-G 6
Rub al-Chāli, poušť - = Ar-Rub'al-Hāli 180-181 F 7-G 6
Rub' al-Khālī = Ar-Rub'al-Khālī 180-181 F 7-G 6
Rub' al-Khālī, Ar- 180-181 F 7-G 6
Rubanovka 140-141 G 3
Rubcovsk 178-179 P 7
Rubeho 171 D 4
Rubesibe 188-189 c 2
Rubežnoje 140-141 J 2
Rubi 168-169 G 2
Rubia, La - 162 D 4
Rubio [MEX] 154-155 B 6
Rubondo 171 BC 3
Ruby, AK 144-145 EF 5
Ruby Lake 150-151 F 5
Ruby Mountains 150-151 F 5
Ruby Range [USA] 150-151 G 3
Ruby Valley 150-151 F 5
Ruč 138-139 T 3
Rucava 138-139 C 5
Rucheng 190-191 D 9
Ruchlovo = Skovorodino 178-179 XY 7
Rudall 196 BC 4
Rudayyif, Ar- 166-167 F 2
Rūdbār 182-183 N 4
Rudé moře 180-181 D 5-7
Rudensk 138-139 F 7
Rudewa 171 C 5
Rudki 140-141 A 2
Rudn'a [SU] 138-139 H 6
Rudnaja Pristan' 178-179 a 9
Rudnica 140-141 D 2
Rudničnyj 138-139 ST 4
Rudnyj 178-179 L 7
Rudog 184-185 D5
Rudol'fa, ostrov - 178-179 JK 1
Rudong [TJ, Guangdong] 190-191 C 11
Rudong [TJ, Jiangsu] 190-191 H 5
Rūd Sar 182-183 O 4
Rudyard, MI 152-153 O 2
Rudyard, MT 150-151 H 1
Ruffec 134-135 GH 5
Rufiji 168-169 J 4
Rufino 162 D 4
Rufisque 166-167 A 5-6
Rufunsa 168-169 GH 6
Rugao 184-185 N 5
Rugby 132 F 5
Rugby, ND 152-153 FG 1
Rügen 133 FG 1
Rugl'akov = Okt'abr'skij 140-141 L 3
Rugozero 138-139 J 1
Ru He 190-191 E 5
Ru He = Beiru He 190-191 D 4
Ruhnu 130-131 K 9
Ruhnu 138-139 D 5
Ruhr 133 D 3
Ruhudji 171 D 5
Ruhuhu 171 C 5
Rui'an 190-191 H 8
Ruichang 190-191 E 7
Ruidoso, NM 154-155 C 4
Ruijin 184-185 M 6
Ruisui = Jui-sui 190-191 H 10
Ruivo, Pico - 166-167 A 2
Ruiz, Nevado del - 158-159 DE 4
Rujewa 171 C 5
Rūjiena 138-139 E 5
Rujm Ta'at al-Jamā'ah 182-183 F 7
Rukhaimiyah' Ar- = Ar-Rukhaymiyah 182-183 L 8
Rukhaymiyah' Ar- 182-183 L 8
Ruki 168-169 E 2-3
Rukungiri 171 B 3
Rukuru 171 C 5
Rukwa 168-169 H 4
Rukwa, Lake - 168-169 H 4
Rule, TX 154-155 F 4
Ruleville, MS 154-155 K 4
Rum 132 C 3
Ruma 136-137 H 3
Rumāh' Ar- 180-181 F 5
Rumahui 186-187 k 7
Rumania 136-137 K-M 2
Rumänien 136-137 K-M 2
Rumaylah, Ar- 182-183 M 7
Rumaythah, Ar- 182-183 L 7
Rumbalara 194-195 FG 5
Rumberpon, Pulau - 186-187
Rumbik 166-167 K 7
Rum Cay 146-147 M 7
Rumelia = Rumelija 136-137 LM 4
Rumelien = Rumelija 136-137 LM 4
Rumelija 136-137 LM 4
Rumford, ME 148-149 H 2
Rummānah 170 E 2
Rummelsburg in Pommern = Miastko 133 H 1-2
Rumoe = Rumoi 188-189 b 2
Rumoi 184-185 R 3
Rumorosa 150-151 EF 9
Rumpi 171 C 5
Rum River 152-153 K 3
Rumula 194-195 HJ 3
Rumunia 136-137 K-M 2
Rumunsko 136-137 K-M 2
Rumuruti 171 CD 2
Runan 190-191 E 5
Rundu 168-169 E 6
Runga, Dar - = Dar Rounga 166-167 J 6-7
Runge, TX 154-155 G 6
Rungu 171 AB 2
Rungwa [EAT, ~] 171 C 4
Rungwa [EAT, ●] 168-169 H 4
Rungwa East 171 BC 4
Rungwe Mount 168-169 H 4
Runheji 190-191 F 5
Running Water Creek 154-155 DE 3
Runö = Ruhnu 138-139 D 5
Runton Range 194-195 D 4
Ruo Shui 184-185 HJ 3
Ruoxi 184-185 M 6
Rupat, Pulau - 186-187 D 6
Rupert, ID 150-151 G 4
Rupert, Rivière de - 144-145 SW 7
Rupert House = Fort Rupert 144-145 V 7
Ruppert Coast 121 B 21-22
Ruq'i, Ar- 182-183 M 8
Rurkala = Rourkela 180-181 NO 5
Rurrenabaque 158-159 F 7
Rusanovo 178-179 JK 3
Rusape 168-169 H 6
Rusayriș, Ar- 166-167 LM 6
Ruse 136-137 LM 4
Rușetu 136-137 M 3
Rush, CO 152-153 DE 6
Rushan 190-191 H 3
Rush Center, KS 152-153 G 6
Rush City, MN 152-153 K 3
Rush Creek 152-153 E 6
Rushford, MN 152-153 L 4
Rush Springs, OK 154-155 FG 3
Rushville, IL 152-153 L 5
Rushville, IN 152-153 O 6
Rushville, NE 152-153 E 4
Rusia 178-179 L-g 4
Rusk, TX 154-155 H 5
Ruskin, NE 152-153 GH 5
Rusko 178-179 L-g 4
Rusland 178-179 L-g 4
Rusné 138-139 C 4
Ruso, ND 152-153 F 2
Russas 158-159 M 5
Russell [NZ] 194-195 OP 7
Russell, KS 152-153 G 6
Russell, MN 152-153 HJ 3
Russell Island 144-145 R 3
Russell Islands 186-187 j 6
Russell Range 194-195 D 6
Russell Springs, KS 152-153 F 6
Russellville, AL 154-155 M 3
Russellville, AR 154-155 J 3
Russellville, KY 154-155 M 2
Russel Springs, KS 152-153 F 6
Russenberg = Krievu kalns 138-139 CD 5
Russenes 130-131 L 2
Rússia 126-127 Q-V 4
Russia 140-141 K-N 1-4
Rússia 140-141 K 2-M 4
Russia Bianca 138-139 F-H 6-7
Russian River 150-151 B 6
Russie 178-179 L-g 4
Russisi = Ruzizi 168-169 G 3
Russkij, ostrov - [SU, p-ov Tajmyr] 178-179 RS 2
Russkij, ostrov - [SU, Vladivostok] 178-179 Z 9
Russkij Aktaš 138-139 T 6
Russkij Zavorot mys - 178-179 JK 4
Rußland 140-141 K 1-M 4
Rust, De - 174-175 E 7
Rustāq, Ar- 180-181 H 6
Rustavi 140-141 M 6
Rustawi = Rustavi 140-141 M 6
Rust de Winterdam 174-175 H 3
Rustenburg 168-169 G 8
Ruston, LA 154-155 H 4
Rūșū = Al-Quwārib 166-167 A 5
Rusufa = Riṣāfah 182-183 H 5
Rusumu, Chutes - 171 B 3
Rutana 168-169 GH 3
Rutanzige 168-169 G 3
Rutbah, Ar- [IRQ] 180-181 DE 4
Rutbah, Ar- [SYR] 182-183 G 6
Ruth, NV 150-151 F 6
Rutherfordton, NC 148-149 C 7
Ruthin 132 E 5
Ruthven, IA 152-153 J 4
Rutland, ND 152-153 H 2
Rutland, VT 146-147 M 3
Rutshuru 168-169 G 3
Rutul 140-141 N 6
Rutzau = Rucava 138-139 C 5
Ruvo di Pùglia 136-137 G 5
Ruvu [EAT, ~] 168-169 J 4
Ruvu [EAT, ●] 171 D 4
Ruvu = Pangani 168-169 J 3
Ruvuma[EAT, ~] 171 C 5
Ruvuma [EAT, ☼] 168-169 J 5
Ruvuvu 171 B 3
Ruwāq, Jabal ar- 182-183 G 5-6
Ruwenzori 168-169 G 2
Ruwenzori National Park 168-169 GH 3
Ruwu = Pangani 168-169 J 3
Ruyang 190-191 D 4
Ruyuan 190-191 D 9
Ruza [SU, ●] 138-139 KL 6
Ruzajevka 178-179 GH 7
Ružany 138-139 E 7
Ruzizi 168-169 G 3
Ružomberok 133 J 4
Rwanda 168-169 GH 3
Rwashamaire 171 B 3
Ryan, OK 154-155 G 3
Ryanggang-do 188-189 FG 2
Rybačij 133 K 1
Rybačij, poluostrov - 178-179 EF 4
Rybacki, Półwysep - = poluostrov Rybačij 178-179 EF 4
Rybačij 133 K 1
Rybačij, poluostrov - 178-179 EF 4
Rybinsk 178-179 F 6
Rybinskoje vodochranilišče 178-179 FG 6
Rybnica 140-141 D 3
Rybnik 133 J 3
Rybnoje 138-139 M 6
Ryder, ND 152-153 F 2
Ryderwood, WA 150-151 B 2
Rye, CO 152-153 D 7
Ryegate, MT 152-153 B 2
Rye Patch Reservoir 150-151 D 5
Ryga = Riga 138-139 E 5
Rykaartspos 174-175 G 4
Ryke Yseøyane 130-131 m 6
Ryl'sk 140-141 G 1
Rijn = Rhein 133 C 3
Ryn-peski 140-141 OP 2-3
Ryōtsu 188-189 M 3
Rypin 133 J 2
Ryska, Zatoka - = Rigas Jūras Licis 138-139 DE 5
Ryškany 140-141 C 3
Ryūkyū 184-185 N 7-O 6
Ryukyu, Fossa delle - 184-185 O 7-R 6
Ryūkyū, příkop - 184-185 O 7-P 6
Ryūkyū-árok 184-185 Q 7-P 6
Ryūkyūgraben 184-185 O 7-P 6
Ryukyu Trench 184-185 O 7-P 6
Rżaksa 138-139 NO 7
Ržava = Pristen' 140-141 H 1
Rzeszów 133 KL 3
Ržev 138-139 K 5
Ržiščev 140-141 E 2
Rzym = Roma 136-137 E 5

S

Sá [BR] 158-159 L 8
Sáa [DY] 172-173 F 3
Saa [RFC] 172-173 H 4
Saale 133 E 3
Saalfeld 133 E 3
Saar 133 C 4
Saarbrücken 133 C 4
Saaremaa 130-131 K 8
Saaremaa 138-139 CD 4
Saargemünd = Sarreguemines 134-135 L 4
Saarijärvi 130-131 L 6
Saariselkä 130-131 MN 3
Saarland 133 C 4
Saarlouis 133 C 4
Saaz = Žatec 133 F 3
Saba 146-147 O 8
Sabaa, Gebel es - = Qârat as-Sab'ah 166-167 H 3
Šabac 136-137 H 3
Sabadell 134-135 J 8
Sabae 188-189 KL 5
Sabah 186-187 G 5
Sab'ah, Qârat as- 166-167 H 3
Sabaki = Galana 168-169 JK 3
Säbälän, K uhhā-ye 182-183 M 3
Sabana, Archipiélago de - 146-147 KL 7
Sabanalarga [CO, Atlántico] 158-159 DE 2
Sabang [RI, Aceh] 186-187 C 5
Şabanözü 182-183 E 2
Sabará 160-161 L 3
Sabari 180-181 N 7
Şabāyā' Jabal - 180-181 E 7
Sab' Biyār 182-183 G 6
Şabbūrah 182-183 G 5
Sabetha, KS 152-153 HJ 6
Sabhah 166-167 G 3
Sabhah, As- 182-183 H 5
Sabi 168-169 H 7
Sabié [Moçambique] 174-175 K 3
Sabie [ZA] 174-175 J 3
Sabierivier 174-175 J 3
Sabile 138-139 D 5
Sabile 130-131 K 9
Sabina, OH 152-153 P 6
Sabinal 154-155 B 5
Sabinal, TX 154-155 F 6
Sabinas 146-147 F 6
Sabinas, Sierra - = Sierra de la Iguana 154-155 E 7
Sabinas Hidalgo 146-147 F 6
Sabine, TX 154-155 HJ 6
Sabine Lake 154-155 J 6
Sabineland 130-131 k 5
Sabine Peninsula 144-145 OP 2
Sabine River 146-147 H 5
Sabini, Monti - 136-137 E 4
Sabinópolis 160-161 L 3
Sabinoso, NM 154-155 C 3
Sabirabad 140-141 O 6-7
Sābiriyah, As- 182-183 M 8
Sabiyah, Qaşr as- 182-183 N 8
Sable 194-195 M 3
Sable, Cape - [CDN] 144-145 XY 9
Sable, Cape - [USA] 146-147 K 6
Sable Island [CDN] 144-145 Z 9
Sable Island [PNG] 186-187 hj 5
Sables-d'Olonne, les - 134-135 FG 5
Sablinskoje 140-141 L 4
Sablykino 138-139 K 7
Sabon Birni 172-173 G 2
Sabon Gari 172-173 H 3
Sabonkafi 172-173 H 2
Saboûra = Şabbūrah 182-183 G 5
Sabrina Land 121 C 12-13
Sabtang Island 190-191 H 11
Sabun 178-179 P 5
Sabunči 140-141 OP 6
Sabuncu 182-183 D 3
Sabuncupinar = Sabuncu 182-183 D 3
Şabyā', As- 180-181 E 7
Sabzawār = Shindand 180-181 J 4
Sabzewār 180-181 H 3
Sacaba 158-159 F 8
Sacaca 158-159 F 8
Sacajawea Peak 150-151 E 3
Sacami, Lac - 144-145 V 7
Sacanta 162 D 4
Saččhere 140-141 L 5
Sac City, IA 152-153 J 4
Sacedi-Arabië 180-181 D 5-F 6
Sachalin 178-179 b 7-8
Sachalinskij zaliv 178-179 b 7
Sach'ang-ni 188-189 F 2
Šachdag, gora - 140-141 O 6
Sachigo River 144-145 S 6-7
Sachnovščina 140-141 G 2
Šachova kosa 140-141 P 6
Šachovskaja 138-139 K 5-6
Šachrisabz 180-181 K 3
Sachsen 133 FG 3
Šachtinsk 178-179 N 8
Šachty 140-141 K 3
Šachunja 178-179 GH 6
Sack [SU, Rossijskaja SFSR] 138-139 N 6
Sackets Harbor, NY 148-149 EF 3
Saco, ME 148-149 H 3
Saco, MT 152-153 C 1
Sacramento 160-161 J 3
Sacramento, CA 146-147 B 4
Sacramento, Pampa del - 158-159 D 6
Sacramento Mountains 146-147 EF 5
Sacramento River 146-147 B 3-4
Sacramento Valley 146-147 B 3-4
Sac River 152-153 K 7
Şa'dah 180-181 E 7
Sada-misaki 188-189 HJ 6
Sadani 168-169 J 4
Saddle Mountain 150-151 G 4
Saddle Mountains 150-151 CD 2
Saddle Peak 150-151 H 3
Sa Đec 186-187 E 4
Sadgora 140-141 BC 2
Sadıkali = Karahasanlı 182-183 F 3
Sadiola 172-173 C 2
Sādis, Al-Jandal as- 166-167 L 5
Sadiya 180-181 Q 5
Sa'diyah, As- 182-183 L 5
Sa'diyah, Hawr as- 182-183 M 6
Sado 134-135 C 10
Sado 184-185 Q 4
Sadovoje 140-141 M 3
Şadr, Wādī - 170 F 3
Šadrinsk 178-179 LM 6
Sæby 130-131 D 9
Saeki = Saiki 188-189 HJ 6
Safā, As- 182-183 G 6
Şafā, Tulūl aş- 182-183 G 6
Safad = Zĕfat 180-181 D 4
Şafah As- 182-183 J 4
Şafājā 166-167 L 3
Şafājā, Jazirat - 170 F 4
Safaji Island = Jazirat Şafājah 170 F 4
Şafāqis 166-167 FG 2
Şafayn, 'Ard - 182-183 H 5
Safēd Kōh, Selselae - 180-181 JK 4
Şaff, Aş- 170 D 3
Şaffāf, Birkat aş- 182-183 M 7
Saffāf, Hōr as- = Birkat as-Saffāf 182-183 M 7
Saffāniyah 180-181 F 5
Şaffār Kalay 180-181 J 4
Säffle 130-131 E 8
Safford, AZ 150-151 J 9
Saffron Walden 132 G 5-6
Şafi 166-167 C 2
Safid, Kūh-e - = Kūh-e Sefid 182-183 M 5-N 6
Safīd Kuh = Selselae Safēd Kōh 180-181 JK 4
Safīd Rūd = Sefid Rūd 182-183 N 4
Safirah 182-183 G 4
Şāfitā' 182-183 G 5
Safonovo 138-139 J 6
Safranbolu 182-183 E 2
Šafranovo 138-139 U 7
Saga 184-185 P 5
Saga 188-189 MN 3
Sagaing = Sitkaing 186-187 D 2
Sagaing = Sitkaing Taing 186-187 B 2-C 1
Sagala 172-173 D 2
Sagami nada 184-185 Q 4-R 5
Saganoseki 188-189 HJ 6
Šagany, ozero - 140-141 DE 4
Šagany, ozero - 136-137 NO 3
Sagar [IND, Maharashtra] 180-181 M 6
Sagara 188-189 M 5
Saga-ri 188-189 F 5
Sagarmatha 184-185 F 6
Sagavanirktok River 144-145 G 3-4
Sage, WY 150-151 H 5
Sage Creek 152-153 A 1
Sagerton, TX 154-155 F 4
Sage Zong = Sakha Dsong 184-185 F 6
Saghir, Zāb aş- 182-183 K 5
Saghru, Jebel - = Jabal Sārū 166-167 C2
Sagī', Har - 182-183 F 7
Saginaw, MI 146-147 K 3
Saginaw, TX 154-155 G 4
Saginaw Bay 146-147 K 3
Sagiz 178-179 JK 8
Sagobé 172-173 B 1
Saguache, CO 152-153 CD 6
Saguache Creek 152-153 C 6-7
Saguaro National Monument 150-151 H 9
Saguenay, Rivière - 144-145 WX 8
Sagunto 134-135 GH 9
Sagyndyk, mys - 140-141 P 4
Sahagún 134-135 E 7
Sahand, Kūh-e - 182-183 M 4
Sahara-Atlas 166-167 D 2-F 1
Saharanpur 180-181 M 4
Sahara Occidental 166-167 A 4-B 3
Sahara Occidentale 166-167 A 4-B 3
Sahara Well 194-195 D 4
Sahara Zachodnia 166-167 A 4-B 3
Saharský Atlas 166-167 D 2-F 1
Saharunpore = Saharanpur 180-181 M 4
Sahbā', Wādī aş- 180-181 F 6
Sahel = Sāhil 166-167 BC 5
Şāhhāt = Shahhāt 166-167 J 2
Sāhil 166-167 BC 5
Sāhiwāl 180-181 L 4
Şahn, Aş- 182-183 K 7
Şahneh 182-183 M 5
Şahrā', Bi'r - 170 C 6
Şahrā, Jabal - 170 EF 4
Şahrā' al-Gharbiyah, Aş- 170 BC 4
Sahuarita, AZ 150-151 H 10
Sahuayo de José Maria Morelos 146-147 F 7-8
Sahyādri = Western Ghats 180-181 L 6-M 8
Saibai Island 186-187 M 8
Sai Buri 186-187 D 5
Saiburi = Alor Setar 186-187 CD 5
Şa'īd, Aş- 166-167 L 3-4
Saïd, Es- = Aş-Şa' īd 166-167 L 3-4
Saïda = Saydā [RL] 180-181 CD 4
Sa'īdābād = Sirjān 180-181 H 5
Saidaiji 188-189 JK 5
Sa'īd Bundās 166-167 JK 7
Saigō 188-189 J 4
Saigon = Thành Phô Hô Chí Minh 186-187 E 4
Saigón = Thàn Phô Hô Chi Minh 186-187 E 4
Saihūt = Sayhūt 180-181 G 7
Saijo 188-189 J 6
Saikai National Park = Gotō-rettō 188-189 G 6
Saiki 188-189 HJ 6
Šaim 178-179 L5
Saima 188-189 E 2
Saimaa 130-131 MN 7
Sai-ma-chi = Saima 188-189 E 2
Saimbeyli 182-183 FG 3
Sā'in Dezh 182-183 M 4
Sainjang 188-189 E 3
Sāin Qal'eh = Shāhin Dezh 182-183 M 4
Saint Albans, VT 148-149 G 2
Saint Albans, WV 148-149 BC 5
Saint-Amand-Mont-Rond 134-135 J 5
Saint-André, Cap - 168-169 K 6
Saint Andrew, FL 154-155 MN 5
Saint Andrew Bay 154-155 MN 5-6
Saint Andrew Point 154-155 MN 6
Saint Andrews, SC 148-149 CD 8
Saint Anne, IL 152-153 MN 5
Saint Anthony 144-145 Za 7
Saint Anthony, ID 150-151 H 4
Saint Arnaud 196 F 6
Saint Augustin, Baie de - 168-169 K 7
Saint-Augustine, FL 146-147 KL 6
Saint Austell 132 D 6
Saint-Avold 134-135 L 4
Saint Barthélemy 146-147 O 8
Saint-Blaize, Cape - = Kaap Sint Blaize 174-175 E 8
Saint-Boniface 144-145 R 8
Saint-Brieuc 134-135 F 4
Saint Catharines 144-145 UV 9
Saint Catherines Island 148-149 C 9
Saint Charles, ID 150-151 H 4
Saint Charles, MI 152-153 O 4
Saint Charles, MO 146-147 H 4
Saint Charles, Cape - 144-145 Za 7
Saint Clair, MI 152-153 P 4
Saint Clair, MO 152-153 L 6
Saint Clair, Lake - 144-145 U 9
Saint Clair River 152-153 P 4
Saint Clairsville, OH 148-149 C 4
Saint Cloud, FL 148-149 c 2
Saint Cloud, MN 146-147 H 2
Saint Croix 146-147 O 8
Saint Croix Falls, WI 152-153 K 3
Saint Croix River 152-153 K 2-3
Saint David Islands = Kepulauan Mapia 186-187 KL 6
Saint David's Head 132 CD 6
Saint-Denis [F] 134-135 J 4
Saint-Denis [Réunion] 168-169 N 7
Saint-Dié 134-135 L 4
Saint-Dizier 134-135 K 4
Sainte-Agathe-des-Monts 144-145 VW 8
Saint Edward, NE 152-153 GH 5
Sainte Genevieve, MO 152-153 L 6-7
Saint Elias, Mount - 144-145 H 5
Saint Elias Mountains 144-145 J 5-6
Saint-Élie 158-159 J 3-4
Saint Elmo, IL 152-153 M 6
Sainte-Lucie 156 CD 2
Sainte-Lucie 146-147 O 8
Sainte-Marie [CDN] 148-149 H 1
Sainte-Marie [Gabun] 168-169 D 3
Sainte-Marie [Martinique] 146-147 O 9
Sainte-Marie, Cap - 168-169 L 8
Sainte-Marie, Île - = Nosy Boraha 168-169 M 6
Saintes 134-135 G 6
Sainte Thérèse 148-149 FG 2
Saint-Étienne 134-135 JK 6
Saint Faith's 174-175 J 6
Saint-Flour 134-135 J 6
Saint Francis, KS 152-153 EF 6
Saint Francis, ME 148-149 J 1
Saint Francis, Cape - = Sealpunt 174-175 F 8
Saint Francis Bay = Sint Francisbaai 174-175 F 8
Saint Francisbaai Bay = Sint Franziskusbaai 174-175 A 3
Saint Francis River 146-147 H 4
Saint Francisville, IL 152-153 MN 6
Saint Francisville, LA 154-155 K 5
Saint François, Lac - 148-149 H 2
Saint François Island 168-169 M 4
Saint François Mountains 152-153 L 7
Saint-Gaudens 134-135 H 7
Saint George [AUS] 194-195 J 5
Saint George, GA 148-149 B 9
Saint George, SC 148-149 C 8
Saint George, UT 150-151 G 7
Saint George, Cape - [USA] 154-155 N 6
Saint George, Point - 150-151 A 5
Saint George Island 154-155 N 6
Saint-Georges [Französisch-Guyana] 158-159 J 4
Saint George's [WG] 146-147 O 9
Saint-Georges, Canal - = Saint George's Channel 132 C 6-D 5
Saint George's Channel 132 C 6-D 5
Saint George's Channel [PNG] 186-187 h 5-6
Saint-Gilles-sur-Vie 134-135 FG 5
Saint-Girons 134-135 H 7
Saint Govan's Head 132 D 6
Saint Helena 165 F 10
Saint Helena, CA 150-151 B 6
Saint Helena Bay = Sint Helenabaai 168-169 E 9
Saint Helena Range 150-151 B 6
Saint Helena Sound 148-149 CD 8
Saint Helens 132 E 5
Saint Helens [AUS] 196 d 2
Saint Helens, OR 150-151 B 3
Saint Helens, WA 150-151 B 2
Saint Helens, Mount - 150-151 BC 2
Saint Helens Point 196 d 2
Saint Helier 132 E 7
Saint-Hyacinthe 144-145 W 8
Saint Ignace, MI 152-153 O 3
Saint Ignatius, MT 150-151 FG 2
Saint James, MI 152-153 O 3
Saint James, MN 152-153 J 3-4
Saint James, MO 152-153 L 6-7
Saint James, Cape - 144-145 K 7
Saint-Jean 144-145 W 8
Saint-Jean, Lac - 144-145 W 8
Saint-Jean-de-Luz 134-135 FG 7
Saint Jo, TX 154-155 G 4
Saint Joe, AR 154-155 J 2
Saint Joe River 150-151 E 2
Saint John [CDN] 144-145 X 8
Saint John, KS 152-153 G 6-7
Saint John, ND 152-153 FG 1
Saint John, Lake - = Lac Saint Jean 144-145 W 8
Saint John River 144-145 X 8
Saint John's [CDN] 144-145 a 8
Saint John's [West Indies] 146-147 O 8
Saint Johns, AZ 150-151 J 8
Saint Johns, MI 152-153 O 4
Saint Johns = Saint-Jean 144-145 W 8
Saint Johnsbury, VT 148-149 G 2
Saint Johns River 148-149 c 1-2
Saint Joseph, LA 154-155 K 5
Saint Joseph, MI 152-153 N 4
Saint Joseph, MO 146-147 GH 4
Saint Joseph, Lake - 144-145 ST 7
Saint Joseph Bay 154-155 N 6
Saint-Joseph-d'Alma = Alma 144-145 W 8
Saint Joseph Island [SY] 168-169 M 4
Saint Joseph Island [USA] 154-155 G 6-7
Saint Joseph Point 154-155 N 6
Saint-Junien 134-135 H 6
Saint Kilda 132 B 3
Saint Kitts and Nevis 157 D 1
Saint Kitts e Nevis 157 D 1
Saint Kitts e Nevis 156 C 2
Saint Kitts en Nevis 157 D 1
Saint Kitts-et-Nevis 157 D 1
Saint Kitts Nevis 156 C 2
Saint Kitts u. Nevis 157 D 1
Saint Kitts y Nevis 157 D 1
Saint Laurent 144-145 W 8
Saint-Laurent, Fleuve 144-145 W 8-9
Saint-Laurent, Golfe du - = Gulf of Saint Lawrence 144-145 Y 8
Saint Lawrence [AUS] 194-195 J 4
Saint Lawrence, Gulf of - 144-145 Y 8
Saint Lawrence Island 144-145 BC 5
Saint Lawrence River 144-145 X 8
Saint-Lô 134-135 G 4
Saint-Louis [SN] 166-167 A 5
Saint Louis, MI 152-153 O 4
Saint Louis, MO 146-147 H 4
Saint Louis Park, MN 152-153 K 3
Saint Louis River 152-153 K 2
Saint Lucia 146-147 O 9
Saint Lucia, Lake - = Sint Luciameer 168-169 H 8
Saint Lucia Bay - = Sint Luciabaai 174-175 K 5
Saint Magnus Bay 132 EF 1
Saint-Malo 134-135 FG 4
Saint Marc 148-149 G 7
Saint Maries, ID 150-151 E 2
Saint-Marin 136-137 E 4
Saint Marks, FL 154-155 N 5
Saint Martin [☼] 146-147 O 8
Saint Martin, Cape - = Kaap Sint Martin 174-175 B 7
Saint Martins Bay 152-153 O 2-3
Saint Martins Bay 148-149 A 1-2
Saint Martins Point = Kaap Sint Martin 174-175 B 7
Saint Mary Lake 150-151 G 1
Saint Mary Peak 194-195 G 6
Saint Marys [AUS] 194-195 J 8
Saint Mary's [CDN, Ontario] 148-149 C 3
Saint Marys, GA 148-149 C 9
Saint Marys, KS 152-153 HJ 6
Saint Marys, MO 152-153 LM 7
Saint Marys, OH 152-153 O 5
Saint Marys, PA 148-149 D 4
Saint Marys, WV 148-149 C 5
Saint Marys River [USA] 146-147 K 2
Saint Mathieu, Pointe 134-135 E 4
Saint Matthew 178-179 1 5
Saint Matthew Island 144-145 B 5
Saint Matthew Island = Zādetky Kyûn 186-187 C 5
Saint Matthews, SC 148-149 C 8
Saint Matthias Group 186-187 NO 7
Saint-Maurice, Rivière 144-145 W 8
Saint Michael, AK 144-145 D 5
Saint Michaels, AZ 150-151 J 8
Saint-Nazaire 134-135 F 5
Saint-Omer 134-135 HJ 3
Saintonge 134-135 G 6
Saint Paris, OH 152-153 OP 5
Saint Paul [CDN] 144-145 O 7
Saint Paul [Saint Paul] 124-125 NO 7
Saint Paul, MN 146-147 H 2
Saint Paul, NE 152-153 G 5
Saint Paul, VT 148-149 B 6
Saint Paul, Cape - 172-173 F 4
Saint Paul River 166-167 BC 7
Saint Pauls, NC 148-149 D 7
Saint Peter, MN 152-153 JK 3
Saint Peter Port 132 E 7
Saint Petersburg 138-139 H 3-4
Saint Petersburg, FL 146-147 K 6
Saint-Pierre et Miquelon 144-145 Za 8
Saint Pierre Island 168-169 LM 4
Saint-Quentin 134-135 J 4
Saint-Raphaël 134-135 L 7
Saint Regis, MT 150-151 F 2
Saint Sebastian Bay = Sint Sebastianbaai 174-175 D 8
Saint-Sébastien, Cap - 168-169 L 5
Saint Simons Island 148-149 C 9
Saint Simons Island, GA 148-149 C 9
Saint Stephens, SC 148-149 D 8
Saint Thomas [CDN] 148-149 C 3
Saint Thomas [Westindien] 146-147 NO 8
Saint Thomas, ND 152-153 H 1
Saint-Tropez 134-135 L 7
Saint Vincent a. the Grenadines 158-159 G 2
Saint Vincent, MN 152-153 H 1
Saint Vincent, Gulf - 194-195 G 6-7
Saint Vincent e Grenadine 146-147 O 9
Saint Vincent en de Grenadinen 146-147 O 9
Saint-Vincent-et-les-Grenadines 158-159 G 2
Saint Vincent Island 154-155 N 6
Saint Vincent u. die Grenadinesn 146-147 O 9
Saint Xavier, MT 152-153 C 3
Saio = Dembi Dolo 166-167 LM 7
Saipurú 160-161 E 6
Saiqi 190-191 G 8
Sairme 140-141 L 6
Saishū = Cheju-do 188-189 F 6
Saitama 188-189 M 4
Saiteli = Kadınhanı 182-183 E 3
Saito 188-189 H 6
Sai'wun = Say'ūn 180-181 F 7
Sajak 178-179 O 8
Sajama, Nevado de - 158-159 F 8
Sajano-Šušenskoje vodochranilišče 180-181 R 7
Sajari, Bi'r - 182-183 H 6
Sajchin 140-141 N 2
Šajgino 138-139 Q 5
Sajgon = Thành Phô Ho Chi Minh 186-187 JK 4
Saji-dong 188-189 G 2
Šajmak 180-181 L 3
Sajmenskij kanal 138-139 G 3
Sajnšand 184-185 KL 3
Sajo 133 K 4
Sajram nuur 184-185 DE 3
Saka 171 D 3
Sakai 184-185 Q 5
Sakaide 188-189 JK 5
Sakaiminato 188-189 J 5
Sakākah 180-181 E 4-5
Sakakawea, Lake - 146-147 F 2
Sakamachi = Arakawa 188-189 M 3
Sakania 168-169 G 5
Sakarya 180-181 C 2
Sakarya Nehri 180-181 C 2
Sakata 184-185 Q 4
Sakavi = Mercimekkale 182-183 J 3
Sakawa 188-189 J 6
Sakchu 188-189 E 2
Saketa 186-187 J 7
Sakha Dsong 184-185 F 6
Sakht-Sar 182-183 O 4
Saki 140-141 F 4
Sakikdah 166-167 F 1
Sakinohama 188-189 K 6
Sakishima-guntō 188-189 NO 7
Sakisima guntō = Sakishima-guntō 188-185 NO 7
Sâkkâne, 'Erg I-n- 166-167 D 4
Sakon Nakhon 186-187 B 3
Sakonnet Point 148-149 H 4
Sakovlevskoje = Privolžsk 178-179 N 5
Sakrivier [ZA, ~ Agter Roggeveld] 174-175 D 6
Sakrivier [ZA, ~ De Bosbulten] 174-175 D 5
Sakrivier [ZA, ●] 168-169 EF 9
Sal 140-141 K 3
Sala 130-131 G 8
Salacgriva 130-131 KL 9
Salacgriva 138-139 DE 5
Sala Consilina 136-137 F 5
Salada, Laguna - [MEX] 150-151 F 9
Saladillo [RA, Buenos Aires] 162 DE 5
Salado, Rio - [RA, Santa Fe] 162 D 3
Salado, Rio - [USA] 154-155 B 3
Salado, Valle del - 146-147 F 7
Salaga 166-167 D 7
Salah, In- = 'Ayn Şālih 166-167 E 3
Salāhuddin 182-183 KL 5
Salair 178-179 PQ 7
Salairskij kraž 178-179 PQ 7
Salajar = Pulau Selayar 186-187 H 8
Šalakuša 138-139 N 2
Salal 166-167 H 6
Salala 172-173 C 4
Şalālah 180-181 G 7
Şalālah, Jabal - 170 F 7
Salamanca 134-135 E 8
Salamanca, NY 148-149 D 3
Salamat, Bahr - 166-167 H 6-7
Salāmatābād 182-183 M 5
Salamaua 186-187 N 8
Salamis 136-137 K 7
Salamiyah 182-183 G 5
Salamon-medence 186-187 h 6
Salamon-szigetek, ☼ 186-187 h 6-k 7
Salamon-szigetek, ★ 186-187 kl 7
Salamon-tenger 186-187 hj 6
Salang = Ko Phuket 186-187 C 5
Salantai 138-139 CD 5
Salantai 130-131 J 9
Salatan, Cape - = Tanjung Selatan 186-187 F 7
Salatiga 186-187 F 8
Salavat 178-179 K 7
Salaverry 158-159 D 6
Salawati, Pulau - 186-187 K 7
Sala y Gómez 198-199 M 6
Sala-y-Gomez, Dorsale di - 124-125 C-E 7
Salazar, NM 154-155 B 3
Salazar = Ndalatando 168-169 DE
Šalčininkai 138-139 E 6
Saldanha [ZA] 168-169 E 9
Saldus 130-131 K 9
Saldus 138-139 D 5
Sale [AUS] 194-195 J 7
Salé = Slā 166-167 C 2
Salé, Grand Lac - = Great Salt Lake 146-147 D 3
Salechard 178-179 M 4
Saleh, Teluk - 186-187 G 8
Şālehābād [IR ↙ Hamadān] 182-183 N 5
Şālehābād [IR ↙ Īlām] 182-183 M
Salem [IND] 180-181 M 8
Salem [ZA] 174-175 G 7
Salem, AR 154-155 K 2
Salem, FL 146-149 b 2
Salem, IL 152-153 M 6
Salem, IN 152-153 NO 6
Salem, MA 148-149 H 3
Salem, MO 152-153 L 7
Salem, NJ 148-149 F 5
Salem, OH 148-149 C 4
Salem, OR 146-147 B 2
Salem, SD 152-153 H 4

Salem, VA 148-149 C 6
Salem, WV 148-149 C 5
Salemi 136-137 E 7
Sälen 130-131 E 7
Salentina 136-137 GH 5
Salerno 136-137 F 5
Salerno, Golfo di - 136-137 F 5
Saléye 172-173 E 3
Salford 132 E 5
Salgir 140-141 G 4
Salgótarjan 133 J 4
Salgueiro 158-159 M 6
Salhyr = Nižnegorskij 140-141 G 4
Sali [SU] 140-141 MN 5
Salibabu, Pulau - 186-187 J 6
Salida, CO 146-147 E 4
Salif, Aṣ - 180-181 E 7
Ṣāliḥiyah, Aṣ - [ET] 170 DE 2
Ṣāliḥiyah, Aṣ - [SYR] 182-183 J 5
Salihli 182-183 C 3
Salima 168-169 HJ 5
Salimah, Wāḥat - 166-167 K 4
Salina, KS 146-147 G 4
Salina, OK 154-155 H 2
Salina, UT 150-151 H 6
Salina, Ìsola - 136-137 F 6
Salina, La - 150-151 G 10
Salina Cruz 146-147 G 8
Salinas [BR] 158-159 L 8
Salinas [EC] 158-159 C 5
Salinas, CA 146-147 B 4
Salinas, Cabo de - 134-135 J 9
Salinas, Punta de - 158-159 D 7
Salinas, Rio - 160-161 L 2
Salinas Grandes [RA ↖ Cordoba] 162 C 4-D 3
Salinas Peak 154-155 B 4
Salinas River 150-151 C 7-8
Salinas Victoria 154-155 EF 7-8
Saline, LA 154-155 J 4
Saline River [USA, Arkansas] 154-155 JK 4
Saline River [USA, Kansas] 152-153 G 6
Saline Valley 150-151 E 7
Salinópolis 158-159 K 4-5
Salisburg = Mazsalaca 138-139 E 5
Salisbury 132 EF 6
Salisbury, CT 148-149 G 3-4
Salisbury, MD 146-147 LM 4
Salisbury, MO 152-153 K 6
Salisbury, NC 146-147 KL 4
Salisbury = Harare 168-169 H 6
Salisbury, ostrov - = ostrov
Salsberi 178-179 HJ 1
Salisbury Island 144-145 VW 5
Salish Mountains 150-151 F 1-2
Salismünde = Salacgriva 138-139 DE 5
Salitre-cué 160-161 DE 7
Saljany 140-141 O 7
Salkar 140-141 PQ 1
Salkar, ozero - 140-141 P 1
Salkhad 182-183 G 6
Salkum, WA 150-151 B 2
Salla 130-131 N 4
Salle, La -, CO 152-153 D 5
Salle, La -, IL 152-153 M 5
Salley, SC 148-149 C 8
Sallisaw, OK 154-155 H 3
Sallyana 180-181 N 5
Sal'm, ostrov - 178-179 KL 2
Salmah, Jabal - 180-181 E 5
Salmān, As- 182-183 L 7
Salmanlı 182-183 F 3
Salmanlı = Kaymas 182-183 D 2
Salmān Pāk 182-183 L 6
Salmās 182-183 L 3
Salmi 178-179 E 5
Salmon, ID 150-151 FG 3
Salmon Creek Reservoir 150-151 F 4
Salmon Falls 150-151 F 4
Salmon Falls Creek Lake 150-151 F 4
Salmon Gums 194-195 D 6
Salmon River [USA, Idaho] 146-147 CD 2
Salmon River Mountains 146-147 C 3-D 2
Salo 130-131 K 7
Salobel'ak 138-139 R 5
Salomão [Estado] 186-187 kl 7
Salomão [ilhas] 186-187 h 6-k 7
Salomão, Bacia de - 186-187 h 6
Salomão, Mar de - 186-187 hj 6
Salomón [⊙] 186-187 h 6-k 7
Salomón [★] 186-187 kl 7
Salomon, Bassin des - 186-187 h 6
Salomón, Cuenca de las - 186-187 h 6
Salomon, Îles - [⊙] 186-187 h 6-k 7
Salomon, Îles - [★] 186-187 kl 7
Salomón, Mar de las - 186-187 hj 6
Salomon, Mer des - 186-187 hj 6
Salomona, Morze - 186-187 hj 6
Salomona, Wyspy - [⊙] 186-187 h 6-k 7
Salomona, Wyspy - [★] 186-187 kl 7
Salomonbekken 186-187 h 6
Salomone [regione] 186-187 h 6-k 7
Salomone [Stato] 186-187 kl 7
Salomone, Bacino delle - 86-187 h 6
Salomone, Mar delle - 186-187 hj 6
Salomonen, ⊙ 186-187 h 6-k 7
Salomonen, ★ 186-187 kl 7
Salomonenbecken 186-187 h 6
Salomon Sea 192-193 FG 5
Salomonensee 186-187 hj 6
Salomonseilanden [⊙] 186-187 h 6-k 7
Salomonseilanden [★] 186-187 kl 7
Salomonzee 186-187 hj 6
Salonga 168-169 F 3
Salonga Nord, Parc national de la - 168-169 F 3
Salonga Sud, Parc national de la - 168-169F3
Salónica = Thessalonikē 128-129 N 7
Salónica = Thessalonikē 136-137 K 5
Salonicco = Thessaloniké 136-137 K 5
Salonika = Thessalonikē 136-137 K 5
Saloniki = Thessaloniké 136-137 K 5
Salonique = Thessalonikē 136-137 K 5
Salonta 136-137 JK 2
Salor 134-135 D 9
Salpausselkä 130-131 L-O 7
Salsacate 162 CD 4
Salsberi, ostrov - 178-179 HJ 1
Sal'sk 140-141 K 3
Sal'skij 138-139 KL 3
Salso 136-137 E 7
Salsomaggiore Terme 136-137 C 3
Salṭ, As- 182-183 F 6
Salta [RA, ●] 162 CD 2
Salta Ginete, Serra do - 160-161 K 3
Salt Basin 154-155 C 5
Salt Creek 152-153 C 4
Salten 130-131 F 4-G 3
Saltfjord 130-131 EF 4
Salt Flat, TX 146-147 EF 5
Salt Flat 154-155 C 5
Salt Fork Brazos River 154-155 E 4
Salt Fork Red River 154-155 F 3
Saltillo 146-147 FG 6
Salt Lake, NM 150-151 J 8
Salt Lake City, UT 146-147 D 3
Salt Lakes 194-195 CD 5
Salt Lick, KY 152-153 P 6
Salt Marsh = Lake MacLeod 194-195 B 4
Salto [RA] 162 DE 4
Salto [ROU, ●] 162 E 4
Salto, El - 146-147 E 7
Salto da Divisa 158-159 LM 8
Salto Grande [BR] 160-161 H 5
Salto Grande, Embalse - 162 E 4
Saltoluokta 130-131 H 4
Salton, CA 150-151 F 9
Saltón, El - 162 B 7
Salton Sea 146-147 CD 5
Salt River [USA, Arizona] 146-147 D 5
Salt River [USA, Kentucky] 152-153 O 6-7
Salt River [USA, Missouri] 52-153 L 6
Salt River = Soutriver [ZA ◁ Atlantic Ocean] 174-175 B 6
Salt River = Soutriver [ZA ◁ Grootsriver] 174-175 E 7
Salt River Indian Reservation 150-151 H 9
Saltspring Island 150-151 B 1
Saltville, VA 148-149 C 6
Saltykovka 138-139 P 7
Saluda, SC 148-149 BC 7-8
Saluen 184-185 H 6
Saluen = Thanlwin Myit 186-187 C 2-3
Saluen = Thanlwin Myit 186-187 C 2-3
Saluin = Thanlwin Myit 186-187 C 2-3
Salūm, As- 166-167 K 2
Salus, AR 154-155 J 3
Saluzzo 136-137 B 3
Salvador 146-147 J 9
Salvador 158-159 M 7
Salvador, Lake - 154-155 K 6
Salwá Baḥrī 170 E 5
Salwador 146-147 J 9
Salyersville, KY 152-153 P 7
Salween = Thanlwin Myit 186-187 C 2-3
Salwin = Thanlwin Myit 186-187 C 2-3
Salyānā = Sallyana 180-181 N 5
Salzach 133 F 4-5
Salzbrunn 168-169 E 7
Salzburg [A, ●] 133 F 5
Salzburg [A, ☆] 133 F 5
Salzgitter 133 E 2-3
Salzwedel 133 E 2
Sama de Langreo 134-135 E 7
Samāh, Bi'r - 182-183 L 8
Samalayuca 154-155 B 5
Samālūṭ 170 D 3
Samaná, Bahia de - 146-147 N 8
Samānalakanda 180-181 N 9
Samandağı 182-183 F 4
Samandéni 172-173 D 3
Samangān 180-181 K 3
Samani 184-185 R 3
Samar 186-187 J 4
Samara [Ukraina] 140-141 G 2
Samara [~] 178-179 J 7
Samara [●] 178-179 HJ 7
Samarai 186-187 gh 7
Samarga 178-179 ab 8
Samarinda 186-187 G 7
Samarkand 180-181 K 3
Samarkand = Temirtau 178-179 N 7
Sāmarrā' 180-181 E 4
Samatra = Sumatra 126-127 C 6-D 7
Samāwah, As- 180-181 EF 4
Sambala 168-169 F 4
Sambaliung 186-187 G 6
Sambalpore = Sambalpur 180-181 N 6
Sambalpur 180-181 N 6
Sambas 186-187 E 6
Sambava 168-169 M 5
Sambhal 180-181 M 5
Sambia 168-169 G 6-H 5
Sambo 172-173 E 3
Samboja 186-187 G 7
Sambongi = Towada 188-189 N 2
Sambor [K] 186-187 E 4
Sambir [SU] 140-141 A 2
Samborombón, Bahia - 162 E 5
Sambre 134-135 K 3
Šamchal 140-141 N 5
Samch'ŏk 184-185 OP 4
Samch'ŏnp'o 188-189 FG 5
Samdŭng 188-189 F 3
Same [EAT] 168-169 J 3
Samfya 171 B 5
Samḥah 180-181 G 8
Samia [RN] 172-173 H 2
Samia [WAN] 172-173 F 3
Šamkir 140-141 MN 6
Samīm, Umm as- 180-181 H 6
Samnagjin 188-189 G 5
Samoa 186-187 c 1
Samoa, CA 150-151 A 5
Samoa, American 122-123 A 6
Samoa, Amerikaans 122-123 A 6
Samoa, Americana [E.U.A.] 122-123 A 6
Samoa, Americane [E.U.A.] 122-123 A 6
Samoa, Îles - = Samoa Islands 186-187 c 1
Samoa, Wyspy - = Samoa Islands 186-187 c 1
Samoainseln = Samoa Islands 186-187 c 1
Samoa Islands 186-187 c 1
Samoa Orient [E.-U.] 122-123 A 6
Samoded 138-139 N 2
Samora = Zamora de Hidalgo 146-147 F 7-8
Sámos [GR, ⊙] 136-137 M 7
Sámos [GR, ●] 136-137 M 7
Samosir, Pulau - 186-187 C 6
Samothrákē 136-137 L 5
Šamovo 138-139 H 6
S'amozero, ozero - 138-139 J 3
Sampacho 162 CD 4
Sampang 186-187 F 8
Samper de Calanda 134-135 G 8
Sampit 186-187 F 7
Sampit, Teluk - 186-187 F 7
Sampur 138-139 NO 7
Samrah = Mazıdağı 182-183 J 4
Sam Rayburn Lake 154-155 H 5
Samrong 186-187 D 4
Samshui = Sanshui 190-191 D 10
Samson, AL 154-155 MN 5
Sarnsø 130-131 D 10
Samsu 188-189 G 2
Samsun 180-181 D 2
Samter = Szamotuly 133 H 2
Samtredia 140-141 L 5
Samuel, Mount - 194-195 F 3
Samui, Ko - 186-187 D 5
Samutlu = Temelli 182-183 E 3
Samut Prakan 186-187 D 4
Samur 140-141 O 6
Samurskij chrebet 140-141 N 6
S'amža 138-139 N 3
San 133 L 3
San [RMM] 166-167 CD 6
Sanā [Y, Hadramawt] 180-181 FG 7
Ṣan'ā' [Y, Tihāmah] 180-181 EF 7
Sana [YU] 136-137 G 3
Sanaag 166-167 b 2
Sānabād 182-183 N 4
Ṣanabū 170 D 4
Sanae 121 b 36-1
Ṣanāfir, Jazirat - 170 F 4
Sanaga 166-167 G 8
San Agustin [RA, Buenos Aires] 162 E 5
San Agustin, Cape - 186-187 J 5
Sanām, As- 180-181 G 6
Sanām, Jabal - 182-183 M 7
San Ambrosio 157 C 5
Sanana, Pulau - 186-187 J 7
Sanandaj 180-181 F 3
Sanando 172-173 D 2
San Andreas, CA 150-151 C 6
San Andrés [CO, ⊙] 146-147 KL 9
San Andres Mountains 146-147 E 5
San Andres Tuxtla 146-147 GH 8
San Angel 158-159 E 2-3
San Angelo, TX 146-147 FG 5
Sanangyi 190-191 BC 8
Sanankoroba 172-173 CD 2
San Anselmo, CA 150-151 B 7
San Antonio [PY] 160-161 D 5
San Antonio [RCH] 162 B 4
San Antonio, NM 154-155 B 4
San Antonio, TX 146-147 G 6
San Antonio, Cabo - [C] 146-147 K 7
San Antonio Bay 154-155 G 6
San Antonio de Caparo 158-159 E 3
San Antonio de Chacones 154-155 B 6
San Antonio del Mar 150-151 E 10
San Antonio de los Cobres 162 C 2
San Antonio Mountain 154-155 C 5
San Antonio Oeste 162 CD 6
San Antonio Peak 150-151 E 8
San Antonio River 154-155 G 6
San Ardo, CA 150-151 C 7
Sanatorium, TX 154-155 E 5
San Augustine, TX 154-155 HJ 5
Sanāw 180-181 G 7
Sanbalpur = Sambalpur 180-181 N 6
San Benedetto del Tronto 136-137 EF 4
San Benedicto, Isla - 146-147 DE 8
San Benito, TX 146-147 G 6
San Benito Mountain 150-151 C 7
San Bernardino, CA 146-147 CD 5
San Bernardino Mountains 150-151 E 8
San Bernardo [MEX] 154-155 C 7-8
San Bernardo [RCH] 162 BC 4
San Blas, Cape - 146-147 J 6
San Blas, Cordillera de - 146-147 L 10
San Blas, Punta - 146-147 L 10
San Borja 158-159 F 7
Sanborn, MN 152-153 J 3
Sanborn, ND 152-153 G 2
San Buenaventura = Ventura, CA 150-151 D 8
Sancang 190-191 H 5
San Carlos [PY] 160-161 D 5
San Carlos [RCH] 162 B 5
San Carlos [RP, Luzón] 186-187 GH 3
San Carlos [RP, Negros] 186-187 H 4
San Carlos [W, Cojedes] 158-159 F 3
San Carlos, AZ 150-151 H 9
San Carlos [MEX, Coahuila → Torreón] 154-155 D 8
San Carlos [MEX, Coahuila ↓ Villa Acuña] 154-155 E 6
San Carlos, Estrecho de - = Falkland Sound 162 DE 8
San Carlos, Rio - 160-161 C 5
San Carlos Bay 148-149 bc 3
San Carlos de Bariloche 162 B 6
San Carlos de Bolívar 162 D 5
San Carlos de Puno 158-159 EF 8
San Carlos de Río Negro 158-159 F 4
San Carlos de Zulia 158-159 E 3
San Carlos Indian Reservation 150-151 HJ 9
San Carlos Lake 150-151 H 9
San-ch'a = San-i 190-191 H 9
San-chiang = Sanjiang 190-191 B 9
San Clemente, CA 150-151 E 9
San Clemente Island 146-147 BC 5
San Cristóbal [CO] 158-159 E 5
San Cristóbal [RA] 162 D 4
San Cristóbal [Solomons] 186-187 k 7
San Cristóbal [W] 158-159 E 3
San Cristóbal, Isla - 158-159 B 5
San Cristóbal de las Casas 146-147 H 8
San Cristobal Wash 150-151 G 9
San Cristoval = San Cristóbal 186-187 k 7
Sancti-Spíritus [C] 146-147 L 7
Sančursk 138-139 Q 5
Sand 130-131 AB 8
Ṣandafā' 170 D 3
Sandai 186-187 F 7
Sandakan 186-187 G 5
Sandane 130-131 AB 7
Sandanski 136-137 K 5
Sand Arroyo 152-153 E 7
Sanday 132 EF 2
Sandberg [ZA] 174-175 C 7
Sandbult 174-175 G 2
Sandefjord 130-131 D 8
Sanders, AZ 150-151 J 8
Sanderson,TX 154-155 D 5
Sandersville, GA 148-149 B 8
Sandfish Bay = Sandvisbaai 174-175 A 2
Sandfontein 168-169 EF 7
Sandfontein [ZA] 174-175 H 2
Sandfontein [Namibia ↓ Karasburg] 174-175 C 5
Sandhornøy 130-131 EF 4
Sandia 158-159 F 7
Sandia Crest 154-155 BC 3
Sandiao Jiao = Sun-chiao Chiao 190-191 HJ 9
Sandia Peak = Sandia Crest 154-155 BC 3
Sandias 154-155 BC 7
San Diego 154-155 C 6
San Diego, TX 154-155 F 7
San Diego, CA 146-147 C 5
San Diego, Cabo - 162 CD 8
San Diego Aqueduct 150-151 E 9
Sandıklı 182-183 CD 3
Sand Island 152-153 L 2
Sand Key 148-149 b 3
Sand Mountains 146-147 J 5
Sandnes 130-131 A 8
Sandoa 168-169 F 4
Sandomierz 133 K 3
San Donà di Piave 136-137 E 3
Sandouping 190-191 C 6
Sandover River 194-195 FG 4
Sandovo 138-139 L 4
Sandoway = Thandwe 186-187 B 3
Sandpoint, ID 150-151 E 1
Sandringham 194-195 G 4
Sandriver [ZA ◁ Krokodilrivier] 174-175 G 3
Sandriver [ZA ◁ Limpopo] 174-175 H 2
Sandriver [ZA ◁ Vetrivier] 174-175 G 5
Sand Springs, MT 152-153 C 2
Sand Springs, OK 154-155 G 2
Sandspruit [ZA Welkom] 174-175 G 4
Sandstone 194-195 C 5
Sandstone, MN 152-153 K 2
Sand Tank Mountains 150-151 G 9
Sandu 190-191 E 7
Sandu Ao 190-191 GH 8
Sandur 130-131 ab 2
Sandusky, MI 152-153 P 4
Sandusky, OH 152-153 P 5
Sandusky Bay 152-153 P 5
Sandveld [Namibia] 168-169 EF 7
Sandveld [ZA] 174-175 C 6-7
Sandverhaar 174-175 B 4
Sandviken 130-131 G 7
Sandvisbaai 174-175 A 2
Sandwich Australi, Fossa delle - 121 D 34
Sandwich, IL 152-153 M 5
Sandwich Bay = Sandvisbaai 174-175 A 2
Sandwich do Sul, Fossa das - 121 CD 34
Sandwich du Sud, Fosse du - 121 D 34
Sandwich Południowy, Rów - 121 D 34
Sandwich del Sur, Dorsal de las - 121 D 34
Sandy, NV 150-151 F 8
Sandy Cape [AUS, Queensland] 194-195 K 4
Sandy Cape [AUS, Tasmania] 196 ab 2
Sandy City, UT 146-147 D 3
Sandy Creek 150-151 J 4-5
Sandy Hills 146-147 GH 5
Sandy Hook 148-149 G 4
Sandy Hook, KY 152-153 P 6-7
Sandy Key 148-149 c 4
Sandy Lake [CDN, ≈ Ontario] 144-145 S 7
Sandy Ridge 148-149 B 6
Sandy River 150-151 BC 3
San Estanislao 162 E 2
San Esteban de Gormaz 134-135 F 8
San Felipe [CO] 158-159 F 4
San Felipe [MEX, Chihuahua] 154-155 BC 7
San Felipe [RCH] 162 B 4
San Felipe [YV] 158-159 F 2
San Felipe, NM 154-155 B 3
San Felipe, Punta - 150-151 F 10
San Felipe de Puerto Plata = Puerto Plata 146-147 M 8
San Feliu de Guixols 134-135 J 8
San Félix [Desventurados] 157 B 5
San Félix [RCH] 157 BC 5
San Fernando [E] 134-135 D 10
San Fernando [RA] 162 E 4
San Fernando [RCH] 162 B 4
San Fernando [TT] 146-147 L 9
San Fernando [YV] 158-159 F 3
San Fernando, CA 150-151 D 8
San Fernando[RP ↖ Baguio] 186-187 GH 3
San Fernando [RP ↖ Manila] 186-187 H 3
San Fernando de Atabapo 158-159 F 4
San Fernando del Valle de Catamarca 162 C 3
Sånfjället 130-131 E 6
Sanford, FL 146-147 K 6
Sanford, ME 148-149 H 3
Sanford, NC 148-149 D 7
San Francisco [MEX, Coahuila] 154-155 D 7
San Francisco [RA] 162 D 4
San Francisco, CA 146-147 AB 4
San Francisco Bay 150-151 B 7
San Francisco de Borja 154-155 B 7
San Francisco de Conchos 154-155 C 7
San Francisco de la Caleta 146-147 bc 3
San Francisco de Laishi 160-161 C 7
San Francisco del Oro 146-147 E 6
San Francisco del Parapetí 158-159 G 8-9
San Francisco de Macoris 146-147 MN 8
San Francisco Peaks 150-151 GH 8
San Francisco Plateau 146-147 D 4-E 5
San Francisco River 150-151 J 9
San Francisco Solano, Punta - 158-159 D 3
San-Franziskus-Bucht = Sint Franziskusbaai 174-175 A 3
Sangā 186-187 C 2
Sanga = Sangha 168-169 E 2-3
San Gabriel [EC] 158-159 D 4
San Gabriel Mountains 150-151 DE 8
Sangagchhö Ling 184-185 G 6
Šangaly 138-139 O 3
Sangamon River 152-153 LM 5-6
Sangar 178-179 Y 5
Sangarédi 172-173 B 3
Sangários = Sakarya Nehri 180-181 C 2
Sangasār 182-183 L 4
Sangay 158-159 D 5
Sangchih = Sangzhi 190-191 C 7
Sangeang, Pulau - 186-187 GH 8
Sanger, CA 150-151 D 7
Sanger, TX 154-155 G 4
Sanggan He 190-191 E 1
Sanggou Wan 190-191 J 3
Sanggau 186-187 F 6
Sangha 168-169 E 2-3
Sanghaj = Shanghai 184-185 N 5
Sang-i Māsha 180-181 K 4
San Giovanni in Persiceto 136-137 D 3
Sangir, Kepulauan - 186-187 J 6
Sangir, Pulau - 186-187 J 6
Sangju 188-189 G 4
Sang-kan Ho = Sanggan He 190-191 E 1
Sang-kou Wan = Sanggou Wan 190-191 J 3
Sangkulirang 186-187 G 6
Sangkulirang, Teluk - 186-187 G 6
Sāngli 180-181 LM 7
Sangmélima 166-167 G 8
Sangonera, Río - 134-135 G 10
San Gorgonio Mountain 150-151 E 8
Sangre, La - 150-151 H 10
Sangre de Cristo Range 146-147 E 4
Sangre Grande 146-147 OP 9
Sangue, Rio do - 158-159 H 7
Sanguin River = Sehnkwehn River 172-173 C 4
Sangutane, Rio - 174-175 K 2-3
Sangymgort 178-179 M 5
Sangzhi 190-191 C 7
San He [TJ, Anhui] 190-191 FG 5
Sanhe [TJ, Guangdong] 190-191 F 9
Sanhe [TJ, Hebei] 190-191 F 2
Sanho = Sanhe 190-191 F 2
San Hu 190-191 D 6
San-i 190-191 H 9
Sanibel Island 148-149 b 3
San Ignacio [PY] 162 E 3
San Ignacio, NM 154-155 C 3
San Ignacio [BOL ↗ La Paz] 158-159 F 7
San Ignacio [BOL ↗ Santa Cruz 158-159 G 8
Saniquellie 166-167 C 7
San Isidro [RA] 162 E 4
Sanitatas 168-169 D 6
Saniyah, Hawr as- 182-183 M 7
San Jacinto, CA 150-151 E 9
San Jacinto Mountains 150-151 E 9
San Javier [BOL, Santa Cruz] 158-159 G 8
San Javier [MEX] 154-155 B 7
San Javier [RA, Misiones] 162 EF 3
San Jerónimo, Serrania de - 158-159 D 3
Sanjiao 190-1941 C 3
Sanjō 188-189 M 4
San Joaquin [BOL] 158-159 FG 7
San Joaquín [PY, Boquerón] 160-161 B 4
San Joaquín [PY, Caaguazú] 160-161 D 6
San Joaquin River 146-147 BC 4
San Joaquin Valley 146-147 BC 4
San Jon, NM 154-155 D 3
San Jorge, Canal de - = Saint George's Channel 132 C 6-D 5
San Jorge, Golfo - 162 CD 7
San Jorge, Golfo de - 134-135 H 8
San José [CR] 146-147 K 9-10
San José [GCA] 146-147 H 9
San José [PA] 146-147 b 3
San José [PY, Caaguazú] 160-161 D 6
San José [PY, Itapúa] 160-161 E 7
San José [RP] 186-187 H 3
San Jose, CA 146-147 B 4
San José [ROU, ●] 162 E 4
San José, Isla - [MEX] 146-147 DE 6
San José, Isla - = Weddell Island 162 D 8
San José de Buenavista 186-187 H 4
San José de Chiquitos 158-159 G 8
San José de Jáchal 162 C 4
San José de las Salinas 162 CD 4
San José del Cabo 146-147 E 7
San José del Guaviare 158-159 E 4
San José de Ocuné 158-159 E 4
San José de Sextin 154-155 C 7
San José-mi 160-161 D 7
San Jose River 154-155 AB 3
San Juan [MEX] 154-155 E 7
San Juan [PE] 158-159 DE 8
San Juan [Puerto Rico] 146-147 N 8
San Juan [RA, ●] 162 C 4
San Juan, Cabo - [Guinea Ecuatorial] 166-167 F 8
San Juan, Cabo - [RA] 162 D 8
San Juan, Rio - [MEX, Chihuahua] 154-155 B 7
San Juan, Rio - [NIC] 146-147 K 9
San Juan Archipelago 150-151 B 1
San Juan Bautista 134-135 H 9
San Juan Bautista 162 E 3
San Juan Bautista = Villahermosa 146-147 H 8
San Juan Bautista Ñeembucú 160-161 D 7
San Juan de Guía, Cabo de - 158-159 DE 2
San Juan del Norte = Bluefields 146-147 K 9
San Juan del Norte, Bahía de - 146-147 K 9
San Juan de los Morros 158-159 F 3
San Juan Mountains 146-147 E 4
San Juan Nepomuceno [PY] 160-161 E 7
San Juan River 146-147 E 4
San Justo [RA, Santa Fe] 162 D 4
Sankarani 172-173 C 3
Sankeng 190-191 D 10
Sankisen 188-189 cd 2
Sankt Gallen 133 D 5
Sankt-Georgs-Kanal = Saint George's Channel 132 C 6-D 5
Sankt Gotthard 133 D 5
Sankt Jakobi = Pärnu-Jaagupi 138-139 E 4
Sankt Johannis = Järva-Jaani 138-139 EF 4
Sankt Kitts e Nevis 146-147 O 8
Sankt Kitts u. Nevis 157 D 1
Sankt Michel = Mikkeli 130-131 MN 7
Sankt Moritz 133 DE 5
Sankt-Peterburg = Sankt Peterburg 178-179 E 5-6
Sankt Pietroburgo = Sankt Peterburg 138-139 H 3-4
Sankt Pölten 133 G 4
Sankuru 168-169 F 3
San Lázaro 160-161 CD 5
San Lázaro, Cabo - 146-147 D 7
Sanlı Urfa 180-181 D 3
San Lorenzo [EC] 158-159 D 4
San Lorenzo [PY] 162 E 3
San Lorenzo [RA, Santa Fe] 162 D 4
San Lorenzo [YV, Zulia] 158-159 E 3
San Lorenzo [BOL ↙ Riberalta] 158-159 F 7
San Lorenzo [BOL ↑ Tarija] 158-159 FG 9
San Lorenzo, Cabo de - 158-159 C 5
San Lorenzo, Cerro - 162 B 7
San Lorenzo, Isla - [PE] 158-159 D 7
San Lorenzo, Sierra de - 134-135 F 7
Sanlúcar de Barrameda 134-135 D 10
San Lucas, CA 150-151 C 7
San Lucas, Cabo - 146-147 E 7
San Luis, CO 152-153 D 7
San Luis [RA, ●] 162 C 4
San Luis, Sierra de - [W] 158-159 EF 2
San Luis Obispo, CA 146-147 B 4
San Luis Obispo Bay 150-151 C 8
San Luis Pass 154-155 H 6
San Luis Potosí 146-147 FG 7
San Luis Valley 152-153 CD 7
San Manuel, AZ 150-151 H 9
San Marcial, NM 154-155 B 4
San Marco, Capo - 136-137 BC 6
San Marcos [RCH] 162 B 4
San Marcos, TX 146-147 G 6
San Marcos, Sierra de - 154-155 DE 7
San Marino [RSM, ●] 136-137 E 4
San Marino [RSM, ★] 136-137 E 4
San Martín [BOL] 158-159 G 7-8
San Martín [RA, La Rioja] 162 C 3
San Martín, Lago - 162 B 7
San Martín, Río - 158-159 G 8
San Mateo, CA 146-147 B 4
San Mateo Peak 146-147 E 5
San Matías, Golfo - 162 D 6
Sanmen 190-191 H 7
San-mên-hsia = Sanmenxia 184-185 L 5
Sanmenxia 184-185 L 5
San Miguel [ES] 146-147 J 9
San Miguel [MEX] 150-151 H 10
San Miguel [PY, Concepción] 160-161 D 5
San Miguel [PY, Misiones] 160-161 D 7
San Miguel, AZ 150-151 H 10
San Miguel, CA 150-151 C 8
San Miguel, NM 154-155 C 3
San Miguel, Río - [BOL] 158-159 G 7-8
San Miguel de Huachi 158-159 F 8
San Miguel del Monte 162 E 5
San Miguel de Tucumán 162 CD 3
San Miguel Island 150-151 C 8
San Miguelito [PA] 146-147 bc 3
San Miguel River 150-151 JK 6-7
Sanming 190-191 F 8
Sannār 166-167 L 6
San Narciso 186-187 GH 3
Sannaspos 174-175 G 5
San Nicolás de los Arroyos 162 D 4
San Nicolas Island 146-147 BC 5
Sannikova, proliv - 178-179 ab 3
Sanniquellie = Saniquellie 166-167 C7
Sannohe 188-189 N 2
Sannūr, Wādi - 170 D 3
Sanok 133 L 4
San Pablo Balleza 154-155 B 7
San Pablo [RP] 186-187 H 4
San Pablo Bay 150-151 B 6
San Patricio 160-161 D 7
San-Pédro [CI] 172-173 D 4
San Pedro [MEX, Chihuahua] 154-155 C 6
San Pedro [MEX, Durango] 154-155 BC 7-8
San Pedro [RA, Buenos Aires] 162 E 4
San Pedro [RA, Misiones] 160-161 EF 7
San Pedro [RA, Santiago del Estero] 162 C 3
San Pedro [PY, ●] 162 E 2
San Pedro [PY, ☆] 160-161 D 5-6
San Pedro [BOL, Santa Cruz ↗ Santa Cruz] 158-159 G 8
San Pedro [BOL, Santa Cruz ↑ Trinidad] 158-159 G 7
San Pedro, Punta - [CR] 146-147 K 10
San Pedro, Sierra de - 134-135 D 9
San Pedro, Volcán - 158-159 F 9
San Pedro Channel 150-151 D 9
San Pedro-cué 160-161 D 7
San Pedro de las Colonias 146-147 F 6
San Pedro del Paraná 160-161 DE 7
San Pedro de Macoris 146-147 N 8
San Pedro Mártir, Sierra 146-147 CD 5
San Pedro Mountain 154-155 B 2
San Pedro River 150-151 H 9
San Pedro Sula 146-147 J 8
San Perlita, TX 154-155 G 7
San Pietro 136-137 BC 6
San Quintín, Cabo - 146-147 C 5
San Rafael [RA] 162 C 4
San Rafael, CA 146-147 B 4
San Rafael, Rio - 150-151 EF 10
San Rafael del Encanto 158-159 E 5
San Rafael Mountains 150-151 CD 8
San Rafael River 150-151 H 6
San Rafael Swell 150-151 H 6
San Ramón de la Nueva Orán 162 CD 2
Sanrao 190-191 F 10
San Remo 136-137 BC 4
San Román, Cabo - 158-159 EF 2
San Rosendo 162 B 5
San Saba, TX 154-155 F 5
San Saba River 154-155 F 5
Sansalé 172-173 B 3
San Salvador [BS] 146-147 M 7
San Salvador [ES] 146-147 HJ 9
San Salvador, Isla - 158-159 A 5
San Salvador de Jujuy 162 CD 2
Sansanding 166-167 CD 6
Sansading, Barrage - 172-173 D 2
Sansané Haoussa = Sonsoni Haoussa 172-173 F 2
Sansanné-Mango = Mango 166-167 E 6
San Sebastián 134-135 FG 7
San Sebastián [RA] 162 C 8
San Sebastián de la Gomera 166-167 A3
San Severo 136-137 F 5
Sansha Wan 190-191 GH 8
Sansibar = Zanzibar 168-169 JK 4
San Silvestre [W] 158-159 EF 3
San Simeon, CA 150-151 C 8
San Simon, AZ 150-151 J 9
Sansing = Yilan 184-185 OP 2
Sansuan Shan 190-191 H 7
Sansui 190-191 B 8
Santa Adélia 160-161 H 4
Santa Ana [CO, Guainia] 158-159 F 4
Santa Ana [ES] 146-147 HJ 9
Santa Ana [MEX] 146-147 D 5
Santa Ana, CA 146-147 C 5
Santa Ana [BOL ↖ Trinidad] 158-159 F 7
Santa Ana, Ilha - 160-161 M 5
Santa Ana Mountains 150-151 E 9
Santa Anna, TX 154-155 F 5
Santa Bárbara [BR, Mato Grosso] 160-161 C 1
Santa Bárbara [BR, Minas Gerais] 160-161 L 3-4
Santa Bárbara [MEX] 146-147 E 6
Santa Bárbara [RCH] 162 B 5
Santa Barbara, CA 146-147 BC 5
Santa Bárbara [YV ↙ Maturín] 158-159 G 3
Santa Bárbara [YV → San Cristóbal] 158-159 E 3
Santa Bárbara [YV → San Fernando de Atabapo] 158-159 F 4
Santa Bárbara, Serra de 158-159 J 9
Santa Barbara Channel 150-151 CD 8
Santa Barbara Island 150-151 D 9
Santa Catalina [RA, Jujuy] 162 C 2
Santa Catalina = Catalina 162 C 3
Santa Catalina, Gulf of 150-151 DE 9
Santa Catalina Island 146-147 BC 5
Santa Catarina 162 FG 3
Santa Catarina, Ilha de - 162 G 3
Santa Catarina, Valle de 150-151 EF 10
Santa Cecilia 160-161 G 7
Sant Cecilia do Pavão 160-161 G 5
Santa Clara [C] 146-147 KL 7
Santa Clara [CO] 158-159 EF 5
Santa Clara [MEX, Chihuahua] 154-155 C 6
Santa Clara, CA 146-147 B 4
Santa Cruz [BR, Rio Grande do Norte] 158-159 M 6
Santa Cruz [RA, Santa Cruz] 162 BC 7
Santa Cruz, CA 146-147 B 4
Santa Cruz [BOL, ●] 158-159 G 8
Santa Cruz, Îles - = Santa Cruz Islands 186-187 I 7
Santa Cruz, Isla - [EC] 158-159 AB 5
Santa Cruz, Rio de Janeiro - 160-161 L 5
Santa Cruz, Wyspy - = Santa Cruz 186-187 I 7
Santa Cruz Cabrália 158-159 M 8
Santa Cruz das Palmeiras 160-161 J 4
Santa Cruz de Barahona = Barahona 146-147 M 8
Santa Cruz de Goiás 160-161 H 2
Santa Cruz de la Palma 166-167 A 3
Santa Cruz de Tenerife 166-167 A 3
Santa Cruz do Monte Castelo 160-161 F 5
Santa Cruz do Rio Pardo 160-161 H 5
Santa Cruz dos Angolares 172-173 G 5
Santa Cruz do Sul 162 F 3
Santa-Cruz-Inseln = Santa Cruz Islands 186-187 I 7
Santa Cruz Island 146-147 BC 5
Santa Cruz Islands 186-187 I 7
Santa Cruz Mountains 150-151 BC 7
Santa Cruz River 150-151 H 9
Santa Cruz-szigetek = Santa Cruz Islands 186-187 I 7
Santa Elena [BOL] 158-159 G 9
Santa Elena [PE] 158-159 E 5
Santa Elena, Cabo - 146-147 J 9
Santa Elena de Uairén 158-159 G 4
Santa Eudóxia 160-161 J 4
Santa Fe, NM 146-147 E 4
Santa Fe [RA, ●] 162 D 4
Santa Fé des Minas 160-161 K 2
Santa Fé do Sul 158-159 J 9
Santa Fe Railway 146-147 F 4
Santa Filomena 158-159 K 6
Santa Genoveva = Cerro las Casitas 146-147 E 7
Santa Gertrudis 154-155 BC 7
Santa Helena [BR, Maranhão] 158-159 K 5
Santa Helena [BR, Pará] 158-159 H 5-6
Santa Helena [BR, Paraná] 160-161 E 6
Santa Helena de Goiás 160-161 G 2
Santai 184-185 JK 5
Santa Inés [BR, Bahia] 158-159 LM 7
Santa Inés, Isla - 162 B 8
Santa Isabel [RA, La Pampa] 162 C 5
Santa Isabel [Solomon Is.] 186-187 jk 6
Santa Isabel = Malabo 166-167 F 8
Santa Isabel, Ilha Grande de - 158-159 L 5
Santa Isabel, Sierra - 150-151 F 10
Santa Isabel do Araguaia 158-159 K 6
Santa Isabel do Morro 158-159 J 7
Santa Juliana 160-161 J 3
Santa Lidia 160-161 C 5
Santa Lucía 146-147 O 8
Santa Lúcia [WL] 146-147 O 9
Santa Lucia Range 150-151 C 7-8
Santa Luisa, Serra de - 160-161 E 3
Santaluz [BR, Bahia] 158-159 M 7
Santa Luzia [BR, Minas Gerais] 160-161 L 3
Santa Margarida 160-161 LM 4
Santa Margarita, CA 150-151 C 8
Santa Margarita, Isla - 146-147 D 7
Santa Margherita Ligure 136-137 C 3
Santa Maria [BR, Amazonas] 158-159 H 5
Santa Maria [BR, Rio Grande do Sul] 162 EF 3
Santa Maria [PE, Loreto] 158-159 E 5
Santa Maria [RA] 162 C 3
Santa Maria [Vanuatu] 194-195 N 2
Santa Maria [Z] 171 B 5
Santa Maria, CA 146-147 B 5
Santa Maria, Cabo de - 134-135 CD 10
Santa Maria, Cabo de - = Cap Sainte-Marie 168-169 L 8
Santa Maria, Riacho - 160-161 C 5
Santa Maria Asunción Tlaxiaco 146-147 G 8
Santa Maria das Barreiras 158-159 JK 6
Santa Maria de Ipire 158-159 F 3
Santa Maria di Leuca, Capo - 136-137 H 6
Santa Maria do Suaçuí 160-161 L 3
Santa Maria Madalena 160-161 LM 4
Santa Mariana 160-161 G 5
Santa Marta [CO] 158-159 DE 2
Santa Marta, Sierra Nevada de - 158-159 E 2
Santa Marta Grande, Cabo - 160-161 H 8
Santa Monica, CA 146-147 BC 5
Santa Monica, TX 154-155 G 7
Santana 158-159 L 7
Santana, Coxilha da - 162 E 3-F 4
Santana, Ilha de - 158-159 L 5
Santana de Oatos 160-161 J 3
Santa de Patos 160-161 J 3
Santana do Livramento 162 EF 4
Santander 134-135 F 7
Santander [CO, Cauca] 158-159 D 4
Sant' Antioco [I, ⊙] 136-137 BC 6
Sant' Antioco [I, ●] 136-137 BC 6
Santañy 134-135 J 9
Santa Paula, CA 150-151 D 8
Santa Pola, Cabo de - 134-135 GH 9
Santarém [BR] 158-159 J 5
Santarem [P] 134-135 C 9
Santaren Channel 146-147 L 7
Santa Rita [BR, Paraiba] 158-159 MN 6
Santa Rita [YV, Zulia] 158-159 E 2
Santa Rita, NM 150-151 J 9
Santa Rita do Araguaia 158-159 J 8
Santa Rita de Jacutinga 160-161 KL 5
Santa Rita do Passa Quatro 160-161 J 4
Santa Rita do Sapucai 160-161 K 5
Santa Rito do Weil 158-159 F 5
Santa Rosa [BR, Acre] 158-159 EF 6
Santa Rosa [BR, Rio Grande do Sul] 162 F 3
Santa Rosa [CO, Guainia] 158-159 EF 4
Santa Rosa [PE] 158-159 E 5
Santa Rosa [PY, Boquerón] 160-161 B 4
Santa Rosa [PY, Misiones] 160-161 D 7
Santa Rosa [RA, La Pampa] 1 62 CD 5
Santa Rosa [RA, Mendoza] 162 C 4
Santa Rosa [RA, San Luis] 162 C 4
Santa Rosa, CA 146-147 B 4
Santa Rosa, NM 154-155 C 3
Santa Rosa [BOL, Beni ↘ Riberalta] 158-159 F 7
Santa Rosa de Copán 146-147 J 9
Santa Rosa del Palmar 158-159 G 8
Santa Rosa de Viterbo 160-161 J 4
Santa Rosa Island [USA, California] 146-147 B 5
Santa Rosa Island [USA, Florida] 154-155 M 5
Santa Rosalía [MEX] 146-147 D 6
Santa Rosa Range 150-151 E 5
Santa Rosa Wash 150-151 GH 9
Šantarskije ostrova 178-179 a 6-7
Santa Sylvina 162 DE 3
Santa Tecla = Nueva San
Santa Teresa [BR] 160-161 M 3
Santa Teresa [MEX] 154-155 E 7
Salvador 146-147 HJ 9
Santa Vitória 160-161 GH 3
Santa Vitória do Palmar 162 F 4
Santa Ynez, CA 150-151 CD 8
Santee River 148-149 D 8
San Telmo 150-151 EF 10
Sant' Eufèmia, Golfo di - 136-137 FG 6
Santiago [BR] 162 EF 3
Santiago [DOM] 146-147 M 7
Santiago [PA] 146-147 K 10
Santiago [PY] 160-161 D 7
Santiago, Salto - 160-161 F 6
Santiago de Chile 162 B 4
Santiago de Chuco 158-159 D 6
Santiago de Cuba 146-147 L 7-8
Santiago de Compostela 134-135 CD 7
Santiago del Estero [RA, ●] 162 CD 3
Santiago del Estero [RA, ☆] 160-161 AB 7
Santiago Ixcuintla 146-147 EF 7
Santiagoma 158-159 H 8
Santiago Mountains 154-155 D 5-6
Santiago Papasquiaro 146-147 EF 6-7
Santiago Peak 154-155 D 6
Santiam Pass 150-151 BC 3
Santigi 186-187 H 6
Santo, TX 154-155 F 4
Santo Amaro 158-159 M 7
Santo Amaro, Ilha de - 160-161 JK 6
Santo Amaro de Campos 160-161 M 5
Santo Anastácio 160-161 G 4
Santo André 158-159 K 9
Santo André = Isla de San Andrés 146-147 KL 9
Santo Ângelo 162 EF 3
Santo António [São Tomé e Principe] 166-167 F 8
Santo Antônio, Cachoeira - [BR, Rio Madeira] 158-159 FG 6
Santo Antônio, Rio - [BR ◁ Rio Doce] 160-161 L 3
Santo Antônio, Rio - [BR ◁ Rio Iguaçu] 160-161 F 6
Santo Antônio da Platina 160-161 GH 5
Santo Antônio de Jesus 158-159 LM 7
Santo Antônio de Pádua 160-161 LM 4
Santo Antônio de Rio Verde 160-161 J 2
Santo Antônio do Leverger 160-161 DE 1
Santo Antônio do Monte 160-161 K 4
Santo Antônio do Sudoeste 160-161 F 7
Santo Antônio do Zaire = Soyo 168-169 D 4
Santo Corazón 158-159 H 8

248

'afina, NM 154-155 C 3
'am [RI] 186-187 JK 7
'am, Mar de - 186-187 JK 7
'am, Mar de - 126-127 J 7
'am, Mer de - 186-187 JK 7
'am , Morze - 186-187 J 7
'am-Laut, Kepulauan -
186-187 K 7
'ampore 180-181 O 6
'am Sea 192-193 D 5
'amsee 186-187 J 7
'amské moře 186-187 J 7
'am-tenger 186-187 J 7
'amzee 186-187 JK 7
'ang 186-187 E 8
'āyā = Sarāyah 182-183 F 5
'ben = Dzërbene 138-139 E 5
'bia 136-137 H 3-J 4
'bie 136-137 H 3-J 4
'bien 136-137 H 3-J 4
'bka 136-137 O 2
'bka 140-141 E 3
'dar = Kaypak 182-183 G 4
'déles = Sardalas 166-167 G 3
'dobsk 138-139 P 7
'ebr'anka 138-139 T 3
'ebr'ansk 178-179 P 8
'ebr'anyje Prudy 138-139 M 6
'eda [SU, Jaroslavl'] 138-139 N 4
'eda [SU, Moskva] 138-139 K 6
'edina-Buda 138-139 JK 7
'edka 138-139 FG 4
'efiye 182-183 G 2
'eflikoçhişar 182-183 E 3
'egovo 138-139 S 2
'emban 186-187 D 6
'emetjevka 138-139 S 6
'ena, La - [E] 134-135 E 9
'ena, La - [RCH] 162 B 3
'engeti National Park
168-169 HJ 3
'engeti Plain 171 C 3
'enitz = Vasknarva 138-139 F 4
'enje 168-169 GH 5
'et 140-141 B 2
'ga 138-139 V 5
'gač 138-139 P 6
'geja Kirova, ostrova -
178-179 QR 2
'gijev Posad 178-179 F 6
'ginskij 178-179 LM 5
'giopolis = Riṣāfah 182-183 H 5
'gipe 158-159 M 7
'go = Kadijevka 140-141 J 2
'ia 186-187 F 6
'ibu, Kepulauan - 186-187 E 7-8
'ifos 136-137 L 7
'ik 182-183 D 4
'inga, Serra da - 158-159 J 6
'kaly 178-179 M 5
'lovaja Gora 178-179 W 7
'mata, Pulau - 186-187 J 8
'milik 144-145 d 4
'nodovsk 138-139 ST 7
'nur 138-139 R 5
'ov 178-179 L 6
'owe 168-169 G 7
'oža 138-139 O 6
'pa 134-135 D 10
'pa Pinto = Menongue
168-169 E 5
'peddi, Punta - 136-137 C 6
'piente, Boca de la -
158-159 G 2-3
'pnevoje 140-141 D 3
'puchov 138-139 L 6
'puchow = Serpuchov
138-139 L 6
'ra Azul [BR, ●] 160-161 J 4
'ra das Araras [BR, Minas Gerais]
160-161 K 1
'ra Geral [BR, Santa Catarina]
162 F 3
'ra Geral [BR, Rio Grande do
↘ Porto Alegre] 162 F 3
'rai 136-137 K 5
'ra Leoa 166-167 B 7
'ra Leoa, Bacia da -
124-125 HJ 5
'rra Leoa, Patamar da -
124-125 HJ 5
'rrana 160-161 J 4
'rrana Bank = Banco Serrana
158-159 CD 2
'rra Negra [BR, Minas Gerais]
160-161 L 2-3
'rra Negra [BR, São Paulo]
160-161 J 5
'rra Talhada 158-159 M 6
'rrezuela 162 C 4
'rrinha [BR ↑ Feira de Santana]
158-159 M 7
'rro 160-161 L 3
'rtânia 158-159 M 6
'rtanópolis 160-161 G 5
'rtão 158-159 L 7-M 6
'rtãozinho 160-161 HJ 4
'rua, Pulau - 186-187 K 8
'rule 168-169 G 7
'rvia 136-137 H 3-J 4
'rvilletta, NM 154-155 BC 2
'rxū 184-185 H 5
'šča 138-139 J 7
'se Islands 168-169 H 3
'sepe 186-187 J 7
'sfontein 168-169 D 6
'sheke 168-169 FG 6
'simbra 134-135 C 9
'šma 138-139 S 6
'ssa Aurunca 136-137 EF 5
'stakovo 138-139 RS 4
'štokaj 138-139 D 6
'stroreck 178-179 DE 5
'szele 168-169 CD 3
'tana 184-185 Q 3
'te 134-135 J 7
'te Barras 160-161 HJ 6
'téia 136-137 M 8
'te Lagoas 160-161 KL 3
'te Quedas, Salto das -
[BR, Paraná] 160-161 E 6
'te Quedas, Salto das - [BR,
Rio Teles Pires] 158-159 H 6
'termoen 130-131 H 3
'tesdal 130-131 B 8
'tif = Saṭīf 166-167 F 1
'tlagodi 174-175 F 4
'to 188-189 L 5
'to-naikai 184-185 P 5
'ttât = Saṭṭāt 166-167 C 2
'tté Cama 168-169 C 3
'tte-Daban, chrebet- 178-179 a 5
'ttlers 174-175 H 3
'túbal 134-135 C 9
'túbal, Baía de - 134-135 C 9
'túbal, Rio - 160-161 L 2
'uil Néo-zélandais 194-195 M 5-7
'uil Sibérien Oriental 120 B 36-1
'uil = Sōul 184-185 O 4
'ul, Lac - 144-145 S 7
'van 140-141 M 6
'van, ozero - 140-141 M 6
'vastopol' 140-141 F 4
Ševčenkovo = Dolinskaja
140-141 F 2
Seven Emu 194-195 G 3
Seven Islands = Sept-Îles
144-145 X 7-8
Severn 132 E 6
Severn 174-175 F 2
Severnaja 178-179 QR 4
Severnaja Dvina 178-179 G 5
Severnaja Semlja = Severnaja
Zemľa 178-179 ST 1-2
Severnaja Keľtma 138-139 U 3
Severnaja Sos'va 178-179 L 5
Severnaja Zemľa 178-179 ST 1-2
Severni Borneo = Sabah
186-187 G 5
Severni Irsko 132 C 4
Severni ledový oceán
120 AB 132-5
Severní moře 132 F-J 3
severni pól 120 A
Severní Rhodésie = Zambie
168-169 G 6-H 5
Severní středoatlantský hřbet
194-195 C 2
Severnoje [SU, Orenburg]
138-139 T 6
Severnoje [SU ↑ Samara]
178-179 O 6
Severn River 144-145 T 6-7
Severnyj 178-179 LM 4
Severnyj čink = Donyztau
178-179 K 8
Severnyje uvaly 178-179 HJ 5-6
Severnyj Kommunar 138-139 TU 4
Severnyj Ural 178-179 K 5-6
Severobajkal'sk 180-181 UV 6
Severo-Bajkal'skoje nagorje
178-179 UV 6
Severodoneck 140-141 J 2
Severodvinsk 178-179 FG 5
Severofidžijská pánev 194-195 O 3
Severofriské o-vy 133 D 1
Severo-Jenisejskij 178-179 RS 5
Severo-Kuril'sk 178-179 de 7
Severoosetinskajá autonomí
republika 140-141 LM 5
Severo-Osetinskaja Avtonomnaja
Sovetskaja Socialističeskaja
Respublika = Nordossetische
Autonome Republik
140-141 LM 5
Severo-Sibirskaja nizmennosť
178-179 P-X 3
Severo-Vostočnyj Bank = Bank
140-141 O 7
Severozápadní teritoria = Northwest
Territories 144-145 M-U 4
Severo-Zadonsk 138-139 M 6-7
Severy, KS 152-153 H 7
Sevier Desert 150-151 G 6
Sevier Lake 150-151 G 6
Sevier River 146-147 D 4
Sevierville 148-149 B 7
Sevierville, TN 154-155 O 3
Sevilla 134-135 E 10
Sevlievo 136-137 L 4
Sèvre 134-135 G 5
Sevsib 178-179 M 6
Sevsk 138-139 K 7
Sewa 166-167 B 7
Seward, AK 144-145 G 5-6
Seward, KS 152-153 G 6
Seward, NE 152-153 H 5
Seward Peninsula 144-145 CD 4
Sewastopol = Sevastopol'
140-141 F 4
Sewell, Lake - = Canyon Ferry
Reservoir 150-151 H2
Sewilla = Sevilla 134-135 E 10
Seychellen 168-169 L-N 4
Seychelles 165 M 8
Seychelles [SY, Estado] 168 J 3
Seychelles [SY, Îlhas] 165 M 8
Seychelle-szigetek 168-169 LM 4
Seychelles 168-169 L-N 4
Seydhisfjördhur 130-131 fg 2
Seydişehir 182-183 D 4
Seyhan = Adana 180-181 D 3
Seyhan Nehri 180-181 D 3
Seychelles [SY, Estado] 168 J 3
Seychelles [SY, ilhas] 165 M 8
Seychely 168-169 LM 4
Seyitgazi 182-183 D 3
Seyla' = Saylac 166-167 N 6
Seymour [AUS] 196 G 6
Seymour [ZA] 174-175 G 7
Seymour, IA 152-153 K 5
Seymour, IN 146-147 JK 4
Seymour, MO 154-155 J 2
Seymour, TX 154-155 F 4
Seymour, WI 152-153 M 3
Seyne-sur-Mer, la - 134-135 K 7
Sezze 136-137 E 5
Sfax = Ṣafāqis 166-167 FG 2
Sfântu Gheorghe [●] 136-137 LM 3
Sfântu Gheorghe, [~] 136-137 N 3
Sfire = Safirah 182-183 G 4
Sfoŭk = Sufūq 182-183 J 4
Sha Alam 186-187 D 6
Shaanxi 184-185 K 4-5
Shaba 168-169 FG 4
Shabakah, Ash- [IRQ, ≡]
182-183 K 7
Shabakah, Ash- [IRQ, ●]
182-183 K 7
Shabani = Zvishavane
168-169 GH 7
Shabb, Ash- 170 C 6
Shabbona, IL 152-153 M 5
Shabeelle, Webi - 166-167 N 8
Shabellaha Dhexe =
5 ◁ 166-167 b 3
Shabellaha Hoose =
3 ◁ 166-167 N 8
Shabēlle, Webi - = Wabē
Shebelē Weniz 166-167 N 7
Shabunda 168-169 G 3
Shabwah 180-181 F 7
Sha Ch'i 0 Sha Xi 190-191 F 8
Shackleton Ice Shelf 121 C 10
Shackleton Inlet 121 A 19-17
Shackleton Range 121 A 35-1
Shacun 190-191 E 8
Shādegān 182-183 N 7
Shadehill Reservoir 152-153 E 3
Shadi 190-191 E 8
Shafter, CA 150-151 D 8
Shafter, NV 150-151 F 5
Shafter, TX 154-155 C 6
Shagamu 172-173 F 4
Shag Rocks 162 H 8
Shaguotun 188-189 C 2
Shāh, Godār-e - 182-183 MN 5
Shahabad [IND, Maisuru]
180-181 M 7
Shahāmī 182-183 H 6
Shahān, Kūh-e - 182-183 LM 5
Shahan, Wādī - = Wādī Shihan
180-181 G 7
Shahbā 182-183 G 6
Shahbā' ,Harrat ash- 182-183 G 6-7
Shahdād 180-181 H 4
Shahdād, Namakzār-e -
180-181 H 4
Shahe [TJ, Shandong] 190-191 G 3
Sha He [TJ, Hebei ~] 190-191 E 3
Shahe [TJ, Hebei ●] 190-191 E 3
Shahedian 190-191 D 5
Shāhi 180-181 G 3
Shahidulla Mazar 184-185 D 4
Sha-ho = Shahe [TJ, Shandong]
190-191 G 3
Sha Ho = Sha He [TJ, Hebei ~]
190-191 E 3
Shaho = Shahe [TJ, Hebei ●]
190-191 E 3
Sha-ho-tien = Shahedian
190-191 D 5
Shahpura 180-181 L 5
Shahrak 180-181 J 4
Shahr-e Bābak 180-181 GH 4
Shahredā 180-181 G 4
Shahr-e Kord 180-181 G 4
Shahrestānbālā 182-183 NO 4
Shāh Rūd [IR, ~] 182-183 NO 4
Shāhrūd [IR , ●] 180-181 GH 3
Shahsien = Sha Xian 190-191 F 8
Shahu 190-191 D 6
Shāhzand 182-183 N 6
Shā'ib al-Banāt, Jabal - 166-167 L 5
Sha'īt, Wādī - 170 E 5
Shajahanpur 180-181 MN 5
Shajianzi 188-189 E 2
Shaka, Ras - 171 E 3
Shakar Bolāghī = Qara Büteh
182-183 M 4
Shakh yar 184-185 E 3
Shaki 166-167 E 7
Shakir, Jazirat - 166-167 LM 3
Shakopee, MN 152-153 K 3
Shakotan misaki 188-189 b 2
Shakou 190-191 D 9
Shāl 182-183 N 5
Shalaamboot 166-167 N 8
Shala Hayik 166-167 M 7
Shalang 190-191 C 11
Shalar, Nahr - 182-183 L 5
Shalar Rūd = Nahr Shalar
182-183 L 5
Shallāl, Ash- [ET, ~] 166-167 L 3
Shallāl, Ash- [ET, ●] 166-167 L 3
Shallotte, NC 148-149 D 7-8
Shallowater, TX 154-155 DE 4
Shāmah, Ash- = Al-Harrah
182-183 GH 7
Shamāli, Ash- 166-167 KL 5
Shāmbā 166-167 L 7
Shāmiyah, Ash- 182-183 L 7
Shammar, Jabal - 180-181 E 5
Shamo = Gobi 184-185 H-K 3
Shamokin, PA 148-149 E 4
Shamrock, FL 148-149 b 2
Shamrock, TX 154-155 EF 3
Shāmshir = Pāveh 182-183 M 5
Shamva 168-169 H 6
Sha'nabi, Jabal ash- 166-167 F 1-2
Shanchengzhen 188-189 EF 1
Shan-ch'iu = Shenqiu 190-191 E 5
Shandan 184-185 J 4
Shandi 166-167 L 5
Shandish, MI 148-149 AB 3
Shandong 184-185 M 4
Shandong Bandao 184-185 MN 4
Shangani 168-169 G 6
Shangbahe 190-191 E 6
Shangbangcheng 188-189 B 2
Shangcai 190-191 E 5
Shangcheng 190-191 E 6
Shang-chia-ho = Shangjiahe
188-189 E 2
Shang-ch'iu = Shangqiu
184-185 LM 5
Shangchuan Dao 184-185 L 7
Shangcigang = Beijingzi
188-189 DE 3
Shangdachen Shan = Dachen Dao
190-191 HJ 7
Shangfu 190-191 E 7
Shanggang 190-191 H 5
Shanggao 190-191 E 7
Shanghai 184-185 N 5
Shanghang 184-185 M 6-7
Shanghe 190-191 F 3
Shangho = Shanghe 190-191 F 3
Shanghsien = Shang Xian
184-185 KL 5
Shangjao = Shangrao 184-185 M 6
Shangjiahe 188-189 E 2
Shangkan 190-191 C 6
Shang-kang = Shanggang
190-191 H 5
Shang-kao = Shanggao 1
90-191 E 7
Shangkiu = Shangqiu
184-185 LM 5
Shangnan 190-191 C 5
Shangqiu 184-185 LM 5
Shangrao 184-185 M 6
Shangshe 190-191 D 2
Shang Xian 184-185 KL 5
Shangyou 190-191 E 9
Shangyu 190-191 H 6-7
Shang-yu = Shangyou 190-191 E 9
Shang-yü = Shangyu 190-191 H 6-7
Shangzhi 184-185 O 2
Shanhaiguan 184-185 MN 3
Shan-hai-kuan = Shanhaiguan
188-189 BC 2
Shan-hsi = Shaanxi 184-185 L 4-5
Shaniko, OR 150-151 C 3
Shankou [TJ,Guangdong]
190-191 BC 11
Shankou [TJ,Hunan] 190-191 C 7
Shankou [TJ,Jiangxi] 190-191 E 7
Shannon 174-175 G 5
Shannon 132 B 5
Shannon Airport 132 B 5
Shannon Ø 120 B 20
Shannontown, SC 148-149 CD 8
Shan Pyinnei 186-187 C 2
Shanqiu 190-191 E 5
Shanshan 184-185 G 3
Shansi = Shanxi 46-49 L 4
Shan-tan = Shandan 184-185 J 4
Shantangyi 190-191 BC 8
Shantou 184-185 M 7
Shantow = Shantou 184-185 M 7
Shantung = Shandong 184-185 M 4
Shan-tung Chiao = Chengshan Jiao
190-191 J 3
Shanwa 171 C 3
Shanwei 190-191 E 10
Shanxi 184-185 L 4
Shan Xian 190-191 EF 4
Shanyang 190-191 B 5
Shanyin 184-185 L 4
Shaobo 190-191 G 5
Shaodong 190-191 C 8
Shaoguan 184-185 L 6-7
Shaohsing = Shaoxing
184-185 N 5-6
Shao-kuan = Qujiang 190-191 D 9
Shaol Lake 152-153 J 1
Shao-po = Shaobo 190-191 G 5
Shaotze = Wan Xian 184-185 K 5
Shaowu 184-185 M 6
Shaoxing 184-185 N 5-6
Shaoyang 184-185 L 6
Shaqlāwah 182-183 L 4
Shaqqar 166-167 C 3
Shaqrā, 180-181 F 5
Shār, Jabal - [Saudi-Arabien]
170 F 4
Shā'r, Jabal - [SYR] 182-183 GH 5
Sharafkhāneh 182-183 LM 3
Sharāh, Ash- 182-183 F 7
Sharbithāt, Rā's ash- 180-181 H 7
Sharbot Lake 148-149 E 2
Shari 188-189 d 2
Shari = Chari 166-167 H 6
Shāri', Bahr ash- = Buhayrat
Shāri 182-183 L 5
Shāri, Buhayrat - 182-183 L 5
Shari'ah, Nahr ash- 182-183 F 6-7
Shārib, Ma'tan - 170 C 2
Shari-dake 188-189 d 2
Shārigah, Ash- 180-181 GH 5
Shark Bay 194-195 B 5
Sharmah, Ash- 170 F 3-4
Sharmah, Wādī ash- = Wādī Ṣadr
170 F 3
Sharm ash-Shaykh 170 F 4
Sharm esh-Sheikh = Sharm ash-
Shayh 170 F 4
Shar Mörön 190-191 C 1-2
Shar Mörön = Chatan gol
184-185 K 3
Sharon, KS 154-155 F 2
Sharon, PA 146-147 KL 3
Sharon Springs, KS 152-153 F 6
Sharqāṭ, Ash- 182-183 K 5
Sharqī, Ash- 166-167 GH 6
Sharqī, Ash-Shaṭṭ ash-
166-167 DE 2
Sharqī, Jebel esh- = Jabal
Lubnān ash-Sharqī 182-183 G 5-6
Sharrukin, Dur - = Khorsabad
182-183 K 4
Shāsh, 'Irq ash- 166-167 D 3-4
Shashemenē 166-167 M 7
Shashi 184-185 L 5-6
Shasta , Mount - 146-147 B 3
Shasta Lake 150-151 B 5
Sha-ti = Shadi 190-191 E 8
Shaṭrah, Ash- 182-183 LM 7
Shattuck, OK 154-155 F 2
Shau = Wādī Huwār 166-167 K 5
Shaubak, Esh- = Ash-Shawbak
182-183 F 7
Shaw, MS 154-155 K 4
Shawan 190-191 G 8
Shawano, WI 152-153 M 3
Shawatun = Shaguotun
188-189 C 2
Shawbak, Ash- 182-183 F 7
Shawinigan Sud 144-145 W 8
Shawnee, OK 146-147 G 4
Shawneetown, IL 152-153 M 7
Shawo 190-191 E 6
Shaw River 194-195 C 4
Shāwshāw, Jabal - 170 C 5
Shawville 148-149 E 2
Sha Xi [TJ, Fujian] 190-191 F 8
Shaxi [TJ, Jiangxi] 190-191 G 7
Shaxi [TJ, Nanchang] 190-191 E 8
Sha Xian 184-185 M 6
Shayang 190-191 D 6
Shaykh Aḥmad 182-183 J 4
Shaykh Hilāl 182-183 G 5
Shaykh Sa'd 182-183 M 6
Shaykh Ṣalāh 182-183 J 4
Shaykh 'Uthmān, Ash- 180-181
EF 8
Shayōg = Shyog 180-181 M 3-4
Shazhou 190-191 H 6
Shāzī, Wādī ash- 182-183 J 7
Shea 158-159 H 4
She'aiba, Ash- = Ash-Shu'aybah
182-183 M 7
Sheaville, OR 150-151 E 4
Shebelē Weniz, Webi - 166-167 N 7
Sheboygan, WI 146-147 J 3
Shebu 190-191 C 10
Sheenjek River 144-145 H 4
Sheep Creek 152-153 CD 4-5
Sheep Mountain 152-153 D 3
Sheep Mountains 152-153 CD 2
Sheep Peak 150-151 F 7
Sheep Range 150-151 F 7
Sheffield [AUS] 196 c 2
Sheffield [GB] 132 F 5
Sheffield, AL 154-155 LM 3
Sheffield, IA 152-153 K 4
Sheffield, TX 154-155 DE 5
Shefoo = Yantai 184-185 N 4
Shehami = Shahāmī 182-183 H 6
Shehsien = She Xian 138-139 DE 3
Shê-hsien = She Xian [TJ, Anhui]
184-185 M 5-6
Shê-hsien = She Xian [TJ, Hebei]
190-191 E 3
Shekhar Dsong 184-185 F 6
Shekki = Chixi 190-191 D 10-11
Shekkong = Shikang 190-191 B 11
Sheklung = Shilong 190-191 DE 10
Shelär 182-183 N 6
Shelbina, MO 152-153 K 6
Shelburne [CDN, Ontario]
148-149 C 2
Shelburne Bay 194-195 H 2
Shelby, MI 152-153 N 4
Shelby, MS 154-155 K 4
Shelby, MT 150-151 H 1
Shelby, NC 146-147 K 4
Shelby, OH 152-153 P 5
Shelbyville, IL 152-153 M 6
Shelbyville, IN 152-153 O 6
Shelbyville, KY 152-153 O 6
Shelbyville, MO 152-153 KL 6
Shelbyville, TN 154-155 M 3
Sheldon 174-175 FG 7
Sheldon, IA 152-153 HJ 4
Sheldon, MO 152-153 J 7
Sheldon, WI 152-153 L 3
Shelikof Strait 144-145 EF 6
Shell, WY 152-153 C 3
Shell Beach, LA 154-155 L 6
Shell Creek [USA, Colorado]
150-151 J 5
Shell Creek [USA, Nebraska]
152-153 H 5
Shellen 172-173 J 3
Shelley, ID 150-151 GH 4
Shellharbour, Wollongong-
194-195 K 6
Shell Lake, WI 152-153 L 3
Shellman, GA 154-155 N 5
Shellrock River 152-153 K 4
Shelter Cove, CA 150-151 A 5
Shelton, WA 150-151 B 2
Shemankar, River - 172-173 H 3
Shenāfiya, Ash- = Ash-Shināfiyah
182-183 L 7
Shenandoah, IA 152-153 J 5
Shenandoah, PA 148-149 EF 4
Shenandoah, VA 148-149 D 5
Shenandoah Mountains
148-149 D 5
Shenandoah National Park
148-149 DE 5
Shenandoah River 148-149 DE 5
Shenchi 190-191 CD 2
Shenchih = Shenchi 190-191 CD 2
Shên-ching = Shenjing
190-191 D 10-11
Shendam 166-167 FG 7
Shendi = Shandi 166-167 L 5
Shengcai = Shangcai 190-191 E 5
Shenge 172-173 B 4
Sheng Xian 184-185 N 6
Shenhsien = Shen Xian
190-191 E 2
Shenhu 190-191 G 9
Shenjing 190-191 D 10-11
Shenmu 184-185 L 4
Shennongjia 190-191 C 6
Sheno 172-173 J 3
Shenqiu 190-191 E 5
Shensa Dsong 184-185 FG 5
Shensi = Shaanxi 184-185 K 4-5
Shentseh = Shenze 190-191 E 2
Shentuan 190-191 G 4
Shen Xian 190-191 E 2
Shenyang 184-185 NO 3
Shenze 190-191 E 2
Sheopuri = Shivpuri 180-181 M 5
Shepherd, MT 152-153 B 2-3
Shepherd, TX 154-155 H 5
Shepparton 194-195 HJ 7
Sherborne [ZA] 174-175 F 6
Sherbro Island 166-167 B 7
Sherbrooke [CDN, Quebec]
144-145 W 8
Sherburn, MN 152-153 J 4
Shereik = Ash-Shurayk 166-167 L 5
Sheri'ah, Nahr esh- = Nahr ash-
Shari'ah 182-183 F 6-7
Sheridan, AR 154-155 J 3
Sheridan, MT 150-151 GH 3
Sheridan, OR 150-151 B 3
Sheridan, TX 154-155 G 6
Sheridan, WY 146-147 E 3
Sheridan, Mount - 150-151 H 3
Sheridan Lake, CO 152-153 E 6
Sherman, MS 154-155 L 3
Sherman, TX 146-147 G 5
Sherman Inlet 144-145 R 4
Sherman Mills, ME 148-149 JK 2
Sherman Mountain 150-151 EF 5
Sherridon 144-145 Q 6
Sherwood, ND 152-153 F 1
She Shui 190-191 E 6
Shethātha = Shithāthah
182-183 K 6
Shetland 132 FG 1
She Xian [TJ, Anhui] 184-185 M 5-6
She Xian [TJ, Hebei] 190-191 DE 3
Sheyang 190-191 H 5
Sheyang He 190-191 H 5
Sheyenne River 152-153 H 2
Sheykh Hoseyn 182-183 N 7
Shibām 180-181 F 7
Shibarghān 180-181 K 3
Shibata 188-189 M 4
Shibecha 188-189 d 2
Shibei 190-191 G 9
Shibetsu [J ↑ Asahikawa]
188-189 c 1
Shibetsu [J ↖ Nemuro] 188-189 d 2
Shibicha, Ash- = Ash-Shabakah
182-183 K 7
Shibīgā 186-187 C 1
Shibin al-Kawn 170 D 2
Shibin al-Qanāṭir 170 D 2
Shib Kūh 180-181 G 5
Shibushi 188-189 H 7
Shibushi-wan 188-189 H 7
Shibutami = Tamayama
188-189 N 3
Shicheng 190-191 F 8
Shicheng Dao 188-189 D 3
Shichuan Ding 190-191 CD 9
Shickshock, Monts - = Monts
Chic-Choqs 144-145 X 8
Shidād, Umm ash- = Sabkhat
Abā ar-Rūs 180-181 GH 6
Shidao 190-191 J 3
Shiddādī, Ash- 182-183 J 4
Shidiyah, Ash- 182-183 FG 8
Shields, ND 152-153 F 2
Shifshāwn 166-167 CD 1
Shiga 188-189 KL 5
Shigatse = Zhigatse 184-185 F 6
Shihan, Wādī - 180-181 G 7
Shih-ch'êng = Shicheng
190-191 F 8
Shih-ch'êng Tao = Shicheng Dao
144-145 D 3
Shih-ch'ien = Shiqian 184-185 K 6
Shih-chiu-so = Shijiuso
190-191 G 4
Shih-ch'ü = Serxü 184-185 H 5
Shihchuan = Shiquan 184-185 K 5
Shih-chuang = Shizhuang
190-191 H 5
Shih-hsing = Shinxing 190-191 E 9
Shih-k'ang = Shikang 190-191 B 11
Shih-lou = Shilou 190-191 C 3
Shihlung = Shilong [TJ, Guang-
dong] 190-191 DE 10
Shih-lung = Shihlong [TJ, Guangxi
Zhuangzu Zizhiqu] 190-191 B 10
Shihmen = Shimen 190-191 C 7
Shihnan = Enshi 184-185 K 5
Shih-pei = Shibei 190-191 G 8
Shih-p'ing = Shiping 184-185 J 7
Shih-p'u = Shipu 190-191 H 7
Shihr, Ash- 180-181 F 8
Shih-shou = Shishou 190-191 D 7
Shihtai = Shitai 190-191 F 6
Shihtsien = Shiqian 184-185 K 6
Shijiao 190-191 C 11
Shijiazhuang 184-185 L 4
Shijiu Hu 190-191 G 6
Shikang 190-191 B 11
Shikārpūr 180-181 K 5
Shikhartse = Zhigatse 184-185 F 6
Shikine-chima 188-189 M 5
Shikk'ah, Rā's ash- 182-183 F 5
Shikoku 184-185 P 5
Shikoku sammyaku 188-189 JK 6
Shikotan-tō 184-185 S 3
Shikotsu-ko 188-189 b 2
Shikou 190-191 G 3
Shilaong = Shillong 180-181 P 5
Shilchar = Silchar 180-181 P 6
Shilif [DZ, ~] 166-167 E 1
Shilif [DZ, ●] 166-167 E 1
Shilipu 190-191 CD 6
Shillington, PA 148-149 EF 4
Shillong 180-181 P 5
Shiloguri = Siliguri 180-181 O 5
Shiloh National Military Park and
Cemetry 154-155 LM 3
Shilong [TJ, Guangdong]
190-191 DE 10
Shilong [TJ, Guangxi Zhuangzu
Zizhiqu] 190-191 B 10
Shilou 190-191 C 3
Shilyah, Jabal - 166-167 F 1
Shimabara 188-189 H 6
Shimabara hantō 188-189 H 6
Shimada 188-189 M 5
Shima-hantō 188-189 L 5
Shimane 188-189 HJ 5
Shimen 190-191 C 7
Shimenjie 190-191 F 7
Shimizu 184-185 Q 4-5
Shimizu = Tosashimizu 188-189 J 6
Shimla 184-185 D 5
Shimminato 188-189 L 4
Shimo = Kyūshū 184-185 P 5
Shimoda 188-189 M 5
Shimodate 188-189 MN 4
Shimoga 180-181 LM 8
Shimokita-hantō 184-185 R 3
Shimo-Koshiki-chima 188-189 G 7
Shimoni 168-169 JK 3
Shimonoseki 184-185 P 5
Shimono-shima 188-189 G 5
Shimoyaku = Yaku 188-189 H 7
Shimo-Yūbetsu 188-189 cd 1
Shimushiru = ostrov Simušir
178-179 d 8
Shimushu = ostrov Šumšu
178-179 e 7
Shin, Loch - 132 D 2
Shināfiyah, Ash- 182-183 L 7
Shinaibeidong 190-191 H 7
Shinano gawa 188-189 M 4
Shināṣ 180-181 H 6
Shināy, Bi'r - 170 F 6
Shinbwiyan 186-187 C 1
Shindand 180-181 J 4
Shindidāy, Jabal - 170 G 6
Shiner, TX 154-155 G 6
Shingbwiyang = Shinbwiyan
186-187 C 1
Shingishu = Sinŭiju 184-185 NO 3
Shingleton, MI 152-153 N 2
Shingletown, CA 150-151 C 5
Shingu 188-189 KL 6
Shingwedzi 174-175 J 2
Shingwidzi = Shingwedzi
174-175 J 2
Shiniu Shan 190-191 G 9
Shinjiang = Xinjiang Uyghur
Zizhiqu 184-185 D-G 3
Shinji-ko 188-189 J 5
Shinjō 188-189 QR 4
Shinjō = Hsing ch'eng
190-191 HJ 9
Shinkafi 172-173 G 2
Shinko = Chinko 166-167 J 7
Shinkō = Hsing ch'eng
190-191 HJ 9
Shinkolobwe 168-169 G 5
Shin-nan = Enshi 184-185 K 5
Shinnston, WV 148-149 C 5
Shinqīti 166-167 B 4
Shinshār, Sabkhat - 166-167 B 4
Shinshu = Chinju 184-185 O 4
Shinyanga 168-169 H 3
Shiobara 188-189 MN 4
Shiogama 188-189 N 3
Shiono-misaki 188-189 K 6
Shioya-misaki 188-189 N 4
Shiping 184-185 J 7
Ship Island 154-155 L 5
Shippensburg, PA 148-149 DE 4
Shiprock, NW 150-151 J 7
Shipu 190-191 HJ 7
Shiqian 184-185 K 6
Shiqiao 190-191 CD 6
Shiqq, Hāssi - 166-167 B 3
Shiquan 184-185 K 5
Shiquan He = Sengge Khamba
184-185 DE 5
Shirahama 188-189 K 6
Shirakami-saki 188-189 MN 2
Shirakawa 188-189 N 4
Shirane-san 188-189 LM 5
Shiranuka 188-189 cd 2
Shiraoi 188-189 b 2
Shirataka 188-189 MN 3
Shirāz 180-181 G 5
Shiraze-hyōga 121 B 4-5
Shirbīn 170 D 2
Shire 168-169 HJ 6
Shiretoko hantō 188-189 d 1-2
Shiretoko-misaki 188-189 d 1
Shirīn Sū 182-183 N 5
Shiritoru = Makarov 178-179 b 8
Shiriya-saki 188-189 N 2
Shirley, AR 154-155 J 3
Shirley Basin 152-153 C 4
Shiro, TX 154-155 H 5
Shiroishi 188-189 N 3-4
Shirotori 188-189 L 5
Shirqāṭ, Ash- = Ash-Sharqāṭ
182-183 K 5
Shishi 190-191 G 9
Shishikui 188-189 K 6
Shishmaref, AK 144-145 CD 4
Shishou 190-191 D 7
Shitai 184-185 M 5
Shithāthah 182-183 K 6
Shiwālak Pahāriyān = Siwālik
Range 180-181 M 4-N 5
Shivamagga = Shimoga
180-181 LM 8
Shivpuri 180-181 M 5
Shivwits Indian Reservation
150-151 FG 7
Shivwits Plateau 150-151 G 7
Shiwa Ngandu 171 BC 5
Shixing 190-191 E 9
Shiyan 190-191 C 5
Shizhu 190-191 B 6
Shizhuang 190-191 H 5
Shizukawa 188-189 N 3
Shizunai 188-189 c 2
Shizuoka 188-189 LM 5
Shkodër 136-137 H 4
Shkumbin 136-137 J 5
Shmaytiyah 182-183 H 5
Shoa = Shewa 166-167 M 7
Shoals, IN 152-153 N 6
Shōbara 188-189 J 5
Shōdo-shima 188-189 K 5
Shodu 184-185 H 5
Shokā = Chang-hua 190-191 H 9
Shokambetsu-dake 188-189 b 2
Shokotsu 188-189 c 1
Sholāpur = Solapur 180-181 M 7
Shōra, Ash- = Ash-Shūr'a
182-183 K 5
Shorapur 180-181 M 7
Shorewood, WI 152-153 N 4
Shortland Island 186-187 hj 6
Shoshone, CA 150-151 EF 8
Shoshone, ID 150-151 F 4
Shoshone Falls 150-151 FG 4
Shoshone Mountain 150-151 E 7
Shoshone Mountains
146-147 C 3-4
Shoshone River 154-155 B 3
Shoshoni, WY 154-155 BC 4
Shō-Tombetsu 188-189 c 1
Shott el Jerid = Shaṭṭ al-Jarīd
166-167 F 2
Shouchang 190-191 G 7
Shouguang 190-191 G 3
Shou-hsien = Shouguang
190-191 G 3
Shouning 190-191 G 8
Shoup, ID 150-151 F 3
Shou Xian 190-191 F 5
Shouyang 190-191 D 3
Showak = Shuwak 166-167 M 6
Showhsien = Shou Xian
190-191 F 5
Showkwang = Shougang
190-191 G 3
Show Low, AZ 150-151 H 8
Showning = Shouning 190-191 G 8
Showyang = Shouyang
190-191 D 3
Shreveport, LA 146-147 H 5
Shrewsbury 132 E 5
Shrikākulam = Srikakulam
180-181 M 7
Shrirampur = Serampore
180-181 O 6
Shrirangam = Srirangam
180-181 M 8
Shrivardhan = Srivardhan
180-181 L 7
Shuaiba = Ash-Shu'aybah
182-183 M 7
Shuangcheng 184-185 NO 2
Shuang-ch'êng = Shuangcheng
184-185 NO 2
Shuanfeng 190-191 D 8
Shuanggou [TJ, Hubei] 190-191 D 5
Shuanggou [TJ, Jiangsu ↓ Suqian]
190-191 G 5
Shuanggou [TJ, Jiangsu ↘ Xuzhou]
190-191 FG 4
Shuang-kou = Shuanggou [TJ,
Hubei] 190-191 D 5
Shuang-kou = Shuanggou [TJ,
Jiangsu ↓ Suqian] 190-191 G 5
Shuang-kou = Shuanggou [TJ,
Jiangsu ↘ Xuzhou]
190-191 FG 4
Shuangliao 184-185 N 3
Shuangpai 190-191 C 8-9
Shu'aybah, Ash- 182-183 M 7
Shu'bah, Ash- 182-183 L 8
Shubert, NE 152-153 HJ 5
Shubuta, MS 154-155 L 5
Shucheng 190-191 F 6
Shūfah = Qāshqār 184-185 CD 4
Shugra = Shuqrā 180-181 F 8
Shuguri Falls 171 D 5
Shuhekou 190-191 B 5
Shu-ho-k'ou = Shuhekou
190-191 B 5
Shuidong = Dianbai 190-191 C 11
Shuifeng Supong Hu = Supung Hu
188-189 E 2
Shuigoutou = Laixi 190-191 H 3
Shuiji 190-191 G 8
Shuikou 184-185 M 6
Shūkāt ath-Thalātha, Rā's ash-
166-167 D 1
Shullsburg, WI 152-153 LM 4
Shulu 190-191 E 3
Shumagin Islands 144-145 DE 6
Shumla, TX 154-155 E 6
Shumlūl, Ash- = Ma'qalā,
180-181 F 5
Shun'an = Chun'an 190-191 G 7
Shunchang 190-191 FG 8
Shunde 190-191 D 10
Shungnak, AK 144-145 EF 4
Shunhua = Chunhua 190-191 B 4
Shunking = Nanchong
184-185 JK 5
Shunsen = Ch'unch'ŏn
184-185 O 4
Shuntak = Shunde 190-191 D 10
Shunteh = Shunde 190-191 D 10
Shunteh = Xingtai 184-185 L 4
Shuo-hsien = Shuo Xian
190-191 D 2
Shuo Xian 190-191 D 2
Shuqrā' 180-181 F 8
Shūr, Āb-e - 182-183 N 7
Shūr'a, Ash- 182-183 K 5
Shurayf 180-181 D 5
Shurayk 166-167 L 5
Shurugwi 168-169 GH 6
Shūsh 182-183 N 6
Shushan = Susa 182-183 N 6
Shushong 174-175 G 2
Shūshtar 180-181 F 4
Shuwak 166-167 M 6
Shuwayyib, Ash- 182-183 MN 7
Shuyang 184-185 M 5
Shuzenji 188-189 M 5
Shwangcheng = Shuangcheng
184-185 NO 2
Shwangliao = Liaoyuan
184-185 NO 3
Shwebō 186-187 C 2
Shyog 180-181 M 3-4
Shyopur = Shivpuri 180-181 M 5
Siāh, Kūh-e - = Kūh-e Marzu
182-183 M 6
Siāhdehān = Tākestān
182-183 NO 4
Siakiang = Xiajiang 190-191 E 8
Siakwan = Xiaguan 184-185 J 6
Sialcote = Siyālkoṭ 180-181 LM 4
Sialkot = Siyālkoṭ 180-181 LM 4
Siam = Thailand 186-187 CD 3
Siam = Thaïlande 186-187 CD 3
Siam = Thailandia 186-187 CD 3
Siam = Thajsko 186-187 CD 3
Siam, Golfo del - 186-187 D 4-5
Si'an 190-191 G 6
Sian = Xi'an 184-185 K 5
Siangfan = Fangcheng 184-185 L 5
Siangho = Xianghe 190-191 F 2
Siangning = Xiangning
190-191 C 3-4
Siangtan = Xiangtan 184-185 L 6
Siangyang = Xiangyang 184-185 L 5
Siangyin = Xiangning 190-191 D 7
Siangyuan = Xiangyuan
190-191 D 3
Siangiāo = Xiang Jiang 190-191 D 8
Siaofeng = Xiaofeng 190-191 G 6
Siaohsien = Xiao Xian 190-191 F 4
Siaokan = Xiaogan 190-191 D 6
Siaoyi = Xiaoyi 190-191 C 3
Siapa, Rio - 158-159 FG 4
Siargao Island 186-187 J 4-5
Siau, Pulau - 186-187 J 6
Šiauliai 130-131 K 10
Šiauliai 138-139 D 6
Siazan' 140-141 O 6
Sibah, As- 182-183 N 7
Siba'i, Jabal as- 170 EF 5
Sība'iyah, As- 170 E 5
Sibaj 178-179 K 7
Sibasa 174-175 J 2
Sibayameer 174-175 K 4
Sibayi, Lake - = Sibayameer
174-175 K 4
Šibenik 136-137 FG 4
Siberia 178-179 O-X 5
Siberia 178-179 N-W 5
Sibéria 178-179 O-X 5
Siberia Central, Meseta de -
178-179 R-W 4-5
Sibéria Central, Meseta de -
178-179 R-X 4-5
Siberia Centrale, Altopiano della -
178-179 R-X 4-5
Sibéria Oriental, Mar da -
178-179 d-h 3
Siberia Oriental, Mar de -
178-179 c-j 3
Siberia Orientale, Mar della
178-179 d-h 3
Sibéria Oriental, Patamar da -
120 B 36-1
Siberia Orientale, Platea della -
120 B 36-1
Siberia Oriental, Ramal de -
120 B 36-1
Sibeřie 178-179 N-W 5
Sibérie 178-179 N-W 5
Sibérie Centrale, Plateau de -
178-179 R-W 4-5
Sibérie Orientale, Mer de -
178-179 c-j 3
Siberut, Pulau - 186-187 C 7
Siberut, Selat - 186-187 C 7
Sibi 180-181 K 5
Sibiloi National Park 171 D 1-2
Sibiń = Sibiu 136-137 L 3
Sibir'akova, ostrov - 178-179 OP 3
Sibircevo 178-179 Z 9
Sibirien 178-179 N-W 5
Sibiř 178-179 O-X 5
Sibiti [EAT] 171 C 3
Sibiti [RCA] 168-169 D 3
Sibiu 136-137 KL 3
Sibley, IA 152-153 HJ 4
Sibolga 186-187 C 6
Sibu 186-187 F 6
Sibū, Nahr - 166-167 CD 2
Sibū 'Gharb, As- 170 E 6
Sibutu Group 186-187 G 6
Sibuyan Island 186-187 H 4
Sibuyan Sea 186-187 H 4
Siby 172-173 C 2
Sibyŏn-ni 188-189 F 3
Sicasica 158-159 F 8
Sicasso = Sikasso 166-167 C 6
Sichang = Xichang 184-185 J 6
Šichany 138-139 Q 7
Sichem = Nābulus 182-183 F 6
Sichota-Alin = Sichoté Alin'
178-179 a 8-Z 9
Šichoté Alin' 178-179 a 8-Z 9
Sichrany = Kanaš 178-179 H 6
Sichuan 184-185 J 5-6
Sichwan = Xichuan 184-185 L 5
Sicile = Sicilia 136-137 EF 7
Sicilia 136-137 EF 7
Sicily = Sicilia 136-137 EF 7
Sicuani 158-159 E 7
Sidaogou 188-189 F 2
Sideby 130-131 J 6
Sidéradougou 172-173 DE 3
Sidérókastron 136-137 K 5
Sideros, Akrōtērion - 136-137 M 8
Sidi Abd'ar Rahman 170 C 2
Sidi Ban al-'Abbās 166-167 DE 1
Sīdī Barrānī 166-167 K 2
Sidi-bel-Abbès = Sīdī Ban al-
'Abbās 166-167 DE 1
Sīdī Mirwān 166-167 JK 1
Sīdī Qāsim 166-167 CD 2
Sidi Sālim 170 D 2
Sidley, Mount - 121 B 121
Sidnaw, MI 152-153 M 2
Sidney 150-151 B 1
Sidney, IA 152-153 J 5
Sidney, MT 152-153 D 2
Sidney, NE 152-153 E 5
Sidney, NY 152-153 O 5
Sidney, OH 148-149 A 4
Sidney Lanier Lake - 154-155 NO 3
Sidobia 172-173 F 2
Sidorovo 138-139 N 4
Sidr, As- 166-167 H 2
Sidr, Wādī - 170 E 3
Sidra = As-Surt 166-167 H 2-3
Sidra, Golfo de - = Khalij as-
Surt 166-167 H 2
Sidra, Gulf of - = Khalij as-Surt
166-167 H2
Sidra, Khalig - = Khalij as-Surt
166-167 H2
Sidra-öböl = Khalij as-Surt
166-167 GH 2
Sidrolândia 158-159 HJ 9
Siebenbürgen = Transilvania
136-137 KL 2
Siedlce 133 L 2
Sieg 133 C 3
Siegen 133 D 3
Siemiatycze 133 L 2
Siem Reap 186-187 D 4
Siena 136-137 D 4
Sienfeng = Xianfeng 190-191 B 7
Sienku = Xianju 190-191 H 7
Sienning = Xianning 190-191 E 7
Sienyang = Xianyang 184-185 K 5
Sieradz 133 J 3
Sierpc 133 JK 2
Sierra Blanca, TX 154-155 C 5
Sierra Blanca Peak 146-147 E 5
Sierra Colorada 162 C 6
Sierra de Outes 134-135 C 7
Sierra Gorda 162 C 2
Sierra Grande [RA, Rio Negro ●]
162 C 6
Sierra Leona 166-167 B 7
Sierra Leona, Cuenca de -
124-125 HJ 5
Sierra Leona, Ramal de -
124-125 HJ 5
Sierra Leone 166-167 B 7
Sierra Leone, Bacino della -
124-125 HJ 5
Sierra Leone, Bassin de -
124-125 HJ 5
Sierra Leone, Dorsale della -
124-125 HJ 5
Sierra Leone, Seuil de -
124-125 HJ 5
Sierra Leone Basin 124-125 HJ 5
Sierra-Leone-Becken 124-125 HJ 5
Sierra Leonebekken 124-125 HJ 5
Sierra Leonedrempel 124-125 HJ 5
Sierra Leone Rise 124-125 HJ 5
Sierra-Leone-Schwelle
124-125 HJ 5
Sierra Madre [MEX] 146-147 H 8
Sierra Madre [RP] 186-187 H 3
Sierra Madre [USA] 152-153 C 5
Sierra Madre del Sur 146-147 FG 8
Sierra Madre Mountains
150-151 CD 8
Sierra Madre Occidental
146-147 E 5-F 7
Sierra Madre Oriental
146-147 F 6-G 7
Sierra Morena 134-135 D 10-E 9
Sierra Nevada 134-135 F 10
Sierra Nevada [USA] 146-147 BC 4
Sierra Pinta 150-151 G 9

South Fiji Basin 194-195 OP 4-5
South Fork, CO 152-153 C 7
South Fork Clearwater River
150-151 F 3
South Fork Flathead River
150-151 G 2
South Fork Grand River
152-153 E 3
South Fork John Day River
150-151 D 3
South Fork Moreau River
152-153 E 3
South Fork Mountains 150-151 B 5
South Fork Owyhee River
150-151 E 4-5
South Fork Powder River
152-153 C 4
South Fork Republican River
152-153 E 6
South Fork Salmon River
150-151 F 3
South Fork Solomon River
152-153 F 6
South Fork White River 152-153 F 4
South Fox Island 152-153 NO 3
South Gate, CA 150-151 DE 9
South Georgia 162 J 8
South Georgia Ridge
121 D 133-E 34
South Grand River 152-153 JK 6
South Haven, KS 154-155 G 2
South Haven, MI 152-153 N 4
South Henik Lake 144-145 R 5
South Hill, VA 148-149 D 6
South Honshu Ridge 184-185 R 5-6
South Horr 168-169 J 2
South Charleston, WV
148-149 BC 5
South China Basin 186-187 FG 3-4
South China Sea 186-187 E 5-G 3
South Indian Ridge 124-125 OP 8
South Island 194-195 OP 8
South Korea 184-185 OP 4
South Loup River 152-153 FG 5
South Luangwa National Park
171 B 6
South Milwaukee, WI 152-153 N 4
South Mountain 148-149 E 4-5
South Nahanni River 144-145 LM 5
South Ogden, UT 150-151 H 5
South Orkneys 121 C 132
South Ossetian Autonomous
Region 140-141 LM 5
South Pacific Basin 121 D 21-19
South Pacific Ridge 121 D 22-C 20
South Padre Island 154-155 G 7
South Paris, ME 148-149 H 2
South Pass [USA, Louisiana]
146-147 J 6
South Pass [USA, Wyoming]
146-147 E 3
South Plate River 146-147 F 3
Southport [AUS] 196 c 3
Southport, NC 148-149 DE 7-8
South Portland, ME 148-149 HJ 3
South Ronaldsay 132 EF 2
South Saint Paul, MN 152-153 K 3
South Sandwich Islands 121 CD 34
South Sandwich Trench 121 D 34
South Saskatchewan River
144-145 OP 7
South Sea 192-193 HN 5
South Shetlands 121 C 30
South Shields 132 F 4
South Sioux City, NE 152-153 H 4
South Sulphur River 154-155 H 4
South Taranaki Bight 194-195 O 7
South Tent 150-151 H 6
South Tyrol 136-137 D 2
South Uist 132 BC 3
South Umpqua River 150-151 B 4
Southwest Africa = Namibia
168-169 E 7
South West Cape [AUS] 196 bc 3
South West Cape [NZ] 194-195 N 9
Southwest Cay 146-147 KL 9
Southwest Indian Basin
124-125 MN 7
Southwest Pass [USA, Mississippi
River Delta] 146-147 J 6
Southwest Pass [USA, Vermillion
Bay] 154-155 J 6
South Williamsport, PA 148-149 E 4
Soutpansberge 168-169 GH 7
Soutrivier [ZA ◁ Atlantic Ocean]
174-175 B 6
Soutrivier [ZA ◁ Grootrivier]
174-175 E 7
Souzel 158-159 J 5
Sovdozero 138-139 J 2
Sovetsk 133 K 1
Sovetsk [SU, Vjatka] 178-179 H 6
Sovetskaja 140-141 KL 2
Sovetskaja Gavan' 178-179 ab 8
Sovetskij [SU, Rossijskaja SFSR]
138-139 G 3
Sovetskij [SU, Ukrainskaja SSR]
140-141 G 4
Sovetskoje [SU, Saratov]
138-139 Q 8
Soweto, Johannesburg-
174-175 G 4
Sōya [J, Hokkaidō] 188-189 b 1
Sōya-kaikyō 184-185 R 2
Sōya misaki 188-189 bc 1
Söylemez 182-183 JK 3
Soyo 168-169 D 4
Sož 138-139 H 7
Sozopol 136-137 MN 4
Spagna 134-135 D 7-G 9
Spahren = Spāre 138-139 D 5
Spain 134-135 D 7-G 9
Spakovskoje 140-141 L 4
Spalato = Split 136-137 G 4
Spalding 132 FG 5
Spalding [AUS] 196 D 4
Spalding, ID 150-151 E 2
Spalding, NE 152-153 G 5
Spangle, WA 150-151 E 2
Spanien 134-135 D 7-G 9
Spanish Fork, UT 150-151 H 5
Spanish Peak = West Spanish Peak
152-153 D 7
Spanish Head 132 D 4
Spanish Town 146-147 L 8
Spanje 134-135 D 7-G 9
Spanta, Akrōtḗrion - 136-137 KL 8
Spanyolország 134-135 D 7-G 9
Sparbu 130-131 D 6
Spāre 138-139 D 5
Sparkman, AR 154-155 J 3-4
Sparks, GA 148-149 B 9
Sparta, IL 152-153 M 6
Sparta, MI 152-153 O 4
Sparta, GA 148-149 B 8
Sparta, NC 148-149 C 6
Sparta, TN 154-155 N 3
Sparta, WI 152-153 L 4
Sparta = Spártē 136-137 K 7
Spartanburg, SC 146-147 K 4-5
Spártē 136-137 K 7
Spartivento, Capo - [I, Calàbria]
136-137 G 7
Spartivento, Capo - [I, Sardegna]
136-137 G 6
Spasporub 138-139 R 3
Spassk = Spassk-Dal'nij
178-179 Z 9
Spasskaja Guba 138-139 J 2
Spassk-Dal'nij 178-179 Z 9
Spasskoje [SU, Kostroma]
138-139 Q 4
Spassk-R'azanskij 138-139 N 6
Spearfish, SD 152-153 E 3
Spearman, TX 154-155 E 2
Spearville, KS 152-153 G 7
Speke Gulf 168-169 H 3
Spencer, IA 152-153 J 4
Spencer, ID 150-151 G 3
Spencer, IN 152-153 N 6
Spencer, NC 148-149 C 7
Spencer, SD 152-153 H 4
Spencer, WI 152-153 L 3
Spencer, WV 148-149 C 5
Spencer, Cape - [AUS]
194-195 G 7
Spencerbaai 174-175 A 3
Spencer Bay = Spencerbaai
174-175 A 3
Spencer Gulf 194-195 G 6
Spencerville, OH 152-153 OP 5
Spessart 133 D 3-4
Spétsai 136-137 K 7
Spey 132 E 3
Speyer 133 D 4
Spèzia, La - 136-137 C 3
Spezzano Albanese 136-137 G 6
Spicheby 130-131 k
Spicer Islands 144-145 UV 4
Spilimbergo 136-137 E 2
Spin Buldak 180-181 K 4
Spioenberg I 174-175 D 6
Spioenberg II 174-175 CD 6
Spirit Lake, IA 152-153 J 4
Spirit Lake, ID 150-151 E 1-2
Spirit Lake, WA 150-151 BC 2
Spiro, OK 154-155 H 3
Spirovo 138-139 K 5
Spitak 140-141 LM 6
Spithamn = Pöõsaspea
138-139 DE 4
Spitsbergen 130-131 k 6-o 5
Spittal 133 F 5
Spitzberg = Svalbard 134-135 k-m 6
Split 136-137 G 4
Split Rock, WY 152-153 C 4
Splügen 133 D 5
Spofford, TX 154-155 E 6
Spoği 138-139 F 5
Spojené arabské emiráty
180-181 GH 6
Spojené státy americké
146-147 C-K 4
Spokane, WA 146-147 C 2
Spokane Indian Reservation
150-151 DE 2
Spokane River 150-151 DE 2
Spokojnyj 178-179 YZ 6
Špola 140-141 E 2
Spoleto 136-137 E 4
Spooner, MN 152-153 J 1
Spooner, WI 152-153 L 3
Spoon River 152-153 L 5
Sporaden 136-137 M 6-8
Sporades 136-137 M 6-8
Sporades de la Polynésie Centrale
192-193 L 4-M 5
Sporadi 136-137 M 6-7
Sporadi della Polinesia Centrale
192-193 L 4-M 5
Sporady 136-137 M 6-7
Sporyj Navolok, mys -
178-179 M-O 2
Spotted Horse, WY 152-153 D 3
Spotted Range 150-151 F 7
Sprague, WA 150-151 DE 2
Sprague River 150-151 C 4
Sprague River, OR 150-151 C 4
Spratly Islands = Quần Đao
Hoang Sa 186-187 F 5
Spray, OR 150-151 D 3
Spree 133 G 3
Spreewald 133 F 2-G 3
Spremberg 133 G 3
Sprengisandur 130-131 de 2
Spring, TX 154-155 H 5
Spring Bay 150-151 G 5
Springbok 168-169 E 8
Springbokvlakte 174-175 H 3
Spring City, TN 154-155 N 3
Springdale, AR 154-155 HJ 2
Springdale, MT 150-151 HJ 3
Springdale, NV 150-151 E 7
Springdale, UT 150-151 G 7
Springdale, WA 150-151 DE 1
Springer, NM 154-155 C 2
Springerville, AZ 150-151 J 8
Springfield, CO 152-153 E 7
Springfield, GA 148-149 C 8
Springfield, ID 150-151 G 4
Springfield, IL 146-147 HJ 4
Springfield, KY 152-153 O 7
Springfield, MA 146-147 M 3
Springfield, MN 152-153 J 3
Springfield, MO 146-147 H 4
Springfield, OH 146-147 K 3-4
Springfield, OR 150-151 B 3
Springfield, SD 152-153 GH 4
Springfield, TN 154-155 M 2
Springfield, VT 148-149 G 3
Springfontein 174-175 FG 6
Springhill, LA 154-155 J 4
Spring Hill, TN 154-155 M 3
Spring Hope, NC 148-149 DE 7
Spring Mountains 150-151 F 7
Springs 168-169 G 8
Springsure 194-195 J 4
Spring Valley [USA] 150-151 F 6
Spring Valley [ZA] 174-175 G 7
Spring Valley, IL 152-153 M 5
Spring Valley, MN 152-153 K 4
Springview, NE 152-153 G 4
Springville, AL 154-155 M 4
Springville, NY 148-149 D 3
Springville, UT 150-151 H 5
Spruce Knob 146-147 KL 4
Spruce Mountain 150-151 F 5
Spruce Pine, NC 148-149 BC 6-7
Spry, UT 150-151 G 7
Spur, TX 154-155 E 4
Spur Lake, NM 150-151 J 8-9
Squaw Valley, CA 146-147 BC 4
Squillace, Golfo di - 136-137 G 6
Srbsko 136-137 H 3-J 4
Srbija 136-137 H 3-J 4
Sredinnyj chrebet 178-179 f 6-e 7
Sredna gora 136-137 L 4
Sredn'aja Achtuba 140-141 M 2
Srednekolymsk 178-179 d 4
Srednerusskaja vozvyšennost'
138-139 L 6-8
Sredne-Sibirskoje ploskogorje
178-179 R-W 4-5
Srednij Ural 178-179 KL 6
Sredsib 178-179 L 7-P 7
Śrem 133 H 2
Sremska Mitrovica 136-137 H 3
Sremska Rača 136-137 H 3
Sretensk 178-179 W 7
Srê Umbell 186-187 D 4
Sri Jayawardanapura 180-181 N 9
Srikakulam 180-181 N 7
Sri Lanka 180-181 N 9
Sri Lanka 180-181 N 9
Srinagar 180-181 LM 4
Srirangam 180-181 M 8
Srivardhan 180-181 L 7
Środa Wielkopolska 133 HJ 2
Sseu-p'ing = Siping 184-185 N 3
Ssongea = Songea 168-169 J 5
Staateninsel = Isla de los
Estados 162 D 8
Staaten River 194-195 H 3
Stachanov 140-141 J 2
Stackeln = Strenči 138-139 E 5
Stack Skerry 132 D 2
Stade 133 D 2
Städjan 130-131 E 7
Stadlandet 130-131 A 6
Stafford 132 E 5
Stafford, KS 152-153 G 7
Stafford, NE 152-153 G 4
Staicele 138-139 E 5
Staizel = Staicele 138-139 E 5
Staked Plain = Llano Estacado
146-147 F 5
Stalina, pik - = pik
Kommunizma 180-181 L 3
Stalinabad = Dušanbe 180-181 K 3
Stalingrad = Volgograd
140-141 LM 2
Staliniri = Cchinvali 140-141 LM 5
Stalinka = Černovozavodskoje
140-141 FG 1
Stalino = Doneck 140-141 H 2-3
Stalino = Ošarovo 178-179 S 5
Stalinogorsk = Novomoskovsk
138-139 M 6
Stalinsk = Novokuzneck
178-179 Q 7
Stallo, MS 154-155 L 4
Stalowa Wola 133 L 3
Stalwart Point = Stalwartpunt
174-175 G 7
Stalwartpunt 174-175 G 7
Stambul = İstanbul 180-181 BC 2
Stambuł = İstanbul 180-181 BC 2
Stamford [AUS] 194-195 H 4
Stamford, CT 148-149 G 4
Stamford, TX 154-155 F 4
Stampriet 168-169 E 7
Stamps, AR 154-155 J 4
Stamsund 130-131 EF 3
Stanbury, MO 152-153 J 5
Stanbury Mountains 150-151 G 5
Stancy 138-139 G 4
Standerton 168-169 GH 8
Standing Rock Indian Reservation
152-153 F 2-3
Standish, MI 152-153 OP 4
Stane = Stavnoje 140-141 A 2
Stanford, KY 152-153 O 7
Stanford, MT 150-151 H 2
Stanger 174-175 J 5
Stancia Bagajevskaja 140-141 K 3
Stanislau = Ivano-Frankovsk
140-141 B 2
Stanislaus River 150-151 C 6-7
Stanke Dimitrov 136-137 K 4
Stanley [AUS] 196 b 2
Stanley [Falkland Islands] 162 E 8
Stanley, ID 150-151 F 3
Stanley, KY 152-153 N 7
Stanley, ND 152-153 E 1
Stanley, NM 154-155 BC 3
Stanley, WI 152-153 L 3
Stanley, Mount - 194-195 F 4
Stanley Pool = Pool Malebo
168-169 E 3
Stanley Reservoir 180-181 M 8
Stanleyville = Kisangani
168-169 G 2
Stann Creek 146-147 J 8
Stanovoj chrebet 178-179 X-Z 6
Stanovoje nagorje 178-179 VW 6
Stanthorpe 196 KL 2
Stanton, KY 152-153 P 7
Stanton, MI 152-153 O 4
Stanton, ND 152-153 F 2
Stanton, NE 152-153 H 5
Stanton, TX 154-155 DE 4
Stanwood, WA 150-151 B 1
Stany Zjednoczone 146-147 C-K 4
Stapi 130-131 b 2
Staples, MN 152-153 J 2
Stapleton, NE 152-153 F 5
Star' 138-139 JK 7
Star, NC 148-149 D 7
Star, MS 154-155 KL 4
Starachowice 133 K 3
Staraja Buchara = Buchara
180-181 JK 3
Staraja Kulatka 138-139 Q 7
Staraja Ladoga 138-139 HJ 4
Staraja Majna 138-139 R 6
Staraja Matvejevka 138-139 T 6
Staraja Porubežka 138-139 RS 7
Staraja Račejka 138-139 QR 7
Staraja Russa 178-179 E 6
Staraja Toropa 138-139 HJ 5
Stara Pazova 136-137 J 3
Stara Zagora 136-137 L 4
Starbuck [⊙] 198-199 K 5
Star City, AR 154-155 K 4
Stargard Szczeciński 133 G 2
Starica 138-139 K 5
Starigrad 136-137 F 3
Starke, FL 148-149 bc 2
Starkey, ID 150-151 E 3
Starkville, CO 152-153 D 7
Starkville, MS 154-155 L 4
Starkweather, ND 152-153 G 1
Starnberg 133 E 4-5
Starnberger See 133 E 5
Starobel'sk 140-141 J 2
Starodub 138-139 J 7
Starogard Gdański 133 HJ 2
Staroizborsk 130-131 MN 9
Staroizborsk = Izborsk
138-139 FG 5
Staroje 138-139 N 4
Starojurjevo 138-139 N 7
Starokonstantinov 140-141 C 2
Starominskaja 140-141 J 3
Staroščerbinovskaja 140-141 J 3
Starotimoškino 138-139 Q 7
Starotitarovskaja 140-141 H 4
Staroverčeskaja 138-139 QR 4
Staryje Dorogi 138-139 G 7
Staryj Bir'uz'ak 140-141 N 4
Staryj Krym 140-141 G 4
Staryj Oskol 140-141 HJ 1
Staryj Sambor 140-141 A 2
Staryj Terek 140-141 N 5
Staßfurt 133 E 3
Staszów 133 K 3
State College, PA 148-149 DE 4
State Line, MS 154-155 L 5
Staten Island 148-149 FG 4
Statenville, GA 148-149 B 9
Statesboro, GA 148-149 C 8
Statesville, NC 146-147 K 4
Stati Uniti 146-147 C-K 4
Stauffer, OR 150-151 C 4
Staunton, IL 152-153 M 6
Staunton, VA 146-147 KL 4
Stavanger 130-131 A 8
Stavern 130-131 CD 8
Stavka = Urda 140-141 N 2
Stavkoviči 138-139 G 5
Stavnoje 140-141 A 2
Stavropol' 140-141 KL 4
Stavropol' = Togliatti 178-179 H 7
Stavropol'skaja vozvyšennost'
140-141 K-M 4
Stavrós 136-137 K 5
Stawell 194-195 H 7
Stawropol = Stavropol'
140-141 KL 4
Steamboat, NV 150-151 D 6
Steamboat Springs, CO
152-153 C 5
Stearns, KY 154-155 N 2
Steele Island 121 B 130-131
Steele, AL 154-155 M 4
Steele, MO 154-155 L 2
Steele, ND 152-153 FG 2
Steelpoort 168-169 GH 7
Steelpoortrivier 174-175 HJ 3
Steelton, PA 148-149 E 4
Steelville, MO 152-153 L 7
Steenkampsberge 174-175 HJ 3
Steenkool = Bintuni 186-187 K 7
Steensby Inlet 144-145 V 3
Steens Mountain 150-151 D 4
Steenstrups Gletscher
144-145 Za 2
Steep Point 194-195 B 5
Ştefăneşti 136-137 M 2
Stefansson Island 144-145 OP 3
Steflești 136-137 K 3
Stege 130-131 E 10
Steiermark 133 G 5
Steilloopbrug 174-175 H 2
Steinbrück = Zidani most
136-137 F 2
Steinen, Rio - 158-159 J 7
Steinhatchee, FL 148-149 b 2
Steinkjer 130-131 DE 5
Steinkopf 174-175 BC 5
Steinnest 130-131 m 6
Steinort = Akmeņrags 138-139 C 5
Steins, NM 150-151 J 9
Stekl'anka 138-139 N 4
Stella 174-175 F 4
Stellaland 168-169 F 8
Stellenbosch 168-169 EF 9
Stendal 133 E 2
Stende 138-139 D 5
Stenden = Stende 138-139 D 5
Stensele 130-131 G 5
Stepan' 138-139 F 8
Stepanakert = Xankändi
140-141 N 7
Stepana Razina 138-139 P 6
Stepanavan 140-141 LM 6
Stephanie, Lake - = Thew Bahir
166-167 M 8
Stephen, MN 152-153 H 1
Stephens, AR 154-155 J 4
Stephenson, MI 152-153 N 3
Stephensville, TX 154-155 FG 4
Stephenville 144-145 YZ 8
Stepn'ak 178-179 N 7
Štepovka 140-141 G 1
Sterkspruit 174-175 D 6
Sterkstroom 168-169 G 9
Sterkwater 174-175 H 3
Sterkley, TX 154-155 E 3
Sterly, TX 154-155 E 3
Sterling, CO 146-147 F 3
Sterling, IL 152-153 M 5
Sterling, KS 152-153 GH 6
Sterling, ND 152-153 FG 2
Sterling City, TX 154-155 E 5
Sterling Heights, MI 152-153 P 4
Sterlitamak 178-179 K 7
Sternberg = Torzym 133 G 2
Štětin = Szczecin 133 G 2
Stettin = Szczecin 133 G 2
Stettino = Szczecin 133 G 2
Steuben, MI 152-153 N 2
Steubenville, OH 146-147 K 3
Stevenson, AL 154-155 MN 3
Stevenson, WA 150-151 BC 3
Stevenson, The - 194-195 FG 5
Stevens Point, WI 152-153 M 3
Stevensville, MT 150-151 FG 2
Stewart, AK 144-145 KL 6
Stewart, MN 152-153 J 3
Stewart, NV 150-151 D 6
Stewart, Isla - 162 B 8-9
Stewart Island 194-195 N 9
Stewart Islands 186-187 k 6
Stewart River [CDN, ~]
144-145 JK 5
Stewart River [CDN, ●] 144-145 J 5
Stewartsville, MO 152-153 JK 6
Stewartville, MN 152-153 K 4
Steynsburg 174-175 F 6
Steynsrus 174-175 G 4
Steyr 133 G 4
Stickney, SD 152-153 G 4
Stigler, OK 154-155 H 3
Stikine Mountains = Cassiar
Mountains 144-145 KL 6
Stikine Plateau 144-145 K 6
Stikine River 144-145 KL 6
Stilbaai 174-175 D 8
Stiles, TX 154-155 E 5
Stiller Ozean = Pazifischer
Ozean 198-199 GL 4-6
Stillwater, MN 152-153 K 3
Stillwater, OK 154-155 G 2
Stillwater Mountains 150-151 DE 6
Stilwell, OK 154-155 H 3
Stimson, Mount - 150-151 G 1
Stinear Nunataks 121 BC 7
Stinnet, TX 154-155 E 3
Štip 136-137 K 5
Stirling City, CA 150-151 C 6
Stirling Range 194-195 C 6
Stites, ID 150-151 EF 2
Stjernøy 130-131 K 2
Stjørdalshalsen 130-131 D 6
Stobi 136-137 J 5
Stoccolma = Stockholm
138-139 AB 4
Stoccolma = Stockholm
130-131 H 8
Stochod 138-139 E 8
Stockdale, TX 154-155 FG 6
Stockerau 133 G 4
Stockett, MT 150-151 H 2
Stockholm 130-131 GH 8
Stockholm, ME 148-149 JK 1
Stockholms län 130-131 GH 8
Stockport 132 E 5
Stocks, Cima de - 158-159 N 7
Stocks, Crête de - 158-159 N 7
Stocks, Cume de - 158-159 N 7
Stocks-fenékhegy 158-159 N 7
Stockskuppe 158-159 N 7
Stocks-Ondiepte 158-159 N 7
Stocks, Punta - 158-159 N 7
Stocks Seamount 158-159 N 7
Stockton, CA 146-147 BC 4
Stockton, IL 152-153 LM 4
Stockton, KS 152-153 G 6
Stockton, MO 152-153 K 7
Stockton, Island 152-153 L 2
Stockton on Tees 132 F 4
Stockton Plateau 154-155 D 5
Stockville, NE 152-153 FG 5
Stodolišče 138-139 J 6
Stoffberg 174-175 H 3
Stojba 178-179 Z 7
Stoj, gora - 140-141 A 2
Stoke on Trend 132 EF 5
Stokes Point 196 ab 2
Stokkseyri 130-131 c 3
Stokksnes 130-131 f 2
Stolac 136-137 GH 4
Stolbcy 138-139 F 7
Stolbcy 130-131 M 11
Stolbovaja 138-139 L 6
Stolbovoj, ostrov - 178-179 Za 3
Stolin 138-139 F 8
Stolp = Słupsk 133 H 1
Stolzenfels [Namibia] 174-175 C 5
Ston 136-137 G 4
Stone City, CO 152-153 D 6
Stonehaven 132 EF 3
Stonehenge 132 EF 6
Stonehenge [AUS] 194-195 H 4
Stone Mountains 148-149 C 6
Stoner, CO 150-151 J 7
Stonewall, TX 154-155 F 5
Stonington 121 C 30
Stonington, ME 148-149 J 2-3
Stony Creek, VA 148-149 E 6
Stonyford, CA 150-151 B 6
Stony Point [USA] 148-149 E 3
Stony River 144-145 EF 5
Stopnica 133 K 3
Stora Lulevatten 130-131 HJ 4
Stora Sjöfallet 130-131 H 4
Stora-Sjöfallets nationalpark
130-131 GH 4
Storavan 130-131 H 5
Stord 130-131 A 8
Store Bælt 130-131 D 10
Støren 130-131 CD 6
Storfjord 130-131 B 6
Storfjordbotn 130-131 LM 2
Storfjorden 130-131 k 6
Storlien 130-131 E 6
Storm Bay 194-195 J 8
Stormberg 174-175 FG 6
Stormberge 174-175 G 6
Storm Lake, IA 152-153 J 4
Stormsrivier 174-175 E 7-F 8
Stornorrfors 130-131 HJ 6
Stornoway 132 CD 2
Storøya 130-131 n 4
Storoževsk 178-179 J 5
Storsjön 130-131 E 6
Storuman [S, ●] 130-131 G 5
Storuman [S, ≅] 130-131 G 5
Story City, IA 152-153 K 4
Stosch, Isla - 162 A 7
Stoughton, WI 152-153 M 4
Straatsburg = Strasbourg
134-135 L 4
Strabane 132 C 4
Straight Cliffs 150-151 H 7
Strakonice 133 FG 4
Stralsund 133 F 1
Strand 168-169 E 9
Stranda 130-131 c 1-2
Stranraer 132 D 4
Strasbourg 134-135 L 4
Strasbourg = Brodnica 133 J 2
Strasburg, CO 152-153 D 6
Strasburg, ND 152-153 FG 2
Strasburgo = Strasbourg
134-135 L 4
Străşeni 140-141 D 3
Strasburk = Strasbourg
134-135 L 4
Straßburg = Strasbourg
134-135 L 4
Stratford [AUS] 196 H 7
Stratford [CDN] 144-145 U 9
Stratford, CA 150-151 D 7
Stratford, CT 148-149 G 4
Stratford, SD 152-153 GH 3
Stratford, TX 154-155 DE 2
Stratford, WI 152-153 LM 3
Stratford on Avon 132 F 5
Strathgordon 196 bc 3
Strathmore 132 E 3
Strathroy 148-149 C 3
Stratonis Turris = Caesarea
182-183 F 6
Stratton, CO 152-153 E 6
Stratton, ME 148-149 H 2
Stratton, NE 152-153 F 5
Straubing 133 F 4
Straw, MT 152-153 AB 2
Strawberry Mountains 150-151 D 3
Strawberry Point, IA 152-153 L 4
Strawberry River 150-151 H 5
Strawn, TX 154-155 F 4
Streaky Bay [AUS, ◡] 194-195 F 6
Streaky Bay [AUS, ●] 194-195 FG 6
Streator, IL 152-153 M 5
Středozemní moře 136-137 C 7-M 8
Streeter, ND 152-153 G 2
Streetman, TX 154-155 GH 5
Streich Mound 194-195 D 6
Strelka-Čun'a 178-179 T 5
Strenči 138-139 E 5
Stresa 136-137 C 3
Strešen' = Strašeny 140-141 D 3
Strevell, ID 150-151 G 4
Strickland River 186-187 M 8
Stringtown, OK 154-155 GH 3
Strižament, gora - 140-141 L 4
Striži 138-139 R 4
Stroeder 162 D 6
Strofádes 136-137 J 7
Strómboli 136-137 F 6
Stromsburg, NE 152-153 H 5
Strömstad 130-131 D 8
Strömsund 130-131 F 6
Ströms Vattudal 130-131 F 5-6
Stroner, WY 152-153 D 3
Strong, AR 154-155 J 4
Strong City, KS 152-153 H 6
Stronsay 132 EF 2
Stroud 132 EF 6
Stroud, OK 154-155 G 3
Stroudsburg, PA 148-149 F 4
Struer 130-131 C 9
Strugi Krasnyje 138-139 G 4
Struisbaai 174-175 D 8
Struma 136-137 K 5
Strumica 136-137 K 5
Strunino 138-139 M 5
Struys Bay = Struisbaai 174-175 D 8
Strydenburg 174-175 E 5
Strydomsvlei 174-175 E 7
Strydpoortberge 174-175 H 3
Stryj [SU, ~] 140-141 A 2
Stryj [SU, ●] 140-141 A 2
Strymṓn 136-137 K 5
Strzelecki Creek 196 E 2
Strzelno 133 HJ 2
Střdosibiřská vysočina
178-179 R-X 4-5
Střední Atlas = Al-A(tm.)las al-
Mutawassiṭ 166-167 CD 2
Středoafrická republika
166-167 HJ 7
Střelkový mys 168-169 F 9
Stuart, IA 152-153 J 5
Stuart, FL 148-149 c 3
Stuart, NE 152-153 G 4
Stuart, OK 154-155 GH 3
Stuart, VA 148-149 C 6
Stuart Island 144-145 D 5
Stuart Lake 144-145 M 7
Stuart Range 194-195 FG 5
Stubbenkammer 133 FG 1
Studenica 136-137 J 4
Studenka 138-139 G 6
Stumpy Point, NC 148-149 F 7
Stung Treng 186-187 E 4
Stupino 138-139 LM 6
Stura di Demonte 136-137 B 3
Sturge Island 121 C 17
Sturgeon Bay, WI 152-153 N 3
Sturgeon Bay Canal
152-153 N 3
Sturgis, KY 152-153 N 7
Sturgis, MI 152-153 O 5
Sturgis, OK 154-155 D 2
Sturgis, SD 152-153 E 3
Sturt, Mount - 194-195 H 5
Sturt Creek 194-195 E 3
Sturt Desert 194-195 H 5
Sturt Plain 194-195 F 3
Stutterheim 168-169 G 9
Stuttgart 133 D 4
Stuttgart, AR 154-155 K 3
Stuurmen 174-175 CD 6
Stviga 138-139 F 8
Stwiga = Stviga 138-139 F 8
Stykkishólmur 130-131 b 2
Stylis 136-137 K 6
Styr' 140-141 B 1
Šu [~] 184-185 C 3
Suaçuí Grande, Rio - 160-161 L 3
Suākin = Sawākin 166-167 M 5
Suan 188-189 F 3
Suancheng = Xuancheng
190-191 G 6
Suanen = Xuan'en 190-191 B 6-7
Süanhua = Xuanhua 184-185 LM 3
Suanhwa = Xuanhua 184-185 LM 3
Su-ao 184-185 N 7
Su'ao = Su-ao 184-185 N 7
Suazi 168-169 H 8
Suazilândia 169 H 8
Šubarkuduk 178-179 K 8
Šūbāţ, Nahr as- 166-167 L 7
Subate 138-139 EF 5
Subayhah 182-183 H 7
Subbat = Subate 138-139 EF 5
Subiaco 136-137 E 5
Sublett, ID 150-151 G 4
Sublette, KS 152-153 F 7
Subotica 136-137 HJ 2
Subugo 171 C 3
Suceava 136-137 LM 2
Suchaj nuur 184-185 GH 4
Suchana 178-179 W 4
Süchbaatar [MVR, ●] 184-185 JK 1
Süchbaatar [MVR, ☆ = 17]
184-185 L 2
Sucheng = Su Xian 184-185 M 5
Su-chia-t'un = Sujiatun 188-189 D 2
Su-ch'ien = Suqian 184-185 M 5
Suchiniči 138-139 K 6
Suchobezvodnoje 138-139 P 5
Suchoj Liman 140-141 E 3
Suchoj Liman 136-137 O 2
Suchona 178-179 G 6
Suchou = Xuzhou 184-185 M 5
Su-chou = Yibin 184-185 JK 6
Suchow = Xuzhou 184-185 M 5
Suchow = Yibin 184-185 JK 6
Suchumi 140-141 K 5
Sucre [BOL] 158-159 FG 8
Sucuaro 158-159 F 4
Sucun 190-191 G 4
Sucunduri, Rio - 158-159 H
Sucuriú, Rio - 158-159 J 8
Sūd = As-Sudd 166-167 L 7
Suda [SU, ~] 138-139 L 4
Sudafrica 168-169 F-H 8
Sudáfrica, República de -
168-169 F-H 8
Südafrika 168-169 F-H 8
Sudaj 138-139 O 4
Sudak 140-141 G 4
Südamerika 124-125 FG 6
Sudan, TX 154-155 D 3
Sudan, ≅ 166-167 C-K 6
Sudan, ★ 166-167 KL 6
Sudán [≅] 166-167 C-K 6
Szudán [≅] 166-167 C-K 6
Súdan [★] 166-167 J-L 6
Sudán [★] 166-167 J-L 6
Südantillenbecken 124-125 G 8
Sudão 170 B-F 7
Sudão [Estado] 166-167 KL 6
Sudão [região] 166-167 C-K 6
Südatlantischer Rücken
124-125 J 6-8
Südaustralisches Becken
124-125 PQ 8
Sudayr 180-181 EF 5
Südbandabecken 186-187 J 8
Sudbišči 138-139 L 7
Sudbury [CDN] 144-145 U 8
Südchinesisches Becken
186-187 FG 3-4
Südchinesisches Meer
186-187 E 5-G 2
Sudd, As- 166-167 L 7
Suddie 158-159 H 3
Sud-Est Indien, Bassin du -
124-125 OP 7
Sud-Est Indien, Dorsale du -
124-125 OP 8
Süd-Fidschibecken
194-195 OP 4-5
Südgeorgien = South Georgia
162 J 8
Südgeorgienschwelle
121 D 133-E 34
Sudhavik 130-131 b 1
Süd-Honschu-Rücken
184-185 R 5-6
Sudhur-Múla 130-131 f 2
Sudhur-Thingeyjar 130-131 ef 2
Südindischer Rücken 124-125 OP 8
Sudirman, Pegunungan -
186-187 L 7
Sudislavl' 138-139 NO 5
Südkorea 184-185 OP 4
Südlicher Ural = Južnyj Ural
178-179 K 7-L 6
Südlivländische Höhen = Vidzeme
138-139 EF 5
Sudogda [SU, ●] 138-139 N 6
Sudong-ni = Changhang
188-189 F 4-5
Südossetische Autonome Oblast
= 7 ◁ 182-183 H 7
Südossetische Autonome Oblast
140-141 LM 5
Sudost' 138-139 J 7
Südostindisches Becken
124-125 OP 7
Sud-Ouest Indien, Bassin du -
124-125 MN 7
Südpazifischer Rücken
121 D 22-C 20
Südpazifisches Becken
121 D 21-19
Sudr = Rā's as-Sidr 170 E 3
Sudr, Wādī - = Wādī Sidr 170 E 3
Südsandwichgraben 121 CD 34
Südtirol 136-137 D 2
Südwestindisches Becken
124-125 MN 7
Sudža 140-141G 1
Sue = Nahr Sui 166-167 K 7
Sueca 134-135 G 9
Suecia 130-131 F 9-J 10
Suécia 130-131 F 9-K 4
Suède 130-131 F 9-J 10
Sueski, Kanał = Qanat as-
Suways 166-167 L 2
Sueur, Le - MN 152-153 K 3
Suez = As-Suways 166-167 L 3
Sūfān, Qulbān as- 182-183 H 8
Sufeyān 182-183 LM 3
Suffolk, VA 148-149 E 6
Suflíon 136-137 LM 5
Sufu = Qäshqär 184-185 CD 4
Sufūq 182-183 J 4
Šuga 178-179 N 4
Sugar Island 152-153 O 2
Sugarloaf Mountain 148-149 HJ 2
Sugiyasu 188-189 H 6
Suğla Gölü 182-183 DE 4
Šugozero 138-139 K 4
Suguta 171 D 2
Sūhāj = Sawhat. 166-167 L 3
Şuḩār 180-181 H 6
Suhelipāḍ = Suheli Par 180-181 L 8
Suheli Par 180-181 L 8
Suhl 133 E 3
Su-hsien = Su Xian 184-185 M 5
Şuhut 182-183 D 3
Sui'an 190-191 G 7
Suica 126-127 K 6
Suiça 133 CD 5
Suichang 190-191 G 7
Sui-ch'i = Suixi 190-191 C 11
Suichuan 184-185 L 6
Sui Chiang = Sui Jiang
190-191 D 10
Sui-chung = Suizhong 188-189 C 2
Suichwan = Suichuan 184-185 L 6
Suide 184-185 KL 4
Suifenhe 184-185 OP 3
Sui He 190-191 F 4-5
Sui Ho = Sui He 190-191 F 4-5
Suihsien = Sui Xian [TJ, Henan]
190-191 E 4
Suihsien = Sui Xian [TJ, Hubei]
184-185 L 5
Suihua 184-185 O 2
Suihwa = Suihua 184-185 O 2
Sui Jiang 190-191 D 10
Suilai = Manaas 184-185 F 3
Suining [TJ, Hunan] 190-191 BC 8
Suining [TJ, Jiangsu] 190-191FG 5
Suiping 190-191 D 5
Suir 132 C 5
Suisse 133 CD 5
Suiteh = Suide 184-185 KL 4
Suixi [TJ, Anhui] 190-191 F 5
Suixi [TJ, Guangdong]
190-191 C 11
Sui Xian [TJ, Henan] 190-191 E 4
Sui Xian [TJ, Hubei] 184-185 L 5
Suiyuan 184-185 K 4-L 3
Sui-yüan = Suiyuan
184-185 K 4-L 3
Suiza 133 CD 5
Suizhong 188-189 C 2
Šuja [SU, Ivanovo] 178-179 G 6
Šuja [SU, Karel'skaja ASSR]
138-139 J 3
Sujiatun 188-189 D 2
Šujostrov 138-139 K 1
Šujskoje 138-139 M 4
Sukabumi 186-187 E 8
Sukadana 186-187 EF 7
Sukagawa 188-189 MN 4
Sukaraja = Marau 186-187 F 7
Sukch'ŏn 188-189 E 3
Sukhe Bator = Süchbaatar
184-185 JK 1
Şukhnah, As- 182-183 H 5
Sūki, As- 166-167 L 6
Sukkertoppen= Manitsoq
144-145 Za 4
Sukkozero 138-139 J 2
Sukromľa 138-139 K 5
Sukses 168-169 E 7
Sukulu 171 C 2
Sukumo 188-189 J 6
Sukumo wan 188-189 J 6
Sul, Canal do - 158-159 K 4-5
Sula [SU,~] 140-141 F 1
Sula, MT 150-151 FG 3
Sula, Kepulauan - 186-187 HJ 7
Sulak [SU,~] 140-141 N 5
Sulak [SU,●] 140-141 N 5
Sulakyurt 182-183 E 2
Sulan Cheer 184-185 K 3
Sula Sgeir 132 C 2
Šulavery = Šaum'ani 140-141 M 6
Sulawesi 186-187 G 7-H 6
Sulawesi Selatan =
21 ◁ 186-187 G 7
Sulawesi Tengah =
120 ◁ 186-187 H 6
Sulawesi Tenggara =
20 ◁ 186-187 H 7
Sulawesi Utara = 18 ◁ 186-187 H 6
Sulaymān, Kohistān -
180-181 KL 4-5
Sulaymāniyah 180-181 EF 3
Sulaymiyah, As- 180-181 F 6
Sulayyil, As- 180-181 F 6
Şulb, Aş- 180-181 F 5
Šul'ca = Sosnovka 138-139 Q 2
Sule He 184-185 H 4
Sule Skerry 132 D 2
Süleymanli 182-183 G 4
Sulima 166-167 B 7
Sulina 136-137 N 3
Sulina, Braţul - 136-137 N 3
Sulitjelma [N, ▲] 130-131 G 4
Sulitjelma [N, ●] 130-131 FG 4
Sullivan, IL 152-153 M 6
Sulimov = Čerkessk 140-141 L 4
Sullana 158-159 C 5
Sulligent, AL 154-155 L 4
Sullivan, IN 152-153 N 6
Sullivan, MO 152-153 L 6
Šul'mak = Novabad 180-181 L 3
Sulmona 136-137 E 4-5
Su-lo Ho = Sule He 184-185 H 4
Sulphur, NV 150-151 D 5
Sulphur, LA 154-155 J 5
Sulphur, OK 154-155 G 3
Sulphurdale, UT 150-151 G 6
Sulphur River 154-155 HJ 4
Sulphur Springs, TX 154-155 H 4
Sultanabad = Arāk 180-181 F 4
Sultandağı 182-183 D 3
Sultan Dağları 182-183 D 3
Sultan Hamud 171 D 3
Sultanhisar 182-183 C 4
Sultanpur [IND, Uttar Pradesh]
180-181 N 5
Šultus 138-139 M 3
Sulu, Mar de - 186-187 GH 5
Sulu, Mare di - 186-187 GH 5
Sulu, Mer de - 186-187 GH 5
Sulu, Morze - 186-187 GH 5
Sulu Archipelago 186-187 H 5
Suluca = Suluova 182-183 F 2
Sulūk 182-183 H 4
Sülüklü 182-183 E 3
Sul'ukta 180-181 KL 3
Suluova 182-183 F 2
Suluq 166-167 J 2
Sulu Sea 186-187 GH 5
Sulusee 186-187 GH 5
Suluské moře 186-187 GH 5
Sulu-tenger 186-187 GH 5
Suluzee 186-187 GH 5
Sulzberger Bay 121 B 21-22
Šum'ači 138-139 J 7
Šumadija 136-137 J 3-4
Sūmār 182-183 L 6
Sumas, WA 150-151 BC 1
Sumatera = Sumatra
186-187 C 6-D 7
Sumatera Barat = 3 ◁ 186-187 D 7
Sumatera Selatan =
6 ◁ 186-187 D 7
Sumatera Tengah = Riau =
4 ◁ 186-187 D 6
Sumatera Utara = 2 ◁ 186-187 C 6
Sumatra 186-187 C 6-D 7
Sumatra, FL 154-155 N 5
Sumatra, MT 152-153 C 2
Sumaúma 158-159 G 6
Sumba [RI] 186-187 G 9
Sumba, Selat - 186-187 GH 8
Sumbawa 186-187 G 8
Sumbawa Besar 186-187 G 8
Sumbawanga 168-169 H 4
Sumbe 171 C 3
Sümber 184-185 K 2
Sumbu 171 B 5
Sumbu Game Reserve 171 B 5
Sumburgh Head 132 F 2
Šumbut 138-139 S 6
Šumen 136-137 M 4
Šumerľa 138-139 PQ 6
Sumgait [SU,~] 140-141 O 6
Sumgait [SU,●] 140-141 O 6
Sumi 126-127 P 5
Šumicha 178-179 L 6
Sumidouro 160-161 L 5
Šumilino 138-139 G 6
Šumino 138-139 T 3
Sumisu-jima 184-185 R 5
Sumisu zima = Sumisu-jima
184-185 R 5
Şummān, As- [Saudi-Arabien ↑
Ar-Riyāḍ] 180-181F5
Şummān, As- [Saudi-Arabien ↘ 4
Ar-Riyāḍ] 180-181 F 6
Summer Island 152-153 N 3
Summer Lake 150-151 C 4
Summer Lake, OR 150-151 C 4
Summer, Lake - 154-155 C 3
Summerfield, TX 154-155 D 3
Summertown, TN 154-155 M 3
Summerville, SC 148-149 CD 8
Summerville, WV 148-149 C 5
Summit 146-147 b 2
Summit, CA 150-151 E 8
Summit, MS 154-155 K 5
Summit, OR 150-151 B 3
Summit, SD 152-153 H 3
Summit Lake Indian Reservation
150-151 D 5
Summit Mountain 150-151 E 6
Summit Peak 152-153 C 7
Sumner, IA 152-153 K 4
Sumner, MO 152-153 K 6
Sumoto 188-189 K 5
Sumozero 138-139 K 1-2
Šumperk 133 H 3-4
Sumprabum = Hsûmbārabûm
186-187 C 1
Sumpter, OR 150-151 DE 3
Sumrall, MS 154-155 L 5
S'umsi 138-139 ST 5
Sumskij Posad 138-139 K 1
Sumter, SC 146-147 KL 5
S'un' 138-139 T 6
Suna [EAT] 171 C 4
Suna [SU,~] 138-139 J 2
Suna [SU,●] 138-139 S 5
Sunagawa 188-189 b 2
Sunan 188-189 E3
Sunato 171 DE 6
Sunaysilah 182-183 J 5
Sunburst, MT 150-151 H 1
Sunbury, OH 152-153 P 5
Sunbury, PA 148-149 E 4
Sun-chiao Chiao 190-191 HJ 9
Suncho Corral 162 D 3
Sunch'ŏn [Nordkorea]
188-189 E 3
Sunch,ŏn [ROK] 184-185 O 4-5
Sunchow = Guiping 184-185 KL 7
Suncook, NH 148-149 H 3
Sundance, WY 152-153 D 3
Sunda, Fossa de - 124-125 P 6
Sunda, Grandes Ilhas de -
186-187 E-H 7-8
Sunda, Pequenas Ilhas de -
186-187 GH 8
Sunda, Selat - 186-187 E 8
Sundagraben 124-125 P 6
Sundar Bans = Sundarbans
180-181 OP 6
Sundarbans 180-181 OP 6
Sunda Trench 124-125 P 6
Sundays River = Sondagsrivier
174-175 F 7
Sundbyberg 130-131 G 8
Sunderbunds = Sundarbans
180-181 OP 6
Sunderland 132 F 4
Sunderland [CDN] 148-149 D 2
Sündiken Dağları 182-183 D 2-3
Sundown [AUS] 194-195 F 5
Sundsvall 130-131 GH 6
Sun'ga 138-139 K 2
Sungaidareh 186-187 D 7
Sungai Patani 186-187 CD 5
Sungaipenuh 186-187 D 7
Sungari 184-185 N 2-O 3
Sungari Reservoir = Songhua Hu
184-185 O 3
Sung-chiang = Songjiang
184-185 N 5

Sung-hsien = Song Xian 190-191 CD 4
Sung hua Chiang = Songhua Jiang 184-185 N 2-O 3
Sŭngjibaegam 188-189 G 2
Sungkiang = Songjiang 184-185 N 5
Sung-k'ou = Songkou 190-191 G 9
Sung-mên = Songmen 190-191 H 7
Sung-t'ao = Songtao 190-191 B 7
Sungu 168-169 E 3
Sungurlu 182-183 F 2
Sunhing = Xinxing 190-191 D 10
Sun-chiao Chiao 190-191 HJ 9
Sunhwa = Xunhua 184-185 J 4
Suning = Xiuning 190-191 FG 7
Súnion, Atrōtḗrion - 136-137 KL 7
Sunke = Xunke 184-185 O 2
Sunnagyn, chrebet - = Aldano-Učurskij chrebet 178-179 Y 6
Sunndalsøra 130-131 C 6
Sunniland, FL 148-149 c 3
Sunnūris = Sinnūris 170 D 3
Sunnyside, UT 150-151 H 6
Sunnyside, WA 150-151 CD 2
Sunnyvale, CA 150-151 B 7
Suno saki 188-189 M 5
Sunray, TX 154-155 E 2-3
Sunrise, WY 152-153 D 4
Sun River 150-151 GH 2
Sunset Country 196 E 5
Suntar 178-179 W 5
Suntar-Chajata, chrebet - 178-179 ab 5
Suntaži 138-139 E 5
Suntsar 180-181 J 5
Sun Valley, ID 150-151 F 4
Sunyani 166-167 D 7
Sunyang = Xunyang 190-191 B 5
Sunzel = Suntaži 138-139 E 5
Suojarvi 178-179 E 5
Suojoki 138-139 J 2
Suokonmäki 130-131 KL 6
Suolahti 130-131 LM 6
Suomen selkä 130-131 K-N 6
Suomussalmi 130-131 N 5
Suō nada 188-189 H 6
Suonenjoki 130-131 M 6
Supai, AZ 150-151 G 7
Superior, AZ 150-151 H 9
Superior, MT 150-151 F 2
Superior, NE 152-153 GH 5
Superior, WI 146-147 H 2
Superior, WY 152-153 B 5
Superior, Lake - 146-147 HJ 2
Suphan Buri 186-187 CD 4
Süphan Dağı 182-183 K 3
Supiori 186-187 KL 7
Sup'ung-chŏsuji 188-189 E 2
Supung Hu 184-185 NO 3
Šupunskij, mys - 178-179 f 7
Sūq Aḥrās 166-167 F 1
Suq ash-Shuyūkh 182-183 M 7
Suqian 184-185 M 5
Suquṭrā' 180-181 G 8
Ṣūr [Oman] 180-181 H 6
Ṣur [RL] 182-183 F 6
Sur, Point - 150-151 BC 7
Sura 138-139 Q 6
Sura, Raas - = Raas Surud 166-167 b 1
Šurab 180-181 L 2
Surabaia = Surabaya 186-187 F 8
Surabaya 186-187 F 8
Surachany 140-141 P 6
Surakarta 186-187 F 8
Ṣūrān 182-183 G 5
Surat [AUS] 194-195 J 5
Surat [IND] 180-181 L 6
Surate = Surat 180-181 L 6
Surat Thani 186-187 CD 5
Suraž [SU, Belorusskaja SSR] 138-139 H 6
Suraž [SU, Rossijskaja SFSR] 138-139 J 7
Sūrdāsh 182-183 L 5
Šuren'ga 138-139 M 2
Surf, CA 150-151 C 8
Surgut [SU, Chanty-Mansijskaja AO] 178-179 N 5
Surgut [SU, Samara] 178-179 J 7
Surguticha 178-179 PQ 5
Surigao 186-187 J 5
Surin 186-187 D 4
Surinam 158-159 HJ 4
Suriname 158-159 HJ 4
Suriname [SME, Estado] 158-159 HJ 4
Suring, WI 152-153 M 3
Šurma 138-139 RS 5
Sürmene 182-183 J 2
Surnadalsøra 130-131 C 6
Surovikino 140-141 L 2
Surprise Valley 150-151 CD 5
Surrey, ND 152-153 F 1
Sur-Sari = ostrov Gogland 138-139 F 3
Sursk 138-139 PQ 7
Surskoje 138-139 Q 6
Surt 166-167 H 2
Surt, Khalīj - 166-167 H 2
Surt, Saḥrā' - 166-167 H 2-3
Surtsey 130-131 C 3
Sürüç 182-183 H 4
Surud, Raas - 166-167 b 1
Suruga wan 188-189 M 5
Surukrom 172-173 E 4
Surulangun 186-187 D 7
Šuryškary 178-179 M 4
Susa 136-137 B 3
Susa [IR] 182-183 N 6
Susa [J] 188-189 H 5
Šuša [SU] 140-141 N 7
Susa = Sūsah 166-167 G 1
Sušac 136-137 G 4
Sūsah [LAR] 166-167 J 2
Sūsah [TN] 166-167 G 1
Susaki 188-189 J 6
Susami 188-189 K 6
Susan = Susa 182-183 N 6
Susanino 138-139 N 4
Susanville, CA 146-147 B 3
Susč'ovo 138-139 GH 5
Suşehri 182-183 GH 2
Sushui = Xushui 190-191 E 2
Sušice 133 F 4
Susitna River 144-145 FG 5
Suslonger 138-139 R 5
Susong 190-191 F 6
Susquehanna, PA 148-149 EF 4
Susquehanna River 148-149 E 5
Susques 162 C 2
Süssah 182-183 J 5
Sussey 132 FG 6
Susuman 178-179 cd 5
Susung = Susong 190-191 F 6
Susupe 192-193 F 3
Susurluk 182-183 C 3
Sütçüler 182-183 D 4
Sutherland, NE 152-153 F 5
Sutherland [ZA] 168-169 EF 9
Sutherland Reservoir 152-153 F 5
Sutherlin, OR 150-151 B 4
Sutlej = Satlaj 180-181 L 4
Sutsien = Suqian 184-185 M 5
Su-ts'un = Sucun 190-191 G 4
Sutter Creek, CA 150-151 C 6
Sutton, NE 152-153 H 5
Sutton, WV 148-149 C 5
Suttsu 188-189 ab 2
Suurberge [ZA ↑ Winterberge] 174-175 F 6
Suurberge [ZA ↙ Winterberge] 174-175 F 7
Suure-Jaani 138-139 E 4
Suur Manamägi 138-139 F 5
Suur väin 138-139 D 4
Suva 186-187 a 2
Suvainiškis 138-139 E 5
Suvorov [⊙] 198-199 JK 5
Suvorovo [SU] 140-141 D 4
Suvorovo 136-137 N 3
Suwa 188-189 M 4
Suwa-ko 188-189 M 4-5
Suwałki 133 L 1
Suwalki = Vilkaviškis 138-139 D 6
Suwannee River 148-149 b 2
Suwannee Sound 148-149 b 2
Ṣuwār, Aṣ- 182-183 J 5
Suwaybit, As- 182-183 H 6
Suwaydā', As- 180-181 D 4
Suwayḥ 180-181 HJ 6
Suwayqīyah, Hawr as- 182-183 LM 6
Ṣuwayr 182-183 J 7
Ṣuwayrah, Aṣ- 182-183 L 6
Suways, As- 166-167 L 2-3
Suways, Khalīj as- 166-167 L 3
Suways, Qanat as- 166-167 L 2
Suweinischki = Suvainiškis 138-139 E 5
Suweis, Es- = As-Suways 166-167 L 2-3
Suweis, Khalîg es - = Khalīj as-Suways 166-167 L 3
Suweis, Qanât es- = Qanat as-Suways 166-167 L 2
Suwŏn 184-185 P 4
Ṣuwwān,'Arḍ eṣ - = 'Arḍ aṣ-Ṣawwān 182-183 G 7
Su Xian 184-185 M 5
Suxima = Tsushima 188-189 G 5
Sūy, Nahr - 166-167 K 7
Suzaka 188-189 M 4
Suzdal' 138-139 N 5
Suzhou 184-185 N 5
Suzu 188-189 L 4
Suzuka 188-189 L 5
Suzu misaki 188-189 L 4
Svájc 133 CD 5
Svalbard 130-131 k 6-n 5
Svalbard 130-131 k 6-n 5
Svanetskij chrebet 140-141 L 5
Svapa 138-139 K 8
Svappavaara 130-131 J 4
Svartenhuk Halvø 144-145 Za 3
Svartisen 130-131 EF 4
Svatá Lucie 146-147 O 9
Sv'atoj Krest' = Prikumsk 140-141 LM 4
Sv'atoj Nos, mys - 178-179 ab 3
Svatovo 140-141 J 2
Svatý Kryštof a Nevis 146-147 O 8
Svatý Tomaš 166-167 F 8
Svatý Vincenc 146-147 O 9
Svay Rieng 186-187 E 4
Svazijsko 168-169 H 8
Sveča 138-139 Q 4
Sveagruva 130-131 k 6
Svealand 130-131 E-G 7
Svedala 130-131 E 10
Svédország 130-131 F 9-K 4
Sveg 130-131 F 6
Svelvik 130-131 CD 8
Švenčionėliai 138-139 EF 6
Svendborg 130-131 D 10
Svenskøya 130-131 mn 5
Šventoji 138-139 E 6
Sverdlovo [SU, Vologda] 138-139 MN 4
Sverdlovsk 140-141 JK 2
Sverdlovsk = Jekaterinburg 178-179 L 6
Sverdrup, ostrov - 178-179 O 3
Sverdrup Islands 144-145 P-T 2
Sverofriské o-vy 130-131 C 10
Svessa 138-139 JK 8
Svetac 136-137 F 4
Svetlaja 178-179 a 8
Svetlyj [SU → Orsk] 178-179 L 7
Svetlogorsk [SU, Belorusskaja SSR] 138-139 GH 7
Svetlograd 140-141 L 4
Svetogorsk 138-139 G 3
Svetozarevo 136-137 J 3-4
Svezia 138-139 A 2-4
Svezia 130-131 F 9-K 4
Svijaga 138-139 R 6
Svilengrad 136-137 LM 5
Svir 130-131M10
Svir [SU, ~] 178-179 EF 5
Svir' [SU, ●] 138-139 F 6
Svirica 138-139 J 3
Svirsk 178-179 T 7
Svir'stroj 138-139 J 3
Svisloč' [SU,●] 138-139 E 7
Svisloč' [SU,~ ◁ Berezina] 138-139 FG 7
Svištov 136-137 L 4
Svizzera 133 CD 5
Svoboda [SU] 138-139 KL 8
Svobodnyj [SU ↑ Belogorsk] 178-179 YZ 7
Svobodnyj [SU, Saratov] 138-139 PQ 7
Svolvær 130-131 F 3
Swabue = Shanwei 190-191 E 10
Swaib, As- = Ash-Shuwayyib 182-183 MN 7
Swaibit, As- = As-Suwaybit 182-183 H 6
Swain Reefs 194-195 K 4
Swainsboro, GA 148-149 B 8
Ṣwaira, Aṣ- = Aṣ-Ṣuwayrah 182-183 L 6
Swakop 174-175 B 2
Swakopmund 168-169 D 7
Swale 132 F4
Swalferort = Sõrve säär 138-139 CD 5
Swallow Islands 186-187 I 7
Swanage 132 F 6
Swan Hill 194-195 H 7
Swan Hills 144-145 N 7
Swan Lake [USA] 152-153 FG 3
Swan Range 150-151 G 2
Swan River [CDN, ●] 144-145 Q 7
Swansea 132 DE 6
Swansea, SC 148-149 C 8
Swans Island 148-149 J 2-3
Swanton, VT 148-149 G 2
Swanville, MN 152-153 J 3
Swartberg 174-175 H 6
Swartberge 168-169 F 9
Swartkops 174-175 F 7
Swartmodder 174-175 D 5
Swart Nossob 174-175 C 2
Swartplaas 174-175 G 4
Swartrand 174-175 B 3-4
Swartruggens [ZA, Kaapland] 174-175 F 7
Swartruggens [ZA, Transvaal] 174-175 G 3
Swart Umfolozi 174-175 J 4-5
Swasiland 168-169 H 8
Swāt 180-181 L 3-4
Swatow = Shantou 184-185 M 7
Swaziland 168-169 H 8
Swaziland 168-169 H 8
Sweden 130-131 F 9-J 10
Swedru 172-173 E 4
Sweeny, TX 154-155 H 6
Sweetgrass, MT 150-151 GH 1
Sweet Home, OR 150-151 B 3
Sweetwater, TX 146-147 FG 5
Sweetwater River 152-153 B 4
Swellendam 168-169 F 9
Świdnica 133 H 3
Świdwin 133 GH 2
Świebodzin 133 G 2
Świecie 133 HJ 2
Swienta = Šventoji 138-139 E 6
Swift Current 144-145 P 7-8
Swinburne, Cape - 144-145 R 3
Swindon 132 F 6
Swinemünde = Swinoujście 133 G 2
Swinoujście 133 G 2
Switzerland 133 CD 5
Sworbe = Sõrve 138-139 D 5
Sybaris 136-137 G 6
Syberia 178-179 O-X 5
Sybin = Sibiu 136-137 L 3
Sycamore, IL 152-153 M 4-5
Sychellen 168-169 LM 4
Sychem = Nābulus 182-183 F 6
Syč'ovka 138-139 JK 6
Syczuańska, Kotlina - = Sichuan Pendi 184-185 JK 5-6
Sydney [AUS] 194-195 K 6
Sydney [CDN] 144-145 Y 8
Syene = Aswān 166-167 L 4
Syfergat 174-175 G 6
Syjamska, Zatoka - 186-187 D 4-5
Syktyvkar 178-179 J 5
Sylacauga, AL 154-155 M 4
Sylarna 130-131 E 6
Sylhet = Silhat 180-181 P 6
Sylt 133 D 1
Sylva 138-139 V 4
Sylva, NC 148-149 B 7
Sylvan Grove, KS 152-153 G 6
Sylvania, GA 148-149 C 8
Sylvan Pass 150-151 H 3
Sylvester, GA 148-149 B 9
Sylvester, TX 154-155 EF 4
Sylvia, KS 152-153 G 7
Sylviaberg 174-175 A 3
Sylvia Hill = Sylviaberg 174-175 A 3
Sym 178-179 Q 5
Sýmē 136-137 M 7
Synaj, Półwysep - = Sīnā' 166-167 L 3
Syndassko 178-179 UV 3
Syowa 121 C 4-5
Syracuse, KS 152-153 F 6-7
Syracuse, NY 146-147 LM 3
Syracuse = Siracusa 136-137 F 7
Syrakus = Siracusa 136-137 H 7
Syrakuzy = Siracusa 136-137 F 7
Syrdarja 178-179 M 9
Syria 180-181 D 4
Syriam = Thanlyin 186-187 C 3
Syrian Desert 180-181 DE 4
Sýrie 178-179 D 4
Syrië 180-181 D 4
Syrie 180-181 D 4
Syrie, Désert de - 180-181 DE 4
Syrien 180-181 D 4
Syrische Woestijn 180-181 DE 4
Syrische Wüste 180-181 DE 4
Syrjanowsk = Zyr'anovsk 178-179 PQ 8
Sýrna 136-137 M 7
Sýros 136-137 L 7
Syrská poušť 180-181 DE 4
Syrskij 138-139 M 7
Syryjska, Pustynia - 180-181 DE 4
Sysladobsis Lake 148-149 JK 2
Sysola 138-139 S 3
Sysran = Syzran' 178-179 N 7
Syt'kovo 138-139 K 5
Sytynja 178-179 YZ 4
Syzran' 178-179 N 7
Szamos 136-137 K 2
Szamotuly 133 H 2
Szawle = Šiauliai 130-131 KL 10
Szczecin 133 G 2
Szczecinek 133 H 2
Szczytno 133 K 2
Szechuan = Sichuan 184-185 J 6-K 5
Szeged 133 JK 5
Szehsien = Si Xian 190-191 FG 5
Székesfehérvár 133 J 5
Szekszárd 133 J 5
Szemao = Simao 184-185 J 7
Szeming = Xiamen 184-185 M 7
Szentes 133 K 5
Szeping = Siping 184-185 N 3
Szeskie Wzgórza 133 L 1
Szkocja 132 D 3-E 4
Szolnok 133 K 5
Szombathely 133 H 5
Sztokholm = Stockholm 130-131 H 8
Szŭ-an = Si'an 190-191 G 6
Szŭ-mao = Simao 184-185 J 7
Szumawa 133 F 4
Szŭ-ming Shan = Siming Shan 190-191 H 7
Szŭ-nan = Sinan 190-191 B 8
Szŭ-p'ing = Siping 184-185 N 3
Szŭ-shui = Sishui [TJ, Henan] 190-191 D 4
Szŭ-shui = Sishui [TJ, Shandong] 190-191 F 4
Szŭ-tao-kou = Sidaogou 188-189 F 2
Szŭ-t'ing = Siting 190-191 D 3
Szwajcaria 133 CD 5
Szwecja 130-131 F 9-K 4

T

Ta = Da Xian 184-185
Tabaco 186-187 H 4
Tābah, Bi'r - 170 F 3
Tabajé, Ponta - 158-159 LM 5
Tabankort 166-167 D 5
Tabankulu 174-175 H 6
Tabar Islands 186-187 h 5
Tabarka = Ṭabarqah 166-167 F 1
Ṭabarqah 166-167 F 1
Ṭabas 180-181 H 4
Tabasco 146-147 H 8
Tabašino 138-139 QR 5
Tabatinga [BR, Amazonas] 158-159 F 5
Tabatinga [BR, São Paulo] 160-161 H 4
Taber 144-145 O 7
Taberg 130-131 EF 9
Tablas Island 186-187 H 4
Table, Île de la - = Đao Cai Ban 186-187 E 2
Table Bay = Tafelbaai 174-175 C 7
Table Mount = Tafelberg 174-175 BC 8
Table Mountain 150-151 G 3
Table Rock 152-153 B 5
Table Rock Lake 154-155 J 2
Taboco, Rio - 160-161 E 4
Taboga 146-147 b 3
Taboga, Isla - 146-147 bc 3
Taboguilla, Isla - 146-147 bc 3
Tábor 133 G 4
Tabora 168-169 H 4
Tabor City, NC 148-149 D 7
Tabou 166-167 C 8
Tabris = Tabrīz 180-181 F 3
Tabrīz 180-181 F 3
Tabu-dong 188-189 G 4
Tabūk 180-181 D 5
Tabuleiro, Morro do - 160-161 H 7
Täby 130-131 GH 8
Tabyn-Bogdo-Ola = gora Tavan Bogdo Ula 184-185 F 2
Tacau = Kaohsiung 184-185 MN 7
T'ačev 140-141 A 2
Ta-ch'ang-shan Tao = Dachangshan Dao 188-189 D 3
Tacheng = Chuguchak 184-185 E 2
T'a-ch'êng = Chuguchak 184-185 E 2
Ta-chi 190-191 H 9
Tachia 184-185 MN 7
Ta-ch'iao = Daqiao 190-191 E 7
Tachibana-wan 188-189 GH 6
Tachikawa 188-189 M 5
Ta-ching = Dajing 190-191 H 7
Ta-ch'ing Shan = Daqing Shan 184-185 L 3
Tachnoj 178-179 TU 7
Tachta 178-179 a 7
Tachta-Bazar 180-181 J 3
Tachtabrod 178-179 M 7
Tachtojamsk 178-179 de 5
Ta-ch'üan = Daquan 184-185 H 3
Tacloban 186-187 HJ 4
Tacna [PE, ●] 158-159 E 8
Tacoma, WA 146-147 B 2
Taconic Range 148-149 G 3-4
Tacora, Volcán - 162 C 1
Tacuaras 160-161 CD 7
Tacuarembó [ROU, ●] 162 EF 4
Tacuati 160-161 D 5
Tacuru 160-161 E 5
Tadami gawa 188-189 M 4
Tadarimana, Ribeiro - 160-161 E 2
Tademaït, Plateau du - = Haḍbah Tādmayt 166-167 E 3
Tāḍipatri = Tadpatri 180-181 M 7-8
Tadjikistan 184-185 BC 4
Tadjoura 166-167 N 6
Tadjoura, Golfe de - 166-167 N 6
Tādmāyt, Haḅdah - 166-167 E
Tadmur 180-181 D 4
Tadoussac 144-145 X 8
Tadpatri 180-181 M 7-8
Tadschikistan 180-181 KL 3
Tadum = Tradum 184-185 E 6
Tadzjikistan 180-181 KL 3
Tadzikistan 180-181 KL 3
Tádžikistán 180-181 KL 3
Tadžikskaja Sovetskaja Socialističeskaja Respublika = Tadschikistan 180-181 KL 3
Tadżykistan 180-181 KL 3
Tadzsikisztán 180-181 KL 3
T'aean 188-189 F 4
T'aebaek-san 188-189 G 4
T'aebaek-sanmaek 184-185 O 4
Taebu-do 188-189 F 4
T'aech'ŏn 188-189 E 3
Taech'ŏng-do 188-189 E 4
Taedong-gang 188-189 EF 3
Taegu 184-185 O 4
Tae-hŭksan-do 188-189 E 5
Taehwa-do 188-189 E 3
Taejŏn 184-185 O 4
Taejŏng 188-189 EF 6
Tae-muŭi-do 188-189 EF 4
Ta-êrh Hu = Dalaj Nur 184-185 M 3
T'aet'an 188-189 E 3
Tae-yŏnp'yŏng-do 188-189 E 4
Tafalla 134-135 G 7
Ta-fan = Dafan 190-191 E 7
Tafaraut = Ṭarfāyah 166-167 B 3
Tafāsasat, Wādī - 166-167 F 4
Tafassasset, Ouèd - = Wādī Tafāsasat 166-167 F 4
Tafassasset, Ténéré du 166-167 FG 4
Tafdasat 166-167 F 3-4
Tafelbaai 174-175 C 7
Tafelberg [ZA, ▲] 174-175 BC 8
Tafelberg [ZA, ●] 174-175 F 6
Ṭafilah, Aṭ- 182-183 F 7
Tafí Viejo 162 C 3
Tafresh 182-183 N 5
Tafresh, Kūh-e - 182-183 NO 5
Taft, CA 150-151 D 8
Taft, OK 154-155 H 3
Taft, TX 154-155 G 6-7
Taftān, Kūh-e - 180-181 J 5
Tagalgan 184-185 H 4
Taganrog 140-141 J 3
Taganrogskij zaliv 140-141 HJ 3
Tāgau 186-187 C 2
Tagawa = Takawa 188-189 H 6
Tagbilaran 186-187 H 5
Tag-Dheer = Togdheer 166-167 b 2
Tāghit 166-167 D 2
Tagiúra = Tājurā' 166-167 G 2
Tāgu = Taegu 184-185 O 4
Taguatinga [BR, Distrito Federal] 158-159 K 8
Taguatinga [BR, Goiás] 158-159 K 7
Taguedoufat 172-173 H 1-2
Tagula 186-187 h 7
Tagum 186-187 J 5
Tahaa 192-193 M 6
Tahan, Gunung - 186-187 D 6
Tahara 188-189 L 5
Tahat 166-167 F4
Tahiti 198-199 K 5
Tahlequah, OK 154-155 H 3
Tahoe, Lake - 146-147 BC 4
Tahoe City, CA 150-151 C 6
Tahoe Valley, CA 150-151 CD 6
Tahoka, TX 154-155 E 4
Tahola, WA 150-151 A 2
Tahoua 166-167 F 6
Taḥrīr, At- 170 CD 2
Ta-hsi 190-191 H 10
Ta-hsien = Da Xian 184-185 K 5
Ta-hsin-tien = Daxindian 190-191 H 3
Ta Hsü = Ta Yü 190-191 G 10
Ta-hsüeh Shan = Daxue Shan 184-185 J 5-6
Ṭahṭā 166-167 L 3
Tahtacı = Borlu 182-183 C 3
Tahtalı Dağı 182-183 D 4
Tahtali Dağlar 182-183 F 4-G 3
Ta-hu = Tachia 184-185 MN 7
Tahuata 192-193 NO 6
Tahulandang, Pulau - 186-187 J 6
Tahuna 186-187 HJ 6
Ta-hung Shan = Dahong Shan 190-191 D 6
Ta-hu-shan = Dahushan 188-189 D 2
Taï 166-167 C 7
Taï, Parc national de - 172-173 D 4
Tai'an [TJ, Liaoning] 188-189 D 2
Tai'an [TJ, Shandong] 184-185 M 4
Taïba 172-173 A 2
Taibai 190-191 B 3
Taibai Shan 184-185 K 5
Taibei = Taipei 184-185 N 6-7
Taicang 190-191 H 6
T'ai-chou Wan = Taizhou Wan 190-191 H 7
Taichū = Taichung 184-185 MN 7
Taichung 184-185 MN 7
T'ai-chung = Taichung 184-185 MN 7
T'ai-chung-hsien = Fêng-yüan 190-191 H 9
Taiden = Taejŏn 184-185 O 4
Taidong = Taitung 184-185 N 7
Ṭā'if, Aṭ- 180-181 E 6
Taigu 184-185 L 4
Taihang Shan 184-185 LM 4
Taihe [TJ, Anhui] 190-191 E 5
Taihe [TJ, Jiangxi] 184-185 L 6
Taihei yō 188-189 K7-03
Taihing = Taixing 184-185 N 5
T'ai-ho = Taihe [TJ, Anhui] 190-191 E 5
Taiho = Taihe [TJ, Jiangxi] 184-185 L 6
Taihoku = Tai-pei 184-185 N 6-7
Taihsien = Dai Xian 190-191 D 2
Taihu [TJ, ●] 190-191 F 6
Tai Hu [TJ, ≈] 184-185 MN 5
Taikang 190-191 E 4
Taiki 188-189 c 2
Taiku = Taigu 184-185 L 4
Taikyu = Taegu 184-185 O 4
Tailai 184-185 N 2
T'ai-lai = Tailai 184-185 N 2
Tailândia 186-187 CD 3
Tailândia, Golfo da - 186-187 D 4-5
Tailem Bend 194-195 GH 7
Tailie 190-191 B 8
Taim 162 F 4
Tain 132 D 3
Tain [GH] 172-173 E 4
Tai-nan 184-185 MN 7
T'ai-nan = Tai-nan 184-185 MN 7
Tainão = Tai-nan 184-185 MN 7
Tainaron, Akrōtḗrion - 136-137 K 7
Taining 190-191 F 8
Taió 160-161 GH 7
Taiobeiras 160-161 LM 1
T'ai-pai Shan = Taibai Shan 190-191 A 4-5
Taipale 130-131 N 6
Taipeh = Tai-pei 184-185 N 6-7
Tai-pei 184-185 N 6-7
Taiping [MAL] 186-187 CD 5-6
Taiping [TJ, Anhui] 190-191 G 6
Taiping [TJ, Guangdong] 190-191 D 10
Taiping [TJ, Guangxi Zhuangzu Zizhiqu] 190-191 C 10
Taipingshao 188-189 E 2
Taiping Wan 190-191 G 3
Taiping Yang 184-185 O 8-R 5
Taipinsan = Miyako-jima 184-185 O 7
Taisei 188-189 ab 2
Taisha 188-189 J 5
Tai Shan [TJ, ▲▲] 190-191 F 3
Taishan [TJ, ●] 190-191 D 10
Tai Shan = Dai Shan 190-191 HJ 6
Taishan Liedao 190-191 H 8
Taishun 184-185 MN 6
Taisien = Tai Xian 190-191 H 5
Ta'iss = Ta'izz 180-181 E 8
Taitao, Cabo - 162 A 7
Taitao, Península de - 162 AB 7
T'ai-tchong = Tai-chung 184-185 MN 7
Taitō = Tai-tung 184-185 N 7
Taitsang = Taicang 190-191 H 6
Tai-tung 184-185 N 7
T'ai-tzŭ Ho = Taizi He 188-189 D 2
Taivalkoski 130-131 N 5
Taivassalo 130-131 JK 7
Taiwa 188-189 N 3
Taiwan 184-185 N 7
Taiwán 184-185 N 7
Taïwan 184-185 N 7
T'ai-wan Hai-hsia 184-185 M 7-N 6
Taiwan Haixia = T'ai-wan Hai-hsia 184-185 M 7-N 6
T'ai-wan Shan 184-185 N 7
Taiwanský průliv = Taiwan Haihsia 184-185 M 7-N 6
Tai Xian 190-191 H 5
Taixing 184-185 N 5
Taiyuan 184-185 L 4
T'ai-yüan = Taiyuan 184-185 L 4
Taiyue Shan 190-191 CD 3
Taizhong = Taichung 184-185 MN 7
Taizhou 184-185 MN 5
Taizhou Wan 190-191 H 7
Taizi He 188-189 D 2
Ta'izz 180-181 E 8
Tāj, At- 166-167 J 4
Taj, El - = At-Tāj 166-167 J 4
Tajarḥī 166-167 G 4
Tajdžinar nuur 184-185 GH 4
Tajga 178-179 PQ 6
Tajgonos, mys - 178-179 ef 5
Tajgonos, poluostrov - 178-179 f 5
Tajikistan 184-185 BC 4
Tajima 188-189 M 4
Tajique, NM 154-155 B 3
Tajiquistão 180-181 KL 3
Tajis 180-181 G 8
Tajitos 150-151 G 10
Tajlandia 186-187 CD 3
Tajmir (Dolgan-Nyenyec) Autonóm Körzet 178-179 P-U 3
Tajmura 178-179 ST 5
Tajmyr, Circolo Nazionale del - 178-179 P-U 3
Tajmyr, Circunscripción Nacional de - 178-179 P-U 3
Tajmyr, ozero - 178-179 TU 3
Tajmyr, poluostrov - 178-179 R-U 2
Tajmyrský (Dolgansko-něnecký) autonomní okruh 178-179 P-U 3
Tajo 134-135 F 8
Tajšet 178-179 S 6
Tajsir 184-185 H 2
Tajumulco, Volcán de 146-147 H 8
Tajuña 134-135 F 8
Tajūrā' 166-167 G 2
Tajvan 184-185 N 7
Tajvani-szoros = Taiwan Haihsia 184-185 M 7-N 6
Tajwan 184-185 N 7
Tajwańska, Cieśnina - = Taiwan Haihsia 184-185 M 7-N 6
Tak 186-187 C 3
Takāb 182-183 M 4
Takaba 171 E 2
Takachiho = Mitai 188-189 H 6
Takachu 174-175 DE 2
Takada 184-185 Q 4
Takada = Bungotakada 188-189 H 6
Takada = Rikuzen-Takata 188-189 NO 3
Takahagi 188-189 N 4
Takahashi 188-189 J 5
Takahashi-gawa 188-189 J 5
Takahe, Mount - 121 B 25-26
Takalar 186-187 G 8
Takamatsu 184-185 PQ 5
Takamatu = Takamatsu 184-185 PQ 5
Takamori 188-189 H 6
Takanabe 188-189 H 6
Takao = Kao-hsiung 184-185 MN 7
Takaoka 184-185 Q 4
Takapuna 194-195 O 7
Takasaki 184-185 Q 4
Takataka 186-187 k 6
Takawa 188-189 H 6
Takayama 188-189 L 4
Takefu 188-189 KL 5
Takemachi = Taketa 188-189 H 6
Takengon 186-187 C 6
Takéo 186-187 D 4
Take-shima [J, Ōsumi shotō] 188-189 H 7
Take-shima [J ↖ Oki] 188-189 HJ 4
Tākestān 182-183 NO 4
Taketa 188-189 H 6
Takhlīs, Bi'r - 170 CD 6
Ta Khmau 186-187 DE 4
Takht-e Jämshīd = Persepolis 180-181 G 4
Takiéta 172-173 H 2
Takikawa 188-189 b 2
Takinoue 188-189 c 1
Takiyuak Lake 144-145 O 4
Takkuna neem 138-139 CD 4
Takla Lake 144-145 LM 6
Takla Makan 184-185 D-F 4
Takla Makan Chöli 184-185 D-F 4
Tako-bana 188-189 J 5
Takoma Park, MD 148-149 E 5
Ta-ku = Dagu 190-191 F 2
Takua Pa 186-187 C 5
Ta-ku Ho = Dagu He 190-191 H 3
Takum 172-173 H 4
Takumé 192-193 N 6
Tākwayat, Wādī - 166-167 E 4
Takyu = Taegu 184-185 O 4
Talā [ET] 170 D 2
Talacasto 162 C 4
Talaimannar = Taleimannarama 180-181 MN 9
Talak 166-167 EF 5
Talana 174-175 J 5
Talanyené, Rapides de - 172-173 E 3
Tālaqān 182-183 O 4
Talara 158-159 C 5
Talas 178-179 N 9
Talasea 186-187 gh 6
Talata Mafara 172-173 G 2
Talaud, Kepulauan - 186-187 J 6
Talavera de la Reina 134-135 E 8-9
Talawdī 166-167 L 6
Talbingo 196 J 5
Talbot, Cape - 194-195 E 2
Talbot, Mount - 194-195 E 5
Talbotton, GA 154-155 N 4
Talca 162 B 5
Talco, TX 154-155 H 4
Talcuhuano 162 AB 5
Taldykuduk 140-141 O 1
Taldy-Kurgan 178-179 OP 8
Taleimannarama 180-181 MN 9
Tal-e Khosravī = Yasūj 180-181 G 4
Talent, OR 150-151 B 4
Tale Sap = Thale Luang 186-187 D 5
Tali = Dali [TJ, Shaanxi] 190-191 B 4
Tali = Dali [TJ, Yunnan] 184-185 HJ 6
Talia 154-155 D 8
Taliabu, Pulau - 186-187 HJ 7
Talica [SU, Vjatka] 138-139 S 4
Talickij 138-139 Q 4
Ta-lien = Dalian 184-185 N 4
Talihina, OK 154-155 H 3
Ta-li Ho = Dali He 190-191 B 3
Talimã 158-159 H 4
Ta-ling Ho = Daling He 188-189 G 2
Talin Shan = Huaiyu Shan 190-191 F 7
Taliwang 186-187 G 8
Talju, Jabal - 166-167 K 6
Talkeetna Mountains 144-145 G 5
Talkheh Rūd 182-183 M 3
Talladega, AL 146-147 J 5
Tall 'Afar 182-183 K 4
Tallahassee, FL 146-147 K 5
Tall al-Abyaḍ 182-183 H 4
Tallapoosa, GA 154-155 N 4
Tall as-Sam'ān 182-183 H 4
Tallassee, AL 154-155 N 4
Tall Bisah 182-183 G 5
Tall Ḥalaf 182-183 HJ 4
Tallin = Tallinn 178-179 CD 6
Tallinn 178-179 CD 6
Tallinn 130-131 KL 8
Tall Kalakh 182-183 G 5
Tall Kayf 182-183 K 4
Tall Kujik 182-183 JK 4
Tall Tāmir 182-183 J 4
Tallulah, LA 154-155 K 4
Tall 'Uwaynāt 182-183 JK 4
Tal'menka 178-179 PQ 7
Talnach 178-179 QR 4
Tal'noje 140-141 E 2
Talo = Nantong 184-185 N 5
Talōdī = Talawdī 166-167 L 6
Taloga, OK 154-155 F 2
Talovaja 140-141 K 1
Talpa, TX 154-155 F 5
Talsen = Talsi 138-139 D 5
Talsi 138-139 D 5
Taltal 162 B 3
Taltson River 144-145 O 5
Talvār, Rūdkhāneh - 182-183 MN 5
Talvik 130-131 K 2
Talwood 196 J 2
Talyawalka Creek 196 F 3-4
Tama, IA 152-153 K 5
Tamādah 166-167 E 4
Tamala 138-139 O 7
Tamale 166-167 D 7
Taman' [SU, Krasnodar] 140-141 H 4
Taman' [SU, Perm'] 138-139 UV 4
Tamana [J] 188-189 H 6
Tamano 188-189 JK 5
Tamanrāsat 166-167 EF 4
Tamanrāsat, Wādī - 166-167 E 4
Tamaqua, PA 148-149 F 4
Tamarugal, Pampa del - 162 C 1-2
Tamási 133 HJ 5
Tamatave = Toamasina 168-169 LM 6
Tamaulipas 146-147 G 6-7
Tamayama 188-189 N 3
Tambach 171 CD 2
Tambacounda 166-167 B 6
Tambaqui 158-159 G 6
Tambaú 160-161 J 4
Tambej 178-179 N 3
Tambo 194-195 J 4
Tambo, El - [CO, Cauca] 158-159 D 4
Tambo, Río - [PE ◁ Río Ucayali] 158-159 E 7
Tambohorano 168-169 K 6
Tambora, Gunung - 186-187 G 8
Tamboritha, Mount - 196 H 6
Tambov 138-139 N 7
Tambow = Tambov 138-139 N 7
Tamč 184-185 G 2
Tam Cag Bulak = Tamsagbulag 184-185 M 2
Tamdybulak 178-179 L 9
Tâmega 134-135 D 8
Támesis = Thames 132 G 6
Tamgak, Monts - 166-167 F 5
Tamiahua, Laguna de - 146-147 G 7
Tamiami Canal 148-149 c 4
Tamigi = Thames 132 F 6
Tamil Nadu 180-181 M 8-9
Ta'mīn, At- 182-183 KL 5
Taming = Daming 190-191 E 3
Tāmir'z,qīd 166-167 AB 5
Tamisa = River Thames 132 G 6
Tamise = Thames 132 G 6
Tāmīyah 170 D 3
Tamiza = Thames 132 G 6
Tam Ky 186-187 E 3
Tammerfors = Tampere 130-131 K7
Tammisaari = Ekenäs 130-131 K 7
Tampa, FL 146-147 K 6
Tampa Bay 146-147 K 6
Tampelan, Kapulauan - 186-187 E 6
Tampere 130-131 KL 7
Tampico 146-147 G 7
Tampico, MT 152-153 C 1
Tampin 186-187 D 6
Tampoketsa, Plateau du - = Causse du Kelifely 168-169 KL 6
Ṭamrīdah 180-181 G 8
Tamsagbulag 184-185 M 2
Tamsal = Tamsalu 138-139 F 4
Tamsalu 138-139 F 4
Tāmshikiṭ 166-167 BC 5
Tamud = Thamūd 180-181 F 7
Tamworth [AUS] 194-195 K 6
Tamyang 188-189 F 5
Tana [EAK] 168-169 JK 3
Tana [Vanuatu] 194-195 N 3
Tana [N, ~] 130-131 M 2-3
Tana [N, ●] 130-131 N 2
Tanabat 186-187 C 6
Tanabe 188-189 K 6
Tanabi 160-161 H 4
Tanabu = Mutsu 188-189 N 2
Tanacross, AK 144-145 H 5
Ta-n-Adar 166-167 F 5
Tanafjord 130-131 N 2
Tanaga Island 120 D 36-1
Tanágra 136-137 K 6
Ṭana Hayiḳ 166-167 M 6
Tanahbala, Pulau - 186-187 C 7
Tanahgrogot 186-187 G 7
Tanahjampea, Pulau - 186-187 H 8
Tanahmasa, Pulau - 186-187 C 6-7
Tanah Menah 186-187 D 5
Tanahmerah 186-187 LM 8
Tanakeke, Pulau - 186-187 G 8
Tanal 172-173 E 2
Tanami 194-195 E 3
Tanami Desert 194-195 F 3
Tanana, AK 144-145 F 4
Tananarive = Antananarivo 168-169 L 6
Tanana River 144-145 G 5
Tân Ấp 186-187 E 3
Tànaro 136-137 B 3
Ṭanburah 166-167 K 7
Tanchavur = Thanjavar 180-181 MN 8
Tancheng 190-191 G 4
Tan Chiang = Dan Jiang 190-191 C 5
Tanch'ŏn 188-189 G 2
Tanchow = Dan Xian 184-185 K 8
Tancítaro, Pico de - 146-147 F 8
Tandag 186-187 J 5
Tandaho = Tendaho 166-167 N 6
Ţăndărei 136-137 M 3
Tandil 162 E 5
Tandou Lake 196 EF 4
Tandža = Ṭanjah 166-167 C 1
Tanega-shima 184-185 P 5
Tanega sima = Tanega-shima 184-185 P 5
Tanew 133 L 3
Tanezrouft = Tānizruft 166-167 DE 4
Tanf, Jabal at- 182-183 H 6
Tan-fêng = Danfeng 190-191 C 5
Tanga 168-169 J 4
Tangail = Ṭangāyal 180-181 O 6
Tanga Islands 186-187 h 5
Tangale Peak 172-173 H 3
Tanganyika, Lake - 168-169 G 3-H 4
Tangar = Thangkar 184-185 J 4
Tangará 162 F 3
Tangāyal 180-181 O 6
T'ang-chan = Tangshan 184-185 M 4
Tangdukou 190-191 C 8
Tanger = Ṭanjah 166-167 C 1
Tânger = Tanjah 126-127 G 8
Tanggela Youmu Hu = Thangra Yumtsho 184-185 EF 5
Tanggu 184-185 M 4
Tanghe [TJ, ●] 190-191 D 5
Tang He [TJ, ~ ◁ Bai He] 190-191 D 5
Tang He [TJ, ~ ◁ Baiyang Dian] 190-191 E 2
T'ang-ho = Tanghe [TJ, ●] 190-191 D 5
T'ang Ho = Tang He [TJ, ~ ◁ Bai He] 190-191 D 5
T'ang Ho = Tang He [TJ, ~ ◁ Baiyang Dian] 190-191 E 2
T'ang-hsien-chên = Tangxianzhen 190-191 D 6
Tangier Sound 148-149 EF 5-6
Tangjin 188-189 F 4
Tang La [TJ, Himalaya ⇄] 184-185 F 6
Tang La [TJ, Tanglha] 184-185 G 5
Tangla = Tanglha 184-185 FG 5
Tanglha 184-185 FG 5
Tangshan 184-185 M 4
Tangshan = Dangshan 190-191 F 4
Tangshancheng 188-189 DE 2
Tangtou 190-191 G 4
Tangtu = Dangtu 190-191 G 6
T'ang-tu-k'ou = Tangdukou 190-191 C 8
Tanguiéta 172-173 F 3
Tanguj 178-179 T 6
Tangxi 190-191 G 7
Tang Xian 190-191 E 2
Tangxianzhen 190-191 D 6
Tangyiang = Dangyang 190-191 CD 6
Tangyin 190-191 E 4
Tangyuan 184-185 O 2
Tan Ho = Dan He 190-191 D 4
Tanhsien = Dan Xian 184-185 K 8
Tanimbar, Kepulauan - 186-187 K 8
Taning = Daning 190-191 C 3
Ta-ning = Wuxi 190-191 B 6
Taninthāri 186-187 C 4
Taninthāri Taing 186-187 C 4
Tānizruft 166-167 DE 4
Ṭanjah 166-167 C 1
Tanjay 186-187 H 5
Tanjong Malim 186-187 D 6
Tanjor = Thanjavur 180-181 MN 8
Tanjung 186-187 G 7
Tanjungbalai 186-187 CD 6
Tanjungkarang 186-187 DE 8
Tanjungkarang-Telukbetung Bandar Lampung 186-187 DE 8
Tanjungpandan 186-187 E 7
Tanjungpinang 186-187 DE 6
Tanjungpura 186-187 C 6
Tanjungredep 186-187 G 6
Tankersly, TX 154-155 E 5
Tankoro 172-173 F 2
Tankwa 174-175 D 7
Tanlovo 178-179 NO 4
Tännäs 130-131 E 6
Tannūmah, At- 182-183 MN 7
Tannu-Ola, chrebet - 178-179 R 7
Tanoé 166-167 D 7
Tanoso 172-173 E 4
Tanoût 166-167 F 6
Tanqua River = Tankwa 174-175 D 7
Tanque, AZ 150-151 J 9
Tanque Alvarez 154-155 D 7
Tansania 168-169 HJ 4
Tan-shui 184-185 N 6
Tan-shui = Danshui 190-191 E 10
Tan-shui Kang 190-191 H 9
Tansīft, Wādī - 166-167 C 2
Tansilla 172-173 D 2
Ťan-šan 184-185 C-G 3
Ṭanṭā 166-167 KL 2
Tanyang 188-189 G 4
Tanyang = Danyang 190-191 G 6
Tanyeri 182-183 HJ 3
Tanzânia 168 FG 3
Tanzánia 168-169 HJ 4
Tanzania 168-169 HJ 4
Tanzania 169-169 HJ 4
Tanzanie 168-169 HJ 4
Taoan 184-185 N 2
Tao'an = Baicheng 184-185 N 2
T'ao-chou = Lintan 184-185 J 5
Taocun 190-191 H 3
Tao-hsien = Dao Xian 190-191 C 9
Taohua Dao 190-191 J 7
Tao Jiang [TJ, ~] 190-191 E 9
Taojiang [TJ, ●] 190-191 D 7
Taole = Taoluo 190-191 G 4
Tao-li = Daoli 190-191 H 3
Taoluo 190-191 G 4
Taoqi = Taoxi 190-191 F 6
Taormina 136-137 F 7
Taos, NM 146-147 E 4
Tao Shan = Pei-ta-wu Shan 190-191 H 10
Tao Shui = Dao Shui 190-191 E 6
T'ao-ts'un = Taocun 190-191 H 3
Taoudenni 166-167 D 4
Taourirt = Tāwrīrt 166-167 D 2
Taoxi 190-191 F 6
Tao yüan [RC] 190-191 H 9
Taoyuan [TJ] 190-191 C 7
Tapa 138-139 E 4
Tapacaré 160-161 B 3
Tapachula 146-147 H 9
Tapajós, Rio - 158-159 H 5
Tapaktuan 186-187 C 6
Ta-pa Shan = Daba Shan 184-185 KL 5
Tapat, Pulau - 186-187 J 7
Tapauá 158-159 FG 6
Tapauá, Rio - 158-159 F 6
Ta-p'êng = Dapeng 190-191 E 10
Tapepo 171 B 4
Tapera Pesoe 160-161 B 1
Taperoá [BR, Bahia] 158-159 M 7
Tapeta 166-167 C 7
Tāpī = Tapti 180-181 M 6
Ta-pieh Shan = Dabie Shan 184-185 M 5
Tapini 186-187 N 8
Tapiocanga, Chapada do - 160-161 J 2
Tapirapecó, Sierra - 158-159 FG 4
Tapoa 172-173 F 2
Ta-p'o-ti = Dabaidi 190-191 E 8
Tappahannock, VA 148-149 E 5-6
Tappi-saki 188-189 MN 2
Tappita = Tapeta 166-167 C 7
Taps = Tapa 138-139 E 4
Tapti 180-181 M 6
Tapuaenuku 194-195 O 8
Ta-pu-hsün Hu = Dabas nuur 184-185 H 4
Tapuruquara 158-159 FG 5
Taqānat, At- 172-173 C 1
Ṭaqṭaq 182-183 L 5
Taquara, Ponta da - 160-161 HJ 7
Taquara, Serra da - 160-161 F 1
Taquari [BR, Mato Grosso] 160-161 F 2
Taquari, Pantanal do - 160-161 DE 3
Taquari, Rio - [BR ◁ Rio Paranapanena] 160-161 H 5
Taquari, Rio - [BR ◁ Rio Taquari Novo] 160-161 F 3
Taquari Novo, Rio - 158-159 H 8
Taquaritinga 160-161 H 4
Taquarituba 160-161 H 5
Taquaruçu, Ribeira - 160-161 F 4
Tara 136-137 H 4
Tara [AUS] 194-195 K 5
Tara [SU, ~] 178-179 O 6
Tara [SU, ●] 178-179 N 6
Taraba [WAN, ⭑] 172-173 H 3
Taraba, River - 172-173 H 3
Tarabillas, Laguna - 154-155 C 5
Tarabuco 158-159 FG 8
Ṭarabulus 166-167 GH 2
Ṭarābulus al-Gharb 166-167 G 2
Ṭarābulus ash-Shām 180-181 CD 4
Tarago 196 J 5
Tarahumara, Sierra - 146-147 E 6
Tarāī = Terei 180-181 NO 5

Tien Schan 184-185 C-G 3
Tien Shan 184-185 C-G 3
Tien Shan 184-185 C-G 3
Tienshui = Tianshui 184-185 JK 5
Tiensjan 184-185 C-G 3
Tienszan 184-185 C-G 3
Tientai = Tiantai 190-191 H 7
Tientsin = Tianjin 184-185 M 4
Tiên Yên 186-187 E2
Tierfontein 174-175 G 5
Tierp 130-131 G 7
Tierpoortdam 174-175 G 5
Tierra Amarilla, NM 154-155 B 2
Tierra Blanca [MEX, Chihuahua] 154-155 C 7
Tierra Blanca [MEX, Veracruz] 146-147 G 8
Tierra Blanca Creek 154-155 DE 3
Tierra del Fuego 156 C 9
Tie Siding, WY 152-153 P 5
Tiétar 134-135 E 8
Tietê 160-161 J 5
Tietê Rio - 160-161 H 4
Tieton, WA 150-151 C 2
Tifariti = Atfāriti 166-167 B 3
Tiffany Mountain 150-151 CD 1
Tiffin, OH 152-153 P 5
Tiflis = Tbilisi 140-141 M 6
Tifore, Pulau - 186-187 J 6
Tifton, GA 148-149 B 9
Tiger Point 154-155 J 6
Tighina = Bendery 140-141 D 3
Tigieglo = Tayeegle 168-169 K 2
Tigil' 178-179 e 6
Tigre = Nahr Dijlah 180-181 E 3
Tigre, Dent du - = Dông Voi Mêp 186-187 E 3
Tigre, El - [MEX] 150-151 J 10
Tigre, El - [YV] 158-159 G 3
Tigre, Rio - [EC] 158-159 D 5
Tigri = Nahr Dijlah 180-181 E 3
Tigris = Nahr Dijlah 180-181 E 3
Tigui 166-167 H 5
Tiguidit, Falaise de - 172-173 GH 1
Tiguila 172-173 E 2
Tih, Jabal at- 166-167 L 3
Tih, Şahrā, at- 166-167 L 2
Tiham = Tihāmah 180-181 D 6-E 8
Tihāmah 180-181 D 6-E 8
Ti-hua = Ürümchi 184-185 F 3
Tihwa = Ürümchi 184-185 F 3
Tiirismaa 130-131 L 7
Tijeras, NM 154-155 B 3
Tijiqjah 166-167 B 5
Tijoca 158-159 K 5
Tijuana 146-147 C 5
Tijucas 160-161 H 7
Tijucas, Baia de - 160-161 H 7
Tijucas, Rio - 160-161 H 7
Tijuco, Rio - 160-161 H 3
Tikahau 192-193 MN 6
Tikal 146-147 J 8
Tikopia 194-195 N 2
Tikrit 182-183 K 5
Tiksi 178-179 Y 3
Tikšozero 130-131 OP 4
Tilamuta 186-187 H 6
Tilbeşar ovasi 182-183 G 4
Tilburg 134-135 K 3
Tilbury 152-153 P 4
Tilcara 162 CD 2
Tilden, NE 152-153 H 4-5
Tilden, TX 154-155 F 6
Tilemsès 166-167 EF 5
Tilemsi 166-167 E 5
Tiličiki 178-179 g 5
Tilimsān 166-167 D 2
Tillabéry 166-167 E 6
Tillamook, OR 150-151 B 3
Tillamook Bay 150-151 AB 3
Tillery, Lake - 148-149 CD 7
Tillia 166-167 E 5
Tillsonburg 148-149 C 3
Tilogne 172-173 B 2
Tilpa 194-195 H 6
Tilsit = Sovetsk 133 K 1
Tim 140-141 H 1
Timā 170 D 4
Timaná 158-159 D 4
Timane, Rio - 160-161 B 4
Timanskij kr'až 178-179 J 5-H 4
Timar 182-183 K 3
Timaru 194-195 O 8
Timaševo [SU, Samara] 138-139 S 7
Timaševsk 140-141 J 4
Timasova Gora 138-139 Q 3
Timassah 166-167 H 3
Timassanin = Burj 'Umar Idris 166-167 EF 3
Timbalier Bay 154-155 K 6
Timbalier Island 154-155 K 6
Timbédra = Tinbadghah 166-167 C5
Timber, OR 150-151 B 3
Timber Lake, SD 152-153 F 3
Timber Mountain 150-151 F 6
Timbó [BR, Santa Catarina] 160-161 H 7
Timbo [Guinea] 166-167 B 6
Timbó, Rio - 160-161 G 7
Timboulaga 166-167 F 5
Timia 166-167 F 5
Timimoun = Tīmīmūn 166-167 E 3
Timimūn 166-167 E 3
Timiş 136-137 J 3
Timişoara 136-137 J 3
Ti-m-Merhsoï, Oued - 166-167 F 5
Timmins 144-145 U 8
Timmonsville, SC 148-149 D 7
Timmoudi = Timmūdi 166-167 D 3
Timoé 192-193 O 7
Timon 158-159 L 6
Timor 186-187 H 9-J 8
Timor, Fosa de - 186-187 J 8
Timor, Fossa di 186-187 J 8
Timor, Fosse de - 186-187 J 8
Timor, Fossa de - 186-187 J 8
Timor, Mar de - 194-195 E 2
Timor, Mar de - 122-123 Q 6
Timor, Mar di 194-195 E 2
Timor, Mare di 194-195 E 2
Timor, Mer de - 194-195 E 2
Timor, Morze - 186-187 E 2
Timor-árok 186-187 J 8
Timorgraben 186-187 J 8
Timor Sea 194-195 E 2
Timorsee 198-199 F 5
Timorské moře 186-187 E 2
Timorski, Rów - 186-187 J 8
Timorský kaňon 186-187 J 8
Timor-tenger 194-195 E 2
Timor Timur = 23 ◁ 186-187 J 8
Timortrog 186-187 J 8
Timor Trough 186-187 J 8
Timorzee 194-195 E 2
Timošino 138-139 L 3
Timpahute Range 150-151 F 7
Timpas, CO 152-153 E 7
Timpson, TX 154-155 H 5
Timsāh, Buhayrat at- 170 E 2
Timšer [SU, ~] 138-139 U 3
Timšer [SU, ●] 138-139 U 3
Tina 174-175 H 6
Tinah, Khalij at- 170 E 2
Tinajas, Las - 160-161 A 7
Tinakula 186-187 kl 7
Ti-n-Asselak 166-167 E 5
Tinbadghah 166-167 C 5
Tindouf = Tindūf 166-167 C 3
Tindouf, Sebkra de - = Sabkhat Tindūf 166-167 C 3
Tindūf, Sabkhat - 166-167 C 3
Ti-n-Edrine 172-173 E 1
Tineo 134-135 D 7
Tin Essalak = Ti-n-Asselak 166-167 E5
Tingha 196 K 2-3
Tinghing = Dingxing 190-191 E 2
Tinghirt, Hammadat - = Hammādat Tinrirt 166-167 FG 3
Ting-hsi = Dingxi 184-185 J 4
Tinghsien = Ding Xian 190-191 E 2
Ting-hsin = Dingxin 184-185 H 3
Ting-hsing = Dingxing 190-191 E 2
Ting Jiang 190-191 F 9
Tingling Shan = Qin Ling 184-185 KL 5
Ting-nan = Dingnan 190-191 E 9
Tingo Maria 158-159 D 6
Tingpian = Dingbian 190-191 A 3
Tingréla 166-167 C 6
Tingri Dsong 184-185 F 6
Tingsiqiao 190-191 E 7
Tingsryd 130-131 F 9
Ting-szŭ-ch'iao = Tingsiqiao 190-191 E 7
Tingtao = Dingtao 190-191 E 4
Tinguipaya 158-159 F 8
Tingvoll 130-131 BC 6
Tingwon 186-187 g 5
Ting-yüan = Dingyuan 190-191 F 5
Ting-yüan-ying = Bajan Choto 184-185 JK 4
Tinian 192-193 F 3
Tinjil, Pulau - 186-187 E 8
Tinkisso 166-167 BC 6
Tinnevelly = Tirunelveli 180-181 M 9
Tinnin, 'Ayn - 170 C 4
Tinogasta 162 C 3
Tinpak = Dianbai 190-191 C 11
Tinrhert, Hamada de - = Hammādat Tinrirt 166-167 FG 3
Tinrirt, Hammādat - 166-167 FG 3
Tinsukia 180-181 Q 5
Tintah, MN 152-153 H 2-3
Tin Tarābin, Wādi - 166-167 F 4
Ti-n-Tehoun 172-173 E 1
Tintina 162 D 3
Tintinara 196 E 5
Tio, El - 162 D 4
Tioga, CO 152-153 D 7
Tioga, LA 154-155 J 5
Tioga, ND 152-153 E 1
Tioga, TX 154-155 G 4
Tiogo 172-173 E 2
Tioman, Pulau - 186-187 DE 6
Tionesta, CA 150-151 C 5
Tionesta, PA 148-149 D 4
Tipp City, OH 152-153 O 6
Tippecanoe River 152-153 NO 5
Tipperary 132 BC 5
Tipton, CA 150-151 D 7
Tipton, IA 152-153 L 5
Tipton, IN 152-153 N 5
Tipton, MO 152-153 K 6
Tipton, OK 154-155 F 3
Tipton, WY 152-153 B 5
Tipton, Mount - 150-151 F 8
Tiptonville, TN 154-155 L 2
Tiracambu, Serra de - 158-159 K 5
Tiradentes 160-161 KL 4
Tirān, Jazirat - 170 F 4
Tirana = Tiranë 136-137 HJ 5
Tiranë 136-137 HJ 5
Tirasduines 174-175 B 4
Tirasdünen = Tirasduines 174-175 B 4
Tirashochebene = Tirasplato 174-175 B 3-4
Tiras Mountains = Tirasplato 174-175 B 3-4
Tirasplato 174-175 B 3-4
Tiraspol' 140-141 D 3
Tirbande Turkestān 180-181 JK 3
Tire 182-183 B 3
Tirebolu 182-183 H 2
Tiree 132 C 3
Tiree Passage 132 C 3
Tirich Mir 180-181 L 3
Tirikunāmalaya 180-181 N 9
Tirnabos 136-137 K 6
Tiro 172-173 C 3
Tirol 133 EF 5
Tirolo = Tirol 133 EF 5
Tirso 136-137 C 6
Tiruchchendur = Tiruchendur 180-181 M 9
Tiruchchirāppalli = Tiruchirapalli 180-181 M 8
Tiruchendur 180-181 M 9
Tiruchirapalli 180-181 M 8
Tirukkunamalai = Tirikunāmalaya 180-181 N 9
Tirunelveli 180-181 M 9
Tirupati 180-181 M 8
Tiruvanatapuram = Trivandrum 180-181 M 9
Tisa 140-141 A 2
Tisdale 144-145 Q 7
Tishit 166-167 C 5
Tishlah 166-167 AB 4
Tishomingo, MS 154-155 L 3
Tishomingo, OK 154-155 G 3
Tis Isat Fwafwatē 166-167 M 6
Tiškovka 140-141 E 2
Tismana 136-137 K 3
Tisza 133 K 5
Tisza-tó 178-179 H 9
Tiszaújváros 178-179 HJ 9
Tit-Ary 178-179 Y 3
Titemsi 166-167 E 5
Titicaca, Lago - 158-159 F 8
Titov Veles 136-137 JK 5
Titran 130-131 C 6
Tittabawassee River 152-153 OP 4
Titu [EAK] 171 D 2
Titule 168-169 FG 2
Titusville, FL 148-149 c 2
Titusville, PA 148-149 D 4
Tiṭwān 166-167 CD 1
Tivaouane 166-167 A 5
Tiverton 132 E 6
Tivoli 136-137 E 5
Tiyārat [DZ] 166-167 E 1
Tizimin 146-147 J 7
Tizi-Ouzou = Tizi Wazū 166-167 E 1
Tizi Wazū 166-167 E 1
Tiznit 166-167 C 3
Tjakassen, Autonome Republiek = 10 ◁ 178-179 R 7
Tjeggelvas 130-131 GH 4
Tjendana, Pulau - = Sumba 186-187 G 9
Tjertjen = Chārchān 184-185 F 4
Tjirebon = Cirebon 186-187 E 8
Tjörn [IS] 130-131 c 2
Tjörn [S] 130-131 D 8-9
Tjörnes 130-131 e 1
Tjøtta 130-131 E 5
Tjumen = Tumen' 178-179 M 6
Tjuvfjorden 130-131 l 6
Tkibuli 140-141 L 5
Tkvarčeli 140-141 K 5
Tlahualilo, Sierra del - 154-155 D 7
Tlahualilo de Zaragoza 154-155 D 7
Tlaquepaque 146-147 F 7
Tl'arata 140-141 N 5
Tlaxcala 146-147 G 8
Tlaxcala de Xicoténcatl 146-147 G 8
Tlemcen = Tilimsān 166-167 D 2
Tlemcès = Tilemsès 166-167 EF 5
Tlumač 140-141 B 2
Tluste = Tolstoje 140-141 B 2
Tmessa = Timassah 166-167 H 3
Toamasina 168-169 LM 6
Toano, VA 148-149 E 6
Toano Range 150-151 F 5
Toba [J] 188-189 L 5
Toba, Danau - 186-187 C 6
Tobago 146-147 OP 9
Tobalai, Pulau - 186-187 J 7
Tobar, NV 150-151 F 5
Tobarra 134-135 G 9
Tobati 160-161 D 6
Tobelo 186-187 J 6
Tobermorey 194-195 G 4
Tobermory [CDN] 148-149 BC 2
Tobi 186-187 K 6
Tobias, NE 152-153 H 5
Tobin, Mount - 150-151 E 5
Tobi-shima 188-189 M 3
Tobli 172-173 C 4
Tobo 186-187 JK 7
Toboali 186-187 E 7
Tobol [SU, ~] 178-179 M 6
Tobol [SU, ●] 178-179 L 7
Toboli 186-187 H 7
Tobol'sk 178-179 MN 6
Tobruch = Tubruq 166-167 J 2
Tobruk = Tubruq 166-167 J 2
Tobseda 178-179 J 4
T'ob'ulech 178-179 b 3
Tobys' 138-139 T 2
Tocantinia 158-159 K 6
Tocantinópolis 158-159 K 6
Tocantins 158-159 K 7
Tocantins, Rio [~]- 158-159 K 5-6
Toccoa, GA 148-149 B 7
Tochigi 188-189 MN 4
Tochio 188-189 M 4
T'o-chi Tao = Tuoji Dao 190-191 H 2
Toch'o-do 188-189 E 5
Tochta 138-139 R 2
Tockoje 138-139 T 6
Toco [RCH] 162 C 2
Tocopilla 162 B 2
Tocorpuri, Cerro de - 158-159 F 9
Tocqueville = Ra's al-Wād 166-167 E1
Tocra = Tūkrah 166-167 HJ 2
Tocumen, Rio - 146-147 c 2
Tocuyo, El - 158-159 F 3
Todeli 186-187 H 7
Todenyang 171 C 1
Tödi [CH] 133 D 5
Todi [I] 136-137 E 4
Todmorden [AUS] 194-195 FG 5
Todness 158-159 H 3
To-dong 188-189 H 4
Todo-saki 188-189 O 3
Todos os Santos, Baía de - 158-159 M 7
Todos os Santos, Rio - 160-161 M 2
Todos os Santos-öböl = Baia de Todos os Santos 158-159 M 7
Todos Santos [BOL, Cochabamba] 158-159 F 8
Todos Santos [MEX] 146-147 D 7
Todos Santos, Islas de - 150-151 E 10
Todro 171 B 2
Toecé 172-173 E 3
T'oejo 188-189 FG 3
Tōen = Tao-yüan 190-191 H 9
Toeva Autonome Republiek 178-179 RS 7
Tofte, MN 152-153 L 2
Tofua 192-193 K 6
Togdheer 166-167 b 2
Togi 188-189 L 4
Togian, Kepulauan - 186-187 H 7
Togo 166-167 E 7
Togochale = Togotyalē 166-167 N 7
Togotyalē 166-167 N 7
Togtoh = Tugt 184-185 L 3-4
Togye-dong 188-189 G 4
Tŏgyu-san 188-189 FG 5
Tohatchi, NM 150-151 J 8
Tohma Çayı 182-183 G 3
Tohoku 188-189 N 2-4
T'o Ho = Tuo He 190-191 F 5
Toiama = Toyama 184-185 Q 4
Toijala 130-131 K 7
Toili 186-187 H 7
Toi-misaki 188-189 H 7
Toiserivier 174-175 G 7
Toivola, MI 152-153 M 2
Toiyabe Range 150-151 E 6
Tok [SU] 138-139 U 7
Tokachi-dake 188-189 c 2
Tokachi-gawa 188-189 c 2
Tokai 188-189 LM 5
Tokaj 133 K 4
Tōkamachi 188-189 M 4
Tōkar = Tawkar 166-167 M 5
Tokara-kaikyō 184-185 O 5-P 6
Tokara-rettō 184-185 OP 6
Tokarevka 138-139 N 8
Tokat 180-181 D 2
Tŏkchŏk-kundo 188-189 EF 4
Tŏkch'ŏn 188-189 F 3
Tokelau Islands 198-199 J 5
Toki 188-189 L5
Tokio, TX 154-155 D 4
Tokio = Tōkyō 184-185 QR 4
Tokió = Tōkyō 184-185 QR 4
Tōkyō 184-185 QR 4
Tokitsu = Toki 188-189 L 5
Tokko 178-179 WX 6
Tok-kol 188-189 GH 2
Tokmak [SU, Kirgizskaja SSR] 178-179 O 9
Tokmak [SU, Ukrainskaja SSR] 140-141 GH 3
Tōkō = Tung-kang 190-191 H 10
Tokolimbu 186-187 H 7
Tokoro 188-189 cd 1
Tokosun = Toksun 184-185 F 3
Tokra = Tūkrah 166-167 HJ 2
Toksun 184-185 F 3
Tokuno-shima 184-185 O 6
Tokuno sima = Tokuno-shima 184-185 O 6
Tokushima 184-185 PQ 5
Tokusima = Tokushima 184-185 PQ 5
Tokuyama 188-189 HJ 5
Tōkyō 184-185 QR 4
Tōkyō wan 188-189 M 5
Tola, La - 158-159 D 4
Tolar, NM 154-155 D 3
Tolar Grande 162 C 2
Tolbuhin = Dobrič 136-137 MN 4
Toledo [BR, Paraná] 160-161 F 6
Toledo [E] 134-135 EF 9
Toledo, OH 146-147 K 3
Toledo, OR 150-151 B 3
Toledo, Montes de - 134-135 E 9
Toledo Bend Reservoir 154-155 HJ 5
Tolga = Tūljā 166-167 EF 2
Toliary 168-169 K 7
Tolitoli 186-187 H 6
Toljatti 178-179 H 7
Toll'a, zaliv - 178-179 ST 2
Tolleson, AZ 150-151 G 9
Tolley, ND 152-153 EF 1
Tolloche 162 D 3
Tolmač'ovo 138-139 G 4
Tolo, Teluk - 186-187 H 7
Toločin 138-139 G 6
Tolone = Toulon 134-135 KL 7
Tolono, IL 152-153 MN 6
Tolosa 134-135 FG 7
Tolosa = Toulouse 134-135 HJ 7
Tolox, Sierra de - 134-135 E 10
Tolsan-do 188-189 FG 5
Tolstoj, mys - 178-179 e 6
Tolstoje 140-141 B 2
Toltén 162 B 5
Toluca, IL 152-153 M 5
Toluca, Nevado de - 146-147 FG 8
Toluca de Lerdo 146-147 FG 8
To-lun = Doloon Nuur 184-185 LM 3
Toma, La - 162 C 4
Tomah, WI 152-153 L 3-4
Tomahawk, WI 152-153 M 3
Tomakomai 184-185 R 3
Tomakovka 140-141 G 3
Tomamae 188-189 b 1
Tomaniive 186-187 a 2
Tomar 134-135 C 9
Tomar [BR] 158-159 G 5
Tomari 178-179 b 8
Tomarovka 140-141 GH 1
Tomarza 182-183 F 3
Tomašovka 138-139 DE 8
Tomaszów Lubelski 133 L 3
Tomaszów Mazowiecki 133 K 3
Tomazina 160-161 H 5
Tombador, Serra do - [BR, Mato Grosso] 158-159 H 7
Tomball, TX 154-155 H 5
Tombé = Tumbi 166-167 L 7
Tombigbee River 146-147 J 5
Tomboco 168-169 D 4
Tombos 160-161 L 4
Tombouctou 166-167 D 5
Tombstone, AZ 150-151 HJ 10
Tom Burke 174-175 G 2
Tomé 162 B 5
Tömek = Aşağı Pınarbaşı 182-183 E 3
Tomelilla 130-131 EF 10
Tomelloso 134-135 F 9
Tomini 186-187 H 6
Tomini, Teluk - 186-187 H 7
Tominian 172-173 D 2
Tomioka 188-189 N 4
Tomkinson Ranges 194-195 E 5
Tommot 178-179 Y 6
Tomo 158-159 F 4
Tomo, Rio - 158-159 F 3
Tompkinsville, KY 154-155 N 2
Tompo 178-179 a 5
Tom Price 194-195 C 4
Tomra 130-131 B 6
Tomsk 178-179 PQ 6
Toms River, NJ 148-149 FG 5
Tomtabakken 130-131 EF 9
Tonala 146-147 H 8
Tonalea, AZ 150-151 H 7
Tonami 188-189 L 4
Tonantins 158-159 F 5
Tonasket, WA 150-151 D 1
Tonbai Shan 184-185 L 5
Tonbridge 132 G 6
Tonchino = Bắc Bô 186-187 DE 2
Tonchino, Golfo del - 186-187 E 2-3
Tonda 186-187 M 8
Tønder 130-131 C 10
Tondern = Tønder 130-131 C 10
Tondi 180-181 M 9
Tondibi 172-173 EF 1
Tone-gawa 188-189 N 5
Tonekābon 180-181 G 3
Tonga [AUS] 196 F 3
Tonga [Tonga] 186-187 bc 2
Tōngā = Tunjah 166-167 L 7
Tonga, Fosa de - 190-191 c 2
Tonga, Fossa de - 186-187 c 2
Tonga, Fossa delle - 186-187 c 2
Tonga, Fosse des - 186-187 c 2
Tonga, Rów - 186-187 c 2
Tonga-árok 186-187 c 2
Tongaat 174-175 J 5
Tongagraben 186-187 c 2
Tonga Islands 198-199 J 5-6
Tongaland 168-169 H 8
Tong'an 190-191 G 9
Tongareva = Penrhyn 192-193 M 5
Tongatapu 192-193 K 7
Tonga Trench 186-187 c 2
Tongatrog 186-187 c 2
Tongbai 190-191 D 5
Tongch'ang 188-189 EF 2
Tongcheng [TJ, Anhui] 190-191 F 6
Tongcheng [TJ, Hubei] 190-191 DE 7
Tongcheng [TJ, Jiangsu] 190-191 G 5
T'ongch'ŏn 188-189 FG 3
Tongchuan 184-185 K 4
Tongdao 190-191 B 8
Tonggu 190-191 E 7
Tungguan [TJ, Hunan] 190-191 D 7
Tongguan [TJ, Shaanxi] 184-185 L 5
Tonggu Zhang 190-191 F 10
Tonghan-man 184-185 O 4
Tonghua 184-185 O 3
Tongjosŏn-man = Tonghan-man 184-185 O 4
Tongliao 184-185 N 3
Tongling 184-185 M 5
Tonglu 184-185 M 5-6
Tongmun'gŏ-ri 188-189 F 2
Tongoy 162 B 4
Tongphu 184-185 H 5
Tongpu = Tongphu 184-185 H 5
Tongren 184-185 K 6
Tongshan 190-191 E 7
Tongshan = Dongshan 190-191 F 10
Tongshan Dao = Dongshan Dao 190-191 F 10
Tongshannei Ao 190-191 F 10
Tongshi 190-191 F 4
Tongue River 152-153 CD 2-3
Tong Xian 184-185 M 3-4
Tongxiang 190-191 H 6
Tongxu 190-191 E 4
Tongyang 188-189 F 3
Tongyang = Dongyang 190-191 H 7
T'ŏngyŏng = Ch'ungmu 188-189 G 5
Tongyu 184-185 N 3
Tonk 180-181 M 5
Tonkawa, OK 154-155 G 2
Tonkin = Bac Bô 186-187 DE 2
Tonkin, Golfe du - 186-187 E 2-3
Tonkin, Golfo de - 186-187 E 2-3
Tonkin, Golf van - 186-187 E 2-3
Tonkin, Golf von - 186-187 E 2-3
Tonkin, Gulf of - 186-187 E 2-3
Tonking = Bac Bô 186-187 D 2
Tonkini-öböl 186-187 E 2-3
Tonkińska, Zatoka - 186-187 E 2-3
Tonkinský záliv 186-187 E 2-3
Tonlé Sap 186-187 D 4
Tonneins 134-135 GH 6
Tonopah, NV 146-147 C 4
Tonquim = Bac Bô 186-187 D 2
Tonquim, Golfo de 186-187 E 2-3
Tønsberg 130-131 CD 8
Tonstad 130-131 B 8
Tontelbos 174-175 D 6
Tonya 182-183 H 2
Tonžský příkop 186-187 c 2
Tooele, UT 146-147 D 3
Tooligie 196 B 4
Toompine 196 G 1
Toora 196 H 7
Toora-Chem 178-179 S 7
Toowoomba 194-195 K 5
Topeka, KS 146-147 G 4
Topki 178-179 PQ 6
Topko, gora - 178-179 a 6
Toplịţa 136-137 L 2
Topock, AZ 150-151 F 8
Topoli 140-141 P 3
Topolobampo 146-147 E 6
Topolovgrad 136-137 M 4
Toponas, CO 152-153 C 5
Topozero 178-179 E 4
Toppenish, WA 150-151 C 2
Toprakkale 182-183 FG 4
Topsi 174-175 G 2
Ṭoqra = Tūkrah 166-167 HJ 2
Toqsun = Toksun 184-185 F 3
Toquepala 158-159 E 8
Toquerville, UT 150-151 G 7
Tonquim = Bac Bô 186-187 D 2
Tonquim, Golfo de - 186-17 E 2-3
Toquima Range 150-151 E 6
Tor 166-167 L7
Tora 171 B 2
Torbalı 182-183 B 3
Torbali 182-183 B 3
Torbat-e Heydariyeh 180-181 HJ 3-4
Torbat-e Jām 180-181 J 3
Torbat-e Sheikh Jām = Torbat-e Jām 180-181 J 3
Torbay 132 E 6
Torbino 138-139 J 4
Torch Lake 152-173 O 3
Torčin 140-141 B 1
Tordesillas 134-135 E 8
Töre 130-131 K 5
Torekov 130-131 E 9
Torellbreen 130-131 j 6
Torell land 130-131 k 6
Torez 140-141 J 3
Torgau 133 F 3
Torino 136-137 BC 3
Toriñana, Cabo - 134-135 C 7
Tōrit = Turit 166-167 L 8
Torixoréu 160-161 F 2
Torkamān 182-183 M 4
Torkoviči 138-139 H 4
Tormes 134-135 D 8
Tormosin 140-141 L 2
Torneå = Tornio 130-131 L 5
Torne älv 130-131 K 4
Torneträsk 130-131 H 3
Torngat Mountains 144-145 Y 6
Tornio 130-131 L 5
Tornquist 162 D 5
Toro 134-135 E 8
Toro [EAU] 171 B 2
Toro, Cerro del - 162 C 3
Torodi 166-167 E 6
Torodo 172-173 C 2
Torokina 186-187 hj 6
Toroku = Yün-lin 190-191 H 10
Toronto 144-145 UV 9
Toronto, KS 152-153 J 7
Toro Peak 150-151 E 9
Toropec 138-139 H 5
Tororo 168-169 H 2
Toros dağları 180-181 C 3
Toros-hegység 180-181 C 3
Torrance, CA 150-151 D 9
Torre del Greco 136-137 F 5
Torre de Moncorvo 134-135 D 8
Torrelaguna 134-135 F 8
Torrelavega 134-135 E 7
Torrens, Lake - 194-195 G 6
Torrens Creek 194-195 HJ 4
Torrente 134-135 G 9
Torreón 146-147 F 6
Torreón de Cañas 154-155 C 7
Torres 162 G 3
Torres, Détroit de - 194-195 H 2
Torres, Îles - 194-195 N 2
Torres Islands 194-195 N 2
Torres Martinez Indian Reservation 150-151 E 9
Torres Strait 194-195 H 2
Torres Vedras 134-135 C 9
Torrevieja 134-135 G 10
Torrijos 134-135 E 8-9
Torrington, CT 148-149 G 4
Torrington, WY 152-153 DE 4
Torrinha 160-161 HJ 5
Torsås 130-131 FG 9
Torsby 130-131 E 7
Tortillas, Las - 154-155 F 7
Tortola 146-147 O 8
Tortoli 136-137 C 6
Tortona 136-137 C 3
Tortosa 134-135 H 8
Tortosa, Cabo de - 134-135 H 8
Tortue, Île de la - 146-147 M 7
Tortum 182-183 J 2
Ṭorūd 180-181 H 3
Torugart Davan 180-181 L 2
Torul 182-183 I J 2
Toruń 133 J 2
Tõrva 138-139 E 4-5
Törwa = Tõrva 138-139 E 4-5
Tory 132 B 4
Tory Hill 148-149 DE 2
Toržok 178-179 E 6
Torzym 133 G 2
T'oša [SU,~] 138-139 O 6
T'oša [SU,●] 138-139 O 6
Tosan = Chūbu 188-189 L 5-M 4
Tosashimizu 188-189 J 6
Tosa-wan 188-189 J 6
Toscana 136-137 D 4
Toscane = Toscana 136-137 D 4
To-shima 188-189 M 5
Toskana = Toscana 136-137 D 4
Toškent 184-185 B 3
Tosno 138-139 H 4
Tos nuur 184-185 H 4
T'o-so Hu = Tos nuur 184-185 H 4
Tosoncengel 184-185 H 2
T'osovo-Netyl'skij 138-139 H 4
Tostado 162 D 3
Tõstamaa 138-139 D 4
Toston, MT 150-151 H 2
Tosu 188-189 H 6
Tosya 180-181 C 2
Totana 134-135 G 10
Toteng 168-169 F 7
Totes Meer = Baḥr al-Mayyit 180-181 D 4
Tot'ma 178-179 G 5-6
Totonicapán 146-147 HJ 8-9
Totora [BOL, Cochabamba] 158-159 FG 8
Totoya 186-187 ab 2
Totta 178-179 a 6
Tottan Range 121 B 35-36
Totten Glacier 121 C 12
Tottenham [AUS] 194-195 J 6
Tottenham [CDN] 148-149 CD 2-3
Tottenham, London- 132 FG 6
Tottori 184-185 P 4
Tou 172-173 E 2
Ṭouâl, Abâ = Ṭuwāl, Abā' 182-183 H 4
Touamotoubekken 124-125 BC 7
Touat = At-Tuwāt 166-167 DE 3
Touba [CI] 166-167 C 7
Touba [SN] 166-167 A 6
Toubqâl, Jbel - = Jabal Tubqāl 166-167 C2
Toudao Jiang 188-189 F 1-2
Tougan 166-167 D 6
Touggourt = Tūjurt 166-167 EF 2
Tougnifili = Tounyifili 172-173 B 3
Tougouri 172-173 E 2
Tougue 172-173 C 3
Touho 194-195 N 4
Toukley 196 KL 4
Toukoto 166-167 BC 6
Tou-kou = Dougou 190-191 E 5
Toul 134-135 K 4
Tou-lin = Yün-lin 190-191 H 10
Toulépleu 166-167 C 7
Toulon 134-135 KL 7
Toulon [ZA] 174-175 J 3
Toulon, IL 152-153 LM 5
Touloûl, Diret et- = Dirat at-Tulūl 182-183 G 6
Touloûl eṣ Ṣafâ = Tulul aṣ-Ṣafā 182-183 G 6
Toulouse 134-135 HJ 7
Toummo 166-167 G 4
Toumodi 166-167 CD 7
Toumotou, Îles - 198-199 K 5-L 6
Tou-nan 190-191 H 10
Toungo 172-173 HJ 3
Toungoo–Taungngū 186-187 C 3
Toûnis = Tūnis 166-167 FG 1
Tounyifili 172-173 B 3
Toura, Monts du 172-173 D 4
Touraine 134-135 H 5
Tourane = Đa Năng 186-187 E 3
Tournai 134-135 J 3
Tournon 134-135 K 6
Touros 158-159 MN 5-6
Tours 134-135 H 5
Tous les Saints, Baie de - = Baia de Todos os Santos 158-159 M 7
Toussidé, Pic - 166-167 H 4
T'ou-tao Chiang = Toudao Jiang 188-189 F 1-2
Touva, République Autonome des - 178-179 RS 7
Touwsrivier [ZA,~] 174-175 D 7
Touwsrivier [ZA,●] 174-175 D 7
Töv = 12 ◁ 184-185 K 2
Tovarkovskij 138-139 M 7
Tovmač = Tlumač 140-141 B 2
Tovqussaq 144-145 a 5
Tovste = Tolstoje 140-141 B 2
Towada 188-189 N 2
Towada-ko 188-189 N 2
Towanda, PA 148-149 E 4
Towani 174-175 G 2
Tower, MN 152-153 K 2
Towner, CO 152-153 E 6
Towner, ND 152-153 F 1
Townes Pass 150-151 E 7
Townsend, GA 148-149 C 9
Townsend, MT 150-151 H 2
Townshend Island 194-195 K 4
Townsville 194-195 J 3
Towori, Teluk - 186-187 H 7
Towot 166-167 L 7
Towson, MD 148-149 E 5
Towuti, Danau - 186-187 H 7
Toyah, TX 154-155 D 5
Toyahvale, TX 154-155 CD 5
Tōya-ko 188-189 b 2
Toyama 184-185 Q 4
Toyama-wan 184-185 Q 4
Toyohara = Južno-Sachalinsk 178-179 bc 8
Toyohashi 184-185 Q 5
Toyohasi = Toyohashi 184-185 Q 5
Toyoma 188-189 N 3
Toyonaka 188-189 K 5
Toyooka 188-189 K 5
Toyota 188-189 L 5
Toyotama 188-189 G 5
Tôzeur = Tawzar 166-167 F 2
Törökország 180-181 B-E 3
Törökország 136-137 M-O 6
Trabiju 160-161 H 5
Trabzon 180-181 DE 2
Trachéia = Silifke 180-181 C 3
Tra Cu 186-187 E 5
Tracy, CA 150-151 C 7
Tradum 184-185 E 6
Træna 130-131 DE 4
Traer, IA 152-153 K 4
Trafalgar, Cabo de - 134-135 D 10
Trafāwi, Bi'r - 182-183 H 4
Trail 146-147 N 8
Trail, MN 152-153 J 2
Trail City, SD 152-153 F 3
Trajan, Mur inferior de - = Nižnij Trajanov val 136-137 N 3
Trajan, Mur superior de - = Verchnij Trajanov val 136-137 N 2
Trajano Meridional, Muro de - = Nižnij Trajanov val 136-137 N 3
Trajano Septentrional, Muro de = Verchnij Trajanov val 136-137 N 2
Trajanova vrata 136-137 L 4
Trajan's Wall = Verchnij Trajanov val 136-137 N 2
Traka 174-175 E 7
Trakai 138-139 E 6
Trakya 182-183 AB 2
Tralee 132 B 5
Tranås 130-131 F 8
Trancas [MEX] 154-155 C 6
Trancas [RA] 162 CD 3
Trangan, Pulau - 186-187 K 8
Trani 136-137 G 5
Trân Ninh, Cao Nguyên 186-187 D 3
Trans Canada Highway 144-145 P 7
Trans-Himalaia 184-185 EF 5
Transhimálaj 184-185 EF 5
Transhimalaje 184-185 EF 5
Transhimalaya 184-185 EF 5
Transilvania 136-137 K-M 2
Transilvânia 136-137 K-M 2
Transit istasyonu = Doğubayazıt 182-183 KL 3
Transkasp 180-181 H 3
Transkei = 29-31 ◁ 174-175 GH 6
Transsib 178-179 L 6
Transsylvanie 136-137 KL 2
Transturan 178-179 K 7
Transylvánie 136-137 K-M 2
Transylvanie 136-137 KL 2
Transylwania 136-137 K-M 2
Transzhimalája 184-185 EF 5
Trapandé, Baia de - 160-161 J 6
Trápani 136-137 E 6-7
Trapezunt = Trabzon 180-181 DE 2
Trapezûs = Trabzon 180-181 DE 2
Trapper Peak 150-151 F 3
Traralgon 194-195 J 7
Trarza = At-Trārzah 166-167 AB 5
Trārzah, At- 166-167 AB 5
Trasimeno, Lago - 136-137 DE 4
Trás-os-Montes 134-135 D 8
Trás-os-Montes = Cucumbi 168-169 E 5
Trat 186-187 D 4
Traunstein 133 F 5
Trautenau = Trutnov 133 GH 3
Trava, Cachoeira - 158-159 H 5
Traverse, Lake - [USA] 152-153 H 3
Traverse City, MI 146-147 JK 2-3
Tra Vinh 186-187 E 5
Travis, Lake - 154-155 FG 5
Trbovle 136-137 F 2
Treasury = Mono Island 186-187 j 6
Třebíč 133 G 4
Trebinje 136-137 H 4
Trebisonda = Trabzon 180-181 DE 2
Trebizonda = Trabzon 180-181 DE 2
Trébizonde = Trabzon 180-181 DE 2
Trechado, NM 150-151 J 8
Trefâouî , Bîr - = Bi,r Trafāwi 182-183 H 4
Trego, MT 150-151 F 1
Trégorrois 134-135 F 4
Treinta y Tres [ROU, ●] 162 F 4
Trekkopje 174-175 A 2
Trelew 162 C 6
Trelleborg 130-131 E 10
Tremadoc Bay 132 D 5
Tremembé 160-161 K 5
Trèmiti, Ìsole - 136-137 F 4
Tremonton, UT 150-151 G 5
Tremp 134-135 H 7
Trempealeau, WI 152-153 L 3-4
Tren, El - 150-151 G 10
Trenary, MI 152-153 N 2
Trenčín 133 J 4
Trencsén = Trenčín 133 J 4
Trenque Lauquen 162 D 5
Trentino-Alto Àdige 136-137 D 2
Trentino-Südtirol = Trentino-Alto Adige 136-137 D 2
Trento 136-137 D 2
Trenton 148-149 E 2
Trenton, FL 148-149 b 2
Trenton, IA 152-153 K 5
Trenton, MI 152-153 P 4
Trenton, NE 152-153 F 5
Trenton, NJ 146-147 M 3-4
Trenton, TN 154-155 L 3
Tréport, le - 134-135 H 3
Tres Arroyos 162 DE 5
Três Barras 160-161 GH 7
Três Corações 158-159 KL 9
Tres Esquinas 158-159 DE 4
Tres Forcas, Cap - = Rā's Wūruq 166-167 D 1
Três Irmãos, Ilhas - 160-161 H 7
Tres Irmãos, Pontas dos 158-159 M 6-N 5
Treska 136-137 J 5
Três Lagoas 158-159 J 9
Tres Lagos 162 B 7
Três Marias 160-161 K 3
Três Marias, Represa - 160-161 K 3
Tres Montes, Peninsula - 162 A 7
Tres Picos, Cerro - 162 B 6
Tres Ollas 160-161 D 5
Tres Piedras, NM 154-155 C 2
Três Pontas 160-161 K 4
Tres Puntas, Cabo - 162 CD 7
Três Rios 158-159 L 9
Tres Virgenes, Las - 146-147 D 6
Treuburg = Olecko 133 L 1
Treuer River = Macumba 194-195 G 5
Treungen 130-131 C 8
Treviglio 136-137 C 3
Treviño 134-135 F 7
Treviso 136-137 E 3
Treze Quedas 158-159 H 4
Triabunna 196 c 3
Triangle, ID 150-151 E 4
Tribuga, Golfo de - 158-159 D 3
Tribune, KS 152-153 F 6
Trichaty 140-141 E 3
Trichōnis, Limnē - 136-137 J 6
Trichur 180-181 M 8
Trida 194-195 HJ 6
Tridell, UT 150-151 J 5
Trident Peak 150-151 D 5
Trident = Trento 136-137 D 2
Trient = Trento 136-137 D 2
Trier 133 C 4
Triest = Trieste 136-137 E 3
Triëst = Trieste 136-137 E 3
Trieste 136-137 E 3
Trieszt = Trieste 136-137 E 3
Trikala 136-137 JK 6
Trinchera, CO 154-155 CD 2
Trincheras, Las - 158-159 FG 3
Trincomalee = Tirikuṇāmalaya 180-181 N 9
Trincomali = Tirikuṇāmalaya 180-181 N 9
Trindade [BR, Goiás] 160-161 H 2
Trindade = Trinidad [BOL] 158-159 G 7
Trindade = Trinidad [TT] 146-147 O 9
Trindade , Ilha da - 158-159 NO 9
Trinidad [BOL, Beni] 158-159 G 7
Trinidad [C] 146-147 KL 7
Trinidad [CO] 158-159 E 3
Trinidad [PY] 162 E 3
Trinidad [ROU] 162 E 4
Trinidad [TT] 146-147 O 9
Trinidad, CA 150-151 A 5
Trinidad, CO 146-147 F 4
Trinidad, TX 154-155 GH 4
Trinidad, WA 150-151 CD 2
Trinidad e Tobago 146-147 O 9-10
Trinidad = Ilha da Trindade 158-159 NO 9
Trinidad, Bahia - 146-147 b 2
Trinidad, Isla - 162 D 5
Trinidad, Laguna - 160-161 B 4
Trinidad, Rio - 146-147 b 3
Trinidad and Tobago 146-147 O 9-10
Trinidad a Tobago 146-147 O 9-10
Trinidad e Tobago 146-147 O 9-10
Trinidad en Tobago 146-147 O 9-10
Trinidad és Tobago 146-147 O 9-10
Trinidad und Tobago 146-147 O 9-10
Trinidad y Tobago 146-147 O 9-10
Trinité et Tobago 146-147 O 9-10
Trinity, TX 154-155 H 5
Trinity Bay 144-145 a 8
Trinity Center, CA 150-151 B 5
Trinity Islands 144-145 F 6
Trinity Mountains 150-151 B 5
Trinity Range 150-151 D 5
Trinity River [USA, California] 150-151 B 5
Trinity River [USA, Texas] 146-147 G 5
Trion, GA 154-155 N 3
Tripoli, WI 152-153 LM 3
Tripoli = Ṭarābulus al-Gharb 166-167 G 2
Tripolis 136-137 K 7
Tripolis = Ṭarābulus al-Gharb 166-167 G2
Tripolitaine = Ṭarābulus 166-167 GH 2
Tripolitánia = Ṭarābulus 166-167 GH2
Tripolitania = Ṭarābulus 166-167 GH 2
Tripolitânia = Ṭarābulus 166-167 GH 2
Tripolsko = Ṭarābulus 166-167 GH2
Tripp, SD 152-153 GH 4
Tripura 180-181 P 6
Trishshivaperūr = Trichur 180-181 M 8
Tristao, Îles - 172-173 B 3
Triumph, MN 152-153 J 4
Trivandrum 180-181 M 9
Trnava 133 H 4
Trobriand Islands 186-187 h 6
Trofors 130-131 E 5
Trogir 136-137 FG 4
Troglav 136-137 G 4
Tròia [I] 136-137 F 5
Troick [SU ↓ Čel'abinsk] 178-179 L 7
Troickoje [SU, Rossijskaja SFSR] 178-179 a 8
Troickoje [SU, Ukrainskaja SSR] 140-141 HJ 2
Troicko-Pečorsk 178-179 K 5
Troickosavsk = K'achta 178-179 U 7
Trois-Rivières 144-145 W 8
Trojan 136-137 L 4
Trojanski prohod 136-137 L 4
Trojekurovo [SU, Lipeck] 138-139 M 7
Troki = Trakai 138-139 E 6
Trolihättan 130-131 E 8
Trolltindan 130-131 B 6
Trombetas, Rio - 158-159 H 5
Trombudo Cental 160-161 H 7
Tromelin, Île - 168-169 M 6
Trompsburg 174-175 FG 6
Troms 130-131 G-J 3
Tromsø 130-131 H 3
Tron 130-131 D 6
Trona, CA 150-151 E 8
Tronador, Monte - 162 B 6
Trondheim 130-131 D 6
Trondheimfjord 130-131 CD 6
Tróodos 180-181 C 4
Tropic, UT 150-151 GH 7
Tropico del Capricorno 174 A-F 2
Troppau = Opava 133 H 4
Trosa 130-131 G 8
Trost'anec [SU, Sumy] 140-141 G 1
Trost'anec [SU, Vinnica] 140-141 D 2
Trotus 136-137 M 2
Troûmbá = Turumbah 182-183 J 4
Troup, TX 154-155 H 4
Trout Creek 150-151 D 4
Trout Creek, MT 150-151 EF 2
Trout Creek, UT 150-151 G 6
Trout Lake [CDN, Northwest Territories] 144-145 MN 5
Trout Lake [CDN, Ontario] 144-145 S 7
Trout Lake, MI 152-153 O 2
Trout Peak 152-153 B 3
Trouwers Island = Pulau Tinjil 186-187 E 8
Trowbridge 132 EF 6
Troy, AL 146-147 J 5
Troy, ID 150-151 E 2
Troy, KS 152-153 J 6
Troy, MO 152-153 L 6
Troy, MT 150-151 F 1
Troy, NC 148-149 D 7
Troy, OH 152-153 O 5
Troy, NY 146-147 M 3
Troy, OR 150-151 E 3
Troy, PA 148-149 E 4
Troyes 134-135 K 4
Trubčevsk 138-139 J 7
Trubetčino 138-139 M 7
Truckee, CA 150-151 CD 6
Truckee River 150-151 D 6
Trud [SU] 138-139 JK 5
Trudante = Tārūdānt 166-167 C 2
Trudfront 140-141 N 4
Trujillo [E] 134-135 DE 9
Trujillo [Honduras] 146-147 J 8
Trujillo [PE] 158-159 CD 6
Trujillo [YV] 158-159 EF 3
Trumann, AR 154-155 K 3
Trumbull, Mount - 150-151 G 7
Trung Bô 186-187 D 3-E 4
Trung Phân, Cao Nguyên - 186-187 E 4
Trung Phân, Plateau de - = Cao Nguyên Trung Phân 186-187 E 4
Truro 132 D 6
Truro [CDN] 144-145 Y 8
Truro, IA 152-153 K 5
Truscott, TX 154-155 F 4
Truskavec 140-141 A 2
Truth or Consequences, NM 154-155 B 4
Trutnov 133 GH 3
Truva 180-181 B 3
Truxilho = Trujillo 146-147 J 8
Trydent = Trento 136-137 D 2
Trynidad i Tobago 146-147 O 9-10
Tryon, NE 152-153 F 5
Trypolis = Ṭarābulus al-Gharb 166-167 GH2
Trypolitania = Ṭarābulus 166-167 GH2
Trysil 130-131 DE 7
Trysilelv 130-131 DE 7

U

'iedma 162 D 6
'iedma, Lago - 162 B 7
'ieille Castille = Castilla la Vieja 134-135 E 8-F 7
'iejo, Cerro - 150-151 G 10
'iena = Wien 133 H 4
'iena = Wien 128-129 M 6
ienna, GA 148-149 B 8
ienna, IL 152-153 M 7
ienna, MO 152-153 L 6
ienna, SD 152-153 H 3
'ienna, WV 148-149 C 5
'ienna = Wien 133 H 4
'ienne [F, ~] 134-135 H 5
ienne [F, ●] 134-135 K 6
ienne = Wien 133 H 4
'ientiane = Viangchan 186-187 D 3
'ientos, Los - 162 BC 2
'ientos, Paso de los - 146-147 M 7-8
ieques 146-147 N 8
ierfontein 174-175 G 4
ierges, Îles - 146-147 NO 8
ierwaldstätter See 133 D 5
ierzon 134-135 J 5
iesite 130-131 L 9
iesite 138-139 E 5
iesite 136-137 G 5
iêtnam 177 O 8
êtnam 177 O 8
iêtnam 177 O 8
ietname 186-187 D 2-E 4
iêt Tri 186-187 E 2
ievis 138-139 E 6
iew, TX 154-155 F 4
iga 138-139 O 4
igan 186-187 GH 3
igia 158-159 K 5
gia, El - 158-159 E 3
ignola 136-137 D 3
igo 134-135 C 7
ihren 136-137 K 5
iipuri = Vyborg 178-179 DE 5
iitasaari 130-131 LM 6
ijāpur = Bijapur 180-181 LM 7
ijayanagaram = Vizianagaram 180-181 NO 7
ijayawada 180-181 N 7
k 130-131 d 3
ka 130-131 M 4
iking 144-145 O 7
ikna 130-131 D 5
ikøyri 130-131 B 7
ila [SU] 138-139 O 6
ila Arriaga = Bibala 168-169 D 5
ila Artur de Paiva = Cubango 168-169 E 5
ila Bela da Santíssima Trindade 158-159 H 7-8
ila Cabral = Lichinga 168-169 J 5
ila Coutinho 168-169 H 5
ila da Maganja 168-169 J 6
ila de Aljustrel = Cangamba 168-169 E 5
la de Aviz = Oncócua 168-169 D 6
la de João Belo = Xai Xai 168-169 H 8
la de Manica = Manica 168-169 H 6
la de Sena 168-169 HJ 6
ila Fontes = Caia 168-169 J 6
ila Franca de Xira 134-135 C 9
la Gouveia = Catandica 168-169 H 6
la Henrique de Carvalho = Saurimo 168-169 F 4
laine 134-135 F 5
la João de Almeida = Chibia 168-169 D 6
illaller 134-135 H 7
ila Luisa 174-175 K 3
ila Macedo do Cavaleiros = Andulo 168-169 E 5
la Marechal Carmona = Uíge 168-169 E 4
la Mariano Machado = Ganda 168-169 D 5
ilanculos 168-169 J 7
iljāni 130-131 M 9
iljāni 138-139 F 5
la Norton de Matos = Balombo 168-169 D 5
la Nova do Seles 168-169 D 5
la Paiva Couceiro = Gambos 168-169 DE 5
la Pereira d'Eça = Ngiva 168-169 E 6
ila Pery = Manica 168-169 H 6
ila Real 134-135 D 8
la Real de Santo António 134-135 D 10
lar Formoso 134-135 D 8
las, SD 152-153 H 3
la Salazar = Ndalatando 168-169 DE 4
la Teixeira da Silva = Bailundo 168-169 E 5
ila Teixeira de Sousa = Luau 168-169 EF 5
ila Velha [BR, Espírito Santo] 158-159 LM 9
ila Viçosa 134-135 D 9
ilcabamba, Cordillera - 158-159 E 7
il'čeka, zemľa - 178-179 L-N 1
iled' 138-139 R 3
ilejka 138-139 F 6
il'gort 138-139 V 3
il'gort = Vyľgort [SU, Komi ASSR] 138-139 S 3
il'gort = Vyľgort [SU, Syktyvkar] 178-179 HJ 5
ilhelmina 130-131 G 5
ilhena 158-159 G 7
ilija 138-139 EF 6
iljandi 130-131 L 8
iljandi 138-139 E 4
iljoenskroon 174-175 G 4
ilkaviškis 138-139 D 6
il'kickogo, ostrov - [SU, Gydanskij p-ov] 178-179 NO 3
il'kickogo, ostrov - [SU, Novosibirskije o-va] 178-179 de 2
il'kickogo, proliv - 178-179 S-U 2
ilkija 138-139 D 6
ilkovo 140-141 D 4
illa Abecia 158-159 FG 9
lla Acuña 154-155 E 6
lla Acuña, GA 154-155 N 3
lla Ángela 162 D 3
lla Bella 158-159 F 7
llablino 134-135 D 7
llacañas 134-135 F 9
llacarillo 134-135 F 9
llach 133 F 5
llacidro 136-137 C 6
lla Cisneros = Ad-Dakhlah 166-167 A4
llada 134-135 E 7
lla de Cura 158-159 F 2-3
lla de María 162 D 3
Villa Dolores 162 C 4
Villa Federal = Federal 162 E 4
Villa Florida 160-161 D 7
Villa Franca [PY] 160-161 CD 7
Villafranca del Bierzo 134-135 D 7
Villafranca de los Barros 134-135 DE 9
Villafranca del Penedès 134-135 H 8
Villa Frontera 146-147 F 6
Villagarcía de Arosa 134-135 C 7
Villàgio Duca degli Abruzzi = Joowhar 168-169 L 2
Villa Grove, IL 152-153 MN 6
Villaguay 162 E 4
Villa Hayes 160-161 D 6
Villahermosa [MEX] 146-147 H 8
Villajoyosa 134-135 GH 9
Villaldama 154-155 E 7
Villa López 154-155 C 7
Villa Luiza = Vila Luisa 174-175 K 3
Villa María 162 D 4
Villa Matamoros 154-155 C 7
Villa Mazán 162 C 3
Villamil 158-159 A 5
Villa Montes 158-159 G 9
Villa Nora 174-175 GH 2
Villanova i la Geltrú 134-135 HJ 8
Villanueva, NM 154-155 C 3
Villanueva de Córdoba 134-135 E 9
Villanueva de la Serena 134-135 E 9
Villa Ocampo [MEX] 154-155 C 7
Villa Ocampo [RA] 162 DE 3
Villaodrid 134-135 D 7
Villa Ojo de Agua 162 D 3
Villa Olivia 160-161 D 6-7
Villa Rey 160-161 D 6
Villarreal de los Infantes 134-135 GH 9
Villarrica [PY] 162 E 3
Villa San Martín 162 D 3
Villa Unión [MEX, Coahuila] 154-155 E 6
Villa Unión [RA, La Rioja] 162 C 3
Villa Valeria 162 CD 4
Villavicencio [CO] 158-159 E 4
Villaviciosa 134-135 E 7
Villavieja de Yeltes 134-135 D 8
Villefranche-sur-Saône 134-135 K 5-6
Villena 134-135 G 9
Villeneuve-Saint-Georges 134-135 J 4
Villeneuve-sur-Lot 134-135 H 6
Ville Platte, LA 154-155 J 5
Villeurbanne 134-135 K 6
Villiers 174-175 H 4
Villiersdorp 174-175 C 7-8
Villingen-Schwenningen 133 D 4
Villisca, IA 152-153 J 5
Villmanstrand = Lappeenranta 130-131 N 7
Vilnius 130-131 L 10
Vilnius 138-139 E 6
Vilnjus = Vilnius 130-131 L 10
Vilos, Los - 162 B 4
Vilsandi 138-139 C 4
Vil'uj 178-179 W 5
Vil'ujsk 178-179 X 5
Villacañas 134-135 F 9
Vimmerby 130-131 FG 9
Vina, CA 150-151 BC 6
Viña, La - [PE] 158-159 D 6
Viña, La - [RA] 162 C 3
Viña del Mar 162 B 4
Vinalhaven, ME 148-149 J 2-3
Vinaroz 134-135 H 8
Vincennes, IN 146-147 J 4
Vincennes Bay 121 C 11
Vindelälven 130-131 H 5
Vindeln 130-131 HJ 5
Vindhya Range 180-181 L-N 6
Vineland, NJ 148-149 F 5
Vineyard Sound 148-149 H 4
Vinh = Xa-doai 186-187 E 3
Vinh Lo'i 186-187 E 5
Vinh Long 186-187 E 4
Vinho, Pais do - 134-135 CD 8
Vinita, OK 154-155 H 2
Vinje 130-131 B 8
Vinkekuil 174-175 D 7
Vinkovci 136-137 H 3
Vinnica = Vinnycja 140-141 D 2
Vinnycja 140-141 D 2
Vinnicy 138-139 K 3
Vinson, Mount - 121 B 28
Vinton, IA 152-153 KL 4
Vinton, LA 154-155 J 5
Vinton, VA 148-149 D 6
Viña, La - [PE] 158-159 D 6
Viña, La - [RA] 162 C 3
Viña del Mar 162 B 4
Viola, KS 152-153 H 7
Vioolsdrif 174-175 B 5
Vipya Mountains 171 C 5
Virac 186-187 H 4
Viradouro 160-161 HJ 4
Viramgam 180-181 L 6
Viramgaon = Viramgam 180-181 L 6
Virandozero 138-139 KL 1
Viranşehir 182-183 H 4
Virbalis 130-131 K 10
Virbalis 138-139 D 6
Virden, IL 152-153 M 6
Virden, NM 150-151 J 9
Vire 134-135 G 4
Virgem da Lapa 160-161 L 2
Vírgenes, Cabo - 162 C 8
Vírgenes, Islas - 146-147 NO 8
Virgenes, Ilhas - 146-147 NO 8
Virginia [USA] 146-147 KL 4
Virginia [ZA] 174-175 G 5
Virginia, IL 152-153 LM 6
Virginia, MN 146-147 H 2
Virginia Beach, VA 148-149 EF 6
Virginia City, MT 150-151 GH 3
Virginia City, NV 150-151 D 6
Virginia Mountains 150-151 D 6
Virgin Islands 146-147 NO 8
Virgin Mountains 150-151 FG 7
Virginópolis 160-161 L 3
Virgin River 150-151 FG 7
Virgin-sziaetek 146-147 NO 8
Virgolândia 160-161 LM 3
Virihaure 130-131 G 4
Virmond 160-161 FG 6
Viroqua, WI 152-153 L 4
Virovitica 136-137 G 3
Virtaniemi 130-131 MN 3
Virtsu 130-131 K 8
Virtsu 138-139 D 4
Virunga, Parc National - 168-169 G 2-3
Vis 136-137 G 4
Visagapatão = Vishākhapatnam 180-181 NO 7
Visakhapattanam = Vishakhapatnam 180-181 NO 7
Visalia, CA 150-151 D 7
Visayan Sea 186-187 H 4
Visby 130-131 GH 9
Visconde do Rio Branco 160-161 L 4
Viscount Melville Sound 144-145 O-Q 3
Višegrad 136-137 H 4
Višera [SU, ~ ◁ Kama] 138-139 V 3
Višera [SU, ~ ◁ Vyčegda] 138-139 S 2
Viševskij kanal 138-139 HJ 4
Viseu 134-135 D 8
Viseu [BR] 158-159 K 5
Vişeu-de-Sus 136-137 L 2
Vishākhapatnam = Vishakhapatnam 180-181 NO 7
Vishanpur = Bishenpur 180-181 P 6
Visim 138-139 V 4
Višnevec 140-141 B 2
Viso, Monte - 136-137 B 3
Visrivier 174-175 B 4
Vista Reservoir 150-151 F 5
Vistula = Wisła 138-139 D 8
Vistula = Wisła 133 K 3
Vistula = Wisła 138-139 C 8
Vistule = Wisła 133 K 3
Vit 136-137 L 4
Viterbo 136-137 DE 4
Vitias, Fossa de - [Fossa das Marianas] 192-193 F 3
Vitiaz Strait 186-187 N 8
Vitichi 158-159 F 9
Viti Levu 186-187 a 2
Vitim 178-179 V 6
Vitimskoje ploskogorje 178-179 V 7
Vitja, Fosa de - 184-185 S 3
Vitjaz, Abisso - [Fossa delle Curili] 184-185 S 3
Vitjaz, Abisso - [Fossa delle Marianne] 192-193 F 3
Vitjas, Abysse de - 184-185 S 3
Vitjaz Deep 184-185 S 3
Vitória [BR, Espírito Santo] 158-159 LM 9
Vitoria [E] 134-135 F 7
Vitória, Ilha da - 160-161 K 5
Vitória da Conquista 158-159 L 7
Vitoša Planina 136-137 K 4
Vitré 134-135 G 4
Vitry-le-François 134-135 K 4
Vitshumbi 171 B 3
Vittangi 130-131 JK 4
Vittòrio d'Africa = Shalanbod 168-169 KL 2
Vittòrio Vèneto 136-137 E 2
Vitu Islands 186-187 g 5
Vityaz-mélység [Iturup] 184-185 S 3
Vivarais, Monts du - 134-135 K 6
Vivario 136-137 C 4
Vivero 134-135 D 7
Vivi 178-179 S 4
Vivi, ozero - 178-179 R 4
Vivian, LA 154-155 HJ 4
Vivian, SD 152-153 F 4
Vivorata 162 E 5
Vivsta 130-131 G 6
Vižaj 138-139 VW 3
Vižajskij zavod = Krasnovišersk 178-179 K 5
Vizcachas, Meseta de las - 162 B 8
Vizcaíno, Sierra - 146-147 D 6
Vizcaya, Golfo de - 134-135 EF 6
Vizcayai-öböl 134-135 EF 6
Vize 182-183 B 2
Vize, ostrov - 178-179 O 2
Vizianagaram 180-181 NO 7
Vizinga 178-179 HJ 5
Vižnica 140-141 B 2
Vjatka = Kirov 178-179 HJ 6
Vjosë 136-137 HJ 5
Vlaanderen 134-135 J 3
Vladikavkaz 140-141 M 5
Vladimir 178-179 FG 6
Vladimir Iljič Lenina 138-139 Q 7
Vladimirovka [SU, Kazachskaja SSR] 140-141 P 1
Vladimirovka [SU, Rossijskaja SFSR Astrachan'] 140-141 MN 2
Vladimirovka [SU, Ukrainskaja SSR Doneck] 140-141 H 3
Vladimirovka [SU, Ukrainskaja SSR Nikolajevsk] 140-141 F 3
Vladimir-Volynskij 140-141 B 1
Vladislavovka 140-141 G 4
Vladivostok 178-179 Z 9
Vladyčnoje 138-139 M 4
Vlakfontein 174-175 F 4
Vlasenica 136-137 H 3
Vlasotince 136-137 K 4
Vleifontein 174-175 D 7
Vlissingen 134-135 J 3
Vlorë 136-137 H 5
Vltava 133 G 4
Vochma [SU, ~] 138-139 Q 4
Vochma [SU, ●] 138-139 Q 4
Vochtoga 138-139 N 4
Vodla 138-139 L 3
Vodlozero, ozero - 138-139 L 2
Vodnyj 138-139 T 2
Voëleiland 174-175 G 7
Vœune Sai 186-187 E 4
Vogelkop = Cenderawasih 186-187 K 7
Vogel Peak = Dimlang 172-173 HJ 3
Vogelsberg 133 D 3
Vogesen 134-135 L 4-5
Vogézek 134-135 L 4-5
Vogezen 134-135 L 4-5
Vogézy 134-135 L 4-5
Voghera 136-137 C 3
Vohémar = Vohimarina 168-169 M 5
Vohibinany 168-169 LM 6
Vohimarina 168-169 M 5
Vohipeno 168-169 L 7
Voi [EAK, ~] 171 D 3
Voi [EAK, ●] 168-169 J 3
Voinjama 166-167 BC 7
Voiron 134-135 K 6
Vojejkov šelfovyj lednik 121 C 12-13
Vojkovo 140-141 F 4
Vojvodina 136-137 HJ 3
Vojvož 138-139 U 2
Volborg, MT 152-153 D 3
Volcano Islands 177 RS 7
Volchov [SU, ~] 138-139 HJ 4
Volchov [SU, ●] 178-179 E 5-6
Volchovstroj = Volchov 178-179 E 5-6
Volčja 140-141 H 2
Volčki 138-139 N 7
Volda 130-131 B 6
Voľdino 138-139 U 2
Volga [SU, ~] 178-179 F 6
Volga [SU, ●] 138-139 M 5
Volga [SU, río] 178-179 F 6
Volga [SU, fiume] 178-179 F 6
Volgo-Baltijskij kanal 138-139 K 3-L 4
Volgodonsk 140-141 L 3
Volgo-Donskoj kanal 140-141 LM 2
Volgograd 140-141 LM 2
Volgogradskoje vodochranilišče 140-141 MN 1-2
Volgoverchovje 138-139 J 5
Volha = Volga 178-179 F 6
Volin, SD 152-153 DE 7
Volksrepublik China = China 184-185 E-K 5
Volksrust 174-175 H 5
Voľn'ach 140-141 FG 1
Volnovacha 140-141 H 3
Voloč'ok 138-139 NO 2
Voločanka 178-179 R 3
Volodarsk 138-139 O 5
Volodarsk-Volynskij 140-141 D 1
Vologda 178-179 FG 6
Vologino 140-141 P 1
Volokolamsk 138-139 KL 5
Volokonovka 140-141 HJ 1
Voloma 138-139 P 3
Vološka [SU, ~] 138-139 M 3
Vološka [SU, ●] 138-139 MN 3
Volosovo 130-131 N 8
Volosovo 138-139 G 4
Volosskaja Balakleja 140-141 JK 2
Volot 138-139 H 5
Volovec 140-141 A 2
Volovo 138-139 LM 7
Voložin 138-139 F 6
Voľsk 178-179 H 7
Volta [GH] 166-167 E 7
Volta, Lake - 166-167 DE 7
Volta Grande 160-161 L 4
Volta Grande, Represa de - 160-161 HJ 3-4
Volta Noire 166-167 D 6
Volta Redonda 160-161 KL 5
Voltera 136-137 D 4
Voltti 130-131 K 6
Volturino, Monte - 136-137 F 5
Volturno 136-137 F 5
Volubilis 166-167 C 2
Volynskaja Oblast' 138-139 DE 8
Volynskaja vozvyšennosť 140-141 BC 1
Volžsk 178-179 H 6
Volžskij 140-141 M 2
Võma 138-139 D 4
Vona = Perşembe 182-183 G 2
Vonguda 138-139 M 2
Von Martius, Salto - 158-159 J 7
von Otterøya 130-131 15
Voor-Indië 124-125 NO 4
Vop' 138-139 J 6
Vopnafjördhur [IS, ◡] 130-131 fg 2
Vopnafjördhur[IS, ●] 130-131 F 2
Vorarlberg 133 DE 5
Vorderindien 124-125 NO 4
Vorderrhein 133 D 5
Vordingborg 130-131 D 10
Vorenža 138-139 K 2
Vorga 138-139 J 7
Vorjapauľ 178-179 L 5
Vorkuta 178-179 L 4
Vormsi 138-139 D 4
Vormsi 130-131 K 8
Vorochta 140-141 B 2
Vorogovo 178-179 QR 5
Vorona 138-139 O 7
Voroncovo [SU, Dudinka] 178-179 PQ 3
Voroncovo [SU, Pskov] 138-139 G 5
Voronež [SU, Ukrainskaja SSR] 138-139 J 8
Voronež [SU, Rossijskaja SFSR ~] 138-139 MN 7
Voronež [SU, Rossijskaja SFSR ●] 138-139 M 8
Voronežskij zapovednik 138-139 MN 8
Voronino 138-139 P 4
Voronje [SU, Vjatka] 138-139 ST 4
Voronok 138-139 J 7
Voronovo 138-139 E 6
Voropajevo 138-139 F 6
Vorošilov = Ussurijsk 178-179 Z 9
Vorošilovgrad = Lugansk 140-141 JK 2
Voroťkovo 140-141 D 1
Vorožba 140-141 FG 1
Vorskla 140-141 G 2
Vörtsjärv 130-131 LM 8
Vörtsjärv 138-139 E 4
Võru 130-131 M 9
Võru 138-139 F 5
Vorzeľ 140-141 E 1
Vosburg 174-175 E 6
Vosges 134-135 L 4-5
Vosgi 134-135 L 4-5
Vosgos 134-135 L 4-5
Vosgos 133 C 4-5
Voskresensk 138-139 LM 6
Voskresenskoje [SU, Vologda ↑ Čerepovec] 138-139 LM 4
Voss 130-131 B 7
Vostočnyje Karpaty 140-141 AB 2-3
Vostočnyj Sajan 178-179 R 6-T 7
Vostok [Antarktika] 121 B 11
Vostok [○] 198-199 K 5
Vostychoj = Jegyrjach 178-179 M 5
Votice 133 G 4
Votkinsk 178-179 J 6
Votkinskoje vodochranilišče 178-179 JK 6
Votuporanga 160-161 H 4
Vouga 134-135 C 8
Vouonkoro Rapides 172-173 E 3
Vožajeľ 138-139 S 2
Voža'ol 138-139 RS 2
Vože, ozero - 138-139 M 3
Vožega 138-139 N 3
Vožgaly 138-139 S 4
Voznesenje 138-139 KL 3
Voznesensk 140-141 E 3
Voznesensk-Ivanovo= Ivanovo 178-179 FG 6
Voznesenskoje 138-139 O 6
Vozroždenija, ostrov 178-179 KL 9
Vozvraščenija, gora - 178-179 b 8
Vörös-tenger 180-181 D 5-E 7
Vrachos 136-137 K 4
Vradijevka 140-141 E 3
Vrangeľa, ostrov - 178-179 hj 3
Vranje 136-137 J 4
Vratislav = Wrocław 133 H 3
Vrbas [YU, ~] 136-137 G 3
Vrbas [YU, ●] 136-137 H 3
Vrede 174-175 H 4
Vredefort 174-175 G 4
Vredenburg 174-175 B 7
Vreed-en-Hoop 158-159 H 3
Vršac 136-137 J 3
Vryburg 168-169 F 8
Vryheid 168-169 H 8
Vschody 138-139 JK 6
Vsetín 133 J 4
Vukovar 136-137 H 3
Vulcano, Ìsola - 136-137 F 6
Vulture, Monte - 136-137 F 5
Vuotso 130-131 M 3
Vuria 171 D 3
Vurnary 138-139 Q 6
Vuurland 162 C 8
Vyborg 178-179 DE 5
Vyčegda 178-179 J 5
Vyčegodskij 138-139 Q 3
Východní novozemský příkop 178-179 K 3-L 2
Východočínské moře 184-185 N 6-O 5
Východofríské o-vy 130-131 B 11
Východofríské o-vy 133 C 2
Východosibiřské moře 178-179 d-h 3
Vyg 138-139 K 2
Vygoda 140-141 AB 2
Vygozero, ozero - 138-139 K 2
Vyksa 178-179 G 6
Vyľgort 178-179 HJ 5
Vym'138-139 S 2
Vypolzovo 138-139 J 5
Vyrica 138-139 H 4
Vyša 138-139 O 7
Vyšnij Voloč'ok 178-179 EF 6
Vysock 138-139 G 3
Vysokaja, gora - 178-179 a 8
Vysokogornyj 178-179 ab 7
Vysokoje [SU, Belorusskaja SSR] 138-139 D 7
Vysokoje [SU, Rossijskaja SFSR Tver'] 138-139 K 5
Vysokovsk 138-139 KL 5
Vysoký Atlas 166-167 CD 2
Vytegra 178-179 F 5

W

W, Parcs nationaux du - 166-167 E6
Wa 166-167 D 6
Waajid 166-167 a 3
Waal 134-135 K 3
Waar, Meos - 186-187 KL 7
Wabag 186-187 M 8
Wabana 144-145 a 8
Wabasca River 144-145 NO 6
Wabash, IN 152-153 O 5
Wabasha, MN 152-153 K 3
Wabash River 146-147 J 3
Wabasso, MN 152-153 J 3
Wabeno, WI 152-153 M 3
Wabu Hu 190-191 F 5
Wabuska, NV 150-151 D 6
Waccamaw, Lake - 148-149 D 7
Waccasassa Bay 148-149 b 2
Wachan = Wākhān 180-181 L 3
Waco, TX 146-147 G 5
Wād, Al- 166-167 F 2
Wadah, Al- 170 F 6
Wād an-Nayl 166-167 L 6
Wadayama 188-189 K 5
Wād Bandah 166-167 K 6
Waddān 166-167 H 3
Waddington, Mount - 144-145 LM 7
Wadena, MN 152-153 J 2
Wadesboro, NC 148-149 C 7
Wād Hāmid 166-167 L 5
Wadhwān 180-181 L 6
Wādī, Bi'r al - 182-183 K 6
Wādī Halfā 166-167 L 4
Wādī Jimāl, Jazirat - 170 F 5
Wādī Zam 166-167 C 2
Wadley, GA 148-149 B 8
Wād Madanī 166-167 L 6
Wadsworth, NV 150-151 D 6
Waegwan 188-189 G 4-5
Waelder, TX 154-155 G 6
Wa-fang-tien = Fu Xian 184-185 N 4
Wagal-bong = Maengbu-san 188-189 F 2
Wageningen [SME] 158-159 H 3
Wager Bay 144-145 T 4
Wagga Wagga 194-195 J 7
Wagin 194-195 C 6
Wagina 186-187 j 6
Wagner, SD 152-153 G 4
Wagoner, OK 154-155 H 3
Wagon Mound, NM 154-155 C 2
Wagontire, OR 150-151 D 4
Wągrowiec 133 H 2
Wāhah 166-167 H 3
Wahai 186-187 J 7
Wahlbergøya 130-131 k 5
Wahlenbergfjord 130-131 kl 5
Wahoo, NE 152-153 H 5
Wahpeton, ND 152-153 H 2
Wahrān 166-167 D 1
Wah Wah Mountains 150-151 G 6
Waidhofen an der Thaya 133 G 4
Waidhofen an der Ybbs 133 G 5
Waifang Shan 190-191 C 5-D 4
Waigama 186-187 JK 7
Waigeo, Pulau - 186-187 K 6
Waikabubak 186-187 G 8
Waikerie 194-195 GH 6
Waimate 194-195 O 8
Wainganga 180-181 MN 6-7
Waingapu 186-187 GH 8
Waini Point 158-159 H 3
Wainwright, AK 144-145 DE 3
Wairoa 194-195 P 7
Waitaki River 194-195 O 8
Waitara 194-195 OP 7
Waitsap = Huaiji 184-185 L 7
Waitsburg, WA 150-151 D 2
Waitzen = Vác 133 J 5
Waiyeung = Huiyang 184-185 LM 7
Wajh, Al- 180-181 D 5
Wajima 188-189 L 4
Wak, El - 168-169 K 2
Waka 168-169 F 3
Wakamatsu = Aizu-Wakamatsu 188-189 M 4
Wakamatsu-shima 188-189 G 6
Wakasa 188-189 K 5
Wakasa-wan 188-189 K 5
Wakayama 184-185 Q 5
Wake [HV] 172-173 F 3
Wake [○] 198-199 H 4
Wa Keeney, KS 152-153 G 6
Wakefield, KS 152-153 H 6
Wakefield, MI 152-153 M 2
Wakefield, NE 152-153 H 4
Wake Forest, NC 148-149 D 7
Wakeham = Maricourt 144-145 W 5
Wākhān 180-181 L 3
Wākhjir, Kotāle - 180-181 LM 3
Wakinosawa 188-189 N 2
Wakkanai 184-185 R 2
Wakkerstroom 174-175 J 4
Wakool 196 G 5
Wākṣa = Wāqiṣah 182-183 K 7
Wakunai 186-187 j 6
Walachei 136-137 LM 3
Walachije 136-137 LM 3
Wa'lan 166-167 E 4
Walapai, AZ 150-151 G 8
Walātah 166-167 C 5
Wałbrzych 133 H 3
Walcha 196 KL 3
Walcheren 134-135 J 3
Walcott, ND 152-153 H 2
Walcott, WY 152-153 C 5
Wałcz 133 H 2
Waldajhöhen = Valdajskaja vozvyšennost 138-139 H-K 5
Walden, CO 152-153 CD 5
Waldenburg (Schlesien) = Wałbrzych 133 H 3
Walden Ridge 154-155 N 3
Waldo, AR 154-155 J 4
Waldo, FL 148-149 bc 2
Waldport, OR 150-151 A 3
Waldron, AR 154-155 HJ 3
Walencja = Valencia 134-135 H 9
Wales 132 E 5-6
Wales, AK 144-145 C 4
Wales, MN 152-153 L 2
Wales Island 144-145 T 4
Walfischbucht 168-169 D 7
Walfischbucht [ZA, ◡] 174-175 A 2
Walfischrücken 124-125 K 7
Walgett 194-195 J 6
Walgreen Coast 121 B 26
Walhalla, MI 152-153 NO 3-4
Walhalla, ND 152-153 H 1
Walhalla, SC 148-149 B 7
Walia = Wales 132 E 5-6
Waligiro 171 DE 3
Walikale 168-169 G 3
Walk = Valga 138-139 F 5
Walk = Valka 138-139 EF 5
Walker, MN 152-153 J 2
Walker, SD 152-153 F 3
Walkerbaai 174-175 C 8
Walker Bay = Walkerbaai 174-175 C 8
Walker Lake [USA] 146-147 C 4
Walker Mountain 148-149 C 6
Walker Mountains 121 B 126-127
Walker River Indian Reservation 150-151 D 6
Walkerton 148-149 C 2
Walkerton, IN 152-153 N 5
Walkerville, MT 150-151 G 2
Walkite = Welkītē 166-167 M 7
Wall, SD 152-153 E 3-4
Wallace 148-149 DE 2
Wallace, ID 150-151 EF 2
Wallace, MI 152-153 N 3
Wallace, NC 148-149 DE 7
Wallace, NE 152-153 F 5
Wallaceburg 152-153 P 4
Wallal Downs 194-195 D 3-4
Wallangarra 196 KL 2
Wallaroo 194-195 G 6
Wallasey 132 E 5
Walla Walla, WA 146-147 C 2
Wallekraal 174-175 B 6
Wallel = Tulu Welēl 166-167 LM 7
Walili, Sha'ib al- 182-183 H 6
Wallingford, CT 148-149 G 4
Wallis, TX 154-155 G 6
Wallis = Valais 133 D 5
Wallis, Îles - 186-187 b 1
Wall Lake, IA 152-153 J 4
Wallowa, OR 150-151 E 3
Wallowa Mountains 150-151 E 3
Wallowa River 150-151 E 3
Wallula, WA 150-151 D 2
Walmer 174-175 F 7
Walney 132 E 4
Walnut, IL 152-153 M 5
Walnut, KS 152-153 J 7
Walnut, MS 154-155 L 3
Walnut Canyon National Monument 150-151 H 8
Walnut Cove, NC 148-149 C 6
Walnut Creek 152-153 F 6
Walnut Grove, MO 152-153 K 7
Walnut Grove, MS 154-155 L 4
Walnut Ridge, AR 154-155 K 2
Walpole 194-195 NO 4
Walpole, NH 148-149 G 3
Walsall 132 F 5
Walsenburg, CO 152-153 D 7
Walsh, CO 152-153 E 7
Walterboro, SC 148-149 C 8
Walter F. G. Reservation 154-155 N 5
Walters, OK 154-155 F 3
Walthill, NE 152-153 H 4
Waltman, WY 152-153 C 4
Walton, IN 152-153 N 5
Walton, KY 152-153 O 6
Walton, NY 148-149 F 3
Walvisbaai, Dorsale de - 124-125 K 7
Walvis Bay [ZA, ◡] 174-175 A 2
Walvis Bay [ZA, ●] 168-169 D 7
Walvis Ridge 124-125 K 7
Walvisrug 124-125 K 7
Wamanfo 172-173 E 4
Wamba [EAK] 171 D 2
Wamba [WAN] 166-167 F 7
Wamba [ZRE, Bandundu] 168-169 E 4
Wamba [ZRE, Haut-Zaïre] 168-169 G 2
Wamego, KS 152-153 H 6
Wamlana 186-187 J 7
Wanaaring 194-195 H 5
Wān Ahjār, Tās?11 - 166-167 F 3
Wān al-Hajjār, Tāsīlī - = Murtaf'āt Tāsīlī 166-167 E 5-F 4
Wan'an 190-191 E 8
Wanapiri 186-187 L 7
Wanchuan = Zhangjiakou 184-185 L 3
Wanda 160-161 E 7
Wanda Shan 184-185 P X
Wanderama 172-173 DE 3
Wan-do 188-189 F 5
Wandoan 194-195 JK 5
Wanfu 188-189 D 2
Wanfu He 190-191 F 4
Wanganella 196 G 5
Wanganui 194-195 OP 7
Wangaratta 194-195 J 7
Wangary 196 B 5
Wangasi Turu 172-173 E 3
Wang-chia-ch'ang = Wangjiachang 190-191 C 7
Wang-chiang = Wangjiang 190-191 F 6
Wangdu 190-191 E 2
Wangi 171 E 3
Wangjiachang 190-191 C 7
Wangjiang 190-191 F 6
Wangkiang = Wangjiang 190-191 F 6
Wangmudu 190-191 E 9
Wangpang Yang 184-185 N 5
Wangpan Yang 190-191 H 6
Wangtu = Wangdu 190-191 E 2
Wangyemiao = Ulan Hot 184-185 N 2
Wanhsien = Wan Xian = Wan Xian [TJ, Hebei] 190-191 E 2
Wanhsien = Wan Xian [TJ, Sichuan] 184-185 K 5
Wankie = Hwange 168-169 G 6
Wanlaweyn 166-167 NO 8
Wannian 190-191 F 7
Wanning 184-185 L 8
Wanshan Liehtao = Wanshan Qundao 190-191 DE 11
Wanshan Qundao 190-191 DE 11
Wantan 190-191 C 6
Wan-ta Shan-mo = Wanda Shan 184-185 P 2
Wantsai = Wanzai 184-185 LM 6
Wan Xian [TJ, Hebei] 190-191 E 2
Wan Xian [TJ, Sichuan] 190-191 B 6
Wanyuan 190-191 B 5
Wanzai 184-185 LM 6
Wanzhi 190-191 G 6
Wapakoneta, OH 152-153 OP 5
Wapanucka, OK 154-155 G 3
Wapato, WA 150-151 C 2
Wapello, IA 152-153 L 5
Wapiti, WY 152-153 B 3
Wapsipinicon River 152-153 L 5
Wa-pu He = Wabu Hu 190-191 F 5
Waqbá, Al- 182-183 L 8
Waqf,Al- 62 E 4
Wāqif, Jabal al- 170 D 6
Wāqiṣah 182-183 K 7
Waqooyi-Galbeed = Wquooyi-Galbeed 166-167 a 1
War, WV 148-149 C 6
Warab 166-167 K 7
Warān 166-167 BC 4
Warangal 180-181 MN 7
Waratah 196 b 2
Waratah Bay 196 GH 7
Warba, MN 152-153 K 2
Warburton 196 G 6
Warburton, The - 194-195 G 5
Warburton Aboriginal Reserve = Central Australia Aboriginal Reserve 194-195 E 4-5
Wardān, Wādī - 170 E 3
Warden 174-175 H 4
Warden, WA 150-151 D 2
Wardere = Werdēr 166-167 O 7
Wardha [IND, ~] 180-181 M 6
Wardha [IND, ●] 180-181 M 6
Ward Hunt, Cape - 186-187 N 8
Ware 144-145 LM 6
Ware, MA 148-149 GH 3
Waren 133 F 2
Waren [RI] 186-187 L 7
Wari'ah, Al- 180-181 F 5
Warialda 194-195 K 5
Warin Chamrap 186-187 DE 3
Warjalah 166-167 F 2
Warklany = Varakļāni 138-139 F 5
Warland, MT 150-151 F 1
Warmbad [ZA] 168-169 G 7-8
Warmbad [Namibia, ●] 168-169 E 8
Warmbad [Namibia, ☆] 174-175 BC 5
Warmsprings, MT 150-151 G 2
Warm Springs, OR 150-151 C 3
Warm Springs, NV [USA ↓ Cherry Creek] 150-151 F 6
Warm Springs, NV [USA → Tonopah] 150-151 EF 6
Warm Springs Indian Reservation 150-151 C 3
Warm Springs Valley 150-151 C 5
Warna = Varna 136-137 MN 4
Warnemünde, Rostock- 133 F 1
Warner, SD 152-153 G 3
Warner Range 146-147 B 3
Warner Robins, GA 146-147 K 5
Warner Valley 150-151 CD 4
Warnes [BOL] 158-159 G 8
Warnpko 186-187 LM 8
Warqlā = Warjalah 166-167 F 2
Wārqzīz, Jabal - 166-167 C 3
Warra 194-195 K 5
Warracknabeal 196 F 6
Warragul 196 G 7
Warrego River 194-195 J 5
Warren [AUS] 196 HJ 3
Warren, AR 154-155 JK 4
Warren, AZ 150-151 J 10
Warren, ID 150-151 F 3
Warren, IL 152-153 LM 4
Warren, IN 152-153 O 5
Warren, MI 152-153 P 4
Warren, MN 152-153 H 1
Warren, OH 146-147 K 3
Warren, PA 148-149 D 4
Warren, TX 154-155 H 5
Warrensburg, MO 152-153 JK 6
Warrenton 168-169 FG 8
Warrenton, GA 148-149 B 8
Warrenton, MO 152-153 L 6
Warrenton, NC 148-149 DE 6
Warrenton, OR 150-151 AB 2
Warrenton, VA 148-149 E 5
Warri 166-167 F 7
Warriner Creek 196 BC 2
Warrington, FL 154-155 M 5
Warrior, AL 154-155 M 4
Warrnambool 194-195 H 7
Warroad, MN 152-153 J 1
Warsaw, IL 152-153 L 5
Warsaw, IN 152-153 O 5
Warsaw, KY 152-153 O 6
Warsaw, MO 152-153 K 6
Warsaw, NC 148-149 DE 7
Warsaw, NY 148-149 DE 3
Warsaw = Warszawa 133 K 2
Warschau = Warszawa 133 KL 2
Warszawa 133 K 2
Warta 133 HJ 2
Wartrace, TN 154-155 M 3
Warwick 132 EF 5
Warwick [AUS] 194-195 K 5
Warwick, GA 154-155 NO 5
Warwick, RI 148-149 H 4
Wasatch, UT 150-151 H 5
Wasatch Range 146-147 D 3-4
Wasbank 174-175 J 5
Waschbank = Wasbank 174-175 J 5
Wasco, CA 150-151 D 8
Wasco, OR 150-151 C 3
Wase, River - 172-173 H 3
Waseca, MN 152-153 K 3
Wash, The - 132 G 5
Washago 148-149 D 2
Washakie Needles 152-153 B 4
Washburn, ND 152-153 F 2
Washburn, TX 154-155 E 3
Washburn, WI 152-153 L 2
Washburn Lake 144-145 PQ 3
Washington [USA] 146-147 BC 2
Washington, AR 154-155 HJ 4
Washington, DC 146-147 LM 4
Washington, GA 148-149 B 8
Washington, IA 152-153 KL 5
Washington, IN 152-153 N 6
Washington, KS 152-153 H 6
Washington, MO 152-153 L 6
Washington, NC 148-149 E 7
Washington, OH 152-153 P 6
Washington, PA 148-149 C 4
Washington, Mount - 146-147 M 3
Washington Island 152-153 N 3
Washita River 146-147 G 4-5
Washm, Al- 180-181 EF 5-6
Wash Shahrī 184-185 F 4
Wasior 186-187 KL 7
Wasipe 172-173 E 3
Wāsit 182-183 L 6
Wāsiṭah, Al- 166-167 L 3
Waskish, MN 152-153 J 1
Waskom, TX 154-155 H 4
Wassadougou 172-173 D 2
Wassamu 188-189 c 1-2
Wasser 174-175 C 4
Wassou 172-173 B 3
Wassuk Range 150-151 D 6
Wasta, SD 152-153 E 3
Wasum 186-187 g 6
Watampone 186-187 GH 7
Watansopeng 186-187 G 7
Waterberg 168-169 E 7
Waterberge 174-175 GH 3
Waterbury, CT 148-149 G 4
Wateree River 148-149 C 7
Waterford 132 C 5
Waterford [CDN] 148-149
Waterford [ZA] 174-175 F 7
Waterford, CA 150-151 C 7
Waterkloof 174-175 F 6
Waterloo [AUS] 194-195 EF 3
Waterloo [B] 134-135 K 3
Waterloo [CDN, Ontario] 148-149 C 3
Waterloo [WAL] 172-173 B 3
Waterloo, IA 146-147 H 3
Waterloo, IL 152-153 LM 6
Waterloo, MT 150-151 G 3
Waterloo, NY 148-149 E 3
Waterpoort 174-175 H 2
Waterproof, LA 154-155 K 5
Waters, MI 152-153 O 3
Watersmeet, MI 152-153 M 2
Watertown, NY 146-147 LM 3
Watertown, SD 146-147 G 2
Watertown, WI 152-153 M 4
Waterval-Boven 174-175 J 3
Water Valley, MS 154-155 L 3
Water Valley, TX 154-155 E 5
Waterval-Onder 174-175 J 3
Waterville, KS 152-153 H 6
Waterville, ME 146-147 N 3
Waterville, MN 152-153 K 3
Waterville, WA 150-151 CD 2
Waterways 144-145 OP 6
Watford City, ND 152-153 E 2
Watkins Glen, NY 148-149 E 3
Watkinsville, GA 148-149 B 8
Watlam = Yulin 184-185 L 7
Watling Island = San Salvador 146-147 M 7
Watonga, OK 154-155 F 3
Watrous, NM 154-155 C 3
Watsa 168-169 G 2
Watseka, IL 152-153 N 5
Watson, AR 154-155 K 4
Watson, UT 150-151 J 6
Watson Lake 144-145 L 5
Watsonville, CA 150-151 BC 7
Watt, Point - 194-195 E 5
Watts Bar Lake 154-155 N 3
Watubela, Kepulauan - 186-187 K 7
Watykan 136-137 DE 5
Wau 186-187 N 8
Waubay, SD 152-153 H 3
Wauchope 196 L 3
Wauchula, FL 148-149 bc 3
Wau el Kebir = Wāw al-Kabīr 166-167 H3
Waukarlycarly, Lake - 194-195 D 4
Waukeenah, FL 148-149 ab 1
Waukegan, IL 152-153 N 4
Waukesha, WI 152-153 M 4
Waukon, IA 152-153 L 4
Wauneta, NE 152-153 F 5
Waupaca, WI 152-153 M 3
Waupun, WI 152-153 M 4
Waurika, OK 154-155 G 3
Wausa, NE 152-153 H 4
Wausau, WI 146-147 J 2-3
Wausaukee, WI 152-153 MN 3
Wauseon, OH 152-153 OP 5
Wautoma, WI 152-153 M 3
Wauwatosa, WI 152-153 M 4
Wave Hill 194-195 F 3
Waverley 174-175 G 6
Waverly, IA 152-153 K 4
Waverly, NY 148-149 E 3
Waverly, OH 152-153 P 6
Waverly, SD 152-153 H 3
Waverly, TN 154-155 M 2
Waverly, VA 148-149 E 6
Waverly Hall, GA 154-155 N 4
Wāw [Sudan] 166-167 K 7
Waxahatchie, TX 154-155 G 4
Waxell Ridge 144-145 H 5
Way, Lake - 194-195 D 5
Wayan, ID 150-151 H 4
Waycross, GA 146-147 K 5
Wayland, KY 148-149 B 6
Wayland, MI 152-153 O 4
Wayne, NE 152-153 H 4
Wayne, WV 148-149 B 5
Waynesboro, GA 148-149 BC 8
Waynesboro, MS 154-155 L 5
Waynesboro, PA 148-149 E 5
Waynesboro, TN 154-155 M 3
Waynesboro, VA 148-149 D 5
Waynesburg, PA 148-149 CD 5
Waynesville, MO 152-153 KL 7
Waynesville, NC 148-149 B 7
Waynoka, OK 154-155 F 2
Wayside, TX 154-155 E 3
Waza 166-167 G 6
Wāzakhwā 180-181 K 4
Wāzīrābād = Balkh 180-181 K 3
Wazz, Al- 166-167 L 5
Wazzān 166-167 C 2
We, Pulau - 186-187 BC 5
Weatherford, OK 154-155 F 3
Weatherford, TX 154-155 G 4
Weaubleau, MO 152-153 K 7
Weaverville, CA 150-151 B 5
Webb, TX 154-155 F 7
Webbe Shibeli = Wābī Shebelē 166-167 N 7
Webster, MA 148-149 GH 3
Webster, SD 152-153 H 3
Webster City, IA 152-153 K 4
Webster Reservoir 152-153 G 6
Webster Springs, WV 148-149 C 5
Weda 186-187 J 6
Weddell, Mar de - = Weddell Sea 120 BC 132-34
Weddell, Mer de - = Weddell Sea 121 BC 132-34
Weddella, Morze - = Weddell Sea 121 BC 132-34
Weddell Island 162 D 8
Weddellmeer = Weddell Sea 121 BC 132-34
Weddellovo moře = Weddell Sea 121 BC 132-34
Weddell Sea 121 BC 132-34
Weddell-tenger = Weddell Sea 121 BC 132-34
Weddellzee = Weddell Sea 121 BC 132-34
Weddell, Mar de - = Weddell Sea 121 BC 132-34
Wedel Jarlsberg land 130-131 j 6
Wedowee, AL 154-155 N 4
Weed, CA 150-151 B 5
Weedon Centre 148-149 H 2
Weedville, PA 148-149 D 4
Weeks, LA 154-155 K 6
Weeksbury, KY 148-149 B 6

Weenen 174-175 J 5
Weenusk = Winisk 144-145 T 6
Weeping Water, NE 152-153 HJ 5
Wee Waa 194-195 J 6
Wegener-Inlandeis 121 B 36-1
Węgry 133 H-K 5
Wehlau = Znamensk 133 K 1
Weichang 184-185 M 3
Weichou Tao = Weizhou Dao 190-191 B 11
Weichsel = Wisła 133 K 3
Weiden 133 EF 4
Weifang 184-185 MN 4
Weihai 184-185 N 4
Wei He [TJ ◁ Hai He] 184-185 M 4
Wei He [TJ ◁ Huang He] 184-185 K 5
Wei He [TJ ◁ Laizhou Wan] 190-191 G 3
Weihnachtsinsel = Christmas Island 186-187 E 9
Wei Ho = Wei He [TJ ◁ Hai He] 190-191 F 2
Wei Ho = Wei He [TJ ◁ Laizhou Wan] 190-191 G 3
Weihsien = Wei Xian 190-191 E 3
Wei-hsien = Yu Xian 190-191 E 2
Weilmoringle 196 H 2
Weimar 133 E 3
Weimar, TX 154-155 G 6
Weinan 190-191 B 4
Weiner, AR 154-155 K 3
Weining 184-185 JK 6
Weipa 194-195 H 2
Weirton, WV 148-149 C 4
Weisburd 160-161 A 7
Weiser, ID 150-151 E 3
Weiser River 150-151 E 3
Weishan Hu 190-191 F 4
Weishi 190-191 E 4
Weißbrunn = Veszprem 133 HJ 5
Weiße Berge = Witberge 174-175 G 6
Weiße Elster 133 F 3
Weißenbrunn = Witputs 174-175 B 4
Weißenfels 133 E 3
Weißenstein = Paide 138-139 E 4
Weißer Umfolosi = Wit Umfolozi 174-175 J 5
Weißer Volta = White Volta 166-167 D7
Weißes Meer 178-179 FG 4
Weißkirchen = Bela Crkva 136-137 J 3
Weiss Knob 148-149 D 5
Weißrandgebirge = Witrandberge 174-175 C 3
Weissrand Mountains = Witrandberge 174-175 C 3
Weißrußland 138-139 E-H 6-7
Wei Xian [TJ, Hebei] 190-191 E 3
Wei Xian [TJ, Shandong] 190-191 G 3
Weiyang = Huiyang 184-185 LM 7
Weizhou Dao 190-191 B 11
Wejh = Al-Wajh 180-181 D 5
Welbourn Hill 194-195 F 5
Welch, TX 154-155 DE 4
Welch, WV 148-149 C 6
Weldon, NC 148-149 E 6
Weldona, CO 152-153 E 5
Weldon River 152-153 K 5
Weldya 166-167 M 6
Weleetka, OK 154-155 GH 3
Welel, Tulu - 166-167 LM 7
Weleny = Viļani 138-139 F 5
Welgeleë 174-175 G 5
Welikije Luki = Velikije Luki 138-139 H 5
Welķītē 166-167 M 7
Welkom 168-169 G 8
Welland [CDN] 148-149 D 3
Welland Canal 148-149 D 3
Wellesley Islands 194-195 GH 3
Wellington [AUS] 194-195 JK 6
Wellington [CDN] 148-149 E 3
Wellington [NZ] 194-195 OP 8
Wellington [ZA] 174-175 C 7
Wellington, CO 152-153 D 5
Wellington, KS 154-155 G 2
Wellington, NV 150-151 D 6
Wellington, OH 148-149 B 4
Wellington, TX 154-155 E 3
Wellington, Isla - 162 AB 7
Wellington Channel 144-145 S 2-3
Wellman, IA 152-153 L 5
Wellman, TX 154-155 D 4
Wells, MN 152-153 K 4
Wells, NE 152-153 F 4
Wells, NV 146-147 C 3
Wells, TX 154-155 H 5
Wells, Lake - 194-195 D 5
Wellsboro, PA 148-149 E 4
Wellsford 194-195 OP 7
Wells Gray Provincial Park 144-145 MN 7
Wells next the Sea 132 G 5
Wellston, OH 148-149 B 5
Wellsville, KS 152-153 J 6
Wellsville, MO 152-153 L 6
Wellsville, NY 148-149 E 3
Wellton, AZ 150-151 FG 9
Wels 133 FG 4
Welshpool 132 E 5
Wembere 168-169 H 3-4
Wen'an 190-191 F 2
Wenatchee, WA 146-147 BC 2
Wenatchee Mountains 150-151 C 2
Wenchi 172-173 E 4
Wên-chou Wan = Wenzhou Wan 190-191 H 8
Wenchow = Wenzhou 184-185 N 6
Wendel, CA 150-151 CD 5
Wendell, ID 150-151 F 4
Wendell, NC 148-149 D 7
Wenden, AZ 150-151 G 9
Wenden = Cēsis 138-139 E 5
Wendeng 190-191 J 3
Wendling, OR 150-151 B 3
Wendover, UT 150-151 FG 5
Wendover, WY 152-153 D 4
Wendte, SD 152-153 F 3
Wenecja = Venècia 136-137 E 3
Wenen = Wien 133 H 4
Wenezuela 158-159 FG 3
Wengyuan 190-191 DE 9
Wen He 190-191 G 4
Wên-hsi = Wenxi 190-191 C 4
Wenling 190-191 H 7
Wenquan 190-191 B 6
Wenshan 184-185 JK 7
Wenshang 190-191 F 4
Wenshan Zhuangzu Miaozu Zizhizhou 184-185 JK 7
Wenshi 190-191 C 9
Wên-shih = Wenshi 190-191 C 9
Wenshui 190-191 CD 3
Wên-su = Aqsu 184-185 E 3
Wenteng = Wendeng 190-191 J 3
Wentspils = Ventspils 138-139 C 5
Wentworth 194-195 H 6
Wentworth, SD 152-153 H 3-4
Wentzville, MO 152-153 L 6
Wenxi 190-191 C 4
Wenzhou 184-185 N 6
Wenzhou Wan 190-191 H 8
Wepener 168-169 G 8
Werdër [ETH] 166-167 O 7
Werder = Virtsu 138-139 D 4
Wernecke Mountains 144-145 JK 5
Wernigerode 133 E 3
Werona = Verona 136-137 D 3
Werra 133 D 3
Werribee, Melbourne- 196 FG 6
Werris Creek 194-195 K 6
Werro = Võru 138-139 F 5
Werschetz = Vršac 136-137 J 3
Wesel 133 C 3
Wesenberg = Rakvere 138-139 F 4
Weser 133 D 2
Weserbergland 133 D 2-3
Weskan, KS 152-153 F 6
Wesleyville, PA 148-149 CD 3
Wessel, Cape - 194-195 G 2
Wessel Islands 194-195 G 2
Wesselsbron 174-175 G 4
Wessington, SD 152-153 G 3
Wessington Hills 152-153 G 3
Wessington Springs, SD 152-153 G 3-4
Wesson, MS 154-155 K 5
West 172-173 E 4
West, MS 154-155 L 4
West, TX 154-155 G 5
Westall, Point - 196 AB 4
West Allis, WI 152-153 MN 4
Westaustralian Basin 124-125 P 7
Westaustralisch Bekken 124-125 P 7
Westaustralisches Becken 124-125 P 7
West Bay 154-155 L 6
West Bend, IA 152-153 J 4
West Bend, WI 152-153 MN 4
West Bengal 180-181 O 6
West Blocton, AL 154-155 M 4
Westboro, WI 152-153 L 3
West Branch, MI 152-153 OP 3
Westbrook, ME 148-149 H 3
Westbrook, TX 154-155 E 4
West Butte 150-151 H 1
Westby, MT 152-153 D 1
Westby, WI 152-153 L 4
West Caroline Basin 124-125 QR 5
West-Carolinenbekken 124-125 QR 5
Westcliffe, CO 152-153 D 6
West Columbia, SC 148-149 C 8
West Columbia, TX 154-155 GH 6
West Des Moines, IA 152-153 JK 5
Westelijke Sahara 166-167 AB 4-3
Westerland 133 D 1
Westerly, RI 148-149 H 4
Western [EAK] 168-169 H 2
Western [Z] 168-169 F 6
Western Area 172-173 B 3
Western Australia 194-195 C-E 4-5
Western Bahr al- Ghazal 166-167 JK 7
Western Cape 174-175 C 7
Western Dafur 166-167 HJ 6
Western Dvina = Daugava 130-131 LM 9
Western Dvina = Daugava 138-139 E 5
Western Equatoria 166-167 K 7
Western Ghats 180-181 L 6-M 8
Western Kordofan 166-167 K 6
Western Port 194-195 HJ 7
Westernport, MD 148-149 D 5
Western Sahara 166-167 A 4-B 3
Western Shoshone Indian Reservation 150-151 E 4-5
Westerschelde 134-135 J 3
Westerville, OH 152-153 P 5
Westerwald 133 CD 3
Westeuropäisches Becken 124-125 HJ 3
West European Basin 124-125 HJ 3
Westeuropees Bekken 124-125 HJ 3
West Falkland 162 D 8
Westfall, OR 150-151 E 3-4
Westfield, MA 148-149 G 3
Westfield, NY 148-149 D 3
Westfield, PA 148-149 E 4
West Fork, AR 154-155 HJ 3
West Fork Des Moines River 152-153 J 4
West Fork Poplar River 152-153 CD 1
West Fork White River 152-153 N 6
West Frankfort, IL 152-153 M 7
Westfriesische Inseln 134-135 KL 2
West Frisian Islands 134-135 KL 2
Westgate 194-195 J 5
Westham, London- 132 FG 6
West Haven, CT 148-149 G 4
Westhoff, TX 154-155 G 6
Westhope, ND 152-153 F 1
West Ice Shelf 121 C 9
West-Indië 146-147 LM 7
Westindien 146-147 L-O 7
West Indies 146-147 LM 7
Westirian 186-187 K 7-L 8
West Jefferson, NC 148-149 C 6
West-Karolinenbecken 124-125 QR 5
West-Karolinenbecken 198-199 FG 4
West Lafayette, IN 152-153 N 5
Westlake, LA 154-155 J 5
Westlake, OR 150-151 A 4
Westleigh 174-175 G 4
West Liberty, IA 152-153 L 5
West Liberty, KY 152-153 P 7
Westlicher Großer Erg = Al-'Irq al-Gharbi al-Kabir 166-167 D 3-E 2
Westlicher Sajan = Zapadnyj Sajan 178-179 Q-S 7
West Memphis, AR 146-147 H 4
Westminster 174-175 G 5
Westminster, CO 152-153 D 6
Westminster, MD 148-149 E 5
West Monroe, LA 154-155 J 4
Westmoreland, KS 152-153 H 6
Westmorland, CA 150-151 F 9
West Mountain 148-149 FG 3
West Nicholson 168-169 GH 7
Weston [CDN] 148-149 D 3
Weston [MAL] 186-187 G 5
Weston, CO 152-153 D 7
Weston, ID 150-151 GH 4
Weston, MO 152-153 J 6
Weston, OR 150-151 D 3
Weston, WV 148-149 C 5
Weston-super-Mare 132 E 6
Westover, TX 154-155 F 4
West Palm Beach, FL 146-147 KL 6
West Pass 154-155 N 6
West Plains, MO 154-155 JK 2
West Point [AUS] 194-195 F 7-G 6
West Point, GA 154-155 N 4
West Point, KY 152-153 O 7
West Point, MS 154-155 L 4
West Point, NE 152-153 H 5
West Point, NY 148-149 G 4
West Point, VA 148-149 E 6
Westport [IRL] 132 AB 5
Westport [NZ] 194-195 O 8
Westport, CA 150-151 AB 6
Westport, OR 150-151 B 2
Westray 132 E 2
West-Sahara 166-167 A 4-B 3
Westsahara 166-167 A 4-B 3
West Scotia Basin 124-125 G 8
West Spanish Peak 152-153 D 7
West Union, IA 152-153 KL 4
West Union, OH 152-153 P 6
West Union, WV 148-149 C 5
West Unity, OH 152-153 O 5
West Virginia 146-147 KL 4
Westville, IL 152-153 N 5-6
Westville, OK 154-155 H 2-3
Westwater, UT 150-151 J 6
Westwego, LA 154-155 KL 6
Westwood, CA 150-151 C 5
West Wyalong 196 H 4
West Yellowstone, MT 150-151 H 3
Wetar, Pulau - 186-187 J 8
Wetaskiwin 144-145 NO 7
Wete 168-169 JK 4
Weti = Wete 168-169 JK 4
Wetmore, OR 150-151 D 3
Wet Mountains 152-153 D 6-7
Wetonka, SD 152-153 G 3
Wetter = Pulau Wetar 186-187 J 8
Wetumpka, AL 154-155 MN 4
Wewahitchka, FL 154-155 N 5-6
Wewak 186-187 M 7
Wewela, SD 152-153 G 4
Wewnętrzne Morze Japońskie = Seto-naikai 184-185 P 5
Wewoka, OK 154-155 G 3
Wexford 132 C 5
Weyb = Wabē Gestro Weniz 166-167 N7
Weyburn 144-145 Q 8
Weymouth 132 EF 6
Weymouth, Cape - 194-195 HJ 2
Weyprecht, Kapp - 130-131 l 5
Whakatane 194-195 P 7
Whaleback, Mount - 194-195 CD 4
Whales, Bay of - 121 B 19-20
Whalsay 132 F 1
Whangarei 194-195 OP 7
Wharton, TX 154-155 GH 6
Wharton, Bacino di - 124-125 OP 6
What Cheer, IA 152-153 K 5
Wheatland, CA 150-151 C 6
Wheatland, WY 152-153 D 4
Wheatley, AR 154-155 K 3
Wheaton, MN 152-153 H 3
Wheeler, OR 150-151 AB 3
Wheeler, TX 154-155 E 3
Wheeler Lake 154-155 M 3
Wheeler Peak [USA, Nevada] 146-147 CD 4
Wheeler Peak [USA, New Mexico] 146-147 E 4
Wheeler Ridge, CA 150-151 D 8
Wheeling, WV 146-147 KL 4-5
Whewell, Mount - 121 B 17-18
Whichaway Nunataks 121 A 34-1
Whidbey, Point - 196 B 5
Whidbey Island 150-151 B 1
Whipore 196 L 2
Whitby [CDN] 148-149 D 3
White, Lake - 194-195 E 4
White, SD 152-153 H 3
White Bay 144-145 Z 7
White Bear Lake, MN 152-153 K 3
White Bird, ID 150-151 EF 3
White Castle, LA 154-155 K 5
White City, FL 148-149 C 3
White City, KS 152-153 H 6
White Cliffs 194-195 H 6
White Cloud, MI 152-153 O 4
White Deer, TX 154-155 E 3
White Earth, ND 152-153 E 1
White Earth Indian Reservation 152-153 J 2
Whiteface, TX 154-155 D 4
Whiteface Mountain 148-149 FG 2
Whitefish, MT 150-151 F 1
Whitefish Bay 152-153 O 2
Whitefish Bay, WI 152-153 N 4
Whitefish Lake [USA, Minnesota] 152-153 JK 2
Whitefish Point 152-153 O 2
Whitefish Point, MI 152-153 O 2
Whitefish Range 150-151 F 1
Whiteflat, TX 154-155 E 3
White Hall, IL 152-153 LM 6
Whitehall, MI 152-153 N 4
Whitehall, MT 150-151 GH 3
Whitehall, NY 148-149 G 3
Whitehall, WI 152-153 L 3
Whitehaven 132 DE 4
Whitehorse 144-145 JK 5
White Horse, CA 150-151 C 5
White Horse Pass 150-151 FG 5
White Lake [USA] 154-155 J 6
White Lake, SD 152-153 G 4
White Lake, WI 152-153 M 3
Whiteland, TX 154-155 F 5
Whitemark 196 cd 2
White Mountain, AK 144-145 D 5
White Mountains [USA, California] 150-151 D 7
White Mountains [USA, New Hampshire] 148-149 H 2
White Nile 166-167 L 6
White Nossob = Wit Nossob 174-175 C 2
Whiteoak Swamp 148-149 E 7
White Owl, SD 152-153 E 3
White Pine, MT 150-151 F 2
White Pine Mountains 150-151 F 6
White Plains, NY 148-149 FG 4
White River, SD 152-153 F 4
White River = Witrivier 174-175 J 3
White River [CDN, Yukon Territory] 144-145 H 5
White River [USA, Arkansas] 146-147 H 4
White River [USA, California] 150-151 F 7
White River [USA, Colorado] 152-153 BC 5
White River [USA, Indiana] 152-153 N 6
White River [USA, South Dakota] 146-147 F 3
White River [USA, Texas] 154-155 E 4
White River Plateau 152-153 C 6
White River Valley 150-151 F 6
White Rock, SD 152-153 H 3
White Salmon, WA 150-151 C 3
Whitesands = Witsand 174-175 D 8
White Sands National Monument 154-155 B 4
White Springs, FL 148-149 b 1
White Sulphur Springs, MT 150-151 H 2
White Swan, WA 150-151 C 2
Whitetail, MT 152-153 D 1
White Umfolozi = Wit Umfolozi 174-175 J 5
Whiteville, NC 148-149 D 7
Whiteville, TN 154-155 L 3
White Volta 166-167 D 7
Whitewater, CO 152-153 B 6
Whitewater, KS 152-153 H 7
Whitewater, MT 152-153 C 1
Whitewater, WI 152-153 M 4
Whitewater Baldy 146-147 E 5
Whitewood, SD 152-153 DE 3
Whitewright, TX 154-155 G 4
Whitfield 196 H 6
Whithorn 132 DE 4
Whiting, NJ 148-149 F 5
Whitley City, KY 154-155 N 2
Whitmire, SC 148-149 C 7
Whitman, ND 152-153 GH 1
Whitman, NE 152-153 F 4
Whitmore Mountains 121 A
Whitney, NE 152-153 E 4
Whitney, OR 150-151 DE 3
Whitney, TX 154-155 G 5
Whitney, Mount - 146-147 C 4
Whitsett, TX 154-155 F 6
Whitsunday Island 194-195 JK 4
Whittier, AK 144-145 G 5
Whittlesea 196 G 6
Whitwell, TN 154-155 N 3
Wholdaia Lake 144-145 PQ 5
Whyalla 194-195 G 6
Wiang Phran = Mae Sai 186-187 CD 2
Wiarton 152-153 Q 3
Wiaźma = V'az'ma 138-139 JK 6
Wibaux, MT 152-153 D 2
Wichian Buri 186-187 D 3
Wichita, KS 146-147 G 4
Wichita Falls, TX 146-147 FG 5
Wichita Mountains 154-155 F 3
Wick 132 E 2
Wickenburg, AZ 150-151 G 8-9
Wickersham, WA 150-151 BC 1
Wickes, AR 154-155 H 3
Wickliffe, KY 154-155 L 2
Wickham, Cape - 196 b 1
Wicklow 132 CD 5
Wicklow Mountains 132 C 5
Widen, WV 148-149 C 5
Widgiemooltha 194-195 D 6
Wi-do 188-189 F 5
Widyan, Al- 180-181 E 4
Widze = Vidzy 138-139 F 6
Więcbork 133 H 2
Wiedeń = Wien 133 H 4
Wiegnaarspoort 174-175 E 7
Wielkie Łuki = Velikije Luki 138-139 H 5
Wielka Brytania i Irlandia Północna 132 F-H 4-5
Wielka Ławica Bahamska 146-147 L 6-7
Wielka Rafa Koralowa = Great Barrier Reef 194-195 H 2-K 4
Wielka Syrta, Zatoka - = Khalij as-Sūrt 166-167 H 2
Wielka Zatoka Australijska = Great Australian Bight 194-195 E 6-G 7
Wielki Chingan 184-185 M 3-N 1
Wielkie Antyle 146-147 K 7-N 8
Wielkie Jezioro Gorzkie = Al Buhayrat al-Murrat al-Kubrá 170 E 2
Wielkie Jezioro Niedźwiedzie 144-145 MN 4
Wielkie Jezioro Niewolnicze 144-145 NO 5
Wielkie Jezioro Słone = Great Salt Lake 146-147 D 3
Wielki Erg Wschodni = Al-'Irq al Kabir ash-Sharqi 166-167 F 2-3
Wielki Erg Zachodni = Al-Irq al Gharbi al-Kabir 166-167 D 3-E 2
Wielki Erg Zachodni = Al-'Irq al-Kabir al-Gharbi 166-167 D 3-E 2
Wielki Chingan 184-185 M 3-N 1
Wielki Mur 184-185 K 4
Wieluń 133 J 3
Wien 133 G 4
Wiener Neustadt 133 GH 5
Wienerwald 133 GH 4
Wieprz 133 L 3
Wierzbołowo = Virbalis 138-139 D 6
Wiesbaden 133 CD 3
Wiese Island = ostrov Vize 178-179 O 2
Wietnam 186-187 D 2-F 4
Wigadēn 166-167 NO 7
Wiga Hill = Ogadēn 172-173 H 3
Wigan 132 E 5
Wiggins, CO 152-153 D 5
Wiggins, MS 154-155 L 5
Wight, Isle of - 132 F 6
Wijdefjorden 130-131 j 5
Wiktoria = Victoria 194-195 HJ 7
Wiktoria, Wodospad - = Mosi Oa-Toenja 168-169 FG 6
Wilber, NE 152-153 H 5
Wilborn, MT 150-151 G 2
Wilbourn Hill 196 B 1
Wilbur, WA 150-151 D 2
Wilburton, OK 154-155 H 3
Wilcannia 194-195 H 6
Wilcox, NE 152-153 G 5
Wilczek, zemľ'a - = zemľ'a Vil'čeka 178-179 L-N 1
Wilczek land = zemľ'a Vil'čeka 178-179 L-N 1
Wilderness = Wildernis 174-175 E 7-8
Wildernis 174-175 E 7-8
Wild Horse Reservoir 150-151 F 5
Wild Rice River 152-153 HJ 2
Wildrose, ND 152-153 E 1
Wild Rose, WI 152-153 M 3
Wildwood, FL 148-149 bc 2
Wildwood, NJ 148-149 F 5
Wilejka = Vilejka 138-139 F 6
Wilge 174-175 H 4
Wilgena 196 B 3
Wilhelm, Mount - 186-187 M 8
Wilhelmina Gebergte 158-159 H 4
Wilhelmøya 130-131 l 5
Wilhelmshaven 133 CD 2
Wilhelmstal 174-175 B 1
Wilija = Vilija 138-139 EF 6
Wilkes 121C 12
Wilkes Barre, PA 146-147 L 3
Wilkes Land 121 BC 12-14
Wilkie 144-145 P 7
Wilkinsburg, PA 148-149 D 4
Wilkinson Lakes 194-195 F 5
Wilkomir = Ukmergė 138-139 E 6
Willacoochee, GA 148-149 B 9
Willamette River 146-147 B 3
Willandra Billabong Creek 196 G 4
Willapa Bay 150-151 AB 2
Willard, CO 152-153 E 5
Willard, MT 152-153 D 2
Willard, NM 154-155 BC 3
Willard, OH 152-153 P 5
Willard, UT 150-151 GH 5
Willcox, AZ 150-151 HJ 9
Willemstad [NA] 146-147 N 9
Willeroo 194-195 F 3
William Creek 194-195 G 5
Williams, AZ 150-151 G 8
Williams, CA 150-151 B 6
Williamsburg, IA 152-153 KL 5
Williams Lake 144-145 M 7
Williamson, WV 148-149 B 6
Williamsport, PA 146-147 L 3
Williamsport, IN 152-153 N 5
Williamston, NC 148-149 E 6-7
Williamstown, KY 152-153 O 6
Willimantic, CT 148-149 G 4
Willis, TX 154-155 H 5
Willis Group 194-195 K 3
Williston 168-169 F 9
Williston, FL 148-149 b 2
Williston, ND 146-147 F 2
Williston, SC 148-149 C 8
Willits, CA 150-151 B 6
Willmar, MN 152-153 J 3
Willoughby, OH 148-149 C 4
Willow 144-145 F 5
Willow Creek [USA, California] 150-151 C 5
Willow Creek [USA, Oregon] 150-151 D 3
Willow Lake, SD 152-153 H 3
Willowlake River 144-145 MN 5
Willowmore 168-169 F 9
Willow Ranch, CA 150-151 C 5
Willow River, MN 152-153 K 2
Willow Run, MI 152-153 P 4
Willows, CA 150-151 B 6
Willow Springs, MO 154-155 JK 2
Willsboro, NY 148-149 G 2
Wills Point, TX 154-155 GH 4
Willunga 196 D 5
Wilmer, AL 154-155 L 5
Wilmington [AUS] 196 D 4
Wilmington, DE 146-147 LM 4
Wilmington, IL 152-153 MN 5
Wilmington, NC 146-147 L 5
Wilmington, OH 152-153 P 6
Wilmot, AR 154-155 K 4
Wilmot, SD 152-153 H 3
Wilna = Vilnius 138-139 EF 6
Wilna = Vilnius 130-131 L 10
Wilno = Vilnius 130-131 L 10
Wilsall, MT 150-151 H 3
Wilson, AR 154-155 K 3
Wilson, NC 146-147 L 4
Wilson, NY 148-149 D 3
Wilson, OK 154-155 G 3
Wilson Lake 154-155 M 3
Wilson, Mount - 152-153 BC 7
Wilson Bluff 194-195 EF 6
Wilson Creek, WA 150-151 D 2
Wilson Creek Range 150-151 F 6
Wilson River 194-195 H 5
Wilsons Promontory 194-195 J 7
Wilsonville, NE 152-153 FG 5
Wilton, ND 152-153 F 2
Wilton, WI 152-153 L 4
Wilton River 194-195 F 2
Wiluna 194-195 D 5
Wimbledon, ND 152-153 G 2
Wimbledon, London- 132 F 6
Wimmera 194-195 H 7
Wina = Ouina 166-167 G 7
Winamac, IN 152-153 N 5
Winburg 168-169 G 8
Winchell, TX 154-155 F 5
Winchester 132 F 6
Winchester [CDN] 148-149 F 2
Winchester, ID 150-151 E 2
Winchester, IL 152-153 LM 6
Winchester, IN 152-153 O 5
Winchester, KY 152-153 OP 6-7
Winchester, TN 154-155 M 3
Winchester, VA 146-147 L 4
Winchester, WY 152-153 BC 4
Winchester Bay, OR 150-151 A 4
Windau = Venta 138-139 CD 5
Windau = Ventspils 138-139 C 5
Windber, PA 148-149 D 4
Wind Cave National Park 152-153 E 4
Winder, GA 154-155 O 3-4
Windesi 186-187 K 7
Windhoek 168 E 7
Windhuk = Windhoek 168-169 E 7
Windom, MN 152-153 J 4
Windorah 194-195 H 5
Wind River [USA, Wyoming] 152-153 B 4
Wind River, WY 152-153 B 4
Wind River Indian Reservation 150-151 J 4
Wind River Range 146-147 DE 3
Windsor [AUS] 196 K 4
Windsor [CDN, Ontario] 144-145 U 9
Windsor [GB] 132 F 6
Windsor, CO 152-153 D 5
Windsor, MO 152-153 K 6
Windsor, NC 148-149 E 6
Windsor, ND 152-153 G 2
Windsor, VT 148-149 G 3
Windsorton 174-175 F 5
Windward Islands [West Indies] 146-147 O 9
Winfield, AL 154-155 M 3-4
Winfield, IA 152-153 L 5
Winfield, KS 146-147 G 4
Winfred, SD 152-153 H 3-4
Wing, ND 152-153 F 2
Wingham 152-153 Q 4
Wingo, KY 154-155 L 2
Winifred, MT 152-153 B 2
Winisk 144-145 T 6
Winisk Lake 144-145 T 7
Winisk River 144-145 T 7
Wink, TX 154-155 D 5
Winkelman, AZ 150-151 H 9
Winkelpos 174-175 G 4
Winlock, WA 150-151 B 2
Winneba 166-167 D 7
Winnebago, MN 152-153 JK 4
Winnebago, Lake - 152-153 M 3-4
Winnemucca, NV 146-147 C 3
Winnemucca Lake 150-151 D 5
Winner, SD 152-153 G 4
Winnetka, IL 152-153 N 4
Winnett, MT 152-153 B 2
Winnfield, LA 154-155 J 5
Winnibigoshish Lake 152-153 JK 2
Winnie, TX 154-155 H 6
Winning 194-195 B 4
Winnipeg 144-145 R 7
Winnipeg, Lake - 144-145 R 7
Winnipegosis, Lake - 144-145 R 7
Winnipeg River 144-145 RS 7
Winnipesaukee, Lake - 148-149 H 3
Winnsboro, LA 154-155 K 4
Winnsboro, SC 148-149 C 7
Winnsboro, TX 154-155 H 4
Winona, AZ 150-151 H 8
Winona, KS 152-153 F 6
Winona, MI 152-153 M 2
Winona, MN 146-147 H 3
Winona, MO 154-155 K 2
Winona, MS 154-155 KL 4
Winona, TX 154-155 H 4
Winona, WA 150-151 DE 2
Winschoten 134-135 L 2
Winslow, AR 154-155 H 3
Winslow, AZ 146-147 DE 4
Winslow, IN 152-153 N 6
Winslow, ME 148-149 J 2
Winsted, CT 148-149 G 4
Winston, MT 150-151 GH 2
Winston, OR 150-151 B 4
Winston-Salem, NC 146-147 KL 4
Winterberg 133 D 3
Winterberge 174-175 FG 7
Winter Garden, FL 148-149 c 2
Winterhaven, CA 150-151 F 9
Winter Haven, FL 148-149 c 2
Winter Park, CO 152-153 CD 6
Winter Park, FL 148-149 c 2
Winters, CA 150-151 C 6
Winters, TX 154-155 F 5
Winterset, IA 152-153 JK 5
Winterthur 133 D 5
Winterton [ZA] 174-175 H 5
Winterveld 174-175 E 6
Winthrop, ME 148-149 HJ 2
Winthrop, MN 152-153 J 3
Winthrop, WA 150-151 C 1
Winton [AUS] 194-195 H 4
Winton [NZ] 194-195 N 9
Winton, MN 152-153 L 2
Winton, WA 150-151 C 2
Winton, WY 150-151 J 5
Winyah Bay 148-149 D 8
Wirāj, Wādi al- 170 D 3
Wirballen = Virbalis 138-139 D 6
Wirginia = Virginia 146-147 KL 4
Wirrulla 194-195 FG 6
Wirzsee = Võrtsjärv 138-139 E 4
Wiscasset, ME 148-149 J 2
Wisconsin 146-147 H 2-J 3
Wisconsin Dells, WI 152-153 M 4
Wisconsin Rapids, WI 152-153 LM 3
Wisconsin River 146-147 HJ 3
Wisdom, MT 150-151 G 3
Wiseman, AK 144-145 FG 4
Wishek, ND 152-153 G 2
Wisła 133 K 3
Wislana, Mierzeja - 133 J 1
Wislany, Zalew - 133 J 1
Wisłok 133 KL 4
Wisłoka 133 K 4
Wismar 133 E 2
Wisner, LA 154-155 K 4-5
Wisner, NE 152-153 H 4-5
Wissel, Danau - = Danau Paniai 186-187 L 7
Wissembourg 134-135 LM 4
Wissmann, Chutes - 168-169 EF 4
Wister, OK 154-155 H 3
Wiswila 171 AB 5
Witbank 168-169 GH 8
Witberge 174-175 G 6
Witdraai 174-175 D 4
Witebsk = Vitebsk 138-139 H 6
Witelsbos 174-175 F 8
Witerna = Emmaste 138-139 D 4
Witfonteinrand 174-175 G 3
Withernsea 132 FG 5
Witjasdiep 184-185 S 3
Witjastief 184-185 S 3
Witkop 174-175 D 4
Witkoppies 174-175 H 4
Wit Nossob 174-175 C 2
Witpoort 174-175 G 4
Witputs 168-169 E 8
Witrandberge 174-175 C 3
Witrivier 174-175 J 3
Witsand 174-175 D 8
Witteberge 174-175 D 7
Witte-Els-Bosch = Witelsbos 174-175 F 8
Witten, SD 152-153 FG 4
Wittenberg 133 F 3
Wittenberg, WI 152-153 M 3
Wittenberge 133 EF 2
Wittenoom Gorge 194-195 C 4
Witte Zee 178-179 FG 4
Wittlich 133 C 4
Wittmann, AZ 150-151 G 9
Wittpütz = Witputs 174-175 B 4
Wittstock 133 F 2
Witu 168-169 JK 3
Wit Umfolozi 174-175 J 5
Witvlei 168-169 E 7
Witwatersrand 174-175 G 3-H 4
Wiwŏn 188-189 F 2
Wjasma = Vaz'ma 138-139 JK 6
Wkra 133 JK 2
Wladyslawow = Naumiestis 138-139 D 6
Włocławek 133 J 2
Włodawa 133 L 3
Wladywostok = Vladivostok 178-179 Z 9
Włochy 136-137 C 3-F 5
Wöbs = Vööpsu 138-139 F 4
Wodonga 196 H 6
Wogezy 134-135 L 4-5
Wohlau = Wołów 133 H 3
Wohlthatmassiv 121 B 2
Wokam, Pulau - 186-187 KL 8
Wolbach, NE 152-153 G 5
Wolcott, NY 148-149 E 3
Woleai 186-187 M 5
Wolf Creek, MT 150-151 G 2
Wolf Creek, OR 150-151 B 4
Wolf Creek Pass 152-153 C 7
Wolfe City, TX 154-155 G 4
Wolfenbüttel 133 E 2
Wolff, Chutes - 168-169 F 4
Wolfforth, TX 154-155 D 4
Wolf Mountains 152-153 C 3
Wolf Point, MT 152-153 D 1
Wolf River 152-153 M 3
Wolfsburg 133 E 2
Wolga = Volga 178-179 F 6
Wolhuterskop 174-175 G 3
Wolhynien = Volynskaja Oblast' 138-139 DE 8
Wolin 133 G 2
Wolin = Volyně 130-131 F 10
Wolkitte = Welķītē 166-167 M 7
Wollaston, Islas - 162 C 9
Wollaston Lake 144-145 PQ 6
Wollaston Peninsula 144-145 NO 3-4
Wollega = Welega 166-167 LM 7
Wollo = Welo 166-167 MN 6
Wollogorang 194-195 G 3
Wollongong 194-195 K 6
Wolmar = Valmiera 138-139 E 5
Wolmaransstad 174-175 F 4
Wołów 133 H 3
Wolseley [AUS] 194-195 GH 7
Wolseley [ZA] 174-175 C 7
Wolsey, SD 152-153 G 3
Wolsk = Vol'sk 138-139 Q 7
Wolstenholme 144-145 VW 5
Wolstenholme, Cape - 144-145 VW 5
Wolsztyn 133 GH 2
Wolverhampton 132 E 5
Wolverine, MI 152-153 O 3
Wolynien = Volynskaja Oblast' 138-139 DE
Wolynische Oblast = Volynskaja Oblast' 138-139 DE 8
Wołga = Volga 178-179 F 6
Wołoszczyzna 136-137 K-M 3
Wonder, OR 150-151 B 4
Wonderfontein 174-175 HJ 3
Wonderkop 174-175 G 4
Wongrowitz = Wągrowiec 133 H 2
Wŏngsŏng-dong 188-189 DE 3
Wŏnju 184-185 O 4
Wonosari 186-187 F 8
Wŏnsan 184-185 O 4
Wonthaggi 194-195 HJ 7
Woocalla 196 C 3
Wood, SD 152-153 F 4
Wood, Mount - [USA] 150-151 J 3
Wood Bay 121 B 17-18
Woodbine, GA 148-149 C 9
Wood Buffalo National Park 144-145 O 6
Woodburn, OR 150-151 B 3
Woodbury, GA 154-155 N 4
Woodbury, NJ 148-149 F 5
Woodend 196 G 6
Woodfjorden 130-131 j 5
Woodlake, CA 150-151 D 7
Wood Lake, NE 152-153 FG 4
Woodland, CA 150-151 BC 6
Woodland, WA 150-151 B 3
Woodland Park, CO 152-153 D 6
Woodlark Island 186-187 h 6
Wood River, IL 152-153 LM 6
Wood River, NE 152-153 G 5
Woodroffe , Mount - 194-195 F 5
Woodruff, SC 148-149 BC 7
Woodruff, UT 150-151 H 5
Woodruff, WI 152-153 M 3
Woods, Lake - 194-195 F 3
Woods, Lake of the - 144-145 R 8
Woodsboro, TX 154-155 G 6
Woodsfield, OH 148-149 C 5
Woodside 194-195 J 7
Woodside, UT 150-151 H 6
Woodson, AR 154-155 JK 3
Woodstock [AUS] 194-195 H 3
Woodstock [CDN, Ontario] 148-149 C 3
Woodstock, IL 152-153 MN 4
Woodstock, VA 148-149 D 5
Woodstock, VT 148-149 G 3
Woodsville, NH 148-149 GH 2
Woodville 194-195 P 8
Woodville, MS 154-155 K 5
Woodville, TX 154-155 H 5
Woodward, OK 146-147 G 4
Woolgoolga 196 L 3
Wooltana 196 DE 3
Woomera 194-195 G 6
Woonsocket, RI 148-149 GH 4
Woonsocket, SD 152-153 GH 3
Wooramel River 194-195 C 5
Wooster, OH 148-149 C 4
Woqooyi Galbeed 166-167 a 1
Worcester [GB] 132 E 5
Worcester [ZA] 168-169 EF 9
Worcester, MA 146-147 M 3
Worcester Range 121 B 17-15
Worden, OR 150-151 BC 4
Workington 132 E 4
Worland, WY 152-153 C 3
Worms 133 CD 4
Worms = Vormsi 138-139 D 4
Worny = Varniai 138-139 D 6
Woronesch = Voronež 138-139 M 8
Woronów = Voronovo 138-139 E 6
Woropajewo = Voropajevo 138-139 F 6
Woroschilowgrad = Vorošilovgrad 140-141 JK 2
Wortel [Namibia] 174-175 B 2
Wortham, TX 154-155 G 5
Worthing 132 FG 6
Worthington, MN 152-153 J 4
Wōru = Võru 138-139 F 5
Wotho 192-193 H 4
Wotje 192-193 J 4
Wou-han = Wuhan 184-185 L 5
Wou-hou = Wuhu 184-185 M 5
Wour 166-167 H 4
Wou-tcheou = Wuzhou 184-185 L 7
Wowoni, Pulau - 186-187 H 7
Wrakpunt 174-175 B 5
Wrangel, ostrov - = ostrov Vrangel'a 178-179 hj 3
Wrangell, AK 144-145 K 6
Wrangell Mountains 144-145 H 5
Wrath, Cape - 132 D 2
Wray, CO 152-153 E 5
Wreck Point = Wrakpunt 174-175 B 5
Wrens, GA 148-149 B 8
Wright, Lake - 194-195 EF 5
Wright City, OK 154-155 H 3
Wrightson, Mount - 150-151 H 10
Wrightsville, GA 148-149 B 8
Wrigley 144-145 M 5
Wrigley Gulf 121 B 121
Wrocław 133 H 3
Września 133 HJ 2
Wschodniochińskie, Morze - 184-185 N 6-O 5
Wschodniofryzyjskie, W-y- 130-131 B 11
Wschodniofryzyjskie, W-y- = Ostfriesische Inseln 133 C 2
Wschodniosyberyjskie, Morze - 178-179 d-h 3
Wschowa 133 H 3
Wszystkich Świętych, Zatoka - = Baia de Todos os Santos 158-159 M 7
Wu'an 190-191 E 3
Wubin 194-195 C 5-6
Wubu 190-191 C 3
Wuchai = Wuzhai 190-191 C 2
Wuchang 184-185 O 3
Wuchang, Wuhan- 184-185 LM 5
Wucheng [TJ, Shandong] 190-191 EF 3
Wucheng [TJ, Shanxi] 190-191 C 3
Wu-ch'i = Wuxi [TJ, Sichuan] 190-191 B 6
Wu Chiang = Wu Jiang [TJ, ~] 184-185 K 6
Wu-chiang = Wujang [TJ, ●] 190-191 H 6
Wu-ch'iang = Wuqiang 190-191 E 2
Wu-ch'iao = Wuqiao 190-191 F 3
Wu-chih = Wuzhi 190-191 D 4
Wu-chou = Wuzhou 184-185 L 7
Wuchow = Wuzhou 184-185 L 7
Wuchuan [TJ, Guangdong] 190-191 C 11
Wuchuan [TJ, Guizhou] 184-185 K 6
Wuchuan [TJ, Nei Monggol Zizhiqu] 184-185 L 3
Wu-chung-pao = Wuzhong 184-185 K 4
Wu Chiang = Wu Jiang [TJ, ~] 184-185 K 6
Wudang Shan 190-1911 C 5
Wudaogou 188-189 EF 1
Wudi 184-185 M 4
Wudian 190-191 D 6
Wuding He 190-191 C 3
Wudu 184-185 J 5
Wuduhe 190-191 C 6
Wufeng 190-191 C 6
Wugang 184-185 L 6
Wugong 190-191 AB 4
Wugong Shan 190-191 D 8
Wuhan 184-185 L 5
Wuhe 190-191 F 5
Wu hei 184-185 K 4
Wu-ho = Wuhe 190-191 F 5
Wu-hsi = Wuxi 184-185 MN 5
Wu-hsiang = Wuxiang 190-191 D 3
Wu-hsüan = Wuxuan 190-191 B 10
Wuhu 184-185 M 5
Wuhua 190-191 E 10
Wu Chiang = Wu Jiang [TJ, ~] 184-185 K 6
Wu-i = Wuyi [TJ, Anhui] 190-191 G 5
Wu-i = Wuyi [TJ, Zhejiang] 190-191 G 7
Wu-i Shan = Wuyi Shan 184-185 M 6
Wu Jiang [TJ, ~] 184-185 K 6
Wujiang [TJ, ●] 190-191 H 6
Wujin = Changzhou 184-185 MN 5
Wukang 190-191 GH 6
Wukari 166-167 F 7
Wuki = Wuxi 190-191 B 6
Wukiao = Wuqiao 190-191 F 3
Wu-kung = Wugong 190-191 AB 4
Wuleidao Wan 190-191 HJ 3
Wuli 184-185 K 7
Wulian 190-191 G 4
Wuliang Shan 184-185 J 7
Wu Ling 190-191 CD 4
Wuling He 184-185 P 2
Wuling Shan 190-191 B 8-C 7
Wulongji = Huaibin 190-191 E 5
Wulumuqi = Ürümchi 184-185 F 3
Wulun He = Dingzi Wan 190-191 H 3
Wumei Shan 190-191 E 7
Wuning 190-191 E 7
Wunstorf 133 D 2
Wupatki National Monument 150-151 GH 8
Wuping 190-191 F 9
Wuppertal 133 C 3
Wuppertal [ZA] 174-175 C 7
Wūqbá, Al- = Al-Waqbá 182-183 L
Wuqi 190-191 B 3
Wuqiang 190-191 E 2
Wuqiao 190-191 F 3
Wur = Wour 166-167 H 4
Wurno 166-167 EF 6
Wūruq, Rā's - = Rā's ash-Shūkāt ath-Thalātha 166-167 D
Würzburg 133 DE 4
Wushan 190-191 BC 6
Wusheng 190-191 G 7
Wushi [TJ ↓ Shaoguan] 184-185 L 7
Wushi [TJ ↙ Zhanjiang] 190-191 BC 11
Wushi = Üchturpan 184-185 DE 3
Wu Shui [TJ ◁ Bei Jiang] 190-191 D 9
Wu Shui [TJ ◁ Yuan Jiang, Hongjian] 190-191 BC 8
Wu Shui [TJ ◁ Yuan Jiang, Qiancheng] 190-191 B 8
Wusi = Wuxi 184-185 M N 5
Wusiang = Wuxiang 190-191 D 3
Wusong 184-185 N 5
Wusu 184-185 EF 3
Wusuli Jiang 184-185 P 2
Wutai 190-191 D 2
Wutai Shan 184-185 L 4
Wu-tang Shan = Wudang Shan 190-191 C 5
Wuti = Wudi 184-185 M 4
Wu-ting = Huimin 190-191 F 3
Wu-ting Ho = Wuding He 190-191 C 3
Wutong 190-191 B 9
Wutongqiao 184-185 J 6
Wutong Shan = Wugong Shan 190-191 D 8
Wutsing = Wuqing 190-191 F 2
Wu-tu = Wudu 184-185 J 5
Wu-tu-ho = Wuduhe 190-191 C 6
Wuvulu 186-187 M 7
Wuwei [TJ, Anhui] 190-191 F 6
Wuwei [TJ, Gansu] 184-185 J 4
Wuxi 184-185 MN 5
Wuxian = Suzhou 184-185 N 5
Wuxiang 190-191 D 3
Wuxing 184-185 MN 5
Wuxue = Guangji 184-185 M 6
Wuyang [TJ, Henan] 190-191 D 5
Wuyang [TJ, Hunan] 190-191 C 8
Wuyi [TJ, Anhui] 190-191 G 5
Wuyi [TJ, Zhejiang] 190-191 G 7
Wuyiling 184-185 OP 2
Wuying 184-185 OP 2
Wuyi Shan 184-185 M 6
Wuyou 190-191 H 5
Wu-yu = Wuyou 190-191 H 5
Wuyuan [TJ, Jiangxi] 190-191 FG 7
Wuyuan [TJ, Nei Monggol Zizhiqu] 184-185 K 3
Wu-yüan = Wuyuan [TJ, Jiangxi] 190-191 FG 7
Wu-yüan = Wuyuan [TJ, Nei Monggol Zizhiqu] 184-185 K 3
Wuyun 184-185 O 2
Wu-yün = Wuyun 184-185 O 2
Wuz, El- - = Al-Wazz 166-167 L 5
Wuzhai 190-191 C 2
Wuzhang = Wuchang 184-185 O 3
Wuzhen 190-191 C 6
Wuzhi 190-191 D 4
Wuzhong 184-185 K 4
Wuzhou 184-185 L 7
Wyandotte, MI 152-153 P 4
Wyandra 194-195 HJ 5
Wyanet, IL 152-153 M 5
Wyangala Reservoir 194-195 J 6
Wyarno, WY 152-153 C 3
Wybrzeże Kości Słoniowej [≅] 166-167 CD 8
Wybrzeże Kości Słoniowej [★] 166-167 CD 7
Wye 132 E 5
Wymore, NE 152-153 H 5
Wynbring 194-195 F 6
Wyndham 194-195 E 3
Wyndmere, ND 152-153 H 2
Wynne, AR 154-155 K 3
Wynne Wood, OK 154-155 G 3
Wynniatt Bay 144-145 O 3
Wynyard [AUS] 194-195 HJ 8
Wyola, MT 152-153 C 3
Wyoming 146-147 D-F 3
Wyoming, IL 152-153 M 5

Zagorsk = Sergijev Posad 178-179 F 6
Zágráb = Zagreb 136-137 FG 3
Zagreb 136-137 FG 3
Zágros, Kühhä-ye - 180-181 F 3-4
Zagrzeb = Zagreb 136-137 FG 3
Žagubica 133 J 3
Zagura = Zäkürah 166-167 C 2
Záhedän 180-181 J 5
Zahl, ND 152-153 E 1
Zahlah 182-183 F 6
Zahrän 180-181 E 7
Zährän, Az- 180-181 FG 5
Zaidam = Tsaidam 184-185 GH 4
Zair 168-169 FG 3
Zaire [Angola] 168-169 D 4
Zaïre = Demokratische Republik Kongo 64-65 FG 3
Zaječar 136-137 JK 4
Zajsan, ozero - 178-179 P 8
Zajsan 178-179 P 8
Zakamsk, Perm 138-139 UV 4
Zakarpatskaja Oblasť 140-141 A 2
Zakataľskij zapovednik 140-141 N 6
Zakataly 140-141 N 6
Zákhü 180-181 E 3
Zako 166-167 J 7
Zakopane 133 JK 4
Zakouma 168-169 HJ 6
Zakroczym 133 K 2
Zäkürah 166-167 C 2
Zákynthos [GR, ○] 136-137 J 7
Zákynthos [GR, ●] 136-137 J 7
Zala 133 H 5
Zalabiyah 182-183 HJ 5
Zalaegerszeg 133 H 5
Zalanga 172-173 H 3
Zaläu 136-137 K 2
Zalazna 130-131 T 4
Zálinjay 166-167 J 6
Zaltan 166-167 H 3
Zaľtyr, ozero - 140-141 P 3
Zalučje 138-139 H 5
Zambeze, Rio - 168-169 H 6
Zambezi 168-169 GH 6
Zambézia 168-169 G 6-H 5
Zámbia 168 E 5-F 4
Zambia 168-169 G 6-H 5
Zambie 168-169 G 6-H 5
Zamboanga 186-187 H 5
Zamboanga Peninsula 186-187 H 5
Zametčíno 138-139 O 7
Zamfara, River - 168-169 F 6
Zamjany 140-141 NO 3
Zamkova, gora - 138-139 EF 7
Zammär 182-183 K 4
Zamora 134-135 E 8
Zamora, CA 150-151 BC 6
Zamora [EC, •] 158-159 D 5
Zamora de Hidalgo 146-147 F 7-8
Zamość 133 L 3
Zamzam, Wädi - 166-167 G 2
Zanaga 168-169 D 3
Zanapa 182-183 F 4
Zanasu 140-141 O 3
Žanatas 178-179 MN 9
Žanbaj 140-141 P 3
Záncara 134-135 F 9
Zandbult = Sandbult 174-175 G 2
Zandrivier = Sandrivier 174-175 G 3
Zanesville, OH 146-147 K 4
Žarietty, ostrov - 178-179 ef 2
Zang = Xizang Zizhiqu 184-185 EF 5
Zanhuang 190-191 E 3
Zania 174-175 C 2
Zanjän 180-181 F 3
Zanjänrüd 182-183 MN 4
Zanthus 194-195 D 6
Zanulje 138-139 R 3
Zanzibar 168-169 JK 4
Zanzibar 168-169 J 4
Zanzibar and Pemba 168-169 JK 4
Zanzibar Island 168-169 JK 4

Zaokskij 138-139 L 6
Zaoshi 190-191 C 7
Zaouatallaz 166-167 F 3-4
Zaouia-el-Kahla = Burj'Umar Idris 166-167 EF 3
Zaoyang 190-191 D 5
Zaozerje, Perm - 138-139 UV 4
Zaozhuang 190-191 FG 4
Zap = Çigli 182-183 K 4
Zapadnaja Dvina [SU,~] 138-139 FG 6
Zapadnaja Dvina [SU,●] 138-139 HJ 5
Zapadnaja Dvina = Daugava 138-139 E 7
Zapadna Morava 136-137 HJ 4
Západní Irian 186-187 K 7-L 8
Západni Sahara 166-167 A 4-B 3
Zapadno-Sibirskaja ravnina 178-179 L-Q 5-6
Západoevropská pánev 134-135 B-D 6
Západofriské o-vy 133 BC 2
Zapala 162 BC 5
Zapata, TX 154-155 F 7
Zapaleri, Cerro - 162 C 2
Zape, El - 154-155 C 8
Zapiga 162 BC 1
Zapiškis 138-139 D 6
Zapokrovskij 178-179 W 7
Zaporižžja 140-141 G 3
zapovednik Belovežskaja Pušča 138-139 E 7
Zaqäziq, Az- 166-167 KL 2
Zara 182-183 G 3
Zara = Zadar 136-137 F 3
Zarajsk 138-139 M 6
Zarand-e Kohneh 182-183 O 5
Zarasai 131 LM 10
Zarasai 138-139 EF 6
Zárate 162 E 4
Zaraza 158-159 F 3
Zarbatiya = Zurbatiyah 182-183 LM 6
Zardob 140-141 NO 6
Zareq 182-183 N 5
Zarghün Shahr 180-181 K 4
Zari 172-173 J 2
Zaria 166-167 F 6
Zarisberge 168-169 E 7-8
Zarizyn = Volgograd 140-141 LM 2
Žarkamys 178-179 K 8
Žarkovskij 138-139 J 6
Žarma 178-179 P 8
Zarrinäbäd 182-183 N 5
Zarrineh Rüd 182-183 LM 4
Zarskoje Selo = Puškin 178-179 DE 6
Zarubino 138-139 JK 4
Zaruşat = Arpaçay 182-183 K 2
Zary 133 G 3
Žaryk 178-179 N 8
Žašejek [SU, Kandalakša] 130-131 O 4
Žašejek [SU, Kandalakša] 130-131 P 4
Žaškov 140-141 E 2
Zasla 130-131 M 10
Zaslav = Iz'aslav 140-141 C 1
Zaslaví 138-139 F 6
Zastron 174-175 G 6
Zatab ash-Shamah 182-183 GH 7
Žataj 178-179 YZ 5
Zatec 133 F 3
Zatir, Az- 180-181 E 6-7
Zatišje 136-137 NO 2
Zatišje [SU, Odesska] 140-141 DE 3
Zatoka 140-141 E 3
Žáuiet el Beidä' = Al-Baydä' 166-167 J2
Zavalla, TX 154-155 H 5
Zavetnoje 140-141 L 3
Zavety Iljiča 178-179 ab 8
Zavidovicí-136-137 GH 3
Zavitinsk 178-179 Y 7

Zäviyeh 182-183 L 3
Zavodoukovsk 178-179 M 6
Zavolžje 178-179 G 6
Zavolžsk 138-139 O 5
Zawi 166-167 HJ 7
Zawia = Az-Zäwiyah 166-167 G 2
Zawilah 166-167 H 3
Zäwiyah, Az- 166-167 G 2
Zäwiyah, Jabal az- 182-183 G 5
Zäwiyat al-Muthniyän 170 B 2
Zäwiyat Shammäs 170 B 1-2
Zawr, Az- 182-183 N 8
Zayb, Bi'r - 182-183 K 6
Zaydün, Wädi - 170 E 5
Zaytün, Az- 170 AB 3
Zbarazd 140-141 B 2
Zbąszyn 133 GH 2
Zborov 140-141 B 2
Zbruč 140-141 C 2
Zdanov = Mariupoľ 140-141 H 3
Zdolbunov 140-141 C 1
Zduńska Wola 133 J 3
Zebedäni = Zabdäni 182-183 G 6
Zebediela 174-175 H 3
Zeebrugge, Brugge- 134-135 J 3
Zeehan 194-195 H 7
Zeekoegat = Seekoegat 174-175 E 7
Zeekoe River = Seekoerivier 174-175 F 6
Zeeland, MI 152-153 NO 4
Zeerust 168-169 G 8
Zéfat 180-181 D 4
Zeghortä = Zaghartä 182-183 F 5
Zeidün, Wädi - = Wädli Zaydün 170 E 5
Zeil, Mount - 194-195 F 4
Zeila = Seyla' 166-167 N 6
Žeimelis 138-139 DE 5
Zeitz 133 EF 3
Zeja [SU, ~] 178-179 Y 7
Zeja [SU, ●] 178-179 Y 7
Zejskoje vodochranilišče 178-179 Y 7
Zeľabova 138-139 L 4
Zelebiyé = Zalabiyah 182-183 HJ 5
Zelenaja Rošča 138-139 T 6
Zelenčukskaja 140-141 K 5
Zelenga 140-141 O 3
Zelenoborskij 130-131 P 4
Zelenodoľsk 178-179 HJ 6
Zelenogorsk 138-139 GH 3
Zelenograd 138-139 J 5
Zelenogradsk 133 H 1
Zelenokumsk 140-141 LM 4
Železnik 130-131 J 2
Železnodorožnyj [SU, Komi ASSR] 178-179 J 5
Železnogorsk 138-139 KL 7
Železnovodsk 140-141 L 4
Zelinograd = Celinograd 178-179 MN 7
Zella = Zillah 166-167 H 3
Žeľudok 138-139 E 7
Zelwa = Zeľva 138-139 E 7
Zemcy 138-139 J 5
Zemetčino = Zametčino 138-139 O 7
Zemio 166-167 JK 7
Zemiandskij poluostrov 133 K 1
Zemiandski p-ov 130-131 J 10
Zemland 133 K 1
Zemmer = Zämmär 182-183 M 8
Zemmür = Zammär 182-183 K 4
Zemongo 166-167 J 7
Zempoaltepec, Cerro 146-147 GH 8
Zemun, Beograd- 136-137 HJ 3
Zemzen, Uádi - = Wädi Zamzam 166-167 G 2
Zengcheng 190-191 D 10
Zenia, CA 150-151 B 5
Zenica 136-137 G 3

Zen'kov 140-141 G 1
Zenshü = Chŏnju 184-185 O 4
Zentralafrica 167 HJ 7
Zentralafrikanische Republik 166-167 HJ 7
Zentralarktisches Becken 120 A
Zentralindischer Rücken 124-125 N 5-7
Zentralindisches Becken 124-125 NO 6
Zentralmassiv 134-135 JL 4-5
Zentralpazifisches Becken 124-125 BC 5
Zentralpazifisches Becken 198-199 KL 4
Zentralpolynesische Sporaden 192-193 L 4-M 6
Zephyrhills, FL 148-149 bc 2
Zeravšan 180-181 K 3
Zeravšanskij chrebet 180-181 K 3
Žerdevka 138-139 N 8
Žerev 140-141 K 3
Žernograd 140-141 K 3
Žésart 138-139 RS 2
Zestoienín = Sesfontein 168-169 D 6
Zeshou = Jieshou 190-191 G 5
Zestafoni 140-141 L 5
Zevgári, Akrótérion - 182-183 E 5
Zeydikän = Zidikän 182-183 K 3
Zeytin Burnu 182-183 F 5
Zeytinlik 182-183 JK 2
Žézere 134-135 CD 9
Žezkazgan 184-185 B 2
Zgierz 133 J 3
Zgorovka 140-141 E 1
Zhahang = Tsethang 184-185 G 6
Zhajiang 190-191 D 8
Zhajin 190-191 E 7
Zhaling Hu = Kyaring Tsho 184-185 F 5
Zhang He 190-191 E 3
Zhangbei 190-191 E 2
Zhangdu 190-191 B 9
Zhangguangcai Ling 184-185 O 2-3
Zhanghua = Changhua -190-191 H 9
Zhanghuang 190-191 B 10
Zhangjiakou 184-185 L 3
Zhangjiapeng 190-191 B 7
Zhangling 184-185 N 1
Zhangmutou 190-191 D 10
Zhangping 190-191 F 9
Zhangpu 190-191 F 9
Zhangqiao 190-191 F 5
Zhangqiu 190-191 F 3
Zhangsanta 190-191 C 2
Zhangsanying 188-189 AB 2
Zhangwu 184-185 N 2
Zhangye 184-185 J 4
Zhangzhou 184-185 M 7
Zhangzi Dao 188-189 D 3
Zhanhua 190-191 FG 3
Zhanjiang 184-185 L 7
Zhanjiang Gang 184-185 L 7
Zhao'an 190-191 F 10
Zhao'an Wan 190-191 F 10
Zhaocheng 190-191 C 3
Zhaocheng = Jiaocheng 190-191 CD 3
Zhaoping 190-191 C 9
Zhaoqing 190-191 D 10
Zhaotong 184-185 J 6
Zhao Xian [TJ, Hebei] 190-191 E 3
Zhaoxian [TJ, Shandong] 190-191 G 4
Zhaoyuan 190-191 H 1
Zhapo 190-191 C 11
Zhashui 190-191 B 5
Zhaxigang 184-185 DE 5
Zhaxilhünbo 184-185 F 6
Zhecheng 190-191 E 4
Zhegao 190-191 F 5
Zhejiang 184-185 MN 6
Zhelang Jiao 190-191 E 10
Zheling Guan 184-185 L 6
Zhen'an 190-191 B 5

Zheng'an = Cheng'an 190-191 E 3
Zhengding 190-191 E 2
Zhenghe 190-191 G 8
Zhengjiayi 190-191 C 7
Zhengzhou 184-185 LM 5
Zhenhai 184-185 N 5-6
Zhenjiang 184-185 L 7
Zhenping 190-191 D 5
Zhen Shui 190-191 DE 9
Zhentong 190-191 F 5
Zhenxi = Bar Köl 184-185 G 3
Zhenyuan [TJ , Guizhou] 184-185 K 6
Zhenyuan [TJ, Yunnan] 184-185 J 7
Zherong 190-191 GH 8
Zhidan 190-191 B 3
Zhigatse 184-185 F 6
Zhijiang [TJ, Hubei] 190-191 C 6
Zhijiang [TJ, Hunan] 184-185 KL 6
Zhili 190-191 E 3-F 2
Zhongcun 190-191 FG 4
Zhongdian 184-185 HJ 6
Zhongdu 190-191 B 9
Zhongmou 190-191 DE 4
Zhongshan 184-185 L 7
Zhongtiao Shan 190-191 CD 4
Zhongwei 184-185 JK 4
Zhongxiang 190-191 D 6
Zhongxin 190-191 F 7
Zhongyang 190-191 C 3
Zhoukou 190-191 C 3
Zhorelec = Görlitz 133 G 3
Zhoucun 190-191 FG 3
Zhoudangfan 190-191 E 6
Zhoujiakou = Zhoukou 184-185 LM 5
Zhoukou 184-185 LM 5
Zhouning 190-191 H 6
Zhouzhi 190-191 AB 4
Zhuanghe 188-189 D 3
Zhucheng 184-185 MN 4
Zhudong = Chu-tung 190-191 H 9
Zhuguang Shan 190-191 DE 8-9
Zhuhe = Shangzhi 184-185 O 2
Zhuji 184-185 N 6
Zhujia Jian 190-191 J 7
Zhujiang Kou 190-191 D 10
Zhulong He 190-191 E 2
Zhumadian 190-191 DE 5
Zhuolu 190-191 E 1
Zhuo Xian 190-191 E 1
Zhuozhang He 190-191 D 3
Zhushan 184-185 KL 5
Zhushui He 190-191 EF 4
Zhutan 190-191 F 7
Zhuting 190-191 D 8
Zhuxi 190-191 BC 5
Zhuzhou 184-185 L 6
Zia 172-173 D 4
Zibär, Az- 182-183 KL 4
Zibo 184-185 M 4
Zichang 190-191 B 3
Zichuan 190-191 FG 3
Zidani most 136-137 F 2
Zidikän 182-183 K 3
Zid'ki 140-141 H 2
Zielona Góra 133 GH 2-3
Zifta 170 D 2
Žigalovo 178-179 U 7
Žigansk 178-179 X 4
Zigong 184-185 JK 6
Ziguey 166-167 H 6
Zigui 190-191 C 6
Žiguinchor 166-167 A 6
Žiguli 138-139 R 7
Žiguľovsk 138-139 R 7

Zihu = Bajan Choto 184-185 JK 4
Žjenbet 140-141 N 2
Žljin 184-185 M 7
Zikhrōn-Ya'aqov 182-183 F 6
Zilä 182-183 G 6
Zilair 178-179 K 7
Zilalet 172-173 GH 1
Zile 182-183 F 2
Žilina 133 J 4
Zillah 166-167 H 3
Zillah, WA 150-151 C 2
Žiloj 140-141 P 6
Žilti, Az- 180-181 EF 5
Žilupe 138-139 FG 5
Zima 174-175 D 7
Zimane 174-175 K 2
Zimbabwe 168-169 H 7
Zimbabwe 168-169 H 7
Zimbabwe [*] 168-169 GH 6
Zimbabwe [ZW, Estado] 168 EF 5
Zimbabwe [ZW, ruinas] 168 H 7
Zimbabwe [ZW, Stato] 168-169 GH 6
Zimi 172-173 C 4
Zimkän, Äb-e - 182-183 LM 5
Zimme = Chiang Mai 186-187 CD 3
Zimnicea 136-137 L 4
Žimovniki 140-141 L 3
Zinder 166-167 G 6
Ziniaré 172-173 E 2
Zinqiang 190-191 F 4
Zintenhof = Sindi 138-139 E 4
Zion, IL 152-153 N 4
Zion National Monument 150-151 G 7
Zion National Park 150-151 G 7
Zionsville, IN 152-153 NO 6
Zipaquirá 158-159 E 3-4
Ziqiu 190-191 C 6
Žir'atino 138-139 J 7
Zirke 136-137 F 4
Zirkel, Mount - 152-153 C 5
Žirnov 140-141 K 2
Žirnovsk 140-141 M 1
Zirräh, Gaud-e - = Gawdezereh 180-181 J 5
Zixi 190-191 F 8
Zixing 190-191 D 9
Ziya He 190-191 F 2
Ziyamet 182-183 F 5
Ziyang 190-191 B 5
Ziyang = Yanzhou 190-191 F 4
Ziyuan 190-191 C 8
Zizhong 184-185 JK 5-6
Zizhou 190-191 B 3
Zižo-zaki 188-189 J 5
Zjednoczone Emiraty Arabskie 180-181 GH 6
Zlatica 136-137 KL 4
Zlatograd 136-137 L 5
Zlatonosné pobřeží 166-167 DE 8
Zlatopoľ 140-141 E 2
Zlatoust 178-179 K 6
Zlin 133 H 4
Zitan 166-167 GH 2
Žlobin 138-139 GH 7
Złoczew 133 J 3
Zlotów 133 H 2
Złote Wybrzeże 166-167 DE 8
Žluté moře 184-185 N 4
Zlynka 138-139 H 7

Žmerinka 140-141 D 2
Žmijiv 138-139 L 7
Znaim = Znojmo 133 GH 4
Znamenka [SU, Rossijskaja SFSR Smolensk] 138-139 K 6
Znamenka [SU, Rossijskaja SFSR Tambov] 138-139 N 7
Znamenka [SU, Ukrainskaja SSR] 140-141 F 2
Znamensk 133 K 1
Znamenskoje 138-139 KL 7
Znojmo 133 GH 4
Zóbuè 168-169 H 6
Žochova, ostrov - 178-179 de 2
Zogirma 172-173 FG 2
Zohreh, Rüd-e - 180-181 G 5
Zola Chäy 182-183 L 3-4
Zoločev [SU, Char'kov] 140-141 G 1
Zoločev [SU, L'vov] 140-141 B 2
Zolotaja Gora 178-179 XY 7
Zolotar'ovka 138-139 P 7
Zolte, Morze - 184-185 N 4
Zolotonoša 140-141 F 2
Zomba 168-169 J 6
Zombi Nzoro 171 B 2
Zongcun 190-191 D 8
Zongo 168-169 E 2
Zonguldak 180-181 C 2
Zonüz 182-183 L 3
Zoo Baba 172-173 J 1
Zorgo 172-173 E 2
Zorra, Isla - 146-147 b 2
Zortman, MT 152-153 B 2
Zorzor 166-167 C 7
Zou 172-173 F 4
Zou Xian 190-191 F 4
Zouping 190-191 F 3
Zoushi 190-191 D 7
Zoutpansberge = Soutpansberge 168-169 H 7
Zuar = Zouar 166-167 H 4
Zubaydiyah, Az- 182-183 L 6
Zubayr, Jabal - 170 E 4
Zubayr, Az- 182-183 M 7
Zubayr, Jazä'ir az- 180-181 E 7-8
Zubayr, Khawr az- 182-183 MN 7
Zubcov 138-139 K 5
Zubova Poľana 138-139 O 6
Zubovo 138-139 Q 3
Zubovskaja = Ali-Bajramly 140-141 O 7
Žudev, ostrov - 140-141 O 4
Zuénoula 166-167 C 7
Zuera 134-135 G 8
Zufär 180-181 J 5
Zug 133 D 5
Zugdidi 140-141 KL 5
Zugspitze 133 E 5
Zuid-Afrika 168-169 F-H 8
Zuid-Amerika 124-125 FG 6
Zuid-Antillenbekken 124-125 G 8
Zuidaustralisch Bekken 124-125 PQ 8
Zuid-Bandabekken 186-187 J 8
Zuidchinees Bekken 186-187 F 3-4
Zuidchinese Zee 186-187 E 5-G 3
Zuid-Georgië = South Georgia 162 J 8
Zuid-Georgiëdrempel 121 D 133-E 34
Zuid-Honjoerug 184-185 R 5-6
Zuidindische Rug 124-125 OP 8

Zuid-Korea 184-185 OP 4
OP 7
Zuidoostindisch Bekken 124-125 OP 7
Zuidpacifisch Bekken 121 D 21-1
Zuidpacifische Rug 121 D 22-C 2
Zuid-Sandwichtrog 121 D 34
Zuidwest-Afrika = Namibie 168-169 E 7
Zuidwestindisch Bekken 124-125 MN 7
Zuidzee 192-193 H-N 5
Zújar 134-135 E 9
Zujevka 138-139 S 4
Zujevo, Orechovo- 178-179 FG 6
Z'uk, mys - 140-141 H 4
Žukovka 138-139 U 4
Žukovskij 138-139 M 6
Zukur 166-167 N 6
Žuldyz 140-141 O 2
Zululand 174-175 J 5-K 4
Zumbo 158-159 D 5
Zumbo 168-169 GH 6
Zumbrota, MN 152-153 K 3
Zumul, Umm az- 180-181 GH 6
Zungeru 166-167 F 6
Zunhua 190-191 F 1
Zuni, NM 150-151 J 8
Zuni Indian Reservation 150-151
Zuni Mountains 150-151 JK 8
Zuo'an 190-191 E 4
Zuoquan 190-191 D 3
Zuoyun 190-191 D 2
Župania 136-137 H 3
Žüq, Hässi - 166-167 B 4
Zuqar = Zukur 166-167 N 6
Züräbäd 182-183 L 6
Zurak 172-173 H 3
Zurbatiyah 182-183 LM 6
Zürich 133 D 5
Zürichsee 133 D 5
Zurmi 172-173 G 2
Zuru 166-167 F 6
Zurych = Zürich 136-137 C 2
Zurzuna = Cildir 182-183 K 2
Žuša 138-139 L 7
Žutovo = Okt'abr'skij 140-141 L 3
Zuwärah 166-167 G 2
Zuwe 174-175 F 2
Zvenigorodka 140-141 E 2
Zvenigovo 138-139 QR 6
Zviaheľ = Novograd-Volynskij 140-141 C 1
Zvishavane 168-169 H 7
Zvolen 133 J 4
Zvornik 136-137 H 3
Žwai, Lake - = Ziway 166-167 M 7
Zwartberg = Swartberg 174-175 E 6
Zwarte Zee 140-141 EJ 5
Zwartkops = Swartkops 174-175 F 7
Zwartmodder = Swartmodder 174-175 D 5
Zweden 130-131 F 9-J 10
Zweibrücken 133 C 4
Zwelitsha 174-175 G 7
Zwettl 133 G 4
Zwickau 133 F 3
Zwiebelhochebene = Nananibplat 174-175 J 3
Zwiesel 133 F 4
Zwitserland 133 CD 5
Zwolle 134-135 L 2
Zwolle, LA 154-155 J 5
Żydowski Obwód Autonomiczny = 12 ◁ 178-179 Z 8
Zýohana 188-189 L 4
Zypern 180-181 C 3
Zyr'anovsk 178-179 PQ 8
Żyrardów 133 K 2
Žytomyr 126-127 O 5